THE STRATEGY READER

The Open University Business School

The Open University Business School offers a three-tier ladder of opportunity for managers at different stages of their careers: the Professional Certificate in Management; the Professional Diploma in Management; and the Master of Business Administration. If you would like to receive information on these open learning programmes, please write to the Open University Business School, The Open University, Milton Keynes MK7 6AA, UK.

This volume is the Course Reader for the Open University Business School's MBA course *Strategy* (B820).

THE STRATEGY READER

EDITOR
Susan Segal-Horn

First published 1998 by Blackwell Publishers Ltd in association with The Open University

Reprinted 1999 (twice), 2000, 2001 (twice), 2002 (twice)

The Open University
Walton Hall
Milton Keynes MK7 6AA, UK

Blackwell Publishers Ltd
108 Cowley Road
Oxford OX4 1JF
UK

Blackwell Publishers Inc.
350 Main Street
Malden, Massachusetts 02148
USA

British Library Cataloguing in Publication Data

A CIP catalogue record for this book is available from the British Library.

Library of Congress Cataloging in Publication Data

The strategy reader/editor, Susan Segal-Horn.
p. cm.
ISBN 0-631-20900-X (hardcover).
ISBN 0-631-20901-8 (pbk.)
1. Strategic planning. I. Segal-Horn, Susan.
HD30.28.S73969 1998
658.4'012–dc21   97-45215
                                                                                            CIP

Typeset in Sabon 10 on 11 point by The Open University
Printed in Great Britain by T. J. International Ltd., Padstow, Cornwall

This book is printed on acid-free paper.

CONTENTS

LIST OF FIGURES

LIST OF TABLES

FOREWORD

ROBERT M. GRANT

My transition from economics to strategic management occurred formally in 1983 when I joined London Business School's newly-formed Centre for Business Strategy. At that time the field was woefully under-developed. We were deeply segmented by discipline: those of us with an economics background had a difficult time conversing with those who had come to strategy from organizational science. Cognitive psychologists and systems scientists further added to the Tower of Babel. Meanwhile progress in building frameworks and theories was impeded by those who upheld the dictum: *If it can't be expressed in a 2 × 2 matrix, it's too complicated for managers to comprehend.*

What a lot has happened in the past decade and a half! In industry analysis we have gone beyond Porter's 'five forces' analysis to apply game theory, develop Schumpeter's ideas of creative destruction, apply ecological and evolutionary models to industry development, and recognize the role of standards. The analysis of competitive advantage has looked behind simple classifications of strengths and weaknesses to develop a rich analysis of the strategic characteristics of firms' resources and capabilities and their relationships with profitability. Our understanding of what strategy is has broadened and deepened. The debate between those who saw strategic management in terms of rationally designing optimal strategies (the 'design school'), and those who saw strategy as the outcome of a complex, often unpredictable organizational process (the 'process school') has subsided. It is acknowledged that strategy is a multifaceted concept which gives rise to different questions calling for different analytic approaches.

During the 1990s, the focus of strategic management thinking has shifted to within the firm. The impetus for this has been provided by interest in the resources and capabilities of the firm. As competitive advantage has been increasingly viewed in terms of organizational capabilities and competencies, questions arise as to how capabilities are built and exercised. To maintain its success, it is not enough for McDonald's to efficiently supply millions of absolutely identical hamburgers each day under meticulously hygienic conditions and accompany them with efficient, friendly service. McDonald's must adjust to very different customer preferences in India, Japan and South Africa; to supply chain difficulties in Russia; to 'mad cow' disease in Britain; to intensifying competition from Burger King, Wendy's and smaller chains; to legal challenges from disgruntled franchisees in the USA and environmentalists in England; and to the continual need to innovate and introduce new products. Firms are under continuous pressure to marshal a broader range of capabilities. A company must strive for efficiency, but it must also be innovative and responsive to changing customer needs, it must plan for the long term while being flexible in adapting to the short term, it must be entrepreneurial and responsive at the local level while achieving high levels of integration. The result has been an explosion of interest in the organizational requirements for competitive advantage: the role of routines, the mechanisms for transferring know-how and best practice, the implications of information technology for business processes and co-operation with other companies, and the implications of strategy for leadership style and the composition of top management teams.

The result has been continuous expansion of the boundaries of strategic management. No longer is strategic management focused on a narrow range of issues to do with industry selection, competitive positioning and diversification. Strategy is now embracing areas of interest that were once the preserve of other fields of study: organization theory and design, the management of technology, marketing, and operations management. This colonization is a consequence of the sheer dynamism of the field. While some areas of management are dominated by a single discipline – finance by economics, organization theory by sociology – strategic management is driven by practical issues: what will the telecommunications industry look like in ten years time? Which technologies and standards will dominate recorded music? How can Kodak build the capabilities in digital imaging it needs to maintain its competitive position within the world photographic industry? Can networks of cooperating firms achieve the benefits of scale and scope traditionally associated with large, diversified corporations?

To address these issues strategic management has been forced to be inclusive and eclectic with regard to the concepts, ideas and theories which it draws upon. Over recent years strategy has looked beyond economics and organization theory to draw inspiration from biology, population ecology and the mathematics of chaos and complexity. Strategy's 'coal face,' however, is at the interface between the companies which formulate the strategies and the markets within which they deploy them. It is here that strategy innovations occur. It is within business schools that we try to make sense of these innovations, to identify patterns in firms' responses to new challenges, and to fit them within a broader analytical framework.

The readings in this book mark milestones in the development of strategic management over the past decade (almost all the readings date from the 1990s) and point towards the future of the field. The readings represent the contributions of some of the most influential thinkers in the field and reflect both the power of the ideas which have shaped thinking about strategy, and the rich variety of its intellectual heritage. If we look behind the readings to the events which shaped the ideas expressed, the power of practical experience is evident. Recognition of emergent strategies and the complex organizational processes of strategy-making was a reflection of the disillusionment with strategic planning in the 1970s and 1980s. Interest in, and recognition of, the role of standards and the strategic importance of controlling them was stimulated by battles between VHS and Betamax in video cassette players, Mac and Wintel, and other contests between rival standard-bearers. Questioning orthodox views about industry maturity was stimulated by the remarkable performance of companies such as Coca-Cola in soft drinks, Nucor in steel, and innovative retailers such as IKEA, Body Shop and Wal-Mart. The rapid advance in the analysis of global strategies and multinational organization reflects the internationalization of the past few decades: notably the proliferation of Japanese multinationals and the challenge of global integration to companies such as Unilever and Ford.

This is an exciting subject area. *The Strategy Reader* is a uniquely stimulating, wide-ranging, and useful set of key readings for anyone wishing to be at the forefront of current thinking in strategy and needing the conceptual tools to make a difference in practising strategic management.

Robert M. Grant
Georgetown University
Washington DC
September 1997

INTRODUCTION

SUSAN SEGAL-HORN

THE DEVELOPMENT OF STRATEGIC MANAGEMENT THINKING

Before we pursue the ideas contained in these readings, it may be useful to review some of the background and history of strategy and so begin to enter the strategist's way of thinking. The idea of strategy is very ancient indeed. It has been around for thousands of years as a way of thinking about survival and of achieving success through leadership in war or politics. Political and military rulers or leaders have always had to make choices: about direction and policy; about the resources at their disposal; about how best to distribute those resources in pursuit of objectives. So, although the term 'strategic management' only began to be popularized in the 1960s through the American business schools, activities which most modern managers would now think of as 'strategic' have been understood and acted upon in all the world's great civilizations.

Classic texts such as Sun Tzu's *The Art of War,* written in China 2,500 years ago, the political strategy of Machiavelli who wrote *The Prince* in 1513, or German military strategists such as Clausewitz in the nineteenth century, are still well known and highly influential. However in this century, the subject of strategic management has been particularly applied to organizations, most typically to business firms and corporations.

One of the most readable texts to discuss the historical development of the field of strategy from the 1960s is Whittington (1993). At that time it was more likely to be called 'business policy' and had its roots in the ideas of Alfred Chandler, a business historian; Igor Ansoff, a management theorist; and Alfred Sloan, a businessman and renowned industrialist who was the founder of the giant American car firm General Motors.

Ansoff was then a professor at the Carnegie Institute of Technology in the USA. His job title is instructive. He was professor of 'Industrial Administration'. His best-known and most influential book, published in 1965, was called *Corporate Strategy* and subtitled 'an analytic approach to business policy for growth and expansion'. This gives a clear feel for the approach to management which he espoused and which was one of the first coherent statements of this relatively new field of business strategy. Together with Chandler (1962, 1977) and Sloan (1963), they established a perspective which Whittington (1993) calls the 'Classical' school of strategic thinking. The focus for them was strategy as deliberate and rational, directed towards profit-maximization, and very much the restricted domain of top management. It drew heavily on notions of military leadership and viewed corporations as hierarchies to be directed from the top. For a more modern example of this genre see Ohmae (1983) and Porter (1980, 1985). Chandler's definition of strategy was:

> the determination of the basic long-term goals and objectives of an enterprise, and the adoption of courses of action and the allocation of resources necessary for those goals.
> (1962 p.13)

This represented a view of strategy as planning. The focus of Chandler's work then, not surprisingly, was the organizational structures that would enable these managerial hierarchies to work efficiently by allowing top managers to allocate resources as they saw fit to achieve their strategic objectives. Companies and organizations were seen as efficient and rational resource-allocating mechanisms. Strategy in the Classical school is thus seen as a rational process of analysis which is designed to achieve (in the phrase popularized by Porter, 1985) 'competitive advantage' of one organization over another in the long term.

Since then, strategy has progressed through at least three further phases. To use Whittington's (1993) terminology, these may be called the Evolutionary, Processual and Systemic perspectives on strategy. The Evolutionary approach to strategy (Nelson and Winter, 1982; Henderson, 1989) sees rational planning as frequently irrelevant, due to permanent environmental turbulence. Markets are seen as dynamic and businesses (and their strategies) must evolve or die. In this school of thought, it is markets not managers, which force choices. Successful strategies emerge in response to environmental turbulence and the role of managers is to fit their strategies as well as possible to the turbulence.

The Processual approach to strategy, like the Evolutionary approach, perceives 'long-range planning' (also the title of one of the best-known practitioner journals in the strategy field) as of less relevance than the *process* by which strategy emerges from a combination of influences within the organization. From this perspective, whose best-known exponent is Henry Mintzberg (1987), strategy is emergent, rather than deliberate, rational and top down as the Classical school would argue. Strategy as process not only reflects the views of top management, but represents a set of pragmatic compromises between various stakeholders in the organization (Pettigrew, 1985). The implication of this Processual view of strategy, is that those strategies which are imposed top-down, without incorporating other organizational constituencies, are unlikely in practice to be effective, realized strategies.

Systems thinkers (Granovetter, 1985; Shrivastava, 1986) see strategy as the child of context: social context, geographic context, political context, cultural context, etc. It follows that strategy must always be *contingent* on that context rather than absolute: therefore Asian or Middle Eastern strategic thinking may vary considerably from Western European or Eastern European strategic thinking. Viable strategies will therefore be context-specific.

Finally, this brief summary of the developing field of strategic management, should indicate the dominant perspective on strategy which has emerged in the 1990s. That is the approach known as the 'resource-based' view of strategy

(Prahalad and Hamel, 1990; Grant, 1991). This takes the view that organizations are bundles of resources which managers have to develop and build towards achieving their strategic objectives. These basic resources constitute inputs into more complex resource clusters built up within each organization. How effectively these complex resource clusters are built and managed is determined by managerial competencies or capabilities. Since such managerial competencies will vary, this suggests that two firms with the same physical resources but with different managerial or organizational talent will generate different levels and types of performance. In the same industry therefore, firms may pursue different strategies and achieve different performance levels, as a result of similar resources but differing competencies. This places a premium on the role of management in creating relevant processes for competence-building within their organizations.

Overall in developmental terms, there has been a gradual evolution in strategic management as a subject away from a rational planning view of strategy and towards an emergent, incremental, Processual view of strategy. In these more recent schools of thought, industry type does not of itself determine strategic possibilities. Innovation and learning are as relevant in mature industries as in growth industries, and possibly more so. Strategic management now offers many differing views on how to compete for resources and for customers. This suggests, rightly, that strategic decision-making is complex and difficult and has to take place in contexts which are continuously dynamic. The gradual development of theories of learning and complexity within strategy show a vibrant subject continuously responding to organizational changes and managerial needs.

Having discussed some of the history and development of strategic management as a subject, let us consider the reasons why such a subject should have arisen at all.

WHAT IS STRATEGY FOR?

'At some time in the life-cycle of virtually every organization, its ability to succeed in spite of itself runs out.' (Brier's First Law)

I am indebted to my colleague Professor John Constable for introducing me to Brier's First Law. Neither he nor I were ever sure of Brier's identity or if there ever was a second 'Law', but he deserves his fifteen minutes of fame just for the First. It is saying something essential about the purpose of strategy. The existence of a clear strategy is what gives drive and strategic intent to an organization (Hamel and Prahalad, 1989). It defines a target for where the organization wants to be in the future. There can be only a very poor second place for an organization which addresses operational processes in isolation from strategic intent.

Strategy is a practical subject. That does not mean that it contains no concepts, frameworks or methodologies to provide pathways for analysis and implementation. It means that it has emerged as an academic subject because a practical need exists to better understand processes of strategy-making and strategy implementation. That is because in modern societies strategy is most strongly associated with economic life and business organizations and is thus closely identified with economic growth and job and wealth creation. On that basis, effective (and ineffective) strategies have social, political and economic consequences. As Rumelt *et al.* (1994) have said:

> Strategic management as a field of enquiry is firmly grounded in practice and exists because of the importance of its subject.

Strategy is about choice, which affects outcomes. Organizations can often survive, and indeed do well, for periods of time in conditions of relative stability, low environmental turbulence and little competition for resources. Virtually none of these conditions prevail in the modern world for any organization or sector, public or private. Hence the rationale for strategic management: to enable an organization to identify, build and deploy resources most effectively towards the attainment of its objectives. To achieve this, Henderson (1984) suggested the following were necessary:

- a critical mass of knowledge concerning the competitive process
- the ability to integrate this knowledge and understand cause and effect
- imagination to foresee alternative actions and logic to analyse their consequences
- availability of resources beyond current needs in order to invest in future potential.

Although this list of factors emphasizes the analytical part of strategic thinking and seems to ignore the process of strategy-making, the view taken in this book is that the purpose of analysis is to help understand the issues. It does not of itself provide the answers. Managers must discover these for themselves. I would agree with Henderson that it is in their use of their 'imagination to foresee alternative actions' and deciding in which possible futures to invest that the true test of their strategic thinking will emerge. Although there are many reliable frameworks for carrying out strategic analysis, there are no recipes for good strategy. Analysis is a necessary but not a sufficient condition for strategic thinking. Strategic thinking is about making judgements which are then translated into decisions. Judgements are not context-free and neither is strategic decision-making. Ultimately it depends on exercising judgement.

THE STRUCTURE OF THIS BOOK

The readings in this book are organized into six sections. Each section contains a mixture of papers: some develop the conceptual ideas and frameworks of strategic management; others describe broad empirical research findings or particular industry or company practice. All are part of the continuous critical debate within strategy.

The collection of papers in Part 1, 'What is strategy?', explores the nature and the purpose of strategy, how it is generated within an organization and who 'owns' or controls it. Are strategies used to further the aspirations of an organization or to limit them? These articles were chosen because they support the view that organizations make their own strategy: that strategic thinking is at least as important, and may be more important, than industry or context. In Part 2, 'The role of industry in strategy?', the theme of strategic thinking is continued, but in terms of the question of external influences on strategy. How influential is industry context on strategy? If environmental context is important for strategy, then which are the most important environmental domains and why? Part 3 of the book, 'The resource-based view of strategy', introduces an approach to strategy which challenges the industry- and market-positioning strategy paradigm popularized by Michael Porter in the 1980s which regarded strategy as driven by differences in market structure. By contrast, the resource-based view looks at the organization in terms of internal features and the resources which it owns or controls as the key to strategy. The articles in Part 4, 'Connections between strategy, structure and process', address strategy implementation. They seek to reflect both the creativity and constraints on implementation, of strategy as a process within a structure, culture and context and the need to harness leadership, vision, knowledge, learning and cognition as equal parts of effective strategy-making.

All of the views discussed in the previous sections of the book will reappear as bit players in Part 5, 'Developing corporate and international strategy'. This reflects the fact that corporate and international strategy have to deal with all the standard strategy issues of structure, culture, design and process as well as a further range of problems arising from cross-border management co-ordination and integration. However, it also shows where future sources of advantage available to international organizations pursuing international strategies are likely to be found.

The book ends with the 'Postscript' in Part 6, which returns to the overview of different types of historical approaches to strategy, where such future perspectives might come from and what ideas they might contain. It also traces the curious process by which some strategy ideas, propagating certain types of strategic thinking, have become popularized. This final section is not designed to neatly close issues down but instead to open them wide to the complexity, diversity and paradox that make up organizational life.

THE PURPOSE OF THIS BOOK

If this book has a message it is that management matters and that organizations are heterogeneous and that these two factors are intimately related. The book has been designed to stimulate the imagination and inform the judgement of all those engaged in strategic decision-making, either currently or in the future, since it is assumed that the quality of their judgement matters. All of the contributions in their separate ways are challenging strategic thinking. Some are already regarded as classics in the field and others are more unusual, or less well-known contributions, which have been chosen for their additional insight and perspective. It is a collection which provides an overview of where strategy is going and what the emerging issues are for strategic thinking for the next decade. Strategy in the future must be able to deal with complexity, learning and flexibility. Managers must be prepared and able to change their thinking and aspirations accordingly:

> ...if the times and conditions change, he will be ruined because he does not change his methods of procedure ... because he cannot be persuaded to depart from a path, having always prospered by following it.
>
> (Machiavelli, 1513)

The book has been designed to present both the past and the future of strategy. It has done this by selecting topics that, in the view of the editor, are substantive rather than merely fashionable or transitory and from which the reader should emerge with an excitement about what it means when we call something 'strategic'.

REFERENCES

Chandler, A.D. (1962) *Strategy and Structure*, MIT Press, Cambridge, MA.

Chandler, A.D. (1977) *The Visible Hand*, Harvard University Press, Cambridge, MA.

Granovetter, M. (1985) 'Economic action and social structure: the problem of embeddedness', *American Journal of Sociology*, Vol. 91, No. 3, pp. 481–510.

Grant, R.M. (1991) 'The resource-based theory of competitive advantage: implications for strategy formulation', *California Management Review*, Spring, pp. 114–35.

Hamel, G. and Prahalad, C.K. (1989) 'Strategic intent', *Harvard Business Review*, May–June, pp. 63–76.

Henderson, B.D. (1984) *The Logic of Business Strategy*, Cambridge, MA, Ballinger.

Henderson, B.D. (1989) 'The origin of strategy', *Harvard Business Review*, November–December, pp. 139–43.

Machiavelli, N. (1513/1984) *The Prince*, Oxford University Press, Oxford.

Mintzberg, H. (1987) 'Crafting strategy' *Harvard Business Review*, July–August, pp. 65–75.

Nelson, R. and Winter, S. (1982) *An Evolutionary Theory of Economic Change*, Harvard University Press, Cambridge, MA.

Ohmae, K. (1983) *The Mind of the Strategist*, Penguin, Harmondsworth.

Pettigrew, A. (1985) *The Awakening Giant: continuity and change in ICI*, Blackwell, Oxford.

Porter, M.E. (1980) *Competitive Strategy*, The Free Press, New York.

Porter, M.E. (1985) *Competitive Advantage*, The Free Press, New York.

Prahalad, C.K. and Hamel, G. (1990) 'The core competence of the corporation', *Harvard Business Review*, May–June, pp. 71–91.

Quinn, J.B. (1992) *Intelligent Enterprise*, The Free Press, New York.

Rumelt, R.P., Schendel, D.E. and Teece, D.J. (1994) *Fundamental Issues in Strategy: a research agenda*, Harvard Business School Press, Boston, MA.

Shrivastava, P. (1986) 'Is strategic management ideological?', *Journal of Management*, Vol. 12, No. 3, pp. 363–77.

Sloan, A.P. (1963) *My Years With General Motors,* Sedgwick and Jackson, London.

Sun Tzu (1983) *The Art of War,* Dell Publishing, New York.

Whittington, R. (1993) *What is Strategy – and Does it Matter?*, Routledge, London.

PART 1

WHAT IS STRATEGY?

INTRODUCTION

The article by Mintzberg and Waters which opens Part 1 asks the fundamental question: 'How do strategies form in organizations?'. They draw the important distinction between leadership plans and intentions (*intended* strategy) and what the organization actually did (*realized* strategy). By comparing the two they are able to provide a basic framework of types of strategy-making processes, in the form of a continuum. At one end of the continuum is planned strategy, where intentions are clearly formulated and subsequently translated into actions. The further the authors move along the continuum away from planned to entrepreneurial, ideological and umbrella strategies, the less precisely articulated is the strategy and the looser the central control. At the far end of the continuum are the emergent strategies, such as the consensus strategy arrived at through mutual adjustment. Using the continuum as their framework, Mintzberg and Waters are able to show powerfully that there is no 'one best way' of formulating strategy. The process appropriate for one type of organization may be wholly inappropriate for another facing a different environment, and different task and stakeholder expectations. Theirs, then, is a 'contingency' view of strategy. The gap that they reveal between intended and realized strategy will be returned to later in Part 4.

The article by Prahalad and Hamel has broken new ground for strategic thinking in the 1990s. It is one of a series of six articles published by Hamel and Prahalad in the Harvard Business Review from the mid-1980s to the mid-1990s. In those articles a distinct body of work has been set out which has acquired a wide readership amongst both academics and practitioners. Their perspective on strategy extends the traditional conceptual strategy frameworks as follows:

Traditional approach	Hamel and Prahalad
Strategy as fit	Strategy as stretch
Resource allocation	Resource leverage
Portfolio of businesses	Portfolio of competencies
Competition as confrontation	Competition as collaboration

Their work asks: 'why do some companies redefine the industries in which they compete, while others take the existing structure as given?'. They specifically emphasize the role of senior management in setting ambitious targets and being creative in their internal and external view of resources. It provides its own most effective illustration of the concept of 'stretch' in strategic thinking. Their stance on strategy is that managerial aspirations should drive resources rather than vice versa. We will return to their ideas in Part 3.

Hamel and Prahalad answer their own question about the aspirations and objectives of companies in terms of what they call 'managerial frames of reference' – the assumptions and received wisdom which 'frame' a company's understanding of itself and its industry and which drives its managers' competitive strategy. Continuing this exploration of 'managerial frames of reference', the chapter by

Eccles and Nohria deals with the internal management of strategy: how language forms a climate of meaning which can create, persuade and reinforce different organizational 'conversations'. Eccles and Nohria discuss the potential power of language in generating, or failing to generate, action. They argue that for leadership and vision to be effective in inspiring and guiding action, they must be grounded in a clear understanding of what motivates people (their individual 'identity') in any given organizational context – a contingency view once again.

Eccles and Nohria describe managers as living in a universe where language is constantly used not only to communicate, but also to persuade and even to create climates of meaning. Language can therefore be used to shape the way that people think and act. They argue that since strategy is ultimately about 'the kinds of conversations' people have in organizations, shaping such conversations is critical to realized strategy. They see strategy as the pursuit of a metaphor for collective identity for an organization. Such a metaphor is often provided by a common language that captures this potential for collective identity, and hence collective purpose, within any organization. One of the most famous examples of such a metaphor is the slogan 'Maru C' ('Surround Caterpillar') developed by the Japanese earth-moving equipment company Komatsu to serve as the rallying cry for their successful attack on their seemingly invincible American rival Caterpillar.

The final chapter in Part 1 is a powerful restatement and development by Michael Porter of the 'positioning' school of strategy. Porter stresses his anxiety that managers are no longer distinguishing between operational effectiveness and strategy and that as a result, 'bit by bit, almost imperceptibly, management tools have taken the place of strategy'. Porter argues that *both* are essential to superior performance but that they work in very different ways. In Porter's terms, having a strategy means deliberately exercising choice: 'choosing a particular set of activities to deliver a unique mix of value'. He considers this to be the reason why Japanese corporations are becoming less successful. Their success was based predominantly on operational efficiency and their lead has been narrowed and in some sectors wiped out. Porter argues that they will now 'have to learn strategy', by which he means making hard choices about which markets, which customers, which service levels, etc. to target. Imitating each other's improvements in quality, outsourcing or partnerships leads to a convergence of strategies and 'a series of races down identical paths no one can win'. Continuous improvement in operational effectiveness alone is not the basis of advantage. Porter argues that choices and trade-offs are essential in strategy. It is important to choose and deliberately limit what an organization offers. Operational effectiveness is critical but it is not a substitute for strategic thinking or a substitute for choosing a strategy.

In this article Porter is dismissive of the Evolutionary school of strategy and the current and the popular view of 'hypercompetition' – extreme environmental turbulence – as driving strategy. He also sees Hamel and Prahalad's ideas as at best difficult to implement, and at worst unrealistic. Hamel and Prahalad are more concerned to enrich the strategy process, the way in which organizations can renovate their strategic thinking, while Porter is concerned that organizations should make strategic choices and then focus coherently on the consequences of that choice for the way the organization is managed.

CHAPTER 1

OF STRATEGIES, DELIBERATE AND EMERGENT

HENRY MINTZBERG AND JAMES A. WATERS

INTRODUCTION

How do strategies form in organizations? Research into the question is necessarily shaped by the underlying conception of the term. Since strategy has almost inevitably been conceived in terms of what the leaders of an organization 'plan' to do in the future, strategy formation has, not surprisingly, tended to be treated as an analytic process for establishing long-range tools and action plans for an organization; that is, as one of formulation followed by implementation. As important as this emphasis may be, we would argue that it is seriously limited, that the process needs to be viewed from a wider perspective so that the variety of ways in which strategies actually take shape can be considered.

For over 10 years now, we have been researching the process of strategy formation based on the definition of strategy as 'a pattern in a stream of decisions' (Mintzberg, 1972, 1978; Mintzberg and Waters, 1982, 1984; Mintzberg *et al.*, 1986; Mintzberg and McHugh, 1985; Brunet, Mintzberg and Waters, 1986). This definition was developed to 'operationalize' the concept of strategy, namely to provide a tangible basis on which to conduct research into how it forms in organizations. Streams of behaviour could be isolated and strategies identified as patterns or consistencies in such streams. The origins of these strategies could then be investigated, with particular attention paid to exploring the relationship between leadership plans and intentions and what the organizations actually did. Using the label strategy for both of these phenomena – one called *intended*, the other *realized* – encouraged that exploration.
[...]

Comparing intended strategy with realized strategy, as shown in Figure 1.1, has allowed us to distinguish *deliberate* strategies – realized as intended – from *emergent* strategies – patterns or consistencies realized despite, or in the absence of, intentions.
[...]

This paper sets out to explore the complexity and variety of strategy formation processes by refining and elaborating the concepts of deliberate and emergent strategy. We begin by specifying more precisely what pure deliberate and pure emergent strategies might mean in the context of organization, describing the

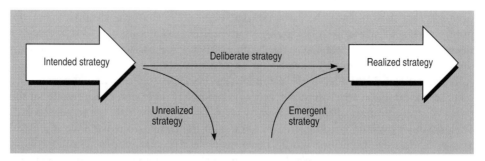

Figure 1.1 Types of strategies

conditions under which each can be said to exist. What does it mean for an 'organization' – a collection of people joined together to pursue some mission in common – to act deliberately? What does it mean for a strategy to emerge in an organization, not guided by intentions? We then identify various types of strategies that have appeared in our empirical studies, each embodying differing degrees of what might be called deliberateness or emergentness. The paper concludes with a discussion of the implications of this perspective on strategy formation for research and practice.

PURE DELIBERATE AND PURE EMERGENT STRATEGIES

For a strategy to be perfectly deliberate – that is, for the realized strategy (pattern in actions) to form exactly as intended – at least three conditions would seem to have to be satisfied. First, there must have existed precise intentions in the organization, articulated in a relatively concrete level of detail, so that there can be no doubt about what was desired before any actions were taken. Secondly, because organization means collective action, to dispel any possible doubt about whether or not the intentions were organizational, they must have been common to virtually all the actors: either shared as their own or else accepted from leaders, probably in response to some sort of controls. Thirdly, these collective intentions must have been realized exactly as intended, which means that no external force (market, technological, political, etc.) could have interfered with them. The environment, in other words, must have been either perfectly predictable, totally benign, or else under the full control of the organization. These three conditions constitute a tall order, so that we are unlikely to find any perfectly deliberate strategies in organizations. Nevertheless, some strategies do come rather close, in some dimensions if not all.

For a strategy to be perfectly emergent, there must be order – consistency in action over time – in the absence of intentions about it. (No consistency means no strategy or at least unrealized strategy – intentions not met.) It is difficult to imagine action in the *total* absence of intention – in some pocket of the organization if not from the leadership itself – such that we would expect the purely emergent strategy to be as rare as the purely deliberate one. But again, our research suggests that some patterns come rather close, as when an environment directly imposes a pattern of action on an organization.

Thus, we would expect to find tendencies in the directions of deliberate and emergent strategies rather than perfect forms of either. In effect, these two form the poles of a continuum along which we would expect real-world strategies to fall. Such strategies would combine various states of the dimensions we have discussed above: leadership intentions would be more or less precise, concrete and explicit, and more or less shared, as would intentions existing elsewhere in the organization; central control over organizational actions would be more or less firm and more or less pervasive; and the environment would be more or less benign, more or less controllable and more or less predictable.

Below we introduce a variety of types of strategies that fall along this continuum, beginning with those closest to the deliberate pole and ending with those most reflective of the characteristics of emergent strategy. We present these types, not as any firm or exhaustive typology (although one may eventually emerge), but simply to explore this continuum of emergentness of strategy and to try to gain some insights into the notions of intention, choice and pattern formation in the collective context we call organization.

THE PLANNED STRATEGY

Planning suggests clear and articulated intentions, backed up by formal controls to ensure their pursuit, in an environment that is acquiescent. In other words, here (and only here) does the classic distinction between 'formulation' and 'implementation' hold up.

In this first type, called *planned strategy*, leaders at the centre of authority formulate their intentions as precisely as possible and then strive for their implementation – their translation into collective action – with a minimum of distortion, 'surprise-free'. To ensure this, the leaders must first articulate their intentions in the form of a plan, to minimize confusion, and then elaborate this plan in as much detail as possible, in the form of budgets, schedules and so on, to pre-empt discretion that might impede its realization. Those outside the planning process may act, but to the extent possible they are not allowed to decide. Programmes that guide their behaviour are built into the plan, and formal controls are instituted to ensure pursuit of the plan and the programmes.

But the plan is of no use if it cannot be applied as formulated in the environment surrounding the organization so the planned strategy is found in an environment that is, if not benign or controllable, then at least rather predictable. Some organizations, as Galbraith (1967) describes the 'new industrial states', are powerful enough to impose their plans on their environments. Others are able to predict their environments with enough accuracy to pursue rather deliberate, planned strategies. We suspect, however, that many planned strategies are found in organizations that simply extrapolate established patterns in environments that they assume will remain stable. In fact, we have argued elsewhere (Mintzberg and Waters, 1982) that strategies appear not to be *conceived* in planning processes so much as elaborated from existing visions or copied from standard industry recipes (see Grinyer and Spender, 1979); planning thus becomes programming, and the planned strategy finds its origins in one of the other types of strategies described below.

Although few strategies can be planned to the degree described above, some do come rather close, particularly in organizations that must commit large quantities of resources to particular missions and so cannot tolerate unstable environments. They may spend years considering their actions, but once they decide to act, they commit themselves firmly. In effect, they deliberate so that their strategies can be rather deliberate. Thus, we studied a mining company that had to engage in a most detailed form of planning to exploit a new ore body in an extremely remote part of Quebec. Likewise, we found a very strong planning orientation in our study of Air Canada, necessary to co-ordinate the purchase of new, expensive jet aircraft with a relatively fixed route structure.

[...]

THE ENTREPRENEURIAL STRATEGY

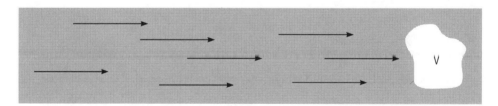

In this second type of strategy, we relax the condition of precise, articulated intentions. Here, one individual in personal control of an organization is able to impose his or her vision of direction on it. Because such strategies are rather common in entrepreneurial firms, tightly controlled by their owners, they can be called *entrepreneurial strategies*.

In this case, the force for pattern or consistency in action is individual vision, the central actor's *concept* of his or her organization's place in its world. This is coupled with an ability to impose that vision on the organization through his or her personal control of its actions (e.g. through giving direct orders to its operating personnel). Of course, the environment must again be co-operative. But entrepreneurial strategies most commonly appear in young and/or small organizations (where personal control is feasible), which are able to find relatively safe niches in their environments. Indeed, the selection of such niches is an integral part of the vision. These strategies can, however, sometimes be found in larger organizations as well, particularly under conditions of crisis where all the actors are willing to follow the direction of a single leader who has vision and will.

Is the entrepreneurial strategy deliberate? Intentions do exist. But they derive from one individual who need not articulate or elaborate them. Indeed, for reasons discussed below, he or she is typically unlikely to want to do so. Thus, the intentions are both more difficult to identify and less specific than those of the planned strategy. Moreover, there is less overt acceptance of these intentions on the part of other actors in the organization. Nevertheless, so long as those actors respond to the personal will of the leader, the strategy would appear to be rather deliberate.

In two important respects, however, that strategy can have emergent characteristics as well. First, as indicated in the previous diagram, vision provides only a general sense of direction. Within it, there is room for adaptation: the details of the vision can emerge *en route*. Secondly, because the leader's vision is personal, it can also be changed completely. To put this another way, since here the formulator is the implementor, step by step, that person can react quickly to feedback on past actions or to new opportunities or threats in the environment. He or she can thus reformulate vision, as shown in the figure below.

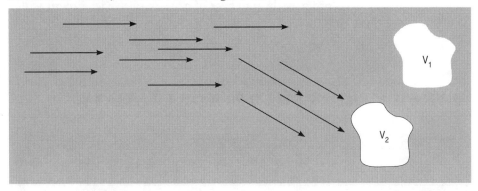

It is this adaptability that distinguishes the entrepreneurial strategy from the planned one. Visions contained in single brains would appear to be more flexible, assuming the individual's willingness to learn, than plans articulated through hierarchies, which are composed of many brains. Adaptation (and emergentness) of planned strategies are discouraged by the articulation of intentions and by the separation between formulation and implementation. Psychologists have shown that the articulation of a strategy locks it into place, impeding willingness to change it (e.g. Keisler, 1971). The separation of implementation from formulation gives rise to a whole system of commitments and procedures, in the form of plans, programmes and controls elaborated down a hierarchy. Instead of one individual being able to change his or her mind, the whole system must be redesigned. Thus, despite the claims of flexible planning, the fact is that organizations plan not to be flexible but to realize specific intentions. It is the entrepreneurial strategy that provides flexibility, at the expense of the specificity and articulation of intentions. [...]

THE IDEOLOGICAL STRATEGY

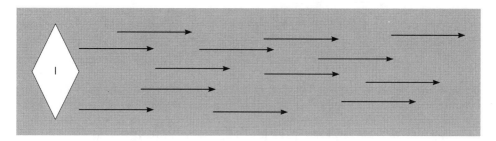

Vision can be collective as well as individual. When the members of an organization share a vision and identify so strongly with it that they pursue it as an ideology, then they are bound to exhibit patterns in their behaviour, so that clear realized strategies can be identified. These may be called *ideological strategies*.

Can an ideological strategy be considered deliberate? Since the ideology is likely to be somewhat overt (e.g. in programmes of indoctrination), and perhaps even articulated (in rough, inspirational form, such as a credo), intentions can usually be identified. The question thus revolves around whether these intentions can be considered organizational and whether they are likely to be realized as intended. In an important sense, these intentions would seem to be most clearly organizational. Whereas the intentions of the planned and entrepreneurial strategies emanate from one centre and are accepted passively by everyone else, those of the ideological strategy are positively embraced by the members of the organization.

As for their realization, because the intentions exist as a rough vision, they can presumably be adapted or changed. But collective vision is far more immutable than individual vision. All who share it must agree to change their 'collective mind'. Moreover, ideology is rooted in the past, in traditions and precedents (often the institutionalization of the vision of a departed, charismatic leader: one person's vision has become everyone's ideology). People, therefore, resist changing it. The object is to interpret 'the word', not defy it. Finally, the environment is unlikely to impose change: the purpose of ideology, after all, is to change the environment or else to insulate the organization from it. For all these reasons, therefore, ideological strategy would normally be highly deliberate, perhaps more so than any type of strategy except the planned one.

[...]

THE UMBRELLA STRATEGY

Now we begin to relax the condition of tight control (whether bureaucratic, personal or ideological) over the mass of actors in the organization and, in some cases, the condition of tight control over the environment as well. Leaders who have only partial control over other actors in an organization may design what can

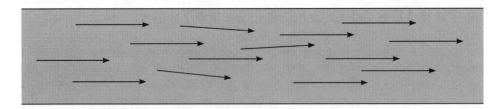

be called *umbrella strategies*. They set general guidelines for behaviour – define the boundaries – and then let other actors manoeuvre within them. In effect, these leaders establish kinds of umbrellas under which organizational actions are expected to fall – for example that all products should be designed for the high-priced end of the market (no matter what those products might be).

When an environment is complex, and perhaps somewhat uncontrollable and unpredictable as well, a variety of actors in the organization must be able to respond to it. In other words, the patterns in organizational actions cannot be set deliberately in one central place, although the boundaries may be established there to constrain them. From the perspective of the leadership (if not, perhaps, the individual actors), therefore, strategies are allowed to emerge, at least within these boundaries. In fact, we can label the umbrella strategy not only deliberate and emergent (intended at the centre in its broad outlines but not in its specific details), but also 'deliberately emergent' (in the sense that the central leadership intention-ally creates the conditions under which strategies can emerge).

[...]

We have so far described the umbrella strategy as one among a number of types that are possible. But, in some sense, virtually all real-world strategies have umbrella characteristics. That is to say, in no organization can the central leadership totally pre-empt the discretion of others (as was assumed in the planned and entrepreneurial strategies) and, by the same token, in none does a central leadership defer totally to others (unless it has ceased to lead). Almost all strategy making behaviour involves, therefore, to some degree at least, a central leadership with some sort of intentions trying to direct, guide, cajole or nudge others with ideas of their own. When the leadership is able to direct, we move towards the realm of the planned or entrepreneurial strategies, when it can hardly nudge, we move towards the realm of the more emergent strategies. But in the broad range between these two can always be found strategies with umbrella characteristics.

In its pursuit of an umbrella strategy – which means, in essence, defining general direction subject to varied interpretation – the central leadership must monitor the behaviour of other actors to assess whether or not the boundaries are being respected. In essence, like us, it searches for patterns in streams of actions. When actors are found to stray outside the boundaries (whether inadvertently or intentionally), the central leadership has three choices: to stop them, ignore them (perhaps for a time, to see what will happen), or adjust to them. In other words, when an arm pokes outside the umbrella, you either pull it in, leave it there (although it might get wet), or move the umbrella over to cover it.

In this last case, the leadership exercises the option of altering its own vision in response to the behaviour of others. Indeed, this would appear to be the place where much effective strategic learning takes place – through leadership response to the initiatives of others. The leadership that is never willing to alter its vision in such a way forgoes important opportunities and tends to lose touch with its environment (although, of course, the one too willing to do so may be unable to sustain any central direction). The umbrella strategy thus requires a light touch, maintaining a subtle balance between proaction and reaction.

THE PROCESS STRATEGY

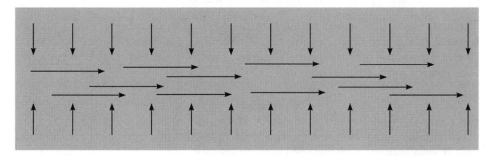

Similar to the umbrella strategy is what can be called the *process strategy*. Again, the leadership functions in an organization in which other actors must have considerable discretion to determine outcomes, because of an environment that is complex and perhaps also unpredictable and uncontrollable. But instead of trying to control strategy content at a general level, through boundaries or targets, the leadership instead needs to exercise influence indirectly. Specifically, it controls the *process* of strategy making while leaving the *content* of strategy to other actors. Again, the resulting behaviour would be deliberate in one respect and emergent in others: the central leadership designs the system that allows others the flexibility to evolve patterns within it.

The leadership may, for example, control the staffing of the organization, thereby determining who gets to make strategy if not what that strategy will be (all the while knowing that control of the former constitutes considerable influence over the latter). Or it may design the structure of the organization to determine the working context of those who get to make strategy.
[...]

Divisionalized organizations of a conglomerate nature commonly use process strategies: the central headquarters creates the basic structure, establishes the control systems and appoints the division managers, who are then expected to develop strategies for their own businesses (typically planned ones for reasons outlined by Mintzberg, 1979: 384–392); note that techniques such as those introduced by the Boston Consulting Group to manage the business portfolios of divisionalized companies, by involving headquarters in the business strategies to some extent, bring their strategies back into the realm of umbrella ones.

THE UNCONNECTED STRATEGIES

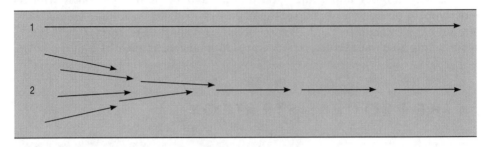

The *unconnected strategy* is perhaps the most straightforward one of all. One part of the organization with considerable discretion – a sub-unit, sometimes even a single individual – because it is only loosely coupled to the rest, is able to realize its own pattern in its stream of actions.

[...]

Unconnected strategies tend to proliferate in organizations of experts, reflecting the complexity of the environments that they face and the resulting need for considerable control by the experts over their own work, providing freedom not only from administrators but sometimes from their own peers as well. Thus, many hospitals and universities appear to be little more than collections of personal strategies, with hardly any discernible central vision or umbrella, let alone plan, linking them together. Each expert pursues his or her own strategies – method of patient care, subject of research, style of teaching. On the other hand, in organizations that do pursue central, rather deliberate strategies, even planned ones, unconnected strategies can sometimes be found in remote enclaves, either tolerated by the system or lost within it.

[...]

THE CONSENSUS STRATEGY

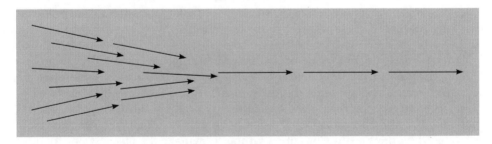

In no strategy so far discussed have we totally dropped the condition of prior intention. The next type is rather more clearly emergent. Here many different actors naturally converge on the same theme, or pattern, so that it becomes pervasive in the organization, without the need for any central direction or control. We call it the *consensus strategy*. Unlike the ideological strategy, in which a consensus forms around a system of beliefs (thus reflecting intentions widely accepted in the organization), the consensus strategy grows out of the mutual adjustment among different actors, as they learn from each other and from their various responses to the environment and thereby find a common, and probably unexpected, pattern that works for them.

In other words, the convergence is not driven by any intentions of a central management, nor even by prior intentions widely shared among the other actors. It just evolves through the results of a host of individual actions. Of course, certain actors may actively promote the consensus, perhaps even negotiate with their colleagues to attain it (as in the congressional form of government). But the point is that it derives more from collective action than from collective intention.
[...]

THE IMPOSED STRATEGIES

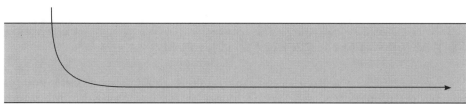

All the strategies so far discussed have derived in part at least from the will (if not the intentions) of actors within the organization. The environment has been considered, if not benign, then at least acquiescent. But strategies can be *imposed* from outside as well; that is, the environment can directly force the organization into a pattern in its stream of actions, regardless of the presence of central controls. The clearest case of this occurs when an external individual or group with a great deal of influence over the organization imposes a strategy on it. We saw this in our study of the state-owned Air Canada, when the minister who created and controlled the airline in its early years forced it to buy and fly a particular type of aircraft. Here the imposed strategy was clearly deliberate, but not by anyone in the organization. However, given its inability to resist, the organization had to resign itself to the pursuit of the strategy, so that it became, in effect, deliberate.

Sometimes, the 'environment' rather than people *per se* impose strategies on organizations, simply be severely restricting the options open to them. Air Canada chose to fly jet aeroplanes and later wide-body aeroplanes. But did it? Could any 'world class' airline have decided otherwise? Again the organization has internalized the imperative so that strategic choice becomes a moot point.
[...]

Reality, however, seems to bring organizations closer to a compromise position between determinism and free choice. Environments seldom pre-empt all choice, just as they seldom offer unlimited choice. That is why purely determined strategies are probably as rare as purely planned ones. Alternatively, just as the umbrella strategy may be the most realistic reflection of leadership intention, so too might the partially imposed strategy be the most realistic reflection of environmental influence. As shown in the figure below, the environment bounds what the organization can do, in this illustration determining under what part of the umbrella the organization can feasibly operate.

[...]

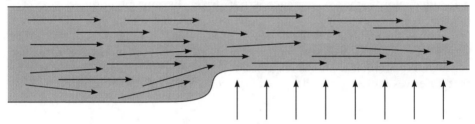

This completes our discussion of various types of strategies. Table 1.1 summarizes some of their major features.

EMERGING CONCLUSIONS

This article has been written to open up thinking about strategy formation, to broaden perspectives that may remain framed in the image of it as an *a priori*, analytic process or even as a sharp dichotomy between strategies as either deliberate or emergent. We believe that more research is required on the process of strategy formation to complement the extensive work currently taking place on the content of strategies; indeed, we believe that research on the former can significantly influence the direction taken by research on the latter (and vice versa).

One promising line of research is investigation of the strategy formation process and of the types of strategies realized as a function of the structure and context of organizations. Do the various propositions suggested in this article, based on our own limited research, in fact hold up in broader samples, for example, that strategies will tend to be more deliberate in tightly coupled, centrally controlled organizations and more emergent in decentralized, loosely coupled ones?

It would also be interesting to know how different types of strategies perform in various contexts and also how these strategies relate to those defined in terms of specific content. Using Porter's (1980) categories, for example, will cost leadership strategies prove more deliberate (specifically, more often planned), differentiation strategies more emergent (perhaps umbrella in nature), or perhaps entrepreneurial? Or using Miles and Snow's (1978) typology, will defenders prove more deliberate in orientation and inclined to use planned strategies, whereas prospectors tend to be more emergent and more prone to rely on umbrella or process or even unconnected, strategies? It may even be possible that highly deliberate strategy making processes will be found to drive organizations away from prospecting

Table 1.1 Summary description of types of strategies

Strategy	Major features
Planned	Strategies originate in formal plans: precise intentions exist, formulated and articulated by central leadership, backed up by formal controls to ensure surprise-free implementation in benign, controllable or predictable environment; strategies most deliberate.
Entrepreneurial	Strategies originate in central vision: intentions exist as personal, unarticulated vision of single leader, and so adaptable to new opportunities; organization under personal control of leader and located in protected niche in environment; strategies relatively deliberate but can emerge
Ideological	Strategies originate in shared beliefs: intentions exist as collective vision of all actors, in inspirational form and relatively immutable, controlled normatively through indoctrination and/or socialization; organization often proactive *vis-à-vis* environment; strategies rather deliberate
Umbrella	Strategies originate in constraints: leadership, in partial control of organizational actions, defines strategic boundaries or targets within which other actors respond to own forces or to complex, perhaps also unpredictable environment; strategies partly deliberate, partly emergent and deliberately emergent
Process	Strategies originate in process: leadership controls process aspects of strategy (hiring, structure, etc.), leaving content aspects to other actors; strategies partly deliberate, partly emergent (and, again, deliberately emergent)
Unconnected	Strategies originate in enclaves: actor(s) loosely coupled to rest of organization produce(s) patterns in own actions in absence of, or in direct contradiction to, central or common intentions; strategies organizationally emergent whether or not deliberate for actor(s)
Consensus	Strategies originate in consensus: through mutual adjustment, actors converge on patterns that become pervasive in absence of central or common intentions; strategies rather emergent
Imposed	Strategies originate in environment: environment dictates patterns in actions either through direct imposition or through implicitly re-empting or bounding organizational choice; strategies most emergent, although may be internalized by organization and made deliberate

activities and towards cost leadership strategies whereas emergent ones may encourage the opposite postures.

The interplay of the different types of strategies we have described can be another avenue of inquiry: the nesting of personal strategies within umbrella ones or their departure in clandestine form from centrally imposed umbrellas; the capacity of unconnected strategies to evoke organizational ones of a consensus or even a planned nature as peripheral patterns that succeed pervade the organization; the conversion of entrepreneurial strategies into ideological or planned ones as vision becomes institutionalized one way or another; the possible propensity of imposed strategies to become deliberate as they are internalized within the organization; and so on. An understanding of how these different types of strategies blend into each other and tend to sequence themselves over time in different contexts could reveal a good deal about the strategy formation process.

At a more general level, the whole question of how managers learn from the experiences of their own organizations seems to be fertile ground for research. In our view, the fundamental difference between deliberate and emergent strategy is that whereas the former focuses on direction and control – getting desired things done – the latter opens up this notion of 'strategic learning'. Defining strategy as intended and conceiving it as deliberate, as has traditionally been done, effectively precludes the notion of strategic learning. Once the intentions have been set, attention is riveted on realizing them, not on adapting them. Messages from the environment tend to get blocked out. Adding the concept of emergent strategy, based on the definition of strategy as realized, opens the process of strategy making up to the notion of learning.

Emergent strategy itself implies learning what works – taking one action at a time in search for that viable pattern or consistency. It is important to remember that emergent strategy means, not chaos, but, in essence, *unintended order*. It is also frequently the means by which deliberate strategies change. As shown in Figure 1.2, in the feedback loop added to our basic diagram, it is often through the identification of emergent strategies – its patterns never intended – that managers and others in the organization come to change their intentions. This is another way of saying that not a few deliberate strategies are simply emergent ones that have been uncovered and subsequently formalized. Of course, unrealized strategies are also a source of learning, as managers find out which of their intentions do not work, rejected either by their organizations themselves or else by environments that are less than acquiescent.

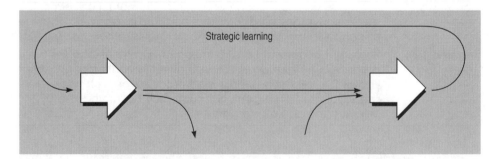

Figure 1.2 Strategic learning

We wish to emphasize that emergent strategy does not have to mean that management is out of control, only – in some cases at least – that it is open, flexible and responsive, in other words, willing to learn. Such behaviour is especially important when an environment is too unstable or complex to comprehend, or too imposing to defy. Openness to such emergent strategy enables management to act before everything is fully understood – to respond to an evolving reality rather than having to focus on a stable fantasy. For example, distinctive competence cannot always be assessed on paper *a priori*; often, perhaps usually, it has to be discovered empirically, by taking actions that test where strengths and weaknesses really lie. Emergent strategy also enables a management that cannot be close enough to a situation, or to know enough about the varied activities of its organization, to surrender control to those who have the information current and detailed enough to shape realistic strategies. Whereas the more deliberate strategies tend to emphasize central direction and hierarchy, the more emergent ones open the way for collective action and convergent behaviour.

Of course, by the same token, deliberate strategy is hardly dysfunctional either. Managers need to manage too, sometimes to impose intentions on their organizations – to provide a sense of direction. That can be partial, as in the cases of umbrella and process strategies, or it can be rather comprehensive, as in the cases of planned and entrepreneurial strategies. When the necessary information can be brought to a central place and environments can be largely understood and predicted (or at least controlled), then it may be appropriate to suspend strategic learning for a time to pursue intentions with as much determination as possible (see Mintzberg and Waters, 1984).

Our conclusion is that strategy formation walks on two feet, one deliberate, the other emergent. As noted earlier, managing requires a light deft touch – to direct in order to realize intentions while at the same time responding to an unfolding pattern of action. The relative emphasis may shift from time to time but not the requirement to attend to both sides of this phenomenon.

REFERENCES

Brunet, J.P., Mintzberg, H. and Waters, J. (1986) 'Does planning impede strategic thinking? the strategy of Air Canada, 1937–1976', in Lamb, R. (ed.) *Advances in Strategic Management*, Vol. 4, Prentice-Hall, Englewood Cliffs, NJ.

Galbraith, J.K. (1967) *The New Industrial State*, Houghton Mifflin, Boston.

Grinyer, P.H. and Spender, J.C. (1979) *Turnaround: the fall and rise of the Newton Chambers Group*, Associated Business Press, London.

Kiesler, C.H. (1971) *The Psychology of Commitment: experiments linking behaviour to belief*, Academic Press, New York.

Miles, R. and Snow, C. (1978) *Organizational Strategy, Structure and Process*, McGraw-Hill, New York.

Mintzberg, H. (1972) 'Research on strategy-making', *Proceedings of the 32nd Annual Meeting of the Academy of Management*, Minneapolis.

Mintzberg, H. (1978) 'Patterns in strategy formation', *Management Science*, Vol. 24, pp. 934–48.

Mintzberg, H. (1979) *The Structuring of Organizations*, Prentice-Hall, Englewood Cliffs, NJ.

Mintzberg, H. and McHugh, A. (1985) 'Strategy formation in adhocracy', *Administrative Science Quarterly.*

Mintzberg, J. and Waters, J.A. (1982) 'Tracking strategy in an entrepreneurial firm', *Academy of Management Journal*, pp. 465–99.

Mintzberg, H. and Waters, J.A. (1984) 'Researching the formation of strategies: the history of Canadian Lady, 1939–1976', in Lamb, R. (ed.) *Competitive Strategic Management*, Prentice-Hall, Englewood Cliffs, NJ.

Mintzberg, H., Otis, S., Shamsie, J. and Waters, J.A. (1986) 'Strategy of design: a study of "architects in co-partnership"', in Grant, J. (ed.) *Strategic Management Frontiers*, JAI Press, Greenwich, CT.

Porter, M.E. (1980) *Competitive Strategy: techniques for analyzing industries and competitors*, The Free Press, New York.

CHAPTER 2

STRATEGY AS STRETCH AND LEVERAGE

GARY HAMEL AND C.K. PRAHALAD

General Motors versus Toyota. CBS versus CNN. Pan Am versus British Airways. RCA versus Sony. Suppose you had been asked, 10 or 20 years ago, to choose the victor in each of these battles. Where would you have placed your bets? With hindsight, the choice is easy. But at the time, GM, CBS, Pan Am, and RCA all had stronger reputations, deeper pockets, greater technological riches, bigger market shares, and more powerful distribution channels. Only a dreamer could have predicted that each would be displaced by a competitor with far fewer resources – but far greater aspirations.

Driven by the need to understand the dynamics of battles like these, we have turned competitiveness into a growth industry. Companies and industries have been analysed in mind-numbing detail, autopsies performed, and verdicts rendered. Yet when it comes to understanding where competitiveness comes from and where it goes, we are like doctors who have diagnosed a problem – and have even found ways to treat some of its symptoms – but who still don't know how to keep people from getting sick in the first place.

Consider the analogy. The first step in understanding competitiveness is to observe competitive outcomes: some companies gaining market share, others losing it, some companies in the black, others bleeding red ink. Like doctors taking a patient's blood pressure or temperature, we can say whether the patient is well or ill, but little more.

The next step is to move from observation to diagnosis. To diagnose competitive problems, we rely on industry structure analysis. A company's market position – the particular market segments in which the company participates – broadly determines the potential for profitability and growth. Within any particular market segment, it is the company's relative competitive advantage that determines actual profitability and growth.

Industry structure analysis points us to the *what* of competitiveness: *what* makes one company more profitable than another. As new whats have been discovered, companies have been exhorted to strive for six sigma quality, compete on time, become customer led, and pursue a host of other desirable advantages. In diagnosing a specific competitive disease, we may conclude that a company is in an unattractive industry segment with a cost disadvantage and subpar quality. This is a bit like determining that a patient has Parkinson's disease: the diagnosis may point to a cure, but it isn't the cure itself and certainly won't prevent disease.

To find a cure, the medical researcher must unravel the workings of disease. The competitive analogy lies in studying organizational structure and process: for example, what are the administrative attributes of a speedy product-development process or a successful total quality management programme? But however deeply we understand the various elements of a company's competitive advantage, we are still addressing the what of competitiveness, not the *why*.

Understanding the what of competitiveness is a prerequisite for catching up. Understanding the why is a prerequisite for getting out in front. Why do some companies continually create new forms of competitive advantage, while others watch and follow? Why do some companies redefine the industries in which they compete, while others take the existing industry structure as a given?

To answer these questions, another layer of understanding must be peeled back. If the goal of medicine is to prevent rather than simply cure disease, a doctor must search for the reason some people fall ill while others do not. Differences in life style and diet, for instance, predispose some to sickness and others to wellness. A company's institutional environment is the industrial corollary here. Monetary and fiscal policy, trade and industrial policy, national levels of education, the structure of corporate ownership, and the social norms and values of a particular nation all have an impact on how well that nation's industries will compete.

But often too much attention is paid to these factors, especially by managers eager to externalize the causes of competitive decline – and the responsibility for it. After all, we regularly see companies that fail to benefit from the inherent advantages of their institutional context and others that manage to escape the disadvantages. Why hasn't Japan, with more snow skiers than any country on earth, produced a world-class manufacturer of ski equipment? Conversely, why did Yamaha, a Japanese company, become the world's largest producer of high-quality grand pianos, which are not suited to the homes or traditional musical tastes of Japanese customers? And why do US computer manufacturers, competing in an industry targeted by Japan's industrial policymakers, thrive around the world when US automakers often wilt in the face of Japanese competition? Institutional factors are only part of the story.

BREAKING THE MANAGERIAL FRAME

To understand why some people contract a disease while others do not, a medical researcher must finally confront genetics. Just as genetic heritage manifests itself as a susceptibility to some diseases and an ability to resist others, managerial frames of reference – the assumptions, premises, and accepted wisdom that bound or 'frame' a company's understanding of itself and its industry and drive its competitive strategy – determine in large part which diseases a company will fall prey to and which it will avoid.

Managers acquire their frames of reference invisibly from business school and other educational experiences, from peers, consultants, and the business press, and, above all, from their own career experiences. But invisible as the frames themselves may be, their consequences are visible at every turn in how a company's senior managers understand what it means to be 'strategic', in their choice of competitive stratagems, in their relationships with subordinates. In this sense, managerial frames, perhaps more than anything else, bound a company's approach to competitive warfare and thus determine competitive outcomes.

Failure to reckon with managerial frames was understandable as long as competition took place mostly between companies whose managers graduated from the same universities, hired the same consultants, subscribed to the same trade journals, and job-hopped among the same few companies. After all, it wasn't Ford that challenged GM's long-held managerial precepts, nor Thomson that compelled Philips to discard once-sacrosanct organizational tenets. Today such blindness is inexcusable. Just as the health of biological species depends, over time, on genetic variety, so it is with global companies: long-term competitiveness depends on managers' willingness to challenge continually their managerial frames.

The term 'head-to-head competition' is literal. Global competition is not just product versus product, company versus company, or trading bloc versus trading bloc. It is mind-set versus mind-set, managerial frame versus managerial frame.

FROM FIT TO STRETCH

A good place to begin deconstructing our managerial frames is with the question, 'What is strategy?' For a great many managers in large Western companies, the answer centres on three elements: the concept of fit, or the relationship between the company and its competitive environment; the allocation of resources among competing investment opportunities; and a long-term perspective in which 'patient money' figures prominently. From this perspective, 'being strategic' implies a willingness to take the long view, and 'strategic' investments are those that require a large and pre-emptive commitment of resources – betting bigger and betting earlier – as well as a distant return and substantial risk.

This dominant strategy frame is not wrong, only unbalanced. That every company must ultimately effect a fit between its resources and the opportunities it pursues, that resource allocation is a strategic task, and that managers must often countenance risk and uncertainty in the pursuit of strategic objectives all go without saying. But the predominance of these planks in corporate strategy platforms has obscured the merits of an alternative frame in which the concept of stretch supplements the idea of fit, leveraging resources is as important as allocating them, and the long term has as much to do with consistency of effort and purpose as it does with patient money and an appetite for risk.

To illustrate the effects of these opposing frames, imagine two companies competing in the same industry. Alpha, the industry leader, has accumulated a wealth of resources of every kind – human talent, technical skills, distribution access, well-known brands, manufacturing facilities, and cash flow – and it can fund just about any initiative it considers strategic. But its aspirations to remain atop its present perch, to grow as fast as its industry, and to achieve a 15 per cent return on equity are modest. 'Where do you go,' Alpha's managers ask themselves, 'when you're already number one?'

Beta, its rival, is a relative latecomer to the industry. It is much smaller than Alpha and has no choice but to make do with fewer people, a smaller capital budget, more modest facilities, and a fraction of Alpha's R&D budget. Nevertheless, its ambitions belie its meagre resource base. Beta's managers have every intention of knocking Alpha off its leadership perch. To reach this goal, they know that they must grow faster than Alpha, and build a worldwide brand franchise and a presence in every major market, all while expending fewer resources. The misfit between Beta's resources and its aspirations would lead most observers to challenge the feasibility of its goals, if not the sanity of its managers.

But consider the likely effects of Alpha's abundance and Beta's ambition on how the two companies frame their competitive strategies and marshal their resources.

Clearly, Alpha is much better placed to behave 'strategically': to pre-empt Beta in building new plant capacity, to outspend Beta on R&D, to buy market share through aggressive pricing, and so on. Alpha's managers are likely to rest easily, confident that they can overpower their smaller rival in any confrontation. They are also likely to approach their battles with a mind-set reminiscent of World War I trench warfare – 'Whoever runs out of ammunition first is the loser' – however resource-inefficient this approach may be.

Beta, on the other hand, is likely to adopt the tactics of guerrilla warfare in hopes of exploiting the orthodoxies of its more powerful enemy. It will search for undefended niches rather than confront its competitor in well-defended market segments. It will focus investments on a relatively small number of core competencies where management feels it has the potential to become a world leader. It might even find itself compelled to invent lean manufacturing with an emphasis on doing more with less.

The argument here is substantially more subtle than the oft-made point that small companies are more nimble. What distinguishes Beta from Alpha is not Beta's smaller resource base but the greater gap that exists between Beta's resources and its aspirations. In contrast, Alpha's problem is not that it is large – there's no inherent virtue in being small – but that it has insufficient stretch in its aspirations. Alpha's managers will not think and behave as if they were in a small, resource-restrained company. What bedevils Alpha is not a surfeit of resources but a scarcity of ambition.

The products of stretch – a view of competition as encirclement rather than confrontation, an accelerated product-development cycle, tightly knit cross-functional teams, a focus on a few core competencies, strategic alliances with suppliers, programmes of employee involvement, consensus – all are elements of a managerial approach typically labelled 'Japanese'. But as the less than sterling performance of Japan's well-endowed banks and brokerage houses reminds us, there is no magic simply in being Japanese. Indeed, so-called Japanese management may have less to do with social harmony and personal discipline than it does with the strategic discipline of stretch. Companies like NEC, CNN, Sony, Glaxo, and Honda were united more by the unreasonableness of their ambitions and their creativity in getting the most from the least than by any cultural or institutional heritage. Material advantages are as poor a substitute for the creativity stretch engenders in Japan as they are in the United States or Europe. Creating stretch, a misfit between resources and aspirations, is the single most important task senior management faces.

FROM ALLOCATION TO LEVERAGE

'If only we had more resources, we could be more strategic.' Every experienced manager will recognize that lament. Yet it is clear that copious resources cannot guarantee continued industry leadership. Tens of billions of dollars later, no one can accuse GM of not being 'strategic' in its pursuit of factory automation. If anything, GM was *too* strategic. The company's ability to invest outpaced its ability to absorb new technology, retrain workers, re-engineer work flows, rejuvenate supplier relationships, and discard managerial orthodoxies.

Conversely, if modest resources were an insurmountable deterrent to future leadership, GM, Philips and IBM would not have found themselves on the defensive with Honda, Sony and Compaq. NEC succeeded in gaining market share against AT&T, Texas Instruments and IBM despite an R&D budget that for most of its history was more modest in both absolute and relative terms than those of its rivals. Toyota developed a new luxury car for a fraction of the resources required by Detroit. IBM challenged Xerox in the copier business and failed, while Canon, a company only 10 per cent the size of Xerox in the mid-1970s, eventually displaced Xerox as the world's most prolific copier manufacturer. CNN in its adolescence managed to provide 24 hours of news a day with a budget estimated at one-fifth that required by CBS to turn out one hour of evening news. Performance like this isn't just lean manufacturing; it's lean everything.

Allocating resources across businesses and geographies is an important part of top management's strategic role. But leveraging what a company already has rather than simply allocating it is a more creative response to scarcity. In the continual search for less resource-intensive ways to achieve ambitious objectives, leveraging resources provides a very different approach from the downsizing and delayering, the restructuring and retrenchment that have become common as managers contend with rivals around the world who have mastered the art of resource leverage.

There are two basic approaches to gathering greater resource productivity, whether those resources be capital or human. The first is downsizing, cutting investment and head count in hopes of becoming lean and mean – in essence, reducing the buck paid for the bang. The second approach, resource leveraging, seeks to get the most out of the resources one has – to get a much bigger bang for the buck. Resource leverage is essentially energizing, while downsizing is essentially demoralizing. Both approaches will yield gains in productivity, but a company that continually ratchets down its resource base without improving its capacity for resource leverage will soon find that downsizing and restructuring become a way of life – until investors locate a new owner or demand a management team with a better track record. Indeed, this is happening in the United States and in Europe as an increasing share of human and physical capital falls through acquisition, joint venture and surrender of market share to competitors who are better at getting more from less.

THE ARENAS OF RESOURCE LEVERAGE

Management can leverage its resources, financial and non-financial, in five basic ways: by *concentrating* them more effectively on key strategic goals; by *accumulating* them more efficiently; by *complementing* one kind of resource with another to create higher order value; by *conserving* resources wherever possible; and by *recovering* them from the market-place in the shortest possible time. Let us look, one by one, at some of the components that make up these broad categories and ask the questions that managers must ask to assess the scope within their company for further resource leverage.

> *Convergence* – Have we created a chasm between resources and aspirations that will compel creative resource leverage? Have we been loyal to our strategic goals and consistent in their pursuit?

Concentrating resources: convergence and focus. Leverage requires a strategic focal point, or what we have called a strategic intent, on which the efforts of individuals, functions, and businesses can converge over time. Komatsu's goal of 'encircling Caterpillar', President Kennedy's challenge to 'put a man on the moon by the end of the decade', British Airways' quest to become the 'world's favourite airline', and Ted Turner's dream of global news all provided a strategic intent.

Yet in many, probably most, companies there is neither a strategic focal point nor any deep agreement on the company's growth trajectory. As a result, priorities shift constantly. Resources are squandered on competing projects. Potentially great ideas are abandoned prematurely. And the very definition of core business changes often enough to confuse both investors and employees. It is hardly surprising then that in many companies there is little cumulativeness to month-by-month and year-by-year strategic decisions.

Compare NEC's relentless pursuit of 'computers and communication' with IBM's on-again, off-again affair with telecommunications. While NEC was first a telecommunications equipment manufacturer and IBM first a computer maker, both have long recognized that the two industries are converging. Yet IBM's Satellite Business Systems, dalliances with MCI and Mitel, and the acquisition of Rolm have come and, for the most part, gone, while its communications business remains a poor relation to its computer business. NEC, on the other hand, is the only company in the world that is a top-five producer of both computer and communications equipment. NEC achieved this not by outspending IBM but rather through its strategic focus. In the mid-1970s, management established the goal of becoming a leader in both computers and communications; next it elaborated the implications of that goal in terms of the skills and capabilities it would require; and finally, it pursued its ambition unswervingly for the next decade and a half.

As NEC's experience suggests, convergence requires an intent that is sufficiently precise to guide decisions. Converging resources around an amorphous goal – becoming a $100 billion company, growing as fast as the industry, achieving a 15 per cent return on equity – is difficult if not impossible.

Resource convergence is also unlikely if strategic goals fail to outlive the tenures of senior executives. Even with a high degree of resource leverage, the attainment of worldwide industry leadership may be a ten-year quest. Recasting the company's ambition every few years virtually guarantees that leadership will remain elusive. The target has to sit still long enough for all members of the organization to calibrate their sights, take a bead on the target, fire, adjust their aim, and fire again.

> *Focus* – Have we clearly identified the next competitive advantage that we must build? Is top management's attention focused firmly on the task until it is accomplished?

If convergence prevents the diversion of resources over time, focus prevents the dilution of resources at any given time. Just as a general with limited forces must pick his targets carefully, so a company must specify and prioritize the improvements it will pursue. Too many managers, finding their companies behind on cost, quality, cycle time, customer service, and other competitive metrics, have tried to put everything right at the same time and then wondered why progress was so painfully slow. No single business, functional team, or department can give adequate attention to all these goals at once. Without focused attention on a few key operating goals at any one time, improvement efforts are likely to be so diluted that the company ends up as a perpetual laggard in every critical performance area.

Consider Komatsu. Starting with products that were judged only half the quality of Caterpillar's, Komatsu won Japan's highest quality award, the Deming Prize, in three years. Many other companies have been wrestling with quality for a decade or more and still cannot lay claim to world-class standards. What accounts for this difference? When Komatsu initiated its total quality control programme, every manager was given explicit instructions to vote quality in a choice between cost and quality. Although quality may be free in the long run, Komatsu's managers recognized that the pursuit of quality is anything but free in the short run. Thus Komatsu focused almost exclusively on quality until it had achieved world standards. Then, and only then, did it turn successively to value engineering, manufacturing rationalization, product-development speed, and the attainment of variety at low cost. Each new layer of advantage provided the foundation for the next.

Dividing meagre resources across a host of medium-term operational goals creates mediocrity on a broad scale. Middle managers are regularly blamed for failing to translate top-management initiatives into action. Yet middle management often finds itself attempting to compensate for top management's failure to sort out priorities, with the result that mixed messages and conflicting goals prevent a sufficient head of steam from developing behind any task.

> *Extraction* – Are we willing to apply lessons learned on the front line, even when they conflict with long-held orthodoxies? Have we found a way to tap the best ideas of every employee?

Accumulating resources: extracting and borrowing. Every company is a reservoir of experiences. Every day, employees come in contact with new customers, learn more about competitors, confront and solve technical problems, and discover better ways of doing things. But some companies are better than others at extracting knowledge from those experiences. Thus what differentiates companies over time may be less the relative quality or depth of their stockpile of experiences than their capacity to draw from that stockpile. Because experience comes at a cost, the ability to maximize the insights gained from every experience is a critical component of resource leverage. Being a 'learning organization' is not enough; a company must also be capable of learning more efficiently than its competitors.

Take Mazda, for example. The Japanese automaker has launched a fraction of the new models created by Ford or GM, yet it seems capable of developing new products in a fraction of the time it takes the other two and at a fraction of the cost. Mazda's experience mocks the experience curve because it suggests that the rate of improvement in a company's capabilities is determined not by some lockstep relationship with accumulated volume but by the relative efficiency with which the company learns from experience. The smaller a company's relative experience base, the more systematic its managers must be in searching for clues to where and how improvements might be made.

The capacity to learn from experience depends on many things: employees who are both reflective and well schooled in the art of problem solving; forums (such as quality circles) where employees can identify common problems and search for higher order solutions; an environment in which every employee feels responsible for the company's competitiveness; the willingness to fix things before they're broken; continuous benchmarking against the world's best practice. But learning takes more than the right tools and attitudes. It also requires a corporate climate in which the people who are closest to customers and competitors feel free to challenge long-standing practices. Unless top management declares open season on precedent and orthodoxy, learning and the unlearning that must precede it cannot begin to take place.

Borrowing – Are we willing to learn from outsiders as well as from insiders? Have we established borrowing processes and learning goals for employees working within alliances and joint ventures?

'Borrowing' the resources of other companies is another way to accumulate and leverage resources. The philosophy of borrowing is summed up in the remark of a Japanese manager that 'you [in the West] chop down the trees, and we [in Japan] build the houses.' In other words, you do the hard work of discovery, and we exploit those discoveries to create new markets. It is instructive to remember that Sony was one of the first companies to commercialize the transistor and the charge-coupled device, technologies pioneered by AT&T's Bell Laboratories. Increasingly, technology is stateless. It crosses borders in the form of scientific papers, foreign sponsorship of university research, international licensing, cross-border equity stakes in high-tech start-ups, and international academic conferences. Tapping into the global market for technology is a potentially important source of resource leverage.

At the extreme, borrowing involves not only gaining access to the skills of a partner but also internalizing those skills. Internalization is often a more efficient way to acquire new skills than acquiring an entire company. In making an acquisition, the acquirer must pay both for the critical skills it wants and for skills it may already have. Likewise, the costs and problems of integrating cultures and harmonizing policy loom much larger in an acquisition than they do in an alliance.

NEC relied on hundreds of alliances, licensing deals, and joint ventures to bolster its product-development efforts and to gain access to foreign markets. Alliances with Intel, General Electric, Varian, and Honeywell, to name a few, multiplied NEC's internal resources. Indeed, NEC managers have been forthright in admitting that without the capacity to learn from their partners, their progress towards the goal of computers and communication would have been much slower.

Borrowing can multiply more than technical resources. Companies such as Canon, Matsushita, and Sharp sell components and finished products on an OEM basis to Hewlett-Packard, Kodak, Thomson, Philips and others to finance their leading-edge research in imaging, video technology and flat-screen displays. Almost every Japanese company we have studied had a bigger share of world development spending in core competence areas and a bigger share of world manufacturing in core components than its brand share in end-product markets. The goal is to capture investment initiative from companies either unwilling or unable to invest in core competence leadership, in order to gain control of critical core competencies. Think of this as borrowing distribution channels and market share from downstream partners to leverage internal development efforts and reduce market risks.

In leveraging resources through borrowing, absorptive capacity is as important as inventive capacity. Some companies are systematically better at borrowing than others are, not least because they approach alliances and joint ventures as students, not teachers. Suffice it to say, arrogance and a full stomach are not as conducive to borrowing as humility and hunger. Captives of their own success, some companies are more likely to surrender their skills inadvertently than to internalize their partners' skills. We might call this negative leverage!

Borrowing can take a myriad of forms: welding tight links with suppliers to exploit their innovations; sharing development risks with critical customers; borrowing resources from more attractive factor markets (as, for example, when Texas Instruments employs relatively low-cost software programmers in India via a satellite hook-up); participating in international research consortia to borrow foreign taxpayers' money. Whatever the form, the motive is the same, to supplement internal resources with resources that lie outside a company's boundaries.

> *Blending* – Have we created a class of technology generalists who can multiply our resources? Have we created an environment in which employees explore new skill combinations?

Complementing resources: blending and balancing. By blending different types of resources in ways that multiply the value of each, management transforms its resources while leveraging them. The ability to blend resources involves several skills: technological integration, functional integration, and new-product imagination.

It is possible that GM or Ford could outspend Honda in developing engine-related technologies like combustion engineering, electronic controls, and lean burn – and perhaps even attain scientific leadership in each area – but still lag Honda in terms of all-around engine performance because the US companies were able to blend fewer technologies. Blending requires technology generalists, systems thinking, and the capacity to optimize complex technological trade-offs. Leadership in a range of technologies may count for little and the resources expended in such a quest may remain under-leveraged if a company is not as good at the subtle art of blending as it is at brute-force pioneering.

Successfully integrating diverse functional skills like R&D, production, marketing and sales is a second form of blending. Where narrow specialization and organizational chimneys exist, functional excellence is rarely translated into product excellence. In such cases, a company may outinvest its competitors in every functional area but reap much smaller rewards in the marketplace. Again, what is required is a class of generalists who understand the interplay of skills, technologies, and functions.

The third form of blending involves a company's ingenuity in dreaming up new-product permutations. Sony and 3M, for example, have demonstrated great imagination in combining core technologies in novel ways. Sony's 'Walkman' brought together well-known functional components – headphones and an audiotape playback device – and created a huge market if not a new life style.

Yamaha combined a small keyboard, a microphone and magnetically encoded cards to create a play-along karaoke piano for children. In these cases, the leverage comes not only from better amortizing past investments in core competencies but also from combining functional elements to create new markets.

> *Balancing* – Have we pursued high standards across the board so that our ability to exploit excellence in one area is never imperilled by mediocrity in another? Can we correct our imbalances?

Balancing is another approach to complementing resources. To be balanced, a company, like a stool, must have at least three legs: a strong product-development capability; the capacity to produce its products or deliver its services at world-class levels of cost and quality; and a sufficiently widespread distribution, marketing and service infrastructure. If any leg is much shorter than the others, the company will be unable to exploit the investments it has made in its areas of strength. By gaining control over the missing resources, however, management can multiply the profits extracted from the company's unique assets.

To illustrate, consider the situation EMI faced in the early 1970s when it invented computerized axial tomography, or the CAT scanner. Although the British company had a ground-breaking product, it lacked a strong international sales and service network and adequate manufacturing skills. As a result, EMI found it impossible to capture and hold onto its fair share of the market. Companies like GE and Siemens, with stronger distribution and manufacturing capabilities, imitated the concept and captured much of the financial bonanza. As for EMI, it ultimately abandoned the business.

Today many small, high-tech companies are unbalanced the way EMI was. While they can enter partnerships with companies that have complementary resources, the innovators are likely to find themselves in a poor bargaining position when it comes to divvying up profits. This imbalance explains why so many Japanese companies worked throughout the 1980s to set up their own worldwide distribution and manufacturing infrastructures rather than continue to borrow from their downstream partners. They realized they could fully capture the economic benefits of their innovations only if they owned all complementary resources. Today, in contrast, Japanese companies are acquiring innovators to complement their strong brand and manufacturing skills. Of the more than 500 small, high-tech US companies sold to foreign interests between 1988 and 1991, Japanese companies bought about two-thirds.

Whatever the nature of the imbalance, the logic is the same. A company cannot fully leverage its accumulated investment in any one dimension if it does not control the other two in some meaningful way. Rebalancing leads to leverage when profits captured by gaining control over critical complementary assets more than cover acquisition costs.

Recycling – Do we view core competencies as corporate resources rather than the property of individual businesses? Have we created lateral communication to ensure that ideas aren't trapped?

Conserving resources: recycling, co-opting, and shielding. The more often a given skill or competence is used, the greater the resource leverage. Sharp exploits its liquid-crystal-display competence in calculators, electronic pocket calendars, mini-TVs, large-screen-projection TVs and laptop computers. Honda has recycled engine-related innovations across motorcycles, cars, outboard motors, generators, and garden tractors. It is little wonder that these companies have unmatched R&D efficiency. The common saying in Japan is, 'No technology is ever abandoned, it's just reserved for future use.' Honda and Sharp are proof of that maxim.

Recycling isn't limited to technology-based competencies. Brands can be recycled too. Familiarity with a high-quality 'banner' brand can predispose customers at least to consider purchasing new products that bear the 'maker's mark.' Think of the leverage Sony gets when it launches a new product, thanks to the relatively modest incremental cost of building credibility with retailers and consumers and the implicit goodwill with which the product is imbued simply because it carries the Sony brand.

Banner branding cannot turn a loser into a winner. In fact, a lousy product will undermine the most respected brand. And in companies such as Unilever and Procter & Gamble, with a long history of product branding, it would be foolish to abandon well-loved brands for an unknown corporate banner. Yet even these companies are more and more apt to use their corporate monikers along with well-known product brands. For example, in working to build a strong presence in Japan, P&G recognized the added oomph its efforts would receive from a judicious use of its corporate name. Building brand leadership in a new market is always a slow and expensive process. But it becomes even more so when advertising budgets and customer awareness are fragmented across multiple brands.

Walk through an international airport and note the billboards bearing the corporate logos of Japan's and Korea's industrial giants. For these companies, brand building is a corporate responsibility. No one expects each business to bear the costs of building global share of mind. A few years ago, a major US company took what, for it, was an unusual step. It erected an illuminated billboard at Heathrow with its logo and a slogan. The billboard didn't stay up long, however; none of the business units was willing to pay for the sign. A few days later, that piece of English sky belonged to a Japanese competitor.

Opportunities for recycling hard-won knowledge and resources are manifold. The ability to switch a production line quickly from making widgets to making gadgets, known as flexible manufacturing, is one. Others include sharing merchandising ideas across national sales subsidiaries, transferring operating improvements from one plant to another, using the same subsystem across a range of products, quickly disseminating ideas for better customer service, and lending experienced executives to key suppliers. But recycling will not occur without a strong organizational foundation. It requires a view of the corporation as a pool of widely accessible skills and resources rather than a series of fiefdoms.

> *Co-option* – Have we identified the industry players who are dependent on us for some critical skill or for their very livelihood? Do we understand how to enroll others in the pursuit of our goals?

Co-option provides another route to conserving resources. Enticing a potential competitor into a fight against a common enemy, working collectively to establish a new standard or develop a new technology, building a coalition around a particular legislative issue – in these and other cases, the goal is to co-opt the resources of other companies and thereby extend one's own influence. In borrowing resources, management seeks to absorb its partners' skills and make them its own; in co-opting resources, the goal is to enroll others in the pursuit of a common objective.

The process of co-option begins with a question: 'How can I convince other companies that they have a stake in my success?' The logic is often, 'My enemy's enemy is my friend.' Philips has a knack for playing Sony and Matsushita against each other, enrolling one as a partner to block the other. Being slightly Machiavellian is no disadvantage when it comes to co-opting resources.

Sometimes co-option requires a stick as well as a carrot of common purpose. Typically, the stick is control over some critical resource, and the unstated logic here is, 'Unless you play the game my way, I'll take my ball and go home.' Fujitsu's relationship with its partners in the computer business is a good example. Each of these partners – ICL in Britain, Siemens in Germany, and Amdahl in the United States – shares a common objective to challenge the dominance of IBM. That is the carrot. The stick is the substantial, in some cases almost total, dependence of these companies on Fujitsu's semi-conductors, central processors, disk drives, printers, terminals, and components.

> *Shielding* – Do we understand competitors' blind spots and orthodoxies? Can we attack without asking retaliation? Do we know how to explore markets through low-cost, low-risk incursions?

To understand shielding, the third form of resource conservation, think about military tactics. Wise generals ensure that their troops are never exposed to unnecessary risks. They disguise their true intentions. They reconnoitre enemy territory before advancing. They don't attack heavily fortified positions. They feint to draw the enemy's forces away from the intended point of attack. The greater the enemy's numerical advantage, the greater the incentive to avoid a full frontal confrontation. The goal is to maximize enemy losses while minimizing the risk to one's own forces. This is the basis for 'resource shielding.'

Attacking a competitor in its home market, attempting to match a larger competitor strength-for-strength, accepting the industry leader's definition of market structure or 'accepted industry practice' are strategies akin to John Wayne taking on all the bad guys single-handedly – and they work better in Hollywood than they do in global competition. In business, judo is more useful than a two-fisted brawl. The first principal in judo is to use your opponent's weight and strength to your own advantage: deflect the energy of your opponent's attack; get him off balance; then let momentum and gravity do the rest.

Dell Computer, America's fastest growing personal computer company, could never have matched Compaq's dealer network or IBM's direct sales force, so the company chose to sell its computers by mail. Computer industry incumbents have found it almost impossible to match Dell, not because they don't have the resources but because these companies face powerful constituents who have a big stake in the status quo. Critical success factors become orthodoxies when a competitor successfully changes the rules of engagement. Such competitive innovation is an important way of shielding resources.

Searching for underdefended territory is another way to shield resources. Honda's success with small motorbikes, Komatsu's early forays into Eastern Europe and Canon's entry into the 'convenience' copier segment all failed to alert incumbents whose attention was focused elsewhere. Understanding a competitor's definition of its 'served market' is the first step in the search for underdefended competitive space. The goal is to build up forces just out of sight of stronger competitors. This may be one reason why Toyota chose to launch the Lexus, its challenge to Mercedes Benz, not in Germany but in California, where buyers are technologically sophisticated, value conscious and not overly swayed by brand loyalty.

Recovery – Have we shortened product-development, order-processing, and product-launch times? Have we built global brands and distribution positions that allow us to pre-empt slower rivals?

Recovering resources: expediting success. The time between the expenditure of resources and their recovery through revenues is yet another source of leverage – the more rapid the recovery process, the higher the resource multiplier. A company that can do anything twice as fast as its competitors, with a similar resource commitment, enjoys a twofold leverage advantage. This rudimentary arithmetic explains, in part, why Japanese companies have been so intent on accelerating product-development times. Consider the effects of the two-to-one development-time advantage Japanese automakers traditionally held over their US and European rivals. This lead not only allowed them to recoup investments more quickly but also gave them more up-to-date products and gave customers more excuses to abandon their brand loyalties.

But fast-paced product development is only one way of expediting recovery time. A company that has built a highly esteemed global brand will find customers eager to try out new products. This predisposition to buy can expedite recovery dramatically, since recovery time is measured not from product concept to product launch but from product concept to some significant level of world-market penetration.

STRETCH WITHOUT RISK

The essential element of the new strategy frame is an aspiration that creates by design a chasm between ambition and resources. For many managers great ambition equals big risk. If managers at Ford, for instance, were simply to extrapolate past practices, they might believe that developing a car five times as good as the Escort (a potential Lexus beater, say) would require five times the resources. But stretch implies risk only when orthodox notions dictate how the ambition is to be achieved.

Stretch can beget risk when an arbitrarily short time horizon is set for long-term leadership goals. Impatience brings the risk of rushing into markets not fully understood, ramping up R&D spending faster than it can be managed, acquiring companies that cannot be digested easily, or rushing into alliances with partners whose motives and capabilities are poorly understood. Trouble inevitably ensues if resource commitments outpace the accumulation of customer and competitor insights. The job of top management is not so much to stake out the future as it is to help accelerate the acquisition of market and industry knowledge. Risk recedes as knowledge grows, and as knowledge grows, so does the company's capacity to advance.

The notion of strategy as stretch helps to bridge the gap between those who see strategy as a grand plan thought up by great minds and those who see strategy as no more than a pattern in a stream of incremental decisions. On the one hand, strategy as stretch is strategy by design, in that top management has a clear view of the goal line. On the other hand, strategy as stretch is strategy by incrementalism, in that top management must clear the path for leadership metre by metre. In short, strategy as stretch recognizes the essential paradox of competition: leadership cannot be planned for, but neither can it happen without a grand and well-considered aspiration.

CHAPTER 3

STRATEGY AS A LANGUAGE GAME

ROBERT G. ECCLES AND NITIN NOHRIA

> For we live not in a settled and finished world, but in one which is going on ...
> John Dewey, Democracy and Education

Management has a lot to do with the use of language, both in the sense of how language is used *in* organizations and in the sense of how it is used in ways – such as business books and journalism – that *span* organizations. Unfortunately, the use of language is such an everyday activity that it tends to be almost invisible. A manager may spend the better part of her day talking to people or deciding how to talk about certain actions in her organization, yet she may nonetheless be unaware of the extent to which language creates the context for everything she does. Similarly, managers may read and hear all kinds of arguments about new practices or changing times, yet be unaware of how the authors of these arguments actively use and abuse language to try to provide a certain picture of the world.

In a nutshell, managers live in a rhetorical universe – a universe where language is constantly used not only to communicate but also to *persuade*, and even to *create*. The first step in taking a fresh perspective towards management is to take language, and hence *rhetoric*, seriously – to understand rhetoric as a powerful force always at work in our understanding of organizations. [...]

In its traditional meaning, rhetoric refers to the formal field of study that examines how language is used to shape the way people think and act – a study that needs to be properly understood as one of the central concerns of effective management. In his translation of Aristotle's *On Rhetoric* (a book that has more than passing relevance for today's manager despite the two millennia that have elapsed since its writing), George Kennedy defines rhetoric as 'the energy inherent in emotion and thought, transmitted through a system of signs, including language, ... to influence [people's] decisions or actions.'[1] By this definition, almost every situation that a manager faces has something to do with rhetoric: one-on-one conversations, small group discussions, presentations to large audiences, written documents and memos, articles in newsletters, project proposals, capital appropriation requests, management information reports, committee proposals, strategic plans, vision statements, magazine articles, best-selling management books – all are examples of situations where managers must actively wrestle with language in the service of decision and action.

We suspect that, to some readers, our use of the term *rhetoric* is something of a red flag. After all, most of us are accustomed to thinking of rhetoric in a negative sense, often as verbal trickery that blurs the distinction between words and reality. Yet it is partially for this reason that we have chosen to use this term in the first place. True, most of us today have a negative connotation of the word *rhetoric*, as exemplified in such phrases as 'mere rhetoric' and 'inflammatory rhetoric'. But rhetoric has a positive component as well, as in the 'powerful' or 'moving' rhetoric that can force us to see the world in new and enlightening ways. This understanding of rhetoric is usually confined to the world of politics – for example, it is often associated with leaders such as Mahatma Gandhi, Martin Luther King, John F. Kennedy, Margaret Thatcher and Winston Churchill. When we agree with the message, the effective use of rhetoric can profoundly influence how we lead our lives. And even when we do not, we are forced to acknowledge the impact that rhetoric can have in shaping the actions of others.

While this latter example is closer to what we mean by the term, our position on rhetoric goes even further. Taking our cue from a variety of recent writers, we argue that rhetoric is not the kind of thing one can be for or against – it is simply the way of the world, the way human beings interact and get things done.[2] It exists everywhere and on many different levels – from individual conversations to entire systems of thinking and speaking. Rhetoric is something that can be used and abused, but it *cannot* be avoided. Rather, it constantly serves to frame the way we see the world. In our view, rhetoric is used well when it mobilizes actions of individuals in a way that contributes both to the individuals as people and to the performance of organizations as a whole. It is abused when it remains unconnected to action or when it leads to actions that are detrimental to individuals and the organization.[3]

To see this distinction more concretely, take the example of the way one kind of rhetoric – corporate vision statements, say – is received in different organizations. Clearly, in some companies the distribution of a corporate vision statement by senior management is seen as a very positive gesture which influences people's actions and the way in which they think and talk about the organization. In other companies – perhaps the majority, we are afraid – the distribution of such a statement is seen simply as a meaningless exercise, one that merely promotes trite phrases indistinguishable from those found in similar statements in other companies. Clearly, the particular words chosen to express the corporate vision can make a difference – often a significant one. But given the similarity in many of the statements we have seen ('produce high-quality products', 'pay attention to customers', 'treat employees fairly', 'provide a good return to shareholders,' and so forth), it cannot be merely the words alone that explain these differences.

Taking action

Whether words and the concepts they represent are old or new, their efficacy is judged by how well they are used to generate *action*. The fundamental problem with the 'flavour of the month' phenomenon so common in many American companies today – e.g. 'If it's March, it must be "Vision 2000"' – is that words are used carelessly without ever being connected to action. In organizations, words without deeds are less than empty since they can potentially undermine the power of all the words that follow them.

[...] Action is always the final test. But there are many kinds of action, and simply to urge action is futile and meaningless. *How*, for example, should managers think about action? What kinds of guidelines can help the manager take action and make decisions day by day? We argue that managers should be taking a particular kind of action, which we call *robust action*. Simply stated, robust action is action that accomplishes short-term objectives while preserving long-term flexibility. Because future problems and opportunities are always uncertain, present actions should not constrict a manager's ability to adapt to new situations as they evolve.

Robust action depends upon the timing of making – and *not* making – decisions. Harvard Business School's Dean, John McArthur, once brought to our attention an insight Chester Barnard made over sixty years ago, one that corresponds perfectly to our notion of robust action. 'The fine art of executive decision,' Barnard instructed, 'consists in not deciding questions that are not now pertinent, in not deciding prematurely, in not making decisions that cannot be made effective, and in not making decisions that others should make.'[4] And as we will see, rhetoric is crucial to robust action at every stage in the game.

But how does a manager *know* what questions are pertinent and what times are right? In the end, we believe, robust action fundamentally depends upon the exercise of judgement: each manager must eventually decide for herself what needs to be done. Like everything else in management, robust action is about finding out what works in particular contexts and situations – it is about the pragmatic know-how gleaned from actual experience. In light of the fact that companies differ in terms of size, industry, strategy, culture, geographical location, people, and history, this advice may seem obvious – though not exactly comforting. Nevertheless, much contemporary writing about management does little to qualify the circumstances under which its principles apply. Excellent companies, Japanese companies, and leading-edge companies are all championed as if they somehow hold the keys to competitive success. This dubious proposition is especially questionable if one asks how unique competitive advantage could be obtained if the trick were ever as simple as to mimic what other companies were doing.

Of course, most managers know better than this, as expressed in the common observation that 'our situation here at FAD Corporation, Inc. is unique.' In some sense this is always true. No two situations are exactly the same, if for no other reason than spatial separation and the passage of time. But it *is* possible to find lessons or practices that are applicable across a number of situations. Managers are aware of this and are therefore constantly searching for universal principles, which consultants and academics are only too eager to provide. Yet as soon as a manager has been given a general model, if she is reflective she immediately sets to thinking about how it needs to be qualified for her particular situation.

Ultimately, it is the manager on the line who is in the best position to decide if something makes sense in her particular situation. In doing so, she needs to be aware of and resist the pressures to adopt an action based on the perceived expertise of the person who is advocating it. Put frankly, there is no escaping the need to exercise judgement at every turn. And in this there are no easy guidelines. Judgement comes from experience, wisdom, and a willingness to admit mistakes.

Recognizing individual identities

The final component of our action perspective on management is the importance of individual *identity*. As every manager soon learns, taking effective action requires understanding the unique identities of the people with whom one deals. Regardless of the issue at hand, treating individuals simply as an 'organizational resource' ignores many of the important specifics that must be taken into account for action to happen.

Of course, a concern for individuals is not new – and it is a quality that most managers are quick to claim. An action perspective, however, means more than simply taking individuals into account. It means considering how identities get built and maintained in organizations, and how the quest for personal identity – in contemporary society perhaps more than ever – is an inseparable aspect of everything that occurs within them. [...]

In the sense we are using the term, identity is not to be confused with the narrower notion of self-interest. Our notion of identity is broader and more robust insofar as it stresses that human action takes place along multiple, often vaguely defined dimensions. Since identity is something that must be understood and managed in the particular, the question of 'what motivates people' must always be grounded in specific contexts. While general models of human behaviour can provide useful orienting frameworks, each person in an organization is truly unique and must be dealt with as such. Robust action, which takes account of situational specifics, requires a robust concept of human behaviour based on identity, which takes account of individual specifics. [...] Adopting such a view may actually require moving away from the idea that 'motivation' is the proper way to frame the issue in the first place.

Taking a rhetorical stance

As should be clear by now, our perspective on management – based as it is on the themes of rhetoric, action, and identity – is an *action perspective*. We intend it to be understood as a kind of wide-angle view of management, one that might allow the reader to start thinking differently about what the dynamics of successful managing really are. Basically, the action perspective sees the reality of management as a matter of *actions* and *processes* – rather than as a matter of things, states, structures or [...] *designs*.

[...]

Seeing strategy from an action perspective – that is, through the prism of rhetoric, action, and identity – is what allows a manager to craft strategy most effectively. Perhaps most important, looking at strategy as a special kind of rhetoric gives us important insights into the role strategy really plays in the manager's world. Visions, mission statements, objectives, goals, and strategic plans are all examples of how rhetoric is used to impart meaning to past and present actions and to create purposeful energy for future ones.[5] The rhetoric of strategy provides a common language used by people at all levels of an organization in order to determine, justify and give meaning to the constant stream of action that the organization comprises.

In fact, seen from a rhetorical stance, all forms of strategy might be seen as having the character of what the philosopher Ludwig Wittgenstein called *'language games.'* Dissatisfied with the traditional view that language simply 'draws pictures' of an existing reality, Wittgenstein introduced the idea of a language game to explain that there isn't any one right way to view the world. By his account, all we really have are different language games that define the conventions by which we agree to talk and act. Each different language, he argued, was at heart simply a different 'form of life' that expressed itself in different ways of speaking and acting.[6] Seen from this perspective, it does not really make sense to ask whether a chosen language game is a true or false representation of reality. [...] What matters instead is the extent to which people find the conventions and rules of their language game a *useful* way to conduct their business. And of course, different language games can prove more or less useful, depending on the situation at hand and the purposes of the players.

[...]

THE EFFECTIVE USE OF STRATEGIC RHETORIC

In the struggle to create effective strategic rhetoric, realizing that strategy is a language game may be half the battle. After all, while strategies may be codified in three-ring binders or certain design concepts, in the end they are about the *kinds of conversations* people have in organizations. With this in mind, the strategist's main task in shaping the game is to pay attention to four key rhetorical issues – and one important caveat.

Issue 1: defining powerful core concepts

The core concepts of any strategic language should be chosen for their ability to provide fresh and useful insights. It is this essential step that makes concepts like strategic business units and core competencies so powerful.[7] What such concepts offer is a powerful way to visualize the organization, to take stock of it, and to act on it. Interestingly enough, although their proponents may claim to have defined these core concepts precisely, their value often lies precisely in their ambiguity. In adopting them, effective managers deliberately keep their interpretations very general, open, and fairly ambiguous. From detailed case studies of how managers articulate strategies, James Brian Quinn concludes that:

> [Effective strategists] initially work out only a few integrating concepts, principles, or philosophies that can help rationalize and guide the company's overall actions. They proceed step by step from early generalities toward later specifics, clarifying the strategy as events both permit and dictate. In early stages, they consciously avoid overprecise statements that might impair the flexibility or imagination needed to exploit new information and opportunities.[8]

Fred Borch, General Electric's CEO from 1963 to 1972, is a good example of someone whose strategic rhetoric masterfully walked this line between incisiveness and ambiguity. Concerned about the decline in GE's profitability despite its phenomenal growth in the 1950s and 1960s, Borch in 1969 commissioned McKinsey & Company to analyse the problem and come up with a new strategy for GE. McKinsey proposed that GE be reorganized into strategic business units that could subsequently be managed as a portfolio.[9] Even though Borch was impressed with the McKinsey solution as a way of strategically analysing GE's businesses, he used the SBU approach flexibly by consciously keeping the concept ambiguous at General Electric. Technically, an SBU could be a GE group, division, or department. According to McKinsey's proposal, about 80% of the SBUs could be readily agreed upon. The remaining 20% required considerable judgement – and in these cases Borch's choices were based on the specifics of the business and the specific identity of the manager running it. By allowing the particulars of each situation to determine how the SBU was defined, Borch was thus able to use the powerful SBU concept flexibly.

Issue 2: defining clear guides for action

While Borch introduced the language of visualizing units as SBUs, it was his 1972 successor Reginald Jones who defined the rules by which specific strategic actions were taken with respect to these SBUs. With McKinsey's help, Jones built a portfolio-planning model to deal with GE's problem of unbridled diversification. In this new model, SBUs were classified [...] according to the attractiveness of the industry they were in and their strength in that industry. Based on this classification, the model recommended a suitable investment strategy and course of action for each business.

According to a senior GE executive, the attractiveness of Jones's portfolio planning model was that 'it not only compressed a lot of data, but contained enough subjective evaluation to appeal to the thinking of GE management.'[10] While it was ambiguous enough to be flexible, the model also had the virtue of clear and specific decision rules to guide action. Once an SBU was categorized, [...] the model provided a clear recommendation to build, hold, or harvest the investment in the business. Jones found this model very useful in taking the strategic actions he wished to take in order to build the 'new GE'. In all, GE exited from seventy-three product lines during his tenure and entered into several others, most notably the 1976 acquisition of Utah International, a billion-dollar mining company with substantial holdings of metallurgical coal. GE entered the 1960s with 80% of its revenues coming from electrical equipment. By 1979, the ratio had fallen to 47%, and company earnings were up to between 6 and 7% of sales.

Issue 3: communicating and exemplifying the rhetoric

Since strategy is intended to define a purpose for the entire organization and to guide collective action, finding a way to communicate the strategy and make its action implications clear is of the utmost importance. Whenever possible, managers should try to articulate simple maxims and slogans that capture the main thrust of the strategy. One superb example is Komatsu's slogan 'Maru C', or 'Surround Caterpillar', which served as the rallying cry for the company's successful attack against the then seemingly invincible Caterpillar.[11]

Because of the vividness conveyed by images, another powerful technique is some kind of pictorial representation of the strategy. Portfolio planning does this through the growth/share matrix, within which circles represent businesses. The core competence approach does this through a tree-like diagram picture of the company's strategic architecture, described as the 'broad map of the evolving linkages between customer functionality requirements, potential technologies, and core competencies.'[12] Such diagrams summarize a great deal of information in an organized way. When accompanied by a few simple rules, these pictures can be used to clearly communicate resource allocation decisions. For example, in BCG's growth/share or 'barnyard' matrix – of which more soon – the rule is milk cash cows, invest in stars and question marks, and divest dogs.

Again, Jack Welch has displayed an intuitive knack for the skilful use of rhetoric in this sense. As GE built and divested businesses in the 1980s, Welch grappled with the problem of finding a concise way of talking about GE to managers and outsiders. What he wanted was a concept that would have strategic meaning for GE and that would provide a simple description of what the company was and what it was not. With his typical flair, he drew up what came to be known as the three circle concept of GE's strategy (see Figure 3.1).[13] Welch's inventive representation visualized all of GE's businesses in terms of whether they were in or out of three overlapping circles. To be in any one of the circles, a business had not only to meet Welch's definition of what constituted 'core', 'high technology' and 'services', but also to meet the criterion of being number one or number two in its relevant market-place.

Communicating strategy vividly is undoubtedly important. But it is not as important as persuading people that the strategy is for real and not a passing fancy. After all, what use is a good strategy if people fail to act in accordance with it? In order for a strategy to be persuasive and be taken seriously, it often requires a highly visible and symbolic action that serves as an exemplar of the strategy in action. For instance, when Jones was CEO of GE, he used the divestiture of GE's computer business and the acquisition of Utah International as symbolic exemplars to create momentum for his strategy. Similarly, when Welch became CEO, it was his sales of Utah International and of GE's Housewares Division (which had been established at the turn of the century and was considered almost sacred) that drove home the message that when he said 'number one or number two', he meant it.[14]

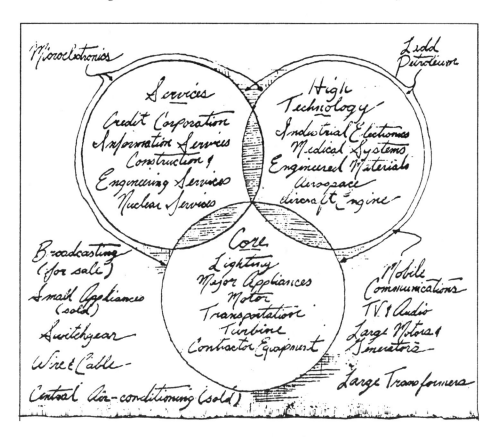

Figure 3.1 Jack Welch's representation of the new GE. (His) shorthand rundown of GE is based on three circles, covering the traditional 'core' businesses (around 33% of profits), the high-technology businesses (30% but rising) and the services (29%). Around these main groupings lie the remainder of the businesses. Some are profitable, some lose money. Among them, they account for around 13% of sales. These are the businesses that Welch has told to fix themselves, to become top players in their league, or they'll be sold or closed. Some, like microelectronics or Ladd Petroleum, have links to all three main businesses circles. They are not on the threatened list. Some, like small appliances or central air-conditioning, have already been sold or are planned to be. (Source: 'General Electric – going with the winners', *Forbes*, March 26, 1984, p. 106.)

Issue 4: using strategy rhetoric for multiple purposes

Effective managers often adapt the strategic rhetoric they find in the world to suit their purposes and to mobilize a wide range of actions they wish to take. For instance, management theorist Richard Hamermesh found that portfolio planning, at the height of its popularity, was used to take a surprisingly wide variety of very different actions. Against the seemingly safe intuition that portfolio planning is simply portfolio planning, Hamermesh found that CEOs used the technique to accomplish *all kinds* of strategic objectives at both the corporate and business unit levels, objectives that went beyond the simple allocation of resources issue with which portfolio planning is usually associated.[15] Citing companies such as Mead Corporation, General Electric and Memorex as examples, Hamermesh concluded that exactly how portfolio planning was used in each situation depended on the particular problem the CEO was trying to solve at the time. Sometimes it was used in the firmwide allocation of resources. At other times it was used for strategizing at the business unit level. In still others it was used to stimulate corporate management's understanding of the corporate portfolio in general.[16]

Indeed, the most effective managers will even find ingenious ways to use strategic tools that might otherwise be branded as 'mere rhetoric'. For example, one manager we know told us that although the consensus in her organization was that the company vision statement was hackneyed at best, she would often half-seriously invoke it to build support for specific actions that might otherwise meet resistance. Once she had identified the action as consistent with the company's avowed vision, she explained, those around her were far more likely to accept it. Of course, this inventive use of 'pre-packaged' rhetoric might be labelled hypocritical, but when one thinks about it, why should a manager refrain from using tools that are there for the using? Building consensus is *always* a matter of using the rhetorical means at one's disposal. Certainly, there are situations when rhetoric used in this way is abusive and manipulative. Most of the time, however, such use of rhetoric is simply a fact of life, a powerful way of mobilizing action that often leads to improved performance.

The caveat: maintaining a rhetorical stance

To realize that strategy is a language game is one thing – but to remember it, and remember it constantly, is another. While strategists must heed these four issues, they must be equally conscious that any rhetorical framework tends to become dogmatic and ineffective once its rhetorical nature is forgotten. And it is this lesson that presents the most serious peril for the manager. Once a given way of speaking about the world has settled in, it is all too easy to forget that a *different* language game could have been chosen, and that this other game would have framed issues in a slightly different way. Gradually, the world may seem as if it is actually *composed* of the concepts one espouses. Instead of seeing the BCG growth/share, or 'barnyard' matrix [...] as simply one among many useful ways to represent businesses and take actions with respect to them, the world actually is perceived *as* a barnyard of businesses. When this happens, the truly crucial questions go unasked: 'Is this *really* a dog business? Is there any way in which it can have a future?' According to some observers, it was precisely this rote application of the portfolio framework that led American businesses to exit certain industries – steel, textiles, and consumer electronics, for example – in droves, while foreign competitors eyed them differently and took actions that turned dogs into profitable businesses.[17]

A related, equally dangerous tendency in strategy 'games' is for form to overtake function. Welch describes this danger well in his description of what happened to the planning system that Jones had established and used with great success. '[The planning system] was dynamite when we first put it in,' Welch explained. 'The thinking was fresh; the form was little – the format got no points – it was idea-oriented. Then we hired a head of planning and he hired two vice presidents and then he hired a planner and the books got thicker and the printing got more sophisticated and the covers got harder and the drawings got better....'[18] The scenario Welch depicts is a fine example of what we call *creeping formalization*, a tendency managers must vigorously resist. (And of course, Welch's very invocation of the problem has everything to do with his own rhetorical strategy for mobilizing change at GE.)

While any system for producing or defining strategy must be taken seriously if it is to be of any value, system-building for its own sake can lead to disaster. The concepts must be believable, but they must not be sacrosanct. The legitimacy of the concepts should not be based upon their consistency with the past, but rather on their utility to direct present actions for accomplishing future purpose.

How does the world look when we view strategy this way? We think that taking this stance toward strategy means recognizing a constant dynamic: an ongoing process of establishing shared sets of assumptions that are treated as real until experience shows that they are not – that they are, after all, only assumptions and can easily (in theory at least) be changed. Without these shared assumptions, common purpose is difficult to establish at the rhetorical level and collective action becomes difficult. At the same time, if the assumptions are simply treated as reality, collective action can end up moving in the wrong direction. In short, what is required is a rhetorical stance that locates itself between total cynicism and naive acceptance of strategic language.

Maintaining this gentle scepticism is crucial if the strategic rhetoric a manager adopts is to be robust enough to give meaning to actions and events as they unfold. Since no manager has a crystal ball, what is most important is not predictive power, but an ability to make ongoing sense of what has happened. This is especially important because strategies rarely emerge as the grand ideas they may often seem. Usually, strategy is the product of complex sequences of action. Effective managers recognize this and accordingly exercise their judgement in prodding initiatives along, providing support and momentum when required, and using rhetoric to cast emergent actions as strategic initiatives. Robust rhetoric is used to take robust action.

STRATEGY AS ROBUST ACTION

Viewing strategy as robust action requires abandoning what might be called the grand view of strategy. Strategy should not be visualized as a cognitive activity that takes place at the upper levels of management and results in ingenious forward-looking plans for taking action that are in turn implemented at lower levels of organization with the hope of gaining a huge competitive advantage. Strategy is instead a complex system of acting and talking, a system that occasionally manifests itself in rational designs but that more typically has to do with the entire network of conversations that exists within a firm – and with the way action is continually pursued through this network. Understood in this manner, effective strategies have the following characteristics:

1 *Effective strategies act as a bridge between the past and the future.* As corporate strategist, a manager is certainly responsible for shaping a vision of the firm's future. But she must also always think deeply about the organization's past and understand the constraints and opportunities afforded by the capabilities and language games that have been handed down. Good strategy is never ahistorical – it is always *path-dependent*. At any moment in time, the viable strategic options available to a manager are influenced by the commitments, choices and conversations that have already occurred. This is not to say that strategic courses of action from which a manager can choose are so constrained by the past as to be deterministic.[19] Managers can certainly alter the strategic course of the firm and will oftentimes do so quite dramatically through a major acquisition or divestiture. Yet a manager must recognize that, in the words of Henry Mintzberg, the strategist 'sits between a past of corporate capabilities and a future of market opportunities.'[20]

   Of course, managers cannot afford to spend *too* much time playing the twin roles of historian and visionary. Try as they may, they cannot escape the real and pressing demands of the present. On this count, however, they may be helped by the recognition of something that too often goes unsaid: that the oft-cited trade-off between taking actions for the short term and taking them for the long term may present a false choice to begin with – false because every short-term strategic choice, however robust, shapes the range of long-term options available. Every strategic action a manager undertakes affects the path of future strategy; like it or not, the manager is pulled into the future with every action and speech, regardless of its scale.

2 *Effective strategies are both planned and opportunistic.* Regardless of the impressions one may receive, there is no one 'best' way to formulate and implement strategy. The attractiveness of any particular approach depends largely on how it is framed. Those who extol the techniques and virtues of formal planning decry the disorder and confusion that come with informal entrepreneurialism. Those who favour the latter point to the energy it can unleash and depict formal planning as a sterile, meaningless exercise.

In practice, strategy is a messy combination of both of these perspectives – or of what Stanford's Robert Burgelman has called 'induced' and 'autonomous' processes.[21] rational, top-down 'strategic plans' *can* effectively set the context for individual action. But people in firms always pursue their own strategic agendas as well, and many of these autonomous initiatives can end up as an important part of firm-wide strategy. Formal plans must be flexible enough to accommodate these emergent actions, which typically rely on individual intuition, timing and circumstances.

3 *Effective strategies involve a wide variety of actions.* Contrary to the recent proposal of Pankaj Ghemawat, we argue that effective strategies do not boil down to a matter of periodically making key resource commitments.[22] Nor do they boil down – as Amar Bhide, another colleague of ours, has argued – to maintaining constant hustle in pursuing and seizing opportunities.[23] *The word 'strategy' covers all kinds of things* – it is simply a word we use as part of the larger language game of management, and as such, it is not really reducible to a single essence of one kind of action or another.[24] Effective strategy simply involves combining the kinds of action listed above with a variety of other types of action. And of course, in some periods a particular form of action – and hence a particular form of strategy – may be more appropriate than in another.

In an uncertain and competitive world – and when has the world been otherwise? – managers have to use their judgement to know when to take different actions. As Elizabeth Teisberg points out, strategy involves judgements about when to commit and be willing to bet, when to delay making a commitment, when to kill something, when to hedge and ensure a bet, when to hustle, and when to try to change the rules of the game.[25] Of course, there are no easily generalizable answers for when managers should pursue which of these actions because so much depends on the particulars of the situation at hand. Quinn, for instance, notes that even if one has made a commitment to pursue a strategy of diversification through acquisition, 'so much depends on the availability, sequencing, conditions of purchase, and specific management characteristics of the individual companies that [one can] only proceed flexibly and opportunistically, interactively reshaping initial visions and strategies as concrete potentials emerge.'[26] And all actions taken will have to be dressed in and mobilized through the appropriate use of rhetoric.

STRATEGY IN PRACTICE: THE STORY OF BIOGEN

The evolution of Biogen's strategy since the firm's founding in 1978 is an interesting example of the challenges of crafting an effective strategy over time. The founding vision of Dan Adams and Ray Schafer, the two venture capitalists whose impetus set the ball rolling towards Biogen's creation, was to create a trans-Atlantic firm that would pursue a broad range of commercial applications of biotechnology. When founded, the firm was basically a group of scientists scattered throughout

Europe and the United States who used the initial venture funding to pursue the ongoing research projects in their own labs that appeared to hold the largest commercial potential. In practice at least, Biogen's initial strategy was thus determined largely by the identities and research interests of the scientists who agreed to join the firm, either as members of the founding team or as collaborators and members of the firm's Scientific Board.

Positioning the firm

Encouraged by the early results of some of these projects, the founders of Biogen raised additional capital and set up laboratories and manufacturing facilities in Geneva, Switzerland, and Cambridge, Massachusetts, to pursue the further commercialization of these projects. The strategy at this stage could best be described as a diversified strategy aimed at exploring all possible avenues of biotechnology. Joe Rosa, currently the head of Biogen's department of Protein Chemistry, recalls that when he joined the firm in 1981, 'Every problem was up for grabs as an area to apply this technology. It was a time to dream up great ideas. Then we developed aspartame [an artificial sweetener] using biotechnology and even though we were successful at doing it, we realized that we would never be able to match the economies of Searle.' (G.D. Searle currently produces aspartame, under the tradename Nutrasweet, using conventional technology.) Rosa added: 'That was one of the first times that we realized the commercial side of research.'

As Biogen's original CEO, Wally Gilbert remembers always pursuing the strategic goal of building a fully integrated biotechnology firm that would develop, manufacture, and market a broad range of products. But to support the wide-ranging exploratory work that he wanted to see continue, Gilbert felt it necessary to position Biogen initially as a contract research firm, a firm that undertook research and development on projects that were licensed to be manufactured and sold by other firms. By 1983, however, Gilbert had placed his bets on gamma interferon, a cancer-fighting drug that he hoped would be the first proprietary product that Biogen would bring to market independently. To raise the capital necessary to make the transition from a contract research firm to an independent fully integrated company, Biogen went public in 1983.

Unfortunately, gamma interferon ran into unforeseen difficulties during the critical clinical trial process. This setback – when combined with the aggressive and diversified R&D strategy adopted by Biogen during these years – led to huge losses as the firm consumed cash and generated little by way of revenues. By 1985, Biogen's 'burn rate' (or negative cash flow) had reached such dangerous proportions that for a time it seemed questionable whether the firm would be able to survive. Concerned about expenditures they felt were running out of control, Biogen's board of directors recruited Jim Vincent to replace Gilbert as CEO, although Gilbert stayed on the firm's board of directors and Scientific Board.

Biogen in transition

Had Gilbert failed? While Gilbert had certainly not been very disciplined about the manner in which he allocated the firm's resources, his broad exploratory strategy had nonetheless allowed Biogen to navigate and survive the enormous uncertainty that surrounded the field of biotechnology during this period. His intuitive approach to strategy had sown the seeds for important benefits that would be derived in the future, including royalties on patents filed on the large number of projects that he had undertaken and the European presence that would offer Biogen the option of starting clinical trials in Europe (where the regulatory restrictions were more lax during the early stages), thus speeding up product development. But when Vincent took over, he faced a daunting challenge. Not only did he have to address certain immediate issues if the firm was to survive, Vincent also had to come up with a vision of the firm's future while building upon its past. In his actions, Vincent displayed all the flair of a great strategist and organizational builder. First, he redefined the purpose of Biogen. Unlike Gilbert whose vision was to build a diversified biotechnology firm, Vincent redefined Biogen as a 'biopharmaceutical' company focused on the area of human therapeutics.

With the idea of becoming a biopharmaceutical company as a guiding vision, Vincent launched an ambitious restructuring programme at Biogen. He cut costs by divesting the firm's European operations and by concentrating resources only on those projects where there was exceptional commercial promise. AIDS therapy, cancer therapeutics, and anti-inflammatory agents received top priority because they reflected Biogen's traditional expertise and also offered exciting opportunities for long-term growth. To build revenue, Vincent (along with the help of vice president of marketing Alan Tuck) negotiated a number of aggressive licence contracts that substantially increased royalty revenues. In addition, Vincent actively explored new avenues for programmes such as gamma interferon that had got stuck in clinical trials. The results: by 1988, the company had a stable recurring revenue stream that matched its expenses, $50 million in cash in the bank, and a healthy product pipeline. Having turned the company around, Vincent placed his main strategic bets on CD4, an AIDS treatment drug he had targeted over gamma interferon as Biogen's best chance for an independent product.

While Vincent's rhetoric during this turnaround period was openly critical of Biogen's undisciplined past, he did not make the mistake of rejecting the past completely. Indeed, as outlined above, he tried as far as possible to build upon and leverage the firm's previous strategic initiatives even as he made tough decisions like selling off the European operations. And by letting the Scientific Board continue to play an active role in overseeing the research being done at Biogen, he maintained an important link with the firm's past

In all, Vincent brought a new approach to how strategy was shaped at Biogen. Building on his experience as a manager and his familiarity with a wide variety of analytic tools, Vincent introduced a more analytic and deliberate approach to strategic thinking at Biogen. Under Gilbert's leadership, Biogen had been guided primarily by intuition and experimentation. Vincent brought disciplined analysis to bear on the resource allocation process and implemented project planning, budgeting, and reviews as a way of prioritizing and controlling resources spent on the various projects. Through Vincent's approach was undoubtedly directive, he was careful not to completely squelch the autonomous and free-wheeling culture of Biogen. He continued to allow scientists to pursue their own pet projects under the '20% free time' plan. He also continued Biogen's traditional Friday evening party and 'beer bust.'

An unexpected direction

In late 1987, a young research scientist John Maraganore took advantage of the 20% plan to begin working on an interesting side project. At the start, Maraganore was trying to build the blood clot-preventing protein hiruden by combining the protein building blocks known as amino acids. The idea of building proteins this way was based on a suggestion by Jeremy Knowles, a prominent scientist on Biogen's Scientific Board, who felt that it might be a clever way to get around patented proteins by creating their mirror images. All the same, Maraganore's reasons for choosing the project weren't strategic in any grand sense. For him, it was largely an opportunity to pursue an interest he had before joining Biogen. He chose hiruden in particular because it was a small, well-defined protein with well-known application in the cardiovascular area – in short, it was a good place to start. The project was launched on little more than an interesting idea.

As it turned out, the original idea did not work. In the process, however, Maraganore discovered a related molecule that showed impressive anticlotting activity. Excited by this discovery, Maraganore set out to build support for this new molecule, dubbed Hirugen. He knew that treating Hirugen as a potential drug candidate would represent a radical departure from Biogen's usual strategy of making drugs based on genetic engineering techniques. Strictly speaking, Hirugen was not a biotechnology product at all. A synthetic peptide, it couldn't even be manufactured in-house by Biogen. Maraganore later remembered a fellow scientist telling him at the time: 'Even if you are successful in proving your peptide works, this is the kind of product that Biogen will just licence out because it is not within the boundaries of the firm's strategy.'

Responding to the noticeable lack of excitement among many fellow scientists, Maraganore started laying the foundations that would make it more likely for a formal development effort to be initiated. He contacted several of the leading outside experts in the area and roused their enthusiasm about his discovery. He even managed to persuade a scientist in a university to test the peptide on baboons and provide him with performance data for free. Meanwhile, he worked on implementation inside the company by winning the support of Rosa and also that of Bill Kelley, who headed Product Development and Manufacturing. All the while, Maraganore was 'trying to make it as easy as possible for Vicki Sato [Biogen's vice president of Research] to support the project.' As he put it, 'I knew that Vicki was not an expert in this area and would ask people outside and inside Biogen whom she trusted about the merits of the project. I tried as best as I could to make sure that I had built enthusiasm among all the people she was likely to ask.' By simultaneously working on formulation and implementation concerns, Maraganore was pursuing a robust strategy. He had prepared himself to take advantage of any fortuitous opportunity.

Sato, for her part, remembers having inherited an empty pipeline when she took over as the head of Biogen's research group and remembers feeling the pressing need to put something new in it. In her view, the research group at Biogen had already begun questioning the traditional technological paradigm on which the firm's early strategy had been based. Moreover, Sato was concerned about putting all her chips on the increasingly chancy CD4. As Sato put it, 'The ground was fertile for something new.' Hirugen offered a potential hedge, and even though Sato was personally not wild about it, she lent Maraganore her support – 'in part,' she explained, 'because he beat me up until I had no choice, and in part because he had been good at building the support of the outside opinion leaders.'

Bolstered by Sato's support and by the data he had gathered, Maraganore arrived at the firm's annual planning and budgeting exercise in November 1988 requesting a budget of $200K to procure enough Hirugen to initiate clinical trails. Yet to Maraganore's dismay, Vincent refused his request on the grounds that Hirugen had an indefensibly weak patent position since another company had been pursuing the project for years and had already filed for numerous broad rights. Vincent decided to use Hirugen in his own way – as an example in his continuing attempts to articulate a policy of not committing resources to the development of any drug that did not have a strong patent position. For Vincent, the issue was a no-brainer. He had already tried to initiate discussions with the other company, an effort which led nowhere. Knowing the company would aggressively defend its patent, Vincent could tell that pursuing Hirugen was a mistake unless the patent issue was first addressed. Yet even though he put up a wall against immediate development, Vincent did not kill the Hirugen programme. He kept the door open and his options alive and gave Maraganore the funds to see if he could find a way to circumvent the patent issue.

From autonomous effort to official strategy

Though discouraged to the point that he considered leaving Biogen, Maraganore persevered. In August 1989, his perseverance paid off and he filed a patent for Hirulog, a compound that involved a clever modification of the original Hirugen molecule. Not only did Hirulog have a stronger patent position, it also showed more activity than Hirugen. In the Scientific Board's quarterly review of research programmes in November 1989, a number of board members – including Jeremy Knowles, always a Maraganore champion – applauded Maraganore's genius in developing Hirulog. The board's enthusiasm, according to Maraganore, helped catch Vincent's attention and suddenly Hirulog was no longer an idea run afoul but a serious candidate for a new drug. Again, Vincent was practising robust action, exploring any and all options and getting as much information as possible. In the annual planning meeting which followed the Scientific Board review, Vincent approved the $200K that Maraganore requested to file an IND (an application for 'investigational new drug' status) to begin clinical trials on Hirulog.

Once he received the necessary funding, Maraganore moved fast. By May 1990, Hirulog was in first-stage clinical trails – having set an industry record for the fastest time between drug discovery and clinical trials. This record speed was accomplished in no small measure because of Maraganore's ability to pull together a team of people from Marketing, Development, and Regulatory and Clinical Affairs who together formulated and executed the drug's strategy. In devising this strategy, Maraganore embraced all the precepts of robust action. 'We always kept as many contingencies as possible in mind,' he explained. 'It's not as if I could draw a decision tree. But at each point, I was acutely aware of trying to keep as many different branches of the tree as open as possible that could serve as alternate routes to achieving my goal. In fact, I deliberately built options at each stage.'

As coincidence would have it, while Hirulog showed promising results in the first stage of clinical trials, the results of the second stage of CD4's clinical trials proved disappointing. (In Vincent's words, it was a 'dead turkey.') In the November 1990 annual planning exercise, Maraganore exploited this advantage to the fullest. During the two-day exercise, he pressed hard for resources that would permit a very aggressive development schedule for Hirulog. The CD4 program, which had entered the planning meeting with almost 60% of the firm's expenditures allocated to it, emerged at meeting's end only a shadow of its former strategic significance. In two days' time, Hirulog had essentially replaced it as Biogen's leading drug candidate. This dramatic shift in Biogen's drug development strategy became the overt, public strategy in January 1991, when Vincent made it the centrepiece of an important meeting with the investment community. Biogen's strategy for accomplishing its redefined mission of 'building a global research-based pharmaceutical company' now hinged on a new bet – Hirulog.

By 1992, Hirulog had progressed to second-stage clinical trials and continued to move at an unprecedented rate through the testing and approval process. At the same time, Hirulog had become an exemplar for a corporate strategy now based on rational drug design. Under this newer strategic rhetoric – which Vincent had been advocating for some time – earlier research using conventional biotechnology methods of recombinant DNA and monoclonal antibody research continued, but a new emphasis was placed on research into peptides and protein chemistry. Maraganore himself was made the manager of this new strategic thrust, selected to head a thrombosis unit focused on identifying and developing opportunities for new products in the cardiovascular area.

Clearly, Hirulog's progress had been spectacular, but Vincent was still confronted with difficult strategic choices. While he was hoping that through aggressive hustle Biogen would be able to bring Hirulog to market in record time, the comprehensiveness of clinical testing meant that it would still be 1994 before the drug came to market. Meanwhile, the other leading biotechnology firms founded at about the same time as Biogen were already bringing their first products to market. To keep up, Vincent wondered if he needed to make a big move, such as a major acquisition. In addition to this short-term concern, he was also contemplating what new technological competencies Biogen had to acquire in order to stay abreast of a fast-moving scientific field and to lay the foundation for the next generation of products. He knew that the choices he made would have a crucial bearing on the evolution of Biogen's strategy and would continue to shape the firm's identity. Under Vincent's tenure, Biogen's identity as a firm – the shared sense of where the firm stood in the world – had already changed considerably from the days of Gilbert. Vincent also knew that depending on how he envisioned the firm's future place in the world, some of his managers would stay or leave.

STRATEGY IN THE PURSUIT OF COLLECTIVE IDENTITY

If Biogen's story doesn't seem typical of how strategy happens in organizations, it is perhaps because we are not accustomed to looking at strategy formation from an action perspective. The Biogen story isn't one of models, matrices, or strategic 'Eureka!!'s' – just a steady shifting of different actions and reactions, interpretations and reinterpretations. During slightly more than a decade, the identity of Biogen changed incrementally – sometimes in surprising directions – to yield a highly successful firm that nonetheless was probably unlike anything the company's founders would have predicted at the outset.

Crafting identity: a metaphor

The Biogen story may not reveal any definitively new tricks for how to corner competitive advantage. What it *does* reveal, however, is that strategy is a *process* rather than a thing – and this is no small fact to recognize. In particular, strategy as we have seen it here is a process by which a firm goes about a building its identity in the world in much the same way that individuals inside the firm do. The process is neither a clean nor a quiet one: there is much talking, acting, trying on of possibilities. Seen this way, the hallmark of strategy is not the grand rational gesture, but the constant dealing with the vagaries of action and the constant need to build, and often rebuild coherent meaning in the face of uncertainty.

To employ a metaphor, the strategic process we have encapsulated above might be understood as akin to the strategic process that goes into wine making. Expert wine makers are the world's most under-recognized strategists: they deal with contingencies from start to finish, they make an enormous number of different judgements – and yet, when all is said and done, they produce a wine with distinctive identity almost year after year. How do they do it? To begin with, good wine makers think in terms of situations rather than formulas. There are unending, path-dependent decisions that wine makers must manage with good situational judgement as their main strategic weapon. In fact, Michel Lafarge, one of the most respected wine makers from France's Burgundy region, has been described as liking to change his entire strategy of fermentation in order to meet the specific conditions of each growing season: 'You must ask yourself each year, "What type of vinification will bring quality?" Each year we vinify differently and may change the length or vary the temperatures.'[27] In all, producing a wine with a winning and distinctive identity demands constant attention to an enormous range of factors and a willingness to exercise one's own judgement about what action is right for each particular moment in the process. And depending on how the process evolves, one may have to be willing to make a number of spontaneous about-faces along the way.

With organizations, things are really no different, and we tend to think that most organizations would do well to take the wine maker's approach to heart. The identity of a firm is not something that can be decided once and for all; it arises as the result of a continuous steam of strategic decisions that have no real bedrock other than judgement itself. Choices are constantly made, each one adding in some way to an identity that, like individual identity, is always a work-in-progress. What business the firm is in, where it sells its products and services, how it interacts with other firms in its environment, what kinds of public stances it takes on certain important issues, what kind of people it employs – all these dimensions contribute to the building of collective identity inside a firm, to how individuals form a view of the firm's role in the world.[28]

Finding identity in diversity

Of course, building a distinctive and coherent identity for what is essentially no more than an assortment of people and resources is no easier than turning a heap of crushed grapes into a distinctive bottle of *premier cru* Burgundy. Like individuals themselves, firms can exist along so many dimensions that developing a sense of collective identity can seem a hopeless task. Yet the task is a crucial one: through an interesting quirk of organizational feedback, it is only by first projecting a coherent identity that a firm can command support of the resources necessary to maintain it. Employees, for example, partially define their own identities, and hence their actions, in terms of identification (or lack thereof) with the firm's identity. Organizational theorist Mats Alvesson notes that "by strengthening the organization's identity – its experienced distinctiveness, consistency, and stability – it can be assumed that individuals' identities and identifications will be strengthened with what they are supposed to be doing at their workplace."[29] Statements of vision, mission values, and beliefs are all rhetorical devices designed to give employees a sense of the identity of their company. [...]

At the same time, collective identity can never fully override the diversity of personal identities within an organization. As we have seen, lurking just beneath the surface of calm, rational discussions about strategic choice are powerful opinions regarding whether individual and collective identities are in conflict or confluence with one another. Especially in a world where individuals define their lives and lifestyles along numerous dimensions, building collective identity is always a delicate game of finding identity in differences – of providing a common language of purpose that manages to capture salient dimensions of collective meaning. The power of strategic rhetoric, and the basis of our eternal fascination with it, lies as much with how it creates a common meaning for individual and collective identity as it does with the competitive positioning of the firm.

[...]

Strategy in the social world

Building and sustaining collective identity is always a social process. It is common to hear managers describe and compare companies in the same way they do people. Conversations among peers, consultants, and academics are a marketplace where notions of collective identity are explored and refined. Industry trade journals, membership in trade associations, and transfers by managers between firms also contribute to generating information which makes these comparisons possible.[30] The mechanisms of identification and comparison are so pervasive that it is hard to find examples where strategy and identity are articulated without reference to them. For instance, Vincent frequently described Biogen's cautious growth strategy – in which the firm's use of resources was held in check until near the time of product launch – as similar to the one followed by Amgen but very different from the strategy adopted by Cetus and Genentech.

Suppliers, customers, shareholders, alliance partners, and others are also involved in a process of mutual identity formation with the firm. Like friends and relatives, they play an important role in determining exactly 'who' a firm is in the world. For example, suppliers take pride in having leading-edge firms as their customers, customers emphasize that they require suppliers to practise total quality, shareholders may only invest in socially responsible companies, and alliances may only be made with companies (including competitors) that have similar cultures. The mutual identity formation at the organizational level carries down to the individual level since these relationships are ultimately based on those between people.

Perhaps what this means is that as the identities of individuals become more complex and multidimensional, it will be harder for firms to articulate a collective identity that a broad spectrum of people can identity with. And of course, we are already seeing how the proliferation of such identities leads to an interesting set of strategic choices for managers. On the one hand, there will be more opportunities to carve out narrow strategic niches that appeal to individuals with particular identities – companies such as Anita Roddick's The Body Shop, a firm that makes cosmetics that appeal to those who are against animal testing.[31] On the other hand, there will continue to be firms that will try to shape their strategies to appeal to as broad a cross-spectrum of identities as possible. Only time will tell which of these approaches will be more robust. Much will depend upon how the present conundrums of identity play themselves out. Meanwhile, managers will have to continue much as they always have – by using language to craft strategies that are as robust to evolving situations as possible.

NOTES

1 Aristotle, *On Rhetoric*, tr. and ed., George Kennedy (New York: Oxford University Press: 1991), 22.

2 In recent decades there has been a resurgence of interest in the concept of rhetoric which has resulted in several works that might be seen as forerunners of our discussion here. For example, in economics, see Donald N. McCloskey, *The Rhetoric of Economics* (Milwaukee: University of Wisconsin Press, 1985); in literature, see Wayne Booth, *The Rhetoric of Fiction* (Chicago: University of Chicago Press, 1961) and 'The revival of rhetoric' in Martin Steinmann, ed., *New Rhetorics* (New York: Charles Scribner's Sons, 1967); and in science, see Alan G. Gross, *The Rhetoric of Science* (Cambridge, MA: Harvard University Press, 1990). An important, less-disciplinary treatment of rhetoric is in Chaim Perelman and L. Olbrechts-Tyteca, *The New Rhetoric: a treatise on argumentation*, John Wilkinson and Purcell Weaver, trs. (Notre Dame, IN: University of Notre Dame Press, 1958, 1971).

3 Now over two millennia old, the debate over rhetoric has been a remarkably constant one. Indeed, Plato's fascinating dialogues (written in the fourth century BC) use a highly rhetorical style to argue that rhetoric is (mainly) a bad thing, thus laying the foundation for most contemporary attitudes about language. See in particular the 'Gorgias' and 'Phaedrus' dialogues, in Edith Hamilton and Huntington Cairns, eds, *Plato: The Collected Dialogues* (Princeton, NJ: Princeton University Press, 1961). For an overview of the debate that seeks to restore rhetoric's good name, see Chapter 20, 'Rhetoric', in Stanley Fish, *Doing What Comes Naturally: change, rhetoric, and the practice of theory in literary and legal studies* (Durham, NC: Duke University Press, 1989).

4 Chester I. Barnard, *The Functions of the Executive* (Cambridge, MA: Harvard University Press, 1938, 1968), 194.

5 The rhetorical nature of strategic language has received consideration before, although usually not in these terms. See Kenneth R. Andrews, *The Concept of Corporate Strategy*, 3rd ed. (Homewood, IL: Richard D. Irwin, 1987), 15–16: 'Whether you wish to think of a view of the total corporation as its *vision*, or a statement of purpose as its *mission statement* ... is up to you. The language for describing so central an activity as choice of purpose is infinitely varied.... In the meantime, remember that what you are doing has no meaning for yourself or others unless you can sense and convey to others what you are doing it for.'

6 See Ludwig Wittgenstein, *Philosophical Investigations*, tr., G.E.M. Anscombe (Oxford: Basil Blackwell, 1974). The *Investigations* – written toward the end of Wittgenstein's life – forms a sharp break with his earlier work, which attempted to trace just the kind of logical view of thought and language he would later criticise. The notion of language games has since been used in various capacities in the management literature, most notably in Louis R. Pondy, 'Leadership Is a Language Game', in Morgan W. McCall, Jr., and Michael M. Lombardo, eds., *Leadership: where else can we go?* (Durham, N.C.: Duke University Press, 1978).

7 For a discussion of how to define strategic business units, see Derek F. Abell, *Defining the Business: the starting point of strategic planning* (Englewood Cliffs, N.J.: Prentice-Hall, 1980); for the value chain.

8 James Brian Quinn, 'Managing Strategies Incrementally', in Robert B. Lamb, ed., *Competitive Strategic Management* (Englewood Cliffs, N.J.: Prentice-Hall, 1984), 37–38.

9 Francis J. Aguilar and Richard Hamermesh, 'General Electric: Strategic Position 1981', Case Study 9-381-174. Boston: Harvard Business School, 1981, 2–3. In McKinsey's

definition, an SBU was defined as having 'a unique set of competitors, a unique business mission, a competitor in external markets …, the ability to accomplish integrated strategic planning, and the ability to call the shots on the variables crucial to the success of the business.'

10 Francis J. Aguilar, Richard Hamermesh, and Caroline Brainard, 'General Electric: Reg Jones and Jack Welch', Case Study 9-391-144. Boston: Harvard Business School, 1991.

11 See Christopher A. Bartlett and V.S. Rangan, 'Komatsu Ltd.', Case Study 9-385-277. Boston: Harvard Business School, 1985.

12 Prahalad and Hamel, 'The Core Competence of the Corporation', 89.

13 See Aguilar, Hamermesh, and Brainard, 'General Electric: Reg Jones and Jack Welch'.

14 Ibid.

15 See Richard G. Hamermesh, *Making Strategy Work: how senior managers produce results* (New York: John Wiley, 1986), 21–22. Hamermesh's findings were later confirmed by Philippe Haspeslagh in a larger survey. He too found that managers used portfolio planning in a wide variety of ways, often improvising and adapting the technique to make it suit their particular needs. It is perhaps because of these virtues of being a legitimate and flexible tool for action that Haspeslagh estimated that a full 45% of the *Fortune 500* companies had introduced the portfolio planning approach to some extent. (See Haspeslagh, 'Portfolio Planning'.)

16 Hamermesh, *Making Strategy Work*, 67.

17 The dangers of how the BCG matrix came to be used are discussed at length by Stuart St. P. Slatter, 'Common pitfalls in using the BCG product portfolio matrix', *London Business School Journal* (Winter, 1980): 18–22. For one of the most provocative arguments about how the rote application of such models led to the decline of American competitiveness, see Robert H. Hayes and William J. Abernathy, 'Managing our way to economic decline', *Harvard Business Review*, 58 (July–August 1980): 67–77. Also see Ronald Henkoff, 'How to Plan for 1995', *Fortune* (December 31, 1990): 70–77.

18 Francis J. Aguilar, Richard G. Hamermesh, and Caroline Brainard, 'General Electric, 1984', Case Study 9-385-315. Boston: Harvard Business School, 1985.

19 The path-dependence of strategy is most apparent from a reading of Penrose, *The Theory of the Growth of the Firm*.

20 Henry Mintzberg, 'Crafting strategy', *Harvard Business Review*, 65 (July–August 1987): 66.

21 Robert A. Burgelman, 'Intra-organizational ecology of strategy making and organizational adaptation: theory and field research', *Organization Science*, 2 (1991): 239–262. On this, see also Quinn, 'Managing Strategies Incrementally', 36: 'The processes used to generate major strategies are typically fragmentary and evolutionary with a high degree of intuitive content. Although one usually finds in these fragments some very refined pieces of formal analysis, overall strategies emerge as a series of conscious internal decisions blend and interact [*sic*] with changing external events to slowly mutate key managers' broad consensus about what patterns of action make sense for the future.'

22 See Ghemawat, *Commitment*.

23 See Amar Bhide, 'Hustle as strategy', *Harvard Business Review*, 64 (September–October 1986): 59–65.

24 To make this point about strategy as a concept is to stay close to Wittgenstein's later ideas about language games and the very concept of language itself. For example, in the *Philosophical Investigations*, Wittgenstein poses the example of the concept of 'games' and shows that the great variety of different kinds of games cannot be subsumed under a single, definable concept of what a game is. The concept is simply defined by practice – by

the variety of different situations in which people use the word *game* to describe what they are doing. See section 66 in Wittgenstein, *Philosophical Investigations*. See also the discussion in Stanley Cavell's essay, 'The availability of Wittgenstein's later philosophy', in Stanley Cavell, ed., *Must We Mean What We Say?* (New York: Cambridge University Press, 1976), 44–72. According to Cavell: 'There is no one set of characteristics ... which everything we call "games" shares.... Language has no essence' (Cavell, 50). Our argument here has certain parallels to what management theorist Louis Pondy has already argued about the nature of 'leadership' as a concept – namely, that it is best seen as a language game that covers a 'pastiche' of different practices rather than a single essence. See Pondy, 'Leadership Is a Language Game'.

25 Elizabeth Olmstead Teisberg, 'Strategic Responses to Uncertainty' (Harvard Business School Working Paper, 1990).

26 Quinn, 'Managing Strategies Incrementally', 40.

27 Per-Henrik Mansson, 'Volnay's veteran vintner,' *The Wine Spectator* (January 31, 1992), 30.

28 For a discussion of corporate identity, see Walter P. Marguiles, 'Make the Most of Your Corporate Identity,' *Harvard Business Review*, 55 (July–August 1977):66–74 Also see Wally Olins, *Corporate Identity: making business strategy visible through design* (Boston: Harvard Business School, 1990).

29 Mats Alvesson, 'Organization: from substance to image?', *Organization Studies*, 11 (1990): 373–394.

30 There are numerous ways in which companies are compared with each other that shape their reputations. An explicit attempt to judge the relative reputations of firms is to be found in *Fortune* magazine's annual Corporate Reputations survey which in 1990 covered 305 companies in 32 industry groups and ranked them in terms of reputations along the dimensions of management, quality, innovation, investment value, financial soundness, people development, social responsibility, and use of assets. For more, see Sarah Smith, 'America's most admired corporations,' *Fortune* (January 29, 1990):58-92.

31 The story of Roddick's store is told in Anita Roddick, Body and Soul: profits with principles, the amazing success story of Anita Roddick and the Body Shop (New York: Crown, 1991).

CHAPTER 4

WHAT IS STRATEGY?

MICHAEL E. PORTER

Michael E. Porter is the C. Roland Christensen Professor of Business Administration at the Harvard Business School in Boston, Massachusetts.

OPERATIONAL EFFECTIVENESS IS NOT STRATEGY

For almost two decades, managers have been learning to play by a new set of rules. Companies must be flexible to respond rapidly to competitive and market changes. They must benchmark continuously to achieve best practice. They must outsource aggressively to gain efficiencies. And they must nurture a few core competencies in the race to stay ahead of rivals.

Positioning – once the heart of strategy – is rejected as too static for today's dynamic markets and changing technologies. According to the new dogma, rivals can quickly copy any market position, and competitive advantage is, at best, temporary.

But those beliefs are dangerous half-truths, and they are leading more and more companies down the path of mutually destructive competition. True, some barriers to competition are falling as regulation eases and markets become global. True, companies have properly invested energy in becoming leaner and more nimble. In many industries, however, what some call *hypercompetition* is a self-inflicted wound, not the inevitable outcome of a changing paradigm of competition.

The root of the problem is the failure to distinguish between operational effectiveness and strategy. The quest for productivity, quality and speed has spawned a remarkable number of management tools and techniques: total quality management, benchmarking, time-based competition, outsourcing, partnering, reengineering, change management. Although the resulting operational improvements have often been dramatic, many companies have been frustrated by their inability to translate those gains into sustainable profitability. And bit by bit, almost imperceptibly, management tools have taken the place of strategy. As managers push to improve on all fronts, they move further away from viable competitive positions.

Operational effectiveness: necessary but not sufficient

Operational effectiveness and strategy are both essential to superior performance, which, after all, is the primary goal of any enterprise. But they work in very different ways.

A company can outperform rivals only if it can establish a difference that it can preserve. It must deliver greater value to customers or create comparable value at a lower cost, or do both. The arithmetic of superior profitability then follows: delivering greater value allows a company to charge higher average unit prices; greater efficiency results in lower average unit costs.

Ultimately, all differences between companies in cost or price derive from the hundreds of activities required to create, produce, sell, and deliver their products or services, such as calling on customers, assembling final products, and training employees. Cost is generated by performing activities, and cost advantage arises from performing particular activities more efficiently than competitors. Similarly, differentiation arises from both the choice of activities and how they are performed. Activities, then, are the basic units of competitive advantage. Overall advantage or disadvantage results from all a company's activities, not only a few.[1]

Operational effectiveness (OE) means performing similar activities *better* than rivals perform them. Operational effectiveness includes but is not limited to efficiency. It refers to any number of practices that allow a company to better utilize its inputs by, for example, reducing defects in products or developing better products faster. In contrast, strategic positioning means performing *different* activities from rivals' or performing similar activities in *different ways*.

Differences in operational effectiveness among companies are pervasive. Some companies are able to get more out of their inputs than others because they eliminate wasted effort, employ more advanced technology, motivate employees better, or have greater insight into managing particular activities or sets of activities. Such differences in operational effectiveness are an important source of differences in profitability among competitors because they directly affect relative cost positions and levels of differentiation.

Differences in operational effectiveness were at the heart of the Japanese challenge to Western companies in the 1980s. The Japanese were so far ahead of rivals in operational effectiveness that they could offer lower cost and superior quality at the same time. It is worth dwelling on this point, because so much recent thinking about competition depends on it. Imagine for a moment a *productivity frontier* that constitutes the sum of all existing best practices at any given time. Think of it as the maximum value that a company delivering a particular product or service can create at a given cost, using the best available technologies, skills, management techniques and purchased inputs. The productivity frontier can apply to individual activities, to groups of linked activities such as order processing and manufacturing, and to an entire company's activities. When a company improves its operational effectiveness, it moves towards the frontier. Doing so may require capital investment, different personnel, or simply new ways of managing.

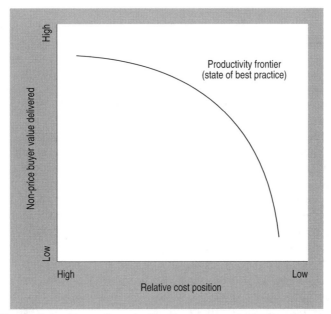

Figure 4.1 Operational effectiveness v. strategic planning

The productivity frontier is constantly shifting outward as new technologies and management approaches are developed and as new inputs become available. Laptop computers, mobile communications, the Internet, and software such as Lotus Notes, for example, have redefined the productivity frontier for sales-force operations and created rich possibilities for linking sales with such activities as order processing and after-sales support. Similarly, lean production, which involves a family of activities, has allowed substantial improvements in manufacturing productivity and asset utilization.

For at least the past decade, managers have been preoccupied with improving operational effectiveness. Through programmes such as TQM, time-based competition, and benchmarking, they have changed how they perform activities in order to eliminate inefficiencies, improve customer satisfaction and achieve best practice. Hoping to keep up with shifts in the productivity frontier, managers have embraced continuous improvement, empowerment, change management, and the so-called learning organization. The popularity of outsourcing and the virtual corporation reflect the growing recognition that it is difficult to perform all activities as productively as specialists.

As companies move to the frontier, they can often improve on multiple dimensions of performance at the same time. For example, manufacturers that adopted the Japanese practice of rapid changeovers in the 1980s were able to lower cost and improve differentiation simultaneously. What were once believed to be real trade-offs between defects and costs, for example turned out to be illusions created by poor operational effectiveness. Managers have learned to reject such false trade-offs.

Constant improvement in operational effectiveness is necessary to achieve superior profitability. However, it is not usually sufficient. Few companies have competed successfully on the basis of operational effectiveness over an extended period, and staying ahead of rivals gets harder every day. The most obvious reason for that is the rapid diffusion of best practices. Competitors can quickly imitate management techniques, new technologies, input improvements, and superior ways of meeting customers' needs. The most generic solutions – those that can be used in multiple settings – diffuse the fastest. Witness the proliferation of OE techniques accelerated by support from consultants.

OE competition shifts the productivity frontier outward, effectively raising the bar for everyone. But although such competition produces absolute improvement in operational effectiveness, it leads to relative improvement for no one. Consider the $5 billion-plus US commercial printing industry. The major players – R.R. Donnelley & Sons Company, Quebecor, World Color Press, and Big Flower Press – are competing head to head, serving all types of customers, offering the same array of printing technologies (gravure and web offset), investing heavily in the same new equipment, running their presses faster, and reducing crew sizes. But the resulting major productivity gains are being captured by customers and equipment suppliers, not retained in superior profitability. Even industry leader Donnelley's profit margin, consistently higher than 7% in the 1980s, fell to less than 4.6% in 1995. This pattern is playing itself out in industry after industry. Even the Japanese, pioneers of the new competition, suffer from persistently low profits. (See the insert 'Japanese Companies Rarely Have Strategies.')

Japanese companies rarely have strategies

The Japanese triggered a global revolution in operational effectiveness in the 1970s and 1980s' pioneering practices such as total quality management and continuous improvement. As a result, Japanese manufacturers enjoyed substantial cost and quality advantages for many years.

But Japanese companies rarely developed distinct strategic positions of the kind discussed in this article. Those that did – Son, Canon and Sega, for example – were the exception rather than the rule. Most Japanese companies imitate and emulate one another. All rivals offer most if not all product varieties, features and services; they employ all channels and match one another's plant configurations.

The dangers of Japanese style competition are now becoming easier to recognize. In the 1980s, with rivals operating far from the productivity frontier, it seemed possible to win on both cost and quality indefinitely. Japanese companies were all able to grow in an expanding domestic economy and by penetrating global markets. They appeared unstoppable. But as the gap in operational effectiveness narrows, Japanese companies are increasingly caught in a trap of their own making. If they are to escape the mutually destructive battles now ravaging their performance, Japanese companies will have to learn strategy.

To do so they may have to overcome strong cultural barriers. Japan is notoriously consensus oriented, and companies have a strong tendency to mediate differences among individuals rather than accentuate them. Strategy, on the other hand, requires hard choices. The Japanese also have a deeply ingrained service tradition that predisposes them to go to great lengths to satisfy any need a customer expresses. Companies that compete in that way end up blurring their distinct positioning, becoming all things to all customers.

(This discussion of Japan is drawn from the author's research with Hirotaka Takeuchi, with help from Mariko Sakakibara.)

The second reason that improved operational effectiveness is insufficient – competitive convergence – is more subtle and insidious. The more benchmarking companies do, the more they look alike. The more that rivals outsource activities to efficient third parties, often the same ones, the more generic those activities become. As rivals imitate one another's improvements in quality, cycle times, or supplier partnerships, strategies converge and competition becomes a series of races down identical paths that no one can win. Competition based on operational effectiveness alone is mutually destructive, leading to wars of attrition that can be arrested only by limiting competition.

The recent wave of industry consolidation through mergers makes sense in the context of OE competition. Driven by performance pressures but lacking strategic vision, company after company has had no better idea than to buy up its rivals. The competitors left standing are often those that outlasted others, not companies with real advantage.

After a decade of impressive gains in operational effectiveness, many companies are facing diminishing returns. Continuous improvement has been etched on managers' brains. But its tools unwittingly draw companies toward imitation and homogeneity. Gradually, managers have let operational effectiveness supplant strategy. The result is zero-sum competition, static or declining prices, and pressures on costs that compromise companies' ability to invest in the business for the long term.

STRATEGY RESTS ON UNIQUE ACTIVITIES

Competitive strategy is about being different. It means deliberately choosing a different set of activities to deliver a unique mix of value.

Southwest Airlines Company, for example, offers short-haul, low-cost, point-to-point service between midsize cities and secondary airports in large cities. Southwest avoids large airports and does not fly great distances. Its customers include business travellers, families and students. Southwest's frequent departures and low fares attract price-sensitive customers who otherwise would travel by bus or car, and convenience-oriented travellers who would choose a full-service airline on other routes.

Most managers describe strategic positioning in terms of their customers: 'Southwest Airlines serves price- and convenience-sensitive travellers', for example. But the essence of strategy is in the activities – choosing to perform activities differently or to perform different activities than rivals. Otherwise, a strategy is nothing more than a marketing slogan that will not withstand competition.

A full-service airline is configured to get passengers from almost any point A to any point B. To reach a large number of destinations and serve passengers with connecting flights, full-service airlines employ a hub-and-spoke system centred on major airports. To attract passengers who desire more comfort, they offer first-class or business-class service. To accommodate passengers who must change planes, they co-ordinate schedules and check and transfer baggage. Because some passengers will be travelling for many hours, full-service airlines serve meals.

Southwest, in contrast, tailors all its activities to deliver low-cost, convenient service on its particular type of route. Through fast turnarounds at the gate of only 15 minutes, Southwest is able to keep planes flying longer hours than rivals and provide frequent departures with fewer aircraft. Southwest does not offer meals, assigned seats, interline baggage checking, or premium classes of service. Automated ticketing at the gate encourages customers to bypass travel agents, allowing Southwest to avoid their commissions. A standardized fleet of 737 aircraft boosts the efficiency of maintenance.

Southwest has staked out a unique and valuable strategic position based on a tailored set of activities. On the routes served by Southwest, a full-service airline could never be as convenient or as low cost.

Ikea, the global furniture retailer based in Sweden, also has a clear strategic positioning. Ikea targets young furniture buyers who want style at low cost. What turns this marketing concept into a strategic positioning is the tailored set of activities that make it work. Like Southwest, Ikea has chosen to perform activities differently from its rivals.

Consider the typical furniture store. Showrooms display samples of the merchandise. One area might contain 25 sofas; another will display five dining tables. But those items represent only a fraction of the choices available to customers. Dozens of books displaying fabric swatches or wood samples or alternative styles offer customers thousands of product varieties to choose from. Salespeople often escort customers through the store, answering questions and helping them navigate this maze of choices. Once a customer makes a selection, the order is relayed to a third-party manufacturer. With luck, the furniture will be delivered to the customer's home within six to eight weeks. This is a value chain that maximizes customization and service but does so at high cost.

In contrast, Ikea serves customers who are happy to trade off service for cost. Instead of having a sales associate trail customers around the store, Ikea uses a self-service model based on clear, instore displays. Rather than rely solely on third-party manufacturers, Ikea designs its own low-cost, modular, ready-to-assemble furniture to fit its positioning. In huge stores, Ikea displays every product it sells in roomlike settings, so customers don't need a decorator to help them imagine how to put the pieces together. Adjacent to the furnished showrooms is a warehouse section with the products in boxes on pallets. Customers are expected to do their own pickup and delivery, and Ikea will even sell you a roof rack for your car that you can return for a refund on your next visit.

Although much of its low-cost position comes from having customers 'do it themselves', Ikea offers a number of extra services that its competitors do not. Instore child care is one. Extended hours are another. Those services are uniquely aligned with the needs of its customers, who are young, not wealthy, likely to have children (but no nanny), and, because they work for a living, have a need to shop at odd hours.

The origins of strategic positions

Strategic positions emerge from three distinct sources, which are not mutually exclusive and often overlap. First, positioning can be based on producing a subset of an industry's products or services. I call this *variety-based positioning* because it is based on the choice of product or service varieties rather than customer segments. Variety-based positioning makes economic sense when a company can best produce particular products or services using distinctive sets of activities.

Jiffy Lube International, for instance, specializes in automotive lubricants and does not offer other car repair or maintenance services. Its value chain produces faster service at a lower cost than broader line repair shops, a combination so attractive that many customers subdivide their purchases, buying oil changes from the focused competitor, Jiffy Lube, and going to rivals for other services.

The Vanguard Group, a leader in the mutual fund industry, is another example of variety-based positioning. Vanguard provides an array of common stock, bond and money market funds that offer predictable performance and rock-bottom expenses. The company's investment approach deliberately sacrifices the possibility of extraordinary performance in any one year for good relative performance in every year. Vanguard is known, for example, for its index funds. It avoids making bets on interest rates and steers clear of narrow stock groups. Fund managers keep trading levels low, which holds expenses down; in addition, the company discourages customers from rapid buying and selling because doing so drives up costs and can force a fund manager to trade in order to deploy new capital and raise cash for redemptions. Vanguard also takes a consistent low-cost approach to managing distribution, customer service and marketing. Many investors include one or more Vanguard funds in their portfolio, while buying aggressively managed or specialized funds from competitors.

The people who use Vanguard or Jiffy Lube are responding to a superior value chain for a particular type of service. A variety-based positioning can serve a wide array of customers, but for most it will meet only a subset of their needs.

A second basis for positioning is that of serving most or all the needs of a particular group of customers. I call this *needs-based positioning,* which comes closer to traditional thinking about targeting a segment of customers. It arises

Finding new positions: the entrepreneurial edge

Strategic competition can be thought of as the process of perceiving new positions that woo customers from established positions or draw new customers into the market. For example, superstores offering depth of merchandise in a single product category take market share from broad-line department stores offering a more limited selection in many categories. Mail-order catalogues pick off customers who crave convenience. In principle, incumbents and entrepreneurs face the same challenges in finding new strategic positions. In practice, new entrants often have the edge.

Strategic positionings are often not obvious, and finding them requires creativity and insight. New entrants often discover unique positions that have been available but simply overlooked by established competitors. Ikea, for example, recognized a customer group that had been ignored or served poorly. Circuit City Stores' entry into used cars, CarMax, is based on a new way of performing activities – extensive refurbishing of cars, product guarantees, no-haggle pricing, sophisticated use of in-house customer financing – that has long been open to incumbents.

New entrants can prosper by occupying a position that a competitor once held but has ceded through years of imitation and straddling. And entrants coming from other industries can create new positions because of distinctive activities drawn from their other businesses. CarMax borrows heavily from Circuit City's expertise in inventory management, credit and other activities in consumer electronics retailing.

Most commonly, however, new positions open up because of change. New customer groups or purchase occasions arise; new needs emergs as societies evolve; new distribution channels appear; new technologies are developed; new machinery or information systems become available. When such changes happen, new entrants, unencumbered by a long history in the industry, can often more easily perceive the potential for a new way of competing. Unlike incumbents, newcomers can be more flexible because they face no trade-offs with their existing activities.

when there are groups of customers with differing needs, and when a tailored set of activities can serve those needs best. Some groups of customers are more price sensitive than others, demand different product features, and need varying amounts of information, support and services. Ikea's customers are a good example of such a group. Ikea seeks to meet all the home furnishing needs of its target customers, not just a subset of them.

A variant of needs-based positioning arises when the same customer has different needs on different occasions or for different types of transactions. The same person, for example, may have different needs when travelling on business than when travelling for pleasure with the family. Buyers of cans – beverage companies, for example – will likely have different needs from their primary supplier than from their secondary source.

It is intuitive for most managers to conceive of their business in terms of the customers' needs they are meeting. But a critical element of needs-based positioning is not at all intuitive and is often overlooked. Differences in needs will not translate into meaningful positions unless the best set of activities to satisfy them *also* differs. If that were not the case, every competitor could meet those same needs, and there would be nothing unique or valuable about the positioning.

In private banking, for example, Bessemer Trust Company targets families with a minimum of $5 million in investable assets who want capital preservation combined with wealth accumulation. By assigning one sophisticated account officer for every 14 families, Bessemer has configured its activities for personalized service. Meetings, for example, are more likely to be held at a client's ranch or yacht than in the office. Bessemer offers a wide array of customized services, including investment management and estate administration, oversight of oil and gas investments, and accounting for racehorses and aircraft. Loans, a staple of most private banks, are rarely needed by Bessemer's clients and make up a tiny fraction of its client balances and income. Despite the most generous compensation of account officers and the highest personnel cost as a percentage of operating expenses, Bessemer's differentiation with its target families produces a return on equity estimated to be the highest of any private banking competitor.

Citibank's private bank, on the other hand, serves clients with minimum assets of about $250,000 who, in contrast to Bessemer's clients, want convenient access to loans from jumbo mortgages to deal financing. Citibank's account managers are primarily lenders. When clients need other services, their account manager refers them to other Citibank specialists, each of whom handles pre-packaged products. Citibank's system is less customized than Bessemer's and allows it to have a lower manager to client ratio of 1:125. Biannual office meetings are offered only for the largest clients. Both Bessemer and Citibank have tailored their activities to meet the needs of a different group of private banking customers. The same value chain cannot profitably meet the needs of both groups.

The third basis for positioning is that of segmenting customers who are accessible in different ways. Although their needs are similar to those of other customers, the best configuration of activities to reach them is different. I call this *access-based positioning*. Access can be a function of customer geography or customer scale, or of anything that requires a different set of activities to reach customers in the best way.

Segmenting by access is less common and less well understood than the other two bases. Carmike Cinemas, for example, operates movie theatres exclusively in cities and towns with populations under 200,000. How does Carmike make money in markets that are not only small but also won't support big-city ticket prices? It does so through a set of activities that result in a lean cost structure. Carmike's small-town customers can be served through standardized, low-cost theatre complexes requiring fewer screens and less sophisticated projection technology than big-city theatres. The company's proprietary information system and management process eliminate the need for local administrative staff beyond a single theatre manager. Carmike also reaps advantages from centralized purchasing, lower rent and payroll costs (because of its locations), and rock-bottom corporate overhead of 2% (the industry average is 5%). Operating in small communities also allows Carmike to practice a highly personal form of marketing in which the theatre manager knows patrons and promotes attendance through personal contacts. By being the dominant if not the only theatre in its markets – the main competition is often the high school football team – Carmike is also able to get its pick of films and negotiate better terms with distributors.

Rural versus urban-based customers are one example of access driving differences in activities. Serving small rather than large customers or densely rather than sparsely situated customers are other examples in which the best way to configure marketing, order processing, logistics, and after-sale service activities to meet the similar needs of distinct groups will often differ.

Positioning is not only about carving out a niche. A position emerging from any of the sources can be broad or narrow. A focused competitor, such as Ikea, targets the special needs of a subset of customers and designs its activities accordingly. Focused competitors thrive on groups of customers who are overserved (and hence overpriced) by more broadly targeted competitors, or underserved (and hence underpriced). A broadly targeted competitor – for example, Vanguard or Delta Air Lines – serves a wide array of customers, performing a set of activities designed to meet their common needs. It ignores or meets only partially the more idiosyncratic needs of particular customer groups.

The connection with generic strategies

In *Competitive Strategy* (The Free Press, 1985), I introduced the concept of generic strategies – cost leadership, differentiation, and focus – to represent the alternative strategic positions in an industry. The generic strategies remain useful to characterize strategic positions at the simplest and broadest level. Vanguard, for instance, is an example of a cost leadership strategy, whereas Ikea, with its narrow customer group, is an example of cost-based focus. Neutrogena is a focused differentiator. The bases for positioning – varieties, needs, and access – carry the understanding of those generic strategies to a greater level of specificity. Ikea and Southwest are both cost-based focusers, for example, but Ikea's focus is based on the needs of a customer group, and Southwest's is based on offering a particular service variety.

The generic strategies framework introduced the need to choose in order to avoid becoming caught between what I then described as the inherent contradictions of different strategies. Trade-offs between the activities of incompatible positions explain those contradictions. Witness Continental Lite, which tried and failed to compete in two ways at once.

Whatever the basis – variety, needs, access, or some combination of the three – positioning requires a tailored set of activities because it is always a function of differences on the supply side; that is, of differences in activities. However, positioning is not always a function of differences on the demand, or customer, side. Variety and access positioning, in particular, do not rely on *any* customer differences. In practice, however, variety or access differences often accompany needs differences. The tastes that is, the needs of Carmike's small-town customers, for instance, run more towards comedies, Westerns, action films and family entertainment. Carmike does not run any films rated NC-17.

Having defined positioning, we can now begin to answer the question, 'What is strategy?' Strategy is the creation of a unique and valuable position, involving a different set of activities. If there were only one ideal position, there would be no need for strategy. Companies would face a simple imperative win the race to discover and pre-empt it. The essence of strategic positioning is to choose activities that are different from rivals'. If the same set of activities were best to produce all varieties, meet all needs, and access all customers, companies could easily shift among them and operational effectiveness would determine performance.

A SUSTAINABLE STRATEGIC POSITION REQUIRES TRADE-OFFS

Choosing a unique position, however, is not enough to guarantee a sustainable advantage. A valuable position will attract imitation by incumbents, who are likely to copy it in one of two ways.

First, a competitor can reposition itself to match the superior performer. J.C. Penney, for instance, has been repositioning itself from a Sears clone to a more upscale, fashion-oriented, soft-goods retailer. A second and far more common type of imitation is straddling. The straddler seeks to match the benefits of a successful position while maintaining its existing position. It grafts new features, services, or technologies onto the activities it already performs.

For those who argue that competitors can copy any market position, the airline industry is a perfect test case. It would seem that nearly any competitor could imitate any other airline's activities. Any airline can buy the same planes, lease the gates, and match the menus and ticketing and baggage handling services offered by other airlines.

Continental Airlines saw how well Southwest was doing and decided to straddle. While maintaining its position as a full-service airline, Continental also set out to match Southwest on a number of point-to-point routes. The airline dubbed the new service Continental Lite. It eliminated meals and first-class service, increased departure frequency, lowered fares, and shortened turnaround time at the gate. Because Continental remained a full-service airline on other routes, it continued to use travel agents and its mixed fleet of planes and to provide baggage checking and seat assignments.

But a strategic position is not sustainable unless there are trade-offs with other positions. Trade-offs occur when activities are incompatible. Simply put, a trade-off means that more of one thing necessitates less of another. An airline can choose to serve meals adding cost and slowing turnaround time at the gate or it can choose not to, but it cannot do both without bearing major inefficiencies.

Trade-offs create the need for choice and protect against repositioners and straddlers. Consider Neutrogena soap. Neutrogena Corporation's variety-based positioning is built on a 'kind to the skin,' residue-free soap formulated for pH balance. With a large detail force calling on dermatologists, Neutrogena's marketing strategy looks more like a drug company's than a soap maker's. It advertises in medical journals, sends direct mail to doctors, attends medical conferences, and performs research at its own Skincare Institute. To reinforce its positioning, Neutrogena originally focused its distribution on drugstores and avoided price promotions. Neutrogena uses a slow, more expensive manufacturing process to mould its fragile soap.

In choosing this position, Neutrogena said no to the deodorants and skin softeners that many customers desire in their soap. It gave up the large volume potential of selling through supermarkets and using price promotions. It sacrificed manufacturing efficiencies to achieve the soap's desired attributes. In its original positioning, Neutrogena made a whole raft of trade-offs like those, trade-offs that protected the company from imitators.

Trade-offs arise for three reasons. The first is inconsistencies in image or reputation. A company known for delivering one kind of value may lack credibility and confuse customers – or even undermine its reputation – if it delivers another kind of value or attempts to deliver two inconsistent things at the same time. For example, Ivory soap, with its position as a basic, inexpensive everyday soap would have a hard time reshaping its image to match Neutrogena's premium 'medical' reputation. Efforts to create a new image typically cost tens or even hundreds of millions of dollars in a major industry – a powerful barrier to imitation.

Second, and more important, trade-offs arise from activities themselves. Different positions (with their tailored activities) require different product configurations, different equipment, different employee behaviour, different skills and different management systems. Many trade-offs reflect inflexibilities in machinery, people, or systems. The more Ikea has configured its activities to lower costs by having its customers do their own assembly and delivery, the less able it is to satisfy customers who require higher levels of service.

However, trade-offs can be even more basic. In general, value is destroyed if an activity is overdesigned or underdesigned for its use. For example, even if a given salesperson were capable of providing a high level of assistance to one customer and none to another, the salesperson's talent (and some of his or her cost) would be wasted on the second customer. Moreover, productivity can improve when variation of an activity is limited. By providing a high level of assistance all the time, the salesperson and the entire sales activity can often achieve efficiencies of learning and scale.

Finally, trade-offs arise from limits on internal co-ordination and control. By clearly choosing to compete in one way and not another, senior management makes organizational priorities clear. Companies that try to be all things to all customers, in contrast, risk confusion in the trenches as employees attempt to make day-to-day operating decisions without a clear framework.

Positioning trade-offs are pervasive in competition and essential to strategy. They create the need for choice and purposefully limit what a company offers. They deter straddling or repositioning, because competitors that engage in those approaches undermine their strategies and degrade the value of their existing activities.

Trade-offs ultimately grounded Continental Lite. The airline lost hundreds of millions of dollars, and the CEO lost his job. Its planes were delayed leaving congested hub cities or slowed at the gate by baggage transfers. Late flights and cancellations generated a thousand complaints a day. Continental Lite could not afford to compete on price and still pay standard travel agent commissions, but neither could it do without agents for its full-service business. The airline compromised by cutting commissions for all Continental flights across the board. Similarly, it could not afford to offer the same frequent-flier benefits to travellers paying the much lower ticket prices for Lite service. It compromised again by lowering the rewards of Continental's entire frequent-flier program. The results: angry travel agents and full-service customers.

Continental tried to compete in two ways at once. In trying to be low cost on some routes and full service on others, Continental paid an enormous straddling penalty. If there were no trade-offs between the two positions, Continental could have succeeded. But the absence of trade-offs is a dangerous half-truth that managers must unlearn. Quality is not always free. Southwest's convenience, one kind of high quality, happens to be consistent with low costs because its frequent departures are facilitated by a number of low-cost practices – fast gate turnarounds and automated ticketing, for example. However, other dimensions of airline quality – an assigned seat, a meal, or baggage transfer – require costs to provide.

In general, false trade-offs between cost and quality occur primarily when there is redundant or wasted effort, poor control or accuracy, or weak co-ordination. Simultaneous improvement of cost and differentiation is possible only when a company begins far behind the productivity frontier or when the frontier shifts outward. At the frontier, where companies have achieved current best practice, the trade-off between cost and differentiation is very real indeed.

After a decade of enjoying productivity advantages, Honda Motor Company and Toyota Motor Corporation recently bumped up against the frontier. In 1995, faced with increasing customer resistance to higher automobile prices, Honda found that the only way to produce a less expensive car was to skimp on features. In the United States, it replaced the rear disc brakes on the Civic with lower cost drum brakes and used cheaper fabric for the back seat, hoping customers would not notice. Toyota tried to sell a version of its best-selling Corolla in Japan with unpainted bumpers and cheaper seats. In Toyota's case, customers rebelled, and the company quickly dropped the new model.

For the past decade, as managers have improved operational effectiveness greatly, they have internalized the idea that eliminating trade-offs is a good thing. But if there are no trade-offs companies will never achieve a sustainable advantage. They will have to run faster and faster just to stay in place.

As we return to the question, What is strategy? we see that trade-offs add a new dimension to the answer. Strategy is making trade-offs in competing. The essence of strategy is choosing what *not* to do. Without trade-offs, there would be no need for choice and thus no need for strategy. Any good idea could and would be quickly imitated. Again, performance would once again depend wholly on operational effectiveness.

FIT DRIVES BOTH COMPETITIVE ADVANTAGE AND SUSTAINABILITY

Positioning choices determine not only which activities a company will perform and how it will configure individual activities but also how activities relate to one another. While operational effectiveness is about achieving excellence in individual activities, or functions, strategy is about *combining* activities.

Southwest's rapid gate turnaround, which allows frequent departures and greater use of aircraft, is essential to its high-convenience, low-cost positioning. But how does Southwest achieve it? Part of the answer lies in the company's well-paid gate and ground crews, whose productivity in turnarounds is enhanced by flexible union rules. But the bigger part of the answer lies in how Southwest performs other activities. With no meals, no seat assignment, and no interline baggage transfers, Southwest avoids having to perform activities that slow down other airlines. It selects airports and routes to avoid congestion that introduces delays. Southwest's strict limits on the type and length of routes make standardized aircraft possible: every aircraft Southwest turns is a Boeing 737.

What is Southwest's core competence? Its key success factors? The correct answer is that everything matters. Southwest's strategy involves a whole system of activities, not a collection of parts. Its competitive advantage comes from the way its activities fit and reinforce one another.

Fit locks out imitators by creating a chain that is as strong as its *strongest* link. As in most companies with good strategies, Southwest's activities complement one another in ways that create real economic value. One activity's cost, for example, is lowered because of the way other activities are performed. Similarly, one activity's value to customers can be enhanced by a company's other activities. That is the way strategic fit creates competitive advantage and superior profitability.

Types of fit

The importance of fit among functional policies is one of the oldest ideas in strategy. Gradually, however, it has been supplanted on the manage merit agenda. Rather than seeing the company as a whole, managers have turned to 'core' competencies, 'critical' resources, and 'key' success factors. In fact, fit is a far more central component of competitive advantage than most realise.

Fit is important because discrete activities often affect one another. A sophisticated sales force, for example, confers a greater advantage when the company's product embodies premium technology and its marketing approach emphasizes customer assistance and support. A production line with high levels of model variety is more valuable when combined with an inventory and order processing system that minimizes the need for stocking finished goods, a sales process equipped to explain and encourage customization, and an advertising theme that stresses the benefits of product variations that meet a customer's special needs. Such complementarities are pervasive in strategy. Although some fit among activities is generic and applies to many companies, the most valuable fit is strategy-specific because it enhances a position's uniqueness and amplifies trade-offs.[2]

There are three types of fit, although they are not mutually exclusive. First-order fit is *simple consistency* between each activity (function) and the overall strategy. Vanguard, for example, aligns all activities with its low-cost strategy. It minimizes portfolio turnover and does not need highly compensated money managers. The company distributes its funds directly, avoiding commissions to brokers. It also limits advertising, relying instead on public relations and word-of-mouth recommendations. Vanguard ties its employees' bonuses to cost savings.

Consistency ensures that the competitive advantages of activities cumulate and do not erode or cancel themselves out. It makes the strategy easier to communicate to customers, employees, and shareholders, and improves implementation through single-mindedness in the corporation.

Second-order fit occurs when *activities are reinforcing*. Neutrogena, for example, markets to upscale hotels eager to offer their guests a soap recommended by dermatologists. Hotels grant Neutrogena the privilege of using its customary packaging while requiring other soaps to feature the hotel's name. Once guests have tried Neutrogena in a luxury hotel, they are more likely to purchase it at the drugstore or ask their doctor about it. Thus Neutrogena's medical and hotel marketing activities reinforce one another, lowering total marketing costs.

In another example, Bic Corporation sells a narrow line of standard, low-priced pens to virtually all major customer markets (retail, commercial, promotional, and give-away) through virtually all available channels. As with any variety-based positioning serving a broad group of customers, Bic emphasizes a common need (low price for an acceptable pen) and uses marketing approaches with a broad reach (a large sales force and heavy television advertising). Bic gains the benefits of consistency across nearly all activities, including product design that emphasizes ease of manufacturing, plants configured for low cost, aggressive purchasing to minimize material costs, and in-house parts production whenever the economics dictate

Yet Bic goes beyond simple consistency because its activities are reinforcing. For example, the company uses point-of-sale displays and frequent packaging changes to stimulate impulse buying. To handle point-of-sale tasks, a company needs a large sales force. Bic's is the largest in its industry, and it handles point-of-sale activities better than its rivals do. Moreover, the combination of point-of-sale activity, heavy television advertising, and packaging changes yields far more impulse buying than any activity in isolation could.

Third-order fit goes beyond activity reinforcement to what I call *optimization of effort*. The Gap, a retailer of casual clothes, considers product availability in its stores a critical element of its strategy. The Gap could keep products either by holding store inventory or by restocking from warehouses. The Gap has optimized its effort across these activities by restocking its selection of basic clothing almost daily out of three warehouses, thereby minimizing the need to carry large instore inventories. The emphasis is on restocking because the Gap's merchandising strategy sticks to basic items in relatively few colours. While comparable retailers achieve turns of three to four times per year, the Gap turns its inventory seven and a half times per year. Rapid restocking, moreover, reduces the cost of implementing the Gap's short model cycle, which is six to eight weeks long.[3]

Co-ordination and information exchange across activities to eliminate redundancy and minimize wasted effort are the most basic types of effort optimization. But there are higher levels as well. Product design choices, for example, can eliminate the need for after-sale service or make it possible for customers to perform service activities themselves. Similarly, co-ordination with suppliers or distribution channels can eliminate the need for some in-house activities, such as end-user training.

In all three types of fit, the whole matters more than any individual part. Competitive advantage grows out of the *entire system* of activities. The fit among activities substantially reduces cost or increases differentiation. Beyond that, the competitive value of individual activities or the associated skills, competencies, or resources cannot be decoupled from the system or the strategy. Thus in competitive companies it can be misleading to explain success by specifying individual strengths, core competencies, or critical resources. The list of strengths cuts across many functions, and one strength blends into others. It is more useful to think in terms of themes that pervade many activities, such as low cost, a particular notion of customer service, or a particular conception of the value delivered. These themes are embodied in nests of tightly linked activities.

Fit and sustainability

Strategic fit among many activities is fundamental not only to competitive advantage but also to the sustainability of that advantage. It is harder for a rival to match an array of interlocked activities than it is merely to imitate a particular sales-force approach, match a process technology, or replicate a set of product features. Positions built on systems of activities are far more sustainable than those built on individual activities.

Consider this simple exercise. The probability that competitors can match any activity is often less than one. The probabilities then quickly compound to make matching the entire system highly unlikely ($0.9 \times 0.9 = 0.81$; $0.9 \times 0.9 \times 0.9 \times 0.9 = 0.66$, and so on). Existing companies that try to reposition or straddle will be forced to reconfigure many activities. And even new entrants, though they do not confront the trade-offs facing established rivals, still face formidable barriers to imitation.

The more a company's positioning rests on activity systems with second- and third-order fit, the more sustainable its advantage will be. Such systems, by their very nature, are usually difficult to untangle from outside the company and therefore hard to imitate. And even if rivals can identify the relevant

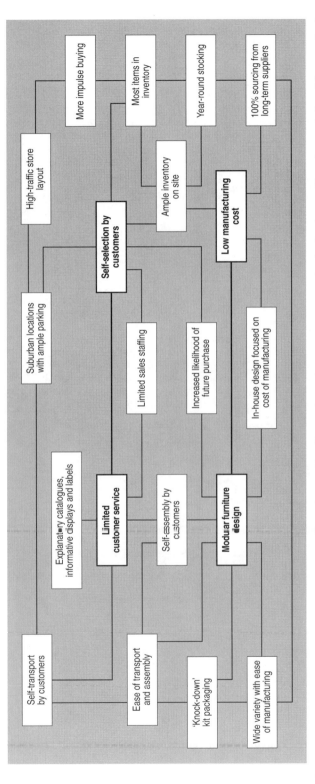

Figure 4.2 Activity-system maps, such as this one for Ikea, show how a company's strategic position is contained in a set of tailored activities designed to deliver it. In companies with a clear strategic position, a number of higher-order strategic themes (in darker tint) can be identified and implemented through clusters of tightly linked activities (in lighter tint).

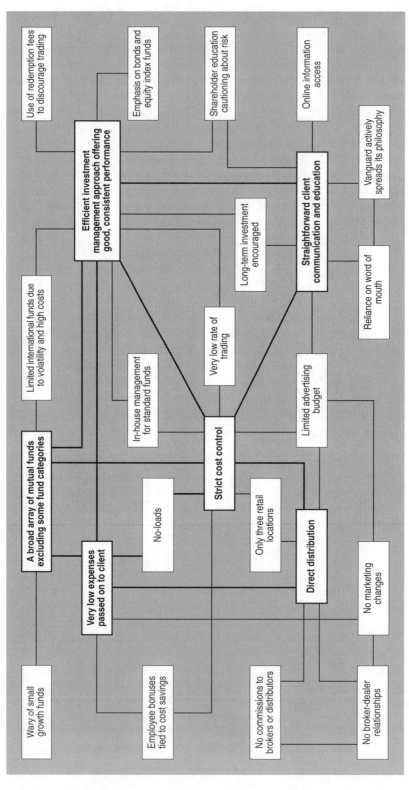

Figure 4.3 Activity system maps can be useful for examining and strengthening strategic fit. A set of basic questions. should guide the process. First, is each activity consistent with the overall positioning the varieties produced, the needs served, and the type of customers accessed? Ask those responsible for each activity to identify how other activities within the company improve or detract from their performance. Second, are there ways to strengthen how activities and groups of activities reinforce one another? Finally, could changes in one activity eliminate the need to perform others?

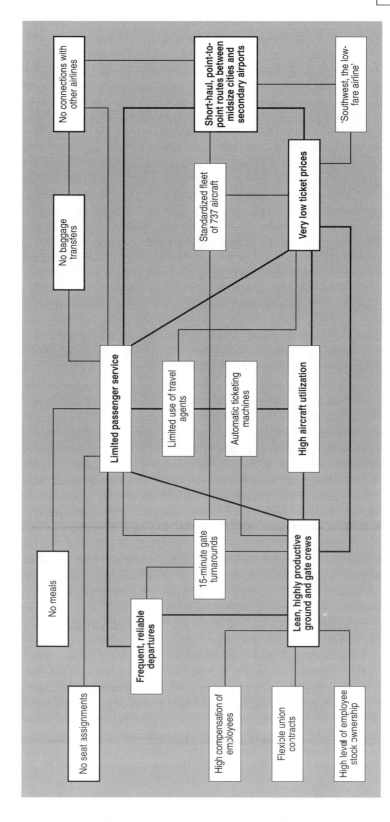

Figure 4.4 Southwest Airlines' activity system

interconnections, they will have difficulty replicating them. Achieving fit is difficult because it requires the integration of decisions and actions across many independent sub-units.

A competitor seeking to match an activity system gains little by imitating only some activities and not matching the whole. Performance does not improve; it can decline. Recall Continental Lite's disastrous attempt to imitate Southwest.

Finally, fit among a company's activities creates pressures and incentives to improve operational effectiveness, which makes imitation even harder. Fit means that poor performance in one activity will degrade the performance in others, so that weaknesses are exposed and more prone to get attention. Conversely, improvements in one activity will pay dividends in others. Companies with strong fit among their activities are rarely inviting targets. Their superiority in strategy and in execution only compounds their advantages and raises the hurdle for imitators.

When activities complement one another, rivals will get little benefit from imitation unless they successfully match the whole system. Such situations tend to promote winner-take-all competition. The company that builds the best activity system – Toys R Us, for instance – wins, while rivals with similar strategies – Child World and Lionel Leisure – fall behind. Thus finding a new strategic position is often preferable to being the second or third imitator of an occupied position.

The most viable positions are those whose activity systems are incompatible because of trade-offs. Strategic positioning sets the trade-off rules that define how individual activities will be configured and integrated. Seeing strategy in terms of activity systems only makes it clearer why organizational structure, systems and processes need to be strategy-specific. Tailoring organization to strategy, in turn, makes complementarities more achievable and contributes to sustainability.

One implication is that strategic positions should have a horizon of a decade or more, not of a single planning cycle. Continuity fosters improvements in individual activities and the fit across activities, allowing an organization to build unique capabilities and skills tailored to its strategy. Continuity also reinforces a company's identity.

Conversely, frequent shifts in positioning are costly. Not only must a company reconfigure individual activities, but it must also realign entire systems. Some activities may never catch up to the vacillating strategy. The inevitable result of frequent shifts in strategy, or of failure to choose a distinct position in the first place, is 'me-too' or hedged activity configurations, inconsistencies across functions, and organizational dissonance.

What is strategy? We can now complete the answer to this question. Strategy is creating fit among a company's activities. The success of a strategy depends on doing many things well – not just a few – and integrating among them. If there is no fit among activities, there is no distinctive strategy and little sustainability. Management reverts to the simpler task of overseeing independent functions, and operational effectiveness determines an organization's relative performance.

Alternative views of strategy	
The implicit strategy model of the past decade	Sustainable competitive advantage
One ideal competitive position in the market	Unique competitive position for the company
Benchmarking of all activities and achieving best practice	Activities tailored to strategy
Aggressive outsourcing and partnering to gain efficiencies	Clear trade-offs and choice vis-à-vis competitors
Advantages rest on a few key success factors, critical resources, core competencies	Competitive advantage arises from fit across activities
Flexibility and rapid responses to all competitive and market changes	Sustainability comes from activity system, not the parts
	Operational effectiveness a given

REDISCOVERING STRATEGY

The failure to choose

Why do so many companies fail to have a strategy? Why do managers avoid making strategic choices? Or, having made them in the past, why do managers so often let strategies decay and blur?

Commonly, the threats to strategy are seen to emanate from outside a company because of changes in technology or the behaviour of competitors. Although external changes can be the problem, the greater threat to strategy often comes from within. A sound strategy is undermined by a misguided view of competition, by organizational failures, and, especially, by the desire to grow.

Managers have become confused about the necessity of making choices. When many companies operate far from the productivity frontier, trade-offs appear unnecessary. It can seem that a well-run company should be able to beat its ineffective rivals on all dimensions simultaneously. Taught by popular management thinkers that they do not have to make trade-offs, managers have acquired a macho sense that to do so is a sign of weakness.

Unnerved by forecasts of hypercompetition, managers increase its likelihood by imitating everything about their competitors. Exhorted to think in terms 'of revolution, managers chase every new technology for its own sake.

The pursuit of operational effectiveness is seductive because it is concrete and actionable. Over the past decade, managers have been under increasing pressure to deliver tangible, measurable performance improvements. Programs in operational effectiveness produce reassuring progress, although superior profitability may remain elusive. Business publications and consultants flood the market with information about what other companies are doing, reinforcing the best-practice mentality. Caught up in the race for operational effectiveness, many managers simply do not understand the need to have a strategy.

Companies avoid or blur strategic choices for other reasons as well. Conventional wisdom within an industry is often strong, homogenizing competition. Some managers mistake 'customer focus' to mean they must serve all customer needs or respond to every request from distribution channels. Others cite the desire to preserve flexibility.

Organizational realities also work against strategy. Trade-offs are frightening, and making no choice is sometimes preferred to risking blame for a bad choice. Companies imitate one another in a type of herd behaviour, each assuming rivals know something they do not. Newly empowered employees, who are urged to seek every possible source of improvement, often lack a vision of the whole and the perspective to recognize trade-offs. The failure to choose sometimes comes down to the reluctance to disappoint valued managers or employees.

The growth trap

Among all other influences, the desire to grow has perhaps the most perverse effect on strategy. Trade-offs and limits appear to constrain growth. Serving one group of customers and excluding others, for instance, places a real or imagined limit on revenue growth. Broadly targeted strategies emphasizing low price result in lost sales with customers sensitive to features or service. Differentiators lose sales to price-sensitive customers.

Managers are constantly tempted to take incremental steps that surpass those limits but blur a company's strategic position. Eventually, pressures to grow or apparent saturation of the target market lead managers to broaden the position by extending product lines, adding new features, imitating competitors' popular services, matching processes, and even making acquisitions. For years, Maytag Corporation's success was based on its focus on reliable, durable washers and dryers, later extended to include dishwashers. However, conventional wisdom emerging within the industry supported the notion of selling a full line of products. Concerned with slow industry growth and competition from broad-line appliance makers, Maytag was pressured by dealers and encouraged by customers to extend its line. Maytag expanded into refrigerators and cooking products under the Maytag brand and acquired other brands – Jenn-Air, Hardwick Stove, Hoover, Admiral, and Magic Chef – with disparate positions. Maytag has grown substantially from $684 million in 1985 to a peak of $3.4 billion in 1994, but return on sales has declined from 8–12% in the 1970s and 1980s to an average of less than 1% between 1989 and 1995. Cost cutting will improve this performance, but laundry and dishwasher products still anchor Maytag's profitability.

Neutrogena may have fallen into the same trap. In the early 1990s, its US distribution broadened to include mass merchandisers such as Wal-Mart Stores.

Reconnecting with strategy

Most companies owe their initial success to a unique strategic position involving clear trade-offs. Activities once were aligned with that position. The passage of time and the pressures of growth, however, led to compromises that were, at first, almost imperceptible. Through a succession of incremental changes that each seemed sensible at the time, many established companies have compromised their way to homogeneity with their rivals.

The issue here is not with the companies whose historical position is no longer viable; their challenge is to start over, just as a new entrant would. At issue is a far more common phenomenon: the established company achieving mediocre returns and lacking a clear strategy. Through incremental additions of product varieties, incremental efforts to serve new customer groups, and emulation of rivals' activities, the existing company loses its clear competitive position. Typically, the company has matched many of its competitors' offerings and practices and attempts to sell to most customer groups.

A number of approaches can help a company reconnect with strategy. The first is a careful look at what it already does. Within most well-established companies is a core of uniqueness. It is identified by answering questions such as the following:

- Which of our product or service varieties are the most distinctive?
- Which of our product or service varieties are the most profitable?
- Which of our customers are the most satisfied?
- Which customers, channels or purchase occasions are the most profitable?
- Which of the activities in our value chain are the most different and effective?

Around this core of uniqueness are encrustations added incrementally over time. Like barnacles, they must be removed to reveal the underlying strategic positioning. A small percentage of varieties or customers may well account for most of a company's sales and especially its profits. The challenge, then, is to refocus on the unique core and realign the company's activities with it. Customers and product varieties at the periphery can be sold or allowed through inattention or price increases to fade away.

A company's history can also be instructive. What was the vision of the founder? What were the products and customers that made the company? Looking backwards, one can re-examine the original strategy to see if it is still valid. Can the historical positioning be implemented in a modern way, one consistent with today's technologies and practices? This sort of thinking may lead to a commitment to renew the strategy and may challenge the organization to recover its distinctiveness. Such a challenge can be galvanizing and can instil the confidence to make the needed trade-offs.

Under the Neutrogena name, the company expanded into a wide variety of products – eye make-up remover and shampoo, for example – in which it was not unique and which diluted its image, and it began turning to price promotions.

Compromises and inconsistencies in the pursuit of growth will erode the competitive advantage a company had with its original varieties or target customers. Attempts to compete in several ways at once create confusion and undermine organizational motivation and focus. Profits fall, but more revenue is seen as the answer. Managers are unable to make choices, so the company embarks on a new round of broadening and compromises. Often, rivals continue to match each other until desperation breaks the cycle, resulting in a merger or downsizing to the original positioning.

Profitable growth

Many companies, after a decade of restructuring and cost-cutting, are turning their attention to growth. Too often, efforts to grow blur uniqueness, create compromises, reduce fit, and ultimately undermine competitive advantage. In fact, the growth imperative is hazardous to strategy.

What approaches to growth preserve and reinforce strategy? Broadly, the prescription is to concentrate on deepening a strategic position rather than broadening and compromising it. One approach is to look for extensions of the strategy that leverage the existing activity system by offering features or services that rivals would find impossible or costly to match on a stand-alone basis. In other words, managers can ask themselves which activities, features or forms of competition are feasible or less costly to them because of complementary activities that their company performs.

Deepening a position involves making the company's activities more distinctive, strengthening fit, and communicating the strategy better to those customers who should value it. But many companies succumb to the temptation to chase 'easy' growth by adding hot features, products or services without screening them or adapting them to their strategy. Or they target new customers or markets in which the company has little special to offer. A company can often grow faster and far more profitably by better penetrating needs and varieties where it is distinctive than by slugging it out in potentially higher growth arenas in which the company lacks uniqueness. Carmike, now the largest theatre chain in the United States, owes its rapid growth to its disciplined concentration on small markets. The company quickly sells any big-city theatres that come to it as part of an acquisition.

Globalization often allows growth that is consistent with strategy, opening up larger markets for a focused strategy. Unlike broadening domestically, expanding globally is likely to leverage and reinforce a company's unique position and identity.

Companies seeking growth through broadening within their industry can best contain the risks to strategy by creating stand-alone units, each with its own brand name and tailored activities. Maytag has clearly struggled with this issue. On the one hand, it has organized its premium and value brands into separate units with different strategic positions. On the other, it has created an umbrella appliance company for all its brands to gain critical mass. With shared design, manufacturing, distribution, and customer service, it will be hard to avoid homogenization. If a given business unit attempts to compete with different positions for different products or customers, avoiding compromise is nearly impossible.

The role of leadership

The challenge of developing or re-establishing a clear strategy is often primarily an organizational one and depends on leadership. With so many forces at work against making choices and trade-offs in organizations, a clear intellectual framework to guide strategy is a necessary counterweight. Moreover, strong leaders willing to make choices are essential.

In many companies, leadership has degenerated into orchestrating operational improvements and making deals. But the leader's role is broader and far more important. General management is more than the stewardship of individual functions. Its core is strategy: defining and communicating the company's unique position, making trade-offs, and forging fit among activities. The leader must provide the discipline to decide which industry changes and customer needs the company will respond to, while avoiding organizational distractions and maintaining the company's distinctiveness. Managers at lower levels lack the perspective and the confidence to maintain a strategy. There will be constant pressures to compromise, relax trade-offs, and emulate rivals. One of the leader's jobs is to teach others in the organization about strategy – and to say no.

Strategy renders choices about what not to do as important as choices about what to do. Indeed, setting limits is another function of leadership. Deciding which target group of customers, varieties, and needs the company should serve is fundamental to developing a strategy. But so is deciding not to serve other customers or needs and not to offer certain features or services. Thus strategy requires constant discipline and clear communication. Indeed, one of the most important functions of an explicit, communicated strategy is to guide employees in making choices that arise because of trade-offs in their individual activities and in day-to-day decisions.

Improving operational effectiveness is a necessary part of management, but it is *not* strategy. In confusing the two, managers have unintentionally backed into a way of thinking about competition that is driving many industries toward competitive convergence, which is in no one's best interest and is not inevitable.

Managers must clearly distinguish operational effectiveness from strategy. Both are essential, but the two agendas are different.

The operational agenda involves continual improvement everywhere there are no trade-offs. Failure to do this creates vulnerability even for companies with a good strategy. The operational agenda is the proper place for constant change, flexibility, and relentless efforts to achieve best practice. In contrast, the strategic agenda is the right place for defining a unique position, making clear trade-offs,

Emerging industries and technologies

Developing a strategy in a newly emerging industry or in a business undergoing revolutionary technological changes is a daunting proposition. In such cases, managers face a high level of uncertainty about the needs of customers, the products and services that will prove to be the most desired, and the best configuration of activities and technologies to deliver them. Because of all this uncertainty, imitation and hedging are rampant: unable to risk being wrong or left behind, companies match all features, offer all new services, and explore all technologies.

During such periods in an industry's development, its basic productivity frontier is being established or re-established. Explosive growth can make such times profitable for many companies, but profits will be temporary because imitation and strategic convergence will ultimately destroy industry profitability. The companies that are enduringly successful will be those that begin as early as possible to define and embody in their activities a unique competitive position. A period of imitation may be inevitable in emerging industries, but that period reflects the level of uncertainty rather than a desired state of affairs.

In high-tech industries, this imitation phase often continues much longer than it should. Enraptured by technological change itself, companies pack more features – most of which are never used – into their products while slashing prices across the board. Rarely are trade-offs even considered. The drive for growth to satisfy market pressures leads companies into every product area. Although a few companies with fundamental advantages prosper, the majority are doomed to a rat race no one can win.

Ironically, the popular business press, focused on hot, emerging industries, is prone to presenting these special cases as proof that we have entered a new era of competition in which none of the old rules are valid. In fact the opposite is true.

and tightening fit. It involves the continual search for ways to reinforce and extend the company's position. The strategic agenda demands discipline and continuity; its enemies are distraction and compromise.

Strategic continuity does not imply a static view of competition. A company must continually improve its operational effectiveness and actively try to shift the productivity frontier; at the same time, there needs to be ongoing effort to extend its uniqueness while strengthening the fit among its activities. Strategic continuity, in fact, should make an organization's continual improvement more effective.

A company may have to change its strategy if there are major structural changes in its industry. In fact, new strategic positions often arise because of industry changes, and new entrants unencumbered by history often can exploit them more easily. However, a company's choice of a new position must be driven by the ability to find new trade-offs and leverage a new system of complementary activities into a sustainable advantage.

This article has benefited greatly from the assistance of many individuals and companies. The author gives special thanks to Jan Rivkin, the co-author of a related paper. Substantial research contributions have been made by Nicolaj Siggelkow, Dawn Sylvester and Lucia Marshall. Tarun Khanna, Roger Martin and Anita McGahan have provided especially extensive comments.

NOTES

1 I first described the concept of activities and its use in understanding competitive advantage in *Competitive Advantage* (New York: The Free Press, 1985). The ideas in this article build on and extend that thinking.

2 Paul Milgrom and John Roberts have begun to explore the economics of systems of complementary functions, activities and functions. Their focus is on the emergence of 'modern manufacturing' as a new set of complementary activities, on the tendency of companies to react to external changes with coherent bundles of internal responses, and on the need for central co-ordination – a strategy – to align functional managers. In the latter case, they model what has long been a bedrock principle of strategy. See Paul Milgrom and John Roberts, 'The economics of modern manufacturing: technology, strategy, and organization,' *American Economic Review* 80 (1990): 511–28; Paul Milgrom, Yingyi Qian and John Roberts, 'Complementarities, momentum, and evolution of modern manufacturing,' *American Economic Review* 81 (1991) 84–8; and Paul Milgrom and John Roberts, 'Complementarities and fit: strategy, structure, and organizational changes in manufacturing,' *Journal of Accounting and Economics,* vol. 19 (March–May 1995): 179–208.

3 Material on retail strategies is drawn in part from Jan Rivkin, 'the rise of retail category killers,' unpublished working paper, January 1995. Nicolaj Siggelkow prepared the case study on the Gap.

PART 2

THE ROLE OF INDUSTRY IN STRATEGY?

INTRODUCTION

The stance taken in Part 2 is that the quality of strategy and the effective harnessing of organizational resources outweigh industry context and industry characteristics as determinants of firm performance. In so far as context drives strategy and performance, the more significant contextual factors are cultural and regulatory. Industry context should not, and does not, determine the profitability of firms, nor does industry maturity preclude innovative strategy.

Part 1 emphasized the impact of idiosyncratic organizational styles and purposes on strategy. It ended with a strong restatement from Michael Porter of the 'positioning' school of strategy where differences in market positioning are seen as governing differences in profit potential. One of the early consequences of the positioning school was that much academic research and much managerial effort went into analyses of the relative 'attractiveness' of various industries. Since it is usually unrealistic (due to various combinations of entry, exit and mobility barriers) for firms to move easily out of one industry sector and into another, most firms make do with the sector they are in. Indeed, had they all attempted to move into attractive industries, certain sectors were likely to be overcrowded and profitability (and their attractiveness) affected.

Rumelt's research and data (Chapter 5) return to the question of the relative emphasis to be placed in strategy on the characteristics of the organization, or the characteristics of the industry: which has the more powerful impact on performance. He argues that 'long-term rates of return are not associated with industry, but with the unique endowments, positions and strategies of individual businesses'. The implications of Rumelt's findings are exciting. He shows that businesses differ from one another in their performance and profitability a great deal more than industries differ from one another. Industries are not homogeneous; they are heterogeneous. Performance is more homogeneous between industries than within industries. He thus provides evidence that managerial action greatly outweighs the importance of industry structure on long-term organizational returns. The quality of strategic thinking matters.

Baden-Fuller and Stopford (Chapter 6) follow and reinforce Rumelt's arguments regarding the importance of the quality of strategic thinking in firm performance. Their research specifically looked at the performance of firms located within 'mature' industries. They discovered groups of managers who believed 'that industry and environmental factors determine business performance' and who felt imprisoned by their environments, and others who did not. These latter believed and demonstrated that 'rejuvenation' is possible within the framework of a mature industry. Baden-Fuller and Stopford state as their central theme that 'managers need to take control of their destiny'. They do not see strategy as being about fit with the current environment, leaving the organization merely a passive actor. Like Hamel and Prahalad, they view strategy-making as dynamic. They argue that there are no mature industries, only passive, unimaginative managers, substituting worn-out industry recipes for genuine strategic thinking.

The remaining two chapters in Part 2 deal with the effect on strategic decision-making of the organization's cultural, institutional and regulatory contexts. Biggart and Hamilton take the Asian 'economic miracle' of the 1960s to the 1990s and review it in order to challenge assumptions about the social, cultural, business and economic structure of the Asian economies, and in particular to explore the differences between the Western and the Asian versions of capitalism and competition.

Markets and industries are the operational contexts for firms. All firms have to determine the industries and markets they wish to address. The importance of Biggart and Hamilton's analysis is in showing the gulf between Asian and Western notions of industries and markets and therefore the contrasting organizations, values, social relations and ultimately strategies, that each generates. The assumptions of Western economic individualism and its resultant social, legal and institutional structures are that social relations in a market lead only to such uncompetitive practices as price-fixing and various other forms of collusion. In other words 'keeping economic actors apart is a crucial condition of capitalism' in the neo-classical ('Western') view. Individual competence is seen as the just way of selecting and rewarding people and organizations. Personal relations in the workplace or between organizational members are seen as collusion and favouritism. Asian economies by contrast are organized through networks. Just as Western economies have legal and regulatory frameworks for maintaining autonomy, so Asian economies have institutions that encourage and maintain ties between actors. In other words, Asian nations have built economic policies around the presence of social relations among market actors. What Western governments, organizations or managers regard as impediments to free trade express an ethnocentric view of the economic institutions of capitalism. Asian history and experience has led to the institutionalization of networks in governments and organizations. The beliefs and institutions of individual autonomy are deeply Western in origin and history. The pervasiveness of networks (social, economic, organizational and institutional) is equally deeply Asian. The implications for managerial practice and strategic thinking and decision-making are profound.

By contrast with this sweeping comparative overview of Western and Asian economic and social contexts, Grindley looks in detail at one specific regulatory problem and its impact on industries and organizations: the process for setting compatible international standards. Such standards may be for anything from plugs and railway gauges to satellite broadcasting and telecommunication links. Grindley's statement of the problem will resonate with managers everywhere: how to find an effective balance between the use of official bodies and regulatory authorities to set such standards and the desire to leave it to market forces. The article focuses on compatibility standards for the interface between two products, rather than minimum standards for such things as health and safety. Grindley's conclusion is strongly researched and argued. His results show clearly that standards are hard to set and that when a regulating authority is involved, the results are worse than when the market is left alone. He suggests that markets are effective at setting standards which pass the important test of user acceptability and that the role of standards bodies may therefore more usefully be to provide conditions in which the market can work and to correct potential excesses. He further argues that standard-setting should not be seen as a backdoor way of supporting national industries or firms, or of implementing national or international industrial policies. Since these approaches most often result in poor standards, there is no benefit to industries, firms or customers.

CHAPTER 5

HOW MUCH DOES INDUSTRY MATTER?

RICHARD P. RUMELT

This study partitions the total variance in rate of return among FTC Line of Business reporting units into industry factors (whatever their nature), time factors, factors associated with the corporate parent, and business-specific factors. Whereas Schmalensee (1985) reported that industry factors were the strongest, corporate and market share effects being extremely weak, this study distinguishes between stable and fluctuating effects and reaches markedly different conclusions. The data reveal negligible corporate effects, small stable industry effects, and very large stable business-unit effects. These results imply that the most important sources of economic rents are business-specific; industry membership is a much less important source and corporate parentage is quite unimportant.

Because competition acts to direct resources towards uses offering the highest returns, persistently unequal returns mark the presence of either natural or contrived impediments to resource flows. The study of such impediments is a principal concern of industrial organization economics and the dominant unit of analysis in that field has been the *industry*. The implicit assumption has been that the most important market imperfections arise out of the collective circumstances and behaviour of firms. However, the field of business strategy offers a contrary view: it holds that the most important impediments are not the common property of collections of firms, but arise instead from the unique endowments and actions of individual corporations or business-units. If this is true, then industry may not be the most useful unit of analysis. Consequently, there should be considerable interest in the relative sizes of inter-industry and intra-industry dispersions in long-term profit rates.

Despite these arguments for this issue's salience, surprisingly little work addressed it until Schmalensee's (1985) estimation of the variance components of profit rates in the FTC Line of Business (LB) data. Schmalensee decomposed the total variance of rates of return on assets in the 1975 LB data into industry, corporate, and market-share components. He reported that: (1) corporate effects did not exist; (2) market-share effects accounted for a negligible fraction of the variance in business-unit rates of return; (3) industry effects accounted for 20 per cent of the variance in business-unit returns; (4) industry effects accounted for at least 75 per cent of the variance in industry returns.[1] He concluded, 'the finding that industry effects are important supports the classical focus on industry-level analysis as against the revisionist tendency to downplay industry differences' (1985: 349).

Schmalensee's study was innovative and technically sophisticated. Nevertheless, there are difficulties with it traceable to the use of a single year of data. In this article I perform a new variance components analysis of the FTC LB data that corrects this weakness. I analyse the four years (1974–1977) of data available and include components for overall business cycle effects, stable and transient industry effects, as well as stable and transient business-unit effects.[2] Like Schmalensee, I find that corporate effects are negligible. However, I draw dramatically different conclusions about the importance of industry effects, the existence and importance of business-level effects, and the validity of industry-level analysis.

The most straightforward way to review my analysis is to start with what Schmalensee's results left undecided. The first major incertitude is that, although 20 per cent of business-unit returns are explained by 'industry effects', we do not know how much of this 20 per cent is due to stable industry effects rather than to transient phenomena. For example, in 1975 the return on assets of the passenger automobile industry was 6.9 per cent and that of the corn wet milling industry was 35 per cent. But this difference was far from stable: in the following year the industries virtually reversed positions, auto's return rising to 22.1 per cent and corn wet milling's return falling to 11.5 per cent (Federal Trade Commission, 1975, 1976). The presence of industry-specific fluctuations like these adds to the variance in industry returns observed in any *one* year. Thus, Schmalensee's snapshot estimate of the variance of 'industry effects' is the variance among stable industry effects *plus* the variance of annual fluctuations. But the 'classical focus' is surely on the stable differences among industries, rather than on random year-to-year variations in those differences.

My analysis of the FTC LB data shows that stable industry effects account for only 8 per cent of the variance in business-unit returns. Furthermore, only about 40 per cent of the dispersion in industry returns is due to stable industry effects.

The second incertitude concerns the variance not explained by industry effects. Schmalensee noted (p. 350) 'it is important to recognize that 80 per cent of the variance in business-unit profitability is unrelated to industry or share effects. While industry differences matter, they are clearly not all that matters.' If this intra-industry variance is due to transient disequilibrium phenomena, then the 'classical focus on industry' would still be a contender; although it explains only 8 per cent of the variance, it would be the only stable pattern in the data. But, if a large portion of the intra-industry variance is due to stable differences among business-units within industries, then the 'classical focus on industry' may be misplaced.

In this study, I find that the majority of this 'residual' variance is due to stable long-term differences among business-units rather than to transient phenomena. Using Schmalensee's sample, I find that stable business-unit effects account for 46 per cent of the variance. Indeed, the stable business-unit effects are six times more important than stable industry effects in explaining the dispersion of returns. Business-units differ from one another within industries a great deal more than industries differ from one another.

The conceptual conclusions are straightforward. The 'classical focus on industry analysis' is mistaken because these industries are too heterogeneous to support classical theory. It is also mistaken because the most important impediments to the equilibration of long-term rates of return are not associated with industry, but with the unique endowments, positions, and strategies of individual businesses.

The empirical warning is equally striking. Most of the observed differences among industry returns have nothing to do with long-term industry effects; they are due to the random distribution of especially high- and low-performing business-units across industries. As will be shown, an FTC industry return must be at least 15.21 percentage points above the mean to warrant a conclusion (95 per cent confidence) that the true stable industry effect is positive. Fewer than one in forty industry returns are high enough to pass this test.

BACKGROUND

Most industrial organization research on business, corporate, and industry profitability tests propositions about the causes of differential performance. The primary tradition made industry the unit of analysis and sought a link between industry concentration (and entry barriers) and industry profitability (usually measured with pooled data).[3] A second tradition focused on inter-firm differences in performance, seeking explanation first in terms of firm size and later in terms of market share.[4] The early reaction against the mainline tradition viewed the concentration–profitability correlation as an artefact induced by the deeper share–profitability link.[5] Finally, the *stochastic* and *efficiency* views explain both firm profitability and market-share, and thus concentration, in terms of exogenous differential firm efficiencies.[6]

In contrast to economics, business strategy research began with the presumption of heterogeneity within industries and has only recently come to grips with the question of how differences in efficiency are sustained in the face of competition. Thus, the earliest case research informed by the 'strategy' concept focused on the different approaches to competition adopted by firms within the same industry. As the field matured, attention turned towards developing quantitative measures of this diversity[7] and, more recently, to its explanation in economic terms.[8] Each of these streams of work presumes different causal mechanisms and employs different units of analysis. Claims about whether profit-rate dispersion reflects collusion, share-based market power, or difficult-to-imitate resources are coupled with claims that the more aggregate phenomena are spurious or counter-claims that less aggregate phenomena are noise. My intention here is to suppress concern with *causal* mechanisms and focus instead on the question of *locus*. Put differently, my concern here is with the existence and relative importance of time, corporate, industry, and business-unit effects, *however generated*, on the total dispersion of reported rates of return.

Most prior work touching on the issue of *locus* has done so tangentially, rough measures of intra-industry dispersions in return being mentioned in passing within a study on a different topic. Stigler, for example, studying the convergence of profit rates over time, used the relative proportions of positive-profit and loss corporations to construct rough estimates of intra-industry variances in the rate of return by IRS size class (his estimates unavoidably confound inter-period and inter-firm variances). He remarked in passing (1963: 48) that these values were much larger than inter-industry variances, but drew no implications. Fisher and Hall (1969) measured the long-term (1950–1964) dispersion in rates of return about industry averages in order to obtain a measure of risk that could be regressed against industry profitability. Although they did not remark the fact, they obtained estimates that were approximately double their reported standard deviation in inter-industry rates of return.

McEnally (1976), in an analysis of results obtained by Conrad and Plotkin (1968), showed that industries with larger average return tend also to have larger dispersions in long-term inter-firm rates of return. His figures[9] show inter-firm variances that are two to five times as large as inter-industry variances.

As part of a re-examination of the concentration–profitability relationship, Gort and Singamsetti (1976) were apparently the first to explicitly ask whether or not 'the profit rates of firms cluster around industry means.' Assigning firms to 3-digit and 4-digit industries, they found to their surprise that the data failed to support the hypothesis that industries have different characteristic levels of profitability. Furthermore, they noted that the proportion of the total variance explained by industry was low (approximately 11 per cent, adjusted), did not increase as they moved from 3-digit to 4-digit industry definitions, and did not increase as the sample was restricted to more specialized firms.

In an unpublished working paper I performed a variance components analysis of corporate returns using 20 years of Compustat data (Rumelt, 1982). Although problems of industry definition and firm diversification prevented definitive results, here again the intra-industry effect dominated the inter-industry effect: the measured intra-industry variance in long-term firm effects was three to ten times as large as the variance due to industry-specific effects.

Schmalensee's (1985) study was the first published work aimed squarely at these issues and is the direct ancestor of the work presented here. Looking at the 1975 FTC LB data, Schmalensee estimated the following random-effects model:[10]

$$r_{ik} = \mu + \alpha_i + \beta_k + \eta S_{ik} + \epsilon_{ik} \tag{1}$$

where r_{ik} is the rate of return of corporation k's activity in industry i, S_{ik} is the corresponding market share, α_i and β_k are industry and corporate effects respectively, and ϵ_{ik} is a disturbance. Schmalensee used regression to conclude that corporate effects were non-existent ($\beta_k = 0$), and variance components estimation to show that industry effects were significant and substantial ($\sigma_\alpha^2 > 0$), and that share effects were significant but not substantial ($\eta > 0$ and $s_a^2 \geq h^2 \sigma_S^2$).

Kessides (1987) re-analysed Schmalensee's data, excluding corporations active in less than three industries. He found statistically significant corporate effects in the restricted sample, suggesting that inclusion of the less-diversified corporations had lowered the power of Schmalensee's test. In a related vein, Wernerfelt and Montgomery (1988) estimated a model patterned after Schmalensee's, replacing return on assets with Tobin's q and replacing the numerous corporate dummy variables with a single continuous measure of 'focus' (the inverse of diversification). They found industry effects and share effects of about the same magnitudes as Schmalensee found, and also found a small, but statistically significant, positive association between corporate focus and performance.

Cubbin and Geroski (1987) attacked the question of the relative strength of industry and firm effects with a different methodology. Using a sample of 217 large UK firms, they measured how much of firms' profitability *movements* over time were unique, how much were related to other firms' movements, and how much were related to common industry movements. Nearly one-half of the companies in their sample exhibited no common industry-wide response to dynamic factors.

Hansen and Wernerfelt (1989) studied the relative importance of economic and organizational factors in explaining inter-firm differences in profit rates. They found that industry explained 19 per cent of the variance in profit rates, but that organizational characteristics were roughly twice as important.

DATA

Because the impetus for this study comes from the existence of the unique FTC LB data, and because the statistical work performed is fundamentally descriptive rather than hypothesis testing, I break with convention and discuss the data before introducing the model.

Data on the operations of large US Corporations are available from a variety of sources. However, there is only one source of disaggregate data on the profits of corporations by industry – the FTC's Line of Business Program. The FTC collected data on the domestic operations of large corporations in each of 261 4-digit FTC manufacturing industry categories. Information on a total of 588 different corporations was collected for the years 1974–1977; because of late additions, deletions, acquisitions, and mergers, the number of corporations reporting in any one year ranged from 432 to 471. The average corporation reported on about eight business-units.

Schmalensee's sample was constructed by starting with Ravenscraft's (1983) data-set of 3,186 stable and meaningful business-units – those which were not in miscellaneous categories and which were neither newly created nor terminated during the 1974–1976 period. He then dropped business-units in 16 FTC industries judged to be primarily residual classifications, dropped business-units with sales less than 1 per cent of 1975 FTC industry total sales, and excluded one outlier.

Two data sets were used in this research, labelled A and B. Sample A was constructed by starting with Schmalensee's sample of 1,775 business-units from the 1975 file and appending data on the same business-units from the 1974, 1976 and 1977 files. After this expansion, one business-unit was judged to have unreliable asset measures (in 1976–77) and was dropped. Eight other observations were eliminated because assets were reported as zero. Sample A then contained 6,932 observations provided by 457 corporations on 1,774 business-units operating in a total of 242 4-digit FTC industries.

Sample B was constructed by adding to Sample A the 1,070 'small' business-units which had failed Schmalensee's size criterion. After adjoining the 1974, 1976 and 1977 data for these business-units, 34 were excluded due to (apparent) measurement problems: negative or zero assets, sales-to-assets ratios over 30, and extreme year-to-year variations in assets that were unconnected to changes in sales. Sample B then contained 10,866 observations provided by 463 corporations on 2,810 business-units operating in a total of 242 4-digit FTC industries.

The rate of return was taken to be the ratio of profit before interest and taxes to total assets, expressed as a percentage. In sample A the average return was 13.92 and the sample variance was 279.35. In sample B, the average and sample variance of return were 13.17 and 410.73 respectively.

The FTC defined operating income as total revenues (including transfers from other units) less cost of goods sold, less selling, advertising, and general and administrative expenses. Both expenses and assets were further divided into 'traceable' and 'untraceable' components, the traceable component being directly attributable to the line of business and the untraceable component being allocated by the reporting firm among lines of business using 'reasonable procedures'. In 1975, 15.8 per cent of the total expenses and 13.6 per cent of total assets of the average business unit were allocated.

A number of scholars have advanced arguments that accounting rates of return are systematically biased measures of true internal rates of return.[11] Whatever the merits of this position, the purpose of this study is to partition the variance in reported business-unit rates of return. If different industry practices or corporate policies do induce systematic biases in reported returns, the estimated variance components will reflect these facts and, therefore, help in estimating their importance.

A VARIANCE COMPONENTS MODEL

In discussing the heterogeneity within industries the term 'firm' has an ambiguity that easily leads to confusion. In economics a 'firm' is usually an autonomous competitive unit within an industry, but the term is also often used to indicate a legal entity: a 'company' or 'corporation'. Because most empirical studies are of large corporations, and because most large corporations are substantially diversified, legal or corporate 'firms' are, at best, amalgams of individual theoretical competitive units. Confusion can arise if one author uses the term 'firm effects' to indicate intra-industry dispersion among theoretical 'firms', and another author uses the same term to denote differences among corporations which are not explained by their patterns of industry activities.

To reduce the ambiguity in what follows I avoid the term 'firm'. Instead, I use the term *business-unit* to denote that portion of a company's operations which are wholly contained within a single industry.[12] I use the term *corporation* to denote a legal company which owns and operates one or more business-units. Thus, both industries and corporations are considered to be sets of business-units.

In this regard, note that Schmalensee (1985) used the term 'firm-effects' to denote what I call corporate effects. Thus, his first proposition, 'firm effects do not exist' (p. 349), refers to what are here termed corporate effects. Consequently, as he noted, finding insignificant corporate effects does not rule out the presence of substantial intra-industry effects. However, unless more than one year of data are analysed, intra-industry effects pool with the error and cannot be detected.

Taking the unit of analysis to be the business-unit, assume that each business-unit is observed over time and is classified according to its industry membership and its corporate ownership. Let r_{ikt} denote the rate of return reported in time period t by the business-unit owned by corporation k and active in industry i. A particular business-unit is labelled ik, highlighting the fact that it is simultaneously a member of an industry and a corporation. Working with this notation, I posit the following descriptive model:

$$r_{ikt} = \mu + \alpha_i + \beta_k + \gamma_t + \delta_{it} + \phi_{ik} + \epsilon_{ikt} \qquad (2)$$

where the α_i are industry effects ($i = 1, ..., l_\alpha$), the β_k are corporate effects ($k = 1, ..., l_\beta$), the γ_i are year effects ($t = 1, ..., l_\gamma$) the δ_{it} are industry–year interaction effects (l_δ distinct *it* combinations), and the ϕ_{ik} are business-unit effects (l_ϕ distinct *ik* combinations). The ϵ_{ik} are random disturbances (one for each of the N observations). Each corporation is only active in a few industries, so $l_\phi < l_\alpha l_\beta$. Because a few industries may not be observed over all years, $l_\delta \leq l_\alpha l_\gamma$. The model takes the assignment of business-units to corporations and industries as given and is essentially descriptive. In particular, it offers no causal or structural explanation for profitability differences across industries, years, corporations, or business-units – it simply posits the existence of differences in return associated with these categories.

There are two key differences between this model and Schmalensee's. First, the terms γ_t, and δ_{it} have been added to deal with year-to-year variations in overall returns and year-to-year variations in industry-specific returns. Second, the market-share term has been replaced by ϕ_{ik}. In this regard, it is useful to recall Schmalensee's persuasive reasons for turning to a nominal measure of industry. He argued (1985: 343) that conventional market-level variables (e.g. concentration) are very imperfect measures of the theoretical constructs (perceived interdependence) they are supposed to represent. Therefore, the fact that these variables perform poorly, relative to market-share, in cross-sectional regressions may not mean that 'industry' is unimportant. Hence, Schmalensee sought to measure the importance of *all* industry effects, using nominal industry categories, and compare it to the importance of market-share. But, just as concentration is an imperfect measure of industry structure, so market-share is an imperfect measure of resource heterogeneity among businesses. Comparing *all* industry effects to market-share effects may unfairly load the dice in favour of industry. Consequently, in this study I extend Schmalensee's argument to the business-unit and, rather than give special attention to market-share, I measure the importance of *all* stable industry effects, and *all* stable business-unit effects.

Were this a *fixed-effects* model, the usual assumption would be that the ϵ_{ikt} are random disturbances, drawn independently from a distribution with mean zero and unknown variance σ_ϵ. In this model I make the additional assumption that all of the other effects, like the error term, are realizations of random processes with zero means and constant, but unknown variances $\sigma_\alpha^2, \sigma_\beta^2, \sigma_\gamma^2, \sigma_\delta^2$, and σ_ϕ.

Note that this *random effects* assumption does not mean that the various effects are inconstant. Instead, for example, each business-unit effect ϕ_{ik} is seen as having been independently generated by a random process with variance σ_ϕ^2, and, having once been set, remaining fixed thereafter.

The random-effects assumption says nothing about why effects differ from one another – effects may differ from one another in either fixed-effects or random-effects models. The real substance of the random-effects assumption is that the differences among effects, whatever their source, are 'natural', not having been controlled or contrived by the research design, and are independent of other effects. That is, the effects in the data represent a *random* sample of the effects in the population. Independence implies that knowing the value of a particular ϕ_{ik}, for example, is of no help in predicting the values of other business-unit effects or the values of any industry, corporate, or year effects. An important exception to this assumption, involving an association between industry and corporate effects, is discussed below.

Readers familiar with fixed-effects regression models may be concerned that the effects posited in this model are not estimable. Such a concern is well placed – the individual effects cannot be estimated. Furthermore, regression methods cannot deliver unambiguous estimates of the relative importance of classes of effects. However, the statistical problem is not to estimate the thousands of effects, but to estimate the six variances. Despite the nesting in the model, the variance components are estimable. Note that it is the assumption that the underlying effects are realizations of random processes that allows a measure of their relative 'importance'. Were they assumed to be 'fixed', one could test for statistical significance, but there would be no reliable way of assessing importance. *It is only by estimating the variances of effects that relative importance can be assessed.*

The α_i represent all persistent industry-specific impacts on observed rates of return. Differences among the α_i reflect differing competitive behaviour, conditions of entry, rates of growth, demand-capacity conditions, differing levels of risk, differing asset utilization rates, differing accounting practices, and any other industry-specific impacts on the rate of return. The fundamentally descriptive model used here offers no hypotheses as to the nature of these industry differences – the α_i represent their total collective impact.

Corporate effects β_k should arise from differences in the quality of monitoring and control, differences in resource sharing and other types of synergy, and differences in accounting policy. Total corporate returns will, of course, also be affected by the industry memberships of their constituent businesses. However, the unit of analysis here is the business-unit, not the corporation.

The ϕ_{ik} represent persistent differences among business-unit returns other than those due to industry and corporate membership. That is, they are due to the presence of business-specific skills, resources, reputations, learning, patents, and other intangible contributions to stable differences among business-unit returns. Such differences may also arise from persistent errors in the allocation of costs or assets among a corporation's business-units. (Note, however, that corporate-wide or industry-wide biases in accounting will appear as corporate or industry effects.) The Section on Empirical Results presents the results of a test for the presence of allocation errors.

Are the differences among business-unit returns within industries simply disequilibrium phenomena? Until recently, rates of return were thought to converge fairly rapidly to 'normal' levels. Consequently, the idea of business-unit effects had little currency. If they surfaced empirically, they were treated as an autocorrelation problem. However, researchers using more disaggregate data have discovered that abnormal profit rates do not rapidly fade away; Mueller (1977, 1985) and Jacobson (1988) have found them to be extraordinarily persistent. This consideration, and the fact that the FTC LB data covers only four years, leads to modelling the business-unit effects as fixed. If this assumption is incorrect, and the business-unit effects decay over time, then the estimated residuals will display positive autocorrelation. Such a finding would signal the need for a more complex autoregressive model. As will be seen, no such autocorrelation was found in the data studied here.

The γ_t represent year-to-year fluctuations in macroeconomic conditions that influence all business-units equally. The δ_{it} represent industry-specific year-to-year fluctuations in return. Finally, there is an ϵ_{ikt} associated with each observation. Although these effects have been named 'error', they may equally well be thought of as year-to-year variations that are specific to each business-unit.

In an important exception to the independence assumption, Schmalensee (1985: 344) argued that corporations which are more skilful at operating businesses might also be more skilled at having identified and entered more profitable industries, thereby inducing a dependence between the values of β and α observed across business-units. Incorporating this presumption, and maintaining elsewhere the assumption of independence, the total variance σ_r of returns may be decomposed into these variance–covariance components:

$$\sigma_r^2 = \sigma_\alpha^2 + \sigma_\beta^2 + \sigma_\gamma^2 + \sigma_\delta^2 + \sigma_\phi^2 + \sigma_\epsilon^2 + 2C_{\alpha\beta} \tag{3}$$

where $C_{\alpha\beta}$ is the covariance between α_i and β_k, given that corporation k is active in industry i (i.e., $E(\alpha_i\beta_k) = C_{\alpha\beta}$ if business-unit ik exists, and 0 otherwise). [...]

EMPIRICAL RESULTS

Table 5.1 displays the estimated variance–covariance components for the full model. The procedure used does not prohibit negative estimates. The normal practice is to replace small negative estimates with zero and take large negative estimates as an indication of specification error. In sample A, $\sigma_\gamma^2 = -2.82$, and in sample B, $2C_{\alpha\beta} = -0.01$, results surely indistinguishable from zero.

Treating the model as one with fixed, rather than random, effects provides additional information on its adequacy. Table 5.2 shows sequential analyses of variance with business-unit effects entering last and then again with industry-year effects entering last. The R^2 for the sample A regression is 0.765 (0.632 corrected) and for the sample B regression it is 0.696 (0.549 corrected). Both regressions are highly significant overall. Additionally, in both samples the estimates of σ_ϵ^2 obtained from the fixed-effect regressions are quite close to those obtained from the variance components procedure. This confirmatory test provides an indication that the model is adequately specified.

Table 5.1 Variance–covariance components estimates: Full model

Component	Sample A	Sample B
Year	−2.82	0.20
Industry-year	24.74	21.89
Industry	20.49	16.62
Corporation	0.19	6.75
Business unit	131.69	181.49
$2C_{\alpha\beta}$	2.13	−0.01
Error	102.51	184.06

The fixed-effects estimations provide residuals that can be examined for autocorrelation. The correlation between the residuals and their lagged values was −0.018 in sample A and 0.001 in sample B. Thus, there is no evidence in these data that business-unit effects decay. The lack of autocorrelation confirms the decision to model business-unit effects as fixed over the 4-year sample period.

It is important to note that with fixed-effects estimation, strict tests for the presence of effects are possible only for the last effects fitted. Thus, Table 5.2 shows that business-unit effects and industry-year effects are quite significant. However, because of the nesting in the model, it is not possible to fit industry or corporate effects *after* fitting business-unit effects. Put differently, in analysis-of-variance one cannot hold business-unit effects 'constant' and then estimate industry or corporate effects. Thus, the significance attaching to the entry of 'corporation' in Table 5.2 (F-value = 6.13) does not necessarily mean that corporate effects are significantly different from zero.[13] Thus, analysis of variance or regression cannot reveal whether the apparent explanatory power of corporation is due to real corporate effects or whether it reflects differences among corporate returns induced by large uncontrolled business-unit effects. The same problem arises in interpreting the results on industry effects.

Table 5.2 Fixed-effects ANOVA results

Business-Unit Entering Last

Source	df	Sample A Incr. R^2	F-Value	df	Sample B Incr. R^2	F-Value
Year	3	0.0003	1.78	3	0.0008	6.09[b]
Industry	241	0.179	14.03[a]	241	0.103	10.28[a]
Industry* Year	721	0.098	2.57[a]	721	0.071	2.36[a]
Corporation	456	0.148	6.13[a]	462	0.109	5.70[a]
Business-unit	1076	0.339	5.94[a]	2106	0.413	4.72[a]
Total Model	2497	0.765	5.78[a]	3533	0.696	4.75[a]
Error	4434	0.235		7332	0.304	
Total	6931			10865		

Industry-Year Entering Last

Source	df	Sample A Incr. R^2	F-Value	df	Sample B Incr. R^2	F-Value
Year	3	0.0003	1.78	3	0.0008	6.09[b]
Corporation	456	0.176	7.27[a]	462	0.116	6.05[a]
Industry	241	0.153	11.98[a]	241	0.098	9.76[a]
Business-unit	1076	0.340	5.95[a]	2106	0.414	4.74[a]
Industry- Year	721	0.096	2.52[a]	721	0.068	2.26[a]
Total Model	2497	0.765	5.78[a]	3533	0.696	4.75[a]
Error	4434	0.235		7332	0.304	
Total	6931			10865		

[a] Significant at 0.0001 level.
[b] Significant at 0.0005 level.

This ambiguity is a central reason for turning to variance components estimation; unlike regression, variance components procedures can assess the independent importance of nested business-unit, corporate and industry effects. Indeed, as Table 5.1 shows, corporate effects are essentially nil (in Sample A). Thus, the apparent significance attached to the introduction of corporate effects in the fixed-effect estimation is wholly due to the dispersion among corporate returns induced by the deeper business-unit effects. This case is an excellent illustration of the problem associated with using R^2 or 'incremental' R^2 as a measure of a factor's importance. In Sample A (Table 5.2) the marginal R^2 of the industry and corporate effects are roughly comparable at 18 and 15 per cent respectively (the adjusted marginal R^2s are about 14 and 10 per cent). Yet Table 5.1 shows that the corporate variance component is only one-hundredth as large as the industry variance component.

The results strongly suggest that $\sigma_\gamma^2 = 0$ and $C_{\alpha\beta} = 0$ in both samples. Accordingly, the model was re-estimated with these restrictions. The results are shown in Table 5.3. The restrictions produce only slight changes in the estimates of the remaining variance components.[14]

Table 5.3 Variance components estimates: restricted model (year effects and $C_{\alpha\beta}$ removed)

Component	Sample A			Sample B		
	Est.	Std. Error	Per cent	Est.	Std. Error	Per cent
Industry-Year	21.92	2.04	7.84	22.09	2.31	5.38
Industry	23.26	4.72	8.32	16.55	4.26	4.03
Corporation	2.25	3.84	0.80	6.74	3.31	1.64
Business-unit	129.63	6.91	46.37	181.50	7.04	44.17
Error	102.51	2.18	36.87	184.06	3.04	44.79
Total	279.56		100.00	410.95		100.00

Since σ_ϵ^2 was also obtained by fixed-effects regression, the variance of this estimate is available from standard regression theory and is reported in Table 5.3. However, the sampling distributions of the other variance components estimators are not known and, even under normality assumptions, usable expressions for the variances of the estimates are not available. To provide some guidance on this matter I provide standard errors of the estimates that would be observed were the true variance components equal to their estimated values and were the underlying distributions normal. These estimates were obtained by simulation: taking the variance components at their estimated values, a realization of each effect in the model was generated by a draw from the appropriate normal distribution, these effects were then combined according to the original data structure, and the variance components estimation procedure was then re-applied to the simulated data set. The standard errors shown are based on 1000 such trials. The values obtained offer convincing evidence that the estimates of the larger variance components are not overly noisy. With regard to the corporate effect, I conclude that there is no evidence of non-zero corporate effects in sample A, whereas the inclusion of the smaller business-units (sample B) provides some evidence of (small) corporate effects.

As has been noted, the estimate of the variance among business-unit effects reflects both 'real' differences in return and any persistent errors in the corporate allocation of costs and assets among business-units. If allocation error is an important phenomenon in these data it should be detectable through the induced statistical dependence among business-unit returns within corporations. That is, an allocation error which increases one business-unit's return must also decrease the returns of other business-units in the same corporation.

More formally, assume that errors in a corporation's allocation policy add u_i to the ith business-unit's return and that these allocations are constrained such that $\sum w_i u_i = 0$, where the w_i are positive constants. If the *unconditional* distribution of each u_i is normal with mean zero and variance σ_u^2, it is not hard to show that the distribution of the ui, *conditional* on the constraint, is joint (singular) normal such that

$$cov(u_i, u_j) = Eu_i u_j = -k_{ij}\sigma_u^2,$$

where $k = w_i w_j / \sum_m w_m^2$. Thus, instead of independence, allocation error implies that $E\phi_{ik}\phi_{jk} < 0$.

To examine this question, it is useful to first 'adjust' returns for industry-year effects so that attention may be focused on business-unit phenomena. Accordingly, the deviation in return d_{ikt} from the average for that industry in that year was defined:

$$d_{ikt} = r_{ikt} - r_{i.t}/n_{i.t},$$

one pair of these measures was randomly selected from each corporation (in each year) with two or more business-units. To a first approximation, $d_{ikt} \approx \phi_{ik} + \epsilon_{ikt}$. If, within corporations, ϕ_{ik} is independent of ϕ_{jk} and ϵ_{ikt} is independent of ϵ_{jkt}, the covariance between the 1,321 paired measures should be zero. The calculated covariance was 0.007, providing no reason to doubt independence. Looking further, and taking the weight w_i to be the fraction of a corporation's assets utilized in the ith business, the regression of the products of the paired measures $(d_{ikt}d_{jkt})$ on the k_{ij} (defined above) was then computed: the coefficient of k_{ij} is a direct estimate of σ_u^2. Neither the constrained ($m = 0$) nor the unconstrained regression was significant ($t = -0.43$ and $t = -0.6$). These results do not support the view that allocation errors are an important source of heterogeneity in the FTC LB data.

DISCUSSION AND IMPLICATIONS

The variance in business-unit profitability in sample A (B) may be partitioned approximately as follows: 8 (4) per cent industry effects, 1 (2) per cent corporate effects, 46 (44) per cent business-unit effects, 8 (5) per cent industry-year effects, and 37 (45) per cent residual error.

The fundamental differences between the two samples is that in sample B the non-industry variances are substantially larger, making industry relatively less important. Whereas the industry and industry-year components are comparable in both samples, in sample B business-unit variance component is 40 per cent larger than in sample A and the residual error is 80 per cent larger. (The corporate variance component is three times as large but its magnitude is small in both samples.) If the components are expressed as percentages, the opposite pattern emerges: the contribution of industry falls from 8.29 per cent in sample A to 4.01 per cent in sample B, whereas the percentage contribution of the business-unit component is virtually unchanged.

Table 5.4 compares the variance partition for sample A with that reported by Schmalensee (1985). Schmalensee estimated that 19.59 per cent of the total variance was due to industry effects. In this study, I find that somewhat less, 16.12 per cent, is due to all industry effects (stable plus year-to-year fluctuations). The difference between the estimates arises mainly because 1975 was an abnormal year – repeating Schmalensee's one-year analysis in 1976 and 1977 yields smaller industry components. More importantly, I find that only one-half of this variance is due to stable effects. Long-term industry effects account for only 8.28 per cent of the observed variance among sample A business-unit returns.

Table 5.4 Comparison with Schmalensee's results (percentage of total variance by source)

Source	This Study Sample A	Schmalensee (1985)
CORPORATE	0.80	x
Industry	8.28	x
Industry-Year	7.84	x
ALL INDUSTRY	16.12	19.46
Share	x	0.63
Share-Industry Covariance	x	−0.62
Business-Unit	46.38	x
Business-Unit-Year	36.70	x
ALL INTRA-INDUSTRY	83.08	80.54
TOTAL	100.00	100.00

x Component not estimated

Turning to the intra-industry variance, Schmalensee reported that 80.41 per cent of the variance was unexplained by industry; the comparable figure in this study is 83.08 per cent. However, my partition of this intra-industry variance into stable and year-to-year components reveals that over one-half is due to stable business-unit effects. Indeed, the variance among stable business-unit effects is six times as large as the variance among stable industry effects – business-units differ from one another within industries much more than industries differ from one another.

Despite the fact that this is a descriptive study, some strong general results can be reported:

1 There are significant business-unit effects in US manufacturing activities that strongly outweigh industry and corporate membership as predictors of profitability. The variance among business-unit effects is much larger than the variance among industry effects (six times larger in sample A and eleven times larger in sample B).
2 Corporate effects, although present in sample B, are not important in explaining the dispersion in observed rates of return among business-units.

Business-unit effects

The large observed variance component for business-unit effects overshadows the other variance components. Although this model cannot reveal the sources of this dispersion, some insight can be gained by examining Schmalensee's results on the importance of market share. His study of sample A for 1975 measured a variance component due to share of 2.2. This amounts to 1.7 per cent of the business-unit variance component estimated for sample A data in this study. Hence, it seems safe to conclude that only a very small part of the large business-unit effects can be associated with differences in the relative sizes of business-units.

The large business-unit effects indicate that there is more intra-industry heterogeneity than has been commonly recognized. Whereas economists are quick to refer to *inframarginal rents* when this issue arises, the unspoken presumption is that these effects are small, or related to scale. The results are otherwise. The business-unit effects are large and owe only a small fraction of their strength to market share. Some portion of these effects may, of course, be due to measurement biases. But the most obvious sources of bias, differences in industry accounting and differences in corporate policy, should appear as industry or corporate effects.

The presence of strong business-unit effects is consonant with the presumptions in portions of the *business strategy* literature. Beginning with Caves and Porter's mobility barriers concept, based on the hypothesis that 'sellers within an industry are likely to differ systematically in traits other than size,' (1977: 250) ideas in this area have evolved in the direction of recognizing increasingly disaggregate sources of resource immobility or specificity.[15] According to this view, product-specific reputation, team-specific learning, a variety of first-mover advantages, causal ambiguity that limits effective imitation, and other special conditions permit equilibria in which competitors earn dramatically different rates of return. Although this study cannot discriminate among the various theories regarding the sources of intra-industry heterogeneity, it necessarily gives broad support to this class of theory and should encourage further work in this vein.

What do industry returns measure?

If business-units within industries have large and persistent differences in return, it becomes necessary to ask what the 'industry returns' measures used in many industrial organization studies actually represent. That is, when industries exhibit differing levels of overall return, to what extent are such differences due to systematic industry effects and to what extent are such differences the veiled result of differences in individual business-unit performance? I undertake a very simple exploration of this question by examining the variance of $\gamma_i = \sum_{k \cdot t} r_{i \cdot \cdot} / n_{i \cdot \cdot}$, the average return observed for industry i over all four years, so that

$$y_i = \mu + \alpha_i + \sum_t \frac{n_{i \cdot t}}{n_{i \cdot \cdot}} \delta_{it} + \sum_k \frac{n_{ik \cdot}}{n_{i \cdot \cdot}} \phi_{ik} + \sum_{k \cdot t} \frac{n_{ikt}}{n_{i \cdot \cdot}} \epsilon_{ikt}. \tag{14}$$

The sample variance s_γ^2 of industry returns was 61.9 in sample A and 58.1 in sample B. Extending the development of (10) to cover industry-year effects, the expected value of this measure can be written

$$E\left(s_y^2\right) = s_a^2 + \left(\sum_{i \cdot t} \frac{n_{i \cdot t}^2}{l_a n_{i \cdot \cdot}^2}\right) s_d^2 + \left(\sum_{i \cdot k} \frac{n_{ik \cdot}^2}{l_a n_{i \cdot \cdot}^2}\right) s_f^2 + \left(\sum_i \frac{1}{l_a n_{i \cdot \cdot}}\right) s_\epsilon^2.$$

This equation, and the Table 5.3 estimates of $\sigma_\alpha^2, \sigma_\delta^2, \sigma_\phi^2$ and σ_ϵ^2 allow the construction of a partitioned estimate of $E(s_y^2)$; the result is shown in Table 5.5. The agreement between the sample values and the total expected values appears to be good.

Table 5.5 Estimated components of sample variance among industry average returns

	Sample A		Sample B	
Source	Component	Per cent	Component	Per cent
Industry	23.3	39.3	16.6	29.8
Industry * Year	5.5	9.3	5.6	10.0
Business-Unit	25.3	42.7	26.6	47.7
Error	5.2	8.7	7.0	12.5
Total	59.27	100.0	55.8	100.0
Actual Sample Variance	61.9		58.1	

This partition reveals that only 40 per cent of the variance among industry returns is actually due to stable industry effects. In sample A an additional 40 per cent of s_y^2 is due to business-unit effects which randomly combine to affect industry averages; in sample B the corresponding proportion is close to one-half. The remaining variance (one-fifth in sample A, one-eighth in sample B) is due to various industry-year and business-unit-year fluctuations. (This portion would be smaller had the averages been taken over more than 4 years.) Because only 40 per cent of the variance in industry returns is due to industry effects, industry returns are noisy estimates of the true industry effects.

How large does an industry return have to be in order to justify a conclusion that the corresponding industry effect is positive? From (14), it should be clear that

$$y_i = \mu + \alpha_i + e_i$$

where e_i is a weighted average of industry-year, business-unit, and error effects, and where α_i and e_i are independent. To simplify matters, assume that μ is known. Then $E(y_i) = \mu$, $E(\alpha_i) = 0$, and $\text{cov}(y_i, \alpha_i) = E(\alpha_i^2) = \sigma_\alpha^2$.

Let $x = [\alpha_i, \gamma_i]$, so that $Ex = [0\mu]$, and

$$\text{var}(x) = \begin{bmatrix} V_{11} & V_{12} \\ V_{21} & V_{22} \end{bmatrix} = \begin{bmatrix} s_\alpha^2 & s_\alpha^2 \\ s_\alpha^2 & s_y^2 \end{bmatrix}.$$

Now consider the conditional distribution of α_i given γ_i. Assuming that x is bivariate normal, the desired conditional distribution is normal with these parameters:

$$E(\alpha_i|y_i) = V_{11}(\gamma_i - \mu)/V_{22} = \zeta(y_i - \mu)$$

$$\text{Var}(\alpha_i|y_i) = V_{11} - V_{12}^2/V_{22} = (1 - \zeta)\sigma_\alpha^2,$$

where $\zeta = \sigma_\alpha^2/\sigma_y^2$. Table 5.3 indicates that $\sigma_\alpha^2 \approx 23$ and Table 5.5 shows that $\zeta \approx 0.4$. Therefore, $\sigma_{\alpha_i|y_i} = \sqrt{0.6 \cdot 23} = 3.71$.

Thus, if γ_i is 10 percentage points above the mean, the expectation is that $\alpha_i = 0.4 \cdot 10 = 4$. But the conditional distribution of α_i has a standard deviation of 3.71 – although the expectation is of a 4-point industry effect, this estimate is only 1.08 standard deviations above zero. Using the normal distribution, $F_N(-1.08) = 0.14$. That is, although industry i has an average return that is 10 percentage points above the mean, there remains a 0.14 probability that α_i is actually negative.

To reduce the chance of this type of error to 0.05 or less, the conditional estimate of α_i must be at least 1.64 standard deviations above zero ($F_N(1.64) = 0.95$). That is, if one is to conclude $\alpha_i > 0$ with 95 per cent confidence, the inequality

$$0.4(y_i - \mu) > 1.64 \cdot 3.71$$

must be satisfied. It follows that $\gamma_i - \mu > 13.21$ is required.

Thus, in order to have 95 per cent confidence that $\alpha_i > 0$, the observed industry average must be at least 15.21 percentage points above the mean. How often will this happen? The standard deviation σ_y of industry returns has the approximate value $\sqrt{23/0.4} = 7.58$. Obviously, the 'typical' industry return does not pass the 15.21 point criterion. Indeed, the 15.21 point cut-off lies two standard deviations above the mean! Hence, only one in forty industries ($F_N(2) = 0.977$) will exhibit a return large enough to warrant a conclusion that the true industry effects is positive. Put differently, industry returns are such noisy measures of industry effects that only about six of the 242 FTC industries studied could be judged (95 per cent confidence) to have positive industry effects.

Corporate effects

Turning to the issue of corporate effects, corporations exhibit little or no (differential) ability to affect business-unit returns. It is not that corporate effects do not exist – it appears that $s_\beta^2 > 0$ in sample B – but rather that corporate effects are astonishingly small. Put differently, if one business-unit within a corporation is very profitable, there is little reason to expect that any of the corporation's other business-units will be performing at other than the norms set by industry, year, and industry-year effects.

Corporate returns will, of course, differ from one another for reasons other than corporate effects. Corporate returns will differ because of their differing patterns of participation in industries. More importantly, corporate returns will differ because their portfolios of business-units differ. But the results indicate that the dispersion among corporate returns can be fully explained by the dispersions of industry and business-unit effects; there is no evidence of 'synergy'.

Given the extent of the literature on corporate strategy, corporate culture, the number of consulting firms that specialize in corporate management, and the focus on senior corporate leaders in the business world, it is surprising to find only vanishingly small corporate effects on these data. This result, first obtained by Schmalensee, remains a puzzle and deserves further investigation.

Implications

To the extent that accounting returns measure the presence of economic rents, the results obtained here imply that by far the most important sources of rents in US manufacturing businesses are due to resources or market positions that are specific to particular business-units rather than to corporate resources or to membership in an industry. Put simply, business-units within industries differ from one another a great deal more than industries differ from one another.

Empirical results are rarely definitive and there are a number of issues left unresolved in this study. It may be, for example, that the FTC 4-digit industries are simply too broad to reveal the true strength of industry effects. Or, it may be that the assumption of a constant σ_ϕ is unjustified, some industries being much more heterogeneous than others. Nevertheless, most empirical work within the industrial organization paradigm has been conducted on data at this or higher levels of aggregation and persistent intra-industry heterogeneity has been generally assumed away rather than measured. Consequently, it seems worthwhile to sharply and clearly state the implications of this study:

1 The neoclassical model of industry as composed of firms that are homogeneous (but for scale) does not describe 4-digit industries: these data show real industries to be extremely heterogeneous.
2 The simple revisionist model in which business-units differ in size due to differences in manufacturing efficiency is incorrect – only a small portion of the large observed variance among business-unit effects can be associated with differences in relative size.

3 Theoretical or statistical explanations of business-unit performance that use industry as the unit of analysis can, at best, explain only about eight per cent of the observed dispersion among business-unit profit rates.
4 Theoretical or statistical explanations of business-unit performance that use the corporation as the unit of analysis can, at best, explain only about 2 per cent of the observed dispersion among business-unit profit rates.
5 Theoretical or statistical work seeking to explain an important portion of the observed dispersion in business-unit profit rates must use the business-unit (or even less aggregate entities) as the unit of analysis and must focus on sources of heterogeneity within industries other than relative size.

REFERENCES

Caves, R.E. and Porter, M.E. (1977) 'From entry barriers to mobility barriers: conjectural decisions and contrived deterrence to new competition', *Quarterly Journal of Economics*, Vol. 91, pp. 241–61.

Conrad, G.R. and Plotkin, I.H. (1968) 'Risk/return: U.S. industry pattern', *Harvard Business Review*, March–April, pp. 90–9.

Cubbin, J. and Geroski, P. (1987) 'The convergence of profits in the long run: inter-firm and inter-industry comparisons', *Journal of Industrial Economics*, Vol. 35, pp. 427–42.

Demsetz, H. (1973) 'Industry structure, market rivalry, and public policy', *Journal of Law and Economics*, Vol. 16, pp. 1–9.

Federal Trade Commission, *Statistical Report: Annual Line of Business Reports, 1975, 1976*. Published in 1981 and 1982.

Fisher, I.N. and Hall, G.R. (1969) 'Risk and corporate rates of return', *Quarterly Journal of Economics*, Vol. 83, pp. 79–92.

Fisher, F. and McGowan, J. (1983) 'On the misuse of accounting rates of return to infer monopoly profits', *American Economic Review*, Vol. 73, pp. 82–97.

Gort, M. and Singamsetti, R. (1976) 'Concentration and profit rates: new evidence on an old issue', *Occasional Papers of the National Bureau of Economic Research: Explorations in Economic Research*, Vol. 3, Winter, pp. 1–20.

Hansen, G.S. and Wernerfelt, B. (1989) 'Determinants of firm performance: the relative importance of economic and organizational factors', *Strategic Management Journal*, Vol. 10, pp. 399–411.

Hatten, K.J. and Schendel, D.E. (1977) 'Heterogeneity within an industry', *Journal of Industrial Economics*, Vol. 26 pp. 97–113.

Jacobson, R. (1988) 'The persistence of abnormal returns', *Strategic Management Journal*, Vol. 9, pp. 415–30.

Kessides, I.N. (1987) 'Do firms differ much? Some additional evidence', Working Paper, Department of Economics, University of Maryland.

Lippman, S.A. and Rumelt, R.P. (1982) 'Uncertain imitability: an analysis of inter-firm differences in efficiency under competition', *Bell Journal of Economics*, Vol. 13, pp. 418–38.

Mancke, R.B. (1974) 'Causes of interfirm profitability differences: a new interpretation of the evidence', *Quarterly Journal of Economics*, Vol. 88, pp. 181–93.

McEnally, R.W. (1976) 'Competition and dispersion in rates of return: a note', *Journal of Industrial Organization*, Vol. 25, pp. 69–75.

McGee, J. and Thomas, H. (1986) 'Strategic groups: theory, research and taxonomy', *Strategic Management Journal*, Vol. 7, pp. 141–60.

Mueller, D.C. (1977) 'The persistence of profits above the norm', *Economica*, Vol. 44, pp. 369–80.

Mueller, D.C. (1985) *Profits in the Long Run*, Cambridge University Press, Cambridge.

Ravenscraft, D.J. (1980) 'Price-raising and cost reducing effects in profit-concentration studies: a Monte-Carlo simulation analysis', PhD thesis, Northwestern University.

Ravenscraft, D.J. (1983) 'Structure–profit relationships at the line of business and industry level', *Review of Economics and Statistics*, Vol. 65, pp. 22–31.

Rumelt, R.P. (1982) 'How important is industry in explaining firm profitability?' unpublished working paper, UCLA.

Rumelt, R.P. (1984) 'Toward a strategic theory of the firm', in R.B. Lamb, (ed.) *Competitive Strategic Management*, Prentice-Hall, Englewood Cliffs, NJ, pp. 557–70.

Rumelt, R.P. (1987) 'Theory, strategy and entrepreneurship', in D. Teece (ed.) *The Competitive Challenge: strategies for industrial innovation and renewal*, Ballinger, Cambridge, MA, pp. 137–58.

Schmalensee, R. (1985) 'Do markets differ much?' *American Economic Review*, Vol. 75 pp. 341–51.

Searle, S.R. (1971) *Linear Models*, Wiley & Sons, New York.

Scherer, F.M. (1980) *Industrial Market Structure and Economic Performance* (2nd edn), Rand-McNally, Chicago, IL.

Stigler, G.J. (1963) *Capital and Rates of Return in Manufacturing Industries*, National Bureau of Economic Research, New York.

Teece, D.J. (1982) 'Toward an economic theory of the multi-product firm', *Journal of Economic Behaviour and Organization*, Vol. 3, pp. 39–63.

Weiss, L.W. (1974) 'The concentration-profits relationship and antitrust', in H.J. Goldschmid *et al.*, (eds), *Industrial Concentration: The New Learning*, Little, Brown, Boston.

Wernerfelt, B. (1984) 'A resource-based view of the firm', *Strategic Management Journal*, April–June, pp. 171–80.

Wernerfelt, B. and Montgomery, C.A. (1988) 'Tobin's q and the importance of focus in firm performance', *American Economic Review*, Vol. 78, pp. 246–51.

NOTES

1 Industry and corporate 'effects' are (unobserved) components of business-unit returns that are associated with membership in each particular industry and corporation. An 'Industry return' is the calculated average return of the business-units in that industry.

2 'Stable' industry effects are the (unobserved) time-invariant components of business-unit returns associated with membership in each industry. 'Stable' business-unit effects are the (unobserved) time-invariant components of business-unit returns that are not due to industry or corporate membership.

3 See Weiss' (1974) survey of this line of work.

4 See Scherer's (1980) review of prior work on this topic.

5 Ravenscraft (1980, 1983) is the best example of this line.

6 See Demsetz (1973) and Macke (1974), as well as Lippman and Rumelt (1982).

7 Hatten and Schendel (1977) provided early contributions; see McGee and Thomas (1986) for a review of the strategic groups literature.

8 See Teece (182), Rumelt (1984) and Wernerfelt (1984).

9 Conrad and Plotkin computed intra-industry variances directly from deviations about industry averages. Because they are not based on true variance components estimation, their results may over estimate intra-industry variances and produce substantially upwards biased estimates of inter-industry variances (although the latter was not of direct interest to them or to McEnally).

10 I have altered his notation to preserve consistency within this paper.

11 In particular, see Fisher and McGowan (1983).

12 It is common practice among FTC LB researchers to refer to a business-unit as an 'LB'. I avoid this usage because many others naturally, but erroneously, believe that the term 'Line of Business' refers to an industry group rather than to an individual business-unit within a larger firm.

13 Formally, neither β, nor $\beta_i - \beta_j$, $i \neq j$, is estimable. A common practice is to force estimability by imposing the 'usual' restrictions – in this case an assumption that the average business-unit effect in each industry is zero. The problem with that approach is that it 'deals' with the potential distortions caused by the unobserved business-unit effects by simply assuming them away.

14 Because the sample variance s_r^2 is computed about the sample average, rather than about the true mean μ, the sum of the variance components is not the sample variance. However, it is very close in both cases and the difference will be ignored in what follows.

15 See Rumelt (1987) for a summary of the *isolating mechanisms* viewpoint.

CHAPTER 6

MATURITY IS A STATE OF MIND

CHARLES BADEN-FULLER AND JOHN STOPFORD

Mature businesses are those whose managers believe they are imprisoned by their environments and are unable to succeed. At best, they seem doomed to give poor service to customers and barely adequate financial returns to shareholders. In contrast, dynamic businesses are able to sustain above-average performance, introduce new products and processes, and create new markets. They challenge the conventional norms and managerial beliefs pervading many mature businesses.

Mature and dynamic businesses exist uneasily side by side in many traditional, well-established industries. For example, Banc One is among the United States' most profitable and fastest-growing banks, with more than $76 billion in assets. Creative and innovative in the retail market and in the services it offers to other financial institutions, it is highly successful, while many in the banking industry, led by Citibank and Chase Manhattan, are racked by falling margins and bad loans.[1] Benetton, with more than $3 billion in retail sales, is Europe's first truly multinational textile retailer-producer.[2] Inventive in its approach to young fashion-conscious consumers, it is fast growing and very profitable in contrast to many of the textile businesses in northern Europe, which are continuing to struggle against imports from low-wage areas in southern Europe and less-developed countries.

Can a mature business turn itself into a successful one? It is amazing that a caterpillar can turn into a butterfly. The caterpillar creeps along the ground, has limited horizons, and is unable to move quickly. Yet that small furry larva can become one of nature's most graceful creatures, able to fly and traverse a much wider terrain. Naturally, one might doubt that a mature firm could become dynamic and entrepreneurial, yet such a metamorphosis is possible.

Most of us know that change is usually painful, slow, and immensely difficult. Of the many mature businesses that have tried to rejuvenate, some show improved results for a short time before the effects evaporate, and only a few succeed in holding on to improved performance for any length of time.[3] We found and examined many that tried and failed; we studied carefully a group that did succeed, and an even smaller number that went on to become industry leaders.[4] Firms in the last category did more than transform themselves; they transformed their industries and created new competitive rules. Such transformations are rare, but inspirational, and their rich histories suggest many valuable lessons. [...]

Our successful transformations share a common feature: rejuvenation was generated from within, using limited outside resources. Like the caterpillar, they seemed almost self-sufficient in their metamorphoses. They demonstrated that organizations could counter their own history of poor profitability and low growth and operate successfully in the same, often hostile, environment that weighed so heavily on their rivals.

For example, the rejuvenated Edwards High Vacuum, a British-based company, is the world's second largest producer of high-vacuum pumps and arguably the most successful, while its counterparts fight to stay alive. Edwards has had great success in the three major markets of the world – Japan, the United States, and Europe – beating local competition in these tough sectors and overcoming customer preferences to buy local products; yet in the early 1970s, Edwards was broke and near extinction.[5] Edwards is an obvious example of successful rejuvenation, but it may not remain successful forever, as more than sixteen Japanese firms have entered its industry since the mid-1980s.

Another rejuvenator is Hotpoint, the European appliance producer owned by General Electric of the United States and GEC of the United Kingdom, one of Europe's most successful appliance firms and one of the most profitable in the world. It was not always so: in the early 1970s, Hotpoint was almost broke, and Philips was Europe's largest and second most successful producer. Hotpoint has hauled itself from oblivion to become the industry's exemplar, while the European arm of the merged Philips-Whirlpool struggles to succeed. It appears that Hotpoint provides its customers with more reliable, more imaginatively designed products at lower cost. Hotpoint's position is constantly being challenged, but so far it has managed to stay with the leaders in terms of profitability and influence.

Butterflies die; so, eventually, do most organizations. We do not claim that our rejuvenators will be different in this respect. Our note of caution is well intended, for if rejuvenators can challenge leaders, they, too, can be challenged. Our focus is not on sustaining success, [...] but on attaining it. The achievements of our rejuvenators should not be minimized for they required great courage and determination. Showing that there is hope for mature businesses, that rejuvenation is possible on limited resources, we describe a pathway to renewal. In doing this we challenge much conventional wisdom about the capacity of firms to rejuvenate, the management of change, and the determinants of business performance.

PERCEPTIONS

What is a mature business? Is it defined by poor financial performance? It is true that many mature businesses do perform poorly, but this is neither a complete nor a satisfactory definition. Many factors distinguish mature businesses from dynamic or rejuvenated competitors, but the key is perception. Our actions are driven in part by our beliefs, just as our beliefs are informed by our actions and experiences. For a firm to rejuvenate, its managers must learn to act and think differently. Correcting perceptions is a hard task and central to instilling new kinds of behaviour; its importance is obvious from contrasting the beliefs of managers in mature and dynamic businesses.

Managers of mature businesses often told us, 'Our industry is mature' and 'We face many adverse outside pressures' and 'Failure is not our fault.'[6] They felt imprisoned by their environments. They often said that they experienced poor profitability and low organic growth because demand was growing slowly and the competitive environment was tough. They told us of the impossibility of improving their position significantly or dramatically, and typically rejected the suggestion that their strategy was defective and that they should try something different. 'Our industry is not like that', they cried. They seemed to believe that industry and environmental factors determine business performance. They would not accept that stable shares of the market, stable costs, and stable sales – the usual measures of maturity – mask turmoil and change in sub-markets, driven by such factors as changing consumer choice and new technology.

In every case we found managers in competing dynamic organizations with quite different views. 'We have to ride the waves of the seesaw nature of the environment'; 'Outside pressures must be overcome'; and 'Failure is always [the managers'] responsibility'. These managers thought more positively than their 'mature' counterparts; they did not see the environment as a prison or constraint, yet they believed that understanding the detail of their industries was critical. They invested heavily in building specific knowledge of how their technology, customers, and environment work.

The managers in our dynamic firms said that the environment has to be understood, mastered, and subdued. For them, strategies were not fixed in stone but creative and dynamic, to be moulded and changed through time. The dynamic firms seemed able to ride their industry's ups and downs. To be sure, recessions and booms affected them, but not in the same way as they did their mature rivals. [...]

The difficulty faced by mature firms is that their perceptions influence what managers do. One senior executive of a major French appliance firm explained that his firm had undertaken an extensive analysis of the environment, but that the analysis had been limited to firms operating or selling in the French market. This analysis showed that the firm was in a mature and hostile industry, that poor performance was inevitable, and that the business was not out of line with its perceived competitors. Even though customer surveys and profit figures were disappointing, the top team saw no need for radical action. But its analysis had ignored the activities of firms such as Hotpoint, which were neither world scale nor in direct competition. Hotpoint was doing things quite differently; its actions showed that the industry was not mature, that hostile factors could be overcome, and that its performance was remarkably good in comparison with the French firm and its competitors. Because the French managers believed that they could learn nothing from examining non competing firms, they had ignored the evidence.

Once this data block had been removed, it became clear that many aspects of the French firm were inefficient and inflexible and that it had misread the trends in customer desires and technological possibilities. The organization was able to rescue itself from its trapped thinking and realize that action was urgently needed to change its performance. It also became clear that its mediocre performance was not the result of 'outside forces beyond our control' but internal routines and behaviours 'which we can do something about'.

In some mature firms, the data have been collected, but then ignored or rejected. Rejection of data was a problem in a mature pump firm competing with Edwards.

Its team was shown data on the performance of Edwards and some of the other firms in the sector, which suggested that alternative ways of operating would improve performance. Management rejected the data. It could neither believe the facts nor accept their consequences. It fell into the common trap of refusing to accept that it could do things differently.

[...]

Even when some individuals in such firms find that external signals for change need to be addressed, they may face insuperable obstacles in persuading their colleagues to share their views. It is all too easy to be lulled into continuing inaction by plausible arguments – typically based on past experience – even when the reasoning is superficial and demonstrably false. Resistance can arise from personal unwillingness to face the uncomfortable fact that all one's professional experience might count for little in the future. The prospect of having to relearn how to manage or, worse, of losing relative status can be a powerful obstacle to changing one's mind and perspective. Further, it is often difficult to prove before the event that a deep-seated belief about how to compete has become obsolete. A lone voice on these matters can readily be ignored in a collective determination to uphold the traditional perspectives of the 'if it ain't broke, don't fix it' variety.

CREATING VALUE

Not only do perceptions about the environment distinguish mature firms from successful ones but beliefs about how value is created also differ fundamentally. In mature firms people seem to believe that if one group is doing well, it must be at the expense of another. When management is paid well, workers feel that it is at their expense; when shareholders are doing well, managers feel that they must be exploited, and many firms are suspicious of their suppliers and customers. These beliefs are linked to actions. When shareholders complain that returns are not high enough, managers in mature firms downgrade service to customers, tell staff to work longer hours, and attempt to extract larger discounts from suppliers. They see this as the only way to deliver extra profit. They seem unable to detect a positive connection between doing something differently to give better service to customers, getting staff to work more effectively rather than just longer hours, and integrating suppliers to better effect rather than just looking for the cheapest source.

Managers in dynamic businesses seem quite different. They believe it essential to satisfy all interest groups and treat them fairly and equally. Even in adverse and turbulent environments, successful firms are not only able to give good service and value to customers and a good and fair return to shareholders, but also to improve the lot of their employees and treat their suppliers and distributors properly. Our argument is not the obvious point that the more profitable the firm, the greater the largesse it can distribute. Ours concerns the perception of how value is created.

At the time of their crisis in maturity, many of our rejuvenating organizations had poor profits, bad service, poor staff relations, and a bad image with suppliers.

The awakening managers saw the way out through rethinking the business, and they typically started with the customer. [...]

For example, Richardson Sheffield rose from being an almost bankrupt UK knife producer to becoming a world leader in profits and market share by its novel approach to customers. It built customer value in stages in an industry whose service was traditionally dreadful. It began by giving speedier service and ensuring that goods always arrived on time. The more accurate service pointed up inefficiencies in the production and operating systems as well as encouraging customers to pay on time and in full. Almost simultaneously, product quality was improved by eliminating errors and reducing rejects. Although this required investment, much of it was modest, especially in the early stages of rejuvenation, and costs were quickly lowered. Rapid innovation and new product introduction came much later, but again the focus was on giving customers more value. Because Richardson became so much better than its rivals, it could produce new and attractive knives with excellent performance at comparable or even lower prices than rivals and still seek better and rising profitability.[7] This customer-slanted approach was central to its purpose and actions; but management did not use it as an excuse to treat other stakeholders badly. On the contrary, building customer value not only improved profitability, but also was consistent with treating the staff better, raising their wages, and giving them better working conditions.[8]

[...]

Managing stakeholders

Some argue that Western shareholders discourage a long-term horizon by encouraging short-term financial results, making rejuvenation very difficult. Our firms did not find that emphasis on the short term prevented their recovery. Although several complained about the demands for constantly improving financial ratios, they appreciated that their past history had often made shareholders understandably sceptical of their abilities. They all realized that trust had to be created by delivering results and learned how to manage the expectations of their shareholders. They also understood that getting things right for the customers, staff, suppliers, and distributors was the route to financial health. Value must be built as well as extracted.

Initially our rejuvenators had to be content with limited resources. Although some were part of large diversified firms, they did not benefit from generous handouts from their owners. Richardson was typical in that it was allowed to reinvest its profits in the business, but until recently its parent never gave it any other cash. Hotpoint was owned by one of the most frugal financially oriented companies in the United Kingdom, GEC Limited.[9] This parent expected cash and growth. In every case, there was pressure on the top team to deliver good financial results and to justify the usage of cash and capital. They all realized that modern accounting rules prevent their smoothing out some of the earnings fluctuations. All had difficulties, yet they achieved impressive long-run growth in profits and profitability in comparison to that attained elsewhere in the industry. On an absolute standard, they achieved a consistent record of before-tax profits close to 25 per cent of capital employed, an enviable distinction even among excellent performers.[10]

Motivating staff to perform differently and better was an essential step in rejuvenation. [...] All our rejuvenators recorded low staff turnover, high morale, and a line of people waiting to join their organizations. Most kept track of employee concerns, using surveys to complement unusual internal information flows. Many spoke of that elusive feature, the ability to work hard and have fun.

Understanding the need to create value among suppliers and distributors was common among our firms.[11] Long before supply partnerships became fashionable, Benetton managed its suppliers and distributors differently. It formed close strategic alliances, involving its partners with many aspects of its business and teaching them the skills they needed. This attitude was quite different from those adopted by many mature firms in the sector.[12] The results were remarkable. A typical Benetton shop is a low-capital, high-turnover operation, and its owner can expect to pay back her capital investment in three or four years. Benetton's agents organize distribution, and they average close to $1 million a year per person in remuneration. Benetton also contracts to many firms in northern Italy and around the world. Life for the subcontractors is not a bed of roses, but relative to others in the industry they do well. Since the early 1970s, nearly half the European textile business has disappeared in the face of import competition, yet Benetton has managed to grow its European textile base, allowing many of its subcontractors to prosper.

Many of our rejuvenators took the approach of delivering perceived value to multiple interest groups. This had the effect of growing the overall value created, increasing the size of the 'cake' so that all the stakeholders' shares could be larger. They were not concerned merely with profitability for shareholders, for that group was only one of many parties. This approach to business was in marked contrast to that of some firms which did not manage to rejuvenate, which argued about the division of the cake rather than taking care that all the slices of the cake should grow. The cynical may think that creating value among multiple interest groups is impractical idealism for the longer term, especially for mature firms. History is reassuring here, for over the longer time span there is no doubt that Western countries have achieved real wealth creation for all interest groups.

INNOVATION IN STRATEGY

Organizations can challenge maturity and create value for all their interest groups through strategic innovation. This means that they adopt a creative and novel approach to how they compete, where they compete, and with whom they compete. Such creativity does not come easily to mature firms, whose managers are often trapped into thinking that only one set of recipes is appropriate. Typically, they project the past into the future, believing that old approaches which once made leaders rich and enviable are still relevant. Thinking that their industry is stable, they believe that competitive battles are played by a single set of rules and that the winners are those with the greatest resources. They fail to recognize that all industries, especially traditional ones like airlines, automobiles, banking, retailing, and textiles, are capable of flux and that the real competitive battles are fought by those with different approaches. In these battles, the winners are often the less-well-resourced firms, sometimes the entrants, sometimes the rejuvenators, that have chosen to do something different.

Aspiring rejuvenators do well to learn from the past, studying those firms which have changed their industries. Ford was one of the greatest innovators of the century; in the early 1900s it pioneered the cheap production of standardized cars.[13] Henry Ford grew his company from relatively modest resources and soon the Tin Lizzie, or Model T, was in almost every household in the United States and in many in Europe. Industry progress has altered and transcended Ford's paradigm. As is well known, the idea of mass-produced variety was introduced in the 1920s by Alfred Sloan, the founder of General Motors (GM), but in his case variety was limited. For the next half-century, there were many innovations, but since the 1970s the US auto industry has found itself increasingly in trouble, and the firms appear to be stuck in maturity. During the 1980s American automakers invested many billions of dollars in new equipment and training, yet by the beginning of the 1990s they had made little progress in changing their basic cost structure, and their products were similar in many respects. It seems that, despite the investment, they still cling to old beliefs and habits and struggle with old methods of operating. American Motors has disappeared, Chrysler has seen its fortunes seesaw, and although Ford is showing signs of life, even GM seems to be in deep trouble. Both Ford and GM are trying to renew by radically changing the way they operate: both may rise again.[14]

US auto producers' difficulties appear to stem mainly from two quarters: the consumers and the Japanese. Consumers, who have shown an increasing reluctance to value unreliable cars that emphasize gimmicks and the annual model changes so long beloved of the US giants, have turned their attention to reliable compact cars offered first by the Europeans and then by the Japanese. This change in consumer behaviour, unanticipated by the major US firms, had profound effects on their fortunes. As important, if not more so, was the power of the Japanese competitors.[15]

In the 1950s, the Japanese automakers, neither well endowed nor well positioned, were saddled with a history of underperformance. On limited resources, they have risen to challenge the mighty US and European giants. The Japanese challenge has been revolutionary: better-quality cars, better appreciation of consumer needs, faster and more creative responses. Even more impressive was that the Japanese made the cars at less cost. They seem to have unlocked the secret of delivering *quality with high productivity*, and they are making good progress on delivering *variety, speed, and flexibility*. They have undermined the economic position of their US rivals by finding innovative and hard-to-copy ways of competing.

Japanese firms have no monopoly on strategically innovative behaviour. Bank One, Columbus, Ohio, for example, has developed and refined the idea of service to customers, including consumers, small businesses, and other financial institutions.[16] It was the first US bank to install an automated teller machine; it pioneered the idea of a financial service shopping mall, where a complete range of financial services is offered through retail outlets open, like ordinary shopping malls, seven days a week. Bank One has also been a market leader in developing banks within grocery stores in its region. Its development of services to other financial institutions has been more significant in terms of profits: processing credit card transactions at a greater speed, with greater flexibility and accuracy than most of its competitors. Its systems are sold to other banks around the world. Bank One, a driving force for change, forced many of its competitors to adjust, be taken over, or fail.

[...]

In Europe, a well-established service firm, British Airways, became one of the most profitable airlines in the world by adopting a new approach to the market. It was ailing and performing badly after years of state ownership and politicization. Under new leadership, it undertook a massive alteration program, changing the destinations it served, cutting out people and routes to focus its activities on a smaller territory. It also changed its procedures. Reassigning 31,000 of its 51,000 people to the newly redesigned marketing organization, it took customer service very seriously. With little real cost, it transformed its ability to deliver quality service and became more flexible and more responsive. The effects on its revenues, market share, and financial performance were dramatic.[17]

Our examples serve to illustrate the great range of possibilities for creating new value by choosing new ways to compete. [...] In mature organizations, such features as greater variety, higher quality, or faster reaction are commonly considered incompatible with one another and with low cost. Dynamic businesses resolve these dilemmas to deliver new combinations: *variety and efficiency; quality and productivity; speed and flexibility, and mass fashion.* These innovations involve more than product or process change, both of which are vital to progress; they combine many new or better actions to create an alternative approach to providing goods or services. [...]

Our rejuvenators followed the same path as the more famous British Airways, Japanese automobile producers, and Banc One. Edwards challenged its industry's values with durable pumps delivered quickly to the proper specification. Richardson made knives that were not only inexpensive, but also durable and fun. Courtelle delivered a wide range of multicolour fibres in small lots. While the achievements of each organization were specific to its context, all could be classified as capturing one or more new combinations.

Rejuvenating organizations have to complement their creativity in how they compete with new thinking about where and with whom to compete. Decisions about the scope of a business include selecting location, range of products or services, and channels of supply and distribution. We expound the guiding principles for rejuvenators: selecting a manageable scope and exploiting a market or technological trend ignored by the competition.

Hotpoint's rejuvenation was the result of a combination of factors. Not only did it lower costs and raise quality, but it adopted a creative approach to the scope of its business. It chose to compete in a single country when its rivals were in many countries and becoming Pan-European. Within the United Kingdom, it adopted an even-handed approach to selling through small and chain stores. This policy annoyed the chain stores, which demanded preferential treatment, and surprized competitors, which thought that small stores were an unimportant part of the market. By choosing unusual places to compete, Hotpoint was able to exploit ignored consumer trends and competitors' weaknesses.

RETHINKING THE ORGANIZATION

In rejuvenating a business, not only top managers have to change their thinking; everyone in the organization has to act and think differently. The most important and difficult things to change are people and their routines and, as Joseph Schumpeter pointed out, real progress can be achieved only by making people perform differently *inside* the business.[18]

Consider, for example, the change in tasks undertaken at the lower levels in an assembly operation when there is a shift from the old method of homogeneous mass production to the new focus on variety at low cost. The nature of the work changes as do the skills and thinking required. These include ability to create team skills to change tools, alter equipment settings, and reduce the number of substandard items in production. Performance measures change as well. The old order emphasized simple measures of productivity, often of individuals, and focused on maximising production-run lengths. In the new order, inventory is no longer an efficient buffer and production runs must be adjusted to market needs. Productivity in the single function of, say, production or selling is no longer dominant: the goal of the firm is to maximize responsiveness within the overall constraint of limited resources. [...]

A service organization also requires changes in thinking when there is a shift from standardization to a focus on speed and responsiveness. Old systems typically required specialization of tasks by function. The placing of an order for a service might go through several functions. The first checked the creditworthiness of the customer, the second checked the availability of capacity, the third looked for the part, and the fourth scheduled an engineer to do the work in a customer location; finally, the customer was informed of this appointment. It was a slow, cumbersome, and inflexible system. Although the time taken at each station was short, the elapsed time often amounted to days or even weeks because the work waited in lines or piles at each workstation. Worse, the customer was often given short notice of the service call; if it was not convenient, the system found it hard to cope. In some cases it was easier to start again! New systems typically assign one person or a team to take charge of all the work and be responsible for co-ordination with the customer. Such a process must provide a new way of thinking about data bases (they have to be readily accessible to do the checks), new views about who is allowed to complete schedules (the order taker has to have this power or else the system fails), and new views of authority (the order taker's decisions must not be over-ruled). Once these systems are running smoothly – usually no easy task – the overall costs fall as much waste and error are eliminated.

Such changes in operating tasks, commonly labelled process re-engineering, are not confined merely to production or service operations; they occur in every sphere of the organization. The work of the financial control department alters because the strategic task is different. Many of the reports generated under the old system need to be replaced by reports measuring the new needs. The tasks of the logistics department also change. In both services and manufacturing, orders are no longer processed and dispatched at the convenience of an outdated system but are tailored to customer requirements.[19]

It is not enough to change tasks and processes. Rejuvenating businesses have to rebalance the way their departments interrelate. In many industries, such as cars, steel, fibres, appliances, and cutlery, the old practice was to sell what was produced. That has to change to making what customers order or purchase. The sales department is no longer subservient to production; the two have to work together. The nature and span of the functions also change. In many cases the sales department has to become more active in marketing and new forms of co-ordination must exist among product development, production, and sales. With an emphasis on speed to market, the traditional isolation of research and development changes, too. Brand-new departments emerge and other functions collapse. As a consequence of the changes within functions, in processes and routines, and in rebalancing the parts, the rejuvenated organization both looks and thinks very differently from its mature former self.

BUILDING STRATEGIC STAIRCASES

Our rejuvenators had to change the mind-sets in their organizations to create value. The change had to be radical and incremental. [...] The change was radical in the sense that beliefs were altered, structures torn down, skills modified, and new technology introduced. Yet it was incremental in the sense that building new competencies, new capabilities, and new resources was not the work of a moment, but was deeply embedded. Starting with relatively modest beginnings, such as lowering the cost of making existing products or improving the quality and reliability of existing services, our organizations moved only a step at a time to more ambitious goals. They built capabilities that permitted them to challenge and resolve dilemmas and achieve sustained renewal. A few of our organizations reached a position of industry leadership in which they set new standards for a whole industry; for them the process from initial steps to achieving global leadership often took as long as a decade. There were no quick fixes.

The experience of our rejuvenators points to a way forward for others. Renewal can come from the process of successive creation of new capabilities we call *building and climbing a strategic staircase*.[20] For our rejuvenators, the labels on the stairs were often similar, but the sequence of steps varied by organization, even within the same industry. Stairs, such as lower cost, quality, speed, flexibility,

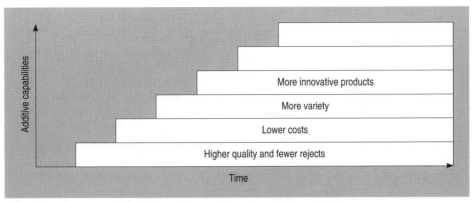

Figure 6.1 A hypothetical strategic staircase of capabilities

variety, and so forth, were built as the result of effort and initiatives. (See Figure 6.1.)

We talk of staircases, not ladders, to emphasize the need for durability and signal that organizations must work continually at their abilities to maintain their value. Since competitors are always close behind, failure to reinforce the capabilities – or steps – means that their value will diminish and the organizations quickly become sloppy. Building a staircase is difficult because the capabilities have to be kept in balance simultaneously. It is easy to build one step, but the next is harder, and each addition becomes harder still, unless the first are on secure foundations.

Although building takes time, the experience of our firms suggests that mature businesses have to feel a sense of urgency. Tom Peters and Robert Waterman spoke of the bias for action,[21] and our rejuvenators were quick to ensure that things which could be done today were not put off to tomorrow. Things like big projects have to be done in a measured way. Others, like small initiatives in the early stages, can be decided quite quickly. The pace of competition, the impatience of stakeholders, the uncertainties of office, and the politics of organizations mean that there must be sense of urgency in renewal. As one chief executive of a recently renewed organization put it:

> My life is a series of first hundred days. Like the US president, everyone has a hundred days to put a plan into action and make it work. Each hundred days, I have to have a new and better plan which builds on the last one. When I run out, either I shall be dead or else I shall quit.

Results do not always follow effort simply. Success usually comes in lumps, sometime later. In a new building, work on the foundations produces few noticeable results, but as the walls go up progress looks dramatic; the same applies to rebuilding an organization. This discontinuity of outcomes gives an illusion that rapid results can be achieved quickly, but builders know that walls without foundations do not make a secure house; the same is true in rejuvenated organizations.

Consider, for example, the innovation and production of the Laser knife by Richardson. [...] This invention was the source of a dramatic increase in the profitability of the firm. The team that worked on the knife produced the inventions in about six months, and the knife was in mass production within a year. This highly successful item, which spawned other innovations, appears to have all the hallmarks of rapid transformational change. But without the laborious effort of building skills in the organization, the invention would not have been produced so quickly. It took more than five years of work to perfect the grinding technology that makes Richardson knives among the best in quality and lowest in cost in the world.

The example of incremental building looking like radical change was common across all our companies. Securing effective change is laborious, and we found many examples of firms that tried to shortcut a change process and failed because they did not alter beliefs or failed to give people the skills and tools to do the task better.

WHO ARE THE REJUVENATORS?

Rejuvenation is not the work of just a few top managers; building a strategic staircase requires effort and creativity from all who work in a business. The task is not impossible, because most mature and poorly performing organizations do have spirited entrepreneurial individuals. The difficulty lies in entrepreneurial behaviour being individualistic and unconnected and having little overall effect. [...] The process of renewal involves connecting the existing and disjointed individual activities and spreading them through the business.

Renewal is not a final goal; many firms aspire to attain industry leadership. That also requires entrepreneurial behaviour which is more extensive, more deeply embedded and connected across the whole organization, including even suppliers and distributors. [...]

The problem faced by many mature organizations is that renewal and change appear very risky, much more risky than the status quo. This perception has to be altered. The real risks of rejuvenation, especially if it is undertaken in stages, are less than imagined. Clever rejuvenators manage their risks most carefully. They all understand that when one is far behind, only innovative plays will succeed in radically altering their positions. Just as in a sailing race or sports event where the distant follower can catch the leader only if he or she tries a new tactic, so too in industry. The trick in the real world of business is to make creative plays with low risk and with limited resources, something only entrepreneurial organizations can do.

At the start, constrained by their history and their resource limitations, our organizations looked for creative plays that did not expose them unduly. [...] Our organizations simplified their businesses so that costs could be reduced and the whole managed better. This could be seen as an attempt to reduce risk. They also encouraged many small investments, each of which could fail without causing serious damage, but each of which, if it succeeded, would further progress. These initiatives were especially aimed to encourage individual and small-team entrepreneurial behaviour. We therefore depict the first phases of rejuvenation – *galvanizing and taking many new initiatives* – as of low risk.

As each organization made progress on its strategic staircase, it became more imperative to create new competitive advantages and to take the steps required to secure the renewal. These initiatives were aimed at connecting functions and teams to form a more business-driven entrepreneurial activity. [...] Usually much larger moves than those of the first stage, the risks, although greater, were acceptable because the organization had a more secure foundation and was better resourced. These frame-breaking investments could not have been successfully undertaken earlier; they required a level of skills and capabilities coupled with aspirations and beliefs not previously in evidence.

The few rejuvenators that succeeded in attaining and maintaining industry leadership faced the biggest risk.[22] To get in front, they had to find new patterns of activity that required the whole organization to work together. To stay in front required fending off competitors and, from time to time, undertaking radical reshaping. Teamwork on an organizational scale is risky as well as rewarding. Successful industry leaders have the resources and capabilities to bear these risks, but they too can fail.

Figure 6.2 is a diagrammatic attempt to capture these differential risks and spheres of activities and emphasize the staircase of progress from renewal to

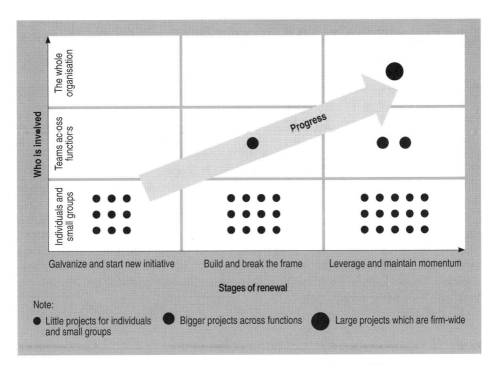

Figure 6.2 The locus of activity in different stages of rejuvenation

industry leadership. At the start, many small initiatives (small circles) are undertaken by individuals and small groups throughout the organization, each of which generally involves only small resources. In renewal, the entrepreneurship becomes more prevalent, the smaller initiatives more numerous and supplemented by bigger collective projects (medium-size circles) that cross functional divides. At the third stage, major projects are required which involve all parts of the organization working together entrepreneurially, hence the large circles. These projects supplement other, more numerous individual initiatives and, collectively, permit the business to master its industry.

Those who take risks and succeed know that they have to appreciate the role of fortune, and all our rejuvenators claimed, 'We were lucky.' Hotpoint was lucky that its rivals ignored it and that the chain stores eventually fell into line. Edwards was lucky that just as it launched a new pump, designed originally for the chemical industry, the US semiconductor market boomed and created new demand for which this pump was best suited. Richardson was lucky with its remarkable owner who set the challenge of the Laser knife. But luck is exploited best by those who are well prepared. As Arnold Palmer once said of his putting performance, 'The more I practice, the luckier I become.' Or, as Louis Pasteur, the world-famous French scientist, observed more than a century ago, 'Chance favours the prepared mind.' So Danny Rozenkranz at Edwards made the luck possible by seeing the boom early and recognizing the potential of the new pump.

REJUVENATORS AIM TO CONTROL THEIR DESTINY

Whereas managers in mature businesses are imprisoned by their beliefs and feel powerless to alter their destiny, rejuvenated firms seek to control their industries and their future. The central theme of our [work] is that managers need to take control of their destiny; strategy is not a question of fit where the economic environment is uppermost and the firm largely a passive actor. In our view, the firm is a dynamic actor shaping its environment. In this conception, the task of the firm is to read the economic signals and recognize the potential opportunities to shape and harness tastes, technology, and competitor behaviour.

Put simply, we suggest that for the dynamic firm the direction of causality is from the organization to the market. It recognizes the role of innovative strategy, choosing territories, building staircases, and using entrepreneurship to shape the environment. In contrast, the mature business sees the causality as the other way around. For such managers, the environment is beyond control, old recipes are best, and value is a subtraction game.

NOTES

1 Banc One is the holding company for its member Bank One banks. For information on Banc One Corporation and Bank One, Ohio, we are grateful for interviews with executives and numerous articles, including R. Teitelman, 'The magnificent McCoys', *Institutional Investor*, July 1991.

2 We thank G. Lorenzoni for his research into Benetton, some of which is reported in The Benetton Case, London Business School Case Series, 4, 1988.

3 It will be clear that we are concerned with business units. It is obvious that a corporation with a portfolio of poorly performing business can improve its statistics by closing some units and purchasing better performers – this of course is not the same as rejuvenating a business. There is a large literature on the turnaround of businesses, much of which is referred to in this book. It is not possible to summarize it here, but note that some of the most valuable studies are of individual organizational transformations, such as R.L. Shook, *Turnaround: The New Ford Motor Company* (New York: Prentice Hall, 1990). Typically these studies look internally. More external studies include P.H. Grinyer, D.G. Mayes, and P. McKiernan, *Sharpbenders: The Secrets of Unleashing Corporate Potential* (Oxford: Basil Blackwell, 1988), which studies both corporate and business sharpbending as well as a few genuine rejuvenations.

4 For reasons of confidentiality, we cannot list the many who tried to rejuvenate but failed. They came from the sectors of appliances, chemicals, cutlery, fibres, pumps, steel, and textiles. Those which renewed include vibrant organizations such as Wolsey of Courtaulds Textiles, Merloni Electrodomestici, TEM of Thomson (now Ocean). Those which renewed and achieved industry leadership include Edwards High Vacuum (part of BOC, the large industrial gases group), Hotpoint (part of GE-GEC), Cook (the Sheffield casting firm), Richardson (once independent and now part of McPherson's), and Weir pumps (part of the Weir Group).

5 Much of the evidence on Edwards High Vacuum is reported in J.M. Stopford, *Edwards High Vacuum International*, London Business School, 1989.

6 An exploration of such statements in the context of appliances appeared in M.R.S. Green 'Beliefs, actions and strategic change: a study of paradigms in UK domestic appliances industry', in *Papers and Proceedings of Academy of Management Conference*, New Orleans, August 1987.

7 Much of the information about Richardson is reported in R.M. Grant and C.W.F. Baden-Fuller, *The Richardson Sheffield Story*, London Business School Case Series, 2, 1987. The company has been acquired by the Australian group McPherson's, which now holds 15 percent of the world market.

8 The staff, of course, had to change their work practices and style of operating. Not all were able to adjust, but those who did found the changes were rewarded. Richardson claims that it pays above the average for its local market.

9 See M. Goold and A. Campbell, *Strategies and Styles: The Role of the Centre in Managing Diversified Corporations* (Oxford: Basil Blackwell, 1987).

10 Where possible, we used internal accounting records for the relevant business unit, cross-checked with public accounts.

11 R. Lamming, *Beyond Partnership: Strategies for Innovation and Lean Supply* (Hemel Hempstead: Prentice Hall, 1993), provides an up-to-date review of these issues.

12 An exception is Marks and Spencer, the UK retailer, which for decades has followed a policy of close links with its suppliers. But until more recently, Marks and Spencer did not involve its suppliers in its strategic thinking.

13 See also D. Hounshell, *From the American System to Mass Production* (Baltimore: Johns Hopkins University Press, 1984).

14 Shook, *Turnaround*, describes some of Ford's progress. J.P. Womak, D.T. Jones, and D. Roos, *The Machine that Changed the World* (New York: Rawson Associates, 1990), confirms the slow emergence of the results.

15 There is an extensive literature on the causes of the demise of the US automobile companies. Of particular note are Womak, Jones, and Roos, *The Machine That Changed the World*, and Shook, *Turnaround*.

16 Bank One is a subsidiary of Banc One Corporation.

17 We are grateful to Nick Georgiardis, former director of British Airways, for the background information on its transformation. Many of the details have appeared elsewhere.

18 In highlighting the importance of innovations we owe our intellectual debt to J.A. Schumpeter, whose *Theory of Economic Development*, which first appeared in German in 1912, is better known in the 1934 English version. Schumpeter emphasized the role of innovation in the dynamics of competition and, in particular, in the way in which successful firms emerge. It was here that he coined the famous phrase, 'the perennial gale of creative destruction.'

19 All our rejuvenators re-engineered their business processes. The nature of such changes is documented in several books, including T.H. Davenport, *Process Innovation* (Boston: Harvard Business School Press, 1993); H.J. Johansson, P. McHugh, A.J. Pendlebury, and W.A. Wheeler, *Business Process Re-engineering* (New York and Chichester: Wiley, 1993).

20 The need to create multiple advantages is an old idea, and the concept of this being a staircase is neatly captured by our colleagues P. Williamson and M. Hay in 'Strategic staircases', *Long Range Planning* 24, no. 4, 1991: 36–43.

21 T.J. Peters and R.H. Waterman, Jr., *in Search of Excellence* (New York: Harper & Row, 1982).

22 This point is also made persuasively by R.T. Pascale, *Managing on the Edge* (New York: Touchstone, Simon & Schuster, 1990).

CHAPTER 7

ON THE LIMITS OF A FIRM-BASED THEORY TO EXPLAIN BUSINESS NETWORKS: THE WESTERN BIAS OF NEO-CLASSICAL ECONOMICS

NICOLE WOOLSEY BIGGART AND GARY G. HAMILTON

INTRODUCTION

The leading business success story of the last two decades cannot be disputed: the tremendous growth and economic development of the East Asian economies. During the fifteen-year period from 1965 to 1980, Japan and the newly industrialized countries (NICs) of South Korea, Taiwan, Hong Kong, and Singapore grew at an average annual rate of 8.8%. At the same time, the US economy grew 2.9%. In the period from 1980 to 1985, a time of world recession, Japan grew 3.8%, while the Asian NICs 'slowed' to 6.6%. The comparable figure for all industrial market economies for that five-year period was 2.5%.

Both the popular and the scholarly press have lauded the economic development of Asia using such hyperbole as 'miracle' and 'astounding' to describe nations whose economies were little more than rubble after World War II and the Korean War. Observers have marvelled at the ability of countries with poor resources not only to grow, but also to become world-class competitors in the most advanced industrial sectors, including automobiles, steel, shipbuilding, electronics, and pharmaceuticals.

It is no small irony that precisely those countries that Westerners have marvelled at have come under severe attack for their patterns of economic development and international trade practices. Analysts and trade negotiators describe Japan and her neighbours as being 'unfair' in bilateral trading relations, and suffering 'imperfections' that 'distort' their domestic economies. These criticisms are most often levelled at the dense networks of ties between firms in Asia, ties that look like cartels to Westerners. Network ties link major industrial firms into groups, such as Sumitomo in Japan and Samsung in Korea, as well as the myriad small manufacturers in the Taiwanese economy.

Why the paradox? Why should Asian economies that have been extraordinarily successful by every economic measure at the same time be described as unprincipled and distorted? Is it merely a reflection of Westerners' sense of fair play or perhaps even their own inadequacy in the face of vigorous economic competition? Or is it a fundamental misunderstanding of the patterns of Asian capitalism?

While it is no doubt frightening to have one's economic well-being challenged by other nations' competitive success, we do not believe that this is the primary reason for the strong American critique of Asian economies. For example, the United States has had substantial trade deficits with its second-largest trading partner, Canada, for years with little public outcry. The recent heavy investment by the Japanese in the United States has met with far more invective than has US investment by the British or the Dutch, two economies that have higher levels of American investment than Japan does.

We believe, rather, that the response to Asian capitalism as unfair and distorted is primarily the result of ethnocentrism, a Western-based view of the proper organization and functioning of a market economy. American economic thinking is largely grounded in the neo-classical economic tradition. This perspective views competition between autonomous economic actors, both individual capitalists and firms acting as fictive individuals, as a necessity of mature capitalism. In numerous ways the United States has institutionalized competitive individualism in its market structure. Asian economies, in contrast, are organized through networks of economic actors that are believed to be natural and appropriate to economic development. Likewise, Asian nations have institutionalized policies and practices that flow from a network vision of correct market relations.

We argue two points in this chapter. First, Western academic and popular conceptualizations of Asia, particularly those based on the neo-classical model, are biased portrayals of Asian economic dynamics. A Western perspective leads analysts to conclude that Asia's network capitalism rests on market imperfections, and therefore that the vibrant capitalism of the region has been artificially induced and maintained. Second, and more important, the successful network structure of Asian capitalism reveals the neo-classical model to be not a general theory of capitalism, but rather an ethnocentric model developed from Western experience and applicable only to Western economies. We will not argue that neo-classical economics is wrong, merely that its utility is limited to settings where its institutional assumptions are in force.

MARKETS ARE NOT ALL ALIKE

The neo-classical economic paradigm conceives of ideal conditions for perfect competition: a large number of firms making substitutable products so that buyers have no reason to prefer one firm's output over another, independent and dispersed firms, and complete knowledge of all offers to buy and sell (Stigler 1968).

This model of competitive economic relations conceives of actors as isolated units. Capitalists, both buyers and sellers, ideally are independent and mindless of one another and indifferent as to the parties from whom they buy or whom they sell. Price is the only criterion for a transaction. This is an asocial conceptualization of economic action (Abolafia and Biggart 1990) in the sense that it believes meaningful social relations are unimportant to competitive outcomes under idealised conditions. Where social relations are recognized to occur, they are viewed pejoratively and called 'friction'. Social relations in a market can lead only to such anticompetitive practices as price-fixing, restriction of output, and other forms of collusion. Keeping economic actors apart is a crucial condition of capitalism in the neo-classical view.

Western markets, particularly the Anglo-American economies, attempt to approximate tenets of the neo-classical paradigm at the level of both firms and individuals. Laws, including corporate and employment regulations, stress individual rights and obligations. Contracts, for example, bind only on the parties involved and not on their families or communities. Employers for the most part hire, promote, and otherwise reward workers based on their personal efforts. Seniority, to many Americans, does not seem a just way of determining pay or promotion. Affirmative action laws similarly express a belief that employment decisions should be made regardless of social characteristics or connections; it is individual competence and effort that should be the basis of selection.

Americans are fearful of hiring spouses, blood relatives, and even friends into the same company. Many firms have antinepotism rules to limit the effects of personal relations in the workplace, effects assumed to be detrimental. Employers may require disclosure of stock ownership and other ties, even through relatives, to outside firms. Disclosure guards against favouritism in awarding contracts, something most Americans think is wrong.

An individualistic institutional structure exists at the corporate level as well. State regulatory agencies, such as the Federal Trade Commission, prevent firms from colluding with each other. Strong antitrust laws enforced by the Attorney General limit monopoly power and the formation of cartels, except under very unusual situations (such as public utilities, where there exists what economists call a 'natural' monopoly). The role of the US government in the economy is largely a regulatory one. Government does not have a co-ordinated planning role, and does not have a strategic management plan for the United States' place in the world economy. Its primary function is to maintain competitive – that is, autonomous – conditions between economic actors.

At both the level of individuals and the level of corporations, people in the United States act to maintain an 'open' market in which independent buyers, sellers, and workers can pursue their own interests in arm's-length transactions. In the United States 'open' means free from social relations between individuals and firms.

MARKET CONDITIONS IN ASIA

The free market conditions Westerners think are crucial technical requisites for a successful capitalist economy are frequently not in evidence in Asia. In fact, they are often not even presumed to be necessary. Asian economies espouse different institutional logics from Western economies, ones rooted in connectedness and relationships: Asians believe that social relations between economic actors do not impede market functioning, but rather promote it. Just as Western economies have institutionalized ways of maintaining autonomy between actors, Asian economies are rooted in institutions that encourage and maintain ties.

For example, the crucial economic actor in Asian societies is typically not the individual, but rather the network in which the individual is embedded. In major Japanese firms, cohorts are often hired, compensated, and promoted, with individual performance differences having little import until late in a career (Clark 1979). Korean firms encourage workers to nominate their friends and relatives for vacant jobs; Koreans believe that social relations exert pressure on workers to perform well and to work hard for fear of embarrassing their nominators. The major source of venture capital in Taiwan, a country noted for its economy of small-scale entrepreneurial concerns, is friends and relatives (Biggs 1988). Impersonal sources of funds, such as banks and unknown investors, are far less important in Taiwan than in Western societies. In all three countries, buyers favour suppliers with whom they have an established relation, rather than the least-cost supplier. They routinely violate the neo-classical expectation that price is the critical factor in purchase decisions.

Although relationships are manifest in multiple ways at the interpersonal level in Asian business, they are seen dramatically and most importantly in business networks between Asian firms. It is impossible to underestimate the importance of business networks – sometimes called enterprise or business groups – to the development of Asian capitalism. The Japanese economy is dominated by *kigyo shudan*, modern-day descendants of pre-World War II *zaibatsu*, family-controlled conglomerates. Kigyo shudan are networks of firms in unrelated businesses that are joined together, no longer by family ties, but by central banks or trading companies. Michael Gerlach (1992) has recently argued that these inter-market networks constitute a form of capitalism that he calls 'alliance capitalism'. Many of the largest firms in Japan are members of these major business networks: Mitsubishi, Mitsui, Sumitomo, Fuji, Dai-Ichi, and Sanwa. Other forms of networks link Japanese businesses. For example, a major manufacturer and its affiliated subcontractors (e.g., the Toyota 'independent group'), and small neighbourhood retailers (*gai*) that may invest together (Orru, Hamilton, and Suzuki 1989).

The South Korean economy is dominated by networks that on the surface resemble Japan's, but in fact have substantial differences (Amsden 1989; Whitley 1990; Kim 1991; Biggart 1990; Orru, Biggart, and Hamilton 1991; Hamilton and Biggart 1988). South Korean *chaebol* are networks of firms owned and controlled by a single person or family and organized through a central staff, which may be a holding company or 'mother' firm. By far the most powerful actors in the Korean economy are the major chaebol networks, which include Samsung, Hyundai, Lucky-Goldstar, Daewoo.

The Japanese and Korean economies are ruled by networks of medium-sized to very large firms. Networks are important in Taiwan, too, but they link smaller numbers of smaller firms (Numazaki 1986; Hamilton and Kao 1990; Hamilton and Biggart 1988). The leading economic actor in Taiwan, although occupying a less central position than the kigyo shudan or chaebol, is the family firm and family-owned conglomerates, which are called *jituanqiye*. Chinese business networks are usually based on family and friendship ties between owners and partners who often cross-invest in businesses, hold multiple positions throughout the network, and act as suppliers or upstream producers to downstream firms.

What the American economy works so studiously to prevent – connections between individuals, links between firms – Asian economies accept as appropriate and inevitable. Moreover, Asian nations have institutionalized networks and built economic policies around the presence and presumption of social relations among market actors.

EXPLAINING DIFFERENCES

With the extraordinary success of Asian economies, both business people and scholars have attended to the apparent differences between Asian and Western business practices. Analysts hope to understand the differences in order to explain success, to project patterns of growth, and to predict likely competitive outcomes of Asian economic practices. There are diverse explanations for Asian economic differences from the west, but three types of theories are most influential: development theories, culture theories, and market imperfection theories.

Development theory

Development theories are concerned with the factors that aid or impede economies in their presumed march toward industrialization. In their earliest form, 'modernization' theories assumed a linear progression that all nations passed through on the path toward development into a modern capitalist economy, epitomised by the United States and industrialized Europe. There was the presumption that stages of development were more or less alike and that at some unspecified future moment there would be a convergence, with all market economies having similar market institutions – for example, a capitalist class, a freely accessible money and banking system, a rational orientation toward economic matters.

More recent versions of modernization theory argue that learning is possible; countries can skip stages by observing and emulating more advanced nations, or by having 'modern' economic practices imposed on them through colonial subjugation, for example, or as a precondition for development loans. Alice Amsden's

Asia's Next Giant: South Korea and Late Industrialization (1989) is in this genre, arguing that South Korea was able to rapidly industrialize, leapfrogging early development stages, by appropriating technologies and processes formulated by more advanced nations.[1]

Alternatively, another set of development theories, conventionally labelled 'dependency' theories, argues that the more-developed industrial economies are systemically linked to and impede the development of the less-developed economies (Evans and Stephens 1988). Powerful advanced nations maintain the dependency of less-developed economies by enforcing, for example, unfavourable trading relations or lending policies. A web of political relations shapes nations' differential possibilities for advancement.

There are a number of criticisms of development theories (Evans and Stephens 1988). It is increasingly clear, for example that there is no convergence toward a single model of capitalism as exemplified by the West. It is also equally apparent that the world economy is neither a monolithic economic system nor easily divided into core and peripheral areas (Gereffi and Hamilton 1990). Moreover, Asia's differences, as well as those of some other industrialising nations, are not disappearing as they become more developed (Orru, Biggart, and Hamilton 1991). While it is certainly true that nations can learn from more developed economies, the learning thesis is not especially useful because it cannot predict which countries can or will learn, or indeed which models they will choose to emulate. For example, both Taiwan and South Korea were colonies of Japan, and both received substantial economic aid and policy directives from the United States. Neither economy looks very much like the United States or Japan, although Korea has adopted some elements of Japanese industrial organization.

One branch of development economics, the endogenous growth models, does ask why differences in the fact and rate of economic growth and well-being persist over time. Neo-classical economic models predict that capital, both labour and financial, flows to the most efficient locales, eventually limiting nation-state differences. In fact, there is great diversity in per capita economic well-being and national growth rates, and the differences endure. Endogenous growth models posit that variations are attributable to differences in trade policies and human capital differences – that is, the differential investment in learning by various labour forces. Labour forces are not all the same in their approach to hard work, learning, and productivity. Endogenous growth models go beyond an earlier individualistic approach to human capital, which focused on the returns on investment in learning by individuals, to posit that there are social returns on effects, at the level of groups such as families and firms, to the acquisition of new skills and orientations by labour. It seems to us that this perspective is important in raising the unit of observation from the individual to the group, showing the cumulative effects of individual economic decisions (for example, to invest in school rather than to take a low-skilled job). By focusing on effects, however, endogenous growth models do not seek answers as to why observably different patterns are pursued in different locales, whether they be trade policies or human capital decisions. R. E. Lucas, for example, dismisses the possibility of identifying the social impulse for human capital acquisition: 'We can no more directly measure the amount of human capital a society has, or the rate at which it is growing, than we can measure the degree to which a society is imbued with the Protestant Ethic' (1988:35).

Culture theory

Culture theories do precisely what the endogenous growth models leave aside: attempt to account for the differential bases for economic action and organization. They are popular in journalistic accounts of Asian management practice, but also have academic standing (e.g., Berger and Hsiao 1988). Culture – the beliefs, values, symbols – of a society is understood to be the basis for economic practices and institutions. For example, the Japanese penchant for involving all members of a firm in decision making is seen to be an expression of a belief in the importance of consensus and harmony (*wa*) (Alston 1986). In contrast, the American CEO is expected to make independent decisions, probably after consulting subordinates, but ultimately to take individual responsibility. The two sets of decision-making practices, common in their respective economies, are explained by culture theory as respective expressions of the cultural values of communitarianism and individualism.

Cultural explanations have much truth in them; clearly, a preference for groupness or individualism will be reflected in commercial practices. Culture, though, is a problematic basis for comparative analysis (Hamilton and Biggart 1988: S69–S74). American culture, even if one could define it, cannot explain the differences in business practice one encounters in the United States. Is IBM's strong hierarchical management style the 'true' organizational expression of American culture? Or is Apple Computer's decentralized and team-based system the 'real' exemplar of American ideals? When comparing Japan with the West, which Western practices form the basis of comparison? Culture theories, by building up from rich and diverse data in a single society, make generalizations – and hence comparisons – difficult.

Market imperfection theory

Market imperfection theory is based on the logic of neo-classical economics and is the most important explanation of Asian distinctiveness. Under perfectly competitive market conditions, optimal firm size is a function of the demand for and the economies of scale to produce a product (Stigler 1968:1). When markets are not fully competitive, that is, when they suffer from constraints, then firm size is influenced by the constraints as well as by production and demand requirements. For example, when there is no market, as in a socialist command economy, then decrees by the state will influence the size and structure of the firm. Although economists recognise that a fully competitive market is an ideal condition that does not exist anywhere in reality, they use this conception of the ideal market and the optimal firm as a model against which to assess real conditions. They can then compare actual markets and firms to see how well they conform to the ideal. Deviations are either more or less 'perfect'.

This conceptualization of the perfect market, with its conditions of autonomy and impersonality and its resultant 'optimal' firms, was developed as a means to understand the structure and functioning of Western societies, primarily the British and American economies. Economists, however, do not regard this model as an abstract, ethnocentric representation of these economies, but rather as a general model of capitalism that can be applied worldwide.

According to neo-classical theory there are only two forms of economic organization: markets and firms (also called hierarchies). Economists have difficulty applying this model of markets and firms to Asia with its developed interfirm networks (Aoki 1984, 1990; Goto 1982). Networks are neither independent market actors, nor hierarchically governed firms. Nonetheless, Western economists attempt to interpret Asian economic organization in terms of this dualistic neo-classical conceptualization. Alfred Chandler, for example, describes the Japanese zaibatsu, the historical precursor to the kigyo shudan, as an 'organization comparable to the M-form', or multidivisional firm that originated in the United States (1982, p. 22). Nathaniel Leff (1976, 1978) writes that Asian firms, as well as firms in other non-Western societies, actually constitute a single firm organized on a 'group principle'. 'The group is a multicompany firm which transacts in different markets but which does so under common entrepreneurial and financial control' (Leff 1978, p. 644). Others endorse the idea that despite some differences, the Asian business group is the functional equivalent of the Western firm. Like Western firms, some groups are large and monopolistic while others are small or operate in competitive markets in which the group principle allows economies of scale without actually expanding the size of firms.

Several Japanese economists (Aoki 1984; Goto 1982) have slightly qualified this view. Knowing Japan well, they argue that Japanese business groups are neither firms nor markets, but constitute an intermediate phenomenon that exists between the two. They argue that Japanese business groups do not operate like a single firm. They have neither a single set of owners, nor a tightly integrated system of financial controls. They are not independent, competitive firms, nor do they constitute a single megafirm. They are networks, according to Goto (1982), that buffer and channel market forces.

Despite some disagreement about how to categorize Asian business groups, economists do concur on how to explain their presence. Virtually all use a theory of market imperfections that to neo-classical economists seems self-evident. States Leff:

> The group pattern of industrial organization is readily understood as a micro-economic response to well-known conditions of market failure in the less-developed countries. In fact, the emergence of the group as an institutional mode might well have been predicted on the basis of familiar theory and a knowledge of the environment in these countries (1978:666).

Chandler (1982) explains the differences between the Japanese zaibatsu and the M-form American and European conglomerates by citing 'undeveloped' capital markets in Japan. Even Goto explains Japanese business group networks the same way:

> The group is an institutional device designed to cope with market failure as well as internal organizational failure. Under certain circumstances, transactions within a group of firms are more efficient than transactions through the market or transactions through the internal organization of the firm (1982, p. 69).

More recently, but using the same logic, Jorgensen, Hafsi, and Kiggundu (1986) argue that in developing countries, a category in which they place Japan, market imperfections occur in the course of 'striving for self-sufficiency' and the absence of an adequate 'density of market transactions' (424). In promoting a 'rational', risk-controlling policy for industrialization, governments promote such market 'distortions' as tariffs to protect infant industries, exchange controls to create price advantages, and administrative hierarchies to co-ordinate resource allocation and other forms of market imperfections (426). They note four common 'aberrations' in developing economies: the entrepreneurial family firm, the industrial cluster, the multinational corporation subsidiary, and the state-owned enterprise (427–32). All four of these so-called aberrations are common in Asian economies, even the most developed, and are not disappearing.

There are other variants of the market imperfection thesis. Political economists emphasize the importance of the 'developmental state' in creating systemic distortions, both in the economy and in the society, that allow for concentrated capital accumulation and rapid development. Such theorists thus create a link between market imperfection and development theories. American trade negotiators likewise argue that Japan has created 'structural impediments' to 'free' trade that prevent American access to Japanese markets; most notable of the alleged impediments are business groups that limit competition. Although they focus more on political factors that create distortions, the logic of both political economists and trade negotiators is much the same as the market-imperfections thesis: Asian economies deviate from the Western ideal and therefore suffer imperfections.

We believe that market imperfection theories, like developmental and cultural theories, do not explain the Asian 'difference' very well. The neo-classical paradigm is a framework that assumes one fundamental 'perfect' economy against which real economies can be gauged. Although it does not exist anywhere in reality, the model is an approximation of the market economies that developed during Western industrialization. It is not a theory of Asian capitalism but a theory of Western capitalism applied to Asia, and its logic is akin to the logic of Henry Higgins' question in *My Fair Lady*: 'Why can't a woman be more like a man?' Answers to a question so framed can only detail the ways in which a woman deviates from a man; they cannot lead to discovery of what a woman is. A market imperfection theory can describe the ways in which Asian capitalism deviates from the neo-classical ideal, but it cannot discover the principles of Asian capitalism.

Evidence of the economic vitality of Asia leads us to advance two points. First, a model of Asian capitalism based on Asia's institutional foundations is overdue. It stretches credibility to describe Japan, the world's second-largest economy, as 'imperfect' or 'deviant', even for analytic purposes. Second, the poor fit of the neo-classical model to the Asian case, suggests to us not an imperfect economy, but rather an inappropriate theory. Asia calls into questions the presumption that this model is a general theory of capitalism. We will argue that the neo-classical model is more suited to the institutional arena that it was developed to explain: England and the United States. In fact, neo-classical economics rests on an institutional theory of firm autonomy that displays great power in explaining Western economic dynamics. It is not, however, a general theory of capitalism.

THE DEVELOPMENT OF MARKETS IN THE WEST

The neo-classical model is based on a central idea: the autonomy of economic actors, both individuals and firms, who seek their self-interest in economic matters. Actors go into the marketplace and, mindless of all social and moral considerations, rationally calculate exchanges based only on price. This portrait of economic actors as individuated, asocial, and rational is the useful fiction that economists have drawn to provide a parsimonious behaviourist model of economic action. While few economists would argue that any real person acts exactly this way, it is assumed that this is the ideal that most people, at least in the aggregate, approximate.

Homo economicus is a generic individual distinguished not by sex, ethnicity, religion, age, or any other social characteristic. The presumption is that any person, in any place, at any time would behave more or less the same way – that is, as a rational individual. In building on this central idea, neo-classical economics assumes that social relations and characteristics do not make significant differences in economic choice. To the extent that these assumptions have a universal reality, they support claims that the neo-classical paradigm is a general theory of capitalism.

Recently, a number of scholars have attempted to question tenets of the neo-classical paradigm. For example, the individual decision-making studies of psychologists Tversky and Kahneman (1974) suggest that people are not the hyperrational actors assumed by the model. Economic sociologist Amitai Etzioni (1988) has marshalled substantial evidence that people consider moral as well as economic factors in making economic choices. Anthropologist Richard Shweder's (1986) anthropological studies of a community in India demonstrate that economic rationality is based on substantive beliefs, not abstract calculus. Similarly, Mark Granovetter has argued that the economy is embedded in social relationships and is not the aggregate activity of isolated individuals (1985). Our own studies (Hamilton and Biggart 1988; Orru, Biggart, and Hamilton 1991) have suggested, as we do in this chapter, that Asian economic action is based on different principles of social action, principles developed through the historical experience of Asian nations.

While these and other studies question crucial elements of the neo-classical model, particularly as they apply to non-Western locales, it remains clear that the model does describe in important ways the aggregate dynamics of Western economies, especially those of the United States.

We believe that it is possible to reconcile the power of the neo-classical paradigm in understanding much of the West, with its limitations in explaining micro-economics phenomena, especially in non-Western settings: The neo-classical model assumes and tacitly incorporates many of the features of the Western societies it was developed to explain. Its 'ideal-typical' premises aptly characterize the institutional setting in which Anglo-American capitalism developed.[2]

The institutional foundations of western markets

The rise of markets in Western Europe followed what Barrington Moore (1966) called the 'routes' that Western nations took in moving from feudalism to modernity. At the first of the period, sometime before the thirteenth century, markets were embedded in *oikos* economy dominated by aristocratic households. A market city either comprised a part of the manor and was actually owned by the lords of the land (Koebner, 1964), or existed as a free city, characterized by Weber (1968, pp. 1212–36) as a 'non-legitimate' enclave located at the margin of a manorial economy. Although it varied from region to region, the feudal economy was embedded in the political structure of Western Europe, and when that structure began to change decisively with the rise of absolutism, market economies also began to change.

Absolutism gradually moved the organizing locus of the economy from manors to cities, particularly national cities such as London and Paris that were dominated by kings. Mercantilism followed an economic policy designed to fill royal treasuries, which were used mainly to pay for navies and land armies needed to defend or expand territory. When European kings had difficulty gaining revenues from territory owned by their fellow aristocrats, they tried to compensate by creating royal companies, such as the East India Company, designed to generate royal surplus from overseas adventures. Mercantilistic policies created national urban-centred, consumer-oriented economies. Urban-centred consumption in turn fostered an integrated marketing system linking urban, rural, and overseas areas and nurtured rural industries that produced raw resources and handicraft items for urban consumption (Jones 1987). Although commercial markets were certainly growing and prospering, the mercantilistic economy rested on royal institutions, including the kings' courts and the kings' companies.

The revolutionary period, starting in the last half of the eighteenth century, entirely changed the institutional structure of Western economies and accelerated the growth of 'free market' capitalism. Social scientists have described the changes from a mercantilistic to a free market economy as a 'great transformation' (Polanyi 1957). The phrase is somewhat hyperbolic for economic activity but quite accurate for the institutional change that occurred after these revolutions, a period in which all the major economic institutions that we associate with capitalism first developed.

The change in government from absolutism to democracy marked a pivotal switch from an institutional environment based on centralized public spheres to one dispersed through decentralized private spheres. With great insight, Michel Foucault (1979) has described this shift in connection with the institutions for criminal justice, but an even larger and more profound shift occurred in the regulation and conduct of the economic activity. Isomorphic with the shift in other institutional spheres, the shift in the economic sphere in Western Europe and the United States moved from centrally instituted economies through royal banks, companies, courts, market taxes – all institutions against which Adam Smith (1991) inveighed in his *Wealth of Nations* – to a 'self-regulating' economy. The economic counterpart of Bentham's Panopticon that so intrigued Foucault (1979) was the commodity and equity markets created in the same period as circular Panopticon prisons. Both institutional structures embodied the principles of self-regulation: in the circular market pit, where all buyers and all sellers exchange simultaneously, everyone sees everything.

The institutionalization of firm autonomy

Underlying self-regulation in markets, as in prisons, was the notion of the autonomy of individual units. In the criminal justice system, as in society in general, rested the presumption that every individual was distinct and responsible for his or her own actions. The same principles applied in the economy: every firm was distinct and responsible for its own actions.

This belief in individual autonomy, as applied to both people and their businesses, arose out of an intellectual tradition that is characteristically Western. The strands of this tradition can be traced to antiquity, particularly to the Roman legal system, which had decisive effects on modern Western European state structure, citizenship, commercial law, and to Christianity, which conceptualized each individual as a distinct soul-bearing entity. Despite the many strands, however, the institutionalization of individual autonomy did not occur until after absolutism gave way to democracy.

The cornerstone of self-regulating markets based on firm autonomy came from the Enlightenment philosophers' reconceptualization of private property. In Western Europe, with the enactment of the constitutional state based on natural laws, ownership and control of property were not so much an economic issue as a political issue with economic implications. Property rights became a crucial principle in the articulation of democracy, an idea used by citizens to claim rights over jurisdictions that formerly had been held by absolutist monarchs. The writings of eighteenth-century philosophers, such as John Locke and slightly later Adam Smith, are rife with the notion of private property and its implications for individual political control vis-à-vis an authoritarian stage. Therefore, when constitutional states were enacted, the right to property was embodied in individualism, in the very conception of what an individual was.

The idea of individual autonomy in a society is the principle of nineteenth-century democracy, and the idea of firm autonomy in the economy is the principle of self-regulating markets in a democratic society. These ideas were not only abstract philosophies, but also working principles gradually instituted throughout society to conform to changing social and economic conditions. Such abstract ideas have a very technical dimension when they are used to order everyday reality.

The legal assignment of private rights requires a clear delineation of who claims ownership and what is owned. When non-state businesses in the West were subsumed under the legal definition of private property, business firms became in principle separate, distinct, and independent. They became conceptualized as a person–as autonomous, legally indivisible units that could form contractual links with people and with other firms. The clearest demonstration of this occurred in the United States, where under the Fourteenth Amendment corporations were held to be a person and could not be 'deprived of life, liberty, or property' without due process.

In the early nineteenth century, when businesses were small and individually or family owned, firms were equated with property and due process applied to their owners, and not to the firms as separate entities. With the growth of American capitalism and large firms with multiple owners, the firm itself took on the status of an individual. The test case in the US. Supreme Court in 1882 was a conflict between a California county and the Southern Pacific Railway Company. The issue was who owed taxes to the government. The Court upheld the idea, already established, that 'incorporation' created a unified entity – literally, a body – that had an existence over and above the parts that made it up.

This legal formulation had far-reaching effects on the development of Western business practices. Importantly, the law required the individuation of firms. Each firm was conceptualized as a separate body, a single entity distinct from all others. Business practices conformed to this principle, not because it was efficient or necessary, but because it was the law and deeply rooted in Western political and social ideas. The principle of individual corporateness established an institutional environment that formed a basis for Western capitalism's organizational structure and dynamics.

As legislated by most Western countries, and independently by states in the United States, laws of incorporation require firm autonomy, require the specification of ownership and corporate assets. National and state laws of taxation demand accounting procedures that delineate ownership and income. Capital markets assume that firms are autonomous: the loan provisions of the banking system, the equity provisions of the stock markets, the insurance provisions of industry all have institutionalized the principle of firm autonomy. Antitrust legislation, in working to prevent cartels and monopolies, provides sanctions to sustain autonomous corporations.

Firm autonomy has been institutionalized in many ways. A part of this process has been to work out legally and procedurally modes of legitimate interfirm linkages. That firms are really autonomous from all other firms or that individuals are entirely independent of one another is, of course, a fiction. But it is a fiction that was created historically as a means to specify institutionally the interrelation among people in the creation of a democratic political order. The fiction of autonomy became true, with time, for firms as well as for people. Interrelationships between businesses and people in the West are specified in legal terms, through contracts–that is, through autonomous entities exercising their free will to make agreements. Firm autonomy and personal autonomy are not independent of the institutions that reinforce such autonomy.

Therefore, to see firm autonomy as a universal element of capitalism, as something inherent to it in all time and all places, is really a misreading of history and of economies. It is a profoundly ethnocentric point of view.

THE DEVELOPMENT OF MARKETS IN ASIA

It is incorrect to think that Asian economies 'matured' only after being exposed to Western capitalism. While it is certainly the case that they changed considerably after the nineteenth century opening of Chinese and Japanese economies, it is not the case that the respective economies were undeveloped before the nineteenth century. The dazzling innovation in, and virtual explosion of, Western societies and economies after the seventeenth century has obscured the fact that Asian societies were economically quite advanced and quite complex. Although neither was heading toward industrial capitalism, both Japanese and Chinese economies were quite dynamic and quite old. They had been mature for a long time.

The organization of these economies, like the organization of society, rested on principles quite different from those found in the West. The great historian of Chinese science, Joseph Needham, has clarified these differences by contrasting Chinese 'associative thinking' with what he calls the Western 'billiard ball' conception of reality. Westerners, he says, see their world in terms of 'rational' cause and effect: like billiard balls bounding off each other, one motion causes another motion, which causes another motion in turn. Had he written later, he might have called this the 'rational choice' model of human behaviour: reduced to individual units, causative, and lawlike.

According to Needham (1956, pp. 279–91), a Chinese world-view is completely unlike a Western one. Although highly developed and more advanced than Western science until the seventeenth and eighteenth centuries, Chinese science did not rest on correlations based on cause and effect, on first principles, or on lawlike assertions. Instead, Chinese science rests on a conception of order. In the Chinese thinking, order rests on a stable relationship among things. There is order in a family when all the relationships in a family are obeyed; there is order in a country when all the reciprocal relationships between subjects and rulers are fulfilled; there is order in the universe when mankind fulfils its relationship with heaven and earth. Needham (1956, p. 286) compares this Chinese notion of order to a dance that has no beginning and no ending and in which all partners dance in time to the music: 'an extremely and precisely ordered universe, in which things "fitted" so exactly that you could not insert a hair between them.' Everything causes everything else.

Therefore, what is essential in life is not the individual cause and effect, but the order in the group as a whole.

In Asian societies the principle informing human behaviour is not for people to obey the law, whether God's laws or natural laws or economic laws. Instead it is for people to create order by obeying the requirements of human relationships as these are manifest in a situational context. The person is Asia is always embedded in ongoing relationships and is not an abstract entity that exists outside society, not even for purposes of rational calculation.

Just as individualism is institutionalized in the Western societies, social relationships are institutionalized in Asian societies. Legal codes in Asia, as many have argued, are in fact codifications of morality embedded in social relationships. For instance, the Tang Dynasty legal codes, which influenced Japan's legal codes and were passed down more or less intact through all the remaining dynasties in China, made unfilial behaviour to one's parents one of the 'Ten Abominations', and a crime punishable by death. Other relationships, such as those outlined in the *wulun* (five relationships: parent/child, emperor/subject, husband/wife, older sibling/younger sibling, and friend), were upheld in the magistrate's courts as well as in quasi-legal settings such as the lineage, village, and merchant associations. Because everyone has a responsibility for order in a group, failure to uphold one's responsibility in a relationship could lead not only to personal punishment, but also to the punishment of others in one's group. In this way mutual surveillance has come to be an essential part of the institutionalization of social relationships in East Asian societies. The Western concept of an individual's 'right to privacy' has no meaning in an Eastern setting.

The eminent Chinese sociologist Fei Xiaotong (1992) shows that this relational logic produces a society that rests on social networks. Every person is a part of multiple networks: family, friends, neighbours, co-workers–the list goes on and on. Each person is not an independent, self-willed actor, but rather is responsible simultaneously for the order within multiple networks; Fei shows that network ties are ranked, with family ties taking precedence over more distant kinship ties, which in turn may (or may not, depending on the context) have priority over ties with other types of people. Fei also shows that every institutional sphere, including the economy, is based on a structure of networks of relationships.

The institutional foundations of Asian markets

Using these insights, we can show that network organization is an institutional feature of Asian capitalism. These networks precede the modern era. For instance, in China during the Ming and Qing Dynasties (extending from the sixteenth to the twentieth centuries), commercial activities and handicraft industries were highly developed with a level of production and a volume of movement exceeding all other locations in the world until the eighteenth century. This level of complexity was achieved without support from the state, even in such matters as maintaining a currency, establishing weights and measures, and creating commercial laws. In short, creating order within the worlds of merchants and artisans was not a function undertaken by the imperial state, but one that remained in the hands of those actually engaged in business.

Through *huiguan,* associations of fellow regionals, merchants and artisans themselves established and enforced economic standards that created predictability and continuity in the marketplace (Hamilton 1985). Huiguan were literally meeting halls, places where people from the same native place would congregate. As a number of researchers have shown (Fewsmith 1983; Golas 1977; Hamilton 1979; and Skinner 1977) all the main merchant groups in late imperial China were out-of-towners organized through huiguan. Within the huiguan, people with common origins were pledged to a moral relationship *(tongxiang guanxi)* that generated sufficient trustworthiness for them to monopolize an area or areas of business for themselves. They would set and enforce standards for the trade as well as moral standards for fellow regionals in the trade.

Although the regional associations mediated the trading relationships, the actual firms engaged in business were always family firms. The family firms, through their ties with other firms, often owned by fellow regionals, stretched beyond any one locale. In fact, through using native place ties as the medium of organization, merchants were able to monopolize commerce in a commodity for an entire region, as the Swatow merchants did for the sugar trade for all of China. The success of the overseas Chinese in Southeast Asia in the nineteenth century was organizationally based on regional networks.

In the premodern era, Japanese merchants were organized quite differently from the Chinese merchants. Japanese merchants were organized as members of city-based guilds. Unlike Chinese firms, which would come and go, Japanese merchant and artisan firms were members of stable communities of firms, each one of which would be passed from father to eldest son or to a surrogate for him. Whereas Chinese firms would often be dissolved at the death of the owner because of partible inheritance, many Japanese firms continued intact for generations. Moreover, as members of stable networks of urban-based firms, Japanese merchants often developed long-term creditor-debtor relationships with members of the samurai class.

In the modern era, the same general network configurations persist both in overseas Chinese communities, including Taiwan, Hong Kong and Southeast Asia, and in modern Japan. Continually changing patrilineal networks of small firms that connect near and distant kin, and frequently friends, into production-and-supply networks characterize modern Chinese economies. Likewise, relatively stable business networks of large firms dominate the modern Japanese economy. Neither Asian social sphere has ever had a legacy of autonomous firms comparable to those of the West, nor are they likely to develop. Recent scholarship confirms that the institutional environments that support associative network relationships remain strong in Asia at the interpersonal, business, and state levels.

CONCLUSION: THE NEO-CLASSICAL PARADIGM AS AN INSTITUTIONAL THEORY

The fundamental assumptions of neo-classical economics include the idea that economic actors are rational and autonomous, and that they seek their self-interest independent of social relations or characteristics. Even a brief examination of the history of Western Europe demonstrates that these characteristics of individuals, to the extent that they are true now, were not always evident. In feudal society, people were not autonomous but were bound by traditional ties of fealty and homage. In absolutist Europe, people belonged to the 'body politic' that was personified by the king himself (Kantorowicz 1957). Kings 'embodied' nations, so that individuals within those jurisdictions were presumed to have no ultimate autonomy. Only after the institutionalization of the constitutional states in the West did an order arise in which the building blocks of societies and economies–people and firms–became rationally and systematically individuated.

The factors that neo-classical economics assumes are universal traits of the human condition are, in fact, part of the development of the modern West. Western institutions are embodiments of beliefs in individual autonomy and economic rationality. Now institutionalized, these principles are reproduced by individuals and firms who go about acting 'rationally' and 'autonomously'. Neo-classical economics captures, at least at some level, institutional characteristics of American and European societies, and it would be surprising if this theory did not work well in explaining important aspects of Western economic activity. Nonetheless, this paradigm cannot sustain a claim to universal status. It fits poorly the Asian economies that do not have the same institutional heritage. Asian societies have never had a Western-style legal system that treated each person as a separate entity, equal to all others. Asia has had no salvationist religion from which to derive a principle of individual rights. Individuals are not the basic social, economic, or political units in Asia. Rather, networks of people linked together through differentially categorized social relationships form the building blocks of Asian social orders and derive from Asia's institutional history. Individuals play roles in these networks, to be sure, but it is the networks that have stability. The presence of networks – of kin, of friends, of fellow regionals – is institutionalized in business and other social practices.

Persuasive explanations for the success of Asian business will ultimately come from an institutional analysis of Asian societies and the economies that are embedded in them. Explanations will not come–indeed, cannot come–from an attempt to apply a theory rooted in Western experience to an alien institutional arena. That can only result in explaining Asia as 'imperfect' and 'distorted'.

REFERENCES

Abolafia, M, and Biggart, N.W. (1990) 'Competition and markets.' In Etzioni, A. and Lawrence, P. (eds) *Perspectives on Socio-Economics*, M.E. Sharpe, Armonk, NY.

Alston, J. (1986) *The American Samurai*, De Gruyter, Berlin.

Amsden, A. (1989). *Asia's Next Giant: South Korea and Late Industrialization*, Oxford University Press, Oxford.

Aoki, M. (1984) *The Economic Analysis of the Japanese Firm*, North-Holland, Amsterdam.

Aoki, M. (1990) 'Toward an economic model of the Japanese firm.' *Journal of Econonmic Literature*, Vol. 28, pp. 1–27.

Berger, P.L. and Hsin-Huang Michael Hsiao (eds) (1988). *In Search of an East Asian Development Model*, Transaction Books, New Brunswick, NJ.

Biggart, N.W. (1990). 'Institutionalized patrimonialism in Korean business', in Calhoun, C. (ed.) *Comparative Social Research*, 12. Greenwich, CT: JAI Press, pp. 113–133.

Biggs, T.S. (1988) 'Financing the emergence of small and medium enterprises in Taiwan: financial mobilization and the flow of domestic credit to the private sector.' Working paper.

Chandler, A.D. and Daems, H. (1980) *Managerial Hierarchies: comparative perspectives on the rise of the modern industrial enterprise*, Harvard University Press, Cambridge, MA.

Clark, R. (1979). *The Japanese Company*, Yale University Press, New Haven, CT.

Dore, R. (1973). *British Factory–Japanese Factory: the origins of national diversity in industrial relations*, University of California Press, Berkeley.

Etzioni, A. (1988) *The Moral Dimension: toward a new economics*, The Free Press, New York.

Evans, P.B. and Stephens, J.D. (1988). 'Development and the world economy', in Smelser, N. (ed.) *Handbook of Sociology*, Sage, Newbury Park, CA.

Fei Xiaotong (1992) *Up From the Soil: the foundations of Chinese society*, Hamilton, G. and Wang Zheng (trans.) University of California Press, Berkeley.

Fewsmith, J. (1983) 'From guild to interest group: the transformation of public and private in late Qing China.' *Comparative Studies in Society and History*, Vol. 25, pp. 617–40.

Foucault, M. (1979) *Discipline and Punish: the birth of the prison*, Vintage, New York.

Friedman, M. (1953) *Essays in Positive Economics*, University of Chicago Press, Chicago, IL.

Gereffi, G. and Hamilton, G. (1990) 'Modes of incorporation in an industrial world: the social economy of global capitalism.' Unpublished paper presented at the American Sociological Association meetings, Washington, DC, August.

Gerlach, M. (1992) *Alliance capitalism: the social oganization of Japanese business*, University of California Press, Berkeley.

Golas, P.J. (1977) 'Early Ch'ing guilds', in Skinner, W. (ed.) *The City in Late Imperial China*, Stanford University Press, Stanford, pp. 555–80.

Goto, A. (1982) 'Business groups in a market economy', *European Economic Review*, Vol. 19, pp. 53–70.

Granovetter, M. (1985) 'Economic action and social structure.' *American Journal of Sociology*, Vol. 91, pp. 393–426.

Hamilton, G., and Biggart, N.W. (1988). 'Market, culture, and authority: a comparative analysis of management and organization in the Far East.' *American Journal of Sociology*, Vol. 94, pp. S52–S94.

Hamilton, G., and Cheng-shu Kao (1990) 'The institutional foundations of Chinese business: the family firm in Taiwan.' *Comparative Social Research*, Vol. 12, pp. 95–112.

Jones, E.L. (1987) *The European Miracle*, Cambridge University Press, Cambridge.

Jorgensen, J.J., Taieb Hafsi and Kiggundu, M.N. (1986) 'Towards a market imperfections theory of organizational structure in developing countries', *Journal of Management Studies*, Vol. 24, pp. 419–42.

Kantorowicz, E. (1957) *The King's Two Bodies*, Princeton University Press, Princeton.

Kim, Eun Mee (1991) 'The industrial organization and growth of the Korean chaebol: integrating development and organizational theories', in Hamilton, G. (ed.) *Business Networks and Economic Development in East and Southeast Asia*, Centre of Asian Studies, Hong Kong.

Koebner, R. (1964) 'German towns and Slav markets,' Thupp, S. (ed.) *Change in Medieval Society*, Appleton-Century-Crofts, New York.

Leff, N. (1976) 'Capital markets in the less developed countries: the group principle', in McKinnon, R.I. (ed.) *Money and Finance in Economic Growth and Development: essays in honor of Edward S. Shaw*, M. Decker, New York, pp. 97–122.

Leff, N. (1978) 'Industrial Organization and entrepreneurship in the developing countries: the economic groups.' *Economic Development and Cultural Change*, Vol. 26, pp. 661–75.

Levy, M. (1972) *Modernization: latecomers and survivors*, Basic Books, New York.

Lucas, R.E. (1988) 'On the mechanics of economic development.' *Journal of Monetary Economics*, Vol. 22, pp. 3–42.

Moore, B. (1966). *Social Origins of Dictatorship and Democracy: lord and peasant in the making of the modern world*, Beacon Press, Boston.

Needham, J. (1956) *The Grand Titration*, Toronto University Press, Toronto.

Numazaki, I. (1986) 'Networks of Taiwan big business', *Modern China*, Vol. 12, pp. 487–534.

Orru, M., Biggart, N.W. and Hamilton, G. (1991) 'Organizational isomorphism in East Asia', in Powell, W.W. and DiMaggio, P. (eds.) *The New Institutionalism in Organizational Analysis*, University of Chicago Press, Chicago.

Orru, M., Hamilton, G. and Suzuki, M. (1989) 'Patterns of inter-firm control in Japanese business', *Organization Studies*, Vol. 10, pp. 549–574.

Polanyi, K. (1957) *The Great Transformation*, Beacon Press, Boston.

Schweder, R. (1986) 'Divergent rationalities', in Fiske, R.W. and Schweder, R. (eds) *Metatheory in the Social Sciences: pluralisms and subjectivities*, Chicago University Press, Chicago.

Skinner, W.F. (1977) *The City in Late Imperial China*, Stanford University Press, Stanford.

Smith, A. (1991) *The Wealth of Nations*, Knopf, New York.

Stigler, G. (1968) *The Organization of Industry*, Irwin, Homewood, IL.

Tversky, A. and Kahneman, D. (1974) 'Judgement under uncertainty: heuristics and biases', *Science*, Vol. 185, pp.1124–31.

Weber, M. (1968). *Economy and Society*, University of California Press, Berkeley.

Whitley, R.D. (1990) 'Eastern Asian enterprise structures and the comparative analysis of forms of business organization', *Organization Studies*, Vol. 11, pp.47–74.

NOTES

1 Earlier versions of this theory include Marion Levy (1972) and the very sophisticated treatment of Ronald Dore (1973) as applied to Japan.

2 This point requires a short digression into what the methods of what Milton Friedman calls 'positive economics'. Friedman (1953) makes it clear that not even those economists who believe fully in the utility of models of perfect competition would argue for the universality and the validity of these theories. Friedman argues for the utility of economic models, but at the same time says that they are not valid or universal in an absolute sense. In this regard, economic models resemble Weberian ideal types more than they resemble natural laws. Economic models represent a slice of reality from which a few causal factors or processes are reformulated at a more abstract plane and are made more precise and internally logical. The model is then applied back to the same or like contexts from which the main elements have been abstracted in order to see how well the model predicts the actual behaviour. 'The ideal types,' says Friedman (1953, p. 36), 'are not intended to be descriptive; they are designed to isolate the features that are crucial for a particular problem.' In this role economic models, logically, neither make a truth claim nor require an assumption of universality. The model merely has to meet the test of usefulness.

CHAPTER 8

REGULATION AND STANDARDS POLICY: SETTING STANDARDS BY COMMITTEES AND MARKETS

PETER GRINDLEY

INTRODUCTION

A major problem for the regulator is how to set standards. Compatibility standards are vital for telecommunications, where equipment must match the network, for television services, where receivers need broadcasts, and for mobile phones, where handsets need base stations. They are equally important in more mundane areas such as plugs and sockets, electric supply voltages, railway gauges and even which side of the road we drive on. It may seem that the advantages of everyone using the same standard should be clear and it would be a simple matter to agree a standard. Yet the recent history of some spectacular failures to establish standards, for high-definition television, cordless telephone, and satellite broadcasting, show that standards are hard to set, and that results when a regulating authority is involved are often worse than when the market is left alone.

The difficulty is co-ordinating the decisions of the various firms and users involved in deciding standards for a new product. Standards for private goods such as video cassette recorders or computers, which need compatible pre-recorded tapes or computer software, are usually determined efficiently by market competition. In other areas, where the public interest is seen as more pressing or where the standard overlaps with other regulation, such as the allocation of radio spectrum, it is often believed that the regulating authority should co-ordinate if not decide standards.

The problem for the policy-maker is how to find a balance between the use of official standards bodies and market forces to set standards, called *de jure* and *de facto* standards. The worry with market determined standards is that there are often costly standards wars and these may result in fragmented standards, with some stranded users of a losing standard. Owners of Betamax VCRs discover that there are few pre-recorded tapes for rent, and owners of non-DOS compatible personal computers have difficulty finding software and pay high prices for it.

Though these costs are usually manageable and can be dealt with within the market, the costs of confusion in other areas may be more severe and call for public intervention. Social costs are high if each television station uses a different transmission method or a group of drivers tries to drive on the wrong side of the road. Official standards committees try to avoid these problems by deciding standards before firms and users make irreversible decisions. However, official standards may bring more problems than they solve. Vested interests and other organizational problems may block the committees. With crucial commercial interests involved it is often impossible to reach agreement purely by committee, and the time scales involved may be too long in areas of rapid technological change. Also the authority is tempted to add other policy aims which can ruin the standard. As a result either agreement is not reached or the official standard may fail in the market-place.

For these reasons it may be better to make more use of markets for standards setting, despite the risks, even in regulated industries. Where total reliance on markets is not appropriate, hybrid mechanisms for greater involvement of market forces may be possible to reduce the problems of co-ordination by committees. In either case the role of the authority becomes more one of facilitating rather than selecting standards.

The standards of most concern here are compatibility standards for the interface between two products. These differ from the perhaps more familiar type of standards for minimum quality, such as health and safety regulations, or weights and measures. European Single Market legislation, for example, more often refers to quality standards than compatibility standards. Minimum-quality standards regulate the market and protect the consumer. As such they benefit the market as a whole and do not have the same strategic importance for the firms and users as compatibility standards. They may be dealt with effectively over longer time horizons by the standards bodies.

In this paper we first outline three major recent cases, for high-definition television, cordless telephone and satellite broadcasting, where official standards have been to some degree unsuccessful, to illustrate the potential problems involved. We then summarize the policy problems for both official and market standards. We analyse the causes of these problems and suggest some remedies. Finally we summarize the implications for standards policy.

SETTING REGULATED STANDARDS

High-definition television

The original High Definition Television (HDTV) system was developed by the Japanese broadcasting service, NHK, in the 1980s. It provides greatly improved picture definition over colour television and a larger, wider screen. To be adopted a television standard needs agreement between programme producers, broadcasters and equipment manufacturers, as well as being acceptable to viewers. The official forum for deciding the standard is within the national and international broadcasting authorities. With no other systems in sight either in Europe or the USA, the Japanese proposal at first seemed well on the way to being adopted as a world-wide standard. It had gained the endorsement of the US national standards committee and no opposition had surfaced from Europe. However, this was not to be. At the crucial meeting of the International Radio Consultative Committee (CCIR) in Dubrovnik in 1986, the Europeans refused to accept the standard. Led by the French, they quickly put together proposals for their own HDTV system, called MAC. With the prospect of a single global standard gone, the USA reopened their national standard to fresh proposals and began developing more advanced systems. It now looks as though there will be three incompatible systems world-wide. This repeats the fragmentation of current colour TV standards into three regional groups (NTSC, PAL, and SECAM) which occurred thirty years ago (Pelmans and Beuter, 1987). Serving the smaller regional markets none of these is likely to have the great success once predicted for HDTV and at best the introduction of the service has been delayed by several years.

This outcome is unsatisfactory for several reasons. The benefits of having one world-wide standard for programme production, transmission, and manufacture have been lost, with few compensations. The aim of the Europeans was to protect the remnants of their consumer electronics industry. It is unlikely to do this. MAC development is many years behind the Japanese, who are bound to provide most of the studio equipment and also much of the transmission equipment and receivers whatever standard is used. Moreover, major private satellite broadcasters, such as Sky Television in the UK, are rejecting MAC in favour of the existing PAL colour system, and the prospects for MAC are highly uncertain. The USA has also been concerned to protect its national manufacturers, but as most of these are foreign-owned, a more powerful influence has been the terrestrial broadcasters. These are threatened by HDTV, which is best delivered by satellite or cable, and they have persuaded the US Federal Communications Commission that the standard should be transmittable from land-based stations. This will restrict performance, while the delays in the screening process will delay HDTV in the USA by at least five years. Either of these may ruin its chances of success. An unplanned benefit of the delay is that more advanced all-digital proposals have been developed, though this may not significantly add to HDTV's chances. As with MAC, even if a system is developed, most of the equipment will be Japanese made (for further discussion see Grindley, 1991; Farrell and Shapiro, 1992).

In a case such as this is it not easy to compare what might have happened had the choice of HDTV system been left to market forces, as regulators are involved to some extent even if only in allocating radio bandwidth. However, compared with the delays and fragmented standards following the official route, it is likely that left to themselves satellite and cable services would have introduced the NHK system when and if they felt there was a market for it. They have been restrained from doing this in Europe by licensing conditions and in the USA by the prospect of an FCC-backed terrestrial standard. Market introduction would probably have been gradual, as it has been in Japan, where even with official support the manufacturers are now using an intermediate stage with Extended Definition TV. Given this gradualism, HDTV is probably not as great a threat to western industry as it has been portrayed.

This case shows the ineffectiveness of standards bodies in obtaining agreement when faced with major clashes of commercial interests, here from the manufacturers and broadcasters. Also industrial and political aims have crowded out those of finding efficient standards. The official standards process has actually made fragmented standards more likely than would giving the market a freer hand, with ultimately few visible benefits.

Cordless telephone

Cordless telephone provides a useful contrast between an attempt to involve markets in the standards-setting process in the UK and the more traditional committee approach to standards used for the European Community as a whole. The UK experiment failed dismally, due partly to operator errors but mainly to product restrictions and low commitment inherent in the policy, which did not give the market process a chance to work. The European standard should eventually provide a workable standard, but this is taking a long time and it is unlikely that any public cordless services will be promoted enthusiastically there.

Telepoint is a UK public cordless-telephone system, launched in 1989 as the 'poor man's mobile phone', which uses radio base-stations to access the public network. Objectively there should have been a market for a low-cost system but it was handicapped by product limitations, which allowed only outgoing calls and restricted use to within a hundred metres of a base-point, and by slow installation rates. It attracted almost no users and services were withdrawn within just two years. The policy setting up Telepoint aimed to mix market and official mechanisms for setting standards. The problem was that the policy left technical details to the operators to decide after issuing the licences, but still laid out the main rules for the system. Two-way calling was barred as the licensing authority did not want this to compete with its plans for the more sophisticated Personal Communications Network (PCN) to follow. It insisted on four operators to ensure a high level of competition, leaving little incentive for investment, especially as it was clear that market shares would have to remain roughly balanced. Finally the means of determining a common standard were never made clear and it was eventually set a year after the start of operations not by market competition but by the authority. In fact each service remained incompatible to the end, which guaranteed fragmented standards and made it even harder for users to find a base-station. Not surprisingly the operators lacked commitment and the public were confused, killing the services (Grindley and Toker, 1992).

Behind this, the main policy aim of the regulator was to use Telepoint to develop a standard for cordless telephone which, being proven in the market-place, would be well-placed for adoption as the European standard. The Telepoint standard was developed very quickly, within two years, but the failure of the services was a poor recommendation and left it with little chance of adoption.

In contrast the European Commission has used a traditional committee approach to setting cordless standards. This is the opposite to the market by selecting between standards submitted for approval. The process has been under way for about five years and is expected to be complete in another five. The main standard being studied is from a consortium of major European manufacturers. Once a standard is set any public services would probably be the responsibility of the national Public Telecommunications Operators who, with the exception of France, have shown little interest in them. There has been some flexibility here in that Telepoint was allowed as an interim standard and had it been more successful this could have led to its adoption.

Telepoint shows the problems caused by trying to bring external policy aims into the standards process. These may distort the standard to such an extent as to make it unworkable. The apparently more successful European procedure still shows major problems with committee standards in the time taken to approve a technology which has essentially been available for years and with no assurance that services will be provided. The process is vulnerable to being bypassed by more quickly developed standards from outside. Rather than disproving the value of market standards Telepoint indicates that if markets are to be used they should be given broad freedom to determine the standard by competition and not just used for technical design. Getting the balance right in hybrid policies of this kind is clearly difficult.

Satellite broadcasting

Satellite television in the UK has seen a contest between two systems, one licensed by the broadcasting authority and the other operating independently. The official service, British Satellite Broadcasting (BSB), was licensed in 1986 but only began broadcasting in 1990. This crucial delay was caused by the long approval process and waiting for the development of MAC, the first stage of the European HDTV standard, which BSB was required to use. The other service, Rupert Murdoch's Sky Television, took advantage of the delay and pre-empted BSB. It started broadcasts over a year earlier in 1989. Sky avoided the licensing requirements by transmitting from Luxembourg on non-restricted channels. It used the existing PAL standard so did not need to wait for MAC. By the time BSB services were launched, Sky had an audience of two million homes. BSB could not attract new users quickly enough and within six months it collapsed into merger with Sky.

Standards are crucial because of the MAC requirement and because users would only be prepared to invest in one or other system, which needed separate receiver dishes. Given Sky's lead there could only be one standards winner. Its installed base of viewers already made Sky look like a winner and was beginning to attract significant advertising. BSB tried to differentiate its service with high-quality programming but this was ineffective and expensive. Being tied to MAC was a further disadvantage as there were no MAC television sets and an additional decoding stage was needed. When they merged, BSB services were transferred to Sky and the stranded BSB viewers were given help switching their equipment.

In this case the official standard was clearly bypassed by a market-generated one. Adoption by the standards authority was a hindrance as it delayed the service and restricted it to a technology which was not fully developed. The UK government had thought that it had a controlled policy experiment on its hands and wanted to use this to promote high-definition television. If UK plans for HDTV have suffered, this is partly the result of viewers electing against it in this way. Sky's victory shows how effective a flexible and fast-moving market standard may be against an official one. The contest was not cheap. BSB spent £700 million and Sky £550 million in its first two years, but it was resolved rapidly. As for other policy concerns, at least some viewers and UK manufacturers of receiving equipment have benefited from Sky's success.

REGULATED AND MARKET STANDARDS

Market standards

For many standards government intervention is not needed or appropriate, and standards setting may safely be left to market competition. A large part of the success of products such as video cassette recorders and personal computers has been due to the efficiency and speed with which product design converged to a single main standard. Once the common standard became clear in these products, complementary software markets in pre-recorded tapes or computer programs grew up to support them and the main markets then grew rapidly. The availability of tape rentals and PC software packages were the keys to the growth of these markets (for these and other cases see Grindley, 1992).

Market standards work by competition between alternative designs. This is the reason for their effectiveness but is also a source of problems. While it is extremely valuable to have a range of alternatives generated by the market, the ensuing standards wars are costly and to some extent unpredictable. The dynamics are that a small advantage early on may be the signal to the market that this will be the winning standard. Complementary support snowballs and although it may not be technically the most advanced standard it is very hard for another one to dislodge it. For example, the arrangement of the typewriter keyboard was already obsolete when it was introduced a hundred years ago, but has lasted to this day (David, 1985). Alternatively, if a leader does not emerge until later, there may be several standards each with a small installed base, large enough to survive but not to attract adequate support. Fragmented standards divide the market so that no one standard is truly successful. The expansion of railway traffic in nineteenth-century England was retarded by the different railway gauges which had evolved for regional services, and one of these, Brunel's Great Western Railway, resisted conformity for over fifty years. Similar compatibility problems have reappeared recently on a European-wide scale with the introduction of high-speed train services. Also, users who have invested in a losing, minority standard are 'stranded' with little software and service, as owners of Betamax VCRs discovered. Finally, if the standard is proprietary the design owner may restrict access and use its monopoly power to charge high prices (Farrell and Saloner, 1986; David, 1986; Grindley, 1990*b*, 1992).

These problems of stranding, fragmentation, technical obsolescence, duplication of effort, and monopoly power often occur with market standards but it is possible to overstate the risks and in most cases the market itself finds ways to minimize them. Many historical cases of fragmented standards occurred because they grew up under a different set of conditions when, say, international transport and communications were less important than today. If the issues are understood from the beginning markets usually converge to a single standard. If the costs of fragmentation and stranding are high then all the more reason for us to support a single standard, so the numbers involved may be small. Thus only about 2 per cent of the VCR machines in existence are now the losing Betamax standard. In any case technical change may soon give an opportunity to switch to the leading standard with the next upgrade. Converters may be developed to help stranded users, as happened with BSB subscribers in UK satellite broadcasting where the merged Sky service was anxious to build up its audience and subsidize the conversion of receiver dishes. An 'obsolete' standard may have outlived its technical shelf-life but still give great value to users through their investment in software and training, as MS-DOS continues to do in personal computers. Competition and duplicated development effort may be necessary to generate new technology, while proprietary standards are becoming more of a rarity in a world where open standards are more effective in attracting broad support and winning contests, as seen in VCR and PC. A sense of proportion is needed in assessing the costs.

Even so there are areas where the costs of the standards chaos possible under the market are more serious. Markets can be harsh on the loser. The costs of being stranded may be more than an individual can bear and may fall not on the firms making the decisions but on society as a whole. For example, the costs of replacing expensive medical equipment which no longer has maintenance support or of retraining specialized skills in technology made obsolete by a standards war, may be beyond what individuals can afford. Confusion in the use of the radio spectrum with several transmission standards makes broadcasting difficult for everyone, not just the maverick broadcasters. There are also some standards which may be beneficial but need to be co-ordinated centrally by an authority which sees the whole picture, particularly for changes to a standard. A change in the side of the road a nation drives on clearly has to be arranged by government ruling, individuals cannot change it themselves. In cases such as these there may be a need for government intervention to co-ordinate and regulate the standards process. The government may already be involved as a regulator of the industry, as in telecommunications and broadcasting.

The questions are how best to achieve standards co-ordination and where to draw the line between using market and official or committee standards. Some of the factors in this decision are given in Figure 8.1. Before we are ready to make an evaluation, however, we need to explain some of the difficulties of using regulation and the committee process.

	Market	Committee
Favouring markets	+ Clear decision Fast Commercial goals Acceptable to market Open process Product focus Design variety Global	– Agreement difficult Slow Technical bias Remote from market Covert lobbying External policy agenda Monolithic Local/national
Favouring committees	– Standard wars Duplicate devel. costs Fragmented standards Stranding Locked-in obsolescence	+ Orderly process Single launch Unified standard Provision for losers Technically superior

Figure 8.1 Comparison factors for market and committee standards

Problems with regulated standards

An official standards authority aims to set standards outside the market, if possible before products are developed and launched. This is achieved by a process of negotiation and selection using committees representing manufacturers, complementary producers, users, and government. Standards bodies are of various types, from voluntary industry associations with no direct legal powers to regulatory authorities with strong enforcement capability. However, they all co-ordinate standards by some form of consultative, consensus process and most have some policy overtones, otherwise we have a market standard. They may also perform many other functions in addition to defining standards, including information exchange, providing a discussion forum, drafting standards, testing and documentation. We are concerned with their role setting new standards and take the supporting functions as given.

The intent is that if a standard can be set first, before substantial development takes place, then this avoids duplicated R&D costs, standards wars, and stranding. It reduces the uncertainty about the new standard, so that manufacturers and complementary producers can then develop products in a stable environment. On this reading the only problem is whether deciding a standard too early reduces variety and cuts off potential technologies before they have a chance to develop.

Unfortunately the process does not work as well as this. It may introduce as many problems as it solves and the net results are often worse than leaving things to the market, with all its risks. Some prominent failures are described above. These are not unconnected cases but stem from the inherent difficulties of using committees to make decisions for new technology. The variables are numerous and fast changing and the outcomes are crucial to the firms' commercial interests, so that it is hardly surprising that consensus is less effective than market competition.

The problems are in four areas. First, it is very hard to get agreement in committee. Even if reached it may not be upheld in practice. Vital commercial interests are involved and these are too important to the firms' futures to be decided purely by committee. Firms are bound to compete in product development and possibly to try to pre-empt the decision by launching products on the market. If a decision goes against them they may attempt to bypass the official standard in the market. We have seen Sky do this to British Satellite Broadcasting. Also, in HDTV the Japanese system has become the de facto studio standard if not the broadcasting standard. Thus the agreement itself may be of little value unless it is backed up by market forces.

Second, the official standards bodies tend to concentrate on technical rather than commercial aspects and so use too narrow criteria. They are often surprised when the most advanced standard is not adopted by the market. This bias is partly a response to the difficulties of obtaining commercial information and partly historical. Standards contests show us that the most advanced standard often does not win, and that it takes other aspects such as obtaining broad support, complementary investment, and distribution to establish a standard. Yet technical excellence may be relatively unimportant once a basic level of user-acceptability is reached. VHS was technically inferior to Betamax VCR, and the IBM PC was less advanced than other systems, yet both were huge successes.

Third, the official process changes the focus of competition from the product itself to influencing the standards authority. It introduces an additional player in the game, the authority itself. Firms' efforts are diverted into finding out what the regulator is thinking and trying to influence it in their favour. The merits of the product may get overlooked. Also the authority is usually poorly equipped to make the commercial judgements needed for success in the market-place. As a government body it has different objectives than the firms and cannot have all the information, especially business information. It must rely on the firms to supply this information, which apart from being at second hand will also be selective regarding the merits and costs of alternatives. The only way to fully understand the product is intimate involvement at the firm level. The game for the firms becomes to lobby rather than win users. Yet relying on adoption by the standards authority is often a bad strategy for the firms. It may be no guarantee of success, as was the case for Telepoint and BSB, and looks set to be for MAC, and possibly the US HDTV standard.

Most important is that the authority may bring in its own policy agenda beyond setting an efficient standard. It is hard to resist the temptation to use standards to promote national industry. Such policy looks costless, as the standard is sensitive to small nudges one way or another in the early stages. However this is not costless. For the same reasons of sensitivity, distorting the standard to fit other policy aims easily makes it unacceptable to the market. Telepoint is a case where the standard was restricted to fit other policy aims to promote UK manufacturers and orchestrate mobile telephone competition, and this led to an unworkable standard.

Finally, the committee process takes a very long time, and one of the crucial elements in setting a new standard is speed. There is a narrow window of opportunity to establish a standard. An official standard may find it hard to meet the pace. This gives a chance for a faster moving market solution to pre-empt the official standard and establish itself as the *de facto* standard before the official standard appears. The process is also inflexible, so that needed modifications to the standard which become apparent as the product is being introduced either cannot be made or take too long. For Telepoint, vital changes to correct basic product errors by adding pagers and two-way calling took over a year to be approved and were still not introduced when the services failed.

This combination of problems may mean that the standard is unattractive or, worse, that the process is so confused and delayed that the product fails when launched. Telepoint and BSB standards both failed. HDTV has been damaged, possibly terminally, by fragmentation and delay. The committee may also fail to avoid the costs of market solutions. There is little saving of duplicated development costs as firms still compete. The competition is distorted as the object is adoption by the authority not what is most attractive to the market. The chances of fragmentation still exist as firms may launch products ahead of time or try to bypass the official standard. Where different authorities are involved, as they are for international standards, the chances of fragmentation are actually increased by official standards, as they have been with HDTV, colour TV, and most national telecommunications standards. Finally an official standard may be just as likely as the market to confer monopoly power on the winner.

These are not only problems for regulated standards. Many of the difficulties using committees apply equally to voluntary industry standards bodies. Committees became a focus for disagreement between manufacturers and music companies for Digital Audio Tape (DAT) standards, and also made little progress on agreeing Unix open computer software standards until commercial pressures became strong (Grindley and McBryde 1992; Grindley 1990a). Markets do not always work. In digital audio the DAT standard has been squeezed out by Compact Discs though in many ways it is the more useful product. However many of the failures to establish a standard (video disc, mini-CD) may be attributed to unwanted products rather than the standards process.

COMBINING MARKETS AND REGULATION

Why committees fail

Setting standards is a co-ordination exercise, to get manufacturers, complementary producers and users to adopt a common interface design. The larger the installed base of a standard, the more complementary products are supplied, and the greater the demand for it by users. The standard benefits each group and the more widespread the adoption the greater its value. Though there may be some reduction in variety and possible monopoly effects associated with the standard, the network benefits usually far outweigh these costs. The problem is that the benefits are not evenly distributed. If the winning standard is proprietary then the owner may restrict use or charge high licence fees to other producers. Even if, as is more likely, the standard is open and made available to all producers, so there are no net losers, some firms may gain more than others. The developer of the standard has a first move advantage on the market and the others can only follow after a delay. The leader may be able to hold on to its position by making further technical improvements. With this uneven distribution of gains firms will compete to have their standard adopted by the committee. It is a negotiation game in which players may never agree on a standard as each wants to lead and will continue to argue the merits of his own standard. This is why the standard may need to be taken to the market to decide either with or without the involvement of the committee.

The contest is a 'battle of the sexes' game, well-known in game theory in which two players both gain by agreeing to do the same thing but one gains more than the other. The players vie with one another to be first to choose and unless the game is expanded to include other factors there may be no resolution to an endless argument. Most of the usual ways out of this impasse do not work for compatibility standards (see Kay, 1993, for the application of game theory to business strategy). The regulator tries to adjudicate the decision, and this is one reason for the technical bias of committees, but it cannot evaluate the conflicting claims effectively for the reasons we have given above. If it makes a selection it is almost bound to please nobody. Similarly this cannot be a repeat game (in which case players could take turns to lead) as once the standard is set it is locked in for the duration. Deciding the outcome by hierarchy, such as following the largest firm, is also unsuitable with new technology where the market is new and leadership often changes, though it may be used after the fact once standards exist to decide which of several incompatible standards should become the common standard.

The only way out of the dilemma is for one or more of the players to make a commitment to a standard. This means making a sunk-cost investment in the market-place. The other players must then decide whether to compete with the standard in the market or follow the committed standard. This clears the impasse. It may be combined with continued negotiations in committee to help smooth competition by exchanging information, but once the players have decided to compete in the market the game has changed and must be followed to its conclusion. The effectiveness of market competition is that it cannot continue endlessly. Costly investments (decisions) are made and these are tested against the market. Because of the costs involved the process must be finite and the results decisive. It is very clear whether the market has adopted or reflected the standard and this point is reached after a short time. Market competition allows great flexibility so the standard can be quickly modified if it is not meeting any demand. In Japan, with no regulatory obstacles, HDTV strategy was soon changed in response to slow consumer adoption to introduce it via Extended Definition TV. For Telepoint the UK market rejected the system decisively. If the licensing terms had not been so restrictive the system could have been revised in time and perhaps been successful.

Using markets

This helps explain the effectiveness of markets in setting standards and the value of bringing them into the process in some way. This includes the option of using fully market determined standards, which years of regulation should not make as 'unthinkable' as we may imagine. Often we do not want to go this far and we should first consider hybrid policies for cases where some public control over standardization is necessary, as when the risks of stranding and fragmentation are too high. It has been shown that under some conditions a hybrid policy combining committee negotiations with market commitments may be better than either the committee or the market on their own (Farrell and Saloner, 1988). The question is finding the right balance. At this point we can only suggest some possible approaches and more experience is needed before we can make any clear recommendations.

At one level, market mechanisms may be used to improve the selection process, while still leaving the authority to make the final decision. Firms are likely to withhold some information to improve their standard's chances of selection. This is especially so for cost information, which is harder to verify than technical. As a result the regulator often chooses a technically excellent but expensive standard. One way to induce firms to reveal their true costs is by auctioning the rights to set the standard (Farrell and Shapiro, 1991). This motivates firms to optimize the costs and features of the product. To avoid monopoly problems this should also include the condition that the final standard be licensed at 'reasonable' (low) royalties to other producers. Unfortunately a problem with this approach is that there are usually few suppliers for large systems, and there is unlikely to be an effective market bidding for the standard. The recent experience of the UK in auctioning television programme franchises has not been encouraging for this kind of auction with widely varied bids and threats of lawsuits to follow.

Having clear rules for selection may also help avoid strategic game playing. Options are to decide a winner by a date deadline, by the first to establish a clear lead, or by the first to surpass a performance threshold. All have problems but the first, deadline, has the best chance of cutting short the to- and fro- tournament between the firms.

Although we may improve the committee process in these ways the basic problems of evaluation, lobbying, and external agendas remain. It may be necessary to go to the next level and turn over the standard decision more completely to market competition, on the basis that the committee can never resolve the differences. The questions are where to draw the boundary and how much influence the authority retains. On the basis of our experience so far the boundary probably needs to move a long way towards the market. If market competition is used for the main decisions then it needs a minimum of interference. This does not mean that the authority takes no part in the standard but it lays out only broad rules within which the market develops and establishes the standard on its own. It retains its traditional roles of facilitating standards and providing channels for information exchange and negotiation within market competition. This has always been a major part of what standard bodies do (Sanders 1972; Verman 1973). If there is a change it is to encourage firms to make more use of this facility. The authority also still needs to try to correct possible market problems. It should almost undoubtedly require that the standard is openly licensed, with reasonable royalties, to avoid giving monopoly power to the winner and discourage standards wars. It may include incentives or provisions for taking care of stranded users.

Beyond this the authority should not treat standards as an opportunity to pursue an external agenda for other industrial policy. Standards setting is a delicate business and is easily disturbed, and should as far as possible be kept separate. Competition policy may be pursued by an open licensing requirement to avoid monopoly rather than by forcing the number of competitors or other powerful restrictions. Market structure, including the number of competitors, may remain the concern of existing anti-monopoly rules. Trade and infant industry arguments may also best be dealt with aside from standards. The market cases show that strong standards flow from well-managed firms, not the other way round. Standards are not robust enough to be general policy tools. At an international level, policies to support national champions are probably the main reason for globally fragmented standards, rather than any market mechanism. Changing this may have to wait for some basic realignment of international thinking.

Market standards for AM Stereo

One of the few examples of what can happen in turning over regulated standards to the market is AM stereo radio in the USA, described in Berg, 1987. The FCC had evaluated proposals through committees for over twenty years from 1961 to 1982 without coming to a decision. Possibly because external pressure for a decision for this non-vital product was weak, the committees went round in circles trying to decide between a number of standards. This was brought to a halt in 1982, when in a surprise policy change the FCC announced that stations would be allowed to choose what standards they wished provided it fitted within their bandwidth allocations. The first system (Kahn) was launched within two months and began recruiting local radio stations. Others followed quickly. The main competitor (Motorola C-QUAM) was introduced about six months later. This had superior technology, support and financial backing and overtook Kahn. AM stereo became an established service within a three year period. Standards converged on the C-QUAM standard but left a sizeable minority stranded with Kahn, which held on to the installed base it had built up before C-QUAM entered.

The market was able to establish a standard quickly, in three years compared with the previous twenty years of fruitless negotiation, but the case also shows the problems of fragmentation. Markets are harsh on the losers and lawsuits against the FCC are a possibility. However, the fragmentation was in part a hold-over from the previous delay. When this was unexpectedly lifted it did not give all the alternatives an equal start. Those who had been counting on FCC adoption were ready to begin broadcasting immediately and knew their only chance against better funded rivals was to try to get in first. As the geographic coverage does not overlap very much the costs of fragmentation from the user side may not have been excessive.

CONCLUSION

The roles of official standards bodies have evolved for historical reasons. Their traditional concern has been with the technical functioning of a network or the maintenance of quality and service standards across an industry. The technical approach, working through layers of committees towards consensus, is well-suited to this kind of regulation. It does not work well for the fast decision-making needed with interface standards and new technology. Co-ordinating the various interests involved may need market competition. The outcomes of several recent officially mediated standards have compared poorly with the successes of some private standards set in the market-place. Indeed standards bodies may be better equipped to deal with negotiations after standards have evolved to move towards a common standard as painlessly as possible, than to set them in the first place.

We need to re-evaluate how market forces may be brought into the standardization process. So far attempts to combine markets and regulation have not always been successful. In some cases this has been because attempts have not gone far enough. In Telepoint, details were left to the market but the main decisions remained with the regulator. Where the market has been allowed enough freedom, as in satellite television (inadvertently) and AM stereo, a standard has been set efficiently, if not perfectly. Left to themselves markets have shown that they will set some standard very efficiently, and whatever may be said about its technical merits the standard has passed an important test of user acceptability. The role of the authority then becomes to provide the conditions for the market to work and if necessary correct potential excesses. If it tries to do more, to orchestrate the standard, it is as likely to hinder as help.

Finally, standards should not be seen as a simple way to implement industrial policy. It is too easy to ruin a standard's chance of success. Providing information and alternatives via standards bodies is beneficial to all parties, but once this becomes direct manipulation the risk is that the standard becomes unworkable. Policy to support national industry should be kept separate from the actual standards setting. Market standards cases have shown that a successful standard depends on the committed backing of strong firms, rather than the other way round. Concerns such as trade protectionism or industrial development should be dealt with directly, if possible, and not made part of the standards. After all, good standards benefit and support industrial users as much as manufacturing, and these are also at risk with poor standards.

REFERENCES

Berg, S. (1987) 'Public policy and corporate strategies in the AM stereo market', in Gabel, L. (ed.), *op. cit.*

David, P. (1985) 'CLIO and the economics of QWERTY', *American Economic Review*, Vol. 75, No. 2, pp. 332–7.

David, P. (1986) 'Narrow windows, blind giants and angry orphans: the dynamics of system rivalries and dilemmas of technology policy', in Arcangel, F. *et al.* (eds), *Innovation Diffusion*, iii, Oxford University Press, New York.

Farrell, J. and Saloner, G. (1986) 'Economic issues in standardization' in Miller, J. (ed.) *Telecommunications and Equity*, North-Holland, New York.

Farrell, J. (1988) 'Coordination through committees and markets', *Rand Journal of Economics*, Vol. 19, No. 2, pp. 235–52.

Farrell, J. and Shapiro, C. (1991) 'Standard setting in high definition television', mimeo, University of California, Berkeley, CA.

Gabel, L. (ed.) (1987) *Product Standardization as a Tool of Competitive Strategy: INSEAD Symposium*, North-Holland, Paris.

Grindley, P. (1990a) 'Standards and the open systems revolution in the computer industry', in Berg, J. and Shumny, H. (eds), *An Analysis of the Information Technology Standardization Process*, Elsevier, Amsterdam.

Grindley, P. (1990b) 'Winning standards contests: using product standards in business strategy', *Business Strategy Review*, Vol. 1, pp. 71–84.

Grindley, P. (1991) 'Replacing a product standard: the case of high-definition television', Working Paper No. 100, Centre for Business Strategy, London Business School.

Grindley, P. (1992) *Standards, Business Strategy and Policy: a casebook*, Centre for Business Strategy Report, London Business School.

Grindley, P. and McBryde, R. (1992) 'The standards contest for digital audio: compact disc and digital audio tape', Working Paper No. 114, Centre for Business Strategy, London Business School.

Grindley, P. and Toker, S. (1992) 'Regulators, markets and standards co-ordination: policy lessons from Telepoint', Working Paper No. 112, Centre for Business Strategy, London Business School.

Kay, J. (1993) *The Foundations of Corporate Success*, Oxford University Press, Oxford.

Pelkmans, J. and Beuter, R. (1987) 'Standardization and competitiveness: private and public strategies in the EC colour TV industry', in Gabel, L. (ed.) *op. cit.*

Sanders, T. (1972) *The Aims and Principles of Standardization*, International Organization for Standardization, Geneva.

Verman, L. (1973) *Standardization: a new discipline*, Arden Books, Hamden, CN.

PART 3

THE RESOURCE-BASED VIEW OF STRATEGY

INTRODUCTION

The articles in Part 3 present the resource-based view (RBV) of strategy. It is an approach which has a long provenance, but has only recently come into prominence in strategic thinking as the dominant strategy paradigm of the 1990s. The most important emphasis in RBV is the issue of 'heterogeneity'. This means that each firm consists of a unique cluster of resources (both tangible and intangible) and capabilities. These will differ between firms in the same industry and will make possible different strategies and different performance. The RBV places the firm rather than the industry at the centre of strategy formulation and strategic decision-making. RBV is therefore able to explain some of the factors contributing to Rumelt's results described in Part 2. It has an internal resource focus rather than an external industry or market focus for strategic thinking. It is most productive however, not to place the RBV and the positioning schools in opposition to each other but rather to see them as complementary perspectives on strategy and how to compete.

The chapters by Grant, and Amit and Schoemaker, both present this idea of the organization as bundles of resources and capabilities. Grant gives the simplest and best definition that I have read of the distinction between resources and capabilities. He argues:

> There is a key distinction between resources and capabilities. Resources are inputs into the production process – they are the basic units of analysis.... But, on their own, few resources are productive. Productive activity requires the co-operation and co-ordination of teams of resources. A capability is the capacity for a team of resources to perform some task or activity. While resources are the source of a firm's capabilities, capabilities are the main source of its competitive advantage.

Such teams of resources are certainly not just human teams. They are any cluster of buildings, ideas, systems, staff, equipment, technology, finance and managerial talent, the combining of which makes different organizations different. Grant is arguing for strategies which 'exploit to maximum effect each firm's unique characteristics'. Amit and Schoemaker present the economist's view of resources. They agree with Grant that organizations differ in their ability to secure advantage from resources and capabilities. Furthermore they argue that uncertainty, complexity and conflict, both inside and outside the organization, constitute the normal conditions under which managers have to manage. However, this leaves room for 'discretionary managerial decisions on strategy crafting'. In other words, it is precisely such uncertainties that create the opportunity for differences between firms to develop, often as a result of better or worse decision-making by managers about the external environment or the internal resource mix. Their chapter suggests that the challenge facing managers is to identify and nurture a set of 'strategic assets' directly arising from the firm's resources and capabilities. They will have the following characteristics:

they should be scarce, durable, not easily traded and difficult to imitate, thus enabling the firm to secure a revenue stream from them over time and generate superior economic returns from superior performance.

That is an important set of points about what makes certain resources and capabilities valuable. Resources and capabilities which are common, short-lived and easy to imitate must be less valuable to an organization than those which are scarce, durable and difficult to imitate. It is the latter which form the basis of sustainability in strategy.

We end Part 3 with another of the series of ground-breaking *Harvard Business Review* articles of Prahalad and Hamel. In this paper they set out to redefine the corporation to work *across* traditionally defined internal organizational boundaries. They see this as crucial to the practice of core competence-based strategy which involves many levels of people and all functions. Their concern is with managers 'trapped in the strategic business unit (SBU) mindset'. By definition, potential core competencies cannot be realized where top management is 'unable to conceive of the corporation as anything other than a collection of discrete businesses'. Prahalad and Hamel urge managers to think of organizations as 'repositories of skills rather than portfolios of products'. They have enlarged the concept of 'relatedness' in corporate strategy. Organizational coherence is to be found in corporate portfolios of competencies rather than just portfolios of related businesses. This should help to generate unconventional options for corporate direction. It has shifted the role of top management from resource allocation to building strategic architecture to map future core competencies, and their constituent technologies, to safeguard the future of the corporation.

CHAPTER 9

THE RESOURCE-BASED THEORY OF COMPETITIVE ADVANTAGE: IMPLICATIONS FOR STRATEGY FORMULATION

ROBERT M. GRANT

Strategy has been defined as 'the match an organization makes between its internal resources and skills ... and the opportunities and risks created by its external environment.'[1] During the 1980s, the principal developments in strategy analysis focused upon the link between strategy and the external environment. Prominent examples of this focus are Michael Porter's analysis of industry structure and competitive positioning and the empirical studies undertaken by the PIMS project.[2] By contrast, the link between strategy and the firm's resources and skills has suffered comparative neglect. Most research into the strategic implications of the firm's internal environment has been concerned with issues of strategy implementation and analysis of the organizational processes through which strategies emerge.[3]

Recently there has been a resurgence of interest in the role of the firm's resources as the foundation for firm strategy. This interest reflects dissatisfaction with the static, equilibrium framework of industrial organization economics that has dominated much contemporary thinking about business strategy and has renewed interest in older theories of profit and competition associated with the writings of David Ricardo, Joseph Schumpeter, and Edith Penrose.[4] Advances have occurred on several fronts. At the corporate strategy level, theoretical interest in economies of scope and transaction costs have focused attention on the role of corporate resources in determining the industrial and geographical boundaries of the firm's activities.[5] At the business strategy level, explorations of the relationships between resources, competition, and profitability include the analysis of competitive imitation,[6] the appropriability of returns to innovations,[7] the role of imperfect information in creating profitability differences between competing firms,[8] and the means by which the process of resource accumulation can sustain competitive advantage.[9]

Together, these contributions amount to what has been termed 'the resource-based view of the firm'. As yet, however, the implications of this 'resource-based theory' for strategic management are unclear for two reasons. First, the various contributions lack a single integrating framework. Second, little effort has been made to develop the practical implications of this theory. The purpose of this article is to make progress on both these fronts by proposing a framework for a resource-based approach to strategy formulation which integrates a number of the key themes arising from this stream of literature. The organizing framework for the article is a five-stage procedure for strategy formulation: analysing the firm's resource-base; appraising the firm's capabilities; analysing the profit-earning potential of firm's resources and capabilities; selecting a strategy; and extending and upgrading the firm's pool of resources and capabilities. Figure 9.1 outlines this framework.

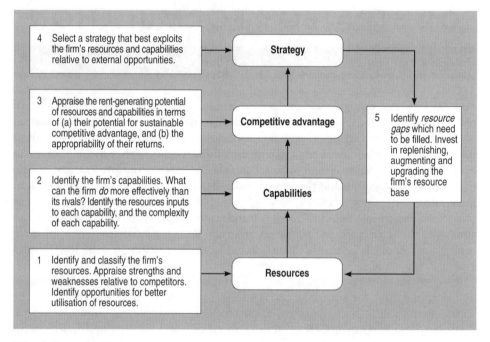

Figure 9.1 A resource-based approach to strategy analysis: a practical framework

RESOURCES AND CAPABILITIES AS THE FOUNDATION FOR STRATEGY

The case for making the resources and capabilities of the firm the foundation for its long-term strategy rests upon two premises: first, internal resources and capabilities provide the basic direction for a firm's strategy; second, resources and capabilities are the primary source of profit for the firm.

Resources and capabilities as a source of direction

The starting point for the formulation of strategy must be some statement of the firm's identity and purpose – conventionally this takes the form of a mission statement which answers the question: 'What is our business?' Typically the definition of the business is in terms of the served market of the firm: e.g., 'Who are our customers?' and 'Which of their needs are we seeking to serve?' But in a world where customer preferences are volatile, the identity of customers is changing, and the technologies for serving customer requirements are continually evolving, an externally focused orientation does not provide a secure foundation for formulating long-term strategy. When the external environment is in a state of flux, the firm's own resources and capabilities may be a much more stable basis on which to define its identity. Hence, a definition of a business in terms of what it is capable of doing may offer a more durable basis for strategy than a definition based upon the needs which the business seeks to satisfy.

Theodore Levitt's solution to the problem of external change was that companies should define their served markets broadly rather than narrowly: railroads should have perceived themselves to be in the transportation business, not the railroad business. But such broadening of the target market is of little value if the company cannot easily develop the capabilities required for serving customer requirements across a wide front. Was it feasible for the railroads to have developed successful trucking, airline, and car rental businesses? Perhaps the resources and capabilities of the railroad companies were better suited to real estate development, or the building and managing of oil and gas pipelines. Evidence suggests that serving broadly defined customer needs is a difficult task. The attempts by Merrill Lynch, American Express, Sears, Citicorp and, most recently, Prudential-Bache to 'serve the full range of our customers' financial needs' created serious management problems. Allegis Corporation's goal of 'serving the needs of the traveller' through combining United Airlines, Hertz car rental and Westin Hotels was a costly failure. By contrast, several companies whose strategies have been based upon developing and exploiting clearly defined internal capabilities have been adept at adjusting to and exploiting external change. Honda's focus upon the technical excellence of 4-cycle engines carried it successfully from motorcycles to automobiles to a broad range of gasoline-engine products. 3M Corporation's expertise in applying adhesive and coating technologies to new product development has permitted profitable growth over an ever-widening product range.

Resources as the basis for corporate profitability

A firm's ability to earn a rate of profit in excess of its cost of capital depends upon two factors: the attractiveness of the industry in which it is located, and its establishment of competitive advantage over rivals. Industrial organization economics emphasizes industry attractiveness as the primary basis for superior profitability, the implication being that strategic management is concerned primarily with seeking favourable industry environments, locating attractive segments and strategic groups within industries, and moderating competitive pressures by influencing industry structure and competitors' behaviour. Yet empirical investigation has failed to support the link between industry structure and profitability. Most studies show that differences in profitability within industries are much more important than differences in profitability between industries.[10] The reasons are not difficult to find: international competition, technological change, and diversification by firms across industry boundaries have meant that industries which were once cosy havens for making easy profits are now subject to vigorous competition.

The finding that competitive advantage rather than external environments is the primary source of inter-firm profit differentials between firms focuses attention upon the sources of competitive advantage. Although the competitive strategy literature has tended to emphasize issues of strategic positioning in terms of the choice between cost and differentiation advantage, and between broad and narrow market scope, fundamental to these choices is the resource position of the firm. For example, the ability to establish a cost advantage requires possession of scale-efficient plants, superior process technology, ownership of low-cost sources of raw materials, or access to low-wage labour. Similarly, differentiation advantage is conferred by brand reputation, proprietary technology, or an extensive sales and service network.

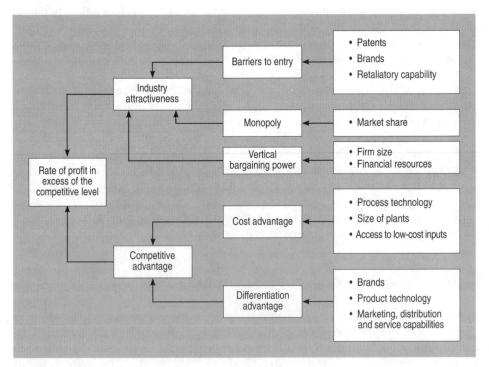

Figure 9.2 Resources as the basis for profitability

This may be summed up as follows: business strategy should be viewed less as a quest for monopoly rents (the returns to market power) and more as a quest for Ricardian rents (the returns to the resources which confer competitive advantage over and above the real costs of these resources). Once these resources depreciate, become obsolescent, or are replicated by other firms, so the rents they generate tend to disappear.[11]

We can go further. A closer look at market power and the monopoly rent it offers, suggests that it too has its basis in the resources of firms. The fundamental prerequisite for market power is the presence of barriers to entry.[12] Barriers to entry are based upon scale economies, patents, experience advantages, brand reputation, or some other resource which incumbent firms possess but which entrants can acquire only slowly or at disproportionate expense. Other structural sources of market power are similarly based upon firms' resources: monopolistic price-setting power depends upon market share which is a consequence of cost efficiency, financial strength, or some other resource. The resources which confer market power may be owned individually by firms, others may be owned jointly. An industry standard (which raises costs of entry), or a cartel, is a resource which is owned collectively by the industry members.[13] Figure 9.2 summarizes the relationships between resources and profitability.

TAKING STOCK OF THE FIRM'S RESOURCES

There is a key distinction between resources and capabilities. Resources are inputs into the production process – they are the basic units of analysis. The individual resources of the firm include items of capital equipment, skills of individual employees, patents, brand names, finance, and so on.

But, on their own, few resources are productive. Productive activity requires the co-operation and co-ordination of teams of resources. A capability is the capacity for a team of resources to perform some task or activity. While resources are the source of a firm's capabilities, capabilities are the main source of its competitive advantage.

Identifying resources

A major handicap in identifying and appraising a firm's resources is that management information systems typically provide only a fragmented and incomplete picture of the firm's resource base. Financial balance sheets are notoriously inadequate because they disregard intangible resources and people-based skills – probably the most strategically important resources of the firm.[14] Classification can provide a useful starting point. Six major categories of resource have been suggested: financial resources, physical resources, human resources, technological resources, reputation, and organizational resources.[15] The reluctance of accountants to extend the boundaries of corporate balance sheets beyond tangible assets partly reflects difficulties of valuation. The heterogeneity and imperfect transferability of most intangible resources precludes the use of market prices. One approach to valuing intangible resources is to take the difference between the stock market value of the firm and the replacement value of its tangible assets.[16] On a similar basis, valuation ratios provide some indication of the importance of firms' intangible resources. Table 9.1 shows that the highest valuation ratios are found among companies with valuable patents and technology assets (notably drug companies) and brand-rich consumer-product companies.

Table 9.1 Twenty companies among the US Top 100 companies with the highest ratios of stock price to book value on 16 March 1990

Company	Industry	Valuation Ratio
Coca Cola	Beverages	8.77
Microsoft	Computer software	8.67
Merck	Pharmaceuticals	8.89
American Home Products	Pharmaceuticals	8.00
Wal Mart Stores	Retailing	7.51
Limited	Retailing	6.65
Warner Lambert	Pharmaceuticals	6.34
Waste Management	Pollution control	6.18
Marrion Merrell Dow	Pharmaceuticals	6.10
McGaw Cellular Communications	Telecom equipment	5.90
Bristol Myers Squibb	Pharmaceuticals	5.48
Toys R Us	Retailing	5.27
Abbot Laboratories	Pharmaceuticals	5.26
Walt Disney	Entertainment	4.90
Johnson & Johnson	Health care products	4.85
MCI Communications	Telecommunications	4.80
Eli Lilly	Pharmaceuticals	4.70
Kellogg	Food products	4.58
H.J. Heinz	Food products	4.38
Pepsico	Beverages	4.33

Source: *The 1990 Business Week Top 1000*

The primary task of a resource-based approach to strategy formulation is maximising rents over time. For this purpose we need to investigate the relationship between resources and organizational capabilities. However, there are also direct links between resources and profitability which raise issues for the strategic management of resources:

- *What opportunities exist for economising on the use of resources?* The ability to maximize productivity is particularly important in the case of tangible resources such as plant and machinery, finance, and people. It may involve using fewer resources to support a larger volume of business. The success of aggressive acquirors, such as ConAgra in the US and Hanson in Britain, is based upon expertise in rigorously pruning the financial, physical and human assets needed to support the volume of business in acquired companies.
- *What are the possibilities for using existing assets more intensely and in more profitable employment?* A large proportion of corporate acquisitions are motivated by the belief that the resources of the acquired company can be put to more profitable use. The returns from transferring existing assets into more productive employment can be substantial. The remarkable turnaround in the performance of the Walt Disney Company between 1985 and 1987 owed much to the vigorous exploitation of Disney's considerable and unique assets: accelerated development of Disney's vast landholdings (for residential development as well as entertainment purposes); exploitation of Disney's huge film library through cable TV, videos, and syndication; fuller utilization of Disney's studios through the formation of Touchstone Films; increased marketing to improve capacity utilization at Disney theme parks.

IDENTIFYING AND APPRAISING CAPABILITIES

The capabilities of a firm are what it can do as a result of teams of resources working together. A firm's capabilities can be identified and appraised using a standard functional classification of the firm's activities.

For example, Snow and Hrebiniak examined capabilities (in their terminology, 'distinctive competencies') in relation to ten functional areas.[17] For most firms, however, the most important capabilities are likely to be those which arise from an integration of individual functional capabilities. For example, McDonald's possesses outstanding functional capabilities within product development, market research, human resource management, financial control and operations management. However, critical to McDonald's success is the integration of these functional capabilities to create McDonald's remarkable consistency of products and services in thousands of restaurants spread across most of the globe. Hamel and Prahalad use the term 'core competencies' to describe these central, strategic capabilities. They are 'the collective learning in the organization, especially how to co-ordinate diverse production skills and integrate multiple streams of technology.'[18] Examples of core competencies include:

- NEC's integration of computer and telecommunication technology
- Philips' optical-media expertise
- Casio's harmonization of know-how in miniaturization, microprocessor design, material science, and ultrathin precision casting

- Canon's integration of optical, microelectronic, and precision-mechanical technologies which forms the basis of its success in cameras, copiers and facsimile machines
- Black and Decker's competence in the design and manufacture of small electric motors.

A key problem in appraising capabilities is maintaining objectivity. Howard Stevenson observed a wide variation in senior managers' perceptions of their organizations' distinctive competencies.[19] Organizations frequently fall victim to past glories, hopes for the future, and wishful thinking. Among the failed industrial companies of both America and Britain are many which believed themselves world leaders with superior products and customer loyalty. During the 1960s, the CEOs of both Harley-Davidson and BSA-Triumph scorned the idea that Honda threatened their supremacy in the market for 'serious motorcycles'.[20] The failure of the US steel companies to respond to increasing import competition during the 1970s was similarly founded upon misplaced confidence in their quality and technological leadership.[21]

The critical task is to assess capabilities relative to those of competitors. In the same way that national prosperity is enhanced through specialization on the basis of comparative advantages, so for the firm, a successful strategy is one which exploits relative strengths. Federal Express's primary capabilities are those which permit it to operate a national delivery system that can guarantee next day delivery; for the British retailer Marks and Spencer, it is the ability to manage supplier relations to ensure a high and consistent level of product quality; for General Electric, it is a system of corporate management that reconciles control, co-ordination, flexibility and innovation in one of the world's largest and most diversified corporations. Conversely, failure is often due to strategies which extend the firm's activities beyond the scope of its capabilities.

Capabilities as organizational routines

Creating capabilities is not simply a matter of assembling a team of resources: capabilities involve complex patterns of co-ordination between people and between people and other resources. Perfecting such co-ordination requires learning through repetition. To understand the anatomy of a firm's capabilities, Nelson and Winter's concept of 'organizational routine' is illuminating. Organizational routines are regular and predictable patterns of activity which are made up of a sequence of co-ordinated actions by individuals. A capability is, in essence, a routine, or a number of interacting routines. The organization itself is a huge network of routines. These include the sequence of routines which govern the passage of raw material and components through the production process, and top management routines which include routines for monitoring business unit performance, for capital budgeting and for strategy formulation.

The concept of organizational routines offers illuminating insights into the relationships between resources, capabilities and competitive advantage:

- *The relationship between resources and capabilities.* There is no predetermined functional relationship between the resources of a firm and its capabilities. The types, the amounts, and the qualities of the resources available to the firm have an important bearing on what the firm can do since they place constraints upon the range of organizational routines that can be performed and the standard to which they are performed. However, a key ingredient in the relationship between resources and capabilities is the ability of an organization to achieve co-operation and co-ordination within teams. This requires that an organization motivate and socialize its members in a manner conducive to the development of smooth-functioning routines. The organization's style, values, traditions and leadership are critical encouragements to the co-operation and commitment of its members. These can be viewed as intangible resources which are common ingredients of the whole range of corporation's organizational routines.
- *The trade-off between efficiency and flexibility.* Routines are to the organization what skills are to the individual. Just as the individual's skills are carried out semi-automatically, without conscious co-ordination, so organizational routines involve a large component of tacit knowledge, which implies limits on the extent to which the organization's capabilities can be articulated. Just as individual skills become rusty when not exercised, so it is difficult for organizations to retain co-ordinated responses to contingencies that arise only rarely. Hence there may be a trade-off between efficiency and flexibility. A limited repertoire of routines can be performed highly efficiently with near-perfect co-ordination – all in the absence of significant intervention by top management. The same organization may find it extremely difficult to respond to novel situations.
- *Economies of experience.* Just as individual skills are acquired through practice over time, so the skills of an organization are developed and sustained only through experience. The advantage of an established firm over a newcomer is primarily in the organizational routines that it has perfected over time. The Boston Consulting Group's 'experience curve' represents a naive, yet valuable attempt to relate the experience of the firm to its performance. However, in industries where technological change is rapid, new firms may possess an advantage over established firms through their potential for faster learning of new routines because they are less committed to old routines.
- *The complexity of capabilities.* Organizational capabilities differ in their complexity. Some capabilities may derive from the contribution of a single resource. Du Pont's successful development of several cardiovascular drugs during the late 1980s owed much to the research leadership of its leading pharmacologist Pieter Timmermans.[22] Drexel Burnham Lambert's capability in junk bond underwriting during the 1980s resided almost entirely in the skills of Michael Milken. Other routines require highly complex interactions involving the co-operation of many different resources. Walt Disney's 'imagineering' capability involves the integration of ideas, skills, and knowledge drawn from movie making, engineering, psychology, and a wide variety of technical disciplines. As we shall see, complexity is particularly relevant to the sustainability of competitive advantage.

EVALUATING THE RENT-EARNING POTENTIAL: SUSTAINABILITY

The returns to a firm's resources and capabilities depend upon two key factors: first, the sustainability of the competitive advantage which resources and capabilities confer upon the firm; and, second, the ability of the firm to appropriate the rents earned from its resources and capabilities.

Over the long term, competitive advantage and the returns associated with it are eroded both through the depreciation of the advantaged firm's resources and capabilities and through imitation by rivals. The speed of erosion depends critically upon the characteristics of the resources and capabilities. Consider markets where competitive advantage is unsustainable: in 'efficient' markets (most closely approximated by the markets for securities, commodities, and foreign exchange) competitive advantage is absent; market prices reflect all available information, prices adjust instantaneously to new information, and traders can only expect normal returns. The absence of competitive advantage is a consequence of the resources required to compete in these markets. To trade in financial markets, the basic requirements are finance and information. If both are available on equal terms to all participants, competitive advantage cannot exist. Even if privileged information is assumed to exist ('weakly efficient' markets), competitive advantage is not sustainable. Once a trader acts upon privileged information, transactions volume and price movements signal insider activity, and other traders are likely to rush in seeking a piece of the action.

The essential difference between industrial markets and financial markets lies in the resource requirements of each. In industrial markets, resources are specialized, immobile, and long-lasting. As a result, according to Richard Caves, a key feature of industrial markets is the existence of 'committed competition – rivalrous moves among incumbent producers that involve resource commitments that are irrevocable for non-trivial periods of time.'[23] The difficulties involved in acquiring the resources required to compete and the need to commit resources long before a competitive move can be initiated also implies that competitive advantage is much more sustainable than it is in financial markets. Resource-based approaches to the theory of competitive advantage point towards four characteristics of resources and capabilities which are likely to be particularly important determinants of the sustainability of competitive advantage: *durability*, *transparency*, *transferability*, and *replicability*.

Durability

In the absence of competition, the longevity of a firm's competitive advantage depends upon the rate at which the underlying resources and capabilities depreciate or become obsolete. The durability of resources varies considerably: the increasing pace of technological change is shortening the useful life spans of most capital equipment and technological resources. On the other hand, reputation (both brand

and corporate) appears to depreciate relatively slowly, and these assets can normally be maintained by modest rates of replacement investment. Many of the consumer brands which command the strongest loyalties today (e.g. Heinz sauces, Kellogg's cereals, Campbell's soup, Hoover vacuum cleaners) have been market leaders for close to a century. Corporate reputation displays similar longevity: the reputations of GE, IBM, Du Pont, and Proctor and Gamble as well-managed, socially responsible, financially sound companies which produce reliable products and treat their employees well has been established over several decades. While increasing environmental turbulence shortens the life spans of many resources, it is possible that it may have the effect of bolstering brand and corporate reputations.

Firm capabilities have the potential to be more durable than the resources upon which they are based because of the firm's ability to maintain capabilities through replacing individual resources (including people) as they wear out or move on. Rolls Royce's capability in the craft-based manufacture of luxury cars and 3M's capability in new product introduction have been maintained over several generations of employees. Such longevity depends critically upon the management of these capabilities to ensure their maintenance and renewal. One of the most important roles that organizational culture plays in sustaining competitive advantage may be through its maintenance support for capabilities through the socialization of new employees.[24]

Transparency

The firm's ability to sustain its competitive advantage over time depends upon the speed with which other firms can imitate its strategy. Imitation requires that a competitor overcomes two problems. First is the information problem: What is the competitive advantage of the successful rival, and how is it being achieved? Second is the strategy duplication problem: How can the would-be competitor amass the resources and capabilities required to imitate the successful strategy of the rival? The information problem is a consequence of imperfect information on two sets of relationships. If a firm wishes to imitate the strategy of a rival, it must first establish the capabilities which underlie the rival's competitive advantage, and then it must determine what resources are required to replicate these capabilities. I refer to this as the 'transparency' of competitive advantage. With regard to the first transparency problem, a competitive advantage which is the consequence of superior capability in relation to a single performance variable is more easy to identify and comprehend than a competitive advantage that involves multiple capabilities conferring superior performance across several variables. Cray Research's success in the computer industry rests primarily upon its technological capability in relation to large, ultra-powerful computers. IBM's superior perform-ance is multi-dimensional and is more difficult to understand. It is extremely difficult to distinguish and appraise the relative contributions to IBM's success of research capability, scale economies in product development and manufacturing, self-sufficiency through backward integration, and superior customer service through excellence in sales, service, and technical support.

With regard to the second transparency problem, a capability which requires a complex pattern of co-ordination between large numbers of diverse resources is more difficult to comprehend than a capability which rests upon the exploitation of a single dominant resource. For example, Federal Express's next-day delivery capability requires close co-operation between numerous employees, aircraft, delivery vans, computerized tracking facilities and automated sorting equipment, all co-ordinated into a single system. By contrast, Atlantic Richfield's low-cost position in the supply of gasoline to the California market rests simply on its access to Alaskan crude oil. Imperfect transparency is the basis for Lippman and Rumelt's theory of 'uncertain imitability': the greater the uncertainty within a market over how successful companies 'do it', the more inhibited are potential entrants, and the higher the level of profit that established firms can maintain within that market.[25]

Transferability

Once established firm or potential entrant has established the sources of the superior performance, imitation then requires amassing the resources and capabilities necessary for a competitive challenge. The primary source of resources and capabilities is likely to be the markets for these inputs. If firms can acquire (on similar terms) the resources required for imitating the competitive advantage of a successful rival, then that rival's competitive advantage will be short lived. As we have seen, in financial markets the easy access by traders to finance and information causes competitive advantage to be fleeting. However, most resources and capabilities are not freely transferable between firms; hence, would-be competitors are unable to acquire (on equal terms) the resources needed to replicate the competitive advantage of an incumbent firm. Imperfections in transferability arise from several sources:

- *Geographical immobility.* The costs of relocating large items of capital equipment and highly specialized employees puts firms which are acquiring these resources at a disadvantage to firms which already possess them.
- *Imperfect information.* Assessing the value of a resource is made difficult by the heterogeneity of resources (particularly human resources) and by imperfect knowledge of the potential productivity of individual resources.[26] The established firm's ability to build up information over time about the productivity of its resources gives it superior knowledge to that of any prospective purchaser of the resources in question.[27] The resulting imperfection of the markets for productive resources can then result in resources being either underpriced or overpriced, thus giving rise to differences in profitability between firms.[28]
- *Firm-specific resources.* Apart from the transactions costs arising from immobility and imperfect information, the value of a resource may fall on transfer due to a decline in its productivity. To the extent that brand reputation is associated with the company which created the brand reputation, a change in ownership of the brand name erodes its value. Once Rover, MG, Triumph and Jaguar were merged into British Leyland, the values of these brands in differentiating

automobiles declined substantially. Employees can suffer a similar decline in productivity in the process of inter-firm transfer. To the extent that an employee's productivity is influenced by situational and motivational factors, then it is unreasonable to expect that a highly successful employee in one company can replicate his/her performance when hired away by another company. Some resources may be almost entirely firm-specific – corporate reputation can only be transferred by acquiring the company as a whole, and even then the reputation of the acquired company normally depreciates during the change in ownership.[29]

- *The immobility of capabilities.* Capabilities, because they require interactive teams of resources, are far more immobile than individual resources – they require the transfer of the whole team. Such transfers can occur (e.g. the defection of 16 of First Boston's managers and acquisitions staff to Wasserstein, Perella and Company).[30] However, even if the resources that constitute the team are transferred, the nature of organizational routines – in particular, the role of tacit knowledge and unconscious co-ordination – makes the recreation of capabilities within a new corporate environment uncertain.

Replicability

Imperfect transferability of resources and capabilities limits the ability of a firm to buy in the means to imitate success. The second route by which a firm can acquire a resource of capability is by internal investment. Some resources and capabilities can be easily imitated through replication. In retailing, competitive advantages which derive from electronic point-of-sale systems, retailer charge cards, and extended hours of opening can be copied fairly easily by competitors. In financial services, new product innovations (such as interest rate swaps, stripped bonds, money market accounts, and the like) are notorious for their easy imitation by competitors.

Much less easily replicable are capabilities based upon highly complex organizational routines. IBM's ability to motivate its people and Nucor's outstanding efficiency and flexibility in steel manufacture are combinations of complex routines that are based upon tacit rather than codified knowledge and are fused into the respective corporate cultures. Some capabilities appear simple but prove exceptionally difficult to replicate. Two of the simplest and best-known Japanese manufacturing practices are just-in-time scheduling and quality circles. Despite the fact that neither require sophisticated knowledge or complex operating systems, the co-operation and attitudinal changes required for their effective operation are such that few American and European firms have introduced either with the same degree of success as Japanese companies. If apparently simple practices such as these are deceptively difficult to imitate, it is easy to see how firms that develop highly complex capabilities can maintain their competitive advantage over very long periods of time. Xerox's commitment to customer service is a capability that is not located in any particular department, but it permeates the whole corporation and is built into the fabric and culture of the corporation.

Even where replication is possible, the dynamics of stock-flow relationships may still offer an advantage to incumbent firms. Competitive advantage depends upon the stock of resources and capabilities that a firm possesses. Dierickx and Cool show that firms which possess the initial stocks of the resources required for competitive advantage may be able to sustain their advantages over time.[31] Among the stock-flow relationships they identify as sustaining advantage are: 'asset mass efficiencies' – the initial amount of the resource which the firm possesses influences the pace at which the resource can be accumulated; and 'time compression diseconomies' – firms which rapidly accumulate a resource incur disproportionate costs ('crash programs' of R&D and 'blitz' advertising campaigns tend to be less productive than similar expenditures made over a longer period).

EVALUATING RENT-EARNING POTENTIAL: APPROPRIABILITY

The returns to a firm from its resources and capabilities depend not only on sustaining its competitive position over time, but also on the firm's ability to appropriate these returns. The issue of appropriability concerns the allocation of rents where property rights are not fully defined. Once we go beyond the financial and physical assets valued in a company's balance sheet, ownership becomes ambiguous. The firm owns intangible assets such as patents, copyrights, brand names, and trade secrets, but the scope of property rights may lack precise definition. In the case of employee skills, two major problems arise: the lack of clear distinction between the technology of the firm and the human capital of the individual; and the limited control which employment contracts offer over the services provided by employees. Employee mobility means that it is risky for a firm's strategy to be dependent upon the specific skills of a few key employees. Also, such employees can bargain with the firm to appropriate the major part of their contribution to value added.

The degree of control exercised by a firm and the balance of power between the firm and an individual employee depends crucially on the relationship between the individual's skills and organizational routines. The more deeply embedded are organizational routines within groups of individuals and the more they are supported by the contributions of other resources, then the greater is the control that the firm's management can exercise. The ability of IBM to utilize its advanced semiconductor research as an instrument of competitive advantage depends, in part, upon the extent to which the research capability is a team asset rather than a reflection of the contribution of brilliant individuals. A firm's dependence upon skills possessed by highly trained and highly mobile key employees is particularly important in the case of professional service companies where employee skills are the overwhelmingly important resource.[32] Many of the problems that have arisen in acquisitions of human-capital-intensive companies arise from conflicts over property rights between the acquiring company and employees of the acquired company. An interesting example is the protracted dispute which followed the acquisition of the New York advertising agency Lord, Geller, Fredrico, Einstein by WPP Group in 1988. Most of the senior executives of the acquired company left to form a new advertising agency taking several former clients with them.[33] Similar conflicts have arisen over technology ownership in high-tech start-ups founded by former employees of established companies.[34]

Where ownership is ambiguous, relative bargaining power is the primary determinant of the allocation of the rents between the firm and its employees. If the individual employee's contribution to productivity is clearly identifiable, if the employee is mobile, and the employee's skills offer similar productivity to other firms, then the employee is well placed to bargain for that contribution. If the increased gate receipts of the LA Kings ice hockey team can be attributed primarily to the presence of Wayne Gretzky on the team and if Gretzky can offer a similar performance enhancement to other teams, then he is in a strong position to appropriate (as salary and bonuses) most of the increased contribution. The less identifiable is the individual's contribution, and the more firm-specific are the skills being applied, the greater is the proportion of the return which accrues to the firm. Declining profitability among investment banks encouraged several to reassert their bargaining power vis-à-vis their individual stars and in-house gurus by engineering a transfer of reputation from these key employees to the company as a whole. At Citibank, Saloman Brothers, Merrill Lynch, and First Boston, this resulted in bitter conflicts between top management and some senior employees.[35]

FORMULATING STRATEGY

Although the foregoing discussion of the links between resources, capabilities, and profitability has been strongly theoretical in nature, the implications for strategy formulation are straightforward. The analysis of the rent-generating potential of resources and capabilities concludes that the firm's most important resources and capabilities are those which are durable, difficult to identify and understand, imperfectly transferable, not easily replicated, and in which the firm possesses clear ownership and control. These are the firm's 'crown jewels' and need to be protected; and they play a pivotal role in the competitive strategy which the firm pursues. The essence of strategy formulation, then, is to design a strategy that makes the most effective use of these core resources and capabilities. Consider, for example, the remarkable turnaround of Harley-Davidson between 1984 and 1988. Fundamental was top management's recognition that the company's sole durable, non-transferable, irreplicable asset was the Harley-Davidson image and the loyalty that accompanied that image. In virtually every other area of competitive performance – production costs, quality, product and process technology, and global market scope – Harley was greatly inferior to its Japanese rivals. Harley's only opportunity for survival was to pursue a strategy founded upon Harley's image advantage, while simultaneously minimising Harley's disadvantages in other capabilities. Harley-Davidson's new models introduced during this period were all based around traditional design features, while Harley's marketing strategy involved extending the appeal of the Harley image of individuality and toughness from its traditional customer group to more affluent professional types. Protection of the Harley-Davidson name by means of tougher controls over dealers was matched by wider exploitation of the Harley name through extensive licensing. While radical improvements in manufacturing efficiency and quality were essential components of the turnaround strategy, it was the enhancing and broadening of Harley's market appeal which was the primary driver of Harley's rise from 27 to 44 percent of the US heavyweight motorcycle market between 1984 and 1988, accompanied by an increase in net income from £6.5 million to $29.8 million.

Conversely, a failure to recognize and exploit the strategic importance of durable, untransferable, and irreplicable resources almost inevitably has dire consequences. The troubles of BankAmerica Corporation during the mid-1980s can be attributed to a strategy that became increasingly dissociated from the bank's most important assets: its reputation and market position in retail banking in the Western United States. The disastrous outcome of US Air Group's acquisition of the Californian carrier, PSA, is similarly attributable to US Air's disregard for PSA's most important asset – its reputation in the Californian market for a friendly, laid-back style of service.

Designing strategy around the most critically important resources and capabilities may imply that the firm limits its strategic scope to those activities where it possesses a clear competitive advantage. The principal capabilities of Lotus, the specialist manufacturer of sports cars, are in design and engineering development; it lacked both the manufacturing capabilities or the sales volume to compete effectively in the world's auto market. Lotus's turnaround during the 1980s followed its decision to specialize upon design and development consulting for other auto manufacturers, and to limit its own manufacturing primarily to formula one racing cars.

The ability of a firm's resources and capabilities to support a sustainable competitive advantage is essential to the time frame of a firm's strategic planning process. If a company's resources and capabilities lack durability or are easily transferred or replicated, then the company must either adopt a strategy of short-term harvesting or it must invest in developing new sources of competitive advantage. These considerations are critical for small technological start-ups where the speed of technological change may mean that innovations offer only temporary competitive advantage. The company must seek either to exploit its initial innovation before it is challenged by stronger, established rivals or other start-ups, or it must establish the technological capability for a continuing stream of innovations. A fundamental flaw in EMI's exploitation of its invention of the CT scanner was a strategy that failed to exploit EMI's five-year technical lead in the development and marketing of the X-ray scanner and failed to establish the breadth of technological and manufacturing capability required to establish a fully fledged medical electronics business.

Where a company's resources and capabilities are easily transferable or replicable, sustaining a competitive advantage is only feasible if the company's market is unattractively small or if it can obscure the existence of its competitive advantage. Filofax, the long-established British manufacturer of personal organizers, was able to dominate the market for its products so long as that market remained small. The boom in demand for Filofaxes during the mid-1980s was, paradoxically, a disaster for the company. Filofax's product was easily imitated and yuppie-driven demand growth spawned a host of imitators. By 1989, the company was suffering falling sales and mounting losses.[36] In industries where competitive advantages based upon differentiation and innovation can be imitated (such as financial services, retailing, fashion clothing, and toys), firms have a brief window of opportunity during which to exploit their advantage before imitators erode it away. Under such circumstances, firms must be concerned not with sustaining the existing advantages, but with creating the flexibility and responsiveness that permits them to create new advantages at a faster rate than the old advantages are being eroded by competition.

Transferability and replicability of resources and capabilities is also a key issue in the strategic management of joint ventures. Studies of the international joint ventures point to the transferability of each party's capabilities as a critical determinant of the allocation of benefits from the venture. For example, Western companies' strengths in distribution channels and product technology have been easily exploited by Japanese joint venture partners, while Japanese manufacturing excellence and new product development capabilities have proved exceptionally difficult for Western companies to learn.[37]

IDENTIFYING RESOURCE GAPS AND DEVELOPING THE RESOURCE BASE

The analysis so far has regarded the firm's resource base as predetermined, with the primary task of organizational strategy being the deployment of these resources so as to maximize rents over time. However, a resource-based approach to strategy is concerned not only with the deployment of existing resources, but also with the development of the firm's stock of resources and to augment resources in order to buttress and extend positions of competitive advantage as well as broaden the firm's strategic opportunity set. This task is known in the strategy literature as filling 'resource gaps'.[38]

Sustaining advantage in the face of competition and evolving customer requirements also requires that firms constantly develop their resource bases. Such 'upgrading' of competitive advantage occupies a central position in Michael Porter's analysis of the competitive advantage of nations.[39] Porter's analysis of the ability of firms and nations to establish and maintain international competitive success depends critically upon the ability to continually innovate and to shift the basis of competitive advantage from 'basic' to 'advanced' factors of production. An important feature of these 'advanced' factors of production is that they offer a more sustainable competitive advantage because they are more specialized (therefore less mobile through market transfer) and less easy to replicate.

Commitment to upgrading the firm's pool of resources and capabilities requires strategic direction in terms of the capabilities that will form the basis of the firm's future competitive advantage. Thus, Prahalad and Hamel's notion of 'core competencies' is less an identification of a company's current capabilities than a commitment to a path of future development. For example, NEC's strategic focus on computing and communications in the mid-1970s was not so much a statement of the core strengths of the company as it was a long-term commitment to a particular path of technological development.

Harmonising the exploitation of existing resources with the development of the resources and capabilities for competitive advantage in the future is a subtle task. To the extent that capabilities are learned and perfected through repetition, capabilities develop automatically through the pursuit of a particular strategy. The essential task, then, is to ensure that strategy constantly pushes slightly beyond the limits of the firm's capabilities at any point of time. This ensures not only the perfection of capabilities required by the current strategy, but also the development of the capabilities required to meet the challenges of the future. The idea that, through pursuing its present strategy, a firm develops the expertise required for its future strategy is referred to by Hiroyuki Itami as 'dynamic resource fit':

> Effective strategy in the present builds invisible assets, and the expanded stock enables the firm to plan its future strategy to be carried out. And the future strategy must make effective use of the resources that have been amassed.[40]

Matsushita is a notable exponent of this principle of parallel and sequential development of strategy and capabilities. For example, in developing production in a foreign country, Matsushita typically began with the production of simple products, such as batteries, then moved on to the production of products requiring greater manufacturing and marketing sophistication:

> In every country batteries are a necessity, so they sell well. As long as we bring a few advanced automated pieces of equipment for the processes vital to final product quality, even unskilled labor can produce good products. As they work on this rather simple product, the workers get trained, and this increased skill level then permits us to gradually expand production to items with increasingly higher technology level, first radios, then televisions.[41]

The development of capabilities which can then be used as the basis for broadening a firm's product range is a common feature of successful strategies of related diversification. Sequential product addition to accompany the development of technological, manufacturing, and marketing expertise was a feature of Honda's diversification from motorcycles to cars, generators, lawnmowers, and boat engines; and of 3M's expansion from abrasives to adhesives, video tape, and computer disks.

In order both to fully exploit a firm's existing stock of resources, and to develop competitive advantages for the future, the external acquisition of complementary resources may be necessary. Consider the Walt Disney Company's turnaround between 1984 and 1988. In order for the new management to exploit more effectively Disney's vast, under-utilized stock of unique resources, new resources were required. Achieving better utilization of Disney's film studios and expertise in animation required the acquisition of creative talent in the form of directors, actors, scriptwriters, and cartoonists. Putting Disney's vast real estate holdings to work was assisted by the acquisition of the property development expertise of the Arvida Corporation. Building a new marketing team was instrumental in increasing capacity utilization at Disneyland and Disney World.

CONCLUSION

The resources and capabilities of a firm are the central considerations in formulating its strategy: they are the primary constants upon which a firm can establish its identity and frame its strategy, and they are the primary sources of the firm's profitability. The key to a resource-based approach to strategy formulation is understanding the relationships between resources, capabilities, competitive advantage, and profitability – in particular, an understanding of the mechanisms through which competitive advantage can be sustained over time. This requires the design of strategies which exploit to maximum effect each firm's unique characteristics.

NOTES

1 Charles W. Hofer and Dan Schendel, *Strategy Formulation: Analytical Concepts* (St. Paul, MN: West, 1978), p. 12.
2 Robert D. Buzzell and Bradley T. Gale, *The PIMS Principles: Linking Strategy to Performance* (New York, NY: Free Press, 1987).
3 See, for example, Henry Mintzberg, 'Of Strategies, Deliberate and Emergent', *Strategic Management Journal*, 6 (1985): 257–272; Andrew M. Pettigrew, 'Strategy formulation as a political process', *International Studies of Management and Organization*, 7 (1977): 78–87; J.B. Quinn, *Strategies for Change: Logical Incrementalism* (Homewood, IL: Irwin, 1980).
4 David Ricardo, *Principles of Political Economy and Taxation* (London: G. Bell, 1891); Joseph A. Schumpeter, *The Theory of Economic Development* (Cambridge, MA: Harvard University Press, 1934); Edith Penrose, *The Theory of the Growth of the Firm* (New York, NY: John Wiley and Sons, 1959).
5 David J. Teece, 'Economies of scope and the scope of the enterprise', *Journal of Economic Behavior and Organization*, 1 (1980): 223–247; S. Chatterjee and B. Wernerfelt, 'The link between resources and types of diversification: theory and evidence', *Strategic Management Journal*, 12 (1991): 33–48.
6 R.P. Rumelt, 'Towards a Strategic Theory of the Firm', in R.B. Lamb, ed., *Competitive Strategic Management* (Englewood Cliffs, NJ: Prentice Hall, 1984); S.A. Lippman and R.P. Rumelt, 'Uncertain imitability: an analysis of interfirm differences in efficiency under competition', *Bell Journal of Economics*, 23 (1982): 418–438; Richard Reed and R.J. DeFillippi, 'Causal ambiguity, barriers to imitation, and sustainable competitive advantage', *Academy of Management Review*, 15 (January 1990): 88–102.

7 David J. Teece, 'Capturing value from technological innovation: integration, strategic partnering and licensing decisions', *Interfaces*, 18/3 (1988): 46–61.

8 Jay B. Barney, 'Strategic factor markets: expectations, luck and business strategy', *Management Science*, 32/10 (October 1986): 1231–1241.

9 Ingemar Dierickx and Karel Cool, 'Asset stock accumulation and the sustainability of competitive advantage', *Management Science*, 35/12 (December 1989): 1504–1513.

10 R. Schmalensee, 'Industrial economics: an overview', *Economic Journal*, 98 (1988): 643–681; R.D. Buzzell and B.T. Gale, *The PIMS Principles* (New York, NY: Free Press, 1987).

11 Because of the ambiguity associated with accounting definitions of profit, the academic literature increasingly uses the term 'rent' to refer to 'economic profit'. 'Rent' is the surplus of revenue over the 'real' or 'opportunity' cost of the resources used in generating that revenue. The 'real' or 'opportunity' cost of a resource is the revenue it can generate when put to an alternative use in the firm or the price which it can be sold for.

12 W.J. Baumol, J.C. Panzer and R.D. Willig, *Contestable Markets and the Theory of Industrial Structure* (New York, NY: Harcourt Brace Jovanovitch, 1982).

13 In economist's jargon, such jointly owned resources are 'public goods' – their benefits can be extended to additional firms at negligible marginal cost.

14 Hiroyuki Itami (*Mobilizing Invisible Assets*, Cambridge, MA: Harvard University Press, 1986) refers to these as 'invisible assets'.

15 Based upon Hofer and Schendel, op. cit., pp. 145–148.

16 See, for example, Iain Cockburn and Zvi Griliches, 'Industry Effects and the Appropriability Measures in the Stock Market's Valuation of R&D and Patents', *American Economic Review*, 78 (1988): 419–423.

17 General management, financial management, marketing and selling, market research, product R&D, engineering, production, distribution, legal affairs, and personnel. See Charles C. Snow and Lawrence G. Hrebiniak, 'Strategy, Distinctive Competence, and Organizational Performance', *Administrative Science Quarterly*, 25 (1980): 317–336.

18 C.K. Prahalad and Gary Hamel, 'The core competence of the corporation' *Harvard Business Review* (May/June 1990), pp. 79–91.

19 Howard H. Stevenson, 'Defining corporate strengths and weaknesses', *Sloan Management Review* (Spring 1976), pp. 51–68.

20 Richard T. Pascale, 'Honda (A)', Harvard Business School, Case no. 9–384–049, 1983.

21 Paul R. Lawrence and Davis Dyer, *Renewing Amercian Industry* (New York, NY: Free Press, 1983), pp. 60–83.

22 'Du Pont's "drug hunter" stalks his next big trophy', *Business Week*, November 27, 1989, pp. 174–182.

23 Richard E. Caves, 'Economic Analysis and the Quest for Competitive Advantage', *American Economic Review*, 74 (1984): 127–128.

24 Jay B. Barney, 'Organizational culture: can it be a source of sustained competitive advantage?' *Academy of Management Review*, 11 (1986): 656–665.

25 Lippman and Rumelt, op. cit.

26 This information problem is a consequence of the fact that resources work together in teams and their individual productivity is not observable. See A.A. Alchian and H. Demsetz, 'Production, Information costs and economic organization', *American Economic Review*, 62 (1972): 777–795.

27 Such asymmetric information gives rise to a 'lemons' problem. See G. Akerlof, 'The market for lemons: qualitative uncertainty and the market mechanism', *Quarterly Journal of Economics*, 84 (1970): 488–500.

28 Barney, op. cit.

29 The definition of resource specificity in this article corresponds to the definition of 'specific assets' by Richard Caves ('International corporations: the industrial economics of foreign investment', *Economica*, 38, 1971: 1–27); it differs from that used by O.E. Williamson (*The Economic Institutions of Capitalism*, New York, NY: Free Press, 1985, pp. 52–56). Williamson refers to assets which are specific to particular transactions rather than to particular firms.

30 'Catch a falling star', *The Economist*, April 23 1988, pp. 88–90.

31 Dierickx and Cool, op. cit.

32 The key advantage of partnerships as an organizational form for such businesses is in averting conflict over control and rent allocation between employees and owners.

33 'Ad world is abuzz as top brass leaves Lord Geller agency', *Wall Street Journal*, March 23, 1988, p. A1.

34 Charles Ferguson ('From the people who brought you voodoo economics', *Harvard Business Review*, May/June 1988, pp. 55–63) has claimed that these start-ups involve the individual exploitation of technical knowledge which rightfully belongs to the former employers of these new entrepreneurs.

35 'The decline of the superstar', *Business Week*, August 17, 1987, pp. 90–96.

36 'Faded fad', *The Economist*, September 30, 1989, p. 68.

37 Gary Hamel, Yves Doz, and C.K. Prahalad, 'Collaborate with your competitors – and win', *Harvard Business Review* (January/February 1989), pp. 133–139.

38 Stevenson (1985), op. cit.

39 Michael E. Porter, *The Competitive Advantage of Nations* (New York, NY: Free Press, 1990).

40 Itami, op. ict., p. 125.

41 Arataroh Takahashi, *What I learned from Konosuke Matsushita* (Tokyo: Jitsugyo no Nihonsha, 1980 (in Japanese)). Quoted by Itami, op. cit., p. 25.

CHAPTER 10

STRATEGIC ASSETS AND ORGANIZATIONAL RENT

RAPHAEL AMIT AND PAUL J.H. SCHOEMAKER

We build on an emerging strategy literature that views the firm as a bundle of resources and capabilities, and examine conditions that contribute to the realization of sustainable economic rents. Because of (1) resource-market imperfections and (2) discretionary managerial decisions about resource development and deployment we expect firms to differ (in and out of equilibrium) in the resources and capabilities they control. This asymmetry in turn can be a source of sustainable economic rent. The paper focuses on the linkages between the industry analysis framework, the resource-based view of the firm, behavioural decision biases and organizational implementation issues. It connects the concept of Strategic Industry Factors at the market level with the notion of Strategic Assets at the firm level. Organizational rent is shown to stem from imperfect and discretionary decisions to develop and deploy selected resources and capabilities, made by boundedly rational managers facing high uncertainty, complexity, and intrafirm conflict.

INTRODUCTION

However they phrase them, executives often examine such questions as, 'What makes us distinctive or unique?' 'Why do some and not other customers buy from us?' 'Why are we profitable?' Typical answers might refer to the firm's 'technical know-how', 'responsiveness to market needs', 'design and engineering capability', or 'financial resources'. The common theme among these responses is that management deems some firm-specific resources and capabilities to be crucial in explaining a firm's performance.

While empirical models may, ex post, point to a limited set of resources and capabilities that explain some of the firm's past performance, *ex ante* such models offer limited insight into the dimensions of competition that will prevail in the future. For managers, the challenge is to identify, develop, protect, and deploy resources and capabilities in a way that provides the firm with a sustainable competitive advantage and, thereby, a superior return on capital.

Managerial decisions concerning such resources and capabilities are ordinarily made in a setting that is characterized by: (1) *Uncertainty* about (a) the economic, industry, regulatory, social, and technological environments, (b) competitors' behaviour, and (c) customers' preferences; (2) *Complexity* concerning (a) the interrelated causes that shape the firm's environments, (b) the competitive interactions ensuing from differing perceptions about these environments; and by (3) *Intraorganizational conflicts* among those who make managerial decisions and those affected by them. These conditions of uncertainty, complexity, and conflict are usually difficult to articulate or model. For example, the exact relationships between the firm's bundle of capabilities and its performance may be unclear in the present, let alone the future.[1]

By explicitly addressing these dimensions of the managerial challenge, our paper attempts to link the 'industry analysis framework' with the 'resource view of the firm' and highlight the human limitations in crafting firm strategy. We start by briefly reviewing the existing literature on the resource-based view and defining the terms we use. We proceed by articulating our view and contribution to the theory. We end by examining the theory in the context of multiple dimensions and emphasising the heuristic nature of organizational rent creation.

LITERATURE AND DEFINITIONS

A growing body of empirical literature points to the importance of firm-specific factors in explaining variations in economic rent[2] (Jacobson 1988; Hansen and Wernerfelt, 1989). For example, Cool and Schendel (1988) reported significant and systematic performance differences among firms belonging to the same strategic group within the US pharmaceutical industry. Additionally, Rumelt (1991) found that business units differ far more within than across industries. Theorists have long recognized the importance of firm differences and distinctive competencies (Selznick, 1957, Ansoff, 1965, Andrews, 1971, Hofer and Schendel, 1978). Current managerial writings such as Irvin and Michaels (1989), Wernerfelt (1989), Prahalad and Hamel (1990), Grant (1991), or Stalk, Evans, and Shulman (1992) further evidence a continuing interest in core skills and capabilities as a source of competitive advantage.

Vasconcellos and Hambrick (1989) recently conducted an empirical, ex post test of the long-standing strategy premise that an organization's success depends on the match between the strengths and the Key Success Factors (KSF)[3] in its environment. Using a range of mature industrial product industries, their empirical findings showed that organizations which rated highest on industry KSF clearly outperformed their rivals.

Although this analysis provides an important test of a core thesis in strategy, it also raises further questions. First, the Vasconcellos and Hambrick (1989) study considers the industry as the primary unit of analysis, whereas managers operate from a firm perspective. Second, the empirical analysis is ex post, whereas managers need to make resource deployment decisions exante, which involves uncertainty, complexity and organizational conflict. Third, it should be recognized that if all firms score high on the presumed KSF, these factors will cease to be KSF. Thus, we need to introduce sustainable asymmetry into the analysis, possibly stemming from mobility barriers, organizational inertia, heterogeneous expectations, failures in resource markets, and so forth.

The use of KSF as a core concept in strategy was recently critiqued by Ghemawat (1991a) as lacking: (1) identification (there may be many success factors, making it hard to decide which ones to focus on); (2) concentrates (ambiguity about the causal processes that tie the firm's success factors to its performance); (3) generality (to be success factors they must be undervalued; i.e., the cost benefit ratio associated with their development must be less than one); and (4) necessity (the failure of the success factor approach to account for dynamic aspects of strategy). Whereas we agree with Ghemawat (1991a) about these challenges, it should be pointed out that without uncertainty, complexity, and conflict, there would be no room for discretionary managerial decisions on strategy crafting. Only differences in initial endowments, or luck, could underlie asymmetric performance in that case.

Since KSF notions are commonly used by strategy scholars and managers alike, they need to be related more carefully to strategy theory. An emerging theoretical perspective – that of the firm as a collection of resources and capabilities required for product/market competition – provides one such underpinning. This Resource View of the firm (Coase, 1937; Penrose, 1959; Nelson and Winter, 1982; Teece, 1982; Rumelt, 1984; Wernerfelt, 1984; Barney, 1986a, 1986b, 1989, 1991; Dierickx and Cool, 1989a, 1989b, 1990; Teece, Pisano, and Shuen, 1990; Conner, 1991; Ghemawat, 1991b; Peteraf, 1991) focuses on factor market imperfections and highlights the heterogeneity of firms, their varying degrees of specialization, and the limited transferability of corporate resources. The resource perspective complements the industry analysis framework (Porter, 1980; Schmalensee, 1985). The latter focuses on product markets; it views the sources of profitability to be the characteristics of the industry as well as the firm's position within the industry. The resource view holds that the type, magnitude, and nature of a firm's resources and capabilities are important determinants of its profitability.

In developing the theoretical foundations, we shall build on both perspectives: The resource view of the firm and the industry analysis framework. In addition, we introduce a third perspective, that of Behavioural Decision Theory (BDT). This new field explicitly acknowledges that managers often make sub-optimal choices, be it in personnel selection or in crafting their firm's strategy. BDT can shed light on how boundedly rational managers cope with the kinds of uncertainty and complexity referred to above. Unlike the resource view, which focuses on failures in resource markets, the BDT perspective highlights cognitive imperfections that, while internal to the firm (e.g. internal conflict, cognitive biases of managers, etc.[4]), have a great impact on the firm's approach to its external environment. To date, few links have been drawn between the BDT literature, the industry analysis framework and the resource view of the firm (for an exception, see Zajac and Bazerman, 1991). Before proceeding to the theory section, where these perspectives are examined and integrated, we clarify below the key terms and concepts we use.

Definitions

The firm's *Resources* will be defined as stocks of available factors that are owned or controlled by the firm. *Resources* are converted into final products or services by using a wide range of other firm assets and bonding mechanisms such as technology, management information systems, incentive systems, trust between management and labour, and more. These *Resources* consist, *inter alia*, of know-how that can be traded (e.g., patents and licenses), financial or physical assets (e.g., property, plant and equipment), human capital, etc.[5]

Capabilities, in contrast, refer to a firm's capacity to deploy *Resources*, usually in combination, using organizational processes, to effect a desired end. They are information-based, tangible and intangible processes that are firm-specific and are developed over time through complex interactions among the firm's *Resources*. They can abstractly be thought of as 'intermediate goods' generated by the firm to provide enhanced productivity of its *Resources*, as well as strategic flexibility and protection for its final product or service. Unlike *Resources*, *Capabilities* are based on developing, caring, and exchanging information through the firm's human capital. Itami (1987) refers to information-based Capabilities as 'invisible assets'. He notes that some of the firm's invisible assets are not carried by its employees but rather depend on the perceptions of the firm's customer base (as brand names may do). *Capabilities* are often developed in functional areas (e.g., brand management in marketing) or by combining physical, human, and technological Resources at the corporate level. As a result, firms may build such corporate *Capabilities* as highly reliable service, repeated process or product innovations, manufacturing flexibility, responsiveness to market trends, and short product development cycles.

Some of the firm's *Resources*, but especially its *Capabilities*, may be subject to market failure; that is, an inability to trade these factors in perfect markets. Multiple sources of market failure have been suggested: Williamson (1975) points to small numbers, opportunism, and information impactedness; Klein, Crawford and Alchian (1978) focus on factor specialization in terms of use or location; Caves (1984) highlights sunk costs, and suggests that a factor's value is inversely related to the extent of its specialization for a particular [SMT1] industry or setting.[6] We thus define the firm's *Strategic Assets* as the set of difficult to trade and imitate, scarce, appropriable and specialized *Resources and Capabilities* that bestow the firm's competitive advantage.

When the industry (or product market) is the unit of analysis, one may observe that, at a given time, certain *Resources* and *Capabilities* which are subject to market failures, have become the prime determinants of economic rents. These will be referred to as *Strategic Industry Factors* (SIF). For instance, Ghemawat (1991b) suggests that one may classify industries in terms of the 'strategic factors that drive competition in them by virtue of dominating the structure of sunk costs incurred in the course of competition'. *Strategic Industry Factors*, in this context, are characterized by their proneness to market failures and subsequent asymmetric distribution over firms. By definition, *Strategic Industry Factors* are determined at the market level through complex interactions among the firm's competitors, customers, regulators, innovators external to the industry, and other stakeholders.

Their main characteristics are articulated in Table 10.1. It is important to recognize that the relevant set of *Strategic Industry Factors* changes and cannot be predicted with certainty ex ante.[7]

Table 10.1 General characteristics of strategic industry factors (SIF)

a Stock type *Resources* and *Capabilities* that ex post are shown to be key determinants of firm profitability in an industry:

b Determined at the market level through complex interactions among industry rivals, new entrants, customers, regulators, innovators, suppliers, and other stakeholders:

c Strategic in that they are subject to market failures and may be the basis for competition among rivals:

d The bundle of SIF changes over time and is not known ex ante:

e Their development takes time, skill, and capital; they may be specialized to particular uses:

f Investments in them are largely irreversible (i.e., entail sunk costs):

g Their values deteriorate or appreciate, over time, at varying rates of change:

h Their pace of accumulation may be affected by a range of managerial actions (policy levers) and by the magnitude of other *Resources* and *Capabilities* that are controlled by industry rivals. One cannot easily speed up their development (e.g. doubling the investment will not usually halve the time);

i Their value to any particular firm may depend on its control of other factors – the complementarity property. For instance, the value of a firm's product design capability may depend upon the effectiveness of its distribution network;

j Not all aspects of their development and interactions will be known or controllable.

This table synthesizes notions from Penrose, 1959; Nelson and Winter, 1982; Teece, 1982; Rumelt, 1984; Wernerfelt, 1984; Barney, 1989, 1991; Dierickx and Cool, 1989a, 1989b, Teece *et. al.*, 1990; Conner, 1991; Ghemawat, 1991b, Peteraf, 1991.

The challenge facing a firm's managers is to identify, ex ante, a set of *Strategic Assets* (SA) as grounds for establishing the firm's sustainable competitive advantage, and thereby generate *Organizational Rents*. These are economic rent that stem from the organization's *Resources and Capabilities*, and that can be appropriated by the organization (rather than any single factor). This requires managers to identify the present set of *Strategic Industry Factors* (SIF) as well as to assess the possible sets of SIF that may prevail in the future. Also, decisions on the further development of existing and new *Strategic Assets* – those that are most likely to contribute to the creation and protection of economic rents – need to be made. Not every firm will succeed with its targeted set of SA, as their applicability and relevance ultimately hinges on the complex interaction referred to above. Examples of possible SA include: Technological capability; fast product development cycles; brand management; control of, or superior access to, distribution channels; a favourable cost structure; buyer-seller relationships; the firm's installed user base; its R&D capability; the firm's service organization; its reputation and so forth. The relationships between industry determined *Strategic Industry Factors*, and firm level *Resources*, *Capabilities*, and *Strategic Assets*, are depicted in Figure 10.1.[8]

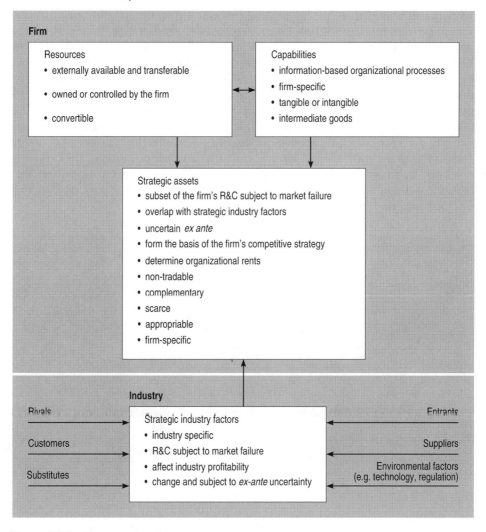

Figure 10.1 Key constructs

A RESOURCE VIEW OF STRATEGIC ASSETS

By focusing on the firm as the relevant unit of analysis, managers are concerned with the creation of a bundle of tangible as well as intangible *Resources and Capabilities* (R&C), whose economic returns are appropriable by the firm. The basic idea that underlies this perspective, cited earlier as the *Resource-Based View Of The Firm*, is that marshalling a set of complementary and specialized *Resources and Capabilities* which are scarce, durable, not easily graded, and difficult to imitate, may enable the firm to earn economic rents. Thus, according to the resource perspective, the value of a firm's *Strategic Assets* extends beyond their contribution to the production process. It depends on a wide range of characteristics (see Figure 10.2), and varies with changes in the relevant set of *Strategic Industry Factors*, as depicted by Figure 10.1. The supposition is that, even in equilibrium, firms may differ in terms of the *Resources and Capabilities* they control, and that such asymmetric firms may coexist until some exogenous change or Schumpeterian shock occurs (Schumpeter, 1934).[9]

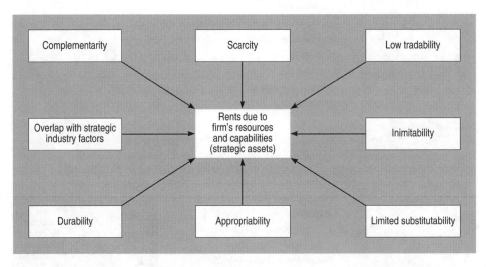

Figure 10.2 Desired characteristics of the firm's resources and capabilities

Economic rents, in this setting, derive from asymmetry in initial resource endowments, resource scarcity, limited transferability of *Resources*, imperfect substitutability, and appropriability.[10] Barney (1986a, 1986b, 1989, 1991), Dierickx and Cool (1989a, 1989b, 1990), and Ghemawat (1991b) provide incisive discussions of desired attributes of such firm *Resources*. Figure 10.2 summarizes the primary determinants of the rent producing capacity of a firm's Strategic Assets.

In general, the strategic value of a firm's *Resources and Capabilities* is enhanced the more difficult they are to buy, sell, imitate or substitute. For example, invisible assets such as tacit organizational knowledge or trust between management and labour cannot be traded or easily replicated by competitors since they are deeply rooted in the organization's history. Such firm-specific and often tacit assets accumulate slowly over a period of time (i.e., they are history-dependent state variables. See Dierickx and Cool 1989a, 1989b, 1990). The focus here is not just on the material aspects of Resources and Capabilities, but especially on their transformational characteristics. These are often specific to a firm and/or to a particular industry at a given point in time. This idiosyncrasy makes them difficult to imitate and their development time cannot be easily compressed.

In addition, the applicability of the firm's bundle of *Resources and Capabilities* to a particular industry setting (i.e., the overlap with the set of *Strategic Industry Factors*), will determine the available rent. Managers influence the development and deployment of *Strategic Assets* by adopting a process perspective (in contrast to an input-output model). This perspective recognizes distinct phases of development, the importance of feedback, and the need for vision. It also entails careful scripting of how *Resources*, information and people are combined and sequenced over time in order to evolve specific *Capabilities*. In this sense, the viewpoint is essentially an institutional one (de Gregori, 1987). Dierickx and Cool (1989a, 1989b) especially highlight the importance of processes for asset accumulation and their impact on inimitability of the firm's *Resources*.

The firm's *Strategic Assets* may further exhibit *complementarity* in deployment or application (Barnard, 1938); that is, the strategic value of each asset's relative magnitude may increase with an increase in the relative magnitude of other *Strategic Assets* (also known as positive externalities; see Dierickx and Cool, 1990). An example is Teece's (1986) notion of co-specialized assets – those for which there is a bilateral dependence in application. Under complementarity, the combined value of the firm's *Resources and Capabilities* may be higher than the cost of developing or deploying each asset individually. Conversely, the strategic value of the firm's *Resources and Capabilities* declines to the extent that they are substitutes.[11]

The more *firm specific, durable and scarce Strategic Assets* are, the more valuable to the firm can be their deployment, for at least three reasons. First, if few other firms have R&C that are in high demand and are difficult to imitate, fewer firms will pursue market strategies based thereon, since others would find these strategies too costly and time consuming.[12] Second, firm-specificity and the presence of transaction costs suggest that the value of some *Resources and Capabilities* will be lower for certain firms. Third, the more durable they are, the smaller will be the investment required to offset their depreciation, if any.[13]

These characteristics of the firm's assets emphasize the trade-off between the specialization of assets (a necessary condition for rent) and the robustness of these assets across alternative futures (see Schoemaker, 1992a). The trade-off between specialization and robustness is only partial, as specialization can be of two kinds: (1) limited use or (2) unique use. Limited use entails reduced robustness in that the asset is of little value in particular states of nature. Uniqueness, in contrast, is defined relative to other players (rather than to states of nature) and need not be restricted in scope or by circumstance. Due to competitive pressures, the kinds of specialization that can yield positive rents tend to entail limited use (and hence, risk). Uniqueness, in contrast, may reflect historical accident or heterogeneous expectations as the primary reasons for non-imitation.

In essence, firms develop specialized assets to enhance profits at the price of reduced flexibility in the face of Schumpeterian shocks. This trade-off is, in our view, a core issue in deciding which R&C to develop. Sustainable advantage is obtained when existing and potential competitors (new entrants) lack either the ability or desire to imitate the rent-producing R&C. A firm's managers can lessen the incentives of competitors to imitate or develop close substitutes by, for example, erecting entry or mobility barriers or by building 'isolating mechanisms' (Rumelt, 1984). Like Ghemawat (1986), we focus here on aspects that relate to the firm's superior *access* to *Resources*. (Of course, competitive advantage may also arise from size and scope, as well as legal or other restrictions on competition.)

Given the competitive and changing context in which managers must decide which R&C to develop as their firm's basis for competition, it is doubtful that decisions about which SA to develop and deploy can be optimally deduced from a general normative theory. More likely, continually changing heuristics will emerge that strive to better incorporate the uncertainty, complexity and organizational conflicts confronting managers.[14] As such, our view extends that of Porter's (1980) by emphasising not only the industry environment in determining future profit but especially the importance of managerial discretion and innovation in SA decisions. The latter are by no means foregone conclusions; the external environment is only one part of the economic rent story.

DECISIONS ABOUT STRATEGIC ASSETS

In making investment decisions about *Strategic Assets*, managers face the daunting tasks of (1) anticipating possible futures, (2) assessing competitive interactions within each projected future, and (3) overcoming organizational inertia and internal dispute in order to realign the firm's bundle of SA. Recent psychological literature (Kahneman, Slovic, and Tversky, 1982) suggests that managers will approach this uncertainty, complexity, and conflict with considerable bias, illusion, and suboptimality. Even if highly simplified and abstracted, the associated SA decisions may not be solvable in close-form equilibrium terms (although, see Camerer, 1991).[15]

Uncertainty

Under rational expectations, the SA challenge will largely vanish as managers will hold the same expectations about the set of SIF that will prevail in the future. Since they will maximize the expected value of returns, their initial SA endowments are the only source of variance regarding their behaviour. In reality, however, managers face considerable uncertainty and ambiguity, stemming from new proprietary technologies, economic and political trends, competitive actions, changes in societal values, and corresponding shifts in consumer preferences. Pervasive uncertainty and ambiguity make it probable that mangers will hold diverse expectations about such key variables as demand growth, price levels, costs, and consumer tastes. Further, their judgements and choices are likely to exhibit idiosyncratic aversions to risk and ambiguity (Kahneman and Tversky, 1979; Einhorn and Hogarth, 1986).[16] The joint effects of heterogeneous beliefs and manager-specific decision processes (and biases) make equilibrium analyses hard to conduct for both managers and researchers. Coupled with overconfidence (Lichtenstein, Fischhoff, and Phillips, 1982) and a penchant for confirming over disconfirming evidence (Klayman and Ha, 1987), Strategic Assets choices under uncertainty may entail opposing biases whose net effects are hard to assess. For example, ambiguity aversion and underweighting of medium and high probabilities will normally lead to risk aversion. However, this tendency may be countered or mitigated by overconfidence and ambitious targets, either of which can induce strong risk-seeking.[17] Consequently, the final SA investment decisions are hard to predict without detailed micro-level knowledge of managers' reference points, problem framing, degrees of overconfidence, non-linear weighting of probabilities, etc. (see Schoemaker, 1992b).

A bounded rationality view (Simon, 1979) may nonetheless predict some overriding biases. For example, managers will probably over-emphasize past *Strategic Industry Factors*, and the SA associated therewith. People generally tend to repeat what was rewarded before. Consequently, managers might be too focused on past competitors and pay too much attention to recent experience. The latter is known as the recency effect which is closely linked to the more general notion of the availability heuristic (Tversky and Kahneman, 1974). If perceptions about strategy are unduly anchored on past SA, rent opportunities arise for firms that approach the future more flexibly and imaginatively. These may be new firms or incumbent ones that vigorously challenge their own beliefs. Past success may especially bias managers toward an illusion of control (Langer, 1975). Recent emphasis on the strategic importance of continual organizational learning (de Geus, 1988; Senge, 1990) underscore the special challenges posed by uncertainty and complexity, whether the firm has been successful or not.

Complexity

To keep SA decisions within cognitive bounds, managers must often and extensively simplify (Russo and Schoemaker, 1989). The kinds of simplification they engage in may lead to additional biases. Tversky and Kahneman (1981) offer persuasive examples of how simplified framing (such as isolating alternatives or expressing outcomes relatively) can lead to inconsistent decisions. Specifically, frames may (1) bound out important futures, competitors, or new technologies; (2) dictate the reference point relative to which SAs are measured (e.g., Chrysler comparing its quality control capability to GM's rather than to Japan's Honda); and, (3) specify the yardsticks or metric used to measure SA (e.g., measuring quality in terms of defective parts per thousand vs. number and type of consumer complaints).

In hindsight, chance and skill are often confused (Fischhof and Beyth, 1975). Judgements about correlation or relative importance frequently miss important cues and interactions (Jennings, Amabile, and Ross, 1982; Hammond, 1955; Hogarth, 1987), especially if not driven by a causal theory. Imputations about causality, in turn, may be overly sensitive to temporal and spatial contiguity, covariation, and similarity of cause and effect (Einhorn and Hogarth, 1986). Unless aided by formal analyses, managers may easily misconstrue the industry's success factors and persist in erroneous beliefs about their firm's SA until proven wrong by competitors.

Lindblom (1959) and Quinn (1980), among others, have highlighted the incremental way in which managers usually deal with complexity. Writers on policy formation have, in general, emphasized the contextual and labile nature of organizational decision making (Mintzberg, 1978; Isenberg, 1987, MacCrimmon and Wehrung, 1986). An example is Cohen, March, and Olsen's (1972) garbage can model, in which problems, solutions, hidden agendas, coalitions and so on mesh in complex ways to yield decisions. Mintzberg (1978) and Mintzberg and Waters (1983) further highlight the role for the firm's unconscious past. They view a firm's realized strategy (e.g., its SA decisions) to be a blend of rational, or at least intentional choices, and implicit or tacit forces within organizations (see also Hamel and Prahalad, 1989). The litany of biases mentioned above serves to underscore our main point here: Discretionary managerial decisions that relate to *Strategic Assets* are affected by a wide range of cognitive biases about the handling of uncertainty and complexity. This, in turn, creates sub-optimality, imperfect imitability, and organizational rents for some firms.

Conflict

Intraorganizational conflict is another serious challenge encountered by management in making SA decisions. Any change in the existing bundle of SA may benefit some employees and hurt others. Not only do complex agency problems (Jensen and Meckling, 1976; Fama and Jensen, 1983a, 1983b) exist in obtaining the necessary information and judgements concerning SA selection, but also issues of co-operation, trust, and competence must be factored into the decision of which *Resources and Capabilities* to develop and how. Allison's (1971) classic treatment of the Cuban Missile Crisis illustrates clearly the importance of organizational and political dimensions, in addition to rational ones, for setting policy.

The key point is that organizations are complex social entities with their own inertia and constraints. The issue is not simply to select the subset of *Resources and Capabilities* that is most likely to yield high rents, but to make organizational participants an integral part of such decisions. Among other things, this poses problems of nestedness; for example, SBU level choices impact divisional as well as corporate *Capabilities* and vice versa. The convenient view that organizations have carefully solved their principal-agent problems and need only select from the implicit market for *Resources and Capabilities*, which and how much of each to buy, denies the crucial role of asymmetric *Resources and Capabilities* as well as the complex decisions managers face.

In sum, as the firm's environment changes, different sets of *Strategic Assets* may have to be developed by firms. Core *Capabilities*, by definition, cannot be purchased off the shelf but require strategic visions, development time, and sustained investment. Decisions about *Strategic Assets* (e.g., the subset of *Resources and Capabilities* that bestows sustainable competitive advantage) are among the most complex that managers encounter. They are characterized by high uncertainty, complexity, and conflict, to an extent that defines optimizetion. Indeed, this lack of solvability is a necessary condition for their strategic importance and positive rent potential.

STRATEGIC ASSETS DEVELOPMENT: A MULTIDIMENSIONAL VIEW

The above analysis of *Strategic Assets* underscores the need for a multidimensional approach; one that includes internal and external elements, static and dynamic aspects, and rational as well as behavioural considerations.[18] Each perspective sheds a different light on the *Strategic Assets* challenge as captured below.

Industry Analysis excels in assessing the profit potential of various industry participants by focusing on the external competitive forces and barriers that prevail in different product/market segments. Further, it is essential in deriving a set of *Strategic Industry Factors*. It is incomplete, however, in that it treats the firm largely as a black box (i.e., a faceless, unitary actor), while de-emphasising the role of managerial discretion. Assuming high rationality and substitutability of executive talent, industry analyses logically deduces the end-game consequences of differences in participants' initial conditions (for a particular industry structure, technology, and action space). Thus, the focus is on rent distribution in equilibrium, given initial firm asymmetries, industry structure, and known rules of the game.

The Resource View, in contrast, highlights imperfections in factor markets, resulting in systematic firm differences. Limited transferability of *Resources*, scarcity, complementarity and appropriability in turn give rise to rent opportunities. Economic rents, in this view, derive from properties unique to the firm's *Resources and Capabilities*. The focus is thus more internal and institutional, recognizing the often slow and evolutionary path by which firm-specific *Capabilities* develop (e.g., see Nelson and Winter, 1982.) These *Capabilities* may include executive talent, culture and other less tangible dimensions that in standard models of rational behaviour have received limited attention.[19] Also, the exclusive focus on equilibrium and structural dimensions is absent. Instead, disequilibrium and process dynamics loom primary.

Behavioural Decision Theory (BDT) complements the resource perspective in explicitly acknowledging bounded rationality and, in particular, the crucial roles of problem framing and heuristic decision-making. Differences in decision frames and heuristics give rise to 'variable rationality' among and within players over time (see Schoemaker, 1990). A rational end-game analysis would largely ignore such factors since it generally assumes constant rationality.[20] In actuality, however, managers are hardly playing a well-defined end game. Logical consequences of moves are seldom ascertainable and equilibrium solutions are not usually transparent in complex strategy decisions. Because the rules of the game, the number of players, and the action space are seldom fixed, creative changes and innovations are permitted, which makes predictions of outcomes especially difficult.

Reliance on heuristics and on a limited repertoire of responses, punctuated by occasional bold or creative moves, introduces complexities whose net effects are hard to assess. Players generally harbour imperfect comprehension's of the deeper relationships operative in the industry or indeed, within their firm. In this view, strategy becomes partly a shot in the dark and partly an exercise in heuristic creativity aimed at overcoming biases and blind spots (Zajac and Bazerman, 1991). These biases will not be just individual or cognitive; many concern group biases (e.g., groupthink) and may be affective in nature, such as wishful thinking, dissonance reaction, etc. (see Russo and Schoemaker, 1989).

The BDT perspective is especially important in light of the pervasive *uncertainty and complexity* surrounding SA decisions. Any industry or market segment will undergo Schumpeterian shocks such that mostly equilibria (if computable at all) will have finite lives. Robust strategies thus must pay attention to disequilibrium, uncertain futures and ambiguous relationships. Without ambiguity and complexity, the SA questions would perhaps be reducible to a rational end-game analysis. In practice, however, it is about the fashioning and deployment of firm-specific *Capabilities* whose rents depend partly on unfathomable futures.

In terms of theoretical underpinnings, various attempts have been made to model the effects of uncertainty or ambiguity on individual decision making (Einhorn and Hogarth, 1986) as well as markets (Kleindorfer and Kunreuther, 1982). The dimension of complexity has yet to see significant formal treatment (although, see Rosenhead, 1980). In psychology, however, various models and techniques exist to depict how people represent complex problem situations, ranging from scripts and schema to cognitive maps (for a review see Klayman and Schoemaker, 1992). Also, numerous heuristic guidelines exist for managers on how to cope with and manage complexity, such as scenario analysis (Wack, 1985a, 1985b; Schoemaker, 1991).

Our further emphasis on *conflict and organization inertia* brings to the fore implementation and other intraorganizational problems in the development and deployment of *Strategic Assets*. The resource and behavioural perspectives refer to these organizational issues but do not develop them. Principal-agent theory provides a highly rational treatment of incentive problems, with abstract links to the origin, scope and organizational form of firms (e.g., U-vs. M-form) and scope, while placing greater emphasis on bounded rationality and internal firm complexity. Organizational theory, in contrast, has been more descriptive and process oriented in seeking to understand how firms control and co-ordinate activities. Rather than making conflict or transactions the unit of analysis, organization theory focuses on systemic aspects, in particular the interactions among such subsystems as the firm's structure, processes, rewards, culture, people and technology. These can explain firm interia and the adaptation difficulties encountered when the environment changes and managers attempt to redirect their firm's *Strategic Assets*.

CONCLUSION

We have sought to replace the strategy field's concept of Key Success Factors with the notions of : (1) *Strategic Industry Factors*, the set of *Resources and Capabilities* that has become the prime determinant of economic rents for industry participants; and (2) *Strategic Assets*, a firm level construct, referring to the set of firm specific *Resources and Capabilities* developed by management as the basis for creating and protecting their firm's competitive advantage. The rent producing capacity of these *Strategic Assets* depends, in part, on their own unique characteristics as well as on the extent to which they overlap with the industry-determined *Strategic Industry Factors*.

Building on insights from the Resource View of the firm, and Behavioural Decision Theory, we identified important theoretical features of *Strategic Assets* and the conditions under which they could produce organizational rents. The managerial difficulty of identifying, developing, and deploying an appropriate mix of SA was highlighted in the discussion. Owing to uncertainty, complexity, and conflict (both in and outside the firm), different firms will employ different *Strategic Assets*, without any one set being provably optimal or easily imitated. At best, managers can devise heuristic solutions that navigate between the numerous cognitive and affective biases characteristic of humans and organizations. We articulated a multidimensional view for the crafting of *Strategic Assets*, in relation to market-determined *Strategic Industry Factors*. Its dimensions consist of (1) industry analysis, (2) the resource perspective and (3) behavioural decision theory. The latter perspective emphasizes the pervasive uncertainty and complexity faced by managers, often resulting in sub-optimal *Strategic Assets* decisions. In this context, the role of intraorganizational conflict and inertia were identified as important barriers to implementing changes to the firm's bundle of *Strategic Assets*.

Throughout, *Strategic Assets* decisions were examined in light of resource market imperfections, bounded and variable rationality within and across firms. If optimal solutions were derivable for a firm's *Strategic Assets*, the latter would largely vanish. Barring market or cognitive imperfections, all firms would envision and pursue an optimal strategy with zero expected rents. As such, the existence of *Strategic Assets* and presence of bounded rationality are closely linked. A normative *Strategic Assets* theory that could systematically lead to the creation of sustainable rents is implausible due to competitive pressures. Our paper instead sought to develop a behavioural view of *Strategic Assets*, with limited prescriptive advice on how to target, develop and employ firm-specific *Strategic Assets*.

In concluding, it may be useful to place our view of organizational rent creation by firms within the larger framework articulated by Conner (1991). We share with the resource view, as well as the transaction cost view, an emphasis on the uniqueness and limited mobility of *Resources and Capabilities*. However, it is not market power (IO view) *per se*, or greater operating efficiency (neo-classical and Chicago school views) that produces organizational rents, although these may be consequences. In this paper uniqueness and low mobility of *Resources and Capabilities* stem from imperfect and hard to predict decisions by boundedly rational managers facing high uncertainty (a la Schumpeter), complexity, and intrafirm conflict. We thus strengthen the resource view by adding behavioural decision making biases and organizational implementation aspects as further impediments to the transferability or imitability of a firm's *Resources and Capabilities*.

ACKNOWLEDGEMENTS

Karen Cool, Ingemar Dierickx, James Emery, Robin Hogarth, Margaret Peteraf, Birger Wernerfelt and two anonymous reviewers are acknowledged for their helpful comments on earlier versions. Insightful discussions with Jay Barney and Chaim Fershtman contributed to the development of this paper and are gratefully acknowledged.

REFERENCES

Allison, G. (1971) *Essence of Decision: explaining the Cuban Missile Crisis*, Little, Brown, Boston, MA.

Andrews, K. R. (1971) *The Concept of Corporate Strategy*, Irwin, Homewood, IL.

Ansoff, H. I. (1965) *Corporate Strategy*, McGraw Hill, New York.

Barnard, C. I. (1938) *The Functions of the Executive*, Harvard University Press, Cambridge, MA.

Barney, J. B. (1986a) 'Strategic factor markets: expectations, luck, and business strategy', *Management Science*, Vol. 42, pp. 1231–41.

Barney, J. B. (1986b) 'Organization culture: can it be a source of sustained competitive advantage?', *Academy of Management Review*, Vol. 11, pp. 656–65.

Barney, J. B. (1989) 'Asset stocks and sustained competitive advantage: a comment', *Management Science*, Vol. 35, pp. 1511–13.

Barney, J. B. (1991) 'Firm resources and sustained competitive advantage', *Journal of Management*, Vol. 17, No. 1, pp. 90–120.

Baumol, W. I., Panzar, J.C. and Willing, R.C. (1982) *Contestable Markets and the Theory of Industry Structure*, Harcourt Brace Jovanovitch, New York.

Camerer, C. F. (1991) 'Does strategy research need game theory?', *Strategic Management Journal*, Vol. 12, pp. 137–52.

Camerer, C.F. and Vepsalainen A. (1988) 'The economic efficiency of corporate culture', *Strategic Management Journal*, Vol. 9, pp. 115–26.

Caves, R. E. (1984) 'Economic analysis and the quest for competitive advantage', *American Economic Review*, Vol. 74, No. 2, pp. 127–32.

Coase, R. H. (1937) 'The nature of the firm', *Economica*, Vol. 4, pp. 331–51.

Cohen, M.D., March, J.G. and Olsen J.P. (1972) 'A garbage can model of organizational choice', *Administrative Science Quarterly*, Vol. 17, pp. 1–25.

Conner, K.R. (1991) 'A historical comparison of resource-based theory and five schools of thought within industrial organizational economics: do we have a new theory of the firm?', *Journal of Management*, Vol. 17, No. 1, pp. 121–54.

Cool, K. and Schendel, D. (1988) 'Performance differences among strategic group members', *Strategic Management Journal*, Vol. 9, No. 3, pp. 207–24.

De Geus, A. (1988) 'Planning as learning', *Harvard Business Review*, March–April, pp. 70–4.

De Gregori, T. R. (1987) 'Resources are not; they become: an institutional theory', *Journal of Economic Issues*, Vol. 21, pp. 1241–63.

Dierickx, I. and Cool, K. (1989a) 'Asset stock accumulation and sustainability of competitive advantage', *Management Science*, Vol. 35, pp. 1504–11.

Dierickx, I. and Cool, K. (1989b) 'Competitive strategy resource accumulation and firm performance', Mimeo, INSEAD, May.

Dierickx, I. and Cool, K. (1990) 'A resource based perspective on competitive strategy', Mimeo, INSEAD, September.

Einhorn, H. and Hogarth, R. (1986) 'Judging probable cause', *Psychological Bulletin*, Vol. 99, pp. 3–19.

Fama, E.F. and Jensen, M.C. (1983a) 'Separation of ownership and control', *Journal of Law and Economics*, Vol. 26, p. 301.

Fama, E.F. and Jensen, M.C. (1983b) 'Agency problems and residual claims', *Journal of Law and Economics*, Vol. 26, pp. 327–49.

Fischhoff, B. and Beyth, R. (1975) 'I knew it would happen – remembered probabilities of once-future things', *Organizational Behaviour and Human Performance*, Vol. 13, pp. 1–6.

Ghemawat, P. (1986) 'Sustainable advantage', *Harvard Business Review*, Vol. 64, pp. 53–8.

Ghemawat, P. (1991a) *Commitment*, The Free Press, New York.

Ghemawat, P. (1991b) 'Resources and Strategy: an IO perspective', Mimeo, Harvard Business School, May.

Grant, R.B. (1991) 'A resource based theory of competitive advantage: implications for strategy formulation', *California Management Review*, Vol. 33, No. 3, pp. 114–35.

Hamel, G. and Prahalad, C.K. (1989) 'Strategic intent', *Harvard Business Review*, Vol. 89, No. 3, pp. 63–76.

Hammond, K.R. (1955) 'Probabilistic functioning and the clinical method', *Psychological Review*, Vol. 62, pp. 255–62.

Hansen, G.S. and Wernerfelt, B. (1989) 'Determinants of economic and organizational factors', *Strategic Management Journal*, Vol. 10, pp. 399–411.

Hofer, C.W. and Schendel, D. (1978) *Strategy Formulation: analytical concepts*, West Publishing Company, St. Paul, MN.

Hogarth, R.M. (1987) *Judgement and Choice*, Wiley, Chichester.

Irvin, R.A. and Michaels, E.G. III (1989) 'Core skills: doing the right things right', *The McKinsey Quarterly*, Summer, pp. 4–19.

Isenberg, D.J. (1987) 'The tactics of strategic opportunism', *Harvard Business Review*, Vol. 65, No. 2, pp. 92–7.

Itami, H. (1987) *Mobilising Invisible Assets*, Harvard University Press, Boston, MA.

Jacobson, R. (1988) 'The persistence of abnormal returns', *Strategic Management Journal*, 9, pp. 41–58.

Jennings, D.L., Amabile, T.M. and Ross, L. (1982) 'Informal conversation assessment: data-based versus theory-based judgements' in D. Kahneman, P. Slovic and A. Tversky (eds),

Judgement Under Uncertainty: heuristics and biases, Cambridge Press, Cambridge, MA, pp. 211–30.

Jensen, M.C. and Meckling, W. (1976) 'Theory of the firm: managerial behaviour, agency costs and ownership structure. *Journal of Financial Economics*, pp. 305–60.

Kahneman, D., Slovic, P. and Tversky, A. (1979) 'Prospect theory', *Econometrica*, 47 (2), pp. 263–292.

Kahneman, D., Slovic, P. and Tversky, A. *(1982) Judgement Under Uncertainty: heuristics and biases*, Cambridge Press, Cambridge, MA.

Klayman, J. and Schoemaker, P. J. H. (1992) 'Thinking about the future: a cognitive perspective', *Journal of Forecasting.*

Klayman, J. and Ha, Y. (1987) 'Confirmation, disconfirmation and information in hypothesis testing', *Psychological Review*, 94 (2), pp. 211–228.

Klein, B., Crawford, R. and Alchian, A. (1978) 'Vertical integration, appropriable rents, and the competitive contracting process', *Journal of Law and Economics*, Vol. 21, pp. 297–326.

Kleindorfer, P.R. and Kunreuther, H. (1982) 'Misinformation and equilibrium in insurance markets' in J. Finisinger (ed.) *Issues in Pricing and Regulation*, Lexington Books, Lexington, MA, pp. 67–90.

Langer, E. (1975) 'The illusion of control', *Journal of Personality and Social Psychology*, Vol. 32, pp. 311–28.

Lichtenstein, S., Fischhoff, B. and Phillips, L.D. (1982) 'Calibration of probabilities: the state of the art to 1990' in D. Kahneman, P. Slovic and A. Tversky (eds). *Judgement Under Uncertainty: heuristics and biases.* Cambridge Press, Cambridge, MA, pp. 306–34.

Lindblom, C.E. (1959) 'The science of muddling through', *Public Administration Review*, Vol. 19, pp. 79–88.

Lippman, S. and Rumelt, R. (1982) 'Uncertain imitabiltiy: an analysis of interfirm difference in efficiency under competition', *Bell Journal of Economics*, pp. 418–38.

MacCrimmon, K.R. and Wehrung, D.A. (1986) *Taking Risks*, The Free Press, New York.

Mintzberg, H. (1978) 'Patterns in strategy formation', *Management Science*, Vol. 24, pp. 934–48.

Mintzberg, H. and Waters, J.A. (1983) 'The mind of the strategist(s)' in S. Srivasta (ed.), *The Executive Mind*, Jossey-Bass, San Francisco, CA, pp. 58–83.

Nelson, R. and Winter, S. *An Evolutionary Theory of Economic Change*, Harvard University Press, Cambridge, MA.

Penrose, E.T. (1959) *The Theory of Growth of the Firm*, Wiley, New York.

Peteraf, M.A. (1991) 'The cornerstone of competitive advantage: a resource based view', Northwestern University, J.L. Kellogg Graduate School of Management, General Motors Research Center for Strategy in Management, Discussion Paper No. 90.

Porter, M. (1980) *Competitive Strategy.* The Free Press, New York.

Prahalad, C.K. and Hamel, G. (1990) 'The core competence of the corporation', *Harvard Business Review*, Vol. 68, No. 3, pp. 79–91.

Quinn, J.B. (1980) *Strategies for Change: logical incrementalism*, Irwin, Homewood, IL.

Rosenhead, J. (1980) 'Planning under uncertainty (II): a methodology for robustness analysis', *Journal of Operational Research Society*, Vol. 31, pp. 331–41.

Rumelt, R.P. (1984) 'Towards a strategic theory of the firm', in R.B. Lamb (ed.) *Competitive Strategic Management*, Prentice Hall, Engelwood Cliffs, NJ, pp. 556–70.

Rumelt, R.P. (1991) 'How much does industry matter?', *Strategic Management Journal*, Vol. 12, No. 3, pp. 167–85.

Russo, J.E. and Schoemaker, P.H. (1989) *Decision Traps: ten barriers to brilliant decision making and how to overcome them*, Doubleday, New York.

Schmalensee, R. (1985) 'Do markets differ much?', *American Economic Review*, Vol. 75, pp. 341–51.

Schoemaker, P.H. (1990) 'Strategy, complexity and economic rent', *Management Science*, Vol. 36, No. 10, pp. 1178–92.

Schoemaker, P.H. (1991) 'When and how to use scenario planning', *Journal of Forecasting*, Vol. 10, pp. 549–64.

Schoemaker, P.H. (1992a) 'Developing strategic vision: a core capabilities approach applied to Apple Computer', *Sloan Management Review*.

Schoemaker, P.H. (1992b) 'Determinants of risk-taking: behavioural and economic views', *Journal for Risk and Uncertainty*.

Schumpeter, J. (1934) *The Theory of Economic Development*, Harvard University Press, Cambridge, MA.

Selznick, P. (1957) *Leadership in Administration: a sociological interpretation*, Harper and Row, New York.

Senge, P. (1990) 'The leader's new work: building learning organizations', *Sloan Management Review*, Fall, pp. 7–23.

Simon, H.A. (1979) *Models of Thought*, Yale University Press, New Haven, CT.

Stalk, G., Evans, P. and Shulman, E. (1992) 'Competing on capabilities: the new rules of corporate strategy', *Harvard Business Review*, March–April, pp. 57–69.

Teece, D.J. (1982) 'Towards an economic theory of the multiproduct firm', *Journal of Economic Behaviour and Organization*, Vol. 3, pp. 39–63.

Teece, D.J. (1986) 'Profiting from technological innovation', *Research Policy*, Vol. 15, pp. 285–305.

Teece, D.J., Pisano, G. and Shuen, A. (1990) 'Firm capabilities, resources, and the concept of strategy'. Mimeo, University of California at Berkeley, Haas School of Business, September.

Thompson, A.A. and Strickland, A.J. (1990) *Strategic Management: concepts and cases*, Irwin, Homewood, IL.

Tversky, A. and Kahneman, D. (1974) 'Judgement under uncertainty: heuristics and biases', *Science*, Vol. 185, pp. 1124–31.

Tversky, A. and Kahneman, D. (1981) 'The framing of decisions and the psychology of choice', *Science*, Vol. 211, pp. 453–58.

Vasconcellos, J.A. and Hambrick, D.C. (1989) 'Key success factors: test of a general framework in the mature industrial-product sector' *Strategic Management Journal*, Vol. 10, No. 4, pp. 367–82.

Wack, P. (1985a) 'Scenarios: uncharted waters ahead', *Harvard Business Review*, Vol. 63, No. 5, pp. 72–89.

Wack, P. (1985b) 'Scenarios: shooting the rapids', *Harvard Business Review*, Vol. 63, No. 6, pp. 139–50.

Weigelt, K. and Camerer, C. (1988) 'Reputation and corporate strategy', *Strategic Management Journal*, Vol. 9, pp. 443–54.

Wernerfelt, B. (1984) 'A resource based view of the firm', *Strategic Management Journal*, Vol. 5, pp. 171–80.

Wernerfelt, B. (1989) 'From critical resources to corporate strategy', *Journal of General Management*, Vol. 5, pp. 171–80.

Williamson, O. (1975) *Markets and Hierarchies*, The Free Press, New York.

Zajac, E.J. and Bazerman, M.H. (1991) 'Blind spots in industry and competitor analysis', *Academy of Management Review*, Vol. 16, pp. 37–56.

NOTES

1 Lippman and Rumelt (1982) refer to this as 'causal ambiguity.'

2 Economists commoly distinguish among three types of rent: Ricardian rents are extraordinary profits earned from resources that are in fixed or limited supply. Parento rents (or quasi rents) refer to the difference between the payments to a resource in its best and second best use. Lastly, Monopoly rents stem from collusion or government protection. Klein, Crawford and Alchian (1978) examine quasi-rents in the context of vertical integration.

3 There are numerous interpretations in the Marketing and Strategic Management literature concerning the meaning of KSF. See for example Thompson and Strickland (1990).

4 Penrose's (1959) seminal work also addresses some of these intrafirm issues.

5 See Grant (1991) for a detailed description of various types of both tangible and intangible resources of the firm.

6 The roles of factor specialization and sunk costs in a firm's ability to earn economic rents have been examined by Klein *et al.* (1978), as well as by Baumol, Panzar, and Willig (1982).

7 While it may not be possible to identify ex ante the relevant set of strategic assets, one can screen out those assets that are *not* strategic.

8 Note that we abandon from hereon the term *Key Success Factors*, because of its many possible interpretations and uses.

9 The assumption of heterogeneous firms controlling resources that are not perfectly mobile (i.e., that cannot be easily bought, sold or imitated) is essential to the existence of such an equilibrium. Lippman and Rumelt (1982) and Barney (1986a, 1986b) articulate some of the reasons for imperfect imitability. These include unique historical conditions, causal ambiguiy, and complexity. Ghemawat (1991b) refers to these conditions as intrinsic inimitability and therefore the firm's factor combinations are viewed as intrinsically heterogeneous. He suggests that less stringent conditions (e.g., imitations being costly but not infeasible) may be sufficient for sustainabiltity. Relatedly, Peteraf (1991) equates resource heterogeneity to differential levels of factor efficiency.

10 Whereas Industrial Organization economics often looks outside the firm to explain sustained superior performance by examining, for example, various market structures, alternative regulatory settings, collusive relationships, or substitute technologies, the source of rents according to the resource perspective is internal.

11 Dierickx and Cool (1989b, 1990) have introduced the notion of complementarity in asset accumulation (or interconnectedness) which refers to economies of scope in asset accumulation. This distinction highlights the dynamic nature of asset accumulation, whereas complementarity in asset deployment is a static notion.

12 The strategic value of R&C may not lie merely in the scarcity of natural resources such as land and oil reserves, but also in the ability to deploy concurrently in multiple uses such invisible firm-specific assets as culture, reputation, and relationships with suppliers and buyers.

13 Unlike physical capital, most capabilties are enhanced with use as more experience is gained.

14 Economic rent may accrue to firms with superior or more timely heuristics, thereby capitalising on variable as well as bounded rationality (see Schoemaker, 1990).

15 For example, when modeled as a differential game, the problem will probably not be tractable. Closed or even open-loop solutions are generally unattainable when confronted

with a multiplicty of state and control variables in non-co-operative multiplayer games. An added complication in our case arises from the difficulty of specifying the game in terms of the number of players, as well as the state, action, and pay-off spaces.

16 When gambles entail well-defined probabilities, most people exhibit risk aversion (except for low probability and pure loss gambles). If probabilities are ill defined (the case of ambiguity), even greater risk-aversion is encountered due to people's dislikes to unknown risk. Most managerial decisions entail risk as well as ambiguity.

17 The predicted bias is towards risk-*seeking* for R&C that are deemed to be below some chosen reference point and towards risk-*aversion* for those that exceed this aspiration level (see Kahneman and Tversky, 1979). Thus, unrealistic goals or ambitious targets will likely result in unduly risky R&C decisions. For additional biases and indeterminacies in risk-taking see MacCrimmon and Wehrung (1986).

18 While we hold that these dimensions need to be reflected in any comprehensive analyses of a firm's *Strategic Assets*, there may well be other relevant dimensions (e.g., ecological, sociological, political, anthropological). To integrate these additional dimensions, however, is beyond our present scope.

19 Some of this is changing. For instance rational models have been devleoped concerning the role of culture (Camerer and Vepsalainen, 1988) and reputation (Weigelt and Camerer, 1988).

20 Some of this is changing. For instance rational models have been developed concerning the role of culture (Camerer and Vepsalainen, 1988) and reputation (Weigelt and Camerer, 1988).

CHAPTER 11

THE CORE COMPETENCE OF THE CORPORATION

C.K. PRAHALAD AND GARY HAMEL

The most powerful way to prevail in global competition is still invisible to many companies. During the 1980s, top executives were judged on their ability to restructure, declutter, and delayer their corporations. In the 1990s, they'll be judged on their ability to identify, cultivate, and exploit the core competencies that make growth possible – indeed, they'll have to rethink the concept of the corporation itself.

RETHINKING THE CORPORATION

Once, the diversified corporation could simply point its business units at particular end-product markets and admonish them to become world leaders. But with market boundaries changing ever more quickly, targets are elusive and capture is at best temporary. A few companies have proven themselves adept in inventing new markets, quickly entering emerging markets, and dramatically shifting patterns of customer choice in established markets. These are the ones to emulate. The critical task for management is to create an organization capable of infusing products with irresistible functionality or, better yet, creating products that customers need but have not yet even imagined.

This is a deceptively difficult task. Ultimately, it requires radical change in the management of major companies. It means, first of all, that top managements of Western companies must assume responsibility for competitive decline. Everyone knows about high interest rates, Japanese protectionism, outdated antitrust laws, obstreperous unions, and impatient investors. What is harder to see, or harder to acknowledge, is how little added momentum companies actually get from political or macro-economic 'relief'. Both the theory and practice of Western management have created a drag on our forward motion. It is the principles of management that are in need of reform.

THE ROOTS OF COMPETITIVE ADVANTAGE

In the short run, a company's competitiveness derives from the price/performance attributes of current products. But the survivors of the first wave of global competition, Western and Japanese alike, are all converging on similar and formidable standards for product cost and quality – minimum hurdles for continued competition, but less and less important as sources of differential advantage. In the long run, competitiveness derives from an ability to build, at lower cost and more speedily than competitors, the core competencies that spawn unanticipated products. The real sources of advantage are to be found in management's ability to consolidate corporate-wide technologies and production skills into competencies that empower individual businesses to adapt quickly to changing opportunities.

Senior executives who claim that they cannot build core competencies either because they feel the autonomy of business units is sacrosanct or because their feet are held to the quarterly budget fire should think again. The problem in many Western companies is not that their senior executives are any less capable than those in Japan or that Japanese companies possess greater technical capabilities. Instead, it is their adherence to a concept of the corporation that unnecessarily limits the ability of individual businesses to fully exploit the deep reservoir of technological capability that many American and European companies possess.

The diversified corporation is a large tree. The trunk and major limbs are core products, the smaller branches are business units; the leaves, flowers, and fruit are end products. The root system that provides nourishment, sustenance, and stability is the core competence. You can miss the strength of a tree if you look only at its leaves (see Figure 11.1).

Core competencies are the collective learning in the organization, especially how to co-ordinate diverse production skills and integrate multiple streams of technologies.

Consider Sony's capacity to miniaturize or Philips' optical-media expertise. The theoretical knowledge to put a radio on a chip does not in itself assure a company the skill to produce a miniature radio no bigger than a business card. To bring off this feat, Casio must harmonize know-how in miniaturization, microprocessor design, materials science, and ultrathin precision casing – the same skills it applies in its miniature card calculators, pocket TVs, and digital watches.

If core competence is about harmonising streams of technology, it is also about the organization of work and the delivery of value. Among Sony's competencies is miniaturization. To bring miniaturization to its products, Sony must ensure that technologists, engineers, and marketers have a shared understanding of customer needs and of technological possibilities. The force of core competence is felt as

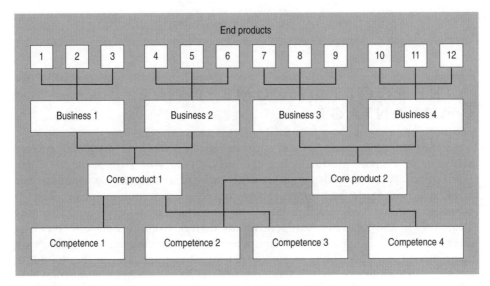

Figure 11.1 Competencies as the roots of competitiveness

decisively in services as in manufacturing. Citicorp was ahead of others investing in an operating system that allowed it to participate in world markets twenty-four hours a day. Its competence in systems has provided the company the means to differentiate itself from many financial service institutions.

Core competence is communication, involvement, and a deep commitment to working across organizational boundaries. It involves many levels of people and all functions. World-class research in, for example, lasers or ceramics can take place in corporate laboratories without having an impact on any of the businesses of the company. The skills that together constitute core competence must coalesce around individuals whose efforts are not so narrowly focused that they cannot recognise the opportunities for blending their functional expertise with those of others in new and interesting ways.

Core competence does not diminish with use. Unlike physical assets, which do deteriorate over time, competencies are enhanced as they are applied and shared. But competencies still need to be nurtured and protected; knowledge fades if it is not used. Competences are the glue that binds existing businesses. They are also the engine for new business development. Patterns of diversification and market entry may be guided by them, not just by the attractiveness of markets.

Consider 3M's competence with sticky tape. In dreaming up businesses as diverse as 'Post-it' note pads, magnetic tape, photographic film, pressure-sensitive tapes, and coated abrasives, the company has brought to bear widely shared competencies in substrates, coatings, and adhesives and devised various ways to combine them. Indeed, 3M has invested consistently in them. What seems to be an extremely diversified portfolio of businesses belies a few shared core competencies.

In contrast, there are major companies that have had the potential to build core competencies but failed to do so because top management was unable to conceive of the company as anything other than a collection of discrete businesses. General

Electric sold much of its consumer electronics business to Thomson of France, arguing that it was becoming increasingly difficult to maintain its competitiveness in this sector. That was undoubtedly so, but it is ironic that it sold several key businesses to competitors who were already competence leaders – Black & Decker in small electrical motors, and Thomson, which was eager to build its competence in microelectronics and had learned from the Japanese that a position in consumer electronics was vital to this challenge.

Management trapped in the strategic business unit (SBU) mind-set almost inevitably finds its individual businesses dependent on external sources for critical components, such as motors or compressors. But these are not just components. They are core products that contribute to the competitiveness of a wide range of end products. They are the physical embodiments of core competencies.

HOW NOT TO THINK OF COMPETENCE

Since companies are in a race to build the competencies that determine global leadership, successful companies have stopped imagining themselves as bundles of businesses making products. Canon, Honda, Casio, or NEC may seem to preside over portfolios of businesses unrelated in terms of customers, distribution channels, and merchandising strategy. Indeed, they have portfolios that may seem idiosyncratic at times: NEC is the only global company to be among leaders in computing, telecommunications, and semiconductors *and* to have a thriving consumer electronics business.

But looks are deceiving. In NEC, digital technology, especially VLSI and systems integration skills, is fundamental. In the core competencies underlying them, disparate businesses become coherent. It is Honda's core competence in engines and power trains that gives it a distinctive advantage in car, motorcycle, lawn mower, and generator businesses. Canon's core competencies in optics, imaging, and microprocessor controls have enabled it to enter, even dominate, markets as seemingly diverse as copiers, laser printers, cameras, and image scanners. Philips worked for more than fifteen years to perfect its optical-media (laser disc) competence, as did JVC in building a leading position in video recording. Other examples of core competencies might include mechantronics (the ability to marry mechanical and electronic engineering), video displays, bioengineering, and microelectronics. In the early stages of its competence building, Philips could not have imagined all the products that would be spawned by its optical-media competence, nor could JVC have anticipated miniature camcorders when it first began exploring videotape technologies.

Unlike the battle for global brand dominance, which is visible in the world's broadcast and print media and is aimed at building global 'share of mind', the battle to build world-class competencies is invisible to people who aren't deliberately looking for it. Top management often tracks the cost and quality of competitors' products, yet how many managers untangle the web of alliances their Japanese competitors have constructed to acquire competencies at low cost? In how many Western boardrooms is there an explicit, shared understanding of the competencies the company must build for world leadership? Indeed, how many senior executives discuss the crucial distinction between competitive strategy at the level of a business and competitive strategy at the level of an entire company?

Let us be clear. Cultivating core competence does not mean outspending rivals on research and development. In 1983, when Canon surpassed Xerox in worldwide unit market share in the copier business, its R&D budget in reprographics was but a small fraction of Xerox's. Over the past twenty years NEC has spent less on R&D as a percentage of sales than almost all of its American and European competitors.

Nor does core competence mean shared costs, as when two or more SBUs use a common facility – a plant, service facility, or sales force – or share a common component. The gains of sharing may be substantial, but the search for shared costs is typically a *post hoc* effort to rationalize production across existing businesses, not a premeditated effort to build the competencies out of which the businesses themselves grow.

Building core competencies is more ambitious and different than integrating vertically, moreover. Managers deciding whether to make or buy will start with end products and look upstream to the efficiencies of the supply chain and downstream towards distribution and customers. They do not take inventory of skills and look forward to applying them in non-traditional ways. (Of course, decisions about competencies *do* provide a logic for vertical integration. Canon is not particularly integrated in its copier business, except in those aspects of the vertical chain that support the competencies it regards as critical.)

IDENTIFYING CORE COMPETENCIES – AND LOSING THEM

At least three tests can be applied to identify core competencies in a company. First, a core competence provides potential access to a wide variety of markets. Competence in display systems, for example, enables a company to participate in such diverse businesses as calculators, miniature TV sets, monitors for laptop computers, and automotive dashboards – which is why Casio's entry into the handheld TV market was predictable. Second, a core competence should make a significant contribution to the perceived customer benefits of the end product. Clearly, Honda's engine expertise fills this bill.

Finally, a core competence should be difficult for competitors to imitate. And it will be difficult if it is a complex harmonization of individual technologies and production skills. A rival might acquire some of the technologies that comprise the core competence, but it will find it more difficult to duplicate the more-or-less comprehensive pattern of internal co-ordination and learning. JVC's decision in the early 1960s to pursue the development of a videotape competence passed the three tests outlined here. RCA's decision in the late 1970s to develop a stylus-based video turntable system did not.

Few companies are likely to build world leadership in more than five or six fundamental competencies. A company that compiles a list of twenty to thirty capabilities has probably not produced a list of core competencies. Still, it is probably a good discipline to generate a list of this sort and to see aggregate capabilities as building blocks. This tends to prompt the search for licensing deals and alliances through which the company may acquire, at low cost, the missing pieces.

Most Western companies hardly think about competitiveness in these terms at all. It is time to take a tough-minded look at the risks they are running. Companies that judge competitiveness, their own and their competitors', primarily in terms of the price/performance of end products are courting the erosion of core competencies – or making too little effort to enhance them. The embedded skills that give rise to the next generation of competitive products cannot be 'rented in' by outsourcing and original equipment manufacturer (OEM) supply relationships. In our view, too many companies have unwittingly surrendered core competencies when they cut internal investment in what they mistakenly thought were just 'cost centres' in favour of outside suppliers.

Of course, it is perfectly possible for a company to have competitive product line up but be a laggard in developing core competencies – at least for a while. If a company wanted to enter the copier business today, it would find a dozen Japanese companies more than willing to supply copiers on the basis of an OEM private label. But when fundamental technologies changed or if its supplier decided to enter the market directly and become a competitor, that company's product line, along with all of its investments in marketing and distribution, could be vulnerable. Outsourcing can provide a shortcut to a more competitive product, but it typically contributes little to building the people-embodied skills that are needed to sustain product leadership.

Nor is it possible for a company to have an intelligent alliance or sourcing strategy if it has not made a choice about where it will build competence leadership. Clearly, Japanese companies have benefited from alliances. They've used them to learn from Western partners who were not fully committed to preserving core competencies of their own. Learning within an alliance takes a positive commitment of resources – travel, a pool of dedicated people, test-bed facilities, time to internalize and test what has been learned. A company may not make this effort if it doesn't have clear goals for competence building.

Another way of losing is forgoing opportunities to establish competencies that are evolving in existing businesses. In the 1970s and 1980s, many American and European companies – like General Electric, Motorola, GTE, Thorn, and General Electric Company (GEC) – chose to exit the colour television business, which they regarded as mature. If by 'mature' they meant that they had run out of new product ideas at precisely the moment global rivals had targeted the TV business for entry, then yes, the industry was mature. But it certainly wasn't mature in the sense that all opportunities to enhance and apply video-based competencies had been exhausted.

In ridding themselves of their television business, these companies failed to distinguish between divesting the business and destroying their video media-based competencies. They not only got out of the TV business but they also closed the door on a whole stream of future opportunities reliant on video-based competencies.

There are two clear lessons here. First, the costs of losing a core competence can be only partly calculated in advance. The baby may be thrown out with the bath water in divestment decisions. Second, since core competencies are built through a process of continuous improvement and enhancement that may span a decade or longer, a company that has failed to invest in core competence building will find it very difficult to enter an emerging market, unless, of course, it will be content simply to serve as a distribution channel.

American semiconductor companies like Motorola learned this painful lesson when they elected to forgo direct participation in the 256k generation of DRAM chips. Having skipped this round, Motorola, like most of its American competitors, needed a large infusion of technical help from Japanese partners to rejoin the battle in the 1-megabyte generation. When it comes to core competencies, it is difficult to get off the train, walk to the next station, and then reboard.

FROM CORE COMPETENCIES TO CORE PRODUCTS

The tangible link between identified core competencies and end products is what we call the core products – the physical embodiments of one or more core competencies. Honda's engines, for example, are core products, linchpins between design and development skills that ultimately lead to a proliferation of end products. Core products are the components or sub-assemblies that actually contribute to the value of the end products. Thinking in terms of core products forces a company to distinguish between the brand share it achieves in end-product markets (for example, 40 per cent of the US refrigerator market) and the manufacturing share it achieves in any particular core product (for example, 5 per cent of the world share of compressor output).

It is essential to make this distinction between core competencies, core products, and end products because global competition is played out by different rules and for different stakes at each level. To build or defend leadership over the long term, a corporation will probably be a winner at each level. At the level of core competence, the goal is to build world leadership in the design and development of a particular class of product functionality – be it compact data storage and retrieval, as with Philips's optical-media competence, or compactness and ease of use, as with Sony's micromotors and microprocessor controls.

To sustain leadership in their chosen core competence areas, these companies *seek to maximize their world manufacturing share in core products*. The manufacture of core products for a wide variety of external (and internal) customers yields the revenue and market feedback that, at least partly, determines the pace at which core competencies can be enhanced and extended. This thinking was behind JVC's decision in the mid-1970s to establish VCR supply relationships with leading national consumer electronics companies in Europe and the United States. In supplying Thomson, Thorn, and Telefunken (all independent companies at that time) as well as US partners, JVC was able to gain the cash and the diversity of market experience that ultimately enabled it to outpace Philips and Sony. (Philips developed videotape competencies in parallel with JVC, but it failed to build a worldwide network of OEM relationships that would have allowed it to accelerate the refinement of its videotape competence through the sale of core products.)

JVC's success has not been lost on Korean companies like Goldstar, Samsung, Kia, and Daewoo, who are building core product leadership in areas as diverse as displays, semiconductors, and automotive engines through their OEM-supply contracts with Western companies. Their avowed goal is to capture investment initiative away from potential competitors, often US companies. In doing so, they accelerate their competence-building efforts while 'hollowing out' their competitors. By focusing on competence and embedding it in core products, Asian competitors have built up advantages in component markets first and have then leveraged off their superior products to move downstream to build brand share. And they are not likely to remain the low-cost suppliers forever. As their reputation for brand leadership is consolidated, they may well gain price leadership. Honda has proven this with its Acura line, and other Japanese carmakers are following suit.

Control over core products is critical for other reasons. A dominant position in core products allows a company to shape the evolution of applications and end markets. Such compact audio disc-related core products as data drives and lasers have enabled Sony and Philips to influence the evolution of the computer-peripheral business in optical-media storage. As a company multiplies the number of application arenas for its core products, it can consistently reduce the cost, time, and risk in new product development. In short, well-targeted core products can lead to economies of scale and scope.

THE TYRANNY OF THE SBU

The new terms of competitive engagement cannot be understood using analytical tools devised to manage the diversified corporation of twenty years ago, when competition was primarily domestic (GE versus Westinghouse, General Motors versus Ford) and all the key players were speaking the language of the same business schools and consultancies. Old prescriptions have potentially toxic side effects. The need for new principles is most obvious in companies organized exclusively according to the logic of SBUs. The implications of the two alternative concepts of the corporation are summarized in Table 11.1.

Table 11.1 Two concepts of the corporation

	SBU	**Core competence**
Basis for competition	Competitiveness of today's products	Interfirm competition to build competencies
Corporate structure	Portfolio of businesses related in product-market terms	Portfolio of competencies, core products, and business
Status of the business unit	Autonomy is sacrosanct; the SBU ``owns'' all resources other than cash	SBU is a potential reservoir of core competencies
Resource allocation	Discrete businesses are the unit of analysis; capital is allocated business by business	Businesses and competencies are the unit analysis: top management allocates capital and talent
Value added of top management	Optimising corporate returns through capital allocation trade-offs among businesses	Enunciating strategic architecture and building competencies to secure the future

Obviously, diversified corporations have a portfolio of products and a portfolio of businesses. But we believe in a view of the company as a portfolio of competencies as well. United States companies do not lack the technical resources to build competencies, but their top management often lacks the vision to build them and the administrative means for assembling resources spread across multiple businesses. A shift in commitment will inevitably influence patterns of diversification, skill deployment, resource allocation priorities, and approaches to alliances and outsourcing.

We have described the three different planes on which battles for global leadership are waged: core competence, core products, and end products. A corporation has to know whether it is winning or losing on each plane. By sheer weight of investment, a company might be able to beat its rivals to blue-sky technologies yet still lose the race to build core competence leadership. If a company is winning the race to build core competencies (as opposed to building leadership in a few technologies), it will almost certainly outpace rivals in new business development. If a company is winning the race to capture world manufacturing share in core products, it will probably outpace rivals in improving product features and the price/performance ratio.

Determining whether one is winning or losing end-product battles is more difficult because measures of product market share do not necessarily reflect various companies' underlying competitiveness. Indeed, companies that attempt to build market share by relying on the competitiveness of others, rather than investing in core competencies and world core-product leadership, may be treading on quicksand. In the race for global brand dominance, companies like 3M, Black

& Decker, Canon, Honda, NEC, and Citicorp have built global brand umbrellas by proliferating products out of their core competencies. This has allowed their individual businesses to build image, customer loyalty, and access to distribution channels.

When you think about this reconceptualization of the corporation, the primacy of the SBU – an organizational dogma for a generation – is now clearly an anachronism. Where the SBU is an article of faith, resistance to the seductions of decentralization can seem heretical. In many companies, the SBU prism means that only one plane of the global competitive battle, the battle to put competitive products on the shelf *today*, is visible to top management. What are the costs of this distortion?

Underinvestment in developing core competencies and core products

When the organization is conceived of as a multiplicity of SBUs, no single business may feel responsible for maintaining a viable position in core products or be able to justify the investment required to build world leadership in some core competence. In the absence of a more comprehensive view imposed by corporate management, SBU managers will tend to underinvest. Recently, companies such as Kodak and Philips have recognized this as a potential problem and have begun searching for new organizational forms that will allow them to develop and manufacture core products for both internal and external customers.

SBU managers have traditionally conceived of competitors in the same way they've seen themselves. On the whole, they've failed to note the emphasis Asian competitors were placing on building leadership in core products or to understand the critical linkage between world manufacturing leadership and the ability to sustain development pace in core competence. They've failed to pursue OEM-supply opportunities or to look across their various product divisions in an attempt to identify opportunities for co-ordinated initiatives.

Imprisoned resources

As an SBU evolves, it often develops unique Competences. Typically, the people who embody this competence are seen as the sole property of the business in which they grow up. The manager of another SBU who asks to borrow talented people is likely to get a cold rebuff. SBU managers are not only unwilling to lend their competence carriers but they may actually hide talent to prevent its redeployment in the pursuit of new opportunities. This may be compared to residents of an underdeveloped country hiding most of their cash under their mattresses. The benefits of competencies, like the benefits of the money supply, depends on the velocity of their circulation as well as on the size of the stock the company holds.

Western companies have traditionally had an advantage in the stock of skills they possess. But have they been able to reconfigure them quickly to respond to new opportunities? Canon, NEC, and Honda have had a lesser stock of the people and technologies that compose core competencies but could move them much quicker from one business unit to another. Corporate R&D spending at Canon is not fully indicative of the size of Canon's core competence stock and tells the casual observer nothing about the velocity with which Canon is able to move core competencies to exploit opportunities.

When competencies become imprisoned, the people who carry the competencies do not get assigned to the most exciting opportunities, and their skills begin to atrophy. Only by fully leveraging core competencies can small companies like Canon afford to compete with industry giants like Xerox. How strange that SBU managers, who are perfectly willing to compete for cash in the capital budgeting process, are unwilling to compete for people – the company's most precious asset. We find it ironic that top management devotes so much attention to the capital budgeting process yet typically has no comparable mechanism for allocating the human skills that embody core competencies. Top managers are seldom able to look four or five levels down into the organization, identify the people who embody critical competencies, and move them across organizational boundaries.

Bounded Innovation

If core competencies are not recognized, individual SBUs will pursue only those innovation opportunities that are close at hand – marginal product-line extensions or geographic expansions. Hybrid opportunities like fax machines, laptop computers, handheld televisions, or portable music keyboards will emerge only when managers take off their SBU blinkers. Remember, Canon appeared to be in the camera business at the time it was preparing to become a world leader in copiers. Conceiving of the corporation in terms of core competencies widens the domain of innovation.

DEVELOPING STRATEGIC ARCHITECTURE

The fragmentation of core competencies becomes inevitable when a diversified company's information systems, patterns of communication, career paths, managerial rewards, and processes of strategy development do not transcend SBU lines. We believe that senior management should spend a significant amount of its time developing a corporate-wide strategic architecture that establishes objectives for competence building. A strategic architecture is a road map of the future that identifies which core competencies to build and their constituent technologies.

By providing an impetus for learning from alliances and a focus for internal development efforts, a strategic architecture like NEC's C&C (computers and communication) can dramatically reduce the investment needed to secure future market leadership. How can a company make partnerships intelligently without a clear understanding of the core competencies it is trying to build and those it is attempting to prevent from being unintentionally transferred?

Of course, all of this begs the question of what a strategic architecture should look like. The answer will be different for every company. But it is helpful to think again of that tree, of the corporation organized around core products and, ultimately, core competencies. To sink sufficiently strong roots, a company must answer some fundamental questions: How long could we preserve our competitiveness in this business if we did not control this particular core competence? How central is this core competence to perceived customer benefits? What future opportunities would be foreclosed if we were to lose this particular competence?

The architecture provides a logic for product and market diversification, moreover. An SBU manager would be asked: Does the new market opportunity add to the overall goal of becoming the best player in the world? Does it exploit or add to the core competence? At Vickers, for example, diversification options have been judged in the context of becoming the best power and motion control company in the world.

The strategic architecture should make resource allocation priorities transparent to the entire organization. It provides a template for allocation decisions by top management. It helps lower-level managers understand the logic of allocation priorities and disciplines senior management to maintain consistency. In short, it yields a definition of the company and the markets it serves. 3M, Vickers, NEC, Canon, and Honda all qualify on this score. Honda knew it was exploiting what it had learned from motorcycles – how to make high-revving, smooth-running, lightweight engines – when it entered the car business. The task of creating a strategic architecture forces the organization to identify and commit to the technical and production linkages across SBUs that will provide a distinct competitive advantage.

It is consistency of resource allocation and the development of an administrative infrastructure appropriate to it that breathes life into a strategic architecture and creates a managerial culture, teamwork, a capacity to change, and a willingness to share resources, to protect proprietary skills, and to think long term. That is also the reason the specific architecture cannot be copied easily or overnight by competitors. Strategic architecture is a tool for communicating with customers and other external constituents. It reveals the broad direction without giving away every step.

REDEPLOYING TO EXPLOIT COMPETENCIES

If the company's core competencies are its critical resource and if top management must ensure that competence carriers are not held hostage by some particular business, then it follows that SBUs should bid for core competencies in the same way they bid for capital. We've made this point glancingly. It is important enough to consider more deeply.

Once top management (with the help of divisional and SBU managers) has identified overarching competencies, it must ask businesses to identify the projects and people closely connected with them. Corporate officers should direct an audit of the location, number, and quality of the people who embody competence.

This sends an important signal to middle managers: core competencies are corporate resources and may be reallocated by *corporate* management. An individual business doesn't own anybody. SBUs are entitled to the services of individual employees so long as SBU management can demonstrate that the opportunity it is pursuing yields the highest possible payoff on the investment in their skills. This message is further underlined if each year in the strategic planning or budgeting process, unit managers must justify their hold on the people who carry the company's core competencies.

Also, reward systems that focus only on product-line results and career paths that seldom cross SBU boundaries engender patterns of behaviour among unit managers that are destructively competitive. At NEC, divisional managers come together to identify next-generation competencies. Together they decide how much investment needs to be made to build up each further competency and the contribution in capital and staff support that each division will need to make. There is also a sense of equitable exchange. One division may make a disproportionate contribution or may benefit less from the progress made, but such short-term inequalities will balance out over the long term.

Incidentally, the positive contribution of the SBU manager should be made visible across the company. An SBU manager is unlikely to surrender key people if only the other business (or the general manger of that business who may be a competitor for promotion) is going to benefit from the redeployment. Co-operative SBU managers should be celebrated as team players. Where priorities are clear, transfers are less likely to be seen as idiosyncratic and politically motivated.

Transfers for the sake of building core competence must be recorded and appreciated in the corporate memory. It is reasonable to expect a business that has surrendered core skills on behalf of corporate opportunities in other areas to lose, for a time, some of its competitiveness. If these losses in performance bring immediate censure, SBUs will be unlikely to assent to skills transfers next time.

Finally, there are ways to wean key employees off the idea that they belong in perpetuity to any particular business. Early in their careers, people may be exposed to a variety of businesses through a carefully planned rotation programme.

Competence carriers should be regularly brought together from across the corporation to trade notes and ideas. The goal is to build a strong feeling of community among those people. To a great extent, their loyalty should be to the integrity of the core competence area they represent and not just to particular businesses. In travelling regularly, talking frequently to customers, and meeting with peers, competence carriers may be encouraged to discover new market opportunities.

Core competencies are the wellspring of new business development. They should constitute the focus for strategy at the corporate level. Managers have to win manufacturing leadership in core products and capture global share though brand-building programmes aimed at exploiting economies of scope. Only if the company is conceived of as a hierarchy of core competencies, core products, and market-focused business units will it be fit to fight.

Nor can top management be just another layer of accounting consolidation, which it often is in a regime of radical decentralization. Top management must add value by enunciating the strategic architecture that guides the competence acquisition process. We believe an obsession with competence building will characterize the global winners of the 1990s. With the decade underway, the time for rethinking the concept of the *corporation is already overdue.*

PART 4

CONNECTIONS BETWEEN STRATEGY, STRUCTURE AND PROCESS

INTRODUCTION

The articles in Part 4 span three types of strategy context: the design and structure of the organization and its particular strategy/structure configuration; the cultural contexts in which the organization is itself embedded; and the mental processes and cognitive perspective of the individual strategist. The contexts thus narrow from the structural to the personal.

As strategies evolve in response to shifting macro-environmental and competitive contexts, so the organizations through which those strategies are to be delivered must themselves evolve and change. It is unlikely that an organization structure developed under one set of conditions will be equally effective and appropriate under a different set of conditions, or if required to deliver a different type of strategy. The articles by Mintzberg and Miller on the relationship between strategy and organizational structure are two of the most-quoted writings on this aspect of strategic management. Indeed Danny Miller was awarded the *Strategic Management Journal* 1995 Best Paper Prize for this paper, originally published in 1986. The *SMJ* is the premier academic journal in the field of strategic management and its awards are by nomination and intensive peer review and evaluation. Award winners are selected for their impact over a significant period of time and Miller's paper has had a remarkable impact on thinking and teaching in the field since its publication.

In the extended chapter by Mintzberg, he suggests that the 'characteristics of organizations appear to fall into natural clusters or configurations'. Mintzberg is therefore arguing beyond a simple 'contingency' approach to the strategy/structure relationship (i.e. that context will determine structure). Instead he argues that 'no one factor – structural or situational – determines the others; rather all are often logically formed into tightly-knit configurations'. He sees a convergence around six structurally distinct configurations and the situations in which they are likely to be found.

The article explains the key features of Mintzberg's influential contribution to our understanding of organization structure. He describes six basic parts of the organization, then its basic co-ordinating mechanisms (such as standardization of work processes) and essential parameters of organizational design (such as job specialization, training and indoctrination, unit groupings and unit size, etc.). He then explains the situational factors influencing the choice of these designs (such as age and size of the organization; its technical system, environment and power structure). All these strands are pulled together to provide the six basic 'configurations'. These six represent logically consistent groupings of design parameters consistent with the situational factors facing the organization. The six configurations are: the simple structure, the machine bureaucracy, the professional bureaucracy, the divisionalized form, the 'adhocracy' and the missionary structure.

Miller takes Mintzberg's six configurations and links them to Porter's generic strategies. He subdivides Porter's differentiation strategy into three: innovative differentiation, marketing differentiation and niche differentiation and then draws together empirical data and theory to indicate matches between particular strategies and particular structures. The configurations Miller proposes are not intended to be exhaustive but are merely illustrative of important relationships. He identifies some common configurations of strategy and structure and then sets about exploring their 'internal complementarities'. He is concerned with common alignments, by which he means strategy/structure combinations that occur frequently (and can now be empirically validated) and therefore represent strong and sensible strategy/structure pairings for the pursuit of specific types of strategies. Thus Miller has himself suggested that 'configuration ... can be defined as the degree to which an organization's elements are orchestrated and connected by a single theme.' The benefits of such complementarity may include: attention and resources being focused on one primary goal and the actions for achieving that goal; systems, procedures, culture, routines and management practice which all reflect the core focus. A high degree of configuration may contribute to competitive advantage by reinforcing commitment, synergy, high levels of co-ordination and a resultant complexity which is difficult for rival organizations to imitate.

Our discussion of Miller's configurations ended with a statement of the benefits of complementarity – directing all elements onto a single focus. For many firms this central focus is distilled in their mission statements. For Campbell and Yeung there must be an emotional logic as well as a commercial logic to placing effective mission statements in support of effective strategies. They argue that 'mission' is an intellectual concept, but that 'a sense of mission' is an emotional concept; an organization with a clear mission does not necessarily have employees with a sense of mission. Managing mission is therefore a long-term process which involves not just strategy but purpose, behaviour standards and values.

Mission statements should capture the vision of the organization. Senge (Chapter 15) sees the role of leadership in organizations as: 'seeing clearly where we want to be (the "vision") and telling the truth about where we are ("current reality")'. He sees the organizational leader as designer and teacher, helping to move current reality closer to their vision. He focuses on 'developing leaders who can develop organizations'; who know how and when to intervene, and when to refrain from intervening; who can see where a minimum change would lead to lasting, significant improvement. Echoing Campbell and Yeung is this quote in Senge: 'Achieving return on equity does not, as a goal, mobilize the most noble forces of our soul.'

Of all resources which are durable and difficult to imitate, Senge discusses the most complex and sophisticated: 'the learning organization'. Senge suggests two fundamental sources of energy that can motivate in organizations: fear and aspiration. He argues strongly that while fear can produce impressive short-term changes, aspiration is what provides motivation for continuous learning and growth, on which resource renewal depends. Strategic leadership is thus about aspiration as well as analysis.

In Chapter 16, Daniels and Henry describe the impact of cognition and managers' 'mental models' on the interpretation and processing of information. These mental models constitute the personal perceptions and judgements which precede strategic thinking and decision-making. They explain the biases (including emotional bias) that can affect the way that managers process information and how this impacts on both their analysis and their judgement as strategists. Too much strategic thinking occurs 'inside the box' of people's existing perceptions and experience. They provide a diagnostic decision matrix to help managers understand better their own type of strategic thinking and its suitability to different organizational and environmental contexts. This diagnostic matrix should help individual managers not only to identify both their own and alternative mental models, but possibly also to move towards new ones. The purpose of such diagnosis is to help managers break free of both current organizational context, and individual and cultural history, to adapt existing mental models. Daniels and Henry provide a rationale for the use of strategic retreats and external consultants to challenge assumptions or point out connections that remain ignored or unchallenged within existing mental models.

CHAPTER 12

THE STRUCTURING OF ORGANIZATIONS

HENRY MINTZBERG

INTRODUCTION

[...]

This [reading] argues that [...] spans of control, types of formalization and decentralization, planning systems, and matrix structures should not be picked and chosen independently, the way a shopper picks vegetables at the market or a diner a meal at a buffet table. Rather, these and other parameters of organizational design should logically configure into internally consistent groupings. Like most phenomena – atoms, ants and stars – characteristics of organizations appear to fall into natural clusters, or configurations.

We can, in fact, go a step farther and include in these configurations not only the design parameters but also the so-called contingency factors. In other words, the organization's type of environment, its production system, even its age and its size, can in some sense be 'chosen' to achieve consistency with the elements of its structure. The important implication of this conclusion, in sharp contrast to that of contingency theory, is that organizations can select their situations in accordance with their structural designs just as much as they can select their designs in accordance with their situations. Diversified firms may divisionalize, but there is also evidence that divisionalized firms have a propensity to further diversity [...] Stable environments may encourage the formalization (bureaucratization) of structure, but bureaucracies also have a habit of trying to stabilize their environments. And in contrast, entrepreneurial forms, which operate in dynamic environments, need to maintain flexible structures. But such forms also seek out and try to remain in dynamic environments in which they can outmanoeuvre the bureaucracies. In other words, no one factor – structural or situational – determines the others; rather, all are often logically formed into tightly knit configurations.

When the enormous amount of research that has been done on organizational structuring is looked at in the light of this conclusion, much of its confusion falls away, and a convergence is evident around several configurations, which are distinct in their structural designs, in the situation in which they are found, and even in the periods of history in which they first developed.

To understand these configurations, we must first understand each of the elements that make them up. Accordingly, the first four sections of this [reading] discuss the basic parts of organizations, the mechanisms by which organizations co-ordinate their activities, the parameters they use to design their structures, and their contingency, or situational, factors. The final section of this reading introduces the structural configurations. [...]

I SIX BASIC PARTS OF THE ORGANIZATION

Different parts of the organization play different roles in the accomplishment of work and of these forms of co-ordination. Our framework introduces six basic parts of the organization, shown in Figure 12.1 and listed below:

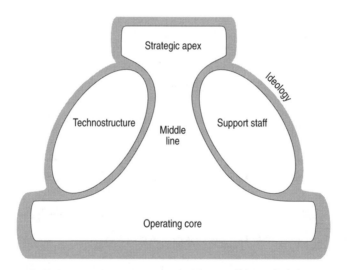

Figure 12.1 The six basic parts of the organization

1 The *operating core* is where the basic work of producing the organization's products and services gets done, where the workers assemble automobiles and the surgeons remove appendices.
2 The *strategic apex* is the home of top management, where the organization is managed from a general perspective.
3 The *middle line* comprises all those managers who stand in direct line relationships between the strategic apex and the operating core.
4 The *technostructure* includes the staff analysts who design the systems by which work processes and outputs of others in the organization are formally designed and controlled.

5 The *support staff* comprises all those specialists who provide support to the organization outside of its operating workflow – in the typical manufacturing firm, everything from the cafeteria staff and the mailroom to the public relations department and the legal counsel.
6 The *ideology* forms the sixth part, a kind of halo of beliefs and traditions that surrounds the whole organization.

II SIX BASIC CO-ORDINATING MECHANISMS

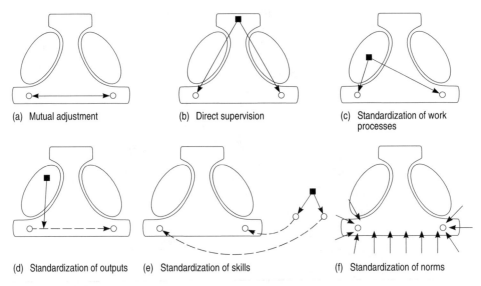

(a) Mutual adjustment

(b) Direct supervision

(c) Standardization of work processes

(d) Standardization of outputs

(e) Standardization of skills

(f) Standardization of norms

Figure 12.2 The basic mechanisms of co-ordination

Six mechanisms of co-ordination seem to describe the fundamental ways in which organizations co-ordinate their work. Two are *ad hoc* in nature; the other four involve various forms of standardization.

1 *Mutual adjustment* achieves co-ordination of work by the simple process of informal communication. The people who do the work interact with one another to co-ordinate, much as two canoeists in the rapids adjust to one another's actions. Figure 12.2a shows mutual adjustment in terms of an arrow between two operators. Mutual adjustment is obviously used in the simplest of organizations – it is the most obvious way to co-ordinate. But, paradoxically, it is also used in the most complex, because it is the only means that can be relied upon under extremely difficult circumstances, such as trying to figure out how to put a man on the moon for the first time.

2 *Direct supervision* in which one person co-ordinates by giving orders to others, tends to come into play after a certain number of people must work together. Thus, fifteen people in a war canoe cannot co-ordinate by mutual adjustment; they need a leader who, by virtue of his instructions, co-ordinates their work, much as a football team requires a quarterback to call the plays. Figure 12.2b shows the leader as a manager with his instructions as arrows to the operators.

Co-ordination can also be achieved by *standardization* – in effect, automatically – by virtue of standards that predetermine what people do and so ensure that their work is co-ordinated. We can consider four forms – the standardization of the work processes themselves, of the outputs of the work, of the knowledge and skills that serve as inputs to the work, or of the norms that more generally guide the work.

3 *Standardization of work processes* means the specification – that is, the programming – of the content of the work directly, the procedures to be followed, as in the case of the assembly instructions that come with many children's toys. As shown in Figure 12.2c, it is typically the job of the analyst to so program the work of different people in order to co-ordinate it tightly.

4 *Standardization of outputs* means the specification not of what is to be done but of its results. In that way, the interfaces between jobs is predetermined, as when a machinist is told to drill holes in a certain place on a fender so that they will fit the bolts being welded by someone else, or a division manager is told to achieve a sales growth of 10% so that the corporation can meet some overall sales target. Again, such standards generally emanate from the analyst, as shown in Figure 12.2d.

5 *Standardization of skills*, as well as knowledge, is another, though looser way to achieve co-ordination. Here, it is the worker rather than the work or the outputs that is standardized. He or she is taught a body of knowledge and a set of skills which are subsequently applied to the work. Such standardization typically takes place outside the organization – for example in a professional school of a university before the worker takes his or her first job – indicated in Figure 12.2e. In effect the standards do not come from the analyst; they are internalized by the operator as inputs to the job he takes. Co-ordination is then achieved by virtue of various operators' having learned what to expect of each other. When an anaesthetist and a surgeon meet in the operating room to remove an appendix, they need hardly communicate (that is, use mutual adjustment, let along direct supervision); each knows exactly what the other will do and can co-ordinate accordingly.

6 *Standardization of norms* (Figure 12.2f) means that the workers share a common set of beliefs and can achieve co-ordination based on it, as implied in Figure 12.2d. For example, if every member of a religious order shares a belief in the importance of attracting converts, then all will work together to achieve this aim.

Bear these six co-ordinating mechanisms in mind; we shall be returning to them repeatedly. Every organization must divide up its work among individuals (known as 'division of labour') to get it done. These co-ordinating mechanisms as the basic means to knit together the divided labour of the organization, serve as the most basic elements of structure – the glue that holds the organization together.

III THE ESSENTIAL PARAMETERS OF DESIGN

In the structuring of organizations, design means turning those knobs that influence the division of labour and co-ordination. In this section we shall be discussing ten such knobs or 'design parameters', which fall into four basic groups. The first deals with the design of individual positions in the organization and includes the specialization of jobs, the formalization of behaviour, and the establishment of requirements for the training and indoctrination associated with each job. The second concerns the designs of 'superstructure', or skeleton of the organization, and includes the determination of the bases on which positions and units are grouped, as well as establishment of the size of units. The third deals with the design of lateral linkages to flesh out the superstructure, and includes two design parameters called planning and control systems and liaison devices. The last concerns the design of the decision-making system in the organization. and includes the design parameters we call vertical decentralization and horizontal decentralization.

Job specialization

The first order of business in organizational design is to decide what each person will do. Key here is the determination of how specialized each job is to be – how many distinct tasks it is to contain – and how much control over those tasks the person who does the job should have. In determining these aspects of job specialization, the organization designer is essentially establishing the division of labour in the organization.

Jobs that have few and 'narrow' tasks are generally referred to as *horizontally specialized*, those with many and 'broad' ones as *horizontally enlarged*. A worker bolts on a bumper every few seconds all day long; a maintenance man nearby is a jack-of-all-trades, shifting from one problem to another. Jobs that involve little control by those who do them – carried out without thinking how or why – are called *vertically specialized*; those which are thoroughly controlled by the worker are referred to as *vertically enlarged*. [...]

Jobs must often be specialized vertically because they are specialized horizontally: the work is so narrow that worker control of it would preclude the necessary co-ordination. These are generally *unskilled* jobs. On the other hand, many so-called *professional* jobs are horizontally specialized yet vertically enlarged – the worker has a narrow repertoire of programs, but because these are highly complex, he must have a good deal of control over them.

Behaviour formalization

The next issue of the design of individual positions is the determination of the extent to which the work content of tasks will be specified – in other words, the behaviour or the job 'formalized'.

Organizations formalize the behaviour of their workers in order to reduce its variability, ultimately to predict and control it. Thus behaviour formalization is also a means to achieve specialization in the vertical direction. A prime motive for formalizing behaviour is, of course, to co-ordinate work very tightly, specifically through the mechanism we have called standardization of work processes. Airline pilots, for example, cannot figure out emergency landing procedures when the need arises and then co-ordinate by mutual adjustment with the ground staff; those have to be very carefully prescribed in advance.

Organizations that rely primarily on the formalization of behaviour to achieve co-ordination are generally referred to as 'bureaucracies', a word that has become highly charged in everyday speech. We shall, however, use a neutral definition here. A structure is *bureaucratic* to the extent that it relies on standardization for -co-ordination. Note that this definition includes any form of standardization, not just that of work processes. [...]

Training

The behaviour required of some tasks is too complex to be rationalized and then formalized directly by the analysts of the technostructure. And so the people who are to do the tasks must be extensively trained before they begin their work. In other words, they must acquire some standardized body of knowledge and set of skills. Such training can, of course, be designed in the organization itself, but more often it must take place in some formal institution (unless it must be learned under an apprenticeship system as a craft). And so this third aspect of position design entails deciding what formal training the organization will require in its different positions and then selecting the appropriately trained 'professionals' to fill them (or establishing its own training programs where it can).

We noted above that formalization and training are basically substitutes for one another. [...] Both are designed to program the work of the individual, but one focuses on unskilled work, while the other is oriented toward complex, professional work. And herein lies the essential difference between the two, for while one takes power from the worker and puts it into the technostructure, the other takes power from all the other parts of the organization and puts it into the hands of the professional workers themselves. In other words, professional tasks must be controlled by those who actually perform them. [...]

Indoctrination

Socialization refers to the process by which a new member learns the value system, the norms, and the required behaviour patterns of the society, organization, or group which he is entering [...] A good deal of socialization takes place informally and unofficially in the organizations, as new members interact with old. But some also takes place more formally, for the organization's own benefit, through the process known as *indoctrination*. As a parameter in the design of individual positions, indoctrination resembles training in many ways. It too takes place largely outside the job – often before it begins – and is also designed for the internalization of standards. But the standards differ. They relate not to formal bodies of knowledge and sets of skills, but to the norms of the organization itself – its values, beliefs, manners of doing things, what is generally referred to as its internal 'culture'. And because these standards are unique to each organization, indoctrination must take place within its own walls under full control of its own personnel. [...]

Unit grouping

Given a set of positions duly designed in terms of specialization, formalization, training, and indoctrination, the next issue in organization design relates to the establishment of a managerial 'superstructure' to knit it all together. In other words, positions are grouped into units, each under its own manager, and units clustered into ever larger units under their own managers, until the whole organization comes under a single manager – the chief executive officer at the strategic apex. Thus, a hierarchy of authority is constructed through which flows the *formal* power to control decisions and actions.

That hierarchy is generally represented by an organizational chart, what we shall call (borrowing from the French) an *organigram* [...] The organigram is a much maligned document, rejected by many as an inadequate picture of what really takes place in organizations. True enough, since it represents the flow of official power – formal authority – which is often superseded by informal power. Yet the organigram is inevitably the first thing asked for by anyone interested in the organization, and for good reason: like a map, it is a useful portrayal of certain surface features of the organization and their linkages. In particular, it tells at a glance how labour is divided into positions in the organization, who fills these positions, how they are grouped into units, and how formal authority flows among these units.

Two major questions arise in the design of the superstructure which are dealt with by our next two design perameters. First, on what basis are positions and units grouped into larger units, and second, what size should each of the units be?

Grouping is not simply a convenience for the sake of creating an organigram, a handy way to keep track of everyone who works for the organization. Rather, it is a fundamental way to co-ordinate work in the organization, for four reasons: (a) it establishes a system of common supervision among positions and units, (b) it typically requires positions and units to share common resources and (c) to be assessed on common measures of performance (i.e. output standards), and (d) as a result of the tendency to put the members of given units into close physical proximity with one another, it encourages mutual adjustment among them.

Positions and units can be grouped [...] by *function* (including knowledge, skill, work process work function), and by *market* (output, client, and place). In one we have grouping by *means*, by the intermediate functions the organization uses to produce or support the production of its final outputs, in the other, grouping by *ends*, by the features of the markets served by the organization – the products or services it markets, the clients it serves, the places where it serves them. [...]

Unit size

On the question of the size of units – historically described in terms of the 'span of control' of their managers – the classical literature was clear: [...] 'No supervisor can supervise directly the work of more than five or, at the most, six subordinates whose work interlocks.' Yet effective units containing dozens – sometimes even hundreds – of people or subunits have been reported. The problem as we shall see, seems to stem from the assumption in the classical literature that co-ordination was synonymous with direct supervision, in other words, that mutual adjustment and the various forms of standardization did not exist as co-ordinating mechanisms. Thus, the focus was on the span of 'control' of the manager, instead of the size of the unit, as if managerial control were the only factor in determining the size of units.

When we turn to an analysis of the co-ordinating mechanisms other than direct supervision, we get the clearest explanation of variation in unit size Two relationships in particular explain a good deal. First the greater the use of standardization (of any kind) for co-ordination, the larger the size of the work unit. It stands to reason that the more co-ordination within a unit can be achieved by standardization – in effect, automatically, without direct managerial intervention – the less time its manager need spend on direct supervision and so the greater the number of employees that can report to him. Thus we find examples of 50 and 100 assembly line workers reporting to a single foreman; similarly, I report together with fifty colleagues directly to one dean.

The second relationship is that the greater the need for mutual adjustment, the smaller must be the size of the work unit. When tasks are rather complex yet tightly coupled, neither direct supervision nor any form of standardization suffices to effect the necessary co-ordination. The specialists who perform the various tasks must co-ordinate by virtue of informal, face-to-face communication among themselves. As we noted at the very outset of this [reading], mutual adjustment is the favoured co-ordinating mechanism for the most complex of endeavours, like putting a man on the moon for the first time. Now, what effect does reliance on mutual adjustment have on unit size? For mutual adjustment to work effectively, the work unit must be small enough to encourage convenient, frequent, and informal interaction among all its members – typically less than ten people and often of the order of five, six or seven. [...]

Planning and control systems

With the establishment of positions and the construction of the superstructure, we have the skeleton of the organizational structure. But the design is still not complete. We need other parameters to flesh it out, to create other kinds of linkages among the component parts. Specifically, we need planning and control systems to standardize outputs and liaison devices to encourage mutual adjustment.

The purpose of formal planning is to specify – standardize – outputs ahead of time, and the purpose of formal control is to determine later whether or not the standards have in fact been met. The two go together, like the proverbial horse and carriage. Nevertheless, we can distinguish *action planning systems* – which focus on before-the-fact determination of outputs – from *performance control systems* – which are more oriented to after-the-fact monitoring of results. [...]

Liaison devices

Mutual adjustment may occur naturally in the small, face-to-face work unit. But how to encourage it across units, when grouping has the known tendency to discourage *inter*unit communication even as it encourages *intra*unit communications? In the past, the resolution of this problem was left to chance. But in recent years, as it has become more and more serious, a whole series of what we shall call *liaison devices* – formal parameters of structural design – have developed to stimulate mutual adjustment across units. These, in fact, represent the most significant – development in structural design in the past fifteen or twenty years. Four are of particular importance, presented in ascending order of their capacity to encourage mutual adjustment.

- *Liaison positions* are jobs created to co-ordinate the work of two units directly, without having to pass through vertical managerial channels. They carry no formal authority *per se*; rather, those who serve in them must use their powers of persuasion, negotiation, etc. to bring the two sides together. Typical liaison positions are the purchasing engineer who sits between purchasing and engineering or the sales liaison person who mediates between the sales force and the factory.
- *Task forces and standing committees* are institutionalized forms of meetings which bring members of a number of different units together on a more intensive basis, in the first case to deal with a temporary issue, in the second, in a more permanent and regular way to discuss issues of common interest. Thus a task force may be formed of engineering, sales and production personnel to redesign a given product and then disband, while line and technocratic personnel may form a standing committee to meet weekly to plan production.
- *Integrating managers* – essentially liaison personnel with formal authority – provide for stronger co-ordination by mutual adjustment than either of the first two devices. These 'managers' are not given authority over the units they link –

each of these still has its own managers. But they are given authority over something important to those units, for example, approval of certain of their decisions or control over their budgets. One example is the unit managers in the hospital, responsible for integrating the efforts of doctors, nurses, and support staff in a particular ward; another is the brand manager in a consumer goods firm who is responsible for a certain product but who must negotiate its production and marketing with different functional departments.

- *Matrix structure* carries liaison to its natural conclusion. No matter what the bases of grouping at one level in an organization, some interdependencies always remain. Functional groupings pose work-flow problems; market-based ones impede contacts among like specialists. Standardization may help, but problems often remain. As shown in Figure 12.3, we have seen three ways to deal with the 'residual interdependencies'; a different type of grouping can be used at the next level in the hierarchy; staff units can be formed next to line units to advise on the problem; or one of the liaison devices already discussed can be overlaid on the grouping. But in each case, one basis of grouping is favoured over the others. The concept of matrix structure is to balance two (or more) bases of grouping, for example functional with market (or for that matter, one kind of market with another – say, regional with product). This is done by the

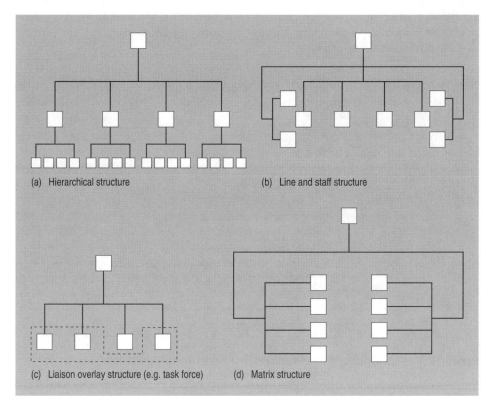

(a) Hierarchical structure

(b) Line and staff structure

(c) Liaison overlay structure (e.g. task force)

(d) Matrix structure

Figure 12.3 Structures to deal with residual interdependencies

creation of a dual authority structure – two (or more) managers, units, or individuals are made jointly and equally responsible for the same decisions. We can distinguish a *permanent* form of matrix structure, where the units and the people in them remain more or less in place, as shown in the example of a whimsical multinational firm in Figure 12.4, and a *shifting* form, suited to project work, where the units and the people in them move around frequently. Shifting matrix structures are common in high technology industries, which group specialist in functional departments for housekeeping purposes (process interdependencies, etc.) but deploy them from various departments in project teams to do the work, as shown in Figure 12.5.

How do these liaison devices relate to the other design parameters we have already discussed? One point seems clear. As means to encourage mutual adjustment, these are most logically used with work that is: (a) horizontally specialized, since specialization impedes natural co-ordination, (b) complex, in other words, professional, and (c) interdependent, so that co-ordination is in fact necessary. Thus, the liaison devices – especially the stronger ones, such as task forces, integrating managers and matrix structure – seem most appropriate to the second kind of professional work we discussed earlier, where the professionals must work together in small units. These liaison devices, as agents of mutual adjustment instead of standardization, are obviously associated with organic structures – indeed, in overriding formal authority or bifurcating it, they tend to destroy bureaucratic priority.

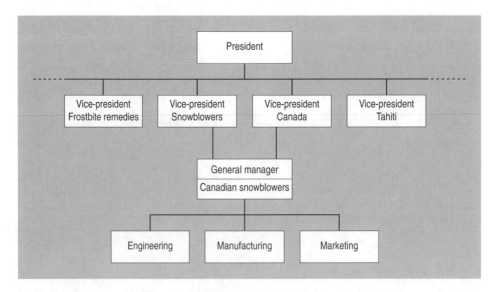

Figure 12.4 A permanent matrix structure in an international firm

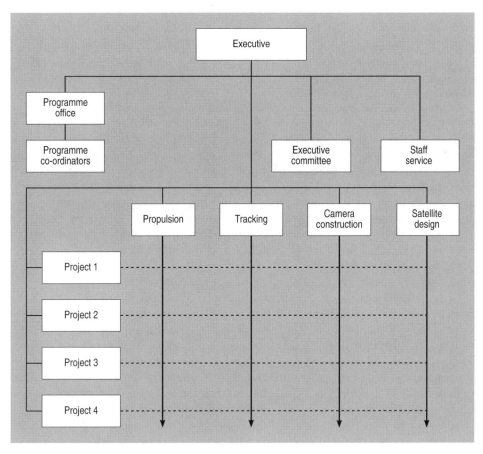

Figure 12.5 Shifting matrix structure in the NASA weather satellite program

Vertical and horizontal decentralization

Finally we come to the most extensively discussed yet least understood of the parameters of structural design, those related to *decentralization*. What does the word really mean? To some, it describes the physical location of facilities: a library is 'centralized' in one location or 'decentralized' to many. To others, it describes the delegation of formal power down the hierarchy of authority. We shall use a broader definition than the second one, but different from the first, associating the term with the sharing of decision making power. When all the power rests at a single point in the organization, we shall call the structure centralized; to the extent that the power is dispersed among many individuals, we shall call the structure relatively decentralized. Notice that our definition of decentralization is not restricted to formal power. In fact we shall distinguish *vertical decentralization* – the delegation of *formal* power down the hierarchy to line managers – from *horizontal decentralization* – the extent to which *formal or informal* power is dispersed out of the line hierarchy to non-managers (operators, analysts, and support staffers). We also introduce another distinction: between *selective* decentralization – the dispersal of power over one or a few kinds of decisions to the same place in the organization – from *parallel* decentralization – the dispersal of power for many kinds of decisions to the same place.

Centralization has one great advantage in the organization. By keeping all the power in one place, it ensures the very tightest form of co-ordination. All the decisions are made in one head, and then implemented through direct supervision. So then why bother to decentralize? Primarily because one brain is often not big enough. It cannot understand all that must be known. Also, decentralization allows the organization to respond quickly to local conditions in many different places, and it can serve as a stimulus for motivation, since capable people require considerable room to manoeuvre if they are to perform at full capacity. [...]

Let us consider decentralization in terms of the six co-ordinating mechanisms because, as we shall see, each inherently leads to a different form and a different degree of decentralization. By considering them all together, in the context of our preceding discussion, we can derive six basic types of decentralization.

Direct supervision clearly constitutes full horizontal centralization, since all the power rests with the managers. In fact, it also constitutes vertical centralization since a dependence on direct supervision for co-ordination means that each manager tightly controls those below him such that all the power eventually ruses to the top of the hierarchy, where it rests in the hands of the chief executive at the strategic apex. What we call *centralization* – in effect, horizontal and vertical as well as parallel – is shown as Type 1 decentralization in Figure 12.6 (where the size of the shaded parts designate their influence in decision making).

The various forms of standardization can, as we have seen, lead to different degrees of decentralization. When the organization relies on the standardization of work processes for co-ordination, as we have seen, the unskilled operators and lower level line managers lose power to the managers higher up in the hierarchy and also to some extent to the analysts of the technostructure who design the systems of behaviour formalization that control others. The result is centralization in the vertical dimension, with a limited and selective degree of decentralization in the horizontal dimension (to the analysts, who control only the design of the systems of standardization). What we call *limited horizontal decentralization* (selective) is shown as Type II in Figure 12.6.

We have also seen that a reliance on standardization of output goes with the delegation of power over many decisions to the managers of market-based units. This is a form if vertical decentralization, but as we noted earlier, only a very limited form, since a few division managers can retain the lion's share of the power. Thus our Type III decentralization is referred to as *limited vertical decentralization (parallel)*. (Some power is shown in the technostructure, because it is the analysts who design the planning and control systems to standardize outputs.)

Next, we have decentralization based on the two kinds of professional work. Because, as noted earlier, experts who do complex work must control it to a large degree, these represent – in contrast to our first three types – rather extensive forms of decentralization.

In the first, the standardization of skills (based on extensive training) is relied upon for co-ordination. As a result, the professionals can work rather autonomously in large units, relatively free of the control of line managers and in control of most of the decisions that affect their work directly. In other words, here we have an extreme form of *horizontal decentralization (parallel)*, shown as Type IV in Figure 12.6, with much of the power residing at the bottom of the hierarchy. Note that we have in types II and IV our two kinds of bureaucracies, the first relatively centralized, the second relatively decentralized.

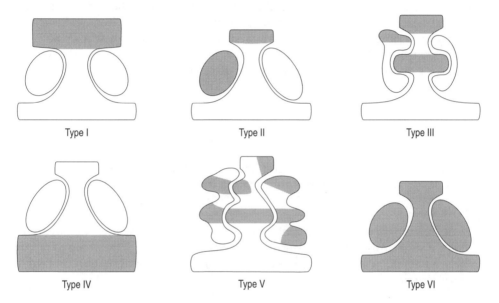

Type I   Type II   Type III

Type IV   Type V   Type VI

Figure 12.6 Six types of decentralization

In the second kind of professional work, the experts work in small units and co-ordinate by mutual adjustment (encouraged by the use of the liaison devices), which gives them a good deal of power. Here we have a combination, in both cases selective, of vertical decentralization – delegation to work groups at different levels in the hierarchy – and horizontal decentralization – a varying distribution of power within each group, of managers and non-managers, with the different decisions being controlled by whoever happens to have the necessary expertise. We end up with *selective horizontal and vertical decentralization*, Type V in Figure 12.6. Note that in Types 1 and V we have essentially two kinds of organic structures, one based on direct supervision for co-ordination, the other on mutual adjustment.

Finally, we come to the form of decentralization dictated by a reliance on the standardization of norms for co-ordination. As noted earlier, when an organization socializes and indoctrinates its members to believe in its strong ideology, it can then allow them considerable freedom to act, since they will in fact act in accordance with the prevailing norms. The result can be the purest form of decentralization – in one sense, the most democratic form of structure. Everyone shares power more or less equally – managers, staff person, operator – hence we have just plain *decentralization.*

IV THE SITUATIONAL FACTORS

A number of contingency or situational factors influence the choice of these design parameters, and vice versa. These include the age and size of the organization; its technical system of production; various characteristics of its environment, such as stability and complexity; and its power system, for example, whether or not it is tightly controlled from the outside. Some of their influences on the design parameters as found in an extensive body of research are summarized below as hypotheses.

Age and size

Five hypotheses seem to cover a good deal of the findings in the research on the effects of the age and size of the organization itself on its own structure.

H1
The older the organization, the more formalized its behaviour What we have here is the 'we've-seen-it-all-before' syndrome. As organizations age, they tend to repeat their behaviours; as a result, these become more predictable and so more amenable to formalization.

H2
The larger the organization the more formalized its behaviour Just as the older organization formalizes what it has seen before, so the larger organization formalizes what it sees often. ('Listen mister, I've heard that story at least five times today. Just fill in the form like it says.')

H3
The larger the organization, the more elaborate its structure; that is, the more specialized its tasks, the more differentiated its units, and the more developed its administrative components As organizations grow in size, they are able to specialize their tasks more finely. (The big barbershop can afford a specialist to cut children's hair; the small one cannot.) As a result, they can also specialize – or 'differentiate' – the work of their units more extensively. This leads to greater homogeneity of work within units, but greater diversity between them, which necessitates more efforts at co-ordination. And so the larger organization tends also to enlarge its hierarchy to effect direct supervision or its technostructure to co-ordinate by standardization, or to include more liaison or integrating positions to encourage co-ordination by mutual adjustment.

H4

The larger the organization, the larger the size of its average unit This finding relates to the previous two, the size of units growing larger as organizations themselves grow larger because: (a) as behaviour becomes more formalized, and (b) as the work of each unit becomes more homogeneous, managers are able to supervise more employees.

H5

Structure reflects the age of founding of the industry This is a curious finding, but one that we shall see holds up remarkably well. Organizational structure seems to reflect not just the age of the organization itself, but the age of the industry in which it operates, no matter what its own age. Industries that predate the industrial revolution seems to favour one kind of structure, those of the age of the early railroads another, and so on. We should obviously expect different structures in different periods; the surprising thing is that these structures seem to carry through to new periods, old industries remaining relatively unaffected by innovations in structural design.

Technical system

Technical system refers to the instruments used in the operating core to produce the outputs. (This should be distinguished from 'technology' which refers to the knowledge base of the organization.) Three hypotheses are especially important here.

H6

The more regulating the technical system – that is, the more it controls the work of the operators – the more formalized the operating work and the more bureaucratic the structure of the operating core Technical systems that regulate the work of the operators for example, mass production assembly lines render that work highly routine and predictable, and so encourage its specialization and formalization, which in turn create the conditions for bureaucracy in the operating core.

H7

The more complex the technical system, the more elaborate the administrative structure, especially the larger and more professional the support staff, the greater the selective decentralization (to that staff), and the greater the use of liaison devices to co-ordinate the work of that staff Essentially, if an organization is to use complex machinery it must hire staff experts who can understand that machinery – who have the capability to design, select, and modify it. And then it must give them considerable power to make decisions concerning that machinery, and encourage them to use the liaison devices to ensure mutual adjustment among them.

H8

The automation of the operating core transforms a bureaucratic administrative structure into an organic one. When unskilled work is co-ordinated by the standardization of work processes, we get bureaucratic structure. But it is not only the operating core that gets bureaucratized. The whole organization tends to take on characteristics of bureaucracy, because an obsessive control mentality pervades the system. But when the work of the operating core gets automated, social relationships change. Now it is machines, not people, that are regulated. So the obsession with control disappears – machines do not need to be watched over – and with it go many of the managers and analysts who were needed to control the operators. In their place come the support specialists, to look after the machinery. And they, as described in the last hypothesis, gain a good deal of power and co-ordinate by mutual adjustment. In other words, the result of automation is a reduction of line authority in favour of staff expertise and a tendency to rely less on standardization for co-ordination, more on mutual adjustment. Thus, ironically, organizations tend to get humanized by the automation of their operating work.

Environment

Environment is a catch-all term that has been used in the literature to describe the general conditions that surround an organization. We shall discuss five hypotheses here, each one dealing with a different condition.

H9

The more dynamic the environment, the more organic the structure It stands to reason that in a stable environment – when nothing changes – an organization can predict its future conditions and so, all other things being equal, can easily rely on standardization for co-ordination. But when conditions become dynamic – when sources of supply are uncertain, the need for product change frequent, labour turnover high, political conditions unstable – the organization cannot standardize, but must instead remain flexible through the use of direct supervision or mutual adjustment for co-ordination. In other words, it must have organic structure. Thus, for example, armies which tend to be highly bureaucratic institutions in peacetime, can become rather organic when engaged in highly dynamic, guerrilla-type warfare.

H10

The more complex the environment, the more decentralized the structure We saw earlier that the prime reason to decentralize a structure is that all the information needed to make decisions cannot be comprehended in one head. For example, when the operations of the organization are based on a complex body of technical knowledge (as in a hospital), then the organization must engage professionals (the physicians) and grant them a good deal of power over their own work. Note that Hypotheses 9 and 10 are independent of one another. A simple environment can be stable or dynamic (the manufacturer of dresses faces a simple environment yet cannot predict style from one season to another). A complex one likewise can be stable or dynamic (the specialist in perfected open heart surgery faces a complex task, yet knows exactly what to expect).

H11

The more diversified the organization's markets, the greater the propensity to split it into market-based units, or divisions, given favourable economies of scale When an organization can identify distinct markets – geographical regions, clients, but especially products and services – it will be predisposed to split itself into high-level units on that basis, and to give each a good deal of control over its own operations (that is, to use what we called 'limited vertical decentralization'). In simple terms, diversification breeds divisionalization. In this way, the organization can reduce the co-ordination needed across units: each has all the functions associated with its own markets. But this assumes favourable economies of scale. If the operating core cannot be divided (as in the case of an aluminium smelter), or if some critical function must be centrally co-ordinated (as in purchasing in a retail chain), then full divisionalization may simply be impossible.

H12

Extreme hostility in its environment drives any organization to centralize its structure temporarily Evidence from the social psychological laboratory suggests that when threatened by extreme hostility in its environment, the tendency for groups (and, presumably, organizations) is to centralize power, in other words, to fall back on the tightest co-ordinating mechanism they know, direct supervision. Here a central leader can ensure fast and highly co-ordinated response to the threat (at least temporarily).

H13

Disparities in the environment encourage the organization to decentralize selectively to differentiated work constellations When an organization faces very different kinds of environments – one dynamic, requiring organic structure, another stable, requiring bureaucratic structure, and so on – the natural tendency is to differentiate the structure, to create different pockets, or 'work constellations', to deal with each. Each constellation is given the power to make the decisions related to its own 'subenvironment', with the result that the structure becomes decentralized selectively.

Power

Our fourth set of situational factors relates to power. Thus impact of external control of the organization, the power needs of the members, and fashion are discussed below.

H14

The greater the external control of the organization, the more centralized and formalized its structure This important hypothesis claims that to the extent that an organization is controlled externally – for example, by a parent firm or a government – it tends to centralize power at the strategic apex and to formalize its behaviour. The reason is that the two most effective ways to control an organization from the outside are to hold its chief executive officer responsible for its actions and to impose clearly defined standards on it. Moreover, external control forces the organization to be especially careful about its actions; because it must justify its behaviours to outsiders, it tends to formalize the structure when it imposes special demands for rationalization, for example, when a parent firm insists that all its subsidiaries use a common set of purchasing procedures. The important point about this hypothesis is that the centralization of power in society – as independent organizations lose their power to larger systems – means centralization of power at the organizational level, and bureaucratization in the use of that power.

H15

The power needs of the members tend to generate structures that are excessively centralized. All members of the organization – operators, support staffers, analysts, managers – seek to enhance their own power, or at least to keep others from having power over them. But the dice are loaded in this game, the line managers and especially those at the strategic apex being favoured by the existence of an authority structure that aggregates formal power up the hierarchy of command. And so we would expect that to the extent that the members seek personal power, excessively centralized structures would tend to be the most common result.

H16

Fashion favours the structure of the day (and of the culture), sometimes even when inappropriate Ideally, the design parameters are chosen according to the dictates of age, size, technical system, and environment. In fact, however, fashion seems to play a role too, encouraging many organizations to adopt currently popular design parameters that are inappropriate for themselves. Paris has its salons of haute couture; likewise New York has its offices of 'haute structure', the consulting firms that sometimes tend to oversell the latest in structural fashion.

V THE CONFIGURATIONS

This completes our discussion of the elements of structure. So far – and especially in our presentation of the situational factors – we have tended to look at structure the way a diner looks at a buffet table. But in fact these elements seem to cluster naturally in a certain number of ways, which we have called configurations. A number may have been evident to the reader in the discussion. In particular, we have six basic parts of the organization, six basic mechanisms of co-ordination, six basic types of decentralization. These in fact all fit together, to describe the essence of six basic configurations, as can be seen in Table 12.1, which also lists the design parameters and situational factors associated with each configuration.

We can explain this correspondence by considering the organization as being pulled in six different directions, one by each of its parts, as shown in Figure 12.7. When conditions favour one of these pulls over the others, a particular organization is drawn to structure itself as one of the configurations as described below.

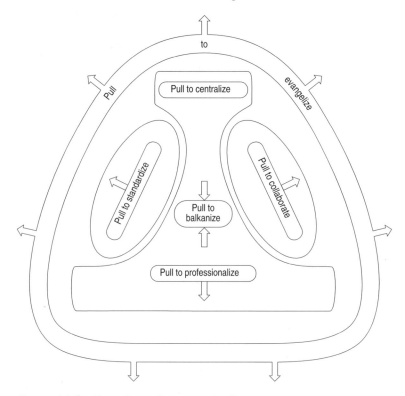

Figure 12.7 Six pulls on the organization

The simple structure

The name tells it all. And Figure 12.8 shows it all. The structure is simple, not much more than one large unit consisting of one or a few top managers, one of whom dominates by the pull to centralize, and a group of operators who do the basic work. Little of the behaviour in the organization is formalized and minimal use is made of planning, training, or the liaison devices. The absence of standardization means that the structure is organic and has little need for staff analysts. Likewise there are few middle line managers because so much of the co-ordination is handled at the top. Even the support staff is minimized, in order to keep the structure lean, the organization flexible.

Table 12.1 Basic dimensions of the six configurations*

	Simple structure	Machine bureaucracy	Professional bureaucracy	Divisionalized form	Adhocracy	Missionary
Key co-ordinating mechanism	Direct supervision	Standardization of work	Standardization of skills	Standardization of outputs	Mutual adjustment	Standardization of norms
Key part of organization	Strategic apex	Technostructure	Operating core	Middle line	Support staff	Ideology
Design parameters:						
Specialization of jobs	Little specialization	Much horizontal and vertical specialization	Much horizontal specialization	Some horizontal and vertical specialization (between divisions and HQ)	Much horizontal specialization	Little specialization
Training	Little	Little	Much	Little	Much	Little
Indoctrination	Little	Little	Little	Some of divisional managers	Some	Much
Formalization of behaviour, bureaucratic, organic	Little formalization, organic	Much formalization, bureaucratic	Little formalization, bureaucratic	Much formalization (within divisions), bureaucratic	Little formalization, organic	Little formal, bureaucratic
Grouping	Usually functional	Usually functional	Functional and market	Market	Functional and market	Market
Unit size	Wide	Wide at bottom narrow elsewhere	Wide at bottom, narrow elsewhere	Wide at top	Narrow throughout	Wide in enclaves of limited size
Planning and control systems	Little planning and control	Action planning	Little planning and control	Much perf. control	Limited action planning	Little planning and control

Liaison devices	Few liaison devices	Few liaison devices	Liaison devices in administration	Few liaison devices	Many liaison devices throughout	Few liaison devices
Decentralization	Centralization	Limited horizontal decentralization	Horizontal decentralization	Limited vertical decentralization	Selective decentralization	Decentralization
Situational factors:						
Age and size	Typically young and small (first stage)	Typically old and large (second stage)	Varies	Typically old and very large (third stage)	Often young	Typically neither very young nor very old; large only through many small enclaves
Technical system	Simple, not regulating	Regulating but not automated, not very sophisticated	Not regulating or sophisticated	Divisible, otherwise typically like Mach. Bur.	Very sophisticated, often automated, or else not regulating or sophisticated	Simple not regulating
Environment	Simple and dynamic; sometimes hostile	Simple and stable	Complex and stable	Relatively simple and stable; diversified markets (esp. products and services)	Complex and dynamic; sometimes disparate	Simple and usually stable
Power	Chief executive control; often owner-managed; not fashionable	Technocratic and external control; not fashionable	Professional operator control; fashionable	Middle line control; fashionable (esp. in industry)	Expert control; very fashionable	Ideological control; coming fashion

* Italic type within columns designates key design parameter

Figure 12.8 The simple structure

The organization must be flexible because it operates in a dynamic environment, often by choice since that is the only place where it can outsmart the bureaucracies. But that environment must be simple, as must the production system, or else the chief executive could not for long hold on to the lion's share of the power. The organization is often young, in part because time drives it toward bureaucracy, in part because the vulnerability of simple structures causes many of them to fail. And many are often small, since size too drives the structure toward bureaucracy. Not infrequently the chief executive purposely keeps the organization small in order to retain his personal control.

The classic simple structure is of course the entrepreneurial firm, controlled tightly and personally by its owner. Sometimes, however, under the control of a very clever autocratic leader who refuses to let go of the reins, a simple structure can grow large. Sometimes under crisis conditions, large organizations also revert temporarily to simple structures to allow forceful leaders to try to save them.

The machine bureaucracy

The machine bureaucracy is the offspring of the Industrial Revolution, when jobs became highly specialized and work became highly standardized. As can be seen in Figure 12.9, in contrast to simple structure, the machine bureaucracy elaborates its administration. First, it requires a large technostructure to design and maintain its systems of standardization, notably those that formalize its behaviours and plan its actions. And by virtue of the organization's dependence on these systems, the technostructure gains a good deal of informal power, resulting in a limited amount of horizontal decentralization, reflecting the pull to standardize. A large hierarchy of middle line managers emerges to control the highly specialized work of the operating core. But that middle line hierarchy is usually structured on a functional

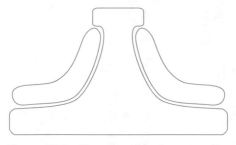

Figure 12.9 The machine bureaucracy

basis all the way up to the top, where the real power of co-ordination lies. So the structure tends to be rather centralized in the vertical sense.

To enable the top managers to maintain centralized control, both the environment and the production system of the machine bureaucracy must be fairly simple, the latter regulating the work of the operators but not itself automated. In fact, machine bureaucracies fit most naturally with mass production. Indeed it is interesting that this structure is more prevalent in industries that date back to the period from the Industrial Revolution to the early part of this century.

The professional bureaucracy

There is another bureaucratic configuration, but because this one relies on the standardization of skills rather than of work processes or outputs for its co-ordination, it emerges as dramatically different from the machine bureaucracy. Here the pull to professionalize dominates. In having to rely on trained professionals – people highly specialized, but with considerable control over their work, as in hospitals or universities – to do its operating tasks, the organization surrenders a good deal of its power not only to the professionals themselves but also to the associations and institutions that select and train them in the first place. So the structure emerges as a highly decentralized horizontally; power over many decisions, both operating and strategic, flows all the way down the hierarchy, to the professionals of the operating core.

Above the operating core we find a rather unique structure, as can be seen in Figure 12.10. There is little need for a technostructure, since the main standardization occurs as a result of training that takes place outside the organization. Because the professionals work so independently, the size of operating units can be very large, and few first line managers are needed. The support staff is typically very large too, in order to back up the high priced professionals.

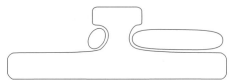

Figure 12.10 The professional bureaucracy

Professional bureaucracy is called for whenever an organization finds itself in an environment that is stable yet complex. Complexity requires decentralization to highly trained individuals, and stability enables them to apply standardized skills and so to work with a good deal of autonomy. To ensure that autonomy, the production system must be neither highly regulating, complex, nor automated.

The divisionalized form

Like the professional bureaucracy, the divisionalized form is not so much an integrated organization as a set of rather independent entities coupled together by a loose administrative structure. But whereas those entities of the professional bureaucracy are individuals, in the divisionalized form they are units in the middle line, generally called 'divisions', exerting a dominant pull to Balkanize. The divisionalized form differs from the other four configurations in one central respect: it is not a complete structure, but a partial one superimposed on others. Each division has its own structure.

An organization divisionalizes for one reason above all, because its product lines are diversified. And that tends to happen most often in the largest and most mature organizations, the ones that have run out of opportunities – or have become bored – in their traditional markets. Such diversification encourages the organization to replace functional by market-based units, one for each distinct product line (as shown in Figure 12.11), and to grant considerable autonomy to each to run its own business. The result is a limited form of decentralization down the chain of command.

How does the central headquarters maintain a semblance of control over the divisions? Some direct supervision is used. But too much of that interferes with the necessary divisional autonomy. So the headquarters relies on performance control systems, in other words the standardization of outputs. To design these control systems, headquarters creates a small technostructure. This is shown in Figure 12.11, across from the small central support staff that headquarters sets up to provide certain services common to the divisions such as legal counsel and public relations.

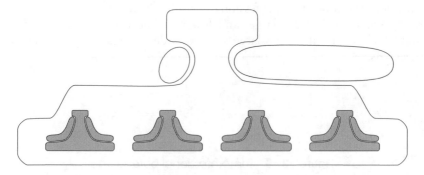

Figure 12.11 The divisionalized form

The adhocracy

None of the structures so far discussed suits the industries of our age, industries such as aerospace, petrochemicals, think tank consulting, and film making. These organizations need above all to innovate in very complex ways. The bureaucratic structures are too inflexible, and the simple structure too autocratic. These industries require 'project structures', structures that can fuse experts drawn from different specialities into smoothly functioning creative teams. That is the role of our fifth structural configuration, adhocracy, dominated by the experts' pull to collaborate.

Adhocracy is an organic structure that relies for co-ordination on mutual adjustment among its highly trained and highly specialized experts, which it encourages by the extensive use of the liaison devices – integrating managers, standing committees, and above all task forces and matrix structure. Typically the experts are grouped in functional units for housekeeping purposes but deployed in small market based project teams to do their work. To these teams, located all over the structure in accordance with the decisions to be made, is delegated power over different kinds of decisions. So the structure becomes decentralized selectively in the vertical and horizontal dimensions, that is, power is distributed unevenly, all over the structure, according to expertise and need.

All the distinctions of conventional structure disappear in the adhocracy, as can be seen in Figure 12.12. With power based on expertise, the line-staff distinction evaporates. With power distributed throughout the structure, the distinction between the strategic apex and the rest of the structure blurs.

Adhocracies are found in environments that are both complex and dynamic, because those are the ones that require sophisticated innovation, the type of innovation that calls for the co-operative efforts of many different kinds of experts. One type of adhocracy is often associated with a production system that is very complex, sometimes and so requires a highly skilled and influential support staff to design and maintain the technical system of the operating core. (The dotted lines of Figure 12.12 designate the separation of the operating core from the adhocratic administrative structure.) Here the projects take place in the administration to bring new operating facilities on line (or when a new complex is designed in a petro-chemical firm). Another type of adhocracy produces its projects directly for its clients (as in a think tank consulting firm or a manufacturer of engineering prototypes). Here, as a result, the operators also take part in the projects, bringing their expertise to bear on them; hence the operating core blends into the administrative structure (as indicated in 23.12 above the dotted line). This second type of adhocracy tends to be young on average, because with no standard products or services, many tend to fail while others escape their vulnerability by standardizing some products or services and so converting themselves to a form of bureaucracy.

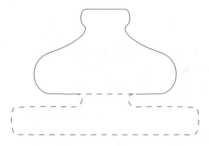

Figure 12.12 The adhocracy

The missionary

Our sixth configuration forms another rather distinct combination of the elements we have been discussing. When an organization is dominated by the pull to evangelize, its members are encouraged to pull together, and so there tends to be loose division of labour, little job specialization as well as reduction of the various forms of differentiation found in the other configurations – of the strategic apex from the rest, of staff from line or administration from operations, between operators, between divisions, and so on.

What holds the missionary together – that is, provides for its co-ordination – is the standardization of norms, the sharing of values and beliefs among all its members. And the key to ensuring this is their socialization, effected through the design parameter of indoctrination. Once the new member has been indoctrinated into the organization – once he or she identifies strongly with the common beliefs – then he or she can be given considerable freedom to make decisions. Thus the result of effective indoctrination is the most complete form of decentralization. And because other forms of co-ordination need not be relied upon, the missionary formalizes little of its behaviour as such and makes minimal use of planning and control systems. As a result, it has virtually no technostructure. Likewise, external professional training is not relied upon, because that would force the organization to surrender a certain control to external agencies.

Hence, the missionary ends up as an amorphous mass of members, with little specialization as to job, differentiation as to part, division as to status. Beyond a certain size, however, as indicated in Figure 12.13, it tends to divide itself, like the amoeba, into smaller units, best thought of as 'enclaves', with perhaps a nominal headquarters in one of the enclaves – a loose strategic apex to serve as the depository of the official manifestations of the ideology (the 'archives').

Figure 12.13 The missionary

Missionaries tend not to be very young organizations – it takes time for a set of beliefs to become institutionalized as an ideology. Many missionaries do not get a chance to grow very old either (with notable exceptions, such as certain long-standing religious orders). Size, as we saw, is also not very clear-cut. On one hand, there is a clear limit to the size of each enclave; on the other hand, nothing stops the organization from spinning off enclave after enclave, since each is a rather independent entity. Neither the environment nor the technical system of the missionary can be complex, because that would require the use of highly skilled specialists, who would hold a certain power and status over others and thereby serve to differentiate the structure. Nor can the technical system be regulating, because that would lead to the formalizing of the operating work. Thus we would expect to find the simplest technical systems in missionaries, usually hardly any at all, as in religious orders or in the primitive farm co-operatives. And the environment of the missionary, in addition to being simple, can also typically be described as stable, in that the organization tends to function in a placid environment that makes few demands on it.

This completes a rather lengthy discussion of the structuring of organizations. As we have seen, what appears to be an enormously complex subject – comprising organizational parts, co-ordinating mechanisms, design parameters, and situational factors – can be made manageable by considering how all these many dimensions cluster to form distinct types of organizations. This may seem like an artificial reduction of the complexity, but in important ways it is far more realistic than trying to consider all of the permutations and combinations of these dimensions (an impossible, or at least awfully confusing task, in any event), or of giving up and dealing with this material in a fragmented way (as has been done in much of the traditional academic literature).

In fact, a good deal of experience with this 'typology' (the common label for a set of types developed logically) in both university teaching and business practice has suggested much use for it. In no way do all organizations fit one type or another. But having the set of them as a conceptual framework can help enormously to cut through, not only the complexities of structure, but of strategy and power and almost any other factor associated with organizations. [...]

CHAPTER 13

CONFIGURATIONS OF STRATEGY AND STRUCTURE: TOWARDS A SYNTHESIS

DANNY MILLER

INTRODUCTION

[...]

In recent years the field of business strategy/policy has made some very significant advances. The conceptual work of Porter (1980) and the empirical studies of the PIMS data by Hambrick and his collaborators (1983, 1983a) are among the most interesting. These authors have derived extremely suggestive conceptual typologies and empirical taxonomies of strategy, focusing on variables that have enjoyed much attention from industrial economists – variables that were shown repeatedly to influence performance; those that can often be manipulated by managers. These include *differentiation* (e.g. innovation, advertising, product quality); *cost leadership* (capacity utilization, relative direct costs); *focus* (breadth of product lines, heterogeneity of clientele); and *asset parsimony* (fixed assets to revenue). Dimensions of market power are also considered (market share rank, barriers to entry, dependence on suppliers and customers), as are performance variables (ROI, earnings variability, growth in market share). The importance of some of these dimensions had already been suggested by Hofer and Schendel (1978) and Henderson (1979).

A central gap in the literature to date is that the rich content of strategies has never been related to structure. It may be, for example, that strategies of differentiation through innovation would not be easy to implement within a bureaucratic or mechanistic structure (Burns and Stalker, 1961). It also seems incongruous that bureaucratic structures could give rise to differentiation through innovation. By the same token, organizations that have embraced a cost leadership strategy pursue extremely efficient, low cost production to lower prices. They might then require bureaucratic, 'mechanistic' structures that place a great deal of emphasis on sophisticated cost controls; standard, repetitive procedures; cost information systems, etc. Organic structures could be too flexible and inefficient to appropriately serve cost leaders. These conjectures are worthy of further study as the match between strategy and structure may vitally influence performance.

The theme we wish to pursue here is that there are ties that unite strategy and structure; that given a particular strategy there are only a limited number of suitable structures and vice versa. The theme is, of course, anything but novel. But it seems to require development in its particulars. Specifically, it would be useful to relate the rather sophisticated conceptions of recent strategic theorists – particularly those of Porter (1980), Hambrick (1983a, b) and Miles and Snow (1978) – to those of the major structural theorists – notably Lawrence and Lorsch (1967), Burns and Stalker (1961), Woodward (1965), Thomson (1967), Galbraith (1973) and Mintzberg (1979). A guiding philosophy that motivates the integration is that all of these authors, whose works have been so very well received, have identified extremely crucial slices of organizational reality. Also, most have tended to do so in terms of ideal or common types. That is, they have isolated frequently occurring configurations of organizational elements. The elements seem to form common gestalts such that each can best be understood in relation to the other elements in the configuration. It is the very fact that we conceive of such configurations that makes it possible for us to order our world of organizations in a rich and holistic way.

[...]

THE CASE FOR CONFIGURATION

[...]

There are three interrelated arguments for configuration. Recent literature on the population ecology of organizations (Hannan and Freeman, 1977; Aldrich, 1979; McKelvey, 1981) contends that the environment selects out various common organizational forms. There are only a rather limited number of possible strategies and structures feasible in any type of environment. A few favoured strategies and structures cause the organizations pursuing them to thrive at the expense of competing organizations. Competitors must therefore either begin to move toward the superior strategies, or perish. In either event the repertoire of viable strategic and structural configurations is reduced. Miller (1982), Astley (1983), Tushman and Romanelli (1983) and Hinings *et al.*, (1984) argue that this convergence upon viable configurations will tend to happen relatively quickly – in short bursts – and that, once reached, a fairly stable set of configurations will exist over a long period.

A second, related argument for the existence of configurations is that organizational features are interrelated in complex and integral ways. In other words the organization may be driven toward a common configuration to achieve internal harmony among its elements of strategy, structure and context. A central theme is pursued which marshals and orders the individual elements. Consider Miller and Mintzberg's (1984, p. 21) description of the machine bureaucracy:

> The organization has highly specialized, routine operating tasks, very formalized procedures, and large units in its operations. The basis for grouping tasks ... is by function and co-ordination is effected by rules and hierarchy. Power for decision making is quite centralized, and there exists an elaborate administrative structure with a clear hierarchy of line authority.

Here standardization, rules and regulations, formal communications, and tight controls are emphasized. These large organizations can only function in stable and simple environments in which their inflexibility is not overly limiting.

Clearly many of these attributes are complementary and mutually reinforcing. The stable environment enables the operating procedures to be routinized and formalized, but the procedures in turn cause the organization to seek out a stable environment. Large size encourages standardization since procedures repeat and controls must be impersonal – but standardization in turn encourages growth to boost economies of scale. Cost leadership strategies (Porter, 1980) come to be favoured. Large size causes inflexibility which then prompts the search for stability in the environment. But the reverse causal direction may also apply since stability encourages growth to a scale that can optimally exploit opportunities. Thus each element makes sense in terms of the whole – and together they form a cohesive system (Miller and Friesen, 1984b:22). Cohesive configurations reduce the number of possible ways in which the elements combine. They make it that much more likely that common configurations will account for a sizeable proportion of organizations.

This brings us to our third argument for the prevalence of common configurations: that organizations tend to change their elements in a manner that either extends a given configuration, or moves it quickly to a new configuration that is preserved for a very long time. Piecemeal changes will often destroy the complementarities among many elements of configuration and will thus be avoided. Only when change is absolutely necessary or extremely advantageous will organizations be tempted to move concertedly and rapidly (to shorten the disruptive interval of transition) from one configuration to another that is broadly different. Such changes, because they are so expensive, will not be undertaken very frequently. Consequently organizations will adhere to their configurations for fairly long periods. Astley (1983), Miller (1982), Miller and Friesen (1984b) and Tushman and Romanelli (1983), have given more detailed arguments for this quantum view of change. Miller and Friesen (1980, 1982) have found corroborating empirical evidence.

So much for the conceptual arguments in favour of configurations. But there is also strong empirical evidence to support the existence of configurations. This is to be found in the well-known works by Woodward (1965), Lawrence and Lorsch (1967), Burns and Stalker (1961) and others, all of whom found integral structural configurations in their data. Hambrick (1983b) and Miller and Friesen (1984a) have also found configurations among elements of strategy in the PIMS data – largely corresponding to Porter's (1980) strategies and appearing in different environments. Dess and Davis (1984) and Miller and Friesen (1984a) showed that firms pursuing Porter's three generic strategies are quite common, and also that they outperform firms that are 'stuck in the middle'.

One of the most heartening developments is that there is considerable overlap between the structural and strategic typologies and taxonomies. Even though the authors were looking at different parts of the proverbial elephant, their work seems to converge considerably so that it is becoming increasingly possible to construct pictures of the whole beast. For example, our bureaucracy described earlier seems to be reflected by Lawrence and Lorsch's (1967) container firms, Burns and Stalker's (1961) mechanistic organizations, Woodward's (1965) mass producers, Perrow's (1971) routine manufacturers and Mintzberg's (1979) machine bureaucracy. The adhocracy of Mintzberg (1979) recalls Lawrence and Lorsch's (1967) plastics firms, Burns and Stalker's (1961) organic organizations, Perrow's (1971) non routine manufacturers, and so on.

Turning to the literature on strategic types there are notable similarities among Porter's (1980) differentiators, Miller and Friesen's (1978) adaptive firms, and Miles and Snow's (1978) prospectors. By the same token, Porter's (1980) cost leaders roughly recall Miles and Snow's (1978) defenders and Miller and Friesen's (1978) giants under fire.

We do not wish to argue that these typologies are substitutes for one another. They do indeed have different emphases. But there seem to be important areas of commonality that suggest some natural links between types of structures and types of strategies.

SELECTION OF STRATEGIC CONFIGURATIONS

[...]

The conceptual work by Porter (1980), Scherer (1980), Miles and Snow (1978) and MacMillan and Hambrick (1983) suggests four broad categories of variables or 'dimensions' that reflect important competitive strategies. They are *differentiation*, *cost leadership*, *focus* and *asset parsimony*. These dimensions can be used to compare firms' competitive advantages within and across industries. Table 13.1 shows some of the many representative variables that are subsumed by each dimension. The empirical work by Hambrick (1983b), Miller and Friesen (1984a) and Dess and Davis (1984) shows how reliably the individual variables cluster together to form the fundamental dimensions. The dimensions do not exhaust the concept of strategy – but they do reflect many of its important elements. We shall discuss each dimension in turn.

Differentiation aims to create a product that is perceived as uniquely attractive. It emphasizes strong marketing abilities, creative, well-designed products, a reputation for quality, a good corporate image, and strong co-operation from marketing channels.

Notwithstanding Porter's (1980) discussion, there appear to be at least two varieties of differentiators – each, as we shall see, with different structural and environmental co-requisites. The *innovating* differentiators are really much like Miles and Snow's (1978) prospectors, and Miller and Friesen's (1984b) S_{1B} adaptive firms. They differentiate by coming out with new products and new technologies. They lead their competitors in innovation and can charge fairly high prices. There is a strong emphasis on R&D and pioneering. In contrast, the *marketing* differentiators are more like Miller and Friesen's (1984b) S_{1A} firms which offer an attractive package, good service, convenient locations, and good

Table 13.1 Representative strategic variables within each dimension

---

Differentiation

Innovation
Percentage of sales from products introduced over last 2 or 3 years.
R&D as a percentage of sales.
Average age of products.
Frequency of major product changes.

Marketing

Product quality.
Product image.
Marketing expenses.
Advertising and promotion.
Sales force.
Services quality.

Focus

Product line breadth.
Breadth of customer types.
Geographic coverage.

Cost leadership

Relative directive costs unit.
Newness of plant and equipment.
Product pricing.
Capacity utilization.
Backward vertical integration.
Process R&D.

Asset parsimony

Fixed asset intensity (gross book value of plant and equipment revenues).
Current asset intensity (current assets/revenues).

---

product/service reliability. These firms are very forceful marketers – spending large sums on advertising, salesmen, promotion, and distribution. They are rarely the first out with new products.

Cost leadership is a strategy that strives to produce goods or services more cheaply than competitors. It stresses efficient scale facilities, the pursuit of cost reductions in manufacture, and the minimization of expenses of product R&D, services, selling and advertising. Cost leaders try to supply a standard, no-frills, high-volume product at the most competitive possible price. They do very little product innovation since this is disruptive of efficiency. The innovations of competitors will only be imitated after a considerable risk-reducing lag. Process R&D, backward vertical integration, and production automation may be pursued to reduce costs. Variants of the cost leadership strategy have been discussed by Buzzell, Gale and Sultan (1975), Henderson (1979), Miles and Snow (1978) and Miller and Friesen (1984b). Porter (1980) claims that differentiation and cost leadership do not usually go well together – that their joint pursuit could lead to a 'stuck-in-the-middle position' which fails to realize the advantages of either strategy.

Focus has been used by Porter (1980) to designate a niche strategy that concentrates the firm's attention on a specific type of customer, product or geographic locale. The firm uses either a differentiation or a cost leadership strategy (or some combination of the two) within a specialized part of the industry. We believe that focus can best be treated as a dimension with both ends of the continuum – very highly focused and very *un*focused – having rather different implications. The highly focused firms pursue Miller and Friesen's (1978) niche strategy. The highly diversified firms recall Miller and Friesen's (1984b) conglomerate strategy, and Rumelt's (1974) unrelated diversification strategy. In all cases focus complements, but does not substitute for, differentiation and cost leadership.

It is worthwhile noting that the focus dimension can refer to a business-level strategy or a corporate-level strategy. In the first instance focus measures the degree to which a firm covers one specific industry.

At the corporate level, however, focus describes the extent to which the firm has diversified into different industries. In fact, the same firm may employ highly focused business strategies in two very different industries. It could then be said to have an unfocused (diversified) corporate strategy and two focused business strategies. Although our typology will deal with strategy at the business level, we shall make a single exception in the case of the discussion of Divisionalized Conglomerates that pursue an unfocused corporate strategy. This common corporate strategy has important implications both for structure and for business-level strategies, and this warrants some discussion.

Asset parsimony is our final strategic category. It refers to the fewness of assets per unit output (MacMillan and Hambrick, 1983). Initially, the literature on strategy showed that capital intensity seemed to impede performance in many different industries (Schoeffler, Buzzell and Heany, 1974; Gale, 1980; MacMillan, Hambrick and Day, 1982). It tends to reduce flexibility and increase competition when an industry reaches over capacity. But MacMillan and Hambrick (1983) discovered that asset intensity, because it can provide for greater efficiency, may be quite suitable for cost leaders operating in stable environments. In contrast, where the organization must be flexible, as is often the case with differentiators, asset parsimony is most necessary (MacMillan and Hambrick, 1983).

How do these four strategic dimensions interact to produce effective strategic types or configurations? There are probably many ways, so just a few important ones will be isolated. Three rules of thumb were used as guides in deriving five common strategic configurations. The first rule has already been referred to. It is that successful firms tend to pursue either cost leadership or differentiation strategies, but usually not both (Porter, 1980). The second rule is that asset parsimony is desirable for differentiators who must remain flexible, but less suitable for cost leaders who must pursue efficiency (MacMillan and Hambrick, 1983). The third rule is that most strategies can have various degrees of focus, subject, of course, to a few constraints: most cost leaders cannot be too narrowly focused because of their need for economies of scale (Scherer, 1980); innovators cannot be too broadly focused or they will deplete their resources trying to lead in too many markets; but they also should not be too narrowly focused as their innovations can take them into new and profitable markets (Miles and Snow, 1978); conglomerates that are completely unfocused at the *corporate* level can have divisions that pursue most other business-level strategies – but our subsequent analysis will indicate that they will often do best with marketing differentiation and cost leadership strategies.

In light of the above, our five strategic configurations are presented in Figure 13.1.

Corporate focus	Business focus: Differentiation and asset parsimony	Business focus: Cost leadership and asset intensity	
High	A1 Niche marketers (see, e.g., Miller and Friesen's (1984b) S1 and S5 strategies; Miller's (1983) entrepreneurial firms)		Business-level strategy
Moderate to low	A2 Innovators (Miles and Snow's (1978) prospectors, Miller and Friesen's (1984b) S1B firms, Hambrick's (1983b) prospectors)	B Cost leaders (Porter's (1980) cost leaders; Hambrick's (1983b) disciplined makers of capital goods)	
Low	C Conglomerates (Miller and Friesen's (1984b) conglomerates; Rumelt's (1974) unrelated diversifiers		Corporate-level strategy

Figure 13.1 Five successful configurations of strategy

Having identified some common strategic types we shall proceed to examine the structures which can adequately support them, and the environments in which they may thrive.

BRIDGING STRATEGY AND STRUCTURE

The literature has shown that there are very many types of organization structures and environments. There are also many elements or variables that can be used to characterize them. So we shall again concentrate on only a selection of elements that has already been shown to be important in its possible consequences for strategy. We shall, using the literature, synthesize these elements into common types, and relate each to our five strategic configurations. We must stress at the outset that we do not by any means, believe that there are only five successful matches between strategy and structure. These are to be taken as representative, not exhaustive.

Mintzberg's (1979) five structural types provide an excellent synthesis of the literature on structure. While his professional bureaucracies are usually not business firms and therefore are beyond our scope, his other types are quite relevant: they are the simple structure, the machine bureaucracy, the divisionalized form and the adhocracy. We shall adapt and extend Mintzberg's framework somewhat to make it more easy to relate it to the common strategies. The dimensions of each type are summarized in Table 13.2.

SIMPLE NICHE MARKETERS

Simple structure

The simple structure is used by small firms run by a dominating chief executive, often an owner-manager. The structure is highly informal with co-ordination of tasks accomplished via direct supervision, and all strategies made at the top. There is little specialization of tasks, a low degree of bureaucratization and formalization (few programs, rules or regulations) (Pugh, Hickson and Hinings, 1969), and information systems are extremely primitive. Because there is a low level of differentiation in the goals, interpersonal orientations, methods and time horizons of the various departments, there is little need for sophisticated integrative or 'liaison' devices (Lawrence and Lorsch, 1967). Power is centralized at the top. Technology is often of Perrow's (1971) engineering or non-routine manufacturing, or Woodward's (1965) custom variety.

Clearly, simple structures cannot be appropriate in all environments and industries. They typically exist where the industry is fragmented (low concentration) and comprised of small highly competitive firms. Competitive rivalry restricts the munificence of the environment and boosts firms' vulnerability. Because simple technologies are often used to produce products, barriers to entry are very low. Market share instability and cost-price squeezes can therefore be major threats. Firms usually have very little bargaining power over their customers in such a competitive setting (see Table 13.2). Indeed, the environment recalls Hambrick's (1983a) 'unruly mob'.

Niche marketing strategy

Given the simple structure and the competitive environment, which of our five strategic types would be most suitable? Typically, simple firms must pursue some sort of differentiation strategy in order to succeed. They are too small and vulnerable to become fixed asset intensive. This would be extremely risky in the light of the substantial industry instability (MacMillan and Hambrick, 1983). Also, simple technologies and small size generally do not allow for cost leadership. Finally, structures are too primitive, too undifferentiated, and too centralized to support *complex* innovation (although very simple, CEO-driven innovations can be common). Thus firms with simple structures must generally pursue a niche or a marketing differentiation strategy. They may flourish by producing a somewhat distinctive product for a niche of the market that is the least competitive. This minimizes some of the disadvantages of smallness. To defend their niche these firms may differentiate their offerings by providing greater convenience, more reliable service, or a more appealing – higher visibility or better quality – product to a select group of customers (strategies A_1 or A_3 on Figure 3.1). None of these competitive strengths require much structural complexity. To conclude, niche or marketing differentiation strategies and simple structures should probably go together (see Table 13.2). Table 13.3 summarizes some of the reasons for the matches and mismatches between the simple structure, its setting, and the five strategic types.

MECHANISTIC COST LEADERS

Machine bureaucracy structure

The mechanistic (Burns and Stalker, 1961) or machine bureaucracy structure has been alluded to earlier. It is a very rigid structure in which the co-ordination of tasks is done via standardisation of work. A key part of the organization is the technostructure (Mintzberg, 1979) which designs the production system. The technology is somewhat automated and integrated and is normally of the line or large batch variety (Woodward, 1965). The firm is highly specialized as tasks are finely broken down. As its name implies, the structure is exceedingly bureaucratic and hierarchical with its many formal rules, programs and procedures (Burns and Stalker, 1961; Pugh, Hickson and Hinings, 1969). The information systems are quite well developed – but mainly for reporting cost and output rather than market information. The departmental, functionally organized structure is only moderately differentiated as the emphasis throughout is on following programs and plans. Integration is affected mainly through these programs (Lawrence and Lorsch, 1967).

Power rests in the hands of the top executives and the designers of workflow processes. Very little authority resides at lower or middle management levels.

The environments of these firms are quite different from those of the niche marketers. Mechanistic firms can thrive only in stable settings. Industries are often highly concentrated and mature, and all the firms are quite large. There is relatively little uncertainty since competitor and customer behaviour is fairly predictable. Demand is quite stable, as are market shares. Hambrick's (1983a) 'orderly producers' environments are recalled (see Table 13.2).

Table 13.2 Structures, environments and strategies

Structural dimensions	Simple structure	Machine bureaucracy	Organic	Divisionalized
Power centralization	All at the top	CEO and designers of workflow	Scientists, technocrats and middle managers	Divisional executives
Bureaucratisation	Low-informal	Many formal rules, policies and procedures	Organic	Bureaucratic
Specialization	Low	Extensive	Extensive	Extensive
Differentiation	Minimal	Moderate	Very high	High
Integration and co-ordination of effort	By CEO via direct supervision	By technocrats via formal procedures	By integrating personnel, task forces via mutual adjustment	By formal committees via plan and budgets
Information Systems	Crude, informal	Cost controls and budgets	Informal scanning, open communications	Management information systems and profit centres

Environmental dimensions				
Technology	Simple, custom	Mass production, large batch/line	Sophisticated product, automated or custom	Varies
Competition	Extreme	High	Moderate	Varies
Dynamism/ uncertainty	Moderate	Very low	Very high	Varies
Growth	Varies	Slow	Rapid	Varies
Concentration ratio	Very low	High	Varies	Varies
Barriers to Entry	None	Scales barriers	Knowledge barriers	Varies
		Business-level strategies		*Corporate-level strategy*
Favoured strategy	*Niche differentiation*	*Cost leadership*	*Innovative differentiation*	*Conglomeration*
Marketing emphasis	Quality, service, convenience	Low price	New products, high quality	Image
Production emphasis	Economy	Efficiency	Flexibility	Vertical integration
Asset management	Parsimony	Intensity	Parsimony	Varies
Innovation and R&D	Little	Almost none	Very high	Low to moderate
Product-market scope	Very narrow	Average	Average	Very broad

COST LEADERSHIP STRATEGY

Clearly the strategic options open to these firms are quite limited. The structures are extremely inflexible and geared to efficiency; so strategies of innovation are out of the question. Also, because markets are not growing much (due to maturity) and because firms are large, it is unwise to focus on too small a segment of the industry. This would increase the risk of declines in demand and under-utilization of facilities. There are thus only two possible strategies that remain promising – marketing differentiation and cost leadership. The second is very natural since it requires the least flexibility and the greatest production efficiency – characteristics which inhere in these structures. Some firms are able to make excellent use of their machine-like structures. They cut costs to the bone and either earn margins superior to the competition or else build up market share by selling very cheaply. Although it is less likely that mechanistic structures can support a marketing differentiation strategy, this is not totally out of the question. This might happen when the firm sells a fairly standard product in high volume but offers services, convenience or quality that exceed the competition's. It is important that this firm not be placed in a position of having to react quickly to competitors. It must therefore differentiate in a way that does not interfere with efficient and mechanical operations, and is not easy to imitate. For example, a poor differentiation tactic would be to fragment the product line by customising products. This would immediately boost costs and invite retaliation. Better alternatives might be to integrate forward (perhaps by buying distributorships), to improve quality, or to boost brand image through advertising. None of these tactics requires structural flexibility and all are facilitated by large size. The theme is clear: these structures and settings favour cost leadership. Only under special conditions can they support a strategy of marketing differentiation (see Table 13.3).

INNOVATING ADHOCRACIES

Organic structure

The organic form (Burns and Stalker, 1961) or adhocracy (Mintzberg, 1979) is a structure that is extremely different from – one might almost say opposite to – the machine bureaucracy. It is ideal for performing unusual and complex tasks which tend to change continually. Such tasks confront Perrow's (1971) R&D firms where there are 'many exceptions' in production and no obvious way of accomplishing the job. Typically, groups of highly trained specialists from a variety of areas work together intensively to design and produce complex and rapidly changing products. Representatives from R&D, marketing and production departments, collaborate face-to-face, via mutual adjustment (Thomson, 1967) in order to co-ordinate their

Table 13.3 Matching strategy and structure

Structure and rationale	Match/conflict	Strategy
Simple structure		
Can offer quality, convenience, and better service since this will not tax the structure	M	Marketing differentiation
Avoids some competition in hostile environment; reduces liability of being small	M	Niche differentiation
Complex innovation impossible in centralized, monolithic structure	C	Innovative differentiation
Insufficient scale; overly primitive structure	C	Conglomeration
Insufficient scale	C	Cost leadership
Machine bureaucracy		
Substantial scale economies possible; emphasis on efficiency good in stable setting	M	Cost leadership
Suitable only if differentiation does not upset production regularity and efficiency (e.g. advertising, good service)	M	Marketing differentiation
Structure too inflexible	C	Innovative differentiation
Functional – departmental structure inappropriate	C	Conglomeration
Inflexibility, capital intensity	C	Niche differentiation
Organic structure		
Flexible, innovative structure	M	Innovative differentiation
May be suitable if niche wide enough to make use of innovation potential; need for caution	M	Niche differentiation
Should not squander resources on selling since state-of-art product is already highly desirable to customers	C	Marketing differentiation
Structure is too inefficient	C	Cost leadership
Would spread innovative efforts too thinly; also, structure is not divisionalized	C	Conglomeration
Divisionalized structure		
Divisions, profit centres, head office controls, formal plans, etc. suitable for diversification	M	Cost leadership
Consistent with bureaucratic tendency; scale economies and vertical integration if divisions use related inputs	M	Cost leadership
Where cost leadership contraindicated marketing differentiation may be suitable for intermediate level of bureaucracy	M	Marketing differentiation
Generally, divisions are forced by head office to be too bureaucratic to be innovative	C	Innovative differentiation

contributions. A high degree of differentiation prevails as people with different skills, goals and time horizons work together (Lawrence and Lorsch, 1967). Frequent meetings, integrating personnel, committees, and other liaison devices are used to ensure effective collaboration (Galbraith, 1973). Power is decentralized as much of it resides with the technocrats and scientists responsible for innovation. Authority is thus situational and based on expertise (Burns and Stalker, 1961). There are few bureaucratic rules or standard procedures since these are too confining and would in any event rapidly become obsolete. Sensitive information gathering systems are developed for analysing the environment, and vertical and horizontal communications are open and frequent. Production technology varies both in its degree of automation and its complexity. It is, for example, highly automated and complex in the semiconductor industry, but of a job shop, custom nature in some aerospace firms.

The environment tends to be very complex and dynamic. Technologies change rapidly, as do product designs and customer needs. A high percentage of production may be exported. Advanced industry capabilities create 'knowledge barriers' to entry (Scherer, 1980). As a result, competitive rivalry is usually not quite as intensive as for the simple structures. Competition is further reduced by a fairly brisk rate of demand growth. But market share instability may arise as firms leapfrog one another with their new creative advances. Product sophistication is often substantial. To summarize, the environment is dynamic, uncertain and moderately competitive (see Table 13.3).

INNOVATIVE DIFFERENTIATION STRATEGY

One of our strategies immediately comes to mind as a fine match for this structure and environment. It is differentiation through innovation (A_2). The structure is flexible and allows for the collaboration among specialists so necessary to create new products. Burns and Stalker (1961), Lawrence and Lorsch (1967) and Mintzberg (1979), have already stressed this theme. The information and scanning systems keep managers and technocrats up to date with scientific and competitive developments. Intensive collaboration and liaison devices, open communications, and decentralization of power (in fact, the reliance on expertise-based power) facilitate complex and continual innovation. Rapid adaptation to the dynamic environment is essential, and this can only be accomplished with a strategy of innovation. Asset parsimony may be useful as high capital intensity dramatically reduces flexibility (MacMillan and Hambrick, 1983). (The cost leadership strategy is clearly inappropriate since it impedes innovation and inhibits adaptiveness. See Table 13.3.)

Innovating adhocracies would do well not to focus too broadly or too narrowly in their selection of markets. While geographic expansion and exporting may be advisable because of barriers to entry and product sophistication, other types of broadening should probably be restricted. For example, if the firm enters too many markets which have different competitive conditions and customer requirements, it may find its efforts spread too thin to do very well in any one of them. Recall that market dynamism places a premium of flexibility, innovation and product sophistication. This entrails a large administrative and structural burden even in a limited market. On the other hand, firms probably should not focus as narrowly as the simple niche marketers. This might increase their dependence on a small cyclical market and prevent them from commercialising their discoveries in a new and growing domain. Diversification could allow firms to more easily shift into safer niches when attacked.

We have discussed only the innovation aspects of differentiation as these can best be exploited by adhocracies. The marketing differentiation variables generally should play a smaller role. Customers want state-of-the-art, sophisticated products. If these are not supplied, no amount of advertising, or promotion will help. In fact, firms may benefit from holding down their marketing expenses to conserve the resources necessary for innovation. One marketing differentiation strategy that might succeed here stresses high quality. Some customers might be willing to trade off novelty for reliability.

DIVISIONALIZED CONGLOMERATES

Divisional structure

An organization may be split into divisions that are responsible for producing and marketing a discrete type of product. Usually these divisions are self-contained profit centres run by an executive whose responsibilities are similar to those of the chief executive of most independent enterprises. The individual divisions may in fact be quite different from one another – a few employing organic structures, many more using bureaucratic structures. Therefore we must shift our focus from business-level structures and strategies to those that apply at the corporate level.

Mintzberg (1979) argues that most divisions in his 'divisionalized form' are driven to become somewhat bureaucratic and formalized. The head office standardizes procedures and methods whenever possible to improve control over the divisions (Chandler, 1962; Channon, 1973). It emphasizes performance control through sophisticated management information systems, cost centres, and profit centres. However, a good deal of decision-making power remains in the hands of the divisional managers who know the most about their markets. The divisions tend to operate fairly independently of one another, with company-wide issues being handled by interdivisional committees and head office staff departments (see Table 13.2).

Environments vary from one division to the next. Mintzberg (1979) believes that the bureaucratic orientations of the divisions require that the environment be stable and simple. Clearly, however, there are exceptions as some divisionalized firms operate in rather turbulent sectors of the economy.

Conglomeration and diversification strategy

The literature agrees overwhelmingly that corporate-level conglomerate strategies that embrace very different industries require divisionalized structures. The administrative complexity caused by diversification gets divided up so that each significant market is dealt with by its own specialist and generalist managers. The head office is concerned only with controlling and appraising the divisions, allocating capital, and scouting out new diversification ventures.

This relationship between diversification and divisionalization has given rise to Chandler's (1962) famous dictum that 'structure follows strategy'. We are not all sure, however, that this is always true. A corporate strategy of conglomeration and a divisional structure may well be part of the same gestalt – diversification creates the need for divisionalization; but divisionalized structures, with their head office venture groups and planning departments, seek out new acquisitions. Often, then, strategy may follow structure. One thing, however, is certain: divisionalized structures tend to be matched by corporate strategies that are the least focused – irrespective of the source of the match (see Table 13.3).

We mentioned earlier that the divisions experience pressures of control of the head office, which often induce bureaucratization, formalization, and a loss of flexibility. This precludes business-level strategies of differentiation through innovation. But marketing differentiation strategies and cost leadership business strategies may be quite useful. Their appropriateness will be a function of the degree of stability in the environment, the prospects of economies of scale, and, of course, the degree of bureaucratization in the divisions. The more prevalent these qualities, the greater the appropriateness of cost leadership. The less prevalent the qualities (all other things being equal) the more suitable the strategy of marketing or even niche differentiation. Of course different divisions may pursue different business strategies.

One element of cost leadership – backward vertical integration at the corporate level – may be quite appropriate for some conglomerates. In cases where divisions use similar raw material inputs, their collective demand for supplies may warrant backward integrations. This can allow economies of manufacture for the total organization without reducing the possibilities of differentiation for the division. The same argument might hold for integration forward.

CONCLUSION

Our arguments throughout have been somewhat crude, the principal aim having been to propose a new method of relating strategy to structure and to suggest some illustrative configurations and linkages. No doubt there are many effective matches between strategies and structures other than the ones we have discussed. Also, the appropriateness of a strategy in general, as well as the relative effectiveness of its various elements, will be a function of much more than structure. It will depend on economic, competitive and customer factors, as well as conditions in international markets. Our arguments, therefore, must be viewed as tentative because we still know so little about the subject. We very much hope that this does not alienate readers but rather spurs them on to more thoroughly investigate the relationships between common structural and strategic configurations and their implications for performance in different environments. More encompassing empirical taxonomies should be of considerable help in this quest.

REFERENCES

Aldrich, H. E. (1979) *Organizations and Environments*, Prentice-Hall, Englewood Cliffs, NJ.

Astley, W. G. (1983) 'The dynamics of organizational evolution: critical reflections on the variation-selection-retention model'. Working Paper, The Wharton School, Philadelphia.

Burns, T. and Stalker, G. (1961) *The Management of Innovation*, Tavistock, London.

Buzzell, R.D., Gale, B. and Sultan, R. (1975) 'Market share: a key to profitability', *Harvard Business Review*, Vol. 51, No. 1, pp. 97–106.

Chandler, A. (1962) *Strategy and Structure*, MIT Press, Cambridge, MA.

Channon, D. (1973) *Strategy and Structure in British Enterprise*, Harvard University Press, Boston, MA.

Dess, G. and Davis, P. (1984) 'Porter's generic strategies as determinants of strategic group membership and organizational performance' *Academy of Management Journal*, Vol. 27, pp. 467–88.

Galbraith, J. (1973) *Designing Complex Organizations*, Addison-Westley, Reading, MA.

Gale, B. (1980) 'Can more capital buy higher productivity?' *Harvard Business Review*, Vol. 58, No. 4, pp. 67–77.

Hambrick, D. C. (1983a) 'An empirical typology of mature industrial product environments', *Academy of Management Journal*, Vol. 26, pp. 213–30.

Hambrick, D. C. (1983b) 'High profit strategies in mature capital goods industries: a contingency approach', *Academy of Management Journal*, Vol. 26, pp. 687–707.

Hambrick, D. and Schecter, S. (1983) 'Turnaround strategies for mature industrial-product business units', *Academy of Management Journal*, l. Vol. 26, pp. 231–48.

Hannan, M. and Freeman, J. (1977) 'The population ecology of organizations', *American Journal of Sociology*, Vol. 83, pp. 929–64.

Henderson, B. (1979) *Henderson on Corporate Strategy*, ABT Books, Cambridge, MA.

Hinings, C.R., Greenwood, R., Ranson, S. and Walsh, K. (1984) 'Reform reorientation and change: the designing of organizational change', unpublished manuscript, Department of Commerce, University of Alberta, Edmonton.

Hofer, C. and Schendel D. (1978) *Strategy formulation: Analytical concepts*, West, St Paul, MN.

Lawrence, P.R. and Lorsch, J.W. (1967) *Organization and Environment*, Harvard University Press, Boston, MA.

MacMillan, I.C. and Hambrick, D.C. (1983) 'Capital intensity, market share instability and profits – the case for asset parsimony', working paper, Columbia University Strategy Research Center, New York.

MacMillan, I.C., Hambrick, D.C. and Day, D. (1982) 'The product portfolio and profitability: a PIMS-based analysis of industrial-product businesses', *Academy of Management Journal*, Vol. 25, pp. 733–55.

McKelvey, W. (1981) *Organizational Systematics*, University of California Press, Los Angeles.

Miles, R. and Snow, C. (1978) *Organizational Strategy, Structure and Process*, McGraw-Hill, New York.

Miller, D. (1982) 'Evolution and revolution: a quantum view of structural change in organizations', *Journal of Management Studies*, Vol. 19, pp. 131–51.

Miller, D. (1983) 'The correlates of entrepreneurship in three types of firms', *Management Science*, Vol. 29, pp. 770–91.

Miller, D. and Friesen, P.H. (1978) 'Archetypes of strategy formulation', *Management Science*, Vol. 24, pp. 921–33.

Miller, D. and Freisen, P.H. (1980) 'Momentum and revolution in organizational adaptation', *Academy of Management Journal*, Vol. 23, pp. 591–614.

Miller, D. and Friesen, P.H. (1982) 'Structural change and performance: quantum vs. piecemeal-incremental approaches', *Academy of Management Journal*, Vol. 25, pp. 867–92.

Miller, D. and Friesen, P.H. (1984a) 'Porter's generic strategies and performance', working paper, McGill University, Montreal.

Miller, D. and Friesen, P.H. (1984b) *Organizations: A Quantum View*, Prentice-Hall, Englewood Cliffs, NJ.

Miller, D. and Mintzberg, H. (1984) 'The case for configuration' in D. Miller and P. Friesen (eds) *op cit.*

Mintzberg, H. (1979) *The Structuring of Organizations* Prentice-Hall, Englewood Cliffs, NJ.

Perrow, C. (1971) *Organizational Analysis: A Sociological View*, Wadsworth, Belmont, CA.

Porter, M. (1980) *Competitive Strategy*, Free Press, New York.

Pugh, D.S., Hickson, D.J. and Hinings, C.R. (1969) 'An empirical taxonomy of structures of work organizations', *Administrative Science Quarterly*, Vol. 14, pp. 115–26.

Rumelt, R.P. (1974) 'Strategy, Structure, and Economic Performance', Division of Research, Graduate School of Business Administration, Harvard University, Cambridge, MA.

Scherer, F. (1980) *Industrial Market Structure and Economic Performance,* Rand McNally, Chicago, IL.

Schoeffler, S., Buzzell, R.D. and Heany, D.F. (1974) 'Impact of strategic planning on profit performance', *Harvard Business Review*, Vol. 52, No. 2, pp. 137–45.

Thompson, J. (1967) *Organizations in Action*, McGraw-Hill, New York.

Tushman, M.L. and Romanelli, E. (1983) 'Organizational evolution: a metamorphosis model of convergence and reorientation', working paper, Columbia University Center for Strategy Research, New York.

Woodward, J. (1965) *Industrial Organization: Theory and Practice*, Oxford University Press, Oxford.

CHAPTER 14

CREATING A SENSE OF MISSION

ANDREW CAMPBELL AND SALLY YEUNG

Many managers misunderstand the nature and importance of mission, while others fail to consider it at all. As far back as 1973, Peter Drucker[1] observed: 'That business purpose and business mission are so rarely given adequate thought is perhaps the most important cause of business frustration and failure'. Unfortunately, his comment is as true today as it was then.

UNDERSTANDING MISSION?

The reason for this neglect is due in part to the fact that mission is still a relatively uncharted area of management. Most management thinkers have given mission only a cursory glance, and there is little research into its nature and importance. What research there is has been devoted to analysing mission statements and attempting to develop checklists of items that should be addressed in the statement.[2] Indeed, a major problem is that mission has become a meaningless term – no two academics or managers agree on the same definition. Some speak of mission as if it is commercial evangelism, others talk about strong corporate cultures and still others talk about business definitions. Some view mission as an esoteric and somewhat irrelevant preoccupation which haunts senior managers, while others see it as the bedrock of a company's strength, identity and success – its personality and character.

Despite the diversity of opinion about mission, it is possible to distinguish two schools of thought. Broadly speaking, one approach describes mission in terms of business strategy, while the other expresses mission in terms of philosophy and ethics.

The strategy school of thought views mission primarily as a strategic tool, an intellectual discipline which defines the business's commercial rationale and target market. Mission is something that is linked to strategy but at a higher level. In this context, it is perceived as the first step in strategic management. It exists to answer two fundamental questions: 'What is our business and what should it be?'
[...]

Recently, it has become common for companies to include a statement of what their business is in the annual report. [...]

The first page of the 1989 annual report of British Telecom reads: 'British Telecom's mission is to provide world class telecommunications and information products and services and to develop and exploit our networks at home and overseas'.

[...]

In contrast, the second school of thought argues that mission is the cultural 'glue' which enables an organization to function as a collective unity. This cultural glue consists of strong norms and values that influence the way in which people behave, how they work together and how they pursue the goals of the organization. This form of mission can amount to a business philosophy which helps employees to perceive and interpret events in the same way and to speak a common language. Compared to the strategic view of mission, this interpretation sees mission as capturing some of the emotional aspects of the organization. It is concerned with generating co-operation among employees through shared values and standards of behaviour.

IBM seems to subscribe to the cultural view of mission. The company describes its mission in terms of a distinct business philosophy, which in turn produces strong cultural norms and values. In his book, *A Business and its Beliefs* Thomas J. Watson Jr asserted: 'The only sacred cow in an organization should be its basic philosophy of doing business'. For IBM, 'the basic philosophy, spirit and drive of the business' lies in three concepts: respect for the individual, dedication to service and a quest for superiority in all things. The importance of other factors which contribute to commercial success, such as technological and economic resources, is 'transcended by how strongly the people in the organization believe in its basic precepts and how faithfully they carry them out'.[3]

Is it possible to reconcile these two different interpretations? Are they conflicting theories or are they simply separate parts of the same picture? We believe these theories can be synthesized into a comprehensive single description of mission. We also believe that some of the confusion over mission exists because of a failure to appreciate that it is an issue which involves both the hearts (culture) and minds (strategy) of employees. It is something which straddles the world of business and the world of the individual.

In the pages that follow we outline a framework that defines mission. The value of this framework is that it helps managers to think clearly about mission and, more importantly, it helps them to discuss mission with their colleagues. Previously, managers have had an intuitive understanding of mission. Intuition is not, however, enough. Mission needs to be managed and it can be managed better if it is clearly defined.

BUILDING A DEFINITION OF MISSION

We have developed our theory of mission both through an intellectual, top-down process and through discussions with managers and employees. Through this approach, we have tried to build an understanding of mission that is firmly grounded in the day-to-day realities of corporate life. [...]

We focused on managers in companies with a strong sense of purpose and a strong culture. We wanted to know why they were committed to their organizations, and if they had a sense of the company's mission. They responded by telling us about the behaviour patterns and behaviour standards in their companies.

They brimmed with stories about why their companies were special. In Marks and Spencer, a retailer known for its high quality and value for money, employees talked about quality and value. They described the high standards they demanded of themselves and their suppliers. [...]

At British Airways, staff spoke of the new pride and professionalism among employees as the result of the effort in the 1980s to build a service culture: 'I feel proud to work for BA', said one individual. 'People outside BA recognize the achievement, especially when they travel on the airline.'

Pride and dedication were also evident in Egon Zehnder, an executive search firm. Consultant after consultant spoke of concepts and values which the company holds dear: the primacy of the client's interest, teamwork and the 'one firm' concept. [...]

In these companies the commitment and enthusiasm among employees seem to come from a sense of personal attachment to the principles on which the company operates. To them mission has more to do with living out behaviour standards than with achieving goals. To the managers we spoke to, their mission appeared to be to follow the standards and behaviours their companies ask of them. [...]

We were hearing managers talk primarily about the standards and behaviours in their companies and why these are important to them. They gave two reasons. They are committed to the standards because, to them, they are worthwhile and elevating. They are also committed to the standards because they can see the practical good sense behind them; they can see that the standards add up to a superior business strategy.

We have attempted to make sense of these responses by developing a definition of mission. Our definition, which we have illustrated in Figure 14.1, includes four elements – purpose, strategy, behaviour standards and values. A strong mission, we believe, exists when the four elements of mission link tightly together, resonating and reinforcing each other.

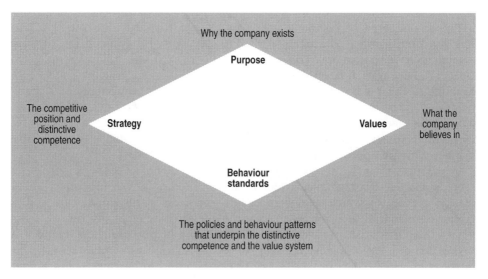

Figure 14.1 The Ashridge mission model

Purpose

What is the company for? For whose benefit is all the effort being put in? Why should a manager or an employee do more than the minimum required? For a company these questions are the equivalent of a person asking 'Why do I exist?' The questions are deeply philosophical and can lead boards of directors into heated debate. Indeed, many companies do not even attempt to reach a conclusion about the nature of their overall purpose.

However, where there does appear to be an overall idea of purpose, companies fall into three categories. First there is the company that claims to exist for the benefit of the shareholders. For these companies the purpose is to maximize wealth for the shareholders. All decisions are assessed against a yardstick of shareholder value. Hanson, a conglomerate focused on Britain and the USA, is one example. Lord Hanson repeatedly states: 'The shareholder is king.' Unlike many companies whose chairmen claim to be working primarily for the shareholders, Lord Hanson believes what he says and manages the business to that end. Hence [one Hanson] director feels quite free to say: 'All of our businesses are for sale all of the time. If anyone is prepared to pay us more than we think they are worth we will sell. We have no attachment to any individual business.'

Most managers, however, are not as single-minded as Lord Hanson. They do not believe that the company's only purpose is to create wealth for shareholders. They acknowledge the claims of other stakeholders such as customers, employees, suppliers and the community. Faced with the question, 'Is your company in business to make money for shareholders, make products for customers or provide rewarding jobs for employees?', they will answer yes to all three.

The second type of company, therefore, is one that exists to satisfy all its stakeholders. In order to articulate this broader idea of purpose many of these companies have written down their responsibility to each stakeholder group. Ciba-Geigy is an example. It has published the company's business principles under four headings – the public and the environment, customers, employees and shareholders. Under the heading of the public and the environment it has five paragraphs describing principles such as: 'We will behave as a responsible corporate member of society and will do our best to co-operate in a responsible manner with the appropriate authorities, local and national.' [...]

In practice it can be argued that the multiple-stakeholder view of purpose is more a matter of pragmatism than arbitrary choice. In a competitive labour market, a company which totally ignored its employees' needs would soon find its labour costs soaring as it fought to stem the tide of rising employee turnover. But what is important is the psychology of statements of purpose. Lord Hanson is saying that he is expecting his managers to put the allegiance of employees after the interests of shareholders in their list of priorities. Other companies say they have equal priority. For employees this makes them very different companies.

Managers in the third type of company are dissatisfied by a purpose solely aimed at satisfying stakeholder needs. They have sought to identify a purpose that is greater than the combined needs of the stakeholders, something to which all the stakeholders can feel proud of contributing. In short, they aim towards a higher ideal. [...]

At The Body Shop, a retailer of cosmetics, managers talk about 'products that don't hurt animals or the environment'. At Egon Zehnder the purpose is to be the worldwide leader in executive search. Whether these companies have an almost moral crusade, like The Body Shop, or whether they just aspire to be the best, like Egon Zehnder, they have all reached beyond the stakeholder definition of purpose. Each stakeholder, whether shareholder, employee or supplier, can feel that doing business with the company supports some higher-level goal.

We believe that leaders will find it easier to create employees with commitment and enthusiasm if they choose a purpose aimed at a higher ideal. We have met individuals committed to shareholders or to the broader definition of stakeholders, but we believe that it is harder for this commitment to grow. Purposes expressed in terms of stakeholders tend to emphasize their different selfish interests. Purposes aimed at higher ideals seek to deny these selfish interests or at least dampen their legitimacy. This makes it easier to bind the organization together.

Strategy

To achieve a purpose in competition with other organizations, there needs to be a strategy. Strategy provides the commercial logic for the company. If the purpose is to be the best, there must be a strategy explaining the principles around which the company will become the best. If the purpose is to create wealth, there must be a strategy explaining how the company will create wealth in competition with other companies.

Strategy will define the business that the company plans to hold in that business and the distinctive competence or competitive advantage that the company has or plans to create.

Egon Zehnder provides a good example of a strategy which explains how the firm will achieve its purpose. Egon Zehnder wants to be the most professional, although not necessarily the biggest, international executive search firm. Its competitive advantage comes, it believes, from the methods and systems it uses to carry out search assignments and from the 'one-firm', co-operative culture it has so carefully nurtured.

Marks and Spencer's strategy in textiles is a second example. In its clothes retailing business, Marks and Spencer seeks to offer the best value for money in the high street by providing a broad range of classic quality clothes. The company's competitive advantage comes from its dedication to quality through managing suppliers, its high levels of service, and the low overheads generated by high sales per square foot.

Behaviour Standards

Purpose and strategy are empty intellectual thoughts unless they can be converted into action, into the policy and behaviour guidelines that help people to decide what to do on a day-to-day basis.

British Airways provides a good example of how the company's purpose and strategy have been successfully converted into tangible standards and actions. It promotes itself as the 'world's favourite airline' and declares as its aim, 'to be the best and most successful company in the airline industry'. The strategy to achieve this is based on providing good value for money, service that overall is superior to its competitors and friendly, professional managers who are in tune with its staff. These strategic objectives are translated into policies and behaviour guidelines such as the need for in-flight services to be at least as good as those of competing airlines on the same route, and the requirement that managers and employees should be helpful and friendly at all times.

By translating purpose and strategy into actionable policies and standards senior managers at British Airways have dramatically changed the performance of the airline. Central to this effort was the training and behaviour change connected with the slogan 'Putting People First'.

[...]

Egon Zehnder provides another example of the link between strategy and policies. Egon Zehnder's strategy is to be more professional than other executive search consultants. Connected with this it has a set of policies about how consultants should carry out assignments, called the 'systematic consulting approach'. One of the policies is that consultants should not take on a search assignment unless they believe it will benefit the client. Another policy is that there should be a back-up consultant for every assignment in order to ensure a quality

service to the client. Supporting this systematic approach are behaviour standards about co-operation. These are ingrained into the culture rather than written on tablets of stone. An Egon Zehnder consultant willingly helps another consultant within his or her office or from other offices around the world.
[...]

The logic for the co-operation [...] is a commercial logic. The firm wants to be the best. This means being better at co-operation than its competitors. As a result it needs a behaviour standard that makes sure consultants help each other. This commercial logic is the left-brain logic of the firm.

Human beings are emotional, however, and are often driven more by right-brain motives than left-brain logic. To capture the emotional energy of an organization the mission needs to provide some philosophical or moral rationale for behaviour to run alongside the commercial rationale. This brings us to the next element of our definition of mission.

Values

Values are the beliefs and moral principles that lie behind the company's culture. Values give meaning to the norms and behaviour standards in the company. [...]

In many organizations corporate values are not explicit and can only be understood by perceiving the philosophical rationale that lies behind management behaviour. For example, consultants in Egon Zehnder believe in co-operative behaviour because they are committed to the firm's strategy. But they also believe in co-operative behaviour because they feel that it is 'right'. Egon Zehnder people are naturally co-operative. They have been selected for that quality. They believe that people ought to be co-operative. 'It makes a nicer place to work and it suits my style', explained one consultant. 'And it's a better way to work', he added with the faintest implication of a moral judgement.

Egon Zehnder people can also be moral about certain aspects of the systematic approach. The policy of not taking on an assignment unless the consultant believes it is good for the client highlights a moral as much as a commercial rationale. Other executive search companies will take on any assignment, they argue. But Egon Zehnder puts the interests of the client first and will advise the client against an assignment even if it means lost revenues. It is a professional code of behaviour. As professionals they feel a moral duty to advise the client to do what is best for the client rather than what is best for Egon Zehnder. There is a commercial rationale for this behaviour, but the moral rationale is stronger.
[...]

Values can provide a rationale for behaviour that is just as strong as strategy. It is for this reason that the framework in Figure 14.1 has a diamond shape. There are two rationales that link purpose with behaviour. The commercial rationale [...] is about strategy and what sort of behaviour will help the company outperform competitors in its chosen arena. The emotional, moral and ethical rationale [...] is about values and what sort of behaviour is ethical: the right way to treat people, the right way to behave in our society.

Our definition of mission includes both these rationales linked together by a common purpose.

CREATING A STRONG MISSION

A strong mission exists when the four elements of mission reinforce each other. This is most easily perceived by looking at the links between the strategy and the value system and whether both can be acted out through the same behaviour standards. Are the important behaviour standards central to both the strategy and the value system?

In Egon Zehnder, British Airways and Hewlett-Packard they are. We looked at only one or two behaviour standards for each company, but we would find much the same reinforcement of both strategy and values if we examined other behaviour standards. Hewlett-Packard's commercial strategy depends on attracting and keeping high-quality committed employees. This means it has to demonstrate a set of values which desirable employees will find attractive. So, for example, it has an 'open door' policy that encourages dissatisfied employees to approach senior managers; a policy of high integrity and open communications with stakeholders; a belief in informality and in decentralization; a policy of promoting from within; and a commitment to teamwork. Each of these policies and behaviour standards has a rationale both in the company's strategy and in its value system. They work cumulatively to create a strong mission.

Marks and Spencer is another company where the most important behaviour standards are essential pillars of both the strategy and the value system. One of the platforms of Marks and Spencer's philosophy is good human relations. As one manager explained: 'Marcus Sieff gave many presentations both in the company and outside. But he only ever gave one speech, about good human relations.' Part of Marks and Spencer's strategy is to have employees who take more care, particularly in relation to customer service. By caring for employees, Sieff would argue, the company will create employees who will care for the company and its customers. As a result Marks and Spencer is famous for its services and support for employees, from the quality of the toilets to things like dental care. The policy of good human relations is a good standard of management behaviour referred to by one manager as 'visible management'. [...] Visible management requires that managers, even at the highest level, spend time visiting stores and talking to staff and customers. As one board member explained: 'In a normal week, the 12 board members will probably between them visit about 25 stores. These are not red-letter days. We will just go in and talk with some of the management, supervisors and staff. It's about getting out and listening to the organization.'

In companies like Egon Zehnder, Marks and Spencer and Hewlett-Packard, the management philosophy and value system dovetail with the strategy so that the company's policies and behaviour standards reinforce both the strategy and the philosophy. The whole has integrity. These companies have strong missions. Strong missions come, therefore, from a clear fit between the four elements in the framework.

A SENSE OF MISSION: THE EMOTIONAL BOND

A sense of mission is an emotional commitment felt by people towards the company's mission. But even in companies with very strong missions there are many people who do not feel an emotional commitment. We were told, for example, that even at the height of Hewlett-Packard's success an employee survey revealed a large minority of employees who did not have a strong belief in the capabilities of the senior management team, implying that they lacked a sense of mission.

A sense of mission occurs, we believe, when there is a match between the values of an organization and those of an individual. Because organization values are rarely explicit, the individual senses them through the company's behaviour standards. For example, if the behaviour standard is about co-operative working, the individual will be able to sense that helpfulness is valued above individual competition. If the individual has a personal value about the importance of being helpful and co-operative, then there is a values match between the individual and the organization. The greater the link between company policies and individual values, the greater the scope for the individual's sense of mission.

We see the values match (illustrated in Figure 14.2) as the most important part of a sense of mission because it is through values that individuals feel emotional about their organizations. Commitment to a company's strategy does not, on its own, constitute a sense of mission. It is not unusual for groups of managers to discuss their company's purpose and strategy and reach an intellectual agreement. However this intellectual agreement does not necessarily translate into an emotional commitment and hence the strategic plan does not get implemented. The emotional commitment comes when the individual personally identifies with the values and behaviours lying behind the plan, turning the strategy into a mission and the intellectual agreement into a sense of mission.

[...]

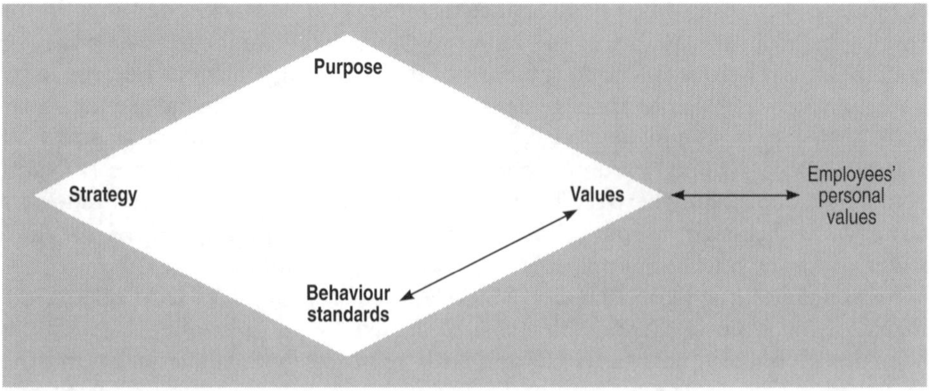

Figure 14.2 Meaning comes mainly from values

Recognizing the personal nature of a sense of mission is important because it has two implications. First, no organization can hope to have 100 per cent of its employees with a sense of mission, unless it is very small. People are too varied and have too many individual values for it to be possible for a large organization to achieve a values match for all its employees. Second, careful recruitment is essential. People's values do not change when they change companies. By recruiting people with compatible values, companies are much more likely to foster a sense of mission.

We have pointed out that even in companies with a strong mission, many people lack a sense of mission. This may be because they have few strong values and, therefore, feel very little for the company. It may also be because their values conflict with those of the company. These individuals may not be poor performers or disruptive but their motivation is more self-interested and their attitudes are likely to be more cynical. These individuals may give good service to the company but there are benefits to a company that only come through having individuals with a sense of mission.

We have defined the terms mission and sense of mission at some length and been at pains to draw a distinction between these two concepts because we believe managers are frequently confused by them.

Mission is an intellectual concept that can be analysed and discussed unemotionally. Like strategy, mission is a set of propositions that can be used to guide the policies and behaviours of a company. However, mission is a larger concept than strategy. It covers strategy and culture. The strategy element of mission legislates what is important to the commercial future of the company. The values element of mission legislates what is important to the culture of the company. When the two are in tune, reinforcing each other and bound by a common purpose, the mission is strong. When there are contradictions and inconsistencies, the mission is weak.

Sense of mission is not an intellectual concept: it is an emotional and deeply personal feeling. The individual with a sense of mission has an emotional attachment and commitment to the company, what it stands for and what is trying to do.

A company with a clear mission does not necessarily have employees with a sense of mission. Some individuals may have a sense of mission with varying degrees of intensity. Many will not. Over time the number of employees with a sense of mission will increase as the policies of the mission become implemented and embedded in the company culture. But even a company like Hewlett-Packard, that has had a clear mission for 30 or more years, will not have more than 50 per cent of employees with what we would recognize as a sense of mission.

IMPLICATIONS OF THE MISSION MODEL

Mission thinking has implications at all levels in business as well as for those connected to business. Our greatest hope is that our research will stimulate management teams to give the subject some executive time.

First, the model states that organization values need to be compatible with employee values. This compatibility or lack of it can be analysed and measured, bringing objectivity to the discussion of culture and human resource issues. Will the member of the executive team have a values conflict with the proposed mission? Will the marketing department have a values conflict? [...]

Moreover, since values must be embedded in behaviour standards, values conflicts become exposed when managers or employees react to behaviour instructions. It may be hard to analyse whether the managers of the chemical laboratory believe in 'supportive management'. It is much easier to decide whether these managers are likely to implement a standard of managing by wandering around. The model's strength, therefore, is that it defines the relationship managers need to create between organization values and employee values.

Second, the model demands that strategy and values resonate and reinforce each other. It is possible to identify many values that are compatible with a particular strategy, but it is hard to analyse whether these are the right values, whether they resonate with strategy sufficiently strongly.

The mission model's emphasis on behaviour standards helps to bridge this analytical gap. By insisting that strategy and values are converted into a few behaviour standards acting as beacons of the mission, the degree of resonance between strategy and values is exposed. If it is possible to condense the mission into a few symbolically important behaviour standards, then we can be confident that the strategy and the values resonate strongly. If not, if no powerful behaviour standards can be identified, then the fault almost certainly lies in a lack of resonance between strategy and values. Further mission planning, further experimentation and further insight are needed.

[...]

Managing mission is, therefore, a continuous, ongoing process. Few companies will be able articulate the behaviour standards that drive their mission without working at the problem over a number of years. By being clear about the need to have a mission, the need to create a relationship between strategy and values and the need to articulate behaviour standards, managers can avoid a superficial attitude to mission and continue the analysis, thinking and experimentation for long enough to develop the mission that will build a great company.

Acknowledgement

This article is drawn from *A Sense of Mission*, Andrew Campbell, Marion Devine and David Young, Economist Publications/Hutchinson (1990).

FURTHER READING

Campbell, A. and Towadey, K. (1990) *Mission and Business Philosophy: winning employee commitment*, Heinemann, Oxford.

Campbell, A. and Yeung, S. (1990) *Do You Need a Mission Statement?* Special Report No. 1208, The Economist Publications Management Guides, London.

NOTES

1 Peter Drucker, *Management: tasks, responsibilities, practices*, Harper & Row, New York (1973).

2 he main academic work on the contents of mission statements has been done by Fred David and Jack Pearce (J.A. Pearce II and F.R. David, 'Corporate mission statements: the bottom line', *Academy of Management Executive*, 1 (1987); D. Cochran and F.R. David, 'The communication effectiveness of organizational mission statements', *Journal of Applied Communication Research* (1987); F.R. David, 'How companies define their mission', *Long Range Planning*, Vol. 22, No. 1 (1989).

3 Thomas J. Watson Jr. *A Business and Its Beliefs*, McGraw-Hill, New York (1963).

CHAPTER 15

THE LEADER'S NEW WORK: BUILDING LEARNING ORGANIZATIONS

PETER M. SENGE

The prevailing view of learning organizations emphasizes increased adaptability. Given the accelerating pace of change, or so the standard view goes, 'the most successful corporation of the 1990s', according to *Fortune* magazine, 'will be something called a learning organization, a consummately adaptive enterprise'.[1]

But increasing adaptiveness is only the first stage in moving toward learning organizations. The impulse to learn in children goes deeper than desires to respond and adapt more effectively to environmental change. The impulse to learn, at its heart, is an impulse to be generative, to expand our capability. This is why leading corporations are focusing on generative learning, which is about creating, as well as adaptive learning, which is about coping.[2]

Generative learning, unlike adaptive learning, requires new ways of looking at the world, whether in understanding customers or in understanding how to better manage a business. For years, US manufacturers sought competitive advantage in aggressive controls on inventories, incentives against overproduction, and rigid adherence to production forecasts. Despite these incentives, their performance was eventually eclipsed by Japanese firms who saw the challenges of manufacturing differently. They realized that eliminating delays in the production process was the key to reducing instability and improving cost, productivity, and service. They worked to build networks of relationships with trusted suppliers and to redesign physical production processes so as to reduce delays in materials procurement, production set up, and in-process inventory – a much higher-average approach to improving both cost and customer loyalty.

THE LEADER'S NEW WORK

Our traditional view of leaders – as special people who set the direction, make the key decisions, and energize the troops – is deeply rooted in an individualistic and non-systemic world view. Especially in the West, leaders are heroes – great men (and occasionally women) who rise to the fore in times of crisis. So long as such myths prevail, they reinforce a focus on short-term events and charismatic heroes rather than on systemic forces and collective learning.

Leadership in learning organizations centres on subtler and ultimately more important work. In a learning organization, leaders' roles differ dramatically from that of the charismatic decision maker. Leaders are designers, teachers, and stewards. These roles require new skills: the ability to build shared vision, to bring to the surface and challenge prevailing mental models, and to foster more systemic patterns of thinking. In short, leaders in learning organizations are responsible for building organizations where people are continually expanding their capabilities to shape their future – that is, leaders are responsible for learning.

CREATIVE TENSION: THE INTEGRATING PRINCIPLE

Leadership in a learning organization starts with the principle of creative tension.[3] Creative tension comes from seeing clearly where we want to be, our 'vision', and telling the truth about where we are, our 'current reality'. The gap between the two generates a natural tension.

Creative tension can be resolved in two basic ways: by raising current reality toward the vision, or by lowering the vision toward current reality. Individuals, groups and organizations who learn how to work with creative tension learn how to use the energy it generates to more reality move reliably forward towards their visions.

The principle of creative tension has long been recognized by leaders. Martin Luther King, Jr., once said, 'Just as Socrates felt that it was necessary to create a tension in the mind, so that individuals could rise from the bondage of myths and half truths ... so must we ... create the kind of tension in society that will help men rise from the dark depths of prejudice and racism.'[4]

Without vision there is no creative tension. Creative tension cannot be generated from current reality alone. All the analysis in the world will never generate a vision. Many who are otherwise qualified to lead fail to do so because they try to substitute analysis for vision. They believe that, if only people understood current reality, they would surely feel the motivation to change. They are then disappointed to discover that people 'resist' the personal and organizational changes that must be made to alter reality. What they never grasp is that the natural energy for changing reality comes from holding a picture of what might be that is more important to people than what is.

But creative tension cannot be generated from vision alone; it demands an accurate picture of current reality as well. Just as King had a dream, so too did he continually strive to 'dramatize the shameful conditions' of racism and prejudice so that they could no longer be ignored. Vision without an understanding of current reality will more likely foster cynicism than creativity. The principle of creative tension teaches that an accurate picture of current reality is just as important as a compelling picture of a desired future.

Leading through creative tension is different from solving problems. In problem solving, the energy for change comes from attempting to get away from an aspect of current reality that is undesirable. With creative tension, the energy for change comes from the vision, from what we want to create, juxtaposed with current reality. While the distinction may seem small, the consequences are not. Many people and organizations find themselves motivated to change only when their problems are bad enough to cause them to change. This works for a while, but the change process runs out of steam as soon as the problems driving the change become less pressing. Without problem solving, the motivation for change is extrinsic. With creative tension, the motivation is intrinsic. This distinction mirrors the distinction between adaptive and generative learning.

NEW ROLES

The traditional authoritarian image of the leader as 'the boss calling the shots' has been recognized as oversimplified and inadequate for some time. According to Edgar Schein, 'Leadership is intertwined with culture formation.' Building an organization's culture and shaping its evolution is the 'unique and essential function' of leadership.[5] In a learning organization, the critical roles of leadership – designer, teacher, and steward – have antecedents in the ways leaders have contributed to building organizations in the past. But each role takes on a new meaning in the learning organization and, as will be seen in the following sections, demands new skills and tools.

Leader as designer

Imagine that your organization is an ocean liner and that you are 'the leader.' What is your role?

I have asked this question of groups of managers many times. The most common answer, not surprisingly, is 'the captain'. Others say, 'The navigator, setting the direction.' Still others say, 'The helmsman, actually controlling the direction,' or, 'The engineer down there stoking the fire, providing energy,' or, 'The social director, making sure everybody's enrolled, involved, and communicating.' While these are legitimate leadership roles, there is another which, in many ways, eclipses them all in importance. Yet rarely does anyone mention it.

The neglected leadership role is the designer of the ship. No one has more sweeping influence than the designer. What good does it do for the captain to say, 'Turn starboard 30 degrees' when the designer has built a rudder that will only turn to port, or which takes six hours to turn to starboard? It's fruitless to be the leader in an organization that is poorly designed.

The functions of design, or what some have called 'social architecture', are rarely visible; they take place behind the scenes. The consequences that appear today are the result of work done long in the past, and work today will show its benefits far in the future. Those who aspire to lead out of a desire to control, or gain fame, or simply to be at the center of the action, will find little to attract them to the quiet design work of leadership.

But what, specifically, is involved in organizational design 'Organization design is widely misconstrued as moving around boxes and lines,' says Hanover's O'Brien. 'The first task of organization design concerns designing the governing ideas of purpose, vision, and core values by which people will live.' Few acts of leadership have a more enduring impact on an organization than building a foundation of purpose and core values.

In 1982, Johnson & Johnson found itself facing a corporate nightmare when bottles of its best-selling Tylenol were tampered with, resulting in several deaths. The corporation's immediate response was to pull all Tylenol off the shelves of retail outlets. Thirty-one million capsules were destroyed, even though they were tested and found safe. Although the immediate cost was significant, no other action was possible given the firm's credo. Authored almost forty years earlier by president Robert Wood Johnson, Johnson & Johnson's Credo states that permanent success is possible only when modern industry realizes that:

- service to its customers comes first;
- service to its employees and management comes second;
- service to its stockholders, last.

Such statements might seem like motherhood and apple pie to those who have not seen the way a clear sense of purpose and values can affect key business decisions. Johnson & Johnson's crisis management in this case was based on that credo. It was simple, it was right, and it worked.

If governing ideas constitute the first design task of leadership, the second design task involves the policies, strategies, and structures that translate guiding ideas into business decisions. Leadership theorist Philip Selznick calls policy and structure the 'institutional embodiment of purpose.'[6] 'Policy making (the rules that guide decisions) ought to be separated from decision making,' says Jay Forrester.[7] 'Otherwise, short-term pressures will usurp time from policy creation.'

Traditionally, writers like Selznick and Forrester have tended to see policy making and implementations as the work of a small number of senior managers. But that view is changing. Both the dynamic business environment and the mandate of the learning organization to engage people at all levels now make it clear that this second design task is more subtle. Henry Mintzberg has argued that strategy is less a rational plan arrived at in the abstract and implemented throughout the organization than an 'emergent phenomenon'. Successful organizations 'craft strategy' according to Mintzberg, as they continually learn about shifting business conditions and balance what is desired and what is possible.[8] The key is not getting the right strategy but fostering strategic thinking. 'The choice of individual action is only part of ... the policy maker's need,' according to Mason and Mitroff.[9] "More important is the need to achieve insight into the nature of the complexity and to formulate concepts and world views for coping with it."

Behind appropriate policies, strategies, and structures are effective learning processes; their creation is the third key design responsibility in learning organizations. This does not absolve senior managers of their strategic responsibilities. Actually, it deepens and extends those responsibilities. Now, they are not only responsible for ensuring that an organization has well-developed strategies and policies, but also for ensuring that processes exist whereby these are continually improved.

Leader as teacher

'The first responsibility of a leader' writes retired Herman Miller CEO Max de Pree, 'is to define reality.'[10] Much of the leverage leaders can actually exert lies in helping people achieve more accurate, more insightful and more empowering views of reality.

Leader as teacher does not mean leader as authoritarian expert whose job it is to teach people the 'correct' view of reality. Rather, it is about helping everyone in the organization, oneself included, to gain more insightful views of current reality. This is in line with a popular emerging view of leaders as coaches, guides, or facilitators.[11] In learning organizations, this teaching role is developed further by virtue of explicit attention to people's mental models and by the influence of the systems perspective.

The role of leader as teacher starts with bringing to the surface people's mental models as important issues. No one carries an organization, a market, or a state of technology in his or her head. What we carry in our heads are assumptions. These mental pictures of how the world works have a significant influence on how we perceive problems and opportunities, identify courses of action, and make choices.

One reason that mental models are so deeply entrenched is that they are largely tacit. Ian Mitroff, in his study of General Motors, argues that an assumption that prevailed for years was that, in the United States, 'Cars are status symbols. Styling is therefore more important than quality.'[12] The Detroit automakers didn't say, 'We have a *mental model* that all people care about is styling.' Few actual managers would even say publicly that all people care about is styling. So long as the view remain unexpressed, there was little possibility of challenging its validity or forming more accurate assumptions.

But working with mental models goes beyond revealing hidden assumptions. 'Reality,' as perceived by most people in most organizations, means pressures that must be borne, crises that must be reacted to, and limitations that must be accepted. Leaders as teachers help people restructure their views of reality to see beyond the superficial conditions and events into the underlying causes of problems – and therefore to see new possibilities for shaping the future.

Specifically, leaders can influence people to view reality at three distinct levels: events, patterns of behaviour, and systemic structure.

Systemic Structure
(Generative)
⇩
Patterns of Behaviour
(Responsive)
⇩
Events
(Reactive)

The key question becomes where do leaders predominantly focus their own and their organization's attention?

Contemporary society focuses predominantly on events. The media reinforces this perspective, with almost exclusive attention to short-term, dramatic events. This focus leads naturally to explaining what happens in terms of those events: 'The Dow Jones average went up sixteen points because high fourth-quarter profits were announced yesterday.'

Pattern-of-behaviour explanations are rarer, in contemporary culture, than event explanations, but they do occur. 'Trend analysis' is an example of seeing patterns of behaviour. A good editorial that interprets a set of current events in the context of long-term historical changes is another example. Systemic, structural explanations go even further by addressing the question, 'What causes the patterns of behaviour?'

In some sense, all three levels of explanation are equally true. But their usefulness is quite different. Event explanations - who did what to whom – doom their holders to a reactive stance toward change. Pattern-of-behaviour explanations focus on identifying long-term trends and assessing their implications. They at least suggest how, over time, we can respond to shifting conditions. Structural explanations are the most powerful. Only they address the underlying causes of behaviour at a level such that patterns of behaviour can be changed.

By and large, leaders of our current institutions focus their attention on events and patterns of behaviour, and, under their influence, their organizations do likewise. That is why contemporary organizations are predominantly reactive, or at best responsive – rarely generative. On the other hand, leaders in learning organizations pay attention to all three levels, but focus especially on systemic structure; largely by example, they teach people throughout the organization to do likewise.

Leader as steward

This is the subtlest role of leadership. Unlike the roles of designer and teacher, it is almost solely a matter of attitude. It is an attitude critical to learning organizations.

While stewardship has long been recognized as an aspect of leadership, its source is still not widely understood. I believe Robert Greenleaf came closest to explaining real stewardship, in his seminal book *Servant Leadership*.[13] There, Greenleaf argues that 'The servant leader *is* servant first ... It begins with the natural feeling that one wants to serve, to serve *first*. This conscious choice brings one to aspire to lead. That person is sharply different from one who is leader first, perhaps because of the need to assuage an unusual power drive or to acquire material possessions.'

Leaders' sense of stewardship operates on two levels: stewardship for the people they lead and stewardship for the larger purpose or mission that underlies the enterprise. The first type arises from a keen appreciation of the impact one's leadership can have on others. People can suffer economically, emotionally, and spiritually under inept leadership. If anything, people in a learning organization are more vulnerable because of their commitment and sense of shared ownership. Appreciating this naturally instils a sense of responsibility in leaders. The second type of stewardship arises from a leader's sense of personal purpose and commitment to the organization's larger mission. People's natural impulse to learn is unleashed when they are engaged in an endeavor they consider worthy of their fullest commitment. Or, as Lawrence Miller puts it, 'Achieving return on equity does not, as a goal, mobilize the most noble forces of our soul.'[14]

NEW SKILLS

New leadership roles require new leadership skills. These skills can only be developed, in my judgement, through a lifelong commitment. It is not enough for one or two individuals to develop these skills. They must be distributed widely throughout the organization. This is one reason that understanding the disciplines of a learning organization is so important. These disciplines embody the principles and practices that can widely foster leadership development.

Three critical areas of skills (disciplines) are building shared vision, surfacing and challenging mental models, and engaging in systems thinking.[15]

Building shared vision

The skills involved in building shared vision include the following:

Encouraging personal vision
Shared visions emerge from personal visions. It is not that people only care about their own self-interest – in fact, people's values usually include dimensions that concern family, organization, community, and even the world. Rather, it is that people's capacity for caring is personal.

Communicating and asking for support
Leaders must be willing to continually share their own vision, rather than being the official representative of the corporate vision. They also must be prepared to ask, 'Is this vision worthy of your commitment?' This can be difficult for a person used to setting goals and presuming compliance.

Visioning as an ongoing process

Building shared vision is a never-ending process. At any one point there will be a particular image of the future that is predominant, but that image will evolve. Today, too many managers want to dispense with the 'vision business' by going off and writing the Official Vision statement. Such statements almost always lack the vitality, freshness, and excitement of a genuine vision that comes from people asking, 'What do we really want to achieve?'

Blending extrinsic and intrinsic visions

Many energising visions are extrinsic – that is, they focus on achieving something relative to an outsider, such as a competitor. But a goal that is limited to defeating an opponent can, once the vision is achieved, easily become a defensive posture. In contrast, intrinsic goals like creating a new type of product, taking an established product to a new level, or setting a new standard for customer satisfaction can call forth a new level of creativity and innovation. Intrinsic and extrinsic visions need to coexist; a vision solely predicated on defeating an adversary will eventually weaken an organization.

Distinguishing positive from negative visions

Many organizations only truly pull together when their survival is threatened. Similarly, most social movements aim at eliminating what people don't want: for example, anti-drugs, anti-smoking, or anti-nuclear arms movements. Negative visions carry a subtle message of powerlessness: people will only pull together when there is sufficient threat. Negative visions also tend to be short term. Two fundamental sources of energy can motivate organizations: fear and aspiration. Fear, the energy source behind negative visions, can produce extraordinary changes in short periods, but aspiration endures as a continuing source of learning and growth.

Surfacing and testing mental models

Many of the best ideas in organizations never get put into practice. One reason is that new insights and initiatives often conflict with established mental models. The leadership task of challenging assumptions without invoking defensiveness requires reflection and inquiry skills possessed by few leaders in traditional controlling organizations.[16]

Seeing leaps of abstraction

Our minds literally move at lightning speed. Ironically, this often slows our learning, because we leap to generalizations so quickly that we never think to test them. We then confuse our generalizations with the observable data upon which they are based, treating the generalizations as if they were data. The frustrated sales rep reports to the home office that 'customers don't really care about quality, price is what matters,' when what actually happened was that three consecutive large customers refused to place an order unless a larger discount was offered. The sales rep treats her generalization, 'customers care only about price,' as if it were absolute fact rather than assumption (very likely an assumption reflecting her own views of customers and the market). This thwarts future learning because she starts to focus on how to offer attractive discounts rather than probing behind the customers' statements. For example, the customers may have been so disgruntled with the firms' delivery or customer service that they are unwilling to purchase again without larger discounts.

Balancing inquiry and advocacy

Most managers are skilled at articulating their views and presenting them persuasively. While important, advocacy skills can become counterproductive as managers rise in responsibility and confront increasingly complex issues that require collaborative learning among different, equally knowledgeable people. Leaders in learning organizations need to have both inquiry and advocacy skills.[17]

Specifically, when advocating a view, they need to be able to:

- explain the reasoning and data that led to their view;
- encourage others to test their view (e.g., Do you see gaps in my reasoning? Do you disagree with the data upon which my view is based?);
- encourage others to provide different views (e.g., Do you have either different data, different conclusions, or both?)

When inquiring into another's views, they need to:

- seek actively to understand the other's view, rather than simply restating their own view and how it differs from the other's view;
- make their attributions about the other and the other's view explicit (e.g., Based on your statement that ...; I am assuming that you believe...; Am I representing your views fairly?).

If they reach an impasse (others no longer appear open to inquiry), they need to:

- ask what data or logic might unfreeze the impasses, or if an experiment (or some other inquiry) might be designed to provide new information.

Distinguishing espoused theory from theory in use

We all like to think that we hold certain views, but often our actions reveal deeper views. For example, I may proclaim that people are trustworthy, but never lend friends money and jealously guard my possessions. Obviously, my deeper mental model (my theory in use), differs from my espouse theory. Recognising gaps between espoused views and theories in use (which often requires the help of others) can be pivotal to deeper learning.

Recognising and defusing defensive routines

As one CEO in our research program puts it, 'Nobody ever talks about an issue at the 8:00 business meeting exactly the same way they talk about it at home that evening or over drinks at the end of the day.' The reason is what Chris Argyris calls 'defensive routines', entrenched habits used to protect ourselves from the embarrassment and threat that come with exposing our thinking. For most of us, such defences began to build early in life in response to pressures to have the right answers in school or at home. Organizations add new levels of performance anxiety and thereby amplify and exacerbate this defensiveness. Ironically, this makes it even more difficult to expose hidden mental models, and thereby lessens learning.

The first challenge is to recognize defensive routines, then to inquire into their operation. Those who are best at revealing and defusing defensive routines operate with a high degree of self-disclosure regarding their own defensiveness (e.g., I note that I am feeling uneasy about how this conversation is going. Perhaps I don't understand it or it is threatening me in ways I don't yet see. Can you help me see this better?)

Systems thinking

We all know that leaders should help people see the big picture. But the actual skills whereby leaders are supposed to achieve this are not well understood. In my experience, successful leaders often are 'systems thinkers' to a considerable extent. They focus less on day-to-day events and more on underlying trends and forces of change. But they do this almost completely intuitively. The consequence is that they are often unable to explain their intuitions to others and feel frustrated that others cannot see the world the way we do.

One of the most significant developments in management science today is the gradual coalescence of managerial systems thinking as a field of study practice. This field suggests some key skills for future leaders:

Seeing interrelationships, not things, and processes, not snapshots
Most of us have been conditioned throughout our lives to focus on things and to see the world in static images. This leads us to linear explanations of systemic phenomenon. For instance, in an arms race each party is convinced that the other is the cause of the problems. They react to each new move as an isolated event, not as part of a process. So long as they fail to see the interrelationships of these actions, they are trapped.

Moving beyond blame
We tend to blame each other or outside circumstances for our problems. But it is poorly designed systems, not incompetent or unmotivated individuals, that cause most organizational problems. Systems thinking shows us that there is no outside – that you and the cause of your problems are part of a single system.

Distinguishing detail complexity from dynamic complexity
Some types of complexity are more important strategically than others. Detail complexity arises when there are many variables. Dynamic complexity arises when

the cause and effect are distant in time and space, and when the consequences over time of interventions are subtle and not obvious to many participants in the system. The leverage in most management situations lies in understanding dynamic complexity, not detail complexity

Focusing on areas of high leverage

Some have called systems thinking the 'new dismal science' because it teaches that most obvious solutions don't work – at best, they improve matters in the short run, only to make things worse in the long run. But there is another side to the story. Systems thinking also shows that small, well-focused actions can produce significant, enduring improvements, if they are in the right place. Systems thinkers refer to this idea as the principle of 'leverage.' Tackling a difficult problem is often a matter of seeing where the high leverage lies, where a change – with a minimum of effort – would lead to lasting, significant improvement.

Avoiding symptomatic solutions

The pressures to intervene in management systems that are going awry can be overwhelming. Unfortunately, given the linear thinking that predominates in most organizations, interventions usually focus on symptomatic fixes, not underlying causes. This results in only temporary relief, and it tends to create still more pressures later on for further, low-leverage intervention. If leaders acquiesce to these pressures, they can be sucked into an endless spiral of increasing intervention. Sometimes the most difficult leadership acts are to refrain from intervening through popular quick fixes and to keep the pressure on everyone to identify more enduring solutions.

NEW TOOLS

Developing the skills described above requires new tools – tools that will enhance leaders' conceptual abilities and foster communication and collaborative inquiry. What follows is a sampling of tools starting to find use [sic] in learning organizations.

System archetypes

One of the insights of the budding managerial systems-thinking field is that certain types of systematic structures recur again and again. Countless systems grow for a period, then encounter problems and cease to grow (or even collapse) well before they have reached intrinsic limits to growth. Many other systems get locked in runaway vicious spirals where every actor has to run faster and faster to stay in the same place. Still others lure individual actors into doing what seems right locally, yet which eventually causes suffering for all.[18]

Some of the system archetypes that have the broadest relevance include the following.

Balancing process with delay

In this archetype, decision makers fail to appreciate the time delays involved as they move toward a goal. As a result, they overshoot the goal and may even produce recurring cycles.

Classic example: Real estate developers who keep starting new projects until the market has gone soft, by which time an eventual glut is guaranteed by the properties still under construction.

Limits to growth

A reinforcing cycle of growth grinds to a halt, and may even reverse itself, as limits are approached. The limits can be resource constraints, or external or internal responses to growth.

Classic examples: Product life cycles that peak prematurely due to poor quality or service, the growth and decline of communication in a management team, and the spread of a new movement.

Shifting the burden

A short-term 'solution' is used to correct a problem, with seemingly happy immediate results. As this correction is used more and more, fundamental long-term corrective measures are used less. Over time, the mechanisms of the fundamental solution may atrophy or become disabled, leading to even greater reliance on the symptomatic solution.

Classic example: Using corporate human resource staff to solve local personnel problems, thereby keeping managers from developing their own interpersonal skills.

Eroding goals

When all else fails, lower your standards. This is like 'shifting the burden,' except that the short term solution involves letting a fundamental goal, such as quality standards or employee morale standards, atrophy.

Classic example: A company that responds to delivery problems by continually upping its quoted delivery times.

Escalation

Two people or two organizations, who each see their welfare as depending on a relative advantage over the other, continually react to the other's advances. Whenever one side gets ahead, the other is threatened, leading it to act more aggressively to re-establish its advantage, which threatens the first, and so on.

Classic examples: Arms race, gang warfare, price wars.

Tragedy of the commons[19]

Individuals keep intensifying their use of a commonly available but limited resource until all individuals start to experience severely diminishing returns.

Classic examples: Sheepherders who keep increasing their flocks until they overgraze the common pasture; divisions in a firm that share a common salesforce and compete for the use of sales reps by upping their sales targets, until the salesforce burns out from overextension.

Growth and underinvestment

Rapid growth approaches a limit that could be eliminated or pushed into the future, but only by aggressive investment in physical and human capacity. Eroding goals or standards cause investment that is too weak, or too slow, and customers get increasingly unhappy, slowing demand growth and thereby making the needed investment (apparently) unnecessary or impossible.

Classic examples: Countless once-successful growth firms that allowed product or service quality to erode, and were unable to generate enough revenues to invest in remedies.

Charting strategic dilemmas

Management teams typically come unglued when confronted with core dilemmas. A classic example was the way US manufacturers faced the low cost-high quality choice. For years, most assumed that it was necessary to choose between the two. Not surprisingly, given the short-term pressures perceived by most management, the prevailing choice was low cost. Firms that chose high quality usually perceived themselves as aiming exclusively for a high quality, high price market niche. The consequences of this perceived either/or choice have been disastrous, even fatal, as US manufacturers have encountered increasing international competition from firms that have chosen to consistently improve quality and cost.

In a recent book, Charles Hampden-Turner presented a variety of tools for helping management teams confront strategic dilemmas creatively.[20]

He summarized the process in seven steps.

1 Eliciting the Dilemmas. Identifying the opposed values that form the 'horns' of the dilemma, for example, cost as opposed to quality, or local initiative as opposed to central coordination and control Hampden-Turner suggests that humour can be a distinct asset in this process since 'the admission that dilemmas even exist tends to be difficult for some companies'.
2 Mapping. Locating the opposing values as two axes and helping managers identify where they see themselves, or their organization, along the axes.
3 Processing. Getting rid of nouns to describe the axes of the dilemma. Present particles formed by adding 'ing' convert rigid nouns into processes that imply movement. For example, central control versus local control becomes 'strengthening national office' and 'growing local initiatives'. This loosens the bond of implied opposition between the two values. For example, it becomes possible to think of 'strengthening national services from which local branches can benefit'.
4 Framing/Contextualising. Further softening the adversarial structure among different values by letting 'each side in turn be the frame or context for the

other.' This shifting of the 'figure-ground' relationship undermines any implicit attempts to hold one value as intrinsically superior to the other, and thereby to become mentally closed to creative strategies for continuous improvement of both.

5 Sequencing. Breaking the hold of static thinking. Very often, values like low cost and high quality appear to be in opposition because we think in terms of a point in time, not in terms of an on-going process. For example, a strategy of investing in new process technology and developing a new production-floor culture of worker responsibility may take time and money in the near term, yet reap significant long-term financial rewards.

6 Waving/Cycling. Sometimes the strategic path toward improving both values involves cycles where both values will get 'worse' for a time. Yet, at a deeper level, learning is occurring that will cause the next cycle to be at a higher plateau for both values.

7 Synergising. Achieving synergy where significant improvement is occurring along all axes of all relevant dilemmas. (This is the ultimate goal, of course.) Synergy, as Hampden-Turner points out, is a uniquely systemic notion, coming from the Greek *syn-ergo* or 'work together.'

DEVELOPING LEADERS AND LEARNING ORGANIZATIONS

In a recently published retrospective on organization development in the 1980s, Marshall Sashkin and W. Warner Burke observe the return of an emphasis on developing leaders who can develop organizations.[21] They also note Schein's critique that most top executives are not qualified for the task of developing culture.[22] Learning organizations represent a potentially significant evolution of organizational culture. So it should come as no surprise that such organizations will remain a distant vision until the leadership capabilities they demand are developed. 'The 1990s may be the period,' suggest Sashkin and Burke, 'during which organization development and (a new sort of) management development are reconnected.'

I believe that this new sort of management development will focus on the roles, skills, and tools for leadership in learning organizations. Undoubtedly, the ideas offered above are only a rough approximation of this new territory. The sooner we begin seriously exploring the territory, the sooner the initial map can be improved – and the sooner we will realize an age-old vision of leadership:

The wicked leader is he who the people despise.
The good leader is he who the people revere.
The great leader is he who the people say,
'We did it ourselves.'

NOTES

1 B. Domain, *Fortune*, 3 July 1989, pp. 48–62

2 The distinction between adaptive and generative learning has its roots in the distinction between what Argyris and Schön have called their 'single-loop' learning, in which individuals or groups adjust their behaviour relative to fixed goals, norms, and assumptions, and 'double-loop' learning, in which goals, norms, assumptions, as well as behaviour, are open to change (e.g. see C. Argyris and D. Schön, *Organizational Learning: A Theory-in-Action Perspective* (Reading, Massachusetts: Addison-Wesley, 1978).

3 The principle of creative tension comes from Robert Fritz' work on creativity. See R. Fritz, *The Path of Least Resistance* (New York: Ballantine, 1989) and *Creating* (New York: Ballantine, 1990).

4 M. L. King, Jr., 'Letter from Birmingham Jail', *American Visions*, January–February 1986, pp. 52–9.

5 E. Schein, *Organizational Culture and Leadership* (San Francisco: Jossey, 1985). Similar views have been expressed by many leadership theorists. For example, see: P. Selznick, *Leadership in Administration* (New York: Harper W. Bennis and B. Nanus, *Leaders* (New York: Harper and N. M. Tichy and M. A. Devanna, *The Transformational Leader* (New York: John Wiley & Sons, 1986).

6 Selznick (1957).

7 J.W. Forrester, 'A new corporate design,' *Sloan Management Review* (formerly *Industrial Management Review*), Fall 1965, pp. 5–17.

8 See, for example, H. Mintzberg, 'Crafting strategy,' *Harvard Business Review*, July–August 1987, pp. 66–75.

9 R. Mason and I. Mitroff, *Challenging Strategic Planning Assumptions* (New York: John Wiley & Sons, 1987), p. 16.

10 M. de Pree, *Leadership is an Art* (New York: Doubleday, 1989) p. 9.

11 For example, see T. Peters and N. Austin, *A Passion for Excellence* (New York: Random House, 1985) and J. M. Kouzes and B. Z. Posner, *The Leadership Challenge* (San Francisco: Jossey-Bass, 1987).

12 I. Mitroff, *Break-Away Thinking* (New York: John Wiley 7.

13 R.K.Greenleaf, *Servant Leadership:A Journey into the Nature of Legitimate Power and Greatness* (New York: Paulist Press, 1977).

14 L.Miller, *American Spirit: Visions of a New Corporate Culture* (New York: William Morrow, 1984), p. 15.

15 These points are condensed from the practices of the five disciplines examined in Senge (1990).

16 The ideas below are based to a considerable extent on the work of Chris Argyris, Donald Schon, and their Action Science colleagues: C. Argyris and D. Schon, *Organizational Learning: A Theory-in-Action Perspective* (Reading, Massachusetts: Addion-Wesley, 1978); C. Argyris, R. Putnam, and D. Smith, *Action Science* (San Francisco: Jossey-Bass, 1985); C. Argyris, *Strategy, Change, and Defensive Routines* (Boston: Pitman, 1985); and C.Argyris, *Overcoming Organizational Defenses* (Englewood Cliffs, New Jersey: Prentice-Hall, 1990).

17 I am indebted to Diana Smith for the summary points below.

18 The system archetypes are one of several systems diagramming and communication tools. See D.H. Kim, 'Toward learning organizations: integrating total quality control and systems thinking' (Cambridge, Massachusetts: MIT Sloan School of Management, Working Paper No. 3037-89-BPS, June 1989).

19 This archetype is closely associated with the work of ecologist Garrett Hardin, who coined its label: G. Hardin, 'The tragedy of the commons,' *Science,* 13 December 1968.

20 C. Hampden-Turner, *Charting the Corporate Mind* (New York: The Free PRess, 1990).

21 M. Sashkin and W. W. Burke, 'Organization development in the 1980s' and 'An end-of-the-eighties retrospective,' in *Advances in Organization Development,* ed. F. Masarik (Norwood, New Jersey: Ablex, 1990).

22 E. Schein (1985).

CHAPTER 16

STRATEGY: A COGNITIVE PERSPECTIVE

KEVIN DANIELS AND JANE HENRY

INTRODUCTION

During the process of formulating strategy, consultants and academics often advise managers to undertake thorough, rational and objective analysis of the industrial or institutionalized environment, competitors, organizational strengths and organizational weaknesses (Hofer and Schendel, 1978). Such analyses can be useful, but they are limited in that the information gathered is rarely sufficient for the needs of managers and is very often ambiguous. In addition, in so far as strategy involves conflicting interests, the formation and implementation of strategy are political, as well as analytic exercises (Allison, 1971). The picture emerges of the strategist inferring patterns from incomplete information and making judgements about which information to ignore, whilst balancing the concerns of different stakeholder groups. The practice of strategy requires judgement, as well as analysis.

To understand more fully how managers use information gathered from strategic analyses and their own knowledge, some writers on strategic management have adopted a cognitive perspective upon strategic management (Walsh, 1995). Roughly speaking, 'cognition' is a term that refers to the mental processes of perception, attention, memory, learning, problem-solving and decision-making (Eysenck and Kean, 1990). This chapter applies these processes to strategic management. We begin with a discussion of the two ways in which we process information and introduce the concept of 'mental models' as the main method by which strategists interpret strategic information and hence take strategic decisions. We then explain the biases that can affect the way managers process information, some of the sources of strategic knowledge, how managers learn, how managers develop 'insight' and how their habitual cognitive style affects information processing. Finally, we offer a diagnostic tool with which managers can attempt to tailor their own cognitive processes to meet the demands of strategic decision-making in any situation.

TWO MODES OF HUMAN INFORMATION PROCESSING

At any given time, we can only pay attention to a limited amount of information. The manager involved in making strategy is constrained in being able to attend only to some information when taking decisions. Moreover, strategists also have to make sense of this ambiguous, conflicting and complex strategic information. To do this, they must rely on experience and learning to help them select the most relevant information to attend to and to interpret this information. Therefore, strategists not only use information from the environment, but also their memory when taking decisions. These two types of information processing that characterize strategic thought are known as 'bottom-up' processing and 'top-down' processing (Walsh, 1995). Bottom-up processing is 'information-driven'. For example, in a management situation, the manager would examine all the available information from strategic analyses, bit by bit, consider all possibilities and make a decision based upon detailed consideration. The problem with pure bottom-up processing is that it takes a long time, because our attention span is limited.

In all but the most novel situations, people make use of top-down information processing. Top-down information processing is 'theory-driven'. People derive their own theories of how the world works from their own knowledge, accumulated through learning and experience. These theories are simplified, generalized and abstract representations and go under many names; here we shall use the title 'mental models' (after Johnson-Laird, 1989). People develop their mental models through a set of organizing principles that group associated concepts together. Mental models can contain knowledge that provides categories or labels (e.g. 'Elko is our major European competitor'), or describes processes (e.g. 'To become a major European competitor, it is necessary to provide a full range or products'). When managers are confronted with a situation, they simply recall the mental models that seem most appropriate to that situation at that time. Once recalled, the mental model then helps to identify which information is most important for the task at hand, eventually influencing subsequent behaviour. For instance, mental models may influence subsequent predictions about future events, decision-making and communication (Rips, 1975; Anderson, 1991; Cherniak, 1984; Edwards, 1991).

A mental model does not have to be in the conscious mind to influence subsequent cognition and behaviour. In some instances, recall may be entirely unconscious: managers may apply a mental model to a situation without being aware of it (Dutton, 1993). People really synthesize mental models, rather than simply recalling them from memory: They recall several generalized and abstracted mental models and combine them in new ways to be relevant to the given context (Barsalou, 1982). For example, in responding to a competitor's new advertising campaign, a manager may recall knowledge about that competitor's marketing strengths and weaknesses, synthesising this with knowledge about his or her own company's marketing strengths and weaknesses to form a mental model to help guide information-search and decision-making.

The manner in which mental models are constructed and how they help guide attention during the process of strategic thinking are illustrated in Figure 16.1 (cf. Anderson, 1983). The most important part of the model shown in Figure 16.1 is that part of memory called *working memory*. Working memory is connected to both attention and to long-term memory, and it is working memory that stores the information and knowledge eventually used in taking strategic decisions. Working memory is a dynamic system, in which the exact contents are constantly changing; but it is also a system with a very limited capacity (Miller, 1956). Figure 16.1 shows that during top-down processing, mental models are constructed in working memory by synthesising knowledge stored in longer-term memory. These mental models then influence which information from the environment is attended to, ultimately influencing which knowledge and information is held in working memory when decisions are taken. During pure bottom-up processing, information that has been attended to is let into working memory, and decisions are made on that information alone.

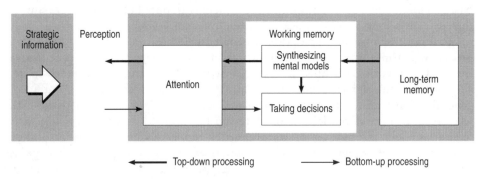

Figure 16.1 The process of strategic thinking

Top-down and bottom-up processing are not mutually exclusive; in any situation both modes of information processing are likely to operate to a greater or lesser degree. However, in any managerial situation, top-down processing is likely to predominate (Walsh, 1995) for many reasons, two of which are: (a) top-down processing is quick: (b) top-down processing can help fill information gaps which are so common in strategic analysis; (managers infer what the missing information is likely to be from their mental models).

BIASES IN COGNITION

The way in which strategists process information can, in some instances, be biased. Such bias can lead to inappropriate decisions being taken, which in extreme circumstances can lead to organizational break down. Most typically, these biases are concerned with top-down information processing, although not always. One common bias is known as 'confirmation bias' (Mynatt, Doherty and Tweney,

1977). This occurs when managers are too sure of the accuracy of their mental models, and thus ignore or misinterpret information that is not consistent with their mental models (Johnson, 1988). The danger of confirmation bias may be great when industry and organizational environments have changed, but the cognitive processes of managers have not (Reger and Palmer, in press). Similar to the problem of confirmation bias is a problem known as 'anchoring' (Tversky and Kahneman, 1974). Anchoring occurs when managers revise their mental models, but not sufficiently. For example, a strategist may predict that an adopted strategy may lead to an increase in market share by 10%. When the strategist notices some information that suggests the adopted strategy may increase market share by only 2%, the strategist may revise the initial estimate downwards, but only to 7%. In this case, a strategy could be adopted on the basis of over-optimistic predictions about its success.

Tversky and Kahneman (1974) studied two other cognitive biases, known as the 'representativeness heuristic' and the 'availability heuristic'. The representativeness heuristic occurs when managers do not have enough information about an important issue, so they infer that information by constructing mental models based on knowledge of similar issues. For example, a manager may attempt to make a prediction about the behaviour of a new entrant to the industry. Having little information about this new competitor, the manager guesses that this organization will behave like organizations with similar characteristics (e.g. of the same nationality, technology base, size or distribution channels). In this case, the problem is that the new competitor does not have to behave like similar organizations. Similarly, the availability heuristic can lead to inappropriate decisions, since managers may act on knowledge that is easily recalled, rather than knowledge that is necessarily relevant. For example, a competitor's new marketing campaign may have attracted some attention; however, the strategist easily recalls that the competitor's last marketing campaign was a complete disaster – leading the strategist to conclude that the competitor has few marketing strengths. The strategist therefore decides that his or her company does not need to respond to this competitive move. However, the strategist has not recalled that, after the failure of the last marketing campaign, the competitor appointed a new managing director and a new marketing director, both with a history of substantial success.

The emotions of strategists can also lead to cognitive bias (Daniels, in press). Sadness appears to affect the construction of mental models in working memory, in such a way that more negative information is recalled. This may lead to pessimistic predictions about the success of a strategy. In contrast, feeling happy may lead to over-optimistic predictions, since more positive information is recalled. People who feel anxious tend to focus their attention on threatening information, which may again lead to over-pessimistic predictions of the success of a strategy. The emotions of strategists can effect the information they attend to and the knowledge they recall, both affecting the eventual choice of strategy.

SOURCES OF MANAGERIAL KNOWLEDGE: THE ROLE OF STRATEGIC FRAMES

Since many managers have only limited individual experience of all the strategic possibilities that may confront an organization, they can draw upon collective knowledge as well as individual experience in constructing mental models of strategic issues. This collective knowledge is based on the experiences and beliefs of individual managers that are communicated to other managers through, for example, interacting with them in the same organization or industry, or by reading trade journals. Therefore, strategists do not just rely on their own experiences in constructing their mental models – they will also recall articles they have read or conversations they have had with other managers, and use the knowledge gained from these sources.

Huff (1982) has used the term 'strategic frame' to describe collective knowledge in a strategic management context: strategic frames are the common beliefs and knowledge of managers from similar backgrounds. She suggested that strategists draw upon multiple strategic frames in constructing mental models of strategic issues – the strategic frames that strategists draw upon are influenced by their backgrounds. There may be shared strategic frames within national cultures (Hughes *et al.*, in press), within industries (Spender, 1989), within organizations (Daniels, *et al.*, 1994), within the same management levels (Ireland *et al.*, 1987) and within professional groups or managers with the same functional background (Hodgkinson and Johnson, 1994; Bowman and Daniels, 1995).

Therefore, managers may draw upon a wide range of individual and collective knowledge in constructing their mental models during the processes of strategy formation. However, differences in individual knowledge and the strategic frames used to construct mental models mean that members of a senior management team can hold very different mental models of the correct course of strategic action. Whilst this may prevent some of the biases outlined above, since divergent perspectives are debated, it may also lead to conflict within the senior management team, as agreement may be hard to achieve. Also, middle managers may draw upon different strategic frames when interpreting a strategy, thus leading to divergence in how the strategy is implemented in different parts of the organization.

BREAKING FREE OF THE 'COGNITIVE' PAST: LEARNING AND INSIGHT

While the previous discussion might imply that managers are slaves to their individual and collective knowledge, we are not dependent upon our mental models in every circumstance, for a number of reasons. One is that managers use bottom-up as well as top-down processing; current context is important as well as recalled mental models. Perhaps the most important reason is that we are capable of both learning new information to increase our knowledge and restructuring our current knowledge to adapt or radically change our mental models.

Numerous studies have demonstrated that learning is an active process: learners assimilate information in terms of their existing mental models. Thus, the information gleaned from the same meeting is likely to be very different for different individuals. It will also be stored and accessed in different ways, since recall involves reconstructing mental models anew each time, as shown in Figure 16.1. Kolb (1985) developed a theory of learning which emphasizes the active involvement of the learner. He conceived of learning as comprising a series of stages: experiencing a situation, making observations and reflecting on that experience, abstracting elements of the situation to form mental models about what went on and generalising from these, then testing out the implications of these models in new situations.

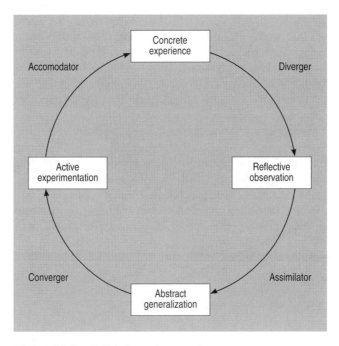

Figure 16.2 Kolb's learning cycle

Historically, much management thinking, especially the rational school that emphasizes strategic planning, has focused around analysing independent elements – the type of thinking highlighted in the lower half of Kolb's learning cycle shown in Figure 16.2. The thinking skills relating to perceiving interdependent relationships highlighted in the upper half of this figure have been neglected, but the increasing pace of change, which necessitates procedures suitable for decision making under uncertainty, is now giving them more prominence (Henry, 1993).

There is considerable evidence that people prefer particular cognitive styles, with the implication that most individuals are more comfortable with some approaches to thinking and learning than others. Kolb proposes that learning style is based on two dimensions – a tendency to be active or reflective, and a tendency to be preoccupied by concrete or abstract issues. These create four learning styles – the *Diverger, Assimilator, Converger* and *Accommodator*. These categories reflect style, not ability, as all styles have their strengths and weaknesses. As shown in Figure 16.2, people with a preference for reflection and experience (as opposed to action and abstraction) are Divergers. Divergers are imaginative, understand people and recognize problems, but can be paralysed by alternatives. People with a preference for reflection and abstraction are Assimilators. Assimilators are good planners, like to define problems and develop models, but their models may have no practical application. Those with a preference for action and abstract generalization are Convergers. Convergers are good at making decisions and solving problems but may make hasty decisions and solve the wrong problem. Those with a preference for action and experience are Accommodators. Accommodators are good at taking risks and getting things done but can get caught up in an endless round of trivial activities. The distribution of favoured learning styles varies across professions. For example, Kolb (1985) finds personnel staff are more likely to have a Diverger style, researchers to be assimilators, marketing executives to favour accommodation, and engineers prefer the Converger style.

Our mental models can change through 'insight', as well as through learning. Insight occurs where you become aware of a solution without being aware of the steps you took to reach the solution. Insight often involves reframing or seeing the problem in a new way. This generally involves reconceputalising a problem – developing a new mental model. A classic insight problem is the 'nine dot problem'. See if you can join up the nine dots in Figure 16.3 with four straight lines without taking your pen off the paper. The answer is given at the end of this chapter.

Figure 16.3 The nine dot problem

Most adults unfamiliar with this problem cannot solve it, since they assume the lines must be within a square frame bounded by the dots. No such assumption or boundary is specified in the problem statement. Here, as in real life, we define the limits of the problem incorrectly. Creativity techniques are often designed to help people break out of this type of restrictive mental model (Henry and Martin, 1993).

Insight is about making a correct judgement without conscious awareness. This is not the province of a chosen few but a common process in everyday cognitive function. The popular conception of insight (after Koestler, 1970; de Bono, 1972) is that insight arises through associating ideas from different fields. Sternberg (1985) has offered a more sophisticated version suggesting that there are three kinds of insight involving 'selective encoding', 'selective comparison' and 'selective combination' – all three of which are important in strategic thinking. Insight based on selective encoding involves distinguishing relevant from irrelevant information or problems (for example, Spencer's discovery of the use of microwaves for heating). Selective comparison involves applying new related information through analogy, for example Kekule's dream of a snake biting its tail acted as a parallel for the chemical structure of the benzene ring. Selective combination involves combining existing information from diverse areas, as Darwin did with the theory of evolution. Insight can be wrong and needs to be verified. Though 40 years of rational thought failed to produce a plausible structure for benzene until Kekule's insight, it took another 70 years to verify how this structure could be stable!

Studies of insightful people have suggested that relevant experience is at least as important as mental flexibility. Experts demonstrate more insight than novices in their domains of expertise, suggesting that years of practice have enabled them to organize their knowledge base in a more sophisticated manner, so as to access key patterns more quickly (Simon, 1988; Perkins, 1981). It is interesting that many of the leaders who have managed to turn organizations around have been working in related fields for years. For example, Jan Carlson had gained much experience in the travel industry before transforming SAS; Lee Iacocca had worked in the car industry for years before he played his part in Chrysler's renewal; and Sir John Harvey-Jones' industrial career had been solely with ICI, before he was widely credited with ICI's regeneration.

COGNITIVE STYLE

In addition to preferred ways of learning, people have relatively enduring preferences for particular ways of thinking. Kirton's (1987) theory of *Adaptation–Innovation* offers a theory of differences in creativity, problem-solving and decision-making. Kirton proposes that everyone can be located on a continuum from the highly adaptive to the highly innovative. High adapters are characterized by a preference for doing things better, building on existing frameworks and favouring conventional approaches. Innovators are characterized by a preference for doing things differently, stepping outside the problem frame and using new approaches. Each differs in their preferred problem-solving style, with adaptors tending to prefer familiar problems and to search within a limited area, and innovators preferring to work with novel situations and gather ideas from many areas. In consequence, those with an adaptive preference tend to offer a fuller account of one or two possible solutions whereas innovators may present many less well-worked-out solutions. Innovators often find it hard to attend to detail and can be seen as abrasive. Adaptors tend to be cautious, but work well in teams. Organizations tend to favour the adaptive approach. Interestingly, Kirton sees these tendencies as relative, so someone who does not have a particularly strong preference for adaptation or innovation, will be perceived as innovative by a high adaptor and adaptive by a high innovator.

Though people prefer a particular cognitive style, they learn to cope and think in ways other than their preferred style. However, it is stressful to behave in ways other than your preferred style over a long period. Kirton and others also suggest that people tend to revert to their natural style under pressure.

Different occupations tend to have different profiles of adaptors and innovators. For example, bank managers and accountants tend to be more adaptive than engineers, who, on average, are neither strongly adaptive nor innovative. Marketing and finance managers tend to be more innovative. Kirton suggests that those whose style is very different from the group norm are more likely to leave than those with similar styles. He also indicates that people whose styles are very different will have difficulty communicating with each other. For example, extreme innovators will have difficulty communicating with adaptors, and *vice versa*. Despite this, research suggests groups containing people with a mix of cognitive styles produce better solutions than those containing people with similar cognitive styles (Belbin, 1981).

CONCLUSION: A MATRIX FOR STRATEGIC ISSUE DIAGNOSIS

Up to this point, we have discussed the nature of managerial thought – the role of bottom-up and top-down processing, the nature of mental models, cognitive biases, strategic frames, learning, insight and cognitive style. How can we apply this to strategy? Consider a manager who must diagnose a strategic situation. The context within which the manager must make the diagnosis varies along two dimensions; the required speed of diagnosis (quick vs. slow) and the stability of the environment. Figure 16.4 shows these decision contexts in the form of a matrix.

Figure 16.4 shows that there are four contingencies: the type of strategic thinking that is most appropriate in each context labels each contingency. In the first box, the manager is 'safe'; rigorous analysis and bottom-up processing in a static and predictable environment help to ensure the 'correct' diagnosis. Managers with an 'adaptor' style of thinking are suited to strategy-forming in this type of environment, one which allows steady improvement on existing strategies, without fundamentally rethinking them.

The second box is also relatively 'safe' for strategists. In this case, the knowledge of the manager (derived from personal experiences), learning and strategic frames are used to make the correct diagnosis. Since the diagnosis is made on the basis of mental models, rather than bottom-up processing, the strategist runs the risk of committing errors caused by the cognitive biases outlined earlier – a particular problem for people with a 'converger' style who like to make fast decisions. Here

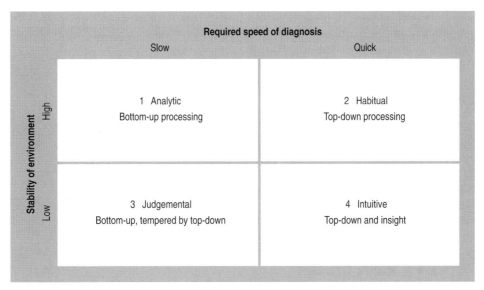

Figure 16.4 Decision matrix

the strategist must make sure he or she is drawing upon the right knowledge. Discussions with colleagues, drawing upon knowledge that complements the individual manager's own knowledge, may help to prevent these biases.

In the third box, the environment is not amenable to finding the 'right' answer through the application of planning systems; the strategist must decide the worth of the messy data by drawing upon personal and collective knowledge through strategic frames. In this situation, the strategist may draw upon knowledge that is inappropriate, leading to an erroneous diagnosis. Here too, cognitive bias is a danger and may be avoided through discussions with colleagues. However, the situation allows enough time to experiment with different scenarios based upon different configurations of knowledge.

In the fourth box, planning systems are of little use – the strategic environment changes too quickly and/or the data from strategic analyses are poor quality. Moreover, because the environment changes so quickly, managers' mental models are soon out of date: the manager who relies purely on mental models runs the risk of incorrect diagnosis. Perhaps the correct diagnosis will come from chance or insight. To increase the chances of making the correct diagnosis, strategists must increase their chances of creating insight. They must be able to connect different pieces of knowledge in completely new mental models. One way to do this is to leave the everyday surroundings that may influence the way we think. (This may explain the popularity of strategic retreats.) Another way is to use external consultants to facilitate discussions, to point out connections that have previously been ignored, or to challenge assumptions that have remained unquestioned. People who favour a Diverger style of learning may be suited to this context, since the situation requires imagination – although there is a danger Divergers may suggest many possible solutions but fail to develop them in sufficient detail or to decide between them. Managers with an Innovator style of thinking also may be particularly suited to strategy formation in these conditions, since the conditions demand complete rethinking of strategy.

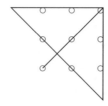

Figure 16.5 Solution to the nine dot problem

REFERENCES

Allison, G.T. (1971) *Essence of Decision: explaining the Cuban Missile Crisis*, Little Brown and Company, New York.

Anderson, J.R. (1991) *The Adaptive Character of Thought*, Erlbaum, Hillsdale NJ.

Anderson, J.R. (1983) *The Architecture of Cognition*, Harvard University Press, Cambridge, MA.

Barsalou, L.W. (1982) 'Context-independent and context-dependent information in concepts', *Memory and Cognition,* Vol. 10, pp. 397–418.

Belbin, R.M. (1981) *The Management Teams: why they succeed or fail*, Heinemann, London (reprinted by Butterworth Heinemann, Oxford).

Bowman, C. and Daniels, K. (1995) 'The influence of functional experience on perceptions of strategic priorities' *British Journal of Management*, Vol. 6, pp. 157–67.

Cherniak, C. (1984) 'Prototypical and deductive reasoning', *Journal of Verbal Learning and Verbal Behaviour*, Vol. 23, pp. 625–42.

Daniels, K. (in press) 'The emotional strategist? A discussion of the potential effects of emotion during strategic analysis', *Iconoclastic Papers*, No. 1.

Daniels, K., Johnson, G., de Chernatony, L. (1994) 'Differences in managerial cognitions of competition', *British Journal of Management*, Vol. 5, Special Issue, pp. S21–S29.

de Bono, E. (1972) *Lateral Thinking for Management*, Penguin, Harmondsworth.

Dutton, J.E. (1993) 'Interpretations on automatic: a different view of strategic issue diagnosis', *Journal of Management Studies*, Vol. 30, pp. 339–57.

Edwards, D. (1991) 'Categories are for talking: on the cognitive and discursive bases of categorization', *Theory and Psychology*, Vol. 1, pp. 515–42.

Eysenck, M. and Keane, M.T. (1990) *Cognitive Psychology*, Erlbaum, London.

Henry, J. (1993) 'Creative capability and experiential and experiential learning', in Mulligan, J. and Griffeths, C. (eds), *Empowerment Through Experiential Learning*, Kogan Page, London.

Henry, J. and Martin, J.N. (1993) *Creative Problem Solving Guide*, Open University Press, Buckingham.

Hodgkinson, G.P.and Johnson, G. (1994) 'Exploring the mental models of competitive strategists: the case for a processual approach', *Journal of Management Studies*.

Hofer, C.W. and Schendel, D. (1978) *Strategy Formulation: analytical concepts.* West Publishing Company, St Paul, MN.

Huff, A.S. (1982) 'Industry influences on strategy formulation', *Strategic Management Journal*, Vol. 3, pp. 119–30.

Hughes, P., Asch, R. and Daniels, K. (in press) 'The diversity of individual level managerial mental models of competition', in Eden, C. and Spender, J-C. (eds), *Managerial and Organizational Cognition: new directions in theory, methods and research*, Sage, London.

Ireland, R.D., Hitt, M.A., Bettis, R.A. and Auld de Porras, D. (1987) 'Strategy formulation processes: differences in perception of strength and weaknesses indicators and environmental uncertainty by managerial level', *Strategic Management Journal*, Vol. 8, pp. 469–85.

Johnson, G. (1988) 'Re-thinking incrementalism', *Strategic Management Journal*, Vol. 9, pp. 75–91.

Johnson-Laird, P.N. (1989) 'Mental models', in Posner, M.I. (ed.), *Foundations of Cognitive Science*, MIT Press, Cambridge, MA.

Kirton, M.J. (1987) *Adaptors and Innovators: styles of creativity and problem solving*, Routledge, London.

Koestler, A. (1970) *The Act of Creation*, Pan Books, London.

Kolb, D. (1984) *Experimental Learning*, Prentice-Hall, Englewood Cliffs, NJ.

Miller, G.A. (1956) 'The magic number seven, plus or minus two: some limitations on our capacity for processing information', *Psychological Review*, Vol. 63, pp. 81–97.

Mynatt, C.R., Doherty, M.E. and Tweney, R.D. (1977) 'Confirmation bias in a simulated research environment: an experimental study of scientific inference', *Quarterly Journal of Experimental Psychology*, Vol. 29, pp. 89–95.

Perkins, D.N. (1981) *The Mind's Best Work*, Harvard University Press, Cambridge, MA.

Reger, R.K. and Palmer, T.B. (in press) 'Managerial categorization of competitors: using old maps to navigate new environments' *Organization Science*.

Rips, L.J. (1975) 'Inductive judgements about natural categories' *Journal of Verbal Learning and Verbal Behaviour*, Vol. 14, 665–81.

Simon, H. (1988) 'Understanding creativity and creative management', in Kuhn, R. (ed.), *Handbook for Creative and Innovative Managers*, McGraw-Hill, New York.

Spender, J.-C. (1989) *Industry Recipes: an enquiry into the nature and sources of managerial judgement*, Blackwell, Oxford.

Sternberg, R.J. (1985) *Beyond IQ: a triarchic theory of human intelligence*, Cambridge University Press, Cambridge.

Tversky, A.T. and Kahneman, D. (1974) 'Judgement under uncertainty: heuristics and biases', *Science*, Vol. 185, pp. 1124–31.

Walsh, J.P. (1985) 'Managerial and organizational cognition: notes from a trip down memory lane', *Organization Science*, Vol. 6, pp. 280–321.

PART 5

DEVELOPING CORPORATE AND INTERNATIONAL STRATEGY

INTRODUCTION

The resource-based view of strategy, covered in Part 3, is the basis of competence-based strategy. It marks the beginning of an evolution of strategy theories towards greater integration of positioning, resources, capabilities and learning to create a more holistic theory of the dynamics of strategy. Core competence management is not about cost-based approaches to maximizing economies of scale for individual businesses. These are a necessary, but no longer distinctive, source of advantage. Instead it is about consolidating corporate-wide skills, expertise and technologies, harnessing collective learning, and co-ordinating them into multiple streams of products and services. It is concerned with the potential for synergy in corporations across portfolios of businesses and the problems of achieving its advantages in practice. It is therefore about exploiting economies of scope across the multibusiness units of the corporation.

Many developments both external to the organization (such as shifting or collapsing industry boundaries) or internal (such as a focus on competencies) require radical managerial responses. The following three chapters in Part 5 all deal with ways of managing competencies, synergies and sources of advantage derivable from strategic thinking at a corporate level. In times of internal and external turbulence, a 'wide-angle lens' is needed for managing the resulting organizational paradoxes: centralization combined with decentralization; control with flexibility; focus with responsiveness; standardization with adaptability; each organization attempts its own balance between these conflicting requirements. In their different ways each of these articles is about rethinking accepted principles of management and rethinking the concept of the corporation.

Chapters 17–19 all deal with ways of benefiting from scale, scope, knowledge, innovation and learning. Ghoshal shows us how to apply these concepts to the evaluation of a global strategy for the corporation. Bartlett and Ghoshal show us a new organizational form in which these resources and processes may be more effectively developed and deployed. Segal-Horn shows us their relevance and applicability to the strategies of service organizations. Let me present their ideas a little more fully.

Ghoshal creates a framework which can be used as a 'road map' to guide managers of multinational corporations through their choices for global strategic management. He clarifies what it means to 'manage globally' and sets out options on which decisions about global strategy should be based. Global strategy is much discussed but poorly understood. Ghoshal reminds us that corporations often 'have globalness thrust upon them' by the initiatives of competitors, and their managers may have little grasp themselves of how to manage under these particular industry conditions. His framework is simple to understand, yet a powerful aid to decision-making. He argues that the objectives of a multinational corporation are threefold: 'to achieve efficiency in its current activities; to manage the risk that it assumes in carrying out those activities; and to develop capabilities for internal learning so as to be able to innovate and adapt to future changes'. Effective global strategies enable the corporation to optimize the interactions between these strategic objectives and the means available to multinationals for achieving those objectives.

Three types of tools ('means') are available: exploiting differences in the many national markets in which the corporation operates; scale economy benefits; and synergy (scope economy) benefits arising from the organizational and business unit diversity of the corporation. Managers may use Ghoshal's framework to generate a checklist of factors to consider if attempting to design and manage a global strategy for their own corporation.

The conclusions reached by Bartlett and Ghoshal are that a new model of the organization is emerging: a 'managerial theory of the firm' which will 'illuminate the corporate world *as seen by managers*'. I have put this last phrase in italics since it an important aspect of what Bartlett and Ghoshal are saying: they argue for the corporate world to be seen more 'from the perspective of those within it' in order to better understand the practice of new managerial roles and organizational tasks. Their research has shown that current assumptions concerning organization structure and decision-making processes are different from what is actually evolving in many advanced corporations. They give examples of new structures, systems and processes. They describe an organizational form which has evolved beyond the administrative focus of the multidivisional ('M-form'), which was designed primarily for vertical integration of vertical information-processing and decision-making. Instead, as management attention has shifted towards processes that add value (such as building core competencies) other processes have overtaken administrative functions in importance. These now include the management of flexibility (rather than management as direction and control); the management of integration and co-ordination without which economies of scope are unattainable (the need for horizontal information-processing, not just vertical); and the management of renewal to prevent 'strategic commitment at the cost of organizational adaptability'. Bartlett and Ghoshal emphasize the importance of an organizational context which positively reinforces the individual, without which the 'adaptability' and 'responsiveness' which is the core of the new organizational form cannot be realized.

Strategy research has been dominated by an over-emphasis on manufacturing organizations at the expense of services. Segal-Horn sets out to redress the balance. Many service industries have experienced prolonged and extreme turbulence in recent years. External developments such as technological and regulatory change have created collapsing or 'fuzzy' industry boundaries which have created opportunities for new types of services supported by new types of strategies, structures, systems and processes for service corporations. Segal-Horn explains how service corporations are developing asset structures, resources and potential synergies which parallel those in manufacturing corporations. She shows how the increasing emphasis on large-scale 'back-office' resources and capabilities (such as data-processing by banks, airlines or retail chains) and the search for sources of advantage from 'know-how', information and knowledge management in services have created international service corporations designed to benefit from scale, scope, innovation and learning, in ways which reflect Ghoshal's framework.

CHAPTER 17

GLOBAL STRATEGY: AN ORGANIZING FRAMEWORK

SUMANTRA GHOSHAL

Global strategy has recently emerged as a popular concept among managers of multinational corporations as well as among researchers and students in the field of international management. This paper presents a conceptual framework encompassing a range of different issues relevant to global strategies. The framework provides a basis for organizing existing literature on the topic and for creating a map of the field. Such a map can be useful for teaching and also for guiding future research in this area. The article, however, is primarily directed at managers of multinational corporations, and is aimed at providing them with a basis for relating and synthesizing the different perspectives and prescriptions that are currently available for global strategic management.

Over the past few years the concept of global strategy has taken the world of *multinational corporations* (MNCs) *by storm. Scores of articles in the* Harvard Business Review, Fortune, The Economist *and other popular journals have urged multinationals to 'go global' in their strategies. The topic has clearly captured the attention of MNC managers. Conferences on global strategy, whether organized by the Conference Board in New York,* The Financial Times *in London, or Nomura Securities in Tokyo, have invariably attracted enthusiastic corporate support and sizeable audiences. Even in the relatively slow-moving world of academe the issue of globalization of industries and companies has emerged as a new bandwagon, as manifest in the large number of papers on the topic presented at recent meetings of the Academy of Management, the Academy of International Business and the Strategic Management Society. 'Manage globally' appears to be the latest battlecry in the world of international business.*

MULTIPLE PERSPECTIVES, MANY PRESCRIPTIONS

This enthusiasm notwithstanding, there is a great deal of conceptual ambiguity about what a 'global' strategy really means. As pointed out by Hamel and Prahalad (1985), the distinction among a global industry, a global firm, and a global strategy is somewhat blurred in the literature. According to Hout, Porter and Rudden (1982), a global strategy is appropriate for global industries which are defined as those in which a firm's competitive position in one national market is significantly affected by its competitive position in other national markets. Such interactions between a firm's positions in different markets may arise from scale benefits or from the potential of synergies or sharing of costs and resources across markets. However, as argued by Bartlett (1985), Kogut (1984) and many others, those scale and synergy benefits may often be created by strategic actions of individual firms and may not be 'given' in any *a priori* sense. For some industries, such as aeroframes or aeroengines, the economies of scale may be large enough to make the need for global integration of activities obvious. However, in a large number of cases industries may not be born global but may have globalness thrust upon them by the entrepreneurship of a company such as Yoshida Kagyo KK (YKK) or Procter and Gamble. In such cases the global industry–global strategy link may be more useful for *ex post* explanation of outcomes than for *ex ante* predictions or strategizing.

Further, the concept of a global strategy is not as new as some of the recent authors on the topic have assumed it to be. It was stated quite explicitly about 20 years ago by Perlmutter (1969) when he distinguished between the geocentric, polycentric and ethnocentric approaches to multinational management. The starting point for Perlmutter's categorization scheme was the world-view of a firm, which was seen as the driving force behind its management processes and the way it structured its worldwide activities (see Robinson, 1978 and Rutenberg, 1982 for detailed reviews and expositions). In much of the current literature, in contrast, the focus has been narrowed and the concept of global strategy has been linked almost exclusively with how the firm structures the flow of tasks within its worldwide value-adding system. The more integrated the flow of tasks appears to be, the more global the firm's strategy is assumed to be (e.g. Leontiades, 1984). On the one hand, this focus has led to improved understanding of the fact that different tasks offer different degrees of advantages from global integration and national differentiation and that, optimally, a firm must configure its value chain to obtain the best possible advantages from both (Porter, 1984). But, on the other hand, it has also led to certain dysfunctional simplifications. The complexities of managing large, worldwide organizations have been obscured by creating polar alternatives between centralization and decentralization, or between global and multidomestic strategies (e.g. Hout *et al.*, 1982). Complex management tasks have been seen as composites of simple global and local components. By emphasizing the importance of rationalizing the flow of components and final products within a multinational system, the importance of internal flows of people, technology, information, and values has been de-emphasized.

Differences among authors writing on the topic of global strategy are not limited to concepts and perspectives. Their prescriptions on how to manage globally have also been very different, and often contradictory.

1 Levitt (1983) has argued that effective global strategy is not a bag of many tricks but the successful practice of just one: product standardization. According to him, the core of a global strategy lies in developing a standardized product to be produced and sold the same way throughout the world.

2 According to Hout *et al.* (1982), on the other hand, effective global strategy requires the approach not of a hedgehog, who knows only one trick, but that of a fox, who knows many. Exploiting economies of scale through global volume, taking pre-emptive positions through quick and large investments, and managing interdependently to achieve synergies across different activities are, according to these authors, some of the more important moves that a winning global strategist must muster.

3 Hamel and Prahalad's (1985) prescription for a global strategy contradicts that of Levitt (1983) even more sharply. Instead of a single standardized product, they recommend a broad product portfolio, with many product varieties, so that investments on technologies and distribution channels can be shared. Cross-subsidization across products and markets, and the development of a strong worldwide distribution system, are the two moves that find the pride of place in these authors' views on how to succeed in the game of global chess.

4 If Hout *et al.*'s (1982) global strategist is the heavyweight champion who knocks out opponents with scale and pre-emptive investments, Kogut's (1985b) global strategist is the nimble-footed athlete who wins through flexibility and arbitrage. He creates options so as to turn the uncertainties of an increasingly volatile global economy to his own advantage. Multiple sourcing, production shifting to benefit from changing factor costs and exchange rates, and arbitrage to exploit imperfections in financial and information markets are, according to Kogut, some of the hallmarks of a superior global strategy.

These are only a few of the many prescriptions available to MNC managers about how to build a global strategy for their firms. All these suggestions have been derived from rich and insightful analyses of real-life situations. They are all reasonable and intuitively appealing, but their managerial implications are not easy to reconcile.

THE NEED FOR AN ORGANIZING FRAMEWORK

The difficulty for both practitioners and researchers in dealing with the small but rich literature on global strategies is that there is no organizing framework within which the different perspectives and prescriptions can be assimilated. An unfortunate fact of corporate life is that any particular strategic action is rarely an unmixed blessing. Corporate objectives are multidimensional, and often mutually contradictory. Contrary to received wisdom, it is also usually difficult to prioritize them. Actions to achieve a particular objective often impede another equally important objective. Each of these prescriptions is aimed at achieving certain objectives of a global strategy. An overall framework can be particularly useful in identifying the trade-offs between those objectives and therefore in understanding not only the benefits but also the potential costs associated with the different strategic alternatives.

The objective of this paper is to suggest such an organizing framework which may help managers and academics in formulating the various issues that arise in global strategic management. The underlying premise is that simple categorization schemes such as the distinction between global and multidomestic strategies are not very helpful in understanding the complexities of corporate-level strategy in large multinational corporations. Instead, what may be more useful is to understand what the key strategic objectives of an MNC are, and the tools that it possesses for achieving them. An integrated analysis of the different means and the different ends can help both managers and researchers in formulating, describing, classifying and analysing the content of global strategies. Besides, such a framework can relate academic research, that is often partial, to the totality of real life that managers must deal with.

THE FRAMEWORK: MAPPING MEANS AND ENDS

The proposed framework is shown in Table 17.1. While the specific construct may be new, the conceptual foundation on which it is built is derived from a synthesis of existing literature.

The basic argument is simple. The goals of a multinational – as indeed of any organization – can be classified into three broad categories. The firm must achieve efficiency in its current activities; it must manage the risks that it assumes in carrying out those activities; and it must develop internal learning capabilities so as to be able to innovate and adapt to future changes. Competitive advantage is developed by taking strategic actions that optimize the firm's achievement of these different and, at times conflicting, goals.

A multinational has three sets of tools for developing such competitive advantage. It can exploit the differences in input and output markets among the many countries in which it operates. It can benefit from scale economies in its different activities. It can also exploit synergies or economies of scope that may be available because of the diversity of its activities and organization.

The strategic task of managing globally is to use all three sources of competitive advantage to optimize efficiency, risk and learning simultaneously in a worldwide business. The key to a successful global strategy is to manage the interactions between these different goals and means. That, in essence, is the organizing framework. Viewing the tasks of global strategy this way can be helpful to both

Table 17.1 Global strategy: an organizing framework

	Sources of competitive advantage		
Strategic objectives	*National differences*	*Scale economies*	*Scope economies*
Achieving efficiency in current operations	Benefiting from differences in factor costs – wages and cost of capital	Expanding and exploiting potential scale economies in each activity	Sharing of investments and costs across products, markets and businesses
Managing risks	Managing different kinds of risks arising from market or policy-induced changes in comparative advantages of different countries	Balancing scale with strategic and operational flexibility	Portfolio diversification of risks and creation of options and side-bets
Innovation learning and adaptation	Learning from societal differences in organizational and managerial processes and systems	Benefiting from experience – cost reduction and innovation	Shared learning across organizational components in different products, markets or businesses

managers and academics in a number of ways. For example, it can help managers in generating a comprehensive checklist of factors and issues that must be considered in reviewing different strategic alternatives. Such a checklist can serve as a basis for mapping the overall strategies of their own companies and those of their competitors so as to understand the comparative strengths and vulnerabilities of both. Table 17.1 shows some illustrative examples of factors that must be considered while carrying out such comprehensive strategic audits. Another practical utility of the framework is that it can highlight the contradictions between the different goals and between the different means, and thereby make salient the strategic dilemmas that may otherwise get resolved through omission.

In the next two sections the framework is explained more fully by describing the two dimensions of its construct, *viz.* the strategic objectives of the firm and the sources of competitive advantage available to a multinational corporation. Subsequent sections show how selected articles contribute to the literature and fit within the overall framework. The paper concludes with a brief discussion of the trade-offs that are implicit in some of the more recent prescriptions on global strategic management.

THE GOALS: STRATEGIC OBJECTIVES

Achieving efficiency

A general premise in the literature on strategic management is that the concept of strategy is relevant only when the actions of one firm can affect the actions or performance of another. Firms competing in imperfect markets earn different 'efficiency rents' from the use of their resources (Caves, 1980). The objective of strategy, given this perspective, is to enhance such efficiency rents.

Viewing a firm broadly as an input–output system, the overall efficiency of the firm can be defined as the ratio of the value of its outputs to the costs of all its inputs. It is by maximizing this ratio that the firm obtains the surplus resources required to secure its own future. Thus it differentiates its products to enhance the exchange value of its outputs, and seeks low cost factors to minimize the costs of its inputs. It also tries to enhance the efficiency of its throughput processes by achieving higher scale economies or by finding more efficient production processes.

The field of strategic management is currently dominated by this efficiency perspective. The generic strategies of Porter (1980), different versions of the portfolio model, as well as overall strategic management frameworks such as those proposed by Hofer and Schendel (1978) and Hax and Majluf (1984) are all based on the underlying notion of maximizing efficiency rents of the different resources available to the firm.

In the field of global strategy this efficiency perspective has been reflected in the widespread use of the integration–responsiveness framework originally proposed by Prahalad (1975) and subsequently developed and applied by a number of authors including Doz, Bartlett and Prahalad (1981) and Porter (1984). In essence, the framework is a conceptual lens for visualising the cost advantages of global integration of certain tasks *vis-à-vis* the differentiation benefits of responding to national differences in tastes, industry structures, distribution systems, and government regulations. As suggested by Bartlett (1985), the same framework can be used to understand differences in the benefits of integration and responsiveness at the aggregate level of industries, at the level of individual companies within an industry, or even at the level of different functions within a company (see Figure 17.1, reproduced from Bartlett, 1985). Thus the consumer electronics industry may be characterized by low differentiation benefits and high integration advantages, while the position of the packaged foods industry may be quite the opposite. In the telecommunications switching industry, in contrast, both local and global forces may be strong, while in the automobile industry both may be of moderate and comparable importance.

Within an industry (say, automobile), the strategy of one firm (such as Toyota) may be based on exploiting the advantages of global integration through centralized production and decision-making, while that of another (such as Fiat) may aim at exploiting the benefits of national differentiation by creating integrated and autonomous subsidiaries which can exploit strong links with local stakeholders to defend themselves against more efficient global competitors. Within a firm, research may offer greater efficiency benefits of integration, while sales and service may provide greater differentiation advantages. One can, as illustrated in Figure 17.1, apply the framework to even lower levels of analysis, right down to the level of individual tasks. Based on such analysis, a multinational firm can determine the optimum way to configure its value chain so as to achieve the highest overall efficiency in the use of its resources (Porter, 1984).

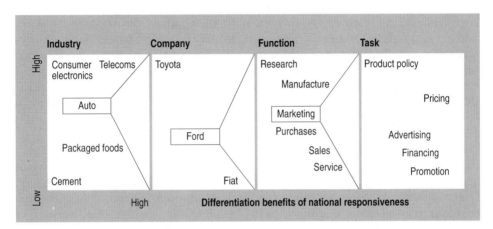

Figure 17.1 The integration–responsiveness framework (reproduced from Bartlett, 1985)

However, while efficiency is clearly an important strategic objective, it is not the only one. As argued recently by a number of authors, the broader objective of strategic management is to create value which is determined not only by the returns that specific assets are expected to generate, but also by the risks that are assumed in the process (see Woo and Cool (1985) for a review). This leads to the second strategic objective of firms – that of managing risk.[1]

Managing risks

A multinational corporation faces many different kinds of risk, some of which are endemic to all firms and some others are unique to organizations operating across national boundaries. For analytical simplicity these different kinds of risks may be collapsed into four broad categories.

First, an MNC faces certain *macro-economic risks* which are completely outside its control. These include cataclysmic events such as wars and natural calamities, and also equilibrium-seeking or even random movements in wage rates, interest rates, exchange rates, commodity prices, and so on.

Second, the MNC faces what is usually referred to in the literature as political risks but may be more appropriately called *policy risks* to emphasize that they arise from policy actions of national governments and not from either long-term equilibrium-seeking forces of global markets, nor from short-term random fluctuations in economic variables arising out of stickiness or unpredictability of market mechanisms. The net effect of such policy actions may often be indistinguishable from the effect of macro-economic forces; for example, both may lead to changes in the exchange rate of a particular currency. But from a management perspective the two must be distinguished, since the former is uncontrollable but the latter is at least partially controllable.

Third, a firm also faces certain *competitive risks* arising from the uncertainties of competitors' responses to its own strategies (including the strategy of doing nothing and trying to maintain the status quo). While all companies face such risks to varying extents (since both monopolies and perfect competition are rare), their implications are particularly complex in the context of global strategies since the responses of competitors may take place in many different forms and in many different markets. Further, technological risk can also be considered as a part of competitive risk since a new technology can adversely affect a firm only when it is adopted by a competitor, and not otherwise.[2]

Finally, a firm also faces what may be called *resource risks*. This is the risk that the adopted strategy will require resources that the firm does not have, cannot acquire, or cannot spare. A key scarce resource for most firms is managerial talent. But resource risks can also arise from lack of appropriate technology, or even capital (if managers, for reasons of control, do not want to use capital markets, or if the market is less efficient than finance theorists would have us believe).

One important issue with regard to risks is that they change over time. Vernon (1977) has highlighted this issue in the context of policy risks, but the same is true of the others. Consider resource risks as an example. Often the strategy of a multinational will assume that appropriate resources will be acquired as the strategy unfolds. Yet the initial conditions on which the plans for ongoing resource acquisition and development have been based may change over time. Nissan, for instance, based its aggressive internationalization strategy on the expectation of developing technological, financial and managerial resources out of its home base. Changing competitive positions among local car manufacturers in Japan have affected these resource development plans of the company, and its internationalizing strategy has been threatened significantly. A more careful analysis of alternative competitive scenarios, and of their effects on the resource allocation plans of the company, may have led Nissan to either a slower pace of internationalization, or to a more aggressive process of resource acquisition at an earlier stage of implementing its strategy.

The strategic task, with regard to management of risks, is to consider these different kinds of risks *jointly* in the context of particular strategic decisions. However, not all forms of risk are strategic since some risks can be easily diversified, shifted, or shared through routine market transactions. It is only those risks which cannot be diversified through a readily available external market that are of concern at the strategic level.

As an example, consider the case of currency risks. These can be classified as contractual, semi-contractual and operating risks (Lessard and Lightstone, 1983). Contractual risks arise when a firm enters into a contract for which costs and revenues are expected to be generated in different currencies: for example a Japanese firm entering into a contract for supplying an item to be made in Japan to an American customer at a price fixed in dollars. Semi-contractual risks are assumed when a firm offers an option denominated in foreign currencies, such as a British company quoting a firm rate in guilders. Operating risks, on the other hand, refer to exchange rate-related changes in the firm's competitiveness arising out of long-term commitments of revenues or costs in different currencies. For example, to compete with a Korean firm, an American firm may set up production facilities in Singapore for supplying its customers in the United States and Europe. A gradual strengthening of the Singapore dollar, in comparison with the Korean won, can erode the overall competitiveness of the Singapore plant.

Both contractual and semi-contractual currency risks can be easily shifted or diversified, at relatively low cost, through various hedging mechanisms. If a firm does not so hedge these risks, it is essentially operating as a currency speculator and the risks must be associated with the speculation business and not to its product-market operations. Operating risks, on the other hand, cannot be hedged so easily,[3] and must be considered at the strategic rather than the operational level.

Analysis of strategic risks will have significant implications for a firm's decisions regarding the structures and locations of its cost and revenue streams. It will lead to more explicit analysis of the effects of environmental uncertainties on the configuration of its value chain. There may be a shift from ownership to rental of resources; from fixed to variable costs. Output and activity distributions may be broadened to achieve the benefits of diversification. Incrementalism and opportunism may be given greater emphasis in its strategy in comparison to pre-emptive resource commitments and long-term planning. Overall strategies may be formulated in more general flexible terms, so as to be robust to different environmental scenarios. In addition, side-bets may be laid to cover contingencies and to create strategic options which may or may not be exercised in the future (see Kogut, 1985b; Aaker and Mascarenhas, 1984; and Mascarenhas, 1982).

Innovation, learning and adaptation

Most existing theories of the multinational corporation view it as an instrument to extract additional rents from capabilities internalized by the firm (see Calvet, 1981, for a review). A firm goes abroad to make more profits by exploiting its technology, or brand name, or management capabilities in different countries around the world. It is assumed that the key competencies of the multinational always reside at the centre.

While the search for additional profits or the desire to protect existing revenues may explain why multinationals come to exist, they may not provide an equally complete explanation of why some of them continue to grow and flourish. An alternative view may well be that a key asset of the multinational is the diversity of environments in which it operates. This diversity exposes it to multiple stimuli, allows it to develop diverse capabilities, and provides it with a broader learning opportunity than is available to a purely domestic firm. The enhanced organizational learning that results from the diversity internalized by the multinational may be a key explanator of its ongoing success, while its initial stock of knowledge may well be the strength that allows it to create such organizational diversity in the first place (Bartlett and Ghoshal, 1985).

Internal diversity may lead to strategic advantages for a firm in many different ways. In an unpredictable environment it may not be possible, *ex ante*, to predict the competencies that will be required in the future. Diversity of internal capabilities, following the logic of population ecologists (e.g. Hannan and Freeman, 1977; Aldrich, 1979), will enhance the probability of the firm's survival by enhancing the chances that it will be in possession of the capabilities required to cope with an uncertain future state. Similarly, diversity of resources and competencies may also enhance the firm's ability to create joint innovations, and to exploit them in multiple locations. One example of such benefits of diversity was recently described in the *Wall Street Journal* (April 29, 1985):

> P&G [Procter and Gamble Co.] recently introduced its new Liquid Tide, but the product has a distinctly international heritage. A new ingredient that helps suspend dirt in wash water came from the company's research center near P&G's Cincinnati headquarters. But the formula for Liquid Tide's surfactants, or cleaning agents, was developed by P&G technicians in Japan. The ingredients that fight mineral salts present in hard water came from P&G's scientists in Brussels.

As discussed in the same *WSJ* article, P&G's research centre in Brussels has developed a special capability in water softening technology due, in part, to the fact that water in Europe contains more than twice the level of mineral content compared to wash water available in the United States. Similarly, surfactant technology is particularly advanced in Japan because Japanese consumers wash their clothes in colder waters compared to consumers in the US or Europe, and this makes greater demands on the cleaning ability of the surfactants. The advantage of P&G as a multinational is that it is exposed to these different operating environments and has learned, in each environment, the skills and knowledge that coping with that environment specially require. Liquid Tide is an example of the strategic advantages that accrue from such diverse learning.

The mere existence of diversity, however, does not enhance learning. It only creates the potential for learning. To exploit this potential, the organization must consider learning as an explicit objective, and must create mechanisms and systems for such learning to take place. In the absence of explicit intention and appropriate mechanisms, the learning potential may be lost. In some companies, where all organizational resources are centralized and where the national subsidiaries are seen as mere delivery pipelines to supply the organization's value-added to different countries, diverse learning may not take place either because the subsidiaries may not possess appropriate sensing, analysing and responding capabilities to learn from their local environments, or because the centralized decision processes may be insensitive to knowledge accumulated outside the corporate headquarters. Other companies, in which the subsidiaries may enjoy very high levels of local resources and autonomy, may similarly fail to exploit global learning benefits because of their inability to transfer and synthesize knowledge and expertise developed in different organizational components. Local loyalties, turf protection, and the 'not invented here' (NIH) syndrome – the three handmaidens of decentralization – may restrict internal flow of information across national boundaries which is essential for global learning to occur. In other words, both centralization and decentralization may impede learning.

THE MEANS: SOURCES OF COMPETITIVE ADVANTAGE

Most recent articles on global strategy have been aimed at identifying generic strategies (such as global cost leadership, focus or niche) and advocating particular strategic moves (such as cross-subsidy or pre-emptive investments). Underlying these concepts, however, are three fundamental tools for building global competitive advantage: exploiting differences in input and output markets in different countries, exploiting economies of scale, and exploiting economies of scope (Porter, 1985).

National differences

The comparative advantage of locations in terms of differences in factor costs is perhaps the most discussed, and also the best understood, source of competitive advantage in international business.

Different nations have different factor endowments, and in the absence of efficient markets this leads to inter-country differences in factor costs. Different activities of the firm, such as R&D, production, marketing, etc. have different factor intensities. A firm can therefore gain cost advantages by configuring its value-chain so that each activity is located in the country which has the least cost for the factor that the activity uses most intensely. This is the core concept of comparative advantage-based competitive advantage – a concept for which highly developed analytical tools are available from the discipline of international economics. Kogut (1985a) provides an excellent managerial overview of this concept.

National differences may also exist in output markets. Customer tastes and preferences may be different in different countries, as may be distribution systems, government regulations applicable to the concerned product-markets, or the effectiveness of different promotion strategies and other marketing techniques. A firm can augment the exchange value of its output by tailoring its offerings to fit the unique requirements in each national market. This, in essence, is the strategy of national differentiation, and it lies at the core of what has come to be referred to as the multidomestic approach in multinational management (Hout et al., 1982).

From a strategic perspective, however, this static and purely economic view of national differences may not be adequate. What may be more useful is to take a dynamic view of comparative advantage and to broaden the concept to include both societal and economic factors.

In the traditional economics view, comparative advantages of countries are determined by their relative factor endowments and they do not change. However, in reality one lesson of the past four decades is that comparative advantages change and a prime objective of the industrial policies of many nations is to effect such changes. Thus, for any nation, the availability and cost of capital change, as do the availability of technical manpower and the wages of skilled and unskilled labour. Such changes take place, in the long run, to accommodate different levels of economic and social performance of nations, and in the short run they occur in response to specific policies and regulations of governments.

This dynamic aspect of comparative advantages adds considerable complexity to the strategic considerations of the firm. There is a first-order effect of such changes – such as possible increases in wage rates, interest rates or currency exchange rates for particular countries that can affect future viability of a strategy that has been based on the current levels of these economic variables. There can also be a more intriguing second-order effect. If an activity is located in an economically inefficient environment, and if the firm is able to achieve a higher level of efficiency in its own operations compared to the rest of the local economy, its competitive advantage may actually increase as the local economy slips lower and lower. This is because the macro-economic variables such as wage or exchange rates may change to reflect the overall performance of the economy relative to the rest of the world and, to the extent that the firm's performance is better than this national aggregate, it may benefit from these macro-level changes (Kiechel, 1981).

Consistent with the discipline that gave birth to the concept, the usual view of comparative advantage is limited to factors that an economist admits into the production function, such as the costs of labour and capital. However, from a managerial perspective it may be more appropriate to take a broader view of societal comparative advantages to include 'all the relative advantages conferred on a society by the quality, quantity and configuration of its material, human and institutional resources, including "soft" resources such as inter-organizational linkages, the nature of its educational system, and organizational and managerial know-how' (Westney, 1985, p. 4). As argued by Westney, these 'soft' societal factors, if absorbed in the overall organizational system, can provide benefits as real to a multinational as those provided by such economic factors as cheap labour or low-cost capital.

While the concept of comparative advantage is quite clear, available evidence on its actual effect on the overall competitiveness of firms is weak and conflicting. For example, it has often been claimed that one source of competitive advantage for Japanese firms is the lower cost of capital in Japan (Hatsopoulos, 1983). However, more systematic studies have shown that there is practically no difference in the risk-adjusted cost of capital in the United States and Japan, and that capital cost advantages of Japanese firms, if any, arise from complex interactions between government subsidies and corporate ownership structures (Flaherty and Itami, 1984). Similarly, relatively low wage rates in Japan have been suggested by some authors as the primary reason for the success of Japanese companies in the US market (Itami, 1978). However, recently, companies such as Honda and Nissan have commissioned plants in the USA and have been able to retain practically the same levels of cost advantages over US manufacturers as they had for their production in Japan (Allen, 1985). Overall, there is increasing evidence that while comparative advantages of countries can provide competitive advantages to firms, the realization of such benefits is not automatic but depends on complex organizational factors and processes.

Scale economies

Scale economies, again, is a fairly well established concept, and its implications for competitive advantage are quite well understood. Micro-economic theory provides a strong theoretical and empirical basis for evaluating the effect of scale on cost reduction, and the use of scale as a competitive tool is common in practice. Its primary implication for strategy is that a firm must expand the volume of its output so as to achieve available scale benefits. Otherwise a competitor who can achieve such volume can build cost advantages, and this can lead to a vicious cycle in which the low-volume firm can progressively lose its competitive viability.

While scale, by itself, is a static concept, there may be dynamic benefits of scale through what has been variously described as the experience or learning effect. The higher volume that helps a firm to exploit scale benefits also allows it to accumulate learning, and this leads to progressive cost reduction as the firm moves down its learning curve.

The concept of the value-added chain recently popularized by Porter (1985) adds considerable richness to the analysis of scale as a source of competitive advantage. This conceptual apparatus allows a disaggregated analysis of scale benefits in different value-creating activities of the firm. The efficient scale may vary widely by activity – being higher for component production, say, than for assembly. In contrast to a unitary view of scale, this disaggregated view permits the firm to configure different elements of its value chain to attain optimum scale economies in each.

Traditionally, scale has been seen as an unmixed blessing – something that always helps and never hurts. Recently, however, many researchers have argued otherwise (e.g. Evans, 1982). It has been suggested that scale efficiencies are obtained through increased specialization and through creation of dedicated assets and systems. The same processes cause inflexibilities and limit the firm's ability to cope with change. As environmental turbulence has increased, so has the need for strategic and operational flexibility (Mascarenhas, 1982). At the extreme, this line of argument has led to predictions of a re-emergence of the craft form of production to replace the scale-dominated assembly form (Piore and Sabel, 1984). A more typical argument has been to emphasize the need to balance scale and flexibility, through the use of modern technologies such as CAD/CAM and flexible manufacturing systems (Gold, 1982).

Scope economies

Relatively speaking, the concept of scope economies is both new and not very well understood. It is based on the notion that certain economies arise from the fact that the cost of the joint production of two or more products can be less than the cost of producing them separately. Such cost reductions can take place due to many reasons – for example resources such as information or technologies, once acquired for use in producing one item, may be available costlessly for production of other items (Baumol, Panzer and Willig, 1982).

The strategic importance of scope economies arises from a diversified firm's ability to share investments and costs across the same or different value chains that competitors, not possessing such internal and external diversity, cannot. Such sharing can take place across segments, products, or markets (Porter, 1985) and may involve joint use of different kinds of assets (see Table 17.2).

A diversified firm may share physical assets such as production equipment, cash, or brand name across different businesses and markets. Flexible manufacturing systems using robots, which can be used for production of different items, is one example of how a firm can exploit such scope benefits. Cross-subsidization of markets and exploitation of a global brand name are other examples of sharing a tangible asset across different components of a firm's product and market portfolios.

Table 17.2 Scope economies in product and market diversification

	Sources of scope economies	
	Product diversification	*Market diversification*
Shared physical assets	Factory automation with flexibility to produce multiple products (Ford)	Global brand name (Coca-Cola)
Shared external relations	Using common distribution channel for multiple products (Matsushita)	Servicing multi-national customers worldwide (Citibank)
Shared learning	Sharing R&D in computer and communications businesses (NEC)	Pooling knowledge developed in different markets (Procter and Gamble)

A second important source of scope economies is shared external relations: with customers, suppliers, distributors, governments and other institutions. A multinational bank like Citibank can provide relatively more effective service to a multinational customer than can a bank that operates in a single country (see Terpstra, 1982). Similarly, as argued by Hamel and Prahalad (1985), companies such as Matsushita have benefited considerably from their ability to market a diverse range of products through the same distribution channel. In another variation, Japanese trading companies have expanded into new businesses to meet different requirements of their existing customers.

Finally, shared knowledge is the third important component of scope economies. The fundamental thrust of NEC's global strategy is 'C&C' – computers and communications. The company firmly believes that its even strengths in the two technologies and resulting capabilities of merging them in-house to create new products gives it a competitive edge over global giants such as IBM and AT&T, who have technological strength in only one of these two areas. Another example of the scope advantages of shared learning is the case of Liquid Tide described earlier in this paper.

Even scope economies, however, may not be costless. Different segments, products or markets of a diversified company face different environmental demands. To succeed, a firm needs to differentiate its management systems and processes so that each of its activities can develop *external consistency* with the requirements of its own environment. The search for scope economies, on the other hand, is a search for *internal consistencies* within the firm and across its different activities. The effort to create such synergies may invariably result in some compromise with the objective of external consistency in each activity.

Further, the search for internal synergies also enhances the complexities in a firm's management processes. In the extreme, such complexities can overwhelm the organization, as it did in the case of EMI, the UK-based music, electronics and leisure products company which attempted to manage its new CT scanner business within the framework of its existing organizational structure and processes (see EMI and the CT scanner, ICCH case 9–383–194). Certain parts of a company's portfolio of businesses or markets may be inherently very different from some others, and it may be best not to look for economies of scope across them. For example, in the soft drinks industry, bottling and distribution are intensely local in scope, while the tasks of creating and maintaining a brand image, or that of designing efficient bottling plants, may offer significant benefits from global integration. Carrying out both these sets of functions in-house would clearly lead to internalizing enormous differences within the company with regard to the organizing, co-ordinating, and controlling tasks. Instead of trying to cope with these complexities, Coca-Cola has externalized those functions which are purely local in scope (in all but some key strategic markets). In a variation of the same theme, IBM has 'externalized' the PC business by setting up an almost stand-alone organization, instead of trying to exploit scope benefits by integrating this business within the structure of its existing organization (for a more detailed discussion on multinational scope economies and on the conflicts between internal and external consistencies, see Lorange, Scott Morton and Ghoshal, 1986).

PRESCRIPTIONS IN PERSPECTIVE

Existing literature on global strategy offers analytical insights and helpful prescriptions for almost all the different issues indicated in Table 17.1. Table 17.3 shows a selective list of relevant publications, categorized on the basis of issues that, according to this author's interpretations, the pieces primarily focus on.[4]

Table 17.3 Selected references for further reading

	Sources of competitive advantage		
Strategic objectives	National differences	Scale economies	Scope economies
Achieving efficiency in current operations	Kogut (1985a); Itami (1978); Okimoto, Sugano and Weinstein (1984)	Hout, Porter and Rudden (1982); Levitt (1983); Doz (1978); Leontiades (1984); Gluck (1983)	Hamel and Prahalad (1985); Hout, Porter and Rudden (1982); Porter (1985); Ohmae (1985)
Managing risks	Keichel (1981); Kobrin (1982); Poynter (1985); Lessard and Lightstone (1983); Srinivasulu (1981); Herring (1983)	Evans (1982); Piore and Sabel (1984); Gold (1982); Aaker and Mascarenhas (1984)	Kogut (1985b); Lorange, Scott Morton and Ghoshal (1986)
Innovation, learning and adaptation	Westney (1985); Terpstra (1977); Ronstadt and Krammer (1982)	BCG (1982); Rapp (1973)	Bartlett and Ghoshal (1985)

Pigeon-holing academic contributions into different parts of a conceptual framework tends to be unfair to their authors. In highlighting what the authors focus on, such categorization often amounts to an implicit criticism for what they did not write. Besides, most publications cover a broader range of issues and ideas than can be reflected in any such categorization scheme. Table 17.3 suffers from all these deficiencies. At the same time, however, it suggests how the proposed framework can be helpful in integrating the literature and in relating the individual pieces to each other.

From parts to the whole

For managers, the advantage of such synthesis is that it allows them to combine a set of insightful but often partial analyses to address the totality of a multidimensional and complex phenomenon. Consider, for example, a topic that has been the staple for academics interested in international management: explaining and drawing normative conclusions from the global successes of many Japanese companies. Based on detailed comparisons across a set of matched pairs of US and Japanese firms. Itami concludes that the relative successes of the Japanese firms can be wholly explained as due to the advantages of lower wage rates and higher labour productivity. In the context of a specific industry, on the other hand, Toder (1978) shows that manufacturing scale is the single most important source of the Japanese competitive advantage. In the small car business, for example, the minimum efficient scale requires an annual production level of about 400,000 units. In the late 1970s no US auto manufacturer produced even 200,000 units of any subcompact configuration vehicle, while Toyota produced around 500,000 Corollas and Nissan produced between 300,000 and 400,000 B210s per year. Toder estimates that US manufacturers suffered a cost disadvantage of between 9 and 17 per cent on account of inefficient scale alone. Add to it the effects of wage rate differentials and exchange rate movements, and Japanese success in the US auto market may not require any further explanation. Yet process-orientated scholars such as Hamel and Prahalad suggest a much more complex explanation of the Japanese tidal wave. They see it as arising out of a dynamic process of strategic evolution that exploits scope economies as a crucial weapon in the final stages. All these authors provide compelling arguments to support their own explanations, but do not consider or refute each other's hypotheses..

This multiplicity of explanations only shows the complexity of global strategic management. However, though different, these explanations and prescriptions are not always mutually exclusive. The manager's task is to find how these insights can be combined to build a multidimensional and flexible strategy that is robust to the different assumptions and explanations.

The strategic trade-offs

This, however, is not always possible because there are certain inherent contradictions between the different strategic objectives and between the different sources of competitive advantage. Consider, for instance, the popular distinction between a global and a multidomestic strategy described by Hout et al. (1982). A global strategy requires that the firm should carefully separate different value elements, and should locate each activity at the most efficient level of scale in the location where the activity can be carried out at the cheapest cost. Each activity should then be integrated and managed interdependently so as to exploit available scope economies. In essence, it is a strategy to maximize efficiency of current operations.

Such a strategy may, however, increase both endogenous and exogenous risks for the firm. Global scale of certain activities such as R&D and manufacturing may result in the firm's costs being concentrated in a few countries, while its revenues accrue globally, from sales in many different countries. This increases the operating exposure of the firm to the vicissitudes of exchange rate movements because of the mismatch between the currencies in which revenues are obtained and those in which costs are incurred. Similarly, the search for efficiency in a global business may lead to greater amounts of intra-company, but inter-country, flows of goods, capital, information and other resources. These flows are visible, salient and tend to attract policy interventions from different host governments. Organizationally, such an integrated system requires a high degree of co-ordination, which enhances the risks of management failures. These are lessons that many Japanese companies have learned well recently.

Similarly, consideration of the learning objective will again contradict some of the proclaimed benefits of a global strategy. The implementation of a global strategy tends to enhance the forces of centralization and to shift organizational power from the subsidiaries to the headquarters. This may result in demotivation of subsidiary managers and may erode one key asset of the MNC – the potential for learning from its many environments. The experiences of Caterpillar are a case in point. An exemplary practitioner of global strategy, Cat has recently spilled a lot of red ink on its balance sheet and lost ground steadily to its archrival, Komatsu. Many factors contributed to Caterpillar's woes, not the least of which was the inability of its centralized management processes to benefit from the experiences of its foreign subsidiaries.

On the flipside of the coin, strategies aimed at optimizing risk or learning may compromise current efficiency. Poynter (1985) has recommended 'upgrade', i.e. increasing commitment of technology and resources in subsidiaries, as a way to overcome risk of policy interventions by host governments. Kogut (1985b), Mascarenhas (1982) and many others have suggested creating strategic and operational flexibility as a mechanism for coping with macro-environmental risks. Bartlett and Ghoshal (1985) have proposed the differentiated network model of multinational organizations as a way to operationalize the benefits of global learning. All these recommendations carry certain efficiency penalties, which the authors have ignored.

Similar trade-offs exist between the different sources of competitive advantages. Trying to make the most of factor cost economies may prevent scale efficiency, and may impede benefiting from synergies across products or functions. Trying to benefit from scope through product diversification may affect scale, and so on. In effect these contradictions between the different strategic objectives, and between the different means for achieving them, lead to trade-offs between each cell in the framework and practically all others.

These trade-offs imply that to formulate and implement a global strategy, MNC managers must consider all the issues suggested in Table 17.1, and must evaluate the implications of different strategic alternatives on each of these issues. Under a particular set of circumstances a particular strategic objective may dominate and a particular source of competitive advantage may play a more important role than the others (Fayerweather, 1981). The complexity of global strategic management arises from the need to understand those situational contingencies, and to adopt a strategy after evaluating the trade-offs it implies. Existing prescriptions can sensitize MNC managers to the different factors they must consider, but cannot provide ready-made and standardized solutions for them to adopt.

CONCLUSION

This paper has proposed a framework that can help MNC managers in reviewing and analysing the strategies of their firms. It is not a blueprint for formulating strategies; it is a road map for reviewing them. Irrespective of whether strategies are analytically formulated or organizationally formed (Mintzberg, 1978), every firm has a realised strategy. To the extent that the realised strategy may differ from the intended one, managers need to review what the strategies of their firms really are. The paper suggests a scheme for such a review which can be an effective instrument for exercising strategic control.

Three arguments underlie the construct of the framework. First, in the global strategy literature, a kind of industry determinism has come to prevail not unlike the technological determinism that dominated management literature in the 1960s. The structures of industries may often have important influences on the appropriateness of corporate strategy, but they are only one of many such influences. Besides, corporate strategy may influence industry structure just as much as be influenced by it.

Second, simple schemes for categorizing strategies of firms under different labels tend to hide more than they reveal. A map for more detailed comparison of the content of strategies can be more helpful to managers in understanding and improving the competitive positions of their companies.

Third, the issues of risk and learning have not been given adequate importance in the strategy literature in general, and in the area of global strategies in particular. Both these are important strategic objectives and must be explicitly considered while evaluating or reviewing the strategic positions of companies.

The proposed framework is not a replacement of existing analytical tools but an enhancement that incorporates these beliefs. It does not present any new concepts or solutions, but only a synthesis of existing ideas and techniques. The benefit of such synthesis is that it can help managers in integrating an array of strategic moves into an overall strategic thrust by revealing the consistencies and contradictions among those moves.

For academics this brief view of the existing literature on global strategy will clearly reveal the need for more empirically grounded and systematic research to test and validate the hypotheses which currently appear in the literature as prescriptions and research conclusions. For partial analyses to lead to valid conclusions, excluded variables must be controlled for, and rival hypotheses must be considered and eliminated. The existing body of descriptive and normative research is rich enough to allow future researchers to adopt a more rigorous and systematic approach to enhance the reliability and validity of their findings and suggestions. The proposed framework, it is hoped, may be of value to some researchers in thinking about appropriate research issues and designs for furthering the field of global strategic management.

ACKNOWLEDGEMENTS

The ideas presented in this paper emerged in the course of discussions with many friends and colleagues. Don Lessard, Eleanor Westney, Bruce Kogut, Chris Bartlett and Nitin Nohria were particularly helpful. I also benefited greatly from the comments and suggestions of the two anonymous referees from the *Strategic Management Journal*.

REFERENCES

Aaker, D.A. and Mascarenhas, B. (1984) 'The need for strategic flexibility', *Journal of Business Strategy*, Vol. 9 No. 2, pp. 74–82.

Aldrich, H.E. (1979) *Organizations and Environments*, Prentice Hall, Englewood Cliffs, NJ.

Allen, M.K. (1985) 'Japanese companies in the United States: the success of Nissan and Honda', unpublished manuscript, Sloan School of Management, MIT.

Bartlett, C.A. (1985) 'Global competition and MNC managers', ICCH Note No. 0–385–287, Harvard Business School.

Bartlett, C.A. and Ghoshal, S. (1985)'The new global organization: differentiated roles and dispersed responsibilities', Working Paper No. 9–786–013, Harvard Business School.

Baumol, W.I., Panzer, J.C. and Willig, R.D. (1982) *Contestable Markets and the Theory of Industry Structure*, Harcourt, Brace, Jovanovich, New York.

Boston Consulting Group (1982) *Perspectives on Experience*, BCG, Boston, MA.

Calvet, A.I. (1981) 'A synthesis of foreign direct investment theories and theories of the multinational firm', *Journal of International Business Studies*, Spring/Summer, pp. 43–60.

Caves, R.F. (1980) 'Industrial organization, corporate strategy and structure', *Journal of Economic Literature*, XVIII, March 1980, pp. 64–92.

Doz, Y. I. 'Managing manufacturing rationalization within multinational companies', *Columbia Journal of World Business*, Fall, pp. 82–94.

Doz, Y.I., Bartlett, C.A. and Prahalad, C.K. (1981) 'Global competitive pressures and host country demands: managing tensions in MNCs', *California Management Review*, Spring, pp. 63–74.

Evans, J.S. (1982) *Strategic Flexibility in Business*, Report No. 678, SRI International.

Fayerweather, J. (1981) 'Four winning strategies for the international corporation', *Journal of Business Strategy*, Fall, pp. 25–36.

Flaherty, M. and Itami, H. (1984) 'Finance' in Okimoto, K.R., Sugano and Weinstein F.B. (eds), *Competitive Edge*, Stanford University Press, Stanford, CA.

Gluck, F. (1983) 'Global competition in the 1980s', *Journal of Business Strategy*, Spring, pp. 22–7.

Gold, B. (1982) 'Robotics, programmable automation and international competitiveness', *IEEE Transactions on Engineering Management*, November.

Hamel, G. and Prahalad, C.K. (1985) 'Do you really have a global strategy?' *Harvard Business Review*, July–August, pp. 139–148.

Hannan, M.P. and Freeman, J. (1977) 'The population ecology of organizations', *American Journal of Sociology*, Vol. 82, pp. 929–64.

Hatsopoulos, G.N. (1983) 'High cost of capital: handicap of American industry', Report sponsored by the American Business Conference and Thermo-Electron Corporation.

Hax, A.C. and Majluf, N.S. (1984) *Strategic Management: an integrative perspective*, Prentice-Hall, Englewood Cliffs, NJ.

Herring, R.J. (ed.) (1983) *Managing International Risk*, Cambridge University Press, Cambridge.

Hofer, C.W. and Schendel, D. (1978) *Strategy Formulation: analytical concepts*, West Publishing Co., St. Paul, MN.

Hout, T., Porter, M.E. and Rudden, E. (1982) 'How global companies win out', *Harvard Business Review*, September–October, pp. 98–108.

Itami, H. (1978) 'Japanese–U.S. comparison of managerial productivity', *Japanese Economic Studies*, Fall.

Kiechel, W. (1981) 'Playing the global game', *Fortune*, 16 November, pp. 111–26.

Kobrin, S.J. (1982) *Managing Political Risk Assessment*, University of California Press, Los Angeles.

Kogut, B. (1984) 'Normative observations on the international value-added chain and strategic groups', *Journal of International Business Studies*, Fall, pp. 151–67.

Kogut, B. (1985a) 'Designing global strategies: comparative and competitive value added chains,' *Sloan Management Review*, Summer, pp. 15–28.

Kogut, B. (1985b) 'Designing global strategies: profiting from operational flexibility', *Sloan Management Review*, Fall, pp. 27–38.

Leontiades, J. (1984) 'Market share and corporate strategy in international industries', *Journal of Business Strategy*, Vol. 5, No. 4, pp. 30–37.

Lessard, D. and Lightstone, J. (1983) 'The impact of exchange rates on operating profits: new business and financial responses', mimeo, Lightstone-Lessard Associates.

Levitt, T. (1983) 'The globalization of markets', *Harvard Business Review*, May–June, pp. 92–102.

Lorange, P., Scott Morton, M.S. and Ghoshal, S. (1986) *Strategic Control*, West Publishing Co., St Paul MN.

Mascarenhas, B. (1982) 'Coping with uncertainty in international business', *Journal of International Business Studies*, Fall, pp. 87–98.

Mintzberg, H. (1978) 'Patterns in strategic formation', *Management Science*, Vol. 24, pp. 934–48.

Ohmae, K. (1985) *Triad Power: the coming shape of global competition*, The Free Press, New York.

Okimoto, D.I., Sugano, T. and Weinstein, F.B. (eds) (1984) *Competitive Edge*, Stanford University Press, Stanford, CA.

Perlmutter, H.V. (1969) 'The tortuous evolution of the multinational corporation', *Columbia Journal of World Business*, January–February, pp. 9–18.

Piore, M.J. and Sabel, C. (1984) *The Second Industrial Divide: possibilities and prospects*, Basic Books, New York.

Porter, M.E. (1980) *Competitive Strategy*, Basic Books, New York.

Porter, M.E. (1984) 'Competition in global industries: a conceptual framework', paper presented to the Colloquium in Competition in Global Industries, Harvard Business School.

Porter, M.E. (1985) *Competitive Advantage*, The Free Press, New York.

Poynter, T.A. (1985) *International Enterprises and Government Intervention*, Croom Helm, London.

Prahalad, C.K. (1975) 'The strategic process in a multinational corporation', unpublished doctoral dissertation, Graduate School of Business Administration, Harvard University.

Rapp, W.V. (1983) 'Strategy formulation and international competition', *Columbia Journal of World Business*, Summer, pp. 98–112.

Robinson, R.D. (1978) *International Business Management: a guide to decision making*, Dryden Press, Illinois.

Ronstadt, R. and Krammer, R.J. (1982) 'Getting the most out of innovations abroad', *Harvard Business Review*, March–April, pp. 94–9.

Rutenberg, D.P. (1982) *Multinational Management*, Little, Brown, Boston, MA.

Srinivasula, S. (1981) 'Strategic response to foreign exchange risks', *Columbia Journal of World Business*, Spring, pp. 13–23.

Terpstra, V. (1977) 'International product policy: the role of foreign R&D', *Columbia Journal of World Business*, Winter, pp. 24–32.

Terpstra, V. (1982) *International Dimensions of Marketing*, Kent, Boston, MA.

Vernon, R. (1977) *Storm Over the Multinationals*, Harvard University Press, Cambridge, MA.

Westney, D.E. (1985) 'International dimensions of information and communications technology', unpublished manuscript, Sloan School of Management, MIT.

Woo, C.Y. and Cool, K.O. (1985) 'The impact of strategic management of systematic risk', mimeo, Krannert Graduate School of Management, Purdue University.

NOTES

1   In the interest of simplicity the distinction between risk and uncertainty is ignored, as is the distinction between systematic and unsystematic risks.

2   This assumes that the firm has defined its business correctly and has identified as competitors all the firms whose offerings are aimed at meeting the same set of market needs that the firm meets.

3   Some market mechanisms such as long-term currency swaps are now available which can allow at least partial hedging of operating risks.

4   From an academic point of view, strategy of the multinational corporation is a specialized and highly applied field of study. It is built on the broader field of business policy and strategy which, in turn, rests on the foundation of a number of academic disciplines such as economics, organization theory, finance theory, operations research, etc. A number of publications in those underlying disciplines, and a significant body of research carried out in the field of strategy, in general, provide interesting insights on the different issues highlighted in Table 17.1. However, given the objective of suggesting a limited list of further readings that *managers* may find useful, such publications have not been included in Table 17.3. Further, even for the more applied and prescriptive literature on global strategy, the list is only illustrative and not exhaustive.

CHAPTER 18

BEYOND THE M-FORM: TOWARDS A MANAGERIAL THEORY OF THE FIRM

CHRISTOPHER A. BARTLETT AND SUMANTRA GHOSHAL

Driven by a set of radical changes in their internal and external environments, large global corporations are innovating a new organizational form. Premised on knowledge and expertise rather than capital or scale as the key strategic resource, this new form is fundamentally different from the multidivisional organization that had emerged in the 1920s and had become the dominant corporate model in the post-War years. In this article, we describe this new organization using Asea Brown Boveri (ABB) as an illustration, and highlight its differences from the classic M-form by contrasting its structure, processes and decision-making mechanisms against the models proposed by Chandler (1962), Bower (1970) and Cyert and March (1963). Our conceptualization of this emerging organization is grounded in a managerial perspective that is very different from the disciplinary foundations of existing economic and behavioural theories of the firm. We conclude by arguing for the need to create a 'managerial theory of the firm' that would be more attuned to the premises of the key actors within the firm so as to be able to illuminate the corporate world as seen by managers and encompass the issues that they perceive to be important.

The post-War growth in the United States created an extraordinary new set of opportunities and challenges for the management of companies operating in that era. In turn, as companies developed new strategic approaches, created innovative organizational forms and redefined management roles in response to the changing environment, they stimulated a wave of research that sought to enrich and even redefine the theory of the firm. It was in this golden era of research in the late 1950s through the 1960s that many of the foundations of current management theory were laid.

At MIT, business historian Alfred Chandler had become fascinated by the rapid spread of the new strategies and the organizations needed to manage them, and was tracing the trend to its roots in the pre-War period. His carefully documented research provided a richly textured interpretation of the new multidivision organization that was beginning to dominate corporate structures in the United

States and abroad (Chandler, 1962). At Carnegie Mellon, another extraordinary research effort was building on the foundations laid by Herbert Simon and James March in modelling human behaviour to better understand how decisions were made in the complex new emerging corporations. The resulting behavioural theory of the firm was consolidated and formalized in the work of Cyert and March (1963). Several years later, at Harvard Business School, Joseph Bower's research into business planning and investment decision-making led to a model of the strategic processes in multidivisional organizations, thereby creating a bridge between the new corporate structure described by Chandler and the theory of decision-making proposed by Cyert and March (Bower, 1970).

The decade of the 1970s and the early part of 1980s was a period of refinement and incremental progress, both for management practice and for management theory. While corporate managers expanded their new diversification strategies, elaborated their new divisionalized structures, and fine-tuned their new management processes, streams of research developed behind the seminal work of Chandler, Bower and Cyert and March, building richer and more refined versions of their models and theories.

By the early 1990s, however, new environmental demands – particularly those emanating from the globalization of competition, markets, and technology and the related economic and social consequences – were driving changes in strategy, structure, and management that were probably as widespread and impactful as the diversification/divisionalization changes that drove the post-War managerial revolution. In such an environment, some were beginning to express concern that the existing paradigms of strategy, organization and decision-making, developed to explain an earlier form of the corporate model, might no longer be as relevant or as powerful as they once were (Hamel and Prahalad, 1993; Handy, 1990). Their arguments were buttressed by the widespread problems in companies that had failed to adapt their classic organizational structures and processes. Indeed, by the 1990s, at least two of the four innovators of the multidivisional form at the core of Chandler's study – General Motors and Sears – were making business headlines more as problem cases than as role models.

Over the last five years, we have been engaged in a research project aimed at understanding and analysing this recent change. While lacking the benefit of Chandler's historical perspective, our objective, like his, was to identify emerging organizational forms and their logics, rather than to describe the average or the dominant patterns. And, just as Chandler selected his final sample of DuPont, General Motors, Jersey Standard and Sears from a longer list because their administrative reorganizations were more creative, their businesses were more complex and data about them were more readily available (1962, p.3), our selection of companies for detailed clinical studies was also biased toward those in complex and dynamic businesses that were attempting relatively more radical changes and were willing to give us access to their managers and their files. AT&T, Andersen Consulting, Corning, Intel, Nike and 3M in the United States; Asea Brown Boveri (ABB), Body Shop, Cartier, Electrolux, ISS, IKEA, Royal Dutch Shell, Richardson Sheffield and 'Semco' in Europe; and Canon, Kao Corporation, Komatsu and Toyota in Japan constituted our sample.

Our overall findings from the study suggest that large global corporations are creating a new organizational model in the 1990s that is significantly different from the M-form organization that has dominated corporate structures over the preceding five decades and that has provided the context for much of current management theory. Just as there were many variations within the broader M-form model (Williamson, 1975; Hill, 1988), there are some significant differences among companies pioneering the new form. Yet, underneath those different nuances lies a broad set of commonalities in corporate structure, organizational processes and management roles that distinguish the new model from the divisionalized corporation in much the same way as a broad set of shared principles differentiated the divisionalized company from its functional predecessor.

In a forthcoming monograph, we will provide a detailed report on this study and will describe this new organizational form based on a comparative analysis of the companies in our sample. In this article, our objective is to provide a summary of some of the key features of the new model and to highlight their differences from those of the classic M-form. To do so within the space limitations of an article and yet provide some descriptive richness that is essential for a proper appreciation of the new form, we will borrow an approach that was most powerfully employed by Allison (1971) in his analysis of the Cuban missile crisis. By examining a well-documented situation from three different conceptual perspectives, Allison found that he was not only able to generate a richer understanding of the situation, he was also able to highlight the limitations of each of the conceptual models. Similarly, in this article, we will use the interpretative lenses of Chandler's structural perspective, Bower's process model and Cyert and March's behavioural theory to examine the organizational characteristics of Asea Brown Boveri (ABB), a 215,000 employee company with worldwide operations in what it describes as the 'electrotechnical business' and often cited as a prime example of the emerging corporate form (see, for example, Taylor, 1991). Each of these three authors provides a different yet complementary view of the M-form organization. By assessing ABB's organization against these three perspectives, we hope to both enrich our description of the company and to also show how it fundamentally differs from the model of the divisionalized corporation in which all three perspectives are grounded.

This method of explicating our arguments is not without its limitations. First, given our objective of presenting a new model, we run the risk of presenting ABB as an ideal type. Having grown from $17 billion in revenues in 1988 to $30 billion in 1992 (mostly through acquisitions) and having simultaneously improved its return on assets from less than 10 per cent to almost 19 per cent, ABB is a vigorous and successful company. But it also confronts a range of challenges and problems arising from the slow growth and overcapacity that characterizes most of its businesses and also from the newness and fragility of its own organizational structure and management processes. Our objective here is to use the company as a concrete context for framing a broad new organizational model, rather than to describe the company, *per se*. So, our attention will be selective, highlighting attributes of the ABB organization that are relevant to our model, thereby presenting only a partial picture of this large and complex global organization.

Second, although we will view the same case through three different lenses, unlike Allison, we will focus on different attributes and dimensions of the case in each round of analysis. To anticipate our arguments, we will contrast ABB (i) with Chandler's structural description to explicate the differences in the company's entrepreneurial process from that of the M-form organization; (ii) with Bower's strategic process model to highlight its horizontal integration process in contrast to the M-form's dominant vertical information processing mechanisms; and (iii) with the behavioural theory of the firm to explain the importance of its macrolevel goal-setting and learning mechanisms as complements to the microlevel processes in the M-form that were the focus of Cyert and March's analysis. As we progress through this sequential analysis, each specific element of departure from the M-form model may appear as an extension – a difference of degree rather than of kind. What we hope to show, however, is that while each of the elements of the new model can be obtained through adjustments of emphasis within the M-form organization, taken together they imply a management system that is substantially different from the system described by Chandler, Bower and Cyert and March.

Our overall conclusions from the project go a step beyond describing a new organizational model. We believe that the management of ABB, and of a number of the other companies we studied, is premised on a set of basic assumptions on the part of its managers regarding organization structure, decision-making processes and, ultimately, human behaviour, that are significantly different from those that underlie the economic and behavioural theories that currently dominate academic analysis of business organizations. As a result, these theories are of limited usefulness for analysing the behaviours of and within such companies. This is a serious handicap for management scholars and a major reason for the widening gap between existing management theory and emerging management practice.

To overcome this gap, we believe that management scholars need to develop a new theory of the firm, induced, as suggested by Chandler, 'from the point of view of the busy men responsible for the destiny of the enterprise' (1962, p.7), rather than being deduced from the disciplinary premises of social scientists. Weber also argued for the need to view a system from the perspective of those within it, thereby developing an 'interpretative understanding (Verstehen) of social behaviour in order to gain an explanation of its causes, its courses, and its effects' (1964, p.29). The model we will present in this article describes the operations of ABB as seen by its managers and in terms of their own specific roles and tasks. Such a managerial perspective, as reflected for example in the work of Barnard (1938), is at least as legitimate for the construction of a theory of the firm as those of the economist or the social psychologist. Our belief is that it can provide a useful complement to existing theories for stimulating both managers and students of management to analyse managerial roles, organizational tasks and even the underlying rationale and purpose of the firm in some significantly different ways. Undoubtedly, much more work would be necessary for developing such an alternative theory of the firm that would focus on the perspective of the practitioner and would, therefore, be more useful for the analysis of practice. However, we hope that the model we will present in this article may serve at least as a strawman to hasten the development of a richer and more rigorous 'managerial theory of the firm' to respond to the new organizational developments.

ABB FROM CHANDLER'S PERSPECTIVE: CREATING DISTRIBUTED ENTREPRENEURSHIP

Chandler's study of the adoption of the multidivisional organization structure by 50 of the largest companies in the United States, and his detailed examination of four of the pioneers of that revolutionary structural form, led him to develop his highly influential strategy/structure thesis. His central conclusion was that companies being driven by market growth and technological change to develop greater diversity in their products and markets, were able to manage their new strategies efficiently only if they adopted a multidivisional organizational structure – the so-called M-form.

The reason this structural form proved so powerful was because it defined a new set of management roles and relationships that emphasized the decentralization of responsibility to operating divisions whose activities were planned, co-ordinated and controlled by a strong corporate management – the general office in Chandler's terms – which also made the company's 'entrepreneurial decisions' about resource allocation. He showed how the management process created by this organization allowed companies to apply their resources more efficiently to opportunities created by changing markets and developing technologies.

Before highlighting the differences, we should note that many of the attributes of ABB's organization, management and even its change process fit well with the model proposed by Chandler. First, the process by which the company's new organization and management approach was designed and implemented parallels his description of changes in the companies pioneering the M-form. In both Asea and Brown Boveri – the two companies that were subsequently merged to form ABB – an existing management of 'insiders' had been unable to change the structure sufficiently to create efficient operations out of their respective diversified portfolios of electrical and power-related products, blocked by what Chandler described as 'the psychological hazards of adjusting to new ways, new tempos, and new duties' (1962, p.320). Yet both companies had the rational, analytic and engineering-driven 'institutional ethos' that Chandler had found conducive to organizational change. More importantly, in Asea there was a top-level manager with exactly the profile of Chandler's classic organizational change agent – a young, analytical inclined outsider. Brought in initially to turn around the troubled Swedish company, the 39-year-old Percy Barnevik had attracted considerable attention when, within six years, he had increased Asea's sales fourfold and its profits by a factor of ten. He was the natural candidate to lead the company created by Europe's biggest ever cross-border merger.

At the broadest level, some of the structural elements on which Barnevik built ABB's new organization follow the design principles of the classic M-form. At the corporate centre, he replaced the functionally orientated staff groups that had dominated the headquarters of the two founding companies with a team of capable group executives supported by highly specialized staffs. More important, the strong principle of decentralization of responsibility that Chandler saw as central to the operation of his model, is also central to ABB's management philosophy. As defined in the company document, *ABB's Mission, Values and Policies*, 'our guiding principle is to decentralize the Group into distinctive profit centres and assign individual accountability to each' (1962, p. 25).

Finally, a core element of ABB's approach for co-ordinating and controlling its diverse operations is in keeping with Chandler's prescription for creating reliable information and data flows to support the lines of authority. The fully automated ABACUS system (Asea Brown Boveri Accounting and CommUnication System), designed and installed within 12 months of the merger, is the centrepiece of the formalized information flow. It not only provides accurate and timely data to the field operations, it is also explicitly designed to help the group executives evaluate performance. As the company's much used *Mission, Values and Policies* document states. 'A decentralized organization will only work effectively with a good reporting system that gives higher-level managers the opportunity to react in good time' (1991, p. 42).

While the broad principles of delegation and control have their roots in the organizational model Chandler described, the structural form by which they are implemented begins to diverge from the classic M-form. ABB is structured not in the traditional multidivisional form, but around a business/geography matrix. Figure 18.1 illustrates this structure. Don Jans, the general manager of ABB's relays business in the United States, reports to both Ulf Gundemark, the Sweden-based head of the company's worldwide relays business area (BA in ABB terminology), and Joe Baker, who has overall responsibility for ABB's power transmission and distribution business (of which the relays business is a part) in the United States. Gundemark, in turn, reports to both B-O Svanholm, the Group Executive responsible for all of ABB's business in Sweden, and Goran Lindahl, another Group Executive heading the company's worldwide activities in the power transmission sector. Similarly, Baker reports to Lindahl on the business axis and to Gerhard Schulmeyer, the Group Executive responsible for all ABB operations in North America, on the geographic axis.

Yet a closer examination of this structure, by now quite common among large global corporations, reveals it to be simply a more complex form of the same basic divisionalized model described by Chandler. As such, it probably serves more to confirm the underlying strategy–structure thesis than to demonstrate a substantive difference. In an industry environment driven by technological and competitive forces requiring companies to be globally integrated, while market and governmental pressures demand a more nationally responsive approach (Prahalad and Doz, 1987), ABB's strategy requires it to manage both product and geographic diversity. To do so, it has structured its organization around a matrix with dual reporting channels linking front-line operating units to their global business area

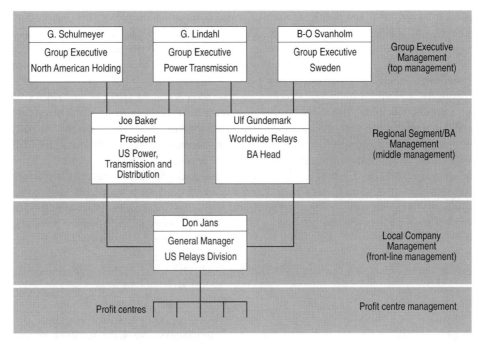

Figure 18.1 ABB's matrix organization

organization on one side and to their national or regional managements on the other.

Despite these similarities, however, there are some core elements in the structure and management of ABB's organization that clearly differentiates it from the model Chandler described. Most immediately obvious are the differences in the extent of decentralization of assets and delegation of responsibilities that both reflect and reinforce a philosophical divergence concerning the locus of entrepreneurship within the organization. It is this philosophical difference that lies at the heart of ABB's structural divergence from the classic M-form.

Barnevik has organized ABB around a principle he describes as 'radical decentralization.' This is more than just a difference of degree from the basic philosophy underlying the creation of the divisionalized organizations at DuPont or General Motors. It is a fundamental difference that is rooted in a very different organizational logic. The ABB organization is based not so much on subdividing the corporate entity into separate divisions to be directed and co-ordinated from the top, as it is on a concept of providing 'self-contained and manageable units with overview.' Translated into action, this philosophy has resulted in an organizational structure and management system in which the basic building block is not the company's seven business segments (groups in Chandler's terms), nor even its 65 business areas (the equivalent of Chandler's divisions). Instead ABB is organized as 'a federation of companies' – 1,300 of them that are structured as separate and distinct businesses and, to the extent possible, as free-standing legal entities. The US relays business headed by Don Jans (see Figure 18.1) is an example of such a company. On average, each of these companies employs 200 people and generates $25 million in annual revenues. In creating such a large number of small entities, Barnevik hoped that employees would lose 'the false sense of security of belonging to a big organization' and would develop the 'motivation and pride to contribute directly to their unit's success.'

Equally striking, and in marked contrast to the classic M-form organization, is the extent to which ABB's hierarchical structure above the individual company level has been stripped to a leanness that Chandler would not recognize. In contrast to the eight or nine layers of management in its predecessor companies, in ABB there is only one intermediate level between the corporate executive committee and the managers of the 1,300 front-line companies. Also, the staff groups supporting that shallow structure are very thin. Barnevik's rule of thumb for restructuring the traditional organizations of the merged and acquired companies from which ABB was created was to remove 90 per cent of all employees at each level above the operating companies. Those individuals or groups that were not required by the companies to increase their self-sufficiency were either set up as independent service centres charging market rates or eliminated. As a result, the entire corporate headquarters of this $30 billion company including the CEO, the seven group executives (such as Lindahl and Schulmeyer) who comprise the executive committee, and the various corporate staff groups together number less than 100 people. Similarly, at the business area level, managers like Ulf Gundemark are supported by a staff of three to five – typically a controller, a technical director and a business development or marketing director, none of whom have any assistants.

This change in basic philosophy to radical decentralization is supported by an equally radical redeployment of human, technological and financial resources. With the corporate HR staff consisting of only one manager, human resources have to be recruited and developed at the level of the front-line companies. Similarly, rather than concentrating its technology in centralized corporate laboratories or even at large group or division-level research facilities, ABB allocates more than 90 per cent of its substantial R&D budget ($2.4 billion in 1992) to support technology development in the front-line companies' centres of excellence whose expertise is then linked with those of centres located in other companies and leveraged broadly across the entire organization.

Finally, each front-line company is given responsibility for its complete balance sheet, and it is explicit corporate policy to allow managers to inherit results over the years through changes in their company's equity. As a result, each unit manages its own treasury function including cash management, foreign exchange exposure and responsibility for borrowing. Coupled with a dividend policy that permits each company to retain a third of its net profits, this policy gives front-line management substantial financial independence by limiting their need to rely on corporate management for funding.

Barnevik's primary objective in making such a radical change to the classic multidivisional structure he inherited was to create a context in which the entrepreneurial activities could be much more widely distributed that in most contemporary companies or indeed in the classic model Chandler described. In Chandler's model, the corporate-level executives were indisputably 'the key men in any enterprise' due to their central role as resource allocators. It was this role that led Chandler to dub them the company's 'entrepreneurs' while those lower in the organization were termed 'managers' and were assumed to focus on the operating activities required to implement the corporate executive's entrepreneurial decisions. Through the radical decentralization of resources to 1,300 front-line units and through the dramatic reductions in the machinery of control, Barnevik has redefined these management roles to create a very different entrepreneurial process that represents the first level of ABB's evolution beyond the classic M-form model.

The entrepreneurial process: aligning and supporting initiatives

This entrepreneurial process, framed and institutionalized by ABB's new organization structure and management philosophy, is embedded in a redefined set of management roles and relationships. Front-line managers – the heads of the 1,300 little companies – have evolved from their traditional role of implementers of top-down decisions to become the primary initiators of entrepreneurial action, creating and pursuing new opportunities for the company. Middle-level managers like Baker and Gundemark are no longer preoccupied with their historic control role, but instead have become a key resource to the front-line manager, coaching and supporting them in their activities. And top management, having radically decentralized the resources and backed them with strong delegated responsibility, focus much more on driving the entrepreneurial process by developing a broad set of objectives and by establishing stretched performance standards that the front-line initiatives must meet (see Figure 18.2).

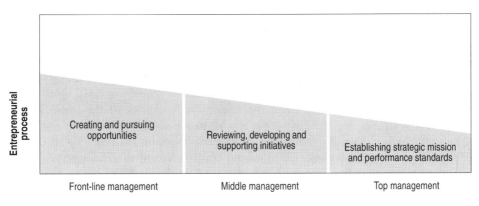

Figure 18.2 The entrepreneurial process

This fundamental difference between the ABB organization and the classic M-form is brought sharply into focus with the changes that occur in organizational processes and management roles every time ABB acquires a company operating in the more traditional mode. With its acquisition of Westinghouse's North American power transmission and distribution business for example, ABB had to overlay its radically decentralized structure and its philosophy of front-line entrepreneurship on a much more hierarchically controlled management system. The impact on the management of the relays division was typical of the changes occurring across this whole acquired business. Because of Westinghouse top management's unwillingness to support investments in what was seen as a mature business, Don Jans – then heading the relays division for Westinghouse – had been unable to convince his bosses to invest to any significant degree in solid-state and microprocessor relays technologies, despite the fact that his ageing electro-mechanical product lines were coming under increasing competitive threat. Under ABB's ownership, however, management roles and relationships changed radically. The relays operation was structured as a separate company and was expected to take responsibility for its own long-term future. Jans, whom ABB retained as the general manager of the company, quickly used his new-found strategic freedom and financial flexibility to start a small-scale effort to develop microprocessor-based products. As the initial experiments yielded some positive results, the scope of the activity was gradually broadened and the company was able to develop innovative new solid-state products in time to head off an aggressive new competitor who had begun to take advantage of the product-market gap.

The stagnation occurring in Westinghouse's power transmission business is not unusual. As has been documented by several observers of large global companies, the hierarchical and staff-led processes in the mature M-form organization tend to dampen front-line initiatives and innovation (Kanter, 1983; Peters, 1992). Evidence over the 1980s suggests that what Williamson (1975) described as the corrupted multidivisional organization is perhaps not an exception but the state to which the internal dynamics of the M-form inevitably lead (see also Chandler, 1991).

One way to prevent this erosion of front-line entrepreneurship is represented by the conglomerate organization labelled by Williamson as the holding company model or the H-form. While the entrepreneurial process developed in ABB is explicitly designed to counter the M-form's tendency to reduce front-line managers to the role of operational implementers, it differs significantly from the management processes of the H-form primarily because of the roles that are played by the company's middle and top managements. Unlike in conglomerates, both these groups in ABB remain involved in the operational realities of the business and contribute directly to the entrepreneurial process. Their actions not only differentiate them from the hands-on substantive decision-making role of the M-form, but also from the hands-off financial control role of the H-form.

The role that Gundemark and Lindahl played in shaping and supporting Jans' initiative can illustrate the point. As head of ABB's worldwide Relays Business Area (BA), Gundemark saw his role as supporting Jans' initiative on microprocessor-based products, incorporating it into the BA's global strategy to lead this technological conversion. As a member of the steering committee that acted as a board for Jans' local company, Gundemark was able to ensure that the proposal was supported and funded within a few days rather than the months or even years it would have taken in Westinghouse for the capital request to work its way up to corporate headquarters for approval and back. Beyond funding approval,

Gundemark provided Jans with advice and support in pursuing a strategy that involved a risk of short-term profit decline. For example, when a US revenue shortfall led Jans' geographic boss, Joe Baker, to push for cuts in the £1.5 million Jans had budgeted for microprocessor product development, Gundemark arranged to provide the technical support from the Swedish relays company.

At the corporate level, Lindahl worked at building a shared commitment from his management team to the ambition of 'conquering the globe in power transmission.' Expecting his BA heads and company managers to take the leadership in developing their business strategies, he saw his role as questioning and challenging the robustness of those strategies by testing them against key issues like environmental legislation or asking them to develop scenarios for dealing with different trade barriers. Beyond such macro exercises, ABB's top management also lived by the motto 'what gets measured gets done.' Yet Lindahl saw his role as much more than defining financial targets; his primary focus was on embedding performance standards that would stretch the organization to achieve extraordinary results. This led him to adopt a style he described as 'fingers in the pie' management, which he contrasted to the 'abstract management' approach of controlling agglomerated units through sophisticated but remote systems. Managing in this way, he had no problem in making direct contract with Jans or other front-line managers to expand their horizons, encourage their initiatives, or offer help when performance was slipping off-track.

The review, support and coaching provided by experienced managers like Gundemark raises the levels of discipline, analysis and judgement in the entrepreneurial initiatives of front-line managers like Jans. Similarly, the strategic mission and performance standards defined by top managers like Lindahl ensure that those initiatives are aligned with the company's overall strategic priorities. This discipline, guidance and support provided by ABB's senior management groups was clearly less constraining than the much more direction- and control-oriented roles played by similar management levels in Westinghouse. At the same time, however, they were much more involved than the remote, measurement-focused management that had allowed front-line entrepreneurs to lead many H-form companies into their incoherent expansions in the 1960s and 1970s (Chandler, 1991). These changes in the roles and tasks of senior managers not only distinguish the entrepreneurial process in ABB from those in both divisionalized and conglomerate organizations, they also lead to a very different process for integrating the knowledge, resources and capabilities lodged in different parts of the company. It is to an analysis of this integration process in ABB that we now turn.

ABB FROM BOWER'S PERSPECTIVE: INTEGRATING RESOURCES AND CAPABILITIES

Bower's intensive study of business planning and investment decision-making in four divisions of a large diversified company he identified as 'National Products' led him to develop a process model of the firm that enriched Chandler's work by challenging and expanding on several of its descriptions and conclusions. He presented a less heroic view of top management than Chandler's description of corporate entrepreneurs determining strategy through their control over resources. Instead, Bower described a process in which the shaping of new strategic initiatives and the investment proposals to support them ('definition' in his terminology) were initiated by front-line managers. Furthermore, in his view, it was the middle-level managers who typically made the resource commitments, since projects reaching the executive committee level with their support (Bower used the term 'impetus') were 'almost never rejected' (1970, p. 57). Thus, the major source of top management's power in Bower's model lay in its control over what he termed the 'structural context' – 'the set of organizational forces that influenced the processes of definition and impetus' (1970, p. 71).

This model of the core management processes in a large, complex organization provides a good yet partial insight into some of the management roles and relationships in ABB. Certainly Percy Barnevik's priorities as he set the course for the newly merged operations were very much orientated towards the context-defining role that Bower described as the top management job of 'constitution writing' (1970, p. 2). Within days of the merger on January 5, 1988, Barnevik convened a three-day meeting of his top 300 managers in Cannes to describe in great detail the operation of the matrix structure, the management philosophy of radical decentralization with strict accountability, and the behavioural expectations based on speed, flexibility and an action orientation. His presentation, communicated through 198 overhead transparencies, was formalized in a widely distributed 21-page *Mission, Values and Policy* booklet referred to inside the company as the 'policy bible'. During the years that followed, he and the other members of the corporate executive committee continued to spend an enormous amount of time elaborating on the management philosophy, refining the structural model, and developing the corporate policies.

Goran Lindahl, member of the corporate executive committee, characterized the resulting management philosophy as one of 'decentralization under central conditions.' In this system, he described the top management role as being 'to provide a framework' within which those lower in the organization could operate and make decisions. It is a philosophy that closely parallels Bower's view that top management's primary role is to define and manage the organization's 'structural context.'

Similarly, at the front-line management level, Bower's description of managers who were the primary developers of new strategic ideas and investment proposals also rings true in ABB, and detailed evidence of this was presented in the previous section. As the 'policy bible' confirms, 'ABB's improvements are generated by thousands of actions taken by both large and small profit centres .... Every ABB manager must be a driving force for change and development' (1991, p. 18). One manager described his role running a profit centre as 'white water rafting management', but was clear that it was his initiative that drove the agenda of his two matrix bosses. Only partly in jest, he declared, 'We are the master of two slaves!'

It is at the critical level of the middle-level manager – like Don Jans' 'two slaves,' Joe Baker, and Ulf Gundemark – that the practices at ABB differ the most from Bower's process model. In Bower's observation, as in Chandler's, the growing size and complexity of organizations required middle managers to focus most of their time and effort on managing the two vital processes of business planning and resource allocation. The challenge at the centre of the division manager's job was to resolve the problems caused by the asymmetry of information in large complex organizations by communicating the corporation's objectives and standards down to front-line managers and transmitting business needs and opportunities up to corporate level managers. As Bower explained:

> Once the gap between the kinds of information, analysis and choice that goes on at the two extreme levels is recognized, it is obvious that some manager has to provide a consistent integration of the parts.... The detail necessary for conducting an evaluation makes it unfeasible for top management to accomplish the task.
>
> (1970, p. 288)

But Bower recognized that this task involved more than being a two-way communication conduit, and he saw the middle manager's key role being focused on the selection, screening and interpretation of information. Like Chandler, he also viewed this task as legitimizing the multitiered, staff-supported hierarchies that were typical of the organizations both researchers studied. While Chandler described the primary role of staffs at department, divisions and corporate levels in analytic terms – 'an independent check on requests, proposals and estimates' (1962, p. 10) – Bower saw their role more from the political perspective that lay at the heart of his model. At the division level, staff played a key role in helping the general manager 'evaluate projects against their understanding of corporate criteria *for evaluating managers*' (1970, p. 78, emphasis added). Thus, the middle management challenge of 'placing bets' and 'building a track record' required them to focus not only on the content of the projects, but also on the process by which they were developed and the credibility and commitment of those proposing them. To ensure that project initiators would 'defend their projects and plans vigorously' (1970, p. 341), Bower's division general managers needed an expert staff whose primary role was 'to perform the adversary role in the planning process' (1970, p. 342).

The centrality that both Bower and Chandler gave to the resource allocation process in their description of the managerial task was appropriate in describing the organizations they were studying. In the rapidly expanding economy of the 1920s and again in the booming markets of the post-War decades, opportunities far exceeded many companies' ability to finance them. Yet, in today's highly competitive, technologically driven environment, the scarce resource that constrains the growth and strategic success of companies like ABB is not so much capital as it is specialized knowledge and expertise, and the organizational capability that embeds it within the company.

Unlike capital, knowledge is a resource that is difficult to accumulate at the corporate level and allocate according to top management's evaluation of strategic need. In ABB and companies like it, there is an increasingly clear recognition that those with the specialized knowledge and expertise most vital to the company's competitiveness are usually located far away from the corporate headquarters – in the front-line units' research laboratories, marketing groups or engineering departments. By decentralizing assets and resources into these small specialized operating units, these companies are trying to create an environment in which this scarce knowledge can be developed and applied most appropriately. However, this creates a greater need for a powerful horizontal integration process to ensure that the entire organization benefits from the specialized resources and expertise developed in its entrepreneurial units. Forced to free-up its middle managers to create and support such horizontal linkages. ABB found it had to reduce the demands placed on them by the intensive vertical information processing tasks and the complex politically driven decision-making processes that were at the heart of Bower's model. This led the company to create a set of alternative organizational mechanisms to address the problem of hierarchical information asymmetry and the need for information screening.

First, the problem of information asymmetry is considerably alleviated by ABB's commitment to system-wide information sharing. As Barnevik described, 'you don't inform, you *over inform*.' It is a philosophy that has been implemented both throughout the company's formal information systems and its informal communication processes. At the foundation of the company's commitment to keep managers at all levels equally well informed lies ABACUS – ABB's sophisticated information system. Governed by strict rules concerning definition, format and timing, this democratic system ensures that managers around the company receive the same information at the same time regardless of their hierarchical level. Coupled with an organizational norm that puts value on managing content and not just process – reflected in Goran Lindahl's 'fingers-in-the-pie management' – this information sharing approach has created a context in which top management continuously remains in touch with front-line operations, thus reducing the need for middle management to constantly play its upward intermediating role.

Similarly, the company's intensive informal communication processes greatly reduce middle management's need to close the information gap in the other direction. Starting with the mission, values and policies detailed in clear, direct and often tough language in the 'policy bible', senior management sees the communication, interpretation and elaboration of ABB's objectives, priorities and philosophies to the lowest levels as a core task. Barnevik sets the standard and provides the role model for this activity, meeting annually with about 5,000 managers with whom he discusses corporate objectives and priorities which he communicates using some of the 200 overhead transparencies he carries with him. Again, the impact is to reduce the burden on middle management to ensure that corporate objectives and standards are properly transmitted down through the organization.

Beyond managing information asymmetry, ABB has had to develop mechanisms to provide an alternative to the vertical information screening process provided by the successive layers of staff-driven challenge and refinement in Bower's model. Compared to the multi-level hierarchies where investment proposals could be defined by managers 'seven or eight levels below the corporate president' (Bower, 1970, p. 9), the ultra-lean ABB structure has only one level between the executive committee and the front-line managers running the independent operating companies. As a result, middle level managers like Gundemark typically have 10 to 20 companies reporting directly to them, yet must manage this wide span of control without sufficient staff support to provide the independent expertise and adversarial challenge that drove the information screening process in Bower's model.

To replicate the discipline and refinement of the M-form's challenge and evaluation processes, ABB has built into its structure a sophisticated system of internal tension that achieves a similar effect. For every key decision, from establishing strategic priorities and setting budget targets to making key investments and restructuring business operations, managers must present, defend, and adjust their proposals to meet the often conflicting interests of two matrix bosses. Through such a process, ABB subjects the overall planning and resource allocation decisions to a filtering and refinement process at least as powerful as the staff-driven challenges of the traditional model. Equally important is the company's extensive use of self-monitoring and self-regulating mechanisms. For example, BA managers routinely create 'performance league tables' ranking all their businesses' operating companies according to the measures or standards that reflect the priority objectives. This creates an environment of internal competition that requires front-line managers to measure their performances and defend their proposals against the standards set by the best performers within the BA.

With their vertical information processing tasks reduced through such mechanisms, middle managers at ABB are able to focus much more of their attention on the horizontal integration tasks. In contrast to the planning and budgeting dominated role they played in Bower's model, this management group spends considerably more time and effort managing activities such as internal benchmarking, best practice identification, and technology transfer – all aimed at linking and leveraging the company's widely distributed resources and capabilities. The development and management of this intensive horizontal integration process is the second major characteristic distinguishing this organization from the classic M-form.

The integration process: linking and leveraging capabilities

Although this vital capability-building and leveraging task is driven by the middle managers, it requires intensive interaction with and support from managers at all levels of the organization (see Figure 18.3). In ABB, the middle managers' pivotal horizontal linkage role is supported by a top management that creates a value-based context to support and reward collaborative behaviour, and by a front-line management that exploits the personal networks such horizontal relationships facilitate. It is a very different process from the vertical planning and resource allocation process at the core of Bower's model, but a vital one for a company competing in an increasingly knowledge-based economy.

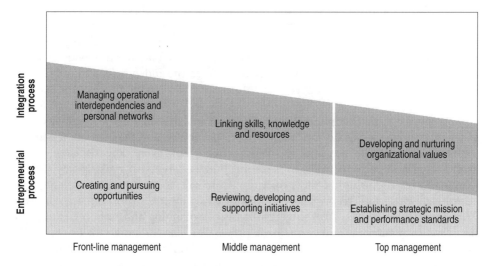

Figure 18.3 The integration process

At the top level, for example, ABB's group executives devote enormous effort to create a sense of shared organizational identity – what Barnevik calls a 'glue' – to bind disparate efforts, as well as organizational norms that value collaboration – a 'lubricant' in Barnevik's terminology – to facilitate the linkages that intensive knowledge transfers require. Without such an organizational context, the centrifugal forces driving independent entrepreneurial units can quickly result in fragmentation, isolation and inter-unit competitiveness to create barriers and defences against internal flow of resources, knowledge and expertise.

Consequently, the first section in ABB's statement of its values is listed as 'Corporate Unity.' Elaborating on this core value the 'policy bible' defines clearly the expectation that individuals and groups would interact 'with mutual confidence, respect and trust ... to eliminate the we/they attitude ... and to remain flexible, open and generous.' Barnevik and his colleagues in the Executive Committee carry the primary responsibility for translating those values into action through their selection and promotion of individuals reflecting such behaviours, their imposition of sanctions against those violating the values, and through their own role-modelling actions.

These strongly ingrained corporate norms and values have created an environment which encourages front-line managers to develop personal networks and operating interdependencies, and rewards them for doing so. Their regular horizontal contacts across formal organizational boundaries create spontaneous transfer of knowledge and expertise that has become a valuable capability of the ABB organization. The linkages are well illustrated by events following the introduction of a time-based management programme by the US relays company as a means of increasing its overall competitiveness in the market. This innovative programme, which required intensive cross-functional co-ordination within the company, was highly successful not only in increasing customer service levels but also in reducing working capital at the same time. At a regular meeting of quality assurance managers held in the premises of the US relays company, the hosts conducted a plant tour as a side event, explaining their just-in-time inventory system and other changes made to reduce throughput time. Without any corporate directive, this programme was transferred to almost every other major relays company in ABB within a year, solely at the initiative of the functional managers and their informal networks.

However, ABB and companies like it cannot rely on such 'spontaneous combustion' to drive the intensive knowledge sharing required in most modern corporations. While the top-level context setting and the front-line personal networks can provide the enabling conditions for this vital horizontal process, it is the middle managers who are the best placed to facilitate these cross-unit linkages. Yet, historically, it has been at this level of the organization where the highest barriers to horizontal transfer of knowledge and expertise has existed, largely due to the structure and management philosophy behind the design of the M-form. By creating divisional managers to carry out the cross-functional integrating task, this successor structure to the functional or U-form organization allowed the top management to devote themselves to the broad corporate-level strategic priorities. In this process, however, the M-form fragmented the company's functional capabilities, while simultaneously creating a norm of divisional autonomy that constrained the reintegration of those capabilities across the divisions.

The integration process framed by ABB's organization structure and management philosophy attempts to overcome this problem of fragmentation of capabilities by avoiding the pitfalls of both the U-form's centralization and consolidation of functional departments and the M-form's decentralization of functions to ensure divisional self-sufficiency. Instead of dividing the company into a small number of independent divisions, ABB has structured itself into 1,300 small companies none of which can ever expect to fully develop or control all required functional capabilities itself. Freed of many of the demands of managing the intensive vertical planning, control and resource allocation processes, and equipped with an intimate knowledge of all the operating companies, the BA managers in ABB are ideally placed to devote substantial time to managing the resulting horizontal interdependencies.

For example, in order to leverage the knowledge and expertise developed in various entrepreneurial units around the world, Gundemark has created a series of additional communication channels and decision-making forums at several levels of the organization. At the lowest level, he has organized functional specialists from the front-line operating companies in the US, Sweden, Finland and Germany into various functional councils, encouraging them to transfer best practice from the leading-edge units to the others. At the next level, he has formed a steering committee for each operating company, nominating to these local boards individuals from the BA management team, the regional staff and others within ABB who could provide the local company with relevant advice or experience. And at the business area level, he has created a BA board with membership drawn from the general managers of his key operating companies, to pool their expertise in shaping the BA's global strategy, management policies and operating objectives. Each of these new structural mechanisms has been managed to maximize its effectiveness as a cross-unit communication channel or decision-making forum, and the company has dramatically increased its use of internal benchmarking and transfer of best practice.

The creation of this broad portfolio of task forces, teams and committees has also had a broader impact on the organizational and management processes: they have served to develop management perspectives and relationships in ways that have helped to prevent isolationism and to break down parochialism, and they have become forums in which managers can negotiate differences and resolve conflicts that are inherent in the matrix structure. These changes in management motivations and behaviours and their consequences for the organizations' goal-setting and learning processes come into sharp focus in the following analysis of ABB from the perspective of Cyert and March's behavioural theory of the firm.

ABB FROM CYERT AND MARCH'S PERSPECTIVE: EMBEDDING PURPOSE AND CHALLENGE

Using clinical field data, experimental studies and computer simulations, Cyert and March formulated a behaviour-based theory of the firm that challenged many of the economists' classic assumptions. By viewing organizations as coalitions of participants with disparate demands, they developed a notion of goal formation in firms that was based on an internal process of bargaining among coalition members. The objectives developed through this process were given stability by internal control mechanisms, particularly by standard operating procedures, yet were adaptable to changes in the external environment and to internal changes in the coalition. To explain decision-making behaviour, Cyert and March developed four key concepts about the way in which firms set objectives, manage expectations, and make choices. In their model, behaviour was driven by the quasi-resolution of conflict, uncertainty avoidance, problemistic search, and organizational learning.

In a global corporation that has very consciously divided itself into 1,300 operating companies which are further fragmented into more than 3,500 profit centres, the notion of an organization as a coalition of diverse interests has a good deal of face validity. And, particularly with regard to the setting of performance targets, Cyert and March's description of organizational objectives being established through a bargaining process provides an accurate description of ABB's system. On the basis of each business's global strategic plan, ABB's executive committee negotiates macrolevel targets for each BA and each geographic area, defining them in terms of broad measures such as growth, profit and return on capital employed. As these macrotargets are transmitted through the organization, each BA and regional manager allocates to each operating company objectives that are defined in terms of more microlevel targets such as new orders, revenue, profit, working capital and headcount. Operating in the matrix, a company manager typically receives different and sometimes conflicting objectives from a BA manager whose priorities may be to maximize global market share and to rationalize worldwide sourcing, and a regional manager who may be working to increase short-term profitability and protect local employment. Forced to agree on a single budget, these three managers then engage in a negotiation that exhibits many of the characteristics of quasi-resolution of conflict. They establish goals on the basis of local rationality, using decision rules based on satisfying rather than maximizing objectives.

Similarly, ABB's management seems to recognize very clearly and explicitly that the tensions in its fragmented organizational system need a strong set of stabilizing mechanisms to reduce complexity, guide action, and control behaviour. Rules of behaviour and guidance on decision-making make up a large part of the company's 'policy bible'. As Cyert and March suggested, these clearly defined 'rules of thumb' and 'standard operating procedures' affect the goals and perceptions of individual ABB managers, as well as the alternatives they consider and decision rules they use in the company's organizational choice process.

For example, it was largely because of its detailed and clearly understood policies and procedures that the company was able to make a large number of vital rationalization decisions in a concentrated two-year period. The speed with which the decisions were made was even more impressive since issues such as the allocation of production capacity and export markets among the companies that had historically competed against one another were obviously highly divisive in nature. Such strategically important and politically sensitive decisions could be agreed on and implemented so quickly only because there was a clear and detailed set of rules laid out in the 'policy bible' relating to such matters as the full utilization of existing facilities before proposing new investments, the principle of locating investments as close as possible to long-term markets, and the mechanics of determining internal sourcing patterns and transfer prices.

Finally, the dynamics underlying ABB's demonstrated market responsiveness and technological adaptability can be captured, at least partially, in Cyert and March's notion of organizational learning. There are scores of examples of the way in which the firm has adapted its practices in response to changes in the highly complex and dynamic global power equipment market. Many of these adjustments have been subsequently institutionalized as new policies, guidelines or rules. To retrieve an earlier example, in 1988, the rule of thumb that guided ABB's major restructuring effort was that every staff group above the operating company level be cut to 10 per cent of its previous size. The prescribed guideline for the remaining 90 per cent was that 30 per cent be retired or laid off, 30 per cent be assigned to independent, self-sufficient service centres, and 30 per cent be redeployed to the decentralized operating companies. Four years later, reflecting the experience of several businesses able to make even deeper cuts, the rule of thumb had changed, and managers were being required to cut the staffs assigned to service centres from 30 per cent to 15 per cent, those in profit centres from 30 per cent to 20 per cent, and the remaining corporate staffs from 10 per cent of their original level to 5 per cent.

Yet, as insightful as many of these concepts are in describing some of the microlevel processes in ABB, they clearly do not capture the main thrust of its management decision-making. In particular, Cyert and March describe an organizational learning process that is fragmented in approach ('with shifts tending to reflect the expansionist inclinations of subunits rather than systematic reviews by top management' [1963, p. 112],) short-term in focus ('so long as the environment of the firm is unstable and unpredictably unstable, the heart of the theory must be the process of short-run adaptive reactions' [p. 100]), and incremental in nature ('because many of the rules change slowly, it is possible to construct models of organizational behavior that postulate only modest changes in decision rules' [p. 101]). This fragmented, short-term focused and incremental learning process is assumed to be captured in and institutionalized by the company's standard operating procedures (SOPs) – 'the memory of an organization' (p. 101). In contrast, our observations suggest that the simplifying nature of SOPs, and the slowness with which they change often make them impediments rather than facilitators of effective renewal in the highly competitive, technologically sophisticated global environment in which companies like ABB operate. As a result, the process of incremental learning at the microlevel tends to be framed by a much more macro process in which top management plays a key role.

Barnevik's ability to continually shake up the internal operations of ABB has, over the years, stimulated a much more dramatic and strategically focused process of organizational learning than the incremental process described by Cyert and March. For example, his decisions to merge the previously separate power generation, power transmission and power distribution businesses, to introduce a company-wide customer focus programme, and to acquire companies that would leverage ABB's environmental protection technologies were all initiated to force such internal adjustment and learning. As he stated, 'These efforts do not represent a one-time project, but will push ABB in the direction of becoming a continuous learning organization.' (President's comments, ABB 1991 Annual Report, p. 9).

The framing of this more macro process of organizational learning occurs within a goal-setting process that is also at variance from the Cyert and March model in which a company's objectives are defined in terms of bargained constraints, its aspirations determined by individuals' past experiences, and its actions primarily driven by a short-term problem-solving process. In contrast to this view that firms 'solve pressing problems rather than develop long-range strategy' (1963, p. 119), ABB managers at all levels place a great deal of importance on developing clear and shared strategic objectives. This process is rooted in a corporate vision that Barnevik presented at the senior management meeting in Cannes marking the formal merging of the two companies. While based on detailed analysis, this vision was hardly the outcome of internally bargained trade-offs. Instead, it reflected Barnevik's strongly held personal beliefs about the power industry and his assessment of the resources and capabilities within ABB. Some of these beliefs, such as his strong commitment to the then stagnant power equipment industry, were indeed contrary to the widely held views among ABB managers that the company needed to diversify away from this business. Yet, that vision became the basis for a massive acquisition activity, a major R&D investment programme, and a variety of related strategic commitments.

To ensure the implementation of this overall blueprint, the company has created new structures and processes to allow managers at all levels to translate the broad objectives into specific business and market strategies. First, within the corporate executive committee, then at BA board meetings, and finally in the operating companies' steering committees, managers examine the implications of Barnevik's vision for their particular areas of responsibility. Overall, these processes of goal formation and organizational learning appear to be much closer to the 'entrepreneurial' and 'consensual' models that Cyert and March rejected. Furthermore, at the business level, the discussions to develop a consensus about strategies and priorities do not result in an outcome that Cyert and March feared would be 'rather vague objectives' under which would lie 'disagreement and uncertainty about subgoals' (1963, p. 28). In fact, the annually updated business strategies become the basis for annual budget targets broken into very specific subgoals that are negotiated and agreed between business, geographic and company managements.

The renewal process: creating purpose and challenge

In sum, ABB has created a much more rational macroframework for goal setting and learning, capturing them both in a third core organizational process we describe as the renewal process (Figure 18.4). Like the entrepreneurial and integration processes, it is defined by a set of top, middle and front-line management roles that not only drive the process but also embed it in the organization's ongoing activities. But, while the front-line managers are the key drivers of the entrepreneurial process and middle management proves the anchor for the integration process, it is the top management of the company that takes the lead in inspiring and energising the renewal process.

This process of purposeful corporate renewal is very different from the individually based, negotiation-driven process by which Cyert and March assumed that companies established their goals and aspiration levels. In fact, many of Barnevik's earliest actions were designed to break the coalitions and redefine the policies that had made ABB's precedent companies operate in such a politically negotiated manner. By reassigning managers, stripping out organization layers, redefining SOPs and shifting the locus of power towards the operating companies, he reshaped coalition membership and redefined the relationships among them. Rather than waiting for the new organization to develop and institutionalize new objectives and behavioural norms through what Cyert and March described as

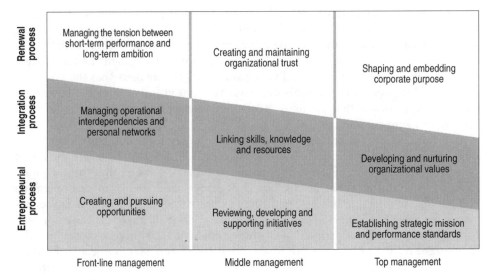

Figure 18.4 The renewal process

'accidents of organizational genealogy' (1963, p. 34), he intervened strongly to define a new common purpose and ambition to shape those objectives and standards.

In doing so, Barnevik seems to reject Cyert and March's assertion that 'people have goals, collectives of people do not' (1963, p. 26) as well as their complementary belief that the organizational aspiration level is determined by the attainable goals aspired to by individual coalition members according to their perceptions of the past. Instead, he has focused ABB on a very ambitious, future-orientated sense of corporate mission that is defined with sufficient conviction and communicated with sufficient intensity that it can result in a simultaneous raising and convergence of individual aspiration levels within the company. It is an activity to which he has devoted an enormous amount of time, first in developing a clearly articulated sense of purpose, and then in overlaying it with a more dynamic sense of challenge.

While many companies have aspired to the voguish objective of 'creating a shared vision,' Barnevik seems to have moved well beyond the rhetoric towards making this an operating reality at ABB. He has done so through several means. The company's mission statement is designed to engage organization members worldwide and to align their interests with ABB's broadly defined corporate purpose 'to contribute to environmentally sound sustainable growth and make improved living standards a reality for all nations around the world' (1991, p. 6). With such a statement, Barnevik has created the sense of 'public interest' and 'social welfare' that Cyert and March saw as providing the common goal of political institutions (1963, p. 28). However, the mission statement then expands that unifying altruistic purpose into a more managerial objective: 'to increase the value of our products based on continuous technological innovation and on the competence and motivation of our employees ... becoming a global leader – the most competitive, competent, technologically advanced and quality minded electrical engineering company in our fields of activity' (1991, p. 6). This translation of the broad mission to a strategic objective lends it a sense of organizational reality and legitimacy, and gives it more managerial power and relevance. Barnevik has further operationalized the broad vision by expressing the goals in financial performance terms – 10 per cent operating profit and 25 per cent return on capital employed by the mid 1990s. Such statements have not only provided a common aspiration level, they have also moved the mission statement beyond the 'ambiguous goals' and 'vague objectives' that led Cyert and March to conclude that such solutions to the goal-setting problem were 'misdirected' (1963, p. 28).

Beyond creating a shared purpose, Barnevik has taken on a major role in providing the organization with a sense of ambition that, on the one hand, legitimizes the company's stretch targets and, on the other hand, creates sufficient strategic turmoil to stimulate organizational learning. For example, recognizing that ABB was too dependent on a stagnant European market, Barnevik set an objective of expanding its North American sales to represent 25 per cent of the company's total. To initiate change, he acquired Combustion Engineering and Westinghouse's power transmission and distribution business in the United States, grafting these operations on to ABB's existing BAs. Not only did such a move boost the North American share of ABB's sales from 12 per cent to 18 per cent, it also exposed the European dominated business to North American technical developments (such as process control automation) and management practices (such as time based management) that were previously neither well understood nor effectively practised in the ABB system.

The dual impact of a clearly defined anchor of corporate purpose juxtaposed against a slightly dissonant corporate ambition is felt particularly strongly in the front-line units. It is here that managers confront the gap between current performance and the aspiration level defined by the visionary purpose statement and the stretching ambition. If this process is to remain in balance, however, this tension created in the front-line units must be resolved. And without a high level of credibility and trust, such resolution can easily degenerate into horse trading or grand compromises. Creating and maintaining credibility and trust in the system, therefore, is a key requirement and these tasks define the main responsibilities of middle management in the renewal process.

One important means for executing these responsibilities lies in their stewardship of the various horizontal co-ordination mechanisms we have described. In contrast to Cyert and March's assumption that 'firms do not resolve potential conflict ... by a procedure of explicit mediation' (1963, p. 27), managers like Ulf Gundemark create and manage a portfolio of boards, committees and project teams that serve not only as channels for the communication and transfer of knowledge, but are also explicitly designated as forums where managers can negotiate differences and resolve conflicts in an open and legitimate manner.

Middle managers also ensure the legitimacy and credibility of this tension-filled process by creating a decision-making context which is both participative and transparent. To ensure the credibility of top management's ambitious objectives, for example, Ulf Gundemark formed a Relays Vision 2000 Task Force of nine operating managers from various front-line companies, and charged them with the task of translating Barnevik's broad vision of ABB's place in the global power equipment industry into specific strategies for the relays business. After six months of intensive effort this task force developed a set of self-funding proposals that ranged from strategic investments to expand into new products (like metering) and new markets (like telecommunications), to plans for increasing employee motivation and organizational effectiveness. With a legitimacy and credibility that came from being defined by peers rather than being imposed by the top management, the strategy was accepted by front line managers like Jans who began trying to meet the ambitious challenges by expanding beyond their existing business boundaries into the new products and markets legitimized by Vision 2000.

The behavioural theory of the firm is, in essence, premised on the absence of leadership, while ABB's renewal process is clearly driven by highly effective leaders at the company's top level. In this specific attribute, the Cyert and March model is fundamentally different from Chandler's conceptualization of the classic M-form organization, which was premised on a strong leadership role of the top management. Alfred Sloan's towering presence in General Motors is perhaps the best known illustration of this role, as reflected in Chandler's (1962) description of him as the architect of GM's strategy, the builder of its structure, and the designer of its systems. Ever since Sloan and his pioneering contemporaries discovered how the then emerging strategy of diversification was facilitated by the divisional structure and how that structure could be supported by some tightly designed planning and control systems, this strategy–structure-systems link has become an article of faith that has shaped top management roles in most large M-form organizations.

While it is clear that the role played by Barnevik and other top managers at ABB is not well captured by Cyert and March's model, it is important to understand how it also has diverged from the top management role described by Chandler. Given their starting point in the midst of a fusion between two large worldwide companies, Barnevik and his colleagues in ABB's group executive management initially focused on these tasks of formulating the merged company's strategy, structure and systems. Over time, however, their roles have evolved to be significantly different from these classic responsibilities of leadership in M-form organizations. From being formulators of corporate strategy, they have become the shapers of an institutional purpose with which all employees can identify and to which they can commit. Instead of being the architects of formal structure, they have come to see themselves as the developers of organizational processes that can capture individual initiative and create supporting relationships. And, rather than being the designers of systems, they have refocused on the individual as the primary unit of analysis in the leadership task and have become the moulders of people.

Leadership in the M-form is fundamentally based on the view of companies as economic entities: managers in ABB and in most of the other companies we studied have premised their role on the recognition that large corporations are also complex social institutions. To capture the energy, commitment and creativity of their people, these managers are replacing the hard-edged strategy–structure–systems paradigm of the M-form with a softer, more organic model built around purpose, process and people. The renewal process we have described challenges the behavioural theory of the firm by the very existence of the leadership role; but it equally challenges Chandler's model of the M-form because of this basic change in the content of that role.

FRAMING THE MODEL: TOWARDS A MANAGERIAL THEORY OF THE FIRM

Chandler, Bower and Cyert and March provided three different and generally complementary views of the same phenomenon – the multi-divisional organization that had first emerged in the 1920s, growing to become the corporate model of the 1950s and 1960s when all three studies were undertaken, and continuing to dominate the assumptions on which most large companies structured their operations into the 1990s. In examining the ABB organization through the perspectives of these three pioneering conceptual models, our objective was not only to develop a richer understanding of the subject of the analysis, but also to derive insights and ideas that would provide the basis for a new model of the large, complex firm more appropriate for companies like ABB.

This new organizational model we have proposed is a product of two interrelated but separate factors, and in this concluding section of the paper we will examine the implications of both. First, it reflects changes in the phenomenon being studied. Over the last decade or so, the operating environments of large global firms have changed significantly, requiring managers not only to rethink the structures and processes of their companies but also their own underlying management philosophies. The model we have presented here describes these emerging organizational characteristics and the new managerial assumptions on which they are built. In other words, the new model represents a real change in the organizations of large firms caused by the changes in their environments and task demands.

But our model also reflects a different research perspective. Despite the obvious fact that organizations are social structures that shape and are shaped by the relationships among actors within their social systems, organizational analysis has historically focused on abstract generalizations of relationships represented by its formal structure. In contrast, in Figure 18.4, we have defined our model in terms of three core processes that are built around a specific set of relationships among the front-line, middle and top management of a company. In this way, we have presented a conceptualization of organizations, not as a scheme for dividing the overall corporate activities among a group of subunits, but as a cluster of roles and their interrelationships. From this perspective, it is the behaviour and actions associated with each of these roles that collectively define the social structure of a company within which its management processes are embedded. Thus, the new model is also the product of a different way of viewing and conceptualizing organizations.

Changes in the phenomenon

Based on his retrospective analysis of business organizations, Chandler concluded that 'historically, administrators have rarely changed their daily routine and their positions of power except under the strongest pressures. Therefore, a study of the creation of new administrative forms and methods should point to urgent needs and compelling opportunities both within and without the firm' (1962, p. 2). Indeed the stability and institutionalization of the M-form organization over more than six decades has provided some significant confirmation of this observation.

In the late 1980s and early 1990s there were several new forces in the environment that were driving firms to develop a different management approach. In many industries, growth was occurring more slowly than earlier optimistic expectations, leaving most firms to contend with serious overcapacities and intensifying their need to reduce costs as a way to protect profits. At the same time, technological change was accelerating, reconfiguring industry structures and boundaries, and increasing the need for speed and flexibility at the firm level. Simultaneously, information processing technologies were transforming internal organizational activities and management roles.

The combined impact of this slowing market growth, accelerating technological change and transforming organizational process was to shift the focus of many firms from allocating capital to managing knowledge and learning as the key strategic task. And, in this overall context of an increasing dependence on knowledge and expertise, the ability to attract and retain the best people was increasingly becoming a key source of competitive advantage. Collectively, these factors created the 'urgent needs and compelling opportunities' that have forced companies like ABB to challenge the basic assumptions about corporate structure and management processes that lay at the core of their multidivisional organizations.

Concerned by the cost of supporting the heavily staffed, multitiered configuration into which such organizations have evolved (for example, Bower's research site showed eight layers of general management from the CEO to the product group manager; ABB's predecessor company, Brown Boveri, had nine), and frustrated by the slowness and inflexibility it caused in decision-making, the most obvious target companies focused on was their basic organizational structure. Managers like Percy Barnevik began to challenge the conventional wisdom that the classic multi-divisional hierarchy was the structural model of choice for large, diversified companies. In doing so, they began to question the basic philosophy underlying that venerable organization form.

Because the M-form typically succeeded the functionally organized U-form company, it built on a management model in which responsibility and authority were concentrated at the apex of the organization in the hands of its only general manager, the CEO. In creating the multidivisional structure, companies were literally dividing the single corporate entity into several entities appropriately called divisions. The new structural units were given legitimacy and power through the allocation of resources and delegation of responsibility to general managers created at this level. In short, the M-form was created through a philosophy of devolution of assets and accountability from the corporate to the divisional level.

The new organizational model we have described, however, represents a radically different structural philosophy. Conceptually, it is based on an assumption that the organization needs to be developed and managed on a principle of *proliferation and subsequent aggregation* of small independent entrepreneurial units from the bottom up, rather than one of *division and devolution* of resources and responsibilities from the top. This structural philosophy implies a significantly different distribution of corporate assets and resources. In contrast to the classic M-form where control over most resources is held at the corporate level, in the new model, resources are decentralized to the front-line units which operate with limited dependence on the corporate parent for technological, financial or human resources, but with considerable interdependence among themselves. In turn, this approach allows a drastic reduction in supervisory layers (like Barnevik at ABB, Jack Welch's objective has been to reduce the number of organizational layers at GE from ten to four) and the size of staff groups each level of management needs.

Beyond driving these changes in the macro-structure, the environmental shifts have also led managers in the new organizations to focus on a very different kind of organizational process compared to those that dominated the operations of traditional divisionalized companies. Chandler's structural perspective concentrated his attention on a set of processes he identified as strategic and tactical decision-making. Bower's model of the firm as a political organizm led him to focus on hierarchical information processing activities that influenced resource allocation decisions. And Cyert and March's view of the firm as a coalition of participants negotiating to achieve their disparate objectives drew their attention to the microlevel processes of setting and adjusting objectives. While shaped by the perspectives of their research, this focus on planning, resource allocation, and objective-setting also reflected the emphasis managers of multidivisional companies placed on these processes. The common characteristics of all these processes was that they were administrative in their focus and function, and were designed primarily to reflect the vertical information processing and decision-making capabilities of the M-form structure. Yet, eventually it was the complexity and inefficiency of these internally focused planning, allocating and controlling activities that forced many companies to make radical changes to their organizations.

In the emerging organizational model, the elaborate planning, co-ordination and control systems have been drastically redesigned and simplified as management time and attention has shifted towards the creation and management of processes more directly related to adding value than on facilitating internal administrative activities. It was this shift in focus that led to the widespread implementation of process-based activities such as total quality implementation, new product development, or customer-focused management for example. At the most strategic level, this has resulted in the development of the three core processes that are at the heart of our model. In many ways, these three processes provide a necessary counterbalance to the biases and limiting assumptions that were increasingly causing difficulties in the classic M-form organization. The entrepreneurial process highlights the need to supplement top management's direction and control with front-line initiative and flexibility; the integration process creates a horizontal information-processing capacity at least as efficient as the previously dominant vertical mechanisms; and the renewal process imposes a dynamic tension into the organization that prevents it from developing strategic commitment at the cost of organizational adaptability. It is a process management orientation quite different from the classic one of ensuring that the allocation of resources matched the strategic priorities and that operating performance met the budgeted objectives.

Just as the largest companies of the time, like General Motors, DuPont, Sears and Jersey Oil, were pioneers of the new M-form organization in the 1920s and 1930s because they experienced the emerging environmental shifts most acutely, so too are the largest global companies of today like General Electric, ABB, 3M, Toyota and Canon acting as the pioneers of the new organizational form we have described. They are often the first to experience the strains because their existing organizations are stretched so thin by the 'urgent needs and compelling opportunities' arising from the emerging internal and external environmental demands.

Documenting a change that had occurred a few decades earlier, Chandler could both describe the multidivisional organization quite precisely and provide some clear evidence of its advantages over the functional form. Not having the benefit of such a retrospective perspective, our description of the new organizational model is considerably less rigorous. However, as we will show in a forthcoming monograph, we observed several companies in our sample independently developing similar organizational characteristics, leading us to conclude that the changes being made at ABB are not an idiosyncratic experiment. Our hypothesis is that these companies and others are laying the basic foundations of an emerging organizational form for large complex corporations.

A different research perspective

Over the last two decades, organizational theory has come to be increasingly dominated by a remote, refined and pessimistic view of large organizations. The remoteness is manifest in theories such as population ecology and transaction cost analysis in which the focal level of analysis either lies in gross aggregations such as organizational populations or in the microlevel detail of specific transactions. With such distant foci, in these theories, organizations have been reduced to refined abstractions, stripped of all the correctness of social actions and relations that define them. At the same time, these theories have presented a view of individual–organization interactions that is grounded in the assumption that the human role in organizations is essentially passive and pathological. This negative assumption about human agency is manifest in the extreme determinism in population ecology (Hannan and Freeman, 1977), the powerful forces of isomorphism that have virtually replaced the role of leadership in institutional theory (contrast, for example, DiMaggio and Powell, 1983 and Selznick, 1957), the denial of purpose and direction in behavioural theory of the firm (Cyert and March, 1963) and the assumptions about shirking, opportunism and inertia in organizational economics (Williamson, 1975; Alchian and Demsetz, 1972). The organizational model we have presented here represents a different perspective on both organizations and on individual–organization interactions.

An organization is fundamentally a social structure. Even though actions of and within organizations may be motivated by a variety of economic and other objectives, they emerge through processes of social interactions that are shaped by the social structure. Over 35 years ago, Merton provided a framework for the analysis of such interactions based on the definitions of statuses and roles within the social structure. As argued by Merton 'status' implies a position in a social system involving designated rights and obligations and 'role' defines the behaviour orientated to the patterned expectations of others. 'In these terms, status and roles become concepts serving to connect culturally defined expectations with the patterned conduct and relationships which make up a social structure' (Merton, 1957, p. 110). Weick (1969) has similarly defined the structure of an organization in terms of 'interlocking behaviours' which are reciprocal actions that are repeated over time. As summarized by Nelson, 'if behaviors between two or more parties are repeated over time to the point where those behaviors are taken for granted as normal or expected, the resulting relationship or tie has become part of the organizational structure' (1986, p. 75). Despite this clearly relational nature of the concept, however, an increasing preoccupation with structural forms has resulted in most organizational analysis focusing not on the network of roles and relationships that define a social structure but on constructs such as centralization, formalization or divisionalization which, at best, represent some broad generalizations about those relationships.

In contrast, in Figure 18.4 we have defined the new organizational model in terms of three core positions within a company's management structure – the front-line, middle and top-level managers – and the behaviours and actions associated with each of them. Each of the three core processes is structured around a specific set of relationships across these three roles; the three processes coexist because of the overall symbiosis within and across those roles. In this way, we have defined the structure of the organization, not in terms of how subunits are composed and decomposed but as a cluster of statuses and associated roles that collectively define the social structure of a company within which its core management processes are embedded.

In explicating its differences from the M-form's structure, processes and decision-making mechanisms, we could have built our arguments not by focusing on the three processes in the new organizational model but by highlighting the very different roles that front-line, middle and top-level managers play in companies like ABB (see Table 18.1). In Chandler's model, the top management is the entrepreneur and resource allocator, middle managers are the administrative controllers, and front-line managers are the operational implementers. For Bower, the top-level manager is the creator of a company's structural context, the middle manager is the vertical information broker, while the front-line manager is the initiator of operating decisions. In Cyert and March's analysis, top-level management is the dominant coalition that establishes the standard operating procedures and resolves conflict, middle managers are the champions and advocates of subunit preferences based on local rationality, while front-line managers are the organization's problem solvers. In the organizational model we have described, while all the three management groups have key roles to play in each of the three core processes, top-level managers are primarily the creators of organizational purpose and the challengers of the *status quo*, middle-level managers are the horizontal integrators of strategy and capabilities, and the front-line managers are the organizational entrepreneurs.

Table 18.1 Roles and tasks of management

	Chandler	Bower	Cyert and March	New model
Top management	Entrepreneur and resource allocator	Creator of structural context	Establisher of SOPs and resolver of conflicts	Creator of purpose and challenger of status quo
Middle management	Administrative controller	Vertical information broker	Advocate of subunit goals	Horizontal information broker and capability integrator
Front-line management	Operational implementer	Initiator	Problem solver	Entrepreneur and performance driver

The second difference in our research perspective relates to the assumptions that are made about the nature of human motivations and interpersonal behaviour within organizations. Particularly in comparison to economic theories that assume a human propensity towards shirking, opportunism and inertia (Williamson, 1975; Alchian and Demsetz, 1972), the managers in the firms we studied took a much less pathological view of human nature. The new model developed from management perspectives reflects that orientation.

The more positive view of human nature on which this model is built, however, does not rely on a fundamental premise of altruism as a stable human disposition. Instead, it reflects more of a relativist view of personal attributes, and more of a situationalist perspective on human behaviour (see Kenrick and Funder, 1988 for a recent review of this perspective). Its assumptions, based on our interpretation of the views most managers we interviewed expressed, is that human beings are capable of both initiative and shirking, that they are given to both collaboration and opportunism, and that they are constrained by inertia but are also capable of learning. Within a firm, actual behaviour is determined in part by the prior disposition of actors (i.e., the location on the spectrum of personal characteristics of the particular individuals involved) and in part by the situation they face (i.e., how the firm's context influences their behaviour) (see Figure 18.5).

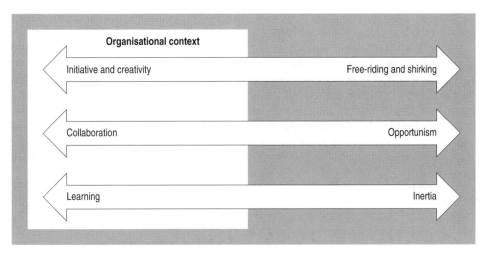

Figure 18.5 Shaping individual behaviour: the role of context

This model assumes that companies ensure positive individual characteristics both by selecting and promoting those whose personal characteristics predispose them towards the desired norms of behaviour, and by creating an internal context that encourages people to act in the way they would as a member of a functional family or a disciplined sporting team. Thus, the entrepreneurial process is built on the assumption that individuals have the capacity of personal agency and initiative, then creates the selection devices and support mechanisms to elicit and encourage such behaviour. Similarly, the integration process both assumes and shapes collaborative behaviour, and the renewal process is designed to capitalize on the human motivation to learn while creating a context that drives them to do so. In short, the same managerial actions that drive the three processes also help create an organizational context that reinforces the effectiveness of the processes by inducing organizational members to take initiative, co-operate and learn. This interactive and mutually reinforcing development of management action, organizational context and individual behaviour is of central importance to the model we have presented here and we will elaborate and illuminate these interactions more thoroughly in a forthcoming article (Ghoshal and Bartlett, 1994).

Towards a managerial theory

We call ours a managerial model for two reasons. First, it describes the firm in terms of the managerial roles necessary to develop and manage the three core processes. Equally important, however, is the fact that the model was developed by analysing the operations of a firm from the perspective and in the language of the managers who live within the system. In this sense, our model is very different from currently dominant theories of the firm which are grounded in the perspectives and languages of different social sciences. The managerial perspective in our model, we believe, is at least as useful for illuminating organizational phenomena as those generated by economists describing the firm in the context of market failure or social psychologists describing it as a higher order aggregation of individual and group behaviour that are typically their focal level of analysis. It is this managerial perspective that we would like to see legitimized in a new theory of the firm that would focus on the distinctive characteristics of large business organizations and illuminate issues that managers of such firms perceive to be important. As we acknowledged in the introductory section, clearly a lot more work has to be done before this initial effort of describing a new organizational form can progress to the stage of presenting an alternative theory of the firm. Our hope is that the model we have proposed in this article might provide some energy to that agenda.

ACKNOWLEDGEMENTS

The authors would like to thank Richard Cyert, Yves Doz, Mitchell Koza, Peter Moran, Nitin Nohria, Richard Rumelt and Jeffrey Williams for their helpful comments on earlier drafts of this paper.

REFERENCES

ABB (1991) *ABB Mission, Values and Policies*, ABB Internal Publications.

Alchian, A.A. and Demsetz, H. (1972) 'Production, information costs, and economic organization', *American Economic Review*, Vol. 62, No. 5, pp. 777–95.

Allison, G.T. (1971) *Essence of Decision*, Little, Brown, Boston, MA.

Barnard, C.I. (1938) *The Functions of the Executive*. Harvard University Press, Cambridge, MA.

Bower, J.L. (1970) *Managing the Resource Allocation Process*, Division of Research, Graduate School of Business Administration, Harvard University, Boston, MA.

Chandler, A.D. (1962) *Strategy and Structure*, The MIT Press, Cambridge, MA.

Chandler, A.D. (1991) 'The functions of the HQ unit in the multibusiness firm', *Strategic Management Journal*, Vol. 12, pp. 31–50.

Cyert, R.M. and March, J.G. (1963) *A Behavioural Theory of the Firm*, Prentice-Hall, Englewood Cliffs, NJ.

DiMaggio, P.J. and Powell, W.W. (1983) 'The Iron Cage revisited: institutional isomorphism and collective rationality in organizational fields', *American Sociological Review*, Vol. 48, pp. 147–60.

Ghoshal, S., and Bartlett, C.A. (1994) 'Linking organizational context and managerial action: the dimensions of quality of management', *Strategic Management Journal*, Summer Special Issue.

Hamel, G. and Prahalad, C.K. (1993) 'Strategy as stretch and leverage', *Harvard Business Review*, March–April, pp. 75–84.

Handy, C. (1990) *The Age of Unreason*, Harvard Business School Press, Boston, MA.

Hannan, M.T. and Freeman, J. (1977) 'The population ecology of organizations', *American Journal of Sociology*, Vol. 82, pp. 929–64.

Hill, C.W. (1988) 'Internal capital market controls and financial performance in multidivisional firms', *Journal of Industrial Economics*, Vol. 37 No. 1, pp. 67–83.

Kanter, R.M. (1983) *The Change Masters*, Simon & Schuster, New York.

Kenrick, D.T. and Funder, D.C. (1988) 'Profiting from controversy: lessons from the person–situation debate', *American Psychologist*, Vol. 43 No. 1, pp. 23–34.

Merton, R.K. (1957) 'The role-set: problems in sociological theory', *British Journal of Sociology*, Vol. 8, pp. 106–20.

Nelson, R.E. (1986) 'The use of Block modelling in the study of organization structure: a methodological proposal', *Organization Studies*, Vol. 7, No. 1, pp. 75–85.

Peters, T. (1992) *Liberation Management*, Knopf, New York.

Prahalad, C.K. and Doz, Y.L. (1987) *The Multinational Mission*, The Free Press, New York.

Selznick, P. (1957) *Leadership in Administration*, Harper and Row, New York.

Taylor, W. (1991) 'The logic of global business: an interview with ABB's Percy Barnevik', *Harvard Business Review*, March–April, pp. 91–105.

Weber, M. (1964) *Basic Concepts in Sociology*, Citadel Press, New York.

Weick, K.E. (1969) *The Social Psychology of Organizing*, Addison-Wesley, Reading, MA.

Williamson, O.E. (1975) *Markets and Hierarchies: analysis and antitrust implications*, The Free Press, New York.

CHAPTER 19

THE INTERNATIONALIZATION OF SERVICE FIRMS

SUSAN SEGAL-HORN

Little of the literature in international business or global strategy addresses the service sector. Indeed, much of the research in service management suggests that services are not easily reproduced across borders and are therefore inappropriate for internationalization. This paper reviews changes in the nature of service characteristics which had led to greater international expansion by service firms. These include the increased availability of scale and scope economies in services and changed asset structures of service firms. The paper then discusses how scale and/or scope economies are differentially distributed across varying types of service businesses. As the potential for scale and scope economies affects competition in services, the result may be the creation of similar types of asset structures and similar industry dynamics to manufacturing.

INTRODUCTION

Service industries are generally regarded as possessing specific characteristics which determine the predominantly 'local' structure of service firms. These include intangibility, perishability, simultaneity of production and consumption, and buyer/supplier interaction in delivery of the service. Traditional assumptions about these service characteristics have been regarded as fundamental to the definition of what constitutes a service (Shostack, 1977; Sasser *et al.*, 1978; Normann, 1984; Daniels, 1985; Albrecht and Zemke, 1985; Heskett, 1986; Hindley, 1987; Carlzon, 1987; Lovelock, 1988; O'Farrell and Hitchens, 1990).

This heavy emphasis on 'front-office' activities in the creation and delivery of a service means that international expansion has represented higher levels of risk and additional difficulties for service businesses compared to those faced by manufacturing businesses (Carman and Langeard, 1980) – especially, the risk of being distant from the customer interface and the problems of maintaining quality control at the point of service delivery. When combined with industry characteristics such as low entry barriers, diseconomies of scale, and close local control, these factors explain why service industries were historically defined as 'local' industries, unsuited to international expansion. However, despite these 'local' assumptions, there exists a degree of *de facto* internationalization of service firms, including multinational enterprises (MNC) and DMNC service firms.

MNCs are expected to standardize or adapt their activities at the optimum level consistent with the most advantageous international cost, scale, and market positions available to them (Hout *et al.*, 1982; Bartlett and Ghoshal, 1986, 1987, 1989; Prahalad and Doz, 1987; Kogut, 1989; Kobrin, 1991). There is a growing view that for service firms, also, MNC operations provide similar competitive opportunities to the firms that utilize them (Dunning, 1989; Enderwick, 1989). The approach taken here builds on the economic literature of the growth of the multinational enterprise (Teece, 1980, 1982; Caves, 1982; Cassno, 1982; Dunning, 1981, 1985, 1989). Since industries are taken as aggregates of firms, and firms as distinctive asset structures, evidence of industry evolution can be based on the evolution of the asset structures of individual firms.

In their international expansion, service firms might be expected to seek to benefit from the same sources of potential advantage as manufacturing firms. These were collected by Ghoshal (1987) under the three headings of: national differences (e.g., to obtain beneficial factor costs or offset country-specific government policies); scale economies (e.g., to spread cost reduction and experience effects across national boundaries, to expand or exploit scale in purchasing, distribution, capital costs, and so forth) and scope economies (e.g., shared investments, knowledge, and learning across products and markets). The issue is whether such benefits from international expansion are as attainable for service firms as for manufacturing firms.

This paper argues that the sources of competitive advantage in service industries are changing. A combination of structural, market, regulatory, and technological changes has provided a shift in the balance of activities within service firms. Greater emphasis on 'back-office' activities may be lowering the levels of perceived risk, and enhancing the potential benefits, attached to international expansion of service firms.

The paper adapts, for service firms, Chandler's model (1977, 1986, 1990) of a 'logic' of manufacturing industry growth to explain the growth of service multinational enterprises. An exploration and development of this framework is used to show the potential of economies of scale and economies scope within a variety of service firms. In addition, some initial criteria are presented for measuring scale and scope in service firms. Of particular interest are variables which drive cost for a service firm, since international expansion of a service firm should involve some efficiency advantages to justify the costs of integration of cross-border operations, compared to provision of the service by a domestic firm. An approach is suggested to understanding how economies of scale and scope actually work in service firms. These appear to be having some impact on the creation of international oligopolies in services.

THE APPLICATION OF CHANDLER'S 'LOGIC' TO SERVICES

Chandler's model, as an explanatory framework for the growth of MNE service firms, suggests a shift in the underlying 'logic' of service industry growth. It implies that the current dynamic of growth of service firms is beginning to parallel that in manufacturing.

The manufacturing 'logic'

Chandler's work (1977, 1986, 1990) addresses the circumstances under which a firm will continue to grow to maintain a position of dominance. The economic basis of Chandler's model is 'the cost advantages that scale and scope provided in technologically advanced, capital-intensive industries' (1990, p. 32). This model of the managerial enterprise was built on manufacturing industry data (e.g., oil, pharmaceuticals, agricultural machinery, steel) from which industries which remained technologically simple and labour-intensive (e.g., textiles, leather, publishing) were excluded. Chandler (1986) showed that in sectors where few large firms appeared their absence was because neither technological nor organizational innovation substantially increased minimum efficient scale. Therefore, in those industries, large plants did not offer significant cost advantages over smaller ones and 'opportunities for cost-reduction through more efficient co-ordination of high-volume throughout by managerial teams remained limited' (1986, p. 417). Hierarchies (Chandler's 'visible hand' (1977)) emerged and spread 'only in those industries or sectors whose technology and markets permitted administrative co-ordination to be more profitable than market co-ordination' (p. 11).

The structure of service industries lay outside Chandler's 'logic'. Despite considerable variance across sectors, service industries have been neither as technologically advanced nor as capital-intensive as manufacturing. They had exhibited minimum efficient scale at low levels, with significant diseconomies of scale reached at modest levels of growth. (For an example of all these industry features, see Dermine and Röller (1990) on the French mutual funds industry, where economies of both scale and scope are demonstrated for small to medium-size firms but disappear for larger firms.) The special characteristics of service businesses have also long been viewed as having an effect on both demand for, and supply of, services (Eiglier and Langeard, 1977; Lovelock and Young, 1979; Grönroos, 1982; Flipo, 1988). In particular, the interaction between buyer and supplier in the supply of the service, often known as 'the moment of truth', the point where service quality is created, (Normann, 1984; Heskett, 1986; Carlzon, 1987; Lovelock, 1988) has dominated thinking about the design and delivery of services. Received wisdom has been that services are 'different.' Thus, the growth paths of service firms have indicated a different 'logic' to manufacturing firms.

For Chandler's model of growth to now be applicable to service industries, the special characteristics of services must have diminished in significance. This paper argues that more capital-intensive asset structures and higher fixed costs have been influential in creating extranational economies of scale. This has encouraged, in turn, high levels of merger and acquisition activity in many service sectors (e.g., hotel chains, accounting and management consultancy firms, airlines, software, information services, telecommunications, financial services, and so forth). Concentration has thereby increased. Service industries are no longer fragmented industries with no clear market leaders. In many sectors, they resemble oligopolies, albeit with a long 'tail' of smaller firms co-existing as local providers in most markets. The result is a greater similarity between manufacturing and service firms.

The rest of this paper will assess the significance of greater potential for economies of scale and economies of scope on the growth strategies of service firms. The research proposition used is that:

> *Proposition* – Where cost advantages of scale and/or scope are available, service firms are likely to internationalize.

Scale and scope in services

Any application of Chandler's 'logic' to service businesses must consider how cost advantages derived from investments in volume may yield economies of scale and scope in services. Table 19.1 lists some of the potential sources of economies of scale and economies of scope in services.

Any asset which yields scale economies can also be the basis for scope economies if it provides input into two or more processes. Economies of scope are usually defined as existing when the cost of producing two outputs jointly is less than the cost of producing each output separately (Teece, 1980, 1982). In clarifying the relationship between economies of scope and the business enterprise, Teece (1980) specified two important circumstances when integration of activities across a multiproduct firm would be needed to capture scope economies: first, where two or more products depend on the same proprietary know-how; second, when a specialized indivisible asset is a common input into two or more products. Both of these conditions are now routinely found in service enterprises.

An obvious example of the interaction between scale and scope benefits deriving from the same proprietary know-how and indivisible asset, is the central role now played by computer reservation systems (CRS) in the activities of airlines, hotel chains, car rental firms and so forth. These not only support the geographic spread of the business and the rapid processing of volumes of transactions but also provide customer databases for cross-marketing of services and the capability to design and deliver completely new services. Table 19.2 gives some illustrations of these information technology-based scale and scope benefits in four different service businesses: a financial services company (American Express), a fashion retailer (Benetton), an airline (British Airways), and an advertising agency (Saatchi & Saatchi).

Table 19.1 Potential sources of economies of scale and scope in services

Economies of scale	Economies of scope
Geographic networks	IT/IS and shared information networks
Physical equipment	Shared learning and doing
Purchasing/supply	Product or process innovation
Marketing	Shared R&D
Logistics and distribution	Shared channels for multiple offerings
Technology/IT/IS	Shared investments and costs
Production resources	Reproduction formula for service system
Management	Range of services and service development
Organization	Complementary services
Operational support	Branding
Knowledge	International franchising
	Training
	Goodwill and corporate identity
	Culture
	Internal exploitation of economies
	Reduced transaction costs
	Common governance
	Know-how effects
	Privileged access to parent services

Source: Authors' judgement and compilation from Normann (1984), Ghoshal (1987), Enderwick (1989)

American Express is able to set and monitor service standards for fast response times for card enquiries, or to provide new and additional services such as 'free' travel arrangements or theatre bookings for cardholders. Benetton has become renowned for its ability to replace inventory in its worldwide outlets and for using real-time information from point-of-sale systems to tailor seasonal production to demand. British Airways has developed sophisticated software to maximize yield from higher-revenue seats on all flights, a major contribution to profitability in a service business with high fixed costs. Saatchi & Saatchi derives economies of scale from bulk purchasing of media time and space, as well as the internal transfer of market and design data in the management of global campaigns for clients.

Dunning (1989) suggests that know-how and specialized assets often combine in service firms, with knowledge featured as a special asset in services (see also Erramilli, 1990). In fact, the capability to acquire, process, and analyse information is the key asset or core competence of many services (e.g., financial, software, brokerage, and professional; also, the agency function of computerized reservation systems linking many service businesses). 'Know-how' here literally consists of the knowledge of how to combine human and physical resources to produce and process information.

Table 19.2 Some scale and scope implications of systems technology on selected service businesses

American Express	Response times
	New products
	Distribution channels
	Add-on services
Benetton	Responsive merchandising
	Inventory elimination
	Customized production
	Credit management
British Airways	Yield management
	Exclusion effect
	Vertical integration
Saatchi & Saatchi	Market information
	Campaign management
	Communications media

Source: Segal-Horn (1990)

Additionally, despite the traditional service industry assumptions, knowledge need not be perishable. It has a shelf life, during which time it may be repeatedly used at little or no cost (e.g., an advertisement, a software program). Many services comprise a firm-specific pool of tacit knowledge. Service firms (e.g., management consultancies and other PSFs, fast food chains hotel chains) are increasingly attempting to codify this inherited knowledge as the basis of standardization of their products, to achieve cost-reduction and increased productivity, as well as reliability of service levels. Some of the strongest brands in services are based on perceived accumulated know-how, for example, McKinsey, Reuters, Neilsen and McDonald's. The trend is for information intensive assets to absorb heavier investment in fixed costs which in itself exerts pressure to lower unit costs by spreading output over larger markets (for scale economies) and a wider variety of products (for scope economies).

In exploring 'know-how', Teece (1982) reviews its 'fungible' character; that is, that individual and organizational knowledge represent a generalizable capability rather than necessarily referring to the particular products and services which the enterprise is currently producing (captured by Prahalad and Hamel (1990) as 'core competences'). This implies that where diversification is based on scope economies, the comparative advantage of the firm is defined in terms of capabilities rather than in terms of outputs. It therefore makes sense for service firms utilizing scope economies to manage their international expansion by means of internationalization (i.e., the internal control of co-ordination of assets and activities) rather than by market transaction. Internalization (Dunning, 1985) enables firms to bring managerial control to bear on internal capabilities, giving greater control over their realization. Thus, internalization is especially important in the growth of service firms in regard not just to efficiency, but also to the harnessing of capabilities and the management of the 'moments of truth' (Normann, 1984; Carlzon, 1987) in which the quality of service firms is experienced by their customers.

The changed services 'logic': Phase 1 – the industry evolution phase

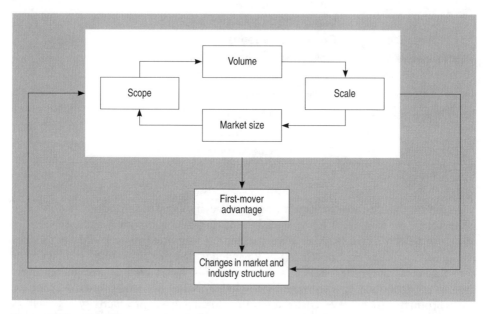

Figure 19.1 Simplified model of Chandler's dynamic of MNE growth: Phase 1

Chandler's 'dynamic logic of growth and competition' occurs at the level of the firm and arises out of the investment and expansion decisions of the management hierarchy. Figure 19.1 is a diagrammatic representation of the path of those decisions showing the early stages of industry evolution.

Chandler's evidence explains the growth of firms to a position of dominance in their sector through the early pursuit of cost advantages derived from volume. Scale and scope are fundamentally volume and cost-driven. Chandler shows that companies which create and sustain dominant position in their industries do so by making pre-emptive investments in scale and scope which enable the firm to strongly influence the evolving structure of the industry and the bases of competition within the industry.

As shown in Figure 19.1, Phase 1 of Chandler's 'logic' consists of four sets of core investments: in volume, to achieve cost advantages of scale; in scope, to achieve consistent capacity utilization; in national, and then international, marketing and distribution networks; and in a management hierarchy to co-ordinate and allocate current and future resource utilization. Firms which moved first to make these co-ordinated sets of large investments could dominate their industries and influence their path of development, both in the short term and longer term. This is because challengers would have to match the first-mover advantages in comparable costs, build distribution and reputation to a point where the dominant incumbent could be effectively challenged, recruit teams of experienced managers, and match specialized experience curve effects.

An illustration: American Express – Phase 1

An example which will be used here as an illustration of the application of this 'logic' in a service firm is American Express (Amex),[1] a financial services company in which scale and scope operate in a massive way. Over time, this company has successively made the investments in marketing, distribution, volume, product, and process outlined by Chandler for manufacturing. In so doing, it has created a world-scale service industry, which it has dominated for more than a century after its first international expansion moves.

The development of American Express involved a series of 'Phase 1' – style investments. The company was founded in New York in 1850 by Wells & Fargo, progressing rapidly from the express carriage of cash and parcels to bonded carrier of freight and finance. It handled European imports to all US Customs interior ports-of-clearance. Investments in its distribution network proceeded beyond national US coverage to the beginnings of its European network in freight forwarding. The company moved from an initial office in Liverpool, England, in 1881 to 3,000 European agencies offices in 1890. Beyond scale expansion of the network, these offices also provided considerable expansion in scope through the increased range of services offered, utilizing additional capacity in the same network of outlets. The company was already benefiting from a virtuous cycle of scale, volume, and scope effects that enabled it to advertise in brochures in Europe at this time that it could:

> pay money on Telegraphic Order, at a moment's notice, between points thousands of miles apart and sell small Drafts or Money Orders which ... can be cashed at 15,000 places.
>
> (American Express company documents, 1991)

American Express began extending its management hierarchy in Europe by beginning its own directly owned chain of European offices in 1895. The freight express business encompassed many developing financial service activities, for example, paying foreign money-order remittances from emigrants, or the commercial credit transactions begun in Rotterdam in 1907. Other major new product development initiatives included:

- Amex Express Money Order (1882)
- Amex Travellers Cheque (1891)

These provide illustrations of Chandler's proposition that incumbent first-mover advantages determine the future structure of an industry. Sale of travellers cheques unleashed demand to provide additional services to tourists, such as itineraries and tickets. A European, and eventually worldwide, travel network was established, uniquely combined with the Amex portfolio of financial products and services to create a new set of asset structures for a specialized segment of the financial services industry. The company introduced the Amex Charge Card in 1958. By the 1960s, 38,000 outlets worldwide sold American Express 'travel-related financial services' (TRS), which is still the source of 70% of the American Express Company's revenues in the 1990s.

The potential for scale and scope economies in different types of service businesses

Moving from a specific illustration of Chandler's 'logic' applied to one service company, some more general observations may be made concerning scale and scope in services.

The grid in Figure 19.2 gives a customary representation of the spread of scale and scope economies available to different types of service businesses. Examples belonging in the top right corner of the grid include financial services companies such as American Express, the major international airlines, travel firms such as Club Med, and information service firms such as Reuters and Dun & Bradstreet. The top left corner covers food retailers, where high-scale effects have arisen from electronic point-of-sale equipment and concentration of retailer buying power, combined with limited scope opportunities, although some large food multiples also trade in clothing, homewares, and even financial services such as in-house credit cards. The bottom right of the grid encompasses management consultancies or other professional service firms (PSFs) such as accountants, surveyors, civil engineers, or head-hunters. PSFs may be high on potential scope economies from assets such as shared client and project databases or shared teams of expertise across national or regional offices, but they have low potential economies of scale since these services are frequently customized, often within different national regulatory frameworks. The bottom left quadrant includes the small-scale, highly location-specific businesses typically defined as services.

Although Figure 19.2 represents the traditional view of varying types of service businesses, what is interesting from the point of view of this paper is the drift of many firms in these different sectors towards the top right of the grid. The creation via mergers (e.g., KPMG Peat Marwick, Ernst & Young, Deloitte Touche) of very large international accounting and consultancy firms, which is mirrored in other PSF sectors, is part of the search for greater efficiencies in capacity utilization of scarce resources and for productivity gains from implementation of standardized methodologies. Equally, food (e.g., Aldi) and non-food (e.g., IKEA, Toys 'R' Us) retailers have begun to operate beyond domestic boundaries (Treadgold, 1989; Segal-Horn and Davison, 1992), seeking scale benefits from volume purchasing and scope benefits from investments in information technology, logistics networks and branding. Insurance companies in Europe (e.g., Allianz of Germany, Generali of Italy, Prudential of the United Kingdom) are building cross-border operations as

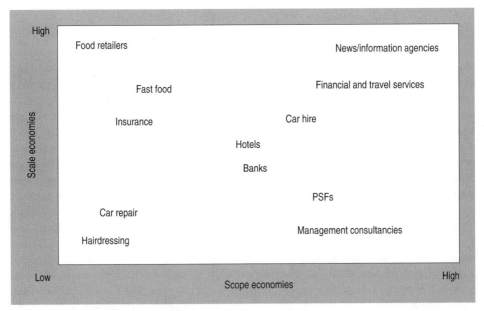

Figure 19.2 Potential for scale and scope economies in different service businesses (source: Segal-Horn, 1992)

regulatory differences become less extreme and types of distribution channels develop and converge. Finally, many erstwhile small service businesses are moving upwards on the grid, seeking volume benefits in purchasing and operations arising from specialization and standardization (e.g., Kwik-Fit Euro, which specializes in the repair of car exhausts or brakes only).

Clearly, none of these shifts would be possible without at least some perceived shift on the demand side in consumer buying behaviour. Economies of scope in services can lower transaction costs for customers. Common examples include: the effect of retailer buying power on quality and price in multiple retail chains (Segal-Horn and McGee, 1989); worldwide reservation systems of hotel chains and airlines; cheaper products in banking, insurance, and brokerage services such as travel agents or investment analysts.

Nayyar (1990) discusses the potential benefit to diversified service firms from leveraging customer relationships across service businesses. He argues that buyers of services will attempt to economize on information acquisition costs by transferring reputation effects to other services offered by a firm, thus enabling the service firm to obtain quasi-rents from firm-specific buyer-seller relationships. This research contributed to our understanding of the growing importance of the branding of services and reinforces, for services, two of the main propositions regarding the competitive advantages of MNEs. First, the ability of MNEs to create and sustain a successful brand image and its concomitant goodwill (Caves, 1982); second, the MNEs ability to monitor quality and reduce buyer transaction costs by offering services from multiple locations (Casson, 1982).

The changed services 'logic': Phase 2 – the industry dynamics phase

Phase 2 of Chandler's model shifts from national to international growth and competition. The applicability to services of Chandler's model of MNE growth rests on the fundamental shifts that have occurred in the historically 'local', domestic and small-scale character of service businesses. There is *de facto* evidence that international chains exist in virtually all types of service businesses, even highly 'local', regulated, and culture-specific services such as education or medical services, (e.g., AMI health care group, EF language schools, international campuses trading on well-known university brand names). The documented examples of national and international concentration and competition in services include professional accountancy firms (Daniels *et al.*, 1989), financial services (Walter, 1988; Wright and Pauli, 1987), retailing (Treadgold, 1989; Segal-Horn and Davison, 1992), contracting (Enderwick, 1989), airlines (McKern, 1990; Olaisen *et al.*, 1990), and news agencies (Boyd-Barrett, 1989).

Underlying these trends is what Levitt (1986) called 'the industrialization of service'. Echoing Chandler's central themes, Levitt argues that the key point in the industrialization of service is 'volume ... sufficient to achieve efficiency, sufficient to employ systems and technologies that produce reliable, rapid and low unit cost results. That in turn requires ... managerial rationality' (Levitt, 1986, p. 61). Services can be industrialized in a variety of ways:

- by automation which substitutes machines for labour (e.g., automatic carwash, automatic toll collection, ATM cash machines, and so forth)
- by systems planning which substitutes organization or methodologies for labour (e.g., self-service shops, fast food restaurants, packaged holidays, unit trust investment schemes, mass-market insurance packages)
- by a combination of the two (e.g., extending scope in food retailing via centralized warehousing and transportation/distribution networks for chilled, fresh, or frozen foods in technically advanced temperature- and humidity-controlled trucks).

Such industrialization of service is based on large-scale substitution of capital for labour in services, together with a redefinition of the technology-intensiveness and sophistication of service businesses. It also assumes a market size sufficient to sustain the push for volume. The point at which a firm is likely to shift to international operations is when the domestic market provides insufficient volume to support minimum efficient scale. This may come earlier for service firms than for manufacturing firms, since for many types of services the option of exporting is not available (Carman and Langeard, 1980; Erramilli, 1990).

The changes in concentration and industrialization of services make Phase 2 of Chandler's model, relating to growth via the international expansion of scale and scope, directly applicable to this sector of the economy.

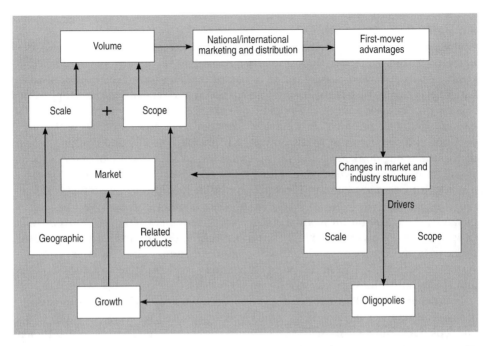

Figure 19.3 An abstract of Chandler's dynamic model of multinational growth and competition: Phase 2 (source: Segal-Horn drawing upon Chandler, 1986, 1990)

Figure 19.3 provides a more extensive representation of Chandler's complete model. Because of their investments in scale, scope, distribution and management, Chandler argues, large firms are able to build dominant positions sufficient to influence the structure, key assets, and capabilities relevant to competing in their industry. Thus, economic advantages of scale and scope lead to national and international concentration, so that competition rapidly becomes oligopolistic. Such oligopolistic competition is based more on innovation than price, although firmly rooted in continuously enhanced cost structures. Growth thus becomes a continuous search for improved quality, sourcing, distribution and marketing (especially branding and advertising), as well as new markets and lower cost. Some growth comes from acquisition, but the main emphasis for long-term growth is two-fold: first, geographic expansion into international markets in the continuous drive for increments in scale and cost advantages; second, related product markets in the pursuit of enhanced scope economies. Together these form a dynamic spiral of volume, scale, scope and cost curves, reinforced by organizational capabilities developed to cope within fierce oligopolistic competition. Chandler emphasizes repeatedly that the opportunity to create such first-mover investments is short-lived. The logic of sustainable international competition is to make long-term scale investments to create organizational capabilities, and then to continue to reinvest in these assets.

To demonstrate this industry concentration phase of the model, the earlier company illustration will be revisited.

An illustration: American Express – phase 2

Many of the innovations made by American Express in new products, new markets, branding, advertising and distribution, have already been referred to above. Amex followed closely the twin routes for long-term growth described by Chandler, geographic expansion into international markets and the development of related product markets in the pursuit of enhanced scope economies. It had the earliest branded products in financial services and advertised these branded products heavily from the 1880s onwards. It invested heavily and continuously in distribution and marketing and in the extension of its network of outlets for its products and services worldwide. There was some growth via acquisition, as in the purchase of Fireman's Fund in 1968 to consolidate its move from a travel company into financial services. Amex's related product markets now cover the express business, the travel business, financial services, movement of goods, movement of people, and the flow of money. These related businesses provide scale and volume, supported by company-wide global communications, data and information systems networks, which in turn support volume, worldwide geographic coverage, and the monitoring of service quality in all outlets.

Following Chandler, Amex does not compete on price but on product innovation, market development, and levels of service. Whether its scale, scope, and cost advantages are still sufficient to fight off the current new efficient competitors in its main markets (e.g., Visa) remains to be seen. It is facing very tough competition and increasing pressure on price and margins from both trade and retail customers.

RETHINKING SERVICES

Chandler's model is of international growth and competition based on firm-specific assets. It is interesting to note that such resource-based theories of the firm are making a comeback in competitive strategy (Rumelt, 1991; Grant, 1991), balancing the industry structure-driven emphasis of strategic thinking of the 1980s. Since such assets may erode over time (Geroski and Vlassopoulos, 1991) and must be continually upgraded to sustain their advantage, it is important to review the implications of this approach to the changing nature of competition in services.

Enderwick (1989) provides insight into firm-specific advantages (FSA) and location-specific advantages (LSA) available to the services multinational enterprise. He builds on the work of Dunning (1981, 1985, 1989), and the eclectic paradigm of international production based on ownership, location, and internalization (OLI) advantages. Ownership incorporates competitive advantages; location incorporates configuration advantages; and internalization incorporates co-ordination advantages. These issues have also been conceptualized in international strategy by Porter (1986) as issues of configuration and co-ordination in the allocation of value chain activities by the firm.

Enderwick includes under FSA factors familiar from the earlier scale and scope debate in services; privileged access to assets such as goodwill and brand name, particularly important in buying decisions for services (some aspects of this were discussed above under 'know-how'); scale economies obtainable from high fixed costs and low variable costs of operation; other economies of common governance available from single hierarchical management of complementary assets; and agglomerate (scope) economies which enable incumbent firms to offer innovatory or complementary services which reinforce their competitive position. Under LSA factors, most significant is the differential between services which are location-specific because production and consumption are inseparable and therefore wide international representation is mandatory (e.g., fast food chains) and services which are tradable and therefore choice of international location results from considerations of comparative advantages (e.g., software houses).

Lastly, the internalization issue is of exceptional importance in reviewing the growth strategies of service firms and must be considered in relation to the special characteristics of service businesses discussed earlier. These characteristics have provided the rationale for one of the most influential models explaining growth paths of service firms. Carman and Langeard (1980) argue that international expansion is the most risky growth strategy for service firms, because of the 'intangibility' and 'simultaneity' characteristics of services. Carman and Langeard have particularly emphasized how the quality-control problems inherent in the daily operational detail of face-to-face service delivery are exacerbated when firms attempt to operate across national boundaries.

However, assumptions concerning the inevitability of 'intangibility' and 'simultaneity' increasingly are being eroded in the services literature. Products may be tangible or intangible or a combination of both (Levitt, 1986, p. 74). O'Farrell and Hitchens (1990) propose a 'a continuum of tangibility' as more accurate. Levitan (1985), Boddewyn et al., (1986), and Dunning (1989) distinguish pure consumer services from producer or intermediate services. Erramilli (1990) makes a distinction between 'hard' and 'soft' services. All of these authors support the separation of production and consumption in many services. For a considerable range of service businesses, therefore, one of the highest risk of international expansion is reduced.

RESOURCE EMPHASIS

The basic argument is that under changed technical and structural conditions, it becomes necessary to reconsider the definition of what constitutes a service and also to consider how firms actually design and deliver their services. One of the biggest changes in service design is reflected in the distinction between 'back-office' and 'front-office' as constituent parts of a service. 'Front-office' is that part of the service which has an interface with the customer. 'Back-office' is any part of the service delivery which may be carried out remote from the customer. Clearly different services contain differing proportions of hard or soft, tangible or intangible, elements. They will vary, therefore, in the balance of front-office to back-office capabilities required to deliver the service.

Figure 19.4 provides a simple illustration of some of these service design and reconfiguration possibilities. It reflects some of the differences in core assets and service delivery between 'hard' and 'soft' services, as well as some of the rethinking of services that has occurred. For example, the location of retail banking in the top left box reflects the capital-intensive, volume-driven transaction-processing part of retail banking operations. These activities are now usually centralized and regionalized. At the same time, the retail banks have been redesigning branch outlets to be more customer-friendly in order to cross-sell other higher-margin financial services. Software houses may sometimes appear also in the top left box if they are selling standardized rather than bespoke software packages.

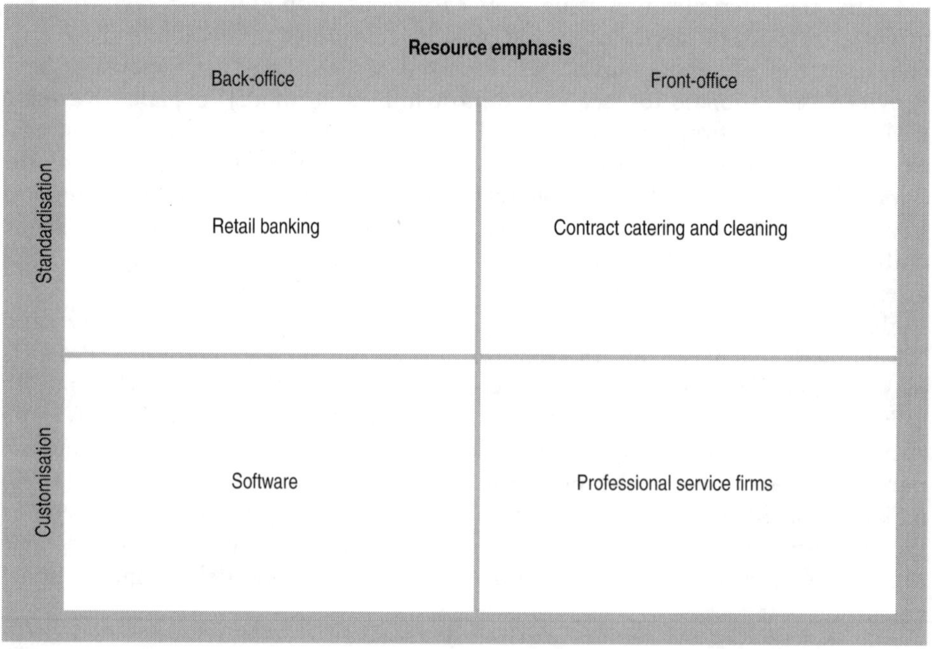

<table>
<tr><td colspan="2"></td><td colspan="2" align="center">Resource emphasis</td></tr>
<tr><td colspan="2"></td><td align="center">Back-office</td><td align="center">Front-office</td></tr>
<tr><td rowspan="2">Standardisation</td><td></td><td align="center">Retail banking</td><td align="center">Contract catering and cleaning</td></tr>
<tr><td></td><td align="center">Software</td><td align="center">Professional service firms</td></tr>
</table>

Figure 19.4 Service standardization (source: Segal-Horn, 1992)

However, the examples in Figure 19.4 are inevitably oversimplified (e.g., it ignores the search by PSFs for methodologies to increase productivity and margins via back-office standardization, an approach for which Arthur Andersen is well-known). Consonant with Chandler's view of international growth and competition as a sustainable dynamic, it is inevitable that continuous shifts such as those between standardization and customization should result in firms continually seeking optimization of such features at the highest level of scale and cost position available to them. It is also to be expected that these positions of optimum efficiencies will be continually shifting.

In short, the continual search for optimization of OLI advantages in services, using the same models and criteria as for manufacturing firms, makes simple distinctions between product and service obsolete. Borrowing from Levitt's (1986) concept of the 'augmented' product, services increasingly cross any definition product/service boundary line whether of tangibility, perishability or simultaneity, in favour of conceptualization of 'augmented' products. Just as Levitt argues that augmented products arise in relatively mature markets or with relatively experienced or sophisticated customers, so augmented products are being developed by service firms. Many services once regarded as highly specialized (e.g., airline seats, bank accounts) have become commodities. This has exerted strong pressures on service providers to simultaneously push down costs and provide additional augmentations (e.g., better in-flight catering; longer bank opening hours). This pressure is itself contributing to the erosion of clear product-service distinctions since, increasingly, manufacturing firms are seeking product augmentation through service features (see Quinn *et al.*, 1988, 1990; Vandermerwe, 1990). Increasingly, advantage comes from exploiting the manu-facturing/services interface.

THE EVOLUTION OF COMPETITION IN SERVICES

Since the Chandler growth model assumes a large enough market size to achieve benefit from scale effects, some consideration of the evolution in both markets and industry structures in services is appropriate. Much of the historic pattern of competition in services occurred within domestic market boundaries as a result of the small-scale, fragmented structure of service industries and their culture-specific patterns of demand and consumption. Under these conditions, clearly scale and volume effects will be limited. However, as has already been argued, in most service sectors restructuring has led to concentration replacing fragmentation in industry structure. In addition, some homogenization of demand in services is also observable.

Evolving patterns of demand in services

There has been a lengthy and vigorous debate about the validity of the argument that an increasing similarity exists between sets of consumers across international markets. The debate centres around the possibility of standardizing products or services for broadly defined international market segments. The belief in consumer homogeneity is controversial, since it co-exists with the view that fragmentation rather than homogenization may more appropriately describe international consumer trends. Much discussion has taken place over the opportunities for, and barriers to, such standardization (Kotler, 1985; Quelch and Hoff, 1986; Douglas and Wind, 1987; Link, 1988; Jain, 1989). It was triggered by Levitt (1983), who argued for convergence as a result of economic and cultural interdependencies across countries and markets. Levitt suggested that old-established differences in national preferences were being reduced by mass culture and communications technologies and urged companies to examine growing similarities between consumer preferences in the markets they served. Lifestyle segmentation has been around for a long time (Sheth, 1983). However, the argument for homogenization means that such segments should be defined internationally. International segmentation does not usually mean providing the same product in all countries, but offering local adaptations around a standardized core.

Well-known examples of this approach in services include the retail chain Benetton, which has built its whole strategy around the standardized 'one unit product' of casual, colour-co-ordinated leisurewear for the 18–25 age group. Although there is some adaptation of such things as colour choice for different domestic markets, consistency is maintained in product range, merchandising, store layout and design, promotion, and use of natural fabrics. Similarly, the restaurant chain Pizza Hut protects the core elements of its brand by copyrighting its individual products' brand names (such as Perfect Pizza) and operating strict specifications of product ingredients. However, the Pizza Hut concept is adapted to suit local needs by varying some elements of the menu (such as desserts), or store design, or the way in which products are served to the customer. Even McDonald's adapts its offering at the margin, for example by selling tea as well as coffee and soft drinks at its UK outlets. In other respects, its brand franchise is maintained virtually intact.

Similar, internationally standardized services would include those of American Express. This company bases much of its marketing on worldwide consistency of quality and range of services, as do the international airlines and hotel chains. International segmentation (e.g., around the business traveller) can give advantages of economies of scale, as well as branding, marketing and reputation benefits. Many services have emerged relatively recently and therefore may have the advantage in establishing cross-national segments. Credit cards, automated teller machines, airlines seats, software, and the automatic car wash, for example, have no prior patterns of usage or acculturation, thereby making them more easily acceptable across national boundaries.

However, alongside social, cultural and technological changes generating homogeneous demand for services, there are additional economic and political pressures on governments to create, or remove, regulatory barriers that can sharply divide markets. The trend is away from such barriers, however, and their removal may have a dramatic impact, as in the deregulation of international trade in financial services, or the 1970s deregulation of US airlines, also being pursued as the 'open skies' policy within [EU] airline competition policy in Europe. The Uruguay GATT round includes services and, if satisfactorily concluded, should greatly simplify many current difficulties affecting international trade in services, such as intellectual copyright protection.

This brief discussion of segmentation and regulatory issues merely indicates some of the most important enabling conditions upon which international market development for services rests. Also of relevance is the way in which the structure of service industries is evolving, often across traditional notions of industry boundaries.

Industry boundaries and firm-specific advantages in services

Reference has already been made to the contribution of fragmented industry structure to the evolution of competition in services, and to the restructuring and concentration which has been exhibited in most service sectors in recent years. Many service industries (such as travel, fast food, some financial services, information services) now meet Kobrin's (1991, p. 18) definition of a global industry, defined in terms of 'the significance of the competitive advantages of international operations' arising mainly from the structural characteristics of scale economies and technological intensity.

Even more important, service-industry growth has often been across traditional industry boundaries (e.g., retail/financial services, retail/leisure, leisure/travel, travel/hospitality, accounting/management consultancy, advertising/public relations, and so forth). This leads to the notion of increasingly 'fuzzy' industry boundaries in service, with industries most appropriately viewed not discretely but as fuzzy sets. American Express, for example, illustrates service-firm growth within a fuzzy industry set of leisure/travel/financial services. It also demonstrates that strong branding across a portfolio of related services arises precisely because Amex operates across this fuzzy set. To generalize, 'growth' for service firms may not involve a deepening of asset structure as in manufacturing companies, but a horizontal accretion of assets across different markets and different industries (i.e., scope).

The point has been made with regard to MNE activity in general (Dunning, 1989), and service MNE activity in particular (Enderwick, 1989) that the way in which firms organize their international activities may itself be a crucial competitive advantage. This is strongly reinforced in recent work by Rumelt (1991), concluding that the most important sources of long-term business rents 'are not associated with industry, but with the unique endowments, positions and strategies of individual businesses' (p. 168). While the issue of change in service-industry structure is central to any discussion of the growth of international competition in services, it therefore may be that the most important factors determining successful international expansion in services should be understood at the level of the firm. This is particularly important with regard to the managerial and organizational capabilities of the firm. The Chandler model of growth used in this paper is especially appropriate because it is a resource-based explanation of successful international competition, driven by sustained investment in the development of firm-specific asset structures.

These points may go some way toward explaining the successes and failures in international expansion undertaken by individual service firms, such as American Express in financial services or Saatchi & Saatchi in advertising.

THE MEASUREMENT OF SCALE AND SCOPE IN SERVICES

In this reassessment of the viability of international strategies for service firms, much emphasis has been placed on the attainability of scale and scope economies. Indeed, the argument can be made that if such benefits are not available for service firms, it must materially reduce the advantages which service MNEs have over local providers of that service. Because they are so important, a systematic framework for tracing the impact of scale or scope variables within the firm is needed. An initial approach to gathering sample data on a specific scale or scope variable is shown in Table 19.3.

A completed data matrix of this type should record all the value chain activities of the firm on the vertical axis. The horizontal axis should capture all resource inputs for each value activity, together with the organizational outputs arising from each input. The resource inputs are recorded at both a minimum level and an optimum level of resource provision. Minimum resources are defined as those which enable the firm to keep operational. Optimum levels of resource provision are defined as those enhancing the ability of the firm to meet its stated strategic objective. The organizational outputs are of three types: first, those that impact other elements in the value chain; second, those that affect the knowledge base of the firm; and third, those that impact the way in which the company defines demand for the service.

Table 19.3 is an illustration of part of the data matrix for an international management consultancy firm. It shows a partial value chain, covering only the activities of marketing to client (which in a service firm usually precedes 'production' i.e., delivery of the service) and R&D, which is often combined with new product development in this type of service firm. As an example of the relationship between resource inputs and outputs, Table 19.3 provides important information for the firm on such things as selection, recruitment, training, and development (including that of senior partners). It also indicates the back-office and front-office resource considerations in the design and delivery of its services, as well as raising many specific issues concerning the firm's products and markets.

This data matrix provides a simple route through a complex set of interrelationships. It enables variables which have significant operational impact to be distinguished from variables with a relatively trivial role, since it discloses variables which recur and can therefore be shown to have a significant impact on many outputs. This approach is also surprisingly powerful in defining and coping with many of the intangible elements of service provision.

Table 19.3: Partial data matrix: international management consultancy

	Inputs		*Outputs*		
Elements in value chain	*Minimum resources*	*Optimum resources*	*Linkage to other elements in chain*	*Linkage to knowledge base*	*Impact on demand conditions*
Market to clients	Informal contacts	Industry database	• Maximize repeat business	• Monitor repeat business	• Review client base
		Client database			
		Market database			
		Product database			
	As above	As above + consultant databases and assignment profiles, etc.	• Standardize skills and procedures	• Client profitability	• Review sector expertise
			• Optimize people quality	• Targeting expertise to opportunity	• Review style and approach to marketing
R&D and NPD			• Maximize training	• Codified knowledge 'manuals'	• Review services offered

Source: Segal-Horn (1992)

CONCLUSION: THE FUTURE FOR SERVICES

This paper has suggested a revised competitive 'logic', explaining the internationalization of service firms. Changes in the nature of service provision which has led service companies to turn more readily to international expansion have been reviewed. It has been argued that the potential availability of a range of economies of scale and/or economies of scope will both reduce the risk, and enhance the advantages of internationalization for service firms. Sources of such scale and scope economies have been suggested, together with a framework for measuring their impact on the firm. Their potential availability across different types of service businesses has been assessed.

The basic argument is that changed technological, market, and regulatory conditions have created more favourable conditions for international expansion of many services, while the special characteristics of services have been diluted in significance. Many services contain 'hard' tangible components which are capital-intensive, amenable to separation from the point of service delivery, and responsive to standardization. In addition, core knowledge and information-based assets of service firms are codifiable and transferable across national boundaries, as is the consumer franchise from strongly branded services.

As a result of this combination of factors, service-industry dynamics are beginning to parallel those of manufacturing. Manufacturing businesses and service businesses appear to be following similar development paths, creating similar types of asset structures and competing in similar ways. Even the most distinctive characteristic of services, the criticality of the interface with the customer, is increasingly something which all types of business are now expecting to handle well. The emphasis on customer service in manufacturing and the emphasis on efficient deployment of back-office assets in services are each trying to capture the advantages the other has traditionally utilized.

REFERENCES

Albrecht, K. and Zemke, R. (1985) *Service America!*, Dow Jones-Irwin, Homewood, IL.

Bartlett, C.A. and Ghoshal, S. (1986) 'Tap your subsidiaries for global reach', *Harvard Business Review*, November–December, pp. 87–94.

Bartlett, C.A. and Ghoshal, S. (1987) 'Managing across borders', *Sloan Management Review*, Vol. 28, No. 4, pp. 7–17; Vol. 29, No. 1, pp.43–53.

Bartlett, C.A. and Ghoshal, S. (1989) *Managing Across Borders*, Hutchinson, London.

Boddewyn, J.J., Halbrich, M.B. and Perry, A.C. (1986) 'Service multinationals: conceptualization, measurement and theory', *Journal of International Business Studies*, Vol. 16, pp. 23–35.

Boyd-Barrett, O. (1989) 'Multinational news agencies', in Enderwick, P. (ed.), *Multinational Service Firms*, Routledge, London.

Carlzon, J. (1987) *Moments of Truth*, Ballinger, Cambridge, MA.

Carman, J. and Langeard, E. (1980) 'Growth strategies for service firms', *Strategic Management Journal*, Vol. 1, pp. 7–22.

Casson, M.C. (1982) 'Transaction costs and the theory of the multinational enterprise', in Rugman,A.M. (ed.) *New Theories of the Multinational Enterprise*, St Martin's Press, New York.

Caves, R.E. (1982) *Multinational Enterprise and Economic Analysis*, Cambridge University Press, Cambridge.

Chandler, A.D. (1977) *The Visible Hand*, Harvard University Press, Cambridge, MA.

Chandler, A.D. (1986) 'The evolution of modern global competition', in Porter, M. (ed.), *Competition in Global Industries*, Harvard Business School Press, Boston, MA.

Chandler, A.D. (1990) 'The evolution of modern global competition', in Porter, M. (ed.), *Competition in Global Industries*, Harvard Business School Press, Boston, MA.

Daniels, P. (1985) *Service Industries: a geographical appraisal*, Methuen, London.

Daniels, P., Thrift, N. and Leyshon, A. (1989) 'Internationalization of professional producer services: accountancy conglomerates', in Enderwick, P. (ed.), *Multinational Service Firms*, Routledge, London.

Dermine, J. and Röller, L.H. (1990) *Economies of scale and scope in the French mutual funds industry* (Working Paper NO. 90/59/FIN) Fontainebleau: INSEAD.

Douglas, S. and Wind, Y. (1987) 'The myth of globalization', *Columbia Journal of World Business*, Vol. 22, No. 4.

Dunning, J.H. (1981) *International Production and the Multinational Enterprise*, Allen and Unwin, London.

Dunning, J.H. (ed.) (1985) *Multinational Enterprise, Economic Structure and International Competitiveness*, Wiley/IRM, Chichester.

Dunning, J.H. (1989) 'Multinational enterprises and the growth of services: some conceptual and theoretical issues', *Service Industries Journal*, Vol. 9, No. 1, pp. 5–39.

Eiglier, P. and Langeard, E. (1977) 'Le marketing des enterprises de services (Marketing in service business)', *Revue Francaise de Gestion*.

Enderwick, P. (1989) *Multinational Service Firms*, Routledge, London.

Erramilli, M.K. (1990) 'Entry mode choice in service industries', *International Marketing Review*, Vol. 7, No. 5, pp. 50–62.

Flipo, J.P. (1988) 'On the intangibility of services', *Service Industries Journal*, No. 8, pp. 286–98.

Geroski, P. and Vlassopoulos, T. (1991) 'The rise and fall of a market leader', *Strategic Management Journal*, Vol. 12, No. 6, pp. 467–78.

Ghoshal, S. (1987) 'Global strategy: an organizing framework', *Strategic Management Journal*, Vol. 8, No. 5, pp. 425–40.

Grant, R. (1991) 'The resource-based theory of competitive advantage: implications for strategy formulation', *California Management Review*, Vol. 33, pp. 114–35.

Grönroos, C. (1982) *Strategic Management and Marketing in the Service Sector*, Svenska Handelshögskolan, Helsinki.

Heskett, J.L. (1986) *Managing the Service Economy*, Harvard Business School Press, Boston, MA.

Hindley, B. *et al.* (1987) 'International trade in services: comments', in Giarini, O. (ed.), *The Emerging Service Economy*, Pergamon Press, Oxford.

Hout, T., Porter, M. and Rudden, E. (1982) 'How global companies win out', *Harvard Business Review*, September–October, pp. 98–108.

Jain, S. (1989) 'Standardization of international marketing strategy: some research hypotheses', *Journal of Marketing*, Vol. 53, pp. 70–9.

Kobrin, S.J. (1991) 'An empirical investigation of the determinants of global integration', *Strategic Management Journal*, Vol. 12, pp. 17–31.

Kogut, B. (1989) 'A note on global strategies', *Strategic Management Journal*, Vol. 10, pp. 383–9.

Kotler, P. (1985) *Global standardization – courting danger* (Panel Discussion 23) American Marketing Association, Washington, DC.

Levitan, S.A. (1985) 'Services and long-term structural change', Economic Impact.

Levitt, T. (1983) The globalization of markets. *Harvard Business Review*, May–June, pp. 92–102.

Levitt, T. (1986) *The Marketing Imagination*, The Free Press, New York.

Link, G. (1988) 'Global advertising: an update', *The Journal of Consumer Marketing*, Vol. 5, No. 2, pp. 69–74.

Lovelock, C.H. (1988) *Managing services*, Prentice-Hall International, London.

Lovelock, C.H. and Young, R.F. (1979) 'Look to consumers to increase productivity', *Harvard Business Review*, May/June, pp. 168–178.

McKern, R.B. (1990) *Evolving strategies in the international airline industry*, Technical Report No. 77, Stanford, CA: Graduate School of Business, Stanford University.

Nayyar, P.R. (1990) 'Information asymmetries: a source of competitive advantage for diversified service firms', *Strategic Management Journal*, Vol. 11, pp. 513–19.

Normann, R. (1984) *Service Management: strategy and leadership in service businesses*, Wiley, Chichester.

O'Farrell, P.N. and Hitchens, D.M. (1990) 'Producer services and regional development: key conceptual issues of taxonomy and quality measurement', *Regional Studies*, Vol. 24, No. 2, pp. 163–71.

Olaison, J., Olsen, G., and Revang, O. (1990) *Bridges and tunnels: strategic alliances and the use of information as components of SAS strategy*, Paper presented at the SMS Annual International Conference, Stockholm.

Porter, M. (1986) *Competition in Global Industries*, Harvard Business School Press, Boston, MA.

Prahalad, C.K., and Doz, Y. (1987) *The Multinational Mission: balancing local demands and global vision*, The Free Press, New York.

Prahalad, C.K. and Hamel, G. (1990) 'The core competences of the corporation', *Harvard Business Review*, May–June, pp. 879–91.

Quelch, J.A., and Hoff, E.J. (1986) 'Customizing global marketing', *Harvard Business Review*, May–June, pp. 59–68.

Quinn, J.B., Baruch, J J. and Paquette, P.C. (1988) 'Exploiting the manufacturing–services interface', *Sloan Management Review*, Vol. 29, No. 4, pp. 45–56.

Quinn, J.B., Doorley, T.L., and Paquette, P.C. (1990) 'Beyond products: services-based strategy', *Harvard Business Review*, May–June, pp. 58–67.

Rumelt, R.P. (1991) 'How much does industry matter?', *Strategic Management Journal*, Vol. 12, pp. 167–85.

Sasser, W.E., Wycoff, D.D. and Olsen, M. (1978) *The Management of Service Operations*, Allyn and Bacon, London.

Segal-Horn, S. (1990) 'The globalization of services', in *Proceedings of the British Academy of Management*, Chichester: Wiley.

Segal-Horn, S. (1992) *The logic of international growth for service firms*, Paper presented at the Fourth Annual Conference of British Academy of Management, Bradford, UK.

Segal-Horn, S. and McGee, J. (1989) 'Strategies to cope with retailer buying power', in Pellegrini, L. and Reddy, S.K. (eds), *Vertical Relationships and the Distribution Trades*, Routledge, London.

Segal-Horn, S. and Davison, H. (1992) 'Global markets, the global consumer and international retailing', *Journal of Global Marketing*, Vol. 5, No. 3, pp. 31–61.

Sheth, J. (1983) 'Marketing megatrends', *Journal of Consumer Marketing*, Vol. 1, pp. 5–13.

Shostack, G.L. (1977) 'Breaking free from product marketing', in Lovelock, C.H. (ed.), *Services Marketing*, Prentice-Hall, Englewood Cliffs, NJ.

Teece, D. (1980) 'Economies of scope and the scope of the enterprise', *Journal of Economic Behaviour and Organization*, Vol. 1, No. 3, pp. 223–47.

Teece, D. (1982) 'Towards an economic theory of the multiproduct firm', *Journal of Economic Behaviour and Organization*, l. Vol. 3, pp. 39–63.

Treadgold, A. (1989) 'The retail response to a changing Europe', *Marketing Research Today*, Vol. 17, No. 3, pp. 161–6.

Vandermerwe, S. (1990) 'The market power is in the services: because the value is in the results', *European Management Journal*, Vol. 8, No. 4, pp. 464–73.

Walter, I. (1988) *Global Competition in Financial Services*, Ballinger, Cambridge, MA.
Wright, R.W. and Pauli, G.A. (1987) *The Second Wave*, Waterlow, London.

NOTE

1 All information concerning American Express is taken from Annual Reports 1983, 1985, 1986, 1988, 1989, 1990; and from internal Company Reports 1990 and 1991.

PART 6

POSTSCRIPT

INTRODUCTION

Strategy as a subject does not have clear boundaries. It has to generate theory capable of informing practice in dynamic rather than static contexts. We have looked at the contrasts and complementarities of a variety of strategy research and the development of new theory for emergent organizational issues such as knowledge management, innovation, learning and cognition. We have argued that strategy is context- and culture-specific, usually contingent to be effective and that many organizations now operate as part of larger networks of resources and capabilities, both across corporations and across geographic boundaries.

The final two chapters complete our look at strategy by discussing critically some of the assumptions built into traditional strategic thinking. We do this not in a negative way but because it is important to ask the questions about how strategy ideas enter the mainstream. Jones does this by providing a general review of ideas and approaches. He suggests that the discipline of strategy meets a managerial need for legitimacy by providing seemingly rational and objective criteria for their exercise of the power of decision-making in corporations. He aims to encourage a healthy debate about strategy and help you to challenge your own ideas and assumptions on many issues within strategy. He reviews many schools of strategic management thinking, beyond the four major schools described by Whittington and mentioned in the Introduction. Jones contrasts their assumptions and prescriptions in some detail. It is possible that strategies are 'not chosen; they are programmed', since they are a way in which managers 'try to simplify and order' a complex world. Strategic planning and strategy reviews offer comforting ritual ('managerial security blankets in a hostile world').

Particularly useful are Jones's discussions of what is wrong with strategy, in which he presents some of the problems that arise from the assumptions that strategy makes: these include the fact that an increasing amount of management education does not automatically lead to improved economic performance; and the difficulties that academics and managers have in valuing equally the practical or experiential and the theoretical. He also provides a stimulating analogy of strategy with drama: each has two 'audiences': those who study it and those who perform or do it. Strategy is largely a 'performance' art. It matters how well it is performed and its performance has serious widespread consequences.

In the book's final chapter, Huczynski investigates the source and provenance of strategy theories that become particularly popular with managers. What makes certain ideas particularly appealing to managers? How do these popular ideas become accepted and widely disseminated? He defines a management idea as 'a fairly stable body of knowledge about what managers ought to do'. He dissects the role of 'management gurus' in propagating certain types of strategic thinking and presents a sceptical approach to their contribution to organized management knowledge. He suggests five prerequisites for a management idea to achieve guru status: timeliness; strong promotion (videos, books and expensive management seminars); sympathy with managers' needs; perceived relevance; engaging presentation (merchandizing, appearance money, in-company programmes). Management ideas which catch on have to pass through two fine filters: acceptability to the corporations which pay the fees; and effective packaging of the idea if it is to be sold by a consultant as a training service. These are important practical issues for the successful dissemination of ideas to the market of practitioners for whom they are intended. Otherwise, what is management research for and how are the models and frameworks carefully chosen and described in the other chapters of this book, to have any impact or readership?

I have a genuine hope that the concepts, ideas and intellectual challenges contained in these articles will, at worst, bring your 'common-sense' approach up-to-date. At best, however, these readings should encourage you to review your own style of strategic thinking and find it enriched.

CHAPTER 20

PERSPECTIVES ON STRATEGY

GEOFF JONES

INTRODUCTION

This chapter is primarily concerned with strategy as a management discipline, what it consists of, what its roots are, what its critics say about it and how it changes. Understanding these things can help us come to our own view and be clearer about what we can and cannot reasonably expect strategy to be able to *do* for us, regardless of the claims made for it by its proponents.

We shall be considering a range of different approaches to strategy in an attempt both to demonstrate its diversity and to highlight some of its dominant assumptions. It is clear that there is no one 'theory' of strategy, or even one definition, but there is what might be considered to be a 'mainstream' of writers and approaches, and certainly many different ideas about what is important in strategy and how strategy research should be conducted. The historic dominance of North American or at least Anglo-American academics, writers and consultants in strategy, with their distinctive concerns and research traditions, has been an important aspect of strategy affecting its global relevance.

Also, because the boundaries of strategy are permeable, there are a number of perspectives, including 'critical' perspectives, which are not part of the mainstream, yet which might become so, or have some influence on how the discipline will change in the future. Here is where some of the biggest challenges to the dominant paradigm(s) may come from. Some of these perspectives will be discussed in this chapter. However, the aim is not to write a compendium but to illustrate the range and scope of the alternatives on offer and place the latest writings on strategy in broader sets of ideas. What might be called the rhetoric of strategy – its persuasive power – is strong, and it is important to be appreciative of its strengths but also to be able to see where they originate, what assumptions they depend on and how they are constructed. One way of doing this is to contrast them with some other management perspectives which are at present not well represented within the discipline.

I begin with a general discussion about the role of different perspectives in strategy and some of the assumptions which underlie them. This is followed by an introduction to some of the ways in which strategy has been divided up into different 'schools'. Problems with these categorizations lead me to consider some perspectives which are more critical of the role of strategy in organizations and of some of its (often undeclared) assumptions. We then introduce some of the less considered approaches to strategy, such as the 'dramaturgical' or 'enactment' approaches which are probably outside the strategy mainstream but which nevertheless are influential in other areas of management and organization studies. We conclude with some brief suggestions about how managers in particular can arrive at their own choices.

PERSPECTIVES ON STRATEGY AND STRATEGY IN PERSPECTIVE

In the period since the end of the Second World War, the discipline of strategy or strategic management has become one of the most powerful elements in the discourse and practice of management. Evidence for this simple statement could no doubt be gathered in many different ways; for example, through surveys of managers and academics, by noting the existence and success of learned journals such as the *Strategic Management Journal*, by analysing the number of books, articles and other media dealing with strategy or strategic issues and so on.

For most readers of this chapter, however, I suspect that no such empirical justification is necessary: strategy self-evidently *is* important. Indeed, one of the ways in which it has achieved its success in becoming such a major part of the management field has been by steadily reinforcing the rough equivalence of 'strategic' and 'important' in the English language. This equivalence gives the management discipline of strategy great power. When any rival formulation of management problems comes along to claim and demand attention, whether it originates in academic research programmes, from accounts of managers' experience or from translation from other fields such as politics or computer science, strategy can immediately make its own claim to appropriate the new ideas, because if they are as important as their proponents say, they must, by definition, be *strategic*, and hence potentially a legitimate part of the domain of strategy. Thus strategy continues to incorporate the best ideas and as it does so it can attract more researchers and fund more research; and so its own power increases along with the knowledge it generates.

In management there can arguably be no more important questions than 'why does this organization exist and what is it trying to achieve?', 'what activities should it undertake?', 'how big should it be?', 'how can it achieve its objectives?' and so on. Strategy claims to be the discipline which deals with these kinds of question. And today we regard these questions as fundamental. Yet in the sociology of knowledge, the kind of questions posed are usually more important than the answers given (Zan, 1995). And the questions strategy poses have not always been conceived in the way we now regard as self-evident, and certainly they have not always been answered in the way we choose to answer them today. The latter may not surprise us if we believe in scientific and academic progress – we simply 'know' more now than we did – but the former perhaps ought to be more persuasive in alerting us to the historical contingency of strategy as a discipline, and that, in turn, should sensitize us to the need to understand the different perspectives and conditions of possibility contained in the dynamics of the discipline today.

Business strategy[1], whether traced from its presumed ancestry in ancient Greece or China (e.g. Ansoff, 1965; Bracker, 1980), from developments in the mid-nineteenth century in North America (Chandler, 1962, 1977; Hoskin, 1990; Hoskin, Macve and Stone, 1997), from the evolution of the 'policy' concept (e.g. Sloan, 1963) or to the industrial economics of the post-World War II era (Rumelt *et al.*,1991), is easily shown to be made up of a wide range of elements. It does not have an 'essence', either in content or method, which is applicable for all time and circumstances. It changes and transforms itself. Yet if we read a book or article about strategy, what is striking about it is its self-confidence, its apparent certainty that the current view is the best view available, that its methods of analysis are capable of being brought to bear on any 'strategic' management issue and that this knowledge is clearly superior to its historical predecessors. And unlike other parts of the social sciences or humanities, the challenge of contemporaneous multiple perspectives seems to be relatively ignored in favour of declaiming the merits of the latest approach (for example, the current prominence of the resource-based view of strategy – see e.g. Grant, 1995).

That is not to say that strategy academics are unaware of different views or unwilling to debate them: there have been some celebrated public disagreements. But as a discipline, like many in management, largely composed of bits of others, there is a rather keen awareness of boundaries, of what is and what is not 'strategy', even if the precise definition is hard to ascertain. There is a certain attempt to promote the discipline and qualify the epithet of 'strategist' (Alvesson and Willmott, 1996:133). This commitment to the discipline tends to obscure some of the assumptions and effects of strategy. Let me start with some widely used yet often undeclared or unexamined assumptions which underpin many writings and courses on strategy.

ASSUMPTIONS AND PREFERENCES IN STRATEGY

It is clear that the style adopted by writers on strategy does not always present any approach or set of ideas uncritically. Many of the models and concepts on offer are qualified in some way so that the reader can form a balanced view of their strengths and weaknesses. Yet it is also clear that particular writers believe that, for example, the resource-based view of strategy has a greater claim on legitimacy and utility than some other views (for example, that organizations should primarily consider and attempt to enter more attractive industries). Also, a number of strategy concepts are underpinned by further concepts which may not always be fully scrutinized. There are various reasons for this in addition to the desire of the writers to legitimize their discipline – for example, you have to start somewhere, with some common understandings, and not need to do a course in philosophy first.

So when considering some of the approaches presented in writings on strategy, I suggest that there are a number of common yet disputable values and assumptions underlying them. These may be summarized as follows:

- The approach is analytical and realistic; that is, it presumes there is some 'reality' 'out there' which can be apprehended and understood with sensitive enough research and conceptual frameworks. Yet there is also recognition of the value of experience and meaning, for example in paradigms and institutions.
- It postulates 'bounded' actors who nevertheless will be 'rational' if 'allowed' to be.
- It stresses the interconnectedness of all elements in the discussion, and implies that these connections can be articulated, mapped in some way and manipulated.
- It conceives of the possibility and desirability of an optimal balance of stakeholder interests while recognizing inevitable imbalances of power.
- It suggests that managers have power to act and change things for the better in accordance with some collective agreement on what 'better' is.
- It is 'positivist' in the sense of claiming (perhaps implicitly) that the knowledge we have now is superior to the knowledge possessed by our predecessors. The present is seen to have emerged from the past in accordance with certain rules (for example, that changes in 'environments' lead to changes in 'organizations') which we believe exist even if we only dimly comprehend them. So it is determinist also, even though we recognize that rationality is bounded.

Many of these assumptions may strike you as being pretty reasonable – even as being 'common sense' (although the strategy material on paradigms (e.g. Johnson, 1987) should alert us to the dangers of taking common sense for granted). But many writers have come to challenge some or all these 'taken-for-granted' assumptions over the last twenty years or so. Later we will consider some of these. First, though, we will look at some of the ways in which strategists have attempted to classify and categorize their own discipline.

APPROACHES TO STRATEGY

A good place to start a review of approaches to strategy is to refer to Richard Whittington's well-regarded and accessible text *What is Strategy and Does it Matter?* (Whittington, 1993). Commenting that there is a fundamental implausibility in the claims made by books on strategy to disclose the 'secrets' of strategy for £25 when top managers are paid so much, he organizes his discussion and theories of strategy into four broad groupings which differ in two fundamental respects: the extent to which organizations seek either profit-maximizing or pluralist outcomes, and the extent to which strategy is deliberately planned rather than emerging incrementally, accidentally or through a more or less muddled and uncertain process. This allows many of the key thinkers in strategy to be located in relation to each other, as in Figure 20.1. The approaches can be roughly characterized as follows:

Classical – Stresses rationality and analysis.

Evolutionary – Stresses the unpredictability of the environment which makes irrelevant much of what is traditionally regarded as strategic analysis. It is analogous to the biological 'survival of the fittest' model.

Processual – A pragmatic view of strategy: the world and our knowledge are imperfect, so organizations have to take account of this in their strategic processes.

Systemic – stresses the importance and, to an extent, the uniqueness of social systems within which diverse attitudes to, and conceptualizations about, strategic issues occur. Strategy will thus, in part, reflect the social system in which it occurs.

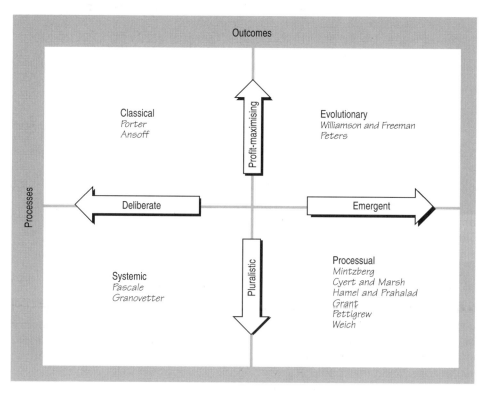

Figure 20.1 Whittington's four generic approaches to strategy with illustrative authors

Although certain writers can be 'placed' in certain 'schools', it is unlikely that any particular view of strategy can be confined entirely within that school, or, indeed that the writings of any particular writer over a long career can be easily classified. It seems even more unlikely that anyone ever set out to be included in any particular category or school. So Whittington's categories are useful primarily as an heuristic device – a way of clarifying or categorizing a complex set of issues. Some people will find his categories too neat and simplistic – for example, categorizing both the Classical and Evolutionary schools as profit-maximizing underrates the Evolutionary approach's emphasis on survival.

There are even simpler ways to categorize approaches to strategy. One common way of dividing up strategy is between the *strategic choice* and *ecological* approaches. Whittington's Classical, Processual and Systemic approaches all in their various ways presume that strategists can make choices which influence outcomes. The ecological approach, on the other hand, tends to see strategists as virtually powerless in the face of uncontrollable, and in many ways unknowable, forces (arising from uncertainty and complexity). Hence, Whittington's Evolutionary category might be considered 'anti-strategy'. But even this distinction is open to challenge: some strategists, particularly those heavily influenced by economics, tend to see macro-economic forces in a similar way to the ecologists, but still believe in strategic choice. They place emphasis on the short-lived nature of advantage and the beneficial effects of this (Rumelt *et al.*, 1991).

In contrast to Whittington's four approaches, there are more elaborate categorizations available, for example, Mintzberg's ten 'schools of strategic thought':

- design
- planning
- positioning
- entrepreneurial
- cognitive
- learning
- political
- cultural
- environmental
- configurational.

(Mintzberg, 1990a)

These schools have been found to differ significantly in the language and concepts they use (Crouch and Basch, 1996) and thus may be genuinely distinctive and incompatible approaches. This possibility ties in well with some of the more critical approaches to strategy (especially strategy as drama and the linguistic aspects of strategy) discussed below.

One important distinction which Whittington's classification draws out is the difference between the Classicists' and the Processualists' attitudes to research and the development of theories of strategy. Classicists stress rational and deliberate processes. This is based on certain commitments to the rules and procedures of science as the only means by which valid and reliable knowledge can be obtained. Their characteristic way of proceeding is to conduct detailed analytical research in an attempt to deduce rules and laws which will work in all (or most) circumstances. The human subject with its vagaries and inconsistencies tends to assume a more subordinate role – unless in the role of strategist, of course!

By contrast, Processual approaches tend to emphasize learning as a means of developing ideas; in particular, learning from experience rather than purely from research. Even this ignores the influential contribution of other modes of learning such as *action research* (Peters and Robinson, 1984). Although it is difficult to criticize the idea of learning as being a 'good thing', learning approaches are not without their difficulties, many of which are recognized by their advocates. Levinthal and March (1993), for example, highlight some of the important limitations of learning processes. They draw attention to the difficulties of coping with confusing experience and the dilemmas involved in deciding whether to explore new knowledge areas or to exploit current competencies. They argue that organizations suffer from three kinds of 'learning myopia': the tendencies to overlook distant times, distant places and failures. For example, strategies which permit survival in the short term may be incompatible with long-run success. Strategies for individual parts of an organization may be incompatible with strategies for the whole. Confidence in control may lead to expectations about outcomes before consequences are observed and interpreted. All this leads to an overinvestment in the exploitation of current capabilities at the expense of exploration of new knowledge. Levinthal and March conclude that expectations about what learning can achieve should be more restrained. This debate between 'science' and 'learning' was the topic of a celebrated exchange between Mintzberg and Ansoff (Mintzberg, 1990, 1991; Ansoff, 1991) representing the Processual and Classical schools of strategy respectively.

The more conventional view of how strategy develops relies on a careful analysis of published studies. For example, Eisenhardt and Zbaracki (1992) reviewed the 'dominant paradigms' of strategy, which they viewed as rationality and bounded validity, politics and power and the 'garbage can' model of strategic choice. They examined the theory and empirical support within each paradigm and concluded that the empirical evidence showed:

1 that strategic decision-makers are boundedly rational
2 that power wins battles of choice, and
3 that chance matters.

But they also argued that 'these paradigms rest on unrealistic assumptions and tired controversies which are no longer very controversial'. A new research agenda in strategy might involve 'creating a more realistic view of strategic decision-making by opening up our conceptions of cognition and conflict to include insight, intuition, emotion and conflict resolution ... [and] emphasizing normative implications'.

So even a view that strategy develops from empirical studies concludes that something may be wrong with the underlying assumptions in the research itself. To assume, therefore, that strategy develops in any particular way – especially a 'scientific' way – is itself an assumption.

There are other approaches which move beyond the categories presented here; for example, some researchers attempt to deal with problems of uncertainty, complexity and non-linearity through theories of *complex adaptive systems* (Stacey, 1995). This approach embraces complexity and 'chaos theory' in an attempt to overcome some of the problems with deterministic approaches. It attempts to model uncertainty and complexity through simulations of randomly formed informal networks. This moves beyond the categories used by Whittington.

These various approaches may influence the kinds of strategy which organizations pursue. Classical approaches stress rationality and clarity and hence are likely to lead to highly analytic and deliberate styles of strategy based in a few expert hands. By contrast, Processual approaches are more likely to recognize a range of factors and inputs leading to a range of outcomes, many of which will be unintentional. This is more likely to involve a wider set of people and to emphasize *learning and bargaining* rather than analysis as the means by which strategic insight is acquired, with *incrementalism* as the typical strategic process.

The Systemic approach draws attention to the effect of local cultures and attitudes, and the Anglo-American roots of strategy itself. It is likely to lead to an interest in different styles of strategy in different cultures and hence to understanding and working with these differences rather than the 'one style fits all' approach characteristic of Classicists. This approach pays attention to differences (in things such as values and governments) and developing strategy accordingly. One rather surprising aspect of Whittington's assessment of this approach is that he seems to regard it as being essentially *deliberate*: there seems to be no particular reason why an emergent stance cannot be adopted here also, or that it might incorporate a Processual outlook.

Another factor not considered by Whittington is the effect of the kind of organization being managed and its type of ownership. For example, small firms are likely to have little or no effect on the environments in which they operate. Also, they may not need to persuade stock markets and analysts that they conform to 'accepted' practices. The Classical rational planning approach, irrespective of its validity otherwise, would just be a waste of time for such an organization.

WHAT'S WRONG WITH STRATEGY?

Most management researchers, although disagreeing with each other about various things (such as dominant theories and methods), do share certain assumptions, particularly generally positive views about the value of strategy and management. These views are not, however, necessarily shared by all researchers, particularly those from the social sciences. Unlike the management researchers, who focus on the actions of managers (often with a view to developing ways of producing 'better' management), many social scientists tend to see management as a wider social phenomenon whose benefits should not be automatically assumed and which is suffering from a range of problems which cast doubt on the bases of management research traditionally underpinning strategy. Some of these problems are:

● The rise of management and in the number of managers does not correspond with cycles of economic prosperity.

- Increasing the amount of management education does not seem to lead automatically to improved economic performance.
- 'Managerialism' is becoming so widespread and influential we find it hard to think of anything except in terms of managing it – our families, our relationships, our time, the environment, etc.
- The world is now seen by some to be too complex and uncertain to be 'managed' in the sense that we ordinarily understand the term (i.e. that managerial actions lead to desired effects and *only* those effects).
- There is a long tradition of valuing the practical and experiential and a distrust of the 'theoretical'.
- There is doubt about whether management practices and meanings can be generalized globally because of fundamental cultural differences. Therefore the idea of management as a science (in the traditional understanding of 'science') is challenged (French and Grey, 1996).

Strategy, because of its claims to be an inclusive and important management discipline, has attracted criticism. This criticism focuses in particular on the *power effects* of strategy and strategic discourse, which I shall discuss next.

CRITICAL APPROACHES

Despite its apparently long history, business strategy has only recently become a subject of its own, and a very powerful one at that (Hoskin, Macve and Stone, 1997). Why is this and what are the consequences? Critics of strategy cite its tendency:

> ...to abstract the politics of strategic decision-making from the wider historical and social contexts of managerial action. Insufficient account is taken of how managers are positioned by historical forces to assume and maintain a monopoly of strategic decision-making responsibility... [t]here is little consideration of how managerial values are laden with ideological assumptions about the 'facts' of strategic management. Corporate strategies are rarely assessed in terms of their wider impact on society.
> (Alvesson and Willmott, 1996: 132)

This argument draws attention to the position and power of the strategist and the consequences of (usually) his actions. It also considers exactly how this power is 'manufactured' – how we come to accept the language of strategy as being 'common sense' and thus accept the power of its speakers as inevitable and deserved. Knights and Morgan (1991) have focused on how strategy has come to be so influential.

They first draw attention to the way in which strategy entered the business field, which they argue was the result of US domination of managerial discourse and the changes which affected US corporations in the post-Second World War period. These changes have three notable features:

1 the gradual restructuring of ownership patterns and the institutional separation of ownership from managerial control which began in the US in the inter-war period (though it had occurred earlier in the UK)
2 changes in international market conditions which gave the USA a stewardship role in the world economy through its multinational corporations
3 changes in the organizational form of these companies, in particular the rise of the multidivisional form, which led to changes in the means of controlling them.

These control requirements led to an opportunity to develop a 'discursive space' which military strategy (with its emphasis on controlling far-flung units through its utilization of communications technology and surveillance techniques, and the prestige acquired through success in war) was able to fill. Academics such as Ansoff (1965) began to articulate the need for corporate strategy. Specialist business practitioners also begin to emerge. Knights and Morgan draw attention to the ways in which, as more and more people come to be involved, it becomes more difficult to think of any alternative. But not everyone is swept along by the power of the discourse. Managers who favour a more instinctive entrepreneurial approach, as well as staff at the lower levels of the organization, are likely to resist, rather than regard strategy as inevitable.

Knights and Morgan identify seven reasons why the discourse of corporate strategy came to be dominant. These are:

1 It provides managers with a rationalization of their successes and failures.
2 It sustains and enhances the prerogatives of management and negates alternative perspectives on organizations.
3 It generates a sense of personal and organizational security for managers.
4 It reflects and sustains a strong sense of gendered masculinity for male management.
5 It demonstrates managerial 'rationality' to colleagues, customers, competitors, government and other significant people in the environment, who are likely to be looking for such signals.
6 It facilitates and legitimizes the exercise of power.
7 It creates a language and practice which enables organizational members to construct an identity for themselves.

Clearly, these kinds of explanation for the development of strategy are far from Ansoff's conception of the 'facts' determining strategy. But what they provide is an explanation which regards the power effects of strategy as being more related to the interests of the people involved than a neutral and objective view of a truth which has become apparent through rigorous and disinterested research techniques.

Knights and Morgan then conduct their own analysis of the assumptions which they say underpin strategy. These are as follows:

• It is characteristic of strategy that everything is explicable in the end. There is nothing in principle which is unknowable.

- Managers are credentialled experts with the ability to both define the problems the organization faces and the solutions it needs to adopt.
- Managers can create a sense of comfort that their destiny is in their own hands.
- Strategic discourse and practice both reflects and reproduces what may be termed a 'masculist conception of power' (Brittan, 1989).
- The construction of managers as competent strategists becomes crucial in coping with the insecurity and the proliferation of information.

These ideas in fact echo some of the Processual school. For example, Pettigrew (1985) draws attention to the construction of power through the creation of expertise. What is different about Knights and Morgan's critique is that it regards the way in which we perceive our roles as managers or customers or strategists as also being the product of these power relations. In other words, the occupation and power of a 'strategist' is a socially constructed, not a natural phenomenon, and depends on there being certain spaces, discourses and power relations available before it can come into existence. Therefore:

> Strategy does not simply respond to pre-existing problems. In the process of its formulation, strategy is actively involved in the constitution, or re-definition, of problems in advance of offering itself as a solution to them.
>
> (Knights and Morgan, 1991: 270)

This discussion may have taken us a long way from the usual discussions found in strategy textbooks. But it is important to appreciate that much debate about strategy – even where there are strong opposing views such as those of Mintzberg and Ansoff – is conducted by 'insiders', those who already accept the boundaries and subject matter of strategy as largely given. What the critical approach does for us, at the very least, is to sensitize us to the existence of a range of views which do not necessarily regard strategy as an inevitable and desirable phenomenon.

What we have discussed is a range of different perceptions of strategy which in turn seem to embody a whole range of different assumptions about human attitudes and behaviour in organizations. The distinctions between Whittington's Classical and Processual schools, the debate between Mintzberg and Ansoff, the critical views of Knights and Morgan, all challenge the idea that strategy is an unambiguously rational activity. The Processualists cast doubt on the feasibility or desirability of the planned, 'rational' approach; the critical theorists draw attention to the role of 'interests' in the development of strategy. The significance of management gurus (Huczynski, 1993) draws attention to another way of looking at strategists – as secular priests or witchdoctors. This suggests a number of different ways of regarding strategy *in terms of* rationality and interests.

One way of conceptualizing this (Thomas, 1993) proposes a framework based on two main dimensions: rationality and sectionalism. Rationality can be divided into the objective (demonstrated through the application of scientific procedures) and the subjective rationality of actions.

Sectionalism contrasts management action as oriented towards 'unitary' ends (in accordance with the interests of all an organization's stakeholders) with that pursued for 'sectional' ends (the interests of specific groups such as shareholders). The resulting matrix (Figure 20.2) defines a conceptual space within which theories of management can be located. This framework would depict Whittington's Classical school as a rational profession and his Processual school as being more concerned with politics. But in addition, we can also include approaches critical of strategy such as those which view strategy as an agency of capitalism, or of a subjectively rational but objectively irrational practice akin to magic or religion.

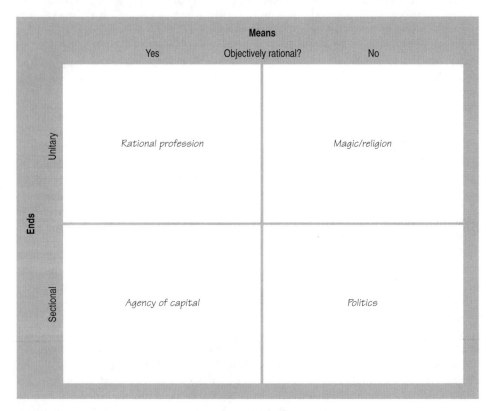

Figure 20.2 An analytical framework for management

This framework allows a different set of concerns from Whittington's about management and strategy to be taken into account. We shall now consider some of these perspectives.

STRATEGY AS DRAMA

Moving towards an outlook which is less analytical than much of mainstream strategic thinking, this section will consider some different emphases which are emerging in the strategy literature. There is an analogy between strategy and drama which leads us to a view of strategy as 'dialogue and doing'. Finally, we consider briefly a kind of criticism which is growing, often under the slippery label of postmodernism, which looks even more carefully than we have so far done at the ways in which management and strategy language and text are constructed.

The discussion in the previous paragraph has drawn attention away from seeing strategy as representing our best interpretation of 'the facts' to seeing it more as a matter of style rather than content. One metaphor which captures this outlook is given by Mockler (1994). In contrast to the 'management guru as witch doctor' (Cleverly, 1971; Clark and Salaman, 1996) he suggests that we need not worry too much about the range of theories and approaches we have been discussing. Mockler claims that strategy is analogous to the field of drama and dramatic literature. Like drama, it has two 'audiences': those who study it as literature and those who perform it. In strategy, the academic or observer perspective prevails despite strategy being largely a performance art acted out by managers. Like strategy, there are many 'schools' of drama – Classical Greek and Roman, sixteenth- and seventeenth-century Elizabethan and Jacobean, seventeenth-century Classical French and so on – which have close ties with the country and era in which they were written, the dramatic genre and author, and other contextual aspects. Drama has a number of factors which separate it from other arts and which allow it to be interpreted in a range of different cultures and situations.

Strategy may also have some common elements which transcend situational context. But in strategy, comparatively little attention is given to the contextual factors themselves. This view directs our attention to three things:

- The futility of trying to decide which general approach to strategy is 'best', because the ideas themselves are not directly comparable to each other. Your view of strategy depends on a whole range of factors to do with you, your stakeholders, the situation, its history and so on. Strategy is judgemental, and therefore uncertain and prone to error.
- That the question of what is 'best' is meaningless since different views can happily co-exist – people just find some kinds of drama/strategy more appealing to their experience and expectations than others. If it 'works' for you – it works.
- Finally, there can be a set of concepts which can be applied to different dramatic situations, whether in the theatre or in organizations, which establish the language in which debates and evaluations can be conducted, yet which do not permit participants to establish privileged positions, because the concepts can be applied to and support many different positions. It is because of these differences that learning can occur, but only if we are sensitive to them and reflective about our own attitude towards them.

THE SOCIAL CONSTRUCTION OF STRATEGY

It is only a short step from seeing strategy as drama to seeing strategy as 'talk' – as a kind of legitimate cultural communication which is actually 'made up' (invented or enacted) in the organizational setting, which makes the participants feel 'in touch', and maybe able to achieve some of the benefits they seek (of being secure, in control, or simply having a role to play). In an article entitled 'Strategy through dialogue and doing', Pye (1995) argues that managing is about dialogue and action – that is, 'through listening and talking, creating, shaping and sharing meaning, things are made to happen and managing is said to have taken place. If, in this process, it is helpful to call this strategic decision-making, so be it. But this should be recognized as a *communicative device* rather than a canon of business: indeed, any search for the principles is ... elusive.'

Weick (1990) sees culture as about sharing certain things. But he points out that sharing can mean either to divide and distribute or to hold things in common. He thinks that we need to refine this and to see sharing as both process and outcome. We need to get away from seeing things in 'I'm right and everybody else is wrong' terms, and more in terms of 'I don't know, let's see...'. The subjects of Pye's study – senior executives from a range of industries such as textile manufacturing, banking, engineering, retailing and conglomerates – practised this kind of orientation. Their readings of situations, their grounding in the language and traditions of the organization differ, yet their ability to craft new languages and meanings, and to maintain relationships through talking and communicating, is what underpins their success – nothing about understanding the principles of strategy. Indeed, Pye goes further and detects a kind of 'halo effect' surrounding senior executives – that is, a tendency on the part of subordinates to *assume* that their discussions with their seniors were based on some set of rules or logic, and to assume that they did not have access to these. Yet Pye argues that it does not matter what these rules are or whether they exist at all, because they are irrelevant to the enactment of management and strategy. People behave *as though* there were principles of management, even though no one can be sure what they are. Yet management 'happens' or is enacted in the talk and transactions between people.

You may recall the story recounted by Weick (1990) of the Hungarian soldiers marooned high in the Alpine snows, who despaired until one of them found a map in his pocket. The soldiers confidently marched down the mountain to safety and only discovered when they got back that the map was of the Pyrenees. This is part of what Pye is saying: strategy may happen *despite* rather than because of the formulations of strategists and gurus. It may not matter whether what they say is 'true' or not. It seems to be more important that we believe that *someone* knows what to do (back to the view of strategists as organizational witch doctors) – but even this may not be what determines whether strategy is successful or not. What matters is the 'talk' and how it is conducted and enacted, and how people interpret and apply what is said in their day-to-day situations – not in the boardroom or the strategy seminars. Strategy is achieved through dialogue and doing.

This seems to sum up much of the world of managing, whether it is called strategic decision-making, executive process, managing or communicating – a search for rules to describe something that is little more than a communicative device. As Pye says, 'every means of appreciating it hinges on dialogue – listening and talking – and *things* may be talked up or down, round or about, over or through. And, ultimately, *things* may be talked out, subsequently to be replaced by different talk. But in this way, *things* are made to happen'. Here we are returning to some themes of management and strategy as symbolic action, as having a value and meaning independent of the facts and theories offered by academics. This approach overcomes some of the problems of strategy in organizations, because an emphasis on constructed meanings applies to all kinds of social interaction, not just to those specialist activities which are undertaken in the kinds of organization included in strategy. It argues that there is no difference between the substantive and the symbolic because all behaviour is symbolic and socially constructed. This line of thought has strong roots in the social sciences (Berger and Luckmann, 1966). There seems no reason why it should not be applied equally to strategy, as Pye suggests.

POSTMODERNISM AND STRATEGY

The debate about strategy and management as 'dialogue' is not the most extreme departure from the more usual ideas about what strategy is. In recent years, a more radical critique of managerial discourses has been developed, drawing from developments in the social sciences and the humanities, and based not on concepts of interests but on linguistic analysis. This approach, still very much a minority interest, considers management disciplines as purely *textual* phenomena – that is, concerned with the relationship between language and thought. As we have seen, there is a range of views on how management or strategy ideas come to be adopted. We have considered a continuum from the 'scientific' at one end, through a behavioural or processual set of views, to views which stress the importance of power and interests, and others which regard the existence of management principles as incidental to the enactment of management and strategy.

The final position I want to consider is what is often controversially labelled a 'postmodern' approach to management and strategy (Cooper and Burrell, 1988). What this concentrates on is not how power or principles come to dominate what is regarded as legitimate management discourse, but how certain assumptions and relations are built into the very language itself that we use to express ourselves. Proponents of postmodernism, such as the French philosopher Derrida (1978), argue that we must attempt to analyse the way in which texts and languages themselves are constructed if we are to understand why our world is the way it seems. This method of analysis, known as *deconstruction*, places at least as much emphasis on what is *not* said as what is said. It is argued that the *presence* of something in a text simultaneously constructs an *absence* of something else, and that attending to these absences will illuminate a lot of our textual practices and hence what we regard as our 'common sense'. Postmodernists go further and argue that there is no *necessary* relationship between our texts and the world 'out there' that can be satisfactorily established: our texts are simply a set of arbitrary signs that only have meaning because we treat them as though they were meaningful. The goal of deconstruction is to expose the inherent contradictions which reside in any text.

This is not the place to explore these ideas in any depth – the postmodernist position is virtually the opposite of that taken in any writing on strategy. It is mentioned here because there seems to be a growing doubt in some quarters about whether the 'science' of management is at all capable of dealing with the issues it claims to be able to, and this has prompted some academics to analyse management from a postmodern perspective (Burrell, 1992). To give some idea of what these writers are interested in, we need to consider some of the ways in which the *concept* of strategy is constructed.

Let us start with a general set of comments. In order for managers to manage we rely on our mutual understanding of certain concepts such as 'organization', 'environment' and 'network'. Most of the time, we do not bother to subject these concepts to any detailed scrutiny unless we want to elaborate them in some way.

There are some other assumptions implicit in these ordinary but unexamined words in strategy and other management fields which may be more problematic than you might think. This is because we are accustomed to their use and may not realize that they are part of our 'paradigm', or way of thinking about these things.

'Environment' is a good example of a concept which seems self-evident to us and which we presume has always existed. But people have only very recently (in historical terms) conceptualized their surroundings in terms of an 'environment'. Does that mean that people have always had an 'environment' even if they did not conceptualize it as such? We tend to think that they did – because we believe in the 'reality' of the concept and its analytical usefulness. Yet 'environment' presupposes something which by definition is *not* environment. Similarly, if we think of an organization, we think also of something which is *not* the organization. These alternations can reveal a lot about the assumptions inherent in the concept itself. This line of thought involves us in questioning the validity (and in some contexts the ethics) of imposing our 'version' of reality on to people who do not share it, arguing that we can only make sense of people's behaviour (and hence formulate programmes of action, such as strategy, which are useful to *us*) if we understand the concepts and categories of thought which were (or are) meaningful to *them*.

Like environment, 'strategy' also has a very recent history in its application to business as against its long use in military discourse. The term is traditionally believed to have its roots in economics and game theory in the post-Second World War period but not to have been widely used in a business context until the 1960s. This ought to make us think about the role that strategy played in the success of organizations before they had things they called strategies. Did, therefore, DuPont or General Motors in the early twentieth century succeed without having any strategy? Or did they have strategies but call them something else?

Strategists tend to make two kinds of responses to these questions. They are likely to argue either:

(a) that the environment (that word again) we exist in today is different from earlier times in particular ways (more uncertainty, complexity, turbulence, rapid change, etc.) which now make strategy vital where it may not have been in the past; or
(b) businesses *did* have strategy in the past in the sense of having purposes, goals, intentions or whatever; they just did not have the benefit of the modern conceptions of it which we have acquired through our research and experience.

In both cases, the modern conception of strategy remains intact and unchallenged. But strategy also has power as a rhetorical device to mobilize support for a particular way of looking at strategic problems (Eccles and Nohria, 1992) and to influence the language in organizational debates. Postmodernists would draw attention to the way in which texts on strategy were constructed regardless of any 'empirical' relationships between the signifier (the language) and the signified (the object being referred to).

So when we 'talk strategy' we should be aware that we are constructing a certain view of the world, mainly in terms of what interests us as strategists; and this construction may not accord with the constructions which non-strategists put on the aspects of the situation which concern them most. The language game itself is one of the areas where power relations are played out.

This general attempt to examine some of the implications of the language and concepts of strategy should facilitate more awareness of a strategist's perspective being a *particular* perspective which might not be shared.

The range of perspectives presented in this chapter is summarized in Figure 20.3, which presents them in terms of their authors' perceptions of the desirability of rationality in management, as defined by Thomas (1993) in Figure 20.2.

WHAT TO DO: THE FOUR FACES OF PRAGMATISM

Given the doubts about, but accepting the continuing demand for, the kinds of offering academics and strategy gurus make available, what should the manager do? Managers need to make up their own minds about how good and how useful is the material they are being offered. The uncritical adoption of the latest management nostrums ('flavour of the month management') has been shown to be harmful to US business over the last 30 years (Locke, 1996). Nohria and Berkley (1994) argue that 'the widespread adoption of trendy management techniques during the 1980s allowed managers to rely on ready-made answers instead of searching for creative solutions'. They call for a 'return to pragmatism' which explicitly recognizes the uncertainties inherent in the managerial environment and the ways in which managers actually try to make sense of it.

To do this, they borrow a well-known concept from anthropology, that of the *bricoleur* ('handyman' in English – but the French connotation is that of an improviser, using anything appropriate for the task). The suggestion is that

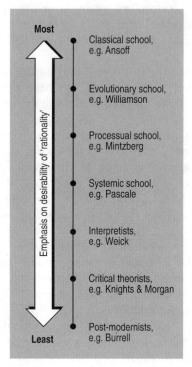

Figure 20.3 The rationality continuum for approaches to strategy

managers should be *bricoleurs* when it comes to management ideas – taking bits and pieces that seem useful to them and welding them into a set of perhaps imperfect tools for the task in hand. Inevitably, as with much management writing, there are some 'guiding principles' (but only four) as follows:

The four faces of pragmatism

- *Sensitivity to context* – Being able to judge the parameters of a particular situation and decide what ideas and actions will work in that context.
- *Willingness to make do* – Experimenting with and using available resources and material to find workable solutions.
- *Focus on outcomes* – Being concerned with getting results, but not being too 'hung-up' on how to get them.
- *Openness to uncertainty* – Recognizing the impossibility of being able to anticipate all circumstances and thereby being required to act out of ignorance.

(Adapted from Nohria and Berkley, 1994)

So we need to consider our own particular 'portfolios' of meaningful concepts, and, given the diversity of approaches this is bound to contain, how we come to accept such a plurality of incongruent actions or techniques in strategy yet remain able to communicate and act effectively. This 'neo-pragmatism' will not be compatible with all the approaches discussed in this chapter, but it probably is compatible with those perspectives which remain convinced that strategy, however defined and with whatever qualification, is an activity worth pursuing.

CONCLUSION

In this chapter, we have taken a journey around the borders of the 'field' of strategy and have occasionally gone through the gate into the world outside and looked back. The aim of this exercise is to assert that no body of knowledge is discrete and sacrosanct, or 'knows all the answers' – even to problems it has itself defined. There is a wide range of approaches to strategy, some of which do not even share basic assumptions. There are some views which are critical of its power, or sceptical about its legitimacy. We need to understand these differences but not be overwhelmed by them. Incompatible approaches can still be melded together in a practical situation even if the mix is likely to vary from one set of problems to another.

The pragmatic model of the conceptual *bricoleur*/handyman and the significance of dialogue and communication in constructing individual strategy models allows us to construct perspectives with which we can be comfortable *and* which also seem to work for us. What is most important is that to achieve this insight it is necessary to have gone through a learning process, and in particular to 'learn how to learn'. Here we return to the propositions put forward at the beginning of the chapter about strategy incorporating ideas from elsewhere, which is one of the key capabilities stressed by the resource-based view of strategy (Grant, 1995). With this capability of learning we might associate the capabilities of choosing and acting, and this chapter has, through its presentation of the wide range of perspectives on strategy which are available, attempted to provide a wider range to choose from than usual. I hope and expect that this will mean that what I have called mainstream strategy becomes in the future a broader rather than narrower discipline and activity than it seems to be at present.

REFERENCES

Alvesson, M. and Willmott, H. (1996) *Making Sense of Management: a critical introduction*, Sage, London.

Ansoff, H.I. (1965) *Corporate Strategy*, McGraw-Hill, New York.

Ansoff, H.I. (1991) 'Critique of Henry Mintzberg's "The design school: reconsidering the basic premises of strategic management"', *Strategic Management Journal*, Vol. 12, pp. 449–61.

Berger, P. and Luckmann, T. (1966) *The Social Construction of Reality*, Penguin, Harmondsworth.

Bracker, J. (1980) 'The historical development of the strategic management concept', *Academy of Management Review*, Vol. 5, pp. 219-224.

Brittan, A. (1989) *Masculinity and Power*, Blackwell, Oxford.

Burrell, G. (1992) 'Back to the future', in Reed, M. and Hughes, M. (eds) *Rethinking Organization*, Sage, London.

Chandler, A. (1962) *Strategy and Structure: chapters in the history of American enterprise*, MIT Press, Cambridge MA.

Chandler, A. (1977) *The Visible Hand: the managerial revolution in American business*, Harvard University Press, Cambridge, MA.

Clark, T. and Salaman, G. (1996) 'The management guru as organizational witchdoctor', *Organizational Studies*, Vol. 9, No.1.

Cleverly, G. (1971) *Managers and Magic*, Longman, London.

Cooper, R. and Burrell, G. (1988) 'Modernism, postmodernism and organizational analysis: an introduction', *Organizational Studies*, Vol. 9, No. 1.

Crouch, A. and Basch, J. (1996) 'The structure of strategic thinking: a lexical and content analysis', Paper presented to the second International Conference on *Organizational Discourse: Talk, Text and Tropes*, London, July.

Derrida, J. (1978) *Writing and Difference*, Routledge, London.

Eccles, R. and Nohria, N. (1992) *Beyond the Hype: rediscovering the essence of management*, Harvard Business School Press, Cambridge MA.

Eisenhardt, K. and Zbaracki, M. (1992) 'Strategic decision making', *Strategic Management Journal*, Vol. 13, pp. 17–37.

French, R. and Grey, C. (eds) (1996) *Rethinking Management Education*, Sage, London.

Grant, R. (1995) *Contemporary Strategy Analysis*, Blackwell, Oxford.

Hoskin, K. (1990) 'Using history to understand theory: a reconceptualization of the historical genesis of "strategy"', Paper presented to the EIASM workshop on *Strategy, Accounting and Control*, Venice.

Hoskin, K., Macve, R. and Stone, J. (1997) 'The historical genesis of modern business and military strategy: 1850–1950', Proceedings of the fifth *Interdisciplinary Perspectives on Accounting Conference*, University of Manchester.

Huczynski, A. (1993) *Management Gurus: what makes them and how to become one*, London, Routledge.

Johnson, G. (1987) *Strategic Change and the Management Process*, Blackwell, Oxford.

Knights, D. and Morgan, G. (1991) 'Corporate strategy, organizations and subjectivity: a critique', *Organizational Studies*, Vol. 12, No. 2, pp. 251–73.

Levinthal, D.A. and March, J.G. (1993) 'The myopia of learning', *Strategic Management Journal*, Vol. 14, pp. 95–112.

Locke, R. (1996) *The Collapse of the American Management Technique*, Oxford University Press, Oxford.

Mintzberg, H. (1990a) 'Strategy formation: schools of thought', in Fredrickson, J. (ed.) *Perspectives on Strategic Management*, Harper Business, New York.

Mintzberg, H. (1990b) 'The design school: reconsidering the basic premises of strategic management', *Strategic Management Journal*, Vol. 11, No. 3, pp. 171–96.

Mintzberg, H. (1991) 'Learning 1, Planning 0, Reply to Igor Ansoff', *Strategic Management Journal*, Vol. 12, p. 462.

Mockler, R. (1994) 'Strategic management research and teaching', *Management Learning*, Vol 25, No. 3 pp. 371–85.

Nohria, N. and Berkley, J.D. (1994) 'Whatever happened to the "take-charge" manager?', *Harvard Business Review*, January–February.

Peters, M. and Robinson, V. (1984) 'The origins and status of action research', *Journal of Applied Behavioural Science*, Vol. 20, pp. 113–24.

Pettigrew, A. (1985) *The Awakening Giant*, Blackwell, Oxford.

Pye, A. (1995) 'Strategy through dialogue and doing', *Management Learning*, Vol. 26, No. 4 pp. 445–62.

Rumelt, R., Schendel, D. and Teece, D. (1991) 'Strategic management and economics', *Strategic Management Journal* Vol. 12, pp. 5–29.

Sloan, A. (1963) *My Years with General Motors*, Sedgewick and Jackson, London.

Stacey, R.D. (1995) 'The science of complexity: an alternative perspective for strategic change processes', *Strategic Management Journal*, Vol. 16, pp. 477–95.

Thomas, A.B. (1993) *Controversies in Management*, Routledge, London.

Weick, K. (1990) 'Cartographic myths in organizations', in Huff, A. (ed.) *Mapping Strategic Thought*, Wiley, London.

Whittington, R. (1993) *What is Strategy and Does it Matter?*, Routledge, London.

Zan, L. (1995) 'Interactionism and systemic view in the strategic approach', *Advances in Strategic Management*, Vol. 12, pp 261–283.

NOTE

1 Within the field of strategic management, 'business strategy' is a discrete specialism of its own concerned with strategy at the level of the business unit as against, say, corporate strategy. But I use the term here simply to differentiate the use of strategy in a business management rather than a military context. The term 'strategic management' which used to denote this distinction is giving way to a more generic use of the term 'strategy' for business or non-military application, yet which excludes certain aspects of strategy in its modern military usage.

CHAPTER 21

MANAGEMENT GURUS: WHAT MAKES THEM AND HOW TO BECOME ONE

ANDRZEJ A. HUCZYNSKI

Management ideas poem

Paul Holland

With Herzberg, Mintzberg and Mr Argyle
I'm desperately trying to develop a style
But will I ever get the chance to Schein
Often I feel I'm in de Klein

I'm looking for a Handy solution I shout
But as soon as I'm interested it just Peters out
I've looked everywhere (at Fielder on the roof and Maslower down)
Till I'm Reddin the face and begin to frown

I'm not as Jung as I used to be (keep it quiet)
But Freud egg and Drucker l'Orange are not my diet
Even in Tescos during Shopenhausers
They Kant stop talking about the brain's mystical powers

I've looked at TA and got my fingers Berned
My cross-transactions have Vroom for improvement – so I learned
Without Fayol when I'm counselled I just get a Block
I get de Board feeling so easily I never take stock

Learning styles may have helped me (but I lied)
However, I discovered, 'Honey, it's Kolb outside'
My search has been rewarded (partial I'd admit)
When asked for my opinion I say it's all Tannenbaum and Schmidt

I'm sorry if the above doesn't scan
But I'm afraid I missed the meter man

(Holland, 1989, p. 96)

INTRODUCTION

Why do certain management ideas achieve widespread popularity and bring fame and fortune to their writers, while others do not? Those authors who have achieved celebrity have had their ideas taught in business schools and on in-company seminars. They are discussed in the books and journal articles of other writers; sections of their writings appear in books of readings. Such a degree of continuing exposure is not limited just to when the authors are alive: their ideas continue to flourish after their deaths. Hence, these management writers achieve fame during their lives, and immortality after it!

Fortune refers to the income that these writers can expect to earn from the sale of their ideas. The income flows come in the form of royalties from their books, from sales of audio and video cassettes, workbooks and associated training materials. Most spectacularly, it can come from personal appearance fees at conferences and company seminars. In 1987, Tom Peters was rumoured to be charging $25,000 per presentation, and Rosabeth Moss Kanter's consultancy fee was $17,000 per hour. Is it luck, or do their ideas have something in common? The author argues that for a management idea to secure fame, fortune and immortality for its writer, it has to meet five prerequisites. Specifically, the idea has:

1 to be timely – that is, it should address itself to the problems of the age
2 to be brought to the attention of its potential audience. Ideas do not promote themselves. Business school academics, management consultancies and training and publishing companies play an important role in the dissemination of the ideas
3 to address organizational requirements in a way that meets the individual needs and concerns of the managers at whom it is addressed
4 to possess the essential ingredients which allow potential users to perceive it as relevant to meeting their needs
5 to be verbally presentable in an engaging way. Not because the majority of managers will learn about it at a public presentation session, but because video and audio-based materials will be developed from the author's presentation of the idea itself.

The analogy of the filter funnel can help to explain why only a very small fraction of all the available management ideas ever achieve popular status. As the ideas are tipped in at the top, they flow down through ever finer filters. These filters have labels such as managers' needs, idea benefits, timeliness, promotion and presentation. Because the majority of the management ideas fail to meet requirements, they get filtered out, only a very small number of them re-emerge at the other end as popular management ideas (see Figure 21.1). This explains why there have only been six truly popular management idea families in the last hundred years.

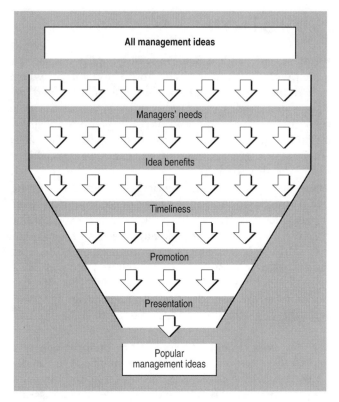

Figure 21.1 Distilling the popular management ideas

The 1980s generated a great interest in management ideas and gurus. During that time, a small number of management commentators attained guru status. Their books sold in their thousands and even millions, royalties flowed in, and their ideas were merchandised through diaries and newsletters, as well as through traditional means such as audio and video cassettes. The appearance money that they charged to make presentations at conferences and on in-company programmes matched that of film, television and pop stars. How can certain management ideas be so attractive and bring such high rewards to those who develop and present them? The purpose of this book is to answer these questions.

Certain ideas such as those of Herzberg *et al.* (1959) continue to be popular even after other writers have demonstrated flaws in the research methods and have challenged them. The fact that newer and methodologically sounder ideas have became available, has not reduced the popularity or discussion of older ones like those of Abraham Maslow (1943), Douglas McGregor (1960) or Rensis Likert (1961). These continue to have a profound effect on management teaching.

Many years ago, John Dryden said that a 'falsehood once received from a famed writer becomes traditional to posterity'. Since then, other authors have commented that the truth or falsehood of an idea was one thing, but that its acceptance and dissemination was another; that there was no apparent correlation between the significance of an idea and its popularity; that what was said was less important than *how* it was said; and that ideas received acclaim not because they were true, but because they were *interesting*.

Since nomenclature represents a potential problem, this will be dealt with immediately. What is collectively referred to as *management thought* in historical accounts of the subject by authors such as Wren (1973) consists of theories, research findings, frameworks, propositions, beliefs, views, saws and suggestions. It is an untidy hotchpotch of diverse offerings. Linguistically, therefore, it is convenient to adopt a set of standardized labels for use throughout this book. The term *management idea* is applied to all abstract thought units or systems of such units. Kramer defined a management idea as a fairly stable body of knowledge about what managers ought to do. He said that it:

> ...derived from inductive and deductive reasoning. It is systematically organized knowledge applicable to a relatively wide area of circumstances. As a system of assumptions, accepted principles and rules of procedures ... [it] assists managers to analyze and explain the underlying causes of a given business situation and predict the outcome of alternate courses of action.
>
> (Kramer, 1975, p. 47)

Where there can be said to be sufficient similarity between these ideas or systems of ideas, then the term *family of management ideas* will be used. Finally, where the idea or idea system spawns a clearly defined set of actions which go beyond mere thought, but actually seek to alter the behaviour of individuals, groups or organizations in some way, then the label *idea technique* will be applied.

Which then are the most popular management ideas of the twentieth century? The results of a survey of academics and practitioners in the field and a content analysis of professional journals, popular texts of selected readings and a reprint series was used to establish this. Matheson (1974) reported the findings of a survey carried out among the 2,123 members of the American Academy of Management which sought to identify contributions that had greatly influenced management thought and research. In the late 1970s Pollard (1974; 1978) summarized the work of forty-two writers on management ideas which gave students 'a fair cross-section of the writings on management'. Books by Pugh, Hickson and Hinings (1983) and Pugh (1984) summarized the contributions of selected management writers and contained extracts from their original books. Authors were chosen because:

> All have attempted to draw together information and distill theories of how organizations function and how they should be managed. Their writings have been theoretical in the sense that they have tried to discover generalizations applicable to all organizations.
>
> (Pugh *et al.*, 1983, p. 9)

Another source with which to identify the popular management ideas comes from Miner (1980; 1982). The management ideas in his book were nominated by 'recognized scholars in the field of organizational study. More than thirty-five individuals suggested theories for consideration. All theories on which most of the scholars were agreed are discussed here' (Miner, 1982, p. 453).

Finally, some more recent texts were consulted (Tosi, 1984; Koontz, 1961 and 1980; Clutterbuck and Crainer, 1988 and 1990; Pierce and Newstrom, 1988 and 1990). The last of these considered the popular texts of the 1980s based on the dimensions of their *market acceptance* (volume of sales achieved); *provocativeness* (presenting viewpoints which run counter to traditional management thought); *distinctiveness* (presenting a variety of interesting topical themes to managers); *author reputation* (those having a strong reputation and the quality of their thinking and the insights they have historically generated). Using these references, each management idea mentioned was held to be 'voted for'. A total of 129 names were identified. More recent writers did not appear often in the voting. The length of the final list indicated that beyond a hard core of writers, there is little consensus as to who the really influential contributors are. The top-ranked management writers are shown in Table 21.1.

Table 21.1 Most popular management writers

Position	Name
1	Henri Fayol
	Douglas McGregor
3	Peter Drucker
	Frederick Herzberg
	Tom Peters
6	Frederick Winslow Taylor
	Rensis Likert
	Chris Argyris

A total of 129 management writers and their votes were grouped into 'families' of management ideas. Table 21.2 lists these families in chronological order. To these five families a sixth is added. This is labelled guru theory. This school acquired prominence in the 1980s. While not yet featuring extensively in management textbooks it has received widespread attention in the financial and business press (Lorenz, 1986; Byrne, 1986; Clutterbuck and Crainer, 1988; Pierce and Newstrom, 1988 and 1990).

These diverse writings which together constitute guru theory include the thoughts of well-known chief executives such as Lee Iacocca, Harold Geneen, John Harvey-Jones and John Scully; of management consultants like Tom Peters and Philip Crosby; and of modern business school academics like Michael Porter, Rosabeth Moss Kanter, Henry Mintzberg and Kenneth Blanchard. Since they are so diverse and since they draw so much of their authority from the idea developers themselves, it was felt that guru theory was an appropriate label. The focus of this book will not be upon the validity or accuracy of these management ideas, but on the reasons for their appeal to practising managers and management students.

Table 21.2 Grouping of the most popular writers into management idea families

Idea family	Writers
Bureaucracy	Blau Scott Brown Crozier Jacques Michels Selznick\ Thompson Weber
Scientific management	Taylor Gantt Gilbreth
Administrative management	Barnard Fayol Follett Mooney Sloan
Human relations	Brown Mayo Roethlisberger and Dickson
Neo-human relations	Argyris Bennis Blake and Mouton Herzberg Likert McGregor Maslow Schein
Guru theory	Blanchard Drucker Iacocca Kanter Peters Porter

Reflecting on the history of management thought, one can discern bodies of organizational practice which draw upon a tradition of research and theorizing (of sorts) which goes back to the work of Taylor at the beginning of the century. Despite the efforts to dignify this body of writing as 'theory', a distinguishing feature of it has been its fierce pragmatism. Such pragmatism reflects both the concern to be applied knowledge and, in the view of many critical observers, the result of a conscious or formulated refusal to ask any fundamental questions about the nature of organization.

A consideration of popular management ideas involves an examination not only of the world of applied theory at the level of subject matter, but also of the enormously lucrative world of management consultancy and training which requires 'touchstone ideas' for its own legitimation and development. This imposes two types of constraint on the nature and form of the evolving management ideas. First, the ideas and their associated techniques must be acceptable to the organizations which pay the fees. Key aspects of organizational life, such as its political nature, thus tend to be excluded. Issues of conflicting attitudes are also frequently displaced into various semi-therapeutic and psychological treatments.

A second limitation of what can be said and written, if it is to achieve popularity, arises from the connection between management thinking and the paying organization. This affects how the management idea is packaged and sold by a consultant as a training service. The popular management ideas [...] are likely to be presented in the form of logos or pseudo-theoretical models which form the basis of a two- or three-day training programmes. Thus, pragmatic ideas in the form of McGregor's 'Theory X and Theory Y', Maslow's Hierarchy of Needs', Herzberg's 'Motivators and Hygiene Factors' and Peters and Waterman's '7-S' model will be included. All of these can be summarized on one page of a course handout in the form of a logo or on an overhead projector transparency.

Critics of the managerialist school (Salaman, 1978; Clegg, 1975; Clegg and Dunkerley, 1980) have argued that an important function of management ideas has been to legitimize the existing structures of power and authority in organizations which would have contested had they been presented directly. For this reason, management ideas have needed to be communicable and comprehensible to a wider group of people other than just top managers.

They have had to be understood by both middle and junior managerial ranks as well as by those being managed. Although the families of management ideas to be investigated appear superficially to differ greatly, they can all be said to represent a broad consensus on the nature of organizational management in a capitalist society that goes back for a hundred years. While there is no formulated agreement on particular areas in the field of management ideas, there is a broadly accepted model and a set of assumptions about organizational structure and technique. This represents a sort of common-sense understanding of what management is or should be in an organization.

Such a high degree of consensus is not surprising. The common underlying agreement referred to might be called the 'capitalist imperative'. The ideas [...] all emerged from Europe and the United States. The capitalist form of organization, therefore, specified objectives such as profit maximization, and the role and power relations between those involved in the production process. It set limits on which goals could be pursued and which forms of work organization were acceptable if the fundamental system was not to break down. Mimicking the communist system of organization, the capitalist system rejected any questioning of either the basic terms on which the management of the organization was conducted, or of the political disposition in which it existed. These potentially troublesome questions were simply bracketed, acknowledged in asides or obliquely referred to in externally determined matters such as the contracts of employment and their regulation by law. The political nature of organization is rarely referred to directly in any of the popular management literature.

REFERENCES

Byrne, J.A. (1986) 'Business fads: what's in and what's out', *Business Week*, 20 January, pp. 40–7.

Clegg, S. (1975) *Power, Rule and Domination: a critical and empirical understanding of power in sociological theory and everyday life*, Routledge, London.

Clegg, S. and Dunkerley, D. (eds) (1980) *Organization, Class and Control*, Routledge, London.

Clutterbuck, D. and Crainer, S. (1988) 'The corporate sages', *Business*, September, pp. 84–95.

Clutterbuck, D. and Crainer, S. (1990) *Masters of Management*, Macmillan, London.

Herzberg, F., Mausner, B. and Snyderman, B. (1959) *The Motivation to Work*, Wiley, New York.

Holland, P. (1989) 'Poem', *Management Education and Development*, Vol. 20, No. 1, p. 96.

Koontz, H. (1961) 'The management theory jungle', *Academy of Management Journal*, Vol. 4, No. 3, pp. 174–88.

Koontz, H. (1980) 'The management theory jungle revisited', *Academy of Management Review*, Vol. 5, No. 2, pp. 175–87.

Kramer, H. (1975) 'The philosophical foundations of management rediscovered', *Management International Review*, Vol. 15, Nos 2–3, pp. 47–55.

Likert, R. (1967) *The Human Organization: its management and values*, McGraw Hill, New York.

Lorenz, C. (1986) 'Europe warms to business punditry', *Financial Times*, 2 July, p. 18.

Maslow, A.H. (1943) 'A theory of human motivation', *Psychological Review*, Vol. 50, No. 4, pp. 370–96.

Matheson, M.T. (1974) 'Some reported thoughts on significant management literature', *Academy of Management Journal*, Vol. 17, pp. 386–9.

McGregor, D. (1960) *The Human Side of Enterprise*, McGraw Hill, New York.

Miner, J.B. (1980) *Theories of Organizational Behavior*, Dryden Press, Hinsdale, IL.

Miner, J.B. (1982) *Theories of Organizational Structure and Process*, Dryden Press, Hinsdale, IL.

Pierce, J.L. and Newstrom, J.W. (1988) *The Manager's Bookshelf*, Harper & Row, New York.

Pierce, J.L. and Newstrom, J.W. (1990) *The Manager's Bookshelf*, (2nd edn) Harper & Row, New York.

Pollard, H.R. (1974) *Developments in Management Thought*, Heinemann, London.

Pollard, H.R. (1978) *Further Developments in Management Thought*, Heinemann, London.

Pugh, D.S. (ed.) (1984) *Organization Theory: selected readings*, Penguin, Harmondsworth.

Pugh, D.S., Hickson, D.J. and Hinings, C.R. (eds) (1983) *Writers on Organization*, Penguin, Harmondsworth.

Salaman, G. (1978) 'Towards a sociology of organizational structure', *Sociological Review*, Vol. 3, pp. 519–54.

Tosi, H.L. (1984) *Theories of Organizations*, Wiley, New York.

Wren, D. (1973) *The Evolution of Management Thought*, Wiley, New York.

INDEX

ACKNOWLEDGEMENTS

Grateful acknowledgement is made to the following sources for permission to reproduce material in this book:

Chapter 1: Mintzberg, H. and Waters, J.A., 1985, 'Of strategies, deliberate and emergent', *Strategic Management Journal*, 6, pp. 257–72, © 1985 by John Wiley & Sons, Ltd. Reproduced by permission of John Wiley & Sons Limited.

Chapter 2: Reprinted by permission of *Harvard Business Review*. From 'Strategy as stretch and leverage' by Hamel, G. and Prahalad, C. K., March–April 1993. Copyright © 1993 by the President and Fellows of Harvard College, all rights reserved.

Chapter 3: Reprinted by permission of Harvard Business School Press. From *Beyond the Hype: Rediscovering the essence of management* by Eccles, R. G. and Nohria, N. Boston, MA 1992, pp. 8–115. Copyright © 1992 by the President and Fellows of Harvard College, all rights reserved.

Chapter 4: Reprinted by permission of *Harvard Business Review*. 'What is strategy?' by Prahalad, M.E. November–December 1996, pp. 61–78. Copyright © 1996 by the President and Fellows of Harvard College. All rights reserved

Chapter 5: Rumelt, R. P. 1991, 'How much does industry matter?', *Strategic Management Journal*, 12, pp. 167–185, © 1991 by John Wiley & Sons, Ltd. Reproduced by permission of John Wiley and Sons Limited.

Chapter 6: Baden-Fuller, C. and Stopford, J. 1992, *Rejuvenating the Mature Business: The competitive challenge*, Second edition, pp. 1–22, Routledge.

Chapter 7: Reprinted by permission of Harvard Business School Press. 'On the limits of a firm-based theory' by Nicole Woolsey Biggart and Gary G. Hamilton from *Networks and Organisation: Structure, from and action* by Nitin Nohria and Robert G. Eccles. Boston, MA. 1992, pp 471–491. Copyright © 1992 by the President and Fellows of Harvard College; all rights reserved

Chapter 8: Grindley, P. 1995, 'Regulation and standards policy: setting standards by committees and markets' reprinted from *The Regulatory Challenge* edited by Bishop, M., Kay, J. and Mayer, C. by permission of Oxford University Press.

Chapter 9: Grant, R. M. 1991, 'The resource-based theory of competitive advantage: implications for strategy formulation'. Copyright © 1991 by The Regents of the University of California. Reprinted from the *California Management Review*, Vol. 33, No. 3. By permission of The Regents.

Chapter 10: Amit, R. and Schoemaker, P. J. H. 1993, 'Strategic assets and organizational rent', *Strategic Management Journal*, 14, pp. 33–46, © 1993 by John Wiley & Sons, Ltd. Reproduced by permission of John Wiley and Sons Limited.

Chapter 11: Reprinted by permission of *Harvard Business Review*. 'The core competence of the corporation' by Prahalad, C.K. and Hamel, G. from *Harvard Business Review*, May–June 1990, pp. 79–91. Copyright © 1990 by the President and Fellows of Harvard College. All rights reserved

Chapter 12: Mintzberg, H. 1979, *The Structuring of Organizations*, Prentice-Hall, Inc.

Chapter 13: Miller, D. 1986, 'Configurations of Strategy and Structure: Towards a synthesis', *Strategic Management Journal*, 7, pp. 233–249. Reproduced by permission of John Wiley and Sons Limited

Chapter 14: Reprinted with permission from *Long Range Planning*, 24(4), pp. 10–20, Campbell, A. and Yeung, S. 'Creating a Sense of Mission', 1991, Elsevier Science Ltd, Oxford, England.

Chapter 15: Reprinted from 'The leader's new work: building learning organisations' by Senge, P. M. *Sloan Management Review*, 32(1) 1990, pp. 7–23, by permission of publisher. Copyright 1990 by Sloan Management Review Association. All rights reserved.

Chapter 17: Ghoshal, S. 1987, 'Global strategy: an organising framework', *Strategic Management Journal*, 8, pp. 425–440, John Wiley and Sons Ltd. By permission of John Wiley and Sons Ltd

Chapter 18: Bartlett, C.A. and Ghoshal, S. 1993, 'Beyond the M-Form: Toward a managerial theory of the firm', *Strategic Management Journal*, 14, pp. 23–46, John Wiley and Sons Ltd. By permission of John Wiley and Sons Ltd

Chapter 19: Segal-Horn, S. 1993, 'The Internationalisation of service firms', *Advances in Strategic Management*, 9, pp. 31–55. Copyright © 1993 by JAI Press Inc., reproduced by permission of the publisher

Chapter 21: Huczynski, A.A. 1993, Management Gurus: what makes them and how to become one, Routledge, Holland, P. 1989, 'Poem', Management Education and Development, 20(1), p. 96.

The Informational City

B

The Informational City

Information Technology, Economic Restructuring, and the Urban–Regional Process

Manuel Castells

BLACKWELL
Oxford UK & Cambridge USA

First published 1989
First published in paperback 1991
Reprinted 1992

Blackwell Publishers
108 Cowley Road, Oxford, OX4 1JF, UK

Three Cambridge Center
Cambridge, Massachusetts 02142, USA

British Library Cataloguing in Publication Data

A CIP catalogue record for this book is available from the British Library.

Library of Congress Cataloging in Publication Data

Castells, Manuel.
    The informational city: information technology, economic
  restructuring, and the urban-regional process/Manuel Castells.
    p.   cm.
    Bibliography: p.
    Includes index.
    ISBN 0–631–115988–6   ISBN 0–631–17937–2 (pbk.)
    1. Information technology.   2. Technology—Social aspects.
  3. High technology industries—Location.   4. Space in economics.
    I. Title.
HC79.I55C37   1989
330.9173′2—dc20

Typeset in 10/12 pt Plantin by Times Graphics
Printed in Great Britain by TJ Press, Padstow

8-2-93

Contents

Acknowledgements

This book has benefited greatly from the support of a number of institutions and people who deserve full credit for it without having to share the author's responsibility for the analyses presented here.

The project of the book was conceived during my year as a Guggenheim Fellow in 1982–3, taking advantage of the intellectual leisure I was able to enjoy thanks to the support of the John H. Simon Guggenheim Memorial Foundation. Throughout the period of research and writing, between 1983 and 1988, I relied on institutional and staff support from the Institute of Urban and Regional Development, from the Berkeley Roundtable on the International Economy, and from the Institute of International Studies, University of California at Berkeley.

A number of colleagues had the patience to read and comment on the various drafts of this work, and they were decisive in influencing the final form of the book. For that my deepest gratitude goes to Norman Glickman, Bennett Harrison, Peter Hall, Allen Scott, Amy Glasmeier, Vicente Navarro, Steve Cohen, Michael Teitz, and the late Philippe Aydalot. Other scholars were extremely helpful in providing ideas and information that are important elements of this book. Among these are Michael Smith, John Mollenkopf, Ed Soja, Saskia Sassen, Martin Carnoy, Derek Shearer, Michael Storper, Anna Lee Saxenian, Peter Schulze, Richard Gordon, Alejandro Portes, Ed Blakely, Susan Fainstein, Norman Fainstein, Richard Sennett, Ira Katznelson, Claude Fischer, and, as always, Alain Touraine.

Finally, this book is, to a great extent, the product of an intellectual milieu generated around my seminar on "The Political Economy of High Technology" in the Department of City and Regional Planning at Berkeley. I want to thank publicly the graduate students who have helped me, over the years, in developing and correcting my own analyses, particularly Jay Stowsky, François Bar, Lionel Nicol, Barbara Baran, Rebecca Skinner, Pei-Hsiung Chin, Lee Goh, Lisa Bornstein, Roberto Laserna, Katharyne Mitchell, Raymond Wu, and Penny Gurstein.

The expression of my gratitude to all the people and institutions who have contributed to the research and thinking formalized in this book amounts to a public recognition of the fact that all intellectual products are, to a large extent, collective enterprises ultimately synthesized in the solitude of authoring.

Berkeley, California
June 1988

To Françoise

Introduction

A technological revolution of historic proportions is transforming the fundamental dimensions of human life: time and space. New scientific discoveries and industrial innovations are extending the productive capacity of working hours while superseding spatial distance in all realms of social activity. The unfolding promise of information technology opens up unlimited horizons of creativity and communication, inviting us to the exploration of new domains of experience, from our inner selves to the outer universe, challenging our societies to engage in a process of structural change.

Yet, as in previous historical instances of major technological transformation, prophecies tend to take the place of analysis in efforts to comprehend the emerging social and spatial forms and processes. Futurologists predict the evolution of society on the basis of linear extrapolation of characteristics of new technologies, without taking into account the historical mediation exercised by social organization between the potential of new technologies and their effects in actuality. We are told, for example, that telecommunications allows work at home in "electronic cottages," while firms become entirely footloose in their location, freed in their operations by the flexibility of information systems and by the density and speed of the transportation network. Or that people can stay at home, and yet be both open to an entire world of images, sounds, and communication flows, and potentially interactive, thus superseding the need for cities as we have known them until the coming of the information age. Historical optimism and moralistic pessimism both convey in different tones an equally simplistic message of technological determinism, be it the liberation of the individual from the constraints of the locale, or the alienation of social life disintegrating in the anonymity of suburban sprawl.

In fact, none of these prophecies stands up to the most elementary confrontation with actual observation of social trends. Telecommunications is reinforcing the commanding role of major business concentrations around the world. Salaried work at home in effect means mainly sweated labor in the garment industry while "telecommuting" is practiced by a negligible fraction of workers in the US. Intensely urban Paris is the success story for the use of home-based telematic systems, while the American equivalent of the French Minitel completely failed to attract customers in the Los Angeles area, the ultimate suburban frontier. High-technology industries are key ingredients of new economic growth in some regions, but are unable to generate a developmental dynamic in other contexts. Societies and economies stubbornly resist being molded by the application of new technologies: in fact, they mold the technologies, selecting their patterns of diffusion, modifying their uses, orienting their functions. New information technologies do have a fundamental impact on societies, and therefore on cities and regions, but their effects vary according to their interaction with the economic, social, political, and cultural processes that shape the production and use of the new technological medium.

This book aims at analyzing the relationship between new information technologies and the urban and regional processes in the broader context of historical transformation in which these technologies emerge and evolve. Our hypothesis is that this context is characterized simultaneously by the emergence of a new mode of socio-technical organization (which we call the *informational mode of development*) and by the restructuring of capitalism, as the fundamental matrix of institutional and economic organization in our societies.

Technological revolutions are always part of a broader process of change in the techno-economic paradigm which forms the basis of the processes of production, consumption, and management. Scientific discovery and technological innovation are both an integral part and a consequential effect of such change. Accordingly, in order to assess the urban and regional impacts of new technologies, we must address the overall transformation of the relationships between production, society, and space, of which new technologies are a fundamental instrument.

Furthermore, in the particular historical period under examination, that is, the emergence and diffusion of new information technologies in the last quarter of the twentieth century, the effects of these technologies on society and space have also been fundamentally conditioned by a substantial modification of the social system that constitutes the structural basis of most of the world – capitalism. The restructuring of capitalism in the late 1970s and 1980s, as a response to the structural crisis of the 1970s, has been accomplished by extensive use of the potential offered by the new technologies, whose maturation reached a crucial point during just that decade: the microprocessor was invented in 1971; gene-splicing techniques were discovered in 1973; the microcomputer was introduced in 1975; and so on. The application of new technologies, and their effects on social organization, were largely conditioned by the characteristics and development of the restructuring process.

It could probably be argued that there are some causal links between the emergence of the informational mode of development, the blossoming of information technologies, and the process of the restructuring of capitalism. However, such an argument pertains to the study of the social sources of technological innovation, and is outside the scope of this book. My approach here is more simple, and is focused on a specific research question. I argue that there is a historically articulated complex of transformations which concerns, simultaneously, capitalism as a social system, informationalism as a mode of development, and information technology as a powerful working instrument. It is this complex socio-economic-technical matrix that is transforming societies, and thus cities and regions. I will analyze the current transformations of spatial forms and processes as a specific manifestation of the interaction between the informational mode of development (in its two dimensions: technological and organizational) and the restructuring of capitalism.

A major methodological issue arises with the attempt to develop this analytical perspective into empirical research. The process of restructuring is not a pure mechanism of adjustment. It is a politically determined process, enacted by governments and organizations. Therefore, by adopting a comprehensive research perspective that embraces both structural transformation and socio-economic restructuring, certain social effects could be attributed to new technologies, or to the informational mode of development, which are in fact linked to the historical circumstances of a given regime, for example the Reagan administration in the US or the Thatcher government in the UK. While it is impossible to discuss fully here the epistemological implications of articulating the analyses of structure and process in explaining social change, it is important to consider the question for the sake of clarity in the presentation of the research findings contained in this book.

While restructuring processes are implemented by social actors, they differ from other policies or decisions in their reference to the overall dynamics of the social system: they are responses to the structural challenges to the expansionary logic of a given system at a particular historical juncture. Crises determine social conflicts and political debates, resulting, sometimes, in restructuring processes which, on the basis of political coalitions and political strategies, modify the rules of the social system while preserving its fundamental logic. Restructuring does not necessarily come about; other outcomes of crises are revolution, or a long period of "muddling through" social inertia. Furthermore, although restructuring cannot happen independently of the political process, when it finally does occur its significance goes beyond the political orientation or the personal interests of the political actors, notwithstanding the importance of those actors for the implementation and final results of the restructuring process. In the 1980s, restructuring clearly took place in the US under Reagan and in the UK under Thatcher; but it also took place in France under a socialist government, with communist participation, the traditional socialist policies to deal with the crisis within the parameters of capitalism having failed in 1981-3. Restructuring took place in most of western Europe: in the Pacific Rim, given impetus by the internationalization of the economy; and in the Third World, as a result of austerity policies often dictated by international financial institutions. Each restructuring process followed a specific path, depending upon the economic, social, and political conditions of the various countries; but in all cases it had to deal with similar policy questions and went through similar political debates, converging on a restricted set of economic policies.

The orientations and outcomes of the restructuring process were not ineluctable, nor had they to develop exactly along the lines they in fact did. However, once they had taken place, they shaped societies, technologies, and space in a particular direction which is now full of historical meaning. Regardless of what could have happened with new information technologies in a different historical context, the fact that they blossomed in their potential applications at the moment when capitalism was transforming itself to enter a new stage of development is of fundamental significance. Capitalist restructuring has been a key force in reshaping cities and regions in the late 1970s and 1980s, in framing the production and use of new information technologies, and in forging the relationships between new technologies and new spatial forms and processes. In turn, technological innovation and territorial restructuring have also deeply modified the emerging socio-economic system. It is this complex generation of a new urban-regional process that I will try to unveil in this book.

The focus of empirical research in this analysis will be on the United States. This is a necessary limit imposed on the study in order to be able to understand the whole set of interactions between restructuring, technology, and space within a relatively homogeneous geographic, cultural, and institutional context. Furthermore, the US is the most advanced society, or at least has been until now, in the production and use of new information technologies, and is the country that has embarked on the boldest process of capitalist restructuring during the 1980s. Given its size and its widespread connections with the international economy, it offers greater potential for in-depth examination of the new spatial processes associated with the inform-ational mode of development than any other country could. The US is of course exceptional on many counts, and the empirical results it provides should not be extrapolated to other contexts without the necessary interpret-ation and adaptation to the specific conditions of other economies and societies. Nevertheless, I would claim wider validity for this analytical perspective than mere empirical observation of the spatial structure of the US alone. It is actually an inquiry into the socio-spatial effects of two macro-processes (restructuring and informationalism) that are fundamental to all advanced capitalist societies. So, while the analysis in this book utilizes almost exclusively American data, the research questions investigated and the relationships propounded are intended to aid understanding of the techno-economic transformation of the urban–regional process in a broad range of social contexts.

A second deliberate limit imposed on this study is the focus on the relationship between information technologies and the spatial dimension of the processes of production and management, leaving aside the study of social life and residential patterns. There is an obvious reason for this, namely, the impossibility of addressing all questions in a book that is already too dense and sufficiently complex. However, there are also methodological and theoretical reasons for this choice. On the former count, very little reliable empirical re-search has been done on the interaction between communication techno-logies and urban social life, in a field particularly biased by ideology, and it is therefore difficult to make any serious assessment of the current transform-ations as they relate to technological change. On the latter, it is my hypothesis that the fundamental impacts of information technologies are taking place in the organization of production and management, and in the sphere of the exercise of power by state institutions. Accordingly, it is necessary first to understand the transformation of the fundamental parameters of the new urban–regional system, before being able to investigate the changes occurring in the private sphere.

The research presented in this book relies on a significant quantity of documents and secondary sources that I have collected over several years in order to examine specific research questions determined at the onset of the inquiry. In a very fundamental way, the studies cited in this text constitute its database. I make no claim to present the arguments of their authors or to dis-cuss alternative interpretations, except when the analytical purpose requires it. I do not undertake a review of the literature on the different subjects exa-mined in the book. My analysis of data and observations is geared toward test-ing a series of specific hypotheses, in the process of building an argument. The reader interested by the various research perspectives referred to in this book should consult these studies directly rather than relying on the interpretation given here. While being extremely careful never to distort the empirical findings reported in this book, their use and their presentation have been selected according to a specific research perspective, without engaging in any major debate, in order to maintain the focus on my particular analytical propositions.

The organization of the book is straightforward. The first chapter presents the theoretical framework, defines what is understood by the "informational mode of development" and by the "restructuring of capitalism," summarizes the characteristics of the current technological revolution, and attempts to formalize the links between captialism, informationalism, and technological change. This theoretical framework is not developed and used in all its dimensions, given the specific purpose of this book, which is to arrive at an understanding of the new urban–regional process. The usefulness of this theoretical construction is in providing a conceptual basis for the specific analyses that are presented, and empirically tested, in the subsequent and substantive chapters of the book.

These substantive chapters examine sequentially the urban–regional transformations determined first by the informational mode of development, and then by the process of capitalist restructuring. Chapter 2 examines the relationship between the production of new information technologies and spatial patterns, while chapter 3 analyzes the territorial effects of the use of information technologies in services and office activities. Chapters 4, 5, and 6 study the impact of the interaction between socio-economic restructuring and information technologies on cities and regions, in the three dimensions proposed as characteristic of the restructuring process: the new relationships between capital and labor; the transformation of the state, with the transition from the "welfare state" to the "warfare state"; and the internationalization of the economy. Throughout these analyses runs, in different forms, a major theme: the emergence of a *space of flows* which dominates the historically constructed space of places, as the logic of dominant organizations detaches itself from the social constraints of cultural identities and local societies through the powerful medium of information technologies. The conclusion examines alternative spatial projects that may be pursued in counteraction of the domination of flows.

Behind the pages of this book lies the unifying intellectual objective: to understand how the interaction between technology, society, and space generates a new urban–regional process as the material basis of our lives at the dawn of the information age. This book is an investigation into the historical rise of the Informational City.

1

The Informational Mode of Development and the Restructuring of Capitalism

Introduction: Modes of Production, Modes of Development, and Social Structure

Technological change can only be understood in the context of the social structure within which it takes place. Yet such an understanding requires something more than historically specific description of a given society. We must be able to locate technology in the level and process of the social structure underlying the dynamics of any society. On the basis of a theoretical characterization of this kind we may then go on to investigate the actual manifestations of the interaction between technology and the other elements of social structure in a process that shapes society and, therefore, space. To proceed along these lines it is necessary to introduce some theoretical propositions and to advance a few hypotheses that attempt to place the analysis of technological change and economic restructuring, as presented in this chapter, within the framework of a broader social theory that informs the overall investigation undertaken in this book.

The analytical focus here is on the emergence of a new mode of development, which I will call the "informational mode," in historical interaction with the process of restructuring of the capitalist mode of production. Therefore, definitions are needed of the concepts of mode of production, mode of development, and restructuring. Such definitions, if they are to be theoretical and not simply taxonomic, require succinct presentation of the broader social theory that lends analytical meaning to such concepts as tools of understanding social structures and social change. For the purposes of this book, the presentation of the overall theoretical framework must be reduced to the few elements indispensable for communicating my hypothesis that the interaction between modes of production and modes of development is at the source of the generation of new social and spatial forms and processes.

This theoretical perspective postulates that societies are organized around human processes structured by historically determined relationships of production, experience, and power.[1] Production is the action of humankind on matter to appropriate and transform it for its benefit by obtaining a product, consuming part of it (in an unevenly distributed manner), and accumulating the surplus for investment in accordance with socially determined goals. Experience is the action of human subjects on themselves within the various dimensions of their biological and cultural entity in the endless search for fulfillment of their needs and desires. Power is that relationship between human subjects which, on the basis of production and experience, imposes the will of some subjects upon others by the potential or actual use of violence.

Production is organized in class relationships that define the process by which the non-producers appropriate the surplus from the producers. Experience is structured around gender/sexual relationships, historically organized around the family, and characterized hitherto by the domination of men over women. Sexuality, in the broad, psychoanalytic sense, and family relationships, structure personality and frame symbolic interaction.

Power is founded upon the state, since the institutionalized monopoly of violence in the state apparatus ensures the domination of power holders over their subjects. The symbolic communication between subjects on the basis of production, experience, and power, crystallizes throughout history on specific territories and thus generates cultures.

All these instances of society interact with one another in framing social phenomena; however, given the particular research interest of this work in the relationship between technological change and economic restructuring, the effort of theoretical definition will here be focused on the structure and logic of the production process.

Production has been defined above as the purposive action of humankind to appropriate and transform matter, thus obtaining a product. It is a complex process because each one of its elements is itself made up of relationships between other elements. Humankind, as a collective actor, is differentiated in the production process between labor and the organizers of production; labor is internally differentiated and stratified according to the role of the producers in the production process. Matter includes nature, human-modified nature, and human-produced matter,[2] the labors of history forcing us to move away from the classic distinction between humankind and nature which has been largely superseded by the reconstruction of our environment through millenia of human action.

The relationship between labor and matter in the process of work is also complex: it includes the use of means of production to act upon matter, on the basis of energy and knowledge. Technology refers to the type of relationship established between labor and matter in the production process through the intermediation of a given set of means of production enacted by energy and knowledge.[3]

The product is itself divided into two main categories, according to its utilization in the overall process of production and reproduction: reproduction and surplus. Reproduction includes three sub-categories: reproduction of labor, reproduction of social institutions (ultimately enforcing relationships of production), and reproduction of means of production and their technological support basis. The surplus is the share of the product that exceeds the historically determined needs for the reproduction of the elements of the production process. It is divided again into two major categories, according to its destination: consumption and investment. Consumption is stratified according to societal rules. Investment is geared toward the quantitative and qualitative expansion of the production process according to the objectives determined by the controllers of the surplus.

Social structures interact with production processes by determining the rules for the appropriation and distribution of the surplus. These rules constitute modes of production, and these modes define social classes on the basis of social relationships of production. The structural principle by which the surplus is appropriated, thus designating the structural beneficiary of such appropriation, namely the dominant class, characterizes a mode of production. In contemporary societies there are two fundamental modes of production: capitalism and statism. Under capitalism, the separation between producers and their means of production, the commodification of labor, and the private ownership of the means of production on the basis of control of commodified surplus (capital), determine the basic principle of appropriation and distribution of surplus by the capitalist class, not necessarily for its exclusive benefit, but for the processes of investment and consumption decided by that class in the specific context of each unit of production under its control. Under statism, the control of the surplus is external to the economic sphere: it lies in the hands of the power-holders in the state, that is, in the apparatus benefiting from the institutional monopoly of violence. In both cases there is expropriation of the producers from their control over the surplus, although criteria for the distribution of consumption and allocation of investment vary according to the respective structural principles of each mode of production. Capitalism is oriented toward profit-maximizing, that is, toward increasing the amount and proportion of surplus appropriated on the basis of the control over means of production. Statism is oriented toward power-maximizing, that is, toward increasing the military and ideological capacity of the political apparatus for imposing its goals on a greater number of subjects and at deeper levels of their consciousness.

Modes of production do not appear as a result of historical necessity. They are the result of historical processes in which a rising social class becomes dominant by politically, and often militarily, defeating its historical adversaries, building social alliances and obtaining support to construct its hegemony. By hegemony I understand, in the Gramscian tradition, the historical ability of a given class to legitimate its claim to establish political institutions and cultural values able to mobilize the majority of the society, while fulfilling its specific interests as the new dominant class.

The social relationships of production, and thus the mode of production, determine the appropriation and distribution of the surplus. A separate, yet fundamental question is the *level* of such surplus, determined by the productivity of a particular process of production, that is, by the ratio of the value of each unit of output to the value of each unit of input. Productivity levels are themselves dependent on the relationship between labor and matter as a function of the use of means of production by the application of energy and knowledge. This process is characterized by technical relationships of production, defining a *mode of development*. Thus, modes of development are the technological arrangements through which labor acts upon matter to generate the product, ultimately determining the level of surplus. Each mode of development is defined by the element that is fundamental in determining the productivity of the production process. In the agrarian mode of development, increases in the surplus result from quantitative increases in labor and means of production, including land. In the industrial mode of development, the source of increasing surplus lies in the introduction of new energy sources and in the quality of the use of such energy. In the informational mode of development, the emergence of which is hypothesized here, the source of productivity lies in the quality of knowledge, the other intermediary element in the relationship between labor and the means of production. It should be understood that knowledge intervenes in all modes of development, since the process of production is always based on some level of knowledge. This is in fact what technology is all about, since technology is "the use of scientific knowledge to specify ways of doing things in a reproducible manner."[4] However, what is specific to the informational mode of development is that here knowledge intervenes upon knowledge itself in order to generate higher productivity. In other words, while in the pre-industrial modes of development knowledge is used to organize the mobilization of greater quantities of labor and means of production, and in the industrial mode of development knowledge is called upon to provide new sources of energy and to reorganize production accordingly, in the informational mode of development knowledge mobilizes the generation of new knowledge as the key source of productivity through its impact on the other elements of the production process and on their relationships. Each mode of development has also a structurally determined goal, or performance principle, around which technological processes are organized: industrialism is oriented toward economic growth, that is, toward maximizing output; informationalism is oriented toward technological development, that is, toward the accumulation of knowledge. While higher levels of knowledge will result in higher levels of output, it is the pursuit and accumulation of knowledge itself that determines the technological function under informationalism.

Social relationships of production, defining modes of production, and technical relationships of production (or productive forces), defining modes of development, do not overlap, although they do interact in contemporary societies. In this sense, it is misleading to pretend that the informational mode of development (or post-industrial society) replaces capitalism, since, as Alain Touraine, Radovan Richta, and Daniel Bell indicated years ago,[5] these are different analytical planes, one referring to the principle of social organization, the other to the technological infrastructure of society. However, there are between the two structural processes complex and significant interactions which constitute a fundamental element in the dynamics of our societies.

Societies are made up of a complex web of historically specific relationships that combine modes of production, modes of development, experience, power, and cultures. Under capitalism, because of its historical reliance on the economic sphere as the source of power and legitimacy, the mode of production tends to organize society around its logic, without ever being able to exhaust the sources of social reproduction and social change within the dynamics of capital and labor. However, given the structural preponderance of capitalist social relationships in the class structure, and the influence they exercise on culture and politics, any major transformation in the processes by which capital reproduces itself and expands its interests affects the entire social organization. Modes of production – and capitalism is no exception – evolve with the process of historical change. In some instances, this leads to their abrupt supersession; more often, they transform themselves by responding to social conflicts, economic crises, and political challenges, through a reorganization that includes, as a fundamental element, the utilization of new technical relationships of production that may encompass the introduction of a new mode of development. By *restructuring* is understood the process by which modes of production transform their organizational means to achieve their *unchanged* structural principles of performance. Restructuring processes can be social and technological, as well as cultural and political, but they are all geared toward the fulfillment of the principles embodied in the basic structure of the mode of production. In the case of capitalism, private capital's drive to maximize profit is the engine of growth, investment, and consumption.

Modes of development evolve according to their own logic; they do not respond mechanically to the demands of modes of production or of other instances of society. However, since technical relationships are historically subordinated to social relationships of production, experience, and power, they tend to be molded in their structure and orientation by restructuring processes. On the other hand, they do have a specific logic that dominant social interests ignore only at the risk of spoiling their technological potential – as, for example, a narrow orientation toward secretive, applied military technology can frustrate scientific advancement. Modes of development emerge from the interaction between scientific and technological discovery and the organizational integration of such discoveries in the processes of production and management. Since these processes are dependent upon the overall social organization, and particularly upon the dynamics of the mode of production, there is indeed a close interaction between modes of development and modes of production. This interaction occurs in different forms according to the pace of historical change. There is a continuous, gradual adaptation of new technologies to the evolving social relationships of production; there are also periods of major historical change, either in technology or in social organization. When historical circumstances create a convergence between social change and technological change, we witness the rise of a new technological paradigm, heralding a new mode of development. This, I contend, is what has brought the rise of the informational mode of development in the last quarter of the twentieth century.

The New Technological Revolution and the Informational Mode of Development

The New Technological Paradigm

During the two decades from the late 1960s to the late 1980s a series of scientific and technological innovations have converged to constitute a new technological paradigm.[6] The scientific and technical core of this paradigm lies in microelectronics, building on the sequential discoveries of the transistor (1947), the integrated circuit (1957), the planar process (1959), and the microprocessor (1971).[7] Computers, spurred on by exponential increases in power and dramatic decreases in cost per unit of memory, were able to revolutionize information processing, in both hardware and software. Telecommunications became the key vector for the diffusion and full utilization of the new technologies by enabling connections between processing units, to form information systems. Applications of these microelectronics-based information systems to work processes in factories and offices created the basis for CAD/CAM (computer aided design/computer aided manufacturing) and Flexible Integrated Manufacturing, as well as for advanced office automation, paving the way for the general application of flexible integrated production and management systems. Around this nucleus of information technologies, a number of other fundamental innovations took place, particularly in new materials (ceramics, alloys, optical fiber), and more recently, in superconductors, in laser, and in renewable energy sources. In a parallel process, which benefited from the enhanced capacity to store and analyze information, genetic engineering extended the technological revolution to the realm of living matter. This laid the foundations for biotechnology, itself an information technology with its scientific basis in the ability to decode and reprogram the information embodied in living organisms.[8]

Although the scientific foundations of these discoveries had already come into existence, over timescales varying from field to field, the relatively simultaneous emergence of these various technologies, and the synergy created by their interaction, contributed to their rapid diffusion and application, and this in turn expanded the potential of each technology and induced a broader and faster development of the new technological paradigm.[9] A key factor in this synergistic process relates to the specific nature of this process of innovation: because it is based on enhanced ability to store, retrieve, and analyze information, every single discovery, as well as every application, can be related to developments in other fields and in other applications, by continuous interactions through the common medium of information systems, and communicating by means of the common language of science, in spite of the persistence of specialization in different scientific fields.

Social, economic, and institutional factors have, as I will argue, been decisive in the coming together of these different scientific innovations under the form of a new technological paradigm.[10] However, the specificity of the new technologies plays a major role in the structure and evolution of this paradigm, and imposes the materiality of their internal logic on the articulation between the process of innovation and the process of social organization. The new technological paradigm is characterized by two fundamental features.[11] First, the core new technologies are *focused on information processing*. This is the primary distinguishing feature of the emerging technological paradigm. To be sure, information and knowledge have been crucial elements in all technological revolutions, since technology ultimately boils down to the ability to perform new operations, or to perform established practices better, on the basis of the application of new knowledge. All major technological changes are in fact based on new knowledge. However, what differentiates the current process of technological change is that *its raw material itself is information, and so is its outcome.* What an integrated circuit does is to speed up the processing of information while increasing the complexity and the accuracy of the process. What computers do is to organize the sets of instructions required for the handling of information, and, increasingly, for the generation of new information, on the basis of the combination and interaction of stored information. What telecommunications does is to transmit information, making possible flows of information exchange and treatment of information, regardless of distance, at lower cost and with shorter transmission times. What genetic engineering does is to decipher and, eventually, program the code of the living matter, dramatically expanding the realm of controllable information processing.

The output of the new technologies is also information. Their embodiment in goods and services, in decisions, in procedures, is the result of the application of their informational output, not the output itself. In this sense, the new technologies differ from former technological revolutions, and justify calling the new paradigm the "informational technological paradigm," in spite of the fact that some of the fundamental technologies involved in it (for example, superconductivity) are not information technologies. But the paradigm itself exists and articulates a convergent set of scientific discoveries by focusing on information processing and by using the newly found informational capacity to enable articulation and communication throughout the whole spectrum of technological innovations. Furthermore, with the progress of the new technological revolution, the machines themselves take second place to the creative synergy made possible by their use as sources of productivity. This trend is often referred to in the literature as the growing importance of software over hardware, a theme stimulated but the promise of research in such fields as artificial intelligence. However, this is still an open debate in scientific terms. Better design of integrated circuits, ever larger-scale integration, enhanced telecommunications capability, and the use of new material in the manufacturing of information-processing devices, are in the medium-term perspective probably more important than artificial intelligence as a basis for information-handling and information-generation capacity. The fundamental trend overall seems to depend not so much on the somewhat obsolete idea of the growing dominance of software over hardware, as on the ability of new information technologies to generate new information, thus emphasizing the specific nature of their output *vis-à-vis* former technological paradigms.

The second major characteristic of the new technologies is in fact common to all major technological revolutions.[12] The main effects of their innovations are on *processes*, rather than on *products*.[13] There are, of course, major innovations in products, and the surge of new products is a fundamental factor in spurring new economic growth. However, the deepest impact of innovation is associated with the transformation of processes.[14] This was also the case with the two industrial revolutions associated with technical paradigms organized respectively around the steam engine and around electricity.[15] In both cases, energy was the pivotal element which, by gradually penetrating all processes of production, distribution, transportation, and management, revolutionized the entire economy and the whole society, not so much because of the new goods and services being produced and distributed, but because of the new ways of performing the processes of production and distribution, on the basis of a new source of energy that could be decentralized and distributed in a flexible manner. The new energy-based industrial and organizational processes gave birth to goods and services, hence products, that could not even have been imagined before the diffusion of energy-processing devices. But it was the revolution in energy, with its influence on all kinds of processes, that created the opportunity for the surge in new products. Process commands products, although functional, economic, and social feedback effects are crucial to an understanding of the historical process.

Similarly, in the current informational revolution, what new information technologies are about in the first place is process. A chip has value only as a means of improving the performance of a machine for an end-use function. A computer is a tool for information handling, whose usefulness for the organization or individual using it depends on the purpose of the information-processing activity. A genetically modified cell will take on its actual significance in its interaction with the whole body. While all social and biological activities are in fact processes, some elements of these processes crystallize in material forms that constitute goods and services, the usual content of economic products. Technological revolutions are made up of innovations whose products are in fact processes.

These two major characteristics of the informational technological paradigm [16] have fundamental effects on its impact on society. (Society itself, as stated above, frames and influences technological innovation in a dialectical relationship of which, at this point, we are only examining one factor, namely, the influence of new technologies on social organization.)

A fundamental consequence is derived from the essential process-orientation of technological innovation. Because processes, unlike products, enter into all spheres of human activity, their transformation by such technologies, focusing on omnipresent flows of information, leads to modification in the material basis of the entire social organization. Thus, new information technologies are transforming the way we produce, consume, manage, live, and die; not by themselves, certainly, but as powerful mediators of the broader set of factors that determines human behavior and social organization.

The fact that new technologies are focused on information processing has far-reaching consequences for the relationship between the sphere of socio-cultural symbols and the productive basis of society. Information is based upon culture, and information processing is, in fact, symbol manipulation on the basis of existing knowledge; that is, codified information verified by science and/or social experience. Thus, the predominant role of new information technologies in the process of innovation is to establish ever more intimate relationships among the culture of society, scientific knowledge, and the development of productive forces. If information processing becomes the key component of the new productive forces, the symbolic capacity of society itself, collectively as well as individually, is tightly linked to its developmental process. In other words, the structurally determined capacity of labor to process information and generate knowledge is, more than ever, the material source of productivity, and therefore of economic growth and social well-being. Yet this symbolic capacity of labor is not an individual attribute. Labor has to be formed, educated, trained, and retrained, in flexible manipulation of symbols, determining its ability constantly to reprogram itself. In addition, productive organizations, social institutions, and the overall structure of society, including its ideology, will be key elements in fostering or stalling the new information-based productive forces. The more a society facilitates the exchange of information flows, and the decentralized generation and distribution of information, the greater will be its collective symbolic capacity. It is this capacity which underlies the enhancement and diffusion of information technologies, and thus the development of productive forces.

In this sense, the new informational technological paradigm emphasizes the historical importance of the Marxian proposition on the close interaction between productive forces and social systems.[17] Perhaps it is only in the current historical period, because of the close connection between information and culture through the human mind, and thus between productivity and social organization, that such inspired anticipation bears its full meaning. However, if this perspective is to be intellectually fruitful it must be purified both from any ideological assumption of historical directionality and from any value judgement. The development of productive forces by the liberation of information flows does not require that capitalism be superseded. In fact, state-planned societies have proved more resistant to the new technological revolution than market-based economies, in contradiction of Marx's prophecy that socialism possessed a superior ability to develop productive forces. Equally unfounded is the opposite ideological position which states that market forces are innately superior in steering development in information technologies. Japan's leadership in the field has been built on strong, systematic state intervention in support of national companies, to raise their technological level in pursuit of the national goal of establishing Japan as a world power on non-military grounds.

The key mechanism for the development of productive forces in the new informational technological paradigm seems to be the ability of a given social organization to educate and motivate its labor force while at the same time setting up an institutional framework that maximizes information flows and connects them to the developmental tasks. The social and political means of achieving such goals vary historically, as do the societal outcomes of the development processes. However, not all these processes are undetermined, and relationships can certainly be found between social structures, techno-economic development, and institutional goals. Nevertheless, the present purpose is more limited and more focused. It is sufficient here to pinpoint the fact that because the new productive forces are information based, their development is more closely related than ever to the characteristics of symbolic production and manipulation in every society, actually fulfilling the hypothesis proposed by Marx on the relationship between social structure and techno-economic development.

From the characteristics of the process-orientation of information-based technological derives a third fundamental effect of the new technological paradigm on social organization: namely, increased *flexibility* of organizations in production, consumption, and management. Flexibility, in fact, emerges as a key characteristic of the new system taking shape;[18] yet it takes place within a context of large-scale production, consumption, and management, generally associated with large organizations and/or extended organizational networks. What happens is that new technologies build on the organizational capacity resulting from the industrial form of production and consumption, particularly during its mature stage (generally associated with what has been labeled in the literature as "Fordism," a very misleading term[19]); but they contribute both to transforming this system and enhancing that organizational capacity by preserving the economies of scale and the depth of organizational power, while overcoming rigidity and facilitating constant adaptation to a rapidly changing context. In this way, the historical oppositions between craft production and large-scale manufacture, between mass consumption and customized markets, between powerful bureaucracies and innovative enterprises, are dialectically superseded by the new technological medium, which ushers in an era of adaptive organizations in direct relationship with their social environments.[20] By increasing the flexibility of all processes, new information technologies contribute to minimizing the distance between economy and society.

The Organizational Transition from Industrialism to Informationalism

The new technological paradigm has fundamental social consequences linked to the specific logic of its basic characteristics. Yet, the new technologies are themselves articulated into a broader system of production and organization, whose ultimate roots are social, but to whose development new technologies powerfully contribute.[21] It is this complex, interacting system of technology and organizational processes, underlying economic growth and social change, that we call a *mode of development*. It is not the product of new technologies, nor are the new technologies a mechanical response to the demands of the new organizational system. It is the convergence between the two processes that changes the technical relationships of production, giving rise to a new mode of development. The previous section presented in summary form the relatively autonomous evolution of technological innovation which has led to the emergence of the informational technological paradigm. This section will examine, even more succinctly, the main organizational and structural trends that characterize the transition from the industrial to the informational mode of development.

The main process in this transition is not the shift from goods to services but, as the two main theorists of the "post-industrial society"[22] proposed many years ago, Alain Touraine in 1969 and Daniel Bell in 1973, the emergence of information processing as the core, fundamental activity conditioning the effectiveness and productivity of all processes of production, distribution, consumption, and management. The new centrality of information processing results from evolution in all the fundamental spheres of the industrial mode of development, under the influence of economic and social factors and structured largely by the mode of production. Specifically, the secular trend toward the increasing role of information results from a series of developments in the spheres of production, of consumption, and of state intervention.

In the sphere of *production*, two major factors have fostered information-processing activities within the industrial mode of development. The first is the emergence of the large corporation as the predominant organizational form of production and management.[23] An economy based on large-scale production and centralized management generated the growing number of information flows that were needed for efficient articulation of the system. The second resides within the production process itself (considering production in the broad sense, that is including production of both goods and services), and is the shift of the productivity sources from capital and labor to "other factors" (often associated with science, technology, and management), as shown by the series of econometric analyses in the tradition best represented by Robert Solow.[24] The hard core of these information-processing activities is composed of knowledge, which structures and provides adequate meaning to the mass of information required to manage organizations and to increase productivity.

In the sphere of *consumption,* two parallel processes have emphasized the role of information. On the one hand, the constitution of mass markets, and the increasing distance between buyers and sellers, have created the need for specific marketing and effective distribution by firms, thus triggering a flurry of information-gathering systems and information-distributing flows, to establish the connection between the two ends of the market.[25] On the other hand, under the pressure of new social demands, often expressed in social movements, a growing share of the consumption process has been taken over by collective consumption, that is, goods and services directly or indirectly produced and/or managed by the state,[26] as a right rather than as a commodity, giving rise to the welfare state. The formation of the welfare state has produced a gigantic system of information flows affecting most people and most activities, spurring the growth of bureaucracies, the formation of service delivery agencies, and consequently the creation of millions of jobs in information handling.[27]

In the sphere of *state intervention*, the past half-century has seen a huge expansion of government regulation of economic and social activities that has generated a whole new administration, entirely made up of information flows and information-based decision processes.[28] Although variations in the mode of production lead to a bureaucratic cycle, with upswings and downturns in the trend toward regulation, state intervention is in more subtle ways a structural feature of the new mode of development, in a process that Alain Touraine has characterized as "la société programmée."[29] This is the process by which the state sets up a framework within which large-scale organizations, both private and public, define strategic goals, which may be geared toward international economic competitiveness or military supremacy, that permeate the entire realm of social activities without necessarily institutionalizing or formalizing the strategic guidance of these activities. To be able to steer a complex society without suffocating it, the modern state relies on a system of "neo-corporatist" pacts, in Philippe Schmitter's terms, [30] which mobilize and control society through a system of incentives and disincentives made up of storage of information, emission of signals, and management of instructions. The state of the informational mode of development, be it under capitalism or under statism, exercises more intervention than ever, but it does so by controlling and manipulating the network of information flows that penetrate all activities. It does not follow that society is doomed to the Orwellian vision, since the intervention of the state will be informed by the political values emerging from the dynamics of the civil society, and thus its enhanced power could be used to counteract the built-in bureaucratic tendencies of state apparatuses.[31] As Nicos Poulantzas wrote ten years ago: "This statism does not refer to the univocal reinforcement of the State, but it is rather the effect of one tendency, whose two poles develop unevenly, toward the simultaneous reinforcing–weakening of the State."[32] The attempt by the state to override the contradiction between its increasing role and its decreasing legitimacy by diffusing its power through immaterial information flows greatly contributes to the dramatic explosion of information-processing activities and organizations. This is because the state sets up a series of information systems that control activities and citizens' lives through the codes and rules determined by those systems.

These structural trends, emerging and converging in a society largely dominated by the industrial mode of development, pave the way for the transformation of that mode, as information processing, with its core in knowledge generation, detracts from the importance of energy in material production, as well as from the importance of goods-producing in the overall social fabric. However, this transformation of the mode of development could not be accomplished without the surge of innovation in information technologies which, by creating the material basis from which information processing can expand its role, contributes to the change both in the structure of the production process and in the organization of society. It is in this sense that I hypothesize the formation of a new, informational mode of development: on the basis of the convergence through interaction of information technologies and information-processing activities into an articulated techno-organizational system.

The Interaction between Technological Innovation and Organizational Change in the Constitution of the Informational Mode of Development

The convergence between the revolution in information technology and the predominant role of information-processing activities in production, consumption, and state regulation, leads to the rise of the new, informational mode of development. This process triggers a series of new structural contradictions which highlight the relative autonomy of technological change in the process of social transformation. In fact, the diffusion of new technologies under the new mode of development calls into question the very processes and organizational forms that were at the basis of the demand for information technologies. This is because these organizational forms were born within the industrial mode of development, under the influence of the capitalist mode of production, and generally reflect the old state of technology. As the new technologies, and the realm of the possibilities they offer, expand, those same organizational forms that were responsible for the demand for new technologies are being rendered obsolete by their development. For instance, the large corporation was critical in fostering the demand for computers. But as microcomputers increase in power and become able to constitute information systems in harness with advanced telecommunications, it is no longer the large, vertical conglomerate but the network which is the most flexible, efficient form of management.

In another crucial development, the old form of the welfare state loses relevance. Previously, its operation had called for the expansion of information-processing activities: but as information itself becomes a productive force, so the social characteristics of labor reproduction (and thus of collective consumption: education, health, housing, etc.) become key elements in the development of productive forces, embodied in the cultural capacity of labor to process information. Thus, the old, redistributive welfare state becomes obsolete, not so much because it is too expensive (this is the capitalist critique, not the informational challenge), as because it has to be restructured to connect its redistributional goals with its new role as a source of productivity by means of the investment in human capital.

A third manifestation of the process of institutional change set in motion by the new technologies concerns the role of the state. The expansion of state regulatory intervention underlay the explosion of government-led information activities, enhancing its dominant role, within the limits of its legitimacy. However, rapid innovation in information technologies has created the facility for two-way information flows, making it possible for civil society to control the state on democratic principles, without paralyzing its effectiveness as a public interest agency. In this situation, the persistence of bureaucratic aloofness, once deprived of its former technical justification, emphasizes authoritarian tendencies within the state, delegitimizes its power, and prompts calls for institutional reform toward more flexible and more responsive government agencies.

The organizational transformation of the mode of development, then, leads to the expansion of information technologies, whose effect triggers pressure for further organizational change. The informational mode of development is not a rigid structure, but a constant process of change based on the interaction between technology and organization. Yet the logic of this process of change does not depend primarily on the interaction between these two planes, for modes of development are conditioned in their historical evolution by the dynamics of specific societies, themselves largely conditioned by the contradictions and transformations of the modes of production that characterize them. More specifically, the evolution of the informational mode of development, with its changing interaction between technology and organizational structures, depends, in our societies, on the restructuring of the capitalist mode of production that has taken place in the past decade. The transition between modes of development is not independent of the historical context in which it takes place; it relies heavily on the social matrix initially framing the transition, as well as on the social conflicts and interests that shape the transformation of that matrix. Therefore, the newly emerging forms of the informational mode of development, including its spatial forms, will not be determined by the structural requirements of new technologies seeking to fulfil their developmental potential, but will emerge from the interaction between its technological and organizational components, and the historically determined process of the restructuring of capitalism.

The Restructuring of Capitalism in the 1980s

When social systems experience a structural crisis, as a result of historical events acting on their specific contradictions, they are compelled either to change their goals, or to change their means in order to overcome the crisis. When the system changes its goals (or structural principles of performance), actually becoming a different system, there is a process of social transformation. When the system changes the institutionalized means by which it aims to achieve its systemic goals, there is a process of social restructuring. Each restructuring process leads to a new manifestation of the system, with specific institutional rules which induce historically specific sets of contradictions and conflicts, developing into new crises that potentially trigger new restructuring processes. This sequence goes on until the social equation underlying both structures and processes makes possible historical change to replace the old system by a new one.

The transformation of the capitalist mode of production on a global scale follows, in general terms, this social logic. The Great Depression of the 1930s, followed by the dislocation of World War II, triggered a restructuring process that led to the emergence of a new form of capitalism very different from the laisser-faire model of the pre-Depression era.[33] This new capitalist model, often characterized by the misleading term "Keynesianism,"[34] relied on three major structural modifications:[35]

(1) A social pact between capital and labor which, in exchange for the stability of capitalist social relationships of production and the adaptation of the labor process to the requirements of productivity, recognized the rights of organized labor, assured steadily rising wages for the unionized labor force, and extended the realm of entitlements to social benefits, creating an ever-expanding welfare state.

(2) Regulation and intervention by the state in the economic sphere: key initiatives in the accumulation process, stimulation of demand through public expenditures, and absorption of surplus labor by increasing public employment.

(3) Control of the international economic order by intervention in the sphere of circulation via a set of new international institutions, organized around the International Monetary Fund and under the hegemony of the United States, with the imposition of the dollar (and to some extent the pound) as the standard international currency. The ordering of world economic processes included the control by the center of the supply and prices of key raw materials and energy sources, most of these being produced by a still largely colonized Third World.

This state-regulated capitalism assured unprecedented economic growth, gains in productivity, and prosperity in the core countries for about a quarter of a century. In retrospect, history will probably consider these years as the golden age of western capitalism.

As I have shown elsewhere,[36] these same structural elements that accounted for the dynamism of this model were the very factors that led to its crisis in the 1970s, under the stress of its contradictions, expressed through rampant inflation that disrupted the circulation process, and under the pressure of social movements and labor struggles whose successful social and wage demands lowered the rate of profit. The oil shocks of 1974 and 1979 were precipitant events which, acting on structurally determined inflation, drove the circulation of capital out of control, prompting the need for austerity policies and fiscal restraint, and thus undermining the economic basis for state intervention. Although in strictly economic terms the increase in oil prices was not the cause of the structural crisis, its impact was crucial in calling into question the post-World War II model of capitalism, because of the pervasive effects of energy cost and supply in an economic system relying on an industrial mode of development based upon energy.

The crisis of the system in the 1970s revealed the declining effectiveness of the mechanisms established in the 1930s and 1940s in ensuring the fulfillment of the basic goals of the capitalist economy.[37] Labor was steadily increasing its share of the product. Social movements outside the workplace were imposing growing constraints on the ability of capital and bureaucracies to organize production and society free from social control. The state entered a fiscal crisis brought on by the contradiction between growing expenditures (determined by social demands) and comparatively decreasing revenues (limited by the need to preserve corporate profits).[38] The international order was disrupted by the surge of Third World nationalism (simultaneously opposed, supported, and manipulated by the strategies of the superpowers), and by the entry into the international economy of new competitive actors. The structural difficulty of making hard choices led companies to pass costs on into prices, the state to finance its intervention through debt and money

supply, and the international economy to prosper through financial speculation and irresponsible lending in the global markets. After a series of
unsuccessful stop-and-go policies, the second oil shock of 1979 revealed the
depth of the crisis and necessitated a restructuring process that was
undertaken simultaneously by both governments and firms, while international institutions such as the IMF imposed the new economic discipline
throughout the world economy.

A new model of socio-economic organization had to be established which
would be able to achieve the basic aims of a capitalist system, namely: to
enhance the rate of profit for private capital, the engine of investment, and
thus of growth; to find new markets, both through deepening the existing
ones and by incorporating new regions of the world into an integrated
capitalist economy; to control the circulation process, curbing structural
inflation; and to assure the social reproduction and the economic regulation
of the system through mechanisms that would not contradict those established to achieve the preceding goals of higher profit rates, expanding
demand, and inflation control.

On the basis of these premises, a new model of capitalism emerged which,
with national variations and diverse fortunes, actually characterizes most of
the international system in the late 1980s. Reducing the new model to its
essentials, we can summarize it in three major features which simultaneously
address the four goals stated above as the fundamental requirements for the
restructuring of capitalism to operate successfully.

(1) *The appropriation by capital of a significantly higher share of surplus from
the production process.* This is a reversal of the historical power relationship
between capital and labor, and a negation of the social pact achieved in the
1930s and 1940s. This fundamental goal is achieved by combining increases
in productivity and increases in exploitation, by means of a fundamental
restructuring of the work process and of the labor market which includes the
following aspects:

(a) Higher productivity derived from technological innovation, combined
with the uneven distribution of the productivity gains in favor of
capital.
(b) Lower wages, reduced social benefits, and less protective working
conditions.
(c) Decentralization of production to regions or countries characterized by
lower wages and more relaxed regulation of business activities.
(d) Dramatic expansion of the informal economy, at both the core and the
periphery of the system. By the informal economy is meant income-
generating activities that are unregulated by the institutional system, in
a context where similar activities are regulated. Much of the development of the informal economy has to do with the dismantling in
practice of many provisions of the welfare state, for example, avoiding

payment of social benefits and contravening the legislation protecting workers.[39]

(e) A restructuring of labor markets to take in growing proportions of women, ethnic minorities, and immigrants, namely, those social groups which, because of institutionalized discrimination and social stigma, are most vulnerable in society and thus in the marketplace.[40] However, it is important to observe that such vulnerability is socially determined. Should the social context change, this supposedly docile labor would not be incorporated into the new labor markets. For example, while immigration has boomed during the restructuring process in the US, it has been practically halted in western Europe. Although part of the difference has to lie in the ability of the US to create millions of new unskilled jobs, a substantial factor is the unionization and rising consciousness of immigrant workers in Europe during the 1970s, to the point where, in countries such as Switzerland and Germany, they have become the militant vanguard among factory workers.[41] It makes little sense for European management to continue to import labor which, despite its social vulnerability, could turn into a focus for militancy while not being responsive to the same mechanisms of integration that are operative with respect to native workers.

(f) The weakening of trade unions – a fundamental, explicit goal of the restructuring process in most countries, and in fact, probably the most important single factor in achieving the overall objective of restoring the rate of profit at a level acceptable for business. By and large this objective has been achieved. Organized labor in most capitalist countries, with the exception of Scandinavia, is at the lowest point of its power and influence in the last thirty years, and its situation is still deteriorating rapidly. Some of the reasons for this decline are structural: for example, the fading away of traditional manufacturing, where the strength of the unions was concentrated, and the parallel expansion of a weakly unionized service economy. Other factors have to do directly with the transformation of labor markets, as noted under (e) above: women, often because of the sexism of the labor unions, are less unionized: many immigrants do not feel that the unions represent them; the informal economy detracts from the socializing effects of the workplace. However, organized labor has also been weakened as a result of targeted policies by both governments and firms, engaging in a deliberate effort at achieving what is perceived as a historical objective that would dramatically increase the freedom of capital to steer the economy and society.[42] Thus, Reagan's tough handling of the 1981 air traffic controllers' strike in the US, ending up with the de-registration of their union (PATCO), and the placement of the names of all the strikers in a blacklist to ban them from future Federal government employment, sent out a powerful signal that was well heard by business. Similarly, Thatcher's merciless repression of the coal miners' strike in the UK ushered in a new era of management–labor relations that put the British Trades Union Congress on the defensive. The historical reversal of the capital–labor power relationship, encapsulated in the gradual decline of the trade union movement, is the cornerstone of the restructuring of capitalism in the 1980s.

(2) *A substantial change in the pattern of state intervention, with the emphasis shifted from political legitimation and social redistribution to political domination and capital accumulation.*[43] Although in the "Keynesian" model regulation of capitalist growth was also a key objective, the means by which such regulation was exercised included widespread expansion of the welfare state, as well as both direct and indirect creation of public sector jobs, stimulating demand and contributing to the reproduction of labor power. The new forms of state intervention are much more directly focused on capital accumulation, and give priority to domination over legitimation in the relationship between state and society, in response to the emergency situation in which the system found itself in the 1970s. However, in contradiction of the ideological self-representation of the restructuring process by its main protagonists, what we are witnessing is not the withdrawal of the state from the economic scene, but the emergence of a new form of intervention, whereby new means and new areas are penetrated by the state, while others are deregulated and transferred to the market. This simultaneous engagement and disengagement of the state in the economy and society is evident in several mechanisms that express the new form of state support of capitalism:

(a) Deregulation of many activities, including relaxation of social and environmental controls in the work process.
(b) Shrinkage of, and privatization of productive activities in, the public sector.
(c) Regressive tax reform, favoring corporations and upper-income groups.
(d) State support for high-technology R&D and leading industrial sectors which form the basis of the new informational economy. This support usually takes the dual form of financing infrastructure and research, and favorable fiscal policies.
(e) Accordance of priority status to defense and to defense-related industries, combining, in pursuit of the objectives of the new state, the reinforcement of military power and the stimulation of a high-technology dominated defense sector. Following an old formula of Herbert Marcuse, I will call this trend the rise of the "warfare state." Defense spending and the development of new defense industries is also a fundamental way of creating new markets to compensate for

retrenchment in other public-sector expenditures, as well as for the loss of demand resulting from the lowering of wages in the production process.

(f) Shrinkage of the welfare state, with variations within and between countries according to the relative power of affected groups.

(g) Fiscal austerity, with the goal of a balanced budget, and tight monetary policy. These are key policies for the new model of capitalism, as the fundamental means of controlling inflation. However, while fiscal conservatism is an integral component of the new capitalism, recent historical experience shows the possibility of huge budget deficits resulting from the contradictions consequent on the implementation of the model in a given country, in particular in the US.

(3) *The third major mechanism of the restructuring of capitalism is the accelerated internationalization of all economic processes, to increase profitability and to open up markets through the expansion of the system.*

The capitalist economy has been, since its beginnings, a world economy, as Braudel and Wallerstein have reminded us.[44] However, what is new is the increasing interpenetration of all economic processes at the international level with the system working as a unit, worldwide in real time. This is a process that has grown steadily since the 1950s and has accelerated rapidly in the 1970s and 1980s as an essential element of the restructuring process. It embraces capital movements, labor migration, the process of production itself, the interpenetration of markets, and the use of nation states as elements of support in an international competition that will ultimately determine the economic fate of all nations.

The internationalization of capitalism enhances profitability at several levels:

(a) It allows capital to take advantage of the most favorable conditions for investment and production anywhere in the world. Sometimes this translates into low wages and lack of government regulation. In other instances, penetration of key markets or access to technology are more important considerations for the firm. But the fact remains that the increasing homogenization of the economic structure across nations allows for a variable geometry of production and distribution that maximizes advantages in terms of opportunity costs.

(b) By allowing round-the-clock capital investment opportunities worldwide, internationalization dramatically increases the rate of turnover of capital, thus enhancing profit levels for a given profit rate, although at the cost of increasing instability built into the system.

(c) The internationalization process also opens up new markets, and connects segments of markets across borders, increasingly differentiating societies vertically while homogenizing markets horizontally. This expansion of demand through new markets is absolutely crucial in a model that relies on the reduction of wages in the core countries, since the loss in potential demand has to be made up by the incorporation of whichever new markets may exist anywhere in the world. This is particularly important in the transitional period of restructuring, when wages have to be kept at the lowest possible level to increase profits and attract investment, while keeping demand high enough to justify new investment.

The process of internationalization offers dynamic expansion possibilities that could substantially benefit the capitalist system. But it can also pose fundamental problems to individual units of that system, be they firms or countries, which are faced with new, tougher competition from the new actors which are incorporated into the system and quickly learn the ruthlessness of the game. This has been the case for the US which has lost market share, in both its domestic market and the international economy, to Japan and the newly industrialized countries. Given the interdependence of economic processes and national policies, the internationalization process prepares the ground for future major crises: on the one hand, any significant downturn has immediate repercussions worldwide, and is thus amplified; on the other hand, competition constantly provokes the threat of protectionism which could wreck the very basis of the system. A system in which the interests of the totality are not necessarily the interests of each competitive unit in every moment in time could become increasingly disruptive. When the "creative destruction" process[45] takes place at the international level, the intermixing of national interests with competitive strategies becomes explosive.

The overpowering of labor by capital, the shift of the state toward the domination–accumulation functions of its intervention in economy and society, and the internationalization of the capitalist system to form a worldwide interdependent unit working in real time are the three fundamental dimensions of the restructuring process that has given birth to a new model of capitalism, as distinct from the "Keynesian" model of the 1945–75 era as that one was from "laisser-faire" capitalism.[46]

These three processes are present in most countries' recent economic policies, but their relative importance may vary considerably according to each country's history, institutions, social dynamics, and place in the world economy. Thus, the UK has emphasized the overpowering of labor as the rallying cry of the Thatcher government; the US has made the emergence of a new "warfare state," based upon high-technology development, the centerpiece of its economic recovery; Japan has saved itself much of the pain of the restructuring process by riding the crest of the internationalization wave. However, since the capitalist system is a world system at the level of the mode of production (although certainly not at the level of societies), the different dimensions of the restructuring process are interconnected across the various regions of the international economy.

Also, the actual practice of restructuring is full of contradictions. Not only social but economic as well. For instance, in the case of the Reagan Administration in the US the dramatic defense build up, combined with a regressive tax reform and the political inability to dismantle Social Security, led to the biggest budget deficit in American history, under one of the most ideologically committed Administrations to fiscal conservatism. The budget deficit was financed to a large extent by foreign capital, attracted by high in-terest rates, driving up the dollar's exchange rate. Together with declining competitiveness of American manufacturing, this evolution resulted in catastrophic trade deficits that weakened the American economy. The twin mega-deficits have spoiled to a large extent the benefits of restructuring for American capitalism and will, most likely, lead to austerity policies in the 1989–91 period that could trigger a world recession. While our purpose here goes far beyond economic forecasting we want to emphasize that the process of restructuring is by no means exempt of contradictions. While fiscal austerity was a must of the new model, and as such was formulated by its sup-ply-side defenders, it could not actually be implemented because the political support for the boldest extremes of restructuring could not be marshalled. The artificial implementation of the model (on the basis of debt-financed military expenditures, a policy we have labeled "perverted Keynesianism"[47] could lead to its demise or to its sharpening through reinforced austerity policies, ushering in a new crisis.

However, in spite of these contradictory trends, a new model of capitalism has emerged that could outlast the forthcoming crises. One of the reasons for its likely durability, we hypothesize, is that it has encompassed in its expansion the informational mode of development that was bursting into life in a process of historical simultaneity. It is the interaction and the articulation between the informational mode of development and the restructuring of capitalism that creates the framework shaping the dynamics of our society and our space.

The Articulation between the Informational Mode of Development and the Restructuring of Capitalism: Reshaping the Techno-Economic Paradigm

The historical coincidence of the restructuring of capitalism and the rise of the informational mode of development has created a structural convergence resulting in the formation of a specific techno-economic paradigm at the very roots of our social dynamics. Because political and organizational decision-makers are always primarily concerned to perpetuate the interests they represent, and therefore concerned with the process of restructuring, it is under the dominance of that process that the merger has taken place. However, the two components of the paradigm are distinguishable only analytically, because while informationalism has now been decisively shaped by the restructuring process, restructuring could never have been accomplished, even in a contradictory manner, without the unleashing of the technological and organizational potential of informationalism.

Given the complexity of the articulation process, I will differentiate between the two dimensions that compose the informational mode of development: the *technological* and the *organizational*. Both have been fundamental in giving rise to a new form of capitalism which, in turn, has stimulated and supported the technological revolution and has adopted new organizational forms.

New *information technologies* have been decisive in the implementation of the three fundamental processes of capitalist restructuring.

(1) *Increasing the rate of profit* by various means:

(a) Enhancing productivity by the introduction of microelectronics-based machines that transform the production process.

(b) Making possible the decentralization of production, and the spatial separation of different units of the firm, while reintegrating production and management at the level of the firm by using telecommunications and flexible manufacturing systems.

(c) Enabling management to automate those processes employing labor with a sufficiently high cost level and a sufficiently low skill level to make automation both profitable and feasible. These jobs happened to be those concentrated in the large-scale factories that had become the strongholds of labor unions, and better remunerated labor, during the industrial era.

(d) Positioning capital in a powerful position *vis-à-vis* labor. Automation, flexible manufacturing, and new transportation technologies provide management with a variety of options that considerably weaken the bargaining position of the unions. Should the unions insist on preserving or improving their levels of wages and benefits, the company can automate or move elsewhere, or both, without losing its connections with the market or with the network of production. Thus, either by using automation to substitute for labor, or by extracting concessions by wielding the threat to automate or relocate, capital uses new technologies to free itself from the constraints of organized labor.

(2) New technologies are also a powerful instrument in weighting the accumulation and domination functions of state intervention. This occurs on two main levels:

(a) On the one hand, rapid technological change makes obsolete the entire existing weapons system, creating the basis for the expansion of the "warfare state" in a political environment characterized by states

striving for military supremacy and therefore engaging in a technological arms race that can only be supported by the resources of the state.
(b) On the other hand, the strategic role played by high technology in
economic development draws the state to concentrate on providing the
required infrastructure, downplaying its role in redistributional
policies.

(3) The process of *internationalization of the economy* could never take
place without the dramatic breakthroughs in information technologies.
Advances in telecommunications, flexible manufacturing that allows simultaneously for standardization and customization, and new transportation
technologies emerging from the use of computers and new materials, have
created the material infrastructure for the world economy, as the construction
of the railway system provided the basis for the formation of national markets
in the nineteenth century. In addition, the economic effects of new
technologies are also crucial in the formation of an international economy.
Their effects on process condition the international competitiveness of
countries and firms. Their effects on new products create new markets in
which the harshest competitive battles are fought, with new economic actors
trying to short-circuit the sequence of development by leapfrogging into
state-of-the-art high-technology markets through dramatic efforts of national
development. The new technological division of labor is one of the
fundamental lines of cleavage in the emerging international economic order.

The *organizational* components of the informational mode of development
are also fundamental features in the restructuring process. Three major
organizational characteristics of informationalism may be distinguished, each
one of them affecting the three dimensions of the restructuring process.

(1) There is a growing *concentration of knowledge-generation and decision-
making processes in high-level organizations* in which both information and the
capacity of processing it are concentrated. The informational world is made
up of a very hierarchical functional structure in which increasingly secluded
centers take to its extreme the historical division between intellectual and
manual labor. Given the strategic role of knowledge and information control
in productivity and profitability, these core centers of corporate organizations
are the only truly indispensable components of the system, with most other
work, and thus most other workers, being potential candidates for automation
from the strictly functional point of view. How far this tendency toward
widespread automation is actually taken in practice is a different matter,
depending on the dynamics of labor markets and social organization.

This concentration of information power in selected segments of the
corporate structure greatly favors the chances of the restructuring process in
the three dimensions presented:

(a) Productive labor can be reduced to its essential component, thus downgrading the objective bargaining power of the large mass of functionally dispensable labor.

(b) The rise of the technocracy within the state displaces the traditional integrative functions of the politically determined bureaucracy, establishing a tight linkage between the high levels of the state and the corporate world through the intermediary of the scientific establishment. The rise of the meritocracy, using the notion advanced by Daniel Bell, establishes new principles of legitimacy in the state, further removing it from the political controls and constituencies represented by the diversity of social interests.

(c) As technology transfer becomes the key to competition in the international economy, that process is controlled by knowledge holders in the centers of the dominant scientific and corporate organizations. It follows that the effective accomplishment of the internationalization process requires access to these knowledge centers, ruling out the adoption of an isolationist stance, which would only lead to the technological obsolescence of those economies and firms holding it.

(2) The second major organizational characteristic of informationalism concerns the *flexibility* of the system and of the relationships among its units, since flexibility is both a requirement of and a possibility offered by new information technologies.[48] Flexibility acts powerfully as a facilitator of the restructuring process in the following ways:

(a) It changes capital–labor relationships, transforming a potentially permanent and protected worker status into a flexible arrangement generally adapted to the momentary convenience of management. Thus, temporary workers, part-time jobs, homework, flexitime schedules, indefinite positions in the corporate structure, changing assignments, varying wages and benefits according to performance, etc., are all creative expedients of management that, while they increase tremendously the flexibility and thus the productivity of the firm, undermine the collective status of labor vis-à-vis capital.

(b) In the restructuring of the state, organizational flexibility contributes to the formation of public–private partnerships and to the blurring of the distinction between the public and private spheres. Segments of the welfare state are being shifted to the private sector, corporations are being brought into the formulation of public policies, and a selective interpenetration of state and capital is diminishing the autonomy of the state, along the lines of the "recapitalization" of the state, characteristic of the restructuring process.[49]

(c) Flexibility is also a necessary condition for the formation of the new world economy, since it is the only organizational form that allows constant adaptation of firms to the changing conditions of the world market.[50]

(3) A third fundamental organizational characteristic of informationalism is the shift from *centralized* large corporations to *decentralized* networks made up of a plurality of sizes and forms of organizational units.[51] Although networking increases flexibility, it is actually a different characteristic, since there are forms of flexibility that do not require networks. These networks, which could not exist on such a large scale without the medium provided by new information technologies, are the emerging organizational form of our world, and have played a fundamental role in ensuring the restructuring process:

(a) They are the prevalent form of the informal economy, as well as of the sub-contracting practices that have disorganized and reorganized the labor process, enhancing capital's profitability.[52]

(b) They have provided the model for the constitution of the new warfare state, as will be argued in chapter 6, on the basis of the interaction between different specialized government agencies, the defence industry, high-technology firms, and the scientific establishment.

(c) They are the organizational form used by major multinational corporations that have established variable strategic alliances to compete in the international economy.[53] Unlike the tendency of the industrial mode of development toward oligopolistic concentration, in the informational era large corporations set up specific alliances for given products, processes, and markets: these alliances vary according to time and space, and result in a variable geometry of corporate strategies that follow the logic of the multiple networks where they are engaged rather than the monolithic hierarchy of empire conglomerates.

Networks, on the basis of new information technologies, provide the organizational basis for the transformation of socially and spatially based relationships of production into flows of information and power that articulate the new flexible system of production and management. The restructuring of capitalism has used the adaptive potential of organizational networking to find breathing room for its "creative–destructive" energy, hitherto constrained by the social and political bonds inflicted upon it by a society reluctant to be but a commodity. The libertarian spirit of capitalism finally found itself at home at the last frontier where organizational networks and information flows dissolve locales and supersede societies. Informationalism and capitalism have historically merged in a process of techo-economic restructuring whose social consequences will last far beyond the social events and political circumstances that triggered the decisions leading to its development in the 1980s.

From this historical synthesis, new social forms and new spatial processes have emerged. My inquiry will explore the territory thus constituted. It will take us into the new world being made up from the contradictions of our past and the promises of our future through the conflicts of our present.

2

The New Industrial Space

The Locational Pattern of Information-Technology Manufacturing and its Effects on Spatial Dynamics

Introduction

The development of new industries, spearheaded by the producers of information technologies, along with the crisis of old line manufacturing, is transforming the economic landscape of the United States; and similar processes are under way in most countries of the industrialized world. This technological revolution has very definite spatial dimensions, with far-reaching consequences for the future of cities and regions. This chapter explores the locational pattern of information technology manufacturing and its effects on spatial dynamics.

In recent years, a growing body of research has focused on the location of high-technology industries, the factors conditioning their spatial pattern, and the consequences of this pattern for regional development.[1] This chapter will build on the results obtained by this research while also attempting to elaborate a broader analytical framework which will incorporate as coherently as possible what we already know of the new industrial space.[2] The perspective presented here starts from the assumption that traditional location theory fails to deal with the novel technological and economic conditions of the new industrialization process.[3] Furthermore, more refined models of regional economic analysis, such as the product cycle–profit cycle model,[4] overlook the historical specificity of the new information-based industries, reducing their spatial logic to a simple manifestation of the stage of the industry in its life cycle. Taking a different view, I argue, with other scholars,[5] that the specific characteristics of the new industries lead to a new and original spatial logic, whose development will reveal itself even more clearly in the future as the organization of knowledge-based production continues to expand in our societies. In turn, this distinctive spatial logic has implications for the inter-regional and international division of labor which affect the world economy, and ultimately, the world itself.[6]

Before presenting the analytical perspective in some detail, it seems useful to summarize the main facts of what we already know on the location of high-technology manufacturing in the US. After reviewing some recent studies on the subject, I will propose an analytical framework whose main elements will then be examined in regard to the available empirical evidence.

Information-Technology Manufacturing and Industrial Location: An Overview

The Spatial Distribution of Information-Technology Manufacturing

Any discussion on the relationship between high-technology industries and spatial structure must be grounded in empirical observation of where such industries are located and what the factors are that seem to be at the roots of their location pattern. However, there are considerable theoretical and methodological problems in appraising the results of such empirical studies. The production of information-technology devices is generally defined in terms of the popular descriptive label "high technology," and questionable operational definitions of high technology bias the findings. Inadequate statistical sources limit the possibilities of refining the analysis. Spatial units of analysis (regions, states, metropolitan areas) are so broad that aggregation of data confuses contradictory coexisting trends, blurring the actual profile of the phenomenon. It is also difficult to distinguish the cumulative effects of long-term location patterns from recent trends emerging from the new industries. In sum, the first impression given by the data on the location of the so-called high-technology industries is one of confusion and indeterminacy in the observed spatial trends. Nevertheless, it is important to start from this overall picture, however complex, in undertaking the task of making analytical sense of the processes constituting the new industrial space.

The most comprehensive empirical study to date is the research by Ann Markusen, Peter Hall, and Amy Glasmeier,[7] and its spin-off, Glasmeier's doctoral dissertation.[8] They define high-technology industries on the basis of a greater-than-average proportion of engineers and scientists in the sector's labor force. Having selected 100 four-digit industrial sectors on this criterion, they studied the distribution of jobs and plants for each sector among 223 metropolitan areas of the US in 1972 and 1977, the most recent year for which Census of Manufacturing data were available in 1985. They also performed a statistical analysis of the main variables associated with the location of these industries.

The first conclusion reached by this study is that the popular sunbelt/snow-belt distinction regarding high-technology development is meaningless. Although California, Texas, and Arizona appear among the states with the largest concentrations of high-technology jobs, so do New England, New Jersey, and Illinois. Furthermore, four of the top five states, ranked in terms of absolute number of high-technology jobs, are states of the old manufacturing belt: Illinois, Pennsylvania, New York, and Ohio (see tables 2.1 and 2.2). Confronted with this finding, one wonders if there is actually a new emergent industrial space or if, on the contrary, the sheer size of the old manufacturing belt means that it simply reproduces itself on the basis of the new industries. To explore this issue, we have to take into consideration *simultaneously* the absolute size of each industry and the share of high-technology industries in each regional economy, as measured by location quotients. By combining the two criteria we arrive at those states which both contain the majority of jobs in

Table 2.1   Leading high-tech states, 1977
(a) In order of absolute high-tech employment

Rank	State	Jobs (000)	Location quotient
1	California	641.3	1.49
2	Illinois	360.3	1.15
3	New York	336.8	0.89
4	Pennsylvania	314.3	0.94
5	Ohio	295.1	0.88
6	Texas	285.7	1.33
7	New Jersey	232.3	1.23
8	Massachusetts	204.6	1.43
9	Michigan	169.4	0.86
10	Connecticut	160.0	1.65
11	Indiana	153.5	0.89
12	Wisconsin	128.8	1.00
13	Florida	119.0	1.39

(b) In order of location quotient

Rank	State	Location quotient	Jobs (000)
1	Arizona	1.80	45.9
2	Connecticut	1.65	160.0
3	Kansas	1.63	62.8
4	Maryland	1.60	48.5
5	Colorado	1.57	52.9
6	California	1.49	641.3
7	Massachusetts	1.43	204.6
8	Florida	1.39	119.0
9	Oklahoma	1.38	53.9
10	Texas	1.33	285.7
11	Utah	1.30	22.9
12	New Jersey	1.23	232.3
13	Louisiana	1.22	56.4

Source: Glasmeier (see note 8).

Table 2.2 Top ranked metropolitan areas, job and plant levels and change, 1972-7

Rank	SMSA	Plants, 1977
1	Los Angeles–Long Beach, California	3,732
2	Chicago, Illinois	3,029
3	Detroit, Michigan	2,291
4	New York, New York/New Jersey	2,149
5	Boston–Lowell–Brockton–Lawrence–Haverhill, Massachusetts	1,484
6	Philadelphia, Pennsylvania/New Jersey	1,455
7	Anaheim–Santa Ana–Garden Grove, California	1,118
8	Newark, New Jersey	1,077
9	Cleveland, Ohio	1,037
10	Nassau–Suffolk, New York	963
11	Dallas–Fort Worth, Texas	942
12	San Francisco–Oakland, California	933
13	San Jose, California	856
14	Houston, Texas	840
15	Minneapolis–St Paul, Minnesota/Wisconsin	740

Rank	SMSA	Jobs, 1977
1	Los Angeles–Long Beach, California	279,293
2	Chicago, Illinois	255,051
3	Boston–Lowell–Brockton–Lawrence–Haverhill, Massachusetts	144,720
4	Philadelphia, Pennsylvania/New Jersey	136,891
5	San Jose, California	106,002
6	Anaheim–Santa Ana–Garden Grove, California	92,726
7	Newark, New Jersey	92,078
8	Dallas–Fort Worth, Texas	87,658
9	Detroit, Michigan	87,180
10	Houston, Texas	81,577
11	New York, New York/New Jersey	80,980
12	Milwaukee, Wisconsin	69,741
13	Minneapolis–St Paul, Minnesota/Wisconsin	68,664
14	Cleveland, Ohio	66,344
15	Nassau–Suffolk, New York	66,335

Rank	SMSA	New plant change 1972-7
1	Anaheim, California	464
2	Los Angeles, California	367
3	San Jose, California	339
4	Dallas, Texas	276
5	Chicago, Illinois	224
6	Houston, Texas	204
7	Boston, Massachusetts	191
8	Minneapolis, Minnesota	158
9	San Francisco, California	151
10	Detroit, Michigan	145
	Median gain	9

Rank	SMSA	Net job change 1972–7
1	San Jose, California	31,909
2	Anaheim, California	30,612
3	Houston, Texas	18,932
4	San Diego, California	16,782
5	Boston, Massachusetts	15,173
6	Dallas, Texas	12,067
7	Worcester, Massachusetts	9,893
8	Oklahoma City, Oklahoma	8,363
9	Lakeland, Florida	8,132
10	Phoenix, Arizona	7,976
	Median gain	248

Rank	SMSA	Percent plant change
1	Lawton, Oklahoma	600.00
2	St Cloud, Minnesota	214.29
3	Laredo, Texas	150.00
4	Santa Cruz, California	137.50
5	Champagne–Urbana, Illinois	118.18
6	Oxnard, California	114.55
7	Fort Meyers, Florida	110.00
8	Billings, Montana	100.00
9	Cedar Rapids, Iowa	100.00
10	Panama City, Florida	100.00

Rank	SMSA	Percent job change
1	Lawton, Oklahoma	2,266.97
2	St Cloud, Minnesota	1,265.08
3	Boise, Idaho	729.31
4	Santa Rosa, California	360.58
5	Lakeland, Florida	266.69
6	Lubbock, Texas	237.44
7	Topeka, Kansas	237.35
8	Laredo, Texas	220.84
9	Savannah, Georgia	204.78
10	McAllen–Pharr–Edinburg, Texas	181.54

Source: Markusen, Hall, and Glasmeier (see note 2).

Table 2.3   States ranked according to their combined position on a scale of (a) high-technology
industries location quotients and (b) their number of
high-technology manufacturing jobs (states ranking
among the top ten on both criteria)

Rank	State
1	California
2	Connecticut
3	Massachusetts
4	Texas
5	Illinois
6	New Jersey
7	Florida

Source: Markusen, Hall, and Glasmeier (note 2) (my
elaboration of their database)

the new industries and seem to be specialized in these industries. Thus, if we
select the states that in 1977 were both among the top ten in terms of high
technology jobs and had location quotients higher than one, we obtain the
ranking given in table 2.3. At a very general level of observation, these states
seem to represent the hard core of high-technology manufacturing under the
terms defined by the Markusen, Hall, and Glasmeier study. This impression is
confirmed by a closer look at the internal composition of the industrial sectors
that account for most of the high-technology manufacturing jobs in these
states: semiconductors, computers, aircraft, telecommunications equipment,
space, and defense-related industries. Simply reading through this list of
high-technology-prone states gives an idea of the geographical, social, and
historical diversity of the new industrial space. Any coherent pattern in
industrial location will have to be found at a deeper analytical level.

Similar findings can be cited concerning the distribution of high-
technology industries among the metropolitan areas. There is an important
difference between those areas that show a concentration of high-technology
jobs because of the sheer size of their industrial history, and those newer areas
that have both a strong quantitative high-technology base and a rapid rate of
growth in these sectors. Thus, if we rank the top ten areas in absolute number
of high-technology jobs *and* the top ten areas in terms of rate of growth in
high-technology jobs between 1972 and 1977, and again combine the two
rankings, we come up with the following top five metropolitan areas: San
Jose, California; Anaheim, California; Boston, Massachusetts; Houston,
Texas; and Dallas, Texas. While this short list also shows a regional and social
diversity, the shift from the state level to the more disaggregated level of the
metropolitan areas gives more specific information about the particular
spatial features of high-technology location. For example, while Los
Angeles–Long Beach had the highest number of high-technology jobs in

1977, Anaheim appears to be the main growth engine for the new industries in Southern California. Also, it would seem that areas such as Chicago and Philadelphia retain their quantitative importance in these high-technology statistics more because of the use of new technologies in the modernization of traditional manufacturing than because of their capacity to retain a significant share of the information-technology producer industries.[9]

Why do high-technology industries locate where they do? According to the regression analysis performed by Markusen, Hall, and Glasmeier, four series of variables explain a sizable proportion of the variance in the distribution of industrial sectors among metropolitan areas:[10]

(1) Amenities (good climate, good educational options, high (?) housing prices).
(2) Access features (airport access, freeway access).
(3) Agglomeration economies (presence of business services; location of headquarters of *Fortune* 500 corporations).
(4) Socio-political factors (importance of defense spending, low percentage of blacks in the resident population).

Other factors frequently cited in the literature, such as wage rates, levels of unionization, or presence of a major university, do not seem to hold a statistical relationship with high-technology location, although these observations will need further qualification as the analysis progresses.

In spite of their interest and importance, the data provided by the Markusen, Hall, and Glasmeier study have two major methodological shortcomings from the point of view of our own analytical purpose. First, since their calculations concern entire sectors, this database does not permit a distinction to be made between innovative functions and assembly-line plants within the same high-technology industry. Given the sharp division of labor within each industry and the extreme differentiation among segments of its labor force, we need to introduce additional criteria to understand the differential spatial dynamics of different segments of the industry. Secondly, the definition of high-technology industries in terms of the proportion of skilled technical labor does not allow differentiation between high-technology producers and high-technology users, since many old line manufacturing companies are also increasing the proportion of engineers and scientists employed in order to be able to use new technologies, regardless of the characteristics of their final products. Although the spatial impact of technological modernization in manufacturing is a very important matter, it is analytically crucial to distinguish it from the spatial logic of the new, information-based industries. The fact that the definition of high technology used in the Markusen, Hall, and Glasmeier study cannot capture this crucial distinction could account for the quantitative importance in their results, in terms of high-technology jobs, of some old industrial areas, such as Illinois and Ohio.

Thus, while the data commented on here present a most interesting overview of the effects of technological change on manufacturing in general, they are not sufficient for an understanding of the potential new spatial dynamics that could exist within the new information-technology industries.

As stated in chapter 2, our hypothesis is that the core of the current technological revolution lies in the development of new information technologies, particularly microelectronics, computers, and telecommunications as well as in biotechnology, with its basis in genetic engineering. From this perspective, studies of particular industries which are clearly a part of the new informational economy, such as semiconductors, computers (hardware and software), and genetic engineering, are crucial to understanding the new spatial logic, if it actually exists. What we lose in comprehensiveness, we gain in deeper insight, thus enhancing the chances of forming the empirical grounding of an analytical model capable of making progress in explaining the process of formation of the new industrial space.

The Evolution of the Locational Pattern of the Semiconductors Industry

Semiconductors manufacturing remains the archetype of information-technology industries. Since it is also the industry on which we have the most detailed information, a synthesis of the main trends of its typical spatial behavior could be a useful step toward understanding the locational pattern of information-technology producers.

First of all, Storper's data[11] show that employment in semiconductors is heavily concentrated in four states: 72.5 per cent of all employment in the industry in 1980 was in California, Massachusetts, Arizona, and Texas. This has been the case since 1969; though not all four states at the top have remained the same, California has been ahead throughout and increased its lead over the years (see table 2.4).

A more recent analysis by Scott and Angel[12] shows a similar tendency, although, according to their calculations, Massachusetts has not been among the top four states since the early 1970s, while New York has maintained a significant share, mainly because of production associated with IBM (see table 2.5). It is important to notice the differences in trend between areas highlighted by Scott and Angel's data: New England and the Mid-Atlantic suffered a significant decline in their shares after an early lead (New England accounted for over 29 per cent of total semiconductors employment in 1958). In contrast, Texas and Arizona displayed impressive gains during the 1970s, and California gradually increased its share to become the undisputed leader in the 1980s. Figure 2.1, elaborated by Scott and Angel, compares the strikingly different evolution in semiconductors employment in, variously, the Mid-Atlantic (New Jersey, New York, Pennsylvania), Massachusetts, and Silicon Valley (Santa Clara County), showing a clear advantage for the last.

These observations emphasize the need for a historical perspective on the formation of the spatial pattern of the industry in generating some hypotheses

Table 2.4 Location of the semiconductor industry

	Production Employment[a] 1980		Production Employment Census, 1977			Value-Added 1977			Establishments 1977		
		%		000	%		$000	%		No.	%
First State	CA	30.4	CA	18.1	28.5	CA	1,172.6	34.4	CA	180	33.0
Second State	AZ	18.3	TX	13.0	20.4	TX	568.6	17.2	NY	59	10.8
Third State	TX	14.6	PA	8.0	12.6	NY	422.4	12.3	MA	46	8.44
Fourth State	MA	9.2	AZ	7.0	11.0	PA	359.9	10.5	TX	36	6.6
Top Four States		72.5		46.1	72.5		2,523.5	74.0		321	58.8
Total	102.9			63.5			3,409.6			545	

[a]SIC 3674 and part of SIC 3679; author's statistics.
Sources: State Industrial Directories, Key Plants, Marketing Economics Incorporated, New York, 1980. Sources gathered and elaborated by Storper (see note 1).

about its underlying logic. To pursue this perspective further, we will turn to Servet Mutlu's pioneering doctoral dissertation, which surveys in great detail the sequence of events that put semiconductors on the economic map of the US.[13]

The first significant fact in this sequence is that the development of semiconductors was actually missed out on by the big companies, which were in the business of making electronic components on the basis of vacuum tube technology. Even when these companies converted to semiconductors in the late 1960s, it was mainly to produce them for their own manufacturing processes, basically focused on consumer durables. They remained located in their original sites in the north-east: Westinghouse in Pittsburgh, Sylvania in Long Island, RCA in New Jersey, and General Electric in northern New York. Since the development of semiconductors was to a large extent

Table 2.5 Percentage distribution of employment in SIC 3674 (semiconductors and related devices) for census divisions and selected states, 1958–1982

	1958	1963	1967	1972	1977	1982
New England	29.1	18.0	n.a.	10.7*	10.6	n.a.
Massachusetts	n.a.	11.2	9.4	4.8	4.4	4.4
Mid-Atlantic	34.5	34.2	30.8	21.8	21.7	16.4
New Jersey	n.a.	6.5	6.2	3.5	2.3	1.9
New York	n.a.	8.1	8.5	5.3	10.6	9.0
Pennsylvania	n.a.	19.6	16.1	13.0	8.8	5.5
East-north-central	n.a.	n.a.	3.1	9.2	2.3	1.9
West-north-central	n.a.	n.a.	0.5	0.8	0.7	n.a.
South Atlantic	n.a.	n.a.	3.5	2.1	2.9	n.a.
Florida	n.a.	n.a.	3.4	1.4	2.6	3.2
East-south-central	n.a.	n.a.	n.a.	0.2	n.a.	n.a.
West-south-central	n.a.	n.a.	3.1	n.a.	14.5	n.a.
Texas	n.a.	n.a.	3.1	18.3	14.5	13.3
Mountain	n.a.	n.a.	6.3	n.a.	n.a.	n.a.
Arizona	n.a.	9.3	6.3	5.8	14.5	10.7
Pacific	n.a.	n.a.	17.5	n.a.	n.a.	n.a.
California	15.9	19.9	17.5	21.0	27.6	28.7

Source: All data for the years 1958 and 1963 taken from US Department of Commerce, Bureau of the Census, *Census of Manufactures.* All data for the years 1967, 1972, 1977, and 1982 taken from US Department of Commerce, Bureau of the Census, *County Business Patterns* (except where marked by an asterik which indicates that the source is the *Census of Manufactures*). Data collected and elaborated by Scott and Angel (see note 12).

dependent on innovation, and none of these companies chose to invest in electronics research, they were gradually pushed aside by the competition.

The only established large firm that could have dominated the innovation process and taken on the leadership of the new industry was obviously ATT–Western Electric, since the New Jersey-based Bell Laboratories were at the very source of the invention of the transistor in 1947, as well as of most of the original R&D in the field of semiconductors. Yet, threatened with anti-trust law suits (particularly the one brought by the Department of Justice against Western Electric in 1956) Bell decided to diffuse its knowledge, organizing conferences to communicate its findings, and liberally licensing the applications of its discoveries. Bell Laboratories, in fact, heavily dependent as it was on government research contracts, became a national research facility. In the long term this turned out to be a brilliant commercial strategy, since telecommunications, largely dominated by ATT, eventually became the highway system of the electronic age. However, it was probably not a conscious decision, but rather a combination of legal and institutional constraints with the research dynamics generated at Bell. This is in fact one of the crucial, new characteristics of a science-based industry: it is very difficult

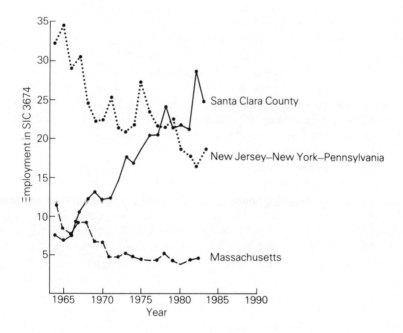

Figure 2.1   Distribution of employment in SIC 3674 (semiconductors and related devices), 1964–1983
Source: US Department of Commerce, Bureau of the Census, County Business Patterns, in Scott and Angel (see note 12)

to play the innovation game and at the same time set up organizational constraints that would undermine the vitality of the research effort, and ultimately its ability to connect with social and commercial applications. Those companies who behaved in such a way as to restrain the process of communicating innovations were left behind in the technological competition, and ultimately lost markets as well.

Interestingly enough, the direct industrial development resulting from Bell's technological discoveries took place elsewhere, when Bell's researchers set up shop in other areas of the country, emphasizing the crucial role of humanly embodied research in the development of the new information-technology industry. Noble Prize winner William Shockley, one of the inventors of the transistor, was appointed Professor of Electrical Engineering at Stanford University by Frank Terman, an entrepreneurial Provost who, in 1951, founded the Stanford Industrial Park and gave high priority to supporting technologically advanced companies. Shockley was a native of Palo Alto, a fact that made his recruitment easier. Yet it was the initiative of the university which created the conditions for bringing together the innovative capacity of one of the leading scientists with the university support and business environment necessary to generate industrial spin-offs and further technological innovation. Shockley's own company was not very successful, since he insisted in engaging himself in what proved to be a dead-end new line of research. But his students and junior partners, more flexible and open to the new avenues of semiconductors technology, quit Shockley to found Fairchild, the source (direct or indirect) of most of the innovative companies that were to provide the basis for the industrial development of Silicon Valley. Spin-offs of Fairchild included Intel, Signetics, and Advanced Micro-Devices. In a similar, though less famous, development, one of the key elements in Texas Instruments' early start in semiconductors was the hiring in 1953 of Gordon Teal, a leading scientist at Bell.

ATT–Bell was able in this way to organize by itself the scientific research milieu in which discoveries were made that triggered the growth of a new and crucial industry; the subsequent spin-offs, however, were not its own, and took place in different locations. New Jersey did not become a major center for semiconductors, in spite of Bell's pre-eminence there, the asset represented by Princeton, the proximity of RCA at Princeton, and the location of the IBM production center in southern New York. Why is it that all these elements never clustered together to generate an industrial complex? First, each one of these companies and institutions constituted a world apart, too arrogant to solicit the others and too self-confident to feel threatened by future competition. Secondly, some basic conditions were lacking which, as we will see, are necessary for the location of advanced electronics industries: the pool of electrical engineers and technicians was not large enough, military markets were simply not present in the region, New York–New Jersey was an area which had strong labor unions, and venture capital was not keen on direct industrial investment, being traditionally channeled through Wall Street. Thus, the world's greatest institution in electronics research could not generate its own manufacturing complex, in spite of its location in a Stanford-like semi-rural area, in the vicinity of the great metropolis, and close to a major university. The seeds of invention were spread by the winds of risk-taking enterprises toward more fertile ground.

A third series of cases revealing the complex dynamics in the historical evolution of semiconductors location is represented by those large companies that dominated semiconductors production from the origins of the technology, constituting isolated, self-sufficient production systems: IBM, Texas Instruments, and Motorola.

IBM started semiconductors production for its own captive market in computer-making. It organized its own production space, with three major research centers in Yorktown Heights, New York; San Jose, California; and Zurich, Switzerland, along with four large plants with integrated production and R&D facilities in East Fishkill, New York; Burlington, Vermont; Manassas, Virginia; and Endicott, New York. Three distinctive features characterize IBM's locational pattern in semiconductors manufacturing in the US.

(1) IBM controlled the rate of obsolescence of the new technology through its dominance of and consequent vertical integration in the computer market. This enabled the company to automate assembly operations from the beginning, thus reducing labor costs without having to disperse production facilities. Therefore, only a relatively small share of production took place off-shore (in semiconductors, not in computers, production of which was decentralized worldwide very early). The two plants located in semi-rural areas (Vermont and Virginia) were the smaller ones: the cost of labor does not seem to have been a major factor in IBM's location.

(2) Access to science and technology was provided by the company itself through its research personnel, network of consultants, and research contracts. Thus, physical proximity to major research centers was not an important criterion, and the location of one of the high-level centers in San Jose was mainly linked to the expansion of the early electronics complex in Silicon Valley.

(3) IBM developed an ethos of isolation and self-sufficiency in relation to its environment, with facilities settled on a campus-like principle. The location of semiconductors production was in fact determined by that of the firm's computer factories and research centers, themselves historically dependent upon the proximity to the market for business services represented by Manhattan, a market to which IBM used, in its early stages, to lease and maintain its machines, requiring daily service contact. This pattern of indifference to its environment (made easier to maintain by a paternalistic policy of high salaries and in-house career prospects which kept IBM's employees away from unions) resulted both in the location of IBM in

environments hardly typical of later high-technology agglomerations, and in the absence of a complex of technologically advanced industries springing up around IBM's production sites.

A different, and very interesting case, is offered by the development of Texas Instruments (TI) in Dallas, and the different courses taken by expansion of semiconductors production, in largely unrelated processes, in Dallas and Austin. Dallas's role in the semiconductors industry appears to be the result of the location of Texas Instruments, following a logic relatively close to IBM's isolationist tactics. In the 1930s, Texas Instruments was a small Dallas company engaged in the oil exploration business. It expanded its electronics capabilities during World War II when it converted itself to the fabrication of anti-submarine detectors. After the war, Texas Instruments decided to build on the recent discovery of the transistor in developing its re-search and production activities in electronic components, mainly aiming at the markets that could develop from its Navy contacts. In 1953, as mentioned above, TI hired Gordon Teal, a leading semiconductors researcher from Bell Laboratories. By 1956 TI had become a leader in silicon transistors, with most of its production geared to military markets. In 1957 Jack Kilby, from TI, co-invented the integrated circuit, simultaneously with Bob Noyce at Intel. Later, TI diversifed its production, becoming a large producer of hand calculators and computers. For a long period, it remained located in Dallas, and in nearby Texas communities, with the major exception of a new plant in Attleboro, Massachusetts, in the early 1970s.

Texas Instruments' location pattern represents a combination of IBM's type of behavior, and of the model represented by a high-technology industrial complex. TI used its isolation in Dallas to generate its own research milieu, tak-ing advantage of its strength in the local market, only challenged by McDonnell Douglas for electronics engineers. It also used its financial and technological capacity to recruit on a nation-wide basis. Yet it did not have the resources that IBM had. So its expansion benefited from a series of factors that were related to its Dallas location: connection with military markets; cheap labor, both skilled and unskilled; a good business climate; and, since the early 1970s, the role of Dallas as a major center of air transportation. However, TI did not generate any significant spin-off activity in Dallas, because the company's policy prevented dissemination of technological know-how to suppliers and customers. To move from the growth of TI to the development of semiconductors production in Texas, then, required a diversification of the new industry and stimulation of the creation of a production complex with scientific and commercial externalities.

At this point, the focus of the action shifted to Austin, which boasted the best university in the state, and where a small number of high energy physics firms had created the germ of a high-technology industrial base. Austin eventually became a major center of semiconductors and electronics manufacturing. Its development was sparked off by the decentralization of the technical branch plants of major electronics companies, with IBM taking the lead in 1967, followed by TI itself, Lockheed, Intel, Control Data, Motorola, Rolm, Hughes, and others. Around these companies developed a network of smaller high-technology firms which provided specialized services.[14] In the 1980s, two major electronics research consortia located in Austin, attracted by good conditions offered by the state government and by the quality of the university. One was MCC, oriented toward microelectronics research and bringing together the technological and financial resources of ten major corporations. The other was SEMATECH, a billionaire facility funded by the Defense Department and operated by major corporations to develop new technologies in semiconductors manufacturing, with the aim of supporting American companies against Japanese competition in technology. Thus, while Austin started as a locus for several decentralized technical branch plants, it was able, unlike Dallas, to generated a network of ancillary companies, and to engage in the upgrading of its technological basis, with government support. Interestingly enough, then, Texas Instruments and Texas do not seem to have shared a common fate in high-technology development, although the accidental location of Texas Instruments in Dallas did generate the first electronics production complex in the state, and provided the sample of the possibilities open to Texas, should the Lone Star be willing to engage itself on the new frontier of manufacturing. Texas Instruments in Dallas, and the Austin industrial complex, represent two locational models, linked in their historical development but clearly distinct in their functional and spatial logic.[15]

An even more clear case of discrepancy between the logic of a major company and that of a region is offered by the expansion of Motorola (the second largest semiconductors company in the US) in Phoenix, Arizona. Here again, Motorola's location in Phoenix (away from its original base as an auto radio producer in Chicago) was accidental, apparently motivated by the advantages of good weather and a pleasant environment in attracting highly skilled engineers. A key factor was the personal preference of David Noble, Vice President for Electronics, who convinced the company to set up an engineering research laboratory in Phoenix in 1949. He took the risk of staking the laboratory's future on the potential of the transistor, shortly after its discovery. According to the case study on Motorola conducted by Glasmeier,[16] by the early 1970s the company was prominent in all aspects of the integrated circuit industry. It then started moving some of its assembly operations off-shore to Mexico, South Korea, and Malaysia, while setting up more advanced facilities in Austin, Texas, and in Chandler, a Phoenix suburb. Yet Motorola's know-how had no real spin-off effects in the Phoenix area. The development of electronics in Phoenix was basically linked to the location there of branch plants of large electronics companies, such as Honeywell, GTE-Microcircuits, Intel, and Sperry. Motorola, nevertheless, remained the dominant employer, with 22,000 workers in Pima County in 1984. Its employment policy included a requirement for all its employees to sign an oath barring the use by them of any knowledge generated while working for the company; in exchange, it was generous toward its skilled personnel.

Among the reasons for Motorola's isolationist attitude Glasmeier cites the following:

(1) The consolidation of purchases of large inputs within the company, precluding local linkages.
(2) The fact that much of the volume of Motorola's inputs is represented by standard materials, such as silicon and special chemicals, delivered by out-of-state suppliers.
(3) New equipment is provided by manufacturing representatives of national companies.
(4) Motorola's market is worldwide, and this limits downstream linkages in the region.

In the absence of local linkages, in both its production and its markets, and with a policy aimed at discouraging new start-ups by former employees, Motorola stands by itself in Phoenix, without being able to spur a process of locally based autonomous technological development. Because of this isolation *vis à vis* its industrial environment, it is dependent on its own scientific and manufacturing potential. Such aloofness, as Glasmeier points out, is detrimental to competitiveness in an industry that is shifting from standardized production into customized products, a trend that requires continuous innovation and strong linkages within a diversified industrial milieu.

A single company, then, however large or technologically well equipped, is not able to generate an industrial milieu reaching beyond its own organization if it does not allow spin-offs and establish backward and forward linkages. The most it can do is to lend visibility to an area which given the proper conditions for high-technology development, could then attract other industries. This is what happened in Arizona. Lacking the scientific base for autonomous innovative development, Phoenix could not become a leading technological center outside Motorola. But, being an ideal location in terms of cheap labor, a pro-business environment, and access to military markets, Arizona became a case of "mitigated success:" a very large complex of advanced manufacturing in standardized electronics products.

It is apparent, then, that the largest companies pioneering in semi-conductors production were not able to create a dynamic of development around them. When the regions where they located were eventually able to develop an advanced technological industrial base, other factors largely autonomous from the companies' presence were generally responsible. As Mutlu writes, "the heart of the American semiconductors industry beats elsewhere."[17] It beats in Silicon Valley (Santa Clara County, California), and along Route 128 near Boston. Why is this so? Although the story is now familiar, it is worthwhile emphasizing those of its elements that bear analytical significance.

In semiconductors, Boston came first. In 1958, of the 55 firms producing semiconductors, 13 were located in Massachusetts, and only 7 in California. Yet by 1967, the San Jose Metropolitan Area employed more workers in semiconductors manufacturing than all of New England. To understand how this came about it will be necessary to explain both the distinguishing characteristics of Boston and Silicon Valley in relationship to the rest of the country, and the differences between the two areas that could account for Silicon Valley's eventual dominance in spite of its late start.[18] The most important common characteristic of the two areas is the fact that they host the top research-oriented university complexes in the US, particularly in electrical engineering and computer sciences, organized around MIT and Harvard in the Boston area, and around Stanford and the University of California at Berkeley in the San Francisco Bay area. As table 2.6 shows, 43 of the 64 science-based electronics firms in the Boston area in 1965 were spin-offs of other research facilities, and 24 of these spin-offs came directly from universities, including 21 from MIT alone. In the case of Silicon Valley there is an even more direct and evident link between the origins of advanced research and manufacturing in semiconductors and the deliberate effort made by Stanford University to develop an industrial park oriented toward high technology. The business-oriented policy of Stanford in the area of electronics received a major boost from Frederick Terman, a professor of engineering who joined Stanford in the 1940s after having directed a military-oriented research program at Harvard, to become Dean and, later, Provost. Under his tenure Stanford not only built an outstanding electrical engineering program and established close ties with the electronics companies, but also played a pioneering role in the formation of a Stanford Industrial Park in 1951, providing low-rent space for 99-year leases of university-owned land to high-technology companies that would benefit, and benefit from, the university. Lockheed's aerospace research facility was one of the first to locate here. From Stanford's Faculty and student body came the majority of researcher/entrepreneurs who started up semiconductors firms in the early stages of formation of the Silicon Valley complex, either directly, or as spin-offs of companies such as Fairchild, itself a creation of William Shockley's Stanford disciples.

The second feature common to the Boston and San Francisco areas is the existence of an active and organized network of financial firms specialized in channeling venture capital toward promising small businesses. This financial sector, boosted by the Small Business Investment Act of 1958, played a major role in the development of a network of small, innovative semiconductors

Table 2.6 Origins of science-based firms in greater Boston, c.1965, by technical area[a]

Company Origin	Electronics	Communication systems, etc.	Computer hardware	Data processing	Instruments	Other	All companies
MIT	21	9	5	5	12	31	(49)
Harvard	3	1			4	4	(7)
Another local university						3	3
Non-local university						3	3
Government laboratory	2	1			1	1	3
Another company	17	4	6	2	10	28	
Total "Spin-offs"	43	15	11	7	27	100	109
Formed a subsidiary	1			1	2	9	
Formed independently	19	10	3	5	8	54	
Other	1						
Total "non-spin-offs"	21	10	3	6	10	63	78
Total, all origins	64	25	14	13	37	135	187

Source: D. Shimshoni, "Regional Development and Science Based Industry," in J.F. Kain and R. Meyer, eds, *Essays in Regional Economics* (Cambridge Mass., Harvard University Press, 1971). pp 111–14, 119. (Cited by Servet Mutlu, see note 13).
[a]A science-based firm is defined as having 20% or more of its employees in R&D. A company can be in more than one technical area. The sample covers 187 firms out of a total of 406 science-based firms in the greater Boston area c.1965.

companies in the two areas. In the early stages of the semiconductors industry, there were low entry barriers in the field of innovative technology production. Because of the relatively small amount of capital required to manufacture a product whose main value came from the knowledge embodied in it, venture capital and personal savings were the main sources of financing in the formative years of Silicon Valley and Route 128. Yet venture capital firms do not spring up in all areas. They require a local society with a profusion of individually wealthy households able and willing to invest outside the traditional avenues of the stock market. Inside knowledge about developments in a new industry, made easy to gain given the local connections of venture capital firms, is a crucial factor that can be exploited by these firms to give them the advantage over the stock exchange or the larger financial institutions. San Francisco and Boston were both particularly suited to the development of such entrepreneurial financial systems. Once the network of venture capital firms was in place, and with the development of the new industry, capital from other sources flowed into it, generally from much larger investors, in particular the pension funds. Ultimately, Wall Street based investment firms joined the rush. But the important element is that, regardless of the origins of the funds, most investment for companies starting up was channeled through the venture capital firms which became a pivotal organizational element of the electronics complex in both Boston and San Francisco.

It is important to emphasize that while venture capital is still a major element in the creation of new firms, its significance has declined in the 1980s under the new conditions of high-technology industries. On the one hand, the capital requirements for entry into the semiconductors business have dramatically escalated, because of the very great research efforts necessary to compete, and the high cost of new semiconductors manufacturing equipment; on the other hand, the downturn of the industry in the mid-1980s diverted much investment attention toward more promising ventures, including the high returns once more available in a speculative, volatile stock market. Yet the organizational linkage between a specific source of high risk–high return financing and the development of semiconductors companies was crucial in the formation of the two major industrial complexes of Santa Clara County and Boston, and set the stage for their joint development as innovative milieux.

A third characteristic common to the two areas, although by no means exclusive to them, is their position as major regional centers and nodal points in a national and international network of telecommunications and air transportation. This enables firms to develop through spatial dispersion in distant locations while maintaining the location of their headquarters and key production facilities close to the core of high-technology centers, actually forming networked milieux of production.

Another feature often cited as common to both areas, although with particular emphasis for Santa Clara County, is their pleasant environment, rich cultural life, proximity to urban amenities and outdoor recreation, and, in the case of Silicon Valley, good weather all year around. In sum, "quality of life:" a crucial asset in attracting the highly educated, demanding personnel that are so important for the development of information-based industries. Yet these images are too vague and too subjective to admit consideration of the so-called "quality of life" factor as a truly distinctive feature of high-technology complexes. Mild weather is certainly not an attribute of New England winters. Sophisticated urban atmosphere does not really describe the rather dull suburban world of Silicon Valley. Active cultural life is generally a correlate of the presence of major universities in an area. The very notion of the attributes of suburbanism as "quality of life" would be challenged by hard-core New Yorkers. While the orchards and beautiful weather of Santa Clara County or the pleasant rural atmosphere of suburban Boston could certainly be an attractive location for nature-loving professionals, a vast number of other places in the United States, including many locations relatively close to major metropolitan areas, would fit the requirements of environmental quality. In fact, the causality seems to operate in the other direction. Most places were quite beautiful before being hit by the first waves of industrialization and urbanization. So, what we are considering are *new* areas of development, which, because they rely on a highly educated, well-paid labor force, could be kept in better environmental condition than the earlier industrial areas, in spite of chemical pollution and traffic jams. Housing prices and industrial real estate prices act as a deterrent for the location of non-desirable activities or lower-income populations. Services catering to a resident population with high social status improve the quality of life in the area for people and activities able to afford it. So, the "quality of life" of high-technology areas is a *result* of the characteristics of the industry (its newness, its highly educated labor force) rather than the *determinant* of its location pattern.

One crucial characteristic of the location of the semiconductors industry that applies in specific and different ways to each of the two leading areas is its relationship to the military markets. In the early stages of the industry these markets were without doubt decisive for its development, although from the mid-1960s to the early 1980s the share of the military in semiconductors sales dramatically decreased. In the formative period of information-technology centers, the assurance of large military markets, more interested in performance than in cost, was the bedrock on which the industry set itself up. In this regard, California clearly enjoyed an advantage. The existence of a complex of large military installations inherited from the Pacific War, the proximity to weapons testing sites in the western deserts, good weather allowing for planes and missiles testing all year round, and the connection to the Los Angeles complex of airframe manufacturers created the basis for a customized relationship between the electronics industry and its military clients. All the data indicate the pre-eminence of California as recipient of the largest proportion of military contracts; Massachusetts did not have the same privileged access to military contracts and the hypothesis has often been formulated that this is what caused the displacement of the center of the semi-conductors industry toward California during the 1960s. In fact, the process seems to be more complex than this. MIT received many very large military contracts, and during World War II played a much greater military role than Stanford. The main northern California connection to weapons-oriented research, the Lawrence Livermore National Laboratory operated by the University of California, did not spin off much industrial development, given the secrecy of its research; neither did its eastern counterpart, the MIT-operated Lincoln Laboratory. It is important to distinguish between military research and military-oriented production, and only in the latter does California appear to have had a historical advantage, maybe accounting for the shift of the semiconductors industry from east to west. Yet once the high-technology complex of Massachusetts took off on its own, based more on computers than on semiconductors, large military markets were accessible to the firms located there, and by the mid-1980s the Route 128 complex was more dependent on military markets than Silicon Valley. In sum, then, Boston – and New England in general – also benefited from military contracts from the very beginning, and the firms there moved more extensively into these markets, regardless of their connection with the military establishment, once their information-generating capability was sufficiently attractive to the Defense Department. On the other hand, the concentration of the military markets in California since the 1950s may have played a role in shifting the main center of semiconductors production westwards, while Boston remained very much on top of the world map of information technology.

There is one further factor to be discussed which is often mentioned as an area of contrast between the two regions, and proposed in explanation of Silicon Valley's prominence in semiconductors: namely, the presence of strong labor unions in Massachusetts, and their absence in Santa Clara County. In fact, the empirical data do not hold up this interpretation. Santa Clara County did have a significant union presence (although proportional to its low industrial base) in the automobile, canneries, transportation, commun-ications, and hospital sectors, *before the growth of the electronics industry*. As with the "quality of life" argument, causality works in the opposite direction: semiconductors, because of its very specific labor requirements, and because it is a new industry, is little unionized anywhere in the world, and therefore the extent of unionization is lower in those areas where it becomes dominant.[19] This interpretation seems to be confirmed by most international experience in the development of the semiconductors industry, including areas with a long labor union tradition, such as Scotland. Furthermore, semiconductors developed first in Massachusetts, in the 1950s and early 1960s, in the heyday of the unions' strength in the Boston area; by the time

Boston's loss of dominance to California at a later stage took place, industrial restructuring had already significantly eroded union power in New England, partly because of the development of the electronics industry.

Most of the locational characteristics that seem to be related to semiconductors production, then, were common to the two major seedbeds of innovation. Those that do not appear to be distinctive of these two areas, also differ between them. Thus it becomes possible to see a tentative pattern in the development of the two locations. Their differential evolution seems to be the result partly of the more direct connection of California to military markets in the 1950s and 1960s; partly of the higher synergetic capabilities of Silicon Valley; and finally, of the ability of Silicon Valley industrialists to build a political business organization that did not face opposition in the region, unlike their counterparts on Route 128 who had to face an old industrial society with conflicting interest groups.[20] The important point, though, is the dominance of *both areas* as centers of technological innovation in the information-based manufacturing industries.

Finally, a crucial element in the locational pattern of the semiconductors industry is the sharp spatial distinction between its innovative production functions, its advanced manufacturing functions and its assembly operations. This has become the central theme for all researchers concerned with the spatial behavior of the new industries.[21] Scott and Angel have provided empirical support for this hypothesis by making a distinction between integrated circuits manufacturing establishments (an indicator of advanced research functions performed in the firm), and discrete devices manufacturing establishments (which tend to be concentrated in the standardized production of less advanced products).[22] As table 2.7 and maps 2.1 and 2.2

Table 2.7   Shipments of discrete semiconductor devices and integrated circuits in 1982 for selected states

	Discrete devices (transistors, diodes and rectifiers)		Integrated circuits	
	(%)	$m	(%)	$m
Arizona	n.a.		6.3	
California	21.8		33.3	
Florida	n.a.		3.1	
Massachusetts	12.5		2.4	
New Jersey	2.4		1.0	
New York	1.9		n.a.	
Pennsylvania	12.5		n.a.	
Texas	n.a.		16.2	
Total US shipments		1102.3		7298.4

Source: US Department of Commerce, Bureau of the Census, *Census of Manufactures,* 1982 (Elaborated by Scott and Angel, see note 12).

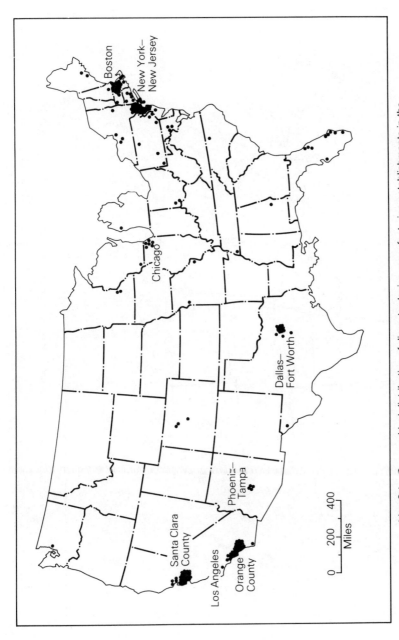

Map 2.1 Geographical distribution of discrete device manufacturing establishments in the US in 1982

Source: Scott and Angel (see note 12)

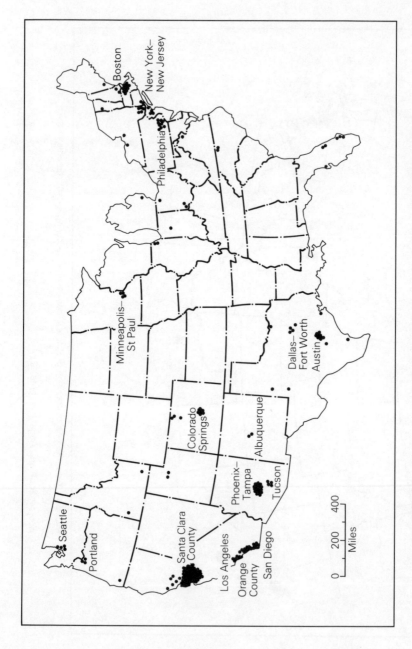

Map 2.2 Geographical distribution of integrated circuit manufacturing establishments in the
US in 1982
Source: Scott and Angel (see note 12)

Boston

New York–
New Jersey

Philadelphia

Minneapolis–
St Paul

Dallas–
Fort Worth
Austin

Colorado
Springs

Albuquerque

Phoenix–
Tampa
Tucson

Seattle

Portland

Santa Clara
County

Los Angeles

Orange
County

San Diego

0   200   400
Miles

show, integrated circuit producers are much more selective in their location, with California, and particularly Silicon Valley, emerging as the core production center, with Massachusetts, Arizona, Texas, and, to a lesser extent, Pennsylvania, New York–New Jersey, and Colorado, holding a solid position in the new industry. Furthermore, the ability of semiconductors production to segment itself between distant spatial locations has made this industry the pioneer of worldwide decentralization; since 1962 it has moved production facilities abroad, first for assembly operations, later for testing and custom design, and in the near future wafer production will follow suit.[23]

Thus, while the semiconductors industry, spearhead of information-technology manufacturing, does show a distinct spatial pattern, that pattern's complexity, its moving boundaries, and its variation throughout its evolution, render inadequate any simplistic images or hasty generalizations, and call for a theoretically based analytical model capable of grasping the new relationship between production and space. Before trying to propose some elements of such an analytical perspective, it will be useful to observe, at a preliminary, descriptive level, the early location pattern of other key industries representative of the current technological revolution.

Computerlands: The Spatial Location of the Computer Industry in its Early Stage

The computer industry is much larger and more diversified than the semiconductors industry. It represents the key linkage between the production of information technology and its widespread use. Unlike semiconductors, it has been dominated, since its beginning, by large companies such as IBM (an industrial universe by itself), Digital, Control Data, Honeywell, Sperry, Burroughs, and Hewlett-Packard, and the initial location of these firms largely determined the spatial profile of the industry in its later stages. For the purpose of this overview, we will focus on the early stages of development of the industry in the 1960s and 1970s, looking for recurring elements that might provide some clues in the process of building an empirically grounded analytical model.[24]

At first sight the evolution of the locational pattern of computer hardware production looks much like that of semiconductors. Tables 2.8 and 2.9, elaborated by Servet Mutlu, show both the autonomy of the industry in relation to the old manufacturing belt and its tendency to cluster in some areas. By ranking order, the largest concentrations of employment in computers manufacturing in the 1970s were: California, Massachusetts, Minnesota, New York, and, well behind, Florida, Texas, Pennsylvania, and Arizona. If we observe the location quotients, indicating spatial specialization, and their evolution over time, we find the largest relative concentration of employment in San Jose Standard Metropolitan Statistical Area (SMSA) as

Table 2.8 Distribution of employment in the electronic computing equipment industry (SIC 3573), by census regions

	1958[a]		1963[a]		1967		1972		1976	
	% of total employment	location quotient	% of total employment	location quotient	% of total employment	location quotient	% of total employment	location quotient	% of total employment	location quotient
US Total Employment (000s)	50.9		96.4		96.9		144.8		176.0	
New England	3.46	0.39	3.63	0.43			12.09	1.59		
Massachusetts	1.50	0.37	3.22	0.81			10.44	3.17	12.08	3.81
Boston SMSA	1.60	0.66	2.28	1.32						
Middle Atlantic	43.86	1.74	35.06	1.46	25.09	1.15	16.55	0.90	15.62	0.62
New York	38.17	3.29	27.90	2.55			13.33	1.51	9.64	1.22
New York-north-eastern New Jersey SMSA	2.34	0.22	2.90	0.28	2.43	0.25	2.97	0.35		
Pennsylvania			4.85	0.57			2.07	0.28	3.37	0.46
East-north-central			27.59	1.04	4.65	0.16	4.56	0.18		
West-north-central			12.03	2.01	19.00	6.04	14.01	2.22		
Minnesota									10.76	11.35
South Atlantic							6.70	0.46		
Florida									4.15	2.25

West-south-central						
Texas					3.88	0.65
Mountain						
Arizona					3.08	5.71
Pacific						
California	11.52	1.51	28.25	3.47		
San Jose SMSA			10.77	15.17	12.19	14.34
San Francisco-Oakland SMSA				1.23		
Los Angeles-Long Beach SMSA	4.59	0.99	9.74	2.37	7.86	1.86
Anaheim-Santa Ana-Garden Grove SMSA					5.79	2.14
San Diego SMSA					2.19	5.334

Sources: For 1958–72, US Bureau of the Census, *Census of Manufactures*, issues for the respective years; for 1976, *Country Business Patterns* (Washington DC, US Government Printing Office, 1978) (processed). Sources gathered and elaborated by Servet Mutlu (see note 13).

[a]Includes accounting machines as well (SIC 3571).

Table 2.9 Location of plants of the main American computing equipment manufacturers

Company	1966 Location		Employment code[1]	1978 Location	
IBM	Burlington[a]	VT	D	*Computers*	
	Endicott[b]	NY	E	Endicott[d]	NY
	Kingston[b]	NY	E	Kingston	NY
	Lexington	KY	D	Poughkeepsie[d]	NY
	Poughkeepsie[b]	NY	E	Brooklyn	NY
	Rochester[e]	MN	D	Burlington[d]	MA
	San Jose[d]	CA	D		
				Small information	
				handling systems	
				and associated	
				peripheral equipment	
				Boca Raton[d]	FL
				Rochester	MN
				Menlo Park[e]	CA
				Peripherals	
				San Jose[d]	CA
				Los Angeles[e]	CA
				Los Gatos[e]	CA
				Boulder[d]	CO
				Endicott[e]	NY
				Kingston[e]	NY
				Mohawsic[e]	NY
				Poughkeepsie[e]	NY
				Burlington[e]	MA
				Gaithesburg[e]	MD
				Manassas	VI
				Raleigh[d]	NC
				Tucson[d]	AZ
				Federal systems	
				Owega[d]	NY
				Manassas[d]	VI
				Gaitherburg[d]	MD
				Houston[f]	TX
				Huntsville[f]	AL
				Cape Kennedy[f]	FL
				Westlake[f]	CA
				Atlantic City[f]	NJ
				Morris Plains[f]	NJ
				Components	
				Burlington[d]	VT
				Manassas[d]	VI
				East Fishkill[d]	NY
				Endicott	NY

Table 2.9   Continued

	1966		Employment code[1]	1978	
Company	Location			Location	
Burroughs[h]	Detroit	MI	D	*Computers*	
	Paoli[d]	PA	B	Santa Barbara	CA
	Pasadena[d]	CA	D	Pasadena	CA
	Plainfield[c]	NY	C	Proctor	
	Plymouth	MI	E	Fredyfifrin	PA
				Dowington	PA
				Plymouth[g]	
				Peripherals	
				Tireman	MI
				Westlake	CA
				Federal systems	
				Paoli	PA
				Components	
				Carlsbad	CA
				Hollywood	CA
Control Data	Cambridge[c]	MN	A	*Computers*	
Corp.	Chatsworth[a]	CA	A	Minneapolis	MN
(CDC)	La Jolla[a]	CA	B	St Paul	MN
	Minneapolis[b]	MN	D		
	Philadelphia	PA	B	*Peripherals*	
	Rockville[a]	MN	B	Campton	KY
	St Paul	MN	D	Washington	DC
	Spring Grove[c]	MN	A	Minneapolis	MN
	Warren[a]	Mi	B		
General	Phoenix	AZ		(exited in 1970)	
Electric	Palo Alto[e]	CA			
Honeywell	Brighton	MA	D	*Computers*	
	Denver	CO	C	Brighton[d]	MA
	Lawrence	MA		Bilterica	MA
	Lowell	MA		Lawrence[d]	MA
				Phoenix[d]	AZ
				Santa Clara	CA
				(microprocessors)	
				Peripheral equipment	
				Northboro	MA
				Lawrence	MA
				Components	
				Santa Clara	CA

Table 2.9   Continued

Company	1966 Location		Employment code[1]	1978 Location	
National	Dayton[b]	OH	E	*Computers*	
Cash	Hawthorne[b]	CA	E	San Diego	CA
Register	Ithaca[a]	NY	D	Wichita[g]	KS
(NCR)				Columbia[g]	SC
				Terminals and subsystems	
				General Purpose Terminals	
				Ithaca	NY
				Retail Terminals	
				Cambridge	OH
				Millsboro	DE
				Financial Terminals	
				Dayton	OH
RCA	Camdem	NY	E	(exited in 1971)	
	Palm Beach Gardens	FL	D		
	Van Nuys	CA	D		
Sperry-Rand	Blue Bell	PA	D	*Computers*	
	Elmira[a]	NY	D	Roseville	MN
	Long Island City	NY	D	St Paul	MN
	St Paul	MN	D	Bristol	TN
	Utica	NY	D	*Small business systems and peripherals*	
				Bristol	TN
				Salt Lake City	UT
				Irvine	CA
Sperry-Rand				*Peripherals and memory systems*	
				Cupertino	CA
				San Jose	CA
				Santa Clara	CA
				Sunnyvale	CA
				Federal systems	
				Clearwater	FL

[a]Only products belonging to SIC 35712 manufactured.
[b]Products of both SIC 35711 and 35712 manufactured.

early as 1972, in spite of the early dominance of New York and Minneapolis–St Paul in the computer industry. We also find a rapid growth of the computer industry in Massachusetts in the 20-year span between 1956 (location quotient 0.37) and 1976 (location quotient 3.81). The industry's development in Arizona and Florida is also striking, while Texas does not perform as well in computers as it does in semiconductors. While Minnesota maintains its significant share of the industry, New York's declines over time, probably because of the worldwide decentralization pattern of IBM. What is the significance of these data?

New York actually means IBM. It emphasizes the characteristics of this firm as a global company, constructing its own environment and inter-linking its different locations. The original reason for the location of IBM in New York can be traced back to the early nature of the firm's operations. Because early IBM machines were so expensive, and computer knowledge so rare, the machines were leased to businesses, with IBM providing service, maintenance, and repair. This meant that close proximity to the large concentration of business and accounting firms in New York was crucial at the beginning of the firm's history. Later, when IBM had achieved domination of the computer market, displacing the initial leader Remington-Rand (makers of the Univac-1, the first commercial computer delivered to the US Census Bureau in 1951) cash-shortage problems (linked to the leasing nature of the business) led to its decision to concentrate most of its production in the facilities it already owned, to avoid new expenditure in plant building. Because of the vertical integration of research and production functions within the firm, and the proprietary nature of its innovation, no industrial milieu developed locally around IBM in suburban New York.

The emergence of a major center of the computer industry in Minneapolis–St Paul, Minnesota, can be likened to the isolated development of semiconductor production in Dallas around Texas Instruments' pioneering activity. The origins of both Remington-Rand (later Sperry-Rand, and since 1986 Unisys), and Control Data can be traced back to a group of particularly

---

cComponents and products belonging to 357112 manufactured.
dHas both laboratories and manufacturing facilities.
eHas only laboratories.
fOperations.
gMinicomputers.
hCirca 1975.
iEmployment code: A: under 100 employees; B: 100–499; C: 500–999; D: 1,006–4,999; E: 5,000 and over.

Sources: For 1966, Fortune, Plant and Product Directory, 1966, Vol. II (1966); Wickham Skinner and David C.D. Rogers, Manufacturing Policy in the Electronics Industry (Homewood, Il, Richard Irwin, Inc., 1968), pp. 109–21; Company Annual Reports: IBM, Employment Fact Sheet, various issues; Burroughs Corporation, Burroughs Corporate Management Systems (Detroit, 1973); Burroughs in Brief (circa 1978); CDC, Committee on Corporate Social Responsibility, Our Corporation's Contributions to Solving Social Needs (1972); CDC, Contact, 3, 9 (August 1977). Sources gathered and elaborated by Servet Mutlu (see note 13).

skilled Navy engineers who created a firm after World War II: Engineering Research Associates. They set up in St Paul because through their Navy contacts they obtained financial support and infrastructural facilities from a businessman in that city. This is not to say that the location of information-technology producers is totally accidental. For instance, a key element in the development of the computer industry in the Twin Cities, founded on this initial technological basis, was the ability of the University of Minnesota to upgrade its engineering and computer sciences programs, and to provide locally the necessary personnel for the industry, overcoming the limitations of a location not outstandingly attractive measured against the traditional image standards for "quality of life." Also, Minneapolis had a long industrial tradition in miniaturization associated with the manufacture of hearing devices; and there was a penny stock market which helped to raise capital for the new companies.[25] The relative isolation of the Minnesota computer seedbed allowed companies (particularly Rand) to enjoy the lack of competition in the *local* labor market for skilled engineers and technicians, while still working within a large, diversified *national* labor market, to which they were selling a transportation- and cost-insensitive product.

As the industry grew and became more competitive, particularly with the introduction of microcomputers in the 1970s, it expanded to take in additional locations, many of which coincided with the preferred locations of semiconductors manufacturing. Again, the major exception was Minnesota, which took the course of further specialization in computers, with the major development of, among others, Cray, the leading manufacturer in super-computers. By as early as 1976 California accounted for about one-third of total US employment in computers manufacturing, with Silicon Valley alone providing about 12 per cent. In the meantime, New York – in other words, IBM – which in 1958 accounted for 38 per cent of total computer-based employment, had fallen in the ratings to offer only 9.6 per cent in 1976. Furthermore, the majority of computer employment in California, particularly in Silicon Valley, is made up of non-production workers, thus concentrating in a few areas the upper tier of the industry. Massachusetts also enjoyed a tremendous expansion in computer manufacturing, increasing its share of total employment from 1.6 percent in 1958 to 12 percent in 1976.[26] Texas and Arizona, on the other hand, leading states in semiconductors employment, lagged behind in the development of their computer industry, emphasizing their mixed character as states with cheap technical labor, and new high-technology centers, the latter feature being still far from dominant. While some of the new locations of the computer industry that emerged during the 1970s seemed to be directly geared toward aerospace and military markets (San Diego, Florida), the main factors that appeared to have formed its locational pattern in the growth period were:

(1) The vertical integration of semiconductor manufacturers, linking the two industries spatially, particularly after the development of the micro-

processor in 1971.[27] In the 1980s, for instance, both Silicon Valley and Route 128 have larger numbers of jobs in the computer industry (both hardware and software) than in semiconductors.

(2) The growing dependence of the industry on the availability of engineers and computer scientists.

(3) The existence of a milieu of innovation, based on the exchange of information and personnel, in areas originally organized around semi-conductors production.

While these factors were leading the computer industry toward concentration in certain areas offering access to technological information and skilled labor, other elements were working toward its worldwide decentralization. Unlike semiconductors, the computer industry decentralized part of its production from the very beginning, in search of markets rather than of cheap labor. IBM set up shop in Europe as early as the 1950s, and most other companies followed as soon as their resources enabled them to do so. Within specific countries, IBM, and other computer companies, located in semi-peripheral regions to take advantage of cheaper labor and government support for regional development – Scotland in the UK, the Midi in France.[28]

A pattern seems to emerge which is distinctive of the computer industry: concentration of research and innovation in a few centers, often vertically integrated with other electronics industries; worldwide markets, insensitive to transportation costs, penetrated by setting up local production facilities to establish a direct relationship to the clients and circumvent trade tariffs; location of assembly plants in areas with cheap technical labor relatively close to some major market. Again, as in the case of the technological origins of semiconductors technology at Bell Laboratories, it has to be noticed that the first industrial milieu of the computer industry did not develop around the pioneering research institution, in this case the University of Pennsylvania, where the first computer was produced for the Army in 1946. Though Pennsylvania does have a computer industry, as much as Texas, for instance, does, it never reached the level of other areas, such as Minnesota, Massachusetts, or California, where scientific innovation is embodied in a network of business organizations. Information-technology production, while being a science-based industry, *remains an industry*, and can only be understood as such. It is the combination of management and research that is reshaping the industrial world. Computers manufacturing does not exactly replicate the spatial distribution of the semiconductors industry; but its locational logic does.

Is Knowledge Placeless? Computer Software, Genetic Engineering, and Beyond

The computer software industry is the fastest growing information-technology sector (with under $1 billion sales in the late 1970s, it is expected to reach 20 billion by 1990), and the ultimate expression of scientific labor-intensive activity. It sells pure knowledge, fabrication being reduced to the minimum material expression, and in theory, therefore, could be an absolutely footloose activity. Yet, according to one of the few locational studies on the industry, [29] by the mid-1980s about 20 percent of employees of all 4,000 firms producing software in the US at that time was concentrated in California; and it was estimated that software employment in that state would increase by 230 percent in the decade 1985–95. Other states with a disproportionately high share of software production are Massachusetts, Texas, and Washington. Within California, although greater Los Angeles accounted for the largest proportion of total employment (about 50 percent of software jobs in California) because of the sheer size of the area, the San Francisco Bay area had the highest relative concentration of these jobs, with over 35 percent of the state total, having increased its leadership during the 1970s. And yet, most of the California software firms interviewed in the study declared that proximity to the market was not the major concern for their location. What seems to account for the location of software firms, particularly for the most technologically advanced of them, are the social and cultural characteristics of the area, in terms valued by their professional employees. According to the study cited:

Eleven out of twenty-eight interviewees said that lifestyle is of major importance. Many firms located where their founders have lived for some time before founding the firm. Many of these firms, plus some others, located where the lifestyle choices of prospective good employees converged with preferences of the firm's founders. These firms said explicitly, and many implied, that they located near available good employees. Another three mentioned "creative atmosphere" as a factor for a full range of business and cultural reasons. [30]

Nevertheless, as argued above, the notion of lifestyle is ambiguous and subjective. Lifestyle for whom? And why is a "desirable" lifestyle associated with some cities or regions rather than with others? Standard preconceptions immediately flash glittering images of sunny California, the Arizona desert, or a daring sail across Seattle Sound. Yet it is very doubtful that the southern charm of New Orleans could attract information-technology production in substantial terms, or that the spectacularly beautiful Ozarks region will ever become a major center of microelectronics. The case of the software industry gives us the chance to try to understand what "lifestyle" or "quality of life" mean in this precise context. The important point is that the reference to such subjective preferences as a determinant of the industry's location underscores the crucial importance of highly skilled scientific labor for the existence of the industry itself. Without software inventors and writers prepared to live in a particular location there would be no such industry. Here the old notion of "milieu" seems to be analytically useful. New York has always been the center of the writing and publishing industry, as Los Angeles kept its early lead in the film production business. Originally, New York's publishing success relied on its vibrant, socially diverse, big-city atmosphere, which attracted intellectuals and creators. Los Angeles was the biggest city with year-round good weather for shooting film. But in each case the original, historical rationale became less important than the milieu that blossomed and expanded over time. The more an industry depends upon information-trained, information-oriented labor, the more this labor itself depends for its development on its continuing relationship with a creative milieu able to generate new ideas and new techniques through the interaction of elements spatially clustered in its inner network. This is why the image of the wired software writer, working in his or her mountain refuge, connected to Silicon Valley over the phone line, is fundamentally a bright advertising spot from futurologists. Software production is heavily dependent on the existence of a consolidated milieu of electronics research and manufacturing, where exchange of ideas and of people is far more important than the beauty of the environment. Once a highly paid, highly educated labor pool is concentrated in a place, its members generally take care of keeping the place beautiful and of improving the social and cultural quality of the area, helped by the protective barrier of real estate prices. And even when the quality of life deteriorates, advanced electronics in general, and software writing in particular, continue to concentrate in the same areas because of the invaluable access to the milieu that generates both the information and the job opportunities. The very basis of computer software production location is an industrial research milieu, generated by an advanced electronics center, often connected to major universities, in the vicinity of a major metropolitan area containing corporate headquarters, around which business services develop.

The connection between science and industry is even more evident in what some experts like to call the "next industrial revolution:" genetic engineering.[31] It is too early to assess the potential of this field and even more problematic to understand its future connection to a new form of science-based manufacturing. In 1977, only 18,489 workers in the US were employed in "manufacturing biological products" (SIC 2831), and only a tiny proportion of these were related to genetic engineering. In 1983, the top 50 American biotechnology companies employed only 6,000 people.[32] We are witnessing the infancy of an industry that could become a major economic force.[33] In 1987, biotechnology in the US is a $3.2 billion industry.[34] The US Office of Technology Assessment predicted that between 1981 and the end of the century, genetic engineering could replace manufactured products worth $27 billion. Dr Glick, President of Genex Corporation, asserts that the market will in fact be worth around $40 billion by the year 2000. When one of the leading genetic engineering firms, Genentech, went public in 1980, its founders, most of them former academic scientists, instantly became multimillionaires. Major pharmaceutical, medical, and energy companies, as well as Wall Street firms, are actively searching for new potential investments in the field. Because the industry is still young, yet already established on solid commercial ground, high returns are expected in a market which still offers relatively low financial barriers to entry. The progression of the industry has been very fast in the last decade. In 1977 only three new biotechnology firms were started up; in 1978 there were 6, and the figure rose to 9 in 1979, 18 in 1980, and 33 in 1981.[35] During the 1980s, the new specialist firms were joined by large pharmaceutical and chemical companies which started to invest in biotechnology, either in their own research departments or by absorbing or contracting with smaller, innovative firms, and by 1987 Cetus' *Bioscan* database identified 512 biotechnology plants in the US.[36] Beyond the smokescreen of science fiction fantasies, biotechnology is becoming a major information-technology industry. The core of this industry, and the truly revolutionary technology, lies in genetic engineering.

The development process of this industry and its spatial pattern are, interestingly enough, very similar to those that characterized the most dynamic firms in semiconductors, computers, and software, namely, small businesses starting as spin-offs of major universities and medical research facilities. While the scientific origins of genetic engineering can be traced back to 1953, when the discovery of the first model of DNA was made by Crick and Watson at Cambridge University, UK, the development of the industry took place only after the discovery in 1973 by Herbert Boyer from the University of California at San Francisco and by Stanley Cohen from Stanford University, on the basis of research by Stanford biologist Paul Berg, of the techniques of gene-splicing, enabling the production of recombinant DNA. However, both the development of this science, and that of its industrial applications, were possible only because of substantial Federal government funding from the National Science Foundation and from the National Institute of Health to medical centers and universities. In 1953 Federal funding accounted for 56.9 percent of all basic research in biotechnology; this proportion increased to 66.5 percent in 1984, when over 48 percent of this went to universities.[37] Thus, the majority of the new companies leading research and production in genetic engineering originated as spin-offs from faculty members and researchers associated with the research centers that were (and are) in the forefront of this scientific field: University of California at San Francisco, Stanford University, Harvard, MIT, Cal Tech in Pasadena, California, Cold Spring Harbor Laboratories in Long Island, New York, University of California at Berkeley, and the National Institute of Health in Washington DC. The three leading firms in the developing stage of the new industry certainly fit the pattern: Genentech (south San Francisco), and Cetus (Berkeley, later moved to nearby Emeryville) were spin-offs from the Stanford and University of California scientific networks: Biogen, with its headquarters in Geneva and its main research activities in Massachusetts, was founded by Nobel Prize-winner Walter Gilbert, a Harvard professor of biology. Most of the new companies have clustered around the Boston–Cambridge area, in the San Francisco Bay area, in the New York–New Jersey area (linked to Cold Spring Harbor, to Princeton University, and to the major hospitals in New York); and around the Washington DC–Baltimore area, closely bound up with the national medical facilities located there.[38] Of all biotechnology companies in the US, 24.4 percent are located in California, 10.6 percent in Massachusetts, and 15.9 percent in New York–New Jersey.[39] Table 2.10, constructed by Hall, Bornstein, Grier, and Webber[40] provides an analysis of the locational pattern of biotechnology firms in the top seven metropolitan areas which account for 44 percent of all biotechnology operations and 60 percent of the firms founded after 1970 (these are assumed to be the most strongly science-based). The location quotients for these areas show their capacity to attract the new industry on the basis of their scientific potential. Thus, the higher location quotients are for Trenton PMSA, which includes Princeton; for Washington DC, which includes various national medical research facilities; for the San Francisco and Oakland PMSAs, which include the University of California campuses at San Francisco and Berkeley; and for the San Diego MSA, linked to the advanced biological research of the University of California at San Diego.

In fact, most of the new companies were directly created by Faculty members. A 1984 survey of 20 percent of all biotechnology companies found 345 scholars represented in these companies. Fifteen members of MIT's biology Faculty were found to have created six different companies.[41] Edward Blakely, in his study on biotechnology in California[42] reports the close links between universities, scientists, and the new biotechnology firms, with northern California accounting for 60 percent of all such firms in the state on the basis of its strong university connections. Firms in northern California are clustered around Palo Alto (site of Stanford), and in the East Bay (around Berkeley).

There is, then, ample evidence that, in the case of biotechnology and genetic engineering, universities and other scientific institutions, such as major research-oriented hospitals, are the principal determinants of location. To be more precise, they are in fact the "mining sites:" the name of the new mineral is knowledge. Universities, Harvard for example, tried to become directly involved in the new and profitable business, but were prevented from doing so by the majority of the Faculty, fearful of the dangers that commercial considerations might interfere in the conduct of scientific research. Nevertheless, business continued as usual for individual Faculty members in all research universities, who more and more often were trying to transform their discoveries into industrial development and personal gain. This evolution illustrates the increasingly intimate connection between advanced university

Table 2.10 US Biotech plants, leading metropolitan areas, 1987

	Total manufacturing plants		Biotech Plants		Post-1971 Biotech plants		Pre-1971 Biotech plants		Location quotient		
	(1982) No.	% of US total	No.	% of US total	No.	% of US total	No.	% of US total	All Biotech plants	Post-1971 plants	Pre-1971 plants
New York CMSA	39100	10.9	74	14.5	29	10.9	5	29.4	1.3	1.0	2.7
New York PMSA	19534	5.5	22	4.3	7	2.6	2	11.8	0.8	0.5	2.2
Newark PMSA	4175	1.2	17	3.3	8	3.0	1	5.9	2.8	2.6	5.0
San Francisco CMSA	10526	2.9	65	12.7	42	15.8	2	11.8	4.3	5.4	4.0
Oakland PMSA	2883	0.8	21	4.1	13	4.9	1	5.9	5.1	6.1	7.3
San Francisco PMSA	3095	0.9	25	4.9	17	6.4		0.0	5.6	7.4	0.0
San Jose PMSA	3326	0.9	16	3.1	11	4.2	1	5.9	3.4	4.5	6.3
Boston–Lawrence NECMA	6798	1.9	41	8.0	28	10.6	1	5.9	4.2	5.6	3.1
Philadelphia CMSA	8700	2.4	32	6.3	19	7.2	0	0.0	2.6	3.0	0.0
Philadelphia PMSA	7495	2.1	17	3.3	12	4.5		0.0	1.6	2.2	0.0
Trenton PMSA	454	0.1	11	2.1	6	2.3		0.0	16.9	17.9	0.0
Washington MSA	2388	0.7	24	4.7	17	6.4	2	11.8	7.0	9.6	17.6
San Diego MSA	2522	0.7	18	3.5	13	4.9		0.0	5.0	7.0	0.0
Seattle–Tacoma CMSA	3669	1.0	14	2.7	10	3.8		0.0	2.7	3.7	0.0
Seattle PMSA	3077	0.9	13	2.5	10	3.8		0.0	3.0	4.4	0.0
USA total	358061	100.0	512	100.0	265	100.0	17	100.0	1.0	1.0	1.0

Source: Hall, Bornstein, Grier and Webber (see note 36).

research and the hottest stocks in the market.[43] Scientific knowledge, at least in some key areas, is now clearly a directly productive force and the source of major profits. In other words, science itself has become an industry.

Thus, in this the purest example of an information technology industry, we observe that the key element in the development of genetic engineering is its relationship to a scientific milieu; a milieu which, in this particular case, itself developed an initial market through government-sponsored contracts to health research institutions.[44] This has clearly been the case in its early stages; will we observe a similar process in the more mature phases of the industry? There are reasonable grounds for hypothesizing that this will be the case for research laboratories, which will either be located in the vicinity of a national or international research community, or absorbed into the closed world of some pharmaceutical or agricultural giant, ready to form a kind of "Bio-Bell Laboratories." The fabrication and diffusion of the products generated by this industry will have no specific space. Its impact will be felt across a broad spectrum of manufacturing and agricultural activities; there will also be applications in energy and, above all, in health services and medical sciences. The real output of genetic engineering, as for electronics, is less a product than a process. In the latter case, it is the process of symbolic information; in the former, the process of information inscribed in living matter.

From specifically located seedbeds of information-technology production emerges a new, pervasive, placeless logic of industrial activity, transforming the economy, the workplace, and the consumer markets, without attaching itself to a particular location. New information technologies organize the space of production along a hierarchy of activities and functions, made up of *networks* and *flows*, which takes the social division between intellectual and manual labor to its extreme limit. To understand this process, whose empirical manifestations we have surveyed without actually explaining, we need a more systematic, explicit, analytical framework to enable us to unveil the logic underlying the formation of the new industrial space.

Investigating the Spatial Pattern of Information-Technology Industries: An Analytical Framework

As argued in chapter 1, the core of the current process of technological change lies in the invention, development, and use of new information technologies. Accordingly, the industries producing information-technology devices are the ones responsible for the new historical trends in the process of restructuring industrial location. Information-technology industries constitute a specific form of productive organization, deriving their specificity from the distinctiveness of their raw material (information), and from the singularity of their product (process-oriented devices with applications across the entire spectrum of human activity).[45] The analytical perspective put forward here contends that the specific spatial pattern of information-technology industries is the result of these two fundamental characteristics. This is not to deny the importance of other factors, such as profit-seeking as the ultimate principle of any capitalist corporation, in determining spatial behavior. Rather, it is to highlight the technological means by which such profit can be obtained as the distinctive feature of the new industries which sets them apart from the old line manufacturing industries. In other words, technology mediates the relationship between the economic rationality embodied in the firm and the attributes of a given space, thus determining locational patterns and the resulting spatial structure.

Let us explore the specific connections between these two fundamental characteristics of information-technology industries and their spatial requirements. First, the reliance on information of these industries means that their basic factor of production is the quality of labor; more precisely, of their scientific and technical labor.[46] Furthermore, this labor requires an organizational environment in which its innovative capacity can be utilized to the full. There are two levels to this organizational environment: the micro-environment of the firm or institution in which the process of innovation occurs; and the macro-environment formed by the network of interactive relationships among innovative organizations and individuals that generate added value in the process of information creation as an outcome of the interaction between the producers.[47] We will call this macro-environment a *milieu*, understood as a specific set of social relationships of production and management, based upon some common instrumental goals, generally sharing a work culture, and generating a high level of organizational synergy.[48] If this analysis is correct, then the spatial logic of information-technology industries will be determined in the first place by the location of innovative labor *and* by the territorial conditions for the formation of innovative milieux.

The second major characteristic of the new industries, namely their production of *process-oriented devices*,[49] has two major spatial consequences. To some extent they contradict each other, underlining the complexity of the spatial logic we are trying to analyze. On the one hand, since the value of the industry's output depends largely on the processing capability embodied in the product, regardless of transportation costs or of general conditions of production, information-technology industries can locate almost anywhere, provided that they keep their access to the sources of innovation, namely innovative labor and a supportive environment.[50] On the other hand, since the effectiveness of the processing devices depends on their capacity to adapt to the users' needs, the general trend in information technology is toward customized devices, and consequently its spatial logic will increasingly depend upon the location of its users. This does not necessarily mean that the industry will have to locate close to its customers: for instance, if an industry has a worldwide market for its customized product, its main locational constraint will be good access to a telecommunications network and to air transportation.[51] If a firm works instead for a very specific client requiring continuous interaction on the use, maintenance, and specification of the processing device (as is frequently the case in defense-related information technologies), then spatial proximity does become a locational requirement. Thus, what seems to characterize the industry is not so much a general, footloose indifference to location as a greater dependence on the spatial characteristics of its markets, because of the intimate relationship between the product of the industry and the process of its users.[52]

A third fundamental spatial implication stems from the *combined* effect of these two basic characteristics: it is the very distinct *internal segmentation of the production process*.[53]

On the one hand, the production of information can be separated from its material support. From this follows a sharp division of labor within the industry, leading to very different requirements in type of labor, and therefore, at least potentially, to different locations for each type, or labor "pool." For instance, in the case of semiconductors manufacturing, so widely discussed in the literature, there are five distinct operations, which can easily be differentiated in time and space[54]: research and design of the circuit, which requires, in general, advanced research engineers and scientists; mask-making, that is, engineering the circuit that will go into the chip and reducing it through lithography, an operation requiring skilled engineers and tech-nicians; wafer fabrication (diffusion), a process in which the circuits receive their material support in the form of wafers which undergo a series of chemical treatments before being divided into individual chips, a process that requires skilled manual workers and quality-control supervision; assembly of the chips to form electronic components (integrated circuits or discrete semiconductor devices), a routine, labor-intensive operation, that can either be performed by unskilled workers or easily automated; finally, testing, a capital-intensive, widely automated process, the main problem of which is quality control. The more pronounced in the electronics industry is the shift from standardized production to custom-designed devices, the more highly skilled, state-of-the art operations increase their strategic importance in the overall production process; yet in all cases, and in all products of the industry, there is a need for material production. This combination leads to very sharply differing labor requirements for each stage of the work process, and allows for separate and distinct organizational environments for each operation. Although in some other information-technology industries the separation between different phases in the production process is less clear than in semiconductors, there remain, as a general trend, basic divisions between knowledge-based research and design, advanced manufacturing, unskilled assembly work, and testing. Some industries, such as computer software and genetic engineering, are almost purely information-production processes, to the point where the very notion of manufacturing loses meaning. Other industries, on the contrary, retain a strong component of skilled factory work; this is the case in robotics and in automated machine-tool industries.[55] In all cases, it is the specific combination of creating information-processing devices and fabricating their material support that determines the process of production in the industry and therefore its labor requirements, which constitute a major determining factor of its location pattern.

Given this strict internal division of labor within the industry, the process-oriented characteristic of its product allows for the spatial differentiation of the various distinct production functions. This is in the first place because of the low sensitivity of the industry to traditional factors influencing location, such as transportation costs or access to bulky raw materials, which makes possible a multilocational pattern in which each production function maximizes its own particular relationship to the spatial conditions of production (particularly labor) or to the location of its markets.[56]

Secondly, information-technology industries are the pioneers in using their products in their own processes of production and management, thereby taking advantage of breakthroughs in automation, telecommunications, and miniaturization of components, to enable themselves to maintain the functional unity of production and management without requiring spatial proximity between the different segments of the organization.[57]

From these three fundamental characteristics of information-technology industries stem four basic spatial processes which I contend to be distinctive of these industries in reflecting a new form of production and a new type of product. These four processes are:

(1) A sharp spatial division of labor within the industry, with each phase of production having distinct labor and functional requirements that translate into specific and different spatial manifestations.

(2) The domination of the industry's technical, social, and spatial hierarchy by the functions of information generation, structured around milieux of innovation which possess specific spatial attributes and are concentrated in a few, exclusive locations.

(3) A process of decentralization of different production functions, reproducing the hierarchical pattern of the industry's internal structure and of its spatial logic.

(4) With the exception of the higher-level innovative milieux, information-technology industries are characterized by extreme flexibility in their actual locations. This flexibility is the result of the close relationship of the industry with its markets, under the conditions of continuous variation in the location of those markets.

The trend toward customized production and the pervasiveness of the industry's products combine to favor a general pattern of centralized generation of technological innovation and decentralized application of the products embodying the processes resulting from such technological discoveries. Figure 2.2 attempts to represent schematically the system of relationships proposed in this analytical framework.

Information-technology industries do not, then, share one single locational pattern; yet they do collectively express a distinctive spatial logic, in a rather

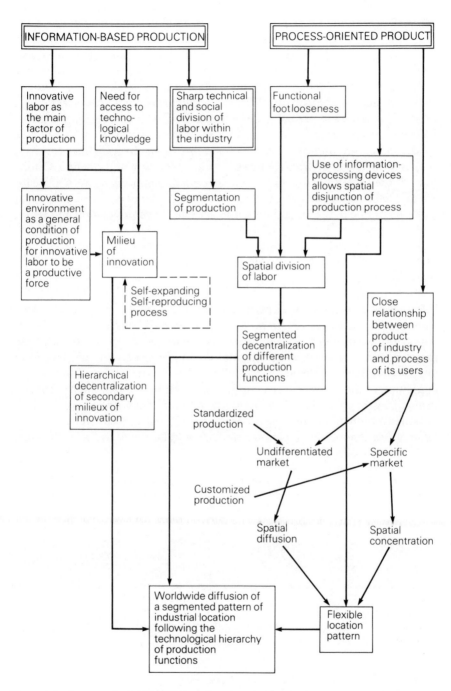

Figure 2.2 System of relationships between the characteristics of information-technology manufacturing and the industry's spatial pattern

complex process of interaction between their fundamental characteristics and the basic processes of the economic structure. The actual location of information-technology manufacturing will depend on the relationship between the specific functions of the industry, along the lines proposed, and the attributes of a given space. If this analytical framework is of any value, it should be able to explain why different segments of the industry are where they are, as well as to predict general trends in their future spatial dynamics. Keeping these goals in mind, we will try to address separately each one of the spatial processes outlined here, confronting their hypothetical logic, as proposed in this analytical framework, with the available evidence. On the basis of the results obtained for each specific spatial process, we will finally attempt to bring together all the elements in a broader perspective which may yield the profile of the emerging relationship between production and space.

The Spatial Division of Labor in Information-technology Manufacturing

Information-technology industries are characterized by sharp distinctions among different stages of the production process.[58] This internal differentiation results in a distinctly polarized occupational structure, with a high proportion of engineers, scientists, and technicians, a sizable proportion of unskilled workers, and a relatively small number of skilled manual workers, in opposition to the pyramidal structure of occupations in traditional manufacturing.[59] Although table 2.11 does not differentiate between skilled and unskilled production workers, it does show the substantial over-representation of professionals and technicians in comparison with average manufac-

Table 2.11   High-technology occupational structure: selected areas

	All US		Massachu-setts	Silicon Valley	Santa Cruz	
	High-tech (%)	Manu-facturing (%)	High-tech (%)	High-tech (%)	Manu-facturing (%)	High-tech (%)
Management	11	7	9	13	7	9
Professional/ Technical[a]	29	12	34	43	14	32
Production	48	70	40	30	68	50
Clerical	12	11	17	14	11	9

[a]Sales workers are included under professional/technical
Sources: Gordon and Kimball, table VI (see note 3); Carnoy (see note 60).

turing industries.[60] In addition it shows a significantly higher proportion of technical labor in the areas with a higher level of technological sophistication, Silicon Valley and Massachusetts. This polarized occupational structure is also characterized by divisions of gender and ethnicity, with women and ethnic minorities being significantly over-represented in unskilled production jobs.

The internal differentiation of the work process, and thus of labor requirements, in information-technology industries, results in a correspondingly sharp spatial differentiation of the various stages of the production process.[61] Higher-level functions tend to be concentrated in certain privileged locations, attracting to those areas the upper tier of the labor force, while assembly functions, employing unskilled labor, are scattered over more and varied locations. Advanced manufacturing occupies an intermediate position, generally clustered around innovation functions in the early stages of the industry, later decentralizing to specific locations on the basis of isolated pools of skilled manual workers, in areas not too far away from the firm's innovative center. This pattern applies to both units of production within a given firm, and to different firms, with their respective locations following the technological hierarchy between the firms. Spatial differentiation occurs among regions, countries, metropolitan areas, and even among specific locations within the same metropolitan area. The technical and social division of labor in information-technology industries not only allows for their spatial segmentation, but actually causes it. Furthermore, it is my hypothesis that the spatial logic of each different segment of the industry not only differs from, but contradicts, that of the others. In other words, the spatial characteristics required by each stage of production and by each type of labor force tend to be reciprocally exclusive, leading to extremely different spatial manifestations of information-technology manufacturing. The new industrial structure will be characterized by locational sprawl, distinct spatial segments, with functional interconnections between the elements of the structure maintained by the means of communication links. Before elaborating on the consequences of this spatial logic, let us examine the evidence supporting the hypothesis of the spatial division of labor in information-technology industries.

First, we will try to assess whether there exists a spatial differentiation among high-technology industries according to their specific occupational levels: namely, are high-technology industries characterized by higher technical levels in their occupational profile disproportionately concentrated in some areas? Amy Glasmeier has tested this hypothesis by conducting a statistical analysis of the distribution of nine occupational categories within five key high-technology industries among the 50 states, in 1977 and 1980.[62] The industries studied were chemicals, non-electrical equipment, electrical equipment, transportation equipment, and professional and scientific instruments. According to Glasmeier:

The results of the analysis for all five industries indicate that the hypothesized spatial division of labor is confirmed in the occupational distribution of employment in high-tech industries. Concentrations of technical, administrative, and professional workers, are present in similar places, while production workers are found in different locations. In general, these results confirm the hypothesis that workers engaged in design and prototype activities are spatially associated with professional and administrative employees . . . The sample high-tech industries also exhibit the tendency for assembly workers to be segmented from both production and technical workers . . . Service workers are found in relatively constant proportions across locations. High-technology industries clearly exhibit a spatial division of labor. States with high proportions of technical and administrative jobs have low proportions of production workers.[63]

Secondly, what is the evidence in support of my contention that there is a spatial differentiation among functions within the same industry, according to the technological level of these functions? Scott and Angel have provided the most accurate empirical test to date of this hypothesis, by comparing the structure and behavior of semiconductor firms located in Silicon Valley to that of firms located in other areas.[64] The group of firms located in Silicon Valley, they found, tended to have a higher percentage of employees engaged in R&D activities, as well as to produce semiconductor wafers with a larger average diameter (an indicator of technological sophistication in the production process). In addition, Scott and Angel performed a similar analysis for two different groups of semiconductor companies: discrete device producers and integrated circuit producers. In general, their earlier findings hold good only for the integrated circuit producers, meaning that the spatial hierarchy of production between Silicon Valley and other locations applies only in the technologically advanced segment of the industry. In other words, the more information-based an industry is, the clearer is the trend toward a hierarchical pattern of segmented location. A general summary of Scott and Angel's findings is presented in table 2.12. As they write:

The correlation coefficients forcefully corroborate our assessment of Silicon Valley as a center of research-intensive, and engineering-intensive forms of leading edge semiconductors production, and above all, complex unstandardized device production. Semiconductor production outside Silicon Valley is more likely to involve high-volume routinized manufacture of standardized integrated circuits and low-technology discrete devices.[65]

This analysis takes one step further the logic of the spatial division of labor in information-technology manufacturing. Not only are there different locations for different functions, but the spatial distribution of the industry follows a very discontinuous pattern, with the concentration of high-level functions in a few locations, most notably Silicon Valley in the case of semiconductors. On the other hand, less sophisticated functions are increasingly dispersed, both nationally and internationally. Yet this locational sprawl must be interpreted within the framework of the technical division of labor within the industry, as shown in maps 2.1 and 2.2, where integrated circuit plants are shown to follow a more concentrated and selective pattern of location than less technologically advanced discrete semiconductor devices.

Other studies of semiconductor manufacturing location at different points in time all reveal the same tendencies; in particular, research conducted by Michael Storper, by Anna Lee Saxenian, and by Servet Mutlu.[66] These studies show that, in addition to their inter-regional division of labor, information-technology industries also pioneered the new international division of labor. There is a vast research literature on this topic, showing how information-technology industries, particularly semiconductors, were among the first to divide their production process over a worldwide variety of locations.[67] Taking advantage of miniaturization, of the light weight of the devices produced, and of advances in air transportation and telecommunication networks, assembly operations in semiconductors and computers began to be relocated offshore in the early 1960s, particularly to cheap labor areas in south-east Asia, and later Mexico. While internationalization of production by multinational corporations was nothing new, the distinguishing feature of this phenomenon was the separation worldwide of the different individual operations of one particular production process within one firm, giving rise to the idea of the "world factory." Although some experts considered this process to be characteristic of the earlier stages of the industry, and expected widespread automation of assembly lines to lead to the "relocation back north" of most plants, most researchers disagree, for reasons we will discuss below. And indeed, the data for the past twenty years show an

Table 2.12   Percentage distribution of semiconductor establishments according to location and type

	Silicon Valley		Non-Silicon Valley		Total	
	Sample[a] (%)	Population[b] (%)	Sample (%)	Population (%)	Sample (%)	Population (%)
Discrete device producers	8.3	5.6	28.3	38.3	36.6	49.3
Integrated circuit producers	31.7	25.3	31.7	30.8	63.4	56.1
Total	40.0	30.9	60.0	69.1	100.0	100.0

[a]Sample of 60 establishments.
[b]The population consists of the 517 establishments (out of a total of 590) that were classifiable by type.
Source: Scott and Angel (see note 12).

increasing tendency for the production of US electronics firms to be located offshore.[68] Information-technology manufacturing is in fact spearheading the formation of a new hierarchical space of production, spread across the world, segmenting countries and differentiating locations, with the connections necessary to the economic and functional logic of the process maintained by the new means of communication. This new industrial space is represented by a variable geometry as firms, regions, and countries move up and down the technological ladder.

Spatial division of labor in these industries also affects labor sub-markets and plant location within individual metropolitan areas. Real estate prices and residential segregation create spatially distinct labor markets and work sub-cultures, as shown by Saxenian[69] and by Keller[70] for Silicon Valley, and by Storper[71] for the "ghetto–peasant worker" communities created in Oregon around decentralized electronics production facilities. Firms' research and design centers tend also to be spatially separate from the main production facility, even when they are in the same area. Yet with a continuous process of deeper spatial differentiation at the inter-regional and international levels taking place, there is a trend toward internal homogenization of technological production functions within each metropolitan area. For example, while what assembly work remains in Silicon Valley tends increasingly to be automated, gradually lowering the proportion of unskilled immigrant workers in its labor force (while employing increasing numbers of foreign *engineers*), the new industrial communities in the western United States resulting from decentralization, such as those analyzed by Storper in Oregon, tend increasingly to specialize in the middle-to-bottom end of the production process.

The reasons behind this strict spatial division of labor in information-technology industries seem to stem from three main factors:

(1) The development of new information technologies, focused on processes of programmable manufacturing and on transmission of information, creates the material conditions for the decentralized location pattern of the industries themselves. Miniaturization of devices means low weight and low transportation costs. Computer automation of manufacturing makes possible high-quality standardization of parts than can be assembled anywhere. Computer-aided flexible manufacturing enables production to be adjusted to market requirements without the different production functions being spatially proximate. Telecommunications and on-line information systems allow for coordination of management of spatially distant units. A dense air transportation network makes possible when necessary quick personal contacts, as well as shipments of equipment and output.

(2) Social control of labor has always been a major condition for the competitiveness of any industry, but it is even more important for information-technology industries whose fate depends on innovation and on the

appropriate timing of such innovation. Any major disturbance in the labor process will slow down the pace of innovation and could result in the firm's loss of its competitive edge. Given the sharp differentiation of the various segments of labor within the industry, processes of social control for each segment are correspondingly different, requiring distinct social spaces for their implementation. In other words, what helps to integrate the high-level engineers into the company's life and work is not necessarily what would be appropriate (or affordable) to achieve similar bonds for workers in isolated rural communities, for immigrants in the US, or for Third World women in offshore locations. Workers' integration into firms depends above all on work culture. In the case of information-technology industries, the differentiation of the labor process into distinct stages leads to a similar differentiation in work sub-cultures, and each of these is likely to be more effective when operating in a specific, isolated space.

(3) Finally, different functions of production and segments of labor in the industry exclude each other in spatial terms, because the upper level of the industry is so valuable, so unique, so irreplaceable, that the locations where such labor performs its functions tend to increase dramatically in quality, and even more in value and price, so becoming exclusive and ruling out the location there of lower-level functions and of strategically less important labor. The mechanisms at work in this process are, on the one hand, real estate prices, and on the other hand, residential and industrial zoning regulations. Local governments, supported by well-to-do residents and business groups (sometimes opposed to each other), tend to draw a restrictive line *vis-à-vis* the activities that are welcome in the privileged land around the high-level information-technology industrial centers. Once a given area of land is declared privileged, demand explodes while supply is limited. Thus, the market achieves the exclusion of lower-level workers – sometimes too fast, outpacing the gradual upgrading of the industrial complex. At the same time, in the less desirable areas, with a low-skilled labor force and scarce technological capabilities, real estate prices are low, representing no barrier to growth, and local governments strive to lure into their area industries labeled "high-technology," regardless of their true technological level. In this way, the spatial division of labor is self-reproductive and self-expansionary. Increasingly valuable spaces first segregate and later expel functions and people that are not worth the cost of keeping them in the gold mines of our technological age. As jobs and economic growth depend more and more upon the performance of high-technology industries, localities fighting for their survival try to compensate for their lack of technological skills by offering convenient conditions for the bottom end of the production process. Functional hierarchy and social segregation are fundamental features of the new industrial space.

The analysis presented here has considerable implications for the method

of investigating the relationship between information-technology manufacturing and the spatial structure of the industry. On the one hand, we cannot
establish any such relationship until we have decided which particular
functions of the industry we are considering, since each stage of the
production process has a specific pattern of location, sometimes contrary to
that of other stages. On the other hand, if there is one factor common to all
elements of the process of high-technology manufacturing, it is precisely
their spatial differentiation, along with the fact that their distinct locations are
functionally connected by a social and technological hierarchy. The process
of industrial decentralization of information-technology producers will tend
to reproduce this spatial hierarchy on a larger scale. We will now turn to
analyze the spatial pattern specific to each stage of production in the information-technology industries, focusing on the dynamics between concentration
and decentralization of their different functions.

Milieux of Innovation

The higher-level production functions of information-technology industries
are concentrated in a few selected areas which we will term *milieux of
innovation*.[72] By a milieu of innovation we understand a specific set of
relationships of production and management, based on a social organization
that by and large shares a work culture and instrumental goals aimed at
generating new knowledge, new processes, and new products. Although the
concept of milieu does not necessarily include a spatial dimension, I will
argue that, in the case of information-technology industries, spatial proximity
is a necessary material condition for the existence of such milieux, because of
the nature of interaction in the innovation process.

There are two different (albeit inter-related) questions concerning the
spatial dimension of innovative milieux: these concern their genesis and their
structure. That is, how and why they are formed in particular locations? and
why and how do they continue to function as specific units of production and
innovation?

In terms of the first question, that is, their coming into existence, the
informational milieux of innovation are not very different from other
industrial milieux of our recent past. They result from the spatio-temporal
convergence of the three fundamental elements of production: labor, capital,
and raw material.[73] The specific characteristics of the new industries result
from the specific characteristics of these three elements in this particular
case. Their raw material is information. Technical labor in these industries,
because of its unique capacity for symbol processing, will require special
methods of generation and reproduction. The nature of this industrial activity
will also influence the type of capital invested during the formative stage of
the innovative milieu: given the high risk of the investment, depending upon

relatively unpredictable technological discoveries, it will be either of a venture capital nature (although not necessarily managed by venture capitalists), expecting high returns, or capital invested on a long-term profit-seeking strategy by a major corporation or institution engaged in a quest for technological superiority, and able to afford a loss on the investment. Different sources of technological and scientific information, of scientific and technical labor, and of adequate capital supply, as well as the combination of all three elements, will determine the different forms taken by milieux of innovation and consequently, their location patterns.

The basic raw material on which the new industries work is innovative technological information. Such information can be found in four different types of organizational environments that are not mutually exclusive:

(1) Leading universities and higher education institutions.
(2) Government-sponsored R&D centers.
(3) Corporate R&D centers linked to technologically advanced large corporations.
(4) A network of R&D centers in an established industrial complex which collectively produce innovative research, creating the critical mass of knowledge necessary to become an autonomous source of generation of technological discovery. These complexes take two forms:
  (a) a traditional manufacturing complex that moves into information technology to keep pace with technological change, as is the case with the aerospace and defense industries;
  (b) the new industrial innovative milieux of information-technology producers, once they become established as such on the basis of any of the sources of information cited above.

The first condition for the development of information-technology industries is access to one of these sources of innovative information. Yet while this is naturally the fundamental condition of production for the new industries, it alone cannot account for the information of an innovative *industrial* milieu since, in principle, the diffusion and communication of science and technology do not require spatial proximity. Nevertheless, as we will see, the spatial dimension becomes an important material condition in linking the source of information to other key components of the production process, namely innovative labor and high-risk capital.

The second major element required for the formation of a milieu of innovation is a large pool of scientific and technical labor. It is important to note that this factor cannot be equated with the first one, access to information, even if information is most often embodied in labor, for there are situations in which one could exist without the other. Examples of this are an isolated research center without connection to a large labor market, such as Los Alamos or Sandia Laboratories in Albuquerque, New Mexico; or a large pool of good quality engineers with little access to companies or institutions able to generate major technological discoveries, such as may be found in some mid-western industrial areas whose high-quality engineering schools export their best graduates to the advanced centers of industrial innovation in the north-east or California. The scientific and technical labor market usually grows up on the basis of major academic institutions, such as the complexes around MIT–Harvard–University of Massachusetts in the Boston area, Stanford–Berkeley–UC San Francisco in the San Francisco Bay area, or Cal Tech–UCLA–USC in Los Angeles. The development of the labor market around the initial nucleus of high-quality professional schools is fostered by a number of conditions which enhance the quality of life for skilled labor, making it attractive to migrate to such areas of opportunity. Among these conditions, good housing and urban services, high-quality educational facilities and urban amenities, including provision for sophisticated leisure and consumption requirements, seem to be important elements in continuing attraction of engineers and scientists to a given area. These conditions relating to the "quality of life" are an important factor in maintaining the attractiveness of a milieu of innovation; however, they are the consequence, rather than the cause, of a sophisticated labor market, as argued above. Furthermore, should they deteriorate, the ultimate fate of the milieu of innovation still depends upon its industrial vitality. For instance, the process of environmental deterioration in Silicon Valley, its skyrocketing housing costs and the gridlock of its highway system, while creating increasing difficulties for residents, have not destroyed its appeal for the most highly qualified electronics engineers from all over the world. As in all truly innovative milieux, the best labor concentrates in the places "where the action is," then trying to make its environment as pleasant as possible. The main factor in the formation of a large technical and scientific labor market is the presence of job opportunities in the most advanced segments of the industry, which amounts to saying that the main factor in attracting highly skilled labor is the location of the milieu itself. The labor requirements for the formative stages of the milieu are generally fulfilled by the presence of good-quality academic and vocational institutions able to train a large pool of skilled personnel. Such institutions also tend to be located in areas of high social status and good urban amenities, able to attract and retain highly valued scientific and technical labor.

The third major element conducive to the formation of an innovative industrial milieu is the availability of investors ready to risk capital in an always uncertain discovery-based activity. While not all information-technology industries can be considered high-risk investments, the early stages of milieux of innovation depend upon the expansion of companies whose products, and even whose future as businesses, are somewhat unpredictable.

These particular features of the investment process lead to three specific sources of funding for the industry:

(1) Long-term investment in R&D by a large company whose assets and position in the market enable it to rationalize its returns over a long span of time, compensating for potential monetary losses with the technological edge which, overall, the company will enjoy as a result of its investment in research.

(2) Direct investment or indirect financing by government in R&D aimed at performance of the product, regardless of cost, as, for example, in the case of Department of Defense subsidies for the development of new technologies for military purposes. There is also a more subtle, and in fact more important way, in which government interests in technological innovation affect the financial basis of the new industries: this is by providing large-scale, secure, profitable markets for untested technological products. While this is not, technically speaking, a source of capital, guaranteed markets eliminate risk, transforming high-risk investments into low-risk ventures and allowing firms to use standard financial sources in spite of the high-risk nature of their business.

(3) The third, and originally the most popular source of high-risk, high-return financing for innovative firms is venture capital, either formal, through investment firms, or informal, that is, from individuals staking their savings on the opportunity represented by a promising start-up. Some high-risk investments (which, for the present analytical purpose, can be taken to mean venture capital) are also made by local commercial banks seeking a high return on the basis of their direct knowledge of a new industry. Without venture capital and the network of financial intermediaries between capital firms and new information-technology companies, much of the dynamism of the new industrial milieux would have never existed. Nevertheless, it is important to differentiate between the functions and origins of venture capital during the initial stages of innovative milieux on the one hand and, on the other, in the later, more mature phases of these industrial areas. In the milieux' formative stages, venture capital firms develop on the basis of the ability of their financial entrepreneurs to identify promising industrial ventures, and to spread the risk among a plurality of small investors betting on the expectation of high returns. In the mature stage, when larger investments are required, and the existence of an established milieux of innovation makes the investment safer, venture capital firms tend to be the financial channels through which major investors, such as pension funds and investment banks, often operate. What is crucial in both cases is the presence of a network of financial intermediaries specializing in transferring resources to the new industries, on the basis of a degree of inside knowledge as to the potential of specific technological projects. In this fundamental sense, the network of

venture capital firms is an indispensable part of the industrial milieu itself.[74]

The important implication for our research purposes is that while capital flows are placeless, the organizational conditions of high-risk investment do have a substantial spatial component: large corporations finance their own research facilities, whose location depends upon the internal logic of the corporation; government contracts, particularly for military expenditure, are biased toward certain regions and metropolitan areas; and venture capital, as argued above, depends upon the existence of a local network of financial firms, itself the expression of a wealthy, entrepreneurial society. Let us examine in some detail the specific spatial implications of these different modes of financing the development of innovative milieux.

Large corporations tend to locate their R&D laboratories close to their headquarters, creating a symbiotic relationship between strategic management and high-level industrial innovation.[75] This is the case for IBM in suburban New York, for ATT and Bell Laboratories in New Jersey, Texas Instruments in Dallas, Motorola in Phoenix, Sperry-Rand, Control Data, and Cray, in Minneapolis-St Paul, Hewlett-Packard in Palo Alto, and so on. It is also the case that, given the global reach of these corporations, they tend to spread their research facilities over a few different locations: for example, IBM's laboratories in San Jose and Zurich are technological centers in their own right. In all cases, the spatial implication of this form of financing, with its corollaries of secrecy and proprietary information (including ATT's Bell after ATT's divestiture) is the confinement of innovation within the boundaries of a given corporation, thus closely following the corporation's own spatial pattern. Considering the broader implications of this trend for the spatial structure of the industry, the connection between headquarters location and R&D centers accounts for the formation of innovative industrial milieux in the largest metropolitan areas, such as New York or Philadelphia.

Concerning direct government financing and indirect financing through guaranteed markets, particularly in defense, there is ample evidence of regional concentration in the distribution of Federal, including military, expenditure, in favor primarily of California and the south-west, but also including Boston, Seattle, Philadelphia, New York–New Jersey, and St Louis among the top beneficiaries of defense and aerospace research funding.[76] It is vital to keep in mind that defense spending favors regions and cities, for cultural, political, functional, and strategic reasons, only to the extent to which these areas are able to provide valuable technological innovation. The existence of a financial source, including defense spending, is an important but not sufficient condition in the formation of an innovative milieu. In other words, defense funding follows the source of information, although it is a very important factor in the development of an original source of technological information into a fully fledged milieu of innovation.

Venture capital is also dependent upon local social and economic characteristics, particularly in the early stages of development of the network of financial intermediaries.[77]A combination of three elements seems to account for favorable conditions for venture capital firms to develop:

(1) A wealthy area with abundance of upper-income households able and willing to invest some of their savings in high-return placements.

(2) An area that is a significant financial center but has no stock exchange or commodities market, since the existence of such powerful financial networks tends to siphon off regional savings from local financial institutions. In other words, what is required is a financial center important enough to generate a network of financial intermediaries but where there is still room for the small investor.

(3) Venture capital firms thrive in areas that have a sound, fast-growing economy, where there is a collective memory of entrepreneurial success, as well as new opportunities opened up by the existence of innovative industrialism.

Interestingly enough, some of the best developed venture capital networks, relative to the size of the regional economies, are in Boston, San Francisco, southern California, and, to a lesser extent, in Texas, that is, in areas that seem to possess the characteristics we have indicated, as opposed to New York or Chicago, traditional financial centers basically geared toward corporate investment (see figure 2.3). In the mature stage of an innovative milieu, in Boston or the San Francisco Bay area, for instance, corporate investment flows in, particularly from New York and Los Angeles, but still generally channeled through the network of venture capital firms established in the formative stage, basically because of their knowledge of the potential of each new development in the industry. In the end, while successful innovative industries go public to raise capital in the stock exchange market, the

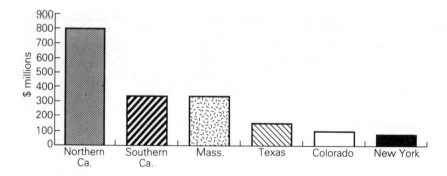

Figure 2.3   Venture capital invested in companies 1985 ($m)
Source: Electronics Business, 1987

dynamism of the milieu remains largely dependent upon the ability of high-risk investors to keep financing quantum-leap innovations. In fact, most of these high-risk investments in the 1980s tend to be made by corporations, including foreign industrial investors, because of the high cost barriers to entry in terms of the capital to undertake major research programs, particularly in microelectronics.

An industrial complex becomes a milieu of innovation when it is able to generate within itself a continuous flow of the key elements that constitute the basis for innovative production of information technologies, namely: new scientific and technological information, high-risk capital, and innovative technical labor. By way of illustration, let us consider the typical case of Silicon Valley, elaborating on the information already provided by Saxenian, Rogers and Larsen, and other researchers.[78] Stanford University's Faculty and graduates played a crucial role in providing the basic technological information on which a group of companies relied during the 1950s. Stanford and Berkeley, with the addition, years later, of the engineering programs at San Jose State University and the University of Santa Clara, provided a very large pool of high-quality electrical engineers. Military markets and government contracts supported the necessary research in the initial stages; and venture capital was decisive in the creation of many innovative companies, including Apple Computers. But during the 1970s the situation changed substantially as Silicon Valley grew and matured as a self-sufficient industrial milieu. Most of the information by this time was generated by the companies' own research efforts; this included the invention of the integrated circuit in 1957, of the planar process in 1959, and of the microprocessor in 1971. Furthermore, this information was diffused and enhanced by informal exchanges between engineers of different companies, as well as continuous spin-offs from existing companies. The military markets' share of the industry's total output plunged, and commercially oriented research became far more important than defense-related subsidized research programs. While markets expanded worldwide, numerous sub-contracting networks developed locally, further integrating Silicon Valley as a production complex. Companies financed most of their expansion themselves, by reinvesting a large share of their profits, by going public in the stock market, or by a combination of both methods, thus reducing the importance of venture capital as a source of finance. While still benefiting from the high-quality labor produced by the San Francisco Bay area universities, Silicon Valley created its own labor pool by becoming a magnet able to attract some of the best engineers and technicians on a national scale.

In this way Silicon Valley became able to generate all the ingredients of a milieu of innovation, while maintaining its lead as an industrial complex at the cutting edge of information-technology production. It is its nature in this respect, as a self-sufficient, self-generating system, that constitutes the strength of a milieu of innovation beyond the ups and downs of business cycles. Around this superior technological capacity, Silicon Valley generated a network of auxiliary companies, as well as a wealth of scientific and business contacts and, ultimately, a distinctive local culture. The concept of "agglomeration economies" does not capture the specificity or the richness of this set of social relationships, because the external economies of an informational production unit are quite different from those of the previous forms of industrialization.[79] For instance, there is little need of spatial proximity because of transportation costs; but there is much need to be able to exchange personal views on last night's software breakthrough, or on a recent visit to Japan. This notion of an innovative industrial milieu is closer to the situation of writers and artists, or stock exchange traders, in New York, or to film and television producers and actors, or financial consultants, in Los Angeles, than to the concentrations of textile or steel mills in the early industrial cities.[80]

Once a milieu of innovation takes shape, it develops its own dynamics, and becomes largely independent of the factors that once converged to give rise to its creation in a particular locality. After coming into being, a milieu of innovation will develop less on the basis of the original locational factors than on that of the overall dynamics of the industry. Nevertheless, it is crucial to understand the original location in terms of bringing together the key factors necessary for the development of innovation in informational production. Where a milieu of innovation locates depends upon the existence in one place of all three main factors as described (information, labor, capital) and upon the process of linking all three factors by the initiative of some key economic or social actors. It is in this sense that the figure of the entrepreneur (capitalist, individual, or institutional) becomes crucial.[81] For instance, the consciously positive attitude of Stanford University toward the creation of an industrial complex of electronics companies was decisive in bringing together the various favorable factors that were present in the San Francisco Bay area for the potential formation of an innovative milieu. It is both the existence of the key factors and the deliberate action by some subjects/entrepreneurs to build an industrial complex, that are necessary to form a milieu of innovation. A very similar story can be told concerning the formation of Boston's Route 128 as the second major center of technological innovation, although in this case the initiative was far more decentralized, and basically took the form of a number of young engineers and scientists starting up their companies on the basis of an entrepreneurially minded academic environment.[82]

Once a milieu is in existence, its evolution closely follows that of the industries clustered in it. Saxenian, in her latest research[83] differentiates three stages in the development of Silicon Valley: the entrepreneurial stage of the 1960s; the era of corporate consolidation and branch plants in the 1970s; and the emergence of networked production in the 1980s. Networked production refers to the formation of a series of linkages among firms and among industries in a given spatially contiguous production complex, under the

Table 2.13   Jobs in electronics industry (excluding defense and aerospace) in Santa Clara County, by sector (annual averages)

	1975		1985		1995[a]	
	(000)	(%)	(000)	(%)	(000)	(%)
Computers	23.0	25	63.1	28	86.4	30
Communications Equipment	10.2	11	25.2	11	32.8	11
Semiconductors	19.6	21	45.5	20	43.2	15
Other electronic components	13.4	15	35.8	16	39.4	14
Instruments	16.9	18	31.8	14	44.5	15
Wholesale electronics	2.5	3	6.6	3	9.9	3
Software development	0.5	1	6.3	3	18.9	6
Research and development	6.1	7	8.1	4	16.2	6
Total	92.2		222.4		291.3	

[a]Projection.
Source: California Employment Development Department.

dominance of system firms. In spatial terms, the first stage represented a period of concentration, leading to the formation of the milieu; the second stage saw a process of decentralization of low-level manufacturing activities, while Silicon Valley continued to grow on the basis of higher-level production functions; the third stage witnessed the re-integration of manufacturing into the Silicon Valley firms, but through automation of assembly and testing. Throughout all three stages, Silicon Valley maintained, and even expanded, its technological leadership, adding new layers of complexity to its industrial structure, but always concentrating the highest technological functions. The net result has been an endless expansion of employment, in spite of downturns in the electronics industry, such that of 1984–6. Table 2.13 and figure 2.4 indicate the trend. Saxenian's latest research reveals that between 1980 and 1986, about 50,000 new high-technology jobs were created in Silicon Valley, more than any other area in the US, ranking second in terms of absolute number of jobs with 234,000 after Los Angeles (297,000), but before Boston (175,000) and Orange Country (114,000).

Silicon Valley and Route 128 have maintained their early technological lead in high-technology manufacturing, continuously enhancing their R&D capabilities, and transforming their industrial organization to cope with the trends of international competition.

The process by which a particular milieu is formed, and therefore the characteristics of the area in which it is located, greatly influence the final outcome of the process, that is, the structure and dynamics of the milieu of innovation itself. In other words, the combination of different sources of innovative information, of different pools of skilled labor, and of different investors of high-risk capital, will result in the formation of *different types of milieux of innovation*, whose location could therefore take place in very different areas. In order to illustrate our approach we will proceed to analyze the relationship between these different sources of information, capital, and technical labor, on the one hand, the location of R&D centers in the US on the other. Admittedly, this is only a very rough, approximate idea of what we understand by milieux of innovation; and moreover, since the data on which we rely concern all R&D, and not just R&D by information-technology producers, we are clearly underplaying the specific nature of the new industry as opposed to traditional manufacturing activities. Corresponding adjustments will therefore have to be made in the interpretation of the data. Nevertheless, we start from the safe assumption that the research function is particularly prominent in information-technology industries; this is especially relevant when the matter in hand is the location of their innovative milieux. It is therefore plausible that there exists some relationship between the spatial logic of information-technology innovative centers and that of R&D centers in general. In any case, at this stage of our investigation we are dependent on the best empirical source available concerning the geography of R&D in the US, namely the research carried out on this subject over a number of years by Edward J. Malecki.[84] While referring to the original

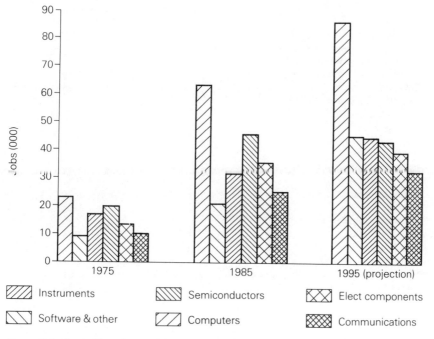

Figure 2.4   Santa Clara County: jobs in electronics, by sector
Source: California Employment Development Department

sources to explain the methodology underlying his data collection, we need to present our own methodology in analyzing that database for the specific purposes of this research.

On the basis of Malecki's data (see tables 2.14–2.16), we have constructed a series of indicators concerning the different potential sources of technological information, high-risk capital, and scientific/technical labor. For each one of these indicators, we have ranked the US metropolitan areas and picked out the top 20 of each ranking. As a criterion for selection we have used absolute values of the variables rather than weighted measures, such as location quotients, or standardized values. The reason for taking this methodological option is our concern with defining the factors that gave birth to the actual innovative milieux that structure industrial space. It is the sheer volume of information generated, of capital invested, and of technical labor available in a given location, that is actually crucially important for the overall spatial structure of information-technology industries, rather than the ability of an

Table 2.14 Location of scientists and engineers employed in R&D or administration of R&D; top 20 metropolitan areas, 1977

Metropolitan area	Number of scientists and engineers employed in R&D	R&D scientists and engineers per thousand population
Los Angeles–Long Beach–Anaheim	32,085	3.13
New York–Newark–Jersey City	26,395	1.65
Washington	20,244	6.95
Philadelphia–Wilmington–Trenton	19,701	3.50
San Francisco–Oakland–San Jose	18,201	4.12
Chicago–Gary	14,834	1.95
Boston–Lawrence–Lowell	14,653	4.16
Detroit–Ann Arbor	11,659	2.50
Seattle–Tacoma	7,683	4.19
Cleveland–Akron–Lorain	7,529	2.51
Houston–Galveston	7,006	3.25
Pittsburgh	6,732	2.80
Minneapolis–St Paul	5,824	2.95
Dallas–Fort Worth	5,568	2.34
Denver–Boulder	5,476	4.42
Hartford–Springfield–Waterbury	5,400	3.21
San Diego	4,939	3.64
St Louis	4,781	1.98
Baltimore	4,726	2.28
Rochester, NY	4,721	4.91

Source: Malecki (see note 75).

area to become innovative on a limited basis, without in fact being able to generate a self-expanding milieu of technological discovery. However, the adoption of this methodological criterion will also introduce a bias in our data in favor of the largest metropolitan areas, a bias that will have to be taken into account in our interpretation.

Furthermore, to attempt a more systematic observation of the location pattern of R&D centers, we have combined the scores of each metropolitan area with respect to the different scales representing sources of information, sources of capital, and sources of research labor. Since areas ranked among the first 20 do not overlap on all indicators, we have analyzed the relative positions of 42 metropolitan areas that can be considered, by various criteria, as forming the backbone of US R&D. Thus, we have been able to assign to each metropolitan area three scores, summarizing its relative position *vis-à-vis* the three main components of a milieu of innovation. Finally, we have combined the three scores to give one global score which is proposed as representative of the rank-order of each metropolitan area in terms of its overall R&D potential. Because of the cumbersome procedures necessary to arrive at this synthetic measure, the reader is referred to the final note to this chapter for the methodological explanation and justification (see p. 366). For present purposes, in order to be able to elaborate on these findings, it is important to note, first, that this analysis is purely illustrative of a research perspective, and therefore does not pretend to set the ranking presented here as hard evidence beyond the significance of Malecki's original findings; secondly, that measurement is limited to that of relative rank-order, and the use of metric numbering is simply an indication of the supposed magnitude of the differences between levels in the scales, not at all a quantitative measure of

Table 2.15 Metropolitan complexes of research and development[a]

Concentrations of both laboratories and employment, 1977

Austin, TX
Boston–Lawrence–Lowell
Denver–Boulder, CO
Huntsville, AL
Lafayette, IN
Madison, WI
Philadelphia–Wilmington–Trenton
Raleigh–Durham, NC
San Francisco–Oakland–San Jose
Washington, DC–MD–VA

[a]Concentration refers to a value over one standard deviation above the average for 177 metropolitan areas.
Source: Malecki (see note 75).

Table 2.16 Location quotients for Federal and private R&D in 50 SMSAs, 1977

Urban area	Total DoD and NASA[a] ($m)	Federal R&D location quotient	Total private R&D Labs[b]	Private R&D location quotient	Speciali-zation in Federal or private R&D
Los Angeles–Long Beach–Anaheim	2,916.3	2.83	446	0.96	Federal
Boston–Lawrence–Lowell	791.1	2.24	264	1.66	Both
San Francisco–Oakland–San Jose	724.1	1.59	187	0.91	Federal
Seattle–Tacoma	548.6	3.03	36	0.44	Federal
Washington	484.0	1.61	214	1.58	Both
Philadelphia–Wilmington–Trenton	432.1	0.77	282	1.11	Private
Dallas–Fort Worth	431.8	1.72	56	0.49	Federal
St Louis	372.1	1.58	71	0.67	Federal
New York–Newark–Jersey City	311.3	0.19	978	1.33	Private
San Diego	284.9	1.81	53	0.75	Federal
Baltimore	228.6	1.07	64	0.66	Federal
Houston–Galveston	210.0	0.86	99	0.89	Private
Detroit–Ann Arbor	183.2	0.39	124	0.59	Private
Orlando	156.5	2.70	4	0.15	Federal
New Orleans	143.2	1.32	8	0.16	Federal
Santa Barbara	141.1	5.07	23	1.83	Both
Cincinnati–Hamilton	139.4	0.86	54	0.74	Federal
Melbourne–Titusville–Cocoa	121.6	5.27	13	1.25	Both
Albany–Schenectady–Troy	85.5	1.08	23	0.64	Federal
Salt Lake City	84.7	1.09	22	0.63	Federal
Binghamton	83.3	2.76	8	0.59	Federal
Bridgeport–New Haven	82.4	1.02	46	1.27	Private
Hartford–Springfield	77.7	0.46	89	1.16	Private
Minneapolis–St Paul	69.5	0.35	53	0.59	Private
Denver–Boulder	60.4	0.43	49	0.93	Private
Huntsville	57.1	2.01	13	1.01	Federal
Dayton	55.1	0.66	32	0.85	Private
Phoenix	50.7	0.42	35	0.64	Private
Columbus	48.1	0.45	44	0.92	Private
Atlanta	43.3	0.24	35	0.44	Private
New London–Norwich	33.6	1.34	5	0.44	Federal
Syracuse	30.9	0.48	22	0.76	Private
Albuquerque	28.0	0.73	10	0.58	Federal
Tampa–St Peterburg	26.5	0.20	14	0.23	Private
Pittsburgh	22.5	0.10	105	1.01	Private
Fort Wayne	21.4	0.58	10	0.60	Private
Pensacola	21.1	0.79	6	0.50	Federal
West Palm Beach	20.5	0.45	8	0.39	Federal
Biloxi–Gulfport	19.1	1.13	2	0.26	Federal
Kansas City	16.8	0.13	37	0.64	Private
Austin	16.6	0.42	18	1.01	Private
Cleveland–Akron–Lorain	16.3	0.06	150	1.76	Private
Indianapolis	16.1	0.14	32	0.63	Private
Buffalo	14.1	0.11	62	1.04	Private
Chicago–Gary	12.1	0.02	390	1.13	Private
Pittsfield	11.6	1.24	3	0.71	Federal

Table 2.16 Continued

Urban area	Total DoD and NASA[a] ($m)	Federal R&D location quotient	Total private R&D Labs[b]	Private R&D location quotient	Speciali- zation in Federal or private R&D
Nashua	11.2	1.12	8	1.76	Private
Utica–Rome	10.5	0.33	12	0.80	Private
Miami–Fort Lauderdale	4.7	0.02	25	0.24	Private
Milwaukee–Racine	0	0	88	1.24	Private

[a]Source: [25, 45].
[b]Source: [4].
Source: Malecki (see note 76).

the statistical intervals between ranks. With all these necessary caveats, we can now look at table 2.17 and try to understand the geography of R&D in the US as it relates to the development of industrial milieux of innovation.

Let us first describe our observations in terms of the spatial location of R&D centers, as they result from the combined criteria we have derived from our analytical model. Los Angeles stands out at the top in a class by itself. This may be surprising, but in fact its ranking is the direct consequence of the combination of a strong corporate basis, government funding (for defense and aerospace work), large, major universities, and a very large pool of technical labor. Since we know from the general literature that this trend has become more marked since 1977, it is probable that, in the mid-1980s, the greater Los Angeles area (including, of course, Orange County) holds, at least quantitatively, the largest concentration of industrial R&D in the US; maybe, with Tokyo–Yokohama, the largest in the world. After Los Angeles comes a group of four major centers of innovation which, in the rank-order given by our elaboration of Malecki's data, are: New York–New Jersey, San Francisco–Oakland–San Jose, Philadelphia–Wilmington–Trenton, and Boston–Lawrence–Lowell. These four represent a mixture of the old and the new industrial R&D centers. On the one hand, the close connection between corporate headquarters and R&D facilities, demonstrated by Malecki in another study, accounts for the renewed importance of old, large metropolitan centers, such as New York and Philadelphia, as R&D locations. On the other hand, the new information-technology centers, such as Boston and San Francisco, are quickly taking up a leading role, on the basis of their strong university presence, their government funding, and their ability to generate a diversified industrial research milieu; it is in fact the last element which is statistically responsible for their presence among the top five areas. This group of just five metropolitan areas appears to form the core of industrial R&D in the US, clearly exhibiting a pattern of concentration that is likely to have consequences for the future manufacturing landscape of America.

Table 2.17 Ranking of 42 metropolitan areas according to their potential as sources of technological innovation, by potential in generating information capital, research labor, with indication of their combined score (ranks only shown for top 20 areas)

Metropolitan Area	Scores for sources[a]				
	Sources of information	Sources of capital	Sources of research labor	Total combined score	Overall rank
Boston	4.25	3.5	3.5	11.25	4
New York–New Jersey	3.33	5.0	1.0	9.33	2
San Francisco–Oakland–San Jose	3.75	4.5	2.5	10.75	3
Los Angeles	3.0	1.5	0.5	5.0	1
Philadelphia–Wilmington–Trenton	4.33	5.0	2.0	11.33	5
Washington, DC–MD–VA	5.0	15.0	3.0	23.0	6
Chicago	7.33	14.0	3.0	24.33	7
Cleveland	16.0	16.0	10.0	42.5	16
Detroit–Ann Arbor	14.0	10.5	4.0	38.5	10
Pittsburgh	2.0	17.0	6.0	43.0	
Houston–Galveston	16.6	11.0	11.0	38.6	11
Hartford–Springfield	20.6	18.0	16.0	54.6	
Milwaukee	21.0	18.5	25.0	64.5	
St Louis	19.33	10.5	9.0	38.83	12
Baltimore	11.33	12.5	9.5	33.33	8
Buffalo, NY	22.0	20.0	25.0	67.0	
Denver–Boulder	11.0	22.5	7.5	41.0	14
Dallas–Fort Worth	22.66	11.5	7.0	41.1	15
Cincinnati–Hamilton	23.0	17.0	25.0	65.0	
Minneapolis–St Paul	18.33	21.5	6.5	46.33	18
San Diego	13.66	14.0	8.5	36.16	9
Huntsville, AL	13.0	25.0	25.0	63.0	
Dayton, OH	18.66	25.0	−25.0	68.66	
Newport–Hampton	20.33	25.0	25.0	70.33	
Portland	18.66	25.0	25.0	68.66	
Knoxville	22.33	25.0	25.0	72.33	
Salt Lake City	22.66	22.5	25.0	70.16	
Sacramento	20.33	25.0	25.0	70.33	
Davenport	23.33	25.0	25.0	73.33	
Madison	14.25	25.0	12.5	51.75	19
Seattle	20.33	14.5	4.5	39.33	13
Champaign–Urbana	21.33	25.0	12.5	58.83	
Austin	16.25	25.0	12.5	53.75	20
Rochester, NY	22.0	25.0	25.0	72.0	
Bridgeport–New Haven	23.33	25.0	25.0	73.33	
Lafayette, IN	18.75	25.0	25.0	68.75	
Raleigh–Durham	18.75	25.0	12.5	56.25	
Orlando, FL	25.0	19.5	25.0	69.5	
New Orleans	25.0	20.0	25.0	70.0	
Santa Barbara, CA	25.0	20.5	25.0	70.5	

Table 2.17   Continued

Metropolitan Area	Scores for sources[a]				
	Sources of information	Sources of capital	Sources of research labor	Total combined score	Overall rank
Melbourne, FL	25.0	21.5	25.0	71.5	
Albany, NY	25.0	22.0	25.0	72.0	

[a]Low score indicates higher potential: level of measure is ordinal. (For scores and procedure for calculating the scores, see note 150.)
Source: Author's elaboration of Malecki's data.

Among other considerations, while New York–New Jersey is still losing manufacturing jobs, even in high technology, it is hardly lagging behind in terms of R&D capabilities, if only because of the sheer size of its financial, institutional, corporate, and technical labor resources.

The leading group is followed by two special cases: Washington DC–Maryland–Virginia, and Chicago, which represent the two opposite poles of the government–corporate spectrum. To some extent, it is clear that R&D is located in Washington because of the Federal government agencies, and that Chicago's R&D is the direct spin-off of headquarters location in the capital of the midwest, as well as of its now fading manufacturing past. Will these two locations be able to shift into the new generation of R&D? This will very much depend on the future of government intervention in research and on the ability of old manufacturing industry to generate new forms of innovation. Activity over the past decade since the mid-1970s suggests that spin-offs from government research centers are in fact generating technological development in Maryland and Virginia, while Chicago is trailing in such developments, despite its strong university base.

Moving down our list, there follows a mixture of areas that combine a university base with a very strong traditional manufacturing structure which is in the process of being revitalized through stepped-up R&D efforts: Baltimore (with outstanding research universities, particularly in health sciences, and the military connection to Johns Hopkins' Applied Physics Laboratory); San Diego, a center for biotechnology, computer industries, and defense-related informational production; Detroit–Ann Arbor, where a large research university complex helps the automobile industry in its transition to robotics and new materials, not forgetting tanks; Houston–Galveston, where the connection is between oil capital and government-supported aerospace research and industrial development; St Louis and Seattle, where the aircraft industry still thrives, supported by government and a solid network of local universities. Denver–Boulder and Dallas–Fort Worth seem to have different stories: while both have medium-level universities (if we include Texas A&M in the Dallas sphere), and well-developed technical labor markets, Denver has government-sponsored research facilities but low research funding, while Dallas relies on its advanced corporate structure funded by government. Next on the list, Cleveland, with the remnants of strong corporate industrial R&D, and Pittsburgh, and advanced university research in robotics and artificial intelligence, witness the persistence of the old manufacturing belt, although not at a level commensurate with its industrial past; Minneapolis remains a major computer industry center and relies on its large, technically oriented public university system to keep pace with industrial research. Finally, Madison and Austin are clear examples of the research vitality that major public universities can generate in an isolated setting. They also demonstrate, however, that university quality by itself cannot generate an industrial complex: Madison was not able to do so in the 1980s, while Austin became a substantial electronics manufacturing area on the basis of government support and corporate decentralization of production facilities.

Outside our list of the top 20 there remain some significant technological centers, such as North Carolina's "research triangle" around the Raleigh-Durham metropolitan area. The 1977 data could not provide the quantitative basis to justify a ranking for this area among the top 20, given our bias toward the effect of absolute size of labor, research facilities, and funding in constituting an innovative milieu. Nevertheless, the "research triangle" does constitute an innovative milieu in the 1980s, on the basis of an original combination of university facilities and government sponsored R&D.[85]

The summary comments above are intended simply to lay the ground for some more analytical conclusions reached on the basis of our elaboration of Malecki's findings. The first of these concerns the necessary distinction between the geography of industrial R&D in the broad sense, as shown here, for the 1976–7 period, and the location of leading information-technology industrial milieux of innovation. Boston and Silicon Valley appear much less clearly dominant in Malecki's data than in the literature specializing in information technology. In fact, Malecki himself provides the explanation, and some empirical data, for this discrepancy. He analyzes the location of headquarters and R&D laboratories for a sample of 54 electronics firms, as shown in table 2.18.[86] The findings are striking: 36 out of the 54 firms have an R&D laborartory either in the Boston area or in California, and the main reason for the other 18 firms *not* having such a facility in either area is related to the location of their headquarters elsewhere. It therefore seems plausible that the location of milieux of innovation in information technology follows the general determinants presented in our analytical framework, but with further determining effect on their spatial location: namely, R&D information, capital, and labor are increasingly targeted to the specific recipient industries. In other words, there seems to be a difference between redesigning the

Table 2.18 Locational characteristics of R&D in three US industries, from a sample of 85 firms

Number of R&D locations	Number of of firms	Firms with a laboratory in the headquarters' area	Firms with a laboratory in the Boston area or California	Firms with headquarters in the Boston area or California
Aerospace				
1	1	1	0	0
2–4	4	4	1	0
5	3	2	3	1
6	3	3	3	1
All aerospace firms	11	10	7	2
Electrical and electronics products				
1	18	16	7	6
2	15	12	10	2
3–5	9	8	8	3
6–10	8	8	7	1
11–36	4	4	4	1
All electronics firms	54	48	36	13
Instruments				
1	11	8	6	4
2	4	4	2	1
3–5	5	4	4	2
All instruments firms	20	16	12	7
All firms	85	74	55	22

Source: Malecki (see note 84).

automobile or steel industries and fostering new breakthroughs in electronics and biotechnology. Thus, within a common matrix of technological and institutional determinants of R&D location there is some specialization in R&D concerned with the new technological frontier that translates into specific spatial locations.

Nevertheless, the importance of R&D facilities in the very large, older metropolitan areas, along with the presence of information-technology manufacturing in these areas, when considered in absolute numbers, calls attention to the diversity of milieux of innovation, away from the simplistic images of the sunrise regions and to the complex reality of the multifaceted process of new industrial development. Because of the variable geometry of sources of information, capital, and labor, linking corporations, government, universities, and industrial complexes, we are clearly in the presence of a variety of high-level innovative milieux that develop along the lines of the specific factors proposed by our analytical framework. To focus more specifically on the innovative milieux of information-technology producers, we can construct a typology on the basis of information already cited, by combining the different structural elements that converge in their formation. Such a typology might provide a basis for comparing innovative information-technology milieux with the location pattern of the overall industrial R&D system, so as to generate some hypotheses on what is specific to the new industrial milieux of innovation.

Type 1, represented by areas such as Silicon Valley and Boston's Route 128, is historically based on a combination of university research, government markets, venture capital, university-produced skilled labor, and start-up companies, ultimately generating through their interaction a self-sustaining milieu. This is the kind of milieu of innovation on which we have focused our analysis, because it is the more distinctively original in the current stage of industrialization, and because it remains the most dynamic configuration in the process of technological development. Yet there are other potential combinations of information, capital, and labor, that have in reality come together to form different kinds of innovative milieux.[87]

Type 2, exemplified by the Los Angeles–Orange Country complex or, on a much smaller scale, by Phoenix or Dallas, directly links large corporations and government funding around defense-related industries that originally recruit from a network of good local engineering schools, to become subsequently a pole of attraction for skilled personnel nationwide.[88]

Type 3, represented by IBM's New York or ATT's New Jersey locations, organizes a self-sustaining milieu behind the closed doors of a very large, innovative corporation. In this particular case it would be difficult to consider that there exists a milieu of innovation as a specific spatial entity. In fact, it is the corporation itself in each case that constitutes the milieu, its component parts sometimes scattered in different locations around the world and interacting via on-line systems. Yet it is important to recognize that the location of such major centers of information-based industrial development do organize the new spatial structure of production, even if the process of innovation takes place generally in a secluded space, and local spin-offs are few.[89]

Type 4, whose closest resemblance could be the Austin, Texas area, mixes the domination of technical branch plants of large corporations, and some level of spin-off able to generate a relatively autonomous dynamic of locally induced firms.[90] In the survey conducted by Amy Glasmeier on 70 high-technology firms in Austin in 1987,[91] half of the firms were manufacturing establishments. Of these, only 4 percent were research oriented. However, 37 percent of them were engaged in some form of R&D on the basis of the technologies of their parent corporations or other outside firms. Austin, until the mid-1980s, was the typical example of a milieu of innovation resulting from the decentralization of corporate R&D to be complemented with a network of ancillary firms.

Type 5, which could be illustrated by the rise of the computer industry in Minneapolis–St Paul, represents an original combination of corporate development, government markets, and self-generation of technological information.[92]

These types do not cover all the variations of innovative milieux that exist in practice, but they provide some standards by which to estimate the originality of other areas. For example, North Carolina's Research Triangle is close in its structure and dynamics to type 1 (Silicon Valley), but with the major difference of a much greater reliance on government contracts and guidance. Pittsburgh and Philadelphia could probably fit well in the same category as Minneapolis (type 5), maybe with the additional features of an even stronger university research basis, particularly in computer software and robotics (Carnegie–Mellon in Pittsburgh), and of a much more highly developed corporate environment.[93]

It is my contention that all types of milieu of innovation are equally at the forefront of the constitution of the new industrial space; and further, that they are all likely to become yet more prominent worldwide because of the cumulative character of knowledge-based uneven development. However, functioning and dynamics of each type of milieu vary according to the specific structure of each. The more a milieu generates its own internal structure, independent of a small group of large corporations or government facilities, the more it fosters its synergetic potential, ultimately enhancing its technological leadership. Where government support plays a leading role in the growth of an innovative milieu, the resources for industry development are larger, accelerating the pace of the milieu's growth; yet, in these cases, milieux tend to be rather unstable and to go through sharp ups and downs, following the uncertain path of government policies.

In terms of the spatial dynamics of innovative milieux, government dominance tends to restrain tendencies toward offshoring, particularly in defense-related industries, and to foster tendencies toward disproportionate concentration in certain areas and regions. Where large corporations are predominant, the linkages of the milieu with the overall international chain of production are emphasized. The highest technological specialization tends to occur in those milieux which rely on a spatially concentrated, functionally decentralized, network-based structure that draws its strength from those very informational/economic externalities that are attached to its clustering pattern.

We are now in a position to assess how the location pattern of informational milieux of innovation has in fact developed over time in relation to the spatial distribution of industrial R&D in general. Ideally, we should be able to compare Malecki's findings to a similar database referring specifically to information-technology industrial R&D. Since no such comparable database is available, we must rely on the general knowledge of the new industries' behavior, particularly in electronics, as presented in a variety of studies already cited.

By and large, the new milieux of innovation occur as specific developments of existing dominant R&D locations. The main reason for this historical overlap is the crucial importance of large metropolitan areas in mobilizing productive resources, including innovative technological capabilities. However, there are three main differences between the traditional R&D areas, as studied by Malecki, and the new emerging centers of innovation:

(1) The technological dominance in information-based industrial R&D, both quantitative and qualitative, has shifted to Silicon Valley and Boston. Their technological advance is the result of a concentration there of all key factors that are fundamental to the process of innovation, as well as of the cumulative character of the knowledge-based process of uneven development. Yet this dominance is not overwhelming, in contrary to what is generally believed, and is in fact shared with at least two other forms of information-based technological centers.

(2) The second type of major center, as described above, is the technological capacity installed in large corporations headquartered in major metropolitan areas such as New York–New Jersey. This is not simply the reproduction of the previous R&D model, but is the spatial expression of the control of innovation by global corporations. In this case, IBM, or ATT, is more important than the area where it is located. The continuity of metropolitan dominance does not mean a continuation in type of industrial milieu.

(3) The third type of center, whose main exemplar is Los Angeles–Orange County, witnesses the entry into the new industrial history of major conglomerates of government programs and large corporations, creating the basis for what may be in the future the fastest and largest

accumulation of technological development, generally organized around defense-related goals.

Thus, the continuity of a pattern of R&D centered on the largest metropolitan areas disguises the shifts in the relative weights of these areas in the new technological era, as well as the very different sources of their developmental potential. Milieux of innovation structure themselves by articulating a major technological revolution to industrial production through the web of relationships among three of the major historical forces of our experience: large corporations, the state, and social networks. They bear the marks of these forces' changing strategies and interests as they unfold according to their developmental logic in the restructuring of the relationship between technology and space.

Decentralization of Production

Information-technology industries are characterized by a strong tendency to decentralize their production operations, both functionally and spatially. This decentralization occurs both within firms and among firms specializing in different segments of the industry. It is important to differentiate between decentralization of production and the spatial dispersion of the industry. The latter is a process that takes place as the industry expands and seeks out new locations and new markets. The former concerns a specific characteristic of the industry's behavior, that has manifested itself since the early stages of its development, as an expression of structural features of information-technology producers. There seem to be four factors that are most important in accounting for the tendency to organize production in a decentralized pattern:[94]

(1) Labor requirements are specific, and different, for each segment of the production process, and there is great difficulty in obtaining and reproducing these very different types of labor in the same functional and spatial unit.[95]

(2) The nature of the product gives it a functional freedom from location: it is indifferent to transportation costs, given its high value/low volume ratio. Different components of the production process can locate in different areas and ship their intermediate output back and forth between those areas.[96]

(3) The industry, being a producer of information-processing devices, is also the main early user of its own products. Advanced devices able to process and telecommunicate information allow for the spatial separation of functions that are reintegrated in the same process of production and management by on-line information systems and programmable manufacturing tools.[97]

(4) The process-orientation of the informational product establishes a very close connection between the industry and the users of its products, since such information processing devices become crucial components of the final product or activity to which they are destined.

The fourth of these factors draws a sharp distinction between standardized production and customized production in the informational industries which is worth discussing in some detail.[98] Those products that are standardized have ubiquitous markets; their production can be centralized, while distribution is potentially decentralized worldwide. The general tendency in the industry, on the other hand, is toward a greater emphasis on customized production, which also accounts for the higher-value products. Customized production, with the associated requirement for a close interaction between producers and users of information-processing devices, translates into strong market dependency in terms of the industry's location pattern. However, the spatial implications of this market dependency may vary according to the characteristics of the market itself. Two main cases must be considered. In the first case, given the general applicability of information-processing devices, most products of the new industry have markets everywhere. In this case, decentralization of production takes place according to the strategies of market penetration, with the only exception being the higher-level R&D functions, which generally remain concentrated in the milieux of innovation. On the other hand, if markets are highly specific, the nature of a process-oriented, customized product requires a very close relationship between the industry and its market, leading to spatial clustering around the market itself, sometimes requiring spatial reintegration of the entire production process. In such cases, market conditions reverse the process of decentralization. This is the case, in particular, with defense-oriented information-technology producers, which tend to cluster around major military–industrial complexes, and end up generating an innovative milieu articulated to the defense complex.[99]

In sum, market conditions in information-technology industries, determined by the process-orientation of their production, call for a *flexible location pattern*, able simultaneously to cater to a worldwide market, to penetrate a specific regional market, or to develop a customized, localized relationship in a given place, according to the changing conditions of an expanding market. Thus, the tendency toward decentralization of production takes place in a context in which flexibility is the most important requirement in the relationship between the industry and its spatial location.[100]

Finally, it is important to keep in mind that decentralization of production, when it occurs, takes place under the commanding logic of the spatial division of labor, with an occupational, functional, and organizational hierarchy separating the different production units and their locations.[101]

On the basis of these hypotheses, we can go on to analyze some of the available empirical evidence on the decentralization of production for US information-technology producers, at both the international and the inter-regional level.

Spatial decentralization of information-technology production industries is exemplified by the behavior of American semiconductor companies, the core of high-technology manufacturing, since the early 1960s. Jeffery Henderson has analyzed the locational pattern of US chip makers, as they spread out their plants in the US, Scotland, and south-east Asia.[102] Table 2.19, constructed by Henderson on the basis of his interviews with company managers, shows the sharp division of labor among research and design functions, concentrated in the innovative milieux of the US; skilled production functions (wafer fabrication), somewhat decentralized in Scotland for the companies studied; assembly and testing, localized in areas such as Hong Kong and Singapore; and finally, predominantly assembly operations in the new periphery, including the Philippines, Malaysia, and Indonesia. Beyond the spatial division of labor, which we have already analyzed, what is significant is the spatial segmentation of the industry, including the shipment back and forth of the various components of its output between different locations. Chips designed in the US go into wafer fabrication in Scotland, then into assembly in south-east Asia, and then, very often, back to Scotland or to the US for final testing and distribution to their markets. Henderson emphasizes the crucial importance of specific labor characteristics in each stage of the production process. The main reason for semiconductors companies to locate in Scotland is the high quality of technical labor trained by Scottish universities, together with the long tradition of skilled industrial workers in the area. In addition, the salaries of these Scottish engineers are 40 percent lower than those of their equivalents in California. Such competitive advantage overrode the supposed concern that companies might have felt about a region with a long tradition of unionzation and class struggle. Once located in Scotland, US companies designed a number of policies aimed at taming labor militancy, such as introducing special advantages for their personnel, and locating in new towns and other isolated areas, bypassing when possible the older industrial agglomerations.

Saxenian's study of Silicon Valley companies[103] shows the same pattern of hierarchical decentralization of production, with control and R&D functions in Silicon Valley, advanced manufacturing in the US, Europe, and Japan, and assembly operations in the Third World (see table 2.20).

Labor force characteristics, together with government support for business, seem to have played a major role, at least originally, in the location of semiconductor companies in south-east Asia. Particularly important was the ability to tap a large pool of unskilled young women, with little protection regarding their health and working conditions. These women provided, and

Table 2.19 American semiconductor companies manufacturing in Scotland and other European and Asian locations

Nature of Operation and Labour Processes

Company	USA	Scotland	England & Wales	France	Germany	Switzer-land	Israel	Japan	Hong Kong	Malaysia	Korea	Singapore	Philippines	Indonesia	Thailand	Taiwan
National Semiconductor	c,rd,w t,ms,m	d,w	r,m				w		a,t, m	a,t		a,t,d,m, r	a	a	a,t	
Motorola	c,rd,w, a,t,ms, m	w,a,t		w,a	w,t	d,r,m	d	w,d	d,t, r,m	a	a		a			a
General Instrument	c,rd,w, ms,m	w	d,m,r	m						a						a,t
Hughes Aircraft	c,rd,w, ms,m,a, t	w,a,t, (ms)	d,r,m						(a)				(a)			
Burr-Brown	c,rd,w, a,t,ms, m	w,a,t, d														

c – corporate control
rd – research & development
d – design centre
ms – mask making
w – wafer fabrication
a – assembly

t – final testing
m – marketing
r – regional/national headquarters
( ) – operation under sub-contract arrangement

Source: Henderson (see note 56) on the basis of interviews with company executives; company reports and data collected by Henderson.

still do provide, the bulk of the workers required for labor-intensive assembly operations, during the industry's period of rapid expansion.[104]

Allen Scott has also conducted a detailed study on the decentralization of US semiconductor manufacturers to south-east Asia.[105] Table 2.21 shows the growing number of such plants in the region, and table 2.22 the growing proportion of semiconductors manufacturing production conducted offshore. Scott reiterates the importance of cheap, unskilled labor in this trend. He also points out the influence of two major institutional factors in the decentralization process: first, US Tariff Schedule legislation, which provided favorable conditions for the firms to reimport output produced offshore; and second, the relative demilitarization of the semiconductors market which enabled it to circumvent the Defense Department's prescription that defense-related manufacturing take place on US soil.

Nevertheless, while labor conditions are important in explaining the *origins* of the process of decentralization in semiconductors production, market-related strategies seem to be a major factor in the *persistence* of this pattern.[106] In the first place, protectionist trends and the dramatic expansion of electronics markets over the long term place a premium on the location of plants within the areas that will become large markets. This clearly applies to western Europe, where Scotland holds the largest concentration of semicon-

Table 2.20 Location of facilities of 11 Santa Clara County-based firms, by phase of production (plants in operation or under construction in 1980)

Location	Phase of production[a]			
	Control	R & D	Advanced manu-facturing[b]	Assembly
Santa Clara County	11	11	35	1
Pacific north-west and south-west	0	0	34	3
Rest of US	0	0	12[c]	0
Europe and Japan	0	3	15[d]	0
Third World	0	0	0	29

[a] This division of the production process is sometimes arbitrary in the case of many older facilities with mixed uses. In particular, all R & D includes prototype production lines and assembly, so therefore includes manufacturing and assembly in the research lab. The guideline for allocation thus is the dominant process occurring in a plant. If the two are of equal importance (e.g. control and R & D are often in the same building), the plant is counted twice; otherwise all plants are counted only once.

[b] Advanced manufacturing refers to wafer fabrication for semiconductor production. Since two of the firms included are electronics, not solely semiconductor firms (Hewlett-Packard and Varian), the term manufacturing is used.

[c] This number would be only three if Hewlett-Packard and Varian were not included.

[d] Facilities established in Europe and Japan are mainly through joint ventures and co-production agreements, and typically are established in order to gain access to foreign markets.

Source: Saxenian (see note 66).

Table 2.21 US semiconductor production and imports under tariff codes 806.30 and 807.00

Year	Value of all US shipments in SIC 3674 ($m)[a]	Total 806.30/807.00 imports ($m)[a]	Total 806.30/807.00 imports as % of US shipments in SIC 3674	Total 806.30/807.00 imports from Asia ($m)[a]	Total 806.30/807.00 imports from Asia as % of total 806.30/807.00 imports
1969	1572.9	127	8.1	77	60.6
1970	1501.2	160	10.7	90	56.3
1971	1599.6	178	11.1	98	55.1
1972	2704.8	254	9.4	170	66.9
1973	3647.7	413	11.3	297	71.9
1974	4305.1	684	15.9	479	70.0
1975	3276.9	617	18.8	469	76.0
1976	4473.8	879	19.6	721	82.0
1977	5322.6	1120	21.0	974	87.0
1978	6435.4	1478	23.0	1300	88.0
1979	8266.7	1916	23.2	1667	87.0
1980	10500.8	2506	23.9	2205	88.0
1981	11701.5	2825	24.1	2458	87.0
1982	12429.9	3131	25.2	2787	89.0
1983	–	3383	–	2876	85.0

[a]All values in current dollars.

Sources: US Department of Commerce, Bureau of the Census, *Census of Manufactures,* and *Annual Survey of Manufactures;* US International Trade Commission (1980, 1981, 1984, 1985); US Tariff Commission (1970); Flamm (see note 23). Data collected by Scott (see note 105).

Table 2.22 Principal sources of assembled semiconductor devices imported into the United States under tariff items 806.30 and 807.00

Year	Hong Kong	Indo-nesia	Korea	Malay-sia	Phili-ppines	Singa-pore	Taiwan	Thai-land	All Asia ($m)[a]
1969	49.2	–	22.9	–	–	9.8	14.8	–	228
1970	44.6	–	23.2	–	–	17.9	8.9	–	254
1971	32.7	–	30.9	–	–	23.6	12.7	–	270
1972	25.4	–	26.9	–	–	37.3	10.4	–	452
1973	19.4	–	23.6	8.3	1.4	33.3	12.5	–	740
1974	17.1	–	22.9	21.4	2.9	22.9	12.9	–	977
1975	11.8	–	17.1	30.3	5.3	26.3	7.9	–	858
1976	13.1	–	20.7	25.6	7.3	28.0	7.3	–	1240
1977	8.0	1.1	21.8	27.6	6.9	24.1	9.2	1.1	1567
1978	6.8	1.1	17.0	34.1	9.1	22.7	5.7	3.4	1948
1979	4.6	2.3	13.8	33.3	11.5	23.0	4.6	2.3	2212
1980	4.5	2.3	10.2	34.1	15.9	25.0	4.5	3.4	2518
1981	3.4	2.3	9.2	34.5	18.4	23.0	4.6	4.6	2536
1982	3.4	2.2	8.9	36.0	20.2	19.1	4.5	3.4	2800
1983	1.2	2.4	16.5	36.5	21.2	12.9	4.7	4.7	2876

[a]All values in constant dollars.

Sources: Calculated by Allen Scott (see note 105) from table 3.7 in Flamm (see note 23).

ductors plants, dominated by US companies thus avoiding the 17 percent EEC tariff on imports. Similar reasons lie behind the development of US-owned electronics production in Ireland, and behind ATT's 1987 decision to locate a design and production facility of advanced integrated circuits in Madrid. Also, US electronics companies in Asia have as their prime target for the 1980s the penetration of crucial and heavily protected markets: mainly Japan (the second largest market in the world), but also Korea, one of the fastest growing, and China. In fact, market conditions are confusing the traditional distinction between the locational behavior of merchant manufacturers and that of the so-called "captive producers," large companies such as IBM and ATT, producing semiconductors for in-house use. While the former typically used decentralization in their early stages, the latter kept most of their production (of semiconductors, not of computers) onshore, close to their own in-house markets. With the expansion of world markets, increasing competition in them, and the trend toward vertical integration, large companies set up production facilities in countries such as Spain and Korea, to establish a firm connection with European and Asian markets, once the basic conditions in terms of local provision of technical labor could be fulfilled. ATT is a good example of a firm practicing this strategy.

Furthermore, the customized relationship between producers and users of semiconductors adds to the reasons for the presence of US companies in those areas that have undertaken a process of industrialization based on intensive use of information technologies. Thus, while the potential for automation of assembly work has provoked considerable speculation about the "relocation back north" of formerly decentralized production functions,[107] there is little evidence of this phenomenon.[108] On the contrary, countries such as Taiwan, Korea, Hong Kong, and Singapore, have upgraded the technological level of their production,[109] and wafer production has started in south-east Asia.[110] Automation of assembly and testing is taking place, but in the same decentralized plants. Western European branch plants are also upgrading their technological capabilities, with customized integrated circuit design taking place in the 1980s in several European countries.[111] Indigenous firms are now joining American companies in local production, although most south-east Asian firms are actually engaged in sub-contracting for US firms, and European companies on the whole, are still limited to protected government and other specialized markets.[112] Nevertheless, overall, market relationships have reinforced the pattern of decentralized production originally built around the quest for specific types of labor.

This process of renewed decentralization gathers momentum given its technological feasibility on the basis of breakthroughs in telecommunications, air transportation networks, and computer-integrated flexible manufacturing. Yet because of the consequent dependence on telecommunications and transportation, most decentralized facilities are clustered in medium-to-large metropolitan areas, close to an airport, and well connected with the US, in a location pattern that is as typical of Europe as of Asia. Scott's study shows the pattern of metropolitan concentration of US semiconductors firms in a few areas such as Singapore, Kuala Lumpur, Penang, Manila, Hong Kong, Taipei, Kaohsiung, and Seoul-Inchon.[113] The study by Breheny, Cheshire and Landgridge points to a similar tendency for British-based US companies.[114] Decentralization of production for information-technology industries is also an inter-regional phenomenon in the US. Saxenian provided one of the first systematic observations of this phenomenon in her 1980 study of a sample of electronics companies in Silicon Valley (see table 2.23).[115] Most of the plants decentralized are advanced manufacturing facilities, generally excluding R&D functions; some companies, such as Intel, did decentralize complete sets of operations, including design functions, but their most advanced research centers always remained in Silicon Valley. Although areas to which companies decentralize are very diverse, a tentative pattern appears from the data collected by Saxenian. The western states are the preferred region for firms decentralizing from Silicon Valley, with an oft-cited criterion for choice of location being a maximum distance from Silicon Valley of three hours by air. Further criteria for selection specify a medium-size city in a semi-rural area with a sufficient level of urbanism and cultural sophistication to attract engineers and technicians with the area's "quality of life," including a rich social life in beautiful surroundings. Proximity to a university is valued, but not so much in terms of a functional need for research (the company brings that with it) as in terms of the cultural and social life associated with it, precluding the isolation that would be attached to a truly rural environment. Of course, an abundant work force, with a suitable level of education and skills, is a must. Educated, unemployed women are the workers preferred by decentralized electronics plants (Saxenian writes of a bias toward employing wives of graduate students in university towns). Companies tend to avoid locating a decentralized facility in the same area as other companies, in order to improve their bargaining position as main employer, both toward the labor force and toward local governments. Although some agglomerations still develop notwithstanding, it is interesting to note that while high-level production facilities in electronics tend to cluster in milieux, whose innovative capacity depends upon interaction and synergistic creativity, their decentralized advanced manufacturing operations look for relative isolation vis-à-vis other industrial plants. This seems to be the reason for the characteristic pattern of decentralized production facilities: location in middle-sized towns in newly industrializing regions.[116]

The study by Markusen, Hall, and Glasmeier provides some contradictory evidence on the decentralization process.[117] They calculated an entropy index for 100 industrial sectors, and then observed the variation of the indexes between 1972 and 1977. According to their findings, while military-related sectors and bulk material processors actually increased their spatial concentration, most rapid growth sectors "showed a modest tendency toward decentralization from original growth centers." Areas with the largest rates of growth in high-technology jobs were precisely those adjacent to states that had the largest concentrations of high-technology industries. Nevertheless, at the same time, some of the most innovative industries did not exhibit a similar trend toward decentralization. Thus, while semiconductors plants spread over the country, semiconductors jobs became more concentrated over the 1972–7 period. Also, high-technology centers such as California increased their share of semiconductors jobs and plants, as well as for computer manufacturing jobs and plants, between the early 1960s and 1977.[118]

Table 2.23   Location of advanced manufacturing facilities of Santa Clara County firms, 1980

Firm	Plant Locations
Hewlett-Packard[a]	McMinnville, Corvallis, Oregon; Boise, Idaho; Fort Collins, Greely, Loveland, Colorado Springs, Colorado; Everett, Spokane, Vancouver, Washington; Roseville, California; Raleigh, North Carolina.
National Semiconductor	Salt Lake City, Utah; Tucson, Arizona; Vancouver, Washington.
Fairchild Camera & Instrument	South Portland, Maine; Worpingers Falls, Massachusetts, Tulsa, Oklahoma (planned).
Intel Corporation	Aloha, Oregon; Chandler, Arizona; Austin, Texas.
Varian Associates[a]	Salt Lake City, Utah; Florence, Lexington, Kentucky; Grove City, Ohio; Geneva, Illinois; Beverly, Danvers, Lexington, Woburn, Massachusetts.
Advanced Micro Devices	Austin, Texas.
American Microsystems, Inc.	Pocatello, Idaho.
Signetics	Orem, Utah.
Intersil	Ogden, Utah.
Memorex[a]	Plano, Texas.
Zilog	Boise, Idaho.
Spectra Physics[a]	Eugene, Oregon.
Siltec[a]	Salem, Oregon.

[a]Not a semiconductor firm.
[b]For semiconductor firms, advanced manufacturing is the same as wafer fabrication. For other firms, the process varies.
Source: Interviews; San Jose Mercury News, Business Section; collected and elaborated by Saxenian (see note 66).

These findings could support two related hypotheses. First, for information-technology industries decentralization of production is a function not of the "age" of the industry, but of the structural characteristics manifested by the industry since its early stages. Therefore, while the period 1960–77 could show a spatial sprawl of industries characterized by a higher than average technological level, the decentralized pattern of information-technology producers simply expanded in size without reversing its location pattern. The original centers of the industry maintained, or even increased, their share, as the continuous upgrading of technological innovation reinforced the role of the higher-level production functions.

Secondly, the decentralization off-shore of low-skilled jobs, and therefore of labor-intensive plants, has been taking place since 1962 at least. Since the entropy index refers only to US counties, it follows that it cannot account for this phenomenon. So, the more an industry decentralizes off-shore, the more its process of decentralization will be under-estimated by a US-specific analysis. As we have observed, off-shoring is especially characteristic of electronics in general, and of semiconductors in particular. This could explain the seemingly contradictory observations of jobs on the one hand and plants on the other: if labor-intensive plants decentralize off-shore, when the industry expands the spatial dispersion of plants in the US will be less than proportional to the expansion of jobs. Thus the growth of the industry on-shore will be biased toward the upper-level productive functions, with most jobs concentrated in the technologically advanced areas. This interpretation seems to fit the available evidence.

Glasmeier's analysis of the trends in decentralization of production also carries this central idea of the selective character of the process.[119] The bulk of new jobs created in the south are in low-skilled production and branch plants from the innovative firms of California and the north-east. According to Glasmeier's data, analysis of the industries on occupational lines to discriminate between higher and lower technological levels within the industry reveals that only 10 states appear to be technological high spots: Arizona, California, Colorado, Connecticut, Florida, Massachusetts, New Jersey, New York, Texas, and Washington. Most of the expansion of high-technology industries in other areas is accounted for by economic and technological subsidiaries of major centers of the new industrial structure. Yet, this new core does not bear out the popular image of a sunbelt/frostbelt opposition, nor does it correspond to the cleavage between old and new areas of industrialization. Some of the traditional industrial regions, such as New England and New Jersey, have transformed themselves into new manufacturing centers, clearly showing that the profile of the new industrial space does not result from some fixed geographical attributes, but from the relationship between the structure of the information-based industry and its socio-economic environment.

In sum, the decentralization of production is a recurrent trend of behavior in technologically advanced industries, and generally takes place within the hierarchical logic of the spatial division of labor among production functions, occupational skills, and organizational levels of the firm. This process of decentralization does not seem to be related to the age of the industry but to its structure since the early stages of its development. Decentralization occurs internationally, inter-regionally and intra-regionally, in a complex web of interaction that reorganizes the industrial landscape while reintegrating its functional and economic logic into a single system.

Growth of Information-technology Industries and Spatial Diffusion of their Location Pattern

Given the remarkable growth of information-technology industries in the past two decades, it is only natural that they should have dispersed their activities over regions and countries. The 1986 study cited above by Markusen, Hall, and Glasmeier found a strong tendency in most of the high-technology sectors they examined in the US to disperse among counties between 1972 and 1977. The extent of their dispersion seemed to be directly related to their rate of job growth. Glasmeier's updated database drawn from the 1982 Manufacturing Census confirms the trend over a longer period.[120] Semiconductors plants were present in 1972 in 120 counties, and in 1977 in 182. Computer manufacturing plants were present in 203 counties in 1977. Similar trends of industrial sprawl can be observed in western Europe, as the new industries continue to thrive, in spite of temporary downturns such as the 1984–6 slump.

A crucial question arises concerning the specificity of the location pattern of information-technology industries once they start dispersing across different regions. In fact, most evidence points to the fact that while production of information-technology devices takes place in an increasing number of places, the proportion of this activity that is concentrated in the main technological centers continues to grow. Furthermore, the spatial diffusion of information-technology production follows, broadly, the spatial logic of the pattern described and analyzed above.

If we consider again the findings of the Markusen, Hall, and Glasmeier study, we see that the most innovative industries were only moderately dispersed, as compared with the "average high-technology industries." Indeed, semiconductors, and other electronic sectors, such as resistors, telephone equipment, and most military-related industries, became more concentrated between 1972 and 1977. Computer manufacturing jobs and plants in 1977 were geographically more heavily concentrated, with the ten top states accounting for 76 percent of jobs and 75 percent of plants;

California alone boasted 30 percent of jobs and 35 percent of plants – an increase of 353 percent in the number of plants since 1967. In semiconductors, the top states maintained their shares of plants between 1963 and 1977, with California actually increasing its lead by 264 percent, compared to a US average increase of 152 percent in 1963–77.[121] Glasmeier's calculations for 1977–82 confirm the trend.

Thus, while the sheer size of the information-technology sector, after two decades of growth at a phenomenal rate, gives rise to its spatial sprawl, the industries remain disproportionately concentrated in the areas that were already the hubs of high-technology activity in the 1960s. There is a cumulative process of uneven development associated with the concentration of information generation and corporate control in the key milieux of innovation.

Furthermore, the spatial diffusion of the industry follows the processes, analyzed above, of hierarchical division of labor and decentralization of production. Specifically, the process of spatial diffusion manifests four main features. First of these is the generation of *secondary milieux of innovation* which articulate themselves to the seedbeds of technology in an asymmetrical, interdependent relationship. These secondary milieux are truly innovative production complexes that specialize in specific technological areas and tend to rely on a network of small, entrepreneurial start-up firms. Gordon and Kimball have analyzed the formation of such a milieu in Santa Cruz, California, since the late 1970s, in close association with nearby Silicon Valley.[122] Yet, as they make clear, Santa Cruz is much more than a set of ancillary firms for Silicon Valley. Most of the firms there tend to engage in innovative R&D for products that they sell, generally, to Silicon Valley companies; they sub-contract most of their production work to other California companies, so that they constitute truly a milieu of innovation of the second order, thus making more complex the chain of interdependence linking innovation, manufacturing, and markets. Secondary milieux of innovation are being generated in areas such as North Carolina's Research Triangle, Colorado Springs, Santa Barbara, and Salt Lake City. The important feature in each case is the direct relationship of these milieu to the higher-order innovation centers, sometimes represented by complexes, such as Route 128 or Silicon Valley, but often also organized around the inner world of large corporations, such as IBM or Motorola.

The second distinctive feature is the decentralization of technical branch plants, subsidiaries of companies located in predominant technological centers. Glasmeier, who has emphasized the role of these plants in the decentralization of high-technology industries, writes:

Technical branch plants represent a new tier in the corporate hierarchy and can be characterized as stand alone profit centers that have spun out of existing concentrations of older and newer vintages in search of pools of technical labor, as well as other factors, such as access to newly developing high-tech agglomerations and final markets. These units are organized often along product lines and are sites where both design and production are carried out.[123]

Thus, they are complete production units, with a large degree of initiative, yet organizationally and technologically dependent on the parent firm. Booming high-technology areas such as Austin and Phoenix are based mainly upon a concentration of large technical branch plants. For instance, Austin's industrial development was based on the location of such plants from IBM, Lockheed, TI, Intel, Control Data, Motorola, Rolm, Tandem, Sperry-Rand, Hughes, and more, attracted to Austin by a good university training large numbers of engineers, relatively cheap labor, good environmental quality, easy air connections, and a direct relationship with the expanding Texas market.

Industrial complexes built around technical branch plants are largely autonomous in their dynamics, yet they remain dependent on the primary milieux of innovation with respect to strategic decisions and access to new discoveries. There are, however, exceptions: for instance, in the case of Austin, the location of the electronics consortium MCC has provided the possibility of access to cutting-edge innovation in advanced microelectronics.[124] It is expected that the location of SEMATECH, a Defense Department-funded major research facility on manufacturing technology for semiconductors, approved in 1987, will further reinforce the potential for high-level research in Austin, which until now has been very limited.[125] Nevertheless, most of MCC's research findings, as well as, most likely, SEMATECH's technology, will constitute proprietary information that is likely to be diffused within the participant corporation networks rather than through the Austin complex.

Technical branch plants are also present in the high-level technological milieux, such as Silicon Valley or Boston, but here they tend to be subsidiaries of a parent company located in a different high-level milieu, set up in the alternative center in an attempt to tap into a competitor's local resources. An example of this would be Intel's branch plant near Boston.

Thirdly, manufacturing continues to be decentralized to less industrialized, relatively isolated areas. This process accounts for the majority of high-technology development in the southern United States, as well as for the location of American companies in the Third World. The evidence reviewed shows that the more industrial sprawl takes place, the more pronounced becomes the separation between advanced manufacturing and assembly manufacturing. The latter is increasingly rare in the US. The distinction between these two tiers of manufacturing tends to be sharper at present in the off-shore production process, with different levels of skill concentrated in different locations in Europe, Asia, and Latin America. For the present analytical purpose it is important to observe the reproduction of the spatial division of labor between different production functions off-shore, with the implication this carries that when information-technology industries expand over the world they do so according to their specific spatial logic.

The fourth feature that would seem to be suggested by the third is that the original milieux of innovation are irreproducible and that the new industrial space is going to be increasingly polarized inter-regionally and internationally. This is indeed the position clearly stated by Gordon and Kimball:

Global high-technology headquarters, once established, are not replicable. First: they were formed under specific historical conditions and circumstances that no longer pertain. Their emergence, far from being reducible to a single, easily replicated origin, was dependent precisely upon the favorable confluence of diverse and complex sources of growth whose simulation, particularly in competition with established headquarters locations, would require new, and impossibly risky governmental and business strategies as well as the concentration of extraordinarily vast resources. Second: rather than other areas creating anew the conditions which made the headquarters successful, the latter's infrastructural advantages act as a magnet for new businesses and skills which continue to be attracted to such areas rather than locating elsewhere. Third, the conversion of competitive entrepreneurial places into dominant technology headquarters renders their duplication unnecessary.[126]

Along similar lines, Oakey also provides a convincing argument about the self-expanding logic of Silicon Valley's pre-eminence.[127]

I tend to concur with these interpretations, yet with two important qualifications. First, the continuous technological upgrading of the industry considerably enhances the technological level of secondary milieux of innovation and technical branch complexes. It also expands the number and size of such complexes. More and more medium-level technological developments can take place away from the upper-level centers of innovation. Thus, the spatial division of labor should be seen no longer as a simple split between innovation and production, but rather as a separation of different levels of innovation and the emergence of different forms of linkage between innovation and production functions. Secondly, the more information-technology products become customized, programmable devices, the more crucial in all sectors is the direct connection between industrial producers and industrial users. While this trend has not reversed the dominance of high-level milieux of innovation, it has nevertheless created an incentive for information-technology producers and technological services to locate close to the major markets, namely the major metropolitan areas, including those of them in the old industrial regions. This is even more evident in the booming European market, where large metropolitan areas are acting as magnets for the location of Japanese and American information-technology firms, superseding the traditional rationale of location in underdeveloped European regions to take advantage of governmental incentives. Most of these new developments take the form of upgraded technical branch plants, including a complete ensemble of production functions. In some cases, research and design centers are being set up for customized prototype production in conjunction with the revitalization of the traditional industrial structure.[128]

The spatial diffusion of information-technology industries, then, basically expands the logic embedded in its structural characteristics. But it also places their location pattern in the context of the unfolding dynamics of economic restructuring and international competition.

Conclusion: The Dynamics of Information-technology Producers and the Transformation of the New Industrial Space

The main theme of this chapter has been the specific nature of the spatial location pattern of information-technology producers, a specificity which stems from the articulation of the structural characteristics of the industry with the dynamics of the firms and institutions that engage in its development. If the analysis presented here is correct, it should hold, in its main elements, for information-technology industries in other national contexts, as well as for future stages of the industry in the United States. This does not necessarily mean that the industry would continue to locate in similar places. The proposition concerns, rather, the replication of the spatial logic of the new productive organizations, namely their characteristic relationship to space, consequent on the dynamics of their process of production and their strategies as firms. To pursue the empirical verification of this proposition would require a comparative, historical, and prospective framework of analysis, and is clearly beyond the limits of this book. The present purpose is limited to defining the profile of a distinctive location pattern, so that its re-producibility can be tested, and the accuracy of the analytical model eventually perfected. Besides, we have made a methodological choice that informs this whole book, namely, to focus on the spatial transformation induced by new information technologies *in the United States*, as a way of testing the broader analytical framework proposed. Accordingly I have in general refrained from analyzing processes in other societies, the description of which could make the content of this book unnecessarily cumbersome at the current stage of development of the theory. Nevertheless, in concluding the treatment of the emergence of the new industrial space, on the basis of the US experience, it seems intellectually useful to consider the validity of the location pattern we have found for information-technology producers in other areas and, even more important, in the subsequent stages of the industry's development.

The only country with a mature information-technology industry at a comparable technological level to that of the US is Japan; and systematic data on Japanese firms' spatial behavior are too sparse to be able to conduct an adequate comparison. At first sight, however, it would seem that the pattern of location of the electronics industry in Japan is quite different from that pertaining in the US. From the beginning, most information-technology industries were located in the greater Tokyo metropolitan area;[129] and until recently, the industry did not present much international and inter-regional division of labor. Of course, geographic specificity has to be taken into consideration along with industrial specificity. Japan being smaller than California, one could hardly expect the same level of spatial differentiation among productive functions and types of firms as exhibited by electronics industries in the US. Yet if the characteristics of each national territory dominate and supersede those of the industry, it would be difficult to argue that we are in the presence of a new logic of industrial space. In fact, the Japanese experience has been more diversified, evolving as it did in different stages of technological development, and has recently become somewhat closer to the location pattern found in America. The key fact in this respect is that, in its initial stage, the Japanese electronics industry did not start from autonomous generation of new technological information.[130] It developed on the basis of manufacturing better information-technology products derived from discoveries made in the US and, to some extent, in Europe.[131] Therefore, since manufacturing quality and low production costs were crucial in gaining a competitive edge in the early stages of the new industry, it was essential to locate in the heart of the Japanese manufacturing areas, where skilled production with skilled workers could take place. There was little room for risking low-quality work in cheaper offshore locations. Besides, governmental support (particularly that of MITI) to large Japanese corporations was vital in the technological upgrading of the industry, as well as in its positioning in domestic and international markets, and Japanese government policy strongly supported location of economically strategic industries on Japanese soil. Given the high concentration of large corporations and government-sponsored research centers in the Tokyo–Yokohama area, this was the obvious location, linking research and manufacturing with the largest domestic market.

Nevertheless, when the industry matured, reaching higher technological status, and dramatically increasing its volume of production and exports, it expanded on the basis of a trend toward decentralization of production inside Japan. This trend has been evident since the early 1970s.[132] The main beneficiary of the process has been the hitherto underdeveloped southern island of Kyushu, which in the mid-1980s accounted for about 40 per cent of Japanese production of integrated circuits, with particularly heavy concentration around the Oita Prefecture.[133] Most of the decentralization concerned technical branch plants of the large corporations, including some American firms. The government also attempted to foster spatial dispersal of R&D by creating the "science and technology city" of Tsukuba,[134] about 60 km north of Tokyo, where in 1988 7,000 researchers worked on advanced research programs, most of them joint ventures between government and corporations.

In the third stage of development, when the Japanese electronics industry raised itself, economically and technologically, to the level of its US counterpart and became a world leader in information-technology production, its location pattern drifted in the direction of that we have found to be typical of the American information-technology industry. First, in a joint initiative between MITI and a number of regional Prefectures, the "technopolis program" was launched, its goal the development of 14 decentralized industrial milieux of innovation and production.[135] These "technopolises" try to reproduce the combination of elements present in Silicon Valley: university and government research centers, manufacturing companies, venture capital, government markets, and a concentration of high-level technical labor, in the hope of generating dynamic synergy among the different factors.[136] Although it is still early to assess the effects of the program, it is already possible to note the significant self-identification of the Japanese industry with the location pattern of milieux of innovation presented in this chapter. In fact, these technopolises are secondary milieux, still dependent on the Tokyo-based higher-level centers. Also, the decentralization of scientists and engineers is only made possible because of the development of a telecommunications infrastructure aimed at linking all milieux on-line, allowing researchers to work together in real time. Another factor favoring decentralization of innovation is a good inter-regional transportation network, based on the bullet-train, which, by increasing the accessibility of Tokyo, makes bearable the engineers' exile from the centers of power and consumption.

Secondly, when cut-throat international competition, the emergence of the newly industralizing countries (NICs) in the electronics market, and new protectionist measures indicated the possibility of a future threat to Japanese hegemony in the world market, the major corporations, among them NEC, Hitachi, and Toshiba, increasingly resorted to the strategy used by their American counterparts years before: offshoring lower-level production functions to the Pacific Rim, particularly to Taiwan, Singapore, Thailand, and Malaysia, to reduce production costs on the basis of cheaper labor, cheaper land, and fewer government taxes and regulations.[137] These plants are, of course, directly dependent on their parent companies. While originally they used to ship their finished products back to Japan, they are now exporting directly to the final markets, in a truly integrated world production chain.

Finally, to circumvent protectionism in other countries, Japanese companies have started to assemble, and sometimes to produce, in their key foreign markets, particularly the US and Europe, in a move parallel to that of American companies in the 1960s.[138]

In spite of obvious geographical contrasts, then, the main difference between the spatial behavior of the US and Japanese electronics industries seems to be related to the time difference in reaching a stage of development at which the firms' strategies had to face similar problems. From this point onwards, similarities in location strategies seem to be greater than the differences resulting from the two countries' specific history and geography. While there are still a great many differences between the American and Japanese industrial location patterns, given their very diverse respective starting points, the unfolding spatial logic of Japanese electronic firms does seem to result from the interaction between the specific structure of their production process and their industrial strategy, along lines not too distant from the spatial behavior observed in the case of the US.

Will this spatial logic persevere in the current stage of development of information-technology industries? Only by answering this question, even tentatively, can we make the distinction between the description of a temporary phenomenon and the analysis of a new process. To address the issue, within the limits of this study, I will conclude by considering the restructuring of the electronics industry during the 1980s and the spatial implication of the trends there displayed.

In 1984–6 the US electronics industry experienced its most serious slump ever, to the point of calling into question standing assumptions on the growth prospects of "sunrise" sectors. Silicon Valley was significantly hurt, with over 12,000 lay-offs, including substantial numbers of researchers and engineers. Vacancies for R&D and industrial space in the Valley jumped to a stunning 35 percent in 1986, a sign that the growth anticipated by the developers had not materialized.[139] The industry did not fully recover its dynamism until late 1987, and even then the potential for future crises was still present, as acknowledged by most observers of the industry. Three major factors appear to account for this crisis:[140]

(1) A process of "creative destruction," in the Schumpeterian sense, in which excess capacity developed by less competitive firms is eliminated, while resources are reoriented toward more productive uses. This is part of the typical cycle of a booming industry reaching a mature stage, a phenomenon that can be understood in the classical terms of the product cycle–profit cycle model. It is not, however, a primary cause of this crisis, which seems to stem mainly from other, more powerful factors.
(2) Increasing international competition, particularly from the Japanese electronics companies, based on lower production costs, higher manufacturing quality, and sustained effort in technological innovation. The arrival of new NIC and European producers in the market forced US companies to revise their structure of production costs as well as their marketing strategies.
(3) The difference in pace between the rate of technological innovation and the rate of diffusion and utilization of information technology in the economy and society at large. This was perhaps the crucial factor. Without wider use of information-technology devices it is impossible for

the electronics industry to keep growing at the same rate and still find markets. But at the same time the drive to innovate is the main competitive strategy hitherto used by information-technology producers, and capital-intensive investments and massive research efforts continue to be the main instruments for winning market shares. It follows that more costly investments and increasingly sophisticated technology need to generate higher returns in a market that, in fact, provides decreasing opportunities for such super-profits to match the expectations of the industry.

This "applications gap" is a particularly serious obstacle to the continuous growth of information-technology producers, because it is deeply entrenched in both the institutions of society and the organization of the industry. Without a massive re-equipping of traditional manufacturing, an upgrading of the educational system, and the appropriation by people and organizations of the full potential of information technologies, the pace of the industry will slow down in the near future, both technologically and economically. It is true that during the 1980s military markets came to the rescue of information-technology producers in the US; high-technology industries experienced a process of remilitarization after a long period of overwhelming dominance by commercial applications. Nevertheless, the military option can hardly be a way out of the potential structural crisis, because of its negative effects on technological diffusion, its limited commercial spin-offs, and its high dependence on budgetary constraints and political conjunctures. The expansion of military markets in the 1980s may have eased the downturn of the industry and allowed it to pick up momentum again, but it cannot absorb in the long term the tremendous productive potential that is boiling up in information technology's cauldrons.

In practice, electronics companies and government industrial polices (at both federal and state level) have tried to respond to the crisis through a number of strategies, leading to a major process of restructuring in the information-technology industries. Most of these new strategic policies can be grouped under four headings:[141]

(1) Establishment of closer and broader linkages with industrial sectors and final users of the technology. Examples are the effort by the computer industry massively to penetrate the school system, or the emphasis of electronics companies on the development of "mechatronics," in connection with the restructuring of old line manufacturing.
(2) Renewed efforts to automate electronics manufacturing, thus lowering production costs. Skilled non-research labor is the main target of cost-saving strategies in the production process. US companies seem to be engaging themselves in a blend of Japanese-inspired emphasis on manufacturing quality and their own traditional concern in finding cheaper sources of labor.

(3) Focus on the technological upgrading of the industry's products, targeting particularly the software component of the new systems, an area in which US science and technology retains a clear technological edge, although still being unable to use effectively the potential of the newest hardware. This strategy includes stepped-up research budgets, joint ventures with universities, sponsored corporate consortia on key technological fields (such as MCC), government-sponsored industrial research facilities, (such as SCI or SEMATECH), and a general call for government support in funding research and providing markets, sometimes on the grounds of protecting national security interests.
(4) An appeal to government support in opening up world markets and helping to protect US markets, under the disguise of free-trade ideology outraged by unfair competition.

The final impact of these strategies on the industry and its spatial manifestation will depend on the broader process of the restructuring of electronics worldwide. Dieter Ernst, having examined this process in detail, foresees four major developments:[142]

(1) A substantial decline of US semiconductors merchant firms will occur relative to huge, diversified electronics systems companies, the so-called "captive producers."
(2) Strategic alliances built around a few major systems corporations will become a key feature of global competition.
(3) There will be a major shift of wafer fabrication capacities to Asia and, more generally, a development of advanced manufacturing capability in that area of the world.
(4) Neo-mercantilist policies will proliferate, increasing protectionism in all economic regions.

Most of the available information points in these directions. However, my purpose here is not to indulge in economic forecasting but to analyze the spatial logic of information-technology industries. For the sake of this analysis, I will assume that the trends presented by Ernst take place, and try to elaborate on their potential spatial implications.

The emphasis on new linkages to be established with traditional manufacturing and information-based service activities is already fostering spatial relocation of some technical branch plants in a closer spatial relationship with the industry's markets.[143] This is also increasingly true for some customized design and prototype production focused on particular applications. The main beneficiaries of this move are large metropolitan areas with a concentration of information services, and old industrial regions in the process of converting their manufacturing basis. Yet only areas that can retain their nodal role in the economy, such as New York, or that are engaged in upgrading the industry's competitiveness in the world economy, such as

Michigan, are actually able to attract electronics industries organized around new strategic linkages.

Protectionist tendencies at the world level accentuate the linkage-induced decentralization of production, adding to the pattern an international dimension, as the need to penetrate growing markets dictates location inside the boundaries of each major economic region. While early decentralization of US electronics companies in Europe favored peripheral areas, such as Scotland or Montpellier, more recent developments tend to be concentrated in large industrial metropolitan areas, business centers, or a combination of both, such as Paris, Milan, Madrid, and Munich;[144] the formerly dominant concentrations of US companies in Scotland and Ireland are likely to be overshadowed by the new, linkage-oriented locations.

The drive toward automation, in terms of both labor cost-saving and manufacturing quality, definitely downplays the importance of cheap, unskilled labor as a location factor. Taking this to its logical extreme, decentralization to the Third World could come to a halt, even eventually be reversed. In fact, a more complex pattern is taking shape, in line with the new industrial strategy:[145] existing offshore locations are being automated and upgraded, and it seems likely, as predicted by Ernst, that advanced manufacturing will eventually take place in Asia. The reason for this development sees to be two-fold: first, the need to penetrate future potential markets, such as China, Korea, and India; secondly, the learning curve of workers in south-east Asian locations and the training of engineers by local institutions makes it possible to upgrade manufacturing and save costs on skilled labor, while keeping in place the existing industrial structure. So the pattern of decentralized production is likely to persist, still along the lines of the technical division of labor, yet with the important qualification of the upgrading of the low end of the technological spectrum. Purely routine tasks will most likely be entirely automated, not so much to save unskilled labor (given its low cost in new potential locations around the world) as to ensure high and consistent quality and smooth production.

The process of technological upgrading, the key element if the US industry is to keep its competitive edge, translates spatially into the reinforcement of high-level innovative milieux, as well as the development of secondary milieux in direct relationship with major centers of innovation. These high-level milieux (Silicon Valley, Boston, North Carolina's Research Triangle, Minneapolis, etc.) concentrate an increasing share of technological knowledge, to the point where we can foresee their evolution into providers of technological services, engaging mainly in design and prototype production, with an attenuation of their manufacturing basis. This trend was already apparent in Silicon Valley in 1987.[146] Companies from all over the world set up shop in Silicon Valley, in many cases by acquiring existing companies, to take advantage of the new technological developments produced there in order to manufacture products resulting from the Valley's discoveries in different, more convenient locations. Thus, in spite of increasingly acute urban problems and occasional economic downturns, these higher milieux will continue to thrive, and are unlikely to be replaced or even replicated at the same level of innovative potential, because of the cumulative character of knowledge generation and the industrial learning process. Only targeted efforts, supported by governments on a very large scale, are able to set up new high-level milieux of innovation in other areas of the world, and even this will become more and more difficult to achieve as the pace of scientific and technological discovery accelerates. High-level milieux of innovation reinforce their own dominance and their exclusiveness on the basis of their self-expanding synergy.

In sum, the spatial implications of the restructuring process in the electronics industry do not reverse the locational logic I have presented and analyzed. In fact, they develop it and give it specific form. Milieux of innovation continue to command the chain of interdependencies, and, if anything, they become more exclusive, more secluded, and more central in the overall production process. Secondary milieux of innovation are developing and will continue to do so, but more as an expression of the process of decentralization of some aspects of innovation functions than as a diffusion of the industry's original seedbeds throughout the country and the world. Decentralization of production still takes place along the lines of the specific requirements of each stage of the labor process. Market-oriented location becomes increasingly important at both domestic and international levels, further decentralizing production to ensure linkages with users of information technology. Spatial division of labor, on the basis of technological level and corporate control functions, is still the pervasive and distinctive characteristic of information-technology industries, although increased automation, upgrading of manufacturing operations, and new technological discoveries have extended the scope of this division both toward the upper end (increasingly exclusive milieux of innovation) and toward the lower end (offshoring of advanced manufacturing).

Thus, although the industry is extending its presence into new locations (for instance, to older manufacturing regions via the "mechatronics connection"), its spatial logic seems to be rooted in its structural characteristics, though the actual location pattern of the industry results from the interaction of that structurally determined logic with the specific orientations of the industry in the changing pattern of world competition. Nevertheless, a major trend in the process of industrial restructuring could decisively effect that spatial logic itself, along with everything else in the world of information-technology producers. I refer here to the evolution, predicted by various authors,[147] toward global strategic alliances between a few major system corporations, together with the dependence of US merchant firms on these large corporations. Could this trend decisively affect the economic, technological, and spatial structure of the industry as I have presented it? Economically, without any doubt, because such is precisely the meaning of the restructuring process. Technologically, less so, because the large corporations have a strong interest in maintaining and enhancing the creativity and synergistic potential of milieux of innovation, while wishing to capture that potential in their corporate structures. Very much in the way that IBM keeps Intel thriving technologically, while making it increasingly dependent commercially, large corporate systems are taking over the world of information technology using a non-traditional approach: the emphasis is on networks and sub-contracting, not on mergers and takeovers. The instruments of domination are technological specification, price-cutting competition, and access to large, secure markets. Large corporations, American as well as Japanese and Europeans, tread a thin line between subduing innovative companies and not destroying their technological potential and entrepreneurial dynamism. Thus, milieux of innovation such as Silicon Valley or Route 128 are becoming increasingly dependent on worldwide corporate conglomerates that internalize their innovative potential in their commercial strategies. In so doing, they do not transform the spatial logic of information-technology industries. IBM, or ATT, or Phillips-Signetics also operate, and will operate, on the basis of spatial division of labor, exclusive milieux of innovation, and decentralization of the production process.[148] Yet there is a major change in the making: the spatial logic of information-technology producers is being drawn inside the organizational structure of large corporations. The internationalization of production, the social and spatial separation of innovation functions, the relocation of production as a basis for market-oriented downward linkages – all these processes increasingly take place within the corporate structures, either inside the corporation itself of within the networks through which the corporate system controls its inputs and expands its output.[149] The emergence of a dominant corporate world in the information-technology industry does not preclude the spatial logic stemming form the industry's structure: it internalizes it, institutionalizing in a network of flows interconnected at a global level the new socio-spatial division of labor. Control over the production of information technology is tantamount to structural domination of the new industrial space.

3

The Space of Flows

The Use of New Technologies in the Information Economy, and the Dialectics between Centralization and Decentralization of Services

Introduction

It would seem obvious that the most direct impact of information techno-logies on the economy and society, and therefore on their spatial structure, occurs in the realm of information-processing activities. Such an elementary observation nevertheless has far-reaching consequences for social and spatial organization, because the processes of production, distribution, and manage-ment of advanced economies rely increasingly on knowledge generation, information exchanges and information handling. The dramatic changes in information technology deeply affect the core of our system, and in so doing lie at the very roots of its pattern of spatial change. The use of information technology by organizations, and particularly by large private corporations and large-scale public bureaucracies, may be the most important immediate source of technological change in our cities and regions. However, the spatial form taken by this change is far from simple. While the prophets of techno-logical determinism have forecast the general dissolution of cities and metro-politan areas in an undifferentiated territorial sprawl, with all communication conducted by satellites and optic fiber networks, the actual processes at work are much more complex because technology is only an instrument, albeit a very powerful one, of the process of organizational restructuring dictated by economic, social, and institutional changes. So, between the new information technologies and the emerging spatial structure, there are a number of fundamental mediating factors: the evolution of services; the rise of the information economy; the impact of automation on office work and office workers; the new organizational, and thus locational, logic of large corpor-ations and public bureaucracies; and the interaction of all these elements with the existing spatial structure and with the social environment in which all these trends articulate with one another. It is this complexity that I will try to reconstruct in this chapter, in order to explain in its final section the dialectics between centralization and decentralization of information-processing activities and the consequences of this process for the overall social and spatial structure. But before we are able to understand the actual meaning of this new spatial logic, we need to examine the impact of office automation in the context of the expansion of an information economy, a process which is at the very core of the shift of employment and output toward service activities.

The Structural Shift to Services and the Rise of the Information Economy

The fundamental transformation of the economic structure in advanced industrial societies, and particularly in the US, is expressed in the continuing shift toward service activities as a source of employment and generation of output.[1] In 1986, in the US, services accounted for 71 per cent of total employment and 68 per cent of GNP.[2] This trend has led to the characterization of such societies as "post-industrial,"[3] a notion that confuses rather than helps the identification of the new historical trends. The notion of post-industrialism is purely negative: it refers to the fact that manufacturing is no more at the center of the economy. This itself is open to question, yet, even accepting that position, we would still need to define what is at the core of the new social and economic dynamics. On both counts (the implicit under-estimation of the structural role of manufacturing industries, and the descriptive negativism of characterizing a major social trend as "post-"), the notion of post-industrialism recognizes, without truly explaining, a major social transformation.[4] It is important to assess this transformation analytically if we are to be able to understand the extent of the impact of information technologies on our socio-spatial structure.

On the one hand, although manufacturing activities have seen their relative importance decline steadily over time, the rise of services cannot be directly correlated with the "demise" of manufacturing.[5] The dramatic increase in service jobs in recent decades (see table 3.1) has taken place mainly as a result of job transfers from agriculture,[6] and of the entry into the labor market of new kinds of workers, particularly women, who account for the great majority of all new jobs in services during the period 1975–85, filling over 82 percent of all new jobs created during that period. There is a direct relationship between the rise of services and the feminization of the labor force.[7]

On the other hand, the declining proportion of jobs in manufacturing, as well as its shrinking share of GNP, do not eliminate its strategic importance in the overall economic picture, in very much the same way as the shrinkage

Table 3.1 Percentage distribution of the labor force by industry sectors and intermediate industry groups 1870–1980

Sectors and industries	1870	1900	1920	1940	1950	1960	1970	1980
Extractive	52.3	40.7	28.9	21.3	14.4	8.1	4.5	4.5
Agriculture	50.8	38.1	26.3	19.2	12.7	7.0	3.7	3.6
Mining	1.6	2.6	2.6	2.1	1.7	1.1	0.8	0.9
Transformative	23.5	27.9	32.9	29.8	33.9	35.9	33.1	29.8
Construction	5.9	5.8		4.7	6.2	6.2	5.8	6.2
Food				2.7	2.7	3.1	2.0	1.8
Textile				2.6	2.2	3.3	3.0	2.1
Metal				2.9	3.6	3.9	3.3	2.7
Machinery	17.6	22.1		2.4	3.7	7.5	8.3	5.2
Chemical				1.5	1.7	1.8	1.6	1.3
Misc. manufacturing				11.8	12.3	8.7	7.7	10.5
Utilities	a	a	a	1.2	1.4	1.4	1.4	1.4
Distributive services	11.5	16.9	18.7	20.4	22.4	21.9	22.3	23.9
Transportation	5.0	7.3	7.6	4.9	5.3	4.4	3.9	6.6
Communication				0.9	1.2	1.3	1.5	1.5
Wholesale				2.7	3.5	3.6	4.1	3.9
Retail	6.5	9.5	11.1	11.8	12.3	12.5	12.8	11.9
Producer services	b	b	2.8	4.6	4.8	6.6	8.2	9.5
Banking				1.1	1.1	1.6	2.6	1.7
Insurance				1.2	1.4	1.7	1.8	1.9
Real Estate				1.1	1.0	1.0	1.0	1.6
Engineering					0.2	0.3	0.4	0.6
Accounting					0.2	0.3	0.4	0.5
Misc. business services				1.3	0.6	1.2	1.8	2.4
Legal services					0.4	0.5	0.5	0.8
Social services	3.4	5.1	8.7	10.0	12.4	16.3	21.9	24.3
Medical					1.1	1.4	2.2	3.3
Hospitals				2.3	1.8	2.7	3.7	4.1
Education	1.5	2.3	2.8	3.5	3.8	5.4	8.6	7.7
Welfare				0.9	0.7	1.0	1.2	1.0
Non-profits					0.3	0.4	0.4	0.6
Postal services				0.7	0.8	0.9	1.0	0.7
Government	0.8	1.0	2.2	2.6	3.7	4.3	4.6	4.7
Misc. social services					0.1	0.2	0.3	2.3
Personal services	9.3	9.4	8.1	14.0	12.1	11.3	10.0	10.8
Domestic Serv.	7.4	6.1	4.1	5.3	3.2	3.1	1.7	1.3
Hotels				1.3	1.0	1.0	1.0	1.1
Eating and drinking	2.0	3.4	4.0	2.5	3.0	2.9	3.3	4.4

Table 3.1   Continued

Sectors and industries	1870	1900	1920	1940	1950	1960	1970	1980
Repair				1.5	1.7	1.4	1.3	1.5
Laundry				1.0	1.2	1.0	0.8	0.4
Barber and beauty				—	—	0.8	0.9	0.7
Entertainment				0.9	1.0	0.8	0.8	1.0
Misc. personal services				1.6	1.2	0.4	0.3	0.4

[a] Utilities included in distributive services.
[b] Finance, insurance, and real estate included in trade.
Source: 1870–1970 US Census; 1980: "Special Labor Force Report 244," U.S. Department of Labor Bureau of Labor Statistics, 1981. Compiled by Singelman (see note 6) and updated by Baran (see note 48).

of the proportion of farmers and agricultural workers to less than 3 percent of total US employment does not preclude agriculture continuing to play a very important role in the economy, both directly, through the provision and pricing of its products, and indirectly, through the manufacturing and service activities it generates. Pursuing this line of reasoning, Cohen and Zysman have argued convincingly the close linkages between manufacturing and service activities.[8] They point out that many service activities, particularly in producer services, the most dynamic in output generation, are in fact support activities to the management, production, and distribution of manufactured goods. In fact, they argue, when a national economy, such as the US, overlooks such linkages, increasingly specializing in services, the loss of competitiveness in manufacturing leads to correspondingly increasing losses in services to the point where service growth cannot compensate in either quantity or quality for the jobs and wealth lost in the process of de-industrialization.

An alternative vision to the classical, and misleading line of argument, Colin Clark's mechanistic and evolutionary distinction between primary, secondary, and tertiary sectors, is to consider the economic structure as made up of *processes*, in which service activities connect agriculture and manufacturing with the consumption of goods and services, and with the management of organizations and institutions of society. Only from this perspective will we be able to understand the diversity of services, a diversity in fact so extreme that it forbids considering services as a single, homogeneous sector of economic activity. Joachim Singelman proposed a few years ago a typology of services that still appears to be the most useful characterization of the different activities arbitrarily merged under the label.[9] Table 3.1 documents the evolution of employment in the US between 1870 and 1980 using Singelman's typology, updated to include the figures of the 1980 Census. A reading of this table shows the great differences among types of services in their relative share of total employment. Thus, between 1960 and 1980, distributive services grew moderately, although still accounting for 23.9 percent of the labor force in 1980. Personal services actually declined, from 11.3 percent to 10.8 percent, with the major exception of eating and drinking activities, which employ 4.4 percent of the labor force – more than agriculture. Producer services almost doubled, while still employing, overall, fewer workers than personal services. And social services literally exploded, jumping from 10 percent in 1940 to 24.3 percent in 1980. Even during the crisis years of the 1970s, the decline in education employment has been more than compensated by employment growth in hospitals and medical services, which in 1980 reached 7.8 percent of the labor force. These trends have continued in the same direction during the 1980s, increasing the gap between expanding service industries and moderate job creation in other sectors. According to calculations by Peter Hall, between 1980 and 1985 4,219,700 new non-farm jobs were added to the US economy.[10] Of these, only 33,200 were in manufacturing, and 3,477,800 were in services. However, within services there were major disparities. For instance, communications grew by over 400,000 jobs, while commerce (wholesale and retail together) actually lost over 66,000 jobs (see table 3.2). Table 3.3 shows the dissimilarity of the evolution of the various types of services in the 1970–84 period in terms of contribution to GNP, with finance, insurance, and real estate, and "other service industries" (including health and education), dramatically increasing their share. Together, these two categories account for 30.7 percent of 1984 GNP, well above the 21 percent accounted for by manufacturing.

The lesson to be drawn from this disparity is very simple: *there is not a service sector*. There are a number of activities, employing people and generating income, that go beyond the extractive and manufacturing activities, and which increase their diversity as our societies grow in complexity.[11] The so-called "services" have grown out of a variety of functional demands and social pressures, many of which derive from social mobilization and political concessions, as I suggested years ago.[12] A substantial part of employment in services, particularly in social services and personal services, is in fact, a way of absorbing the surplus population generated by increased productivity in agriculture and industry, in a society that still requires salaried work to survive, even if we could achieve greater collective output with less collective work. This is why, as Stanback writes:

Productivity is a key issue in assessing the role of services in our economy. There is little evidence of a strong, cumulative shift of demand from goods to services. Yet the shift toward greater shares of employment in services is well established. For services taken as a whole, gains in productivity have failed to match those in non-service activities. Consequently, economic growth has been accompanied by disproportionately large increases in service sector jobs.[13]

Table 3.2 Employment changes by SIC single-digit headings, divisions, 1975–80, 1980–5

(a) 1975–80

	New England	Mid-Atlantic	E.-N.-Cent.	W.-N.-Cent.	S. Atlantic	E.-S.-Cent.	W.-S.-Cent.	Mountain	Pacific	Total US
TOTAL thousands	857.8	1360.0	2071.2	1130.5	2742.5	881.9	2310.5	1180.9	3199.2	15734.5
Mining	1.2	−0.3	10.2	11.7	7.8	15.7	171.2	49.1	14.9	281.5
Construction	12.7	13.6	67.1	37.9	156.4	23.2	186.8	92.6	167.4	757.9
Manufacturing	223.9	38.0	79.9	149.0	414.7	120.7	345.9	141.8	526.6	2039.9
Transportation	31.0	99.6	175.2	121.4	187.9	77.2	166.2	95.7	161.8	1116.0
Communication	27.1	85.9	152.2	100.9	134.5	58.0	119.7	66.3	108.9	852.6
	3.9	13.7	23.0	21.4	53.4	19.2	46.5	28.6	52.9	262.6
Wholesale/retail	168.0	236.7	442.1	222.3	627.4	169.4	494.6	252.5	782.1	3395.1
Finance, Insurance, Real Estate	60.7	109.9	162.3	71.9	163.4	39.3	134.9	75.0	250.9	1068.3
Services	281.7	814.9	906.8	414.9	721.2	283.7	554.1	347.6	1110.3	5435.2
Government	78.6	47.4	227.6	101.4	463.7	152.7	256.8	127.4	185.8	1641.4
Industry	237.3	51.5	157.2	198.6	578.9	159.6	703.9	283.5	708.3	3079.3
Service	620.0	1308.5	1914.0	931.9	2163.6	722.3	1606.6	897.4	2490.9	12655.2
Goods-handling	432.9	374.1	751.5	520.9	1340.8	387.0	1318.2	602.3	1599.3	7327.0
Information-handling	424.9	985.9	1319.7	609.6	1401.7	494.9	992.3	578.6	1599.9	8407.5
Ratio: serv./ind.	2.5	25.4	12.2	4.7	3.7	4.5	2.3	3.2	3.5	4.1
info./goods	1.0	2.6	1.8	1.2	1.0	1.3	0.8	1.0	1.0	1.1

Table 3.2 Continued[1]

(b) 1980–85

	New England	Mid-Atlantic	E.-N.-Cent.	W.-N.-Cent.	S. Atlantic	E.-S.-Cent.	W.-S.-Cent.	Mountain	Pacific	Total US
TOTAL thousands	381.3	39.4	-147.9	19.1	1745.1	265.6	811.8	476.7	628.6	4219.7
Mining	0.7	-7.3	-16.3	-8.1	-23.7	-6.8	-15.4	-44.0	8.8	120.2
Construction	93.2	155.0	31.7	14.8	236.9	24.2	109.8	60.9	102.3	828.8
Manufacturing	64.4	-276.2	-138.0	-39.1	158.6	18.7	-19.0	86.3	177.5	33.2
Transportation	58.0	66.4	91.4	56.6	161.8	68.0	52.2	52.2	140.3	746.9
Transportation	25.1	-2.4	40.7	17.1	48.1	28.0	17.4	21.3	64.8	260.1
Communication	32.9	68.8	50.7	39.5	113.7	40.0	34.8	27.0	44.3	451.3
Wholesale/retail	-55.3	-195.1	-137.0	-66.9	250.5	58.1	120.3	70.5	-111.6	-66.4
Finance, Insurance, Real Estate	105.5	159.4	122.2	63.2	224.8	47.8	159.0	101.8	153.4	1137.3
Services	152.8	204.5	225.5	100.2	794.7	105.3	354.4	119.7	198.2	2255.4
Government	-38.2	-67.4	-327.3	-101.7	-58.5	-49.7	50.4	33.3	-1.0	-560.1
Industry	158.4	-128.4	-122.6	-32.4	371.8	36.1	75.4	103.1	280.5	741.9
Service	222.9	167.8	-25.3	51.5	1373.4	229.5	736.4	373.6	348.0	3477.8
Goods-handling	128.2	-325.9	-218.9	-82.2	670.4	122.2	213.2	194.9	233.7	935.6
Information-handling	253.1	365.3	71.0	101.3	1074.7	143.4	598.6	281.8	394.9	3284.1
Ratios: serv./ind.	1.4	NA	0.2	NA	3.7	6.4	9.8	3.6	1.2	4.7
Info./goods	2.0	NA	NA	NA	1.6	1.2	2.8	1.4	1.7	3.5

Source: Bureau of Labor Statistics, calculated by Peter Hall (see note 10).

Table 3.3 Components of United States Gross National Product

Services	Current $					1972 $ B				
	1970	1975	1980	1983	1984	1970	1975	1980	1983	1984
Total GNP	993	1,549	2,632	3,305	3,663	1,086	1,234	1,475	1,535	1,639
Agriculture, forestry, fisheries	29	53	77	73	91	34	37	40	39	45
Manufacturing	252	358	582	685	776	261	290	351	354	391
Transportation	39	55	99	115	130	43	46	52	47	50
Communication	24	40	67	92	103	26	36	52	59	63
Wholesale trade	68	117	190	229	265	72	88	104	114	130
Retail trade	98	149	238	307	337	104	122	142	152	165
Finance, insurance, real estate	142	216	399	543	598	155	188	236	254	265
Other service industries	114	186	342	478	529	127	148	189	207	219

Source: Quinn (see note 2).

Table 3.4 confirms this statement for the period 1968–78, on the threshold of the technological revolution in information processing. However, here again we find substantial differences among "services." Thus, while communications exhibited spectacular productivity growth during the period under consideration, "other services" (particularly health) and government showed a dismal performance, largely accounting for the low productivity growth overall of the US economy (manufacturing increased by 2.34 percent). Even finance, insurance, and real estate had a lower than average productivity growth, because its major increase in output was accompanied by a significant increase in employment. Yet, this does not imply that service activities, and particularly producer services and social services, are "parasite economic

Table 3.4   Output, employment and productivity growth rates in the US economy 1968–78 (%)

Industry	Output: Constant $ gross product originating	Full-time and part-time employees	Productivity: gross product originating per hour worked
All industries	2.89	1.90	1.41
Private non-farm economy	3.11	2.15	1.42
Agriculture forestry and fishing	1.8	1.18	0.68
Mining	1.40	3.68	−2.29
Construction	−0.54	1.96	−2.28
Manufacturing	2.44	0.34	2.34
Communications	8.36	2.39	5.84
Electric, gas and sanitary services	3.26	1.69	1.59
Wholesale trade	3.97	2.68	1.63
Retail trade	3.06	3.37	0.76
Finance insurance and real estate	4.22	3.50	0.99
Services	3.82	3.37	0.77
Business	5.88	5.95	0.69
Health	4.82	7.04	−1.44
Other	2.82	1.6	1.41
Government	1.31	1.02	0.56

Source: Economic Perspective on Trends in the United States Economy, 1968–1978, US Industrial Outlook, 1981, US Department of Commerce, Bureau of Industrial Economics. Compiled by Baron (see note 48)

activities." The contribution of most services to overall economic growth and social well-being is fundamental. But, until now, the characteristic nature of their labor processes and the institutional framework of service activities (many of them linked to the public sector) made it difficult to obtain the same productivity increases in services that took place in agriculture and manufacturing over the whole of this century. There is a fundamental contradiction building up in advanced economies: on the one hand, support activities, and particularly the handling of information, are at the core of productivity increases in the whole economy;[14] on the other hand, until very recently, many of the information-processing activities were labor-intensive and prone to low labor productivity.[15] Increased productivity in the economy as a whole was being disguised by the expansion of low-productivity, yet indispensable, service activities, particularly in information-handling. This is what explains the apparent mystery illustrated by figure 3.1, constructed by the Bureau of Labor Statistics: between 1948 and 1982, labor output increased substantially, as did, although to a lesser extent, "multifactor productivity" (which accounts for elements other than labor and capital). However, the productivity of capital remained stable.[16] In other words, the overhead costs of production for capital skyrocketed. This trend is partly due to the expansion of government and public services, both in defense and in social expenditures. But a substantial part of these overhead costs is attributable to the management of costs of production, that is, to the processing of information, that for a long time has been difficult to mechanize and rationalize, and even more difficult to automate.[17] Thus, at the center of the expansion of employment in services lies the explosion of information-processing activities.[18]

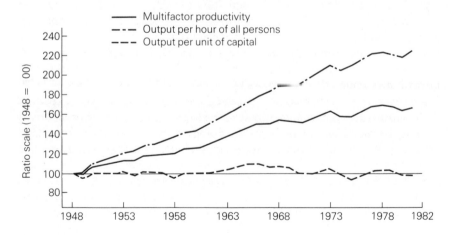

Figure 3.1   Indices of output per hour of all persons, output per unit of capital and multifactor productivity in the private business sector, 1948–1982
Source: Bureau of Labor Statistics

Marc Porat, in his pioneering work on the subject,[19] estimated that by 1970 46 percent of the US work force was employed in the information sector. Building on Porat's work, Kling and Turner have estimated that in 1980 50.5 percent of the US work force was employed in information-handling, up from 41 percent in 1960.[20] Peter Hall estimated that 8 million of the 15.6 million new non-farm jobs generated in the US in 1975–80, and almost 3.3 million of the 4 million new jobs created in 1980–5, were information-handling jobs. This is a most useful catergorization[21] because it cuts across the outmoded distinction between manufacturing and services to address the actual job content of a given occupation, thus avoiding the misleading practice of classifying as manufacturing workers the clerks of an automobile maker company. Kling and Turner have evaluated the distribution of the information work force by occupational categories, showing the increasing relative importance of professionals and semiprofessionals, the stabilization of the proportion of clerical workers (still representing 42.4 percent of the work force in 1980), and the decreasing proportion of sales and supervisory, and of blue-collar workers. It is this information-oriented work force which constitutes the quantitative and qualitative basis of advanced economies. The application of the information generated and processed by this labor force to all sectors, be they extractive, manufacturing, or services, is the main generator of productivity growth and income.[22] Our economies are to be categorized not as "post-industrial," but, as I argued in the first chapter of this book, *informational*, that is to say, the production of surplus derives mainly from the generation of knowledge and from the processing of necessary information. It is the surplus of productivity realized in manufacturing, agriculture, and producer services that allows the secular tendency to the growth of output per unit of input to continue.[23] Service activities mix information processing with the support of production and distribution, the satisfaction of consumer demands, and the management of organizations and institutions of society. Behind the expansion of the service sector, directly in terms of employment, and indirectly in terms of its effects on output, lies the development of the information economy.[24]

However, in a major historical paradox, the more societies have expanded their information-processing activities, the lower has been their productivity growth, because, unlike in high-technology manufacturing, information-processing organizations did not and/or could not extensively use information processing for their own restructuring. With a number of exceptions, mainly related to the use of the telephone, large-scale organizations in advanced economies continued for a long time to work under conditions and procedures close to those of the early periods of industrialization, and in the case of government bureaucracies to those of the pre-industrial age.[25] To be sure, since the mid-1960s some new trends toward greater capital intensity in the service industries did appear, notably in air transport, pipeline and rail transportation, communications, and public facilities.[26] But capital intensity remained low in the core of information industries, even in the financial sector until well into the 1970s.[27] The lack of information-processing technology in the information-processing organizations serving the economy and society at large was (and still largely is) the stumbling block for the unleashing of productive forces in our informational age. When the institutional context of the 1970s and 1980s forced corporations and governments into fully-fledged restructuring, the timely discoveries in information technology of the preceding three decades were at last put to work.[28] The result was the beginning of a dramatic transformation of information-handling activities, and therefore of office work,[29] that is perhaps the true equivalent in our societies to what manufacturing represented *vis-à-vis* craft production during the first industrial revolution.

Office Automation and Organizational Change in the Information Industries

The development of the information economy relies on large-scale organizations, be they private corporations or public bureaucracies.[30] Although small businesses continue to play a dynamic role in investment and job creation,[31] their role is auxiliary in relation to processes that depend largely on the commanding heights of the economy.[32] Both the internal and the external linkages of large organizations have expanded at a dramatic rate in the past quarter of a century, and they continue to do so. Added flexibility in the system, whether by means of decentralization of units of large corporations or by multiple connections with small firms, only increases the number and complexity of the exchanges on which the day-to-day management of the economy is based. In 1985, US offices processed about 500 billion documents, and the volume of paperwork is increasing by 72 billion additional documents per year.[33] It is clear that without a substantial technological overhaul, the system's capacity has arrived at breaking point. Accordingly, in recent years, the bulk of information-technology devices are being installed in the service sector. For instance, in 1982, 80 percent of all computing, communications, and information-technology equipment sold in the US went to services.[34]

The impact of this trend is most significant, and most strongly felt, in relation to office work. By office work, following the definition of the Office of Technology Assessment (OTA), we understand "the processing and use of information for the purpose of tracking, monitoring, recording, directing, and supporting complex human activities."[35] In this context, office automation, again in the OTA's terms, refers to "the application of microelectronic information technology and communication technology to office work."[36]

Two major streams of new information technologies are converging to revolutionize office work and corporate organizations: the computerization of information processing, and the multifaceted application of telecommunications to information exchange. Although for the sake of clarity I will distinguish here between the two processes, they have interacted throughout the evolution of automation, and the most significant recent development is their actual merger into information systems.[37]

The computerization of office work has gone through three different phases.[38] In the first one, mainframe computers were used for batch processing of data, to build corporate databases; centralized computing, handled by specialists in electronic data-processing centers, formed the basis of a system characterized by rigidity and hierarchical control of information flows; data entry operations required substantial efforts since the goal of the system was the accumulation of large amounts of information in a central memory; work was standardized, routinized, and, in essence, de-skilled for the majority of clerical workers, in a process analyzed, and denounced, by Harry Braverman in his pioneer work.[39]

The following stages of automation, however, quite substantially changed this situation in the office and in office work.[40] The second phase, spurred on by the diffusion of microprocessors and the personal computer,[41] is characterized by the emphasis on the handling of microcomputers by the end users, that is the employees in charge of the actual work process; although they can be supported by centralized databases, they interact directly in the process of generating information without the intermediation of computer experts. In fact, by the mid-1980s, the two forms of computerization were merging, under the dominance of the second, with databases being managed mainly through decentralized information-handling processes.

The third phase introduces a more qualitative difference: it relies on networking and integrated office systems, where multiple microcomputers interact among themselves and with mainframes, in a web of generally horizontal exchanges.[42] The process is interactive, and the flows multi-directional. This third phase is made possible by the development of telecommunications. The current impact of telecommunications on the office originates in the dramatic expansion of transmission capacity in recent years, on the basis of the digitization of the telephone network, the use of satellites (which make the cost of transmission independent of the distance involved), microwave systems, coaxial cable, cellular telephony, and, above all, the trend toward the use of laser signals and the installation of optic fiber lines, giving substantially increased carrying capacity as well as much greater speed and accuracy of transmission. It is the combination of these different communication systems, and their gradual integration in an Integrated Service Digital Network (ISDN) which that is projected to become universal, which provides the capability for flexible communication of both voice and data between information-processing units, from anywhere to anywhere, most often simply by using the standard telephone line.[43] It is the merger of computers and telecommunications in the same network that gives birth to *information systems* (IS), which constitute the true foundation of office automation and have already become indispensable tools in the management of our economy and of our society.[44]

New technologies being introduced in the late 1980s will enhance even further the information-processing and transmission capabilities of the automated office.[45] Particularly notable examples are optical character recognition (OCR), already widely used in banking, and speech recognition (SR), which could by the mid-1990s entirely transform the accessibility of sophisticated computing to non-specialist users. Also, the current development of optical disks as storage devices, and more generally the potential of photonics, as well as more powerful chips, will open the way for ultrapowerful microcomputers, rendering less valid the current distinction between mainframe, mini- and microcomputers, and fully decentralizing the information-processing capability. Another major development, related to advances in artificial intelligence, is the setting up of expert systems that synthesize the accumulated knowledge in particular fields (for instance, medical or legal specialties), for use directly by professionals in the field. Coupled with access to centralized or decentralized databases, expert systems allow processing of valuable information by the professionals themselves, bypassing numerous steps of information retrieval and preparation and thus of clerical work.

The effects of these technological changes on office work and office workers are fundamental and complex, and they are not yet fully identified, in part because the process of technological change is only beginning and is rapidly accelerating in pace. However, there are a number of case studies that point consistently toward some fundamental trends.[46] I will leave aside, for the moment, the impact of these trends on employment and on working conditions, aspects that will be analyzed in some detail in chapter 4. Focusing here on the organizational consequences of office automation, the first observation is that there is no such thing as a pure technological effect. The actual effects of automation depend largely on the product of the service industry, as well as on the management of the industry at a particular time. Thus, within one industry, insurance for instance, the underwriting and the selling of the policy do not follow the same logic and are not affected in the same way by automation.[47] Furthermore, life insurance and health insurance also present different effects, given their different markets. Therefore, any specific analysis of office automation will have to consider the interaction between the process and the product, and between the technology and the industry.[48]

With these caveats in mind we can, nevertheless, emphasize some generally observed trends that have particular relevance for the present subject of inquiry. There is a clear tendency to automate the lower end of clerical jobs, those routine tasks that, because they can be reduced to a number of standard steps, can be easily programmed. There is also a movement toward decentralizing as much as possible the process of data entry, gathering the information and entering it into the system as close as possible to the source. For instance, sales accounting will be increasingly connected to automated scanning and storage at the cashier's point-of-sale machine. Bank branches' automated telling machines (ATMs) will be used to update bank accounts' movements constantly without intermediate accounting operations. Insurance claims will be directly stored in memory with respect to all the elements that do not call for a business judgement; and so on. All these trends lead to the elimination of a substantial amount of routine clerical work, and thus, potentially, of clerical jobs (although the matter of the elimination of clerical jobs is a function of social organization and of employment policies, not a direct consequence of technology, and thus will vary among companies and according to varying economic policies).

On the other hand, while routine operations are automated, higher-level operations are concentrated in the hands of skilled clerical workers, middle managers, and professionals, who will make informed decisions on the basis of a considerable amount of information contained in their centralized files. So, while at the bottom of the process there is increasing routinization and automation of data entry, at the middle level, there is reintegration of several tasks into an informed decision-making operation, generally processed, evaluated, and performed by a team made up of clerical workers with some level of autonomy in reaching their decision. Thus, the latest stage of office automation, instead of simply rationalizing the task (which was characteristic of the first phase of batch-processing automation), actually rationalizes the process, because the technology allows the integration of information from many different sources and its redistribution, once processed, to different decentralized units of execution. The pathbreaking studies by Baran and by Baran and Teegarden on the insurance industry have provided systematic evidence of this fundamental process that contradicts the simplistic, Orwellian image of centralized, inflexible office automation.[49] As Baran and Teegarden write:

The first stage of automation in the insurance industry tended to increase office fragmentation, centralize production by narrow function, heighten occupational sex segregation, and make many routine keyboarding functions spatially footloose. More recently however, the greater sophistication of the technologies and transformed market conditions are dictating a new organizational logic which promises to reverse many of the earlier trends. . . . This evolution can be characterized as the gradual movement from functional approaches to systems approaches, that is, from automating discrete tasks (e.g.: typing, calculating) to rationalizing an entire procedure (e.g.: new business insurance, claims processing), to reorganizing and integrating all the procedures involved in a particular decision or product line . . . . As a result, the work process is, in many cases, being functionally reintegrated. Workers who were formerly divided into functional units are being integrated into divisions which serve a particular subset of customers, often on the basis of geographic location and/or market segments.[50]

A similar trend has been observed by Hirschhorn in his case studies of banks.[51] While routine operations are now being processed increasingly by

ATMs (often by the forced procedure of closing down bank branches and re-placing them with automatic machines), the remaining bank clerks are being retrained into the business of selling services to the customers, thus upgrading the work content of a smaller number of employees, and taking a more aggressive, marketing-oriented attitude toward clients.

In another study of the banking industry conducted for the Office of Technology Assessment, Paul Adler obtains similar findings.[52] As the OTA reports:

With computerization, the process of fabricating accounts, the principal activity of the bank, was made internal to the computer. These procedures had previously been done manually, or with the assistance of mechanical accounting machines. The role of human operators then changed from one of doing banking to one of surveillance of the computing as it does banking. Adler points out that "A series of tasks formerly con-sidered the very essence of bank work have been eliminated, including accounting imputation and adjustment, classification of documents, multiple entries of data, manual data search, and supervision by signature . . . . Accountants now diagnose and rectify residues and anomalies listed by the computer system. New types of errors – and fraud – appear." [53]

The automation of tasks is increasingly penetrating the sphere of decision-making, not so much to save labor as to save time, and reach quick decisions in a global financial world where minutes might cost millions. The most important example of this trend, of course, is the automation of stock exchange markets around the world, enabling them to trade in real time at an increasingly faster speed of decision, on a "launch on warning" system of electronically processed financial indicators. The consequences of this process are dramatic and far-reaching. The "Presidential Task Force on Market Mechanisms," appointed by President Reagan to investigate the causes of the collapse of the New York Stock Exchange on 19 October 1987, concluded that the most important single factor immediately behind the crash (apart, of course, from the structural reasons concerning the imbalance of the US economy) was computerized trading by large institutional investors, particularly pension funds. More specifically, the Task Force referred to two computer-trading techniques, portfolio insurance and stock index arbitrage, by which computers can generate transactions that result in orders to sell huge amounts of stock under a number of programmed circumstances. Prompted by a downward market trend, automatic selling orders dramatically amplified that trend and set in motion the 508-point collapse of the Dow Jones index.[54]

In sum, the penetration of computer-and-telecommunications information systems is altering the dynamics of office work and of the information economy in all its dimensions. Quinn has summarized the effects of technology in six major areas:[55] increasing economies of scale; increasing economies of scope; increasing output complexity; furthering functional competition (that is, integrating several industries and activities around a major function, for example, the sales of financial services by department stores such as Sears[56]); enhancing international competitiveness; and increasing wealth through higher productivity in services. In a word, what is facilitated by information technologies is the interconnection of activities, providing the basis for the increasing complexity of service industries, which exchange information relentlessly and ubiquitously. The old separation among different businesses, different markets, different industries, and different organizations disappears in technological terms. Whatever becomes organizationally and legally possible can be technologically implemented, because of the versatility of the technological medium. Such evolution, of course, does not supersede the logic inherent to each specific organization, but minimizes the friction between decision and execution of the organizational goals. What results is the amplification of the problems, conflicts, and errors in the outcome of organizational decisions, but also of the successes and achievements of the strategies and policies that the organization assumes. The technological basis of information systems increasingly frees organizations from their bureaucratic inefficiencies, but brings them into direct confrontation with their built-in shortcomings and strategic failures.

A fundamental effect of a technologically driven organizational logic of this kind is that the operations of many organizations become timeless, because information systems communicate with each other on programmed time patterns, either non-stop in real time or, on the contrary, delayed and recorded. There is a shift, in fact, away from the centrality of the organizational unit to the network of information and decision. In other words, *flows, rather than organizations*, become the units of work, decision, and output accounting. Is the same trend developing in relation to the spatial dimension of organizations? Are flows substituting for localities in the information economy? Under the impact of information systems, are organizations becoming not only timeless but also placeless? These are fundamental questions and require detailed consideration.

Telecommunications, Office Automation, and the Spatial Pattern of Information-processing Activities

Introduction: The Metropolitan Dominance of the Service Economy

Examination of the empirical data on the spatial effects of telecommunications and automation on office work and service activities shows how ill-founded are the simplistic assumptions about the potential for decentralization of activities and businesses under the impetus provided by new technologies able to overcome spatial distance while maintaining communication. There is no direct effect of communication technologies on the location of offices and services. Their effects are mediated through trends in the evolution of service and information activities, and through the changing organizational logic of corporations. Stanback, Noyelle, and their co-workers have systematically studied over a number of years the relationship between the expansion of the service economy and its impact in American cities.[57] Their findings can be summarized in a number of fundamental trends:

(1) Producer services are increasingly concentrated in nodal large metropolitan areas.
(2) These services are further increasingly concentrated within the central business districts (CBDs) of large metropolitan areas.
(3) Both of these tendencies are particularly pronounced for advanced corporate services, as established for the 1970s by Robert Cohen's research. Cohen also showed that the booming sunbelt remained largely dependent on the old established base of headquarters and corporate services in New York, Chicago, San Francisco, and Los Angeles. In particular, the predominance of New York in all advanced corporate services (banking, insurance, financial services, legal services, accounting and auditing, advertising, publishing, consulting, and so on) was, and still is, overwhelming.
(4) There has been a growing tendency toward the suburbanization of secondary offices of major corporations, as well as of some headquarters, unable to or uninterested in sustaining the cost of land and office space in the highly priced CBDs. Most of this suburbanization has occurred in the largest metropolitan areas.
(5) Consumer services, by and large, have followed the suburbanization of middle-class residents, while the high-level entertainment services have stayed in the established elite cores of central cities.
(6) Public services, particularly in health and education, tend to follow the spatial distribution of the population they serve, thus becoming increasingly suburbanized. However, some of these services (major hospitals, for example) can also be export-oriented, and in these cases they tend to dominate a given area, generally in their former location in the inner city.

What Noyelle and Stanback's work shows is, on the one hand, that the spatial consequences of the expansion of the service economy are contradictory, leading at the same time toward centralization and decentralization of activities; and on the other hand, that these processes follow a logic that depends on the function of each organization, and on the hierarchical relationships among the different functions. In order to understand the role played by the use of new technologies in the spatial patterning of information-processing service activities, we must consider their interaction with the characteristics of such activities. I will proceed with this analysis by focusing in turn on the process of centralization and on the different processes of decentralization, attempting in conclusion a synthetic integration of my observations in the formulation of a new spatial logic.

Telecommunications and the Centralization of Information-intensive Industries

At the core of the service economy lies the expansion of information-processing activities. These activities are organized around a nucleus of information-intensive industries whose organizational and spatial logic occupies the top of the functional and economic corporate hierarchy. According to the thorough study of the matter by Drennan,[58] these information-intensive industries (see table 3.5 for an operational definition) accounted in 1985 for 13.9 percent of all US jobs and about 13 percent of GNP. Altogether they were responsible for almost as many jobs as manufacturing (17.6 million in information-intensive industries versus 18.8 million in manufacturing), and they were growing during the 1980s at a much faster rate than the average GNP. Data collected by Drennan show the dramatic expansion between 1975 and 1984 in banking, finance, securities, and insurance. It can be argued convincingly that the emergence of information systems was the technological prerequisite for the dramatic growth of these industries, and that the process will accelerate in the foreseeable future. In turn, it is the growth of these information-intensive industries that drives the demand for advanced information technologies. Consequently, the spatial impact of these technologies will be most clearly manifested in the location of these industries. However, following our methodology of inquiry, in order to assess the impact of new communication technologies, we need first to examine the location patterns of information-intensive industries themselves.

Drennan found that in 1984 there was a significant concentration of these information-intensive jobs in the core counties of the 24 largest metropolitan

Table 3.5   Information-intensive industries

SIC Code	Industry
—	Central administrative offices, all industries
45	Air transportation
47	Transportation services
60	Banking
61	Credit agencies
62	Security and commodity brokers and services
63	Insurance carriers
64	Insurance agents, brokers and services
67	Holding and other investment offices
73	Business services
81	Legal services
82	Educational services (private)
86	Membership organizations
89	Miscellaneous services (engineering and accounting)

Source: US Department of Commerce, Bureau of the Census, County Business Patterns, US Summary, 1983, 1985, elaborated by Drennan (see note 58).

areas: they accounted for 39 percent of information-intensive jobs, while their share of total private employment was only 27 percent, with New York, Los Angeles, and Chicago on top of this list (see table 3.6). Banking is one of the most concentrated industries: one-third of all commercial and savings banks deposits are located in the five largest metropolitan areas, and New York alone has 17 percent of all deposits. Law firms in the top five

Table 3.6   Population, employment, and information-intensive industries' employment, 24 metropolitan areas and United States

Metropolitan Area	Population[a]	Total employment[b]	Information-intensive industries' employment		
			No.	% of total	Rank order
New York	17,677	8,448	1,773	21.0	1
Los Angeles	12,373	5,773	944	16.4	10
Chicago	8,035	3,695	670	18.1	4
Philadelphia	5,755	2,653	404	15.2	
San Francisco	5,685	2,961	524	17.7	5
Detroit	4,316	1,872	247	13.2	
Boston	4,027	2,065	405	19.6	2
Houston	3,566	1,735	276	15.9	
Washington	3,430	1,965	360	18.3	3
Dallas	3,348	1,772	285	16.1	
Miami	2,799	1,274	220	17.3	6
Cleveland	2,788	1,256	167	13.3	
Atlanta	2,380	1,238	200	16.1	
Pittsburgh	2,372	984	150	15.2	
Baltimore	2,245	1,092	184	16.9	7
Minneapolis–St Paul	2,231	1,212	175	14.4	
San Diego	2,064	933	154	16.5	9
Denver	1,791	986	164	16.6	8
Phoenix	1,715	782	123	15.7	
Milwaukee	1,568	763	106	13.9	
Columbus	1,279	614	93	15.1	
Indianapolis	1,195	583	74	12.7	
San Antonio	1,189	530	84	15.8	
Memphis	935	437	55	12.6	
Total 24 areas	94,763	45,623	7,837	17.2	
United States total	235,671	106,891	14,856	13.9	
24 areas as % of US total	40.2	42.7	52.8		

[a] 1984; [b] 1983.

Source: Population data from US Bureau of the Census, Statistical Abstract of the United States, 1986. Total employment (actual) and information-intensive industries employment (partly estimated) from US Department of Commerce, Bureau of Economic Analysis, Survey of Current Business, May 1985, October 1985, and August 1986. Elaborated by Drennan (see note 58).

metropolitan areas earned 39 percent of the receipts of all law firms, and 40 percent of all law firms with more than 50 employees were in the core counties of those five largest metropolitan areas. Here again, New York ranks first with 179 large law offices. For securities and commodities offices, the concentration is even heavier, as one might expect: New York, with 261, and Chicago, with 107, together account for one-third of all large securities firms. Table 3.7 summarizes the data on the relative concentration of information-intensive industries in the top ten areas, as measured by location quotients. Washington DC, New York, and Boston dominate the pack, while, significantly enough, Los Angeles is not among the top ten, emphasizing the greater decentralization of information-intensive industries in southern California (toward Orange County).[59] What is significant is the positive location quotient exhibited by all major metropolitan areas in proportion to the average of information-intensive employment for the US as a whole. Thus, Drennan's recent work on the 1980s, confirming the trends observed by Cohen, Stanback and Noyelle,[60] among others, for the 1970s, suggests that information-intensive industries are disproportionately concentrated in metropolitan areas, in the largest metropolitan areas, and in the cores of the largest metropolitan areas. Since these industries are the main users of new information technologies, it will be important to establish the role played by such technologies in the process of spatial centralization of these industries.

Mitchell Moss has systematically researched this question over a number of years.[61] His data show the close relationship among the internationalization of trade and finance, the centralization of such activities in a few global cities (New York being foremost among them), and the development of the telecommunications infrastructure in these cities. In fact, only through the revolution in telecommunications technology does it become possible to exercise co-ordination and control functions from a given location in a metropolitan CBD over the entire nation or the global economy. On the other hand, the deregulation of telecommunications, with the divestiture of ATT, has made investment in telecommunications even more sensitive to demand. Since the main source of this demand is in the information-intensive industries concentrated in the cores of the largest metropolitan areas, it is in such areas and core locations that most of the new telecommunications infrastructure has been concentrated.

Therefore, in order to exploit the global reach of telecommunications, organizations must locate in certain areas where they will have access to an advanced infrastructure at relatively affordable costs (affordable because of the economies of scale permitted by the extensive use of telecommunication facilities by a large number of customers). Thus, concentration of information industries attracts telecommunications investment which in turn reinforces the pattern of centralization for information-based activities. Furthermore, under the current legal framework in the US, new communication lines have to follow the rights of way already established; and the inter-

Table 3.7 Relative concentration of information-intensive industries, top 10 areas

Population rank	Metropolitan area (rank order)	Information-intensive employment Location quotient	Employment/population ratio	% population college graduates
9	Washington	2.62	58.3	31.9
7	Boston	2.26	56.2	22.6
1	New York	2.06	48.0	19.5
5	San Francisco	1.93	52.6	25.0
13	Atlanta	1.74	53.8	23.8
	Mean (unweighted) – top five	*1.69*	*53.8*	*23.8*
4	Philadelphia	1.59	46.2	17.0
18	Denver	1.43	55.8	25.9
14	Pittsburgh	1.42	41.0	14.1
3	Chicago	1.33	46.1	17.8
11	Miami		45.6	16.1
	Mean (unweighted)	*1.00*	*50.4*	*21.0*
	United States		45.7	16.2

Source: Data on percentage of college graduates from US Bureau of the Census, *State and Metropolitan Area Data Book* 1986. Elaborated by Drennan (see note 58).

city rights of way generally follow the lines of railroads built during the nineteenth century. Thus, the new optic fiber networks are in fact connecting the major areas that were already nodal points during the last century, although when demand is important enough, for example in some new sunbelt locations, they too become integrated into the network.

The creation of a new telecommunications infrastructure in the US is taking place at three levels: (a) long-distance communication; (b) intra-regional communication; and (c) local networks.[62] Concerning *long distance*, the major development is the construction of several optic fiber networks (by different competing companies: ATT, Sprint, MCI) which, because they need to carry a high volume of communication to be profitable, concentrate on communications between the largest metropolitan areas. Thus, the higher the level of existing corporate concentration in an areas, the better and the cheaper the new telecommunications equipment. Satellite-based networks have the edge on optic fiber in terms of versatility of communication flows, being able to communicate, at the same cost, from anywhere to anywhere. However, although optic fiber networks depend on flows that connect two points through a line, their carrying capacity and accuracy are much greater, in particular when satellite signals need to go through the saturated air space of metropolitan CBDs. Therefore, the setting up of optic fiber networks also contributes to reinforcing the inherited pattern of centralization of information-intensive industries.

At the *regional level*, the new companies resulting from ATT's divestiture are also turning to optic fiber, and to the establishment of new facilities for the regionally based organizations. New York also leads in these new developments.[63] By 1984 it accounted for one-third of all optic fiber networks installed in the US. During the 1980s several major telecommunications projects have been developed in the New York area, basically to serve the business agglomeration in Manhattan. The most important project of its kind in the entire world, the Teleport of New York epitomizes the trend. It was developed by the Port Authority of New York and New Jersey, on land leased by the City of New York, and in co-operation with a private partner, Teleport Communications Inc., owned by Merrill Lynch and Western Union. The Port and the City each receive a percentage of the company's profits. The Teleport will provide access to communications satellites through 17 earth stations located on Staten Island, and hooked through an optic fiber line with Manhattan and, in the future, other locations. In addition, Teleport has a developed a 100-acre office park generally used for decentralized back office organizations. The teleport concept is being equated to the harbours of the in-dustrial era, and in the mid-1980s there were under way about 20 similar pro-jects in 12 states in the US. Other intra-regional systems are also being set up, particularly in the New York area, relying on coaxial cable, microwave, digital termination systems, and, increasingly, cellular mobile radio, which extends the office into its transportation vehicles.

At the *local level*, "local area networks" (LANs) and "smart buildings" are establishing telecommunications equipment as an integral part of the structure of the built environment for the office. Increasingly, developers provide built-in telecommunications facilities and wired automated equipment, which are economical because they are shared among different tenants of a particular building or area.[64] This is the best example of the direct relationship with location in a given place as a means of access to the placeless communications network. Telecommunications equipment accounts for most of the increasing capital investment by companies in office workers. According to Jonscher, in 1977 US businesses were investing twice as much capital per worker in blue-collar staff as in white-collar staff.[65] By 1982 the ratios for both had become similar. The "wired city" is now a reality, not only through cable or telephone line networks, but through a variety of telecommunications technologies that lend extraordinary versatility to the system. In addition, it is a business-oriented "wired city," rather than one focused on the "electronic home."[66] As Moss writes:

The emerging telecommunications infrastructure is an overwhelmingly urban-based phenomenon. Although most discussions of new communication technologies emphasize the opportunities presented for decentralization, large cities are the hubs of the new telecommunications systems in the U.S. and are the sites for the most advanced applications of information technology . . . . Although new communications technologies permit geographic dispersal, the economics of the new infrastructure are oriented towards those urban regions that are major information centres . . . . Contrary to much of the popular folklore, new communication technologies have not led to the decline of cities. Rather, new communications technologies have enhanced those cities that serve [in Gottman's words] "the important function of hosting transactional activities."[67]

Interestingly enough, most of the business communications travel a short distance: 60 percent of all communications are intra-facility, and only 8 percent "travel" over 500 miles.

The first impact of the development of telecommunications infrastructure on the location of information-intensive industries, then, is to reinforce their centralization in the higher nodal points of the informational economy, namely, the CBDs of the largest metropolitan areas. (Indeed, it is only because of the existence of automated telecommunications and on-line equipment that offices located in a very few areas are able to extend their global reach without comparable diversification of location.) New York, and particularly Manhattan, is the best illustration of this tendency. In 1958, 35 percent of the city's private jobs were in information-intensive industries. In 1982 the proportion had jumped to 54 percent.[68] The role of telecommunications and office automation in facilitating such concentration while reinforcing the control of New York corporations over the world economy has been crucial.[69] In addition, around the concentration of headquarters of large corporations, whose physical proximity is vital as a way of sustaining the social milieu on which business decisions rely, a constellation of ancillary services has developed, both in business services and in consumer services, from printing and copying to business bars and restaurants. Manhattan hosts an immense concentration of information-technology equipment, as the necessary material condition for processing all the information centralized and decided upon in the Manhattan offices. For instance, to take a simple indicator, in 1984 there were more word processors in Manhattan than in the whole of western Europe. Using another indicator, constructed by Moss in one of his studies, the penetration of facsimile machines for the top US cities (see figure 3.2), shows the overwhelming proportion of these machines to be installed in New York, and in addition a disproportionate concentration of fax machines in major information-industry cities such as San Francisco, Washington DC, Atlanta, and Boston.

The reasons for the persistence of this centralized locational pattern for the top level of information-intensive industries are still the same as those pointed out years ago by the literature on office location:[70] importance of trusted

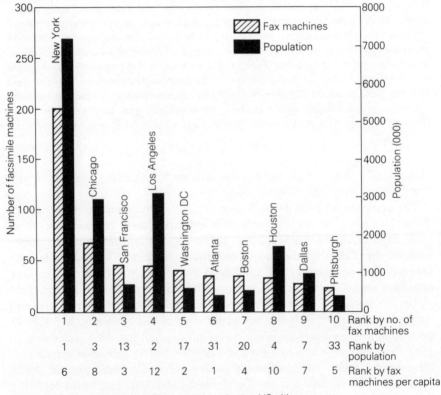

Figure 3.2   Penetration of facsimile machines for top US cities
Source: Official Facsimile Users Guide, 1985; Moss (see note 62)

person-to-person contacts in the decision-making process at the highest level; existence of a business social milieu with strong cultural connotations; prestige of location in a given place; importance of the fixed assets represented by the real estate owned by companies in the CBDs, assets that could be devalued in case of a massive exodus from the area; consolidation of a network of ancillary services around major firms and organizations, a network that provides diversity and versatility of supplies, and which becomes an indispensable working tool for the corporations, at the same time as it is spatially and functionally linked to their concentration. None of these elements is new, and they are largely independent of the development of information technologies, although the telephone was crucial in allowing the formation of such concentrations, as well as making possible vertical communication inside the skyscrapers.[71] However, what is new is that advanced information technologies have made it possible for these concentrations of high-level information-based organizations to operate from the same location while increasing the volume of information they process by a multiple factor, as a result of the large scale of the operations commanded from a particular corporate milieu. In this sense, the large corporation and its network of ancillary services, the world city, the CBD, and information systems based on telecommunications and computers, are all inextricably linked elements of the same system. Raymond Vernon predicted many years ago that the development of telecommunications and air transportation would lead toward increasing concentration of high-level services in a few cities, and particularly in the major metropolitan areas such as New York.[72] He has been proved right.

However, this process is not without its contradictions, nor is it the only spatial trend associated with the new information technologies. On the one hand, the inner cities of large metropolitan areas concentrate not only the corporate headquarters and their support networks, but also the destitute and overexploited segments of the population resulting from the unbalanced restructuring of economy and society, in an increasingly explosive socio-spatial contradiction that will be analyzed in chapter 4.[73] On the other hand, alongside the centralization and metropolitanization of information industries, there is also a process of decentralization of service activities over regions, urban areas, and locations within the major metropolitan areas; and this decentralization is being helped, and sometimes even stimulated, by new information technologies. It is this two-fold process of simultaneous centralization and decentralization, both elements associated with the same techno-economic dynamics, which explains the complexity of our analysis. Beyond a mere formal characterization of the process in terms of concentration/deconcentration of population and activities, we must be able to assess what is being centralized, what is being decentralized, why, and how. Only then we will be able to trace connections between the two processes and come to an understanding of the emerging socio-spatial logic.

Information Technology, Organizational Restructuring, and the
Spatial Decentralization of Office Activities

During the last two decades a process of spatial decentralization of service
activities generally, including the information-processing industries, has
taken place in the United States, although the activities that have been
decentralized are specific in terms of their content and function within the
hierarchy of services. It is received wisdom that new information and
transportation technologies have made this possible; here I will try to assess
the precise role played by technology in these developments. However, we
must differentiate among levels of spatial decentralization, since these differ
both in their origins and in their implications. Decentralization of services is
taking place on at least three different levels: between regions; from
metropolitan to non-metropolitan areas and small cities; from inner cities to
the suburbs of metropolitan areas. In addition, two potential trends will be
discussed, in spite of their current limited impact: the offshoring of service
activities; and the decentralization of office work at home (the so-called
"telecommuting").

Regional decentralization of information-processing activities   Peter Hall has
calculated the regional pattern of distribution of service and informational
jobs for the periods 1975–80 and 1980–5.[74] At a very aggregate level, but in an
analytically useful regional typology, he distinguishes four regional clusters:
the old manufacturing belt (including New England, the mid-Atlantic, and
east–north–central regions); the rural middle (consisting of the west–north–
–central and east–south–central divisions); the sunbelt (south Atlantic,
west–south–central, mountain and Pacific divisions); and what he labels the
"new perimeter," supposedly the new dynamic composite of US economic
geography, made up from the combination of the sunbelt and New England.
53.5 percent of the 15.7 million new non-farm jobs generated during 1975–80
were in information processing. Three out of five of these jobs were created in
the sunbelt and two-thirds of them in the "new perimeter." The period
1980–5 further intensified this regional differentiation, with 96 percent of
all new non-farm jobs created in these years falling in the "new perimeter."
Information-processing jobs accounted for 77.8 percent of all new US jobs in
this period, and of these, 73.2 percent were created in the "new perimeter,"
and 71.6 percent in the sunbelt. Given the former concentration of
information jobs in the older industrial areas of the north-east and north-central regions, there is clearly a major regional restructuring under way.
However, this must be qualified by the analysis of table 3.8, which provides a
more disaggregated view of the trends at the level of individual regions.
According to Hall's index of information jobs/goods-producing jobs, the mid-
Atlantic region (around New York–New Jersey) clearly stands out as the

region with the highest concentration of new information-handling jobs in 1975-80; a trend that, although the index is not calculated in the table, appears even more pronounced for 1980-5. So if, rather than adding New England to the sunbelt to forge the "new perimeter," for the period 1980-5 we add the mid-Atlantic region to the sunbelt, we account for 82.6 percent of all new information-handling jobs. It would seem that the "new perimeter" for information employment should include New York–New Jersey instead of New England. The major decline in share of information jobs has been suffered by the midwest.

In any event, the dramatic increase in the proportion of new information jobs in the sunbelt, and particularly in the south Atlantic region, for the whole decade 1975-85, indicates a clear regional shift in the dynamism of the information-processing sector, as well as in services in general. While we lack the precise data to enable us to identify which activities are being shifted, Peter Hall, recalling findings by Noyelle and Stanback,[75] speculates about three potential sources for the regional decentralization of service and information activities. First is the need to serve the growing population of the sunbelt, given the links of many of the services to residentially based factors. In turn, the decentralization of population to the sunbelt is itself a function of decentralization of economic activities at large, including manufacturing. Secondly, he points to the emergence of a series of new, regionally based industries, such as retirement and tourism, in the south Atlantic region; and his third factor is the dynamism of new regional centers, including such cities as Miami, Atlanta, Houston, Denver, and Phoenix, which have been able to attract corporations to cheaper, more suitable business environments. To these I would add another hypothesis concerning the linkage between manufacturing and information-processing activities. Given the massive scale of the decline in manufacturing jobs in the old manufacturing belt, that decline cannot be compensated for by information-processing jobs except when they deal with higher command and control functions, as is the case in New York. However, the vitality of a number of medium-level information-handling processes is associated with the production and distribution of goods. With a substantial number of manufacturing jobs shifting to the sunbelt and to the "new perimeter," and with the distribution of goods following an expanding population, the linkage factor will tend to induce a similarity in the locational pattern of many information-processing activities to the tendencies shown by the new manufacturing industries.

In sum, it appears that there is a process of regional decentralization of information activities linked to second-rank business services, to producer services of the new industrial perimeter, and to consumer and personal services for the expanding population of the sunbelt areas. Information technologies do play a role in facilitating this movement because the new nodal areas would be unable to compete with the established metropolitan

Table 3.8 Employment changes by SIC single-digit headings, divisions, 1975–80, 1980–5 (% rate of change during the period)

(a) 1975–80

	New England	Mid-Atlantic	E.-N.-Central	W.-N.-Central	S. Atlantic	E.-S.-Central	W.-S.-Central	Mountain	Pacific	Total US
TOTAL	10.8	10.0	14.1	19.6	23.4	20.7	33.0	35.6	32.4	21.0
Mining	38.7	−0.5	13.2	27.7	7.2	20.9	71.3	44.2	36.7	37.3
Construction	7.3	2.8	11.8	13.8	22.4	16.8	39.8	45.5	37.1	21.3
Manufacturing	17.2	1.1	1.7	12.1	15.8	9.7	26.1	33.6	25.7	11.1
Transportation	15.1	12.6	25.7	38.5	30.1	40.5	37.9	52.9	27.7	27.8
Transportation	27.7	19.9	44.0	58.9	42.3	61.0	49.5	82.1	33.9	40.6
Communication	3.6	3.8	6.8	14.7	17.4	20.1	23.7	28.4	20.1	13.7
Wholesale/retail	16.8	8.2	13.4	15.0	24.0	18.7	28.7	31.3	34.7	20.0
Finance, Insurance, Real Estate	22.6	12.1	22.9	23.9	26.7	21.6	37.2	44.6	43.6	26.1
Services	33.2	33.0	41.0	44.1	40.3	52.2	53.0	56.1	66.3	44.7
Government	10.4	1.9	9.0	8.6	17.6	17.2	16.5	15.8	8.2	11.0
Industry	16.1	1.3	3.0	12.8	16.9	10.3	34.6	38.5	27.9	13.6
Service	20.1	13.6	20.3	22.1	26.1	26.6	32.4	34.7	33.9	24.2
Goods-handling	16.8	5.1	8.5	16.3	21.1	15.2	32.9	37.1	31.3	17.6
Information-handling	21.5	15.6	22.8	23.7	26.2	29.0	33.1	34.1	33.6	25.4
Ratios: serv./ind.	1.2	10.5	6.8	1.7	1.5	2.6	0.9	0.9	1.2	1.8
Info./goods	1.3	3.1	2.7	1.5	1.2	1.9	1.0	0.9	1.1	1.4

(b) 1980–85

	New England	Mid-Atlantic	E.-N.-Central	W.-N.-Central	S. Atlantic	E.-S.-Central	W.-S.-Central	Mountain	Pacific	Total US
TOTAL	7.0	0.3	-0.9	0.3	12.1	5.2	8.7	10.6	4.8	4.7
Mining	16.2	-2.6	-10.7	-15.0	-20.5	-7.5	-3.7	-27.5	1.4	-11.6
Construction	50.0	30.4	5.0	4.7	27.7	9.5	16.7	20.6	16.5	19.2
Manufacturing	4.2	-7.8	-3.0	-2.8	5.2	1.4 12.8	-1.1	15.3	6.9	0.2
Transportation	24.5	7.5	10.6	13.0	19.9	25.4	8.6	18.9	18.8	14.6
Transportation	20.1	-0.5	8.2	6.3	10.6	18.3	4.8	14.5	15.0	8.8
Communication	29.4	-8.5	14.1	23.7	31.5	34.9	14.3	20.8	14.0	20.8
Wholesale/Retail	-4.7	-6.2	-3.7	-3.9	7.7	5.4	5.4	6.7	-3.7	-0.3
Finance, Insurance, Real Estate	32.1	-5.6	14.0	17.0	29.0	21.6	31.9	41.9	18.6	22.1
Services	13.5	6.2	7.2	7.4	31.7	12.7	22.2	12.4	7.1	12.8
Government	-4.6	-2.6	-11.9	-7.9	-1.9	-4.8	3.1	3.6	0.0	-3.4
Industry	9.2	-3.1	-2.3	-1.9	9.3	2.1	2.8	10.1	8.7 4.8	2.9
Service	6.0	1.5	-0.2	1.0	13.2	6.7	11.2	10.7	3.5	5.4
Goods-handling	4.3	-4.2	-2.3	-2.2	8.7	4.2	4.0	8.8	3.5	1.9
Information-handling	10.5	5.0	1.0	3.2	15.9	6.5	15.0	12.4	6.2	7.9
Ratios: serv./ind.	0.7	NA	0.1	NA	1.4	3.2	4.0	1.1	0.4	1.9
Info./goods	2.4	NA	NA	NA	1.8	1.5	3.8	1.4	1.8 4.8	4.2

Source: Bureau of Labor Statistics. Calculated and elaborated by Hall (see note 10)

centers were it not for their access to communication and information networks that keep them in close and constant contact with their command and control centers, as well as, for the minority of headquarters in the sunbelt, in direct connection with their national and international markets. Having achieved a minimum density of information complexes, and counting on regional patterns of investment in telecommunications and data processing, the new economic centers lay claim to the advantages of a newer, more flexible, and generally cheaper business environment, with the accessibility to the mainstream of the economy through their integration in the network of information flows.

Suburbanization of business and office activities   While the cores of the dominant metropolitan areas still maintain their function as locations for most of the command and control centers of the economy, a major process of suburbanization of services, and particularly of office activities has been taking place since the late 1960s in most metropolitan areas in the US.[76] The new suburbanization process is in fact business-led rather than purely residential, although the population too is increasingly suburban. What characterizes this new wave of suburbanization is that it relies on the formation of relatively dense business and commercial sub-centers, transforming the metropolitan areas in into multinuclear, multifunctional spatial structures, organized around what Leinberger and Lockwood label new "urban villages."[77] The scale of this phenomenon is unprecedented and constitutes the most important single trend in the transformation of America's built environment. Table 3.9 documents the process of office suburbanization for the 1970s and for 1984 respectively. In the latter year, data computed by Dowall and Salkin for the 19 metropolitan areas under analysis showed that, on average, suburban office construction accounted for 59.3 percent of all new office space in these areas. And the trend is accelerating through the 1980s: between 1982 and 1985 Manhattan gained 23 million square feet of office space, but its share of office space for the whole metropolitan area fell from 67 percent to 60 percent. In 1986 the New York metropolitan suburbs were the location for 261.1 million feet of office space, as compared to 317.6 million for Manhattan. The trend is even more pronounced in the second major metropolitan area of the US, Los Angeles, where the downtown share of the metropolitan area's office market has dropped from 60 percent to 34 percent of new office construction. The new business complex in Orange County (Costa Mesa–Irvine–Newport Beach) contained in 1986 21.1 million square feet of office space; still behind downtown LA with 36.6 million square feet but already the third largest business complex in California.[78]

These new suburban office centers tend to be quite different from their inner-city predecessors. They are generally low-density, either with low-rise buildings or, in the case of major centers, with skyscrapers scattered over a very large area, separated by areas of landscaped open space. Parking lots and the automobile dominate the scenery. In fact, such massive suburban decentralization is closely associated with the expansion of the metropolitan freeway system and the use of the automobile as the prevalent mode of commuting: in 1980, nationwide, 86 percent of all commuting trips were by car, compared with 69.5 percent in 1960. This requires parking space that only an automobile-oriented suburban development can provide, in terms of both physical availability and affordable cost.

It is, then, undeniable that offices are decentralizating, mainly to the suburbs of the largest metropolitan areas. This is taking place both through relocation of existing companies and through new businesses deciding to locate in the suburbs. Let us examine what is being decentralized, and why, and what is the specific effect of the new information technologies on the process.

Table 3.9   Office-dominated industry employment growth in central city and suburban locations: 50 largest and 50 small and mid-sized SMSAs, 1967–1977 (000s)

	Finance, insurance, and real estate		Services		Government	
	Number	% change	Number	% change	Number	% change
Largest SMSAs						
Central city	422	23.5	1177	34.6	1107	44.5
Suburbs	375	172.5	2028	134.2	509	67.3
North-east						
Central city	−16	−2.4	171	14.7	210	36.5
Suburbs	141	152.9	496	109.9	118	42.7
North-central						
Central city	90	20.5	182	20.9	215	37.4
Suburbs	149	176.2	578	151.9	142	96.1
South						
Central city	157	46.2	477	69.9	395	63.3
Suburbs	76	153.0	470	161.0	190	79.0
West						
Central city	192	52.1	347	50.6	288	40.3
Suburbs	62	338.8	485	120.0	60	65.0
Small/Mid-sized SMSAs						
Central city	17	25.0	146	63.5	28	18.3
Suburbs	11	123.5	201	99.0	14	28.6

Source: Phillips and Vidal (1983), tables 6, 7, 9, as compiled by Dowall and Salkin, (see note 79).

Dowall and Salkin have reviewed the available information on this question, and they point to several factors favoring the decentralized location or relocation of office activities.[79] In the first place, they cite the dominance of large, multifunctional, multilocational corporations, whose internal linkages become more important than linkages to their spatial environment. Units of these companies that can be decentralized will be, while maintaining their connections with the other units of the corporation. This functional linkage of the centre and decentralized units is only possible because of the existence of telecommunications and automation technologies that establish an information system able to link the company internally and with its inputs and markets through the communications network. Nevertheless, if corporate structure and information technologies allow for the process of decentralization, with particular emphasis on suburbanization, they do not explain why companies would relocate or locate initially in the suburbs, or, to a lesser extent, in smaller areas. Here a number of inter-related factors emerge to account for most of the preferences for a suburban site over the traditional downtown location:[80]

(1) Land prices and office rents in the suburbs are lower than in downtown locations. Leinberger and Lockwood report that in 1980, the price for suburban office space oscillated between $10 and $50 per square foot, while in downtown areas it jumped to between $50 and $1,000 per square foot.[81] Similarly, office rents were in the range of $18–$42 per square foot for downtown space, while prestige, high-rise suburban office space could be had for between $15 and $24 per square foot.

(2) Suburban offices are more accessible to their workers, most of whom live in the suburbs, and make commuting by car easier.[82]

(3) For retail offices, delivering services directly to the population, suburban locations simply follow the increasing suburbanization of the resident population, as with service activities in general.[83]

(4) One of the most important factors for suburban decentralization is the search for specific labor markets, as a result of the transformation of the labor process by automation, and the redefinition of the type of workers required in the automated office.[84] As we will see, suburban, educated, married women, working part-time or, in any case, for a wage under their level of skill, appears to be the most significant and sought-after labor source for the new type of office work. The case study reported below on the insurance industry will illustrate and elaborate this point. It is important to emphasize here that access to labor markets also works as a negative factor for downtown location, since the new skills required by the automated office are unlikely to be found (or at least, such is the perception of most companies) among the population of minorities that increasingly constitutes the bulk of inner-city residents in the large metropolitan areas.

The process of office decentralization is differentiated according to the different types of office functions and their place in the hierarchy of the corporation. Dowall and Salkin follow the distinction made by Thorngren [85] among orientation, planning, and programming functions in office work, corresponding to the more rigorous traditional sociological distinction of the functions of enterprises among decision, organization, and execution.[86] Nelson adds a more empirical classification separating headquarters, divisional branches, back offices, and retail offices.[87] Tendencies toward spatial decentralization clearly vary according to the three functions and the four categories of office activity. Headquarters of corporations continue, by and large, to be situated in the CBDs of the metropolitan areas, although metropolitan dominance has been eroded in terms both of metropolitan areas themselves and of competition from the suburbs. In 1963 New York City housed 147 of the *Fortune* 500 corporations' headquarters; in 1978 the figure was down to 104. Chicago and Pittsburgh respectively lost six and seven headquarters of major corporations in the same period, while the numbers of headquarters of major firms in Los Angeles, Houston, Atlanta, and San Francisco rose.[88] However, most often, when headquarters relocate they do so over short distances, to the suburbs of the same area.[89] They do so to escape the high costs of doing business in the CBD, and also they are attracted toward the areas where most of their managers and professionals live. Consequently, there is a clear tendency for business suburbanization to take place in upper-middle-class residential areas, such as the Princeton Corridor in the New York–New Jersey area, or the Perimeter Center in the northern suburbs of Atlanta.

Divisional branch offices value connections with the region they serve, or, when they are product divisions, connections with their headquarters.[90] They tend to concentrate in the CBDs of second-tier metropolitan areas or in the suburbs of the largest metropolitan areas. Air transportation links are a fundamental locational factor in this case, since telecommunication linkages do not preclude the need for frequent personal contacts among the managers, as well as for access to courier delivery of important documents.

Retail offices locate according to their need for access to their client base. Consequently they tend to be spatially diffused, following a segregated location pattern specific to each market segment. The higher the social status of an area, the higher the likelihood of increasing density of retail office location. Thus, while retail offices are located wherever there is a concentration of residence and of business, they also tend to follow a pattern of decentralization and suburbanization because of the growing dynamism, both residentially and commercially, of the metropolitan suburbs.

Back offices, in which most of companies' organization and execution work, increasingly automated, is concentrated, are functionally the most footloose office activity, because their main connection is to the company's decision centers, and this is a connection that can easily be maintained through automated information systems.[91] This being the case, it becomes uneconomic to maintain large back-office operations, which generally occupy a lot of space, on expensive downtown sites. Accordingly, back offices account for the bulk of the office decentralization that has taken place since the late 1960s.[92] Most of this decentralization, as we have seen, has taken place into the suburbs of the metropolitan areas, and the main reason for this seems to relate to the presence of a labor market that fulfils the needs of the automated office. The following case study of the insurance industry will clarify this important point, as well as providing a more precise view of the spatial division of labor within the corporation.

On the basis of Barbara Baran's analysis of the impact of office automation on the insurance industry,[93] Jean Marion Ross has analyzed the spatial implications of this transformation, on the basis of both secondary data and her own survey of 37 insurance companies.[94] She shows that the origins of the process lie in the restructuring of the industry as a consequence of increasing deregulation of financial services, putting increasingly competitive pressure on a traditionally regulated industry. Information technologies have played a major role in such restructuring, making insurance the most highly automated white-collar industry. In fact, the characteristics of the industry are particularly suited for information systems: scale economies favor consolidation of information-processing activities, while the requirement of market proximity favors decentralization of sales and service activities. The impact of information technologies on the new spatial pattern of the industry is two-fold. First, telecommunications technology increases the spatial mobility of the industry and lowers the cost of transmission between companies' units. On-line information processing allows geographical separation of activities without losing accessibility to the customers. Secondly, large-scale office automation, particularly in data entry and back-office operations (as described above, on the basis of Baran's study) restructures the occupational profile, increasing the need for skilled clerical labor. This appears to be a major factor in the relocation of back offices, a trend confirmed by Nelson's study of office location in the San Francisco Bay area.[95] The argument is as follows: the reintegration of tasks in the work process, through the use of automated data entry and standardization of routine procedures, calls for the remaining clerical workers to have a higher level of skill, and for team work. Team work is facilitated by similar cultural, ethnic, and gender characteristics in the components of the team. Therefore, insurance companies have increasingly targeted as their preferred labor pool the vast numbers of educated, married women, who can afford to be less demanding in terms of wages, and who will provide skills in information-processing activities at a lower cost than would be incurred by employing men, who were traditionally charged with the more analytical tasks of the

Table 3.10 Survey results: spatial change of insurance employment

Question/response	No. of responses	% response
(I) *Spatial change of operations within the past 10 years*		
Total responses	33	
Yes	22	66.7
No	9	27.3
Planned	2	6.1
(II) *Structural trends in the organization of activities*		
Total responses	23	
Consolidation of functions	8	34.8
Dispersion of functions	4	17.4
Both	11	47.8
(III) *Has there been an increase in the number of operations in small urban or suburban settings?*		
Total responses	24	
Yes	16	66.7
No	8	33.3
(IV) *Criteria affecting choice of location*		
Total responses	22	
Labor cost	12	54.5
Labor force quality	11	50.0
Land/rental cost and availability	12	54.5
Market proximity	7	31.8
Other	3	13.6

Source: Telephone survey of 37 insurance companies, July 1984, by Ross, (see note 94).

business. These women tend to be white and suburban (in one instance, an insurance company targeted a suburban location because of the abundance of educated women of "Dutch and German descent"); their social and cultural homogeneity is supposed to help team work. For many of these women an important factor in looking for a job is to keep time available for family life and child-rearing, and part-time work and/or a location relatively close to their suburban residence is therefore crucial – for them and for the company. Also, easy access by automobile and controlled parking space are key elements in attracting safety-conscious women, likely to be reluctant to commute to downtown areas in the evening hours, as is required by the shift-working of many back offices.

Altogether, back-office work in the insurance industry is being massively decentralized, mainly to the suburbs of the large metropolitan areas. Table 3.10 reports the findings of Ross's survey, indicating the high frequency of the decentralization/relocation process, which has affected over two-thirds of the surveyed companies in the 10 years covered. Of the factors cited as influencing choice of location, land/rental cost and access to labor are clearly

Table 3.11   Insurance employment shifts by city type, 1970–1981

	Percent of SIC 63, 1981	Percent of SIC 63, 1970	Percent change in SIC 63, 1970–81	Percent change in total employment 1970–81
Central cities[a]	32.7	39.1	2.5	3.7
Middle cities[b]	16.6	17.7	14.3	9.7
Small cities[c]	24.3	22.0	35.6	29.7
First ring[d]	13.9	8.1	113.4	34.5
Non-metropolitan[e]	4.9	3.6	67.6	9.3
All other	7.6	9.5	59.6	13.1
Total	100.0	100.0	22.7	30.7

[a] Counties with primary cities ≥ 500,000 population in 1980
[b] Counties with primary cities of 250,000–500,000 population in 1980
[c] Counties with primary cities of 50, 000–250,000 population in 1980
[d] Counties adjacent to or in the same SMSA as central or middle cities
[e] Counties with no city ≥ 50,000 population in 1980

Source: County Business Patterns, 1970 and 1981; compiled by Ross (see note 94).

predominant. It is important to emphasize that labor considerations concern both cost and quality, a finding that is also reported by Kroll and by Nelson in their studies on the San Francisco Bay area. That is to say, the automated office is not looking for cheap labor, but for skilled clerical labor as inexpensive as possible. It is the skill/cost ratio that determines the choice of suburban locations over the potentially even cheaper labor to be found among the inner-city minority populations. In the San Francisco Bay area, insurance companies, and back offices in general, decentralize from San Francisco to the outer suburbs of the East Bay, around Walnut Creek and Concord, skipping Oakland, in spite of the proximity and better infrastructure of this predominantly black city. Indeed, according to Ross, 70 percent of companies are dissatisfied with central city locations, and their main complaint concerns the low quality of the labor force, resulting from the deficiencies of the educational system as suffered by minorities in the public schools of the inner city.

The consequences of these structurally determined locational preferences can be perceived in the overall trend toward decentralization of insurance employment, as shown in Table 3.11. Although in 1981 central cities were still holding 32.7 percent of US insurance employment, the first-ring suburbs showed a dramatic increase in their employment share between 1970 and 1981, followed by non-metropolitan and "other" areas. Thus, office automation at the same time pushes toward the decentralization of back offices, and, to a lesser extent, of headquarters, while making it technologically feasible.

Trends toward further decentralization of office work   The process of decentralization of business and office activities is not limited to the metropolitan suburbs, although to date they account for the largest proportion of the phenomenon. New communication technologies make it possible in principle to relocate operations, particularly back offices, in remote locations, be they non-metropolitan areas, rural localities, or foreign countries.

The trend has been particularly important in the shift of employment shares toward small cities and non-metropolitan areas.[96] In a well publicized move, Citicorp relocated and consolidated a share of its nationwide back-office operations to Sioux Falls, South Dakota, from where most Citibank credit card operations are now managed. And Blue Shield of Northern California moved claim-processing operations to small communities in the California central valley, including Woodland, Sonora, and Turlock. These moves triggered speculation about the dramatic potential for general relocation and dispersal of CBDs' business concentrations. Indeed, during the 1970s small and medium-sized metropolitan areas displayed the highest growth rates in finance, insurance, and real estate jobs. However, as a look back at table 3.9 will remind us, the respective absolute shares of new jobs in the same period still bear no comparison: 797,000 FIRE jobs in the largest SMSAs versus 28,000 in the small and medium-sized SMSAs. Table 3.11 shows a somewhat similar pattern for the insurance industry in 1970–81. While small cities always had a significant share of insurance employment (22 percent in 1970), because of the decentralization of insurance services relative to the industry's customers, the high rates of growth in the non-metropolitan and "all other" categories translate into a mere 12.5 percent of total employment in 1981. So, although the increasing role of small metropolitan areas and non-metropolitan areas in office work is analytically significant, and demonstrates the increasing geographical flexibility provided by information technologies, it does not appear that it will reverse substantially in the near future the overwhelmingly metropolitan character of office location, and the dominance of the largest metropolitan areas.

A number of factors account for the limits of demetropolitanization. Some of them are of a technical nature: the radial pattern of power transmission lines in the US, for examples, which makes remote locations much more vulnerable to power failures, threatening the information systems on which the entire process of decentralization relies; the lack of adequate telecommunications facilities in small areas because of the sufficient market there for sophisticated networks; and insufficient air transportation connections to meet the need for quick personal access to the decision-making centers. The myth of generalized spatial diffusion is confronted with the reality of small communities at a disadvantage in the new communications infrastructure because of their low potential as markets for that infrastructure. The development of technology is dominated by the interests of its providers, in this case determined by the pre-existence of a spatial hierarchy of business locations.

Intense speculation about the future of office work has also been aroused by the offshoring of some routine information-handling operations by American companies to Third World countries,[97] particularly in the Caribbean and Asia, where keyboarding of raw documents is performed by local workers for wages that are between 6 and 20 times lower than those that would be paid in the US. This is a qualitatively most significant phenomenon. I have personally observed the working of one such company in Beijing in 1987. A small Chinese software company finances its development operations by obtaining foreign currency from data entry performed in Beijing for Californian companies. The data are generally law records, sent by several California law firms by air cargo. The documents are keyed onto magnetic tape by temporary workers, teenage girls from high schools who are supposed to obtain their "computer training" through this work for several months, in exchange for a "salary" equivalent to US $15 per month. Quality control and supervision are performed by a male software technician who organizes and supervises the work of about 25 teenagers. The women do not know a word of English, and they transcribe each letter as an ideogramme. The rate of error seems to be lower than in equivalent operations in the US.

Most operations of this kind, however, take place in the Caribbean, fostered in recent years by the Caribbean Basin Initiative Act approved by the US Congress for geopolitical reasons. Barbados, Jamaica, and Haiti have been the main locations for offshoring of data entry work, often used by airlines to process their coupons. Mexico is also a growing location for these activities, as are India, Singapore, and China. While air transport is often used for the exchange of documents for magnetic tapes, some facilities involve one-way or two-way telecommunication links to transmit information where time is a high-priority element in processing. Jamaica is investing heavily in telecommunications facilities, particularly in facsimile transmission, in order to attract US investment in this new, clean industry. Future development of optical character readers and scanning devices could give a boost to the offshoring of routine office jobs. However, in spite of the striking images evoked by this trend, its quantitative importance is very limited. According to the OTA report, in 1985 fewer than 3,000 workers in the Caribbean were employed by US firms on data-entry operations, and just 2,000 more such were predicted for the following decade. Including Mexico and Asia, fewer than 10,000 jobs seem to be involved in the operation overall. In fact, much of the Third World is not suitable for this kind of decentralization of office work because of the inadequacy of telecommunications infrastructure and the unreliability of air connections. This is in fact why the Caribbean was targeted as the expansion area, close to the concentration of business on the US east coast, and enjoying good links with the US on the basis of the communications infrastructure set up by the tourist industry. But even in the closer and more reliable areas, offshore decentralization of office work will remain a marginal phenomenon because the nature of activities that can be decentralized corresponds precisely to those tasks that can be easily automated and will be automated during the 1990s. The same process of technological change that made telecommunicated offshoring possible will cause the phenomenon to be superseded as information-processing capabilities develop further the capacity to operate without requiring a significant amount of unskilled labor.

A more important debate is taking place concerning the extent and potential of the ultimate decentralization of office work: "telecommuting," or, more properly defined in OTA terms, "home-based automated office work."[98] This refers to the ability of workers to perform their work from their homes, using computers connected to information systems networks. Alvin Toffler's prophecy of the "electronic cottage" has fueled speculation that as many as 15 million jobs could be operated from remote locations, including homes, by 1990.[99] However, the data currently available completely contradict such expectations. Around 1985, estimates of the numbers of home-based office workers using electronic equipment ranged between 10,000 and 30,000 for the entire US.[100] Moreover, this includes casual, overtime work; salaried workers "telecommuting" as their main employment for a given company probably number less than 5,000 scattered in experimental programs initiated by about 200 companies in the whole country. These workers fall into two different groups.[101] On the one hand, there are professionals whose job flexibility allows them to perform work from home; and on the other hand, there are clerical workers performing data entry operations, who accept the requirement of higher output for lower pay in exchange for being able to stay home. Most of the workers in the second category are women who stay home to take care of children (although some studies show that many of them eventually find they need to pay for day care for their children in order to be able to perform their work at home). Corporations involved in these experiments are mainly in the financial services and computer business sectors. As Gretzos argues,[102] their main motivation for conducting these experiments seems to be the potential for control of future unionization of clerical office workers, a matter of concern for corporations beginning to face the discontent of the new service working class made up of women clerical workers. This is also the reason why labor unions staunchly oppose home-based work. The findings of case studies conducted on the issue [103] tend to show higher productivity of workers, a tendency toward self-exploitation (putting in more hours of work than are claimed for), and yet higher satisfaction with the work because of increased autonomy in terms of time and space. However, management tends to dislike such arrangements because they largely take workers' activity beyond their control and threaten the traditional organization of the office. The development of home work is also inhibited by the existing legal framework, as it makes fiscal regulations and health and labor legislation more difficult to enforce.

The combination of routine legal obstacles, union hostility, and lack of fundamental motivation on the business side, seem to account for the negligible development of telecommuting in the US during the 1980s. However, the real question for the evolution of the spatial structure, is the extent to which this situation could be reversed. It is obvious that the widespread application of telecommuting on the basis of information technologies could considerably modify not only office work itself, but also the communication and transportation flows in the metropolitan areas, deeply affecting the overall urban system. An assessment of the possibilities here must take into consideration, again, the increasingly bifurcated profile of the occupational structure in information-processing activities. For professionals and managers, electronically-based work at home is already a reality, in the sense that many professionals work overtime at home, increasingly using computers, while still going into the office every day to work. This is , in fact, the continuation of a trend that has always existed for the managerial –professional labor force, with the addition of two relatively new factors: the much greater quantitative importance of this professional stratum; and the facility to access the information network system from home, or from other locations, such as from a hotel room by portable computer during a business trip, that makes professional work a potentially non-stop activity. On the other hand, routine clerical work performed at home, on a full-time or, more often, part-time basis, generally by women combining paid work and unpaid family duties, will tend to develop if workers' control over their labor conditions in the office becomes an important factor, as it will if clerical unionization develops. Unskilled homework is more likely to be associated to the growth of an exploitative underground service economy than with the free worker controlling her or his premises and time. More likely than this is the expansion of electronic home work related to the growth of independent contractors and freelancers, the basis of small business growth in the service sector, for whom automatic information-processing offers the possibility of greater efficiency without investment in hiring employees. But this development, which will probably account for most of business uses of electronic equipment in domestic premises in the next few years, can hardly be equated with telecommuting or to the images generally associated with the electronic cottage. It actually means that small businesses, operating from their various locations, including homes when locations are mixed, will be equipped with information systems machines. The potentially crucial development is the possibility for increasing connections among small businesses, and among corporations and their small business ancillary suppliers, through networks of information systems.[104] Rather than decentralized salaried work at home, we could be witnessing the expansion of sub-contracting and networking, with information technologies reinforcing and making materially feasible the trend toward decentralization of production and organizational flexibility that is one of the main features of the current business dynamics.

Overall, then, we observe a major trend toward spatial decentralization of office work and business activities. This decentralization occurs among regions, among metropolitan areas, from metropolitan areas to smaller cities and rural areas, to a limited extent abroad, and, in the future, to the domestic premises. The most important decentralizing trend is taking place within the largest metropolitan areas, from central cities to suburbia and, increasingly, beyond to exurbia and the creation of multifunctional, multinuclear spatial structures. *This process is not undifferentiated.*[105] It follows a hierarchical and functional logic, with lower-level activities being decentralized to secondary suburban locations, and market-oriented facilities being dispersed close to their segmented markets. New directional centers are also being created, shifting regional and metropolitan locations, thus further complicating the geometry of the corporate structure. Ancillary services follow this decentralization, forming new agglomerations that crystallize at nodal points of the communications structure. However, such major decentralization, best expressed in the process of suburbanization of offices and services, is taking place simultaneously with the reinforcement of centralization of decision-making in the corporate cores of major CBDs, and within the framework of metropolitan dominance reinforced by the new telecommunications infrastructure. It is the dialectics between these processes of centralization and of decentralization that fundamentally characterizes the new spatial logic resulting from the transformation of office activities by the use of new information technologies.

Conclusion: the Information Economy, the New Corporate Structure, and the Space of Flows

Information-processing activities increasingly play a structurally determining role in advanced industrialized countries, be it in services, manufacturing, or agriculture. Our economies should be characterized as information economies, rather than as service economies. Information-processing activities are currently undergoing a profound transformation under the combined effect of organizational changes, economic restructuring, and technological innovation. New spatial forms, and even more important, a new spatial logic, emerge as the result of these transformations.

At the organizational level, four major trends combine to produce a new corporate structure: the growing dominance of the large corporation; the decentralization of management; the sub-contracting of operations to a constellation of ancillary small and medium-sized businesses; and the networking of corporations linking their elements to each other and to their auxiliaries. The result is the formation of a complex, hierarchical, diversified organizational structure that is characterized by a variable geometry depending upon time, place, and realm of activity.

Deregulation, crisis management, and stepped-up worldwide competition have led corporations, and their dependent units, to engage in cost-saving, product diversification, creation of new markets, and reorganization of the labor process, in order to increase profits and win market shares in a new and increasingly challenging environment. As a result, increasing productivity of both labor and capital becomes the bottom line on which will depend the fate of each corporate conglomerate in the struggle for survival.

Major innovations in information technology provide a powerful tool for organizational change and economic restructuring, while at the same time imposing constraints and introducing new processes of management and labor in the workings of business organizations. Increasing automation of routine operations, reintegration of tasks at a higher level, emphasis on decision-making on the basis of expert systems, networking of units within the corporation and between economic units; all these technological trends converge on the growing importance of communication networks and interactive patterns in the life and death of organizations. While technology in the main amplifies the logic built into the organization itself, rather than creating it, it does so at such a fundamental level that it allows for a growing independence of the internal relationships of the organization *vis-à-vis* its external environment. Although the increasing automation of internal procedures allows the corporation to concentrate on the moment of decision from which everything else follows, the velocity and complexity of management tasks in a system of multiple interaction mean that the internal system must be able to process the instructions received from the high level of decision making without referring back to it after the initial input into the system. From this follows a very decentralized, but also extremely hierarchical, division of labor among the different units of the corporate conglomerate and its surrounding network. These complex, decentralized systems are heavily centered, and new information technologies make it possible for them to be at the same time flexible and hierarchical. Moreover, the design of the information systems will generally reflect these hierarchies and priorities in terms of access to information and processing capacity.

The spatial dynamics of information activities express this complex organizational and technological pattern. It is characterized, simultaneously, by the persistent centralization of high-level activities in the CBDs of the largest metropolitan areas, and by the decentralization of back offices to smaller areas, and, above all, to the suburbs of major metropolitan areas. In addition, some limited suburban and regional decentralization of head-quarters locations bears witness to the pervasive presence of information activities in the overall economic geography. Together with the two above-mentioned trends, decentralization of retail services, particularly to the suburbs, reflects the three-fold tendency toward concentration of decision, automation of organization, and diffusion of customized activities across segmented markets. The regional shift of activities, population, and jobs proceeds by reproducing the same basic spatial logic on an expanded geographic scale, as other areas of the national territory are brought into the new developmental dynamics.

In this complex territorial development process, neither centralization nor decentralization is dominant. *What is crucial is the relationship between the two processes.* On the one hand, what matters is what is centralized and what is de-centralized. High-level decision-making is increasingly centralized; organiz-ational management is basically decentralized within major metropolitan areas; and service delivery and customized information retrieval and delivery are diffused throughout the territory. On the other hand, the fundamental characteristic of all these spaces is their interrelationship by means of communication flows. Centralized decision-making can only operate on the basis of customized provision of services and retrieval of information. Back offices are the material basis for decision-making, and large-scale informa-tion-processing organizations can only work on the basis of instructions received from the center. The constellation of services linked to each stage of the process of each industry also depends on access to the corresponding level of the communication network. Thus, the linkages of the intra-organizational network are the defining linkages of the new spatial logic. The space of flows among units of the organization and among different organizational units is the most significant space for the functioning, the performance, and ultimately, the very existence of any given organization. The space of organizations in the informational economy is increasingly a *space of flows*.

However, this does *not* imply that organizations are placeless. On the contrary, we have seen that decision-making continues to be dependent upon the milieu on which metropolitan dominance is based; that service delivery must follow dispersed, segmented, segregated markets; and that large-scale operations in back offices are highly dependent upon specific pools of labor that are concentrated in some suburbs of large metropolitan areas. Thus, each component of the information-processing structure is place-oriented.

Nevertheless, the organizational logic of corporations and their satellite activities is fundamentally dependent upon the network of interaction among the different components of the systems. While organizations are located in places, and their components are place-dependent, the *organizational logic is placeless*, being fundamentally dependent on the space of flows that characterizes information networks. But such flows are structured, not undetermined. They possess directionality, conferred both by the hierarchical logic of the organization as reflected in instructions given, and by the material characteristics of the information systems infrastructure. Organizations establish flows according to their hierarchy within the limits set by the telecommunications and computer infrastructure existing at a particular time in a particular place. The space of flows remains the fundamental spatial dimension of large-scale information-processing complexes.

The consequences of this conclusion are far-reaching, because the more organizations depend, ultimately, upon flows and networks, the less they are influenced by the social contexts associated with the places of their location. From this follows a growing independence of the organizational logic from the societal logic: a trend that we could call "bureaucratization" in the Weberian sense, that is, the predominance of the rationality of means over the rationality of goals. Because access to the network of flows is the basic condition for the performance of any organization, this access will have to take precedence over any other requirement originating from the inputs from a particular location of one of the components of the organization at any given point in the network. In more concrete terms: the interests of a local business elite, or of a local resident working class, or of a local market, will be constantly subordinated to the need for the organization to be connected simultaneously with the financial markets, the pool of professional labor, the strategic alliances in the world economy, and the ability to install and update the necessary technology, to mention just some of the potentially key internal requirements, all of which are dependent upon interactions in the space of flows. Since most organizations (or conglomerates of organizations) tend to connect and interact with other systems, the key element for an organization is, increasingly, to preserve those connections. The organizational flows are connected in a macro-space of flows.

Yet most of these flows are directional, and these directions have a socially specific, place-based component. For instance, the decisions of top financial institutions headquartered in New York are not entirely alien to the social milieu of life and decision-making of the New York-based business elite. However, the more heavily interdependent the world economy and the national economy become, the more information technologies are required to handle instant decision processes, and the more the logic of global organizations, materialized in a series of programmed instructions transmitted to the communications network, becomes largely independent from the cultural values and personal preferences of any particular elite group. While the structural logic embedded in the pattern of flows cannot be entirely abstracted from its originators, given the diversity of sources and the changing pattern of manifestation of dominant interests there is an increasing tension between the individual characteristics of the decision-makers in the corporate world and the structure of flows materialized in the communication networks and the repertoire of computerized instructions. Thus, the dialectics between centralization and decentralization, the increasing tension between places and flows, could reflect, in the final analysis, the gradual transformation of the flows of power into the power of flows.

4

Information Technology, the Restructuring of Capital–Labor Relationships, and the Rise of the Dual City

Introduction: The Impact of New Technologies on Labor and Cities

The impact of new technologies on the level of employment, the quality of work, and the condition of labor, is at the core of the social debate over the technological revolution. As cities are made of and by people, and most people are workers, the relationship between technology and labor is decisive in shaping the urban dynamics.

In order to explore systematically the complex web of interactions between high technology, labor, and cities, I will first address the effects of new technologies on the general level of employment and on the occupational structure. I will then locate the specific impact of technology within the broader restructuring process undergone by labor in recent decades, drawing implications for social stratification and income distribution. On the basis of these analyses it will then be possible to assess the transformation of urban social structure into one that I will characterize as "dual," in a sense that I will try to define precisely in terms of several analytical dimensions, on the basis of case studies of New York City and Los Angeles. Throughout this intellectual journey the central methodological question to be considered is the ability to determine the specific role of high technology in the complex interplay among economic and institutional processes that lies at the roots of a new socio-spatial configuration that I will call the "dual city." The thesis I will try to sustain is that while new technologies are by no means the causal factor in the process leading to the new socio-spatial form, they are a major contributing variable in terms of their instrumental role in the overall process of restructuring of labor. While these trends could be altered, and ultimately reversed, the historical rigidity of spatial forms threatens to consolidate this urban process beyond the time horizon of current economic and technological policies. In this sense, the restructuring of labor could be embodied in our social and spatial organization under the impetus of the technological imperative. Let us examine, in analytical order, the different elements underlying the potential formation of the dual city.

High Technology, Employment, and the Transformation of the Occupational Structure

The potential impact of new technologies on work and employment represents the main source of both hopes and fears for the economy and for people. On the one hand, productivity gains made possible by the diffusion of the technological revolution throughout all sectors of activity could pave the way for economic rejuvenation, leading to a new era of innovation and growth.[1] On the other hand, it is feared that the widespread use of labor-saving process-oriented technologies will worsen unemployment, both functional and structural, at a historical moment when hundreds of thousands of jobs, particularly in manufacturing, are being lost.[2] The debate goes beyond the matter of the quantity of jobs to raise the issue of the quality of work in the new technological environment.[3] Is automation de-skilling workers and reducing them to mindless appendages of computers?[4] Or, on the contrary, is there a process of task reintegration taking place that provides workers with greater autonomy in decision-making and enhances the role of judgmental capacity in the work process?[5] In other words, is technology serving people or further alienating workers, or both? If both, which are the conditions determining each potential outcome of the process of technologyical change?

This polemical background makes it particularly difficult to conduct a serious, objective assessment of the matter in the absence of methodologically indisputable empirical research on a comparative basis, and over a sufficiently long span of time.[6] This is why, while I introduce the subject for the sake of the specific research purpose of this work, it will be necessary to proceed with great caution, pinpointing, one after another, the different questions underlying the general issue of the relationship between information technologies and employment. Indeed, a major reason for the intellectual confusion surrounding this debate is the tendency to tangle several issues in a single question, with that question generally being presented in such a way as to suggest a preconceived answer.

At the most elementary level, it is clear that information technologies, when introduced in the work process, both in factories and in offices, considerably reduce working time per unit of output. Scattered evidence, on the basis of case studies, points in this direction, for instance, studies by Hunt and Hunt on the impact of robotics, and by Maeda, Cockroft, Drennan, and Roessner et al., on office automation.[7] However, labor reduction induced by process technology could be offset by new demand for the products, generated by lower prices and improved quality resulting from technological change. Added demand could also result from the new inputs necessary to the new production processes, as well as from the development of new products made possible by the application of new technologies. Furthermore, for a given firm or for a given national economy, technological innovation may result in enhanced competitiveness, thus enabling that economic unit to win market shares, and thus ultimately to increase employment by providing for a much larger demand, thus requiring a substantially higher output. The transformation of reduced working time into job losses is certainly not the result of technology but of a given form of social organization that cannot be considered historically immutable. After all, in comparison with earlier stages of industralization, workers in advanced industrial societies work fewer hours, produce substantially more output, and receive much higher pay. Productivity increases, as a result of both technological innovation and social change, rather than long, hard working hours, are the fundamental basis for economic growth and social well-being.[8]

The complexity of the issue requires a cautious approach of the kind taken by Kaplinsky in his survey of international experience of the relationship between microelectronics and employment.[9] He carefully emphasized the need to differentiate the interpretation of the findings according to various different levels of discourse, of which he defined eight: process level, plant level, firm level, industry level, region level, sector level, national level, and meta level (meaning the discussion of effects according to specific techno-economic paradigms). After reviewing the evidence for each one of these levels, he concluded:

Insofar as the individual studies offer any clear statement on the issue, it would appear that the quantitative macro and micro studies are drawn to fundamentally different conclusions. Process and plant level investigations generally seem to point to a significant displacement of labour. On the other hand, national level simulations more often reach the conclusion that there is no significant employment problem on hand.[10]

We find a similar level of uncertainty when reviewing available evidence for the United States. Flynn summarized about 200 case studies of the employment impacts of process innovations between 1940 and 1982.[11] According to his conclusions, it appears that while process innovations in manufacturing eliminated high-skill jobs and helped to create low-skill jobs, the opposite was true for information-processing in offices, where technological innovation suppressed low-skill jobs and created high-skill ones. Flynn concluded that the effects of process innovation were variable, depending upon specific situations of industries and firms.

At the industry level, the analysis by Levy and others of five industries showed divergent effects of technological innovation:[12] in three of the industries (iron mining, coal mining, and aluminum), technological change increased output and resulted in higher employment levels; in the other two industries (steel and automobiles), growth of demand did not match reduction of labor per unit of output, and job losses resulted. A matter which this study did not investigate is the consideration that automobiles and steel are both industries in which the loss of American competitiveness has reduced market shares for US firms; here we have pinpointed the crucial role of non-technological factors in determining the evolution of demand and output, and thus of employment levels.

At an aggregate level, a number of simulations, using input–output methodology, constitute the most comprehensive attempt to evaulate the impact of technology on employment, measuring direct and indirect effects over a period of time. Howell evaluated the employment effect of industrial robots on 86 industrial sectors between 1986 and 1990.[13] He concluded that the number of jobs displaced by robotics would range between 168,000 (assuming low diffusion) and 718,000 (assuming fast diffusion). The latter scenario amounts to a displacement level equivalent to about 0.7 percent of total US employment and 3.7 percent of US manufacturing employment, on 1986 figures.

The most ambitious and widely cited study at the national level is the simulation performed by Leontieff and Duchin to evaluate the impact of computers on employment for the period 1963–2000, on the basis of a dynamic input–output matrix of the US economy.[14] They found, in their moderate secenario, that 20 million fewer workers would be required in the year 2000 to fill the expected number of jobs required to achieve the same output, while keeping constant the level of technology. This figure represents a drop of 11.7 percent in required labor. However, according to their calculations, the impact is strongly differentiated among industries and occupations. Interestingly enough, services, and particularly office activities, are predicted to suffer greater job losses than manufacturing, as a result of massive diffusion of office automation. Consequently, clerical workers and managers would see their prospects of employment significantly reduced by new information technologies, while those for professionals would increase substantially, and craftsmen and operatives would maintain their position in the labor force. The methodology of the Leontieff–Duchin study, has, however, been strongly criticized,[15] because it relies on a number of assumptions that, on the basis of limited case studies, maximize the potential impact of computer automation, while limiting technological change to the effect of computers

However, should reductions in labor requirements materialize, it is unlikely that they would be compensated for by high-technology employment induced by demand for new capital goods. High-technology employment projections show these industries growing very fast, but still representing a very small proportion of all new jobs: less than 6 per cent for 1982–95, according to estimates from the Bureau of Labor Statistics (see table 4.1). Following the same line of argument, Gordon and Kimball have shown that high-technology industries will not be able to replace the jobs lost, particularly in manufacturing, because of technological obsolescence and economic restructuring.[16] Employment in electronics in the US tripled between 1960 and 1980, increasing from 1.6 percent of the total labor force in 1965 to 2.1 percent in 1974, and to 2.9 percent in 1986. In that year, with 2,731,000

Table 4.1 Employment and employment growth, by high-tech industries and occupations: 1982–1995

Industries and occupations	Employment, 1982 (000s)	Employment growth, 1982–95[a] (000s)	(%)
All industries[b]	91,950	25,795	28.1
High-tech industries[c]			
Group I (48 industries)	12,350	4,263	34.5
As % of all industries	13.4	16.5	
Group II (6 industries)	2,543	867	34.1
As % of all industries	2.8	3.4	
Group II (28 industries)	5,691	2,029	35.7
As % of all industries	6.2	7.9	
All occupations[d]	101,510	24,600	25.2
High-tech occupations[e]	3,287	1,508	45.9
As % of all occupations	3.2	5.9	

[a]Data for 1995 based on moderate-trend projections.
[b]Employment covers all wage and salary workers.
[c]Group I includes industries where the proportion of workers employed in high-tech occupations[e] is at least 1.5 times the average for all industries. Group II includes industries with a ratio of R & D expenditure to net sales at least twice the average for all industries. Group III includes manufacturing industries in which the proportion of workers employed in high-tech occupations is equal to or greater than the average for all manufacturing industries; two manufacturing industries that provide technical support to high-tech manufacturing industries are also included.
[d]Employment covers all civilian workers.
[e]Engineers, life and physical scientists, mathematical specialists, engineering and science technicians and computer specialists.
Source: Richard W. Riche, Daniel E. Hecker, and John V. Burgan, "High Technology Today and Tomorrow: A Small Slice of the Employment Pie," *Monthly Labor Review,* 106 (November 1983), tables 2 and 4.

workers in the industry, electronics accounted for twice as many jobs as the automobile and the iron and steel industries combined. And yet, electronics in 1986 represented only 12 percent of the total number of manufacturing jobs and 2.9 percent of total US employment. In 1984, eating and drinking places were employing almost twice as many people as electronics, government six times as many and non-government services seven times as many; and this situation will not change in the foreseeable future. The main high-technology electronics industries together are expected to create about 830,000 new jobs between 1984 and 1995. This figure, as Gordon and Kimball write,

constitutes less than half the number of the manufacturing jobs lost in the US economy between 1980 and 1983. High-technology industries will continue to expand more rapidly than total employment but nevertheless are expected to contribute less than 9% of all new jobs in the period 1982–95. In other words, all but a small proportion of the new jobs established in the foreseeable future will originate in spheres outside high-technology industry while high technology itself will have little impact on reducing unemployment in the US, Western Europe or the Third World.[17]

However, the real issue is not the direct trade-off between jobs eliminated by labor-saving technologies and jobs created in high-technology industries, but the overall effect of technological innovation on economic growth and thus on employment in all activities, including services, on the basis of surplus productivity generated in factories and offices and translated into greater demand and greater output. Robert Z. Lawrence has argued that information technologies have a positive effect on employment in a number of ways: by stimulating production and employment in the capital goods sector; by increasing productivity, thus alleviating disputes over redistribution; and by extending productivity increases to the service sector.[18] He considers it unlikely that the impact of information technology on the economy will be disruptive, for at least three major reasons: first, because their introduction proceeds at a relatively slow pace: increases in output per worker attributable to information technology will not be more than 1 per cent per year; secondly, because high rates of investment in new technology will probably take place during expansionary phases of the business cycle, in which disruption is less frequent; and thirdly, and most importantly, the strongest impact will be during the 1990s, when the rate of growth of the labor force will substantially decline (from 3.5 percent in 1970–82 to 2.3 percent in 1982–90 and 1.4 percent in 1990–5). Assuming these conditions, he proceeds with a simulation of employment growth in the US, after which he concludes:

the decline in the US labor force growth of 2.1% is more than twice the rise in output per manhour, but would probably be the maximum due to a rapid increase in information technology. The U.S. economy needs to be no more successful at creating jobs than it has been in the past to absorb the labor potentially displaced by information technology.[19]

Lawrence's analysis, along with a number of other studies, underscores the fundamental flaw in the simulation models used by researchers who come up with predictions of significant job losses, including that built by Leontieff and Duchin: namely, that most of these models assume a fixed level of final demand and output. This is precisely what past experience of technological innovation seems to reject as the most likely hypothesis.[20] If the economy does not grow, it is obvious that labor-saving techniques will reduce the amount of working time required (even on this hypothesis by a somewhat limited amount – less than 12 percent in the Leontieff–Duchin calculations). But in the past, rapid technological change has generally been associated with an expansionary trend that, by increasing demand and output, has generated the need for *more* working time in absolute terms, even if it represents less working time per unit of output. However, in an internationally integrated economic system, expansion of demand and output will depend on the competitiveness of each specific economic unit. Since quality and production costs, the determinants of competitiveness, will largely depend on product and process innovation, and thus on technology, it is likely that faster technological change for a given firm, industry, or national economy, would result in a higher, not a lower, employment level. This is in line with the findings of the Young and Lawson study on the effect of technology on employment and output between 1972 and 1984.[21] In 44 of the 79 industries they examined, the labor-saving effects of new technologies were more than compensated for by higher final demand, so that, overall, employment expanded.

In the most carefully designed recent study, the Bureau of Labor Statistics forecast the impact of technological change on 378 industries and 562 occupations in 1995.[22] Almost all of the 350 occupations with more than 25,000 workers showed employment growth in the simulation. Only 11 occupations showed absolute declines in the number of projected jobs, under the impact of new technologies, and they were concentrated in four areas: office workers performing data entry; communications workers displaced by automation of telecommunications; trucks and tractor operators, linked to containerization and warehouse automation; and gas service station operators. Overall, job losses in the occupation analyzed would amount to 251,000, that is, about 1.6 percent of total employment growth projected for 1984–95.

Thus it seems that, as a general trend, there is no systematic structural correlation between the diffusion of information technologies in the labor process and the evolution of employment levels. Jobs are being displaced and new jobs are being created, but the quantitative relationship between the losses and the gains varies among firms, industries, sectors, regions, and countries, depending upon competitiveness, firms' strategies, government policies, institutional environments, and relative position in the international economy. The specific outcome of the interaction between high technology and employment is largely dominated by macroeconomic factors and economic strategies.

Overall, in the US it does not seem that the aggregate level of employment will be negatively affected by the impact of process-oriented information technologies. Nevertheless, if new jobs are created on the basis of technologically driven productivity and its stimulating effect on demand and output, they are of very different kinds from those phased out by techno-economic restructuring, particularly in manufacturing. Fast-growing high-technology industries are characterized, as reported in chapter 2, by a bipolar distribution

Table 4.2 High-technology occupational structure: gender, ethnicity and race

Occupation type	White female (%)	Minority (male and female) (%)	White male (%)
(a) US high-technology industry			
Production	38.4	24.4	37.2
Technical	15.8	14.3	69.9
Professional	11.9	8.4	79.7
(b) Santa Clara County			
Production	30.2	46.4	23.4
Technical	16.7	28.0	55.3
Professional	13.3	14.4	72.2
(c) Santa Cruz County			
Production	48.4	29.4	22.2
Technical	25.3	23.0	51.7
Professional	24.0	12.7	63.4

Sources: 1980 EEOI Summary Report of Selected Establishments from the Technical Services Division, OSP, Equal Employment Opportunity Commission; R. Gordon and L. Kimball, *Small Town High Technology: The Industrialization of Santa Cruz County,* (1985). The authors are very grateful to Lenny Siegel, Pacific Studies Center, Mountain View for supplying the EEOI raw data from which the US and Santa Clara, figures are calculated.
Compiled and elaborated by Gordon and Kimball (see note 28).

of skills and wages,[23] specified by gender and race, as illustrated in table 4.2, elaborated by Gordon and Kimball.

Concerning the evolution of the occupational structure at large, the projections of the Bureau of Labor Statistics for 1982–95[24] provide some fundamental clues to understanding the emerging social structure (see tables 4.3, 4.4, and 4.5). The bulk of new jobs correspond to low-skilled occupations in the service sector: 779,000 building custodians, 744,000 cashiers, 719,000 secretaries, and so on. While some of the fastest growing categories, as shown in table 4.4, do represent the rise of high-skill occupations related to the process of technological development, their share in the total of new jobs is still limited. Computer systems analysts boast an 85.3 percent growth rate for 1982–95, but this adds only 217,000 new jobs, while the 27.5 percent increase in building custodians translates into 3 million new jobs. A similar argument could be sustained in terms of the projections of job growth by sector. BLS projections for 1982–90 attributed a 27 percent expansion to computers and peripherals, and only 16 percent to "restaurants and other retailing," but these growth rates translated into 200,000 new jobs for the computers sector, and 3 million jobs for "restaurants and other retailing," on top of the 17 million jobs already existing in the latter sector. Similarly, the rate of growth

Table 4.3 Forty occupations with largest job growth, 1982–1995[a]

Occupation	Change in total employment (000s)	% of total job growth	% change
Building custodians	779	3.0	27.5
Cashiers	744	2.9	47.4
Secretaries	719	2.8	29.5
General clerks, office	696	2.7	29.6
Salesclerks	685	2.7	23.5
Nurses, registered	642	2.5	48.9
Waiters and waitresses	562	2.2	33.8
Teachers, kindergarten and elementary	511	2.0	37.4
Truckdrivers	425	1.7	26.5
Nursing aides and orderlies	423	1.7	34.8
Sales representatives, technical	386	1.5	29.3
Accountants and auditors	344	1.3	40.2
Automotive mechanics	324	1.3	38.3
Supervisors of blue-collar workers	319	1.2	26.6
Kitchen helpers	305	1.2	35.9
Guards and doorkeepers	300	1.2	47.3
Food preparation and service workers, fast-food restaurants	297	1.2	36.7
Managers, store	292	1.1	30.1
Carpenters	247	1.0	28.6
Electrical and electronic technicians	222	0.9	60.7
Licensed practical nurses	220	0.9	37.1
Computer systems analysts	217	0.8	85.3
Electrical engineers	209	0.8	65.3
Computer programmers	205	0.8	76.9
Maintenance repairers, general utility	193	0.8	27.8
Helpers, trades	190	0.7	31.2
Receptionists	189	0.7	48.8
Electricians	173	0.7	31.8
Physicians	163	0.7	34.0
Clerical supervisors	162	0.6	34.6
Computer operators	160	0.6	75.8
Sales representatives, non-technical	160	0.6	27.4
Lawyers	159	0.6	34.3
Stock clerks, stockroom and warehouse	156	0.6	18.8
Typists	155	0.6	15.7
Delivery and route workers	153	0.6	19.2
Bookkeepers, hand	152	0.6	15.9
Cooks, restaurants	149	0.6	42.3
Bank tellers	142	0.6	30.0
Cooks, short order, speciality and fast-food	141	0.6	32.2

[a]Includes only detailed occupations with 1982 employment of 25,000 or more.

Data for 1995 are based on moderate-trend projections.

Source: Bureau of Labor Statistics.

Table 4.4   Twenty fastest growing occupations, 1982–1995[a]

Occupation	Growth in employment (%)
Computer service technicians	96.8
Legal assistants	94.3
Computer systems analysts	85.3
Computer programmers	76.9
Computer operators	75.8
Office machine repairers	71.7
Physical therapy assistants	67.8
Electrical engineers	65.3
Civil engineering technicians	63.9
Peripheral EDP equipment operators	63.5
Insurance clerks, medical	62.2
Electrical and electronic technicians	60.7
Occupational therapists	59.8
Surveyor helpers	58.6
Credit clerks, banking and insurance	54.1
Physical therapists	53.6
Employment interviewers	52.5
Mechanical engineers	52.1
Mechanical engineering technicians	51.6
Compression and injection mold machine operators, plastics	50.3

[a]Includes only detailed occupations with 1982 employment of 25,000 or more.
Data for 1995 are based on moderate-trend projections.
Source: Bureau of Labor Statistics.

of secretarial jobs for 1982–90 (28.3 percent) was far below that for data processing mechanics (92.3 percent) but translated into about 700,000 more secretaries, in comparison with 77,000 additional data processing mechanics. Rumberger and Levine have analyzed the wages and skills components of these occupational categories on the basis of BLS projections.[75] Their findings, some of which are displayed in table 4.6, show that occupations with the highest growth in absolute numbers, accounting for the majority of new jobs, are concentrated in low-skilled, low-paid activities with low educational requirements, while three out of the five fastest-declining occupations have high relative earnings.

Bluestone and Harrison have compared the wages and working conditions attached to maufacturing jobs displaced by the restructuring process with those prevailing in the bulk of new manufacturing and service jobs. On the basis of BLS data they report that, in 1982, the average weekly wage was $310 in the declining industries but only $210 in the fastest-growing industries. According to their study, "it was necessary to create 163 electronic components jobs to compensate for the wage bill loss of 100 steel workers. Similarly it takes almost two department store jobs or three restaurant jobs to

Table 4.5   Twenty most rapidly declining occupations, 1982–1995[a]

Occupation	Decline in employment (%)
Railroad conductors	−32.0
Shoemaking machine operatives	−30.2
Aircraft structure assemblers	−21.0
Central telephone office operators	−20.0
Taxi drivers	−18.9
Postal clerks	−17.9
Private household workers	−16.9
Farm laborers	−15.9
College and university faculty	−15.0
Roustabouts	−14.4
Postmasters and mail superintendents	−13.8
Rotary drill operator helpers	−11.6
Graduate assistants	−11.2
Data entry operators	−10.6
Railboard brake operators	−9.8
Fallers and buckers	−8.7
Stenographers	−7.4
Farm owners and tenants	−7.3
Typesetters and compositors	−7.3
Butchers and meatcutters	−6.3

[a]Includes only detailed occupations with 1982 employment of 25,000 or more.
Data for 1995 are based on moderate-trend projections.
Source: Bureau of Labor Statistics.

make up for the earning loss of just one average manufacturing position."[26] Gordon and Kimball advance a similar argument, indicating that in 1984 the average hourly wage of an electronics production worker was $8.89, compared with $13.09 in steel, and $12.54 in the automobile industry.[27] They also report usual starting wages in operative work in electronics in the range of $3.50–$5.50 per hour. Comparable trends in electronics manufacturing are documented by Carnoy for Silicon Valley, Scott for Orange County, and Gordon and Kimball for Santa Cruz, California.[28]

A similar pattern in the evolution of the occupational structure is observed by Michael Teitz in his analysis of prospects for the California economy when he writes:

Electronics, especially production of semiconductors and products derived from them, requires a labor force that differs markedly from that in traditional manufacturing. The proportion of skilled technical and professional workers tends to be much higher than the average in manufacturing, and they are paid correspondingly well. However, production work is highly routinized and selectively low-skilled. Its pay has been below average for manufacturing and it tends to draw on female and immigrant labor

Table 4.6 Employment, education, and relative earnings in the greatest declining and growing occupations, 1982–1995

	Employment (000s)			Relative earnings[a] (%)	Modal education[b] (years)
	1982	1995	1982–95		
Declining occupations					
Farm laborers	1,211	1,019	192	53	<12
Private household workers	1,023	850	173	30	<12
College and university faculty	744	632	112	136	17+
Farm owners and tenants	1,407	1,304	103	119	12
Postal service clerks	307	252	55	122	12
Total	4,692	4,057	635	78	–
Growing occupations					
Building custodians	2,828	3,606	778	69	<12
Cashiers	1,570	2,314	744	49	12
Secretaries	2,441	3,161	720	67	12
General clerks, office	2,348	3,044	696	67	12
Sales clerks	2,916	3,601	685	52	12
Total	12,103	15,726	3,623	61	–

[a]Average weekly earnings during 1979 of workers in each occupation relative to the average weekly earnings of all workers.
[b]Level of education completed by the majority of workers employed in each occupation in the spring of 1980.
Sources: Employment data from Geoge T. Silvestri, John M. Lukasiewicz, and Marcus F. Einstein, "Occupational Employment Projections Through 1995," *Monthly Labor Review* 106 (November 1983), table 1; earnings and education data calculated from the 1980 Public Use sample, US Bureau of the Census. Compiled by R.W. Rumberger (see note 32).

pools that are non-unionized. While this form of employment is undoubtedly critical for low-skilled workers, it is problematic for the long-term. It does not offer income opportunities comparable to those being lost in the older, declining industrial sectors, and therefore provides neither easy transition for displaced workers nor long-term prospects for higher income or career mobility. If anything, it has been argued that the high level of education and technical skill required by the technical/professional part of the labor force tends to decrease prospects that production workers could ever be anything more.[29]

So, while the available empirical evidence does not seem to support the idea of a significant negative impact exercised by information technologies on the aggregate level of employment in the US, there are a number of substantial new trends in the evolution of the occupational structure:

(1) A fast rate of growth of high-technology manufacturing and advanced services-related jobs, yet accounting for only a small propor-

tion of total new jobs, and an even lower share of overall aggregate employment.[30]

(2) A bipolar occupational structure in high-technology manufacturing, as well as in manufacturing industries, fostered by intensive penetration by microelectronics-based process technologies. This bipolar structure is characterized by the juxtaposition of two main groups of workers: professional, engineers, and technicians on the one hand, most of them being white and male; and low-skilled, low-paid direct manufacturing jobs, generally held by women and ethnic minorities.[31]

(3) A massive increase in service jobs, which will account for about 75 percent of all new jobs in the period 1982–95. Most of these jobs will be in low-skill, low-pay occupations, such as building custodians, cashiers, secretaries, waiters, general clerks, etc.[32]

(4) A significant increase in the share of total employment taken by high-level occupations, such as professionals and technicians, from 16.3 percent in 1982 to 17.1 percent in 1995. Meanwhile operatives' share of the total will decline somewhat from 12.8 percent to 12.1 percent.[33]

Along with the proliferation of low-skill service jobs, it appears that the process of bipolarization is not confined to high-technology industries but, on the contrary, increasingly applies across the entire occupational structure. By bipolarization we understand the simultaneous growth of the top and the bottom of the occupational spectrum at a rate such that there is an increase in the relative shares of both extreme positions in the overall population distribution. If these projections are confirmed, and if the characteristics of the growing and declining occupations hold the educational and wage attributes revealed by Levin and Rumberger's analysis, it would seem that the process of restructuring leads to the simultaneous upgrading and downgrading of the occupational structure, although with changing emphasis in different industries and occupations.

Nevertheless, the question arises as to the specific relationship between new technologies and the emerging profile of the occupational structure I have described. In other words, it could be argued that the secular transformation toward the "service economy," and the specific characteristics of a number of service activities, are a more likely source of the new occupational structure than the introduction of new technologies into the work process. A serious attempt to answer this question with recourse to empirical data has been undetaken, for the US, by Ronald Kutscher, Associate Commissioner of the Bureau of Labor Statistics.[34] Kutscher proceeds in two steps. First, he analyzes the specific impact of technological change on employment by industry and by occupation between 1967 and 1978, comparing the actual level of employment to what would have resulted from holding technological input–output coefficients constant at their 1967 level. He then goes on to evaluate the impact of technology on future employment change by calculating a factor analysis of the 1977–95 projections by industry and by occupation, isolating the specific impact of input–output coefficients after having controlled the effect of other factors, in particular GNP growth. It has to be noted that Kutscher's definition of technological change is very broad, and refers to the technical coefficients of the input–output matrix, thus reaching beyond information technologies to include all changes in the goods and services required to produce each industry's goods or services. Nevertheless, his findings still represent a useful approximation for dealing with the question we are analyzing.

Table 4.7 provides Kutscher's estimates of the specific effects of technology on the evolution of employment in the period 1967–78. According to his findings, technology had a significantly negative effect on employment in agriculture and in manufacturing, a positive effect on the construction industry, a slight negative effect on wholesale and retail trade (offsetting the positive effects of the increase in output), and a positive effect on employment in finance, insurance, and real estate, which becomes strongly positive for job creation in "office services." According to data not shown in this table, negative effects on manufacturing employment have been concentrated in textiles, apparel, iron and steel, and motor vehicles. Positive effects have been particularly relevant in "other services," primarily miscellaneous business services. The statistical analysis of occupational change between 1967 and 1978 shows a positive effect on technology on the proportion of professionals

Table 4.7   Employment by Major Sector, % distribution

	Actual 1978	1978 with constant 1967 input–output coefficients	1978 with constant 1967 input–output and employment output coefficients
Agriculture, forestry and fisheries	3.9	3.6	5.5
Mining	0.8	0.8	0.7
Construction	7.0	7.6	5.1
Manufacturing	24.5	24.5	29.6
Durables	14.6	14.7	17.2
Non-durables	9.8	9.6	12.4
Transportation	3.6	3.5	3.0
Communications	1.5	1.3	2.0
Public utilities	1.0	1.1	1.1
Wholesale and retail trade	26.0	27.2	24.2
Finance, insurance and real estate	7.6	7.5	6.8
Other services	20.3	18.2	17.3
Government enterprises	1.8	2.4	2.0
Households	2.2	2.2	1.8

Source: Kutscher (see note 34).

Table 4.8   Largest declines in employment resulting from technological change, as measured by input–output coefficients, 1977–1995

Selected industries	Selected occupations
Iron and ferroalloy mining	Metal-working operatives
Non-ferrous metal ore mining	Factory material repairers
Sugar	Foundry workers
Wooden containers	Metal engineers
	Glassware operators
	Miscellaneous machine operators, binary metals
	Machine operatives, leather and leather goods
	Roadbrake operators
	Automotive engineers
	Road car repairers

Source: Kutscher (see note 34); my selection.

and technicians, a negative effect on operatives and farmers, and a lack of impact on the numbers of clerical workers.

Analysis of future trends is made more complex by the projective nature of the data. Also, because Kutscher kept his database at a high level of disaggregation, to make possible his factor analysis, the trends he shows for 1977–95 are less clear. Still, tables 4.8 and 4.9 provide some hints on the matter by pinpointing those industries and occupations most affected in the decline or increase of their employment by technological factors. It does appear that those most negatively affected by technological progress are the traditional manufacturing industries, and particularly the manual workers in those industries, while clerical work does not appear among the 40 occupations with the largest decline in employment. On the other hand, high technology and advanced services are the industries in which employment is most positively influenced by technological change. Yet the occupations showing the largest increase in employment due to technology are not actually high-technology-related jobs, but service-related occupations. Thus, security-related workers, household repair and maintenance workers, and financial experts outweigh communications mechanics or computer programmers in their rate of increase as a direct effect of technological change. Services are not only the major source of job creation in general, but also the sector whose expansion is most directly related to technological progress, after accounting for the effects of GNP growth, productivity, and staffing patterns. It is worth noting that this overwhelming expansion of service sector employment does not mean the demise of manufacturing. Manufacturing employment grew by 4.5 million jobs between 1959 and 1979, and although it lost 2.2 million jobs in the 1980–2 recession it will, according to BLS projections, gain a further 4.3 million jobs between 1982 and 1995,

Table 4.9   Largest increases in employment resulting from technological change, as measured by input–output coefficients, 1977–1995

Selected industries	Selected occupations
Electronic components	Termite treaters
Communications	Protective signal operators, installers, and repairers
Credit agencies and	Private detectives
financial brokers	Survey workers
Business services	Communications equipment mechanics
	Central office operators and repairers
	Directory assistance operators
	Installers, repairers, section maintainers
	Credit reporters
	Employment interviewers

Source: Kutscher (see note 34): my selection.

maintaining its share of total employment at about the 1982 level, that is, 19 percent. On the other hand, the overwhelming proportion of new job creation (23 million out of 28 million between 1983 and 1995) will take place in the service sector, and particularly in the "other services" category, which includes business services, health, hotels and restaurants, and personal services. This "other services" category will account for about one-third of all new jobs, and will represent in 1995 one-fourth of total US employment.

The interesting point in Kutscher's analysis is that while the general trend toward the increasing share of services in total employment is largely due to GNP growth, it is also attributable in some degree to the specific effect of technological change on the structure of employment, according to the results of his factor analysis. Technology appears to have a two-fold effect on the type of jobs created in the new economy: on the one hand, being a major factor in promoting economic growth, it accelerates the expansion of the service economy; on the other hand, it stimulates employment growth in high-technology manufacturing and in new service activities, as a direct effect of technology itself.

Therefore, on the basis of Kutscher's analysis at least, it seems that there is a statistical relationship between the current process of technological change and the specific profile of the occupational structure emerging in the US. High technology and information processing, in fostering productivity and competitiveness, play a crucial role in creating highly paid new technical and professional jobs. Productivity increases achieved by automation in both factories and offices "frees" labor, which is used by an expansionary service sector whose lower level concentrates most women, minorities, and immigrants in low-skill jobs. These occupations, lacking in organizational strength, become also low-paid, ill-protected jobs.

High technology does not, then, create unemployment by itself, particularly against the background of a declining growth rate of the labor force. On the contrary, when used to foster productivity and economic growth, it contributes to higher demand, investment, and output, ultimately expanding employment, mainly outside the high-technology sector of the economy. Yet high technology does seem to contribute to an occupational structure characterized by polarization and segmentation of the labor force. It probably does so, in spite of the upgrading of much of the labor working in high-technology industries and advanced services, by contributing to the dissolution of the social fabric that for decades protected wage-earners from the unrestrained imposition of the logic of capital. Otherwise it would be difficult to explain why clerical work is less well paid than assembly-line work, or why the wages of electronics production workers do not match those of their counterparts in the automobile industry. It is my hypothesis that the main reason for the current transformation of the occupational structure lies in the dissolution of old industrial forms and activities, and the subsequent creation of new ones, under the powerful impetus of a new, technology-led round of economic growth. It is in this precise sense that high technology appears to exercise a fundamental effect on work and employment: by the role it plays in the broader socio-economic restructuring of the labor process, at the roots of the new social structure.

Information Technology and the Restructuring of the Relationship between Capital and Labor

The introduction of information technology in the work process in factories and offices affects labor deeply. But the specific impact of technological change depends largely on the form in which technology is used and the objectives according to which it is applied. Furthermore, decisions affecting technological diffusion can only be understood within the framework of the restructuring process that has characterized capital–labor relationships in advanced industrial societies since the structural crisis of the 1970s.

The causes and characteristics of the restructuring process that has taken place, under different forms, in most societies, and with special intensity in the US, were presented in chapter 1. The diffusion of information technology in the work process has generally been an instrument, and a powerful one, of restructuring strategy. Therefore, we can only understand the orientations and outcome of technological change in organizations, and its impact on labor, by examining the interaction between the two processes, namely, the restructuring of capital–labor relationships and technological diffusion, under the dominance of the former. However, it should be clearly recognized that the use of information technology is part of a broader set of goals and motivations, and that technology is only one, and not necessarily the most important, of the instruments through which capital reorganizes the labor process.

Capital has had two main goals in pursuing the restructuring of labor in the particular historical circumstances produced by the economic crisis of 1973–4. The first is to change qualitatively the power relationships between management and organized labor in favor of business interests. The second is to enhance substantially the flexibility of labor at all levels, through deregulation, sectoral and geographical mobility, networking and sub-contracting, and constant redefinition of working conditions according to the changing strategies and interests of firms. The two objectives are inter-related, but they remain distinct in terms of their logic as well as of their implementation. The introduction of information technology in the work process plays an instrumental role in fostering both.

The use of information technology enhances capital's bargaining position *vis-à-vis* labor by providing management with a broad range of options: automation of jobs considered to be too expensive or not amenable to management requests; decentralization of production facilities to other regions or other countries, while maintaining links with other productive units and with the markets; sub-contracting of production and distribution to other firms in which labor works under different, generally less favorable conditions. Under these circumstances, capital does not necessarily need to adopt a confrontational strategy. Given its unfavorable position, organized labor will usually be forced to accept wages and working conditions below the historically established standards, just to keep the jobs at their current level. This explains the practice, widespread during the 1980s, of "voluntary" wage cutbacks in union contracts, as well as the two-tier contract system, under which newly hired workers do not benefit from the same wages as senior workers, thus fundamentally splitting the workforce. Also, in many instances, capital has taken a more aggressive stand, and has used technological change as a weapon to automate jobs in those segments of the labor force where organized labor was strongest. As a result of various tactics, backed up by the potential use of the technological medium both as an instrument and as an occasion to change working rules and practices, the position of organized labor has been decisively weakened in the core of manufacturing industries; and it has been unable to organize effectively in the new industries, particularly electronics and in advanced services, the leading sectors of the new economic era.

The second major goal of the restructuring process is to increase labor flexibility. And here also information technology plays a fundamental role, both in intra-firm flexibility and in inter-firm linkages. Within a particular organization, information technology forces a reclassification of job categories to accord with the new tasks, providing for multitask jobs that, while less routinized, are also more open to arbitrary, non-programmed definitions of the performance expected from each particular category. From this follows more direct managerial control, as responsibilities, and related conditions of work, shift with the needs of the company's changing organization of the work process. Flexible manfacturing technologies and microcomputer-based information-processing activities allow for variable volumes of production without increases in production costs. Part-time work, temporary labor contracts, and flexible working schedules become at the same time both possible and convenient for the firm, furthering the trend toward a variable geometry of labor and of labor conditions, able to reflect rapid changes in the market. Organizations certainly become more efficient, leaner, and more productive; but labor loses control over the labor process, and ultimately over its working conditions.

An even more important trend promoted by new technologies is the growing practice of sub-contracting and networking in the production process. The "just in time" system, able to reduce inventories drastically, is the quintessence of this tendency, organizing firms around networks of suppliers that rely on extremely precise information systems. Sub-contracting of entire phases of production to other firms, often in other countries, also allows for a combination of economies of scale and effectively decentralized production and management that increases efficiency and competitiveness. At the same time. labor is made extremely flexible, fitting into the specific conditions required by each unit of the network. Yet this trend also results in the segmentation of labor in a series of distinct organizational situations, while the unity of the production and management processes are largely preserved. Information technologies do not cause the generalized use of networks and sub-contracting in the pursuit of flexible production, or, therefore, the consequent segmentation of labor; but they provide the indispensable material infrastructure for such practices to develop. It is my belief that this trend in the organization of production is irreversible, with mass production being phased out as inefficient, as Piore and Sabel have brilliantly argued.[35] The so-called "Benetton Model" is a prototype of the industrial future of most effective productive organizations.[36] However, the contrast between the networking of capital and the segmentation of labor creates a new historical situation that is clearly undermining the social fabric inherited from earlier stages of industrialization. Considered against the background of organized labor weakened in the restructuring process, these trends clearly have threatening implications for the protection and living conditions of salaried workers, in the absence of a new round of social struggles leading to the formation of a new social contract based on different organizational and technological premises.

A detailed empirical analysis of the themes suggested here clearly exceeds the specific purpose of the research presented in this chapter, namely, to establish the precise connection between the restructuring of labor, infor-mation technology, and the new urban social structure. However, a few illustrations, drawn from available empirical studies on the introduction of new technologies in the labor process, will help to clarify the argument.

Watanabe has shown the different uses of new technology by comparing strategies and results in the process of introducing robots into the automobile industry in the US, in Japan, and in western Europe.[37] While in Japan, the much greater introduction of robots resulted in increased employment, in the US fewer robots displaced more workers, with a large total job loss; and in Ita-ly robots displace more workers than in France (see tables 4.10 and 4.11). The obvious reason for the discrepancies is that, both in the US and in Italy (particularly in Fiat) robots were introduced with the specific aim of saving labor, while in Japan quality considerations and flexibility of production were the main motives for the robotization program. In fact, Watanabe argues that to use robots to trim labor is an ill-conceived strategy, since special-purpose machines, less sophisticated and less expensive, are better suited as direct replacements for assembly-line jobs. His analysis also shows that, in the case of Japan, the competitive edge obtained by a productivity-driven, quality-oriented use of technology resulted in work-amplifying effects of the new technology sufficient largely to offset its labor-saving impact, actually increasing overall employment in the automobile industry. In the US on the other hand, a short-sighted strategy aimed at trimming labor to reduce production costs could not shore up the competitiveness of US manufacturers in their own market. The use and effects of technology depend more on man-agement strategies than on technology itself. By ensuring life tenure of employment to their workers, Japanese automobile companies were able to

Table 4.10   Estimates of labor savings made possible by robotization in the automobile industry (two-shift operation)

Country	(1) No. of robots[a]	(2) No. of workers replaced	(3) Change in employment, 1979–84	(2)/(3) (%)
Japan[b]	10,000	7,000	+60,000	–
United States[c]	5,000–7,000	10,000–15,000	−300,000	3.3–5.0
France	800	1,000	−50,000	2.0
Italy (Fiat)	800	2,400	−68,432	3.3

[a]"Robot" is defined broadly in line with the concept used by the Robotic Industries Association
[b]The Japanese figures relate to playback and higher categories of robots only.
[c]Includes robots installed in Canada.
Source: Watanabe, (see note 37).

Table 4.11   The labor-saving effect of robotization in selected countries

Country	% of robots replacing or substituting for labor	Average gross no. of workers[a] replaced by a robot in 2 shifts where introduced to replace labor	Maintenance staff required per robot[b]
Japan	50	1.4	0.2
United States	Almost 100[c]	2	0.1–0.17
West Germany (Hanover VW)	–	2–4	–
France (Renault)	25–30	4	–
Italy	Almost 100[c]	3	–
Brazil	–	4	–
Sweden (Volvo)	–	2	0.5

[a]Not counting new jobs created in maintenance and programming.
[b]Based on only one or a few observations except for the United States.
[c]Implicitly assumed in the calculation of the employment impact.
Source: Watanable (see note 37).

concentrate on the developmental aspects of technological enhancement, regardless of its labor-saving effects. The inability of US firms to cooperate with labor unions in the process of technological change led them to concentrate on labor costs and on means of undermining the position of organized labor, as a pre-condition for flexibility, thus downgrading the productivity potential of new technologies.

The attitude revealed by this case study is consistent with the traditional approach of American management toward labor unions and toward labor in general. David Noble, in his detailed case studies of technical change in manufacturing, particularly in the analysis of the introduction and development of numerical control machines, has documented the deliberate use of technological change to reduce workers' control over the labor process, actually de-skilling the tasks directly performed by the operative, and seriously limiting the productivity potential of new technologies at the shop-floor level.[38] This is also an argument put forward by Harley Shaiken on the basis of his study of the forms and processes of introduction of computer-aided instruments in manufacturing.[39] He shows that while new technologies could allow for greater work autonomy, enabling higher-quality output and higher productivity, the particular way in which they are introduced is biased by the deliberate goal of limiting machinists' autonomy in performing their work, a basic requirement of the Taylorist organizational principle on which most of American management still relies. Under these historical circumstances, what are the specific effects of new information technologies on the restructuring of the labor process? To illustrate what appear to be the general answers to this fundamental question I will turn to two empirical studies, one concerning manufacturing, the other focusing on office work.

Carol Parsons, in her Berkeley PhD dissertation, studied the role of flexible production technology in the industrial restructuring of the metal-working and apparel industries.[40] In the case of metal-working (including machinery, automobiles, appliances, machine tools, and small metal goods), there has been extensive introduction of microelectronics-based technologies during the 1980s. Among the firms surveyed by Parsons, the reduction of direct labor was the purpose for the use of flexible technology most frequently cited in line with the argument presented above. Firms used new technologies within the framework of their existing management practices and production strategies, without taking advantage of them to modify their position in the industrial structure. Large firms continued to rely on mass production, in spite of the potential offered by new, flexible equipment for economical production on a short-run basis. Small firms remained job shops, whose use of new equipment allowed them to become more efficient suppliers.

Yet the introduction of computer numerical control (CNC) machines and computer-aided manufacturing equipment did have some important effects on the labor processes of the metal-working industries. Plants were closed and the new ones that were opened differed in important respects. First, there was a shift from unionized plants to non-unionized plants. According to Hicks, cited by Parsons, 59.6 percent of the oldest plants (established before 1920) were unionized, while 93.8 percent of those established after 1973 were not unionized.[41] Interestingly enough, companies did not change region when opening a new non-union plant; they remained concentrated in the mid-west, as implementation of the new "just-in-time" method required close proximity to an industrial network. Secondly, most companies engaged in extensive sub-contracting, both regionally and internationally, making use of the new communication facilities and the automated standardization of parts. Thirdly, firms reorganized their internal and external labor processes. Internally, new technologies required the reclassification of jobs with a shift to multiskilled positions. In this way, the content of work was enriched. But, as Parsons writes:

At the same time, however, the over-riding motive for multiskilling was to reduce labor costs. One manager explained that "when one person does five jobs the plant gets more flexible without hiring four more people". Moreover, "not only do I save on the wages and benefits of those other workers but the featherbedding goes way down". Traditional demarcations between jobs, that are the hallmark of American job control unionism and create the featherbedding this manager referred to, are largely incompatible with multiskilling.[42]

As a result of the restructuring process, employment fell substantially in all metal-working industries with the exception of office equipment. Yet net job loss owing to plant turnover was 17 times higher than net job loss owing to layoffs within existing plants during the 1980–2 recession. In other words, rather than introducing new equipment in existing working situations, the restructuring took the form of installing the new machines in a new working environment characterized by transformed labor relationships, the absence of unions being the most notorious change. In terms of the transformation of the occupational structure, following the process of organizational and technological restructuring, there was an acceleration of the shift from direct to indirect labor, partly caused by the use of new technology to reduce direct labor inputs. Holding demand constant, professional, managerial, and technical employment grew rapidly, while production employment declined. And for production workers, the occupational structure showed a trend toward bifurcation, as craft work and simple labor both increased and the number of operatives, most of them assemblers, shrank. Thus, overall, Parsons observes the following features: a reduction in metal-working's manufacturing labor force; an upgrading of the occupational structure, through the trimming of numbers of production workers; and an internal polarization of the remaining production workers between craft workers and simple laborers, while traditional assembly-line operatives are squeezed out by automation. However, she insists that these trends do not result inevitably from the use of flexible production technology, but are the outcome of managerial decisions concerning the use of the technologies, for example, refusing to let machinists program CNC machines by themselves, in spite of their knowledge of the production process and the simplicity of the operation. Parsons also cites alternatives examples of Japanese factories where a more recent version of the same technology has enabled machinists to program their own working tools, with the consequence of added productivity. Within the parameters of the vertical management system, the introduction of new information technologies leads to a reduction of the traditional labor force and to increasing internal segregation of the remaining workers, split between indirect and direct labor, and between craftspeople and unskilled workers.

Parsons' analysis of the US apparel industry is also revealing in the sense that most of the process of technological change here concerns the linkages of the firms with their suppliers and markets, rather than automation of the production process itself. It would seem that, with some exceptions, the majority of apparel firms have decided not to compete with the NICs in terms of production, and are actually relying on foreign suppliers to keep their markets. (I would add, although Parsons does not contemplate this hypothesis, that a substantial element in the decentralization of production in apparel is the existence of the sweatshops of the informal economy in large American cities, particularly in New York and Los Angeles.) The basic element in this industry remains the importance of the network as the organizational form of the surviving companies. The key procedure in this regard is the "quick response" (QR) strategy. As Parsons writes:

A Quick Response strategy is the amalgamation of innovations in interrelated but distinct links in the soft goods chain: one is the textile production–apparel production link; another the retailer–apparel marketing link; and a third the retailer–apparel production link. All of these linkages depend on better flows of information and the use of more flexible manufacturing technology. While a variety of technological innovations are involved in QR electronic data exchange is crucial because, in simple form, a QR system begins with and is driven by information collected by the retailer. ... In principle, this information ripples back to apparel, textile and fiber producers. Thanks to telecommunications advances, textile mills and apparel producers are beginning to forge QR relationships.[43]

The main implication of these technological developments for the labor force in the apparel industry is that direct production workers in the traditional factory are being phased out. These low-paid, low-skilled jobs, generally held by women and minority workers, are rapidly disappearing under the combined impact of technological change, import penetration, and organizational restructuring toward networking and sub-contracting. The industry is rapidly evolving into a dispatching center connecting the demand of the largest market in the world with suppliers that will be increasingly located overseas or established underground in the US. The net result is a complex labor force composed of highly skilled designers, telecommunicated sales managers, and downgraded manufacturing workers either offshore or in domestic sweatshops. Here again technology per se has not determined the fate of the industry and its workers, but it has been a powerful instrument in diffusing apparel factories, symbolic of early industralization, into flows of exchange between hollow firms, their suppliers, and their retailers. In these conditions labor is not only segmented but dispersed and atomized.

A similarly complex web of interaction among technology, restructuring, and labor can be found in current developments in advanced services organizations. The study by Eileen Appelbaum on technology and the redesign of work in the insurance industry provides an interesting insight into the transformations under way in office work.[44]

The insurance industry has led the pace in office automation since the 1970s, in a movement stimulated by the deregulation of financial markets, the need to fight inflation and the wide variation of interest rates. Increasing mobility of capital has been the overarching objective, leading to emphasis on cash-flow management rather than on returns from premiums. Accordingly, versatility becomes crucial for competitiveness in the insurance industry. Instead of the standardized rationalization and mainframe-dependent data entry processes characteristic of the first stages of office automation, insurance companies during the 1980s relied on automation of routine paperwork, greater flexibility and decision-making capacity by a decentralised network of agents, and control and information processing by relatively skilled clerical workers that would handle sales, assess risks, explain procedures to customers, and answer agents' queries, on the basis of the full computerization of underwriting and rating operations.

The impact of these trends on the work force is profound and lasting. On the one hand, unskilled data entry jobs are being massively eliminated through automation. These routine jobs account for the majority of the 22 percent job loss over the next two decades predicted for clerical jobs in the insurance industry.[45] On the other hand, the remaining clerical positions are being re-skilled, by integrating tasks into multidimensional jobs susceptible of greater flexibility and adaptation to the changing needs of an industry that is becoming increasingly diversified. The skills needed for such positions do not necessarily require formal training: high general literacy, verbal communication skills, and an aptitude for arithmetic. On the other hand, professional jobs have been also been differentiated between less skilled tasks, that have been taken on by the upgraded clerical workers, and highly specialized tasks that require formal specialized education, generally on the basis of a college degree.

The resulting configuration of jobs [Appelbaum writes] varies from firm to firm, but in every case job categories have become more abruptly segmented while the avenues of mobility between them have been sharply reduced. . . . As a result of the automation of underwriting and claims estimating for standardized insuranced products, career ladders from skilled clerical to insurance professional positions have been eliminated. The gap between the skills of clerical workers and those of professionals has widened despite the elimination of unskilled clerical work such as coding and sorting mail and much filing, and the reduction of routine keyboarding. Skill requirements for clerical workers have increased at the same time that jobs have become overwhelmingly dead-end. . . . Thus the introduction of microprocessor-based technologies and the dramatic redesign of jobs is altering the distribution of occupations in insurance. Office automation has wiped out thousands of jobs for low skilled clerical workers, created new jobs for skilled clerical workers, and eliminated many professional jobs that comprised the middle of the occupational distribution – and that used to constitute the rungs of a career ladder by which clerical workers could climb up into more highly skilled professional jobs. Declines in unskilled clerical jobs have limited the entry-level job opportunities for minority and working-class women. What is more, the opportunities for advancement by even the more highly skilled clerical workers are being closed. The bottom and the middle of the occupational distribution are both shrinking in the insurance industry.[46]

As in the case of manufacturing, the transformation of the occupational structure in the insurance industry, which could well be indicative of trends in advanced services at large, is not solely the result of office automation: it is the restructuring of the industry and of its labor force that lie behind the process of technological change. Occupational changes are specified by gender, class, and race: while machines are replacing ethnic-minority and uneducated women at the bottom of the scale, white, educated women are in general replacing white men in the upper clerical and lower professional positions –

yet for lower pay and reduced career prospects at a comparable level of skill and responsibility. Multiskilling of jobs and individualization of responsibilities, generally accompanied by ideologically tailored new titles (for example, "assistant manager" instead of "secretary"), also make more difficult the collective grouping of interests in an industry that was never highly unionized and seems unlikely to become so in the near future. The simultaneous re-skilling of job tasks and downgrading of wages and occupational mobility for a given level of responsibility provides a good illustration of the social bias of technological innovation in office work.

The articulation between socio-economic restructuring and the diffusion of information technologies, both in factories and in offices, is transforming labor and the labor process in ways that appear to be consistent when the trends are observed from a macroeconomic as well as from a microsocial perspective. Computer-based automation is not ushering in an era of widespread and indiscriminate unemployment, but a selective redefinition of occupational positions and labor characteristics. While a substantial number of jobs are being upgraded in skills, and sometimes in wages, in the most dynamic sectors an even larger number of jobs are being eliminated in key manufacturing and advanced service industries, and these are generally jobs that are not skilled enough to escape automation but are expensive enough to be worth the investment in technology to replace them. Increasing educational qualifications, either general or specialized, required in the re-skilled positions in the occupational structure further segregate the labor force on the basis of education, itself a highly segregated system because it responds institutionally to a segregated residential structure. Downgraded labor, particularly in the entry positions for a new generation of workers, made up of a majority of women and ethnic minorities, is recycled in the proliferation of low-skill, low-pay activities in the miscellaneous service sector, or integrated in the booming informal economy in both manufacturing and services. The bifurcated and polarized occupational structure reflected in aggregate statistics is not a secular trend linked to the expansion of the service economy. Its profile is socially determined and mangerially designed in the restructuring process taking place at shop-floor level within the framework, and with the help, of fundamental technological change. This restructuring of labor is profoundly affecting the social stratification system, as is shown by recent trends in income distribution. It is to this issue that we now turn.

The Impact of Occupational Change on Wages, Income, and Social Stratification: The Declining Middle

The transformation of the US occupational structure during the 1980s, under the impact of the process of techno-economic restructuring, has had profound consequences on wages and incomes. The polarization of the labor market is reflected in increasingly uneven income distribution, with low-wage jobs expanding much faster than better paid occupations. The job creation capacity of the American economy, which grew by 20 million new jobs in the decade after the 1974 crisis, was attained at the price of lowering the wage rate for the large majority of those new workers. As a consequence of this process, the middle segment of the social stratification system has gradually shrunk, in one of the most debated and politically charged developments of the 1980s.

Bluestone and Harriston have investigated the matter in one of the most important and most controversial studies of recent years, conducted for the Joint Economic Committee of the US Congress.[47] They analyzed the level and distribution of annual real wages earned by American workers for two periods, 1973–9 and 1979–84 (inclusive of 1984). They classified employment in three categories, high-, middle-, or low-wage, and they compared changes in the proportion of workers in each category during the two periods. They also recalculated their findings differentiating the data by industrial sector, region, age, race, gender, education, and working time (part-time versus full-time employment). They found a fundamental change in the wage distribution of new jobs in the second period, 1979–84, which is generally identified as the historical moment of economic restructuring. In that period about 60 percent of all new jobs were created in the low-wage category, paying less than $7,000 per year (in 1984 dollars). In the same period, the number of workers with earnings at least as high as the 1973 median of wage distribution ($14,024 in 1984 dollars) declined by 1.8 million, while workers with wages below the 1973 real median increased by 9.9 million. Overall, 58 percent of all net new employment between 1979 and 1984 paid annual wages less than $7,000. At the same time, there was a decline of 450,000 jobs in the

Table 4.12 Employment levels and employment shares, all US workers (000s)

	Number of Employees			Earnings shares (%)			Shares of net new employment (%)	
	1973	1979	1984	1973	1979	1984	1973–79	1979–84
Low stratum	29,648	32,063	36,750	31.8	30.4	32.4	19.9	58.0
Middle stratum	48,107	55,908	59,745	51.6	53.1	52.7	64.2	47.5
High stratum	15,441	17,374	16,932	16.6	16.5	14.9	15.9	−5.5
Total	93,196	105,345	113,427	100.0	100.0	100.0	100.0	100.0

Source: Uniform CPS (Mare-Winship) data files, calculated by Bluestone and Harrison (see note 47).

high-wage category. Indeed, all of the employment increase between 1979 and 1984 was accounted for by jobs that paid less than the median wage in 1973. The "middle-wage" earnings category did increase, but the growth was concentrated at the bottom end of the category. Table 4.12, and figures 4.1 and 4.2 display the key findings.

Although women and ethnic minorities continued to be concentrated in the low-wage stratum, the biggest losers in relative terms were white men, for whom 97 percent of employment gains were in the low-wage category, in sharp contrast with previous experience. Although young workers were particularly hit by low-wage employment, the trend was also present in workers over 35 years of age, thus contradicting the hypothesis that the expansion of low-wage employment was a temporary phenomenon linked to the entry into the labor market of a large cohort of "baby boomers." Low-wage employment was also the dominant trend throughout all regions of the

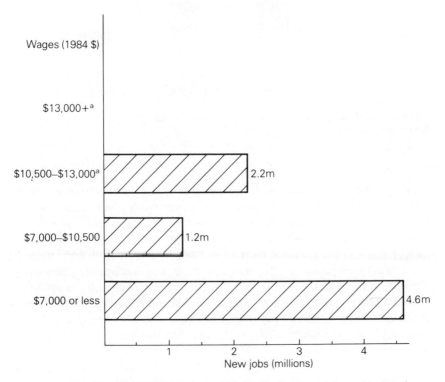

[a] estimated wage level below which 100% of net new jobs were created

Figure 4.1   Net increase in new jobs, 1979–1984, by annual wage grouping
Source: Bluestone and Harrison (see note 47)

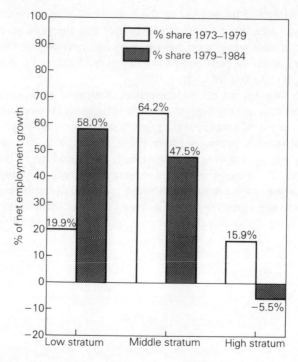

Figure 4.2   Percentage share of new job growth, all workers
Source: Bluestone and Harrison (see note 47)

country, although the mid-west showed the most significant growth in this category, confirming the association between low-wage jobs and the demise of traditional manufacturing. Another important finding is that the tendency toward low wages is valid for both part-time and full-time employment, meaning that lower earnings because of "flexible," part-time arrangements, and downgraded full-time jobs, are cumulative, not overlapping phenomena. These findings are consistent with the sharply increased discrepancies in annual wages and salaries since 1978, as calculated by Bluestone and Harrison in another study. The tendency toward growing inequality remains valid even when the business cycle, the baby boom and the variation of the exchange rate are accounted for.

It is this creation on a massive scale of jobs at the bottom end of the wage spectrum, along with the stagnation of new employment in the upper tier, that underlies the trend towards the "decline of the middle" in the stratification system of American households, as Kuttner pointed out in a notorious and ferociously criticized article in 1983.[48] In fact, the decline of individual wages, as shown by the Bluestone and Harrison study, has been somewhat compensated for in real standards of living by the presence of two wage earners in an increasing proportion of families, particularly in the professional and managerial sector. Yet in terms of the relative distribution of household earnings, the deterioration of wages has resulted in a shrinking proportion of middle-income households in the overall distribution. Thurow calculated that, if percentage income distribution is examined with the age distribution of households kept constant at the 1967 level, the percentage of households with middle-income levels is seen to have declined from 28.2 percent in 1967 to 23.6 percent in 1984.[49] Following the same line of argument, Steven Rose's analysis of the changes in social stratification between 1978 and 1983 showed that while 55 percent of urban families in 1978 fell between the low and high budget lines, in 1983 this figure was down to 40 percent, and the percentage of families below the low budget line had increased from 30 percent to 40 percent.[50]

Given the implications of these analyses, it is not surprising that a host of economists, demographers, and sociologists have made a cottage industry of criticizing the statistical methodology and theoretical assumptions of most of these studies.[51] However, the most standard alternative explanation for the "declining middle" thesis, that is, the suggestion that it is mainly a result of demographic changes in the age structure of the population and in the composition of households, has been refuted by Bradbury in a powerful study. On the whole, as research progresses, there is a growing body of evidence that bears witness to both increasing inequality of income, among both individuals and households, and a tendency toward the decline of the middle-income group, as shown in Nancy Leigh-Preston's doctoral dissertation[52]. It is less clear, however, in empirical terms, what are the causes of the phenomenon. The most solid hypothesis advanced in the literature relates growing inequality and polarization in the stratification system to the changes in industrial and occupational structure as a result of economic restructuring and diffusion of new technologies. Bluestone and Harrison have established an analytical connection between their thesis of the de industrialization of America and the trends they have observed in income inequality.[53] They have also provided some empirical support for their claim that the sources of employment change are structural, and cannot be explained by the effect of the business cycle.[54] From a different theoretical perspective, Lester Thurow advances a similar hypothetical interpretation when he writes:

Part of the change in income distribution is due to the characteristics of America's new growth industries. High-technology industries such as microelectronics tend to have two levels of income distribution – high and low – as opposed to the smokestack industries, like machine-tools, with their high wage, skilled blue collar workers. There is usually a large group of low-wage assemblers, but not many middle-income jobs. To some extent, the reduced number of middle-income jobs is a product of technology and to some extent it is a product of non-union environment. For what unions did in industries such as autos, steel or machine tools was to convert jobs that probably weren't middle-income jobs. Earnings were redistributed within the industry toward those with least skills.[55]

One could not express better the close connection between high technology, socio-economic restructuring, and the emerging system of social stratification.

A new type of labor demand, then, determined by a new occupational structure, is creating new types of jobs, characterized by a bifurcated distribution in which the bulk of new jobs pay lower wages and enjoy less social protection than in recent historical experience. At the same time, to fill jobs a new supply of workers is also changing the characteristics of labor, generally making workers more vulnerable to management requirements in terms of their social characteristics, along the lines of gender, race, nationality, and age discrimination in society at large. As figure 4.3 shows, the new labor of the 1980s and 1990s contains a large majority of women and ethnic minorities. We should also take into account the hundreds of thousands of immigrants arriving each year in the US labor market, most of them undocumented. The downgrading of the majority of jobs and the transformation of the gender and racial characteristics of the main pool of labor go hand in hand, in a process that can only be reversed by the raising of the consciousness and organization of the new breed of workers entering the transformed labor process.

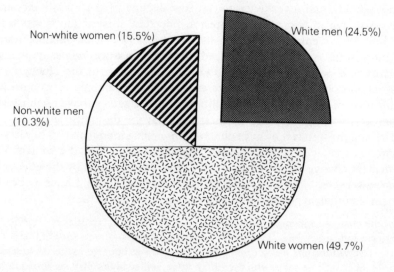

Figure 4.3   Composition of labor force growth, 1984–1995
Source: US Bureau of Labour Statistics

This new, increasingly polarized occupational structure, and the income inequality that results from it, are also territorially specific. As the process of uneven development sees both high-growth activities and downgraded labor concentrated in the largest metropolitan areas, these areas become the spatial expression of the contrasting social conditions into which the effects of the restructuring process are ultimately translated. The trends toward the polarization and segmentation of the social structure underlie the rise of the "dual city."

Toward the Transformation of the Urban Social Structure: The Dual City

Introduction: The Dynamics of Economic Dualism in the Inner City

The polarization and segmentation of the labor force under the impact of the process of techno-economic restructuring has specific spatial manifestations. Although much attention has been given to the regional disparity of the processes of new growth and decline, often simplified under the summary opposition between the sunbelt and the "rustbelt,"[56] probably the most significant spatial expression of the restructuring of labor is taking place within the largest metropolitan areas, and particularly in the dominant world cities, such as New York and Los Angeles.[57] With the exception of some old industrial cities whose fate has been overwhelmingly determined by the old manufacturing industries (Buffalo, NY, for example[58]) processes of sectoral growth and decline, and the reallocation of jobs and labor, are taking place simultaneously within the same metropolitan areas, in a complex pattern that combines the creation of new, highly paid jobs in advanced services and high-technology sectors, the destruction of middle-level jobs in old manufacturing, the gradual shrinkage of protected jobs in the public sector, and the proliferation of new, low-paid jobs both in services and in downgraded manufacturing. At the same time, three inter-related phenomena add complexity to the emerging urban social structure: the explosion of the informal economy, unregulated income-generating activities in a context where similar activities are government-regulated; the reduction of the rate of participation in the labor force, as officially defined, indicative of a growing surplus population in the formal economy; and the proliferation of the criminal economy, particularly in activities related to the drug trade, which becomes the shop floor for a growing proportion of ethnic-minority youth in the largest inner cities.

Interpretations of these trends vary, according to different intellectual traditions. Two predominant theses, nevertheless, formulate a plausible argument, in terms that are largely complementary, in spite of the ideological and theoretical differences between their respective proponents.

One school of thought points to the mismatching of skills between the jobs that are being created and those being destroyed.[59] Advanced services and high-technology industries require a higher level of education than most of the traditional manufacturing and menial jobs that are being phased out, thus substantially changing and upgrading the skills required to obtain employment in the new labor market. With most of the new jobs being created in the advanced services clusters of the large CBDs,[60] and many of the disappearing traditional jobs being concentrated in the old urban industrial cores surrounding these CBDs,[61] it follows that the new expanding labor markets are concentrated in the nodal centers of the large metropolitan areas, as are the pools of obsolete labor, no longer employable, which are made up predominantly of ethnic minorities. John Kasarda, a leading urban scholar forecasting the rise of the dual city,[62] has analyzed the creation of knowledge-intensive jobs and entry-level jobs for nine major US cities between 1970 and 1980 (see table 4.13). His data show the occupational shift in favor of knowledge-intensive jobs, particularly for the largest north-eastern cities. Such a transition could in fact be beneficial for the upgrading of the social structure, were it not for the mismatching of skills determined by inequality in the educational system, itself a result of spatial segregation by class and race. Public schools in the largest inner cities receive proportionally fewer resources than those in the suburbs, and cater to the poorest sectors of the population, with an overwhelming proportion of ethnic minorities with the greatest educational need to overcome a cultural disadvantage in their family background. The majority of the resident population of inner cities, then, cannot match the skill requirements of the new labor market because of the inefficiency and segregated nature of the public school system. In the north-east region in 1982, 42 percent of black males aged 16–64 had not completed high school; the proportion for white males was only 31.4 percent. Adding to this racial discrimination in the labor market, we see that 26.2 percent of those relatively uneducated black males were unemployed in the north-eastern central cities in 1982, against an average of 10.2 percent of white males.[63] For all regions in 1982, 16.5 percent of all black central city residents aged 16–24 were neither in school nor in the labor force, with the same figure increasing to 17.1 percent for the 25–64 age group. The corresponding figures for whites were only 5.4 percent and 9.2 percent. Of these black males not in the labor force and not in school, 40 percent were on welfare, with the proportion increasing to 82 percent for black females. Central cities in the largest metropolitan areas host the majority of the growth in highly paid jobs, while they come to be inhabited mainly by an ethnic-minority population which is increasingly inadequate to fill these jobs. The dual city, manifested in the spatial coexistence of a large sector of professional and managerial middle-class with a growing urban underclass, epitomizes the contradictory development of the new informational economy, and the conflictual appropriation of the inner city by social groups who share the same space while being worlds apart in terms of lifestyle and structural position in society.

Yet while the mismatching thesis underlines a fundamental trend of the new urban social structure, it has some serious methodological and theoretical shortcomings, as has been argued by Norman Fainstein.[64] It also fails to explain why there has been substantial growth in job creation in general, including low-paying jobs, in the largest inner cities, particularly during the 1980s. Indeed, after the 1980–2 recession, unemployment has steadily reduced in most inner cities, even for ethnic minorities, although it remains

Table 4.13 Employment changes by industry's average educational requirements, for nine US cities, 1970–1980 (000s)

City and industrial categorization[a]	Number of jobs, 1980	Change, 1970–80	
		Number	%
New York			
Entry-level	763	−472	−38.2
Knowledge-intensive	462	92	24.9
Philadelphia			
Entry-level	208	−102	−32.9
Knowledge-intensive	91	25	37.8
Baltimore			
Entry-level	108	−52	−32.4
Knowledge-intensive	32	5	20.6
Boston (Suffolk County)			
Entry-level	115	−34	−22.6
Knowledge-intensive	75	19	33.3
St Louis			
Entry-level	103	−23	−18.2
Knowledge-intensive	21	−8	−26.3
Atlanta (Fulton County)			
Entry-level	136	−19	−12.1
Knowledge-intensive	41	11	35.6
Houston (Harris County)			
Entry-level	457	194	73.8
Knowledge-intensive	152	83	119.4
Denver			
Entry-level	110	14	14.5
Knowledge-intensive	44	21	91.4
San Franciso			
Entry-level	142	13	10.2
Knowledge-intensive	65	21	46.8

Sources: US Bureau of the Census, Current Population Survey tape, March 1982, and County Business Patterns, 1970, 1980. Figures are rounded. (Compiled and adapted by Kasarda (see note 62).

[a]Entry-level industries are those where mean schooling completed by employees is less than twelve years; knowledge-intensive industries are those where mean schooling completed is more than fourteen years.

very high for the youth of these minorities. Moreover, this increasing employment rate has taken place in a context where hundreds of thousands of new immigrants have arrived in the metropolitan labor markets, attracted in particular to the booming economies of New York and California.

There are in fact four distinct, though inter-related, processes at work here:

(1)   The decline of some industries and the increasing obsolescence of a segment of semi-skilled labor that is being expelled from the labor force.
(2)   The dynamism of two macro-sectors, one in advanced services and the other in high-technology industries, both of which also include a substantial number of low-paid, low-skill jobs, such as janitors, low-level secretaries, assembly workers.
(3)   The growth of new, downgraded manufacturing activities, many of them informal, which recycle some of the surplus labor expelled from the declining sectors, while incorporating some of the new immigrants, particularly women.
(4)   The expansion of informal and semi-formal service activities spurred on by the overall economic dynamism. These service activities, many of them in consumer services, provide numerous jobs for immigrants, ethnic minorities and women.

This is the analysis put forward by a number of scholars, most notably by Saskia Sassen, in an interpretation that links the thesis of polarization of the occupational structure with the process of restructuring of capital–labor relationships.[65] In this perspective, the dual city is not simply the urban social structure resulting from the juxtaposition of the rich and the poor, the yuppies and the homeless, but the result of simultaneous and articulated processes of growth and decline. Furthermore, according to Sassen's analysis, growth occurs at the same time in the formal and in the informal sectors of the economy, at the top and at the bottom of the newly dynamic industrial sectors, and affects both skilled and unskilled labor, although in segmented labor markets that cater variously to the specific requirements of each segment of capital invested in the different sectors of the local economy. From this follows a highly differentiated social structure, both polarized and fragmented, with segments divided on the basis of class, gender, race, and national origin. Some of the labor surplus is recycled in the dynamic structure of the new informational economy, while the rest leaves the formal labor force, to be distributed among the recipients of welfare, the informal economy, and the criminal economy. This new social dynamics has profound consequences on the spatial organization and processes of the large metro-politan areas. However, since the complexity of these processes makes the analysis hardly comprehensible at a high level of generality, I will introduce here a summary account of the transformation of the urban social structure of

New York and Los Angeles in order to clarify the precise meaning of the rise of the dual city as the new urban form linked to the overall process of techno-economic restructuring.

New York, New York! Dreams and Nightmares of the Restructuring Process

After its dramatic fiscal crisis in 1975–7, New York City bounced back in one of the most spectacular cases of local economic development in recent history.[66] In the decade 1977–87, the city added 400,000 new jobs in an expansion interrupted only by the nationwide recession of 1981–2.[67] Of these jobs, 342,000 were in the private sector, with finance, insurance, real estate, and business services accounting for about 70 percent of new job creation. These industries employed in 1987 664,000 workers, amounting to about one-fifth of all private jobs. At the same time, the building boom linked to the expansion of advanced services, with their demand for office space and upgraded residences for the professional labor force, generated about 64,000 new construction jobs. In addition, growing local revenues and the political needs of the city's patronage system restored, selectively, public services and service jobs, so that by December 1987 local government employment, including education, had risen to 450,000 jobs. However, this process of growth and job creation went hand in hand with a dramatic restructuring process, both among industries and in the labor market. While 153 industries experienced growth in the city in 1977–86, a greater number, 207, actually declined. Most of this decline took place in manufacturing, which shrank in absolute numbers from 539,000 jobs in 1977 to 396,000 in 1986, representing in the latter year slightly over 11 percent of the total labor force (see figure 4.4). In fact, in the 1980s, New York City lost manufacturing jobs at three times the national rate of decline. Furthermore, in the 1982–7 period, the US economy recovered about half the manufacturing jobs lost during the 1980–2 recession, but New York lost an additional 100,000 factory jobs in these years, with the greatest losses concentrated in apparel, miscellaneous manufacturing and electrical–electronic equipment, and the bulk of them being unskilled and semi-skilled jobs. One the other hand, about half of the new jobs were in professional, managerial, and technical positions. As a result, the overall occupational composition of the labor force in New York City has been upgraded. Executives and managers accounted for 11.7 percent of the labor force in 1983 and 13.3 percent in 1986, while the proportion of professionals also increased from 13.9 percent in 1983 to 15.8 percent in 1986. Including technicians, the upper level of the occupational structure in 1986 accounted for 31.3 percent of the total labor force, establishing as a fundamental presence a large group of professional labor that possesses the purchasing power, the demographic weight, and the educational skills to dominate the city economically, culturally, and politically.

This trend is in direct conflict with the changing composition of the New York City population, characterized by a growing proportion of minimally educated minorities, and recent immigrants whose education is hardly marketable in the US. The overall drop-out rate in the city's high schools reached a staggering 37 percent in 1987, 80 percent of which appears to concern ethnic minorities (if we extrapolate the 1980 data for the 16–19 age group). The mismatching of skills is particularly striking in the case of New York. On the one hand, for the American labor force as a whole, one or two years in college seems increasingly to be the norm for obtaining a job: the proportion of the labor force with some college attendance in 1987 stood at 46

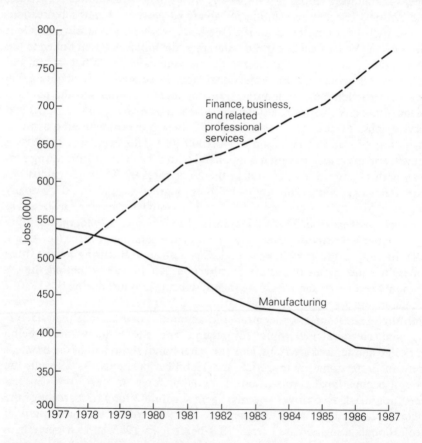

Figure 4.4   Payroll employment in manufacturing and finance, business and related professional services, New York City, 1977–1987
Source: Ehrenhalt (see note 67).

percent, double that of 1970, and it continues to rise. On the other hand, ethnic minorities seem to have accounted for most of net labor force growth in the 1977–87 period and are projected to continue to do so for most of the net increase in New York City's labor force in the 1990s. They accounted in 1987 for 49.5 percent of the total labor force (see figure 4.5); yet ast the same time they exhibit the highest school drop-out rates, and are exposed to the declining quality of the spatially segregated public school system.

Mismatching and racial discrimination in the labor market result in a substantially above-average unemployment level for ethnic minorities, even in the context of sustained economic expansion in the 1980s. In New York in 1987, unemployment levels were 3.1 percent for non-Hispanic whites and 8.5 percent for ethnic minorities. A more important phenomenon, likely to be linked to the inappropriateness of the new labor demand for the urban labor supply, is the low rate of labor-force participation in New York, ten points

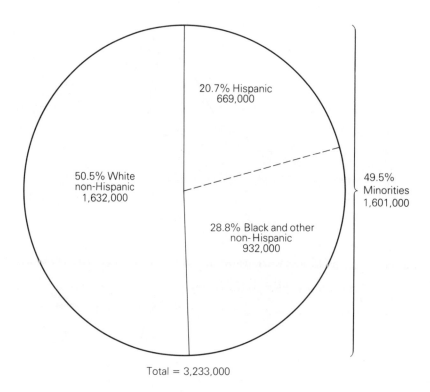

Total = 3,233,000

Figure 4.5   Estimated distribution of the New York City resident labor force by race and Hispanic origin, 1987
Source: Ehrenhalt (see note 67)

below the national average, with the disparity increasing over the past 20 years (see figure 4.6). According to Samuel M. Ehrenhalt, New York Regional Commissioner for the Bureau of Labor Statistics: "It would take something on the order of a half million more New Yorkers in the labor force to lift the New York participation rate to the national average. This points to a considerable job deficit in the local economy and a substantial number of New Yorkers outside the mainstream."[68]

Nevertheless, a great number of jobs have been created, as indicated, showing the strength and the vitality of the new economy. Indeed, most of the ethnic minorities, including recent immigrants, have improved their relative position in the economy.[69] However, this is partly a mere statistical construct: a growing economy, creating a large number of office and service jobs in a

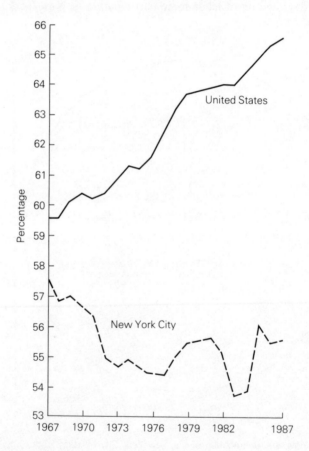

Figure 4.6   Labor force participation rates, United States and New York City, 1967–1987 (total, age 16 years and over)
Source: Ehrenhalt (see note 67).

context of increasing representation of ethnic minorities in the labor market, must necessarily include a higher proportion of minorities in the new service jobs. Yet the tendencies toward polarization described in the preceding sections of this chapter are reflected in an ethnically and gender segregated occupational structure in the new labor force of New York City, as can be seen in the data calculated by John Mollenkopf detailing occupational position by gender and by ethnic group for 1980. As an illustration of these trends, table 4.14 has been constructed on the basis of Mollenkopf's data. Three occupational positions have been selected representative respectively of the top of the occupational scale (managers), of the middle to low position in services (clerical), and of the low-skill manual workers (operatives). For each position, an elementary scale has been built, taking as its zero level the proportion of WASP (white Anglo-Saxon Protestant) males who hold such occupational positions (as a percentage of overall employed WASP males).

Table 4.14   Ethnic composition of occupations in New York City, 1980, by gender (differences in percentage points between proportion of WASPs in each occupational group and proportion of each ethnic group in the same occupation)

	Occupation				
Ethnicity	Managers and professionals	Managers	Clerical	Operatives	% of male/ female population
MALE					
WASP	0.0	0.0	0.0	0.0	2.15
Jewish	+6.0	+1.5	−1.5	−5.9	4.29
Italian	−5.9	−3.1	−1.5	+6.3	16.90
Irish	−5.9	−3.3	+0.9	+2.1	8.18
Black (NY)	−5.9	−4.1	+4.5	+6.1	11.35
Jamaican	−8.4	−4.7	−2.9	+6.5	2.38
Puerto Rican	−10.3	−4.2	−6.5	+14.1	10.46
Dominican	−13.6	−6.2	−10.1	+20.2	3.23
Chinese	−0.6	+0.6	−11.3	−2.6	2.58
FEMALE					
WASP		−2.8	+28.3	−12.3	2.35
Jewish		−3.4	+30.3	−7.7	5.56
Italian		−4.9	+32.4	−14.1	16.14
Irish		−4.2	+33.8	−15.0	9.56
Black (NY)		−5.2	+26.1	−10.0	14.08
Jamaican		−7.7	+9.6	−12.2	3.68
Puerto Rican		−7.7	+7.7	+18.7	8.67
Dominican		−9.5	−6.3	+39.7	3.85
Chinese		−5.4	−6.3	+37.9	2.52

Source: 1980 US Census Public Use Microdata Sample, calculated by John Mollenkopf and elaborated by the author.

The difference has been simply calculated in percentage points between the proportion of WASP males in a given occupational position and the corresponding proportion for each ethnic/gender group. Obviously, positive signs indicative over-representation, while negative signs indicate under-representation. Without going into the details of the table, it can be observed that, for managers, Jewish males and WASP males are over-represented, while all women and ethnic minorities are under-represented, with ethnic-minority women being in the most disadvantaged position.

One apparent anomaly merits explanation: Chinese males are over-represented among the managers, even overtaking WASP males. An analysis of the sectoral distribution of Chinese male workers, provided by Mollen-kopf's database, dissipates the myth of the Chinese male "already making it in corporate business:" 51 percent of Chinese male workers are in "restaurants, hotels, and bars," and thus, they are "managers" of their community-based restaurants. As for employed Chinese women, 67.3 percent are manufacturing workers.

Concerning clerical work, women in general, but particularly Caucasian women, are overwhelmingly over-represented, while recent immigrant, non-English-speaking women are, as one might expect, under-represented. As for operatives, recent immigrants, both male and, even more, female, are concentrated in these jobs, sharing the joys of industrial working-class life in the informational city with the remnants of Italian, Irish, and black workers in the restructured manufacturing sector. Overall, groups privileged by gender and ethnic background (translated into higher education) occupy the top of the hierarchy; women form the bulk of the new white-collar working class of the service economy; and recent immigrants, along with Puerto Ricans, assume the new positions in downgraded manufacturing and low-skill consumer services. To complete our picture of the emerging occupational structure we should add the expansion of new retail commerce (neighbour-hood grocery stores, for example) on the basis of recent immigrants (Koreans, Indians, Chinese), and the growing concentration of blacks in public services: New York blacks in government services (17.1 percent of black males work in public services), and West Indian blacks in health services (11.4 percent of Jamaican males and 29.9 percent of Jamaican females work in health services).

Although the only empirical way of assessing rigorously the polarization of New York City's occupational structure would be to undertake an analysis of income and educational levels for each occupation and industry (which are not available in the published information), the existing data together with most of the specialized research literature on the subject all seem to indicate that the process of growth during the 1980s has generated, at the same time, a significant segment of well paid professionals and technical jobs, a mass of low-paid, semi-skilled clerical jobs for women, and an insufficient but growing number of low-paid jobs for ethnic minorities and immigrants both in downgraded manufacturing and miscellaneous services.[70]

An important element in connecting the new dynamism of the New York economy and the restructuring of labor is the growth of the informal economy. Saskia Sassen has investigated this topic over several years, combining secondary data analysis, ethnographic research, and interviews with key informants.[71] Without being able to estimate the overall size of the phenomenon, in terms of either regional GDP or employment, she has found enough evidence to indicate that it is a sizable economic reality and one that is rapidly expanding to become an indispensable element of the local economy as well as of New Yorkers' way of life. Much of these informal income-generating activities concern manufacturing, particularly in apparel, footwear, toys, sporting goods, and electronic components and accessories. For instance, she reports estimates by labor unions that in 1981 there were in New York about 3,000 sweatshops in the garment industry, employing about 50,000 workers, with a further 10,000 workers doing home work in garments. She also reports, on the basis of data provided by the New York State Labor Department and the Industrial Board of Appeals, considerable informal sub-contracting work in the electronics industry, working out of "garage-shops" and "basement-fronts." She observed that while the furniture industry lost 9 percent of its registered labor between 1982 and 1987, at the same time a number of furniture-making shops were opening in areas that were not zoned for this kind of work, such as Ridgewood Astoria in Queens, and Williamsburg in Brooklyn. In addition, construction work on a small scale is also predominantly informal: Sassen estimates that about 90 percent of all interior remodeling in New York is done without a building permit, by craft workers and contractors who are not registered, most of them recent immigrants. "Gypsy cabs" have taken over the transportation business to the numerous areas of the City where regular cabs refuse to go.[72]

The development of the informal economy is connected to two broader trends of which it is an essential, though certainly not a unique, component. The first of these is the downgrading of manufacturing, with the phasing out or relocation of traditional manufacturing activities, for instance in the garment industry, while low-labour-cost, largely unregulated operations open up in New York to cater to the booming retail market represented by the largest and probably most demanding market in the world. Secondly, there is an explosion in customized services, from gourmet grocery stores to laundry and housekeeping, linked to the new lifestyles of the substantial segment of the population made up of professionals and managers, either single or dual-income households, with little time but high purchasing power and increasingly sophisticated tastes (or, at least, with the idea of being sophisticated, and the desire to become so). As Sassen argues, the new consumption pattern, shifting from middle-level suburban families to high-level urbanite professionals, represents a shift from capital-intensive consumer goods to labor-intensive consumer services, thus stimulating a very large labor demand for customized services, both in high-skill occupations (fashion design, *chefs de cuisine*, in-house "artists") and low-skill occupations ("24-hour tailors," waiters, drivers, security guards).[73] While many of these jobs are by no means part of the informal economy, their definition and their working conditions are usually on the border-line, being extremely flexible, and making part-time, overtime, one-time service, and sub-contracting, the working rule rather than the exception. Hence the polarization and segmentation of an increasing pool of activities, and therefore of labor, on the vibrant New York scene.

A largely unexplored segment of New York's economy is linked to booming criminal activities, particularly related to the drug traffic. While these activities do generate income and a kind of employment for some sectors of the ghetto population, particularly for drop-out youths, they are not limited to the underclass. In fact, the money-laundering activities that are a substantial part of the drug economy lie behind the flourishing of many ephemeral businesses, from restaurants to art galleries, that blossom and disappear in the space of a few months, creating and then destroying a number of jobs that are as ephemeral as their source. Ironically, these money-laundering processes epitomize the oft-praised flexibility of the new economy. While the role of the criminal economy must not be exaggerated, it is important to keep in mind its existence, which adds to the complexity of the overall restructuring process.[74]

The informal economy, and more generally the new flexibility of labor relationships, have greatly contributed to the opening up of job opportunities for the new wave of immigration that has hit New York since the late 1970s, ranking it with Los Angeles and Miami as the most ethnically diverse metropolises in the world. In 1980, 24 percent of New Yorkers were foreign-born (excluding of course Puerto Ricans who are US citizens), and this proportion is predicted to rise to about one-third of the resident population by 1990. Most of these foreign-born residents are recent entrants, a substantial proportion of whom are undocumented.[75] It is estimated that there are about 350,000 Asians (Chinese, Koreans, Vietnamese, Cambodians, Indians), at least 400,000 Dominicans (the largest recent group of immigrants to New York), about 500,000 West Indians, about 250,000 non-Puerto Rican Hispanics (from Colombia, Mexico, Ecuador, Peru, etc.) over 200,000 Europeans (most of them Russian Jews and Italians), and a large number of Arabs, particularly from Egypt and the Lebanon. While living conditions are very harsh for most of the immigrants, particularly for those from Latin America and the Caribbean, they have succeeded in integrating themselves into the labor market, generally in the entry-level jobs, although some groups with financial and educational resources have established small businesses in a number of sectors (for example, middle-class Koreans in the grocery business, Indians in the newspaper stands).[76] Bailey and Waldinger have shown how the living conditions of these immigrants improve in the context of an expanding local economy, sometimes exceeding the achievements of local young blacks and New York Puerto Ricans.[77] However, a number of indications point to the fact that racial discrimination and class barriers are likely to prevent these immigrant families attaining social mobility on a similar level to the non-WASP Caucasian immigrants of former generations, with the potential exception of some middle-class groups, particularly among the Koreans and Chinese.[78] In fact, instead of witnessing the expansion of an informal economy, or of flexible manufacturing and customized services, as a consequence of the drive and entrepreneurialism of the new immigrants, we observe the opposite phenomenon: the new economy, with its flexibility and its polarized occupational structure, has been able to integrate an immigrant labor force that because of its greater vulnerability, linked to racial, class, and language discrimination, and often to its uncertain legal status, is ready to accept working conditions that American workers, including native ethnic minorities, do not accept or are not trusted to accede to by their employers. The new immigration provides the labor supply necessary for the restructuring of labor implicit in the polarized occupational structure of the informational economy.

The process of labor restructuring in New York, proceeding along the lines presented, has specified spatial manifestations. As Saskia Sassen writes:

These processes can be seen as distinct modes of economic organization and their corresponding uses of space: the postindustrial city of luxury high-rise office and residential buildings located largely in Manhattan; the old dying industrial city of low-rise buildings and family type houses, located largely in the outer-boroughs; and the Third World city imported via inmigration and located in dense groupings spread all over the city. . . . Each of these three processes can be seen to contain distinct income-occupational structures and concomitant residential and consumption patterns, well captured in the expansion of a new urban gentry alongside expanding immigrant communities.[79]

Richard Harris has proceeded to a systematic analysis of the spatial differentiation of the New York metropolitan area as an expression of the tendencies toward class, race, and gender polarization in the occupational structure.[80] His data show an increasing functional specialization of the area, with advanced services concentrated in Manhattan, the rest of the core specializing in transportation and public administration, and the inner and outer rings absorbing a growing proportion of manufacturing and retailing. In terms of residence, table 4.15 shows the dramatic trend toward the concentration in Manhattan of managers and professionals, while clericals and the lower occupational groups are over-represented in the inner city outside Manhattan, and the inner and outer rings oscillate moderately around the average, with a slight over-representation of managers and of the middle strata, together with an under-representation of the new and old working classes (clerical, operatives, and laborers). This occupational differentiation of residential patterns is reinforced by distinct lifestyles derived from different

Table 4.15 Occupational specialization of the resident labor force in the New York metropolitan region, 1950, 1970 and 1980

Occupation	Specialization index (NYMR=100)											
	Manhattan			Rest of core			Inner Ring			Outer Ring		
	1950	1970	1980	1950	1970	1980	1950	1970	1980	1950	1970	1980
Managers	93	112	127	93	77	76	122	120	109	84	114	106
Professionals	128	148	163	82	79	74	113	106	99	106	120	107
Clerical	95	94	82	115	117	122	90	90	96	72	74	85
Sales	93	90	94	104	91	87	102	113	109	88	107	106
Crafts	57	50	43	102	101	96	107	107	103	127	128	119
Operatives	94	77	74	104	114	116	92	96	94	109	83	98
Laborers	92	67	57	94	109	117	99	100	100	133	102	94
Service	190	130	105	84	102	116	81	88	90	93	100	94

Source: Hoover and Vernon, *Anatomy of a Metropolis,* 1962, p.148; Kamer, "The Changing Spatial Relationship Between Residence and Workplaces in the New York Metropolitan Region," 1977, pp.448-449; calculated from US Bureau of the Census, *General Social and Economic Characteristics,* Connecticut, New Jersey and New York, table 177 by Richard Harris (see note 80).

household structures. Thus, while the suburbs continue to be based on a typical nuclear family, in Manhattan the average household size (1.7) is lower than in any other country. This single or childless way of life characterizes the consumption patterns and the cultural models of the new professional elite in world cities such as New York.

In terms of income, the core of the city exhibits an interesting bimodal pattern, with the resident population of Manhattan concentrated in the highest and lowest strata of income distribution (see figure 4.7). This stratification pattern is in contrast to that prevailing in the other spatial components of the metropolitan area, as can also be observed from the data displayed in figure 4.7. The outer boroughs of the inner city contain a high concentration of low-income population, while the inner ring is biased toward the upper segments of the distribution, and the outer ring is the closest to the average of the overall income distribution. Thus, there is at the same time intra-metropolitan segregation by income (the suburbs being the privileged space), and intra-urban residential segregation within Manhattan, which hosts both the highest income group and some of the poorest sectors of the population. Ethnic residential segregation closely follows this general pattern, with blacks being the most concentrated and segregated social group, followed by Hispanics. Immigrants of different ethnic groups find their interstitial space either as microcommunities within large segregated areas of other ethnic minorities, or in enclaves inside the predominantly white city, in a symbiotic relationship that is more successful when they provide services to the higher-income resident population.

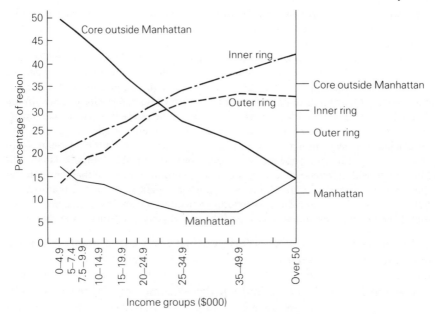

Figure 4.7   Geographic distribution of households by income, New York metropolitan region, 1979
Source: Harris (see note 80)

However, the spatial coexistence of very different social groups in an increasingly valuable space in most of Manhattan is increasingly challenged by the skyrocketing of real estate prices and the increasing functional and social attraction of the central urban space for the professional–managerial segment, representing close to one-third of the employed population. The consequent process of widespread gentrification is gradually, but surely, changing the social characteristics of residential space in the inner city, further segregating social groups and pushing the ethnic minorities into increasingly secluded areas, such as Harlem and the south Bronx. Old white ethnic neighborhoods barricade themselves against both the threat of minorities and their risk of displacement.[81] The urban dynamics resulting from these conflictual processes is characterized both by territorial defensiveness and increasing social and ethnic homogenization of specific neighborhoods. The dual city is a shared space within which the contradictory spheres of the local society are constantly trying to differentiate their territories.

Richard Harris concludes his study on the spatial differentiation of New York with a statement relevant to the present analysis:

The restructuring of New York's economy in the past thirty years has created greater inequality. The contrasts between rich and poor neighborhoods have become greater. Different parts of the metropolitan area have been affected in different ways, and the

City most of all. The loss of manufacturing jobs has had greatest impact upon the boroughs while office growth has been especially important in Manhattan. The changing geography of employment has shaped the emerging social geography of the metropolitan area. Substantial parts of Manhattan have been gentrified, while most areas in the boroughs have suffered a decline. In the process, a new and larger pattern of contrasts between Manhattan, the boroughs, and the outer suburban rings has emerged. . . . Many kinds of informal work have grown up to serve local needs. In the South Bronx this informal work means survival; in the SoHo it means a fashionable way of life; in new ethnic communities scattered throughout the city it helps people to build a home away from home. . . . Life on Long Island or in Fairfield County, as in any American suburbs, depends on a good deal of unpaid domestic labor. But Manhattan, with its towers of apartments and condominiums, more than any place in the continent, is designed to minimize anything but paid work. In this manner, the homes and workplaces of New York together constitute a complex geography of work that embodies the continuing polarities of class and gender, ethnicity and race.[82]

The characterization of New York as a dual city does not simply mean that opposition between executive limousines and homeless people: more fundamentally, it represents an urban social structure that exists on the basis of interaction between opposite and equally dynamic poles of the new informational economy, whose developmental logic polarizes society, segments social groups, isolates cultures, and segregates the uses of a shared space.

The Last Urban Frontier: The Restructuring of Los Angeles

Nowhere is the process of urban restructuring more completely manifested than in Los Angeles, the city where, in the image suggested by its urban analyst, Edward Soja, "it all comes together," as in Borges' Aleph.[83] Like New York, in the past two decades Los Angeles has become a leading financial and business center at the international level, second only to New York in the US, constituting itself the corporate hub for trade and investment in the Pacific Basin.[84] In fact, trans-Pacific trade has surpassed trans-Atlantic trade for the US, and almost half of its volume is concentrated on the LA ports of San Pedro and Long Beach. Around this core of internationally-oriented corporate services, and a still buoyant entertainment and media industry, a number of producer and consumer services have clustered, leading to a spectacular office boom which, together with the residential demand generated by rapid growth in jobs and residents, has fueled one of the largest and most profitable real estate markets in the country.

In addition to this development of advanced services, and in contrast to New York, Los Angeles' manufacturing sector also expanded dramatically during the 1970s and 1980s, to become, in 1984, the largest manufacturing center in the US, in terms of the absolute number of manufacturing jobs in the greater Los Angeles area. This is in sharp contrast with the popular image of Los Angeles as the postindustrial city. Indeed, Los Angeles saw the creation of 250,000 manufacturing jobs in the 1940s, of another 400,000 in the 1950s, of 200,000 in the 1960s, and, in the 1970s, at a moment of slow manufacturing growth in the US, of another 225,000 manufacturing jobs, almost a quarter of total US manufacturing job creation during the decade. The newest manufacturing growth is based on two very different sectors: on the one hand, aerospace and defense-oriented electronics, constituting a booming high-technology sector, concentrated around Los Angeles International Airport and in Orange County, as indicated in chapter 2; and on the other hand, consumer goods, particularly garments and apparel, which account for about 125,000 manufacturing jobs that are low-paid and frequently filled by immigrant women, most of them undocumented. At the same time, as shown by Soja, Morales, and Wolff in their pioneering study on the restructuring of Los Angeles, traditional manufacturing has been phased out. Los Angeles, once boasting the second largest concentration of automobile assembly industries, in the 1980s lost all its automobile factories but one.[85] The city's entire rubber industry, also the second largest US concentration after Akron, also disappeared in the late 1970s. In the 1978–82 period alone 70,000 manufacturing jobs were lost, three-quarters of them in the auto, tire, steel, and civilian aircraft sectors.

The labor force of Los Angeles has altered correspondingly. Unionized labor has been substantially reduced during the 1980s: in Los Angeles County the level of unionization in manufacturing dropped from 30 percent to about 23 percent, and in Orange County from 26.4 percent to 10.5 percent. While the proportion of craft workers and operatives in the labor force substantially decreased, Los Angeles now holds the largest concentration of engineers and scientists anywhere in the US, fueled by its role as the top location, in absolute terms, for defense contracts. At the other end of the employment spectrum, as in New York, corporate services, particularly in finance and law, have created hundreds of thousands of professional and managerial jobs, while low-paid service jobs have increased by about 500,000 in the past twenty years, pushing the region's total to 5.5 million jobs in the mid-1980s.

As in New York, new immigrants to the area have filled many of the jobs in downgraded manufacturing and consumer and personal services, with probably an even greater proportion than in New York of undocumented workers, particularly from Mexico and Central America. Since the late 1960s Los Angeles has received an estimated number of over 1 million Mexicans, 300,000 Salvadoreans, 200,000 Koreans, and several additional hundreds of thousands of Chinese, Indochinese, Filipinos, Thais, Iranians, Arabs, Armenians, Guatemalans, Colombians, and Cubans, among others. Los Angeles blacks have been discriminated against in the labor market, and their levels of unemployment are often above those of the new immigrants, who are considered less threatening by employers in search of flexibility and acquiescence from a socially and politically vulnerable labor force. Soja, Morales, and Wolff report that the ghetto areas of south-central Los Angeles, including Watts, saw their social condition deteriorate during the 1970s, falling below their level of 1965 at the time of the Watts riots.

This process of economic and social restructuring is also spatially specific. While most of the plants closing were concentrated in Los Angeles County and in the Long Beach industrial area, suburban Orange County picked up most of the new, high-technology based manufacturing development. Advanced services organized in a multinuclear urban structure in the downtown area, in the Wilshire Corridor toward the affluent Westside, and are increasingly decentralizing toward Orange County (particularly in the booming Irvine Business Complex[86]), Pasadena, and Glendale–Burbank (see map 4.1). Downgraded manufacturing clustered in whichever spaces could escape administrative controls, generally in low-income areas, such as central and east Los Angeles.

A sharply polarized labor force, with large segments of minority youth excluded from it, has led to a highly segregated residential structure, probably the most ethnically segregated of any major city in the US (only tentatively indicated in map 4.2). Class is also a major factor in residential segregation, as is shown by the clustering of the residences of engineers displayed in map 4.3. An important reason for the high level of spatial segregation in Los Angeles is its extreme administrative fragmentation, for the city of Los Angeles represents a much smaller proportion than New York of its metropolitan area. The fragmentation of a very large, extremely decentralized conurbation (home to over 12 million people) makes possible a strict segregation of public services, in particular of public schools, whose quality, dependent upon local revenue per capita, is a primary factor in determining residential location for concerned middle-class parents. Interestingly enough in such a multi-ethnic local society, class is taking over from ethnicity as the primary criterion for residential segregation, although the large black and Chicano ghettoes (Watts and east Los Angeles respectively) are substantially homogeneous in ethnic terms, largely because class and race reinforce each other as factors leading to the segregation of the overwhelmingly low-income black and Chicano communities.

In these ghettoized communities many youths have no prospect of making it in a an upgraded economy where the low-level jobs are sought after by an increasing pool of downgraded labor coming from all horizons. In the late 1980s, with drop-out rates at an all-time high, these youths often turn to gang formation, most of them simply to build up networks of personal interaction and affirm their identity; too often these gangs also become vehicles for the drug trade, now a multibillion-dollar business. Some of the Los Angeles gangs have won control over national markets for the wholesale distribution of drugs. A surge of violence reminiscent of 1920s Chicago provoked in 1988 a ferocious backlash from public opinion, leading to massive raids by the police, who in several instances arrested hundreds of suspects, detaining them in the Olympic Coliseum Stadium to investigate their gang connections. The police were under instructions to arrest people who could be seen in the streets of some areas (generally in central and south Los Angeles) and who "dressed or

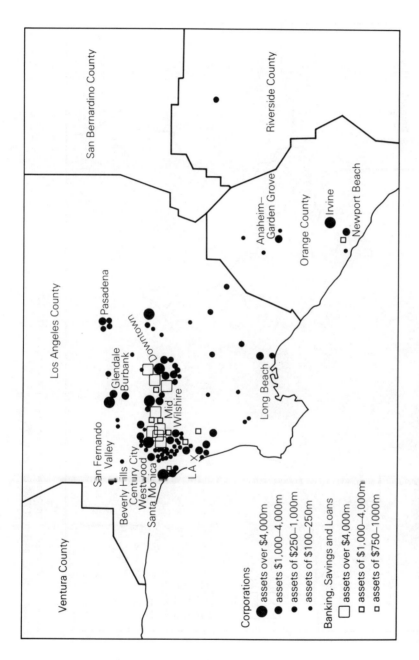

Map 4.1 Corporate and banking headquarters in the Los Angeles region
Source: Soja, Morales, and Wolff (see note 85)

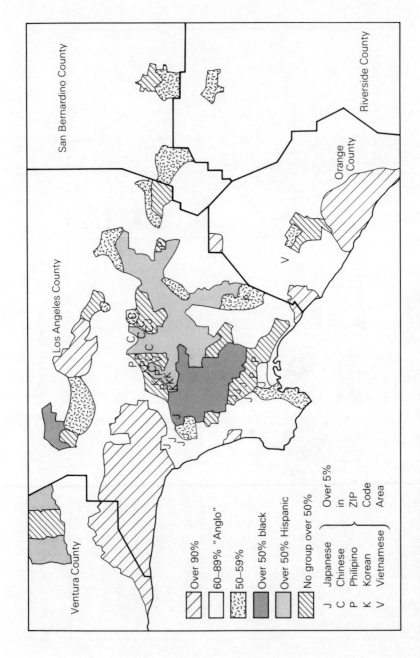

Map 4.2 Distribution of major ethnic groups in the Los Angeles area, 1980
Source: Soja, Morales, and Wolff (see note 85)

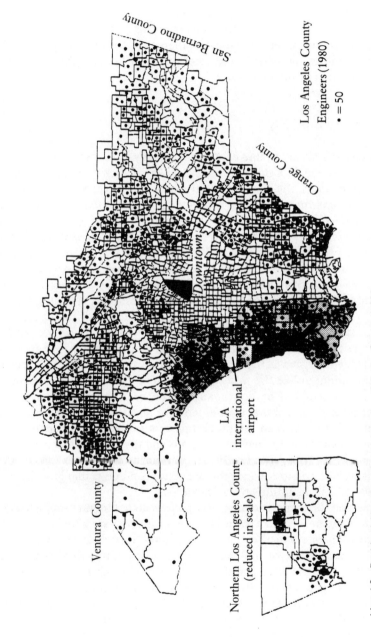

Ventura County

San Bernardino County

Orange County

Los Angeles County
Engineers (1980)
• = 50

Downtown

LA
international
airport

Northern Los Angeles County
(reduced in scale)

Map 4.3   Residential location of engineers, Los Angeles County, 1980
Source: Soja, Morales, and Wolff (see note 85)

acted as gang members."[87] Thus, the boundaries of "normality" and "abnormality" have been traced and enforced. The dual city resorts to policing entire areas of its space that appear to have been lost to social disorder. Although drug trafficking is indeed a murderous activity, the quasi-military occupation by police of large sectors of Los Angeles goes beyond the protection of public order. It indicates alienation between social groups, social norms, and spatial areas. It indicates the outer limits of the restructuring process in the last urban frontier.

The Rise of the Dual City

The dual city is a classic theme of urban sociology.[88] The contrast between opulence and poverty in a shared space has always struck scholars, as well as public opinion. Thus, the coexistence in 1980s Los Angeles of $11 million condominium apartments, sold with a complimentary Rolls Royce, and 50,000 homeless wandering in the streets and on the beaches of the Californian dream, is but an extreme manifestation of an old urban phenomenon, probably aggravated in the 1980s by the removal of the welfare safety net in the wake of neoconservative public policies. Yet there is a new form of urban dualism on the rise, one specifically linked to the restructuring process and to the expansion of the informational economy. It relates, first of all, to the simultaneous processes of growth and decline of industries and firms, processes taking place most intensely at the nodal points in the economic geography, namely, the largest metropolitan areas where most of the knowledge-intensive activities and jobs are concentrated. This occupational transition, unlike the historical shift from agricultural to industrial societies, is characterized by a mismatching between the characteristics of labor being phased out and the requirements for new labor. This is partly due to the contradiction between the much higher knowledge components of a substantial proportion of the new occupations and the institutional capacities of most societies, and specifically of American society, to adapt the educational system and to enhance the structural conditions that give rise to a higher cultural and scientific level of labor.

Yet given that the majority of new occupations do not require sophisticated skills, most of the new characteristics looked for in labor are a function not of technological change but of social and economic restructuring. What is at stake is the dismantling of the capital–labor relationships that were institutionalized during the long, conflictual process by which industrial society was formed. The transition from industrial to informational production processes overlaps with the rise of flexible production, which, under current historical conditions, tends to be equated with de-institutionalized capital–labor relationships. There follows the general demise of traditional labor, not only in manufacturing, and the conditioning of new labor to new organizational conditions, characterized by its relentless adaptation to the needs of firms and agencies as perceived by management, generally under the rule of market logic. Growth and decline do not compensate each other, as they did during the transition toward the industrial society. Part of the new potential labor force, especially among ethnic minority youth, is not integrated into the new labor market, and becomes surplus population. The majority of labor is restructured, both by the imposition upon it of new working conditions, generally in a different sector of activity, and by changing the characteristics of the labor pool itself, increasing the proportion of women, immigrants, and ethnic minorities in the labor force, taking advantage of the greater social vulnerability of these groups in a social context of gender and racial discrimination. Nevertheless, a significant proportion of labor, recruited from the better educated social groups, is upgraded in skills and social status, and becomes the backbone of the new informational economy, both in advanced services and in high-technology manufacturing. The differential reassignment of labor in the process of simultaneous growth and and decline results in a sharply stratified, segmented social structure that differentiates between upgraded labor, downgraded labor, and excluded people. Dualism refers here both to the contradictory dynamics of growth and decline, and to the polarizing and exclusionary effects of these dynamics.

The new dual city can also be seen as the urban expression of the process of increasing differentiation of labor in two equally dynamic sectors within the growing economy: the information-based formal economy, and the downgraded labor-based informal economy. The latter is a highly dynamic, growth-oriented, and often very profitable sector, whose reality is far distant from the survival activities with which it has generally been associated. The informal economy cannot be equated with urban poverty, and in this sense urban dualism does not pertain to the realm of social stratification but to a new socio-economic structure characterized by the different growth dynamics of two distinct, though articulated, components. What differentiates the two sectors, as argued in chapter 1, is the breakdown of state intermediation between capital and labor, resulting in different production relationships, and ultimately in different characteristics of labor, either because it was molded to the requirements of unregulated relationships or because it was selected (or self-selected) in the first place on the basis of its malleability to new working conditions. The widespread observation concerning the entrepreneurialism of the new immigrants fits this model, but so does the adaptation of clerical women to higher skilled jobs at lower rates of pay and without job security, on a part-time basis and without a contract. The informal economy, being concentrated in the largest and most dynamic metropolitan areas, particularly in the central cities, also contributes to the new urban dualism; two equally dynamic sectors, interconnected by a number of symbiotic relationships, define specific labor markets and labor processes in such a way that the majority of workers are unlikely to move upwardly between them. The economy, and thus society, becomes functionally articulated but organiz-ationally and socially segmented.

A third major process of dualization concerns the polarized occupational structure within the rising sectors of advanced services and high technology, with its impact on a stratification system; because of the shrinkage of its middle levels, the system appears to be less open to occupational mobility than in the recent past. Given the relatively large proportion of labor in the upper levels of the occupational structure, the higher levels of the society are no more a secluded elite inevitably forced to interact with the overwhelming majority of the society, but can be functionally and socially self-contained, while the lower tier loses the attraction of the social role model provided by the higher social strata because the privileges, skills, and values of the upper-level, professional class seem to be unreachable for most of the semi-skilled labor force.

Thus the non-complementary processes of informational growth and industrial decline, the downgrading and upgrading of labor, the differen-tiation between the formal and the informal sectors, and the polarization of the occupational structure in the new industries, together produce a highly differentiated labor force that crystallizes in very distinct lifestyles in terms of household structure, inter-gender family relationships, and uses of the urban space. In fact, structural dualism, along the series of dimensions we have indicated, does not result in two social worlds, but in a variety of social universes whose fundamental characteristics are their fragmentation, the sharp definition of their boundaries, and the low level of communication with other such universes. The dual city is a multifaceted reality, but structural dualism manifests itself in the transformation of bipolar dialectics into dual dichotomies. It is in this sense, and only in this sense, that we can speak of dualism.

Structural positions in the relationships of production and distribution crystallize in lifestyles that become less and less communicable, as they presuppose radically different financial means and cultural skills, and so lead to the formation of micro-societies through the patterning of space. Residential areas become exclusionary devices where the dynamics of real estate costs tend to impose social homogeneity, both in terms of class and in terms of ethnicity. The adaptation of a desirable space historically occupied by ethnic minorities or working-class families to its new privileged status as residential location for the new urbanites of the informational society takes place through systematic gentrification and displacement that further segregates the city. What results is a spatial structure that combines segregation, diversity, and hierarchy. The upper tier of the society, mostly white, and largely male-dominated, either by single men or through patriarchal relationships, occupies select spaces, both in the inner core and in exclusive suburbs, and maintains them in a separate circuit of lifestyle, services, and leisure, increasingly protected by both public and private security forces. The vast majority of downgraded workers and new laborers share an excluded space that is highly fragmented, mainly in ethnic terms, building defensive communities that fight each other to win a greater share of services, and to preserve the territorial basis of their social networks, a major resource for low-income communities. Downgraded areas of the city serve as refuges for the criminal segment of the informal economy, as well as reservations for displaced labor, barely maintained on welfare. Newcomers to the dual city often pioneer transformations of these areas, increasing the tension between conflicting social interests and values expressed in territorial terms. On the other hand, a large proportion of the population, made up of low-level labor forming the legions of clerical and service workers of the informational economy, insert themselves into micro-spaces, individualizing their relationship to the city, which becomes reduced, in their living experience, to a tenuous connection between home and work, in the vain hope of not being whirled into the changing dynamics of community structuration and destructuration. Structural dualism leads at the same time to spatial segregation and to spatial segmentation, to sharp differentiation between the upper level of the informational society and the rest of the local residents as well as to endless segmentation and frequent opposition among the many components of restructured and destructured labor.

The territorially based institutional fragmentation of local governments and of schools reproduces these cleavages along the lines of spatial segregation. Since educational and cultural capacity are key elements in labor performance in the informational economy, the system is largely self-reproductive, unless modified by social protest and/or deliberate political intervention.

The social universe of these different worlds is also characterized by differential exposure to information flows and communication patterns. The space of the upper tier is usually connected to global communication and to vast networks of exchange, open to messages and experiences that embrace the entire world. At the other end of the spectrum, segmented local networks, often ethnically based, rely on their identity as the most valuable resource to defend their interests, and ultimately their being.[89] So the segregation of space in one case (for the large social elite) does not lead to seclusion, except regarding communication with the other components of the shared urban area; while segregation and segmentation for defensive communities of ethnic minorities, workers, and immigrants do reinforce the tendency to shrink the world to their specific culture and their local experience, penetrated only by standardized television images, and mythically connected, in the case of immigrants, to tales of the homeland. The dual city opposes, in traditional sociological terms, the cosmopolitanism of the new informational producers to the localism of the segmented sectors of restructured labor.

The series of processes I have shown to be linked to the spatial dimension of labor restructuring in the informational economy converge toward a fundamental outcome of the dual city: its role in restructuring and destructuring social class formation. On the one hand, the recycling, downgrading, and conditioning of labor leads to the configuration of a number of territorially segregated, culturally segmented, socially discriminated communities that cannot constitute a class because of their extremely different positions in the new production relationships, reflected and amplified in their territorial differentiation in the city. On the other hand, a large proportion of the population (between one-fourth and one-third in the largest metropolitan areas) hold the strategic position of information producers in the new economy, enjoy a high cultural and educational level, are correspondingly rewarded in income and status within the stratification system, and control the key to political decision-making in terms of their social influence and organizational capacity. This new professional–managerial class, that by and large is white-dominated and male-dominated, is spatially organized, in terms of residence, work, and consumption activities, and tends to appropriate an increasingly exclusive space on the basis of a real estate market that makes location in that space a most valuable asset. This social group is not a ruling class in the traditional sense. It is a hegemonic social class that does not necessarily rule the state but fundamentally shapes civil society. The spatial articulation of its functional role and its cultural values in a very specific space, concentrated in privileged neighborhoods of nodal urban areas, provides both the visibility and the material conditions for its articulation as a hegemonic actor. In contrast, the endless social and spatial fragmentation of the diversified segments of restructured labor at the lower level fixes their cultural and territorial identities in terms irreducible to other experiences, breaking down the pattern of social communication with other communities and among different positions in the work process. And this is probably the essence of the dual city in our society: an urban form that articulates the rise of the new socially dominant category in the informational mode of development, while disarticulating and opposing the fragments of destructured labor as well as the components of the new labor incorporated into the emerging economic structure. The fundamental contemporary meaning of the dual city refers to the process of spatial restructuring through which distinct segments of labor are included in and excluded from the making of new history.

5

High Technology and the Transition From the Urban Welfare State to the Suburban Warfare State

Introduction: From the Welfare State to the Warfare State

The process of economic restructuring underway in the 1980s is challenging one of the cornerstones of post-1945 industrial democracies: the welfare state. By this term is understood, as in most of the literature,[1] a particular type of state in recent history, characterized by the fact that one of its fundamental principles of legitimacy lies in its redistributive role in delivering goods and services through public institutions, outside the rule of the market, to citizens entitled to such delivery simply by being citizens. I share Morris Janowitz's view that:

.the Welfare State and welfare expenditures are not synonymous. The Welfare State rests on the political assumption that the well-being of its citizens is enhanced not only by allocations derived from their occupations and the marketplace but also from grants regulated by the central government. . . . The Welfare State involves at least two additional elements. First, under the Welfare State, the extent and nature of welfare expenditures are conditioned decisively by parlimentary regimes, that is they political demands and consent and not authoritarian decisions. Second, it is accepted as a legitimate goal of the political system to intervene through governmental institutions in order to create the conditions under which its citizens can pursue their individual goals.[2]

This is to say that the welfare state is above all, as is any form of state, a political phenomenon. Yet it has decisive economic consequences, in terms of both the distribution of the product and its impacts on supply and demand. It would be pretentious to attempt here the analysis, that remains to be undertaken, of the origins, development, and crisis of the welfare state in the US.[3] What is crucial for the present specific analytical purpose is that in the 1970s the welfare state reached its peak in America, at a level that business interests were not ready to accept on economic grounds, and under political conditions that made it possible for conservative forces to mobilize important sectors of the American public against it.[4] Table 5.1 shows the rapid growth of social welfare during the 1960s and its stabilization during the 1970s at a level that greatly contributed to the dramatic decrease of capital's net share of GNP

Table 5.1   Labor and capital share of total output, 1984–1980, as % of GNP[a]

Year	Consumption by labor financed by wages and salaries	Social welfare spending	Capital's gross share	Capital depreciation	Non-social welfare spending	Capital's net share
1948	58	8	34	7	11	16
1950	58	8	34	7	12	14
1955	55	8	37	9	15	13
1959	55	10	35	9	15	9
1965	54	11	35	8	15	12
1972	52	19	29	9	14	6
1977	50	19	31	10	14	6
1979	50	18	32	10	14	8
1980	51	19	30	11	14	5

[a] The total labor consumption share equals column 1 plus column 2; capital's gross share equals 100 minus the total labor consumption share. Capital's net share equals capital's gross share minus capital depreciation minus non-social welfare spending. The net share represents that part of GNP available for net domestic and foreign investment and capitalists' consumption.

Sources: 1948–72: Bowles and Gintis, tables 5 and 6 (see note 5); 1977–80: calculations based on Bowles and Gintis' method, using more recent data. Calculated by Carnoy, Shearer, and Rumberger (see note 7)

from 12 percent in 1965 to 5 percent in 1980.[5] Another important observation from these data is the decline during the 1970s of the proportion of consumption by labor financed by wages, which amounts to an increase in the role played by taxes and social security contributions in financing welfare expenditures. This trend was tantamount to a redistributive process from capital to labor and from middle-income workers to low-income families, including the poor and unemployed. The complexity of this trend is explained by three factors: the growing importance of indirect wages over direct wages in labor's consumption; the process of redistribution in favor of non-working households and low-income families; and the skyrocketing cost of public agencies, particularly because of their role as employers of a growing proportion of the workers, offering better opportunities than the private sector to workers, especially from ethnic minorities. This situation laid the economic ground for an alliance between business interests and middle-class taxpayers to launch a decisive attack against the welfare state. Yet this attack, which was incorporated into the mainstream of conservative politics and, as a result, into the national policies labeled "Reaganomics," was successful only because of the existence of a number of economic, ideological, and political conditions underlying the current transformation of the capitalist state.[6]

Economically, the crisis of the 1970s was partly the consequence of the refusal of business to continue investing under the institutional conditions represented by the welfare state and its regulatory policies. As Carnoy, Shearer, and Rumberger put it:

Government management failed because once big business saw that liberal governments could and would give in to wage earners, the poor, and the old at the expense of profits, it gradually made the New Deal solution unworkable. An important fraction of the business community was and is willing to do whatever is necessary – including bringing on a series of severe recessions, as occured in the 1970s and early 1980s – to get the new and satisfactory conditions of low wages, low welfare spending, low corporate taxes, minimal regulations and weak unions consistent with high profit margins and control over capital formation. Far from wanting government off people's back, business in the 1970s was pushing for government intervention in its favor.[7]

Nevertheless, in a democratic society, economic interests, even when they are structurally dominant, cannot impose their logic unless mediated by ideological and political processes.[8] Ideologically, the reality of bureaucratization of state institutions, and the individualistic, almost libertarian tradition of American culture, favored the deregulation of welfare institutions.[9] Nevertheless, as Vicente Navarro has pointed out,[10] most public opinion polls during the past decade show consistent public support for the fundamental institutions of the welfare state, and particularly for the most costly entitlement program, social security, although rejecting transfers made under the "welfare" label. This is to say that the ideology rooted in individualism and the work ethic rejects the notion of a "free lunch" for the "lazy poor," but is certainly comfortable with major social benefits obtained by and for the working people, such as social security, unemployment benefits, health, and education. The deliberate political attack on the welfare state consists precisely in the ideological confusion of general programs of social benefits with specific programs targeted to the poor.

The relative success of the anti-welfare strategy lies in the differing political origins of two kinds of social programs. In other words, the American welfare state is a two-tier institutional system, originating in two different historical periods around different social actors and political conditions, even if in both cases the Democratic Party came to be its political expression.[11] As we know, the major institutional foundations of the welfare state resulted from the mobilization of the labor unions in the 1930s,[12] when a social contract was reached between business, organized labor, and government, in the form of the New Deal, setting up both the basis for post-World War II economic growth and the political framework for the expansion of the welfare state.[13] These social contracts excluded both ethnic minorities and the new social movements that came to the forefront of collective action during the 1960s, most notably the women's movement, community organizations, environmentalists, countercultural protestors, and ethnic liberation movements, often associated in the anti-war movement.[14] Thus, a new, fragile political coalition appeared in most large US cities toward the end of the 1960s, built upon the concessions made to various minorities and communities by the business–labor political alliances that had controlled the local political institutions in the early 1960s, enlarging and destabilizing the political grouping that John Mollenkopf has characterized as the "pro-growth coalition."[15] To remain in power the pro-growth coalition had to broaden the welfare state to cover poor urban communities, in a movement of such depth that it could be challenged only slightly by the Nixon administration.[16] Once the institutions were in place, by 1969, the bureaucratic logic of the entitlement system pushed them forward, in terms of services, payments, and jobs, turning American inner cities into powerful redistributive machines.[17]

The distinctive features of this new round of welfare state activity were its diversity and its pragmatic specificity. Resulting from uneven development of social struggles, and following the variable geometry of local political coalitions and intergovernment relationships, the urban welfare state was a piecemeal construction of programs and agencies that favored groups and areas whose legitimate entitlement became slowly buried with the passage of time, and the fading of collective memory.[18] Furthermore, the new political alliances were not as firm as that which underlay the New Deal, and basically failed to draw in the new, active middle class, living mainly in the suburbs, as well as the new social movements.[19]

In fact, the political context in which most of the "great society" programs came to maturity, namely the Nixon administration, was no small contributory cause of the lack of consistency of the new liberal coalition. As John Mollenkopf writes.

The conservative counterpoint added to the irrationality, internal inconsistency, and lack of political accountability of the federal urban program delivery system. By undercutting Democratic programs, conservatives reduced the delivery system's responsiveness to the beneficiaries for whom it was initially designed. Since conservatives added new programs more easily than they could terminate old ones, programs increasingly worked at cross purposes. During the periods of conservative ascendency, the number of demoralized and crippled programs also increased, subsequently burdening Democrats as well as Republicans. Over time this build-up of bureauratic ineffectiveness and lack of accountability has become one of the system's primary problems and one that, despite considerable rhetoric about efficiency and reorganization, neither liberals nor conservatives have been able to resolve.[20]

Thus, to some extent, while the mobilizations of the 1930s led to a solid coalition that crystallized in the national institutions of the welfare state, the social movements of the 1960s, while they succeeded in reforming the local state, obtaining welfare programs that expanded during the 1970s, were not able to build stable coalitions that could resist a determined offensive by powerful adversaries such as business, the new middle class, or ideological movements in defense of traditional family values.

This analysis is the basis for one fundamental hypothesis that I will try to substantiate in this chapter: the attack against the welfare state, as a key element of the process of economic restructuring, developed first along the weakest line of defense of welfare institutions, namely, the local welfare state, which was barely sustained by co-opted minority bureaucracies and insulated community organizations, while major entitlement programs, such as social security or unemployment insurance, much more significant in budgetary terms, escaped largely unscathed during the heyday of Reaganomics, in spite of the weakness of organized labor. The historic alliance of the New Deal, along with its powerful ramifications in the Democratic Party, was strong enough to hold much of its ground against the storm of neo-conservatism, while the regulatory institutions conquered by environmentalists and the safety net obtained by the urban poor during the 1960s were what suffered in the blundering attempts to dismantle the welfare state. The urban social landscape was thus much more deeply affected by the turnaround of public policies than was the social wage established by labor-supported reformers in the era of responsible capitalism.

The tentative dismantlement of the welfare state in the process of restructuring is taking place simultaneously with the rise of a new "warfare state." Although I use the term, coined originally by Herbert Marcuse,[21] because of its powerful resonance, I give to it quite a different meaning. I would certainly not imply that the American state, or indeed most states in industrial democracies, are now engaging in active warfare. For one thing, they have already done it, regrettably, in the past decades. Neither do I believe they are aiming to trigger off a new world war. In characterizing the new historic trends under the notion of the warfare state I refer to a number of major social processes. In the first place, on purely empirical grounds, in the 1980s the American state undertook the largest ever defense build-up in peacetime, and in absolute dollar value, the largest military program in the history of mankind (see table 5.2 and figure 5.1). Secondly, and at a more analytical level, one of the main issues at stake is the replacement of the state's principle of legitimacy as economic regulator and social redistributor, forged during the Depression era, by a new principle, powerful enough to justify the reinforcement of the state and the growing budget deficit caused by defense spending and pro-business tax cuts,[22] in spite of the libertarian tone of the discourse targeted against the welfare state. The old conservative justification for the strength of the state as the rampart of national security and the guardian of domestic law and order came to be the main motto of the political program of economic restructuring.Thus, to some extent the demise of welfare and the rise of warfare are intertwined as processes of contradictory political legitimation, whose peaceful coexistence in the 1950s and 1960s became socially and economically untenable in the 1980s.

Furthermore, the political crisis suffered by the American state both domestically (Watergate) and internationally (Vietnam; Iran; the erosion of its political control in Africa and Central America; increasing economic and technological competition from new powers, particularly Japan; strategic parity achieved by the Soviet Union in the arms race) called for a state of emergency in which the greatest power on earth would flex its muscles to show, in a responsible yet determined manner, that it was ready and willing to

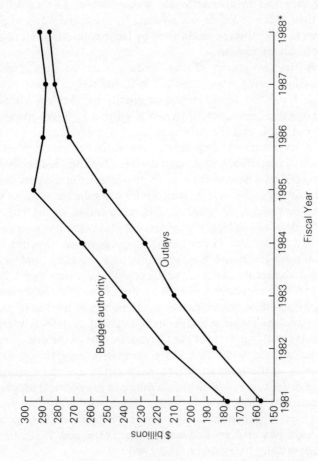

Figure 5.1   The Reagan defense budget, 1981–1988

Table 5.2 Reagan defense budget, 1981–1988

| | 1981 | | 1982 | | 1983 | | 1984 | | 1985 | | 1986 | | 1987 | | 1988[a] | |
	$bn	annual growth rate (%)	$bn	annual growth rate (%)	$bn	annual growth rate (%)	$bn	annual growth rate (%)	$bn	annual growth rate (%)	$bn	annual growth rate (%)	$bn	annual growth rate (%)	$bn	annual growth rate (%)
Budget authority	178.4	–	213.8	19.8	239.5	12.0	265.2	10.7	294.7	11.1	289.1	–1.9	287.4	–0.6	291.4	1.4
Outlays	157.5	–	185.3	17.7	209.9	13.3	227.4	8.3	252.7	11.1	273.4	8.2	282.0	3.1	285.4	1.2

a Projected.

Source: Executive Office of the President, Office of Management and Budget, *Budget of the United States Government*, various years.

engage in sharp confrontations to preserve its status and power. Business interests, both in the US and internationally, redeploying themselves on a planetary scale in the aftermath of the crisis, welcomed this newfound resolution in the leader of the free world, both for its symbolic value and for its global practical consequences.

Together with tax cuts for corporations and upper-income groups, defense spending provided the substitute for the demand and jobs generated by social welfare spending and hence the basis for a new state-led economic policy replacing classical Keynesianism with a "perverted Keynesianism," made up of military expenditures and regressive income redistribution.[23]

To proceed with this new policy, a new power bloc had to be built at the core of the warfare state, able to replace the old liberal coalition which was now deeply in crisis. As Carnoy, Shearer and Rumberger write: "New Deal ideology, fostering an economic development based on a historical compromise among labor, business, and government could not abandon its labor-conscience political base to achieve what business wanted. Neither was it willing to abandon its business ally to strike out in new, imaginative pro-community, pro-labor, pro-consumer directions. It thus collapsed as a viable political ideology."[24]

Business took the initiative in this collapse by breaking the two social contracts achieved during the 1930s and 1940s, and the 1960s, to regain decisive advantages over labor and over the welfare state, and to win a new edge in the international economy. Business enthusiasm for the neo-conservative coalition organized around President Reagan is hardly a mystery. Still, it was not enough decisively to overturn the Democratic majority among the public, and to make them forget so quickly the disturbing tendencies in the Republican administration revealed during the Watergate affair. However, on the basis of the electoral and public opinion data we can hypothesize that the new power bloc was constituted behind the warfare state (without necessarily supporting military action) on the basis of several elements:

(1) The traditional conservative constituency, reinvigorated by the new strength lent by business support and the skills and charisma of a new political leader with good communication skills: Ronald Reagan.

(2) The array of social groups brought together by the backlash against minorities and social movements, particularly among working-class whites reacting against minorities, anti-segregation policies ("busing," for instance) and countercultural movements (feminism, gay liberation, etc.).

(3) Middle-class professionals, reacting against the welfare state because of its benefit of low-income groups at the expense of their tax burden, while supporting the new economy fostered by defense spending and international business, regardless of their ideology as individuals on specific issues.

(4) New regions, benefiting from the new economy in terms of jobs, population, and resources, and emerging as new power-makers outside the traditional alignments generally controlled by the Democratic Party.

Because of the diversity of these interests and their loose socio-political organization, this power bloc had great difficulty in making progress in Congressional and local elections. Yet their social strength was significant enough to coalesce on the national scene around the powerful figure of Ronald Reagan, masterfully dominating the unifying institution of American national politics: the media.

Once in power, the political elite reshaping the Federal government in the direction of the warfare state undertook the task of transforming a conservative current of opinion into a new historic power bloc. However, at least during the 1980s, it failed in this attempt. The causes of this failure are complex and cannot be rigorously examined within the limits of this chapter. It is enough to say here simply that two important factors were the political ineptitude of the President's aides (leading, among other things, to the Iran–Contra affair), and the damaging results of contradictory economic policies that amassed the largest budget deficit and trade deficit in history, prompting demands from business circles for a more rational policy.[25] However, the Reagan administration did set in motion a series of trends that future political leaders will find difficult to reverse: a social and political climate inclined to the deregulation of economic and social activity; the weakening of organized labor, with its corollary in terms of greater freedom on the part of government and business to renounce social programs; a more conservative judiciary, which will be likely to slow down major social changes at the institutional level; an anti-inflationary attitude that will lay the ground for fiscal austerity, once the flow of foreign financing of the deficit decreases; and, above all, a new emphasis on strong defense on the basis of a technological renewal of the armed forces that is likely to be pursued by subsequent administrations, in the form of both strategic policy and industrial policy, in spite of the ups and downs of defense spending.

The process of economic restructuring then, developed on the basis of a socio-political transformation that laid the ground for the transition from the welfare state to the emerging warfare state. Much of this realignment translated into decisive urban and regional restructuring, as a later part of this chapter will go on to analyze. To focus once more on the specific research interest of this work, what was the actual role played by technological change in a process that we have analyzed primarily in economic and political terms?

As in other dimensions of the restructuring process, high technology in fact played a very important role in the transition from the welfare to the warfare state. This is, first of all, because of the technological obsolesence of military equipment brought about by dramatic changes in electronics, communications, and special materials. Certainly, such obsolesence is significant because of the *political* decision to strengthen US defense; once that decision was taken, for reasons that will be discussed briefly in the third section of this chapter, technological modernization of the military became the key instrument for achieving strategic superiority and modifying conventional forces to meet the new international conditions of modern warfare.[26] Although the defense build-up *per se* is independent of technological change, the pace of such change shaped the new defense policy, magnified and accelerated the replacement component of military procurement, and engaged the nation in a number of costly programs aimed at a new generation of sophisticated weapons.[27] Because this rejuvenation of the defense system was given political priority in a period of intended fiscal austerity, it also determined to a large extent the size and characteristics of budget cuts in welfare expenditures. Indeed, it was the combination of tax reductions and defense spending which created the largest federal budget deficit in history, in a paradoxical expression of the internal contradictions of the restructuring process. The obvious complementary policy would have been a dramatic shrinkage of welfare expenditures, as Budget Director David Stockman actually attempted.[28] Yet, as Stockman himself pointed out, many of the institutionalized welfare state programs from the 1930s-1940s legislation, particularly social security entitled payments, by far the largest item in the welfare state, became untouchable, and cuts were concentrated instead on the more recent and politically weaker urban welfare programs. There is, therefore, a systemic connection linking technological modernization of the military, increased defense spending, and selective dismantlement of some institutions of the welfare state.

Also, high-technology-led economic development favors, as has been observed in preceding chapters, the rise of new occupations and new regions to positions of greater wealth and power, undermining the social basis of the New Deal coalition, and fostering the formation of a new power bloc politically more likely to support both the warfare state and the downgrading of the welfare system. This does not mean that new social groups, for instance engineers and upper-level professionals, are warmongers. In fact, many of them were active in the anti-movement, and are often quite liberal in their personal ideology, as the political behavior of "yuppies" seems to indicate. [29] Yet they tend to be distrustful of unions, and scared of minorities, particularly when it comes to sharing public services for their children, and thus they distance themselves from the socio-political coalitions representative of the welfare state. The new model of development based upon high technology and advanced services creates the social conditions for a political realignment of the American public, offering the chance for new policies, such as the strategic project of the warfare state, to find new constituencies. This explains the apparent paradox of seeing one and the same social group, for example middle-class professionals, simultaneously supporting the nuclear freeze and voting for President Reagan, notwithstanding his pro-defense policy. We will see below how technology is used for political ends in the attempt to solve this ideological contradiction in the new power bloc by aiming, at least symbolically, at a non-nuclear, yet strategically superior, new defense system.

This ambiguous combination of liberal ideals and political neo-conservatism disappears in the case of the new regional elites, clearly supportive of the warfare state on the basis of a model of growth that associates closely high technology, the military–industrial complex, and free-wheeling capitalism competing in the international economy.[30] California, Texas, Florida, Arizona, and much of the west, are clearly setting the pace, although New England's liberal stand should sound a note of caution about making a mechanistic association between military industries and political neo-conservatism. All in all, high-technology-led economic restructuring is stimulating the transition from welfare to warfare, through its influence on the transformation of the occupational and regional structures of American society.

There is a third major technological factor that is likely to play an important role in the restructuring of the welfare state. This is the potential of office automation and on-line information systems in the public services.[31] This perspective, still very much undeveloped, could provide the technological basis for reducing public employment while maintaining the level of services, breaking union power, and generalizing the practice of subcontracting to private firms, on the basis of a lean, highly sophisticated public-service sector. Although at present political obstacles and bureaucratic routine to a great extent block the organizational restructuring of the public sector, should the new state prevail and consolidate, such restructuring would certainly be in the logic of the new administrative apparatuses; new information technologies would be a decisive tool in increasing the bureaucratic efficiency of government while insulating it further from citizens' control.

Overall, it is my hypothesis that high technology is an indispensable tool for the fundamental political–economic restructuring taking place in the state institutions of industrial democracies, and particularly in the US, in the last two decades of the twentieth century. This restructuring has roots that go deeper than the ideological preferences of a particular administration. It relates to the emergence of a new power bloc and to the reorganization of economy and society to cope with both new sources of social change and the technological revolution. Given the historical openness of the process, it is impossible to assess the actual extent of its lasting effects. Nevertheless, in about a decade the transition from the welfare to the warfare state will have taken place, producing a substantial, maybe irreversible, impact on the social and spatial structures.

The Rise and Fall of the Urban Welfare State

As stated above, the development of the welfare state in the US results from two major social trends originating in two key historical periods:[32] first, the

1930s, when the economic crisis and labor struggles led to the New Deal and its broad stream of Federal income-transfer programs, ushered in by the 1935 Social Security Act; [33] secondly, the 1960s, when the urban crisis and community struggles forced a realignment of local politics and fostered a new series of collective entitlement programs whose scope went far beyond the Democratic Party's "great society" programs, expanding throughout the 1970s during the conservative Nixon administrations. [34] What characterized this second tier of the welfare state was, on the one hand, its emphasis on the inner cities of large metropolitan areas; and on the other, its decisive role in the dynamics of local governments and in the local political arena. [35] The reversal of historic trends in the orientation of the state in the US, namely, the curtailment of its redistributive functions during the 1980s, is in large part concerned particularly with this urban dimension of the welfare state. [36] This is why the rise and fall of urban social programs are decisive in the shaping of American cities and regions.

In the period extending, approximately, from the mid-1960s to the late 1970s, three parallel trends deeply transformed the urban fabric of the US.[37] First, a substantial increase occurred in the share of total government spending taken by social welfare expenditure, with health, social insurance, and public aid showing the greatest increases. Overall, government domestic expenditures grew from 20.3 percent of GNP in 1969 to 25.9 percent of GNP in 1977. Even more significant, the ratio of domestic to defense spending changed from 2:1 to 4:1, while for much of this period the US was still engaged in the Vietnam War. [38] Social welfare spending as a proportion of total government spending increased from 37 percent in 1948 to 41.1 percent in 1966, 52.8 percent in 1973, and 56.8 percent in 1980. Within social welfare, social insurance increased its share of total social welfare spending from 21 percent in 1950 to 46.5 percent in 1980, while health and medical spending increased over the same period from 13 percent to over 20 percent.

Secondly, a growing flow of funds took place from the Federal government to state and local governments, which became major agents of social redistribution: Federal aid as a percentage of state and local expenditures increased from 18 percent in 1969 to 28 percent in 1977. For every dollar raised locally in 1978 cities received almost 50 cents from the Federal government.[39] In 1972, the Revenue Sharing Act established new financial ties among federal, state, and local governments, reversing the pro-state bias of US federalism in favor of a greater role for local governments.[40] In 1977 total Federal aid to state and local governments was about $70 billion, representing a five-fold increase in one decade. [41] Thirdly, in one of the most original trends of the new urban welfare state, Federal urban programs were developed that were funded and organized for specific localities, constituting what Gelfand calls a "fourth branch of government" [42] in which professionals, community activists, and Federal bureaucrats come together in a unique blend to shape a powerful current of social reform and citizen participation, accused by its conservative critics of causing "maximum feasible misunderstanding." [43] "War on poverty," "Model cities," and a number of categorical programs, targeted particularly on depressed urban areas and ethnic minorities, created a rich and complex geography of social welfare that even after its consolidation in fewer programs during the Nixon administration (particularly under the Community Development Block Programs or CDBG) continued to grow during the 1970s, providing some safety net to those social groups sufficiently deprived to be entitled to and sufficiently well mobilized to win their demands. [44]

To be sure, the budgetary size of most of these programs was (and is) much smaller than major items of the budget, such as defense, social security, or interest payments. Yet, their symbolic value, as a public commitment to people's needs independent of market forces, made these programs the focus of a social debate aimed at restoring social discipline and enhancing the individual work ethic. [45] Furthermore, their targeted distribution made these programs actually significant , in material terms, for their recipients and for the spatial areas they inhabited. [46] Similarly, Federal aid per capita favored bigger cities, that is, generally speaking, cities where social problems tend to more acute. It is true that small cities in depressed regions tend to be poorer than large cities, but research has established that social problems, and thus social welfare, are linked less to the actual level of poverty than to the social visibility of such problems, which is as much as to say, to the capacity for social mobilization of those concerned. [47]

In other words, a fundamental characteristic of the new welfare state that developed during the 1960s and the 1970s in a highly chaotic way, under the variable influence of socio-political factors, was its close association to specific spatial settings. George Vernez provides empirical proof of this hypothesis in one of the few systematic analyses of the spatial impact of Federal spending differentiated by specific programs. [48] His findings are shown in table 5.3. Vernez examined the distribution of Federal outlays by budget function for fiscal year 1976, as well as the evolution over 1970–6, in different spatial areas categorized in terms of income, economic growth, index of social hardship, size, and ecological position within the metropolitan area. He also calculated the distribution of these Federal outlays per region, although I have omitted here the presentation of these details, concentrating on his findings. The reader is referred to Vernez' article for a presentation of his methodology, which follows standard, generally accepted, procedures. A review of the main findings throws up the following points:

In a summary view of the main findings, we observe the following:

(1) Total Federal outlays, Federal outlays by major functions of the Federal budget, and the major individual grant-in-aid programs directed more funds per capita to central cities rather than to the suburbs, with one major exception, namely defense (primarily, according to Vernez, because of a higher concentration of top defense suppliers in suburban areas than in central cities).

Table 5.3 City concentration ratios of Federal outlays by budget function and type of city, fiscal 1976 (values over 1 indicate greater concentration)

(a)

Function	Per capita income, 1970		Population growth, 1970–5			Unemployment rate, 1976	
	Low-income cities (≤$3304)	High-income cities (>$3304)	Declining cities (≤0)	Slow-growth cities (0–15.0)	Rapid-growth cities (>15.0)	Low-unemployment cities (<8.9)	High-unemployment cities (≥8.9)
Development							
Area and regional development	1.32	0.68	1.00	1.01	0.90	1.52	0.69
Community development	1.30	0.70	1.05	0.89	0.87	1.03	0.98
Other advancement and regulation of commerce	0.94	1.05	1.10	0.75	0.89	0.92	1.04
Total 1976	1.26	0.75	1.05	0.89	0.87	1.08	0.95
(1970)	(1.19)	(0.80)	(1.08)	(0.82)	(0.77)	(0.98)	(1.00)
Access infrastructure							
Air transport	1.20	0.80	0.96	1.14	0.82	1.49	0.71
Water transport	0.70	1.28	1.24	0.46	0.56	0.75	1.14
Ground transport	0.85	1.14	1.31	0.38	0.27	0.40	1.34
Other transport	0.39	1.57	0.49	2.58	0.03	0.31	1.39
Total 1976	0.92	1.07	1.17	0.66	0.50	0.81	1.10
(1970)	(0.93)	(1.05)	(1.17)	(0.62)	(0.64)	(0.90)	(1.05)

Human capital							
Manpower training	1.20	0.80	0.98	0.97	1.17	1.13	0.92
Education and social services	0.30	1.66	1.29	0.42	0.23	1.90	0.47
Vocational education	1.08	0.91	0.88	0.99	2.14	1.47	0.72
Higher education, research, and general education aid	1.14	0.86	0.96	0.99	1.34	1.19	0.88
Health	0.48	1.49	1.30	0.36	0.37	0.51	1.27
Total 1976	0.85	1.14	1.12	0.70	0.92	0.89	1.06
(1970)	(1.08)	(0.91)	(1.03)	(0.87)	(1.13)	(1.20)	(0.87)
Relief							
Social services	1.03	0.96	0.97	0.84	1.85	1.49	0.71
Retirement and disability insurance	1.10	0.89	1.03	0.97	0.76	0.89	1.06
Unemployment insurance	1.00	1.00	1.13	0.74	0.57	0.69	1.17
Public assistance and other income supplements	0.87	1.12	1.05	0.81	1.10	0.79	1.11
General revenue sharing and fiscal assistance	1.08	0.92	1.04	0.87	0.99	0.90	1.05
Disaster relief and insurance	0.90	1.09	1.03	1.09	0.25	0.94	1.03
Total 1976	1.07	0.92	1.03	0.95	0.82	0.89	1.06
(1970)	(1.16)	(0.83)	(1.02)	(0.98)	(0.75)	(0.88)	(1.06)
Defense							
Construction	0.61	1.62	0.38	1.42	5.44	1.96	0.44
Supply price contracts	0.80	1.19	0.86	1.32	1.05	1.06	0.96
Payrolls	1.23	0.78	0.63	1.68	1.98	1.39	0.77

Table 5.3 Continued

(a)

Function	Per capita income, 1970		Population growth, 1970-5			Unemployment rate, 1976	
	Low-income cities (≤$3304)	High-income cities (>$3304)	Declining cities (≤0)	Slow-growth cities (0-15.0)	Rapid-growth cities (>15.0)	Low unemployment cities (<8.9)	High unemployment cities (≥8.9)
Total 1976 (1970)	0.95 (1.03)	1.04 (0.96)	0.78 (0.89)	1.45 (1.17)	1.42 (1.34)	1.18 (1.28)	0.89 (0.83)
Other							
Atomic energy defense	1.48	0.54	0.72	1.76	0.81	0.89	1.06
General science, space, and technology	0.68	1.30	0.96	1.17	0.70	0.81	1.10
Water resources and power	1.20	0.80	0.88	1.25	1.16	1.33	0.80
Pollution control and abatement	0.99	1.00	1.03	0.81	1.30	1.05	0.96
Energy	0.93	1.06	0.82	1.37	1.30	1.06	0.96
Recreation	1.00	0.99	0.90	0.80	2.70	1.24	0.85
Law enforcement and justice	1.03	0.96	1.04	0.83	1.14	0.83	1.09
Postal service	1.03	0.96	1.10	0.81	0.68	0.84	1.09
Veterans benefits	1.09	0.91	0.92	1.20	0.98	1.15	0.91
All Federal expenditure (except national debt interest)							
1976	0.98	1.01	0.98	1.04	0.99	1.01	0.98
(1970)	(0.98)	(1.01)	(1.02)	(0.95)	(0.87)	(1.03)	(0.97)

Table 5.3 Continued

(b)

Function	Hardship Index		Size (000s)			Central cities	Suburban cities
	Low-hardship cities (<100)	High-hardship cities (≥100)	Small cities (<100)	Medium-sized cities (100–300)	Large cities (>300)		
Development							
Area and regional development	0.86	1.03	0.83	1.67	0.77	1.18	0.18
Community development	0.81	1.15	0.75	1.33	0.95	1.08	0.63
Other advancement and regulation of commerce	0.75	1.20	0.44	0.79	1.30	1.13	0.38
Total 1976	0.81	1.14	0.72	1.31	0.87	1.10	0.54
(1970)	(0.74)	(1.20)	(0.73)	(1.32)	(0.95)	(1.10)	(0.49)
Access infrastructure							
Air transport	1.22	0.81	0.54	0.74	1.28	1.14	0.35
Water transport	0.32	1.57	0.31	0.29	1.56	1.14	0.37
Ground transport	0.32	1.49	0.17	0.74	1.42	1.18	0.18
Other transport	0.20	1.66	0.18	2.94	0.48	0.40	3.62
Total 1976	0.60	1.30	0.31	0.67	1.39	1.15	0.32
(1976)	(0.66)	(1.26)	(0.41)	(0.50)	(1.43)	(1.14)	(0.34)
Human capital							
Manpower training	0.95	1.02	0.72	1.62	0.83	1.13	0.38
Education and social services	0.38	1.50	0.38	0.61	1.39	1.14	0.37
Vocational education	1.14	0.82	0.81	1.78	0.73	1.16	0.25

Table 5.3 Continued

(b)

Function	Hardship Index		Size (000s)				
	Low-hardship cities (<100)	High-hardship cities (≥100)	Small cities (<100)	Medium-sized cities (100–300)	Large cities (>300)	Central cities	Suburban cities
Higher education, research, and general educational aid	0.91	1.05	0.82	1.38	0.90	1.12	0.45
Health	0.36	1.52	0.19	0.58	1.48	1.17	0.23
Total 1976	0.69	1.23	0.50	1.13	1.13	1.15	0.31
(1970)	(0.88)	(1.05)	(0.66)	(1.39)	(0.95)	(1.09)	(0.55)
Relief							
Social services	1.03	0.95	0.73	1.67	0.81	1.19	0.12
Retirement and disability insurance	0.84	1.12	0.99	1.12	0.95	1.02	0.88
Unemployment insurance	0.70	1.24	0.79	0.93	1.10	1.06	0.71
Public assistance and other income supplements	0.75	1.20	0.69	0.82	1.19	1.10	0.51
General revenue sharing and fiscal assistance	0.79	1.17	–	0.96	1.10	1.08	0.63
Disaster relief and insurance	0.82	1.05	–	1.00	1.17	1.11	0.47
Total 1976	0.83	1.13	–	1.09	0.98	1.04	0.81
(1970)	(0.85)	(1.11)	–	(1.22)	(0.89)	(1.01)	(0.93)

Defense							
Construction	1.72	0.40	—	0.70	1.21	1.15	0.33
Supply price contracts	1.34	0.71	—	1.26	0.78	0.78	1.93
Payrolls	1.31	0.73	—	1.31	0.91	1.06	0.70
Total 1976	1.33	0.72	—	1.27	0.83	0.88	1.48
(1970)	(1.24)	(0.80)	—	(1.28)	(0.90)	(0.94)	(1.24)
Other							
Atomic energy defense	1.12	0.89	—	1.93	0.39	0.82	1.76
General science, space, and technology	0.86	0.90	—	1.95	0.73	0.79	1.90
Water resources and power	0.78	1.18	—	1.35	1.18	1.21	0.07
Pollution control and abatement	0.76	1.19	—	1.41	0.85	1.03	0.84
Energy	1.14	0.81	—	1.80	0.83	1.02	0.88
Recreation	0.92	1.06	—	1.45	0.97	1.02	0.86
Law enforcement and justice	0.76	1.20	—	0.62	1.38	1.08	0.11
Postal service	0.75	1.20	—	0.96	1.13	1.08	0.61
Veterans benefits	1.05	0.95	—	1.04	1.00	1.03	0.85
All Federal expenditure (except national debt interest)							
1976	0.96	1.03	—	1.12	0.99	1.01	0.91
(1970)	(0.93)	(1.04)	—	(1.13)	(1.00)	(1.01)	(0.92)

Source: Vernez (see note 42).

(2) Federal outlays in aggregate and for each major function favor medium-sized cities (population between 100,000 and 300,000) over both large and small cities, with the exception of outlays on transportation infrastruture. However, this trend became weaker between 1970 and 1976, in favor of the large cities rather than the smaller cities. Here again, defense spending has a different pattern: defense oulays *per capita* increased in small cities by 23 percent in 1970-6, while decreasing in large cities by 8 percent.

(3) Outlays in all major categories, again with the exception of defense, favored declining cities over rapidly growing cities, on a per capita basis.

(4) Concerning the distribution between high-income cities and low-income cities, the pattern of Federal outlays is somewhat more diversified by function: more was spent *per capita* on relief expenditures, development outlays, and most individual Federal grant-in-aid programs in low-income cities, while transportation infrastructure, human capital investment, and defense outlays went more than proportionately to high-income cities.

(5) Also diversified are the concentration ratios of Federal outlays regarding cities with high unemployment rates as compared to those with low unemployment rates. The former attract more than their proportional share of outlays for relief, transportation, and human capital, while the latter have a greater concentration of expenditure in defense, development, and most of the largest grant-in-aid programs.

(6) In terms of the regional distribution of Federal spending (not shown in these tables) there is a pro-southern, pro-Pacific bias, related to defense and relief outlays, although Vernez remarks on the broad variation of spending patterns within regions, making almost impossible any serious interpretation of policy orientations on the basis of such an aggregate level of analysis.

Overall, the concentration ratios of Federal spending in the 1970s by type of spatial area appear to support the predominance of a redistributive orientation in Federal policy, with the systematic exception of defense outlays which work at cross-purposes to other budgetary items. Central cities in declining, high-hardship areas received a disproportionately large share of most Federal programs. Other classifications indicate a more complex pattern of resource allocation, as one might expect in a politically determined process. Yet many of the trends point toward defining the role of most Federal urban programs as welfare-related programs, in the broad meaning here given to this concept, fundamentally targeted to the urban areas suffering greater social stress. The decade 1966-76 did witness the rise of an urban welfare state in the US.

Both the critics and the advocates of these developments relate them to the urban fiscal crisis that shook many central cities of the large metropolitan areas in the 1970s, triggering in a policy debate that eventually led to the reversal of the trend toward social redistribution and the prevalence of public interest in urban policy. So much has been written on the "urban fiscal crisis" of American inner cities that it seems unnecessary to reopen a debate both outdated and inconclusive.[49] But for the present analytical purpose, it is important to stress that, whatever the structural causes of the fiscal crisis (suburbanization of affluent populations and of jobs, deindustrialization, uneven regional development, general economic crisis, etc.)[50] the way it developed was determined by policy decisions at various local levels and at national level, as a result of a political process.[51] In other words, one of the reasons for the expansion of the urban welfare state during the 1960s and 1970s was precisely to respond to the structural urban crisis by means of redistributive public policy, either Federally initiated or Federally funded.[52] This accounts for the increasing role of state and local governments in the US economy and in the production and management of the means of collective consumption.

Between 1960 and 1975, while US GNP rose by 200 percent, municipal expenditures increased by 350 percent. Over the same period, city expenditures increased 4.6 times while Federal aid to cities increased 18 times, jumping from a total of $592 million to $10.9 *billion*. Most of these expenses were financed through debt, thus contributing to inflationary pressures, and outstanding municipal debt grew from $23.2 billion in 1960 to $68.8 billion in 1975.[53] There was clearly an economic need, as well as social pressure, to bring public spending under control, particularly at the local level. Middle-class constituencies revolted against tax increases perceived as means to support social programs for the urban poor and to provide for the jobs and benefits of the public sector unions. To reinforce the fiscal protectionism fostered by institutional segregation within metropolitan areas, voters revolted at the state level to avoid both further taxation, and redistribution through state or municipal legislation.[54] 1978 was a turning point, with the passage of California's Proposition 13, establishing by referendum mandatory limits to the increase in local taxes. Other local measures, such as Massachusetts' Proposition 2 1/2 added political pressure to the grassroots resistance to urban social programs in the following years.[55] In the late 1970s, similar votes took place in many cities and states.

Nevertheless, the key element in turning the tide was the adoption of a new social policy at the Federal level that downplayed the emphasis on the well-being of inner cities, by now largely under control, once most of their political leaders had been integrated into the new local political coalitions. Then, as Tomaskovic-Devey and Miller write:

In the late seventies . . . the urban fiscal crisis, national recapitalization, and the social and economic contradictions produced by structural changes in economic activity led to political attacks on urban governments and on the federal government as incompetent, bloated, and a drag on the private sector. High taxes to finance state payrolls and social services, not the movement of private capital, were identified by business, the media, and some academics as the cause of dangerous fiscal gaps in the budgetary process.[56]

The same authors concluded that:

New York City served as the Hiroshima of the welfare state, demonstrating the bankruptcy threat that faced a city profligate enough to provide services to the poor and to have decent salaries.[57]

The fiscal crisis of New York City in the 1975–81 period was indeed exemplary of the attempted dismantlement of the urban welfare state. William Tabb has described it in a powerful, though admittedly controversial, book.[58] New York City was at the forefront of welfare spending, public services delivery, and favorable working conditions for city employees,[59] largely because of the politicization and level of organization of New York citizens. At the same time, the burden of providing municipal services for a business complex as large as the one located in Manhattan put tremendous pressure on the city that had experienced a massive exodus of virtually its entire middle-class population to the suburbs, along with an equally massive influx of minority populations in search of jobs and welfare benefits. The city had to rely increasingly on state and Federal aid, which in 1959 represented 28 percent of its revenues, jumping to 47 percent in 1969. During the 1960s, to cope with New York's aggravated social problems, state aid increased by 250 percent and Federal aid by 706 percent. With taxes already too high, and its political leverage to obtain additional public aid exhausted, New York City turned more and more to borrowing money from New York banks, as indeed it had often done throughout its history. In 1960, tax-exempt municipal bonds accounted for 21.6 percent of bank portfolios; by 1979, that proportion was 50 percent. In June 1975, the city's debt was $12.3 billion, about 40 percent of which was in notes payable within a year.

New York's financial elite came to be increasingly anxious about the city's prospects, both in terms of its solvency, and in terms of the quality of services that could be provided to the essential business quarters of Manhattan, and to its exclusive neighborhoods. Furthermore, the city was blamed for its demagoguery, let alone its corruption and inefficiency, for having given too much attention to its poor population, and for having made excessive concessions to its buoyant public-sector labor unions. As financial expert Roger Starr put it, business saw a growing contradiction between the political city, providing services for which people were unable or unwilling to pay directly, and the economic city, made up of productive citizens, on which the political bureaucracies and their clienteles were living as parasites;[60] a contradiction that had become impossible to sustain. Thus, when in February 1975 the city attempted to issue new securities, the Bankers Trust refused to underwrite the issue, and stopped all new lending. Chase Manhattan refused to form an alternative syndicate. With New York City bound for a default that could trigger a major financial crisis, and the Federal government refusing to provide additional help, the banks designed a rescue plan that included major budgetary and political conditions. The plan developed in three stages. First, in June 1975, a Municipal Assistance Operation was created as a State of New York agency, able to issue bonds to finance the city, backing these bonds with city revenues and the "moral obligation" of the state. Secondly, an Emergency Financial Control Board was created in September 1975 to step up local financial policy in the face of the resistance from municipal workers' unions and to overcome the reluctance of Mayor Beame to the new policy. The Board was made up of the Governor of New York, the Mayor, the State and City Comptrollers, and three representatives from the business world, selected by the Governor. Its function was to control the city's budget and finances. As a symbol of the business community's new political control over the city, in September 1975 a prominent member of that community was appointed as Deputy Mayor in charge of Finance: Mr Kenneth Axelson, from Lazard Freres and J. C. Penney. The Board urged the city to implement an austerity budget, emphasizing major cuts in social programs and the public employees payroll. Still, and thirdly, the Federal government had to be called upon. After tense negotiations, and with the warranty of New York's Governor and the business community, a "New York City Seasonal Financing Act of 1975" provided loans for three years, under a number of financial conditions supervised by the Secretary of the Treasury.

When a new Mayor, Edward Koch, was elected after a campaign that basically espoused the goals and means of the austerity program, new institutional and financial conditions were in place for a dramatic restructuring of New York City policy. In 1978, at a public ceremony, President Carter signed the "New York City Loan Guarantee Act of 1978," signaling the continuity of effort across party lines. For several years, New York City trimmed its social programs while providing tax abatements and business subsidies. Welfare payments decreased, about 25 percent of municipal jobs were eliminated, including 20 percent of the police force, 19,000 teachers, and 2,000 street sweepers, Public workers' unions, after an initial reaction of protest that was rapidly repressed by the city, not only resigned themselves to the measures but contributed about one-third of their pension funds to back the city's finances. Hospitals, schools, transportation, garbage collection, parks and recreation services all suffered drastic reductions in staff and services, while increasing their fees. By 1981–2, Mayor Koch was able to claim a balanced budget, restoring much of the city's financial credibility, albeit at a high social cost.[61]

On the basis of this fiscal and political restructuring the economy of New York City took off during the 1980s, taking advantage of the internationalization of capital flows, the development of advanced services, and the real estate boom triggered off by the new demand for office space and upmarket urban residences (see chapters 4 and 6). Furthermore, with city revenues increasing as a result of the economic bonanza, the Koch administration was able to restore almost all lost public jobs by 1987,[62] and to distribute public funds and support to some community organizations in a reconstruction of the networks of patronage politics.[63] However, the process of new economic growth in New York was highly polarized, and led to an increasingly unbalanced social structure (see chapter 4); and the new public sector did not expand fast enough to meet the new needs generated by this model of growth. The emphasis in city policies was on support for downtown business services (such as the Teleport project), and on improving the living conditions of the professional elite (for example, stepped-up police patrolling in Manhattan). Efforts were more often devoted to cosmetic image-making than to tackling fundamental social problems. Millions of dollars were spent on cleaning graffiti off subway cars, but New York bridges rapidly deteriorated for lack of maintenance: as a result, Williamsburg bridge closed in 1988, causing traffic nightmares. In another illustration of the same logic, the city set up a program to paint the facades of abandoned buildings to disguise dereliction for the benefit of suburban travellers; yet little was done to tackle the problem of the homeless, which went out of control in New York in the second half of the 1980s. In sum, the restoration of the quantitative level of the public sector, in terms both of jobs and of spending, to that of the mid-1970s, was biased socially and functionally toward business interests and middle-class groups. In the face of the mounting needs of the lower segments of the population, the retrenchment of the local welfare state deepened the trends toward the urban–social form that I have called the dual city.[64]

The most important change in the local state in the case of New York was the transformation of the political agenda, as revealed by the treatment of the fiscal crisis of the 1970s. It became clear that, beyond the ups and downs of social spending and clientelistic policies, the city was committed, first and foremost, to the well-being of the professional groups and to fulfilling the needs of the business interests on which the city's health relied, regardless of the social costs involved in the satisfaction of such interests. It is in this precise sense that the politics surrounding the welfare state involve power above everything else, and not just economic redistribution. The welfare state that was particularly present in the expansion of New York social programs in the 1960s and 1970s, was fundamentally a social contract, redistributing power among different social actors, including the organized poor communities. It was this pact that was renounced during the fiscal crisis and never restored during the 1980s, in spite of the excellent condition then of the local economy. The Koch administration played on ethnic divisions to implement class-oriented policies, thus downgrading the status of the local welfare state to pork-barrel politics.[65]

Similar processes, although less well publicized and in some cases more limited, took place at the turn of the decade in several large central cities in America, including among others Cleveland, Detroit, Buffalo, St Louis, Chicago and Philadelphia.[66] However, the restructuring of New York is particularly significant for the present analytical purpose, for two reasons.

First, it took place as early as the mid-1970s, thus signaling that socio-economic restructuring was a structural need of the system, delayed until the 1980s only because of political factors. Secondly, it was implemented, and with the harshest determination, by a Democratic Mayor in a predominantly Democratic city, actually demonstrating that some aspects of the restructuring process are not linked to Reaganism as such, or even to a Republican administration, but to the defense of class interests when threatened by economic crises and social conflicts. However, it took a new Republication President, fully committed to the defense of such interests, and with exceptional ability to build public support on the basis of political image-making, to undertake the assault on the welfare state, with particular focus on its urban dimension.[67]

The different treatment of the various departments in the Federal government by the Reagan administration was indicative not of government restraint, but of selective retrenchment and expansion. If we use a diréct indicator of the expansion of government services, namely the number of employees in each department, between 1980 and 1987 we see the Justice Department *increasing* its labor force by 20 percent, the State Department by 5.4 percent, and the military by 5.2 percent. On the other hand, Health and Human Services experienced personnel *cuts* of 12.4 percent, and Education's work force was cut by 22.4 percent.[68] Beyond the Federal government departments, there was during the Reagan years a reduction in total Federal aid to state and local governments, both in constant dollars, and as a proportion of total Federal spending: the total of such aid fell substantially from 15.5 percent of Federal spending in 1980 to 10 percent in 1987 (see figure 5.2).

The most important issue in the present context, however, is the selective orientation of federal programs toward cities and regions according to the different items in Federal government financing. Norman Glickman has undertaken the most extensive empirical analysis of the restructuring of urban policies under the first Reagan administration (1981–4), with particular emphasis on the urban effects of economic and defense policies what Glickman calls "Reagan's real urban policy."[69] I will examine his findings in some detail, as they are crucial for my argument concerning the crisis of the urban welfare state.

First of all, Glickman combined all urban-related expenditures in the Federal budget, in some itemized detail, and traced their evolution from 1977 to 1984, as shown in table 5.4. From these figures one can observe the generally rapid and consistent increase of the share of urban-related outlays in the Federal budget between 1967 and 1978, in line with the analysis above. Since 1978, on the contrary, we observe a decrease in that proportion, a decrease that accelerates as the trend proceeds. Furthermore, a reading of table 5.4 shows an actual *decrease* in real urban outlays as a whole (− 1.24 percent in 1984 over 1980; − 9.0 percent in 1982 over 1981: − 4.53 percent in

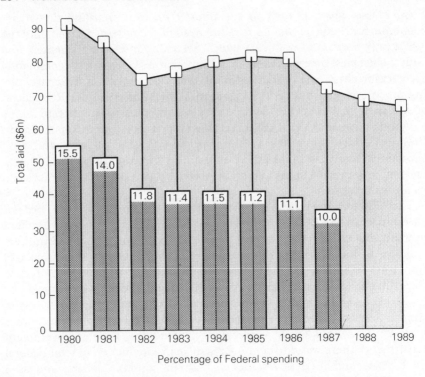

Figure 5.2   Total Federal aid to state and local governments, $bn (constant 1980 $), and aid as percentage of total Federal spending, for fiscal years 1980–1989. Figures for 1988 and 1989 are estimated
Source: Office of Management and Budget and the Brookings Institution

1983 over 1982; −9.36 percent in 1984 over 1983). This trend actually began in 1978, under the last period of the Carter administration, another sign that we are not simply observing a change in the political framework. By the early 1980s at least, a reversal is apparent in the trends concerning the urban welfare state, shifting from its expansion to its decline in absolute terms, as well as in terms of its proportion of the Federal budget.[70] A deepening of these trends during the second Reagan administration has also been observed, although in a less systematic analysis.[71] In addition, the policy of "New Federalism" has transferred a number of programs and responsibilities to state and local governments without allocating corresponding budgetary resources, thus actually reducing the capacity of local governments to meet urban social needs.

The new implicit urban policy has been to stimulate economic growth by creating incentives for private investment, assuming that such growth will solve urban problems. Tax cuts for corporations and upper-income groups

Table 5.4 Detailed description of the urban budget, fiscal years 1977–1984 ($m)

Department and program	1977	1978	1979	1980	1981	1982	1983	1984
Housing and urban development								
Community development block grants	2089	2458	3161	3902	4013	3791	3525	3526
Urban development action grants	–[a]	–	73	225	371	388	488	512
Rehabilitation loan fund	41	47	100	165	60	–23	1	–
Planning assistance	77	67	62	52	39	20	4	–
New communities assistance grants	2	1	*[b]	*	1	1	1	–
Subsidized housing programs	2443	2920	3559	4529	5747	6880	7774	8532
Housing for elderly/handicapped	4	176	459	752	817	742	255	51
Operating payments: low-income housing	506	691	654	824	929	1008	1582	1558
Emergency mortgage purchase assistance	–224	360	271	1039	–74	–37	–227	–
Urban renewal	850	376	281	212	144	90	70	50
Neighborhood self-help development program	–	–	–	2	9	–	–	–
Urban homesteading	–	–	–	–	–	12	20	12
Miscellaneous Appropriations[c]	19	11	15	2	5	1	2	–
Troubled projects operating subsidy	–	–	–12	23	53	29	23	13
Congregate services	–	–	–	*	1	3	5	6
Housing counseling assistance	*	4	5	8	5	3	3	3
FHA fund	492	357	193	151	182	–237	–329	–1546
Low-rent public housing loans and other expenses	–32	11	–3	34	77	–21	102	136
Non-profit sponsor assistance	*	1	1	1	*	*	*	*
Rental housing assistance fund	–7	–12	66	*	3	–	2	–
New communities fund	87	97	31	45	49	16	37	–
Fair housing assistance	–	–	–	–	1	2	11	6
GNMA: Special assistance functions fund	–805	–55	58	396	1303	1666	1433	–
GNMA: Guarantee of mortgage-backed securities	–22	–41	–55	–74	–92	–119	–156	–182
GNMA: Participation sales fund	–4	–21	–12	34	59	–20	–63	–75
Urban-related, HUD	5516	7446	8907	12322	13702	14195	14563	12602
Total HUD Outlays	5838	7589	9213	12576	14033	14491	14853	13737
% Percent Urban-related	94.5	98.1	96.7	98.0	97.6	98.0	98.0	91.7

Table 5.4 Continued

Department and program	1977	1978	1979	1980	1981	1982	1983	1984
Commerce								
Local public works program	585	3057	1741	416	83	40	30	30
Business development loans:								
Econ. Dev. Revolv. Fund	−20	−33	−33	45	−5	46	24	−24
Financial and technical assistance	1	*	–	*	*	*	–	–
Job opportunities program	98	12	2	5	*	1	–	–
Minority business development	54	54	54	56	49	50	57	57
Economic dev. assistance programs	297	330	436	546	502	337	270	207
Urban-related commerce	1015	3420	2200	1068	629	474	381	270
Total commerce outlays	2606	5239	4072	3755	11484	2045	1969	1699
% urban-related	38.9	65.3	54.0	28.4	5.5	23.2	19.3	15.9
Environmental, Protection Agency								
Construction Grants	3530	3187	3756	4343	3881	3756	3100	2800
Urban-related, EPA	3530	3185	3756	4343	3881	3756	3100	2800
Total EPA outlays	4365	4071	4800	5602	5241	5080	4370	4075
% urban-related	80.9	78.3	78.3	77.5	74.1	73.9	70.9	68.7
Transportation								
Federal highway administration (urbanized areas)[d]	861	988	1135	932	808	732	800	800
Urban mass transportation fund	1709	2028	2458	3207	3855	3864	3818	3488
Urban-related, DOT	2570	3016	3593	4139	4663	4596	4818	4288
Total DOT outlays	12514	13452	15486	18963	22509	19917	21157	24370
% DOT-related	20.5	22.4	23.2	21.8	20.7	23.1	21.8	17.6
Small Business Administration								
Business loan and investment fund	464	458	471	721	574	704	270	263
Urban-related, SBA	464	458	471	721	574	704	270	263

Total SBA outlays	700	2766	1631	1899	1913	631	577	262
% SBA-related[e]	66.3	16.6	28.9	38.0	30.0	111.6	46.8	100.4
Community Services Administration								
Community services programs[f]	640	768	780	2170	664	133	39	–
Urban-related CSA	640	768	780	2170	664	133	39	0
Total CSA outlays	640	768	780	2170	664	133	39	–
% CSA-related	100.0	100.0	100.0	100.0	100.0	100.0	100.0	0
Department of Health And Human Services and Education								
Education[g]	2593	3047	3450	1512	4262	3872	3686	3813
Health services administration[h]	1029	1079	1183	1311	1298	1924	1573	786
Grants to states for Medicaid[h]	9713	10680	12407	13957	16833	17391	19326	20799
Assistance payments program[h]	6293	6639	6610	7306	8503	7990	7766	7094
Grants for social and child welfare services[h]	2518	2809	3091	2763	2646	2567	2571	2500
Urban-related, HHS	22146	24254	26741	26851	33542	33744	34922	34922
Total HHS and education outlays	147455	162856	181182	207815	228115	265347	288844	302283
% HHS-related	15.0	14.9	14.8	12.9	14.7	12.7	12.1	11.6
Department of The Treasury								
State and local fiscal assistance trust fund	6760	6823	6848	6829	5137	4569	4567	4567
Anti-recession fiscal assistance fund	1699	1329	*	–	–	–	–	–
Urban-related Treasury	8459	8152	6848	6829	5137	4569	4567	4567
Total Treasury outlays	49560	56355	56044	76691	93372	110521	118025	134997
% Treasury outlays	17.1	14.5	10.5	8.9	5.5	4.1	3.9	3.4
Department of Labor								
Employment and training assistance[i]	3291	4764	6158	7065	6848	4110	3724	3595
Urban-related, DOL	3291	4764	6158	7065	6848	4110	3724	3595
Total DOL outlays	22374	22890	22649	29724	30084	30736	42995	34268
% DOL outlays	14.7	20.8	27.2	23.8	22.8	13.4	8.7	10.5

Table 5.4 Continued

Department and program	1977	1978	1979	1980	1981	1982	1983	1984
Total urban-related outlays	47631	55465	59454	65508	69640	66281	66184	63377
Urban-related outlays								
(without Medicaid)	37918	44785	47047	51551	52807	48890	46858	42578
Total Federal outlays	400506	448368	490097	576674	657204	728375	805202	848483
Urban outlays as % of								
Federal outlays	11.9	12.4	12.1	11.4	10.6	9.1	8.2	7.5
% change urban-related spending	22.94	16.45	7.19	10.18	6.31	-4.82	-0.15	-4.24
% change urban spending								
(without Medicaid)	25.66	18.11	5.05	9.57	2.44	-7.42	-4.16	-9.13
Real urban outlays								
(1972 $)	32795	35346	34762	35016	34583	31469	30043	27230
% change urban outlays	7.13	7.78	-1.65	0.73	-1.24	-9.00	-4.53	-9.36
Real urban outlays								
(without Medicare)	26107	28540	27508	27556	26224	23212	21270	18293
% change real urban outlays								
(without Medicaid)	17.83	9.32	-3.62	0.17	-4.83	-11.49	-8.37	-14.00

[a] No outlays

[b] Less than $500,000.

[c] Miscellaneous appropriations represent the remaining outlays of the model cities program and the community development training and urban fellowship programs. Model cities was terminated in 1975 and the others in 1973.

[d] Dollar amounts for the Federal highway administration's urbanized areas program represent obligations rather than outlays. The *Budget Appendix* does not supply information on outlays at that level of the program.

[e] Urban-related outlays may exceed total outlays for an agency due to additional revenue from other sources. In 1982 and 1984, loan repayments from the disaster loan fund created additional revenue which reduced total outlays.

[f] The increase in 1980 CSA spending results from the energy assistance program which represented $1,160,000 in obligations.

[g] Education outlays are combined in order to simplify the many organizational changes which took place between the Departments of Health, Education and Welfare and Education. Two programs were included in FY 1977 to 1980: elementary and secondary education and emergency school aid. Emergency school aid became the equal educational opportunities program in 1980. The program structure changed in FY 1981 and three new programs replaced the two existing ones. From FY1981 to 1984, compensatory education for the disadvantaged, special programs and populations, and bilingual education have been included in the education category.

[h] The dollar amounts for the health services administration, grants to the states for Medicaid, assistance payments program, and grants for social and child welfare services represent obligations rather than outlays.

[i] Youth programs are included in employment and training assistance.

Source: *US Budget Appendix* (annual). Calculated and elaborated by Glickman (see note 69)

seem to be the cornerstone of this policy, thus favoring social groups and localities that benefit from selective affluence, in a context in which income inequality in the US is increasing substantially, as shown in chapter 4.

Glickman has tried to apply to the 1981–4 data a methodology similar to
that used by Vernez to analyze the spatial impact of Federal spending in the
1970–6 period. Table 5.5 shows some limited calculations for concentration
ratios of Federal spending by ecological characteristics in 1981–4.

We can easily appreciate that practically all urban-welfare-related
expenses, with the exception of the Small Business Administration, are much
more heavily concentrated in central cities than in suburbs; and we have seen
that these programs are the ones that have been cut. Central cities, then, have
suffered proportionally more than suburbs from the shrinkage of the urban
welfare state. Also, although the trends here are somewhat less clear, small
cities have generally higher concentration ratios for most programs, implying
that medium-sized and large cities with their greater social problems have
suffered more also from the cutbacks. Finally, although we do not have
concentration ratios for 1981–84 for the remaining variables, it may be
assumed that the general trends are probably very similar to those calculated
by Vernez for 1970–6. If this were the case, we could observe the relationship
between the variation of Federal spending by program in 1981–4 and the
concentration rate of each program in each type of locality, as presented in
table 5.5.

From these observations we can conclude, in general terms, that programs
having suffered substantial cutbacks in 1981–4 are concentrated more than
proportionally in low-income cities (with the exception of mass transit), in
high-hardship cities (with the exception of vocational education and work-
incentive programs) and in declining cities (with the same exceptions). The
shrinkage of the welfare state tends to be spatially specific: the harder-hit a
type of locality, the more likely it is to receive the burden of budget cuts. On
the contrary, booming defense spending in 1981–4, and particularly procurement, is associated with suburbs rather than with central cities; with small and
medium-sized cities; with high-income, rapidly growing, low unemploy
ment, low-hardship localities.

There is undoubtedly a process of spatial polarization that stems from the
crisis of the urban welfare state and is being spearheaded by the rise of the
new warfare state. Is this a short-term trend or the beginning of a broader
development? To answer this question it will be necessary first to examine the
spatial consequences of defense policy, under the conditions generated by
technological change.

High Technology, Industrial Policy, and the Warfare State

The current technological revolution poses a fundamental challenge to the
warfare state. If it fails to master the formidable discoveries occurring at an

Table 5.5 Concentration ratios for selected programs by city type

Program	Real % outlay change, 1981–4	All cities	Low-income	High-income	Declining	Slow-growing	Rapidly growing
State and local fiscal assistance	−11.5	1.00	1.08	0.92	1.04	0.87	0.99
Employment and training (CETA)	−47.6	2.41	1.22	0.78	0.99	0.94	1.18
Community development block grants	−24.8	1.91	1.41	0.60	1.03	0.92	0.94
Urban mass transit assistance	−21.9	2.24	0.75	1.23	1.35	0.31	0.13
Vocational education	−7.4	2.39	1.19	0.81	0.84	1.04	2.32
Work incentive program (WIN)	−93.9	1.82	1.08	0.91	0.98	1.01	1.04
Small business administration	−88.2	1.50	1.06	0.93	0.96	1.04	1.18
Defense	+37.0		0.95	1.04	0.78	1.45	1.42
Construction	+53.9	0.58	0.61	1.62	0.38	1.42	5.44
Payroll	+11.4	–	1.23	0.78	0.63	1.68	1.98
Procurement	+61.7	–	0.80	1.19	0.86	1.32	1.05

Explanatory note: Columns 1 and 2 represent per capita income in 1970. Low-income cities are defined by per capita income less than or equal to $3.304; high-income cities have per capita income greater than $3,304. Columns 3, 4, and 5 are defined by population growth between 1970 and 1975; declining cities exhibited negative growth, slow growth cities grew by less than 15% over the period, and rapid growth cities grew by greater than 15%. Columns 6 and 7 define 'low' and 'high' unemployment by a 1976 unemployment rate of less than, or greater than or equal to 8.9%, respectively. Columns 8 and 9 are based on a hardship index of 100. Finally, city size is defined by cities with populations of less than 100,000 for small cities. 100,000–300,000 for medium cities, and greater than 300,000 for large cities.
Calculated and elaborated by Glickman (see note 69)

Low-unemployment	High-unemployment	Low-hardship	High hardship	Small	Medium	Large	Central	Suburbs
0.90	1.05	0.79	1.17	0.76	0.96	1.10	1.08	0.63
1.10	0.93	0.97	1.01	0.65	1.59	0.87	1.13	0.42
1.01	0.99	0.81	1.14	0.89	1.45	0.84	1.04	0.80
0.28	1.41	0.26	1.53	0.09	0.60	1.51	1.18	0.17
1.76	0.56	1.26	0.72	0.87	2.19	0.54	1.19	0.13
1.51	0.70	0.99	0.94	0.68	2.07	0.66	1.19	0.13
1.02	0.98	0.91	1.07	0.69	1.11		1.06	1.07
1.18	0.89	1.33	0.72	1.12	1.27	0.83	0.80	1.48
1.96	0.44	1.72	0.40	0.78	0.70	1.21	1.15	0.33
1.39	0.77	1.31	0.73	0.87	1.31	0.91	1.06	0.70
1.06	0.96	1.34	0.71	1.26	1.26	0.78	0.78	1.93

Source: Concentration ratios from Vernez (see footnote 48). Changes in budget outlays are computed from *Special Analyses, the Budget of the United States Government.* Fiscal Years 1983 and 1984. Defense outlays are computed from *The Budget of the United States Government*, fiscal years 1983 and 1984. Calculated and elaborated by Glickman (see note 69)

ever-accelerating pace, its weaponry will become obsolete. As a result, political and diplomatic means would gain the preference as the predominant form of managing international crises, thus undermining the main rationale supporting the institutions of the warfare state. On the contrary, if the state succeeds in finding and utilizing new information technologies, it could dramatically improve its power by gaining a performance edge over its rivals, and by making possible flexible uses of military force adapted to a diversity of geopolitical situations. In sum, its global reach could be decentralized and specifically targeted. The power of technology could substantially enhance the technology of power.[72]

To be sure, the military use of technology has generally been a driving force in the development and application of scientific discoveries, although the case of Japan in the past twenty years shows that there is no universal rule in this matter.[73] In the US, World War II brought together a number of scientific breakthroughs that developed into major applications in such areas as aircraft design, jet propulsion, electronics, communications, and nuclear power. The global arms race triggered off by the cold war stimulated the frantic search for a technological lead that would enable military supremacy to be attained.[74] Given the national priority accorded to such programs, resources were mobilized toward this goal with relative ease, transforming the US into what Daniel Bell calls a "mobilized polity," that is, "a society in which the major resources of the country are concentrated on a few specific objectives defined by the Government."[75] In Bell's words: "In one sense . . . military technology has supplanted the 'mode of production' in Marx's use of the term, as a major determinant of social structure."[76] Between 1945 and 1990, the US will have spent on defense about $3.7 trillion (in constant 1972 dollars),[77] that is, enough to buy everything in America, with the exception of land. Defense spending averaged about 7 percent of US GNP per year.[78] To some extent, "military Keynesianism" has been repeatedly used to stimulate the market during the downturn of the business cycle, particularly during the Reagan administration: defense spending is credited *directly* with at least 0.5 percent of GNP growth and 20 percent of employment gains during the 1982–4 recovery.[79]

Between 1981 and 1985 defense outlays increased by 60 percent and Defense Department spending more than doubled in real terms, the annual increase jumping from 2.8 percent during the Carter administration to an average of about 7.5 percent under the Reagan administration.[80] In the mid-1980s, Defense accounted for, on average, about one-third of the annual Federal budget, a total in excess of $300 billion. In addition to its role in boosting the economy, defense spending is particularly stimulating for US manufacturing in the short term, because, as Ann Markusen has pointed out, the Defense Department requires most of the production to take place in the US, slowing down the tendency toward offshoring by US companies.[81]

The role of defense is particularly important in research, with an emphasis on information technologies. In the mid-1980s, the Department of Defense accounted for about 60 percent of the total research budget of the Federal government. This proportion increased to 90 percent of Federal spending for applied research in electrical engineering, and to 88 percent of applied research in computer sciences.[82] The role of the Defense Department has continued to expand during the 1980s, particularly strongly in the field of research and technological development as a result of the priority accorded to the SDI Program, so that by 1988 the Defense Department accounted for over 70 percent of the Federal R&D Budget.[83] This emphasis on the connection between defense and high technology has already had dramatic effects in the labor market for engineers and scientists. In 1986, estimates from the Congressional Budget Office indicated that the Department of Defense or defense-related industries employed 47 percent of all aeronautical engineers in the US, 30.3 percent of the mathematicians, 24.4 percent of the physicists, 18.3 percent of the electrical engineers, 15.7 percent of the industrial and mechanical technicians, and 28 percent of the total number of science and engineering graduates. However, in 1987–8 defense appropriations were slowed down by political opposition and budgetary constraints, making it unlikely that such dramatic rates of growth in defense spending would continue in the post-Reagan era. Nevertheless, the strong link between high-technology-induced growth and defense policy will remain. The relative containment of defense spending (at a level of about 30 percent of the Federal budget) will feed back into the restructuring of the defense budget itself. There will be lower allocations of funds to personnel, administration, and traditional military procurement, while investment in the design, production, and maintenance of technologically sophisticated weapons systems will be stepped up. Thus, in all likelihood, the new warfare state, with its core in high-technology warfare systems – both strategic and tactical – will continue to expand even in a period of fiscal austerity that will slow down defense spending.

We should not conclude that defense spending and military-oriented research are the result of policies designed to favor economic growth. In fact, most of the existing evidence points to the opposite conclusion: that the predominance of defense interests in economic policies and research programs actually undermines American economic competitiveness and leads technological innovation into commercial dead-ends, contributing to America's economic decline.[84] Leontieff and Duchin have shown that military expenditures are less expansionary than other public expenditures;[85] Gold, Paine, and Shields argue that military expenditures create fewer jobs that other forms of investment;[86] Robert Reich thinks that excessive emphasis on defense spending is at the root of the increasing trade gap with Japan and western Europe;[87] Ann Markusen, while acknowledging the short-term stimulant effect of defense spending, insists on its slow diffusion in the economy and, above all, opposes its racist, sexist biases, and its distorting impacts on regional development;[88] Lloyd J. Dumas shows the limits and deformations inherent in university research on Pentagon-related contracts;[89] David Noble argues that excessive military specification has hampered US technological development, citing as an example the case of numerical machine tools, a key new technology in which the Japanese took over most of the commercial market because of the narrow definition of objectives when the technology was first developed in the US under contract with the Defense Department;[90] Mary Kaldor even objects to the military effectiveness of the "baroque arsenal" produced under the new technological conditions, with "overdeveloped" and unnecessarily sophisticated new weapons.[91] In a more balanced analysis, Jay Stowsky[92] examines different key examples of inter-actions between defense and industry in developing new technologies, to conclude that

the creation of military–industrial firms, of a military-dependent and uncompetitive industry structure, is aided by military programs that focus on the development of specific military product applications instead of promoting the general technological state-of-the-art; that draw the attention of commercial producers away from the development of technological applications consistent with the commercial market requirements of the involved industry toward esoteric, over-sophisticated military applications; that rely on sole-source contracts and cost-plus, weapons-competitive production technologies instead of promoting competitive product development and efficient, generalizable production technologies; that promote small-batch, "one-of-a-kind" custom production instead of mass production or flexible sophistication aimed at creating economies of scale and scope; that disrupt established technological trajectories and investment patterns in mature industries or that skew the techno-logical development trajectory of brand-new industries by pointing them in a single, defense-oriented direction; that routinely reward established suppliers over small, innovative start-ups; that restrict the diffusion of military-sponsored advances through technological oversophistication or direct export and publication controls; and that do all or most of these things in the face of parallel, commercially-oriented R&D projects sponsored by foreign competitors and aimed explicitly at advancing the commercial state-of-the-art over the same time span as the military program.

The problem, then, is how to explain the decisive role of the Defense Department in Federal spending and research policy in spite of its poor contribution to economic performance.[93] The most popular explanation of this trend is the influence of the military–industrial complex,[94] a hypothesis to which President Eisenhower himself contributed when he stated in his 1961 farewell address that "The Military Establishment, not productive of itself, necessarily must feed on the energy, productivity and brain power of the country, and if it takes too much, our total strength declines."[95] Some more sophisticated analyses add to the direct influence of the defense industry the political influence of the defense lobby, that is the several dozen Congressmen and Senators whose constituencies are major recipients of defense spending.[96] Both arguments are true, but neither is sufficient as an explanation. Both implicitly assume a very primitive, almost conspiratorial, theory of the state. State policies and decisions result from the interplay of contradictory social, cultural, and economic interests. But, above all, they result from political decisions, that is, strategies aimed at holding power, either as a means or as a goal. This is particularly true for the state of a major nation with global responsibilities. Thus, the fundamental goal of defense policy, regardless of its economic impact, is the strengthening of US national security, as perceived by its elected leaders. As former Secretary of Defense Caspar Weinberger has said: "Even if achieving the security needed for [peace with freedom] meant some dislocation in the economy – and it does not today – who would suggest any other course?"[97] All other elements in the formation of defense policy, including economic growth and job creation, political clientelism toward some regions, concessions to the defense lobby, the reinforcement of military bureaucracy – all are important, yet all remain subordinate to the primary objective of achieving global supremacy. In pursuit of such supremacy, the Pentagon has been a major force in technology planning, and through the combined effect of spending and shaping technology, has constituted the only systemic industrial policy in the US, as a by-product of its political goals.[98] The evidence and analyses on the relationship between defense, technology, and economic growth may be summarized as follows:

(1) Defense capabilities depend upon technological excellence. Therefore, the Defense Department has concentrated its efforts in R&D in a number of key areas, particularly in aerospace and information technologies.
(2) In so doing, the Pentagon has guided and stimulated technological development, and created huge markets on which hundreds of companies have prospered, some of them among the biggest and most successful in US industry. At the same time, a military–industrial complex, personally and politically linked to the defense-related industrial bonanza, has flourished, creating powerful vested interests in the continuation of such policies.
(3) Nevertheless, the Defense Department's goals are fundamentally to ensure military performance and to reinforce its own bureaucratic power within the state. Personal rewards, economic success, or commercial spin-offs are only by-products of a fundamental political strategy to develop technology in the first instance for its military use.

It is true, then, that defense policy is the major, if implicit, industrial policy in the US; that its core lies in its connection with high-technology industries; that this industrial policy is not the best possible policy, given the short-sightedness of its perspective, its socially undesirable effects, and its poor performance in promoting commercial applications of key technologies; yet that, because the ultimate goals of defense policy are not economic or scientific, but political, defense-oriented industrial technological growth has been, and will most likely continue to be, a fundamental line of development for the US economy, actually constituting the core of high-technology research and manufacturing in the US.

The relationship between defense and the electronics industry was particularly close in the first stage of development of the industry, during the 1950s.[99] Around 1960, government markets represented 90 percent of the US semiconductors market.[100] However, once commercial development of electronic products had taken place, with the entry into the market of new, innovative companies, the proportion plummetted down to about 10 percent in the late 1970s. Indeed, some major discoveries, such as that of the microprocessor by Ted Hoff at Intel in 1971, were totally independent of military support. The trend, however, was once more reversed during the 1980s, and this is what is qualitatively new about the Reagan administration's defense build-up. In quantitative terms, this administration's policy did not depart dramatically from former levels of defense spending when calculated as a percentage of GNP. Even compared with the two previous build-ups, during the Korean and Vietnam wars (see table 5.6), Reagan's defense spending was not significantly higher in relative terms. What was really fundamentally different about policy under Reagan was the concentration of defense spending in military procurement, and its emphasis on new technologies and new weapons systems. In her analysis of the relationship between defense and high-technology industries, whose data are shown in table 5.7, Ann Markusen found that "of the top twenty defense manufacturing sectors, only ship-building and non-ferrous foundries were not high tech. In addition, the military oriented sectors in table [5.7] accounted for 47 percent of all high-tech manufacturing jobs in the 1977 Census of Manufacturers, or approximately 2.25 million jobs. By 1984, given the recent build-up, they undoubtedly account for an even higher percentage."[101]

Table 5.7 shows that the projected defense output growth for computers in the 1982–7 period was 141 percent, well above the average for other defense sectors. Also, the Pentagon has involved itself more deeply in the planning of research on strategic technologies. The Defense Advanced Research Project Agency (DARPA), famed for its managerial flexibility and its bold understanding of scientific research,[102] has launched a number of ambitious programs, connecting leading universities and high-technology companies in defense-targeted research programs, among them, the "Very High Speed Integrated Circuits" program (VHSIC), and the Strategic Computing Initiative (SCI). VHSIC aims at developing advanced custom chips of 1.25 micron and then sub-micron size, through cooperation between researchers and companies coordinated by DARPA.[103] Although Brueckner and Borrus have questioned the commercial value of this program,[104] it does represent a major breakthrough in technological planning in the US. Similarly, the Strategic Computing Initiative aims to achieve a quantum leap in artificial intelligence and development of parallel computer architectures, by distributing research funds and potential markets among different firms and research organizations.[105] In this case, DARPA plays two roles simultaneously: that of the venture capitalist and that of the client setting up product specifications. Here too, criticisms have been levelled against the excessively specialized character of the technologies being developed.[106] Yet, the initiative represents a further step in computer software research and in the guidance of such research by military programs. Finally, in 1987 the Defense Department mobilized its political and financial resources to help major electronics corporations set up a large research facility concentrating on manufacturing technology for semiconductors, a critical area in which the Japanese have taken the lead over the US. Because of the national security implications of this, with the possibility of the US becoming dependent upon Japanese chips in the near future, the Defense Department sponsored the creation of an applied research consortium, SEMATECH, to be located in Austin, Texas. Semiconductors manufacturers supported the initiative enthusiastically despite the significant departure it represented from their libertarian ideas about the undesirability of government interference.[107]

It is clear, then, that the acceleration of the technological revolution, and its particular emphasis on information technologies, represents a qualitatively different stage in the close interaction among the military, technological change, and industrial development. The defense policy of the Reagan administration had in fact three different components: first, and most publicized, a particularly strong defense commitment, linked to Reagan's conservative ideology and explicitly presented to the American public; secondly, a turnaround in US foreign policy toward a more assertive role in the world after the relative decline of US hegemony in the 1970s; thirdly, and perhaps the most lasting element, a renewed effort to use technology as a decisive tool to translate the scientific leadership of the US in the field of in-formation technologies into military superiority. This defense policy is not confined to the ideology and politics of the Reagan administration: in its

Table 5.6   Three US military build-ups: Korean War, Vietnam War, and Reagan

	Change in national defense budget share (%)	Change in military burden (% GNP)	Increase in defense budget outlays ($ bn; 1972 $)
Korean War (1950–3)	29.1–65.6	4.7–13.8	29.7–96.6
Vietnam War (1965–8)	40.1–44.0	7.2– 9.5	69.3–101.7
Reagan (1981–7)	23.2–32.6	5.2– 7.4	71.3–118.9

Source: Office of the Assistant Secretary of Defense (Comptroller), *National Defense Budget Estimates for Fiscal Year 1983*, tables 7.8 and 7.2. Reagan projections from Executive Office of the President, Office of Management and Budget, *Budget of the United States Government, Fiscal Year 1985*, pp. 2–11, 9–61. Defense spending is equivalent to national defense function budget outlays. Compiled by Mosley (see note 23).

Table 5.7 Major Defense Industrial Base Sectors, Employment and Defense Shares

SIC	Industry	Employment (000)		% change 1977-82	Defense 1982 BIE[a]	Defense share 1983 DEIMS[a]	Output growth[b]
		1977	1982				
3721	Aircraft	222.8	286.6	+29	270	65	+59
3761	Missiles	93.9	99.6	+6	68	65	+64
3724	Aircraft engine	106.3	128.6	+21	54	64	+33
3764	Missile propulsion	17.0	25.2	+48	54	64	+33
3728	Aircraft parts	101.9	146.1	+43	41	57	+35
3769	Missile parts	10.9	20.5	+88	41	57	+35
3662	Radio, TV, communications equipment	333.0	471.3	+42	58	61	+54
3811	Engineering and scientific institutions	42.2	43.1	+2	34	49	+60
3674	Semiconductors	114.0	164.5	+44	13	23	+51
3675-9	Other electronic devices	228.0	315.8	+39	17	29	+49
3822	Measuring devices	197.0	246.0	+20	n.a	35	n.a
3883	Optical instruments	29.9	50.6	+69	28	17	+38
3489	Ordnance	19.0	27.4	+44	78	100	+35
3731	Shipbuilding	176.4	168.5	-5	62	75	+24
3483	Ammunition (excl. small arms)	20.6	23.3	+13	91	98	+56
2892	Explosives	11.5	11.9	+3	34	44	+59
3795	Tanks	12.1	18.0	+49	94	99	+47
3484	Small arms	17.5	17.5	0	14	66	-43
3482	Small arms ammunition	12.2	10.1	-17	25	n.a.	+130
3573	Computers	193.7	339.6	+75	7	n.a.	+141

Sources:
[a] Shutt, 1984. From the Department of Defense. DEIMS (Defense Economic Impact Monitoring System), using an input-output model from DRI.

[b] Henry, 1983. From Bureau of Industrial Economics, Department of Commerce, input-output model. These appear to be lower than the following column because of different methods of incorporating foreign sales. Both chart indirect as well as direct demand impacts. Compiled by Markusen (see note 81).

essential aspects it represents the emergence of the new warfare state, reassessing its technological foundations. The Strategic Defense Initiative (SDI) appears to be the most ambitious development along these lines, and the clearest example of the close and politically determined relationship between new technologies and the warfare state. Because of the importance of this program in the present analysis, it will be examined here in some detail. By using "Star Wars" as a case study, we will try to gain a better understanding of the social logic of the new defense policy, its relationship to high technology, and its implications for the economic and spatial restructuring of the United States.

The New Technological Frontier of the Warfare State: The "Star Wars" Program. A Case Study

Introduction

Much has been written, and even more speculated, on the importance of the Strategic Defense Initiative (SDI – popularly known as "Star Wars"), the military–technological program undertaken by the Reagan administration in 1983.[108] Its significance can hardly be overestimated. However impossible it is to achieve its explicit goal (an efficient shield against attacking ICBMs), it is likely to alter the military–political balance of power in the world; if pursued, it would constitute one of the most formidable technological programs in humankind's history, surpassing the ambitions and dimensions of the Manhattan project or the Apollo program. Furthermore, I would argue that it represents a qualitatively new relationship between the dynamics of the state, technological innovation, and economic growth. Thus, its significance goes well beyond its actual implementation. It could well happen that the new administration would limit the scope of SDI as a specific program; but if my analysis is correct, what will probably last for the forseeable future is an increasingly close relationship between the warfare state and the cutting edge of technological development. Advances in information technology, laser, and new materials, and their application to military strategy will be decisive in world power relationships in years to come. Given the political priority of military-oriented technological policies, what SDI truly represents is not so much a strategic doctrine (which could prove unfeasible) as a new organizational–technological formula aimed at harnessing technology and high-technology industry for the assertion of American power in the world against growing challenges to it.

Many of the technologies targeted by SDI were already under development in different sectors of the American defense research complex. What SDI did was to organize these technologies into a system, and to provide political support and greater budgetary resources for their development, within a co-ordinated program directed and implemented by a new, specialized unit within the Pentagon: the SDI Office (SDIO), more flexible and more autonomous than any other bureaucratic unit of the defense establishment. Such a concerted effort is indeed producing significant changes in the defense industry and in research policy in the United States. It also contributes to the emerging shape of the new urban and regional structure, in ways that will be explored in the next section of this chapter.

By focusing on the origins, development, and implications of SDI, and trying to understand its spatial dimension, we are in fact addressing a broader issue: the political determination of the uses to which new technologies are being put in the production of a new socio-economic organization. To present this analysis in a systematic form, I will proceed step by step: first, I will try to substantiate my hypothesis according to which, SDI is, above anything else, a political strategy: secondly, I will examine its actual military and organizational content as it relates to basic technological choices; thirdly, I will examine the industrial policy component of SDI, and its likely impact on the economy; and finally, I will elaborate on the urban and regional dimension of the political–military–technological–economic processes spearheaded and articulated by SDI. (This last analysis will be presented in the next section of this chapter.)

SDI and the State

When, on 23 March 1983, President Reagan wished upon a star, aiming at the obsolescence of strategic nuclear weapons through revolutionary technologies, he may have surprised observers, and even many in the Pentagon; yet he was giving voice to a deliberate, well grounded political strategy that responded to at least six layers of factors, all of them fundamental elements in the dynamics of the modern global state.[109]

First of all, the major technological revolution through which we are living was to become the key factor in determining world power. Of course, technology has always been closely connected to the state and to the military. Yet with the exception of the short period when the US had the monopoly on the A-bomb, this is the first time in recent history in which technological superiority becomes the central factor in achieving military, and thus political, supremacy. The US is aiming at a quantum leap in its warfare capabilities, taking on the Soviet Union in the one area in which the latter's ability to compete is seriously undermined by the very characteristics of its social system: the development of information technologies. By rendering strategic weapons less effective, and by ensuring a technological edge in greatly strengthened armed forces, the US could succeed in stalling the deterioration of its power in the aftermath of the Vietnam War and as a consequence of the Soviet achievement of parity in strategic nuclear terms.[110] New technologies, with all their implications in terms of human, institutional, and economic capabilities to sustain a scientific arms race, became the corner-stone of state power in an increasingly interdependent planet.

Secondly, the array of new technologies envisaged by SDI are not confined to strategic nuclear weapons; they will have a substantial impact on conventional weapons. It is debatable whether SDI, as programmed, is indeed a non-nuclear program (or a 90 percent nuclear-free program) as its advocates claim. But it does represent a shift away from a nuclear-based, strategically oriented military strategy to technologically advanced "smart weapons," susceptible of being used in conventional, non-nuclear warfare. In this sense, it represents the development of the new line of military thinking that emerged after the Vietnam War,[111] when the greatest military power in the world found its ability to react to perceived aggressions or encroachment on its sphere of influence paralyzed because of the combination of two factors: on the one hand, Soviet nuclear power would deter any crisis of major proportions that could risk world peace (the reciprocal argument is, of course, also true); and on the other hand, direct American involvement in military conflicts had become too costly, and generally unacceptable to the American public after the unforgettable tragedy of Vietnam, as demonstrated by strong opposition to direct intervention in Central America. Under these circum-stances, new options were sought to enable American power to exercise itself. Symbolic actions, such as that in Grenada, were effective, but limited. Covert operations, and open support for counter-insurgency (in El Salvador), or to insurgency (the Contras in Nicaragua; Unita in Angola) could be instru-mental in the application of pressure, but could not by themselves deal with major regional military conflicts. US forces still needed the means to intervene "surgically" in any area of the world that might be required; if for no other reason, then to be able to make credible threats that could reinforce the US position in the lower levels of conflict, without necessarily leading to escalation. It is within this perspective that new technologies, and particularly communications, electronics, and a new generation of aircraft armed with precision guided weapons, play a decisive role. To some extent, new technologies are making conventional warfare possible again, at low cost for the holder of superior technology. Advances in microelectronics and computing are required not only to counter Soviet ICBMs, but to overcome the threat posed by Soviet SA-7s or French Exocets in the hands of a hostile Third World army. By assuring its technological superiority, the US military would once more be able to protect the interests of the western world, at a cost politically acceptable to the American public. A striking illustration of this new, "surgical" strategy for military intervention on the basis of advanced conventional weapons was the bombing of Qadhafi's residence in Tripoli, in retaliation for his support of international terrorism. Several observers have pointed to the fact that the actual objective of the raid was to kill the Libyan leader with a high-precision guided bomb fired from a speeding jet. The strategy worked only approximately: the bomb hit the children's room.

The main fact to retain from this analysis is that SDI-induced military technologies are not confined to this illusion of an anti-ballistic shield. They represent a fundamental breakthrough in warfare, mainly because of the precision with which they can be applied, as well as their flexibility in handling. These new military technologies could allow for a greater adaptation of the use of force to the specific conditions under which a global power has to operate at different moments and in different areas, thus linking the military instrument to the new political–military strategy of restrained, but continuous, intervention in the global arena. In this sense, we can use the term of the warfare state literally, because current technological programs are aimed, fundamentally, at returning to the state its warfare capabilities.

In the third place, the political dimension of SDI is not limited to the military expression of state power; it also refers to the search for legitimacy, in one of the most paradoxical twists of world politics in the last decade. SDI was, at least in its origins, a political response from the Reagan administration to the growing strength of the peace movement worldwide, and in the US in particular.[112] Accepting the ideals of eternal peace and of permanent banning of nuclear weapons, it provided a technological solution to the problem that, unlike political negotiations between two sides, relied solely on America's ingenuity and resources. The utopian tone of the White House's proclamations was in quest of new legitimacy among the peace-conscious, anti-nuclear "yuppie" voters, who are becoming the new political mainstream in US elections. Both Reagan himself and the Pentagon insisted on the non-nuclear character of the program, going as far as not to adopt some of the technical proposals made by Edward Teller so as visibly not to comply with his pro-nuclear bias. In spite of later developments that seem to accept a "minor" nuclear component in the program, SDI's officials have systematically emphasized its defensive and non-nuclear characteristics, thus giving in, at least apparently, to the universal demands for peace and nuclear disarmament. The strategy seemed to work, at least initially in the US: public opinion polls in 1984–6 showed *simultaneously* support for SDI and a majority opinion for nuclear disarmament.[113]

Aside from the real purpose of the program, SDI's ideological appeal consists in playing on a very old and deep-rooted American utopian faith in the solution of all problems through a technological fix. Belief in science and technology is the religion of the informational age. Playing powerful roles in terms of both the coercive capacity and the ideological legitimacy of the state, "Star Wars" reveals itself as an attempt at establishing political hegemony on new historical ground.

In 1987 the Reagan administration seized the opportunity offered by greater openness in Soviet policy under Gorbachev and, in spite of all its rhetoric, engaged in nuclear arms reductions agreements with the Soviet Union of historic significance. At the same time, it maintained its commitment to SDI, a commitment that became non-negotiable in the summit meetings. The logic underlying this position is that the nuclear arms race does not allow the US to gain the strategic advantage over the Soviet Union, is militarily risky and politically unpopular; while on the other hand, American technological superiority could gain the upper hand over the USSR's military power in the long term through a gradual process of reducing to obsolescence Soviet military equipment. This is precisely why the Soviet Union is so fearful of "Star Wars," and is also why Pentagon strategists will continue to give the highest priority to the technological weapons race.

The analysis of SDI presented up to this point has focused on the long-term, structurally determined tendencies of the American state, as they express the interests of the social system in which it is rooted. Yet state policies are also the result of the strategies of individual actors defending their own specific interests on the basis of their influence in the power networks to which they have access. It is this interplay between the historical interests of the system and the particular interests of powerful individual actors that generates the complexity of any particular political process, such as that leading to the formulation and implementation of SDI. The fourth factor to be taken into consideration, then, is the influence of the defense lobby, or the military–industrial complex, as it is labeled, in US politics.[114] It is unquestionable that defense contracts, which looked like running out of steam once the last programs (the MX missile, the Midgetman missile, the B-1 bomber) were wound up or cancelled, found in SDI a new driving force with the political strength to foster the defense build-up and, following on down the line, to renew the entire military hardware through induced technological obsolescence. As the spearhead of the new advance in defense procurement, "Star Wars" propels some of the most powerful companies into hyperactivity. According to Seymour Melman, by 1980, for every $100 of capital investment in the civilian economy, the US put $38 into the military. In 1988 the same ratio could be 100:87.[115] Many of the defense contracts are concentrated in only a few companies, with long-established ties to the navy, army, and air force, and this pattern seems to be reproduced in the case of "Star Wars." While the first $2 billion in research contracts for "Star Wars" was spread among 1,500 companies, the top ten "Star Wars" contracts accounted for 60 percent of the funds distribution up to 1985.[116] In 1987, as table 5.8 shows, it is generally the same large companies who specialize in the production of missiles, aircraft, and related electronic equipment, with the addition of the major national laboratories. True, the research money involved is relatively small by Pentagon standards: about $10 billion in 1984–7, maybe $39 billion in 1988–92 (see table 5.9);[117] but should the system come to be deployed, it would be the most expensive military program in history (and, therefore, the largest market ever); estimates widely vary for figures between $400 billion and $1.6 trillion, since no one really knows what such a system would involve. In any event, what is certain is the gigantic scale of such military markets, and their potential spin-offs in a wide range of industries: electronics, materials,

Table 5.8   Top 20 SDI contractors (March 1987)

Rank	Organization	Contracts awarded ($m)
1	Lockheed	1,024
2	General Motors (Hughes Aircraft)	734
3	TRW	567
4	Lawrence Livermore Lab	552
5	McDonnell Douglas	485
6	Boeing	475
7	EG&G	468
8	Los Alamos Lab	458
9	General Electric	420
10	Rockwell International	369
11	Massachusetts Institute of Technology (MIT)	353
12	Raytheon	248
13	LTV	227
14	Fluor	198
15	Grumman	193
16	Gencorp	191
17	Teledyne	189
18	Honeywell	151
19	Martin Marietta	134
20	Textron	118

Source: Federation of American Scientists; reprinted in *High Technology Business* (December 1987). Compiled by Jay Stowsky.

nuclear reactors, weapons procurement and ordnance, etc. This is the reason why companies seek from the outset to position themselves in the research stage of the program: companies with inside knowledge of the technological options adopted for each part of the system will have a decisive advantage in securing future contracts. Given the high business stakes involved, it is not surprising that these interests have been fully mobilized to assure the success of the "Star Wars" policy. A particularly crucial effect is the influence exerted on numerous representatives whose constituencies grow ever more dependent on military-induced funding to shift from traditional manufacturing to high-technology industries. Yet, though this factor is important, it is not the only one, or even the predominant one, that explains the rise of "Star Wars." This is because the defense lobby is a permanent feature of the American political system.[118] Given the opportunity, its influence greatly expands, and it becomes a driving force in obtaining a substantial share of the Federal budget; but this opportunity is itself generated by forces and considerations that go far beyond the defense lobby, as we already stated. True, it is likely that during the Reagan administration a new political elite, with Western and Southern roots, has consolidated its position, and reinforced the access of the defense-related businesses to the higher circles of power. Yet the military–industrial complex is an old feature of the system, and there is no evidence

Table 5.9 Strategic defense Initiative budget authority ($), by types of weapons and services

	Actual					Requested					
	1984	1985	1986	1987	Total 1984–7	1988	1989	1990	1991	1992	Total 1988–92
Surveillance, acquisition, and tracking	367	546	847	911	2,671	1,493	1,859	–	–	–	
Directed energy	323	377	803	844	2,347	1,104	1,246	–	–	–	
Kinetic energy	196	256	596	729	1,777	1,075	1,200	–	–	–	
Systems analysis and battle management	83	100	211	387	781	627	787	–	–	–	
Support	23	118	230	358	729	922	1,190	–	–	–	
DoD total	992	1,397	2,687	3,229	8,305	5,221	6,282	7,400	8,400	9,800	37,103
DoE total	118	224	285	514	1,141	569	390	390	390	390	2,129
SDI total	1,110	1,621	2,972	3,743	9,446	5,790	6,672	7,790	8,790	10,190	39,232

Sources: RDT&E Programs (R-1), Department of Defense Budget for Fiscal Year 1988 and 1989, January 5, 1987. Data for FY 1989–92 from SDIO budget break-down released February 25, 1987, and Congressional Budget office, *Selected Weapons Costs From the President's 1988/1989 Program*, 2 April 1987. (Reproduced from Council on Economic Priorities, *Star Wars: The Economic Fallout* (Cambridge, Mass., Ballinger, 1988), pp. 28–9.

that defense-oriented pork-barrel politics vary very much according to the geographic or social origin of the governing elite: political decision-making is a somewhat more subtle process.

Some analysts, in fact, would argue that in this case a more important factor has been the influence of the scientific and research lobby.[119] By this, I understand an informal network of scientists and research managers that connects leading US universities, national Federal laboratories (these include 775 facilities, with total expenditures of over $15 billion per year), research branches of large companies, specialized private research firms, and Federal government agencies, particularly, though not only, the Pentagon. The most prominent institutions in this complex network are MIT's Lincoln Laboratory in Lexington, Massachusetts, the national laboratories in Livermore, California and Los Alamos, New Mexico, operated by the University of California, and the weapons-development research facility Sandia Laboratory in Albuquerque, New Mexico, initially operated also by the University of California and transferred in 1948 to ATT's management. Together these institutions probably concentrate some of the best scientific potential in the US in terms of a co-ordinated, targeted effort. DARPA, the prospective research agency of the Pentagon, has been crucial in creating bridges among the most advanced research and defense applications through generous funding, flexible procedures, and a generally good understanding of the specific dynamics of basic research.[120]

This scientific network holds tremendous power in an age in which science and technology hold the key to both military and economic superiority. It also has specific interests, namely, the enhancement of the means and resources provided by government to their ever more ambitious scientific programs, which accelerate in scope and scale with the exponential expansion of knowledge during the current technological revolution. Of course, cozy living conditions, special privileges and honors and, sometimes, participation in successful companies, are also among the rewards of the defense-connected, scientific elite. (This elite by no means encompasses the majority of the US scientific community, as widespread scientific and scholarly opposition to "Star Wars" research shows. Indeed, the majority of leading scientists in the US are opposed to "Star Wars.") The most fundamental interest of the scientific lobby, however, is to increase the organization itself, namely, to obtain indefinitely the vast resources they need to engage in activity on the new frontiers of science, in a self-reinforcing spiral of scientific discovery and military power. In the context of priorities, "Star Wars" is the dream program for the scientific lobby. Not that it represents the best way to promote research, as we have already discussed,[121] but what matters for this analysis is that development of "Star Wars" was an effective strategy to win over the US state to a renewed, massive effort in cutting-edge research in key fields of science and technology, very much in the same way that the first Soviet "Sputnik" triggered off the massive expansion of research and higher education in the US during the 1960s. Moreover, when we speak of the "scientific lobby" we are referring, mainly, to those scientists and institutions which have already been engaged in military-related research for many years, a connection that for the most prominent of them can be traced back to the Manhattan project and to work in Los Alamos, the most remarkable spin-off of which was the Lawrence Livermore Laboratory, probably the world's leading center in the design of advanced weapons.

In fact, the day-to-day story of the genesis of "Stars Wars" provides some convincing evidence on the role of the scientific lobby in inspiring the program and urging a favorable Presidential decision on it.[122] A key figure in helping to convince the President was Dr George A. Keyworth, appointed as the President's science adviser in May 1981, a post in which he served until 1985. Dr Keyworth was a nuclear physicist, closely associated with Edward Teller, the father of the H-bomb, and the founder and main supporter of the Livermore National Laboratory. Dr Teller himself appears to have played a major role in conceiving the program in its initial version, and in successfully arguing for it. As the story goes, in 1981 a group of influential scientists, industrialists, military men, and aerospace executives began to meet in Washington DC at the Heritage Foundation, a consevative "think tank." Their goal was to formulate a plan for creating a national system of defense. Among them were Dr Teller, Dr Wood, and such members of the President's "kitchen cabinet" as Joseph Coors, a beer executive; Justin Dart, a wealthy businessman, and Jacqueline Hume, an industrialist. The group's top officer was Karl R. Bendetsen, once Under Secretary of the Army, later chairman of the board of the Champion International Corporation, and a long-term member of the Hoover Institution on War, Revolution, and Peace. He had known Dr Teller, who in addition to his weapons work also held a post at Hoover, since the 1940s. The group's second-in-command was General Daniel O. Graham, now retired from the army and a former head of the Defense Intelligence Agency. All group members received security clearance enabling them to learn about and discuss secret details of new technologies and weapons.

By late 1981, dissension began to arise within the group over differing visions of how to carry out the task of space-based defense. Mr Bendetsen, Dr Teller, and the Reagan "kitchen cabinet" split off into a small group to investigate sophisticated proposals that would require much more research before being ready to apply, while General Graham and his group, known formally as High Frontier, emphasized systems that could be built primarily "off the shelf." Another factor in the split, according to General Graham, was that Dr Teller insisted on the inclusion of third-generation weapons powered by nuclear bombs. "He wanted very much to leave in the nuclear options," the General said. The split had vast implications in terms of Presidential access: Mr Bendetsen and his friends visited the White House with ease; General Graham did not.

This division went to the heart of a dispute that today haunts the Pentagon's search for a defensive shield – the rivalry between pure and applied scientists. On one side are the national laboratories and universities that carry out basic research on such directed-energy weapons as lasers and particle beams. Systems based on their results might be decades away. On the other side are contractors who want to turn dollars into demonstration projects without delay and are pushing for quick deployment of prototypes. The winners have tended to be the barons of basic research. An example can be seen at the Sandia National Laboratory, one of three facilities in the nation for the design and development of nuclear weapons. Based in Albuquerque, in 1986 it invested in a $70 million center to investigate "Star Wars" technologies. About 10 percent of the Strategic Defense Initiative's budget is devoted to the development of nuclear weapons.

The recommendation taken to the President by Mr Bendetsen, Dr Teller and their group was to start a stepped-up program of advanced research rather than trying to create a defense with "off the shelf" technology. Beyond the Teller group's role in the decision-making process, "Star Wars" largely relied on a series of research programs already underway in various laboratories, for instance, radars and computer software at the Lincoln Laboratory, lasers and supercomputers (S-1) at Livermore. The first X-ray laser, powered by a nuclear explosion, was tested as early as 14 November 1980, in the Nevada desert. "Star Wars" was the symbolic and political device that brought together a number of military research programs already underway.[123] By giving them a focus, and by linking all these military technologies to a new, articulate political strategy, it greatly expanded the resources of all the constituent programs and the power of the brains (and bodies) behind them.

At this point the key actor in the "Star Wars" saga enters: President Reagan himself. Reagan's deep personal conviction of both the need for military superiority and the route to its achievement through American-grown technology, are fundamental elements in understanding the scope, the direction, and the resources of the program.[124] In the same way that one cannot understand the French nuclear power policy, with its military dimension, without taking De Gaulle personally into account, so we need to consider Ronald Reagan's role as crucial in the formulation and development of SDI. Not only were the political elements of such a program explicitly contained in the Republican Party Electoral Platform of July 1980; Reagan's commitment to technologically based military development dates back to his period as Governor of California, and to his personal interest in the work conducted at Livermore, and especially in Teller's ideas, as early as 1967. As soon as the opportunity arose he explored the feasibility of concepts that had been hovering over the California military research establishment for many years.[125] In 1981, under the President's instruction, Caspar Weinberger asked the Pentagon's Defense Science Board to study the possibilities of anti-ICBM defense. In January 1982, Edward Teller held the first of four personal meetings with the President to advise him on the feasibility of such a program; and when Reagan announced his decision to propose research aimed at SDI, his call was aimed primarily at American scientists. The circle was closed. This time, the "great communicator" had something of historic relevance to communicate: the dream of eternal peace in a US-dominated world won over by American ingenuity that would also provide markets, jobs, and technology for the nation's industries, as well as substantial rewards for their powerful lobbies. The new warfare state would emerge as the reconstructed coalition of new social groups and old economic interests on the basis of its mastery of technology at the dawn of the informational society.

The Technological Search for a Military El Dorado

SDI is, above all, a military program. Given the media attention that has been lavished on its specific content and its evolution, it is not necessary to recall its characteristics, except when relevant to an understanding of its technological implications. We do, however, need to consider the subject that has dominated public debate concerning "Star Wars:" its feasibility.

Scientists, political leaders, and the media have battled with fury in the arguments for or against the possibility of building a non-nuclear shield.[126] The debate generally has oversimplified extremely complex technical matters that I am not competent to assess. Moreover, each time SDI scientists are forced on to the defensive, they hide behind the classified nature of the technological answers they claim to hold to the gigantic problems faced by an effective space-based defensive system. In fact, informed opinion on both sides of the debate tends to converge toward a realistic assessment of SDI possibilities in the following terms:[127]

(1) The concept of a leak-proof shield seems to be out of the question, particularly because of the difficulty in constructing the software necessary to such a system, and the impossibility of testing it. Nevertheless, taking as read the success of the program, a reasonably effective anti-ICBM system could be deployed, capable of destroying a significant proportion of attacking missiles, increasing uncertainty about the fate of their intended targets, and therefore of enhancing deterrence by achieving strategic superiority.

(2) Consequently, since defense could not completely disregard deterrence, offensive capabilities should be maintained at a significant level, and SDI would be not a defensive system, but a fundamental addition to an offensive system.

(3) Although nuclear weapons would not necessarily be an integral part of the system, a nuclear component would still be present in it, with space-based nuclear reactors as energy sources; possibly, nuclear bombs able to

generate X-ray lasers; and certainly, nuclear warheads in the case of a re-taliatory attack.

Reformulated in these terms, the feasibility of SDI is a much more open technical question. And, given the support for it existing among the defense establishment, the odds are that it will probably be pursued, in a scaled-down form, by the post-Reagan administration.

To some extent, the feasibility question that has taken the forefront of the debate about SDI in its initial stage is largely irrelevant. It was important at the outset because it mobilized public support, or at least non-hostile curiosity, around an apparently peaceful technological utopia. Once the program was underway, however, its proponents and participants became less concerned with the fulfillment of the stated ultimate goal than with the technological breakthroughs to be attained in the pursuit of it, particularly because most of these technological advances have an outstanding import-ance for conventional warfare. For instance, predominance was given to surveillance equipment, especially sophisticated sensors, satellites, and communications, in the first round of funding for SDI. These technologies are fundamental in rapid, precisely targeted strikes carried out by planes or ships in modern warfare; and this is the type of action for which US armed forces are being prepared. Thus, while most of the attention is being focused on the strategic defensive capabilities of "Star Wars," work toward the actual military objectives of the program (strategic offensive superiority, technologi-cal edge in conventional warfare) is well in hand. Witnessing this dynamism are the organizational strength of the program, its growing independence of established administrative channels, its priority in the defense budget, and the flexibility in its management procedures. The management of the SDI program is centralized in one special office within the Department of Defense with large discretionary powers in the use of its $4 billion annual budget. James Abrahamson, an air force general with recognized public relations skills, was appointed as program chief in an effort targeted at winning political support for the program. The SDI office initiates research contracts with universities, national laboratories, and private companies, on the basis of objectives and problems determined by SDI's own technical staff. Additional research for the program is convened and operated by the Department of Energy. To add to this flexibility, in 1986-7 a new SDI Institute was created in Washington, under contract from the Defense Department, to co-ordinate and plan all research and testing activities being performed in literally hundreds of technological units. A very important feature of the SDI program is its systematic effort to enlist the support of for-eign governments and foreign companies, particularly in Japan and in western Europe, offering funding, potential markets, and access to US technology in exchange for the possibility of utilizing for the purposes of SDI some of the best technological teams in each particular field.[128] SDI could be the first step in setting up a comprehensive military-oriented plan for technological development, not only in the US, but on a worldwide scale, by far surpassing the role of Japan's MITI as planner and guide of strategic research programs.

This perspective is particularly relevant when one considers the kind of technologies SDI is trying to advance. The core of the program, in the long term, concerns the development of supercomputers able to process all information at great speed, as well as the writing of adequate software, leading to major progress in artificial intelligence. In this sense, SDI could overwhelm, in both resources and scope, Japan's much-publicized "fifth generation" computing plan. A second major group of technologies centers around communication and sensor satellites, with direct implications for radar and new forms of detection and navigation. A third series of technologies aims at creating new weapons (free-electron lasers, particle-beam weapons, "smart chips," etc.) that represent qualitative breakthroughs in lasers, energy generation, and, most importantly, microelectronics. Advanced materials are also an essential component of the strategy.[129] Including space-related manufacturing and the use of solar energy to power space-based activities, SDI involves all key technologies that matter for future industrial and economic development, with the major exception of genetic engineering (and even in this field, there are also a number of little-known, classified research programs).[130] For instance optical sensors, that are crucial to SDI, are the key element in pushing robotization beyond its current primitive stage in manufacturing. The cost of global communications could be lowered by the technological spin-offs of the program; industrial applications of new forms of lasers are likely to revolutionize precision manufacturing; a new generation of "smart power chips" is in the making; and the breakthrough in artificial intelligence could finally open the era of widespread computer literacy. In sum, SDI brings together *in one system* the the most important new technologies and provides the economic and institutional support for their cumulative development. In this sense, SDI is a major technological program. I am not implying that this is the only or indeed the best way to mobilize research in all these key areas. In fact, a number of leading scientists argue that much talent is being wasted in dead-end research initiatives that are of only marginal interest for the advancement of knowledge, because of their specific military purpose.[131] Yet the fact that an alternative research program could yield better results does not change the basic fact that SDI, regardless of its morality, and in spite of its shortcomings, is a technological program on the grand scale. As the Spanish conquerors explored and colonized the entire American continent in their futile search for the treasures of El Dorado, "Star Wars" scientists and planners are dramatically expanding technological innovation, and framing it into specific applications, while pursuing the military Grail set up for them as a mobilizing goal.

SDI as Industrial Policy

Because of the decisive role of high technology in economic development, SDI as a technological program could become one of the agenda-setting instruments for America's industrial policy.[132] Projected funding for SDI-related R&D is estimated to be about $70 billion for the period 1984–93.[133] But, as stated above, the really important matter concerns the capacity of the first contractors to position themselves favorably for the huge potential offered by the contracts that will follow the research stage, either to deploy an ABM system or to develop the new generation of conventional weapons, or both.

The main beneficiaries of SDI contracts are the major traditional defense contractors in aerospace, missiles, communications, and electronics, as shown in table 5.8. Thus, SDI reforged the close links between high-technology industries and military programs, after their gradual disassociation during the 1970s. There is, however, a fundamental difference from the situation of the 1950s and early 1960s, when high technology was closer than ever to defense markets: namely, that while in the earlier period high-technology industries constituted a very small proportion of total manufacturing, they now represent its most significant component, and the element which determines the overall competitiveness of the US economy. SDI is therefore in a position to guide and frame industrial policy overall.

The influence of SDI has extended far beyond the traditional defense procurement activities. The program has created a large market for information-processing and research firms, which represent the cutting edge of a new form of industrial production in the informational economy.[134] These companies specialize in computer simulations, system analyses, weapons performance assessment, and so on, and include Kaman Corp. (Bloomfield, Connecticut), Rand (Santa Monica, California), SRI (Stanford, California), Mission Research and General Research (both at Santa Barbara, California), Sparta, Inc., and the most prominent in this category, Science Applications International (SAIC), of La Jolla, California. SAIC is an example of the new type of military informational industry fostered by SDI. Its 5,700 workers produce only technical and strategic studies, for an annual revenue of $420 million in 1984, of which 90 percent came from US government contracts. In fact, SAIC was itself very much involved in formulating some of the initial concepts of SDI, beginning in 1981. Its board of directors is an embodiment of the intimate connections among the defense establishment, the defense industry, the scientific community, and the intelligence agencies. It includes former Defense Secretary Melvin R. Laird; former chief of the National Security Agency Admiral Robert R. Inman; former Under Secretary of State Lucy W. Benson; MIT's Provost John M. Deutch; General Welch, formerly with the National Security Agency; and Donald A. Hicks, from Northrop's Corporation, who subsequently resigned from SAIC to become the Pentagon's research director. This company, boasting some of the most sophisticated experts both in technology and in security analysis, is representative of the new breed of defense industry that is being bred by SDI.

Another major new development in information industries directly linked to SDI is the Pentagon's growing role in generating new software.[135] Particularly important here is the creation and diffusion of the ADA language, that allows different software systems to communicate. Tens of thousands of advanced software companies are now being directly funded by the SDI office. In addition, the Defense Department established a new office to provide venture capital for high-technology start-up firms prepared to work in areas of interest to SDI. It is estimated that such SDI funding will account for about 20 percent of all high-tech venture capital in the period 1986–90.[136]

The extent of SDI-inspired activity, then, goes way beyond the traditional realm of the defense industry, to embrace the most advanced research fields, including basic analytical programs. As a result, the personnel employed by SDI-related investment will be in the upper tier of the technical ladder. According to a study by the Council of Economic Priorities, SDI-related production will employ six times as many scientists and engineers as the average industry.[137] This is a development that will affect the high-tech labor market dramatically, creating a shortage of skilled professionals in the civilian markets, and concentrating some of the best talent in the military–industrial sector by paying higher salaries, offering better equipment, and providing better working conditions. From this will follow a gradual technological advantage on the part of the defense industry.[138] These trends are arousing serious concern among economic experts and leading industrialists. It is argued, rightly, that the secrecy surrounding much of the research will inhibit its diffusion, restricting the commercial and civilian spin-offs of the program.[139] Given the slowness of diffusion from military-related innovation, critics argue that increasing dependency on defense-inspired technological change will considerably hamper US economic competitiveness. The analysis by Stowsky already cited[140] on the shortcomings of defense spending as a technological–industrial policy applies also to SDI-related initiatives. The channeling of so large a proportion of technological resources into the defense field will be likely to slow down the rate of innovation and to decrease productive efficiency, to the benefit, for instance, of commercially-oriented Japanese competition.

The response of the Defense Department to this challenge is, of course, to try to universalize SDI, reaching out to foreign companies and opening huge potential markets that could lure into the realm of US defense spending much of the foreign technological potential. Yet it remains most likely that foreign companies, and particularly Japanese firms, will continue to target most of their production to civilian applications, and this offers the prospect of a global bifurcation of high-technology industries, with the US electronics companies being overwhelmed in many areas by Japan, Korea, and western

Europe, while the hard core of US high technology takes refuge in the growing military market. This development could trigger off a new round of economic restructuring within the high-technology industries, as well as a recomposition of the international division of labor.

In sum, SDI has become the core of high-technology defense policy, and could also become an indication of the future industrial policy of the US, both because of its capacity for defining the goals of technological innovation, and because of its potential in creating markets and attracting the most skilled scientific labor force.[141] On the other hand, because of the inherent shortcomings of defense production in relation to civilian industrial development, SDI could trigger off a profound restructuring of the international and national economies from which the US would probably emerge with a shrunk industrial structure, yet with a superior technological edge confined to its own military, statist logic. SDI could choke off the market-driven entrepreneurialism that accompanied the expansion of the American high-tech industries, ushering in a new stage in which economic growth would take second place to the technological exercise of global power. While the warfare state might have important economic consequences and motivations, its ultimate logic is fundamentally political.

Down to Earth: The Urban and Regional Effects of High-technology-based Defense Policy

Technology-driven defense policy is having significant effects on the urban and regional structure of the US. To analyze the resulting spatial forms and processes, it is necessary first to understand the process by which defense industries are geographically located in the US, since much of the current impact is dependent on the established spatial pattern. Special attention will be given here to the role played by technological change in this process, in order to assess the relative likelihood of historical continuity or modification of the existing spatial structure. We will then examine the particular spatial effects of recent defense policies and analyze the specific influence of the new technological factor introduced in these policies.

Much has been written on the regional impact of defense spending in the US,[142] although considerably less is known about the intra-metropolitan and urban effects of military activities or of defense industries. Yet even at the regional level, few studies have approached the issue from the angle that is now crucial according to my hypothesis, namely, the relationship between defense spending and high-technology industries in the formation of a new regional structure.[143] Fortunately, we can rely on the preliminary findings of a major study on this subject, conducted at the University of California by Peter Hall, Ann Markusen, Scott Campbell, and Sabina Dietrick.[144] I am indebted to this study for much of the information underlying the analysis that follows.

The main finding of the study concerns the historical continuity of the location of defense industries since the 1930s, with California (particularly Los Angeles), New England, the north-east, and Texas the main areas of concentration of defense-related industrial jobs. Table 5.10 provides some information on the matter at a very aggregate level. Although a certain degree of regional domination does appear, particularly in the New England and Pacific regions, it is important to analyze the processes of formation of the military–industrial sphere, since spatial continuity may actually disguise the existence of a succession of different processes, whose dynamics could be very distinct, carrying the potential for reversing the spatial patterns over time. This hypothesis seems to be confirmed by the fact that, although most of the sites of the defense industry were already in place in the late 1930s, their relative importance has changed greatly during the past 40 years, with the old manufacturing belt in the mid-west losing out to the west and the south-east, and New England transforming its old industrial base into a new one, definitely connected to defense-related production. Three major factors seem to have accounted for this evolution, and it is my hypothesis that these same factors are the main forces in shaping the regional structure of the US during the current defense build-up. The three factors are:

(1) rapid technological change, organized around new technologies in aerospace and electronics;
(2) the specific nature of the production process in the defense industry; and
(3) the political and institutional process surrounding defense policy and the allocation of defense resources.

It is the interaction among these three specific factors that has redrawn the manufacturing map of America in the past 40 years, on the basis of the critical role played by defense in what is left of manufacturing in the US. Let us examine the specific influence of these factors on spatial processes, one after the other.

Technology entirely transformed military equipment after World War II with the shift of strategic importance to aircraft, then to missiles, as potential vehicles for nuclear weapons (see table 5.11).[145]

Thus, while traditional ordnance (artillery, tanks, mechanized personnel carriers, battleships) was incrementally improved, and was still produced in the mid-western and north-eastern manufacturing belt, the new defense industry expanded around the aircraft industry, itself divided between engine constructors and airframe manufacturers. Production of engines was (and still largely is) located in the New England area, following the tradition of precision engineering in the region since the nineteenth century.[146]

Table 5.10 Distribution of defense procurement, by state and region, 1982

State	Number of employees Total (000s)	As % of US total	Value of shipments Total ($m)	As % of US total
Pacific	281.4	29.70	25,386	29.03
California	267.2	28.20	23,923	27.35
Oregon	3.7	0.39	268	0.31
Washington	9.9	1.04	944	1.08
Alaska	d		d	
Hawaii	d		d	
New England	135.6	14.31	12,405	14.18
Maine	6.2	0.87	545	0.62
New Hampshire	14.1	1.49	911	1.04
Vermont	4.9	0.52	354	0.40
Massachusetts	46.4	5.11	5,058	5.78
Rhode Island	6.1	0.85	706	0.81
Connecticut	51.9	5.48	4,831	5.52
Middle Atlantic	129.3	13.64	11,569	13.23
New York	69.6	7.34	6,261	7.16
New Jersey	25.9	2.73	2,199	2.51
Pennsylvania	33.8	3.57	3,109	3.55
South Atlantic	121.7	12.84	9,060	10.36
Delaware	0.1	0.01	136	0.16
Maryland	26.1	2.75	2,123	2.43
D. of Columbia	D		D	
Virginia	40.0	4.22	2,758	3.15
West Virginia	A		11	0.01
North Carolina	3.5	0.37	245	0.28
South Carolina	1.6	0.17	132	0.15
Georgia	10.9	1.15	1,053	1.20
Florida	39.4	4.16	2,603	2.98
East-North-Central	81.6	8.61	8,331	9.53
Ohio	26.7	2.82	2,848	3.26
Indiana	19.2	2.03	1,907	2.18
Illinois	12.7	1.34	1,125	1.29
Michigan	15.4	1.63	1,819	2.08
Wisconsin	7.6	0.80	632	0.72
West-North-Central	67.3	7.10	8,193	9.37
Minnesota	17.0	1.79	1,603	1.83
Iowa	4.0	0.42	328	0.38
Missouri	31.6	3.33	4,707	5.38
North Dakota	D		D	
South Dakota	D		D	
Nebraska	0.9	0.09	53	0.06

Table 5.10 Continued

State	Number of employees Total (000s)	As % of US total	Value of shipments Total ($m)	As % of US total
Kansas	13.8	1.46	1,497	1.71
East-South-Central	26.0	2.74	2,020	2.31
Kentuky	0.4	0.04	110	0.13
Tennessee	8.0	0.84	620	0.71
Alabama	7.0	0.74	385	0.44
Mississippi	10.6	1.12	905	1.03
West-South-Central	68.6	7.24	6,857	7.84
Arkansas	1.1	0.12	64	0.07
Louisiana	2.6	0.27	468	0.54
Oklahoma	5.6	0.61	499	0.51
Texas	59.1	6.24	5,876	6.72
Mountain	36.2	3.82	3,637	4.16
Montana	A		23	0.03
Idaho	0.1	0.01	13	0.01
Wyoming	A		8	0.01
Colorado	11.0	1.16	1,050	1.20
New Mexico	1.1	0.12	140	0.16
Arizona	16.2	1.71	1,583	1.81
Utah	7.8	0.82	820	0.94
Nevada	A		0	0.00
US total	947.6	100.0	87,458	100.0

Source: US Bureau of Census; US Bureau of Labor Statistics.

Table 5.11 Changes in the composition of military hard goods, 1942–1944 to 1980

Type of military goods	Fiscal year			
	1942–4[a]	1953[a]	1962[b]	1980[b]
Aircraft	27.3	31.5	25.7	31.9
Missiles	0.0	0.5	33.7	19.6
Ships	26.2	6.8	7.4	13.1
Electronics and communication equipment	6.6	11.2	16.6	22.4
Tank-automotive, weapons, ammunition and other	39.9	50.0	16.5	12.9

[a] Composition (%) based on value of deliveries.
[b] Composition (%) based on value of prime contracts.

Source: Malecki (see note 143).

Airframe manufacturers grew up in California, with two major exceptions, which became the two biggest companies, located for accidental reasons, in Seattle (Boeing) and St Louis (McDonnell-Douglas).[147] Southern California saw a flurry of pioneer entrepreneurial activity in aviation as early as the 1920s:[148] Lockheed started in a Hollywood garage moving to Burbank in 1929; Douglas started in an abandoned studio in Santa Monica in 1920; Jack Northrop, after working for both Lockheed and Douglas, set up his own company in Hawthorne in 1939; and in the mid-1930s, Consolidated started operations in Glendale, Convair in San Diego, and North American in Inglewood. All these firms were to become major companies fueled by military contracts during World War II.

Why southern California? Physical conditions have often been cited: large expanses of undeveloped flat land; a sunny, mild climate, favoring flight testing and outdoor industrial work;[149] and a large supply of skilled labor. Yet, Peter Hall and his colleagues[150] argue that the decisive factor was the quality of technical education, particularly for aeronautical engineers, with Cal Tech, in Pasadena, and Stanford being among the only five universities to offer such programs in the 1920s (the others being MIT, University of Washington, and the University of Michigan). Yet in spite of that early start in California, other airframe manufacturers were still located in the old industrial belt: in Buffalo, New York; in Baltimore; in Bridgeport, Connecticut: in Long Island, New York; and, of course, there was the McDonnell plant in St Louis. To explain the continuity of the expansion of the aviation industry in the west and in New England along with its discontinuity in the oldest industrial belt, it is necessary to introduce the factors proposed as explanatory of the defense industry's locational patterns: in particular, the shift to missile technology, which represented both a challenge and an opportunity for the airframe manufacturers.[151] Electronics became a crucial component of the new aerospace industry, particularly after the shock of Sputnik in 1957 launched the race to the moon. Electronics companies positioned themselves strongly in the defense sector, with 90 percent of semiconductors being produced for the government in the 1950s. As we know,[152] major advanced electronics areas were, in temporal sequence, New England, California (particularly northern California), and Texas. Those airframe manufacturers that were able to team up with the new electronics companies, or that developed around them their own electronics suppliers, were able to jump into avionics and missiles, entering the aerospace age as the nucleus of the new defense industry.[153] Southern California was particularly successful in organizing aerospace production around the electronics industry. Texas followed along the same path. New England maintained its position in aircraft engines production and combined this with its strong electronics industry to become the region which, in proportion to its size, most heavily specialized in defense production, in spite of all the ideological discourse about the west;[154] Silicon Valley concentrated mainly on electronics, although it did also become a major missile producer, with the

Lockheed facility in Sunnyvale. The important factor was that by the mid-1960s a fundamental connection had been created between the defense industry (centered around aerospace) and high-technology manufacturing (centered around electronics) that was going to favor decisively the development of those regions able to bring together these two terms of the new techno-military equation, under the dominance of one term or the other (aerospace defense in southern California and Texas, electronics in Silicon Valley, a combination of both in New England).

But why were these particular areas able to maintain their head start in the trade (or even to initiate it, as Texas did), while the mid-west or the north-east (except New England) by and large dropped out of the race? Here two additional factors come into play that will at the same time also help in explaining some other locational developments of the advanced military and space industry, particularly in the south-east.

As stated above, the second major factor determining the location of the defense industry is the specific nature of the industrial organization itself. Defense production is characterized by a close, tight network of day-to-day interaction among companies, their clients (military institutions and government agencies), and the companies' sub-contractors and auxiliary services.[155] Production itself, in the aircraft industry, is largely free of assembly-line operations; instead, it is characterized by batch fabrication, and involves considerable interaction with the researchers and designers of the technological product, as well as with the client, to satisfy detailed specifications.[156] All these elements converge toward the creation of an *industrial milieu* that, once in place, perpetuates itself, reinforcing its prominence and undertaking new initiatives in the new fields of defense as soon as they are opened up by technological innovation. The existence of a tightly knit industrial milieu is also favored by the the fact that the defense industry is characterized by a high level of concentration and dominated by a handful of firms. The top 100 companies control 70 percent of total value of contracts, the top 50 control 50 percent of the market, and the top five, 20 percent.[157] Large defense companies typically obtain multi-million-dollar orders from the Pentagon which they then contract out to many sub-contractors of different sizes and specialties, from metal-work shops to software engineers.[158] It is widely believed that such contracting and sub-contracting involves a great deal of personal contact and face-to-face interaction; the defense industry is a *social* milieu as much as an industrial milieu. High-ranking officers often retire from the military to take up jobs in defense companies, while remaining close to their long-standing friends. A sort of cultural empathy pervades the whole system, sustaining a tight network of values, interests, feelings, and ideas around which major strategic decisions are nurtured, and substantial business deals are agreed upon.[159] Sometimes, critics argue, bribery and pay-offs are almost necessary practices in the sub-contracting business, the famous Lockheed foreign government briberies being of course the most notorious case of what is said to be a structural element of the industry's workings. Whatever the reality, it is quite clear that the defense industry operates as a milieu, requiring spatial clustering of its core activities, regardless of the widespread decentralization of its sub-contracting operations. The existence locally of military installations greatly contributes to the formation of such milieux, particularly when other key elements occur in the same location, such as the presence of aircraft and electronics industries, and the existence of high-level research and technical education institutions. California, of course, and particularly southern California, is also favored in terms of proximity to military bases; and Lockheed's location in Sunnyvale (Silicon Valley) seems to be in direct relationship with Moffit Air Naval Base. Texas also has a comparative advantage on these grounds, particularly because of the army's installations around San Antonio, potentially connecting with the future Austin–San Antonio high-tech corridor.

Nevertheless, the social and industrial milieu of defense activity seems to be all-important by itself, regardless of any spatial connection with military facilities, as demonstrated by the strong defense orientation of New England, in spite of a much less conspicuous military presence there. Once the ingredients of a military–industrial milieu are in place they expand, reinforcing themselves with their technological, commercial, and social externalities; yet the coming together of these elements in a particular area is largely a function of the political and institutional dynamics of the defense establishment, in which ultimately lies the power to decide on particular production lines, and the ability to obtain and allocate the necessary *public* resources.

A vast literature has documented the consistent bias of defense spending toward some regions. For instance, the major study on the subject by Roger Bolton for the period 1952–62 found that defense demand accounted for 21 percent of personal income growth in the Pacific region, while contributing a *negative* 21 percent to that growth in the east-north-central regions. He also showed that defense purchases accounted for 34 percent of current personal income in the Pacific, 23 percent in the Mountain, 23 percent in the south Atlantic region, and 22 percent in New England, while all other regions had shares below 20 percent.[160] Ann Markusen, reviewing the evidence on the regional distribution of defense outlays, states that

especially remarkable has been the regional shift of prime contract awards away from the northeastern and north central states (which, in 1951, received the highest aggregate and per capita amount of such awards and the largest proportion of the national total) toward the southern and western states (which by 1976 received the highest amount and the highest proportion). In addition, the largest number and greatest proportion of installations continued to be located in the southern and western regions up through the mid 1970s.[161]

Table 5.12 presents the top ten states in terms of benefit from direct defense spending in 1959–60 and 1980, showing the continuity of the pattern.

Table 5.12   Top states in receipt of prime defense contracts. 1959–80

Fiscal year 1959–60		Fiscal year 1980	
State	% of US total	State	% of US total
California	24.0	California	20.4
New York	11.4	New York	8.3
Texas	5.8	Texas	8.0
Massachusetts	5.3	Connecticut	5.7
New Jersey	5.0	Massachusetts	5.5
Ohio	4.4	Virginia	4.9
Connecticut	4.2	Missouri	4.8
Washington	4.0	Washington	3.4
Michigan	3.3	Pennsylvania	3.3
Pennsylvania	3.2	Florida	3.0

Source: Malecki (see note 143).

The direction of defense spending to certain regions is obviously, then, a powerful factor in influencing the location of defense industries. But what are the reasons for these regional preferences on the part of the Pentagon? It has been argued that the shift to the west and the south as the home ground of Presidents, and the coming into power of a new Californian and Texan political elite, have played an important role in both reinforcing defense policy, and tying it to the geographic origins of political support for the defense build-up.[162] Markusen and Block have also introduced the argument of political culture, according to which the old manufacturing belt with its strong union tradition and its liberal political climate was not suited to accommodate the national security priorities of the military and of the defense establishment.[163] It is undeniable that local support for military installations, and for related defense expenditures, is an important consideration for any defense agency to feel comfortable setting up in the regions; and that the development of a network of relationships among regional political leaders, public opinion, defense companies, and military settlements creates a strong, sustained basis for defense production in a particular area. Nevertheless, such factors are not overriding, as the case of New England again demonstrates – not exactly a south-western, conservative region, yet one of the most heavily defense-oriented regional economies. There is often a confusion between the location of military bases and test sites (which critically favor the west and the south-west because of their natural conditions: open spaces, depopulated areas, fair weather, sunny skies), and the location of the defense industry. While proximity to military installations is important, it is even more important to have access to the industrial milieu to which I have referred; and this milieu is conditioned largely by the development of high-technology industries and research facilities. It is the combination of a political environment, a technological base, and an industrial milieu which accounts for the development of major defense production in California and Texas, while New England's technological might was sufficient of itself to override the supposed military reluctance to rely on the old industrial regions for building their new productive base.[164]

In fact, it seems that the internal political rivalries of military bureaucracies have been more important than external political factors; namely, the competition among the army, the air force, and the navy to control the technological transition to the new warfare system. Peter Hall and his colleagues have described in some detail what they call "the most extraordinary saga of inter-service rivalry in which the Army and Air Force, in particular, behaved liked competitive capitalist corporations" in trying to secure control of the new missile program between 1953 and 1960.[165] The army had the original mandate for it, and the additional technological advantage of Von Braun and his team. On the other hand, the air force had its strong connection to the aircraft industry and its early lead in electronics equipment. The three services developed in parallel the three first major missile programs: the air force, Atlas, from 1954; the army, Titan and Jupiter, from 1955; and the navy, Polaris, from 1956. Two different organizational logics led to different spatial location patterns. The army favored in-house production of its own equipment, following both the traditional logic of the weapons arsenal, and Von Braun's own experience with the German army. Accordingly, the army organized a major aerospace research and production center in Huntsville, Alabama, connected to the test site at Cape Canaveral, Florida. The air force was more inclined to rely on the private sector, and turned naturally to the Los Angeles complex, and to the research resources of Cal Tech's Jet Propulsion Laboratory. The navy also followed its west coast connection, so that Polaris was developed by Lockheed in Sunnyvale, while Convair built Titan (in Los Angeles), North American (also in LA), built Hounddog, and Boeing, in Seattle, took charge of the Minuteman program, with electronics support from Texas Instruments. To put a halt to waste and inefficiency in the wake of the Sputnik syndrome, the Federal government stepped in, put the air force in charge of most missile programs, quashed the army's stubborn opposition, and in 1958 created NASA around the Alabama–Florida pole of activities, to which were attached some research facilities on the west coast, most notably the Jet Propulsion Laboratory. A number of defense, electronic, and aerospace firms took up locations in Florida and the south-east around the market represented by the Apollo program: most notably Martin Marietta in Orlando and United Technologies in Palm Beach, constituting a new high-tech–defense oriented industrial pole. Yet the real winner of the competition was once again California, and particularly Los Angeles, whose business circles and political influence had been skilfully mobilized by the air force in support of its own programs.

Thus, the location of aerospace and electronic industries, the characteristics of the industrial organization of defense production, and the internal and external politics of military bureaucracies explain most of the location patterns of a defense industry driven and transformed by rapid technological change in the past 30 years.

Only two exceptions remain outside the main preferred locations resulting from the dynamics described above: production of atomic warheads, that for obvious safety reasons is concentrated in remote areas, fundamentally in Oak Ridge, Tennessee, and Amarillo, Texas; and Seattle, which remained a major aerospace production center around the company founded in 1915 by William E. Boeing, a Seattle timberman with a vision of the future, and Conrad Westervelt, a naval officer who, once returned to active duty, may have been crucial in obtaining for Boeing some of its first plane orders from the navy.[166] St Louis also remained at the forefront of aircraft production on the basis of the company founded in 1938 by James Smith McDonnell, an MIT graduate in aeronautical engineering and an air force officer.[167] St Louis' McDonnell-Douglas (as it became after Douglas was absorbed into the business) is the only significant remnant of the early dominance of the mid-west in airframe manufacture, an anomaly attributable to the dynamism of the company and its ability to team up with electronics companies on the west coast and in New England.

From this complex process of development of a powerful defense industry emerged a new economic landscape in the US. Its most extraordinary feature is the formation of the Los Angeles military–industrial complex, probably the largest and most advanced in the world. According to a study by Tiebout in 1966, in the 1960s 7.7 percent of employment in the Los Angeles–Long Beach SMSA was directly tied to defense and space production, a proportion which rose to 43.5 percent when all indirect and induced effects were incorporated. Estimates by the same study for the entire state of California were of 8 percent of employment directly related to defense, and 40 percent with all indirect effects taken into consideration.[168] Since this type of study often relies on arbitrary assumptions about multiplier effects, it is probably inadvisable to take the data too literally. Yet it is unquestionable that the defense industry, and its role in stimulating aircraft production and electronics, had a decisive effect on the growth of the Californian economy, as well as, according to a study by Sabina Dietrick, on the migration of population to California;[169] and it continues to be a major factor in the state's economic prosperity, as borne out by Michael Teitz's analysis of the period 1982–6.[170]

Similarly, the ability of New England, and particularly of Massachusetts, to shift its economy away from its old manufacturing basis in textiles and machine tools to its new high-technology manufacturing and advanced services complex, was and is highly dependent upon the military markets that seem to account for about one-third of the manufacturing work force in the Route 128 area.[171] If we add Texas, Arizona, and Florida to the group of affluent states, and, a later development, the defense-induced industry in Colorado at Denver and Colorado Springs, it is clear that the defense industry's pattern of location is responsible for much of the new uneven regional development in the US. Nevertheless, the dynamics and content of this uneven development are *not* the direct consequence of defense spending, but of the combination of defense policy and high-technology industry,[172] itself resulting from the changes introduced by technological advance in the realm of warfare. The defense industry is driven, as Malecki has put it,[173] by a "technological push" which, by connecting state policy and economic dynamism, becomes a crucial factor in shaping the spatial structure of the nation.

The first major spatial impact of a defense policy driven by global technological competition, then, is the restructuring of regional dominance, accelerating the process of uneven development but revising some of the traditional locational patterns. This regional restructuring does not take place along the simplistic dichotomy between the sunbelt and the snowbelt, but follows, fundamentally, the technological industrial capacity concentrated in each region. The combination of high-tech manufacturing, advanced research, and defense spending seems to be one of the major factors in explaining the new regional dynamics of the US. The result is the displacement of economic and political power to California, Florida, Texas, New England, and, to some extent, certain areas in the west. While New York retains its dominance on the basis of its advanced services complex, much of the urban industrial complex in the north-central and north-eastern regions is suffering a dramatic decline, while the new industrial south appears unable to stand up to international competition.[174] Defense-driven high-technology industries, and technology-driven defense-related industries, are now the core of manufacturing in the US; and because of their spin-off and multiplier effects, they have become a fundamental force underlying the new regional structure.[175]

Within any given metropolitan area, the expansion of the defense industry has taken place in the new suburbs, thus powerfully contributing to the process of suburbanization of manufacturing, and to the economic dynamism of suburbs, as opposed to the central city.[176] The reasons for this trend should be clear as a result of the preceding analysis of the characteristics of the defense industry. The need for large expanses of undeveloped land and easy access to a network of subsidiaries in the area favor a strip-shaped suburban development along the freeway. Proximity to military bases, which are generally located on the outskirts of metropolitan areas, reinforces the pattern. It has also been proposed, by Ann Markusen and Robin Bloch, that the cultural preference of the military, and their related industries, is for seclusion in a separate world, both for security reasons and because of their anti-big-city, anti-cosmopolitan bias.[177] If such a preference exists, it would certainly be reinforced by the co-existence of residence and workplaces within the same suburban world, often through housing procured by the company, or obtained through arrangements with military agencies.

Nevertheless, it is crucial to distinguish between strictly defense industries (for instance, a weapons production facility), and defense-*related* industries (such as aircraft and electronics companies). In the former case, spatial segregation seems to be the tendency; in the latter instance, spatial and social structures are much more diversified, and tend to mingle with the overall social system of the host area. What seems to apply to both is the suburban character of the defense industry, as well as of most of its labor force. But this is also an attribute of high-technology manufacturing and R&D in general. What we are observing is not so much a defense space as the generalization of a new industrial space, with large batch production facilities combined with automated subsidiary plants, in the vicinity of test sites and relatively close to the research and design centers. Access to a large, resource-ful area by means of the freeway system seems to be the main spatial requirement. This is why the defense industry (as with high-technology industry) tends to be peripherally located in large metropolitan areas which are able to provide sufficient diversity and density of interaction to constitute the industrial milieu which is the essential ingredient of the whole process. In fact, the study by a group of Berkeley graduate students on the characteristics of defense-related industries in California[178] shows a great diversity of situations, with, again, the only common factor being their suburban, or even ex-urban, location. The blue-collar community of Vallejo, adjacent to a naval base in the San Francisco area, is in striking contrast to the campus-like community of Livermore, site of the Lawrence National Laboratory. The Los Angeles area complex and Silicon Valley have, of course, highly diversified social and spatial structures that hardly allow for specific social subsets related to defense activity, in contrast to the situation in military–industrial company towns such as, for example, Amarillo, Texas.

The defense industry also presents major differences in occupational structure and its residential manifestation, according to the type of activity involved. Large airframe manufacturers in Los Angeles have a significant proportion of blue-collar workers and a higher share of black workers than manufacturing as a whole in the area. By contrast, Hispanics are underrepresented in the defense industry, and non-US citizens are barred from employment by DoD regulations. Women are particularly under-represented in the industry: as manual workers because these are generally male-dominated occupations, and as engineers, in accordance with the general situation throughout the entire realm of high-technology industries. When industrial location and residential areas coincide spatially, the result is a traditional nuclear family suburb, with men at work and women at home, in higher proportion than in the rest of the area.

In fact, there are two clearly distinct patterns of residence associated with defense industry work. On the one hand are the traditional ordnance and ammunition facilities that, both for safety reasons and by cultural choice on the part of their managers, tend to locate in medium-sized cities in predominantly rural areas, very much following the model of military bases.[179] On the other hand, as table 5.13 shows, in 1983 defense industrial employment was highly concentrated in major urban industrial centers. An observation of the areas included reveals three outstanding features: the overwhelming dominance of the two metropolitan areas of Los Angeles and Anaheim (in fact the same spatial unit) that, together, have 161,800 defense-related jobs, accounting for about one-quarter of all defense-related jobs, at least in the restrictive definition used by Mosely; the extraordinary role played by Boston in the military–industrial complex, in proportion to the size of its work force; and the quantitative importance retained by some old industrial

Table 5.13   Concentration of Department of Defense procurement: top ten metropolitan areas by employment involved and value of shipments, 1983

(a)

Top ten metropolitian areas by employment	No. of employees in establishments involved in DoD procurement (000s)
1 Los Angeles–Anaheim–Riverside, CA	161.8
2 New York–Northern New Jersey–Long Island, NY–NJ	71.9
3 Dallas–Fort Worth, TX	52.0
4 San Francisco–Oakland–San Jose, CA	48.2
5 Boston–Lawrence–Salem, MA–NH	43.9
6 Norfolk–Virginia Beach–Newport News, VA	27.8
7 San Diego, CA	24.3
8 Seattle–Tacoma, WA	22.1
9 Baltimore, MD	20.2
10 Hartford–New Britain–Middletown, CT	20.1

(b)

Top ten metropolitian areas by value of shipments	Value of shipments to DoD ($ m)
1 Los Angeles–Anaheim–Riverside, CA	15,896.3
2 New York–Northern New Jersey–Long Island, NY–NJ	6,541.6
3 San Francisco–Oakland–San Jose, CA	5,465.7
4 Dallas–Fort Worth, TX	4,698.5
5 Boston–Lawrence–Salem, MA–NH	4,540.0
6 Hartford–New Britain–Middletown, CT	2,334.5
7 Philadelphia–Wilmington Trenton, PA–NJ–DE–MD	2,021.2
8 San Diego, CA	1,925.9
9 Norfolk–Virginia Beach–Newport News, VA	1,713.2
10 Baltimore, MD	1,668.7

Source: Department of Commerce, *Current Industrial Reports.*

areas, such as New York–New Jersey, in the defense industry. For defense workers living in such large, complex areas, it is difficult to imagine much specificity in residential pattern. What is significant is that the overwhelming majority of them work and live in the suburbs, and, increasingly, in the newest, most far-flung suburban areas. Therefore, the spatial trend to be associated with the defense build-up is the growth of suburbs, as the location for manufacturing, for related services and for the workers' residences. This trend explains why Glickman's calculations, as cited,[180] show a high concentration of defense spending in suburbs, that is, where the defense procurement industries are located, and where their employees tend to live. This is, of course, hardly a specific spatial behavior; yet the orientation of government policy toward defense greatly encourages the suburbanization process characterizing metropolitan America.

How did recent defense policy, biased toward high technology as represented by the SDI program, fit into this spatial pattern? It is my hypothesis that the industrial dynamics generated by a politically determined defense policy of the SDI type produce specific urban and regional effects that will become increasingly significant with the ever-increasing emphasis on technologically-led defense R&D and manufacturing. To examine this hypothesis I turn to the preliminary findings of a study conducted at Berkeley by Rebecca Skinner on the spatial distribution of SDI contracts, on the basis of information files provided directly by SDIO.[181] At the time of writing, her data refer mainly to all contracts issued by SDIO in 1987, when the program enjoyed full support from the administration and had come to maturity. We must keep in mind that at this stage of SDI, all contracts concern research and development, although it is fair to assume, on the basis of past experience in the defense industry, that research contractors will have a competitive edge when it comes to manufacturing contracts, so that the current pattern of spatial distribution of research by and large foreshadows the future pattern of defense manufacturing production.

Skinner calculated the spatial distribution of SDI contracts using the amount of funds contracted as the accounting unit. Let us first observe the pattern of regional distribution, and try to understand what distinguishes SDI contracts from defense contracts in general, and from all defense contracts concerning "research, development, test, and evaluation" (RDTE). Table 5.14 compares the distribution of SDI contracts for the top ten states in 1987 to that of the other two categories of contracts in 1985 (the last year for which Skinner could construct a complete data set). It appears that there is a very high concentration in a few states, and that this concentration increases with the research component of the program: the top ten states account for 65.2 percent of the value of all defense contracts, 80.6 percent of the RDTE contracts, and 92.9 percent of SDIO contracts. California dominates all three categories, but its leadership increases, in absolute terms, with the research component: California accounts for 20.8 percent of all contracts, 38.8 percent of RDTE contracts, and 40.6 percent of SDIO contracts. States appear in the

Table 5.14   Ranking of top ten states according to the value of defense contracts (SDIO; research (RDTE); prime contracts), 1985 and 1987

(a) Top ten SDI states

State	SDIO 1987 value, $ m	% Total SDIO	% Total top ten
Calfornia	553.965	40.60	42.90
Alabama	170.676	12.00	13.22
New Mexico	142.566	10.10	11.04
Washington	121.928	8.60	9.44
Massachusetts	113.397	8.00	8.78
New York	72.902	5.20	5.65
Colorado	38.079	3.00	2.95
Virginia	29.21	2.00	2.26
Texas	25.654	1.80	1.99
Maryland	23	1.60	1.78
Sum top 10	1291.377	92.90	
Sum other	123.531	8.73	
Sum USA	1414.908	100.00	
Sum, 1st five	1102.532	79.3	85.3
Sum, 2nd five	188.845	20.7	14.6

(b) Top ten DoD states

State	DoD 1985 value, $ m	% Total DoD	% Total top ten
California	29114.5	20.80	31.90
Texas	10561.5	7.50	11.57
New York	10032.7	7.20	10.99
Massachusetts	7713.54	5.50	8.45
Missouri	7612.71	5.40	8.34
Virginia	6166.76	4.40	6.76
Connecticut	5543.44	4.00	6.07
Florida	5271.23	3.80	5.78
Ohio	4648.32	3.30	5.09
Maryland	4608.10	3.30	5.05
Sum top 10	91272.9	65.20	100.00
Sum other	48823.3	34.80	
Sum USA	140096.0	100.00	
Sum, 1st five	65035.0	46.40	71.25
Sum, 2nd five	26237.8	18.80	28.75

(c) Top ten RDTE states

State	RDTE 1985 value, $ m	% Total DoD	% Total top ten
California	5835.949	31.30	38.82
Massachusetts	2125.93	11.40	14.14
New York	1594.241	8.60	10.61
Maryland	995.193	5.30	6.62
Washington	969.504	5.20	6.45
Texas	915.753	4.90	6.09
Virginia	755.163	4.10	5.02
Colorado	691.588	3.70	4.60
New Jersey	640.589	3.40	4.26
Florida	508.754	2.70	3.38
Sum top 10	15032.66	80.60	1
Sum other	3593.74	19.40	
Sum, USA	18626.40	100.00	
Sum, 1st five	11520.81	61.80	76.64
Sum, 2nd five	3511.847	18.80	23.36

Source: Skinner (see note 181).

SDIO top ten list that are not included in the other categories: Alabama, because of the army's Space Center Research and Testing Center at Huntsville; New Mexico, because of the importance of Los Alamos and Sandia National Laboratories; and Washington because of Boeing. On the other hand, states of the old manufacturing belt that are important in terms of general contracts received, such as Missouri and Ohio, are neither in the RDTE top ten nor the SDIO top ten, although Missouri still ranks reasonably high overall because of the continuing significance of McDonnell-Douglas. Table 5.15 presents the location quotients for the three categories of contract and provides a clearer picture of the regional profile of SDIO contracts. Five states stand out in a class by themselves: New Mexico, Alabama, Washington, California, and Massachusetts. These five in fact represent three different types of defense-oriented industrial R&D location, that further specify the logic introduced by SDI-like defense policy. New Mexico and Alabama represent the new secluded, exclusively defense-oriented, RDTE space, isolated from any major metropolitan area; Washington exemplifies the industrial enclave linked to a major corporation, in this case Boeing. California and Massachusetts offer the most significant illustrations of what could be the future defense-oriented industrial space. It is these two areas (Massachusetts should in fact in this context be extended to include most of New England, particularly Connecticut) that we are witnessing the merger between high-technology industries and defense design and manufacturing in the backbone of the US production system. This merger is taking place under the impact of a "technology push"

Table 5.15 Comparison between spatial distribution of SDIO contracts, defense research contracts (RTDE) and DoD prime contracts, 1987 and 1985

Location quotient Greater than 2.0		1.0–2.0		0.5–1.0		0.25–0.5		Less than 0.25	
DoD prime contracts									
Connecticut	2.97	Alaska	1.8	Alabama	0.60	Iowa	0.34		
DC	3.00	Arizona	1.0	Arkansas	0.58	Oklahoma	0.31		
Massachusetts	2.25	California	1.88	Colorado	0.82	Tennessee	0.28		
Missouri	2.57	Georgia	1.0	Delaware	0.71	Wisconsin	0.37		
		Hawaii	1.01	Florida	0.79	Wyoming	0.41		
		Kansas	1.69	Indiana	0.98				
		Maine	1.40	Louisiana	0.82				
		Maryland	1.78	Michigan	0.52				
		New Hampshire	1.15	Minnesota	0.93				
		Texas	1.09	New Jersey	0.87				
		Virginia	1.84	New Mexico	0.57				
		Washington	1.37	New York	0.96				
				North Carolina	0.53				
				North Dakota	0.51				
				Ohio	0.73				
				Pennsylvania	0.62				
				Rhode Island	0.75				
				Utah	0.81				
				Vermont	0.52				
SDIO contracts, 1987									
Alabama	7.16	Colorado	1.98	Maryland	0.88	Indiana	0.44	Alaska	0.13
California	3.545	Connecticut	1.15	New York	0.69	New Jersey	0.32	Arizona	0.04
Massachusetts	3.28	DC	1.16	Virginia	0.86	Minnesota	0.38	Arkansas	0
New Mexico	16.58					Missouri	0.49	Delaware	0
Washington	4.66					Tennessee	0.25	Florida	0.12
						Texas	0.26	Georgia	0.02

RTDE contracts, 1985

State	Value	State	Value	State	Value	State	Value	State	Value	State	Value
California	2.837	Missouri	1.186	Alabama	0.600	Michigan	0.264	Alaska	0.010	Hawaii	0
Colorado	2.743	New Jersey	1.085	Arizona	0.911	N. Carolina	0.321	Arkansas	0.020	Idaho	0
Maryland	2.904	New Mexico	1.267	Connecticut	0.944	Ohio	0.447	Delaware	0.167	Illinois	0.07
Massachusetts	4.680	New York	1.148	DC	0.788	Pennyslvania	0.473	Georgia	0.137	Iowa	0
Washington	2.818	Utah	1.798	Florida	0.573	Rhode Island	0.450	Hawaii	0.130	Kansas	0
		Virginia	1.696	Kansas	0.680	Tennessee	0.279	Idaho	0	Kentucky	0
				Minnesota	0.884			Illinois	0.134	Louisiana	0
				New Hampshire	0.648			Indiana	0.189	Maine	0
				Texas	0.717			Iowa	0.236	Michigan	0
								Kentucky	0.015	Mississippi	0
								Louisiana	0.008	Montana	0
								Maine	0.059	Nebraska	0.01
								Mississippi	0.011	Nevada	0
										New Hampshire	0
										N. Carolina	0.23
										N. Dakota	0

Source: Skinner (see note 181).

from the Pentagon, of which SDI has been the first formal expression, but whose strategic and institutional logic is likely to survive the political avatars of the "Star Wars" mythology.

These new high-technology, defense-oriented industrial milieux are also specific in their urban forms and in their appearance in certain areas. Skinner has analyzed the spatial distribution of SDI contracts within California for 1987 and has found that southern California accounted for 76.7 percent of all funds contracted, with the largest concentration by far in the Los Angeles–Orange County area. She also found that SDI contracts were overwhelming concentrated in the suburbs: 87 percent of them were situated in the suburbs of a large metropolitan area, predominantly Los Angeles. With 84.3 percent of the top twelve defense corporation receiving SDI funds located in suburbs, the destination of SDI contracts fully reflects the metropolitan suburban world of high-technology defense industries. Greater Los Angeles (particularly around Los Angeles International Airport, and in the El Segundo and Redondo Beach areas) and Orange County (around Anaheim) have become the largest, technologically most advanced defense industrial complex in the world, specializing increasingly in manufacturing the material basis of the warfare state on the basis of self-expanding research capabilities in information technologies and aerospace. Similar patterns, although on a much smaller scale, are to be seen along Route 128 in Boston (concentrated on systems design and manufacturing), in Santa Clara County (Silicon Valley), in the Denver area (location of Martin Marietta), in McLean, Virginia (location of BDM), and in Melbourne, Florida (location of Harris) – among others.

The suburban character of SDI-related industrial development also applies to the residential pattern of these industries' labor force. SDI has markedly upgraded the already high level of skills in this particular labor market. SDI-employed scientists and engineers are well paid enough still to be able to afford, as many of the young middle-class professionals cannot, the American dream of the large suburban house in a green suburb. Enjoying relative proximity to their work locations, and the necessary easy access to the freeway, the new high-tech defense workers live very differently from the industrial workers of the large defense procurement plants, who often live in company towns reminiscent of the first industrial cities. Affluent suburbs, secluded communities, and a spatial landscape made up of distinct functional locations around a freeway system are the basic elements of the urban structure associated with a technologically advanced defense industry fostered by SDI.

SDI brings an additional, and more distinctive, urban expression of the new social logic to industrial development: the *space of secrecy*. Perhaps the most distinctive character of the new defense industry organized around SDI is the high level of classified activity it involves.[182] In accordance with its ultimate goal of achieving technological military supremacy, the Defense Department is stepping up its controls to make sure that the Soviet bloc does not receive any technology transfer on time, that is, before the technology has already been rendered obsolete by new discoveries, in an endless race in which the US is intended to enjoy a cumulative lead.[183] This secrecy is perhaps the major obstacle to the industrial and commercial diffusion of results of SDI-inspired technology policy, and is the basis for its critics' most powerful argument. It also has a number of important spatial consequences. Areas where the most advanced high-tech industries are concentrated are likely to become increasingly secluded and kept under surveillance. Each company tends to be isolated from the outside world, both because of the DoD's requirements and because of its own interest in keeping ahead of the competition. The spatial layouts of the companies follow this logic, with discrete buildings scattered along the freeway, isolated from their immediate surroundings. This spatial arrangement does not contradict the tendency toward the formation of a new industrial milieu: it further defines it. On the one hand, each major technological center tends to have its own network of auxiliary enterprises and sub-contractors, most of them in the same spatial area, so that clusters of activities co-exist without necessarily intermixing; on the other hand, the requirement for secrecy leads to a very hierarchical spatial organization within the companies themselves, with the top research centers being segregated from other activities in areas of higher status, provided with better facilities, and more easily isolated and protected. At the very top of the research hierarchy of the SDI-related organizations, major national laboratories constitute their own spaces, in campus-like locations removed from the vicinity of major urban areas, so that social influences can be limited and the physical and cultural distance maintained: such is the case of the Lawrence Laboratory in Livermore, northern California, of Los Alamos and Sandia in New Mexico, and, to a certain extent only, of Lincoln Laboratory in Lexington, Massachusetts.[184] The secrecy of military-related scientific activities fosters the spatial diffusion of the new industrial milieux, emphasizes the importance of the inner world of the company and its network, reinforces the need for face-to-face contact *within* this restricted technical and managerial class, and tends to create a new world of secluded communities that remove themselves both socially and spatially from the context of pre-existing urban organizations.

When SDI's scientific warriors go down to Earth they create a new landscape of specialized, hierarchical, secluded locations, further distinguishing themselves within the already distinct spatial organization of the defense industry.

Conclusion

The transformation of the state in advanced capitalist societies exercises fundamental effects on the shaping of urban and regional processes. The crisis of the urban welfare state and rise of the new warfare state are dramatically altering the structure of cities and regions in different countries, and very especially in the United States. This transformation is a political phenomenon in its origins, characterized by the demise of the New Deal coalition and the emergence of new regional elites and of a new power bloc, based upon the alliance of multinational business and the technical–managerial middle class. In addition, growing challenges to American power and competitiveness on the international scene have called for a more assertive role on the part of the US government in the exercise of its global responsibilities. Altogether, a historical trend has developed in the past decade toward the formation of a specific political dynamic whose essence I have tried to capture under the notion of the transition from the welfare state to the warfare state, in spite of the risks of ideological oversimplification of this formulation. The matter in question is that the primary principle of legitimacy of the new state has shifted from its redistributive role to its power-building function. I believe this to be a fundamental tendency and not limited to a given administration (Reagan) or party (GOP). It is in fact a profound social realignment that has found its expression, and been politically reinforced, in the 1980s under Reagan. Certainly, as in all political processes, the development of the new state is open-ended, and could involve alternative political orientations that would eventually affect again the structure of the state itself. Nevertheless, such conflictive evolution is unlikely to restore the previous situation. We are entering a new political era that in its initial stages is dominated by what I call the warfare state, albeit its future development will be shaped, and may be transformed, by new social movements and political actors yet to enter upon the scene.

As we have seen, new technologies are an important factor in this transformation of the state, although they are by no means at its origin. The technological challenge posed to the institutions of the warfare state has been met with a massive appropriation of scientific and economic resources to the building of a new defense system that would leapfrog over the existing stalemate to achieve military superiority, both strategically and in conventional regional warfare. Budgetary constraints, political priorities, and changing social constituencies all determine the necessary connection between the technology-driven defense build-up and the dismantlement of the urban welfare state. New political coalitions regroup around the ideas of national security, world power, technological progress, and individual well-being, achieved through hard-working entrepreneurship and superior education. The new state is socially exclusive, but ideologically inclusive, with the government's role being reduced to the mediation between the great Americans and the Great America. High technology is presented as the instrument through which both ends meet, economically and functionally. Thus, economic competition in the world arena becomes successful through technological modernization at home and controlled leasing of know-how abroad. Military superiority, and therefore political supremacy, are achieved by the obsolescence of rival armies imposed by leadership in the technological race. And, most importantly, individual well-being is obtained by profound re-tooling of the economy, and by massive reskilling of new workers. This scenario is *not* an ideological artifact; it corresponds to a positive, feasible development policy. What is ideological in this respect is to offer as a general perspective for the whole of society a process that, in reality, will be highly selective, restricted to some social groups, to specific occupations and industries, and to some regions and cities. In this sense, the transformation of the state, which is inherent in the technological revolution, is closely intertwined with the overall process of socio-economic restructuring that has been analyzed in preceding chapters. Changing the principles of political legitimacy, and thus the workings of state institutions, is only possible because of the transformation of the social structure, strongly linked to the new social relationships of production. In turn, the new policies implemented by the state, in particular the technology-driven defense priority, deepen and reinforce the new economic and social organization. The process of restructuring is both multidimensional and interconnected.

The main theme of this chapter has been the impact of such a process of restructuring, and particularly of the transformation of the state, on the urban and regional process. I have also shown how information technologies have played an important role both in the restructuring itself, and in the mediation between the modification of the state and the organization of cities and regions.

First of all, the regional bias of the crisis of the welfare state, damaging further already depressed regions, and the general preference of the warfare state for booming, high-tech-prone areas, have exacerbated uneven regional development. At the same time, some of the traditionally dominant economic regions (for instance the mid-west as opposed to the south-west or the south-east) have been unable to prevail in the new process of growth. So, although the process of uneven development is intensified, the overall spatial pattern does not lead to greater regional disparity, since some of the historical unevenness is now to an extent corrected. What emerges is a much more complex regional structure, with processes of alternate growth and decline, producing an economic space of variable geometry, with acute processes of social dislocation.

Secondly, the demise of the urban welfare state removes the safety net for the large proportion of inner-city residents that fall down the cracks of the new informational economy. In so doing, the new state policies contribute to the process of dualization that characterizes both the labor market and the residential space of large metropolitan areas. The dual city, as an essential part of the informational city, is institutionalized by the state which abandons the spaces of destitution to their own decline, while concentrating resources in and targeting policies on the preserved spaces of functional management and upgraded consumption. Urbanism and the state continue to be tightly linked in the socio-spatial process, although in a direction historically opposite to that which emerged, with the welfare state, during the 1960s.

Thirdly, the rise of a technologically-oriented warfare state has a definite suburban form on the fringe of the large metropolitan areas in expanding regions, for the reasons presented in this chapter on the basis of available empirical evidence. Militarization, high-technology development, and suburbanization seem to be closely related processes, in the specific conditions of the US, and as a consequence of the policies associated with the rise of the warfare state. Given the impetus of this process, the suburban landscape will increasingly be the predominant spatial form of American cities, in spite of all the images of revival of the city cores, a real but limited phenomenon. The suburbanization of residence, of manufacturing, and of services, is now reinforced by the suburbanization of leading industries, associated with defense and high technology, as well as of their relatively affluent workers. It is likely to result in a new type of suburb, more dense, yet extending over a much greater area, in an endless strip served by secondary axes connecting ex-urban dwellings.

The transformation of the state in the informational age deeply affects spatial organization, by exacerbating uneven regional development, reinforcing intra-metropolitan social dualism, and fostering a new breed of suburbanization. In addition, it also influences two key processes at the roots of urban regional dynamics.

On the one hand, the attack on the urban welfare state provokes strong resistance among politically conscious minorities, which organize new local political coalitions in which neighborhoods and minorities have a greater say than in the former pro-growth coalition, in order to retrench themselves in the local state against the predominance of the warfare state logic at Federal and state government level. The example of a large US central city with a populist government, such as Chicago, Washington DC, San Francisco, or Boston, could become general if the demise of the welfare institutions on which patronage resources were based continues, laying the ground for more militant coalitions in which business interests would be secondary to the interests of defending and expanding collective consumption.

On the other hand, the rise of the warfare state is connected to the extension of the logic of military secrecy to the places of work and residence of a substantial proportion of the technological elite. There follows a greater social distance between these exclusive suburban spaces and their surrounding local societies. Cities become more internally segregated, not only socially, but culturally and functionally. Spaces of exclusion, tightly closed communities, co-exist with spatial sprawl of meaningless places structured around their functional activity.

The welfare state was born in the furnaces of life of large inner cities. The warfare state expands over an open space of distance and silence.

6

The Internationalization of the Economy, New Technologies, and the Variable Geometry of the Spatial Structure

Introduction

The internationalization of the economy at an accelerating pace is a fundamental element of the process of economic restructuring now under way. Although the process of internationalization represents a secular trend of capitalism, it has since the 1970s taken on much greater proportions, and has embraced new dimensions, in the attempt by corporations to overcome the contradictions revealed by the structural crisis of the world economy, by increasing the rate at which capital circulates and by constantly searching for the most advantageous location for investment, production, and markets the planet has to offer. National economies have become increasingly inter-dependent through the relentless expansion of world trade and the growing volume of exchange of multidirectional capital flows. While all countries are being drawn into this global network, the internationalization of the US economy is particularly significant because for a long time, while the reach of its companies extended throughout the world, its domestic market had been by virtue of its size and self-sufficiency, relatively insulated from international movements. This process of internationalization proceeds simultaneously on all fundamental dimensions of the economy: markets, investment, means of production, labor, and capital flows. The proportion of exports of goods and services in US GNP was only 5.0 percent in 1950; it increased to 6.78 percent in 1970, then to 12.54 percent in 1981, only to decline subsequently to 8.86 percent in 1986, because of the loss of competitiveness of American industry. Imports' share of GNP increased faster, from 4.26 percent in 1950 to 5.96 percent in 1970, again to 11.42 percent in 1981, and remaining around that level in 1986 (11.37 percent). The importance of foreign trade in goods production and consumption has grown at an even higher rate. In 1970, only 9 percent of goods produced in the US were exported; by 1980, the proportion had climbed to 17 percent. In 1970, 9 percent of goods sold in the US were imported: in 1980 the corresponding figure was 21 percent. About 25 percent of the increase in US consumption of goods during the 1970s was taken up by imports, while 75 percent of American-produced goods must, in the 1980s, face competition in the international market.[1]

Investment and production by American firms have also become increasingly internationalized. Investment overseas by American firms tripled in value between 1970 and 1984. By 1982, US-based multinationals had total assets of about $3.5 billion and employed 20 million workers. Their foreign affiliates had assets of $751 million and employed 6.8 million workers. As early as 1977, American multinationals produced the equivalent of one-third of the US GNP in their offshore facilities. In 1985, the 150 largest US multinationals earned 34 percent of their pre-tax profits abroad, on sales of $415 billion. While the share of world markets for US firms operating in America declined, the exports share of overseas US affiliates increased from 9 percent to 13.4 percent of world exports between 1966 and 1977, indicating a widening gap between the performance of American companies and that of the US economy.[2] Total US direct foreign investment abroad has increased by a factor of five from $51,792 million in 1965 to $259,890 million in 1986 (current dollars), with manufacturing accounting for 40 percent of the total in 1965 and 41.3 percent in 1986. Map 6.1 shows the spatial distribution of employment linked to manufacturing exports in the US.

Offshoring of manufacturing has become an increasingly important feature of US companies in key industries, particularly in electronics, automobiles, textiles, and garments: in 1982, offshore employment accounted for about one-quarter of US manufacturing workers. A particularly important development has been the expansion of offshore production for American companies in northern Mexico, under the protection of Sections 806 and 807 of the US Tariff Code, which permit the export of American components and their re-import after processing in Mexico, with duties to be paid only on the value added. The "maquiladora" plants working in Mexico under such arrangements have increased in number from 300 in 1978 to 760 in 1985, with employment in them growing from 80,000 workers to 300,000. Investments by US firms in these plants and sub-contracting arrangements amounted to $2 billion in 1985 and are still expanding.[3]

Simultaneously, an unprecedented wave of foreign direct investment has swept the US, in all sectors, leading to further interpenetration of the most advanced economies. The value of foreign direct investment in the US in 1985 was $183 billion: 14 times the 1970 level. Between 1979 and 1985 there occurred over seven thousand acquisitions, mergers, and investments in new plants by foreign firms, particularly from the United Kingdom, the Netherlands, Canada, Japan, West Germany, and France. In 1984, foreign firms had $596 billion of total assets, owned 13 million acres of land, and employed 2.7 million workers in the US, including 1.4 million workers in manufacturing, equivalent to 7 percent of total manufacturing employment. Foreign

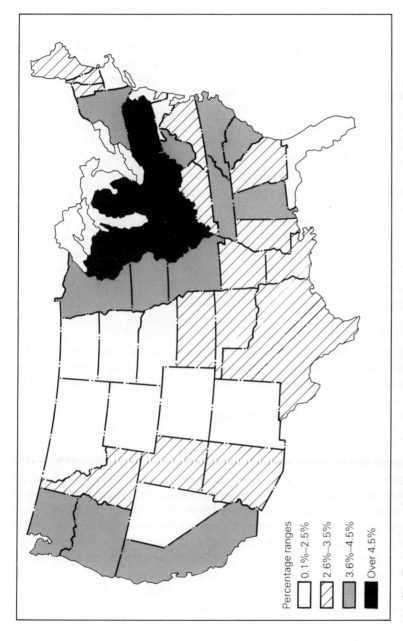

Map 6.1 Employment related to manufacturing exports as a percentage of total civilian employment by state, 1976
Source: Business America, 19 November 1974; compiled by Agnew (see note 1)

Percentage ranges
0.1%–2.5%
2.6%–3.5%
3.6%–4.5%
Over 4.5%

manufacturers further internationalized the patterns of trade, accounting for one-quarter of total exports and one-third of total imports in 1984.[4] In fact, Little[5] has shown that there is a significant correlation between the industries receiving foreign investment in the US and those with the greatest proportion of US investment abroad. What we are witnessing is not the take-over of America but the growing interpenetration of investment patterns within industries between countries, bringing back toward equilibrium the investment flows that for a long time were dominated by movement in one direction only from US firms to other countries.

Also, at the same time, the US has seen its greatest wave of labor immigration since the beginning of the century, in sharp contrast to the scaling down of the pool of immigrant labor in western European countries during the 1980s. Continuing unabated by the recession of 1980–2, immigration to the US from Mexico, Latin America, the Caribbean, Asia, and, to a lesser extent, Europe, has provided an inexhaustible supply of all kinds of labor, assisting in the restructuring of capital–labor relationships, as argued in chapter 4. Most of this immigration bypasses the legal procedures: the number of undocumented workers in the US is estimated at about 7 million, and is believed to represent over three-quarters of the million or so new immigrants who have arrived in the US every year during the 1980s.[6] The fundamental urban impact of this phenomenon has been discussed in chapter 4; here it should just be kept in mind as another dimension of the process of internationalization that includes all aspects of the production and consumption processes.

Finally, internationalization of the process by which capital circulates has reached unprecedented levels. Worldwide capitalization increased from $892 billion in 1974 to a staggering $5.2 trillion in 1986.[7] The US plays a major, albeit decreasing, role in the handling of such capital flows: of the global total of $549 billion of direct foreign investment stock in 1984, the US accounted for 42.5 percent, followed by the UK with 15.5 percent and Japan with 6.9 percent. Total foreign investment in the US to be distinguished, of course, from *direct* foreign investment) doubled from $416 billion in 1979 to $874 billion in 1984, with the largest and fastest-growing category being private portfolios and private deposits, together accounting for almost $500 billion in 1984; private government holdings accounted for an additional $196 billion, the remaining capital being direct foreign investment. In addition, because of its increasing need to borrow foreign capital to finance the budget deficit and to compensate for the trade deficit, the US, as is now well known, has shifted from being a creditor nation in 1980 to become the world's largest debtor nation, with a debt of $250 billion by the end of 1986.[8] The US economy, and US-based financial institutions, are the recipients of a tremendous flow of capital through the combination of three processes: worldwide financial investments handled from the US; massive inflows of foreign investment into the US; and increasing lending from foreign capital to US firms and the US government. Altogether, the American financial system has become entirely interdependent in a global network of capital flows of which the US is indeed a major center, but no longer a dominant one in terms of control over the extent and direction of capital flows. The linkage between capital flows and the balance of trade through the dollar's exchange rate has further constrained domestic fiscal policy, and tied the US inextricably to the interdependent evolution of the world economy.

This multidimensional process of internationalization and growing interdependence has been made possible by widespread utilization of new information technologies.[9] In the same way that the railroads were the indispensable infrastructure for the formation of a national market in the US in the nineteenth century, so the expansion of information systems, based on telecommunications and computers, has provided the technological medium for the formation of a world economy functioning in real time on a day-to-day basis. Without such information systems it would have been impossible to maintain the unity of management while decentralizing worldwide the production and markets of any given firm, at the same time as firms stepped up their interaction in every market. Without information systems, capital mobility could never have reached the volume and velocity illustrated by the data presented above. And without information systems, international trade could hardly constitute the dominant feature of advanced economies.

Furthermore, competitiveness in the new international economy is increasingly determined by the ability to develop and assimilate new technologies in the processes of production and management. Mastery of the technological medium becomes an indispensable requirement to win a competitive edge in a merciless worldwide competition, with new actors entering every day, struggling for survival, searching for domination. Access to technological sources, and ability to use them, adapt them, and improve them, becomes one of the most important forces in shaping the competition and its outcome, that is, the new economic structure. Production of new information-technology devices becomes one of the biggest world markets, whose control largely conditions the performance of firms and countries in all industries. Being the most internationalized industry, the manufacturing of information technologies, and their use, become the backbone of the new international economy, both as a market and as an instrument of competition. The more the economy is internationalized, the more crucial a role information technologies play in its shape and evolution. The technological medium conditions the fate and outcome of economic restructuring by its decisive impact on the process of internationalization, the fundamental feature of the new economy.

From this follows a transformation of spatial processes in all countries, and specifically in the US, whose contours we will examine by focusing in turn on each one of the dimensions of the internationalization process: trade, offshore production, foreign investment, and global financial flows.

International Trade, Competitiveness, and the Rise and Fall of American Regions

The growing integration of the US economy in international trade has far-reaching, and somewhat unsuspected, implications for both the US itself and the world economy at large.[10] Since the mid 1970s manufacturing exports have been growing steadily, as has the share of exports in manufacturing for almost all industries. However, the confrontation of US manufacturers with foreign competition in the world marketplace has proved disastrous for America. In spite of their growing relative importance in US terms, American exports of manufactured goods have declined in proportion to those of other countries, as America's share of world markets in value terms has declined from 26 percent in 1960 to 18 percent in 1980, before the overvaluation of the dollar; and it continued to slip during the 1980s.[11] On the other hand, imports skyrocketed, particularly in consumer electronics, automobiles, textiles, clothing, footwear, and machine tools. The merchandise trade balance, which was positive from 1893 to 1970, turned negative in 1971, and, with the exception of 1973 and 1975, continued negative, with the deficit reaching catastrophic proportions in the 1980s: from a deficit of $38.4 billions in 1982, the negative trade balance set a new record every year, reaching the figure of $171.2 billion in 1987. The extremity of the situation of American trade can be judged by recalling that the trade deficit figures for December 1987 were considered good news, because they showed only a $12.2 billion deficit in just one month!

For some time, losses in manufacturing trade were partially offset by surpluses in agriculture, in services, and in high-technology balances. However, after being stimulated by government policies in the early 1970s, agricultural exports were also exposed to foreign competition, and the surplus was reduced from $30 billion in 1979–80 to just $4 billion in 1986. As for services, the surplus gradually declined as US earnings abroad diminished, and revenues from foreign capital lent to the US increased, until 1985, when the US also posted a deficit in its service account.[12] While the technology chapter of the service account was still positive (but represented only $5 billion), the manufacturing–technology balance deteriorated rapidly over the 1980s.[13] And in 1985 the US imported $463 billion worth of goods and services.

The reasons for this startling loss in competitiveness are rooted in the structure of the American economy. It is true that other factors have to be taken into consideration, in particular the exchange rate: when in 1987 the value of the dollar against the main international currencies plummeted, falling as much as 40 percent from its February 1985 peak, some of the economy's competitiveness was restored and exports started to improve, merchandise exports rising 15 percent in 1987. However, the losses in foreign trade show up during phases when the dollar has been undervalued as well as when it has been overvalued in the last 15 years; and the shares of the US market won by imports have been largely preserved by foreign competitors slashing profit margins to retain their market position. More important in explaining the decline in trade is the role played by the Reagan administration's macroeconomic policy in creating fiscal and monetary conditions that undermined US competitiveness. By artificially stimulating the economy through a runaway budget deficit, Reaganomics stimulated consumer demand for imports by consumers; and by borrowing foreign capital on an unprecedented scale to finance the deficit, it drove the dollar up, which attracted more capital, but made exports more expensive and imports cheaper.[14] Consequently, the *de facto* devaluation of the dollar in 1987 could not be pursued indefinitely because to do so would dry up the sources of capital needed to finance the budget deficit (in this sense the two mega-deficits are interwined). Restoration of competitiveness, then, cannot be achieved by the sole means of manipulating the exchange rate.

The roots of the crisis in competitivness seem to go deeper, and to reach beyond the entry of new economic actors catching up with the US on the international scene. Cohen and Zysman, in a powerful and well informed book,[15] have argued that the decline of American competitiveness lies in a combination of external factors and internal weaknesses. On the one hand, the structure of costs in newly industrializing countries, the state support granted to many foreign firms, and the closing of some major markets, most notably Japan, to American products, certainly placed US firms at a disadvantage. However, the domestic factors seem to be more important. By forgetting the crucial linkage between manufacturing and services, and by concentrating too exclusively on high-technology innovation and services, instead of rooting both in the rejuvenation of industrial production, American companies have created a "hollow economy," dominated by "paper capitalism," that cannot resist the assault of new competitors (Japan, West Germany, and the Asian NICs), who systematically upgrade their production technologies, and concentrate on keeping manufacturing quality up and manufacturing costs down to outpace their competitors in the international market. On this competitive basis they accumulate capital, which ultimately puts them in the position where they control the process of circulation itself. By emigrating to low-cost locations or sub-contracting production internationally, instead of automating and upgrading the production process in the US, American companies have created the conditions of their own demise. Finally, the inability to overhaul the educational system to provide on a sufficiently large scale the new skills required in the informational processes of production and management also places the US behind its competitors, who also do not have to sustain the burden of unproductive, technology-draining military expenditures. Overall, the US is too expensive as a location from which to operate, and too unsophisticated to be worth the investment of staying in the country. Only the attraction of the market remains; but this increasingly has to be shared with foreign investors, and will not last indefinitely, given the precipitous decline in American living standards. While the process is reversible, its unfolding logic shows the contradictions introduced in the economic structure by the processes of internationalization and technological change when, instead of being harnessed within a long-term view, they are approached with a short-term, individualistic strategy aimed at maximizing immediate profits.

The erosion of American competitiveness has had profound effects on the country's economic and occupational structure. Traditional manufacturing, most heavily struck by competition, and by runaway shops trying to reproduce the competitors' cost structure in offshore locations, experienced a substantial decline during the 1976–86 decade. According to the Bureau of Labor Statistics, between 1979 and January 1987, there was a loss of 1.9 million manufacturing jobs, although not all of them can be related to the trade deficit. These losses included 500,000 jobs in primary metals, 450,000 in machinery, 350,000 in textiles and apparel, and 300,000 in fabricated metals. Other sectors that suffered job losses were stone, transportation, leather, chemicals, petroleum, and food.[16] In another study by the Urban Institute, it was estimated that about 2 million jobs were lost because of rising imports between 1979 and 1984, particularly in steel, automobiles, and apparel.[17] High-technology industries were not immune to competition: electronics went into a major slump in 1984–5, with computers being particularly severely hurt. An econometric study by John Lederer relates loss of jobs in California's electronics industry to foreign competition, and more specifically to lower labor costs in the Japanese companies.[18] The more an industry is exposed to competition, the more it is vulnerable to lower production costs, and the more its share of both domestic and international markets will decline. As early as 1979, the US imported 21 percent of its cars, 16 percent of its steel, 50 percent of its televisions, radios, tape recorders, and VCRs, and 90 percent of its knives and forks.[19] Lester Thurow's calculations attribute the loss of 3 million jobs to loss of international competitiveness in overseas markets.[20] An OTA study indicates that half of all workers displaced between 1979 and 1984 worked in manufacturing industries, particularly in those hard hit by foreign competition, such as steel, automobiles, industrial equipment, textiles, and apparel.[21] The effects of loss of competitiveness are not limited to the core manufacturing areas themselves, but, as Cohen and Zysman have argued, are also apparent in related manufacturing and services activities. According to *Business Week*,[22] the total impact on the economy for each billion dollars' worth of imported cars was $2.43 billion, including $1.3 billion lost in auto production, $778 million in manufacturing suppliers, and $387 million in related service industries.

These effects are territorially specific. Since manufacturing, and particularly traditional manufacturing, is unevenly distributed among regions, those areas with industries specially vulnerable to foreign competition will be most hurt by the loss of market share. Map 6.1 shows the concentration of manufacturing exports in 1976, in the early stages of the loss of competitiveness, and table 6.1 exhibits the relative importance of manufacturing exports

Table 6.1 Manufacturing exports by state in the United States. 1976–1984

	Total manufacturing export ($m)		Average annual rate of growth (%)	Export as % of total shipments		Average annual rate of growth (%)
	1976	1984		1976	1984	
Alabama	832	4,198	22.4	4.6	11.6	12.3
Alaska	233	643	13.5	23.5	27.2	1.8
Arizona	639	2,481	18.5	10.3	15.6	5.3
Arkansas	651	2,405	17.7	6.1	10.5	7.0
California	8,072	28,764	17.2	7.9	13.0	6.4
Colorado	616	2,790	20.8	6.5	13.1	9.2
Connecticut	1,598	5,436	16.5	10.7	15.6	4.8
Delaware	188	1,132	25.1	3.7	11.7	15.5
District of Columbia	7	72	33.9	0.7	4.2	25.1
Florida	1,363	5,975	20.3	7.5	12.5	6.6
Georgia	1,364	5,061	17.8	4.8	8.2	6.9
Hawaii	183	414	10.7	9.9	12.1	2.5
Idaho	169	666	18.7	4.9	10.7	10.3
Illinois	6,660	13,332	9.1	8.1	10.6	3.4
Indiana	2,828	9,380	16.2	6.3	12.2	8.6
Iowa	1,500	3,296	10.3	7.2	9.8	3.9
Kansas	635	2,630	19.4	4.3	8.6	9.1
Kentucky	1,137	4,077	17.3	5.6	10.9	8.7
Louisiana	1,383	6,990	22.4	5.5	12.7	11.0
Maine	255	1,215	21.6	5.8	12.2	9.7
Maryland	641	2,328	17.5	4.3	9.9	11.0
Massachusetts	2,502	8,768	17.0	9.3	15.0	6.2
Michigan	6,888	16,662	11.7	8.6	12.8	5.1
Minnesota	1,567	5,294	16.4	7.7	12.4	6.1
Mississippi	698	2,237	15.7	6.4	10.0	5.7

Table 6.1 Continued

Missouri	1,622	5,375	16.2	5.9	10.2	7.1
Montana	44	319	28.2	1.7	8.4	22.1
Nebraska	309	1,328	19.9	3.5	8.7	12.1
Nevada	27	183	26.9	3.8	10.3	13.3
New Hampshire	291	1,129	18.5	8.3	12.9	5.7
New Jersey	2,660	8,024	14.8	5.8	10.3	7.4
New Mexico	69	330	21.6	4.5	8.4	8.1
New York	5,320	15,993	14.7	7.0	11.9	6.9
North Carolina	2,020	8,477	18.4	6.1	10.8	7.4
North Dakota	85	290	16.7	6.8	11.2	6.4
Ohio	5,794	17,381	14.7	6.9	12.3	7.5
Ohlahoma	579	2,288	18.7	5.7	9.3	6.3
Oregon	824	2,709	16.0	6.7	12.9	8.5
Pennsylvania	4,706	12,827	13.4	6.5	11.4	7.3
Rhode Island	269	946	17.1	5.9	11.1	8.2
South Carolina	935	3,982	19.8	5.6	11.7	9.6
South Dakota	68	245	17.3	4.2	7.0	6.6
Tennessee	1,253	5,008	18.9	5.1	10.1	8.9
Texas	5,201	22,093	19.8	6.7	12.6	8.2
Utah	224	1,298	24.6	4.8	12.6	12.8
Vermont	200	617	15.1	9.7	16.2	6.6
Virginia	1,545	4,781	15.2	7.5	10.9	4.8
Washington	3,235	8,632	13.1	17.2	22.4	3.4
West Virginia	447	1,853	19.4	5.6	17.2	15.1
Wisconsin	2,209	5,785	12.8	6.2	9.3	5.2
Wyoming	10	152	40.0	1.2	6.3	23.0
United States, total	83,098	268,278	15.8	7.0	11.9	6.9

Source: US Department of Commerce, *Annual Survey of Manufactures*, 1976, 1984.

by state. If we relate these data to the statistics on job displacement presented in tables 6.2 and 6.3, elaborated by Candee Harris[23] we observe a general correspondence between the regions with a strong trend in manufacturing export-related jobs and those with low replacement ratios for jobs lost and created. Overall, the old manufacturing belt underwent a massive contraction in employment between 1967 and 1980: 24.8 percent down for New York, 11.1 percent for New Jersey, 14.3 percent for Pennsylvania, 11.2 percent for Michigan, 12.5 percent for Illinois, 9.2 percent for Ohio, and 7.3 percent for Indiana.[24]

However, not all these manufacturing jobs disappeared: some moved offshore, and some relocated to other areas, particularly the south and the

Table 6.2 Employment loss in dissolutions of manufacturing establishments by region (%)

Region	1972–4	1974–6	1978–80	1980–2
New England	8.0	8.1	7.4	11.4
Mid-Atlantic	7.9	11.0	7.1	11.5
East-north-central	5.4	8.9	6.4	10.8
West-north-central	7.0	9.9	5.6	10.5
South Atlantic	8.1	11.6	7.3	13.7
East-south-central	7.6	10.3	6.0	13.7
West-south-central	7.8	11.1	7.3	12.6
Mountain	9.2	14.1	7.1	14.7
Pacific	8.6	10.9	9.0	14.0

Sources: 1972–4, 1974–6, David Birch, *The Job Generation Process* (final report to the Economic Development Administration, US Department of Commerce, grant no. OER-608-G78-7, June 1979); 1978–80, 1980–2, unpublished tabulations, US Establishment and Enterprise Microdata Base. Calculated by Harris (see note 23)

Table 6.3 Manufacturing job replacement ratios for all establishments by region

Region	1972–4	1974–6	1978–80	1980–2
New England	1.42	0.45	1.58	0.52
Mid-Atlantic	1.06	0.28	1.45	0.52
East-north-central	1.85	0.57	1.33	0.22
West-north-central	2.15	0.65	2.21	0.57
South Atlantic	1.65	0.61	2.16	0.69
East-south-central	1.97	0.71	1.83	0.32
West-south-central	1.86	1.16	2.94	1.05
Mountain	1.70	1.01	3.01	0.88
Pacific	1.60	1.47	2.10	0.86
US total	1.60	0.67	1.85	0.57

Sources: 1972–4, 1974–6, David Birch *The Job Generation Process;* 1978–80, 1980–2, unpublished tabulations, US Establishment and Enterprise Microdata Base. Calculated by Harris (see note 23).

south-west, trying to find there better conditions with which to fight foreign competition, most notably lower wages and less stringent labor laws. In 1967-80, Texas showed the largest increase in manufacturing employment of any state, in absolute numbers, with particularly high increases in chemicals, petroleum, and primary metals. According to Bluestone and Harrison, for the period 1969-76 the balance between jobs created and jobs destroyed was a positive 8,851,900 million for the whole of the US, of which 6,624,000 were in the sunbelt.[25] Nevertheless, the majority of losses as a result of declining international competitiveness took place after 1976, and Peter Hall's calculations for the 1975-85 period are therefore more relevant.[26] Two sub-periods must be differentiated. In 1975-80, the US economy generated 15.7 million new jobs, of which only 13 percent were in manufacturing, and only 27 percent in the manufacturing belt. Of every five of these new jobs, three were located in the sunbelt, and two-thirds of them in what Hall labels the "new perimeter," meaning the sunbelt and New England together. In fact, 70 percent of new manufacturing jobs in this half-decade were created in the sunbelt, and only an additional 11 percent in New England. In the second half of the decade, 1980-5, only 4.2 million new jobs were created. Of these, 87 percent were in the sunbelt, and 96 percent in the sunbelt plus New England. If New England were to be omitted from the traditional manufacturing belt, this manufacturing belt would be shown to have suffered a net loss of 400,000 manufacturing jobs, although they were more than compensated for numerically by the creation of service jobs. In this sense, the manufacturing belt may be divided into two areas: the mid-Atlantic, which had the worst performance in manufacturing jobs, losing 276,000 of them, but which performed well in terms of creating compensatory numbers of service jobs; and the east-north-central states, which lost fewer manufacturing jobs (138,000) but could not create enough service jobs to compensate for the loss, resulting in a net decline in employment.

Four processes, then, appear to be at work simultaneously: loss of traditional manufacturing, partially linked to foreign competition, both abroad and in the domestic market; relocation of manufacturing jobs in the south, south-west, and west, in search of a labor and regulatory environment that makes competition easier; growth. of manufacturing jobs in new industries, as in the case of New England and California, both established manufacturing regions (although only New England is regionally integrated in the old manufacturing belt); and a capacity of generation of new service jobs, through linkages either with the new expanding regional economy (the sunbelt) or with the nodal metropolitan centers in the international economy (in the north-east and the west). In addition, it must be noted that traditional manufacturing is vulnerable to the new conditions of the international economy wherever it may be located. The automobile industry has been hurt in California as much as it has in the Great Lakes; and the textile and garment industries in the south were devastated by foreign competition, before engineering a comeback on the basis of new technologies.[27]

Regional fortunes have also been linked to the sharp variations in commodity prices on the world markets. When the price of oil in the 1970s appeared to have no limit but the sky, Texas rode on the crest of a spending wave that has left its mark on Houston's architectural monument to self-infatuation. When the administration's policies geared toward offsetting the manufacturing deficit by means of increasing agricultural exports pushed up farm prices in the early 1970s, and encouraged farmers to borrow and expand, the mid-western farm belt believed in the permanence of the earth's bounty. And when one state, such as Oklahoma, was blessed with both agricultural endowments and oil resources, everything seemed possible. But then came the glut of oil and the fall of energy prices, along with fiercer competition in the grain markets from the EEC; and by the mid-1980s there had come into being what has been called a "deflation belt" throughout middle America.[28]

The basic phenomenon, therefore, is not the irreversible demise of certain regions, linked to forms of production that were becoming technologically obsolete in the world economy. Silicon Valley went into a recession in 1984–6, much as Iowa did in the mid-1980s. And while electronics was doing well in 1987, so was agro-business in California. New England taught the world a lesson about how to operate the transition from deindustrialization of old manufacturing to reindustrialization of high technology. Michigan combined depressed areas in Detroit with booming business around Flint and Ann Arbor's "robot alley." The new industrialized south was also losing jobs in textiles, as foreign competition showed its resistance to tariffs by modifying its price structure. All over America's industrial landscape there was a diversity of reactions and adjustments to the new conditions of international competition. Some strategies emphasized upgrading of manufacturing through technology and re-skilling. Others imitated Third World over-exploitation and reinvented the sweatshop. Others still relied on foreign supplies or on Mexican border operations to combine the best of both worlds from a business perspective. The fundamental transformation, common to all industries and to all regions, was the tight linkage between world dynamics and regional dynamics. Never again would the US be able to take refuge in its own land, or to live by its own habits. The law of internationalization, imposed upon the world on an unprecedented scale by American capitalism, was now coming home to roost. Among the corollaries of this process are extreme volatility of production and consumption, and therefore of income and everyday life, according to the state of play in the competition of capital between and within regions. The rise and fall of American regions no longer follows the script written by American capital or the American state. It just happens, in complex interaction among world economic processes, individual firms' strategies, and confused policies from local, state, and Federal governments. The internationalization of the American economy has led to the fragmentation of its regions and to the constant realignment of its processes of regional development; and its reaction, in the attempt to recover autonomy through protectionism at different levels, has triggered the ultimate response from economic competitors worldwide: to penetrate deeply the US economy with foreign investment, some of it dating from the good period of successful exports to the largest market in the world, a time when American companies moved a significant proportion of their own production offshore to enable them to compete in their own market.

Restructuring, Internationalization of Production, and Technological Change: The Case of the American Automobile Industry

The internationalization of the production process itself is one of the dimensions of the process of restructuring. New technologies of telecommunication, transportation, and automation allow firms to separate their different manufacturing operations across boundaries, while reintegrating them into a unified system under the control of the company's management. The resulting locational pattern modifies profoundly the characteristics of the industrial space and its impact on urban and regional development.

In chapter 2 the internationalization of electronics production was analyzed, the pioneer industry in offshoring assembly operations. This section will focus on the automobile industry, a major industrial sector in the American economy, whose direct and indirect employment accounted in 1977 for about 21 percent of the total labor force.[29] Particular attention will be concentrated on the dialectics between offshoring of production and more recent tendencies toward reconcentration in the core, stimulated by newer and more sophisticated automation technologies in manufacturing.

The automobile industry exemplifies the complex interplay between economic and technological restructuring and the internationalization of production and investment. The oil shock of 1973–4 plunged into a worldwide crisis an industry that had been the leading sector in the industrialization process based on mass-production that took place between the 1920s and the 1960s.[30] The effects of that crisis were exacerbated for the US by increased foreign competition from cheaper, better-quality, more fuel-efficient cars. US production represented over 75 percent of total world production of automobiles in 1950, but the proportion was only 29 percent in 1974, and continued to slide down to 19.3 percent in 1982, although it re-covered slightly after that date. Foreign imports' share of passenger cars in the US market rose from 15 percent in 1950 to 28 percent in 1982. The combined impact of oil prices, economic slump, and product obsolescence drove Chrysler to the edge of bankruptcy (from which it was pulled back by the US government), seriously damaged Ford's profitability, and even put the giant

General Motors on the defensive. The industry responded with one of the boldest restructuring processes in recent economic history, focusing at the same time on new products and new processes.[31] New technologies were massively introduced both in factories and in the cars themselves. In the factory, robotization, CAD/CAM, and flexible manufacturing systems rapidly transformed the assembly lines, while computers were introduced in all processes of design and testing.[32] New materials changed the basic characteristics of cars and new electronic systems their operations. The evolution of the automobile from the electrical–mechanical complex to the electronic–plastic product accelerated.[33] At the same time, advances in telecommunications, air transportation, and bulk cargo technologies increased the mobility of parts and vehicles between sites of production, and between production sites and the markets. Altogether, the industry was once again a pioneer in experimenting with new production techniques and, to some extent, with new methods of management. Fifteen years later, it is, by and large, a new industry, whose geographic distribution at the world level has been modified by the scale of its transformation.

The restructuring process went through different stages and revealed different emphases in various countries and firms. In the US the first move, for all companies, was purely defensive. It amounted to retrenchment, with plant closures, massive lay-offs, sales of assets, and reductions in investment. Chrysler liquidated its foreign subsidiaries. The launching of new models, adapted to the new energy circumstances and more highly discriminating consumer tastes, helped to absorb some of the initial shock of the crisis, particularly for GM, which, shielded by its size and financial resources, actually benefited from the catastrophic performance of its US competitors. In the late 1970s, the more positive strategy aimed at surviving the crisis and arriving on more stable ground, came into being along two different lines: stepped-up internationalization of production and distribution; and automation and computerization of the industry, both to save labor and to improve quality, thus enhacing productivity. The two strategies were used simultaneously by all firms, but, as will be explained below, with different emphases from company to company and within different time-frames. They also led to different locational consequences.

The process of internationalization took place on the basis of the decentralization that US companies, and particularly Ford, had effected since the 1950s in Europe, and since the 1960s in Latin America. By 1980, 37.2 percent of the total motor vehicle production of the four leading US manufacturers was located abroad. Indeed, in 1980, the US share of world car production was down to 21.7 percent, but US *manufacturers'* share of world production was still 33.4 percent.[34] The restructuring process initiated in the 1970s saw some additional steps taken along the path toward internationalization of production. The most direct expression of this trend was increased offshoring of sourcing, first of parts, but later of major mechanical elements, including engines. In 1980–3 US imports of engines grew by a factor of about four, from 544,020 units to 2,183,842. Most of these came from Brazil, France, joint-venture operations in Japan, and, particularly, from Mexico. In 1982, all American manufacturers had major engine plants in Mexico: Ford in Chihuahua, producing 400,000 engines (90 percent of them for export to the US and Canada); Chrysler in Ramos Arizpe, with 220,000 engines, equivalent to half of the four-cylinder engines used in Aries and Reliant cars; American Motors in Torreon, producing 300,000 engines for the R-9 built in Kenosha, Wisconsin; and GM in Ramos Arizpe, turning out 360,000 V-6 engines for the "8" and "X" models.[35] In 1984, Mexico exported to the US 700,000 automobile engines. Overall, by 1985, according to UNIDO, agreements to supply engines from offshore sources to US-located manufacturers included 1.5 million engines for Ford, over 1 million for GM, and 1.1 million for Chrysler.[36] The trends are similar for transmissions, cylinder heads, electronic control devices, power train items, and more.[37] Automobile imports, of both vehicles and parts, contributed $40.4 billion to the trade deficit in 1985.[38]

There are basically three reasons for this wholesale move offshore, which increased dramatically from the late 1970s onwards, to Mexico in particular: lower costs of production, mainly because of cheaper labor; government subsidies (in the case of Mexico and Brazil); and better quality (particularly for Japan). The net result is the hollowing out of a substantial part of automobile manufacturing in the US, which comes to be focused on assembling and marketing for the domestic market engines and parts that increasingly have been produced abroad.

The ultimate expression of the internationalization strategy is the "world car" concept, put forward mainly by Ford in the 1970s.[39] It refers to the design of cars that, with some minor modifications, can be sold in many different markets, if not in all countries. Their production takes place in different countries, following the competitive advantages of each location, and the components are assembled close to or in the final markets. The Ford Fiesta was the first example of such a car, with engines made in Valencia, Spain, and components and major parts in England and France, to be assembled in Spain, England, and Germany, and sold in the EC and North America. The strategy avoids duplication of effort in engineering and design, and takes advantage of the best possible location for each phase of the production process, putting into practice the concept of the "global factory." Harley Shaiken[40] has shown the decisive role played by new information technologies in the feasibility of this strategy. On the one hand, computerization of design and sophisticated telecommunications facilities linking engineering centers allow for interaction among research centers in different countries, as well as for the reintegration of the management process despite the multiplicity of production sites and markets. On the other hand, automation of production allows for precision and exact specification of components that can be assembled without being tested in the same plant.

However, the most important element in the "world car" strategy is, in the words of Ford's Chairman, "more common brains than common parts."[41] Ford's Erika Project, according to the company, saved 15,000 engineering/ man years and $150 million, by implementing the "world car" strategy.

The spatial implications of the internationalization process center on decentralization of production and interrelationships both among plants and between plants and markets. Offshoring of component manufacture eliminates jobs in the US and diversifies the location of the industry. Global reintegration through communication channels enables this locational diversity to grow while maintaining the unity of the process. In terms of the regional impacts in the US, Ross and Trachte[42] have shown the dramatic effects of both automation and internationalization on employment in automobile manufacturing. Overall, total US employment in automobile manufacturing reached a peak of 1,004,900 jobs in 1978, to decline by 1983 to 704,800, below its 1951 level. In 1980-1, the industry went into full recession. The three major companies suffered combined losses of $3.5 billion; they laid off 250,000 workers, and an additional 400,000 workers in the supplier companies also lost their jobs.[43] The regions and cities that were the traditional centers of the industry, such as the Great Lakes and the Detroit area, were particularly badly hurt. Total motor vehicle employment in Michigan declined from 411,000 jobs in 1956 to 287,000 in 1982; in Detroit, over the same period, it fell from 252,000 jobs to 167,000. The impact of automobile retrenchment on Detroit was devastating. By 1981, one in every three residents in Detroit was receiving some form of public assistance. Central city infant mortality rates were at the level of Peru or Guyana, standing at four times higher than those of Detroit's suburbs. As Agnew writes:

The history of Detroit captures in one place the history of the American manufacturing belt. From 1870 until 1910 Detroit was one of several multipurpose cities of the industrial belt. From 1910 until the late 1960s the automobile industry and war production made Detroit a major national industrial center. But the country's sixth largest city has now become enmeshed in a web of uneven development spun first by the flow of industrial and commercial capital to the suburbs, and then to the Sunbelt and, more recently, by the reorganization and decentralization of the auto industry on a global scale. . . . Detroit is a victim of the world car.[44]

The impact of restructuring in the automobile industry was by no means limited to the Great Lakes area. In fact, Los Angeles held, after Detroit, the second largest agglomeration of automobile manufacturing in the US. Between 1975 and 1983, California lost 21,835 jobs through the closing of auto-related plants, most of them in northern California. The ratio of production to sales of cars in California went from 0.78 in 1968 to 0.12 in 1983.[45]

Looking beyond the decline of certain regions, what is really significant is the international mobility of capital, which determines the fate of industrial sectors, labor market segments, spatial areas, and local communities.

The global integration process, epitomized by the "world car" strategy, was not the only line pursued by US companies in the restructuring of the automobile industry. As the MIT study on the future of the automobile revealed,[46] a number of alternative options could be, and indeed were, explored. Paramount among them was better use of the possibilities offered by information technologies. Flexible manufacturing technologies make possible short production runs without lower productivity, enabling swift responses to market demand through constant redesign of the product, as well as by reprogramming the production process. The most important development in this transformation of both technology and production techniques is the adoption of the Japanese Kanban or "just in time" system, which enables drastic reduction of inventories by precisely tracking needs for parts and components, so that suppliers can provide those components only when and as they are needed. Besides making for considerable savings by avoiding tying up capital in inventory, the system also makes it possible to define a precise relationship to the market in terms of both time and quality, thus establishing flexible and continuous links between suppliers, assemblers, and markets. Fullest use of the Kanban system became possible only with the introduction of CAD/CAM and FIM (Flexible Integrated Manufacturing) techniques. In addition, automation of routine tasks saves labor costs and enhances quality; and computer design develops engineering capability and marketing adaptability to worldwide demand. An alternative to offshoring production to low-cost location is, following the Japanese example, to concentrate production in core areas of mature industrialization, to automate and upgrade substantially the technological level of manufacturing equipment, and to renovate labor practices through introducing team-work and involving workers in quality control of production, through a re-skilling of their professional capacities. According to this strategy, decentralization to low-skilled areas or countries is self-defeating in the long term, since higher quality and productivity through technological enhancement can only be achieved on the basis of a developed industrial infrastructure and a highly educated and motivated labor force. Moreover, location of manufacturing plants close to the core markets, where the overwhelming proportion of demand will be concentrated for a long time, enables the firm to be responsive to the changing demands of increasingly sophisticated customers in the face of stiff competition from highly flexible and well informed foreign manufacturers. These were the conclusions of the MIT study, in line with observed developments in the industry. Womack, one of the authors of that study, concluded in his analysis of Mexico that the main incentive for US auto makers to locate in the neighboring country would increasingly be the expansion of Mexico's domestic market rather than the off-shoring of production, which would decline as the advantages of flexible automation in the US unfolded.[47] A reconcentration of the industry around core markets and technology-endowed industrial regions is thus foreseen.

GM's strategy since 1979 clearly followed this line of argument, with the whole company adapting to what was perceived to be the secret of Japanese competitiveness: high-technology manufacturing and better management from the home-country platforms. Of course, GM still continued to produce worldwide, particularly in Europe, and still relied on considerable sourcing from foreign countries, mainly Japan, Korea, and Mexico. Nevertheless, the emphasis was on re-equipping the entire company with full use of new technologies and the design of a new generation of cars. In 1979 a new strategy was launched aimed at building complete new plants, and at introducing computerized equipment in all GM factories. By 1987, $60 billion had been spent on this ambitious program – more than one-third over the originally planned $40 billion.[48] The most spectacular example of the new strategy was the project to build a new, small, front-wheel-drive car able to outpace the competition on the basis of its technological advancement, both as a product and in its production process. The "Saturn Project," announced in 1982, contemplated the building of the most advanced automobile factory in the world, at a cost of $5 billion, reducing by $2,000 the production cost of a sub-compact car. The initial production target was 400,000 cars per year, with 1990 as the starting year of production. The site selected for the factory, after major competition among many soliciting cities and states, was a rural southern locality: Spring Hill, Tennessee (close to a Nissan plant). The project was pursued in cooperation with the United Auto Workers labor union, and included relocation from the Detroit area of the majority of the workers to ensure reliance from the onset on an experienced, skilled labor force.

In parallel with production developments, GM also pursued a strategy of innovative management procedures, setting up a joint venture with Toyota to produce under the label of the new company (NUMMI) the US version of the Toyota Corolla. In this case, too, the plant, located in Fremont, a San Franciso suburb, rehired in 1985 most of the unionized auto workers of the GM plant who had been laid off on the closing of the former GM plant in 1982. GM's response to foreign competition was to learn from the successes of its competitors, and to adopt, and adapt for its own purposes, twin measures of better working procedures and better equipment.[49] In addition, an audacious technological program, introducing the most advanced microelectronics technology, was intended to provide the company with a technological edge, based on superior American ingenuity.

The spatial implications of this new, more innovative strategy, are quite different from those of the offshoring process, as shown by Erica Schoenberger in her excellent analysis of the subject.[50] Instead of worldwide decentralization, the new production sites tend toward spatial reconcentration, since linkages within the company and between the company and its quality suppliers are crucial to the functioning of such a complex system. Proximity does not necessarily mean immediate spatial contiguity with the traditional manufacturing regions, as the location of the Saturn factory indicates; but the linkage imperative does require a high degree of accessibility, and therefore good transportation and relative proximity to the main manufacturing complexes and final markets. On the other hand, these new manufacturing complexes are fairly footloose, given that the internal relationships of the company, and its connections with its suppliers, are more important than specific location factors, as exemplifed by the massive relocation of the labor required for the Saturn project. In fact, the location of GM's most advanced production facilities in the US show the diverse geographical expressions that can result from the one spatial logic: in contrast to the examples cited in Spring Hill and in Fremont, the fully automated Orion facility near Detroit, and the Buick–City complex around Flint, Michigan (the company's headquarters), show the persistence of some attachment to the industrial heartland. Yet what is really important is that in all instances the spatial logic remains the same: locational constraints are internalized within the company's own dynamics, in the spatial model that Richard Hill has characterized as typical of the new "company town," best re-presented by Toyota in Nagoya.[51] Thus, Spring Hill, Fremont, Detroit, Flint, are all GM, and it is around these individual sites that the new production complexes are woven, with relationships between these units and their markets following the lines of corporate organization. In this sense, GM's strategy calls for core-based but spatially diversified reconcentration of production, rather than for decentralization and peripheral offshoring, although internationalization remains a support system in the company's global strategy.

It would appear, as the MIT study and Schoenberger's analysis (among other works)[52] suggest, that the process of internationalization of production is being reversed, and decentralization substantially slowed down. However, the process is somewhat more complex than this, for the impact of new technologies on restructuring, and on its spatial consequences, can never be directly inferred from the characteristics of the technology.[53] Several facts challenge the assumption of an irreversible substitution of the flexible automation/spatial reconcentration strategy for the offshore production/ "world car"/decentralization approach that has characterized the strategic debate in the automobile industry during the past decade.

The first fact is that GM's technological restructuring strategy must at the moment be reckoned a failure, while Ford's profits have soared.[54] It should be noticed that the two leading American manufacturers, while combining both strategies, have opted for different emphases. While GM's proportion of production conducted overseas declined from 32.8 percent in 1970 to 28.9 percent in 1980, Ford's jumped from 45.6 percent in 1970 to 57.6 percent in 1980.[55] The net result of these divergent strategies was an increasing productivity advantage by Ford over GM, which translated into a reversal of their relative positions in terms of profits, with Ford overtaking GM in net profits in 1986 for the first time since the 1920s. GM's market share dropped from 48 percent in 1978, at the beginning of its restructuring process, to 41 percent in 1986, yielding ground both to imports and to Ford and Chrysler, in spite of the much greater size and resources of GM (in 1979, when GM launched its technological modernization plan, the $40 billion it invested was equivalent to 14 times Ford's annual pre-tax earnings in that year). Various arguments have been put forward to explain the initial failure of the all-out automation strategy: cheaper gasoline prices, undermining the advantage of fuel-efficient new models; greater foreign competition, particularly from South Korea and Europe, in addition to Japan; organizational mistakes; inability to proceed in parallel with a reform of working processes adapted to the new technological environment; and errors and difficulties in implementing on such a large scale the introduction of information technologies from top to bottom. Whatever the reasons, setting the technological rationality of GM against the business rationality of Ford, it seems that the latter prevails for the moment. Not that the "world car" strategy has been fully implemented to its logical extreme; but the depth of the crisis in Ford forced the company to find, as its first priority, ways of lowering costs and penetrating markets, using information technologies in the service of a short-term survival strategy. On the other hand, GM's long-term view of taking the high technological ground to undermine the competition by using its financial and technological power, has backfired in the short term, actually jeopardizing the long-term strategy. The Saturn project has been scaled down, and some experts foresee its merger in other GM divisions.

The second fact at variance with the assumed predominance of the spatial reconcentration/flexible automation trend is the growing importance of Mexico as a supplier of parts, including engines, and, in the near future, fully assembled cars for US manufacturers, as demonstrated in the thorough study by Hinojosa and Morales. GM itself is the main firm involved in this trade, with about 30 "maquiladora" plants in the border zone in 1987.[56] Between 1979 and 1985 the number of maquiladoras producing transportation equipment in the Mexican border zone rose from 38 to 49, increasing employment from 5,000 to about 34,000. Table 6.4 provides an estimate of the growing importance of production of engines for export for the whole of Mexico. Ford has developed further its strategy in the area since these data were collected by building an advanced plant in Hermosillo, northern Mexico, which started operations in 1988. Ninety percent of the parts to be assembled there will be imported from around the Pacific, and 90 percent of the plant's output will be exported to the US. Three thousand workers will be employed, making about 100,000 cars a year, in a new version of the "world car" strategy; and this in spite of Ford's self-proclaimed abandonment of the term, judged too unpopular with American public opinion.[57]

The third element to be considered in evaluating the balance between the two conflicting tendencies concerns the possibility of increasing the sophistication of offshore production by introducing automated equipment into plants decentralized abroad, including those in developing countries such as Mexico. There is an implicit fallacy in equating the use of flexible automation technologies with US location, consisting in the assumption that neither the

Table 6.4 Principal Mexican export engine plants, 1987

Company	Site	Projected volume	% Export
Chrysler	Saltillo	300,000[a]	85
General Motors	Ramos Arizpe	450,000	95
Ford	Chihuahua	500,000[b]	90
Volkswagen	Puebla	300,000[c]	
Renault	Gomez Palacio	80,000[d]	100
Nissan	Aguascalientes	100,000[e]	

Approximate 1987 total engine exports: 1,600,000

[a]This production is above the plant's capacity of 270,000 annually. The plant has exceeded its rated capacity every year since 1984.
[b]This production is above the plant's capacity of 440,000 annually.
[c]This is the projected 1987 export volume for the plant. An expansion is currently under way to boost capacity to 500,000 annually.
[d]This volume is well under the plant's capacity.
[e]This is entirely an export figure.
Source: Compiled from trade press sources by Shaiken and Herzenberg (see note 58).

industrial infrastructure nor the skills of the labor force would be able to sustain advanced manufacturing processes. Shaiken and Herzenberg, in a remarkable piece of work, have put this assumption to the test of empirical research, analyzing three automobile plants of the same company, each with exactly the same advanced, automated equipment and the same product, but situated respectively in the US, Canada, and Mexico. (Confidentiality forbids identification of the company.)[58] Their results are startling. In spite of a young, inexperienced work force, the Mexican plant achieved, within 18 months, 80 percent of the machine efficiency of the US plant, 75 percent of its labor producitivity, and a level of quality between that of the Canadian and that of the US plant. Figure 6.1 shows the learning curve that brought Mexican workers on a par with their American and Canadian counterparts. They explain the performance by three factors: first, the work force, although inexperienced, was highly educated and highly motivated; secondly, teamwork and control groups were introduced, in line with Ford's Alfa Project on managerial techniques, emphasizing the importance of work procedures if best use is to be made of advanced technology; and thirdly, managers and engineers were brought into the plant from around the world to act as on-site supervisors, training the workers and forming teams with them, so as to avoid a long period of non-supervised, spontaneous learning. Efficient training of an educated labor force accounted for the rapid productivity gains which combined with major savings in labor costs (one-tenth of the equivalent costs in the US) to make the Mexican plant the most profitable of the three, while

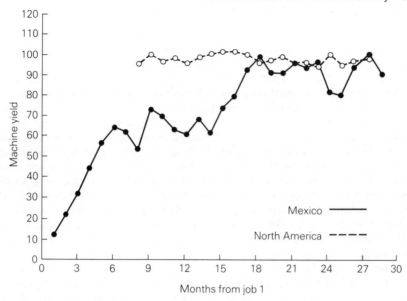

Figure 6.1   Machine yield on the Mexican and North American Block lines, as percentage of 1985 machine yield on North American block line.
Source: Company data complied and elaborated by Shaiken and Herzenberg (see note 58)

still allowing for the introduction of advanced, microelectronics-based equipment. Although these results still leave open the general questions of whether industrial infrastructure is adequate and whether a sufficient pool of educated labor can often be found in such locations, it appears that in principle advanced automation production lines can be moved offshore without a substantial loss of quality. A combination of offshoring and automation strategies thus becomes feasible, and this indeed seems to be Ford's option.

In addition, increasing collaboration among firms of different countries on a world level is blurring the distinction, giving new depth and meaning to the "world car" strategy.[59] American firms, as well as their European and Asian counterparts, have entered into a number of agreements covering co-production, global sourcing, and marketing under another firm's label. Japan and South Korea are the main partners for firms, and these two countries, along with Taiwan, Mexico, and Brazil, are US firms' foremost suppliers in "captive imports," that is, cars produced offshore to be sold under US brand names in the North American market. These captive imports are rapidly increasing, from 6 percent of total auto imports in 1984 to 20 percent in 1988.[60]

Thus, as Richard Hill concludes in his analysis:

What seems to be taking place is a kind of blend of global factory and company town into integrated regional production complexes with some cross-regional, international linkages and coordination. George Maxcy captured this scenario best when he suggested the typical transnational auto company of the future: "... Will have a worldwide network of subsidiaries and affiliates made up of an integrated group of firms in each of the major regions – North America, Europe, Asia–Pacific and Africa – with each regional bloc being more or less self-sufficient. But there will be production as well as technological links between firms in different regions because of worldwide sourcing of components and built-up models in short supply or missing from the range of an individual subsidiary." (Maxcy, 1981: 162) This scenario makes sense of the global net Toyota may eventually weave with General Motors. Toyota executives have indicated that they anticipate possible joint ventures with GM affiliates in South Korea and in the UK. South Korea's Sehan Motor Company is owned in equal part by GM and the local Daewoo group. Sehan produces the subcompact Rekord, and faces strong rivalry from another major Korean automaker, Hyundai Motor Company, which is tied to Japan's Mitsubishi Motor Corporation. A joint venture with Sehan would provide Toyota with a competitive base against foreign companies aiming to use South Korea as a platform from which to penetrate the Asian regional market. In addition, GM's British subsidiary, Vauxhall Motors, which has suffered from continuous deficits over the past few years and is attempting to revitalize its management, would provide Toyota with tariff-free access to the market of the EEC.[61]

The spatial implications of this techno-economic restructuring are, therefore, more complex than is implied by any of the simplified versions of the alternative strategies presented above. Neither generalized decentralization nor general spatial reconcentration is taking place, but rather a global networking of self-sufficient "company towns," that generate around themselves vertically integrated clusters. Because of the different production costs in various specific locations, there will be a hierarchy of relationships among these primary locations, reinforced at the highest level by the technological level of a few engineering centers. Yet the need to relate closely to the markets will disperse these primary places around the main markets of the globe, certainly bypassing most of the Third World. On the other hand, since market penetration will only be achieved on the condition of successful flexible specialization, the importance of the connections among different production centers, following strategic inter-firm alliances, will prevail over any given locational advantage. The net result for the spatial location of the US automobile industry *in the US* will be increasing interdependence with both foreign partners and offshore sources, in order to preserve the command and control functions of primary locations. Flexibility of production will allow independence of specific areas, favoring a process of decentralization from the industrial heartland. This, however, will only be possible to the extent that each firm maintains close relationships with the other units of the firm and with the target markets. Spatial reconcentration and international decentralization are both superseded by their integration, as subsidiary processes, in global networks of design, production, and markets, made possible by information technologies, and constantly restructured by business strategies.

Reverse Flow: Locational Patterns of Foreign Direct Investment in US Manufacturing

At the same time as American manufacturers are locating a significant proportion of their production offshore, foreign direct investment is pouring into the US.[62] In 1984, total assets owned by foreign firms in the US reached $596 billion. In 1985, the value of direct foreign investment for the year was $183 billion, up from $135 billion in 1983. The proportion of this investment that went into manufacturing was about 35 percent in 1983; but a starker picture emerges if one looks at the proportion of employment generated by foreign direct investment accounted for by manufacturing: 52 percent. The expansion of investment in manufacturing has been spectacular, from $2.9 billion in 1962 to $47.8 billion by the end of 1983.[63] The growth rate of direct foreign investment in the US accelerated from an average annual increase of 6.7 percent in real terms in 1962–73, to 9.5 percent in 1973–80, and recent trends show an even greater rate of increase. In 1983, about 33 percent of foreign direct investment in manufacturing was in chemicals, with about 15 percent in food and kindred products, almost 18 percent in machinery, 11.4 percent in primary fabricated metals, and 22 percent in other industries.[64] This major inflow, 77.4 percent of it coming from Europe, 3.5 percent from Japan, and 12.1 percent from other areas, gives rise to an apparent paradox, for simultaneously US firms have been decentralizing production abroad to escape high production costs and a relatively constrained regulatory environment. It certainly shows the complexity of the locational logic in the new international economy, hardly reducible to any single factor, certainly not to labor costs alone.

The major argument for direct foreign investment in US manufacturing is, of course, to assure a presence in the US market, the largest unified market in the world, to pre-empt the potential impact of protectionist measures. But, as Erica Schoenberger argues, a presence in the US market does not necessarily imply actually manufacturing in America.[65] Foreign firms could also decentralize production from the US to lower-cost locations, while still marketing the final assembled products in America. In fact, some Japanese firms are doing just that, locating over the Mexican border to serve the US market from marketing offices headquartered within the US. Yet the bulk of foreign manufacturing firms in the US are setting up complete production lines, sometimes with the exception of the research and development functions that are kept at the home base. Erica Schoenberger, in her doctoral dissertation, investigated the reasons behind this choice of location on the basis of in-depth interviews with a sample of foreign manufacturing firms' executives.[66] Her analysis confirms the widespread view that market consider- ations are the common concern underlying the decisions to locate, at high cost, in the US. But what is more important is the idea that physical presence of production facilities in the market is crucial to penetrating it and to gaining market share. The notion of linkages seems to be essential: linkages among information on market conditions and technologies, the marketing strategy of the firm, and the characteristics of production. Increasingly customized production targeted on specific markets requires a degree of spatial proximity and social affinity that cannot be obtained unless the firm is rooted in the mar- ket it wants to conquer. Also, knowledge obtained through manufacturing in the US is also extremely useful to a firm's efforts to succeed in exports from other locations. Export penetration and direct investment are complementary rather than alternative strategies.

The increasingly important impact of foreign manufacturing investment on the American regional structure has been analyzed by Glickman and Woodward,[67] in the most complete study on the subject to date. Relying on data from the Bureau of Economic Analysis from 1979 to 1983, augmented by data sources from the International Trade Administration, and from Japan's Economic Institute, between 1979 and 1985, Glickman and Woodward provide a detailed account of the spatial pattern of foreign manufacturing investment in the US. The complexity of the trends they observed, and the importance of the subject, require a careful synthesis of their findings, on the basis of which some substantial hypotheses may be proposed.

The regional distribution of foreign employment and foreign manufactur- ing employment for 1974 and 1983 is laid out in tables 6.5 and 6.6. These data show the south-east to be the favored recipient of such investment, followed by the mid-east and by the Great Lakes. Again, the old and new concen- trations of manufacturing employment act as the magnets for new investment from abroad, although the declining share of the old manufacturing belt shows the adaptation of foreign capital to the new industrial space. In terms of emerging trends, the south-west appears to be increasing its attraction much faster than other regions. The west has a relatively modest share of total investment, although this picture changes if Japanese investment alone is examined: 29.5 percent of Japanese-controlled US employment is located in California. Given the likelihood of increased Japanese investment in the second half of the 1980s, it is probable that the west will become substantially more prominent as a home for foreign investment.

Overall, foreign investors created 700,000 new factory jobs in 1974–83, while domestic producers eliminated 2.4 million manufacturing jobs, 93 percent of them in the mid-east and Great Lakes regions. In this sense it con- tributed toward slowing down the process of deindustrialization in the US. But the regional distribution of this new employment could not reverse the

Table 6.5   Regional distribution of total foreign employment, 1974 and 1983

Region	1974		1983		Average annual growth rate (%)
	Employment	Share (%)	Employment	Share (%)	
New England	67,141	6.0	159,924	6.4	10.1
Mid-east	333,867	29.7	561,955	22.6	6.0
Great Lakes	232,179	20.6	425,286	17.1	7.0
Plains	45,351	4.0	111,758	4.5	10.5
South-east	235,588	20.9	615,150	24.8	11.3
South-west	66,725	5.9	255,650	10.3	16.1
Rocky Mountains	17,022	1.5	54,975	2.2	13.9
Far west	128,091	11.4	301,049	12.1	10.0
Total	1,125,964	100.0[a]	2,485,747	100.0	9.2

[a]Because the figures are rounded, regional shares will not add up precisely to 100%.
Source: Coleman (1985), compiled by Glickman and Woodward (see note 67).

Table 6.6   Regional breakdown of foreign manufacturing employment, 1974 and 1983

Region	1974		1983		Average annual growth rate (%)
	Employment	Share (%)	Employment	Share (%)	
New England	41,955	7.2	86,901	6.7	8.4
Mid-east	149,480	25.6	298,313	23.2	8.0
Great Lakes	121,249	20.7	242,105	18.8	8.0
Plains	21,812	3.7	61,486	4.8	12.2
South-east	167,330	28.6	335,424	26.0	8.0
South-west	19,080	3.3	103,037	8.0	20.6
Rocky Mountains	6,682	1.1	24,392	1.9	15.5
Far west	57,574	9.8	137,769	10.7	10.2
Total	585,162	100.0[a]	1,289,427	100.0	9.2

[a]Because the figures are rounded, regional shares will not add up precisely to 100%.
Source: Coleman (1985), calculated by Glickman and Woodward (see note 67).

decline of the Great Lakes area: there is a similar movement toward industrial decentralization to the south-east on the part of both domestic and foreign capital. In the case of foreign capital this is true in terms of both new employment and capital investment, where the south-east ranked first among the recipient regions. In order to enable an assessment of the trends in foreign and domestic investment on a comparative basis, table 6.7 calculates a location quotient that indicates the over- or under-representation of foreign capital for each region. The south-east and the south-west stand up well to

Table 6.7 Regional breakdown of domestic manufacturing employment, 1974 and 1983, and 1983 foreign/domestic location quotients

	1974		1983		1983 Location
Region	Employment	Share (%)	Employment	Share (%)	quotient
New England	1,196.4	7.2	1,323.2	7.8	0.859
Mid-east	4,041.0	20.8	3,087.3	18.1	1.282
Great Lakes	5,037.8	25.9	3,716.6	21.8	0.862
Plains	1,318.6	6.8	1,173.4	6.9	0.696
South-east	4,116.2	21.4	3,910.4	23.0	1.130
South-west	1,111.5	5.7	1,214.4	7.1	1.127
Rocky Mountains	291.2	1.5	320.6	1.8	1.056
Far west	2,099.2	10.8	2,272.1	13.3	0.805
Total	19,461.9	100.0[a]	17,018.0	100.0	

[a]Employment in thousands. Because the figures are rounded, regional shares will not add up precisely to 100%.
Source: US Department of Labor, Bureau of Labor Statistics, 1985, calculated by Glickman and Woodward (see note 67).

this examination, but the mid-east emerges as foreign capital's preferred location in relative terms. This result emerges from the combination of the steep decline in domestic manufacturing in the mid-east (954,000 manufacturing jobs lost in 1974–83) with the number of acquisitions of factories and property in the region by foreign firms exploiting the crisis of American manufacturing to establish their presence in the market.

Nevertheless, in absolute terms, the bulk of foreign investment is increasingly being directed toward the southern states, with the west and New England together in second position, as shown in map 6.2. Higher location indexes are registered in the Carolinas, Tennessee, Virginia, and Texas, but here again Japanese investors present a different pattern, being concentrated on the west coast. An important distinction to be made in investment patterns is that between new plants and acquisitions, the former type of investment generally contributing more to regional development. Overall, 63 percent of the plants are new, but the proportion varies between regions. The south-east dominates in terms of new plants, but New England also exhibits a pattern of new industrialization, confirming the claim that New England's reindustrialization is taking place on a basis quite different from that of traditional industry. On the other hand, as one would expect, the Great Lakes and the mid-east show a greater proportion of acquisitions. Foreign manufacturing is at the same time both participating in the new industrial expansion toward the southern US, and replacing (though only to a limited extent) some of the manufacturing operations in the old industrial belt. Interestingly enough, Japanese investors tend to concentrate more on acquisitions (53 percent of all plants) than do European investors.

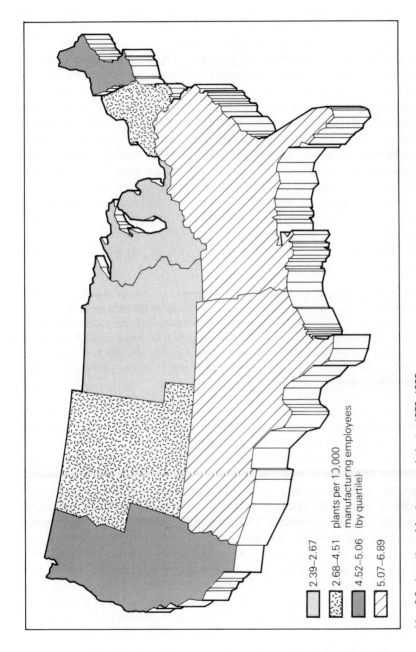

Map 6.2 Location of foreign-owned plants, 1979–1983
Source: Glickmand and Woodward (see note 67)

2.39–2.67

2.68–4.51   plants per 10,000
              manufacturing employees
4.52–5.06   (by quartile)

5.07–6.89

The sectoral composition of foreign manufacturing investment shows a great diversity of investment patterns; however, there is a certain concentration on high-technology industries. This high-technology investment is spread among many states, with greater than average concentrations in the south-east, the Rocky Mountains, the mid-east, and the south-west. The important fact to note is that foreign high-technology companies do not follow the locational pattern of domestic high-technology manufacturers. In fact, the far west and New England come bottom of the ranking of foreign high-technology investment shares. This finding runs contrary to the general perception of foreign companies locating in the US to assimilate new technologies. Although this is probably true for a few research facilities located in Silicon Valley or on Route 128, most of the employment generated by foreign firms seems to be geared toward the growing high-technology *markets* in the US, the only ones sufficiently large to make it possible for a foreign firm to expand its markets at a rate corresponding to its rate of innovation. So, while the innovative centers of most of these firms tend to remain on native soil, their manufacturing operations in the US assure them direct contact with the most sophisticated market in the world. As Glickman and Woodward write:

While technology transfer from the US back to the source country is conceivable, so is a transfer flowing in the opposite direction. The high proportion of new high-tech plants relative to acquisitions indicates that multinational corporations (MNCs) are drawing on ownership advantages to directly compete with domestic high technology firms in the national and regional markets of the US. It is likely that foreign-owned firms add to the technological base of regions as much as they imitate and exploit existing technologies.[68]

The locational pattern of foreign manufacturing in general is also characterized by an "urban bias." Fifty-six percent of the new plants were built in the 10 percent of counties that are highly urbanized, while only 12.5 percent were built in rural counties. Even in the south, where the location pattern was less urban, most plants remained concentrated in the corridors adjacent to large metropolitan areas. The predominant market orientation of this type of investment requires spatial proximity and social affinity to the final destination of its products. Thus, while the pattern of location tends to be regionally scattered, it is also concentrated on metropolitan centers.

Glickman and Woodward have also conducted an econometric analysis of the factors determining location of foreign manufacturing investment, and have compared their results with those of a similar analysis for foreign direct investment. Their findings are revealing. Market location is the most important criterion for both types of investment, followed by rate of market growth. The repositioning of manufacturing in the US is at the same time spearheading and following the opening up of new economically vital regions in the south, south-west, and west. Foreign investment also seems to be willing to take risks in new regions that are less developed, for instance the Rocky Mountains, betting on their potential as new frontiers for further decentralization. It is repelled by the threat of unitary tax legislation, emphasizing the important for multinationals of escaping fiscal controls by diversifying location, but it is not particularly shy of other forms of taxation. On the other hand, foreign investment does not seem to be sensitive to labor costs, or to the presence of unions, in sharp contrast to the priorities of domestic manufacturing investment. Several factors may explain this finding, which runs counter to the usual perception of foreign firms moving south to escape unions and reduce labor costs. Many of them, particularly in Europe, are already used to working in an union environment, and indeed one that is usually more militant than the one they find in the US. Investments in the 1980s have often taken place, as mentioned, through acquisitions (37 percent), many of them in the old industrial belt, under conditons that have saved jobs and helped cities, with the result that wage demands and union pressure have been moderate, even in regions traditionally ranking toward the top of the wage scale. And finally, the apparent lack of concern with labor costs and social environment once more highlights the priority target of foreign investment: market presence. Whatever it takes to consolidate a position in the US market, both through local manufacturing activity, and through the flow of information and contacts that such activity will generate, will be worthwhile, as the American economy continues to be the expansionary segment of the world economy. Another surprising finding, that is nevertheless consistent with the hypothesis concerning the dominance of the market strategy, is the fact that domestic investment is positively correlated with the level of state spending on infrastructure, while foreign capital seems to be indifferent to this attraction. In fact, while American firms are relocating to lower costs, foreign firms put a premium in "being there," namely, locating in the most rapidly expanding areas of the American market, in a bold strategy in which maximizing profit in the long run replaces the short-term view of most American businesses.

In sum, a market-driven flow of direct foreign investment is reviving a substantial share of American manufacturing. Its territorial reach is spreading from its early location on the north-eastern seaboard (the western seaboard for Japanese investors), and moving southward and inland. Being scattered all over the US, including those regions that are not yet developed, foreign investment contributes to the reduction of regional disparity. Foreign investors are also contributing to the slowing down of the process of deindustrialization, particularly in the old industrial belt, by acquiring companies and re-opening formerly closed plants. Overall, foreign capital not only reindustrializes, it also re-equilibrates the US regional structure by concentrating most of its impact on the south. On the other hand, it reinforces metropolitan concentration by investing in the most highly urbanized areas, where it will find the most rapidly expanding markets.

In contrast with the locational pattern of US multinationals abroad, generally to be found clustered in the dominant areas of the already industrialized regions, foreign manufacturing capital in the US is contributing to the decentralization of the American productive structure, revitalizing to some extent the declining regions, and spreading industralization into new areas, away from the traditional manufacturing belt. Yet the price of this dynamic, re-equilibrating effect is the increasingly tight linkage between the evolution of American regions and cities and the movements of capital controlled from a foreign base and deployed on a worldwide strategy. The mobility of capital has now embraced in its uncontrollable spiral the heartland of America. An increasing proportion of manufacturing jobs in the US will be located, as they are in most of the world, at a borrowed place, and will live on borrowed time. The interpenetration of markets and production processes has redefined the meaning of regions at the intersection of flows of capital and labor with the memory of their history and the heritage of their geography.

Global Capital, Global Cities

Capital has always moved throughout the world. But only in the most recent period of our history have individual amounts of capital been able to operate daily on a global scale. This is a fundamental change in our socio-economic organization, and it has been the major contributing force in the formation and consolidation of the new urban entities that Saskia Sassen has labeled "global cities,"[69] in similar vein to the "world city" concept proposed by Friedmann and Wolff a few years ago.[70] Capital mobility has increased dramatically in both volume and velocity in the past decade, as a result of two main interacting processes: the mismatching between capital accumulation and investment opportunities within the same national market; and the restructuring of financial institutions and financial markets, in the context of the broader economic restructuring.

A number of new centers of accumulation have appeared since the mid-1970s. The first and most important was the Eurodollar market which attracted and organized floating capital from around the world. The second, and most publicized, was the concentration of petro-dollars in OPEC countries during the golden period for oil producers of 1974–81, a considerable volume of capital that, to a large extent, was recycled in markets and countries outside OPEC. The third, and the one most likely to have far-reaching consequences, was the emergence of Japan as the major world financial power as a consequence of the capital accumulated in its financial corporations after a quarter of a century of exceptional performance by Japanese companies in the international economy. Along with these three major sources of capital accumulation, other less obvious sources also played a role in generating an unprecedented flow of capital constantly shifting around the world's financial markets. For instance, capital generated by money-laundering operations from drug traffic in Latin America and elsewhere, or government-originated payments resulting from shadow weapons markets, are increasingly important elements in the international cash flow. Altogether, worldwide capitalization in 1986 amounted to $5.2 trillion, up from $892 billion (in constant dollars) in 1974.[71] However, working against this expansionary trend, investment opportunities rapidly declined during the 1970s as core economies implemented austerity policies to fight inflation. As Sassen reports,[72] in the early 1980s most advanced countries saw reduced investment levels and experienced declines in investment inflows. In this general context of restraint, only two markets were open to and potentially profitable for to the massive amount of capital searching for the opportunity to fructify. The first of these was the United States, as the economy came to be artificially stimulated, and the US Treasury sought capital from sources all over the world to finance an increasing budget deficit. The US Treasury market has become the single largest capital market in the world, with $2 trillion in outstanding debt bonds; and about one-third of the bonds issued in the 1980s were purchased by Japanese investors. Also, in 1984, the US received 47 percent of global direct foreign investment, while Japan was the leading lender and the leading foreign investor, worldwide. The second possibility for capital seeking a destination was the international financial markets themselves, increasingly working in their own sphere according to a logic distinct from that of any national economy. In addition to stepped-up capital mobility, we are also witnessing the globalization of capital as a separate entity, with the universe of international finance generating its own investment opportunities by scanning all national economies and, more importantly, by taking advantage of financial transactions and monetary trends, on a rationale increasingly separate from the processes of production and consumption.

However, the transformation of the movements of capital into an interconnected global system depended on a number of key institutional and material conditions, without whose existence the world was at risk of suffering an over-accumulation crisis. These conditions were of three kinds: the restructuring of the financial markets and institutions; the provision of the indispensable technological infrastructure; and the formation of organizational complexes functioning as the material bases for the processing of information and decision-making on the capital flows.

All the major world financial centers went through a period of institutional adjustment during the 1980s, under the guiding principle of deregulation.[73] London went the furthest of any major market and won a competitive edge, consolidating its position as the world's largest financial market. Tokyo was the last, actually waiting until 1987 to organize its offshore investment market. Singapore and Hong Kong had always been more flexible and it was this flexibility that attracted to them an increasing share of global financial flows, although they remained in a secondary position as international centers. Paris, Frankfurt, and Zurich also introduced changes but they needed fewer improvements in terms of flexibility because of their traditional formula of linkage between commercial banks and investment banks. In the US, the need for more flexible instruments, able to enter the global competition, combined with developments in the financial industry, prompted by the need to escape the threat of inflationary pressures through deregulation and disintermediation.[74] Large corporations and institutional investors increasingly bypassed commercial banks and started to sell security-type promissory notes to investors. In 1985, the outstanding value of commercial paper in the US, that hardly existed ten years previously, amounted to $350 billion, that is, about one-quarter of all non-financial corporate debt. Bond markets, investment banks, mutual funds, all entered markets traditionally reserved to the commercial banks. As a result, the commercial banks themselves pushed for deregulation of capital markets and started to offer new financial services. Simultaneously, financial firms exerted pressure to obtain the deregulation of security markets, that took place gradually during the 1980s, including the facility for US commercial banks to serve as dealers in US Treasury bonds. As soon as institutional opportunities were created, the securities trade skyrocketed, spearheading a bull market period on the New York Stock Exchange. Between the mid-1970s and the early 1980s, the number of shares traded in Wall Street leapt from 10 million to 100 million.

This volume of transactions, and the global reach of the restructured financial markets, could not have been attained without the massive introduction of information technologies in the financial industry. Telecommunications and computers, functioning in integrated networks, are the indipensable working tools of global capital. A sophisticated telecommunications and air transportation infrastructure are the precondition for any city to become a production site of the new financial institutions, as argued in chapter 3 when analyzing the impact of technology on information-processing location. But the centers of operation of worldwide financial flows cannot be flows themselves. They have very specific location requirements, that are not reducible to a good telecommunications infrastructure. While the emergence of Hong Kong and Singapore as second-tier financial centers bears witness to the possibility for new locations to emerge on the basis of a deliberate policy to organize a market in a given location, the high-level financial centers, commanding operations on a global scale, have historical and geographical roots, linked to their role in the national and international economies. The major centers, and the ones that are truly global cities, are three:[75] London, as the major financial market in terms of number of transactions; New York, as the major recipient of capital flows and exporter of related services; and Tokyo, as the major lender of capital and headquarters of the largest banks in the world. In 1986, New York, London, and Tokyo together accounted for 80 percent of the world market capitalization, up from 73 percent in 1974, in a process of growing concentration and dominance by the top tier of financial centers. New York alone controlled 44 percent of world capital.

Within the US, New York stands in a class of its own as the dominant global city, followed by Los Angeles as a distant second.[76] The role of New York in international financial networks has its roots in its pre-eminence as host to leading corporate headquarters of the American economy, its Stock Exchange, the concentration in the city of the major commercial banks and security firms, and the network of advanced corporate services required to support and execute the decisions made in the command and control centers of these corporations. Some figures are indicative of the concentration of corporate power in New York City:[77] 454 Manhattan-located headquarters are listed on the US stock exchanges, accounting for one-thirteenth of the publicly owned corporations. In 1986, New York banks' assets were $612 billion, equivalent to 34 percent of cumulated bank assets in the US. It is also the leading foreign banking center, with 405 offices, 60 percent of foreign bank assets, and 56 percent of foreign loan activity in the US. In international terms, New York banks and security firms combined concentrate the highest level of earnings in the world ($5.4 billion in 1985, far ahead of Tokyo and London), and ranks second in cumulated assets behind Tokyo. New York is also the prime location for the world's largest insurers and pension funds, one of the most important sources of capital investment as the deregulation of financial markets progresses. US pension funds accounted in 1985 for $1.5 trillion, compared with $225 million for the UK and $210 million for Japan. Mutual funds in the US accounted for an additional $380 billion. Most of the transactions connecting these pools of capital to the financial markets are conducted in New York. In sum, as the Regional Plan Association of New York writes:

With the growth and transformation of global capital markets, the fields of commercial and investment banking are merging, and the all-important function of intermediation is becoming increasingly dominated by a small band of 25 to 30 financial institiutions. Included in this group are: the twelve major New York commercial banks and investment banks, a small number of UK merchant banks, the four big Japanese securities houses, with Nomura in the lead, and the few European universal banks, including Swiss and German.[78]

The key development in the relationship between the restructuring of the financial system and the location of its information-processing activities is the fact that it has shifted from being corporate-centered to being market-centered. It is the circulation process rather than the investment process that dominates. Increasingly, securities firms have overtaken commercial banks as the nerve centers of the accumulation process. Therefore, the emphasis is less on the internal workings of the financial corporations than on the milieu of exchanges weaved around the financial markets, with its core at the Stock

Exchange. This milieu works on the basis of personal acquaintance and face-to-face interaction, often relying on inside information. It has also given rise to a very large network of ancillary services: financial analysts, management consultants, law firms, at the top level; word-processing pools, computer programming, copy and printing shops, and personal services, at the lower level. The dynamism of this finance-led economy has attracted a vast pool of labor, generating its own labor market with highly specialized segments, whose presence in the city becomes an additional locational factor for the development of the high-level capital management functions.

On the basis of its directional functions and its intermediary role between world capital flows and access to capital and investment in the world's largest economy, New York has fundamentally restructured its regional economy and its local society. While dismantling most of its manufacturing, the New York region gained in 1978–86 about 118,000 new jobs in financial services, about one-third of all new jobs in the area, with brokerage and investment houses experiencing the highest rate of growth of all categories of firms. Employment in the securities industry in New York City rose from 90,000 in 1980 to 138,400 in 1986. Table 6.8 shows the rise in financial services, with spectacular rates of growth in securities and legal services. However, the dependence of this economic dynamism on a highly volatile financial market, sensitive to all variations in the world economy and in world politics, also creates a source of instability for the local economy. After the Wall Street crash of October 1987, the ensuing decline of financial activity led to massive lay-offs in securities and brokerage: the city lost about 50,000 jobs in the three months after the crisis. On the other hand, as argued in chapter 4, the development of high-level information processing is inter-related with the incorporation of low-paid, often immigrant, service labor that caters to the demand in low-skill jobs, and in consumer and personal services. Together

Table 6.8 Employment growth rates, producer services: New York City and Chicago, 1977–1984

SIC	Industry	New York City (%)	Chicago (%)
60	Banking	20.98	18.27
61	Credit agencies	36.62	17.99
62	Securities	71.49	73.17
63	Insurance carriers	−11.24	−11.91
64	Insurance agents	16.15	14.89
65	Real estate	1.57	1.70
73	Business services	36.92	53.01
81	Legal services	50.34	65.79
86	Membership organizations	7.04	0.41
89	Miscellaneous services	28.15	19.39

Source: US Bureau of Census, *County Business Patterns*, Illinois, 1977, 1984; New York 1977, 1984. Compiled by Sassen (see note 69).

with the simultaneous downgrading of manufacturing activities, the two processes create, in the same space of the global city, a highly polarized and segregated social structure. The global city is also the dual city.

The high-level operations of co-ordination and control of world capital flows are performed from a very small area that further specifies the core space of the global city. The Manhattan CBD concentrates 60 percent of New York jobs in 600 million square feet of built space, between 60th Street and the southern tip of the island. The 454 headquarters located in that area control $770 billion in worldwide sales (in 1982 dollars), including 38 financial and securities firms with $100 billion in sales. The same area is also home to half of the foreign branch finance employment of the US which performs 75 percent of all foreign bank business in the country. As Sassen writes: "In brief, much of what constitutes the leading international center for finance multinational headquarters and specialized servicing, is situated in a rather small area in an era of global telecommunications. Since we see this pattern repeated in London and Tokyo it may be indicative of the new forms of centralization required by the new forms of decentralization."[79]

What explains this striking paradox of the increasing concentration of global flows of information, controlling global flows of capital, in a few congested blocks of one particular city? Several elements seem to be at work. The first is the concentration there of high-level directional corporate activity in the US economy, a phenomenon whose logic was analyzed in chapter 3. It is because Manhattan is the CBD of New York, and New York is the corporate center of the largest economy in the world, holding what is still the most important international currency, that capital flows tend to converge on the location of the leading American financial institutions.

Secondly, it is precisely the dependence upon telecommunication networks that requires the concentration of command and control centers in spaces that are provided with the most advanced information systems. And the economies of scale required for the necessary gigantic investments in telecommunications infrastructure are dependent upon a pre-existing concentration of high-level business functions. While terminal points of the telecommunication networks, those required by back offices, can be scattered spatially, the nodal points, requiring the most sophisticated equipment together with round-the-clock repair, maintenance, and reprogramming systems, are concentrated in key locations, where a multiplicity of communication systems complement and reinforce one another. The level of computerization of financial markets can only function on the basis of a technologically highly advanced back-up system.

In the third-place, high-level decision making in an industry entirely dependent upon proper information handling requires access to micro-flows of information, that is to occasional exchanges and to non-public information that translates into a competitive edge in an industry where time is literally money, in billions of dollars. Access to inside information, and speed in gaining and using that information, are crucial characteristics in shaping the macro-flows on the basis of micro-flows. And in the fourth place, around the concentration of high-level functions develops a vast network of suppliers, intermediaries, and implementers in a symbiotic relationship in which they become indispensable to the functioning of the system as a whole.

Once the milieu is consolidated it reproduces its own space; and New York has been the dominant trade and economic center of the US for the past century. However, areas of the city that were well regarded decades ago have since been devastated by social decay and the transformation of its economic base; it is the persistence of the *economically vital* activities in a given space that enhances its value.[80] But when that space affirms itself as a leading corporate center, as is the case for most of Manhattan today, it triggers off a process of continuing re-evaluation, with capital from all over the world investing in its real estate, driving up prices, selecting functions and residents, and transforming the whole area into a highly privileged location. Around such privileges, high-level services develop to provide the global city with the attributes of its power and wealth. Designers come from Europe, imports from anywhere in the world offer the best of everything, and artists perform, compose, paint, sculpt, write, and, above all, sell, for the enjoyment of an elite with increasingly little time to enjoy anything. Ultimately, symbols are attached to location in that space, making the physical presence there of corporate headquarters and high-class residence necessary to credibility as being part of the corporate world or of the high-class population: the functional milieu crystallizes in a social milieu. While New York City has always combined both, its current status as a global city commanding much of the world economy has accentuated the trends toward symbolic recognition of its economic and social dominance, beyond the actual use value of ill-maintained urban services and mediocre French restaurants.

The global city epitomizes the contradictory logic of the space of flows. While reaching out to the whole planet second by second and round the clock, it relies on the spatial proximity of its different command centers, and on the face-to-face interaction of its anonymous masters. Based on telecommunications and information systems that overcome time and distance, it needs a technological infrastructure that can only be provided by agglomeration economies and access to scarce skilled labor. And while determining the destiny of countries and people by spread points in interest rates, it lives in fear of the uncontrolled society generated in its own territory. The global city collapses information flows into social matter.

Conclusion

The growing internationalization of the American economy reshapes cities and regions following the logic of the space of flows. The increasing role played by foreign trade, in a context characterized by loss of competitiveness by US manufacturers, has contributed decisively to the process of deindustrialization in the old manufacturing belt. Faced with decreasing shares of world markets, and loss of domestic markets to foreign imports, American companies have adjusted by relocating a substantial part of their production offshore, as well as in lower-cost areas of the US, particularly in the south. Four phenomena have resulted from this relocation process: an even greater industrial decline in the traditional manufacturing belt; the growing internalization of industrial and commercial flows within corporations, operating across national boundaries; the growth of a border economy along the US–Mexican border, exemplifying the new international division of labor and the close connections among its elements; and the industrialization of the south, that has emerged as the largest manufacturing region in the US, although most of its workers depend upon corporations based in the older industrial cities.

At the same time, other competitive strategies have emphasized the role of automation and upgrading of onshore production, in high-technology manufacturing, and in the automobile and textile industries, among others. Although this movement has contributed toward maintaining some production in the manufacturing belt, most of the automation and modernization of industries is taking place in what Peter Hall calls "the new perimeter," namely the sunbelt and New England.

The threat of massive US protectionism, to halt a trade deficit that has run out of control, and the increasing capital demands of American government and corporations, have caused a massive inflow of foreign direct investment, over one-third of it in manufacturing. Foreign investors have acquired some plants and equipment in the mid-east and Great Lakes regions, helping to slow down the decline of old industries; however, the bulk of new investment has taken place in the southern states, with the addition of the west coast in the case of Japanese capital. Foreign investment has favored high technology, but as a supplier as much as a buyer, actually upgrading the technological level of some southern states. Oriented toward market penetration, foreign firms are reindustrializing America, with emphasis on the "new south."

The combined effects of relocation by US firms and investment by foreign capital is re-equilibrating the economic and demographic balance between regions in the US by reversing the historical dominance of the north-eastern and north-central areas. Although pockets of poverty and underdevelopment still characterize many southern states, for example Mississippi, the overall trend appears to be toward a historic convergence of regions in terms of income and jobs. This is a major trend running against the general assumption that polarized economic growth translates into an acceleration of uneven territorial development. Although there is still great disparity among regions, intra-regional differences seem now to be more important, as the mobility of capital disperses investment, jobs, and income across the American landscape in search of better production locations and newer, more promising markets. While the dislocation of communities in declining regions adds a major social cost to the restructuring process, the new development of formerly depressed areas tends to homogenize America's economic geography.

On the other hand, worldwide capital flows concentrate the operations required for their processing in the directional centers of the higher-level metropolitan areas. New York stands out as the archetypal global city resulting from the formation of a global capital market, but other major cities too are increasingly specializing in financial and international trade activities, as the center of the US economy shifts to advanced corporate services. Los Angeles, with its connection to the Pacific region, and its strong basis in manufacturing, defense , and information industries, stands out clearly as the second global city in the US. Chicago and San Francisco, too, still hold some of their former share of financial power, while Miami (linked to Latin American flows and, to some extent, to the huge but disguised money-laundering operations of the drug trade), Atlanta (financial hub of the new south), Houston, Dallas, and Denver (still relying on the wealth accumulated from oil revenues) are building up their economies and organizing their local societies as regional international capital centers. The more America evolves in the direction of a finance and corporate services economy, the more inter-metropolitan differences supersede regional differentiation. New York suffered a major industrial decline during the 1970s, but emerged during the 1980s wealthier and more powerful than ever on the basis of its international dominance in financial markets and advanced services;[81] on the other hand, most of the Great Lakes region lost industrial competitiveness without being able to connect to the new dominant flows of capital. The process of uneven restructuring within regions and cities also increases disparity within areas rather than among areas. One of the most paradoxical characteristics of the new spatial logic consequent on the internationalization of the economy is the combination of growing regional homogenization with increasing intra-metropolitan inequality. The popular opposition between the frostbelt and the sunbelt is meaningless: the polarization of social dynamics takes place between mid-town Manhattan and the Bronx, or between Westwood and East Los Angeles, rather than between north and south, or east and west. International capital flows segment regional spaces by incorporating them in different ways into the changing geometry of their worldwide logic.

What emerges as the most important characteristic of all cities and regions, regardless of their relative position in the new international division of labor, is the instability of their economic structure and social dynamics, as a consequence of the volatility of movements in the international economy. From Volkswagen's decision to close its plant in Pennsylvania in order to export to the US market from Brazil and Mexico, to the October 1987 Wall Street crash that devastated New York's securities industry, the one feature common to all places in the space of flows is their uncertain fate.

This trend deepens the crisis, while enhacing the importance, of state and local governments. Confronted with worldwide competition and capital mobility, state and local governments in the US have mobilized in the past decade to attract both domestic and foreign capital to their localities, transforming themselves into what, in a perceptive analysis years ago, Robert Goodman labeled "the last entrepreneurs."[82] In order to succeed in this race, they adapted their policies to the perceived needs of business, and re-oriented resources to fostering local economic development, often at the expense of public services and social programs.[83] Even when the strategy succeeded and business-led economic development followed, the benefits of growth, biased toward sustaining a favorable business environment, were not redistributed equally among the population. Thus, local government's entrepreneurship tended to accentuate the polarizing tendencies of the new model of growth, contributing to the extension of the dual city phenomenon. The internationalization of the economy also segments local governments by forcing them to split their constituency between their local voters and their global investors.

A growing social schizophrenia has resulted between, on the one hand, regional societies and local institution and, on the other hand, the rules and operations of the economic system at the international level. The more the economy becomes interdependent on a global scale, the less can regional and local governments, as they exist today, act upon the basic mechanisms that condition the daily existence of their citizens. The traditional structures of social and political control over development, work, and distribution, have been subverted by the placeless logic of an internationalized economy enacted by means of information flows. The ultimate challenge of this fundamental dimension of the restructuring process is the possibility that the local state, and therefore people's control over their lives, will fade away, unless democracy is reinvented to match the space of flows with the power of places.

Conclusion: The Reconstruction of Social Meaning in the Space of Flows

At the end of this analytical journey, we can see a major social trend standing out from all our observations: the historical emergence of the space of flows, superseding the meaning of the space of places. By this we understand the deployment of the functional logic of power-holding organizations in asymmetrical networks of exchanges which do not depend on the characteristics of any specific locale for the fulfillment of their fundamental goals. The new industrial space and the new service economy organize their operations around the dynamics of their information-generating units, while connecting their different functions to disparate spaces assigned to each task to be performed; the overall process is then reintegrated through communication systems. The new professional–managerial class colonizes exclusive spatial segments that connect with one another across the city, the country, and the world; they isolate themselves from the fragments of local societies, which in consequence become destructured in the process of selective reorganization of work and residence. The new state, asserting its sources of power in the control and strategic guidance of knowledge, fosters the development of an advanced technological infrastructure that scatters its elements across undifferentiated locations and interconnected secretive spaces. The new international economy creates a variable geometry of production and consumption, labor and capital, management and information – a geometry that denies the specific productive meaning of any place outside its position in a network whose shape changes relentlessly in response to the messages of unseen signals and unknown codes.

New information technologies are not in themselves the source of the organizational logic that is transforming the social meaning of space: they are, however, the fundamental instrument that allows this logic to embody itself in historical actuality. Information technologies could be used, and can be used, in the pursuit of different social and functional goals, because what they offer, fundamentally, is flexibility. However, their use currently is determined by the process of the socio-economic restructuring of capitalism, and they constitute the indispensable material basis for the fulfillment of this process.

The supersession of places by a network of information flows is a fundamental goal of the restructuring process that has been analyzed. This is because the ultimate logic of restructuring is based on the avoidance of historically established mechanisms of social, economic, and political control by the power-holding organizations. Since most of these mechanisms of control depend upon territorially-based institutions of society, escaping from the social logic embedded in any particular locale becomes the means of achieving freedom in a space of flows connected only to other power-holders, who share the social logic, the values, and the criteria for performance institutionalized in the programs of the information systems that constitute the architecture of the space of flows. The emergence of the space of flows actually expresses the disarticulation of place-based societies and cultures from the organizations of power and production that continue to dominate society without submitting to its control. In the end, even democracies become powerless confronted with the ability of capital to circulate globally, of information to be transferred secretly, of markets to be penetrated or neglected, of planetary strategies of political–military power to be decided without the knowledge of nations, and of cultural messages to be marketed, packaged, recorded, and beamed in and out of people's minds.

What emerges from this restructuring process manifested in the space of flows is not the Orwellian prophecy of a totalitarian universe controlled by Big Brother on the basis of information technologies. It is a much more subtle, and to some extent potentially more destructive, form of social disintegration and reintegration. There is no tangible oppression, no identifiable enemy, no center of power that can be held responsible for specific social issues. Even the issues themselves become unclear, or paradoxically so explicit that they cannot be treated because they constantly refer to a higher level of social causality which cannot be grasped. The fundamental fact is that social meaning evaporates from places, and therefore from society, and becomes diluted and diffused in the reconstructed logic of a space of flows whose profile, origin, and ultimate purpose are unknown, even for many of the entities integrated in the network of exchanges. The flows of power generate the power of flows, whose material reality imposes itself as a natural phenomenon that cannot be controlled or predicted, only accepted and managed. This is the real significance of the current restructuring process, implemented on the basis of new information technologies, and materially expressed in the separation between functional flows and histori-cally determined places as two disjointed spheres of the human experience. People live in places, power rules through flows.

Nevertheless, societies are not made up of passive subjects resigned to structural domination. The meaninglessness of places, the powerlessness of political institutions are resented and resisted, individually and collectively, by a variety of social actors. People have affirmed their cultural identity, often in territorial terms, mobilizing to achieve their demands, organizing their communities, and staking out their places to preserve meaning, to restore whatever limited control they can over work and residence, to reinvent love and laughter in the midst of the abstraction of the new historical landscape. But, as I have shown elsewhere in my cross-cultural investigation of urban social movements, these are more often reactive symptoms of structural contradictions than conscious actions in pursuit of social change. Faced with the variable geometry of the space of flows, grassroots mobilizations tend to be defensive, protective, territorially bounded, or so culturally specific that their codes of self-recognizing identity become non-communicable, with societies tending to fragment themselves into tribes, easily prone to a fundamentalist affirmation of their identity. While power constitutes an articulated functional space of flows, societies deconstruct their historical culture into localized identities that recover the meaning of places only at the price of breaking down communication among different cultures and different places. Between ahistorical flows and irreducible identities of local communities, cities and regions disappear as socially meaningful places. The historical outcome of this process could be the ushering in of an era characterized by the uneasy coexistence of extraordinary human achievements and the disintegration of large segments of society, along with the widespread prevalence of senseless violence – for the impossibility of communication transforms other communities into "aliens," and thus into potential enemies. The globalization of power flows and the tribalization of local comunities are part of the same fundamental process of historical restructuring: the growing dissociation between techno-economic development and the corresponding mechanisms of social control of such development.

These trends are not ineluctable. They can be reversed, and should be reversed, by a series of political, economic, and technological strategies that could contribute to the reconstruction of social meaning in the new historical reality characterized by the formation of the space of flows as the space of power and functional organizations. While the focus of this book has been primarily analytical, outside normative debate about policies, I believe it is important, in concluding, to explore possible ways out of the destructive dynamics identified by this research.

The new techno-economic paradigm imposes the space of flows as the irreversible spatial logic of economic and functional organizations. The issue then becomes how to articulate the meaning of places to this new functional space. The reconstruction of place-based social meaning requires the simultaneous articulation of alternative social and spatial projects at three levels: cultural, economic, and political.

At the cultural level, local societies, territorially defined, must preserve their identities, and build upon their historical roots, regardless of their economic and functional dependence upon the space of flows. The symbolic marking of places, the preservation of symbols of recognition, the expression of collective memory in actual practices of communication, are fundamental means by which places may continue to exist as such, without having to justify their existence by the fulfillment of their functional performance. However, to avert the danger of over-affirmation of a local identity without reference to any broader social framework of reference at least two additional strategies are required: on the one hand, they must build communication codes with other identities, codes that require the definition of communities as sub-cultures able to recognize and to communicate with higher-order cultures; and on the other they must link the affirmation and symbolic practice of cultural identity to economic policy and political practice. They may thereby overcome the dangers of tribalism and fundamentalism.

Localities – cities and regions – must also be able to find their specific role in the new informational economy. This is possibly the most difficult dimension to integrate into a new strategy of place-based social control, since a precise and major characteristic of the new economy is its functional articulation in the space of flows. However, localities can become indispensable elements in the new economic geography because of the specific nature of the informational economy. In such an economy, the main source of productivity is the capacity to generate and process new information, itself dependent upon the symbolic manipulating ability of labor. This informational potential of labor is a function of its general living conditions, not only in terms of education, but in terms of the overall social milieu that constantly produces and stimulates its intellectual development. In a fundamental sense, social reproduction becomes a direct productive force. Production in the informational economy becomes organized in the space of flows, but social reproduction continues to be locally specific. While the overall logic of the production and management system still operates at the level of flows, the connection between production and reproduction – a key element of the new productive forces – requires an adequate linkage to the place-based system of formation and development of labor. This linkage must be explicitly recognized by each locality, so that locally-based labor will be able to provide the skills required in the production system at the precise point of its connection in the network of productive exchanges. Labor – and indeed, individual citizens – must develop an awareness of the precise role of their place-based activities in the functional space of flows. On the basis of such an awareness they will be better placed to bargain for the control of the overall production system as it relates to their interests. Yet this economic bargaining power on the part of the informational labor force is highly vulnerable if it is not backed up by the social strength provided by cultural identity, and if it is not articulated and implemented by renewed political power from local governments.

Local governments must develop a central role in organizing the social control of places over the functional logic of the space of flows. It is only through the reinforcement of this role that localities will be able to put pressure on economic and political organizations to restore the meaning of the local society in the new functional logic. This statement runs counter to the widespread opinion that the role for local governments will diminish in an internationalized economy and within the functional space of flows. I believe that it is precisely because we live in such a world that local governments can and must play a more decisive role as representatives of civil societies. National governments are frequently as powerless as local to handle unidentifiable flows. Furthermore, since the origin and destination of the flows cannot be controlled, the key issue has become flexibility and adaptability to the potential and requirements of the network of flows in each specific situation as it relates to a given locality. Because local governments defend specific interests, linked to a local society, they can identify such interests and respond flexibly to the requirements of the flows of power, so identifying the best bargaining position in each case. In other words, in a situation of generalized lack of control, the more specific the bargaining agenda, and the more flexible the capacity of response, both positive and negative, to the network of flows, the greater will be the chances of restoring some level of social control. It may be instructive to recall that the formation of the world economy in the fourteenth to sixteenth centuries led to the emergence of city-states as flexible political institutions able to engage in worldwide strategies of negotiation and conflictive articulation with transnational economic powers. The current process of total internationalization of the economy may also lead to the renaissance of the local state, as an alternative to the functionally powerless and institutionally bureaucratized nation-states.

Nevertheless, for local governments to assume such a fundamental role they must extend their organizational capacity and reinforce their power in at least two directions. Firstly, by fostering citizen participation they should mobilize local civil societies to support a collective strategy toward the reconstruction of the meaning of the locality in a conflictive dynamics with the placeless powers. Community organization and widespread, active citizen participation are indispensable elements for the revitalization of local governments as dynamic agents of economic development and social control. Secondly, and in so doing, they must connect with other organized, self-identified communities engaged in collective endeavor, taking care to avoid tribalism and acting on the material basis of work and power. Local governments will be unable to control the logic of the space of flows if they remain confined to their locality, while flows-based organizations select their locations at their convenience, playing localized social and political actors one against the other. Local governments attempting to restore social control of the development process need to establish their own networks of information, decision making, and strategic alliances, in order to match the mobility of power-holding organizations. In other words, they must reconstruct an alternative space of flows on the basis of the space of places. In this way they can avoid the deconstruction of their locales by the placeless logic of flows-based organizations.

Interestingly enough both these strategies – active citizen participation and a nation-wide or worldwide network of local governments – could be implemented most effectively on the basis of new information technologies. Citizens' data banks, interactive communication systems, community-based multimedia centers, are powerful tools to enhance citizen participation on the basis of grassroots organizations and local governments' political will. On-line information systems linking local governments across the world could provide a fundamental tool in countering the strategies of flows-based organizations, which would then lose the advantage, deriving from their control of asymmetrical information flows. Information technologies could provide the flexible instrument to reverse the logic of domination of the space of flows built by the process of socio-economic restructuring. However, the technological medium alone will not be able to transform this process in the absence of social mobilization, political decisions, and institutional strategies that would enable local governments to challenge collectively the power of flows and to reinstate the counterpower of places.

These reflections are not intended to provide a specific policy agenda for political action and social change, given the generality of the analysis presented in this book. They aim simply at opening a debate, in both scholarly and political circles, that could begin to address the fundamental challenge posed by the emergence of the space of flows to the meaning of our cities and to the welfare of our societies. The policy orientations I have suggested may appear utopian. But sometimes, a utopian vision is needed to shake the institutions from shortsightedness and stasis and to enable people to think the unthinkable, thus enhancing their awareness and their control of the inevitable social transformation. What we must prevent at all costs is the development of the one-sided logic of the space of flows while we keep up a pretence that the social balance of our cities has been maintained. Unless alternative, realistic policies, fostered by new social movements, can be found to reconstruct the social meaning of localities within the space of flows, our societies will fracture into non-communicative segments whose reciprocal alienation will lead to destructive violence and to a process of historical decline.

However, if innovative social projects, represented and implemented by renewed local governments, are able to master the formidable forces unleashed by the revolution in information technologies, then a new socio-spatial structure could emerge made up of a network of local communes controlling and shaping a network of productive flows. Maybe then our historic time and our social space would converge towards the reintegration of knowledge and meaning into a new Informational City.

Notes

Chapter 1

[1]The social theory underlying this analysis cannot be fully presented in the context of this book, which addresses a specific research topic. However, it is intellectually important to relate this study to the overall theoretical framework that informs it. The elaboration of this theory has built upon several classical traditions: Marx for the analysis of class relationships; Freud and Reich for the understanding of personality on the basis of sexual and family relationships; Weber for the analysis of the state. A number of contemporary social scientists have been crucial to my understanding of links and developments not covered in the classical writings: Nicos Poulantzas, for the recasting of the theory of social classes and the state; Alain Touraine for his analysis on post-industrialism; Nancy Chodorow for the intellectual connection between feminist theory and the psychoanalytical tradition; Agnes Heller, for the understanding of the historical creation of social needs; and Michel Foucault and Richard Sennett for the connection between power and culture. In making explicitly known my theoretical sources, I hope to help place this brief summary of my underlying theoretical framework in the ongoing intellectual debates in social sciences.

[2]Under the term "human-modified matter" I would include what could be called at the risk of paradox, "immaterial matter," that is, the set of symbols and communication codes that are generated by the human mind and which, while they are intangible, are a fundamental part of matter, since they are indeed a material force. One way to understand the informational mode of development, that I will not explore at present, could be the shift from physical matter to mental matter in the process of expansion of nature.

[3]The definition is from Harvey Brooks, cited in Daniel Bell, *The Coming of Post-Industrial Society* (New York, Basic Books, 1973) p. 29 of the 1976 edition.

[4]Ibid.

[5]Alain Touraine, *La Société post-industrielle* (Paris, Denoel, 1969); Radovan Richta, *La Civilisation au carrefour* (Paris, Anthropos, 1969); Bell, *Post-industrial Society*.

[6]For a summary, informed presentation of the rise and implications of information technology see, for instance, Tom Forester, *High Tech Society: The Story of the Information Technology Revolution* (Oxford, Blackwell, 1987); also Bruce R. Guile (ed.), *Information Technologies and Social Transformation* (Washington DC, National Academy Press, 1985).

[7]See E. Braun and S. MacDonald, *Revolution in Miniature* (Cambridge, Cambridge University Press, 1982).

[8]See Edward J. Sylvester and Lynn C. Klotz, *The Gene Age: Genetic Engineering and the Next Industrial Revolution* (New York, Scribner, 1983).

[9]See John S. Mayo, *The Evolution of Information Technologies* in Guile, *Information Technologies*, pp. 7–33.

[10]Nathan Rosenberg, "The Impact of Historical Innovation: A Historical View," in Ralph Landau and Nathan Rosenberg (eds), *The Positive Sum Strategy: Harnessing Technology for Economic Growth* (Washington DC, National Academy Press, 1986).

[11]See Melvin Kranzberg, "The Information Age: Evolution or Revolution," in Guile, *Information Technologies*, pp. 35–55.

[12]See Melvin Kranzberg and Carroll W. Pursell, Jr (eds), *Technology in Western Civilization* (New York, Oxford University Press, 1967), 2 vols.

[13]I. Mackintosh, *Sunrise Europe: The Dynamics of Information Technology* (Oxford, Blackwell, 1986).

[14]Nathan Rosenberg, *Perspectives on Technology* (Cambridge, Cambridge University Press, 1976).

[15]See Eugene S. Ferguson, "The Steam Engine Before 1830," John R. Brae, "Energy Conversion," and Harold I. Sharlin, "Applications of Electricity," in Kranzberg and Pursell, *Technology in Western Civilization*.

[16]For the notion of "technical paradigm" see the analysis in Carlota Perez, "Structural Change and the Assimilation of New Technologies in the Economic and Social Systems," *Futures*, 15 (1983), pp. 357–75.

[17]Marx developed his most far-reaching analysis of the social implications of technology in the *Grundrisse*.

[18]See Robert Boyer and Benjamin Coriat, *Technical Flexibility and Macro Stabilisation*, paper presented at the Venice Conference on Innovation Diffusion, 17–21 March 1986 (Paris, CEPREMAP, 1986).

[19]For an analysis of "Fordism" see Robert Boyer, *Technical Change and the Theory of Regulation* (Paris, CEPREMAP, 1987).

[20]Michael Piore and Charles Sabel, *The Second Industrial Divide* (New York, Basic Books, 1984).

[21]See the fundamental work on the whole series of issues discussed in this chapter, Peter Hall and Paschal Preston, *The Carrier Wave: New Information Technology and the Geography of Innovation, 1846–2003* (London, Unwin Hyman, 1988).

[22]For a discussion of post-industralism, see Manuel Castells, *The Economic Crisis and American Society* (Oxford, Blackwell, 1980), pp. 164–78.

[23]Alfred D. Chandler, *The Visible Hand* (Cambridge, Cambridge University Press, 1977).

[24]Robert Solow, "Technical Changes and the Aggregate Production Function," in *Review of Economics and Statistics*, August 1957. For a summary of the debate on the sources of productivity, see Richard R. Nelson, "Research on Productivity Growth and Productivity Differences: Dead Ends and New Departures," in *Journal of Economic Literature*, XIX (September 1981), pp. 1029–64.

[25]I have relied for this analysis on Nicole Woolsey-Biggart, "Direct Sales and Flexible Market Strategies," forthcoming.

[26]Manuel Castells, "Collective Consumption and Urban Contradictions in Advanced Capitalism," in Leo Lindberg et al. (eds) *Stress and Contradiction in Modern Capitalism* (Lexington, Mass., Heath, 1974).

[27]Morris Janowitz, *Social Control of the Welfare State* (Chicago, University of Chicago Press, 1976).

[28]Michel Aglietta, *Une Théorie de la regulation économique: le cas des Etats-Unis* (Paris, Calmann-Levy, 1976).

[29]Alain Touraine, *La Voix et Le Regard* (Paris, Seuil, 1978).

[30]Philippe Schmitter *Interest Conflict and Political Change in Brazil* (Stanford, Stanford University Press, 1981).

[31]Gordon Clark and Michael Dear, *State Apparatus* (Boston, Allen & Unwin, 1984).

[32]Nicos Poulantzas, *L'Etat, le pouvoir, le socialisme* (Paris, Presses Universitaires de France, 1978), p. 226 (my translation).

[33]See James O' Connor, *Accumulation Crisis* (Oxford, Blackwell, 1984).

[34]Post-depression capitalism did not actually follow the policies proposed by Keynes: the state acted on supply as much as on demand. It would be more appropriate to refer to this form of capitalism as state-regulated capitalism.

[35]See Michel Aglietta, *Regulation et crises du capitalisme* (Paris, Calmann-Levy, 1976).

[36]For the analysis of the causes of the economic crisis of the 1970s and of the potential way out of it through the restructuring process, see Castells, *The Economic Crisis and American Society*.

[37]Samuel Bowles et al., *Beyond the Wasteland* (New York, Doubleday, 1983).

[38]See James O'Connor's classic, *The Fiscal Crisis of the State* (New York, St Martin's, 1973).

[39]See Manuel Castells and Alejandro Portes, "World Underneath: The Origins, Dynamics, and Consequences of the Informal Economy," in Alejandro Portes, Manuel Castells, and Lauren Benton (eds), *The Informal Economy* (Baltimore, Johns Hopkins University Press, 1989).

[40]Michael Reich, *Discrimination in Labor Markets* (Princeton, Princeton University Press, 1982).

[41]Manuel Castells, "Immigrant Workers and Class Struggle in Western Europe," *Politics and Society*, 2 (1975).

[42]Joel Krieger, *Reagan, Thatcher and the Politics of Decline* (New York, Oxford University Press, 1986).

[43]I rely here on an analysis of the state, adapted from Nicos Poulantzas' work, that sees the state's relatively autonomous actions taking place within a dialectical process of ensuring domination and accumulation on the one hand, while trying to maintain legitimation and redistribution on the other. For an attempt at using these concepts in empirical research, see Manuel Castells and Francis Godard, *Monopolville* (Paris, Mouton, 1974).

[44]Fernand Braudel, *Capitalisme et civilisation materielle* (Paris, Armand Colin, 1979); Immanuel Wallerstein, *The Modern World System* (New York, Academic Press, 1974).

[45]By the "creative destruction" of capitalism I refer, of course, to the notion proposed by Schumpeter in his *Business Cycles*.

[46]Robert Boyer (ed.), *Capitalismes fin de siècle* (Paris, Presses Universitaires de France, 1986).

[47]See our analysis of "Reaganomics" in Martin Carnoy and Manuel Castells, "After the Crisis?," in *World Policy Journal*, May 1984.

[48]On the role of flexibility see Boyer and Coriat, *Technical Flexibility*.

[49]The notion of the "recapitalization" of the state has been proposed by S. M. Miller.

[50]For an analysis of flexibility in enhancing competitiveness in the international economy, see Manuel Castells, "Small Business in the World Economy: The Hong Kong Model of Economic Development", Berkeley Roundtable on the International Economy (Berkeley, University of California, forthcoming).

[51]On the analysis of networks see Piore and Sabel, *The Second Industrial Divide* and Woolsey-Biggart, "Direct Sales."

[52]For evidence on the fundamental role of networks in the informal economy, see Portes, Castells, and Benton, *The Informal Economy.*

[53]See Peter Schulze, "Shifts in the World Economy and the Restructuring of Economic Sectors: Increasing Competition and Strategic Alliances in Information Technologies" (Berkeley, University of California, Institute of International Studies, 1987).

Chapter 2

[1]A. J. Scott and M. Storper (eds), *Production Work, Territory: The Geographical Anatomy of Industrial Capitalism* (Boston, London, Allen and Unwin, 1986); Manuel Castells (ed.), *High Technology, Space, and Society* (Beverly Hills, Ca., Sage, 1985); US Congress, Office of Technology Assessment, *Technology, Innovation, and Regional Economic Development* (Washington, DC, Government Printing Office, 1984, OTA-STI-238; Philippe Aydalot (ed.), *Milieux innovateurs en Europe* (Paris, GREMI, 1986); R. Oakey, *High Technology Small Firms: Regional Development in Britain and the United States* (London, Pinter, 1984); Bert Van der Knapp and Egbert Wever (eds), *New Technology and Regional Development* (London, Croom Helm, 1987); M. Storper, *The Spatial Division of Labor: Technology, the Labor Process, and the Location of Industries*, PhD dissertation (Berkeley, University of California, 1982).

[2]See especially Ann Markusen, Peter Hall, and Amy Glasmeier, *High Tech America: The What, How, Where, and Why of the Sunrise Industries* (Boston, London, Allen and Unwin, 1986); M. Breheny, P. Hall, D. Hart, and R. McQuaid, *Western Sunrise: The Genesis and Growth of Britain's High Tech Corridor* (London, Allen and Unwin, 1986); John F. Brotchie, Peter Hall, and Peter W. Newton, *The Spatial Impact of Technological Change* (London, Groom Helm, 1987).

[3]A. J. Scott and M. Storper, "High Technology Industry and Regional Development: A Theoretical Critique and Reconstruction," *International Social Science Journal* (1987); M.D. Thomas, "The Innovation Factor in the Process of Microeconomic Industrial Change: Conceptual Explorations," in Van der Knapp and Wever (eds), pp. 21–44; R. Walker, "Technological Determination and Determinism: Industrial Growth and Location," in Castells, *High Technology, Space, and Society*, pp. 226–64; R. Gordon and L. Kimball, "Industrial Structure and the Changing Global Dynamics of Location in High Technology Industry," in J. Brotchie, P. Hall, and P. W. Newton (eds), *The Spatial Impact of Technological Change* (London, Croom Helm, 1987).

[4]Ann Markusen, *Profit Cycles, Oligopoly, and Regional Development* (Cambridge, Mass., MIT, 1985).

[5]For instance, Edward J. Malecki, "High Technology and Local Economic Development," *Journal of the American Planning Association*, Summer 1984, pp. 262–9; A. J. Scott, "Location Processes, Urbanization, and Territorial Development: An Exploratory Essay," in *Environment and Planning A*, 17, pp. 479–501; M. Taylor,

"Enterprise and the Product-Cycle Model: Conceptual Ambiguities," in Van der Knapp and Wever, *New Technology and Regional Development*, pp. 75–93; Allen Scott, *New Industrial Spaces* (London, Pion, 1988).

[6]See Jeff Henderson and Manuel Castells (eds), *Global Restructuring and Territorial Development* (London, Sage, 1987).

[7]Markusen, Hall, and Glasmeier, *High Tech America*.

[8]A. Glasmeier, *The Structure, Location, and Role of High Technology Industries in U.S. Regional Development*, unpublished PhD dissertation (Berkeley, University of California, 1986).

[9]See John Rees, "Industrial Innovation," in *Economic Development Commentary*, 10, 1 (Spring 1987), pp. 17–21.

[10]See Markusen, Hall, and Glasmeier, *High Tech America*, table 9.1., p. 155.

[11]Storper, *Spatial Division of Labor*.

[12]A. J. Scott and D. P. Angel, *The U.S. Semiconductor Industry: A Locational Analysis*, Department of Geography Research Monograph (Los Angeles, UCLA, 1986).

[13]Servet Mutlu, *Inter-regional and International Mobility of Industrial Capital: The Case of American Automobile and Electronics Companies*, unpublished PhD dissertation (Berkeley, University of California, 1979). Mutlu's work is, to my knowledge, the earliest comprehensive, thorough, and empirical analysis of the spatial implications of high-technology manufacturing in the US.

[14]See Amy Glasmeier, *The Making of High Tech Regions*, forthcoming, ch. 2.

[15]See Glasmeier, *High Technology Industries in U.S. Regional Development*; The Fantus Company, *Local High Technology Initiatives Study* (Washington, DC, US Congress, Office of Technology Assessment, 1983); S. Goodman and V. L. Arnold, "High Technology in Texas," in *Texas Business Review*, Nov.-Dec. 1983.

[16]Glasmeier, *High Technology Industries in U.S. Regional Development*, pp. 316–29.

[17]Mutlu, *Mobility of Industrial Capital*, p. 129.

[18]The major research effort to date on these analytical perspectives is the work conducted by Anna Lee Saxenian since 1980. See, for instance, A. L. Saxenian, "The Genesis of Silicon Valley," in P. Hall and A. Markusen (eds), *Silicon Landscapes* (Winchester, Mass., Allen and Unwin, 1985); A. L. Saxenian, "Silicon Valley and Route 128: Regional Prototypes or Historic Exceptions," in M. Castells, *High Technology, Space, and Society*, pp. 81–105. Mutlu has also analyzed in depth the origins of the two major industrial centers of high technology in *Mobility of Industrial Capital*.

[19]This major fact was brought to my attention by Lenny Siegel, the director of the Pacific Studies Center in Mountain View, Ca. (personal correspondence, 1985).

[20]Anna Lee Saxenian, *In Search of Power: The Organization of Business Interests in Silicon Valley and Route 128*, Department of Political Science Working Paper, (Cambridge, Mass, MIT, 1986).

[21]See Storper, *Spatial Division of Labor*; also J. Henderson and A. J. Scott, "The Growth and Internationalization of the American Semiconductor Industry: Labour Processes and the Changing Spatial Organisation of Production," in M. Breheny and R. McQuaid (eds), *The Development of High Technology Industries* (London, Croom Helm, 1986); A. Sayer, "Industrial Location on a World Scale: The Case of the Semiconductor Industry" in Scott and Storper (eds), *Production Work, Territory*, pp. 107–23.

[22]Scott and Angel, *The U.S. Semiconductor Industry*.

[23]D. Ernst, *The Global Race in Microelectronics* (Frankfurt: Campus, 1983); K. Flamm, "Internationalization in the Semiconductor Industry," in J. Grunwald and K. Flamm (eds), *The Global Factory* (Washington, DC: Brookings Institution, 1985), pp. 38-136.

[24]For data and sources on this section, see Mutlu, *Mobility of Industrial Capital.*

[25]Personal correspondence from Amy Glasmeier, 3 February 1988.

[26]See Markusen, *Profit Cycles*, ch. 9.

[27]See Sarah Kuhn, *Computer Manufacturing in New England: Structure, Location and Labor in a Growing Industry* (Cambridge, Harvard-MIT Joint Center for Urban Studies, 1981).

[28]E. Sciberras, *Multinational Electronics Companies and National Economic Policies* (Greenwich, Conn.: JAI, 1977).

[29]P. Hall, A. Markusen, R. Osborn, and B. Wachsman, *The Computer Software Industry: Prospects and Policy Issues*, Institute of Urban and Regional Development (IURD) Working Paper No. 410 (Berkeley, University of California, 1983).

[30]Ibid., p. 55.

[31]See Edward J. Sylvester and Lynn C. Klotz, *The Gene Age: Genetic Engineering and the Next Industrial Revolution* (New York, Scribner, 1983).

[32]A. Hacking, *Economic Aspects of Biotechnology* (Cambridge, Cambridge University Press, 1986).

[33]N. Simmons, "Biotechnology Industry Offers Specialists a Flurry of Jobs," *New York Times*, 25 March 1984.

[34]Edward J. Blakely, *Developing the Biotechnology Industry: A Case Study of Regional Industrial Planning in the San Francisco Bay Area*, Institute of Urban and Regional Development, Biotech Industry Research Group (Berkeley, University of California, 1988).

[35]M. Kenney, *Biotechnology: The University-Industrial Complex* (New Haven, Yale University Press, 1986).

[36]Peter Hall, Lisa Bornstein, Reed Grier, and Melvin Webber, *Biotechnology: The Next Industrial Frontier*, Institute of Urban and Regional Development, Biotech Industry Research Group (Berkeley, University of California, 1988).

[37]Kenney, *Biotechnology.*

[38]See "Biotech Comes of Age," *Business Week*, 23 January 1984, pp. 84-94.

[39]Hall, Bornstein, Grier, and Webber, *Biotechnology*, p. 14.

[40]Hall, Bornstein, Grier, and Webber, *Biotechnology.*

[41]Kenney, *Biotechnology.*

[42]Edward Blakely with Suzanne Scotchmer and Jonathan Levine, *The Locational and Economic Patterns of California's Biotech Industry: A Preliminary Report*, Institute of Urban and Regional Development, Biotech Industry Research Group (Berkeley, University of California, 1988).

[43]"Biotech Comes of Age."

[44]See Michael Borrus and James Millstein, *Technological Innovation and Industrial Growth: A Comparative Assessment of Biotechnology and Semiconductors*, Research Report prepared for the US Congress, Office of Technology Assessment (Washington, DC, 1982).

[45]See Bruce R. Guile (ed.) *Information Technologies and Social Transformation* (Washington, DC, National Academy Press, 1985).

[46]See US Congress, Office of Technology Assessment, *Information Technology R&D:*

Critical Trends and Issues (Washington, DC, 1985), particularly pp. 139–200.

[47]Ann F. Friedlander, "Macroeconomics and Microeconomics of Innovation: the Role of the Technological Environment," in Ralph Landau and Nathan Rosenberg (eds), *The Positive Sum Strategy: Harnessing Technology for Economic Growth*, (Washington, DC, National Academy Press, 1986), pp. 327–32.

[48]An interesting approach to the analysis of innovative milieux has been proposed by Philippe Aydalot, *L'Aptitude des milieux locaux a promouvoir innovation technologique*, paper delivered at the Symposium on New Technologies and Regions in Crisis, French Language Association of Regional Science, Brussels, 22–3 April 1985. A formal analysis of the notion of innovative technological milieux has been elaborated by W. Brian Arthur, *Industry Location Patterns and the Importance of History*, Food Research Institute Research Paper (Stanford: Stanford University, 1986).

[49]Melvin Kranzberg, "The Information Age: Evolution or Revolution?" in Guile, *Information Technologies*, pp. 35–54.

[50]J. Rees and H. Stafford, *A Review of Regional Growth and Industrial Location Theory: Towards Understanding the Development of High Technology Complexes in the US* (US Congress, Office of Technology Assessment, Washington DC, 1983).

[51]Gordon and Kimball, "Industrial Structure."

[52]This analysis builds on my own contribution to the analysis of the relationship between technology and industrial location in my University of Paris doctoral dissertation (1967). For elaboration on that research, see Manuel Castells, *Sociologie de l'espace industriel* (Paris, Anthropos, 1975).

[53]See M. Carnoy and M. Castells, *Technology and Economy in the U.S.*, paper delivered at the UNESCO Conference on Science and Technology, Athens, September 1985.

[54]See E. Braun and S. MacDonald, *Revolution in Miniature* (Cambridge, Cambridge University Press, 1982).

[55]R. U. Ayres, *The Next Industrial Revolution: Reviving Industry Through Innovation* (Cambridge, Mass., Ballinger, 1984).

[56]Jeff Henderson, "The New International Division of Labour and American Semiconductor Production in South-East Asia," in D. Watts, C. Dixon, and D. Drakakis-Smith (eds), *Multinational Companies and the Third World* (London, Croom Helm, 1986).

[57]Ian Benson and John Lloyd, *New Technology and Industrial Change: The Impact of the Scientific-Technical Revolution on Labour and Industry* (New York, Nichols, 1983); Lionel Nicol, *Communications, Economic Development, and Spatial Structure: A Review of Research*, Institute of Urban and Regional Development, Working Paper No. 404 (Berkeley, University of California, 1983).

[58]The general theme of the spatial division of labor in economic geography has been theorized in masterly fashion by Doreen Massey in *Spatial Divisions of Labour: Social Structures and the Geography of Production* (London, Macmillan, 1984). My own work on this topic is much indebted to Massey's analysis.

[59]R. Gordon and L. Kimball, *High Technology, Employment, and the Challenges to Education*, Silicon Valley Research Group, Working Paper No. 1 (Santa Cruz: University of California, 1985).

[60]M. Carnoy, *The Labor Market in Silicon Valley and its Implications for Education* (Stanford, Ca, Stanford University Institute for Research on Educational Finance and Governance, 1985).

[61]See Scott and Angel, *The US Semiconductor Industry*; Henderson, "New International Division of Labor"; Henderson and Scott, "Growth and Internationalization of the American Semiconductor Industry"; Mutlu, *Mobility of Industrial Capital*; Storper, *Spatial Division of Labor*; Glasmeier, *High Technology Industries in US Regional Development*.

[62]A. K. Glasmeier, "High Tech Industries and the Regional Division of Labor," in *Industrial Relations*, 25, 2 (Spring 1986), pp. 197–211.

[63]Ibid., pp. 202–4.

[64]See Scott and Angel, *The US Semiconductor Industry*.

[65]Ibid., p. 29 of typescript.

[66]See Anna Lee Saxenian, *Silicon Chips and Spatial Structure: The Industrial Basis of Urbanization in Santa Clara County, California*, Institute of Urban and Regional Development, working paper 345 (Berkeley, University of California, 1981); Storper, *Spatial Division of Labor*; Mutlu, *Mobility of Industrial Capital*.

[67]See Henderson and Scott, "Growth and Internationalization of the American Semiconductor Industry."

[68]For a discussion of the evidence on the impact of automation on productive decentralization at the international level, refuting the thesis of "relocation back North," see Manuel Castells, "High Technology and the New International Division of Labor," in *International Labour Review*, October 1988.

[69]Saxenian, *Silicon Chips and Spatial Structure*.

[70]J. Keller, *The Production Worker in Electronics: Industrialization and Labor Development in California's Santa Clara Valley*, PhD dissertation (Ann Arbor, University of Michigan, 1981).

[71]Storper, *Spatial Division of Labor*.

[72]For some key formal and theoretical analyses of milieux of innovation see: W. B. Arthur, *Industry Location and the Economics of Agglomeration: Why a Silicon Valley?* (Stanford, Stanford University Center for Economic Policy Research, 1985); Walter B. Stohr, "Territorial Innovation Complexes," in Aydalot, *L'Aptitude des milieux locaux*, pp. 29–56; A. E. Anderson, *Creativity and Regional Development*, working paper 85–14 (Laxenburg, Austria, International Institute for Applied Systems Analysis, 1985); P. Aydalot, "Trajectoires Technologiques et Milieux Innovateurs," in Aydalot, *L'Aptitude des milieux locaux*, pp. 345–61.

[73]See E. J. Malecki, "Technology and Regional Development: A Survey," *International Regional Science Review*, 8, 2, pp. 89–125.

[74]See George Young, *Venture Capital in High-tech Companies* (London, Pinter, 1985).

[75]E. J. Malecki, "Corporate Organization of R&D and the Location of Technological Activities," in *Regional Studies*, 14 (1980), pp. 219–34.

[76]E. J. Malecki, "Government Funded R&D: Some Regional Economic Implications," in *Professional Geographer*, 33, 1 (1981), pp. 72–82.

[77]Mutlu, *Mobility of Industrial Capital*; John W. Wilson, *The New Ventures: Inside the High-stakes World of Venture Capital* (Reading, Mass., Addison-Wesley, 1985).

[78]Saxenian, *Silicon Chips and Spatial Structure*; Saxenian, *The Political Economy of High Technology Growth Centers: Silicon Valley, Route 128, and Cambridge, England*, PhD dissertation (Cambridge, Mass., MIT, 1988); E. Rogers and J. Larsen, *Silicon Valley Fever* (New York, Basic Books, 1984); Cynthia Kroll and Linda Kimball, *The Santa Clara Valley R&D Dilemma: The Real Estate Industry and High tech Growth*,

Center for Real Estate and Urban Economics, Working Paper (Berkeley, University of California, 1986); Tim Sturgeon, *Industrial Location of the Semiconductor Industry: A Critique*, Honors thesis (Berkeley, University of California, 1987).

[79]See G. A. Van der Knapp, G. J. R. Linge, and E. Wever, "Technology and Industrial Change: An Overview," in Van der Knapp and Wever, *New Technology and Regional Development*, pp. 1–21.

[80]Cf. the analysis by Jay S. Stowsky, *Cultural Industries in the United States*, Department of City and Regional Planning research report (Berkeley, University of California, 1987).

[81]P. Hall, "Innovation: Key to Regional Growth," *Transaction/Society*, 19, 5 (1982).

[82]J. Rees and H. Stafford, *A Review of Regional Growth and Industrial Location Theory: Towards Understanding the Development of High-Technology Complexes in the United States*, Report for the US Congress, Office of Technology Assessment, April 1983.

[83]Saxenian, *Political Economy of High Technology Growth Centers*.

[84]E. J. Malecki, "Dimensions of R&D Location in the United States," in *Research Policy*, 9 (1980), pp. 2–22.

[85]*High Hopes for High Tech* (collective author), (Chapel Hill, University of North Carolina Press, 1985).

[86]See E. J. Malecki, "Corporate Organization of R and D," pp. 227–9.

[87]See Saxenian, "Silicon Valley and Route 128"; Saxenian, "The Genesis of Silicon Valley," in *Built Environment*, 9, 1, pp. 7–17; Lenny Siegel and John Markoff, *The High Cost of High Tech* (New York, Harper and Row, 1985); N. Dorfman, *Massachusetts High Technology Boom in Perspective* (Cambridge, Mass., MIT Center for Policy Alternatives, 1982); Pierre Fischer, Richard Carlson, Jean-Pierre Boespflug, and Pierre Lamond, *Silicon Valley, Anatomie d'Une Reussite* (Paris, Centre de Prospective et d'Evaluation, 1984); Michael Malone, *The Big Score* (New York, Doubleday, 1985).

[88]A. J. Scott, "High Technology Industry and Territorial Development: The Rise of the Orange County Complex, 1955–1984," in *Urban Geography*, 7, 1–43; D. A. Hicks and W. H. Stolberg, *The High-Technology Sectors: Growth and Development in the Dallas–Fort Worth Regional Economy, 1964–84*, Center for Policy Studies Research Report (Dallas, University of Texas, 1985).

[89]F. G. Rodgers, *The IBM Way* (New York, Harper and Row, 1986); Franklin M. Fisher, *IBM and the US Data Processing Industry* (New York, Praeger, 1983); Sonny Kleinfield, *The Biggest Company on Earth: A Profile of AT&T* (New York, Holt, Rinehart, and Winston, 1981).

[90]See Glasmeier, *High Technology Industries in US Regional Development*, pp. 292ff.

[91]A. Glasmeier, *Survey of High Technology Firms in Austin*, unpublished report, Graduate Program in Community and Regional Planning (Austin, University of Texas, 1987).

[92]See Mutlu, *Mobility of Industrial Capital*.

[93]See The City of Pittsburgh, *Strategy 21: Pittsburgh/Allegheny Economic Development Strategy to begin the 21st century*, 1985; Donald S. Shanis, *Transportation Planning for a High-tech Corridor in Suburban Philadelphia*, Delaware Valley Regional Planning Commission, 1985; Ayden Kutay, *Prospects of the Growth of Innovation-based High Technology Clusters in Old Industrial Regions: Pittsburgh as a Case Study*, unpublished research report (Pittsburgh, University of Pittsburgh, 1988).

[94]Henderson and Scott, "Growth and Internationalization of the American Semi-

conductor Industry"; R. P. Oakey, *High Technology Industry and Industrial Location* (Aldershot, Gower, 1981); R. Premus, *Location of High-technology Firms and Regional Economic Development* (Washington, DC, US Congress Joint Economic Committee, 1982).

[95]Storper, *Spatial Division of Labor.*

[96]*International Economic Restructuring and the Territorial Community* (Vienna, UNIDO, 1985).

[97]See Michael Borrus et al., *Telecommunications Development in Comparative Perspective: the New Telecommunications in Europe, Japan, and the US*, BRIE Working Paper (Berkeley, University of California, 1985); U.S. Congress, Office of Technology Assessment, *Computerized Manufacturing: Employment, Education, and the Workplace* (Washington, DC, Government Printing Office, 1984).

[98]See Ernst, *Global Race in Microelectronics*; R. Kaplinsky, *Microelectronics and Employment Revisited: A Review*, A Report for I.L.D. (Brighton, University of Sussex Institute of Development Studies, 1986).

[99]Cf. research in progress by Peter Hall, Ann Markusen, Sabina Dietrick, and Scott Campbell at the Institute of Urban and Regional Development, University of California, Berkeley, supported by the National Science Foundation.

[100]See A. Gillespie (ed.), *Technological Change and Regional Development* (London, Pion, 1983); R. Schmenner, *Making Business Location Decisions* (Englewood Cliffs, NJ, Prentice-Hall, 1982).

[101]Cf. Glasmeier, *High Technology Industries in U.S. Regional Development.*

[102]Jeffrey Henderson, *Semiconductors, Scotland, and the International Division of Labour*, Research Report (Hong Kong, University of Hong Kong Centre of Urban Studies, 1986).

[103]See Saxenian, "The Genesis of Silicon Valley."

[104]On working women in electronics in Asia, see Françoise Sabbah, *Tecnologia Electronica y Trabajo de la Mujer: Una Perspectiva Internacional* (Madrid, Instituto de la Mujer, 1988).

[105]A. J. Scott, "The Semiconductor Industry in South-east Asia: Organization, Location, and the International Division of Labor," in *Regional Studies*, 21 (1987).

[106]Peter W. Schulze, *The Struggle for Future Markets: Sectoral Adaptation and the Internationalization of Production*, discussion paper (Berkeley, Institute of International Studies, 1986)

[107]Juan Rada, *Structure and Behavior of the Semiconductors Industry* (New York, United Nations Center for the Study of Transnational Corporations, 1982).

[108]Manuel Castells and Laura Tyson, "High Technology Choices Ahead: Restructuring Interdependence," in John Sewell (ed.), *Growth, Jobs, and Markets in the International Economy* (Washington DC, Overseas Development Council, 1988).

[109]See Scott, "Semiconductor Industry in South-east Asia"; Dieter Ernst, "Crisis, Technology and the Dynamics of Global Restructuring: The Case of the Electronics Industry," in Henderson and Castells, *Global Restructuring.*

[110]Dieter Ernst, *Micro-electronics and Global Restructuring: The Social Implications of High Tech Neo-Mercantilism*, Discussion Paper (The Hague, Institute of Social Studies, 1986).

[111]J. Northcott, P. Rogers, W. Knetsch, and B. de Lestapis, *Microelectronics in Industry: An International Comparison. Britain, France, and Germany* (London, Policy Studies Institute, 1985).

[112]Scott, "Semiconductor Industry in South-east Asia."

[113]Ibid.

[114]Breheny and McQuaid, *Development of High Technology Industries.*

[115]See Saxenian, *Silicon Chips and Spatial Structure.*

[116]See Storper, *Spatial Division of Labor.*

[117]Markusen, Hall, and Glasmeier, *High Tech America.*

[118]See A. Markusen, *Profit Cycles*, pp. 101–17.

[119]See A. Glasmeier, *High Technology Industries in U.S. Regional Development.*

[120]Amy Glasmeier, personal communication to author of work in progress; see also Glasmeier, *The Making of High Tech Regions.*

[121]See Markusen, Hall, and Glasmeier, *High Tech America*, pp. 80–93.

[122]R. Gordon and L. M. Kimball, *Small Town High Technology: The Industrialization of Santa Cruz County*, (Santa Cruz, University of California Silicon Valley Research Group, forthcoming).

[123]Glasmeier, *High Technology Industries in U.S. Regional Development*, pp. 135–6.

[124]See Norman Glickman, *MCC comes to Austin*, Lyndon B. Johnson School of Public Affairs Working Paper (Austin, University of Texas, 1985).

[125]Amy Glasmeier, *Survey of High Technology Firms in Austin.*

[126]See Gordon and Kimball, "Industrial Structure," pp. 24–5.

[127]See Oakey, *High Technology Small Firms.*

[128]Stephen Cohen and John Zysman, *Manufacturing Matters* (New York, Basic Books, 1987).

[129]See Yasno Miyakawa, "Evolution of the Regional System and Change of Industrial Policy in Japan," in UN Centre for Regional Development, *Regional Development Alternatives* (Tokyo, Maliuze Asia, 1982); Kuniko Fujita, "The Technopolis: High Technology and Regional Development in Japan," in *International Journal of Urban and Regional Research*, 12, 4 (1988), pp. 566–94.

[130]Chalmers Johnson, *MITI and the Japanese Miracle* (Stanford: Stanford University Press, 1982).

[131]M. Borrus et al., *Responses to the Japanese Challenge in High Technology: Innovation, Maturity, and U.S.-Japanese Competition in Microelectronics*, BRIE Working Paper (Berkeley, University of California, 1983).

[132]W. Stohr, "Regional Technological and Institutional Innovation: The Case of the Japanese Technopolis Policy," in J. Federwish and H. Zoller (eds), *Technologie et region, politiques en mutation* (Paris, Economica, 1986).

[133]T. Toda, "The Location of High Technology Industry and the Technopolis Plan in Japan," in Brotchie, Hall, and Newton, *The Spatial Impact of Technological Change*, pp. 271–83.

[134]Ministry of International Trade and Industry (MITI), Japan, *The Technopolis Project in Japan* (Tokyo, MITI, 1981).

[135]Sheridan Tatsuno, *The Technopolis Strategy: Japan, High Technology and the Control of the 21st Century* (Englewood Cliffs, NJ, Prentice Hall, 1986).

[136]See the analysis presented in R. Gordon and L. M. Kimball (eds), *The Future of Silicon Valley*, (Boston, Allen and Unwin, forthcoming).

[137]Dieter Ernst, *U.S.-Japanese Competition and the Worldwide Restructuring of the Electronics Industry: A European View*, Institute of International Studies, Policy Papers, Fall (Berkeley, University of California, 1986).

[138]This is a trend observed and analyzed by key experts on the topic, particularly Okimoto and Ernst.

[139]See Kroll and Kimball, *Santa Clara Valley R&D Dilemma*.

[140]Peter W. Schulze, *Shifts in the World Economy and the Restructuring of Economic Sectors: Increased Competition and Strategic Alliances in the Microelectronics Industries*, paper prepared for the International Seminar on New Technologies, Rio de Janeiro, 26-8 January 1987 (Berkeley, University of California Institute of International Studies).

[141]Ibid.

[142]Ernst, *U.S.–Japanese Competition*.

[143]Carol A. Parsons, *Flexible Production Technology and Industrial Restructuring: Case Studies of the Metalworking, Semiconductor and Apparel Industries*, PhD dissertation (Berkeley, University of California Department of City Planning, 1987).

[144]M. Castells et al., *El Desafio Tecnologico*, (Madrid, Alianza Editorial, 1986).

[145]M. Castells, "High Technology, World Development and Structural Transformation: The Trends and the Debate," *Alternatives*, XI, 3, July 1986, pp. 297–344.

[146]Research in progress by M. Castells and Peter Hall on Silicon Valley's recent spatial restructuring.

[147]Ernst, *Micro-electronics and Global Restructuring*; Ernst, *U.S.–Japanese Competition*; Carnoy and Castells, *Technology and Economy in the U.S.*; Schulze, *Shifts in the World Economy*.

[148]See, for instance, J. Muntendam, "Philips in the World: A View of a Multinational on Resource Allocation," in Van der Knapp and Wever, *New Technology and Regional Development*, pp. 136–44.

[149]See, for instance, the argument put forward in this respect by K. Ohmae, *Triad Power: The Coming Shape of Global Competition* (New York, Free Press, 1985).

[150]Procedure used to rank selected metropolitan areas of the US according to their R&D potential, circa 1977.

(1) The database used is Edward J. Malecki's elaboration of various sources (see notes 75, 76 to Chapter 2).

(2) The first step of the analysis established four rankings for the main sources of information in industrial R&D: universities, government, large corporations, and technological industrial milieux. The indicators used were, respectively: total R&D performed by universities in top 200 (in dollars), with indication of number of universities in top 200 in the metropolitan area; location of federally employed scientists and engineers, top 20 metropolitan areas; number of industrial research laboratories, top 20 metropolitan areas; and 10 top metropolitan areas in terms of both laboratories and employment. On the basis of these indicators, each metropolitan area received a score between 1 and 20 in terms of its position regarding university R&D, government R&D, or corporate research, with 1 representing the highest level of research and 20 the lowest among the top 20 metropolitan areas. Since some areas were among the top 20 in one of the scales but not present in other(s) (for instance, Madison, Wisconsin was seventh in university research but not present in government or corporate research), an arbitrary but systematic criterion was introduced: any area not present in a ranking was given a score of 25.

Another procedural factor must be noted. The indicator for the generation of an industrial milieu is a dichotomic one: it is a closed list of 10 metropolitan areas whose index of concentration in R&D laboratories and R&D employment has a value of one standard deviation above the rankings for 177 metropolitan areas. In this case, I have simply denoted the presence (+) or the absence (−) of such a milieu for any given metropolitan area.

(3) The second step was to rank metropolitan areas according to sources of finance. At this stage of the research there is still no reliable systematic indicator of spatial distribution of venture capital, although work in this direction is in progress. So, metropolitan areas are ranked according to two indicators: total DoD and NASA R&D (in millions of dollars); and total private R&D laboratories. Scores between 1 and 25 were given to each metropolitan area following the same procedure as in the series of indicators in (2) above.

(4) Thirdly, the areas were ranked according to the sources of technical research labor, on the basis of two indicators: for the existence of a self-sustaining technical labor market, we used the absolute number of engineers and scientists employed in R&D or administration of R&D; on the basis of this criterion, each area was given a score between 1 and 25. A second indicator was the presence or absence of a major university complex able to provide highly skilled research personnel. In this case presence (+) or absence (−) was denoted for each area.

(5) Having arrived at eight scores for each area, three synthetic ranking scores were established by combining the four indicators for information, the two indicators for capital, and the two indicators for labor. In the case of capital, it was simple: both scores were added and the total divided by two. In the two other cases (information, labor) it was necessary to combine ordinal scores with nominal scores. Here a systematic criterion was used to project the same influence of the presence of a powerful source of information or of labor in each metropolitan area: in the case of information, the three ordinal scores were added and the total divided by a denominator of four in the case of the presence of an innovative milieu, of three in the case of its absence; for sources of research labor, we divided by two when a major university was present as source of labor, leaving the score unaffected in the case of absence.

(6) Finally, the three synthetic scores were simply added to combine a global score allowing a synthetic overall ranking.

These procedural decisions are admittedly arbitrary, but their systematic use, and their explicit description, provide a basis for evaluating relative rankings of each area within the limits of the *illustrative* purpose of these calculations.

Chapter 3

[1]See Pascal Petit, *Slow Growth and the Service Economy* (London, Pinter, 1986) and the classic work by Victor Fuchs, *The Service Economy* (New York, National Bureau of Economic Research, 1968).
[2]James Brian Quinn, "The Impacts of Technology in the Services Sector," in Bruce

R. Guile and Harvey Brooks (eds), *Technology and Global Industry: Companies and Nations in the World Economy* (Washington DC, National Academy Press, 1987), p. 119.

[3]The notion of a post-industrial society is generally associated in the US with Daniel Bell, *The Coming of Post-industrial Society* (New York, Basic Books, 1973), and in Europe with Alain Touraine, *La Société post-industrielle* (Paris, Denoel, 1969). It is undeniable that both authors have made major contributions to the understanding of fundamental structural change in our societies, regardless of whether and to what extent one agrees with their interpretation of such changes. Here I am not criticizing their theories (to do so would require a longer and more systematic discussion) but rejecting the notion of post-industrialism which, I believe, actually contradicts the analysis put forward by both Bell and Touraine. A knowledge-based society, or a "société programmée," is not simply post-industrial: it opens up a new historic era, a new "mode of development," as I have argued in chapter 1, that is no more post-industrial than the industrial society was post-agrarian. This is why the concept of an informational society, as a result of an informational "mode of development" seems to be more adequate.

[4]For an analysis of the impact of information-based processes on the economic structure, see Tom Stonier, *The Wealth of Information: A Profile of the Post-industrial Economy* (London, Thames Methuen, 1983).

[5]See Thomas J. Stanback, *Understanding the Service Economy* (Baltimore, John Hopkins University Press, 1979).

[6]See the pathbreaking study by Joachim Singelmann, *The Transformation of Industry: From Agriculture to Service Employment* (Beverly Hills, Ca, Sage, 1977).

[7]James P. Smith and Michael P. Ward, *Women's Wages and Work in the 20th Century* (Santa Monica, Ca, Rand Corporation, 1984).

[8]Stephen Cohen and John Zysman, *Manufacturing Matters* (New York, Basic Books, 1987).

[9]Singelmann, *The Transformation of Industry*.

[10]Peter Hall, *Regions in the Transition to the Information Economy*, paper delivered at the Rutgers University Conference on America's New Economic Geography, Washington DC, 29-30 April 1987.

[11]Thomas J. Stanback et al., *Services, The New Economy* (Montclair, NJ, Allanheld, Osman, 1982).

[12]Manuel Castells, "The Service Economy and Postindustrial Society: A Sociological Critique," in *International Journal of Health Services*, 6,4 (1979).

[13]Stanback, *Understanding the Service Economy*, p. 29.

[14]Edward D. Dennison, *Accounting for Slower Economic Growth in the U. S.* (Washington DC, Brookings Institution, 1979).

[15]Stanback, *Understanding the Service Economy*; Petit, *Slow Growth and the Service Economy*.

[16]Jerome A. Mark and William H. Waldorf, "Multifactor Productivity: A New BLS Measure," *Monthly Labor Review*, 106, 12 (December 1983), pp. 3-15.

[17]David Collier, "The Services Sector Revolution: The Automation of Services," in *Long Range Planning*, 16 (December 1983), pp.10-20.

[18]S. Roach, "The Information Economy Comes of Age," in *Information Management Review*, Summer 1985, pp. 9-18.

[19]Marc Porat, *The Information Economy* (Washington DC, Department of Commerce, Office of Telecommunications, 1977).

[20]Rob Kling and Clark Turner, *The Structure of the Information Labor Force: Good Jobs and Bad Jobs* (Irvine, University of California, Department of Information and Computer Science, Public Policy Research Organization, 1987).

[21]For a discussion of the different definitions of the information work force and information industries see Raul L. Katz, "Measurement and Cross-National Comparisons of the Information Work Force," in *The Information Society*, 4, 4 (1986), pp. 231–77. For each specific definition underlying the data presented here I refer to the corresponding source.

[22]See James B. Quinn, "Technology Adoption: The Services Industries," in Ralph Landau and Nathan Rosenberg (eds), *The Positive Sum Strategy: Harnessing Technology for Economic Growth* (Washington DC, National Academy Press, 1986), pp. 357–72.

[23]For the role of information in economic growth, see Nathan Rosenberg and L.E. Birdzell, *How the West Grew Rich: The Economic Transformation of the Industrial World* (New York, Basic Books, 1986).

[24]J. de Bandt (ed.), *Les Services dans les sociétés industrielles avancées*, (Paris, Economica, 1985).

[25]See Micheal L. Dertouzos and Joel Moses, *The Computer Age: A Twenty Year View* (Cambridge, Mass., MIT Press, 1981).

[26]See Quinn, "Impacts of Technology."

[27]Micheal Laub and Charles R. Hoffman, "The Structure of the Financial Services Industry," in *Contemporary Policy Issues*, 2, January 1983; Wallace O. Sellers, "Technology and the Future of the Financial Services Industry,"in *Technology in Society*, 7 (1985), pp. 1–9.

[28]Lionel Nicol, *Information Technology, Information Networks, and On-Line Information Services: Technology, Industrial Structure, Markets, and Potential for Economic Growth*, working paper, Institute of Urban and Regional Development (Berkeley, University of California, 1983).

[29]Theodore J. Gordon, "Computers and Business," in Bruce R. Guile (ed.), *Information Technologies and Social Transformation* (Washington DC, National Academy Press, 1985).

[30]See Alfred D. Chandler, *The Visible Hand: The Managerial Revolution in American Business* (Cambridge, Mass., Harvard University Press, 1977).

[31]See David Birch, *The Job Generation Process* (Cambridge, Mass., MIT Press, 1979).

[32]See Ann Markusen and Michael Teitz, *The World of Small Business: Turbulence and Survival*, working paper no. 408, Institute of Urban and Regional Development (Berkeley, University of California, 1983).

[33]US Congress, Office of Technology Assessment (henceforth OTA), *Automation of America's Offices* OTA-CIT-287 (Washington DC, US Government Printing Office, 1985).

[34]Quinn, "Impacts of Technology," p. 125.

[35]OTA, *Automation*, p. 6.

[36]OTA, *Automation*, p. 7.

[37]Lionel Nicol, "Communications Technology: Economic and Spatial Impacts," in Manuel Castells (ed.), *High Technology, Space, and Society* (Beverly Hills, Ca, Sage, 1985).

[38]See a detailed report of the technological foundations of office automation in OTA, *Automation*, 1985, Appendix A.

[39]Harry Braverman, *Labor and Monopoly Capital* (New York, Monthly Review Press, 1974).

[40]See Larry Hirschhorn, *Beyond Mechanization* (Cambridge, Mass., MIT Press, 1984); International Labour Organization, *The Effects of Technological and Structural Changes on the Employment and Working Conditions of Non-Manual Workers*, 8th Session, Report II (Geneva, ILO, 1981).

[41]Paul A. Strassman, *Information Payoff: The Transformation of Work in the Electronic Age* (New York, Free Press, 1985).

[42]Tora Bikson, Don Manken, and Cathleen Statz, *Individual and Organizational Impacts of Computer Mediated Work: A Case Study*, study prepared for the office of Technology Assessment (Santa Monica, Ca, Rand Corporation, 1985).

[43]Mitchell L. Moss (ed.), *Telecommunications and Productivity* (Reading, Mass., Addison-Wesley, 1981).

[44]On the constitution of information systems, see Nicol, *Information Technology* and "Communications Technology"; also Tom Forester, *High Tech Society* (Oxford, Blackwell, 1987).

[45]See OTA, *Automation*, Appendix.

[46]See Michael Hammer and Michael Zisman, *Design and Implementation of Office Information Systems* (MIT, Laboratory of Computer Science, 1979); Kelly Services Inc., *The Kelly Report on People in the Electronic Office* (Research and Forecasts Inc., 1984); Matthew P. Drennan, *Implications of Computer and Communications Technology for Less Skilled Service Employment Opportunities*, Final Report to the US Department of Labor (New York, Columbia University, 1983).

[47]Barbara Baran, *Technological Innovation and Deregulation: The Transformation of the Labor Process in the Insurance Industry*, PhD dissertation (Berkeley: University of California, 1986).

[48]Barbara Baran, "Office Automation and Women's Work: The Technological Transformation of the Insurance Industry," in Castells, *High Technology, Space, and Society*, pp. 143–71.

[49]Barbara Baran, *The Transformation of the Office Industry*, master's thesis (Berkeley, University of California, 1982); Baran, *Technological Innovation and Deregulation*; Barbara Baran and Suzanne Teegarden, *Women's Labor in the Office of the Future*, Berkeley Roundtable on the International Economy (Berkeley, University of California, 1983).

[50]Baran and Teegarden, *Women's Labor*, p. 13.

[51]Larry Hirschhorn, "Information Technology and the New Services Game," in Castells, *High Technology, Space, and Society*, pp. 172–90.

[52]Paul Adler, *Rethinking the Skill Requirements of New Technologies*, working paper, Graduate School of Business Administration (Cambridge, Mass., Harvard University, 1983).

[53]OTA, *Automation*, p. 104.

[54]*New York Times*, 9 January 1988, p. 1.

[55]Quinn, "Impacts of Technology."

[56]Sellers, "Financial Services Industry."

[57]Thierry Noyelle and Thomas J. Stanback, *The Economic Transformation of American Cities* (Totowa, NJ, Rowman and Allanheld, 1984); Thomas J. Stanback and

Thierry Noyelle, *Cities in Transition* (Totowa, NJ, Allanheld, Osman and Gee, 1982).

[58]Matthew P. Drennan, *Information Intensive Industries: A Metropolitan Perspective* (New York, New York University Graduate School of Public Administration, 1986).

[59]Kling and Turner, *Structure of the Information Labor Force*, 1987.

[60]Robert Cohen, *The Corporation and the City*, Conservation of Human Resources Project (New York, Columbia University, 1979); Noyelle and Stanback, *Economic Transformation of American Cities*.

[61]Mitchell L. Moss., "Telecommunications and the Future of Cities," in *Land Development Studies*, 3 (1986), pp. 33–44; *Telecommunications Policy and World Urban Development*, paper delivered at the Annual Meeting of the International Institute of Communications, Edinburgh, September 1986; *Telecommunications, World Cities, and Urban Policy*, Graduate School of Public Administration (New York, New York University, 1987); "A New Agenda for Telecommunications Policy," in *New York Affairs*, Spring 1986.

[62]Mitchell Moss, *Telecommunications: Shaping the Future*, paper presented at the Rutgers University Conference on America's New Economic Geography, Washington DC, 29–30 April 1987.

[63]Mitchell Moss, *Information Cities: The Example of New York City*, paper presented at the Critical Issues on National Computerization Policy Conference, Honolulu, 31 July 1983; and "New York isn't just New York any more" in *Intermedia*, 12, 4/5 (July–September 1984).

[64]Corporate Design, "OlympiaNet's Gamble on Telecommunications," *Corporate Design*, May/June 1984; Ronald Derven, "Smart Buildings Features Save a Tenant Cash Despite Expensive Buyout of Bell Phone Contract," *Facilities Design and Management*, February/March 1984.

[65]C. Jonscher, *The Impact of Information Technology on the Economy*, paper prepared for the Conference on the Impact of Information Technology on the Service Sector, Philadelphia, University of Pennsylvania, February 1985.

[66]Moss, *Telecommunications: Shaping the Future*.

[67]See Moss, "Telecommunications and the Future of Cities," p. 38.

[68]See Matthew P. Drennan, *Economy of New York State and New York City*, Graduate School of Public Administration (New York, New York University, 1986).

[69]See David Vogel, *The Future of New York City as a Financial Center: An International Perspective*, paper prepared for the Workshops on Metropolitan Dominance, Committee on New York City (New York, Social Science Research Council, 1986).

[70]Peter W. Daniels (ed.), *Spatial Patterns of Office Growth and Location* (New York, Wiley, 1979).

[71]Moss, *Information Cities*.

[72]Raymond Vernon, *New York: Anatomy of a Metropolis* (Cambridge, Mass., Harvard University Press, 1959).

[73]See John D. Kasarda, "Urban Change and Minority Opportunities," in Paul Peterson (ed.), *The New Urban Reality* (Washington DC, Brookings Institution, 1985), pp. 33–67.

[74]Hall, *Regions in the Transition to the Information Economy*.

[75]Noyelle and Stanback, *Economic Transformation of American Cities*.

[76]Edwin S. Mills, *Service Sector Suburbanization*, paper delivered at the Rutgers

University Conference on America's New Economic Geography, Washington DC, 29–30 April 1987.

[77]Christopher B. Leinberger and Charles Lockwood, "How Business Is Reshaping America," in *The Atlantic*, October 1986, pp. 43–63.

[78]Ibid.

[79]David Dowall and Marcia Salkin, *Office Automation and the Implications for Office Development*, IURD Working Paper No. 447 (Berkeley, University of California, 1986).

[80]Peter Daniels, *Service Industries: Growth and Location* (Cambridge, Cambridge University Press, 1982).

[81]Leinberger and Lockwood, "How Business Is Reshaping America."

[82]W. Randy Smith and David Selwood, "Office Location and the Density–Distance Relationship," *Urban Geography*, 4, 4 (1983), pp. 302–16.

[83]Stanback, *Understanding the Service Economy*.

[84]Kristin Nelson, *Back Office and Female Labor Markets: Office Suburbanization in the San Francisco Bay Area*, unpublished PhD dissertation (Berkeley, University of California, 1984).

[85]Cited by Dowall and Salkin, *Office Automation*, p. 113.

[86]Alain Touraine, *Sociologie de l'Action* (Paris, Seuil, 1965).

[87]See Nelson, *Back Office and Female Labor Markets*.

[88]See Daniels, *Service Industries*.

[89]Wolfgang Quante, *The Exodus of Corporate Headquarters from New York City* (New York, Praeger, 1976).

[90]Regina Armstrong, "National Trends in Office Construction, Employment and Headquarters Location in U.S. Metropolitan Areas," in Daniels, *Spatial Patterns*, pp. 61–93.

[91]Cynthia Kroll, *Employment Growth and Office Space Along the 680 Corridor: Booming Supply and Potential Demand in a Suburban Area*, Center for Real Estate and Urban Economics, Working Paper 84–75 (Berkeley, University of California, 1984).

[92]Dowall and Salkin, *Office Automation*.

[93]Baran, *Technological Innovation and Deregulation*.

[94]Jean Marion Ross, *Technology and the Relocation of Employment in the Insurance Industry*, Berkeley Roundtable on the International Economy (Berkeley, University of California, 1985).

[95]Nelson, *Back Office and Female Labor Markets*.

[96]Dowall and Salkin, *Office Automation*.

[97]OTA, *Automation*, pp. 211–30.

[98]OTA, *Automation*, pp. 189–208.

[99]Alvin Toffler, *The Third Wave* (New York, William Morrow, 1980).

[100]OTA, *Automation*, pp. 189–208.

[101]Margrethe H. Olson, *Overview of Work-at-Home Trends in the United States* (New York, New York University Graduate School of Business Administration, Center for Research on Information Systems, 1983).

[102]Paul G. Gretsos, *A Critical Analysis of Telecommuting: The Political Economy of Work at Home*, Graduate Seminar Paper for CP 284, Department of City and Regional Planning (Berkeley, University of California, 1987).

[103]Penny Gurstein, *A Research Proposal on the Implications of the Electronic Home on*

Socio-Spatial Patterns, Graduate Seminar Paper for CP 284, Department of City and Regional Planning (Berkeley, University of California, 1987).

[104]OTA, *Automation*, pp. 283–93.

[105]Allan Pred, "On the Spatial Structure of Organizations and the Complexity of Metropolitan Interdependence," in *Papers of the Regional Science Association*, 35 (1974), pp. 115–43.

Chapter 4

[1]See Nathan Rosenberg, *Perspectives on Technology* (New York, Cambridge University Press, 1976).

[2]See US Congress, Office of Technology Assessment, *Computerized Manufacturing Automation: Employment, Education, and the Workplace* (Washington DC, Government Printing Office, 1984).

[3]See Eli Ginzberg, Thierry J. Noyelle, and Thomas M. Stanback Jr, *Technology and Employment: Concepts and Clarifications* (Boulder, Col., Westview, 1986).

[4]Harry Braverman, *Labor and Monopoly Capital: The Degradation of Work in the Twentieth Century* (New York, Monthly Review Press, 1974).

[5]Larry Hirschhorn, *Beyond Mechanization* (Cambridge, Mass., MIT Press, 1985).

[6]Richard M. Cyert and David C. Mowery (eds), *Technology and Employment: Innovation and Growth in the U.S. Economy*, Report of the Panel on Technology and Employment, National Academy of Sciences, National Academy of Engineering, Institute of Medicine (Washington DC, National Academy Press, 1987).

[7]H. A. Hunt and T. L. Hunt, *Human Resource Implications of Robotics* (Kalamazoo, Mi., W. E. Upjohn Institute for Employment Research, 1983); N. Maeda, "A Fact-finding Study on the Impacts of Microelectronics on Employment," in *Microelectronics, Productivity and Employment* (Paris, OECD, 1980) pp. 155–80; D. Cockroft, "New Office Technology and Employment," *International Law Review*, 119, 6, November–December 1980; M. P. Drennan, *Implications of Computer and Telecommunications Technology for Less Skilled Service Employment Opportunities*, New York, Columbia University, Research Report to the US Department of Labor (New York, Columbia University, 1983); J. D. Roessner et al., *The Impact of Office Automation on Clerical Employment, 1985–2000* (Westport, Conn., Quorum, 1985).

[8]Nathan Rosenberg and L. E. Birdzell, *How the West Grew Rich: The Economic Transformation of the Industrial World* (New York, Basic Books, 1986).

[9]Raphael Kaplinsky, *Microelectronics and Employment Revisited: A Review*, a report prepared for the International Labour Office, World Employment Program (Brighton, University of Sussex, Institute of Development Studies, 1986).

[10]Ibid., p. 153.

[11]P. M. Flynn, *The Impact of Technological Change on Jobs and Workers*, paper prepared for the US Department of Labor, Employment Training Administration, 1985.

[12]R. A. Levy, M. Bowes, and J. M. Jondrow, "Technical Advance and Other Sources of Employment Change in Basic Industry," in E. L. Collins and L. D. Tanner (eds), *American Jobs and the Changing Industrial Base* (Cambridge, Mass., Ballinger, 1984), pp. 77–95.

[13]D. R. Howell, "The Future Employment Impacts of Industrial Robots: An Input–Output Approach," in *Technological Forecasting and Social Change*, 28 (1985), 297–310.

[14]W. Leontieff and F. Duchin, *The Future Impact of Automation on Workers* (New York, Oxford University Press, 1985).

[15]See Cyert and Mowery, *Technology and Employment*, p. 95.

[16]R. Gordon and L. M. Kimball, *High Technology, Employment, and the Challenges to Education*, Silicon Valley Research Group Monograph (Santa Cruz, University of California, 1985).

[17]Ibid., p. 23.

[18]Robert Z. Lawrence, *The Employment Effects of Information Technologies: An Optimistic View*, paper delivered at the OECD Conference on the Social Challenge of Information Technologies, Berlin, 28–30 November 1984.

[19]Ibid., p. 31.

[20]See Ralph Landau and Nathan Rosenberg (eds), *The Positive Sum Strategy: Harnessing Technology for Economic Growth* (Washington DC, National Academy Press, 1986).

[21]K. Young and C. Lawson, *What Fuels U.S. Job Growth? Changes in Technology and Demand on Employment Growth Across Industries, 1972–84*, paper prepared for the Panel on Technology and Employment of the National Academy of Sciences, 1984, as cited by Cyert and Mowery, *Technology and Employment*.

[22]US Bureau of Labor Statistics, *Employment Projections for 1995: Data and Methods* (Washington DC, Government Printing Office, 1986).

[23]See Martin Carnoy, *The Labor Market in Silicon Valley and its Implications for Education*, research report (Stanford, Stanford University, School of Education, 1985).

[24]G. T. Sylvestri, J. M. Lukasiewicz, and M. A. Einstein, "Occupational Employment Projections Through 1995," in *Monthly Labor Review*, November 1983, pp. 37–49.

[25]R. W. Rumberger and H. M. Levin, *Forecasting the Impact of New Technologies on the Future Job Market*, research report (Stanford, Stanford University School of Education, 1984).

[26]Bluestone and Harrison, 1982.

[27]Gordon and Kimball, *Challenges to Education*.

[28]Carnoy, *Labor Market in Silicon Valley*; Allen Scott, *New Industrial Spaces* (London, Pion, 1988); Gordon and Kimball, "Industrial Structure."

[29]Michael Teitz, "The California Economy: Changing Structure and Policy Responses," in John J. Kirlin and Donald R. Winkler (eds), *California Policy Choices* (Los Angeles, University of Southern California, School of Public Administration, 1984), p. 53.

[30]R. W. Riche, D. H. Hecker, and J. D. Burgan, "High Technology Today and Tomorrow: A Small Slice of the Employment Pie," in *Monthly Labor Review*, November 1983, pp. 50–8.

[31]See Myra H. Strober and Carolyn L. Arnold, "Integrated Circuits/Segregated Labor: Women in Computer-Related Occupations and High-Tech Industries," in Heidi I. Hartmann (ed.), *Computer Chips and Paper Clips* (Washington DC, National Academy Press, 1987), 2, pp. 136–84.

[32]Russell W. Rumberger, "High Technology and Job Loss," in *Technology in Society*, 6 (1984), pp. 263–84.

[33]Silvestri, Lukasiewiez, and Einstein, "Occupational Employment Projections."

[34]R. E. Kutscher, *Factors Influencing the Changing Employment Structure of the U.S.*, paper delivered at the Second International Conference of Progetto Milano, Milan, 25 January 1985.

[35]Michael Piore and Charles Sabel, *The Second Industrial Divide* (New York, Basic Books, 1984).

[36]N. Belussi, *Innovation in Production: The Benetton Case*, BRIE Working Paper (Berkeley, University of California, 1986).

[37]Susumu Watanabe, "Labour-saving versus Work-amplifying Effects of Micro-electronics," in *International Labour Review*, 125, 3, May–June 1986, pp. 243–59.

[38]David F. Noble, *Forces of Production: A Social History of Industrial Automation* (New York, Knopf, 1984).

[39]Harley Shaiken, *Work Transformed: Automation and Labor in the Computer Age* (New York, Holt, Rinehart and Winston, 1985).

[40]Carol A. Parsons, *Flexible Production Technology and Industrial Restructuring: Case Studies of the Metalworking, Semiconductor and Apparel Industries*, PhD dissertation (Berkeley, University of California, 1987).

[41]Donald A. Hicks, *Automation Technology and Industrial Renewal: Adjustment Dynamics in the U.S. Metalworking Sector* (Washington DC, AEI, 1986), as cited by Parsons, *Flexible Production Technology*, p. 159.

[42]Parsons, *Flexible Production Technology*, p. 163.

[43]Ibid., p. 324.

[44]Eileen Appelbaum, *Technology and the Redesign of Work in the Insurance Industry*, project report (Stanford, Stanford University, Institute of Research on Educational Finance and Governance, 1984).

[45]Roessner et al., *Impact of Office Automation*.

[46]Appelbaum, *Insurance Industry*, pp. 12–14.

[47]Barry Bluestone and Bennett Harrison, *The Great American Job Machine: The Proliferation of Low Wage Employment in the U.S. Economy*, study prepared for the Joint Economic Committee of the US Congress, December 1986.

[48]Bob Kuttner, "The Declining Middle," in *The Atlantic Monthly*, July 1983, pp. 60–72.

[49]Lester C. Thurow, "The Disappearance of the Middle Class," *New York Times*, 5 February 1984.

[50]Steven Rose, *Social Stratification in the United States* (Baltimore, Social Graphics, 1983).

[51]See, for instance, Fabian Linden, "Myth of the Disappearing Middle Class," *Wall Street Journal*, 23 January 1984.

[52]For a discussion of the relevant research on the "declining middle," and an assessment of the continuing debate, see Nancy Leigh-Preston, National and Regional Change in the Middle of the Earnings and Households Income Distributions, PhD dissertation (in progress) (Berkeley, University of California).

[53]Bennett Harrison, Chris Tilly, and Barry Bluestone, *The Great U-Turn: Increasing Inequality in Wage and Salary Income in the U.S.*, paper presented at the Symposium of the US Congress Joint Economic Committee on "The American Economy in Transition," Washington DC, 16–17 January 1986.

[54]Barry Bluestone, Bennett Harrison, and Alan Matthews, "Structure Vs. Cycle in the Development of American Manufacturing Employment Since the Late 1960s," *Industrial Relations*, 25, 2, Spring 1986.

[55]Thurow, "Disappearance of the Middle Class."

[56]Larry Sawers and William K. Tabb (eds), *Sunbelt/Snowbelt: Urban Development and Regional Restructuring* (New York, Oxford University Press, 1984).

[57]Joe Feagin and Michael Smith (eds), *The Capitalist City* (Oxford, Blackwell, 1986).

[58]Diana Dillaway, *The Politics of Restructuring in a Declining City: Buffalo, NY*, master's thesis (Berkeley, University of California, 1987).

[59]William Wilson, "The Urban Underclass in Advanced Industrial Society," in Paul E. Peterson (ed.), *The New Urban Reality* (Washington DC, Brookings Institution, 1985).

[60]Thierry Noyelle and Thomas J. Stanback, *The Economic Transformation of American Cities* (Totowa, NJ, Rowman and Allanheld, 1984).

[61]B. Bluestone and B. Harrison, *The Deindustrialization of America* (New York, Basic Books, 1982).

[62]John D. Kasarda, "Urban Change and Minority Opportunities," in Paul Peterson (ed.), *The New Urban Reality* (Washington DC, Brookings Institution, 1985).

[63]Ibid., p. 57.

[64]Norman Fainstein, "The Underclass/Mismatch Hypothesis as an Explanation for Black Economic Deprivation," in *Politics and Society*, 15, 4 (1986-7), pp. 403-51.

[65]Saskia Sassen, "Issues of Core and Periphery: Labour Migration and Global Restructuring," in Jeff Henderson and Manuel Castells (eds), *Global Restructuring and Territorial Development* (London, Sage, 1987); and Sassen, The Mobility of Labor and Capital (New York, Cambridge University Press, 1988).

[66]John Mollenkopf, "Economic Development," in C. Brecher and R. Horton (eds), *Setting Municipal Priorities: American Cities and the New York Experience* (New York, New York University Press, 1984).

[67]I have benefited greatly from the perceptive, well documented analysis by Samuel M. Ehrenhalt, *New York City in the New Economic Environment: New Risks and a Changing Outlook* (New York, Regional Commissioner, US Bureau of Labor Statistics, 1988) (paper communicated by the author).

[68]Ehrenhalt, *New York City*, p. 12.

[69]Thomas Bailey and Roger Waldinger, *Economic Change and the Ethnic Division of Labor in New York City*, paper prepared for the Social Science Research Council Committee on New York City, February 1988.

[70]See the studies presented in John H. Mollenkopf and Manuel Castells (eds), *Restructuring New York. Dual City* (forthcoming); see also Gus Tyler, "A Tale of Three Cities – Upper Economy, Lower – and Under," in *Dissent*, special issue: "In Search of New York," Fall 1987, pp. 463-71; Emanuel Tobier, "Population" in Brecher and Horton, *Setting Municipal Priorities*; Roger Waldinger, *Changing Ladders and Musical Chairs: Ethnicity and Opportunity in Post-industrial New York*, paper delivered at the International Conference on Ethnic Minorities, University of Warwick, UK, September 1985.

[71]Saskia Sassen, "The Informal Economy in New York City," in Alejandro Portes, Manuel Castells, and Lauren Benton (eds), *The Informal Economy* (Baltimore: Johns Hopkins University Press, 1989).

[72]Saskia Sassen, "New York City's Informal Economy," paper prepared for the Social Science Research Council Committee on New York City, February 1988.

[73]Saskia Sassen and C. Benamou, *Hispanic Women in the Garment and Electronics Industries in New York Metropolitan Area*, research report to the Revson Foundation, New York, 1985.

[74]For the whole of the US, estimates of cash flow generated by drug traffic oscillate between $60 billion and $120 billion. This capital has to be recycled in the formal economy through laundering. See Jeff Gerth, "Vast Flow of Cash Threatens Currency, Banks and Economies," *New York Times*, 11 April 1988, p. A8.

[75]See Nancy Foner (ed.) *New Immigrants in New York* (New York, Columbia University Press, 1987); Philip Kasinitz "The City's New Immigrants," in *Dissent*, Fall 1987, pp. 497–506.

[76]Roger Waldinger, *Through the Eye of the Needle: Immigrants and Enterprise in New York's Garment Trades* (New York, New York University Press, 1986).

[77]Bailey and Waldinger, *Economic Change and the Ethnic Division of Labor*.

[78]Portes and Bach, *Latin Journey*; Foner, *New Immigrants in New York*; Sassen, "Issues of Core and Periphery."

[79]Sassen *New York City's Informal Economy*, p. 1.

[80]Richard Harris, *Home and Work in New York Since 1950*, paper prepared for the Social Science Research Council Committee on New York City, February 1988.

[81]William Kornblum, *The White Ethnic Neighborhoods in New York City*, paper prepared for the Social Science Research Council on New York City, 1988.

[82]Harris, *Home and Work in New York*, p. 34.

[83]Edward W. Soja, "Taking Los Angeles Apart: Some Fragments of a Critical Human Geography," in *Environment and Planning: D. Space and Society*, special issue on Los Angeles, 4, 3 (September 1986) pp. 255–73.

[84]Edward W. Soja, "Economic Restructuring and the Internationalization of the Los Angeles Region," in Feagin and Smith, *The Capitalist City*.

[85]Edward Soja, Rebecca Morales, and Goetz Wolff, "Urban Restructuring: An Analysis of Social and Spatial Change in Los Angeles," in *Economic Geography*, 59, 2 (April 1983), pp. 195–230.

[86]On suburban office development in Los Angeles, as linked to the process of spatial restructuring, see Tamara Phibbs, *Linkages, Labor, and Localities in the Location of Suburban Office Centers: A Case Study of Office Establishments in Orange County, California*, Master's thesis in Urban Planning (Los Angeles, University of California, 1989).

[87]*Los Angeles Times*, 9 April 1988.

[88]It is, of course a classic theme of the Chicago School of urban sociology. See, for instance Harvey Zorbaugh, *The Gold Coast and the Slum* (Chicago, University of Chicago Press, 1927).

[89]A theme that I have developed in *The City and the Grassroots* (Berkeley, University of California Press, 1983).

Chapter 5

[1]Ian Gough, *The Political Economy of the Welfare State* (London, Macmillan, 1979); Harold L. Wilensky, *The Welfare State and Equality* (Berkeley, University of California Press, 1975); OECD, *The Welfare State in Crisis* (Paris, OECD, 1981); Charles W. Taylor (ed.), *Why Governments Grow* (Beverly Hills, Sage, 1983).

[2]Morris Janowitz, *Social Control of the Welfare State* (Chicago, University of Chicago Press, 1976), p. 3.

[3]Although it has been attempted by some authors; see Gough, *Political Economy of the Welfare State*; Jim O'Connor, *The Fiscal Crisis of the State* (New York, St Martin's, 1973); Vicente Navarro, *The Welfare State and its Distributive Effects: Part of the Problem or Part of the Solution?*, paper delivered at the International Conference on the Economic Crisis and the Welfare State, International University Menendez y Pelayo, Barcelona, Spain, 8–11 April 1987.

[4]For a thorough analysis of the political process surrounding the growth and decline of the welfare state in the US, see Vicente Navarro, "The 1980 and 1984 US Elections and the New Deal: An Alternative Interpretation," in R. Miliband, J. Saville, and M. Liebman (eds), *The Socialist Register 1985* (London, 1985).

[5]Samuel Bowles and Herbert Gintis, "The Crisis of Liberal Democratic Capitalism: The Case of the United States," *Politics and Society*, II, 1 (1982).

[6]For a theoretical analysis of current trends of transformation of the state in advanced capitalism, see Gordon L. Clark and Michael Dear, *State Apparatus* (Boston, Allen & Unwin, 1984); Colin Crouch (ed.), *State and Economy in Contemporary Capitalism* (London, Croom Helm, 1979); Martin Carnoy, *State and Political Theory* (Princeton, NJ: Princeton University Press, 1984).

[7]Martin Carnoy, Derek Shearer, and Russell Rumberger, *A New Social Contract* (New York, Harper and Row, 1983), p. 120.

[8]Allan Wolfe, *Limits of Legitimacy* (New York, Basic Books, 1976); Carnoy, *State and Political Theory*.

[9]Jim O'Connor, *Accumulation Crisis* (Oxford, Blackwell, 1984).

[10]Navarro, "The 1980 and 1984 US Elections."

[11]Peter Marris and Martin Rein, *Dilemmas of Social Reform* (London, Routledge & Kegan Paul, 1972); Frances Piven and Richard Cloward, *Regulating the Poor* (New York, Random House, 1971); Frank Gould, "The Growth of Public Expenditures," in Taylor, *Why Governments Grow*, note 1.

[12]J. David Greenstone, *Labor in American Politics* (Chicago: University of Chicago Press, 1977); Irving Bernstein, *The Lean Years* (Boston, Houghton Mifflin, 1972).

[13]Carnoy, Shearer, and Rumberger, *A New Social Contract*.

[14]See Roderick Aya and Norman Miller (eds), *The New American Revolution* (New York, Free Press, 1971).

[15]John Mollenkopf, *The Contested City* (Princeton, NJ, Princeton University Press, 1983).

[16]Terry N. Clark and Lorna C. Ferguson, *City Money: Political Processes, Fiscal Strain and Retrenchment* (New York; Columbia University Press, 1983).

[17]Douglas Yates, *The Ungovernable City* (New Haven, Yale University Press, 1977).

[18]Manuel Castells, *The City and the Grassroots* (Berkeley, University of California Press, 1983), pp. 49–66.

[19]Mollenkopf, *Contested City*.

[20]Mollenkopf, *Contested City*, p. 20.

[21]Herbert Marcuse, *The One-Dimensional Man* "After the Crisis?".

[22]Martin Carnoy and Manuel Castells, "After the Crisis?," *World Policy Journal*, Spring 1984.

[23]Hugh C. Mosley, *The Arms Race: Economic and Social Consequences* (Lexington, Mass., Lexington, 1985).

[24]Carnoy, Shearer, and Rumberger, *A New Social Contract*, p. 150.

[25]Joel Krieger, *Reagan, Thatcher, and the Politics of Decline* (New York, Oxford University Press, 1986).

[26]J. Coates and M. Killian, *Heavy Losses: The Dangerous Decline of American Defense* (New York, Viking, 1985).

[27]John Tirman (ed.), *The Militarization of High Technology* (Cambridge, Mass., Ballinger, 1984).

[28]David Stockman, *The Triumph of Politics* (New York, Harper and Row, 1986).

[29]I am relying here on current research on "Yuppies as a Social Phenomenon" conducted by Arlene Stein, a sociology graduate at the University of California at Berkeley.

[30]See Joe Feagin, *Houston Boomtown* (New Brunswick, NJ, Rutgers University Press, 1988).

[31]See US Congress, Office of Technology Assessment, *Automation of America's Offices* (Washington DC, Government Printing Office, 1985).

[32]Douglas E. Ashford (ed.), *Financing Urban Government in the Welfare State* (London, Croom Helm, 1980).

[33]Piven and Cloward, *Regulating the Poor*.

[34]Mollenkopf, *Contested City*.

[35]Castells, *City and Grassroots*.

[36]Larry Hirschhorn et al., *Cutting Back: Retrenchment and Redevelopment in Human and Community Services* (San Francisco, Jossey-Bass, 1983).

[37]Mark I. Gelfand, "How Cities Arrived in the National Agenda in the US," in Ashford, *Financing Urban Government*, pp. 28–49.

[38]David H. McKay, "The Rise of the Topocratic State: US Intergovernmental Relations in the 1970s," in Ashford, *Financing Urban Government*, pp. 50–70.

[39]McKay, "The Rise of the Topocratic State."

[40]Gelfand, "How Cities Arrived in the National Agenda."

[41]Douglas E. Ashford, "Political Choice and Local Finance," in Ashford, *Financing Urban Government*, pp. 9–27.

[42]Gelfand, "How Cities Arrived in the National Agenda."

[43]Daniel P. Moynihan, *Maximum Feasible Misunderstanding* (Glencoe, Ill., Free Press, 1969).

[44]Harry C. Boyte, *The Backyard Revolution* (Philadelphia, Temple University Press, 1980).

[45]Robert Leckachmann, *Greed is not Enough: Reaganomics* (New York, Pantheon, 1981).

[46]Marris and Rein, *Dilemmas of Social Reform*; Ralph M. Kramer, *Voluntary Agencies in the Welfare State* (Berkeley, University of California Press, 1981).

[47]Matthew A. Crenson, *Neighbourhood Politics* (Cambridge, Mass., Harvard University Press, 1983).

[48]George Vernez, "Overview of the Spatial Dimensions of the Federal Budget," in Norman Glickman (ed.), *The Urban Impacts of Federal Policies* (Baltimore, Johns Hopkins University Press, 1980), pp. 67–102.

[49]Robert W. Burchell and David Listokin (eds), *Cities Under Stress: The Fiscal Crisis of Urban America* (Piscataway, NJ, Center for Urban Policy Research, 1981); Clark and Ferguson, *City Money*; Hirschhorn et al., *Cutting Back*.

[50]Burchell and Listokin, *Cities Under Stress*.

[51]Peter Marcuse, "The Targeted Crisis: On the Ideology of the Urban Fiscal Crisis and its Uses," *International Journal of Urban and Regional Research*, 5, 3, 330–55.

[52]Roy Bahl (ed.), *Urban Government Finances in the 1980s* (Beverly Hills, Sage, 1981).

[53]Burchell and Listokin, *Cities Under Stress*.

[54]John L. Mikesell, "The Season of Tax Revolt," in John P. Blair and David Nacmias (eds), *Fiscal Retrenchment and Urban Policy* (Beverly Hills, Sage, 1979).

[55]Lawrence Susskind (director), *Proposition 2 1/2: Its Impact on Massachusetts* (Cambridge, Mass., OGH, 1983).

[56]Donald Tomaskovic-Devey and S. M. Miller, "Recapitalization: The Basic US Urban Policy of the 1980s," in Norman I. Fainstein and Susan Fainstein (eds), *Urban Policy Under Capitalism* (Beverly Hills, Sage, 1982), p. 25.

[57]Ibid.

[58]William K. Tabb, *The Long Default: New York City and the Urban Fiscal Crisis* (New York: Monthly Review Press, 1982). For dissenting views of the process, see Daniel P. Moynihan, "On the Origins of New York's Crisis," *The Public Interest*, Spring 1978, and Charles R. Morris, *The Cost of Good Intentions: New York City and the Liberal Experiment* (New York, Norton, 1980).

[59]Of course, Tabb does not consider that the situation in New York was so bright, except for a minority of its residents.

[60]Roger Starr, "Stagnant Metropolis," *Society*, May/June 1976.

[61]For comprehensive analysis of the transformation of New York City, see John Mollenkopf (ed.), *Power, Culture, and Place: Essays on New York City* (New York, Russell Sage Foundation, 1988).

[62]See Charles Brecher and Raymond D. Horton, *Politics in the Postindustrial City*, paper prepared for the Social Science Research Council Committee on New York City, February 1988; and Charles Brecher and Raymond D. Horton (eds), *Setting Municipal Priorities 1988* (New York, New York University Press, 1988).

[63]See John Mollenkopf, *Political Inequality in New York City*, paper prepared for the Social Science Research Council Committee on New York City, February 1988.

[64]See special issue of *Dissent*, "In Search of New York," Fall 1987.

[65]For a socio-political analysis of the evolution of the local state in New York, see Norman I. Fainstein and Susan S. Fainstein, "Stages in the Politics of Urban Development: New York since 1945," in Mollenkopf, *Power, Culture, Place*.

[66]For a political analysis of the fiscal crisis in Cleveland, see Todd Swanstrom, *The Crisis of Growth Politics: Cleveland, Kucinick and the Limits of Local Democracy*, PhD dissertation, Princeton University, 1981); for a comprehensive analysis of urban decline and urban revival see Louise Jezierski, *Urban Politics and Urban Crises: A Comparative Analysis of Pittsburgh and Cleveland*, PhD dissertation (Berkeley, University of California, 1987); for a broader perspective see Paul Kantor, *The Dependent City: The Changing Political Economy and Urban Economic Development in the US*, paper presented at the 1985 annual meeting of the American Political Science Association, 29 August 1985, New Orleans.

[67]Norman J. Glickman, *Economic Policy and the Cities: In Search of Reagan's Real Urban Policy*, paper presented at the North American meetings of the Regional Science Association, Chicago, 11–13 November 1983; published in summarized form in *Journal of American Planning Association*, Autumn 1984, pp. 471–84.

[68]*New York Times*, 16 February 1988.

[69]Glickman, *Economic Policy and the Cities*.

[70]See John L. Palmer and Isabel Sawhill (eds), *The Reagan Experiment* (Washington DC, Urban Institute Press, 1982).

[71]See special issue of *Business Week*, "After Reagan," 1 February 1988.

[72]Frank Barnaby, "Microelectronics and War," in Tirman, *Militarization of High Technology*, pp. 45–62.

[73]Richard R. Nelson, *High Technology Policies: A Five-Nation Comparison* (Washington DC, American Enterprise Institute, 1984).

[74]Seymour Melman (ed.), *The War Economy of the United States* (New York, St Martin's, 1971).

[75]Daniel Bell, *The Coming of Post-industrial Society* (New York, Basic Books, 1973), p. 355.

[76]Bell, *Post-industrial Society*, p. 356.

[77]Fred Hiatt and Rick Atkinson, "Arms and America's Fortunes," *Washington Post*, 12 January 1985, p. A–1.

[78]See the major documented work on the matter: Hugh C. Mosely, *The Arms Race: Economic and Social Consequences* (Lexington, Mass., Lexington, 1985).

[79]Karen Pennar, "Pentagon Spending is the Economy's Biggest Gun," *Business Week*, 21 October 1985, pp. 60–4.

[80]Pennar, "Pentagon Spending."

[81]Ann Markusen, *Defense Spending: A Successful Industrial Policy?* IURD Working Paper 424 (Berkeley, June 1984).

[82]US Congress, Office of Technology Assessment, *Information Technology R&D: Critical Trends and Issues* (Washington DC, Government Printing Office, 1985), pp. 45–6.

[83]Manuel Castells and Rebecca Skinner, *The State and Technological Policy in the U.S.: the Strategic Defense Initiative* (Berkeley, University of California, Institute of International Studies, 1988).

[84]This is particularly the argument forcefully put forward by Seymour Melman in *The Permanent War Economy: American Capitalism in Decline* (New York, Simon and Schuster, 1974).

[85]Wassily Leontieff and Faye Duchin, *Military Spending: Facts and Figures, Worldwide Implications, and Future Outlook* (New York, Oxford University Press, 1983).

[86]David Gold, Christopher Paine, and Gail Shields, *Misguided Expenditure: An Analysis of the Proposed MX Missile System* (New York, Council on Economic Priorities, 1981).

[87]Robert B. Reich, "High Technology, Defense, and International Trade" in Tirman, *Militarization of High Technology*, pp. 33–43.

[88]Markusen, *Defense Spending*; and Ann R. Markusen, *The Economic and Regional Consequences of Military Innovation*, IURD, Working Paper 442 (Berkeley, May 1985).

[89]Lloyd J. Dumas, "University Research, Industrial Innovation, and the Pentagon" in Tirman, *Militarization of High Technology*, pp. 123–57.

[90]David F. Noble, *Forces of Production: A Social History of Industrial Automation* (New York, Knopf, 1984).

[91]Mary Kaldor, *The Baroque Arsenal* (New York, Hill and Wang, 1981).

[92]Jay Stowsky, *Beating Our Plowshares into Double-Edged Swords: The Impact of Pentagon Policies on the Commercialization of Advanced Technologies*, BRIE Working Paper (Berkeley, April 1986), pp. 61–2.

[93]Jacques S. Gansler, *The Defense Economy* (Cambridge, Mass., MIT, 1984); Richard R. Nelson, *High Technology Policies: A Five-Nation Comparison* (Washington DC, American Enterprise Institute, 1984).

[94]Such is the main theme of the major recent book on the subject: Tirman, *Militarization of High Technology*. See particularly the excellent analysis by John Tirman, "The Defense-Economy Debate," pp. 1–32.

[95]Eisenhower, speaking in 1961, as quoted by Dumas, "University Research," p. 149.

[96]Gordon Adams, *The Iron Triangle: The Politics of Defense Contracting* (New Brunswick, NJ, Transaction Books, 1982).

[97]Caspar Weinberger, speech before the Miami Chamber of Commerce, 15 September 1982. Quoted by Tirman, *Militarization of High Technology*, p. 4.

[98]Markusen, *Defense Spending*; Tirman, *Militarization of High Technology*.

[99]Robert DeGrasse, "The Military and Semiconductors," in Tirman, *Militarization of High Technology*, pp. 77–104.

[100]R. Carlson and T. Lyman, *U.S. Government Programs and their Influence on Silicon Valley*, research report (Menlo Park, SRI International, 1984).

[101]Markusen, *Defense Spending*, p. 12.

[102]See a non-partisan description of the structure and activity of DARPA in J. Botkin, D. Dimancescu, and R. Stata, *The Innovators* (New York, Harper and Row, 1984).

[103]Ken Julian, "Defense Program Pushes Microchip Frontiers," *High Technology*, May 1985, pp. 49–57.

[104]Leslie Brueckner and Michael Borrus, *Assessing the Commercial Impact of the VHSIC Program*, BRIE Working Paper, (Berkeley, University of California, November 1984).

[105]Dwight B. Davis, "Assessing the Strategic Computing Initiative," *High Technology*, April 1985, pp. 41–9.

[106]Stowsky, *Beating our Plowshares*.

[107]On the strategic importance of semiconductors production equipment, see Jay Stowsky, *The Weakest Link: Semiconductor Production Equipment, Linkages, and the Limits to International Trade*, BRIE Working Paper (Berkeley, August 1987).

[108]This section summarizes analysis and information presented in our research monograph: Manuel Castells and Rebecca Skinner, *The State and Technological Policy in the U.S.: the SDI Program*, research report (Berkeley, University of California, Berkeley Roundtable on the International Economy, 1989). I refer the reader to this monograph for detailed information and references about SDI as technological policy and as industrial policy.

[109]William J. Broad, "Reagan's Star Wars Bid: Many Ideas Converging," *New York Times*, 4 March 1985, p. 1.

[110]Georges Skelton, "U.S. Fears Soviet Leap in A-Arms," *Los Angeles Times*, 15 February 1985, p. 1; Philip M. Boffrey, "Many Questions Remain as Star Wars Advances," *International Herald Tribune*, 12 March 1985, p. 1.

[111]For a presentation of a reassessment of the American strategic doctrine in the last decade, see the fundamental Pentagon-solicited Report: Fred C. Ikle amd Albert Wohlsletter (co-chairmen), *Discriminate Deferrence: Report of the Commission on Integrated Long-Term Strategy to the Secretary of Defense* (Washington DC, Government Printing Office, January 1988).

[112]E. P. Thompson (ed.), *Star Wars: Science-fiction Fantasy or Serious Probability?* (New York, Pantheon, 1985).

[113]Peter Grier, "U.S. Public Opinion Generally Favors 'Star Wars'," *Christian Science Monitor*, 21 November 1985, p. 3; Kevin Phillips, "Defense Beyond Thin Air: Space Holds the Audience," *Los Angeles Times*, 10 March 1985.

[114]See Thompson, *Star Wars*, pp. 131ff; Ernest Conine, "Star Wars and Economic Power," *Los Angeles Times*, 19 August 1985, p. 115.

[115]Cited by Fred Hiatt and Rich Atkinson, "Arms and America's Fortunes," *Washington Post*, 1 December 1985, p. A1.

[116]David E. Sanger, "But Company Worries Grow," *The New York Times*, 19 November 1985, p. 25.

[117]Council on Economic Priorities, *Star Wars: The Economic Fallout* (Cambridge, Mass., Ballinger, 1988).

[118]G. Adams, *The Iron Triangle: The Politics of Defense Contracting* (New York, Council on Economic Priority, 1981).

[119]William J. Broad, "Scientists Profit from Star Wars," *New York Times*, 5 November 1985, p. 1.

[120]Michael Schrage, "Transporting the Pentagon Into the Future," *Washington Post*, 24 July 1983, p. F6.

[121]See the well documented analysis on the question by Stowsky, *Beating Our Plowshares*; also David Warsh, "Star Wars: Boon or Bane for Economy?" *Boston Globe*, 21 November 1985, p. 57.

[122]See Broad, "Reagan's Star Wars Bid," p. 1.

[123]Robert Scheer, "Star Wars: All-out Publicity Push," *Los Angeles Times*, 29 December 1985, p. 1.

[124]Aaron Wildowsky, "Reagan the Strategist," *Wall Street Journal*, 3 January 1986, p. 10.

[125]As an illustration of the development of the SDI concept in the scientific military establishment prior to the Reagan administration, I can refer to the findings of an investigative report by a journalist, Françoise Sabbah, on the Livermore National Laboratory. She visited Livermore in February 1980 and interviewed a representative of the Laboratory on the research programs under way in that institution. She was told that the priority of the Laboratory had shifted to space-based warfare, with particular emphasis on protecting/destroying the satellite-based communications systems. Most of the concepts that gave birth to the SDI strategy were already at the center of Livermore Laboratory research programs one year before Ronald Reagan's inauguration as President of the United States (personal account from Françoise Sabbah, correspondant for several Spanish newspapers and magazines).

[126]See a good, though partisan, synthesis of the debate in Thompson, *Star Wars*.

[127]David Ignatius, "Analyzing Risks," *Wall Street Journal*, 15 October 1985, p. 1; Bon Oberdofer, "Ex-Defense Chief Calls 'Star Wars' Unrealistic," *Washington Post*, 15 December 1985; Philip M. Boffey, "Dark Side of Star Wars: System Could Also Attack," *New York Times*, 7 March 1985, p. 1; David Perlman, "The Star Wars Scientists Who Doubt It Will Work," *San Francisco Chronicle*, 14 April 1986, p. 8.

[128]Judith Miller, "Allies in West Lend Support to Star Wars," *New York Times*, 30 December 1985, p. 1.

[129]Stowsky, *Beating our Plowshares*.

[130]Stewart Nozette, "A Giant Step Forward in Technology," *New York Times*, 8 December 1985, p. F2.

[131]Ben Thompson, "What is Star Wars?" in Thompson, *Star Wars*, pp. 28–49.

[132]See Walter Zegveld and Christien Enzing, *SDI and Industrial Technology Policy: Threat or Opportunity* (New York, St Martin's, 1987); also the excellent analysis by Mario Pianta, *Star War Economics*, paper presented at the conference "The State of Star Wars," Transnational Institute, Amsterdam, 23–5 January 1987.

[133]Sanger, *But Company Worries Grow*.

[134]Fred Hiatt and Rick Atkinson, "Pentagon's 'Paper Warriors' Find Market for SDI Advice," *Washington Post*, 21 October 1985, p. 1.

[135]Reuters, "Small Firms Capitalize on Pentagon Software," *Los Angeles Times*, 25 November 1985, p. IV1.

[136]Tim Carrington, "Scramble in Space: Star Wars Plans Spur Defense Firms to Vie for Billions in Orders," *Wall Street Journal*, 21 May 1985, p. 1.

[137]Rosy Nimroody and William Hartung, "Putting Industry Even Further Behind," *New York Times*, 8 December 1985, p. F2.

[138]Accentuating the previous trend shown by several authors in Tirman, *Militarization of High Technology*.

[139]Nimroody and Hartung, "Putting Industry even Further Behind."

[140]Schrage, "Transporting the Pentagon."

[141]See Wayne Sandholtz, Jay Stowsky, and Steven K. Vogel, *The Dilemmas of Technological Competition in Comparative Perspective: Is It Guns Vs. Butter?*, Research Report for the UC Berkeley MacArthur Interdisciplinary Group for International Security Studies (Berkeley: University of California, Berkeley Roundtable on the International Economy, April 1988).

[142]Jacqueline Mazza and Dale E. Wilkinson, *The Unprotected Flank: Regional and Strategic Imbalances in Defense Spending Patterns* (Washington DC, Northeast-Midwest Institute, 1980); Roger Bezdek, "The 1980 Economic Impact – Regional and Occupational – of Compensated Shifts in Defense Spending," *Journal of Regional Science*, AS:2 (1975), pp. 183–97; Wassily Leontief et al., "The Economic Impact – Industrial and Regional – of an Arms Cut," *Review of Economics and Statistics*, 47, 3 (1965), pp. 217–44; John Rees, "Defense Spending and Regional Industrial Change," *Texas Business Review*, Jan.–Feb. 1982, 40–4.

[143]Edward J. Malecki, "Military Spending and the US Defense Industry: Regional Patterns of Military Contracts and Subcontracts," *Environment and Planning, C: Government and Policy*, 2 (1984) pp. 31–44.

[144]This is a research program, funded by the NSF, and initiated in 1985 in the Institute of Urban and Regional Development, UC Berkeley. Peter Hall and Ann Markusen are principal investigators. Scott Campbell and Sabina Dietrick, doctoral candidates at UC Berkeley, are research assistants.

[145]G. R. Simonson, *The History of the American Aircraft Industry: An Anthology* (Cambridge, Mass., MIT, 1968).

[146]B. F. Cooling, *War, Business and Society: Historical Perspectives on the Military Industrial Complex* (Port Washington, NY, Kennikat, 1977).

[147]W. G. Cunningham, *The Aircraft Industry: A Study in Industrial Location* (Los Angeles, Morrison, 1951).

[148]J. B. Roe, *Climb to Greatness: The American Aircraft Industry, 1920–1960* (Cambridge, Mass., MIT, 1968).

[149]Interestingly enough, the Pacific War, a factor often cited to explain the west's dominance in the defense industry, does not seem to have been directly a cause for the location pattern. In fact, during the war, the defense industry tended to spread and relocate *inland* for obvious strategic reasons, returning to the west coast, for the most part, at the end of the war. Yet, what was really decisive was the location of the navy and air force bases in the west coast, and the huge contracts provided during World War II to the airframe industries in Los Angeles.

[150]See Peter Hall, "The Creation of the American Aero-Space Complex 1955–65: A

Study in Industrial Inertia," in Michael J. Breheny (ed.), *Defence Expenditure and Regional Development* (London, Mansell, 1988).

[151]B. Bluestone, P. Jordan, and M. Sullivan, *Aircraft Industry Dynamics: An Analysis of Competition, Capital and Labor* (Boston, Auburn House, 1981).

[152]Servet Mutlu, *Inter-regional and International Mobility of Industrial Capital: The Case of American Automobile and Electronics Companies*, unpublished PhD dissertation (Berkeley, University of California, 1979).

[153]R. E. Bilstein, *Flight in America 1900–1983: From the Wrights to the Astronauts* (Baltimore, Johns Hopkins University Press, 1984).

[154]R. C. Estall, *New England: A Study in Industrial Adjustment* (London, G. Bell, 1966).

[155]Paul A. Koistinen, *The Military–Industrial Complex: A Historical Perspective* (New York, Praeger, 1980).

[156]C. D. Bright, *The Jet Makers: The Aerospace Industry from 1945 to 1972* (Lawrence, Ks, The Regents Press of Kansas, 1978).

[157]Gansler, *The Defense Economy*, pp. 36–45.

[158]Adams, *The Iron Triangle*.

[159]Coates and Killian, *Heavy Losses*.

[160]R. E. Bolton, *Defense Purchase and Regional Growth* (Washington DC, Brookings Institution, 1966).

[161]Markusen, *Defense Spending*, p. 21.

[162]Arnold Fleischmann and Joe R. Feagin, "The Politics of Growth-Oriented Urban Alliance: Comparing Old Industrial and New Sunbelt Cities," *Urban Affairs Quarterly*, 23, 2 (December 1987), pp. 207–32.

[163]Ann R. Markusen and R. Bloch, "Defensive Cities: Military Spending, High Technology, and Human Settlements," in Manuel Castells (ed.), *High Technology, Space and Society* (Beverly Hills, Sage, 1985).

[164]N. S. Dorfman, *Massachusetts' High Technology Boom in Perspective: An Investigation of its Dimensions, Causes and the Role of New Firms* (Cambridge, Mass., MIT, Center for Policy Alternatives, 1982).

[165]Hall, "Creation of the American Aero-Space Complex."

[166]Ibid.; P. W. Bowers, *Boeing Aircraft Since 1916* (Fullbrook, Cal., Acre, 1966).

[167]J. J. Horgan, *City of Flight: The History of Aviation in St. Louis* (Gerald, Mo., Patrick Press, 1984).

[168]Charles Tiebout, "The Regional Impact of Defense Expenditures: Its Measurement and Problems of Adjustment," in Roger Bolton (ed.), *Defense and Disarmament* (Englewood Cliffs, NJ, Prentice-Hall, 1984).

[169]Sabina Dietrick, *Military Spending and Migration to California*, unpublished seminar paper (Berkeley, UC Department of City and Regional Planning, 1984).

[170]M. Teitz, "Economic Change and California Public Policy," in Ted Bradshaw and Charles Bell, *The Capacity to Respond: California Political Institutions Face Change* (Berkeley, University of California Institute of Government Studies, 1987).

[171]N. S. Dorfman, "Route 128: the Development of a Regional High Technology Economy," *Research Policy*, 12 (1983), pp. 299–316; the estimate of about one-third of the employment in defense-related jobs has been obtained from J. Markoff, information to the author from the Pacific Studies Center, 1985.

[172]Ann. R. Markusen, *The Economic and Regional Consequences of Military Innovation*, IURD Working Paper 442 (Berkeley, May 1985).

[173]Edward Malecki, "Government-funded R&D: Some Regional Economic Implications," *Professional Geographer*, 33, (1981), pp. 72–82.

[174]Office of Technology Assessment, *Technology and Structural Unemployment: Reemploying Displaced Adults* (Washington DC, US Congress, OTA, 1986).

[175]A. Markusen, P. Hall, and A. Glasmeier, *High Tech America: the What, How, Where and Why of the Sunrise Industries* (Boston, London, Allen & Unwin, 1986).

[176]Ibid.

[177]Markusen and Bloch, "Defensive Cities."

[178]Ann Markusen with G. Clark, C. Curtis, S. Dietrick, G. Fields, A. Henry, E. Ingersoll, J. Levin, W. Patton, J. Ross and J. Schneider, *Military Spending and Urban Development in California*, IURD Working Paper 425 (Berkeley, June 1984).

[179]Markusen and Bloch, "Defensive Cities."

[180]Glickman, "Economic Policy and the Cities."

[181]Rebecca Skinner, *The Urban and Regional Impacts of Defense Oriented Technological Policy: the Case of SDI*, research in progress (Berkeley, University of California, Department of City and Regional Planning, 1988).

[182]Stowsky, *Beating Our Plowshares*.

[183]Committee on Science, Engineering, and Public Policy, *Balancing the National Interest: U.S. National Security Export Controls and Global Economic Competition* (Washington DC, National Academy Press, 1987).

[184]David Fishback, "The Star Wars Laboratory," *Financial Times*, 24 April 1985, p. 9; Charles Stein, "MIT's Lincoln Labs: Unobtrusively Excelling in the Technological World," *Boston Globe*, 15 October 1985, p. 41.

Chapter 6

[1]John Agnew, *The United States in the World Economy: A Regional Geography* (Cambridge, Cambridge University Press, 1987), p. 142.

[2]Ray Marshall and Norman Glickman, *Choices for American Industry*, research report (Austin, University of Texas, Lyndon B. Johnson School of Public Affairs, 1986), p. 11.

[3]Henry B. Schechter, *Imbalances in the Global Economy: Impacts on the United States*, paper delivered at the Rutgers University Conference on America's New Economic Geography, Washington DC, 29–30 April 1987.

[4]Norman J. Glickman, *International Trade, Capital Mobility, and Economic Growth*, a report to the President's Commission For a National Agenda for the Eighties, Washington DC, 3–4 June 1980.

[5]Jane S. Little, "Location Decisions of Foreign Investors in the United States," in *New England Economic Review*, July–August 1978, pp. 43–63.

[6]Alejandro Portes and Robert Bach, *Latin Journey* (Berkeley, University of California Press, 1985).

[7]Regional Plan Association of New York, *New York in the Global Economy: Studying the Facts and the Issues*, research document (New York, April 1987).

[8]Lester Thurow and Laura Tyson, *Adjusting the U.S. Trade Balance: A Black Hole in the World Economy*, BRIE Working Paper, (Berkeley, March 1987).

[9]Bruce R. Guile and Harvey Brooks (eds), *Technology and Global Industry: Companies and Nations in the World Economy* (Washington DC, National Academy Press, 1987).

[10]Laura Tyson, *The U.S. and the World Economy in Transition*, BRIE working paper (Berkeley, July 1986); Robert Z. Lawrence, *Can America Compete?* (Washington DC, Brookings Institution, 1984).

[11]Stephen S. Cohen and John Zysman, *Manufacturing Matters* (New York, Basic Books, 1987).

[12]Thurow and Tyson, *Adjusting the US Trade Balance*.

[13]Michael Borrus, *Chips of State: Microelectronics and American Autonomy*, book manuscript (forthcoming).

[14]Martin Carnoy and Manuel Castells, "After the Crisis?", *World Policy Journal*, Spring 1984.

[15]Cohen and Zysman, *Manufacturing Matters*.

[16]Schechter, *Imbalances in the Global Economy*, p. 24.

[17]Charles Stone and Isabel Sawhill, *Labor Market Implications in the Growing Internationalism of the U.S. Economy*, discussion paper (Washington DC, Urban Institute, 1986).

[18]John Lederer, *High Technology Manufacturing Employment: A Report on Recent Decline in California*, seminar paper for CP 284 (Berkeley, University of California, Department of City and Regional Planning, May 1987).

[19]Agnew, *The United States in the World Economy*, p. 143.

[20]Lester C. Thurow, *The Zero-Sum Society* (New York, Basic Books, 1980).

[21]Cited by Marshall and Glickman, *Choices for American Industry*, box number 7.

[22]*Business Week*, as cited by Marshall and Glickman, *Choices for American Industry*, box number 9.

[23]Candee Harris, "The Magnitude of Job Loss from Plant Closings and the Generation of Replacement Jobs: Some Recent Evidence", *The Annals*, September 1984, pp. 15–27.

[24]Agnew, *The United States in the World Economy*, p. 164.

[25]B. Bluestone and B. Harrison, *The Deindustrialization of America* (New York, Basic Books, 1982).

[26]Peter Hall, *Regions in the Transition to the Information Economy*, paper delivered at the Rutgers University Conference on America's New Economic Geography, Washington DC, 29–30 April 1987.

[27]Leslie Wayne, "U.S. Textile Industry's Turnaround," *New York Times*, 15 February 1988, p. 21.

[28]"America's Deflation Belt," *Business Week*, 9 June 1986, pp. 52–60.

[29]Raul A. Hinojosa and Rebecca Morales, *International Restructuring and Labor Market Interdependence: The Automobile Industry in Mexico and the United States*, paper presented at the Conference on Labor Market Interdependence, El Colegio de Mexico, Mexico DF, 25–7 September 1986.

[30]United Nations Industrial Development Organization (UNIDO), *International Industrial Restructuring and the International Division of Labour in the Automotive Industry* (Vienna, UNIDO, Division for Industrial Studies, 1984).

[31]Alan Altshuler, Martin Anderson, Daniel Jones, Daniel Roos, and James Womak, *The Future of the Automobile: The Report of MIT's International Automobile Program* (Cambridge, Mass., MIT, 1984).

[32]Dennis P. Quinn, *Dynamic Markets and Mutating Firms: The Changing Organization of Production in Automotive Firms*, BRIE working paper (Berkeley, July 1987).

[33]UNIDO, *International Restructuring*.

[34]Ibid., p. 4.

[35]Hinojosa and Morales, *International Restructuring and Labor Market Interdependence*, p. 35.

[36]UNIDO, *International Restructuring*, p. 91.

[37]UNIDO, *International Restructuring*, pp. 92–3.

[38]Hinojosa and Morales, *International Restructuring and Labor Market Interdependence*.

[39]K. Trachte and R. Ross, "The Crisis of Detroit and the Emergence of Global Capitalism," *International Journal of Urban and Regional Research*, 9 (1985), pp. 216–17.

[40]Harley Shaiken, *Work Transformed: Automation and Labor in the Computer Age* (New York, Holt, Rinehart and Winston, 1984).

[41]UNIDO, *International Restructuring*, p. 101.

[42]Trachte and Ross, "The Crisis of Detroit."

[43]Richard C. Hill, *The Auto Industry in Global Transition*, paper presented at the meeting of the American Sociological Association, Detroit, Michigan, 1983.

[44]Agnew, *The United States in the World Economy*, p. 190.

[45]Philip Shapira, *The Crumbling of Smokestack California: A Case Study in Industrial Restructuring and the Reorganization of Work*, IURD working paper (Berkeley, November 1984).

[46]Altshuler et al., *The Future of the Automobile*.

[47]James P. Womack, "Prospects for the U.S. Mexican Relationship in the Motor Vehicle Sector," in Cathryn L. Thorup (ed.), *The U.S. and Mexico: Face to Face with New Technology* (Washington DC, Overseas Development Council, 1987).

[48]"GM: What Went Wrong," *Business Week*, 16 March 1987.

[49]Richard C. Hill, *A Global Marriage of Convenience: General Motors and Toyota at Fremont*, paper presented at the meeting of the society for the Study Social Problems, Detroit, 1983.

[50]Erica Schoenberger, *Technological and Organizational Change in Automobile Production: Spatial Implications*, paper presented at the National Science Foundation/ Hungarian Academy of Sciences Conference on Regional Development, Budapest, 1–7 September 1985.

[51]Richard C. Hill, "Global Factory and Company Town: The Changing Division of Labour in the International Automobile Industry," in Jeff Henderson and Manuel Castells (eds), *Global Restructuring and Territorial Development* (London, Sage, 1987), pp. 18–37.

[52]G. Maxcy, *The Multinational Automobile Industry* (New York, St Martin's, 1981).

[53]Servet Mutlu, *Inter-regional and International Mobility of Industrial Capital: The Case of American Automobile and Electronics Companies*, unpublished PhD dissertation (Berkeley, University of California, 1979).

[54]*Business Week*, 16 March 1987.

[55]UNIDO, *International Restructuring*, p. 23.

[56]Hinojosa and Morales, *International Restructuring and Labor Market Interdependence*, p. 35.

[57]Ibid., p. 36.

[58]Harley Shaiken and Stephen Herzenberg, *Automation and Global Production: Automobile Engine Production in Mexico, the United States, and Canada* (San Diego, University of California, Center for US–Mexican Studies, 1987).

[59]UNIDO, *International Restructuring*.

[60]Shaiken and Herzenberg, *Automation and Global Production*.

[61]Hill, "Global Factory and Company Town," p. 35.

[62]Michael A. Shea, "U.S. Affiliates of Foreign Companies: Operations in 1984," *Survey of Current Business*, 66, 10 (1986), pp. 31–46; Jeffrey Arpan, Edward Flowers, and David Ricks, "Foreign Direct Investment in the United States: The State of Knowledge in Research," *Journal of International Business Studies*, Spring/Summer 1981, pp. 137–54.

[63]Erica Schoenberger, "Foreign Manufacturing Investment in the United States: Competitive Strategies and International Location," *Economic Geography*, 61, 3 (July 1985), pp. 241–59.

[64]Schoenberger, *Foreign Manufacturing Investment in the United States*, p. 241.

[65]Ibid., p. 245.

[66]Erica Schoenberger, "Foreign Manufacturing Investment in the United States: Its Causes and Regional Consequences," PhD dissertation (Berkeley, University of California, Department of City and Regional Planning, 1984).

[67]Norman J. Glickman and Douglas P. Woodward, *Regional Patterns of Manufacturing Foreign Direct Investment in the United States*, special project report prepared for the US Department of Commerce (Austin, University of Texas, Lyndon B. Johnson School of Public Affairs, 1987).

[68]Ibid., p. 37.

[69]Saskia Sassen, *The Global City* (Princeton, NJ, Princeton University Press, forthcoming).

[70]John Friedmann and Goetz Wolff, *World City Formation*, (Los Angeles, UCLA, Comparative Urbanization Studies, 1982).

[71]Regional Plan Association of New York, *New York in the Global Economy*.

[72]Sassen, *The Global City*.

[73]Nigel Thrift, "The Fixers: the Urban Geography of International Commercial Capital," in Jeff Henderson and Manuel Castells (eds), *Global Restructuring and Territorial Development* (London, Sage, 1987), pp. 203–33.

[74]Thierry Noyelle, *The Globalization of New York City*, paper prepared for the Social Science Research Council's Committee on New York City, 1988.

[75]Sassen, *The Global City*.

[76]Regional Plan Association of New York, *New York in the Global Economy*.

[77]Ibid.

[78]Ibid., p. 26.

[79]Sassen, *The Global City*, MS p. 154.

[80]Richard Harris, *Home and Work in New York Since 1950*, paper prepared for Social Science Research Council's Committee on New York City, 1988.

[81]John Mollenkopf, "New York: The Great Anomaly," in R. Browning, D. Marshall and D. Tabb (eds), *Race and Politics in American Cities* (New York, Longman, forthcoming).

[82]Robert Goodman, *The Last Entrepreneurs* (New York, Basic Books, 1979).

[83]Michael P. Smith, "Global Capital Restructuring and Local Political Crises in U.S. Cities," in Henderson and Castells, *Global Restructuring*, pp. 234–50.

Index